This dictionary of German and English is designed to provide the user with wide-ranging and up-to-date coverage of the two languages, and is ideal for both school and reference use.

A special feature of HarperCollins dictionaries is the comprehensive "signposting" of meanings on both sides of the dictionary, guiding the user to the most appropriate translation for a given context. We hope you will find this dictionary easy and pleasant to consult for all your study and reference needs.

ABKÜRZUNGEN

ABBREVIATIONS

Adjektiv	a	adjective
Abkürzung	abk, abbr	abbreviation
Akkusativ	acc	accusative
Adverb	ad	adverb
Landwirtschaft	AGR	agriculture
Akkusativ	akk	accusative
Anatomie	ANAT	anatomy
Architektur	ARCHIT	architecture
Artikel	art	article
Astrologie	ASTROL	astrology
Astronomie	ASTRON	astronomy
attributiv	attr	attributive
Kraftfahrzeuge	AUT	automobiles
Hilfsverb	aux	auxiliary
Luftfahrt	AVIAT	aviation
besonders	bes	especially
Biologie	BIOL	biology
Botanik	BOT	botany
britisch	Brit	British
Chemie	CHEM	chemistry
Film	CINE	cinema
Konjunktion	cj	conjunction
umgangssprachlich (! vulgär)	col(!)	colloquial (! particularly offensive)
Handel	COMM	commerce
Komparativ	comp	comparative
Computer	COMPUT	computing
Kochen und Backen	COOK	cooking
zusammengesetztes Wort	cpd	compound
Dativ	dat	dative
kirchlich	ECCL	ecclesiastical
Eisenbahn	EISENB	railways
Elektrizität	ELEK, ELEC	electricity
besonders	esp	especially
und so weiter	etc	et cetera
etwas	etw	something
Euphemismus, Hüllwort	euph	euphemism
Femininum	f	feminine
übertragen	fig	figurative
Finanzwesen	FIN	finance
Genitiv	gen	genitive
Geographie	GEOG	geography
Geologie	GEOL	geology
Grammatik	GRAM	grammar
Geschichte	HIST	history
unpersönlich	impers	impersonal
unbestimmt	indef	indefinite
nicht getrennt gebraucht	insep	inseparable
Interjektion, Ausruf	interj	interjection
interrogativ, fragend	interrog	interrogative

HarperCollins

GERMAN-
ENGLISH
◆
ENGLISH-
GERMAN

GERMAN DICTIONARY

HarperPaperbacks
A Division of HarperCollinsPublishers

HarperPaperbacks   *A Division of* HarperCollins*Publishers*
10 East 53rd Street, New York, N.Y. 10022

This book was published in Great Britain in 1989 by William Collins Sons & Co. Inc.

First HarperPaperbacks printing: August 1991

Printed in the United States of America

HarperPaperbacks and colophon are trademarks of HarperCollins*Publishers*

10 9 8 7 6 5 4 3 2

ABKÜRZUNGEN

ABBREVIATIONS

unveränderlich	inv	invariable
unregelmäßig	irreg	irregular
jemand	jd	somebody
jemandem	jdm	(to) somebody
jemanden	jdn	somebody
jemandes	jds	somebody's
Rechtswesen	JUR	law
Konjunktion	kj	conjunction
Kochen und Backen	KOCH	cooking
Komparativ	komp	comparative
Sprachwissenschaft	LING	linguistics
wörtlich	lit	literal
literarisch	liter	literary
Literatur	LITER	of literature
Maskulinum	m	masculine
Mathematik	MATH	mathematics
Medizin	MED	medicine
Meteorologie	MET	meteorology
militärisch	MIL	military
Bergbau	MIN	mining
Musik	MUS	music
Substantiv, Hauptwort	n	noun
nautisch, Seefahrt	NAUT	nautical, naval
Nominativ	nom	nominative
Neutrum	nt	neuter
Zahlwort	num	numeral
Objekt	obj	object
oder	od	or
sich	o.s.	oneself
Parlament	PARL	parliament
abschätzig	pej	pejorative
Photographie	PHOT	photography
Physik	PHYS	physics
Plural	pl	plural
Politik	POL	politics
besitzanzeigend	poss	possessive
Partizip Perfekt	pp	past participle
Präfix, Vorsilbe	präf, pref	prefix
Präposition	präp, prep	preposition
Typographie	PRINT	printing
Pronomen, Fürwort	pron	pronoun
Psychologie	PSYCH	psychology
1. Vergangenheit, Imperfekt	pt	past tense
Radio	RAD	radio
Eisenbahn	RAIL	railways
Relativ-	rel	relative
Religion	REL	religion
jemand(-en, -em)	sb	someone, somebody
Schulwesen	SCH	school

ABKÜRZUNGEN

ABBREVIATIONS

Naturwissenschaft	SCI	science
schottisch	Scot	Scottish
Singular, Einzahl	sing	singular
etwas	sth	something
Suffix, Nachsilbe	suff	suffix
Superlativ	superl	superlative
Technik	TECH	technology
Nachrichtentechnik	TEL	telecommunications
Theater	THEAT	theatre
Fernsehen	TV	television
Typographie	TYP	printing
umgangssprachlich (! vulgär)	umg(!)	colloquial (! particularly offensive)
Hochschulwesen	UNIV	university
unpersönlich	unpers	impersonal
unregelmäßig	unreg	irregular
(nord)amerikanisch	US	(North) America
gewöhnlich	usu	usually
Verb	v	verb
intransitives Verb	vi	intransitive verb
reflexives Verb	vr	reflexive verb
transitives Verb	vt	transitive verb
Zoologie	ZOOL	zoology
zusammengesetztes Wort	zW	compound
zwischen zwei Sprechern	—	change of speaker
ungefähre Entsprechung	≃	cultural equivalent
eingetragenes Warenzeichen	®	registered trademark

REGULAR GERMAN NOUN ENDINGS

nom		*gen*	*pl*
-ant	*m*	-anten	-anten
-anz	*f*	-anz	-anzen
-ar	*m*	-ar(e)s	-are
-chen	*nt*	-chens	-chen
-ei	*f*	-ei	-eien
-elle	*f*	-elle	-ellen
-ent	*m*	-enten	-enten
-enz	*f*	-enz	-enzen
-ette	*f*	-ette	-etten
-eur	*m*	-eurs	-eure
-euse	*f*	-euse	-eusen
-heit	*f*	-heit	-heiten
-ie	*f*	-ie	-ien
-ik	*f*	-ik	-iken
-in	*f*	-in	-innen
-ine	*f*	-ine	-inen
-ion	*f*	-ion	-ionen
-ist	*m*	-isten	-isten
-ium	*nt*	-iums	-ien
-ius	*m*	-ius	-iusse
-ive	*f*	-ive	-iven
-keit	*f*	-keit	-keiten
-lein	*nt*	-leins	-lein
-ling	*m*	-lings	-linge
-ment	*nt*	-ments	-mente
-mus	*m*	-mus	-men
-schaft	*f*	-schaft	-schaften
-tät	*f*	-tät	-täten
-tor	*m*	-tors	-toren
-ung	*f*	-ung	-ungen
-ur	*f*	-ur	-uren

PHONETIC SYMBOLS / LAUTSCHRIFT

[ː] *length mark* *Längezeichen* ['] *stress mark* *Betonung*
['] *glottal stop* *Knacklaut*

all vowel sounds are approximate only
alle Vokallaute sind nur ungefähre Entsprechungen

lie	[aɪ]	weit	day	[eɪ]	
now	[aʊ]	Haut	girl	[ɜː]	
above	[ə]	bitte	board	[ɔː]	
green	[iː]	viel	root	[uː]	Hut
pity	[ɪ]	Bischof	come	[ʌ]	Butler
rot	[ɒ,ɔ]	Post	salon	[ɔ̃]	Champignon
full	[ʊ]	Pult	avant (garde)	[ɑ̃]	Ensemble
			fair	[ɛə]	mehr
bet	[b]	Ball	beer	[ɪə]	Bier
dim	[d]	dann	toy	[ɔɪ]	Heu
face	[f]	Faß	pure	[ʊə]	
go	[g]	Gast	wine	[w]	
hit	[h]	Herr	thin	[θ]	
you	[j]	ja	this	[ð]	
cat	[k]	kalt			
lick	[l]	Last	Hast	[a]	mash
must	[m]	Mast	Ensemble	[ã]	avant (garde)
nut	[n]	Nuß	Metall	[e]	meths
bang	[ŋ]	lang	häßlich	[ɛ]	
pepper	[p]	Pakt	Cousin	[ɛ̃]	
sit	[s]	Rasse	vital	[i]	
shame	[ʃ]	Schal	Moral	[o]	
tell	[t]	Tal	Champignon	[õ]	salon
vine	[v]	was	ökonomisch	[ø]	
loch	[x]	Bach	gönnen	[œ]	
zero	[z]	Hase	Heu	[ɔy]	toy
leisure	[ʒ]	Genie	kulant	[u]	
			physisch	[y]	
bat	[æ]		Müll	[ʏ]	
farm	[ɑː]	Bahn	ich	[ç]	
set	[e]	Kette			

[★] r can be pronounced before a vowel; Bindungs-R

DEUTSCH - ENGLISCH
GERMAN - ENGLISH

A

A, a [aː] *nt* A, a.

à [a] *präp* at.

Aal [aːl] *m* -(e)s, -e eel.

Aas [aːs] *nt* -es, -e *od* **Äser** carrion; **~geier** *m* vulture.

ab [ap] ◆ *präp* +*dat* from; **Kinder ~ 12 Jahren** children from the age of 12; **~ morgen** from tomorrow; **~ sofort** as of now ◆ *ad* **1** off; **links ~** to the left; **der Knopf ist ~** the button has come off; **~ nach Hause!** off you go home **2** (*zeitlich*): **von da ~** from then on; **von heute ~** from today, as of today **3** (*auf Fahrplänen*): **München ~ 12.20** leaving Munich 12.20 **4 ~ ~ und zu** *od* **an** now and then *od* again.

Abänderung ['ap'ɛndərʊŋ] *f* alteration.

Abart ['ap'aːrt] *f* (*BIOL*) variety; **a~ig** *a* abnormal.

Abbau ['apbau] *m* -(e)s dismantling; (*Verminderung*) reduction (*gen* in); (*Verfall*) decline (*gen* in); (*MIN*) mining; quarrying; (*CHEM*) decomposition; **a~en** *vt* dismantle; (*MIN*) mine; quarry; (*verringern*) reduce; (*CHEM*) break down.

abbeißen ['apbaisən] *vt unreg* bite off.

Abberufung ['apbəruːfʊŋ] *f* recall.

abbestellen ['apbəʃtɛlən] *vt* cancel.

abbezahlen ['apbətsaːlən] *vt* pay off.

abbiegen ['apbiːgən] *unreg vi* turn off; (*Straße*) bend // *vt* bend; (*verhindern*) ward off.

Abbild ['apbılt] *nt* portrayal; (*einer Person*) image, likeness; **a~en** ['apbıldən] *vt* portray; **~ung** *f* illustration.

Abbitte ['apbıtə] *f*: **~ leisten** *od* **tun** make one's apologies (*bei* to).

abblenden ['apblɛndən] *vti* (*AUT*) dip (*Brit*), dim (*US*).

Abblendlicht *nt* dipped (*Brit*) *od* dimmed (*US*) headlights *pl*.

abbrechen ['apbrɛçən] *vti unreg* break off; (*Gebäude*) pull down; (*Zelt*) take down; (*aufhören*) stop; (*COMPUT*) abort.

abbrennen ['apbrɛnən] *unreg vt* burn off; (*Feuerwerk*) let off // *vi* (*aux sein*) burn down.

abbringen ['apbrıŋən] *vt unreg*: **jdn von etw ~** dissuade sb from sth; **jdn vom Weg ~** divert sb.

abbröckeln ['apbrœkəln] *vti* crumble off *od* away.

Abbruch ['apbrʊx] *m* (*von Verhandlungen etc*) breaking off; (*von Haus*) demolition; **jdm/etw ~ tun** harm sb/sth; **a~reif** *a* only fit for demolition.

abbrühen ['apbryːən] *vt* scald; **abgebrüht** (*umg*) hard-boiled.

abbuchen ['apbuːxən] *vt* debit.

abbürsten ['apbyrstən] *vt* brush off.

abdanken ['apdaŋkən] *vi* resign; (*König*) abdicate.

Abdankung *f* resignation; abdication.

abdecken ['apdɛkən] *vt* uncover; (*Tisch*) clear; (*Loch*) cover.

abdichten ['apdıçtən] *vt* seal; (*NAUT*) caulk.

abdrehen ['apdreːən] *vt* (*Gas*) turn off; (*Licht*) switch off; (*Film*) shoot // *vi* (*Schiff*) change course.

Abdruck ['apdrʊk] *m* (*Nachdrucken*) reprinting; (*Gedrucktes*) reprint; (*Gips~, Wachs~*) impression; (*Finger~*) print; **a~en** *vt* print, publish.

abdrücken ['apdrʏkən] *vt* make an impression of; (*Waffe*) fire; (*Person*) hug, squeeze.

Abend ['aːbənt] *m* -s, -e evening; **guten ~** good evening; **zu ~ essen** have dinner *od* supper; **a~ ad** evening; **~brot** *nt*, **~essen** *nt* supper; **~kasse** *f* box office; **~kurs** *m* evening classes *pl*; **~land** *nt* West; **a~lich** *a* evening; **~mahl** *nt* Holy Communion; **~rot** *nt* sunset; **abends** *ad* in the evening.

Abenteuer ['aːbəntɔyər] *nt* -s, - adventure; **a~lich** *a* adventurous.

Abenteurer *m* -s, - adventurer; **~in** *f* adventuress.

aber ['aːbər] *kj* but; (*jedoch*) however; **das ist ~ schön** that's really nice; **nun ist ~ Schluß!** now that's enough!; ~~~vielen Dank — ~ bitte! thanks a lot — you're welcome // *ad*: **tausend und ~ tausend** thousands upon thousands; **A~glaube** *m* superstition; **~gläubisch** *a* superstitious.

aberkennen ['ap'ɛrkɛnən] *vt unreg*: **jdm etw ~** deprive sb of sth, take sth (away) from sb.

Aberkennung *f* taking away.

abermals ['aːbərmaːls] *ad* once again.

Abf. *abk* (= *Abfahrt*) dep.

abfahren ['apfɑ:rən] *unreg vi* leave, depart // *vt* take *od* cart away; (*Strecke*) drive; (*Reifen*) wear; (*Fahrkarte*) use.

Abfahrt ['apfɑ:rt] *f* departure; (*SKI*) descent; (*Piste*) run; **Abfahrtslauf** *m* (*SKI*) descent, run down; **Abfahrtszeit** *f* departure time.

Abfall ['apfal] *m* waste; (*von Speisen etc*) rubbish (*Brit*), garbage (*US*); (*Neigung*) slope; (*Verschlechterung*) decline; **~eimer** *m* rubbish bin (*Brit*), garbage can (*US*); **a~en** *vi unreg* (*lit, fig*) fall *od* drop off; (*POL, vom Glauben*) break away; (*sich neigen*) fall *od* drop away.

abfällig ['apfɛlɪç] *a* disparaging, deprecatory.

abfangen ['apfaŋən] *vt unreg* intercept; (*Person*) catch; (*unter Kontrolle bringen*) check.

abfärben ['apfɛrbən] *vi* (*lit*) lose its colour; (*Wäsche*) run; (*fig*) rub off.

abfassen ['apfasən] *vt* write, draft.

abfertigen ['apfɛrtɪgən] *vt* prepare for dispatch, process; (*an der Grenze*) clear; (*Kundschaft*) attend to.

Abfertigung *f* preparing for dispatch, processing; clearance.

abfeuern ['apfɔyərn] *vt* fire.

abfinden ['apfɪndən] *unreg vt* pay off // *vr* come to terms; **sich mit jdm ~/nicht ~** put up with/not get on with sb.

Abfindung *f* (*von Gläubigern*) payment; (*Geld*) sum in settlement.

abflauen ['apflauən] *vi* (*Wind, Erregung*) die away, subside; (*Nachfrage, Geschäft*) fall *od* drop off.

abfliegen ['apfli:gən] *unreg vi* (*Flugzeug*) take off; (*Passagier auch*) fly // *vt* (*Gebiet*) fly over.

abfließen ['apfli:sən] *vi unreg* drain away.

Abflug ['apflu:k] *m* departure; (*Start*) take-off; **~zeit** *f* departure time.

Abfluß ['apflʊs] *m* draining away; (*Öffnung*) outlet.

Abfuhr ['apfu:r] *f* -, -en removal; (*fig*) snub, rebuff.

abführen ['apfy:rən] *vt* lead away; (*Gelder, Steuern*) pay // *vi* (*MED*) have a laxative effect.

Abführmittel ['apfy:rmɪtəl] *nt* laxative, purgative.

abfüllen ['apfylən] *vt* draw off; (*in Flaschen*) bottle.

Abgabe ['apgɑ:bə] *f* handing in; (*von Ball*) pass; (*Steuer*) tax; (*eines Amtes*) giving up; (*einer Erklärung*) giving.

Abgang ['apgaŋ] *m* (*von Schule*) leaving; (*THEAT*) exit; (*MED: Ausscheiden*) passing; (*Fehlgeburt*) miscarriage; (*Abfahrt*) departure; (*der Post, von Waren*) dispatch.

Abgas ['apgɑ:s] *nt* waste gas; (*AUT*) exhaust.

abgeben ['apge:bən] *unreg vt* (*Gegenstand*) hand *od* give in; (*Ball*) pass; (*Wärme*) give off; (*Amt*) hand over; (*Schuß*) fire; (*Erklärung, Urteil*) give; (*darstellen, sein*) make; **jdm etw ~** (*überlassen*) let sb have sth // *vr*: **sich mit jdm/etw ~** associate with sb/bother with sth.

abgehen ['apge:ən] *unreg vi* go away, leave; (*THEAT*) exit; (*Baby*) die; (*Knopf etc*) come off; (*abgezogen werden*) be taken off; (*Straße*) branch off; **etw geht jdm ab** (*fehlt*) sb lacks sth // *vt* (*Strecke*) go *od* walk along.

abgelegen ['apgəle:gən] *a* remote.

abgemacht ['apgəmaxt] *a* fixed; **~!** done.

abgeneigt ['apgənaikt] *a* averse to, disinclined.

Abgeordnete(r) ['apgə'ɔrdnətə(r)] *mf* member of parliament; elected representative.

abgeschmackt ['apgəʃmakt] *a* tasteless.

abgesehen ['apgəze:ən] *a*: **es auf jdn/etw ~ haben** be after sb/sth; **~ von ...** apart from ...

abgespannt ['apgəʃpant] *a* tired out.

abgestanden ['apgəʃtandən] *a* stale; (*Bier auch*) flat.

abgestorben ['apgəʃtɔrbən] *a* numb; (*BIOL, MED*) dead.

abgetragen ['apgətra:gən] *a* shabby, worn out.

abgewinnen ['apgəvɪnən] *vt unreg*: **einer Sache etw/Geschmack ~** get sth/pleasure from sth.

abgewöhnen ['apgəvø:nən] *vt*: **jdm/sich etw ~** cure sb of sth/give sth up.

abgleiten ['apglaitən] *vi unreg* slip, slide.

Abgott ['apgɔt] *m* idol.

abgöttisch ['apgœtɪʃ] *a*: **~ lieben** idolize.

abgrenzen ['apgrɛntsən] *vt* (*lit, fig*) mark off; fence off.

Abgrund ['apgrʊnt] *m* (*lit, fig*) abyss.

abhacken ['aphakən] *vt* chop off.

abhalten ['aphaltən] *vt unreg* (*Versammlung*) hold; **jdn von etw ~** (*fernhalten*) keep sb away from sth; (*hindern*) keep sb from sth.

abhanden [ap'handən] *a*: **~ kommen** get lost.

Abhandlung ['aphandlʊŋ] *f* treatise, discourse.

Abhang ['aphaŋ] *m* slope.

abhängen ['aphɛŋən] *vt* (*Bild*) take down; (*Anhänger*) uncouple; (*Verfolger*) shake off // *vi unreg* (*Fleisch*) hang; **von jdm/etw ~** depend on sb/

sth.

abhängig ['aphɛŋɪç] a dependent (von on); **A~keit** f dependence (von on).

abhärten ['aphɛrtən] vtr toughen (o.s.) up; sich gegen etw ~ inure o.s. to sth.

abhauen ['aphauən] unreg vt cut off; (Baum) cut down // vi (umg) clear off od out.

abheben ['aphe:bən] unreg vt lift (up); (Karten) cut; (Masche) slip; (Geld) withdraw, take out // vi (Flugzeug) take off; (Rakete) lift off; (KARTEN) cut // vr stand out (von from), contrast (von with).

abhelfen ['aphɛlfən] vi unreg (+dat) remedy.

abhetzen ['aphɛtsən] vr wear od tire o.s. out.

Abhilfe ['aphɪlfə] f remedy; ~ schaffen put things right.

abholen ['apho:lən] vt (Gegenstand) fetch, collect; (Person) call for; (am Bahnhof etc) pick up, meet.

abhören ['aphø:rən] vt (Vokabeln) test; (Telefongespräch) tap; (Tonband etc) listen to.

Abhörgerät nt bug.

Abitur [abi'tu:r] nt -s, -e German school leaving examination; **Abituri'ent(in** f) m candidate for school leaving certificate.

Abk. abk (= Abkürzung) abbr.

abkanzeln ['apkantsəln] vt (umg) bawl out.

abkapseln ['apkapsəln] vr shut od cut o.s. off.

abkaufen ['apkaufən] vt: jdm etw ~ buy sth from sb.

abkehren ['apke:rən] vt (Blick) avert, turn away // vr turn away.

abklingen ['apklɪŋən] vi unreg die away; (Radio) fade out.

abknöpfen ['apknœpfən] vt unbutton; jdm etw ~ (umg) get sth off sb.

abkochen ['apkɔxən] vt boil.

abkommen ['apkɔmən] vi unreg get away; von der Straße/von einem Plan ~ leave the road/give up a plan; **A~** nt -s, - agreement.

abkömmlich ['apkœmlɪç] a available, free.

abkratzen ['apkratsən] vt scrape off // vi (umg) kick the bucket.

abkühlen ['apky:lən] vt cool down // vr (Mensch) cool down od off; (Wetter) get cool; (Zuneigung) cool.

abkürzen ['apkyrtsən] vt shorten; (Wort auch) abbreviate; den Weg ~ take a short cut.

Abkürzung f (Wort) abbreviation; (Weg) short cut.

abladen ['apla:dən] vt unreg unload.

Ablage ['apla:gə] f (für Akten) tray; (für Kleider) cloakroom.

ablassen ['aplasən] unreg vt (Wasser, Dampf) let off; (vom Preis) knock off // vi: von etw ~ give sth up, abandon sth.

Ablauf ['aplauf] m (Abfluß) drain; (von Ereignissen) course; (einer Frist, Zeit) expiry (Brit), expiration (US); **a~en** unreg vi (abfließen) drain away; (Ereignisse) happen; (Frist, Zeit, Paß) expire // vt (Sohlen) wear (down od out).

ablegen ['aple:gən] vt put od lay down; (Kleider) take off; (Gewohnheit) get rid of; (Prüfung) take, sit; (Zeugnis) give.

Ableger m -s, - layer; (fig) branch, offshoot.

ablehnen ['aple:nən] vt reject; (Einladung) decline, refuse // vi decline, refuse.

Ablehnung f rejection; refusal.

ableiten ['aplaitən] vt (Wasser) divert; (deduzieren) deduce; (Wort) derive.

Ableitung f diversion; deduction; derivation; (Wort) derivative.

ablenken ['aplɛŋkən] vt turn away, deflect; (zerstreuen) distract // vi change the subject.

Ablenkung f distraction.

ablesen ['aple:zən] vt unreg read out; (Meßgeräte) read.

abliefern ['apli:fərn] vt deliver; etw bei jdm/einer Dienststelle ~ hand sth over to sb/in at an office.

Ablieferung f delivery.

abliegen ['apli:gən] vi unreg be some distance away; (fig) be far removed.

ablösen ['aplø:zən] vt (abtrennen) take off, remove; (in Amt) take over from; (Wache) relieve.

Ablösung f removal; relieving.

abmachen ['apmaxən] vt take off; (vereinbaren) agree.

Abmachung f agreement.

abmagern ['apma:gərn] vi get thinner.

Abmagerungskur f diet; eine ~ machen go on a diet.

Abmarsch ['apmarʃ] m departure.

abmelden ['apmɛldən] vt (Zeitungen) cancel; (Auto) take off the road; jdn bei der Polizei ~ register sb's departure with the police // vr give notice of one's departure; (im Hotel) check out.

abmessen ['apmɛsən] vt unreg measure.

Abmessung f measurement.

abmontieren ['apmɔnti:rən] vt take off.

abmühen ['apmy:ən] vr wear o.s. out.

Abnahme ['apna:mə] f -, -n removal; (COMM) buying; (Verringerung) decrease (gen in).

abnehmen ['apne:mən] unreg vt take

off, remove; (*Führerschein*) take away; (*Geld*) get (*jdm* out of sb); (*kaufen, umg: glauben*) buy (*jdm* from sb); (*Prüfung*) hold; (*Maschen*) decrease; **jdm Arbeit ~** take work off sb's shoulders // *vi* decrease; (*schlanker werden*) lose weight.

Abnehmer *m* **-s, -** purchaser, customer.

Abneigung ['apnaɪgʊŋ] *f* aversion, dislike.

abnorm [ap'nɔrm] *a* abnormal.

abnutzen ['apnʊtsən] *vt* wear out.

Abnutzung *f* wear (and tear).

Abonnement [abɔn(ə)'mãː] *nt* **-s, -s** subscription.

Abonnent(in *f*) [abɔ'nɛnt(ɪn)] *m* subscriber.

abonnieren [abɔ'niːrən] *vt* subscribe to.

Abordnung ['ap'ɔrdnʊŋ] *f* delegation.

Abort [a'bɔrt] *m* **-(e)s, -e** lavatory.

abpacken ['appakən] *vt* pack.

abpassen ['appasən] *vt* (*Person, Gelegenheit*) wait for; (*in Größe: Stoff etc*) adjust.

abpfeifen ['appfaɪfən] *vti* *unreg* (SPORT): (**das Spiel**) ~ blow the whistle (for the end of the game).

Abpfiff ['appfɪf] *m* final whistle.

abplagen ['appla:gən] *vr* wear o.s. out.

Abprall ['appral] *m* rebound; (*von Kugel*) ricochet; **a~en** *vi* bounce off; ricochet.

abputzen ['apputsən] *vt* clean.

abraten ['apra:tən] *vi* *unreg* advise, warn (*jdm von etw* sb against sth).

abräumen ['aprɔymən] *vt* clear up *od* away.

abreagieren ['apreagi:rən] *vt* (*Zorn*) work off (*an* +*dat* on) // *vr* calm down.

abrechnen ['aprɛçnən] *vt* deduct, take off // *vi* (*lit*) settle up; (*fig*) get even.

Abrechnung *f* settlement; (*Rechnung*) bill.

Abrede ['apre:də] *f*: **etw in ~ stellen** deny *od* dispute sth.

abregen ['apre:gən] *vr* (*umg*) calm *od* cool down.

Abreise ['apraɪzə] *nf* departure; **a~n** *vi* leave, set off.

abreißen ['apraɪsən] *vt* *unreg* (*Haus*) tear down; (*Blatt*) tear off.

abrichten ['aprɪçtən] *vt* train.

abriegeln ['apri:gəln] *vt* (*Tür*) bolt; (*Straße, Gebiet*) seal off.

Abriß ['aprɪs] *m* **-sses, -sse** (*Übersicht*) outline.

Abruf ['apru:f] *m*: **auf ~** on call; **a~en** *vt* *unreg* (*Mensch*) call away; (COMM: *Ware*) request delivery of.

abrunden ['aprʊndən] *vt* round off.

abrüsten ['aprʏstən] *vi* disarm.

Abrüstung *f* disarmament.

abrutschen ['aprʊtʃən] *vi* slip; (AVIAT) sideslip.

Abs. *abk* (= *Absender*) sender, from.

Absage ['apza:gə] *f* **-, -n** refusal; **a~n** *vt* cancel, call off; (*Einladung*) turn down // *vi* cry off; (*ablehnen*) decline.

absägen ['apzɛ:gən] *vt* saw off.

Absatz ['apzats] *m* (COMM) sales *pl*; (*Bodensatz*) deposit; (*neuer Abschnitt*) paragraph; (*Treppen~*) landing; (*Schuh~*) heel; **~gebiet** *nt* (COMM) market.

abschaben ['apʃa:bən] *vt* scrape off; (*Möhren*) scrape.

abschaffen ['apʃafən] *vt* abolish, do away with.

Abschaffung *f* abolition.

abschalten ['apʃaltən] *vti* (*lit, umg*) switch off.

abschätzen ['apʃɛtsən] *vt* estimate; (*Lage*) assess; (*Person*) size up.

abschätzig ['apʃɛtsɪç] *a* disparaging, derogatory.

Abschaum ['apʃaʊm] *m* **-(e)s** scum.

Abscheu ['apʃɔy] *m* **-(e)s** loathing, repugnance; **a~erregend** *a* repulsive, loathsome; **a~lich** [ap'ʃɔylɪç] *a* abominable.

abschicken ['apʃɪkən] *vt* send off.

abschieben ['apʃi:bən] *vt* *unreg* push away; (*Person*) pack off.

Abschied ['apʃi:t] *m* **-(e)s, -e** parting; (*von Armee*) discharge; **~ nehmen** say good-bye (*von jdm* to sb), take one's leave (*von jdm* of sb); **seinen ~ nehmen** (MIL) apply for discharge; **Abschiedsbrief** *m* farewell letter.

abschießen ['apʃi:sən] *vt* *unreg* (*Flugzeug*) shoot down; (*Geschoß*) fire; (*umg: Minister*) get rid of.

abschirmen ['apʃɪrmən] *vt* screen.

abschlagen ['apʃla:gən] *vt* *unreg* (*abhacken,* COMM) knock off; (*ablehnen*) refuse; (MIL) repel.

abschlägig ['apʃlɛːgɪç] *a* negative.

Abschlagszahlung *f* interim payment.

abschleifen ['apʃlaɪfən] *unreg vt* grind down; (*Rost*) polish off // *vr* wear off.

Abschlepp- ['apʃlɛp] *zW*: **~dienst** *m* (AUT) breakdown service (*Brit*), towing company (*US*); **a~en** *vt* (take in) tow; **~seil** *nt* towrope.

abschließen ['apʃli:sən] *unreg vt* (*Tür*) lock; (*beenden*) conclude, finish; (*Vertrag, Handel*) conclude // *vr* (*sich isolieren*) cut o.s. off.

Abschluß ['apʃlus] *m* (*Beendigung*) close, conclusion; (*von Bilanz*) balancing; (*von Vertrag, Handel*) conclusion; **zum ~** in conclusion; **~prüfung** *f* final exam.

abschmieren ['apʃmi:rən] *vt* (AUT) grease, lubricate.

abschneiden ['apʃnaɪdən] *unreg vt* cut

off // vi do, come off.
Abschnitt ['apʃnɪt] m section; (MIL)
sector; (Kontroll~) counterfoil;
(MATH) segment; (Zeit~) period.
abschnüren ['apʃnyːrən] vt constrict.
abschöpfen ['apʃœpfən] vt skim off.
abschrauben ['apʃraubən] vt unscrew.
abschrecken ['apʃrɛkən] vt deter, put
off; (mit kaltem Wasser) plunge in
cold water; ~d a deterrent; ~des
Beispiel warning.
abschreiben ['apʃraɪbən] vt unreg
copy; (verlorengeben) write off;
(COMM) deduct.
Abschrift ['apʃrɪft] f copy.
Abschuß ['apʃus] m (eines Ge-
schützes) firing; (Herunterschießen)
shooting down; (Tötung) shooting.
abschüssig ['apʃysɪç] a steep.
abschütteln ['apʃytəln] vt shake off.
abschwächen ['apʃvɛçən] vt lessen;
(Behauptung, Kritik) tone down // vr
lessen.
abschweifen ['apʃvaɪfən] vi wander.
Abschweifung f digression.
abschwellen ['apʃvɛlən] vi unreg
(Geschwulst) go down; (Lärm) die
down.
abschwören ['apʃvøːrən] vi unreg
(+dat) renounce.
abseh- ['apzeː] zW: ~bar a foresee-
able; in ~barer Zeit in the foresee-
able future; das Ende ist ~bar the
end is in sight; ~en unreg vt (Ende,
Folgen) foresee // vi: von etw ~en refrain from sth; (nicht berücksichtigen) leave sth out of consideration.
abseits ['apzaɪts] ad out of the way //
präp +gen away from; **A~** nt
(SPORT) offside.
Absend- ['apzɛnd] zW: **a~en** vt unreg
send off, dispatch; ~er m -s, - sender; ~ung f dispatch.
absetz- ['apzɛts] zW: ~en vt (niederstellen, aussteigen lassen) put down;
(abnehmen) take off; (COMM: verkaufen) sell; (FIN: abziehen) deduct;
(entlassen) dismiss; (König) depose;
(streichen) drop; (hervorheben) pick
out // vr (sich entfernen) clear off;
(sich ablagern) be deposited; **A~ung**
f (FIN: Abzug) deduction; (Entlassung) dismissal; (von König) depos-
ing; (Streichung) dropping.
absichern ['apzɪçərn] vtr make safe;
(schützen) safeguard.
Absicht ['apzɪçt] f intention; mit ~ on
purpose; **a~lich** a intentional, deliberate.
absinken ['apzɪŋkən] vi unreg sink;
(Temperatur, Geschwindigkeit) decrease.
absitzen ['apzɪtsən] unreg vi dismount
// vt (Strafe) serve.
absolut [apzo'luːt] a absolute;

A~**ismus** [-'tɪsmʊs] m absolutism.
absolvieren [apzɔl'viːrən] vt (SCH)
complete.
absonder- ['apzɔndər] zW: ~lich
[ap'zɔndərlɪç] a odd, strange; ~n vt
separate; (ausscheiden) give off, secrete // vr cut o.s. off; **A~ung** f
separation; (MED) secretion.
abspalten ['apʃpaltən] vt split off.
abspeisen ['apʃpaɪzən] vt (fig) fob off.
abspenstig ['apʃpɛnstɪç] a: ~ machen
lure away (jdm from sb).
absperren ['apʃpɛrən] vt block off,
close off; (Tür) lock.
Absperrung f (Vorgang) blocking od
closing off; (Sperre) barricade.
abspielen ['apʃpiːlən] vt (Platte, Tonband) play; (SPORT: Ball) pass // vr
happen.
absplittern ['apʃplɪtərn] vt chip off.
Absprache ['apʃpraːxə] f arrangement.
absprechen ['apʃprɛçən] vt unreg
(vereinbaren) arrange; jdm etw ~
deny sb sth.
abspringen ['apʃprɪŋən] vi unreg
jump down/off; (Farbe, Lack) flake
off; (AVIAT) bale out; (sich distan-
zieren) back out.
Absprung ['apʃprʊŋ] m jump.
abspülen ['apʃpyːlən] vt rinse; (Geschirr) wash up.
abstammen ['apʃtamən] vi be de-
scended; (Wort) be derived.
Abstammung f descent; derivation.
Abstand ['apʃtant] m distance; (zeitlich) interval; davon ~ nehmen, etw
zu tun refrain from doing sth; ~
halten (AUT) keep one's distance;
mit ~ der beste by far the best.
abstatten ['apʃtatən] vt (Dank) give;
(Besuch) pay.
abstauben ['apʃtaubən] vti dust;
(umg: stehlen) pinch.
Abstecher ['apʃtɛçər] m -s, - detour.
abstehen ['apʃteːən] vi unreg (Ohren,
Haare) stick out; (entfernt sein)
stand away.
absteigen ['apʃtaɪgən] vi unreg (vom
Rad etc) get off, dismount; (in
Gasthof) put up (in +dat at);
(SPORT) be relegated (in : akk to).
abstellen ['apʃtɛlən] vt (niederstellen)
put down; (entfernt stellen) pull out;
(hinstellen: Auto) park; (ausschal-
ien) turn od switch off; (Mißstand,
Unsitte) stop; (ausrichten) gear (auf
+akk to).
Abstellgleis nt siding.
abstempeln ['apʃtɛmpəln] vt stamp.
absterben ['apʃtɛrbən] vi unreg die;
(Körperteil) go numb.
Abstieg ['apʃtiːk] m -(e)s, -e descent;
(SPORT) relegation; (fig) decline.
abstimmen ['apʃtɪmən] vi vote // vt

(*Instrument*) tune (*auf* +*akk* to); (*Interessen*) match (*auf* +*akk* with); (*Termine, Ziele*) fit in (*auf* +*akk* with) // *vr* agree.

Abstimmung *f* vote.

Abstinenz [apsti'nɛnts] *f* abstinence; teetotalism; ~**ler(in** *f*) *m* -s, - teetotaller.

abstoßen ['apʃto:sən] *vt unreg* push off *od* away; (*verkaufen*) unload; (*anekeln*) repel, repulse; ~**d** *a* repulsive.

abstrakt [ap'strakt] *a* abstract // *ad* abstractly, in the abstract.

abstreiten ['apʃtraitən] *vt unreg* deny.

Abstrich ['apʃtriç] *m* (*Abzug*) cut; (*MED*) smear; ~**e machen** lower one's sights.

abstufen ['apʃtu:fən] *vt* (*Hang*) terrace; (*Farben*) shade; (*Gehälter*) grade.

abstumpfen ['apʃtumpfən] *vt* (*lit, fig*) dull, blunt // *vi* (*lit, fig*) become dulled.

Absturz ['apʃturts] *m* fall; (*AVIAT*) crash.

abstürzen ['apʃtyrtsən] *vi* fall; (*AVIAT*) crash.

absuchen ['apzu:xən] *vt* scour, search.

absurd [ap'zurt] *a* absurd.

Abszeß [aps'tsɛs] *m* -**sses, -sse** abscess.

Abt [apt] *m* -(**e)s, ⁼e** abbot.

Abt. *abk* (= *Abteilung*) dept.

abtasten ['aptastən] *vt* feel, probe.

abtauen ['aptauən] *vti* thaw.

Abtei [ap'tai] *f* -, -**en** abbey.

Abteil [ap'tail] *nt* -(**e)s, -e** compartment; ~**a~en** *vt* divide up; (*abtrennen*) divide off; ~**ung** *f* (*in Firma, Kaufhaus*) department; (*in Krankenhaus*) section; (*MIL*) unit.

abtönen ['aptø:nən] *vt* (*PHOT*) tone down.

abtransportieren ['aptransporti:rən] *vt* take away, remove.

abtreiben ['aptraibən] *unreg vt* (*Boot, Flugzeug*) drive off course; (*Kind*) abort // *vi* be driven off course; abort.

Abtreibung *f* abortion.

abtrennen ['aptrɛnən] *vt* (*lostrennen*) detach; (*entfernen*) take off; (*abteilen*) separate off.

abtreten ['aptre:tən] *unreg vt* wear out; (*überlassen*) hand over, cede (*jdm* to sb) // *vi* go off; (*zurücktreten*) step down.

Abtritt ['aptrit] *m* resignation.

abtrocknen ['aptrɔknən] *vti* dry.

abtun ['aptu:n] *vt unreg* take off; (*fig*) dismiss.

abverlangen ['apfɛrlaŋən] *vt*: **jdm etw** ~ demand sth from sb.

abwägen ['apvɛ:gən] *vt unreg* weigh

up.

abwandeln ['apvandəln] *vt* adapt.

abwandern ['apvandərn] *vi* move away.

abwarten ['apvartən] *vt* wait for // *vi* wait.

abwärts ['apvɛrts] *ad* down.

Abwasch ['apvaʃ] *m* -(**e)s** washing-up; **a~en** *vt unreg* (*Schmutz*) wash off; (*Geschirr*) wash (up).

Abwasser ['apvasər] *nt* -s, -**wässer** sewage.

abwechseln ['apvɛksəln] *vir* alternate; (*Personen*) take turns; ~**d** *a* alternate.

Abwechslung *f* change.

Abweg ['apve:k] *m*: **auf ~e geraten/führen** go/lead astray; **a~ig** ['apve:giç] *a* wrong.

Abwehr ['apve:r] *f* - defence; (*Schutz*) protection; (~**dienst**) counter intelligence (service); **a~en** *vt* ward off; (*Ball*) stop.

abweichen ['apvaiçən] *vi unreg* deviate; (*Meinung*) differ; ~**d** *a* deviant; differing.

abweisen ['apvaizən] *vt unreg* turn away; (*Antrag*) turn down; ~**d** *a* (*Haltung*) cold.

abwenden ['apvɛndən] *unreg vt* avert // *vr* turn away.

abwerfen ['apvɛrfən] *vt unreg* throw off; (*Profit*) yield; (*aus Flugzeug*) drop; (*Spielkarte*) discard.

abwerten ['apve:rtən] *vt* (*FIN*) devalue.

abwesend ['apve:zənt] *a* absent.

Abwesenheit ['apve:zənhait] *f* absence.

abwickeln ['apvikəln] *vt* unwind; (*Geschäft*) wind up.

abwiegen ['apvi:gən] *vt unreg* weigh out.

abwischen ['apviʃən] *vt* wipe off *od* away; (*putzen*) wipe.

Abwurf ['apvurf] *m* throwing off; (*von Bomben etc*) dropping; (*von Reiter, SPORT*) throw.

abwürgen ['apvyrgən] *vt* (*umg*) scotch; (*Motor*) stall.

abzahlen ['aptsa:lən] *vt* pay off.

abzählen ['aptsɛ:lən] *vti* count (up).

Abzahlung *f* repayment; **auf ~ kaufen** buy on hire purchase.

abzapfen ['aptsapfən] *vt* draw off; **jdm Blut** ~ take blood from sb.

abzäunen ['aptsɔynən] *vt* fence off.

Abzeichen ['aptsaiçən] *nt* badge; (*Orden*) decoration.

abzeichnen ['aptsaiçnən] *vt* draw, copy; (*Dokument*) initial // *vr* stand out; (*fig: bevorstehen*) loom.

Abziehbild *nt* transfer.

abziehen ['aptsi:ən] *unreg vt* take off; (*Tier*) skin; (*Bett*) strip; (*Truppen*) withdraw; (*subtrahieren*) take away, subtract; (*kopieren*) run off // *vi* go away; (*Truppen*) withdraw.

abzielen ['aptsiːlən] *vi* be aimed (*auf* +*akk* at).

Abzug ['aptsuːk] *m* departure; (*von Truppen*) withdrawal; (*Kopie*) copy; (*Subtraktion*) subtraction; (*Betrag*) deduction; (*Rauch~*) flue; (*von Waffen*) trigger.

abzüglich ['aptsʏklɪç] *präp* +*gen* less.

abzweigen ['aptsvaɪgən] *vi* branch off // *vt* set aside.

Abzweigung *f* junction.

ach [ax] *interj* oh; ~ **ja!** (oh) yes; ~ **so!** I see; **mit A~ und Krach** by the skin of one's teeth.

Achse ['aksə] *f* -, -n axis; (*AUT*) axle.

Achsel ['aksəl] *f* -, -n shoulder; **~höhle** *f* armpit; **~zucken** *nt* shrug (of one's shoulders).

acht [axt] *num* eight; **sich in ~ nehmen** be careful (*vor* +*dat* of), watch out (*vor* +*dat* for); **etw außer ~ lassen** disregard sth; ~ **Tage a week**; **~bar** *a* worthy; **~e(r, s)** *a* eighth; **~el** *num* eighth; **~en** *vt* respect // *vi* pay attention (*auf* +*akk* to); **darauf ~en, daß** ... be careful that ...

ächten ['ɛçtən] *vt* outlaw, ban.

Achter- ['axtər] *zW:* **~bahn** *f* roller coaster; **~deck** *nt* (*NAUT*) afterdeck.

acht- *zW:* **~fach** *a* eightfold; **~geben** *vi unreg* take care (*auf* +*akk* of); **~los** *a* careless; **~mal** *ad* eight times; **~sam** *a* attentive.

Achtung ['axtʊŋ] *f* attention; (*Ehrfurcht*) respect; **alle ~!** good for you/him *etc* // *interj* look out!; (*MIL*) attention!

achtzehn *num* eighteen.

achtzig *num* eighty.

ächzen ['ɛçtsən] *vi* groan (*vor* +*dat* with).

Acker ['akər] *m* -s, ⁺ field; **~bau** *m* agriculture; **a~n** *vti* plough; (*umg*) slog away.

ADAC [aːdeːʔaːtseː] *abk* (= *Allgemeiner Deutscher Automobil-Club*) ≈ AA, RAC.

addieren [a'diːrən] *vt* add (up).

Addition [aditsi'oːn] *f* addition.

Adel ['aːdəl] *m* -s nobility; **a~ig, adlig** *a* noble.

Ader ['aːdər] *f* -, -n vein.

Adler ['aːdlər] *m* -s, - eagle.

Admiral [atmiˈraːl] *m* -s, -e admiral; **Admiralität** *f* admiralty.

adopt- *zW:* **~ieren** [adɔpˈtiːrən] *vt* adopt; **A~ion** [adɔptsiˈoːn] *f* adoption; **A~iveltern** [adɔptsiˈf-] *pl* adoptive parents *pl*; **A~ivkind** *nt* adopted child.

Adress- *zW:* **~ant** [adrɛˈsant] *m* sender; **~at** [adrɛˈsaːt] *m* -en, -en addressee; **~e** [aˈdrɛsə] *f* -, -n address; **a~ieren** [adrɛˈsiːrən] *vt* address (*an* +*akk* to).

Adria ['aːdria] *f* - Adriatic.

Advent [atˈvɛnt] *m* -(e)s, -e Advent; **Adventskranz** *m* Advent wreath.

aero- [aero] *präf* aero-.

Aerobic [aeˈrɔbɪk] *nt* aerobics.

Affäre [aˈfɛːrə] *f* -, -n affair.

Affe ['afə] *m* -n, -n monkey.

affektiert [afɛkˈtiːrt] *a* affected.

Affen- *zW:* **a~artig** *a* like a monkey; **mit a~artiger Geschwindigkeit** like a flash; **~hitze** *f* (*umg*) incredible heat; **~schande** *f* (*umg*) crying shame.

affig ['afɪç] *a* affected.

Afrika ['aːfrika] *nt* -s Africa; **~ner(in** *f*) [-ˈkaːnər(ɪn)] *m* -s, - African; **a~nisch** [-ˈkaːnɪʃ] *a* African.

After ['aftər] *m* -s, - anus.

AG [aːˈgeː] *abk* (= *Aktiengesellschaft*) (*Brit*) (public) limited company, Ltd; (*US*) corporation, Inc.

ägäisch [ɛˈgɛːɪʃ] *a:* **~es Meer** Aegean.

Agent [aˈgɛnt] *m* agent; **Agentur** [agɛnˈtuːr] *f* agency.

Aggregat [agreˈgaːt] *nt* -(e)s, -e aggregate; (*TECH*) unit; **~zustand** *m* (*PHYS*) state.

Aggress- *zW:* **~ion** [agrɛsiˈoːn] *f* aggression; **a~iv** [agrɛˈsiːf] *a* aggressive; **~ivität** [agrɛsiviˈtɛːt] *f* aggressiveness.

Agitation [agitatsiˈoːn] *f* agitation.

Agrar- [aˈgraːr] *zW:* **~politik** *f* agricultural policy; **~staat** *m* agrarian state.

Ägypt- [ɛˈgʏpt] *zW:* **~en** *nt* -s Egypt; **~er(in** *f*) *m* -s, - Egyptian; **ä~isch** *a* Egyptian.

ah [aː] *interj* ah.

aha [aˈhaː] *interj* aha.

Ahn [aːn] *m* -en, -en forebear.

ähneln ['ɛːnəln] *vi* (+*dat*) be like, resemble // *vr* be alike *od* similar.

ahnen ['aːnən] *vt* suspect; (*Tod, Gefahr*) have a presentiment of.

ähnlich ['ɛːnlɪç] *a* similar (*dat* to); **A~keit** *f* similarity.

Ahnung ['aːnʊŋ] *f* idea, suspicion; presentiment; **a~slos** *a* unsuspecting.

Ahorn ['aːhɔrn] *m* -s, -e maple.

Ähre ['ɛːrə] *f* -, -n ear.

Aids [eːdz] *nt* AIDS.

Akademie [akadeˈmiː] *f* academy.

Akademiker(in *f*) [akaˈdeːmikər(ɪn)] *m* -s, - university graduate.

akademisch *a* academic.

akklimatisieren [aklimatiˈziːrən] *vr* become acclimatized.

Akkord [aˈkɔrt] *m* -(e)s, -e (*MUS*) chord; **im ~ arbeiten** do piecework; **~arbeit** *f* piecework; **Akkordeon**

[a'kɔrdeɔn] *nt* **-s, -s** accordion.
Akrobat(in *f)* [akro'baːt(ɪn)] *m* **-en, -en** acrobat.
Akt [akt] *m* **-(e)s, -e** act; (*KUNST*) nude.
Akte ['aktə] *f* **-, -n** file; **aktenkundig** *a* on the files; **Aktenschrank** *m* filing cabinet; **Aktentasche** *f* briefcase.
Aktie ['aktsiə] *f* **-, -n** share.
Aktien- *zW:* **~emission** *f* share issue; **~gesellschaft** *f* joint-stock company; **~kurs** *m* share price.
Aktion [aktsi'oːn] *f* campaign; (*Polizei~, Such~*) action; **~är** [-'nɛːr] *m* **-s, -e** shareholder.
aktiv [ak'tiːf] *a* active; (*MIL*) regular; **~ieren** [-'viːrən] *vt* activate; **A~i'tät** *f* activity.
Aktualität [aktuali'tɛːt] *f* topicality; (*einer Mode*) up-to-dateness.
aktuell [aktu'ɛl] *a* topical; up-to-date.
Akustik [a'kʊstɪk] *f* acoustics *pl*.
akut [a'kuːt] *a* acute.
AKW [aːkaːveː] *nt abk von* **Atomkraftwerk.**
Akzent [ak'tsɛnt] *m* accent; (*Betonung*) stress.
akzeptieren [aktsep'tiːrən] *vt* accept.
Alarm [a'larm] *m* **-(e)s, -e** alarm; **a~bereit** *a* standing by; **~bereitschaft** *f* stand-by; **a~ieren** [-'miːrən] *vt* alarm.
Alban- [al'baːn] *zW:* **~ien** *nt* **-s** - Albania; **~ier(in** *f) m* **-s,** - Albanian; **a~isch** *a* Albanian.
albern ['albərn] *a* silly.
Album ['albʊm] *nt* **-s, Alben** album.
Algebra ['algebra] *f* - algebra.
Alger- [al'geːr] *zW:* **~ien** *nt* **-s** Algeria; **~ier(in** *f) m* **-s,** - Algerian; **a~isch** *a* Algerian.
alias ['aːlias] *ad* alias.
Alibi ['aːlibi] *nt* **-s, -s** alibi.
Alimente [ali'mɛntə] *pl* alimony.
Alkohol ['alkohɔl] *m* **-s, -e** alcohol; **a~frei** *a* non-alcoholic; **~iker(in** *f)* [alko'hoːlikər(ɪn)] *m* **-s,** - alcoholic; **a~isch** *a* alcoholic; **~verbot** *nt* ban on alcohol.
All [al] *nt* **-s** universe; **a~'abendlich** *a* every evening; **'a~bekannt** *a* universally known.
alle(r, s) ['alə(r, s)] ◆*a* **1** (*sämtliche*) all; **wir ~** all of us; **~ Kinder waren da** all the children were there; **~ Kinder mögen ...** all children like ...; **~ beide** both of us/them; **sie kamen ~** they all came; **~s Gute** all the best; **~s in ~m** all in all **2** (*mit Zeit- oder Maßangaben*) every; **~ vier Jahre** every four years; **~ fünf Meter** every five metres
◆*pron* everything; **~s was er sagt** everything he says, all that he says

◆*ad* (*zu Ende, aufgebraucht*) finished; **die Milch ist ~** the milk's all gone, there's no milk left; **etw ~ machen** finish sth up.
Allee [a'leː] *f* **-, -n** avenue.
allein [a'laɪn] *ad* alone; (*ohne Hilfe*) on one's own, by oneself; **nicht ~** (*nicht nur*) not only // *kj* but, only **A~erziehende(r)** *mf* single parent; **A~gang** *m*: **im A~gang** on one's own; **A~herrscher** *m* autocrat; **~stehend** *a* single.
allemal ['alə'maːl] *ad* (*jedesmal*) always; (*ohne weiteres*) with no bother; **ein für ~mal** once and for all.
allenfalls ['alənfals] *ad* at all events; (*höchstens*) at most.
aller- ['alər] *zW:* **~beste(r, s)** *a* very best; **~dings** *ad* (*zwar*) admittedly; (*gewiß*) certainly.
Allergie [aler'giː] *f* allergy; **allergisch** [a'lɛrgɪʃ] *a* allergic.
aller- *zW:* **~hand** *a inv* (*umg*) all sorts of; **das ist doch ~hand!** that's a bit much; **~hand!** (*lobend*) good show!; **A~'heiligen** *nt* All Saints' Day; **~höchstens** *ad* at the very most; **~lei** *a inv* all sorts of; **~letzte(r, s)** *a* very last; **~seits** *ad* on all sides; **prost ~seits!** cheers everyone!; **~wenigste(r, s)** *a* very least.
alles *pron* everything; **~ in allem** all in all; **~ Gute!** all the best!
allgemein ['algə'maɪn] *a* general; **im ~en** in general; **~gültig** *a* generally accepted; **A~heit** *f* (*Menschen*) general public; (*pl: Redensarten*) general remarks *pl*.
Alliierte(r) [ali'iːrtə(r)] *m* ally.
all- *zW:* **~jährlich** *a* annual; **~mählich** *a* gradual; **A~tag** *m* everyday life; **~täglich** *a, ad* daily; (*gewöhnlich*) commonplace; **~tags** *ad* on weekdays; **~'wissend** *a* omniscient; **~zu** *ad* all too; **~zuoft** *ad* all too often; **~zuviel** *ad* too much.
Almosen ['almoːzən] *nt* **-s,** - alms *pl*.
Alpen ['alpən] *pl* Alps *pl*.
Alphabet [alfa'beːt] *nt* **-(e)s, -e** alphabet; **a~isch** *a* alphabetical.
Alptraum ['alptraʊm] *m* nightmare.
als [als] *kj* **1** (*zeitlich*) when; (*gleichzeitig*) as; **damals, ~ ...** (in the days) when ...; **gerade, ~ ...** just as ... **2** (*in der Eigenschaft*) as; **~ Antwort** as an answer; **~ Kind** as a child **3** (*bei Vergleichen*) than; **ich kam später ~ er** I came later than he (did) *od* later than him; **lieber ... ~ rather ... than; **nichts ~ Ärger** nothing but trouble **4**: **~ ob/wenn** as if.
also ['alzoː] *kj* so; (*folglich*) therefore;

~ **gut** od **schön!** okay then; ~, **so was!** well really!; **na** ~! there you are then!

alt [alt] a old; **alles beim ~en lassen** leave everything as it was; **A~** m -s, -e (MUS) alto; **Altar** [al'taːr] m -(e)s, -äre altar; ~**bekannt** a long-known; **A~'eisen** nt scrap iron.

Alter ['altər] nt -s, - age; (hohes) old age; **im ~ von** at the age of; **a~n** vi grow old, age.

Alternativ- [alterna'tiːf] in zW alternative; ~**e** f alternative.

Alters- zW: ~**grenze** f age limit; ~**heim** nt old people's home; ~**versorgung** f old age pension.

Altertum nt antiquity.

alt- zW: **A~glascontainer** m bottle bank; ~'**hergebracht** a traditional; ~**klug** a precocious; ~**modisch** a old-fashioned; **A~papier** nt waste paper; **A~stadt** f old town.

Aluminium [alu'miːniʊm] nt -s aluminium, aluminum (US); ~**folie** f tinfoil.

am [am] = **an dem;** ~ **Schlafen** (umg) sleeping; ~ **15. März** on March 15th; ~ **besten/schönsten** best/ most beautiful.

Amateur [ama'tøːr] m amateur.

Amboß ['ambɔs] m -sses, -sse anvil.

ambulant [ambu'lant] a outpatient.

Ambulanz [ambu'lants] f outpatients sing.

Ameise ['aːmaɪzə] f -, -n ant.

Amerika [a'meːrika] nt -s America; ~**ner(in** f) [-'kaːnər(ɪn)] m -s, - American; **a~nisch** [-'kaːnɪʃ] a American.

Ampel ['ampəl] f -, -n traffic lights pl.

amputieren [ampu'tiːrən] vt amputate.

Amsel ['amzəl] f -, -n blackbird.

Amt [amt] nt -(e)s, **~er** office; (Pflicht) duty; (TEL) exchange; **a~ieren** [am'tiːrən] vi hold office; **a~lich** a official.

Amts- zW: ~**person** f official; ~**richter** m district judge; ~**stunden** pl office hours pl; ~**zeit** f period of office.

amüsant [amy'zant] a amusing.

amüsieren [amy'ziːrən] vt amuse // vr enjoy o.s.

an [an] ◆präp +dat 1 (räumlich: wo?) at; (auf, bei) on; (nahe bei) near; ~ **diesem Ort** at this place; ~ **der Wand** on the wall; **zu nahe** ~ **etw** too near to sth; **unten am Fluß** down by the river; **Köln liegt am Rhein** Cologne is on the Rhine.

2 (zeitlich: wann?) on; ~ **diesem Tag** on this day; ~ **Ostern** at Easter

3: ~ **arm** ◆ **Fett** low in fat; ~ **etw sterben** die of sth; ~ **(und für) sich** actually

◆präp +akk **1** (räumlich: wohin?) to; **er ging** ~**s Fenster** he went (over) to the window; **etw** ~ **die Wand hängen/schreiben** hang/write sth on the wall

2 (zeitlich: woran?): ~ **etw denken** think of sth

3 (gerichtet ~) to; **ein Gruß/eine Frage** ~ **dich** greetings/a question to you

◆ad **1** (ungefähr) about: ~ **die hundert** about a hundred

2 (auf Fahrplänen): **Frankfurt** ~ **18.30** arriving Frankfurt 18.30

3 (ab): **von dort/heute** ~ from there/ today onwards

4 (~geschaltet, ~gezogen) on; **das Licht ist** ~ the light is on; **ohne etwas** ~ with nothing on

◆siehe auch **am.**

analog [ana'loːk] a analogous; **A~ie** [-'giː] f analogy.

Analyse [ana'lyːzə] f -, -n analysis.

analysieren [analy'ziːrən] vt analyse.

Ananas ['ananas] f -, - od -**se** pineapple.

Anarchie [anar'çiː] f anarchy.

Anatomie [anato'miː] f anatomy.

anbahnen ['anbaːnən] vtr open up.

Anbau ['anbaʊ] m (AGR) cultivation; (Gebäude) extension; **a~en** vt (AGR) cultivate; (Gebäudeteil) build on.

anbehalten ['anbəhaltən] vt unreg keep on.

anbei [an'baɪ] ad enclosed.

anbeißen ['anbaɪsən] unreg vt bite into // vi (lit) bite; (fig) swallow the bait; **zum A~** (umg) good enough to eat.

anbelangen ['anbəlaŋən] vt concern; **was mich anbelangt** as far as I am concerned.

anbeten ['anbeːtən] vt worship.

Anbetracht ['anbətraxt] m: **in** ~ (+gen) in view of.

anbiedern ['anbiːdərn] vr make up (bei to).

anbieten ['anbiːtən] unreg vt offer // vr volunteer.

anbinden ['anbɪndən] vt unreg tie up; **kurz angebunden** (fig) curt.

Anblick ['anblɪk] m sight; **a~en** vt look at.

anbrechen ['anbrɛçən] unreg vt start; (Vorräte) break into // vi start; (Tag) break; (Nacht) fall.

anbrennen ['anbrɛnən] vi unreg catch fire; (KOCH) burn.

anbringen ['anbrɪŋən] vt unreg bring; (Ware) sell; (festmachen) fasten.

Anbruch ['anbrʊx] m beginning; ~ **des Tages/der Nacht** dawn/ nightfall.

anbrüllen ['anbrʏlən] vt roar at.

Andacht ['andaxt] f -, -en devotion; (Gottesdienst) prayers pl.

andächtig ['andɛçtɪç] *a* devout.
andauern ['andauərn] *vi* last, go on; ~**d** *a* continual.
Anden ['andən] *pl* Andes.
Andenken ['andɛŋkən] *nt* -**s**, - memory; souvenir.
andere(r, s) ['andərə(r,z)] *a* other; (*verschieden*) different; ein ~**s** Mal another time; kein ~**r** nobody else; von etw ~**m** sprechen talk about sth else; **andererseits** *ad* on the other hand.
ändern ['ɛndərn] *vt* alter, change // *vr* change.
andernfalls ['andərnfals] *ad* otherwise.
anders ['andərs] *ad* differently (*als* from); wer ~? who else?; jd/ irgendwo ~ sb/somewhere else; ~ aussehen/klingen look/sound different; ~**artig** *a* different; ~**farbig** *a* of a different colour; ~**herum** *ad* the other way round; ~**wo** *ad* somewhere else; ~**woher** *ad* from somewhere else.
anderthalb ['andərt'halp] *a* one and a half.
Änderung ['ɛndəruŋ] *f* alteration, change.
anderweitig ['andər'vaitɪç] *a* other // *ad* otherwise; (*anderswo*) elsewhere.
andeuten ['andɔytən] *vt* indicate; (*Wink geben*) hint at.
Andeutung *f* indication; hint.
Andrang ['andraŋ] *m* crush.
andrehen ['andre:ən] *vt* turn *od* switch on; (*umg*) jdm etw ~ unload sth onto sb.
androhen ['andro:ən] *vt*: jdm etw ~ threaten sb with sth.
aneignen ['an'aignən] *vt*: sich (*dat*) etw ~ acquire sth; (*widerrechtlich*) appropriate sth.
aneinander [an'ai'nandər] *ad* at/on/to *etc* one another *od* each other; ~**fügen** *vt* put together; ~**geraten** *vi* unreg clash.
anekeln ['an'e:kəln] *vt* disgust.
Anemone [ane'mo:nə] *f* -, -**n** anemone.
anerkannt ['an'ɛrkant] *a* recognized, acknowledged.
anerkennen ['an'ɛrkɛnən] *vt* unreg recognize, acknowledge; (*würdigen*) appreciate; ~**d** *a* appreciative; **anerkennenswert** *a* praiseworthy.
Anerkennung *f* recognition, acknowledgement; appreciation.
anfachen ['anfaxən] *vt* (*lit*) fan into flame; (*fig*) kindle.
anfahren ['anfa:rən] *unreg vt* deliver; (*fahren gegen*) hit; (*Hafen*) put into; (*fig*) bawl out // *vi* drive up; (*losfahren*) drive off.
Anfall ['anfal] *m* (*MED*) attack; **a~en** *unreg vt* attack; (*fig*) overcome // *vi* (*Arbeit*) come up; (*Produkt*) be ob-

tained.
anfällig ['anfɛlɪç] *a* delicate; ~ für etw prone to sth.
Anfang ['anfaŋ] *m* -(**e**)**s**, -**fänge** beginning, start; von ~ an right from the beginning; zu ~ at the beginning; ~ Mai at the beginning of May; **a~en** *vti* unreg begin, start; (*machen*) do.
Anfänger(in *f*) ['anfɛŋər(ɪn)] *m* -**s**, - beginner.
anfänglich ['anfɛŋlɪç] *a* initial.
anfangs *ad* at first; **A~buchstabe** *m* initial *od* first letter; **A~stadium** *nt* initial stages *pl*.
anfassen ['anfasən] *vt* handle; (*berühren*) touch // *vi* lend a hand // *vr* feel.
anfechten ['anfɛçtən] *vt* unreg dispute; (*beunruhigen*) trouble.
anfertigen ['anfɛrtɪgən] *vt* make.
anfeuern ['anfɔyərn] *vt* (*fig*) spur on.
anflehen ['anfle:ən] *vt* implore.
anfliegen ['anfli:gən] *vt* unreg fly to.
Anflug ['anflu:k] *m* (*AVIAT*) approach; (*Spur*) trace.
anfordern ['anfordərn] *vt* demand; (*COMM*) requisition.
Anforderung *f* demand (*gen* for).
Anfrage ['anfra:gə] *f* inquiry; **a~n** *vi* inquire.
anfreunden ['anfrɔyndən] *vr* make friends.
anfügen ['anfy:gən] *vt* add; (*beifügen*) enclose.
anfühlen ['anfy:lən] *vtr* feel.
anführen ['anfy:rən] *vt* lead; (*zitieren*) quote; (*umg*: *betrügen*) lead up the garden path.
Anführer *m* leader.
Anführung *f* leadership; (*Zitat*) quotation; **Anführungszeichen** *pl* quotation marks *pl*, inverted commas *pl*.
Angabe ['anga:bə] *f* statement; (*TECH*) specification; (*umg*: *Prahlerei*) boasting; (*SPORT*) service; ~**n** *pl* (*Auskunft*) particulars *pl*.
angeben ['ange:bən] *unreg vt* give; (*anzeigen*) inform on; (*bestimmen*) set // *vi* (*umg*) boast; (*SPORT*) serve.
Angeber *m* -**s**, - (*umg*) show-off; ~**ei** [-'rai] *f* (*umg*) showing off.
angeblich ['ange:plɪç] *a* alleged.
angeboren ['angəbo:rən] *a* inborn, innate (*jdm* in sb).
Angebot ['angəbo:t] *nt* offer; (*COMM*) supply (*an* +*dat* of).
angebracht ['angəbraxt] *a* appropriate, in order.
angegriffen ['angəgrɪfən] *a* exhausted.
angeheitert ['angəhaitərt] *a* tipsy.
angehen ['ange:ən] *unreg vt* concern; (*angreifen*) attack; (*bitten*) approach (*um* for) // *vi* (*Feuer*) light; (*umg*: *beginnen*) begin; ~**d** *a* prospective.
angehören ['angəhø:rən] *vi* belong (*dat* to).

Angehörige(r) *mf* relative.

Angeklagte(r) ['angəkla:ktə(r)] *mf* accused.

Angel ['aŋəl] *f* -, -n fishing rod; (*Tür~*) hinge.

Angelegenheit ['angələ:gənhaɪt] *f* affair, matter.

Angel- *zW:* **~haken** *m* fish hook; **a~n** *vt* catch // *vi* fish; **~n** *nt* -s angling, fishing; **~rute** *f* fishing rod.

angemessen ['angəmesən] *a* appropriate, suitable.

angenehm ['angəne:m] *a* pleasant; **~!** (*bei Vorstellung*) pleased to meet you.

angenommen ['angənɔmən] *a* assumed; **~, wir ...** assuming we ...

angesehen ['angəze:ən] *a* respected.

angesichts ['angəzɪçts] *präp* +*gen* in view of, considering.

angespannt ['angəʃpant] *a* (*Aufmerksamkeit*) close; (*Arbeit*) hard.

Angestellte(r) ['angəʃtɛltə(r)] *mf* employee.

angetan ['angəta:n] *a:* **von jdm/etw ~ sein** be impressed by sb/sth; **es jdm ~ haben** appeal to sb.

angewiesen ['angəvi:zən] *a:* **auf jdn/ etw ~ sein** be dependent on sb/sth.

angewöhnen ['angəvø:nən] *vt:* **jdm/ sich etw ~** get sb/become accustomed to sth.

Angewohnheit ['angəvo:nhaɪt] *f* habit.

angleichen ['anglaɪçən] *vtr unreg* adjust (*dat* to).

Angler ['aŋlər] *m* -s, - angler.

angreifen ['angraɪfən] *vt unreg* attack; (*anfassen*) touch; (*Arbeit*) tackle; (*beschädigen*) damage.

Angreifer *m* -s, - attacker.

Angriff ['angrɪf] *m* attack; **etw in ~ nehmen** make a start on sth.

Angst [aŋst] *f* -, ⁀e fear; **~ haben** be afraid *od* scared (*vor* +*dat* of); **~ haben um jdm/etw** be worried about sb/sth; **a~** *a:* **jdm ist a~** sb is afraid *od* scared; **jdm a~ machen** scare sb; **~hase** *m* (*umg*) chicken, scaredycat.

ängst- [ɛŋst] *zW:* **~igen** *vt* frighten // *vr* worry (o.s.) (*vor* +*dat*, *um* about); **~lich** *a* nervous; (*besorgt*) worried; **Ä~lichkeit** *f* nervousness.

anhaben ['anha:bən] *vt unreg* have on; **er kann mir nichts ~** he can't hurt me.

anhalt- ['anhalt] *zW:* **~en** *unreg vt* stop; (*gegen etw halten*) hold up (*jdm* against sth); **jdn zur Arbeit/ Höflichkeit ~en** make sb work/be polite // *vi* stop; (*andauern*) persist; **~end** *a* persistent; **A~er** *m* -s, - hitch-hiker; **per A~er fahren** hitchhike; **Anhaltspunkt** *m* clue.

anhand [an'hant] *präp* +*gen* with.

Anhang ['anhaŋ] *m* appendix; (*Leute*) family; supporters *pl.*

anhäng- ['anhɛŋ] *zW:* **~en** *vt unreg* hang up; (*Wagen*) couple up; (*Zusatz*) add (on); **A~er** *m* -s, - supporter; (*AUT*) trailer; (*am Koffer*) tag; (*Schmuck*) pendant; **A~erschaft** *f* supporters *pl;* **~lich** *a* devoted; **A~lichkeit** *f* devotion; **A~sel** *nt* -s, - appendage.

Anhäufung ['anhɔyfuŋ] *f* accumulation.

anheben ['anhe:bən] *vt unreg* lift up; (*Preise*) raise.

Anhieb ['anhi:b] *m:* **auf ~** at the very first go; (*kurz entschlossen*) on the spur of the moment.

Anhöhe ['anhø:ə] *f* hill.

anhören ['anhø:rən] *vt* listen to; (*anmerken*) hear // *vr* sound.

animieren [ani'mi:rən] *vt* encourage, urge on.

Anis [a'ni:s] *m* -es, -e aniseed.

Ank. *abk* (= *Ankunft*) arr.

ankaufen ['ankaufən] *vt* purchase, buy.

Anker ['aŋkər] *m* -s, - anchor; **vor ~ gehen** drop anchor; **a~n** *vti* anchor; **~platz** *m* anchorage.

Anklage ['ankla:gə] *f* accusation; (*JUR*) charge; **~bank** *f* dock; **a~n** *vt* accuse; (*JUR*) charge (*gen* with).

Ankläger ['anklɛ:gər] *m* accuser.

Anklang ['anklaŋ] *m:* **bei jdm ~ finden** meet with sb's approval.

Ankleide- ['anklaɪdə] *zW:* **~kabine** *f* changing cubicle; **a~n** *vtr* dress.

anklopfen ['anklɔpfən] *vi* knock.

anknüpfen ['anknypfən] *vt* fasten *od* tie on; (*fig*) start // *vi* (*anschließen*) refer (*an* +*akk* to).

ankommen ['ankɔmən] *vi unreg* arrive; (*näherkommen*) approach; (*Anklang finden*) go down (*bei* with); **es kommt darauf an** it depends; (*wichtig sein*) that (is what) matters; **es darauf ~ lassen** let things take their course; **gegen jdn/etw ~ cope** with sb/sth.

ankündigen ['ankyndɪgən] *vt* announce.

Ankündigung *f* announcement.

Ankunft ['ankunft] *f* -, -künfte arrival; **Ankunftszeit** *f* time of arrival.

ankurbeln ['ankurbəln] *vt* (*AUT*) crank; (*fig*) boost.

Anlage ['anla:gə] *f* disposition; (*Begabung*) talent; (*Park*) gardens *pl;* (*Beilage*) enclosure; (*TECH*) plant; (*FIN*) investment; (*Entwurf*) layout.

Anlaß ['anlas] *m* -sses, -lässe cause (*zu* for); (*Ereignis*) occasion; **aus ~** (+*gen*) on the occasion of; **~ zu etw geben** give rise to sth; **etw zum ~ nehmen** take the opportunity of sth.

anlassen *unreg vt* leave on; (*Motor*) start // *vr* (*umg*) start off.

Anlasser *m* **-s, -** (*AUT*) starter.

anläßlich ['anlɛslɪç] *präp +gen* on the occasion of.

Anlauf ['anlauf] *m* run-up; **a~en** *unreg vi* begin; (*Film*) show; (*SPORT*) run up; (*Fenster*) mist up; (*Metall*) tarnish; **rot a~en** colour; **angelaufen kommen** come running up // *vt* call at.

anlegen ['anle:gən] *vt* put (*an +akk* against/on); (*anziehen*) put on; (*gestalten*) lay out; (*Geld*) invest; (*Gewehr*) aim (*auf +akk* at); **es auf etw** (*akk*) ~ **be out for sth/to do sth**; **sich mit jdm** ~ (*umg*) quarrel with sb // *vi* dock.

Anlegestelle *f*, landing place.

anlehnen ['anle:nən] *vt* lean (*an +akk* against); (*Tür*) leave ajar // *vr* lean (*an +akk* on).

anleiten ['anlaɪtən] *vt* instruct.

Anleitung *f* instructions *pl*.

anlernen ['anlɛrnən] *vt* teach, instruct.

anliegen ['anli:gən] *vi unreg* (*Kleidung*) cling; **A~** *nt* **-s, -** matter; (*Wunsch*) wish; **~d** *a* adjacent; (*beigefügt*) enclosed.

Anlieger *m* **-s, -** resident; **'~ frei'** 'residents only'.

anlügen ['anly:gən] *vt unreg* lie to.

anmachen ['anmaxən] *vt* attach; (*Elektrisches*) put on; (*Zigarette*) light; (*Salat*) dress.

anmaßen ['anma:sən] *vt*: **sich** (*dat*) **etw** ~ (*Recht*) lay claim to sth; **~d** *a* arrogant.

Anmaßung *f* presumption.

anmelden ['anmɛldən] *vt* announce // *vr* (*sich ankündigen*) make an appointment; (*polizeilich, für Kurs etc*) register.

Anmeldung *f* announcement; appointment; registration.

anmerken ['anmɛrkən] *vt* observe; (*anstreichen*) mark; **sich** (*dat*) **nichts** ~ **lassen** not give anything away.

Anmerkung *f* note.

Anmut ['anmu:t] *f* - grace; **a~en** *vt* give a feeling; **a~ig** *a* charming.

annähern ['annɛːərn] *vr* get closer; **~d** *a* approximate.

Annäherung *f* approach; **Annäherungsversuch** *m* advances *pl*.

Annahme ['anna:mə] *f* **-, -n** acceptance; (*Vermutung*) assumption.

annehm- ['anne:m] *zW*: **~bar** *a* acceptable; **~en** *unreg vt* accept; (*Namen*) take; (*Kind*) adopt; (*vermuten*) suppose, assume // *vr* take care (*gen* of); **A~lichkeit** *f* comfort.

Annonce [a'nõ:sə] *f* **-, -n** advertisement.

annoncieren [anõ'si:rən] *vti* advertise.

annullieren [anʊ'li:rən] *vt* annul.

anöden ['an'ø:dən] *vt* (*umg*) bore stiff.

anonym [ano'ny:m] *a* anonymous.

Anorak ['anɔrak] *m* **-s, -s** anorak.

anordnen ['an'ɔrdnən] *vt* arrange; (*befehlen*) order.

Anordnung *f* arrangement; order.

anpacken ['anpakən] *vt* grasp; (*fig*) tackle; **mit** ~ **lend a hand.**

anpassen ['anpasən] *vt* fit (*jdm* on sb); (*fig*) adapt (*dat* to) // *vr* adapt.

Anpassung *f* fitting; adaptation; **anpassungsfähig** *a* adaptable.

Anpfiff ['anpfɪf] *m* (*SPORT*) (starting) whistle; kick-off; (*umg*) rocket.

Anprall ['anpral] *m* collision (*gegen, an +akk* with).

anprangern ['anpraŋərn] *vt* denounce.

anpreisen ['anpraɪzən] *vt unreg* extol.

Anprobe ['anpro:bə] *f* trying on.

anprobieren ['anprobi:rən] *vt* try on.

anrechnen ['anrɛçnən] *vt* charge; (*fig*) count; **jdm etw hoch** ~ value sb's sth greatly.

Anrecht ['anrɛçt] *nt* right (*auf +akk* to).

Anrede ['anre:də] *f* form of address; **a~n** *vt* address; (*belästigen*) accost.

anregen ['anre:gən] *vt* stimulate; **angeregte Unterhaltung** lively discussion; **~d** *a* stimulating.

Anregung *f* stimulation; (*Vorschlag*) suggestion.

anreichern ['anraɪçərn] *vt* enrich.

Anreise ['anraɪzə] *f* journey; **a~n** *vi* arrive.

Anreiz ['anraɪts] *m* incentive.

Anrichte ['anrɪçtə] *f* **-, -n** sideboard; **a~n** *vt* serve up; **Unheil a~n** make mischief.

anrüchig ['anrʏçɪç] *a* dubious.

anrücken ['anrʏkən] *vi* approach; (*MIL*) advance.

Anruf ['anru:f] *m* call; **a~en** *vt unreg* call out to; (*bitten*) call on; (*TEL*) ring up, phone, call.

ans [ans] = **an das.**

Ansage ['anza:gə] *f* **-, -n** announcement; **a~n** *vt* announce // *vr* say one will come; **Ansager(in** *f*) *m* **-s, -** announcer.

Ansammlung *f* collection; (*Leute*) crowd.

ansässig ['anzɛsɪç] *a* resident.

Ansatz ['anzats] *m* start; (*Haar~*) hairline; (*Hals~*) base; (*Verlängerungsstück*) extension; (*Veranschlagung*) estimate; **~punkt** *m* starting point.

anschaffen ['anʃafən] *vt* buy, purchase.

Anschaffung *f* purchase.

anschalten ['anʃaltən] *vt* switch on.

anschau- ['anʃau] *zW*: **~en** *vt* look at;

~lich a illustrative; **A~ung** f (*Meinung*) view; **aus eigener A~ung** from one's own experience.

Anschein ['anʃaın] m appearance; **allem ~ nach** to all appearances; **den ~ haben** seem, appear; **a~end** a apparent.

Anschlag ['anʃlaːk] m notice; (*Attentat*) attack; (*COMM*) estimate; (*auf Klavier*) touch; (*Schreibmaschine*) character; **a~en** ['anʃlaːgən] unreg vt put up; (*beschädigen*) chip; (*Akkord*) strike; (*Kosten*) estimate // vi hit (*an +akk* against); (*wirken*) have an effect; (*Glocke*) ring; (*Hund*) bark.

anschließen ['anʃliːsən] unreg vt connect up; (*Sender*) link up // vir: (sich) an etw (*akk*) ~ adjoin sth; (*zeitlich*) follow sth // vr join (*jdm/etw* sb/sth); (*beipflichten*) agree (*jdm/etw* with sb/sth); **~d** a adjacent; (*zeitlich*) subsequent // ad afterwards.

Anschluß ['anʃlus] m (*ELEK, EISENB*) connection; (*von Wasser etc*) supply; **im ~ an** (+*akk*) following; **~ finden** make friends.

anschmiegsam ['anʃmiːkzaːm] a affectionate.

anschnallen ['anʃnalən] vt buckle on // vr fasten one's seat belt.

anschneiden ['anʃnaıdən] vt unreg cut into; (*Thema*) introduce.

anschreiben ['anʃraıbən] vt unreg write (up); (*COMM*) charge up; (*benachrichtigen*) write to.

anschreien ['anʃraıən] vt unreg shout at.

Anschrift ['anʃrıft] f address.

Anschuldigung ['anʃuldıgʊŋ] f accusation.

anschwellen ['anʃvɛlən] vi unreg swell (up).

anschwemmen ['anʃvɛmən] vt wash ashore.

anschwindeln ['anʃvındəln] vt lie to.

ansehen ['anzeːən] vt unreg look at; **jdm etw ~** see sth (from sb's face); **jdn/etw als etw ~** look on sb/sth as sth; **~ für** consider; **A~** nt -s respect; (*Ruf*) reputation.

ansehnlich ['anzeːnlıç] a fine-looking; (*beträchtlich*) considerable.

ansetzen ['anzɛtsən] vt (*anfügen*) fix on (*an +akk* to); (*anlegen, an Mund etc*) put (*an +akk* to); (*festlegen*) fix; (*entwickeln*) develop; (*Fett*) put on; (*Blätter*) grow; (*zubereiten*) prepare // vi (*anfangen*) start, begin; (*Entwicklung*) set in; (*dick werden*) put on weight // vr (*Rost etc*) start to develop.

Ansicht ['anzıçt] f (*Anblick*) sight; (*Meinung*) view, opinion; **zur ~ on** approval; **meiner ~ nach** in my opinion; **Ansichtskarte** f picture postcard; **Ansichtssache** f matter of opinion.

anspannen ['anʃpanən] vt harness; (*Muskel*) strain.

Anspannung f strain.

Anspiel ['anʃpiːl] nt (*SPORT*) start; **a~en** vi (*SPORT*) start play; **auf etw** (*akk*) **a~en** refer od allude to sth; **~ung** f reference, allusion (*auf +akk* to).

Ansporn ['anʃpɔrn] m -(e)s incentive.

Ansprache ['anʃpraːxə] f address.

ansprechen ['anʃprɛçən] unreg vt speak to; (*bitten, gefallen*) appeal to; **jdn auf etw** (*akk*) (*hin*) ~ ask sb about sth // vi react (*auf +akk* to); **~d** a attractive.

anspringen ['anʃprıŋən] unreg vi (*AUT*) start // vt jump at.

Anspruch ['anʃprʊx] m (*Recht*) claim (*auf +akk* to); **hohe Ansprüche stellen/haben** demand/expect a lot; **jdn/etw in ~ nehmen** occupy sb/take up sth; **anspruchslos** a undemanding; **anspruchsvoll** a demanding.

anstacheln ['anʃtaxəln] vt spur on.

Anstalt ['anʃtalt] f -, -en institution; **~en machen, etw zu tun** prepare to do sth.

Anstand ['anʃtant] m decency.

anständig ['anʃtɛndıç] a decent; (*umg*) proper; (*groß*) considerable; **anstandslos** ad without any ado.

anstarren ['anʃtarən] vt stare at.

anstatt [an'ʃtat] präp +gen instead of // kj: ~ **etw zu tun** instead of doing sth.

Ansteck- ['anʃtek] zW: **a~en** vt pin on; (*MED*) infect; (*Pfeife*) light; (*Haus*) set fire to // vr: **ich habe mich bei ihm angesteckt** I caught it from him // vi (*fig*) be infectious; **a~end** a infectious; **~ung** f infection.

anstehen ['anʃteːən] vi unreg queue (up) (*Brit*), line up (*US*).

anstelle [an'ʃtɛlə] präp +gen in place of; **~n** ['an-] vt (*einschalten*) turn on; (*Arbeit geben*) employ; (*machen*) do // vr queue (up) (*Brit*), line up (*US*); (*umg*) act.

Anstellung f employment; (*Posten*) post, position.

Anstieg ['anʃtiːk] m -(e)s, -e climb; (*fig: von Preisen etc*) increase (*gen* in).

anstift- ['anʃtıft] zW: **~en** vt (*Unglück*) cause; **jdn zu etw ~en** put sb up to sth; **A~er** m -s, - instigator.

anstimmen ['anʃtımən] vt (*Lied*) strike up with; (*Geschrei*) set up.

Anstoß ['anʃtoːs] m impetus; (*Ärgernis*) offence; (*SPORT*) kick-off; **der erste ~** the initiative; **~ nehmen an** (+*dat*) take offence at; **a~en** unreg *vt* push; (*mit Fuß*) kick // *vi* knock, bump; (*mit der Zunge*) lisp; (*mit Gläsern*) drink (a toast) (*auf* +*akk* to).

anstößig ['anʃtøːsɪç] *a* offensive, indecent; **A~keit** *f* indecency, offensiveness.

anstreichen ['anʃtraɪçən] *vt unreg* paint.

Anstreicher *m* -s, - painter.

anstrengen ['anʃtrɛŋən] *vt* strain; (*JUR*) bring // *vr* make an effort; **angestrengt** *ad* as hard as one can; **~d** *a* tiring.

Anstrengung *f* effort.

Anstrich ['anʃtrɪç] *m* coat of paint.

Ansturm ['anʃtʊrm] *m* rush; (*MIL*) attack.

Antarktis [ant''arktɪs] *f* - Antarctic.

antasten ['antastən] *vt* touch; (*Recht*) infringe upon; (*Ehre*) question.

Anteil ['antaɪl] *m* -**s**, -**e** share (*an* +*dat* in); (*Mitgefühl*) sympathy; **~ nehmen an** (+*dat*) share in; (*sich interessieren*) take an interest in; **~nahme** *f* - sympathy.

Antenne [an'tɛnə] *f* -, -**n** aerial.

Anti- ['anti] *in zW* anti; **~alko'holiker** *m* teetotaller; **a~autori'tär** *a* anti-authoritarian; **~biotikum** [anti-bi'oːtikum] *nt* -**s**, -**ka** antibiotic.

antik [an'tiːk] *a* antique; **A~e** *f* -, -**n** (*Zeitalter*) ancient world; (*Kunstgegenstand*) antique.

Antilope [anti'loːpə] *f* -, -**n** antelope.

Antipathie [antipa'tiː] *f* antipathy.

Antiquariat [antikvari'aːt] *nt* -(e)**s**, -**e** secondhand bookshop.

Antiquitäten [antikvi'tɛːtən] *pl* antiques *pl*; **~händler** *m* antique dealer.

Antrag ['antraːk] *m* -(e)**s**, -**träge** proposal; (*PARL*) motion; (*Gesuch*) application.

antreffen ['antrɛfən] *vt unreg* meet.

antreiben ['antraɪbən] *unreg vt* drive on; (*Motor*) drive; (*anschwemmen*) wash up // *vi* be washed up.

antreten ['antreːtən] *unreg vt* (*Amt*) take up; (*Erbschaft*) come into; (*Beweis*) offer; (*Reise*) start, begin // *vi* (*MIL*) fall in; (*SPORT*) line up; **gegen jdn ~** play/fight against sb.

Antrieb ['antriːp] *m* (*lit, fig*) drive; **aus eigenem ~** of one's own accord.

antrinken ['antrɪŋkən] *vt unreg* (*Flasche, Glas*) start to drink from; **sich** (*dat*) **Mut/einen Rausch ~** give oneself Dutch courage/get drunk; **angetrunken sein** be tipsy.

Antritt ['antrɪt] *m* beginning, commencement; (*eines Amts*) taking up.

antun ['antuːn] *vt unreg*: **jdm etw ~** do sth to sb; **sich** (*dat*) **Zwang ~** force o.s.; **sich** (*dat*) **etwas ~** (try to) take one's own life.

Antwort ['antvɔrt] *f* -, -**en** answer, reply; **a~en** *vi* answer, reply.

anvertrauen ['anfertrauən] *vt*: **jdm etw ~** entrust sb with sth; **sich jdm ~** confide in sb.

anwachsen ['anvaksən] *vi unreg* grow; (*Pflanze*) take root.

Anwalt ['anvalt] *m* -(e)**s**, -**wälte**, **Anwältin** ['anvɛltɪn] *f* solicitor; lawyer; (*fig*) champion.

Anwärter ['anvɛrtər] *m* candidate.

anweisen ['anvaɪzən] *vt unreg* instruct; (*zuteilen*) assign (*jdm etw* sth to sb).

Anweisung *f* instruction; (*COMM*) remittance; (*Post~, Zahlungs~*) money order.

anwend- ['anvɛnd] *zW*: **~bar** ['anvɛnt-] *a* practicable, applicable; **~en** *vt unreg* use, employ; (*Gesetz, Regel*) apply; **A~ung** *f* use; application.

Anwesen- ['anveːzən] *zW*: **a~d** *a* present; **die ~den** those present; **~heit** *f* presence.

anwidern ['anviːdərn] *vt* disgust.

Anzahl ['antsaːl] *f* number (*an* +*dat* of); **a~en** *vt* pay on account; **~ung** *f* deposit, payment on account.

Anzeichen ['antsaɪçən] *nt* sign, indication.

Anzeige ['antsaɪgə] *f* -, -**n** (*Zeitungs~*) announcement; (*Werbung*) advertisement; (*bei Polizei*) report; **~ erstatten gegen jdn** report sb (to the police); **a~n** *vt* (*zu erkennen geben*) show; (*bekanntgeben*) announce; (*bei Polizei*) report; **~r** *m* indicator.

anziehen ['antsiːən] *unreg vt* attract; (*Kleidung*) put on; (*Mensch*) dress; (*Schraube, Seil*) pull tight; (*Knie*) draw up; (*Feuchtigkeit*) absorb // *vi* get dressed; **~d** *a* attractive.

Anziehung *f* (*Reiz*) attraction; **Anziehungskraft** *f* power of attraction; (*PHYS*) force of gravitation.

Anzug ['antsuːk] *m* suit; **im ~ sein** be approaching.

anzüglich ['antsyːklɪç] *a* personal; (*anstößig*) offensive; **A~keit** *f* offensiveness; (*Bemerkung*) personal remark.

anzünden ['antsyndən] *vt* light.

Anzünder *m* lighter.

anzweifeln ['antsvaɪfəln] *vt* doubt.

Apathie [apa'tiː] *f* apathy.

apathisch [a'paːtɪʃ] *a* apathetic.

Apfel ['apfəl] *m* -**s**, : apple; **~saft** *m* apple juice; **Apfelsine** [apfəl'ziːnə] *f* -, -**n** orange; **~wein** *m* cider.

Apostel [a'pɔstəl] *m* -**s**, - apostle.

Apostroph [apo'stroːf] *m* -**s**, -**e** apostrophe.

Apotheke [apo'teːkə] *f* -, -**n** chemist's

Apparat [apa'ra:t] *m* -(e)s, -e piece of apparatus; camera; telephone; (*RAD, TV*) set; am ~! speaking!; ~ur [-'tu:r] *f* apparatus.

Appartement [apartə'mãː] *nt* -s, -s flat.

Appell [a'pɛl] *m* -s, -e (*MIL*) muster, parade; (*fig*) appeal; a~ieren [ape'li:rən] *vi* appeal (*an* +*akk* to).

Appetit [ape'ti:t] *m* -(e)s, -e appetite; guten ~ enjoy your meal; a~lich *a* appetizing; ~losigkeit *f* lack of appetite.

Applaus [ap'laus] *m* -es, -e applause.

Aprikose [apri'ko:zə] *f* -, -n apricot.

April [a'prɪl] *m* -(s), -e April.

Aquarell [akva'rɛl] *nt* -s, -e watercolour.

Aquarium [a'kva:riʊm] *nt* aquarium.

Äquator [ɛ'kva:tor] *m* -s equator.

Arab- ['arab] *zW*: ~er(in *f*) *m* -s, - Arab; ~ien [a'ra:biən] *nt* -s Arabia; a~isch [a'ra:bɪʃ] *a* Arabian.

Arbeit ['arbait] *f* -, -en work (*no art*); (*Stelle*) job; (*Erzeugnis*) piece of work; (*wissenschaftliche*) dissertation; (*Klassen~*) test; das war eine ~ that was a hard job; a~en *vi* work // *vt* work, make; ~er(in *f*) *m* -s, - worker; (*ungelernt*) labourer; ~erschaft *f* workers *pl*, labour force; ~geber *m* -s, - employer; ~nehmer *m* -s, - employee; a~sam *a* industrious.

Arbeits- *in zW* labour; ~amt *nt* employment exchange; a~fähig *a* fit for work, able-bodied; ~gang *m* operation; ~gericht *nt* industrial tribunal; ~kräfte *pl* workers *pl*, labour; a~los *a* unemployed, out-of-work; ~losigkeit *f* unemployment; ~platz *m* job; place of work; (*Großraumbüro*) workstation; a~scheu *a* work-shy; ~tag *m* work(ing) day; a~unfähig *a* unfit for work; ~zeit *f* working hours *pl*.

Archäologe [arçɛo'lo:gə] *m* -n, -n archaeologist.

Architekt(in *f*) [arçi'tɛkt(ɪn)] *m* -en, -en architect; ~ur [-'tu:r] *f* architecture.

Archiv [ar'çi:f] *nt* -s, -e archive.

arg [ark] *a* bad, awful // *ad* awfully, very.

Argentin- [argen'ti:n] *zW*: ~ien *nt* -s Argentina, the Argentine; ~ier(in *f*) *m* -s, - Argentinian; a~isch *a* Argentinian.

Ärger ['ɛrgər] *m* -s (*Wut*) anger; (*Unannehmlichkeit*) trouble; ä~lich *a* (*zornig*) angry; (*lästig*) annoying, aggravating; ä~n *vt* annoy // *vr* get annoyed; ~nis *nt* -ses, -se annoyance.

arg- *zW*: ~listig *a* cunning, insidious; ~los *a* guileless, innocent; A~losigkeit *f* guilelessness, innocence; **Argument** [argu'mɛnt] *nt* argument; **A~wohn** *m* suspicion; ~wöhnisch *a* suspicious.

Arie ['a:riə] *f* -, -n aria.

Aristokrat [arɪsto'kra:t] *m* -en, -en aristocrat; ~ie [-'ti:] *f* aristocracy; a~isch *a* aristocratic.

Arktis ['arktɪs] *f* - Arctic.

arm [arm] *a* poor; **A~** *m* -(e)s, -e arm; (*Fluß~*) branch; **Arma'tur** *f* (*ELEK*) armature; **Arma'turenbrett** *nt* instrument panel; (*AUT*) dashboard; **A~band** *nt* bracelet; **A~banduhr** *f* (wrist) watch; **A~e(r)** *mf* poor man/woman; **die A~en** the poor; **Armee** [ar'me:] *f* -, -n army.

Ärmel ['ɛrməl] *m* -s, - sleeve; etw aus dem ~ schütteln (*fig*) produce sth just like that; ~kanal *m* English Channel.

ärmlich ['ɛrmlɪç] *a* poor.

armselig *a* wretched, miserable.

Armut ['armu:t] *f* - poverty.

Aroma [a'ro:ma] *nt* -s, **Aromen** aroma; **aromatisch** [aro'ma:tɪʃ] *a* aromatic.

arrangieren [arã'ʒi:rən] *vt* arrange // *vr* come to an arrangement.

Arrest [a'rɛst] *m* -(e)s, -e detention.

arrogant [aro'gant] *a* arrogant.

Arroganz *f* arrogance.

Arsch [arʃ] *m* -es, -̈e (*umg*) arse, bum.

Art [a:rt] *f* -, -en (*Weise*) way; (*Sorte*) kind, sort; (*BIOL*) species; eine ~ (von) Frucht a kind of fruit; Häuser aller ~ houses of all kinds; es ist nicht seine ~, das zu tun it's not like him to do that; ich mache das auf meine ~ that I do that my (own) way.

Arterie [ar'te:riə] *f* -, artery; **Arterienverkalkung** *f* arteriosclerosis.

artig ['a:rtɪç] *a* good, well-behaved.

Artikel [ar'ti:kəl] *m* -s, - article.

Artillerie [artɪlə'ri:] *f* artillery.

Arznei [arts'nai] *f* medicine; ~mittel *nt* medicine, medicament.

Arzt [a:rtst] *m* -es, -̈e, **Ärztin** ['ɛ:rtstɪn] *f* doctor.

ärztlich ['ɛ:rtstlɪç] *a* medical.

As [as] *nt* -ses, -se ace.

Asbest [as'bɛst] *m* -(e)s, -e asbestos.

Asche ['aʃə] *f* -, -n ash, cinder; **Aschenbahn** *f* cinder track; **Aschenbecher** *m* ashtray; **Aschermittwoch** *m* Ash Wednesday.

Asi- ['a:zi] *zW*: ~en *nt* -s Asia; ~at(in *f*) [azi'a:t(ɪn)] *m* -en, -en Asian; a~atisch [-'a:tɪʃ] *a* Asian.

asozial ['azotsia:l] *a* antisocial; (*Familien*) asocial.

Aspekt [as'pɛkt] *m* -(e)s, -e aspect.

Asphalt [as'falt] *m* -(e)s, -e asphalt; a~ieren [-'ti:rən] *vt* asphalt.

aß *v siehe* essen.

Assistent(in *f)* [asıs'tɛnt(ın)] *m* assistant.

Assoziation [asotsiatsi'o:n] *f* association.

Ast [ast] *m* -(e)s, ⁻e bough, branch; ~er *f* -, -n aster.

ästhetisch [ɛs'te:tıʃ] *a* aesthetic.

Asthma ['astma] *nt* -s asthma; ~tiker(in *f)* [ast'ma:tikər(ın)] *m* -s, - asthmatic.

Astro- [astro] *zW*: ~'loge *m* -n, -n astrologer; ~'lo'gie *f* astrology; ~'naut *m* -en, -en astronaut; ~'nom *m* -en, -en astronomer; ~no'mie *f* astronomy.

Asyl [a'zy:l] *nt* -s, -e asylum; *(Heim)* home; *(Obdachlosen~)* shelter.

Atelier [atəli'e:] *nt* -s, -s studio.

Atem ['a:təm] *m* -s breath; den ~ anhalten hold one's breath; außer ~ out of breath; a~beraubend *a* breathtaking; a~los *a* breathless; ~pause *f* breather; ~zug *m* breath.

Atheismus [ate'ısmʊs] *m* atheism.

Atheist *m* atheist; a~isch *a* atheistic.

Athen [a'te:n] *nt* -s Athens; A~er(in *f)* *m* -s, - Athenian; a~isch *a* Athenian.

Äther ['ɛ:tər] *m* -s, - ether.

Äthiop- [ɛti'o:p] *zW*: ~ien *nt* -s Ethiopia; ~ier(in *f)* *m* -s, - Ethiopian; ä~isch *a* Ethiopian.

Athlet [at'le:t] *m* -en, -en athlete.

Atlant- [at'lant] *zW*: ~ik *m* -s Atlantic (Ocean); a~isch *a* Atlantic.

Atlas ['atlas] *m* - *od* -ses, -se *od* At'lanten atlas.

atmen [a:tmən] *vti* breathe.

Atmosphäre [atmo'sfɛ:rə] *f* -, -n atmosphere.

atmosphärisch *a* atmospheric.

Atmung ['a:tmʊŋ] *f* respiration.

Atom [a'to:m] *nt* -s, -e atom; a~ar [ato'ma:r] *a* atomic; ~bombe *f* atom bomb; ~energie *f* atomic *od* nuclear energy; ~kraftgegner *m* opponent of nuclear power; ~kraftwerk *nt* nuclear power station; ~krieg *m* nuclear *od* atomic war; ~macht *f* nuclear *od* atomic power; ~müll *m* atomic waste; ~sperrvertrag *m* (*POL*) nuclear non-proliferation treaty; ~strom *m* (electricity generated by) nuclear power; ~versuch *m* atomic test; ~waffen *pl* atomic weapons *pl*; a~waffenfrei *a* nuclear-free; ~zeitalter *nt* atomic age.

Attentat ['atənta:t] *nt* -(e)s, -e (attempted) assassination (*auf +akk* of).

Attentäter ['atəntɛ:tər] *m* (would-be) assassin.

Attest [a'tɛst] *nt* -(e)s, -e certificate.

attraktiv [atrak'ti:f] *a* attractive.

Attrappe [a'trapə] *f* -, -n dummy.

Attribut [atri'bu:t] *nt* -(e)s, -e (*GRAM*) attribute.

ätzen ['ɛtsən] *vi* be caustic.

au [au] *interj* ouch!; ~ja! oh yes!

auch [aux] *ad* **1** (*ebenfalls*) also, too, as well; das ist — schön that's nice too *od* as well; er kommt — ich ~ he's coming — so am I, me too; ~ nicht not ... either; ich ~ nicht nor I, me neither; oder ~ or; ~ das noch! not that as well!
2 (*selbst, sogar*) even; ~ wenn das Wetter schlecht ist even if the weather is bad; ohne ~ nur zu fragen without even asking
3 (*wirklich*) really; du siehst müde aus — bin ich ~ you look tired — (so) I am; so sieht es ~ aus it looks like it too
4 (~ *immer*): wer ~ whoever; was ~ whatever; wie dem ~ sei be that as it may; wie sehr er sich ~ bemühte however much he tried.

auf [auf] ◆*präp + dat* (*wo?*) on; ~ dem Tisch on the table; ~ der Reise on the way; ~ der Post/dem Fest at the post office/party; ~ der Straße on the road; ~ dem Land/der ganzen Welt in the country/the whole world
◆*präp +akk* **1** (*wohin?*) on(to); ~ den Tisch on(to) the table; ~ die Post gehen go to the post office; ~ das Land into the country; etw ~ einen Zettel schreiben write sth on a piece of paper
2: ~ deutsch in German; ~ Lebenszeit for my/his lifetime; bis ~ ihn except for him; ~ einmal at once; ~ seinen Vorschlag (hin) at his suggestion
◆*ad* **1** (*offen*) open; das Fenster ist ~ the window is open
2 (*hinauf*) up; ~ und ab up and down; ~ und davon up and away; ~! (*los!*) come on!
3 (~ *gestanden*) up; ist er schon ~? is he up yet?
◆*kj*: ~ daß (so) that.

aufatmen ['auf'a:tmən] *vi* heave a sigh of relief.

aufbahren ['aufba:rən] *vt* lay out.

Aufbau ['aufbau] *m* (*Bauen*) building, construction; (*Struktur*) structure; (*aufgebautes Teil*) superstructure; a~en *vt* erect, build (up); (*Existenz*) make; (*gestalten*) construct; (*gründen*) found, base (*auf +dat* on).

aufbauschen ['aufbauʃən] *vt* puff out; (*fig*) exaggerate.

aufbekommen ['aufbəkɔmən] *vt* *unreg* (*öffnen*) get open; (*Hausaufgaben*) be given.

aufbessern ['aufbɛsərn] *vt* (*Gehalt*) increase.

aufbewahren ['aʊfbəvaːrən] vt keep; (Gepäck) put in the left-luggage office.

Aufbewahrung f (safe)keeping; (Gepäck~) left-luggage office (Brit), baggage check (US).

aufbieten ['aʊfbiːtən] vt unreg (Kraft) summon (up), exert; (Armee, Polizei) mobilize; (Brautpaar) publish the banns of.

aufblasen ['aʊfblaːzən] unreg vt blow up, inflate // vr (umg) become big-headed.

aufbleiben ['aʊfblaɪbən] vi unreg (Laden) remain open; (Person) stay up.

aufblicken ['aʊfblɪkən] vi (lit, fig) look up (zu lit) at, (fig) to).

aufblühen ['aʊfblyːən] vi blossom, flourish.

aufbrauchen ['aʊfbraʊxən] vt use up.

aufbrausen ['aʊfbraʊzən] vi (fig) flare up; ~d a hot-tempered.

aufbrechen ['aʊfbrɛçən] unreg vt break od prize (Brit) open // vi burst open; (gehen) start, set off.

aufbringen ['aʊfbrɪŋən] vt unreg (öffnen) open; (in Mode) bring into fashion; (beschaffen) procure; (FIN) raise; (ärgern) irritate; Verständnis für etw ~ be able to understand sth.

Aufbruch ['aʊfbrʊx] m departure.

aufbrühen ['aʊfbryːən] vt (Tee) make.

aufbürden ['aʊfbyrdən] vt burden (jdm etw sb with sth).

aufdecken ['aʊfdɛkən] vt uncover.

aufdringlich ['aʊfdrɪŋlɪç] a pushy.

aufeinander [aʊfʔaɪˈnandər] ad on top of each other; (schießen) at each other; (vertrauen) each other; ~folgen vi follow one another; ~folgend a consecutive; ~legen vt lay on top of one another; ~prallen vi hit one another.

Aufenthalt ['aʊfʔɛnthalt] m stay; (Verzögerung) delay; (EISENB: Halten) stop; (Ort) haunt; **Aufenthaltsgenehmigung** f residence permit.

auferlegen ['aʊfʔɛrleːgən] vt impose (jdm etw sth upon sb).

Auferstehung ['aʊfʔɛrʃteːʊŋ] f resurrection.

aufessen ['aʊfʔɛsən] vt unreg eat up.

auffahr- ['aʊfaːr] zW: ~en vi unreg vi (Auto) run, crash (auf +akk into); (herankommen) draw up; (hochfahren) jump up; (wütend werden) flare up; (in den Himmel) ascend // vt (Kanonen, Geschütz) bring up; ~end a hot-tempered; **A~t** f (Haus~) drive; (Autobahn~) slip road (Brit), (freeway) entrance (US); **A~unfall** m pile-up.

auffallen ['aʊfalən] vi unreg be noticeable; jdm ~ strike sb; ~d a strik-

ing.

auffällig ['aʊfɛlɪç] a conspicuous, striking.

auffangen ['aʊffaŋən] vt unreg catch; (Funkspruch) intercept; (Preise) peg.

auffassen ['aʊffasən] vt understand, comprehend; (auslegen) see, view.

Auffassung f (Meinung) opinion; (Auslegung) view, concept; (also **Auffassungsgabe**) grasp.

auffindbar ['aʊffɪntbaːr] a to be found.

auffordern ['aʊffɔrdərn] vt (befehlen) call upon, order; (bitten) ask.

Aufforderung f (Befehl) order; (Einladung) invitation.

auffrischen ['aʊffrɪʃən] vt freshen up; (Kenntnisse) brush up; (Erinnerungen) reawaken // vi (Wind) freshen.

aufführen ['aʊffyːrən] vt (THEAT) perform; (in einem Verzeichnis) list, specify // vr (sich benehmen) behave.

Aufführung f (THEAT) performance; (Liste) specification.

Aufgabe ['aʊfgaːbə] f, -, -n task; (SCH) exercise; (Haus~) homework; (Verzicht) giving up; (von Gepäck) registration; (von Post) posting; (von Inserat) insertion.

Aufgang ['aʊfgaŋ] m ascent; (Sonnen~) rise; (Treppe) staircase.

aufgeben ['aʊfgeːbən] unreg vt (verzichten) give up; (Paket) send, post; (Gepäck) register; (Bestellung) give; (Inserat) insert; (Rätsel, Problem) set // vi give up.

Aufgebot ['aʊfgəboːt] nt supply; (Ehe~) banns pl.

aufgedunsen ['aʊfgədʊnzən] a swollen, puffed up.

aufgehen ['aʊfgeːən] vi unreg (Sonne, Teig) rise; (sich öffnen) open; (klarwerden) become clear (jdm to sb); (MATH) come out exactly; (sich widmen) be absorbed (in +dat in); **in Rauch/Flammen** ~ go up in smoke/flames.

aufgelegt ['aʊfgəleːkt] a: **gut/ schlecht** ~ **sein** be in a good/bad mood; **zu etw** ~ **sein** be in the mood for sth.

aufgeregt ['aʊfgəreːkt] a excited.

aufgeschlossen ['aʊfgəʃlɔsən] a open, open-minded.

aufgeweckt ['aʊfgəvɛkt] a bright, intelligent.

aufgießen ['aʊfgiːsən] vt unreg (Wasser) pour over; (Tee) infuse.

aufgreifen ['aʊfgraɪfən] vt unreg (Thema) take up; (Verdächtige) pick up, seize.

aufgrund [aʊfˈgrʊnt] präp +gen on the basis of; (wegen) because of.

aufhaben ['aʊfhaːbən] vt unreg have on; (Arbeit) have to do.

aufhalsen ['aʊfhalzən] vt (umg) jdm

etw ~ saddle od lumber sb with sth.

aufhalten ['aufhaltən] *unreg vt* (*Person*) detain; (*Entwicklung*) check; (*Tür, Hand*) hold open; (*Augen*) keep open // *vr* (*wohnen*) live; (*bleiben*) stay; **sich mit etw ~** waste time over.

aufhängen ['aufhɛŋən] *unreg vt* (*Wäsche*) hang up; (*Menschen*) hang // *vr* hang o.s.

Aufhänger *m* **-s, -** (*am Mantel*) hook; (*fig*) peg.

aufheben ['aufheːbən] *unreg vt* (*hochheben*) raise, lift; (*Sitzung*) wind up; (*Urteil*) annul; (*Gesetz*) repeal, abolish; (*aufbewahren*) keep; **bei jdm gut aufgehoben sein** be well looked after at sb's // *vr* cancel itself out; **viel A~(s) machen** make a fuss (*von* about).

aufheitern ['aufhaitərn] *vtr* (*Himmel, Miene*) brighten; (*Mensch*) cheer up.

aufhellen ['aufhɛlən] *vtr* clear up; (*Farbe, Haare*) lighten.

aufhetzen ['aufhɛtsən] *vt* stir up (*gegen* against).

aufholen ['aufhoːlən] *vt* make up // *vi* catch up.

aufhorchen ['aufhɔrçən] *vi* prick up one's ears.

aufhören ['aufhøːrən] *vi* stop; **~ etw zu tun** stop doing sth.

aufklappen ['aufklapən] *vt* open.

aufklären ['aufklɛːrən] *vt* (*Geheimnis etc*) clear up; (*Person*) enlighten; (*sexuell*) tell the facts of life to; (*MIL*) reconnoitre // *vr* clear up.

Aufklärung *f* (*von Geheimnis*) clearing up; (*Unterrichtung, Zeitalter*) enlightenment; (*sexuell*) sex education; (*MIL, AVIAT*) reconnaissance.

aufkleben ['aufkleːbən] *vt* stick on.

Aufkleber *m* **-s, -** sticker.

aufknöpfen ['aufknœpfən] *vt* unbutton.

aufkommen ['aufkɔmən] *vi unreg* (*Wind*) come up; (*Zweifel, Gefühl*) arise; (*Mode*) start; **für jdn/etw ~** be liable *od* responsible for sb/sth.

aufladen ['auflaːdən] *vt unreg* load.

Auflage ['auflaːgə] *f* edition; (*Zeitung*) circulation; (*Bedingung*) condition; **jdm etw zur ~ machen** make sth a condition for sb.

auflassen ['auflasən] *vt unreg* (*offen*) leave open; (*aufgesetzt*) leave on.

auflauern ['auflauərn] *vi*: **jdm ~** lie in wait for sb.

Auflauf ['auflauf] *m* (*KOCH*) pudding; (*Menschen~*) crowd.

auflegen ['aufleːgən] *vt* put on; (*Telefon*) hang up; (*TYP*) print.

auflehnen ['aufleːnən] *vt* lean on // *vr* rebel (*gegen* against).

Auflehnung *f* rebellion.

auflesen ['aufleːzən] *vt unreg* pick up.

aufleuchten ['auflɔyçtən] *vi* light up.

auflockern ['auflɔkərn] *vt* loosen; (*fig: Eintönigkeit etc*) liven up.

auflösen ['aufløːzən] *vtr* dissolve; (*Haare etc*) loosen; (*Mißverständnis*) sort out; (**in Tränen**) **aufgelöst sein** be in tears.

Auflösung *f* dissolving; (*fig*) solution.

aufmachen ['aufmaxən] *vt* open; (*Kleidung*) undo; (*zurechtmachen*) do up // *vr* set out.

Aufmachung *f* (*Kleidung*) outfit, getup; (*Gestaltung*) format.

aufmerksam ['aufmɛrkzaːm] *a* attentive; **jdn auf etw** (*akk*) **~ machen** point sth out to sb; **A~keit** *f* attention, attentiveness.

aufmuntern ['aufmuntərn] *vt* (*ermutigen*) encourage; (*erheitern*) cheer up.

Aufnahme ['aufnaːmə] *f* **-, -n** reception; (*Beginn*) beginning; (*in Verein etc*) admission; (*in Liste etc*) inclusion; (*Notieren*) taking down; (*PHOT*) shot; (*auf Tonband etc*) recording; **a~fähig** *a* receptive; **~prüfung** *f* entrance test.

aufnehmen ['aufneːmən] *vt unreg* receive; (*hochheben*) pick up; (*beginnen*) take up; (*in Verein etc*) admit; (*in Liste etc*) include; (*fassen*) hold; (*notieren*) take down; (*fotografieren*) photograph; (*auf Tonband, Platte*) record; (*FIN: leihen*) take out; **es mit jdm ~ können** be able to compete with sb.

aufopfern ['aufʔɔpfərn] *vtr* sacrifice; **~d** *a* selfless.

aufpassen ['aufpasən] *vi* (*aufmerksam sein*) pay attention; **auf jdn/etw ~** look after *od* watch sb/sth; **aufgepaßt!** look out!

Aufprall ['aufpral] *m* **-s, -e** impact; **a~en** *vi* hit, strike.

Aufpreis ['aufprais] *m* extra charge.

aufpumpen ['aufpumpən] *vt* pump up.

aufraffen ['aufrafən] *vr* rouse o.s.

aufräumen ['aufrɔymən] *vti* (*Dinge*) clear away; (*Zimmer*) tidy up.

aufrecht ['aufrɛçt] *a* (*lit, fig*) upright; **~erhalten** *vt unreg* maintain.

aufreg- ['aufreːg] *zW*: **~en** *vt* excite // *vr* get excited; **~end** *a* exciting; **A~ung** *f* excitement.

aufreibend ['aufraibənt] *a* strenuous.

aufreißen ['aufraisən] *vt unreg* (*Umschlag*) tear open; (*Augen*) open wide; (*Tür*) throw open; (*Straße*) take up.

aufreizen ['aufraitsən] *vt* incite, stir up; **~d** *a* exciting, stimulating.

aufrichten ['aufrɪçtən] *vt* put up, erect; (*moralisch*) console // *vr* rise; (*moralisch*) take heart (*an* +*dat* from).

aufrichtig ['aʊfrɪçtɪç] a sincere, honest; **A~keit** f sincerity.

aufrücken ['aʊfrʏkən] vi move up; (beruflich) be promoted.

Aufruf ['aʊfruːf] m summons; (zur Hilfe) call; (des Namens) calling out; **a~en** vt unreg (auffordern) call upon (zu for); (Namen) call out.

Aufruhr ['aʊfruːr] m -(e)s, -e uprising, revolt.

aufrührerisch ['aʊfryːrərɪʃ] a rebellious.

aufrunden ['aʊfrʊndən] vt (Summe) round up.

Aufrüstung ['aʊfrʏstʊŋ] f rearmament.

aufrütteln ['aʊfrʏtəln] vt (lit, fig) shake up.

aufs [aʊfs] = auf das.

aufsagen ['aʊfzaːgən] vt (Gedicht) recite.

aufsammeln ['aʊfzaməln] vt gather up.

aufsässig ['aʊfzɛsɪç] a rebellious.

Aufsatz ['aʊfzats] m (Geschriebenes) essay; (auf Schrank etc) top.

aufsaugen ['aʊfzaʊgən] vt unreg soak up.

aufschauen ['aʊfʃaʊən] vi look up.

aufscheuchen ['aʊfʃɔʏçən] vt scare od frighten away.

aufschieben ['aʊfʃiːbən] vt unreg push open; (verzögern) put off, postpone.

Aufschlag ['aʊfʃlaːk] m (Ärmel~) cuff; (Jacken~) lapel; (Hosen~) turn-up; (Aufprall) impact; (Preis~) surcharge; (Tennis) service; **a~en** [-gən] unreg vt (öffnen) open; (verwunden) cut; (hochschlagen) turn up; (aufbauen: Zelt, Lager) pitch, erect; (Wohnsitz) take up // vi (aufprallen) hit; (teurer werden) go up; (Tennis) serve.

aufschließen ['aʊfʃliːsən] unreg vt open up, unlock // vi (aufrücken) close up.

Aufschluß ['aʊfʃlʊs] m information; **a~reich** a informative, illuminating.

aufschnappen ['aʊfʃnapən] vt (umg) pick up // vi fly open.

aufschneiden ['aʊfʃnaɪdən] unreg vt (Geschwür) cut open; (Brot) cut up; (MED) lance // vi brag.

Aufschneider m -s, - boaster, braggart.

Aufschnitt ['aʊfʃnɪt] m (slices of) cold meat.

aufschrecken ['aʊfʃrɛkən] vt startle // vi unreg start up.

Aufschrei ['aʊfʃraɪ] m cry; **a~en** vi unreg cry out.

aufschreiben ['aʊfʃraɪbən] vt unreg write down.

Aufschrift ['aʊfʃrɪft] f (Inschrift) inscription; (auf Etikett) label.

Aufschub ['aʊfʃuːp] m -(e)s, -schübe delay, postponement.

Aufschwung ['aʊfʃvʊŋ] n (Elan) boost; (wirtschaftlich) upturn, boom; (SPORT) circle.

aufsehen ['aʊfzeːən] vi unreg (lit, fig) look up (zu lit at, (fig to); **A~** nt -s sensation, stir; **~erregend** a sensational.

Aufseher(in f) m -s, - guard; (im Betrieb) supervisor; (Museums~) attendant; (Park~) keeper.

aufsetzen ['aʊfzɛtsən] vt put on; (Flugzeug) put down; (Dokument) draw up // vr sit upright // vi (Flugzeug) touch down.

Aufsicht ['aʊfzɪçt] f supervision; die ~ haben be in charge.

aufsitzen ['aʊfzɪtsən] vi unreg (aufrecht hinsitzen) sit up; (aufs Pferd, Motorrad) mount, get on; (Schiff) run aground; **jdm ~** (umg) be taken in by sb.

aufsparen ['aʊfʃpaːrən] vt save (up).

aufsperren ['aʊfʃpɛrən] vt unlock; (Mund) open wide.

aufspielen ['aʊfʃpiːlən] vr show off.

aufspießen ['aʊfʃpiːsən] vt spear.

aufspringen ['aʊfʃprɪŋən] vi unreg jump (auf +akk onto); (hochspringen) jump up; (sich öffnen) spring open; (Hände, Lippen) become chapped.

aufspüren ['aʊfʃpyːrən] vt track down, trace.

aufstacheln ['aʊfʃtaxəln] vt incite.

Aufstand ['aʊfʃtant] m insurrection, rebellion.

aufständisch ['aʊfʃtɛndɪʃ] a rebellious, mutinous.

aufstecken ['aʊfʃtɛkən] vt stick on, pin up; (umg) give up.

aufstehen ['aʊfʃteːən] vi unreg get up; (Tür) be open.

aufsteigen ['aʊfʃtaɪgən] vi unreg (auf etw) get onto; (hochsteigen) climb; (Rauch) rise.

aufstellen ['aʊfʃtɛlən] vt (aufrecht stellen) put up; (aufreihen) line up; (nominieren) put up; (formulieren: Programm etc) draw up; (leisten: Rekord) set up.

Aufstellung f (SPORT) line-up; (Liste) list.

Aufstieg ['aʊfʃtiːk] m -(e)s, -e (auf Berg) ascent; (Fortschritt) rise; (beruflich, SPORT) promotion.

aufstoßen ['aʊfʃtoːsən] unreg vt push open // vi belch.

aufstützen ['aʊfʃtʏtsən] vr lean (auf +akk on) // vt (Körperteil) prop, lean; (Person) prop up.

aufsuchen ['aʊfzuːxən] vt (besuchen) visit; (konsultieren) consult.

Auftakt ['aʊftakt] m (MUS) upbeat;

(fig) prelude.

auftanken ['aʊftaŋkən] *vi* get petrol *(Brit) od* gas *(US)* // *vt* refuel.

auftauchen ['aʊftaʊxən] *vi* appear; *(aus Wasser etc)* emerge; *(U-Boot)* surface; *(Zweifel)* arise.

auftauen ['aʊftaʊən] *vti* thaw; *(fig)* relax.

aufteilen ['aʊftaɪlən] *vt* divide up; *(Raum)* partition.

Aufteilung *f* division; partition.

Auftrag ['aʊftraːk] *m* -(e)s, -träge order; *(Anweisung)* commission; *(Aufgabe)* mission; **im ~ von** on behalf of; **a~en** [-gən] *vt unreg (Essen)* serve; *(Farbe)* put on; *(Kleidung)* wear out; **jdm etw a~en** tell sb sth; **dick a~en** *(fig)* exaggerate; **~geber** *m* -s, - *(COMM)* purchaser, customer.

auftreiben ['aʊftraɪbən] *vt unreg (umg: beschaffen)* raise.

auftreten ['aʊftreːtən] *unreg vt* kick open // *vi* appear; *(mit Füßen)* tread; *(sich verhalten)* behave; **A~** *nt* -s *(Vorkommen)* appearance; *(Benehmen)* behaviour.

Auftrieb ['aʊftriːp] *m (PHYS)* buoyancy, lift; *(fig)* impetus.

Auftritt ['aʊftrɪt] *m (des Schauspielers)* entrance; *(lit, fig: Szene)* scene.

auftun ['aʊftuːn] *unreg vt* open // *vr* open up.

aufwachen ['aʊfvaxən] *vi* wake up.

aufwachsen ['aʊfvaksən] *vi unreg* grow up.

Aufwand ['aʊfvant] *m* -(e)s expenditure; *(Kosten auch)* expense; *(Luxus)* show.

aufwärmen ['aʊfvɛrmən] *vt* warm up; *(alte Geschichten)* rake up.

aufwärts ['aʊfvɛrts] *ad* upwards; **A~entwicklung** *f* upward trend.

aufwecken ['aʊfvɛkən] *vt* wake up, waken up.

aufweisen ['aʊfvaɪzən] *vt unreg* show.

aufwenden ['aʊfvɛndən] *vt unreg* expend; *(Geld)* spend; *(Sorgfalt)* devote.

aufwendig *a* costly.

aufwerfen ['aʊfvɛrfən] *vt unreg (Fenster etc)* throw open; *(Probleme)* throw up, raise.

aufwerten ['aʊfveːrtən] *vt (FIN)* revalue; *(fig)* raise in value.

aufwiegeln ['aʊfviːgəln] *vt* stir up, incite.

aufwiegen ['aʊfviːgən] *vt unreg* make up for.

Aufwind ['aʊfvɪnt] *m* up-current.

aufwirbeln ['aʊfvɪrbəln] *vt* whirl up; **Staub ~** *(fig)* create a stir.

aufwischen ['aʊfvɪʃən] *vt* wipe up.

aufzählen ['aʊftsɛːlən] *vt* list.

aufzeichnen ['aʊftsaɪçnən] *vt* sketch; *(schriftlich)* jot down; *(auf Band)* record.

Aufzeichnung *f (schriftlich)* note; *(Tonband~)* recording; *(Film~)* record.

aufzeigen ['aʊftsaɪgən] *vt* show, demonstrate.

aufziehen ['aʊftsiːən] *vt unreg (hochziehen)* raise, draw up; *(öffnen)* pull open; *(Uhr)* wind; *(umg: necken)* tease; *(großziehen: Kinder)* raise, bring up; *(Tiere)* rear.

Aufzug ['aʊftsuːk] *m (Fahrstuhl)* lift, elevator; *(Aufmarsch)* procession, parade; *(Kleidung)* get-up; *(THEAT)* act.

aufzwingen ['aʊftsvɪŋən] *vt unreg:* **jdm etw ~** force sth upon sb.

Aug- [aʊg] *zW:* **~apfel** *m* eyeball; *(fig)* apple of one's eye; **~e** *nt* -s, -n eye; *(Fett~)* globule of fat; **unter vier ~en** in private; **~enblick** *m* moment; **im ~enblick** at the moment; **a~enblicklich** *a (sofort)* instantaneous; *(gegenwärtig)* present; **~enbraue** *f* eyebrow; **~enweide** *f* sight for sore eyes; **~enzeuge** *m* eye witness.

August [aʊˈgʊst] *m* -(e)s *od* -, -e August.

Auktion [aʊktsiˈoːn] *f* auction.

Aula ['aʊla] *f* -, **Aulen** *od* -s assembly hall.

aus [aʊs] ◆ *präp + dat* **1** *(räumlich)* out of; *(von ... her)* from; **er ist ~ Berlin** he's from Berlin; **~ dem Fenster** out of the window

2 *(gemacht/hergestellt ~)* made of; **ein Herz ~ Stein** a heart of stone

3 *(auf Ursache deutend)* out of; ~ **Mitleid** out of sympathy; ~ **Erfahrung** from experience; ~ **Spaß** for fun

4: ~ **ihr wird nie etwas** she'll never get anywhere

◆ *ad* **1** *(zu Ende)* finished, over; ~ **und vorbei** over and done with

2 *(~geschaltet, ~gezogen)* out; *(Aufschrift an Geräten)* off; **Licht ~!** lights out!

3 *(in Verbindung mit von)*: **von Rom** ~ from Rome; **vom Fenster** ~ out of the window; **von sich** ~ *(selbständig)* of one's own accord; **von ihm** ~ as far as he's concerned.

ausarbeiten ['aʊsarbaɪtən] *vt* work out.

ausarten ['aʊsartən] *vi* degenerate; *(Kind)* become overexcited.

ausatmen ['aʊsaːtmən] *vi* breathe out.

ausbaden ['aʊsbaːdən] *vt:* **etw ~ müssen** *(umg)* carry the can for sth.

Ausbau ['aʊsbaʊ] *m* extension, expansion; removal; **a~en** *vt* extend, expand; *(herausnehmen)* take out, remove; **a~fähig** *a (fig)* worth developing.

ausbessern ['ausbɛsərn] *vt* mend, repair.

ausbeulen ['ausbɔylən] *vt* beat out.

Ausbeute ['ausbɔytə] *f* yield; (*Fische*) catch; **a~n** *vt* exploit; (*MIN*) work.

ausbild- ['ausbild] *zW:* **~en** *vt* educate; (*Lehrling, Soldat*) instruct, train; (*Fähigkeiten*) develop; (*Geschmack*) cultivate; **A~er** *m* **-s, -** instructor; **A~ung** *f* education; training, instruction; development, cultivation.

ausbleiben ['ausblaibən] *vi unreg* (*Personen*) stay away, not come; (*Ereignisse*) fail to happen, not happen.

Ausblick ['ausblik] *m* (*lit, fig*) prospect, outlook, view.

ausbrechen ['ausbrɛçən] *unreg vi* break out; in Tränen/Gelächter ~ burst into tears/out laughing // *vt* break off.

ausbreiten ['ausbraitən] *vt* spread (out); (*Arme*) stretch out // *vr* spread; (*über Thema*) expand, enlarge (*über +akk* on).

ausbrennen ['ausbrɛnən] *unreg vt* scorch; (*Wunde*) cauterize // *vi* burn out.

Ausbruch ['ausbrux] *m* outbreak; (*von Vulkan*) eruption; (*Gefühls~*) outburst; (*von Gefangenen*) escape.

ausbrüten ['ausbry:tən] *vt* (*lit, fig*) hatch.

Ausdauer ['ausdauər] *f* perseverance, stamina; **ausdauernd** *a* persevering.

ausdehnen ['ausde:nən] *vtr* (*räumlich*) expand; (*Gummi*) stretch; (*Nebel*) extend; (*zeitlich*) stretch; (*fig: Macht*) extend.

ausdenken ['ausdɛŋkən] *vt unreg:* sich (*dat*) etw ~ think sth up.

Ausdruck ['ausdruk] *m* expression, phrase; (*Kundgabe, Gesichts~*) expression; (*COMPUT*) print-out, hard copy; **a~en** *vt* (*COMPUT*) print out.

ausdrücken ['ausdrykən] *vt* (*auch vr:* formulieren, zeigen) express; (*Zigarette*) put out; (*Zitrone*) squeeze.

ausdrücklich *a* express, explicit.

ausdrucks- *zW:* **~los** *a* expressionless, blank; **~voll** *a* expressive; **A~weise** *f* mode of expression.

auseinander [aus'ai'nandər] *ad* (*getrennt*) apart; ~ schreiben write as separate words; **~bringen** *vt unreg* separate; **~fallen** *vi unreg* fall apart; **~gehen** *vi unreg* (*Menschen*) separate; (*Meinungen*) differ; (*Gegenstand*) fall apart; (*umg: dick werden*) put on weight; **~halten** *vt unreg* tell apart; **~nehmen** *vt unreg* take to pieces, dismantle; **~setzen** *vt* (*erklären*) set forth, explain // *vr* (*sich

verständigen*) come to terms, settle; (*sich befassen*) concern o.s.; **A~setzung** *f* argument.

auserlesen ['aus'ɛrle:zən] *a* select, choice.

Ausfahrt ['ausfa:rt] *f* (*des Zuges etc*) leaving, departure; (*Autobahn~, Garagen~*) exit, way out; (*Spazierfahrt*) drive, excursion.

Ausfall ['ausfal] *m* loss; (*Nichtstattfinden*) cancellation; (*MIL*) sortie; (*Fechten*) lunge; (*radioaktiv*) fallout; **a~en** *vi unreg* (*Zähne, Haare*) fall od come out; (*nicht stattfinden*) be cancelled; (*wegbleiben*) be omitted; (*Person*) drop out; (*Lohn*) be stopped; (*nicht funktionieren*) break down; (*Resultat haben*) turn out; **a~end** *a* impertinent; **~straße** *f* arterial road.

Ausfertigung ['ausfɛrtigun] *f* drawing up; making out; (*Exemplar*) copy.

ausfindig machen ['ausfindiç maxən] *vt* discover.

ausflippen ['ausflipən] *vi* (*umg*) freak out.

Ausflucht ['ausfluxt] *f* **-, -flüchte** excuse.

Ausflug ['ausflu:k] *m* excursion, outing.

Ausflügler ['ausfly:klər] *m* **-s, -** tripper.

Ausfluß ['ausflus] *m* outlet; (*MED*) discharge.

ausfragen ['ausfra:gən] *vt* interrogate, question.

ausfressen ['ausfrɛsən] *vt unreg* eat up; (*aushöhlen*) corrode; (*umg: anstellen*) be up to.

Ausfuhr ['ausfu:r] *f* **-, -en** export, exportation; in *zW* export.

ausführ- ['ausfy:r] *zW:* **~en** *vt* (*verwirklichen*) carry out; (*Person*) take out; (*Hund*) take for a walk; (*COMM*) export; (*erklären*) give details of; **~lich** *a* detailed // *ad* in detail; **A~lichkeit** *f* detail; **A~ung** *f* execution, performance; (*Durchführung*) completion; (*Herstellungsart*) version; (*Erklärung*) explanation.

ausfüllen ['ausfylən] *vt* fill up; (*Fragebogen etc*) fill in; (*Beruf*) be fulfilling for.

Ausgabe ['ausga:bə] *f* (*Geld*) expenditure, outlay; (*Aushändigung*) giving out; (*Gepäck~*) left-luggage office; (*Buch*) edition; (*Nummer*) issue; (*COMPUT*) output.

Ausgang ['ausgaŋ] *m* way out, exit; (*Ende*) end; (*Ausgangspunkt*) starting point; (*Ergebnis*) result; (*Ausgehtag*) free time, time off; kein ~ no exit.

Ausgangs- *zW:* **~basis** *f*, **~punkt** *m* starting point; **~sperre** *f* curfew.

ausgeben ['ausgeːbən] *unreg vt Geld* spend; *(austeilen)* issue, distribute // *vr:* **sich für etw/jdn** ~ pass o.s. off as sth/sb.

ausgedient ['ausgədiːnt] *a (Soldat)* discharged; *(verbraucht)* no longer in use; ~ **haben** have done good service.

ausgefallen ['ausgəfalən] *a (ungewöhnlich)* exceptional.

ausgeglichen ['ausgəglıçən] *a* (well-balanced; **A~heit** *f* balance; *(von Mensch)* even-temperedness.

Ausgeh- ['ausgeː] *zW:* **~en** *vi unreg* go out; *(zu Ende gehen)* come to an end; *(Benzin)* run out; *(Haare, Zähne)* fall *od* come out; *(Feuer, Ofen, Licht)* go out; *(Strom)* go off; *(Resultat haben)* turn out; **mir ging das Benzin aus** I ran out of petrol *(Brit) od* gas *(US)*; **auf etw** *(akk)* **a~en** aim at sth; **von etw a~en** *(wegführen)* lead away from sth; *(herrühren)* come from sth; *(zugrunde legen)* proceed from sth; **wir können davon a~en, daß** ... we can take as our starting point that ...; **leer a~en** get nothing; **schlecht a~en** turn out badly; **~verbot** *nt* curfew.

ausgelassen ['ausgəlasən] *a* boisterous, high-spirited; **A~heit** *f* boisterousness, high spirits *pl*, exuberance.

ausgelastet ['ausgəlastət] *a* fully occupied.

ausgelernt ['ausgəlɛrnt] *a* trained, qualified.

ausgemacht ['ausgəmaxt] *a (umg)* settled; *(Dummkopf etc)* out-and-out, downright; **es war eine ~e Sache, daß** ... it was a foregone conclusion that ...

ausgenommen ['ausgənomən] *präp* +*gen od dat, kj* except; **Anwesende sind ~** present company excepted.

ausgeprägt ['ausgəprɛːkt] *a* a prominent.

ausgerechnet ['ausgərɛçnət] *ad* just, precisely; ~ **du/heute** you of all people/today of all days.

ausgeschlossen ['ausgəʃlɔsən] *a (unmöglich)* impossible, out of the question.

ausgeschnitten ['ausgəʃnıtən] *a (Kleid)* low-necked.

ausgesprochen ['ausgəʃprɔxən] *a (Faulheit, Lüge etc)* out-and-out; *(unverkennbar)* marked // *ad* decidedly.

ausgezeichnet ['ausgətsaıçnət] *a* excellent.

ausgiebig ['ausgiːbıç] *a (Gebrauch)* thorough, good; *(Essen)* generous, lavish; ~ **schlafen** have a good sleep.

Ausgleich ['ausglaıç] *m* **-(e)s, -e** balance; *(Vermittlung)* reconciliation; *(SPORT)* equalization; **zum** ~ (+*gen*)

in order to offset; **a~en** *unreg vt* balance (out); reconcile; *(Höhe)* even up // *vi (SPORT)* equalize.

ausgraben ['ausgraːbən] *vt unreg* dig up; *(Leichen)* exhume; *(fig)* unearth.

Ausgrabung *f* excavation; *(Ausgraben auch)* digging up.

Ausguß ['ausgus] *m (Spüle)* sink; *(Abfluß)* outlet; *(Tülle)* spout.

aushalten ['aushaltən] *unreg vt* bear, stand; *(Geliebte)* keep // *vi* hold out; **das ist nicht zum A~** that is unbearable.

aushandeln ['aushandəln] *vt* negotiate.

aushändigen ['aushɛndıgən] *vt:* **jdm etw ~** hand sth over to sb.

Aushang ['aushaŋ] *m* notice.

aushängen ['aushɛŋən] *unreg vt (Meldung)* put up; *(Fenster)* take off its hinges // *vi* be displayed // *vr* hang out.

ausharren ['ausharən] *vi* hold out.

ausheben ['aushɛːbən] *vt unreg (Erde)* lift out; *(Grube)* hollow out; *(Tür)* take off its hinges; *(Diebesnest)* clear out; *(MIL)* enlist.

aushelfen ['aushɛlfən] *vi unreg:* **jdm ~** help sb out.

Aushilfe ['aushılfə] *f* help, assistance; *(Person)* (temporary) worker.

Aushilfskraft *f* temporary worker.

aushilfsweise *ad* temporarily, as a stopgap.

ausholen ['aushoːlən] *vi* swing one's arm back; *(zur Ohrfeige)* raise one's hand; *(beim Gehen)* take long strides; **weit ~** *(fig)* be expansive.

aushorchen ['aushɔrçən] *vt* sound out, pump.

aushungern ['aushuŋərn] *vt* starve out.

auskennen ['auskɛnən] *vr unreg* know thoroughly; *(an einem Ort)* know one's way about; *(in Fragen etc)* be knowledgeable.

Ausklang ['ausklaŋ] *m* end.

auskleiden ['ausklaıdən] *vr* undress // *vt (Wand)* line.

ausklingen ['ausklıŋən] *vi unreg (Ton, Lied)* die away; *(Fest)* peter out.

ausklopfen ['ausklɔpfən] *vt (Teppich)* beat; *(Pfeife)* knock out.

auskochen ['auskɔxən] *vt* boil; *(MED)* sterilize; **ausgekocht** *(fig)* out-and-out.

auskommen ['auskɔmən] *vi unreg:* **mit jdm ~** get on with sb; **mit etw ~** get by with sth; **A~** *nt* **-s: sein A~ haben** get by.

auskosten ['auskɔstən] *vt* enjoy to the full.

auskundschaften ['auskuntʃaftən] *vt* spy out; *(Gebiet)* reconnoitre.

Auskunft ['auskunft] *f* **-, -künfte** information; *(nähere)* details *pl*, particulars *pl*; (*Stelle*) information office; (*TEL*) inquiries.

auslachen ['auslaxən] *vt* laugh at, mock.

ausladen ['ausla:dən] *vt unreg* unload; (*umg*: *Gäste*) cancel an invitation to.

Auslage ['ausla:gə] *f* shop window (display); **~n** *pl* outlay, expenditure.

Ausland ['auslant] *nt* foreign countries *pl*; **im/ins** ~ abroad.

Ausländer(in *f*) ['auslɛndər(ın)] *m* **-s, -** foreigner.

ausländisch *a* foreign.

Auslands- *zW*: **~gespräch** *nt* international call; **~korrespondent(in** *f*) *m* foreign correspondent; **~reise** *f* trip abroad.

auslassen ['auslasən] *unreg vt* leave out; (*Wort etc auch*) omit; (*Fett*) melt; (*Kleidungsstück*) let out; (*Wut, Ärger*) vent (*an* +*dat on*) // *vr*: **sich über etw** (*akk*) ~ speak one's mind about sth.

Auslassung *f* omission.

Auslauf ['auslauf] *m* (*für Tiere*) run; (*Ausfluß*) outflow, outlet; **a~en** *vi unreg* run out; (*Behälter*) leak; (*NAUT*) put out (to sea); (*langsam aufhören*) run down.

Ausläufer ['auslɔyfər] *m* (*von Gebirge*) spur; (*Pflanze*) runner; (*MET*: *von Hoch*) ridge; (*von Tief*) trough.

ausleeren ['ausle:rən] *vt* empty.

auslegen ['ausle:gən] *vt* (*Waren*) lay out; (*Köder*) put down; (*Geld*) lend; (*bedecken*) cover; (*Text etc*) interpret.

Auslegung *f* interpretation.

Ausleihe ['auslaıə] *f* **-, -n** issuing; (*Stelle*) issue desk; **a~n** *vt unreg* (*verleihen*) lend; **sich** (*dat*) **etw a~en** borrow sth.

Auslese ['ausle:zə] *f* **-, -n** selection; (*Elite*) elite; (*Wein*) choice wine; **a~n** *vt unreg* select; (*umg*: *zu Ende lesen*) finish.

ausliefern ['ausli:fərn] *vt* deliver (up), hand over; (*COMM*) deliver; **jdm/etw ausgeliefert sein** be at the mercy of sb/sth.

auslöschen ['auslœʃən] *vt* extinguish; (*fig*) wipe out, obliterate.

auslosen ['auslo:zən] *vt* draw lots for.

auslösen ['auslø:zən] *vt* (*Explosion, Schuß*) set off; (*hervorrufen*) cause, produce; (*Gefangene*) ransom; (*Pfand*) redeem.

Auslöser *m* **-s, -** (*PHOT*) release.

ausmachen ['ausmaxən] *vt* (*Licht, Radio*) turn off; (*Feuer*) put out; (*entdecken*) make out; (*vereinbaren*) agree; (*beilegen*) settle; (*Anteil darstellen, betragen*) represent; (*bedeuten*) matter; **macht es Ihnen etwas aus, wenn ...?** would you mind if ...?

ausmalen ['ausma:lən] *vt* paint; (*fig*) describe; **sich** (*dat*) **etw** ~ imagine sth.

Ausmaß ['ausma:s] *nt* dimension; (*fig auch*) scale.

ausmerzen ['ausmɛrtsən] *vt* eliminate.

ausmessen ['ausmɛsən] *vt unreg* measure.

Ausnahme ['ausna:mə] *f* **-, -n** exception; **~fall** *m* exceptional case; **~zustand** *m* state of emergency.

ausnahmslos *ad* without exception.

ausnahmsweise *ad* by way of exception, for once.

ausnehmen ['ausne:mən] *unreg vt* take out, remove; (*Tier*) gut; (*Nest*) rob; (*umg*: *Geld abnehmen*) clean out; (*ausschließen*) make an exception of // *vr* look, appear; **~d** *a* exceptional.

ausnützen ['ausnytsən] *vt* (*Zeit, Gelegenheit*) use, turn to good account; (*Einfluß*) use; (*Mensch, Gutmütigkeit*) exploit.

auspacken ['auspakən] *vt* unpack.

auspfeifen ['auspfaıfən] *vt unreg* hiss/boo at.

ausplaudern ['ausplaudərn] *vt* (*Geheimnis*) blab.

ausprobieren ['ausprobi:rən] *vt* try (out).

Auspuff ['auspuf] *m* **-(e)s, -e** (*TECH*) exhaust; **~rohr** *nt* exhaust (pipe); **~topf** *m* (*AUT*) silencer.

ausradieren ['ausradi:rən] *vt* erase, rub out; (*fig*) annihilate.

ausrangieren ['ausrãʒi:rən] *vt* (*umg*) chuck out.

ausrauben ['ausraubən] *vt* rob.

ausräumen ['ausrɔymən] *vt* (*Dinge*) clear away; (*Schrank, Zimmer*) empty; (*Bedenken*) put aside.

ausrechnen ['ausrɛçnən] *vt* calculate, reckon.

Ausrede ['ausre:də] *f* excuse; **a~n** *vi* have one's say // *vt*: **jdm etw a~n** talk sb out of sth.

ausreichen ['ausraıçən] *vi* suffice, be enough; **~d** *a* sufficient, adequate; (*SCH*) adequate.

Ausreise ['ausraızə] *f* departure; **bei der** ~ when leaving the country; **~erlaubnis** *f* exit visa; **a~n** *vi* leave the country.

ausreißen ['ausraısən] *unreg vt* tear od pull out // *vi* (*Riß bekommen*) tear; (*umg*) make off, scram.

ausrenken ['ausrɛŋkən] *vt* dislocate.

ausrichten ['ausrıçtən] *vt* (*Botschaft*) deliver; (*Gruß*) pass on; (*Hochzeit etc*) arrange; (*erreichen*) get anywhere (*bei* with); (*in gerade Linie bringen*) get in a straight line; (*angleichen*) bring into line; (*TYP*) justify; **ich werde es ihm** ~ I'll tell him.

ausrotten ['aʊsrɔtən] *vt* stamp out, exterminate.

ausrücken ['aʊsrʏkən] *vi* (*MIL*) move off; (*Feuerwehr, Polizei*) be called out; (*umg: weglaufen*) run away.

Ausruf ['aʊsru:f] *m* (*Schrei*) cry, exclamation; (*Verkünden*) proclamation; **a~en** *vt unreg* cry out, exclaim; call out; **Ausrufezeichen** *nt* exclamation mark.

ausruhen ['aʊsru:ən] *vtr* rest.

ausrüsten ['aʊsrʏstən] *vt* equip, fit out.

Ausrüstung *f* equipment.

ausrutschen ['aʊsrʊtʃən] *vi* slip.

Aussage ['aʊsza:gə] *f* -, **-n** (*JUR*) statement; **a~n** *vt* say, state // *vi* (*JUR*) give evidence.

ausschalten ['aʊsʃaltən] *vt* switch off; (*fig*) eliminate.

Ausschank ['aʊsʃaŋk] *m* -(e)s, **-schänke** dispensing, giving out; (*COMM*) selling; (*Theke*) bar.

Ausschau ['aʊsʃaʊ] *f*: ~ **halten** look out, watch (*nach* for); **a~en** *vi* look out (*nach* for), be on the look-out.

ausscheiden ['aʊsʃaɪdən] *unreg vt* separate; (*MED*) give off, secrete // *vi* leave (*aus etw* sth); (*SPORT*) be eliminated *od* knocked out.

Ausscheidung *f* separation; secretion; (*aus Amt*) retiral; elimination.

ausschimpfen ['aʊsʃɪmpfən] *vt* scold, tell off.

ausschlafen ['aʊsʃla:fən] *unreg vir* have a long lie (in) // *vt* sleep off; **ich bin nicht ausgeschlafen** I didn't have *od* get enough sleep.

Ausschlag ['aʊsʃla:k] *m* (*MED*) rash; (*Pendel~*) swing; (*Nadel*) deflection; **den ~ geben** (*fig*) tip the balance; **a~en** [-gən] *unreg vt* knock out; (*auskleiden*) deck out; (*verweigern*) decline // *vi* (*Pferd*) kick out; (*BOT*) sprout; **a~gebend** *a* decisive.

ausschließen ['aʊsʃli:sən] *vt unreg* shut *od* lock out; (*fig*) exclude.

ausschließlich *a, ad* exclusive(ly) // *präp* +*gen* excluding, exclusive of.

Ausschluß ['aʊsʃlus] *m* exclusion.

ausschmücken ['aʊsʃmʏkən] *vt* decorate; (*fig*) embellish.

ausschneiden ['aʊsʃnaɪdən] *vt unreg* cut out; (*Büsche*) trim.

Ausschnitt ['aʊsʃnɪt] *m* (*Teil*) section; (*von Kleid*) neckline; (*Zeitungs~*) cutting; (*aus Film etc*) excerpt.

ausschreiben ['aʊsʃraɪbən] *vt unreg* (*ganz schreiben*) write out (in full); (*ausstellen*) write (out); (*Stelle, Wettbewerb etc*) announce, advertise.

Ausschreitung ['aʊsʃraɪtʊŋ] *f* excess.

Ausschuß ['aʊsʃus] *m* committee, board; (*Abfall*) waste, scraps *pl*; (*COMM: auch ~ware f*) reject.

ausschütten ['aʊsʃʏtən] *vt* pour out;

(*Eimer*) empty; (*Geld*) pay // *vr* shake (with laughter).

ausschweifend ['aʊsʃvaɪfənt] *a* (*Leben*) dissipated, debauched; (*Phantasie*) extravagant.

Ausschweifung *f* excess.

aussehen ['aʊsze:ən] *vi unreg* look; **es sieht nach Regen aus** it looks like rain; **es sieht schlecht aus** things look bad; **A~** *nt* **-s** appearance.

außen ['aʊsən] *ad* outside; (*nach* ~) outwards; ~ **ist es rot** it's red (on the) outside.

Außen- *zW*: **~bordmotor** *m* outboard motor; **~dienst** *m*: **im ~dienst sein** work outside the office; **~handel** *m* foreign trade; **~minister** *m* foreign minister; **~ministerium** *nt* foreign office; **~politik** *f* foreign policy; **~seite** *f* outside; **~seiter** *m* **-s**, - outsider; **~welt** *f* outside world.

außer ['aʊsər] *präp* +*dat* (*räumlich*) out of; (*abgesehen von*) except; ~ **Gefahr** out of danger; ~ **Zweifel** beyond any doubt; ~ **Betrieb** out of order; ~ **sich** (*dat*) sein/geraten be beside o.s.; ~ **Dienst** retired; ~ **Landes** abroad // *kj* (*ausgenommen*) except; ~ **wenn** unless; ~ **daß** except; **~dem** *kj* besides, in addition.

äußere(r, s) ['ɔʏsərə(r,z)] *a* outer, external.

außer- *zW*: **~ehelich** *a* extramarital; **~gewöhnlich** *a* unusual; **~halb** *präp* +*gen*, *ad* outside.

äußerlich *a, ad* external.

äußern *vt* utter, express; (*zeigen*) show // *vr* give one's opinion; (*sich zeigen*) show itself.

außer- *zW*: **~ordentlich** *a* extraordinary; **~planmäßig** *a* unscheduled; **~'stande** *ad* not in a position, unable.

äußerst ['ɔʏsərst] *ad* extremely, most; **~e(r, s)** *a* utmost; (*räumlich*) farthest; (*Termin*) last possible; (*Preis*) highest.

aussetzen ['aʊszɛtsən] *vt* (*Kind, Tier*) abandon; (*Boote*) lower; (*Belohnung*) offer; (*Urteil, Verfahren*) postpone; **jdm/etw ausgesetzt sein** be exposed to sb/sth; **an jdm/etw etwas ~** find fault with sb/sth // *vi* (*aufhören*) stop; (*Pause machen*) drop out.

Aussicht ['aʊszɪçt] *f* view; (*in Zukunft*) prospect; **etw in ~ haben** have sth in view.

Aussichts- *zW*: **a~los** *a* hopeless; **~punkt** *m* viewpoint; **a~reich** *a* promising; **~turm** *m* observation tower.

aussöhnen ['aʊszø:nən] *vt* reconcile // *vr* reconcile o.s., become reconciled.

Aussöhnung *f* reconciliation.

aussondern ['aʊszɔndərn] *vt* separate, select.

aussortieren ['aʊszɔrti:rən] *vt* sort out.

ausspannen ['ausʃpanən] vt spread od stretch out; (Pferd) unharness; (umg: Mädchen) steal (jdm from sb) // vi relax.

aussperren ['ausʃpɛrən] vt lock out.

Aussperrung f lock-out.

ausspielen ['ausʃpiːlən] vt (Karte) lead; (Geldprämie) offer as a prize; jdn gegen jdn ~ play sb off against sb // vi (KARTEN) lead; ausgespielt haben be finished.

Aussprache ['ausʃpraːxə] f pronunciation; (Unterredung) (frank) discussion.

aussprechen ['ausʃprɛçən] unreg vt pronounce; (äußern) say, express // vr (sich äußern) speak (über +akk about); (sich anvertrauen) unburden o.s.; (diskutieren) discuss // vi (zu Ende sprechen) finish speaking.

Ausspruch ['ausʃprux] m saying, remark.

ausspülen ['ausʃpyːlən] vt wash out; (Mund) rinse.

Ausstand ['ausʃtant] m strike; in den ~ treten go on strike.

ausstatten ['ausʃtatən] vt (Zimmer etc) furnish; jdn mit etw ~ equip sb od kit sb out with sth.

Ausstattung f (Ausstatten) provision; (Kleidung) outfit; (Aussteuer) dowry; (Aufmachung) make-up; (Einrichtung) furnishing.

ausstechen ['ausʃtɛçən] vt unreg (Augen, Rasen, Graben) dig out; (Kekse) cut out; (übertreffen) outshine.

ausstehen ['ausʃteːən] unreg vt stand, endure // vi (noch nicht dasein) be outstanding.

aussteigen ['ausʃtaigən] vi unreg get out, alight.

ausstellen ['ausʃtɛlən] vt exhibit, display; (umg: ausschalten) switch off; (Rechnung etc) make out; (Paß, Zeugnis) issue.

Ausstellung f exhibition; (FIN) drawing up; (einer Rechnung) making out; (eines Passes etc) issuing.

aussterben ['ausʃtɛrbən] vi unreg die out.

Aussteuer ['ausʃtɔyər] f dowry.

Ausstieg ['ausʃtiːk] m -(e)s, -e exit.

ausstopfen ['ausʃtɔpfən] vt stuff.

ausstoßen ['ausʃtoːsən] vt unreg (Luft, Rauch) give off, emit; (aus Verein etc) expel, exclude; (Auge) poke out.

ausstrahlen ['ausʃtraːlən] vti radiate; (RAD) broadcast.

Ausstrahlung f radiation; (fig) charisma.

ausstrecken ['ausʃtrɛkən] vtr stretch out.

ausstreichen ['ausʃtraiçən] vt unreg cross out; (glätten) smooth out.

ausströmen ['ausʃtrøːmən] vi (Gas) pour out, escape // vt give off; (fig) radiate.

aussuchen ['auszuːxən] vt select, pick out.

Austausch ['austauʃ] m exchange; a~bar a exchangeable; a~en vt exchange, swop; ~motor m reconditioned engine.

austeilen ['austailən] vt distribute, give out.

Auster ['austər] f -, -n oyster.

austoben ['austoːbən] vr (Kind) run wild; (Erwachsene) sow one's wild oats.

austragen ['austraːgən] vt unreg (Post) deliver; (Streit etc) decide; (Wettkämpfe) hold.

Austral- [aus'traːl] zW: ~ien nt -s Australia; ~ier(in f) m -s, - Australian; a~isch a Australian.

austreiben ['austraibən] vt unreg drive out, expel; (Geister) exorcize.

austreten ['austreːtən] unreg vi (zur Toilette) be excused; aus etw ~ leave sth // vt (Feuer) tread out, trample; (Schuhe) wear out; (Treppe) wear down.

austrinken ['austrɪŋkən] unreg vt (Glas) drain; (Getränke) drink up // vi finish one's drink, drink up.

Austritt ['austrɪt] m emission; (aus Verein, Partei etc) retirement, withdrawal.

austrocknen ['austrɔknən] vti dry up.

ausüben ['aus?yːbən] vt (Beruf) practise, carry out; (Funktion) perform; (Einfluß) exert; (Reiz, Wirkung) exercise, have (auf jdn on sb).

Ausverkauf ['ausfɛrkauf] m sale; a~en vt sell out; (Geschäft) sell up; a~t a (Karten, Artikel) sold out; (THEAT: Haus) full.

Auswahl ['ausvaːl] f selection, choice (an +dat of).

auswählen ['ausvɛːlən] vt select, choose.

Auswander- ['ausvandər] zW: ~er m emigrant; a~n vi emigrate; ~ung f emigration.

auswärtig ['ausvɛrtɪç] a (nicht am/ vom Ort) out-of-town; (ausländisch) foreign.

auswärts ['ausvɛrts] ad outside; (nach außen) outwards; ~ essen eat out; A~spiel nt away game.

auswechseln ['ausvɛksəln] vt change, substitute.

Ausweg ['ausveːk] m way out; a~los a hopeless.

ausweichen ['ausvaiçən] vi unreg: jdm/etw ~ (lit) move aside od make way for sb/sth; (fig) side-step sb/sth; ~d a evasive.

ausweinen ['aʊsvaɪnən] *vr* have a (good) cry.

Ausweis ['aʊsvaɪs] *m* **-es, -e** identity card, passport; (*Mitglieds~, Bibliotheks~* etc) card; **a~en** [-zən] *unreg vt* expel, banish // *vr* prove one's identity; **~papiere** *pl* identity papers *pl*; **~ung** *f* expulsion.

ausweiten ['aʊsvaɪtən] *vt* stretch.

auswendig ['aʊsvɛndɪç] *ad* by heart; **~ lernen** *vt* learn by heart.

auswert- ['aʊsvɛrt] *zW:* **~en** *vt* evaluate; **A~ung** *f* evaluation, analysis; (*Nutzung*) utilization.

auswirk- ['aʊsvɪrk] *zW:* **~en** *vr* have an effect; **A~ung** *f* effect.

auswischen ['aʊsvɪʃən] *vt* wipe out; **jdm eins** ~ (*umg*) put one over on sb.

Auswuchs ['aʊsvuːks] *m* (out)growth; (*fig*) product.

auswuchten ['aʊsvʊxtən] *vt* (*AUT*) balance.

auszahlen ['aʊstsaːlən] *vt* (*Lohn, Summe*) pay out; (*Arbeiter*) pay off; (*Miterbe*) buy out // *vr* (*sich lohnen*) pay.

auszählen ['aʊstsɛːlən] *vt* (*Stimmen*) count; (*BOXEN*) count out.

auszeichnen ['aʊstsaɪçnən] *vt* honour; (*MIL*) decorate; (*COMM*) price // *vr* distinguish o.s.

Auszeichnung *f* distinction; (*COMM*) pricing; (*Ehrung*) awarding of decoration; (*Ehre*) honour; (*Orden*) decoration; **mit** ~ with distinction.

ausziehen ['aʊstsiːən] *unreg vt* (*Kleidung*) take off; (*Haare, Zähne, Tisch* etc) pull out; (*nachmalen*) trace // *vr* undress // *vi* (*aufbrechen*) leave; (*aus Wohnung*) move out.

Auszug ['aʊstsuːk] *m* (*aus Wohnung*) removal; (*aus Buch* etc) extract; (*Konto~*) statement; (*Ausmarsch*) departure.

Auto ['aʊto] *nt* **-s, -s** (motor-) car; ~ **fahren** drive; **~bahn** *f* motorway; **~bahndreieck** *nt* motorway junction; **~bahnkreuz** *nt* motorway intersection; **~fähre** *f* car ferry; **~fahrer(in** *f)* *m* motorist, driver; **~fahrt** *f* drive; **autogen** [-'geːn] *a* autogenous; **~'gramm** *nt* autograph; **Auto'mat** *m* **-en, -en** machine; **auto'matisch** *a* automatic; **autonom** [-'noːm] *a* autonomous.

Autor ['aʊtɔr] *m* **-s, -en**, **Autorin** [aʊ'toːrɪn] *f* author.

Auto- *zW:* **~radio** *nt* car radio; **~reifen** *m* car tyre; **~rennen** *nt* motor racing.

autoritär [aʊtori'tɛːr] *a* authoritarian.

Autorität *f* authority.

Auto- *zW:* **~stopp** *m*: per ~stopp **fahren** hitch-hike; **~unfall** *m* car *od* motor accident; **~verleih** *m* car hire

(*Brit*) *od* rental (*US*); **~wäsche** *f* car wash.

Axt [akst] *f* **-, ¨e** axe.

B

B, b [beː] *nt* B, b.

Baby ['beːbi] *nt* **-s, -s** baby; **~ausstattung** *f* layette; **~sitter** ['beːbizɪtər] *m* **-s, -** baby-sitter.

Bach [bax] *m* **-(e)s, ¨e** stream, brook.

Back- *zW:* **~bord** *nt* **-(e)s, -e** (*NAUT*) port; **~e** *f* **-, -n** cheek; **b~en** *vti unreg* bake; **~enbart** *m* sideboards *pl*; **~enzahn** *m* molar.

Bäcker ['bɛkər] *m* **-s, -** baker; **~ei** [-'raɪ] *f* bakery; (**~laden**) baker's (shop).

Back- *zW:* **~obst** *nt* dried fruit; **~ofen** *m* oven; **~pflaume** *f* prune; **~pulver** *nt* baking powder; **~stein** *m* brick.

Bad [baːt] *nt* **-(e)s, ¨er** bath; (*Schwimmen*) bathe; (*Ort*) spa.

Bade- ['baːdə] *zW:* **~anstalt** *f* (swimming) baths *pl*; **~anzug** *m* bathing suit; **~hose** *f* bathing *od* swimming trunks *pl*; **~kappe** *f* bathing cap; **~mantel** *m* bath(ing) robe; **~meister** *m* baths attendant; **~mütze** *f* bathing cap; **b~n** *vi* bathe, have a bath // *vt* bath; **~ort** *m* spa; **~tuch** *nt* bath towel; **~wanne** *f* bath (tub); **~zimmer** *nt* bathroom.

Bagatelle [baga'tɛlə] *f* **-, -n** trifle.

Bagger ['bagər] *m* **-s, -** excavator; (*NAUT*) dredger; **b~n** *vti* excavate; (*NAUT*) dredge.

Bahn [baːn] *f* **-, -en** railway, railroad (*US*); (*Weg*) road, way; (*Spur*) lane; (*Renn~*) track; (*ASTRON*) orbit; (*Stoff~*) length; **b~brechend** *a* pioneering; **~damm** *m* railway embankment; **b~en** *vt*: sich/jdm einen Weg **b~en** clear a way/a way for sb; **~fahrt** *f* railway journey; **~hof** *m* station; auf dem **~hof** at the station; **~hofsvorsteher** *m* station-master; **~linie** *f* (railway) line; **~steig** *m* platform; **~steigkarte** *f* platform ticket; **~strecke** *f* (railway) line; **~übergang** *m* level crossing, grade crossing (*US*); **~wärter** *m* signalman.

Bahre ['baːrə] *f* **-, -n** stretcher.

Bajonett [bajo'nɛt] *nt* **-(e)s, -e** bayonet.

Bakterien [bak'teːriən] *pl* bacteria *pl*.

Balance [ba'lãːsə] *f* **-, -n** balance, equilibrium.

balan'cieren *vti* balance.

bald [balt] *ad* (*zeitlich*) soon; (*beinahe*) almost; **~ig** ['baldɪç] *a* early, speedy; **~möglichst** *ad* as soon as possible.

Baldrian ['baldriːn] *m* -s, -e valerian.
Balkan ['balkaːn] *m*: der ~ the Balkans *pl.*
Balken ['balkən] *m* -s, - beam; (*Trag~*) girder; (*Stütz~*) prop.
Balkon [bal'kôː] *m* -s, -s *od* -e balcony; (*THEAT*) (dress) circle.
Ball [bal] *m* -(e)s, ̈-s ball; (*Tanz*) dance, ball.
Ballade [ba'laːdə] *f* -, -n ballad.
Ballast ['balast] *m* -(e)s, -e ballast; (*fig*) weight, burden.
Ballen ['balən] *m* -s, - bale; (*ANAT*) ball; **b~** *vt* (*formen*) make into a ball; (*Faust*) clench // *vr* build up; (*Menschen*) gather.
Ballett [ba'lɛt] *nt* -(e)s, -e ballet.
Ballkleid *nt* evening dress.
Ballon [ba'lôː] *m* -s, -s *od* -e balloon.
Ballspiel *nt* ball game.
Bambus ['bambus] *m* -ses, -se bamboo; **~rohr** *nt* bamboo cane.
banal [ba'naːl] *a* banal.
Banane [ba'naːnə] *f* -, -n banana.
band *etc v siehe* **binden.**
Band [bant] *m* -(e)s, ̈-e (*Buch~*) volume // *nt* -(e)s, ̈-er (*Stoff~*) ribbon, tape; (*Fließ~*) production line; (*Faß~*) hoop; (*Ton~*) tape; (*ANAT*) ligament; etw auf ~ aufnehmen tape sth; am laufenden ~ (*umg*) non-stop // *nt* -(e)s, -e (*Freundschafts~ etc*) bond // [bɛnt] *f* -, -s band, group.
Bandage [ban'daːʒə] *f* -, -n bandage.
banda'gieren *vt* bandage.
Bande ['bandə] *f* -, -n band; (*Straßen~*) gang.
bändigen ['bɛndɪgən] *vt* (*Tier*) tame; (*Trieb, Leidenschaft*) control, restrain.
Bandit [ban'diːt] *m* -en, -en bandit.
Band- *zW*: **~maß** *nt* tape measure; **~scheibe** *f* (*ANAT*) disc; **~wurm** *m* tapeworm.
bange ['baŋə] *a* scared; (*besorgt*) anxious; jdm wird es ~ sb is becoming scared; jdm ~ machen scare sb; ~n *vi*: um jdn/etw ~n be anxious *od* worried about sb/sth.
Banjo ['banjo, 'bɛndʒo] *nt* -s, -s banjo.
Bank [baŋk] *f* -, ̈-e (*Sitz~*) bench; (*Sand~ etc*) (sand)bank *od* -bar // *f* -, -en (*Geld~*) bank; **~anweisung** *f* banker's order; **~beamte(r)** *m* bank clerk.
Bankett [baŋ'kɛt] *nt* -(e)s, -e (*Essen*) banquet; (*Straßenrand*) verge (*Brit*), shoulder (*US*).
Bankier [baŋki'eː] *m* -s, -s banker.
Bank- *zW*: **~konto** *m* bank account; **~note** *f* banknote; **~raub** *m* bank robbery.
Bankrott [baŋ'krɔt] *m* -(e)s, -e bankruptcy; ~ machen go bankrupt; **b~** *a*

bankrupt.

Bann [ban] *m* -(e)s, -e (*HIST*) ban; (*Kirchen~*) excommunication; (*fig*: *Zauber*) spell; **b~en** *vt* (*Geister*) exorcise; (*Gefahr*) avert; (*bezaubern*) enchant; (*HIST*) banish; **~er** *nt* -s, - banner, flag.
bar [baːr] *a* (*unbedeckt*) bare; (*frei von*) lacking (*gen* in); (*offenkundig*) utter, sheer; ~e(s) Geld cash; etw (in) ~ bezahlen pay sth (in) cash; etw für ~e Münze nehmen (*fig*) take sth at its face value; **B~** *f* -, -s bar.
Bär [bɛːr] *m* -en, -en bear.
Baracke [ba'rakə] *f* -, -n hut, barracks.
barbarisch [bar'baːrɪʃ] *a* barbaric, barbarous.
Bar- *zW*: **b~fuß** *a* barefoot; **~geld** *nt* cash, ready money; **b~geldlos** *a* non-cash; **~hocker** *m* bar stool; **~kauf** *m* cash purchase; **~keeper** ['baːrkiːpər] *m* -s, - barman, bartender.
barmherzig [barm'hɛrtsɪç] *a* merciful, compassionate; **B~keit** *f* mercy, compassion.
Barometer [baro'meːtər] *nt* -s, - barometer.
Baron [ba'roːn] *m* -s, -e baron; **~esse** [baro'nɛsə] *f* -, -n, **~in** *f* baroness.
Barren ['barən] *m* -s, - parallel bars *pl*; (*Gold~*) ingot.
Barriere [bari'eːrə] *f* -, -n barrier.
Barrikade [bari'kaːdə] *f* -, -n barricade.
Barsch [barʃ] *m* -(e)s, -e perch; **b~** *a* brusque, gruff.
Bar- *zW*: **~schaft** *f* ready money; **~scheck** *m* open *od* uncrossed cheque (*Brit*), open check (*US*).
Bart [baːrt] *m* -(e)s, ̈-e beard; (*Schlüssel~*) bit.
bärtig ['bɛːrtɪç] *a* bearded.
Barzahlung *f* cash payment.
Base ['baːzə] *f* -, -n (*CHEM*) base; (*Kusine*) cousin.
Basel ['baːzəl] *nt* Basle.
BASIC ['beːsɪk] (*COMPUT*) BASIC.
basieren [ba'ziːrən] *vt* base // *vi* be based.
Basis ['baːzɪs] *f* -, **Basen** basis.
Baß [bas] *m* **Basses, Bässe** bass; **~stimme** *f* bass voice.
Bassin [ba'sɛ̃] *nt* -s, -s pool.
Bassist [ba'sɪst] *m* bass.
Bast [bast] *m* -(e)s, -e raffia.
basteln *vt* make // *vi* do handicrafts.
bat *etc v siehe* **bitten.**
Bataillon [batal'joːn] *nt* -s, -e battalion.
Batist [ba'tɪst] *m* -(e)s, -e batiste.
Batterie [batə'riː] *f* battery.
Bau [bau] *m* -(e)s (*Bauen*) building, construction; (*Aufbau*) structure; (*Körper~*) frame; (*Baustelle*) build-

ing site; *pl* ~e (*Tier*~) hole, burrow; (*MIN*) working(s); *pl* ~ten (*Gebäude*) building; **sich im ~ befinden** be under construction; ~arbeiter *m* building worker.

Bauch [baux] *m* -(e)s, Bäuche belly; (*ANAT auch*) stomach, abdomen; ~fell *nt* peritoneum; b~ig *a* bulging; ~redner *m* ventriloquist; ~tanz *m* belly dance; belly dancing; ~schmerzen *pl*, ~weh *nt* stomachache.

bauen ['bauən] *vti* build; (*TECH*) construct; **auf jdn/etw ~** depend *od* count upon sb/sth.

Bauer ['bauər] *m* -n *od* -s, -n farmer; (*Schach*) pawn // *nt od m* -s, - (*Vogel*~) cage.

Bäuerin ['bɔyərɪn] *f* farmer; (*Frau des Bauers*) farmer's wife.

bäuerlich *a* rustic.

Bauern- *zW:* ~fänge'rei *f* deception; ~haus *nt* farmhouse; ~hof *m* farm(yard).

Bau- *zW:* b~fällig *a* dilapidated; ~fälligkeit *f* dilapidation; ~gelände *f* building site; ~genehmigung *f* building permit; ~herr *m* purchaser; ~kasten *m* box of bricks; ~kosten *pl* construction costs *pl*; ~land *nt* building land; b~lich *a* structural.

Baum [baum] *m* -(e)s, Bäume tree.

baumeln ['bauməln] *vi* dangle.

bäumen ['bɔymən] *vr* rear (up).

Baum- *zW:* ~schule *f* nursery; ~stamm *m* tree trunk; ~stumpf *m* tree stump; ~wolle *f* cotton.

Bau- *zW:* ~plan *m* architect's plan; ~platz *m* building site; ~sparkasse *f* building society; ~stein *m* building stone, freestone; ~stelle *f* building site; ~teil *nt* prefabricated part (of building); ~unternehmer *m* contractor, builder; ~weise *f* (method of) construction; ~werk *nt* building; ~zaun *m* hoarding.

Bayer(in *f*) ['baiər(in)] *m* Bavarian.

Bayern ['baiərn] *nt* Bavaria.

bayrisch ['bairiʃ] *a* Bavarian.

Bazillus [ba'tsilus] *m* -, Bazillen bacillus.

beabsichtigen [bə''apziçtigən] *vt* intend.

beachten [bə''axtən] *vt* take note of; (*Vorschrift*) obey; (*Vorfahrt*) observe.

beachtlich *a* considerable.

Beachtung *f* notice, attention, observation.

Beamte(r) [bə''amtə(r)] *m* -n, -n, **Beamtin** *f* official, civil servant; (*Bank*~ *etc*) employee.

beängstigend [bə''ɛŋstɪgənt] *a* alarming.

beanspruchen [bə''anʃpruxən] *vt*

claim; (*Zeit, Platz*) take up, occupy; (*Mensch*) take up sb's time.

beanstanden [bə''anʃtandən] *vt* complain about, object to.

Beanstandung *f* complaint.

beantragen [bə''antra:gən] *vt* apply for, ask for.

beantworten [bə''antvɔrtən] *vt* answer.

Beantwortung *f* reply (*gen* to).

bearbeiten [bə''arbaitən] *vt* work; (*Material*) process; (*Thema*) deal with; (*Land*) cultivate; (*CHEM*) treat; (*Buch*) revise; (*umg: beeinflussen wollen*) work on.

Bearbeitung *f* processing; treatment; cultivation; revision.

Beatmung [bə''a:tmuŋ] *f* respiration.

beaufsichtigen [bə''aufziçtigən] *vt* supervise.

Beaufsichtigung *f* supervision.

beauftragen [bə''auftra:gən] *vt* instruct; **jdn mit etw ~** entrust sb with sth.

bebauen [bə'bauən] *vt* build on; (*AGR*) cultivate.

beben ['be:bən] *vi* tremble, shake; **B~** *nt* -s, - earthquake.

Becher ['bɛçər] *m* -s, - mug; (*ohne Henkel*) tumbler.

Becken ['bɛkən] *nt* -s, - basin; (*MUS*) cymbal; (*ANAT*) pelvis.

bedacht [bə'daxt] *a* thoughtful, careful; **auf etw** (*akk*) **~ sein** be concerned about sth.

bedächtig [bə'dɛçtiç] *a* (*umsichtig*) thoughtful, reflective; (*langsam*) slow, deliberate.

bedanken [bə'daŋkən] *vr* say thank you (*bei jdm* to sb).

Bedarf [bə'darf] *m* -(e)s need, requirement; (*COMM*) demand; supply; **je nach ~** according to demand; **bei ~** if necessary; **an etw** (*dat*) **haben** be in need of sth.

Bedarfs- *zW:* ~artikel *m* requisite; ~fall *m* case of need; ~haltestelle *f* request stop.

bedauerlich [bə'dauərliç] *a* regrettable.

bedauern [bə'dauərn] *vt* be sorry for; (*bemitleiden*) pity; **B~** *nt* -s regret; **bedauernswert** *a* (*Zustände*) regrettable; (*Mensch*) pitiable, unfortunate.

bedecken [bə'dɛkən] *vt* cover.

bedeckt *a* covered; (*Himmel*) overcast.

bedenken [bə'dɛŋkən] *vt unreg* think (over), consider; **B~** *nt* -s, - (*Überlegen*) consideration; (*Zweifel*) doubt; (*Skrupel*) scruple.

bedenklich *a* doubtful; (*bedrohlich*) dangerous, risky.

bedeuten [bə'dɔytən] *vt* mean; signify; (*wichtig sein*) be of importance; ~d *a* important; (*beträchtlich*) considerable.

Bedeutung *f* meaning; significance; (*Wichtigkeit*) importance; **bedeutungslos** *a* insignificant, unimportant; **bedeutungsvoll** *a* momentous, significant.

bedienen [bə'di:nən] *vt* serve; (*Maschine*) work, operate // *vr* (*beim Essen*) help o.s.; (*gebrauchen*) make use (*gen* of).

Bedienung *f* service; (*Kellnerin*) waitress; (*Verkäuferin*) shop assistant; (*Zuschlag*) service (charge).

Bedingung *f* condition; (*Voraussetzung*) stipulation; **bedingungslos** *a* unconditional.

bedrängen [bə'drɛŋən] *vt* pester, harass.

bedrohen [bə'dro:ən] *vt* threaten.

bedrohlich *a* ominous, threatening.

Bedrohung *f* threat, menace.

bedrücken [bədrʏkən] *vt* oppress, trouble.

bedürf- [bə'dʏrf] *zW:* **~en** *vi unreg* +*gen* need, require; **B~nis** *nt* **-ses, -se** need; **B~nisanstalt** *f* public convenience, comfort station (*US*); **~tig** *a* in need (*gen* of), poor, needy.

beeilen [bə'ailən] *vr* hurry.

beeindrucken [bə'aindrukən] *vt* impress, make an impression on.

beeinflussen [bə'ainflusən] *vt* influence.

beeinträchtigen [bə'aintrɛçtigən] *vt* affect adversely; (*Freiheit*) infringe upon.

beend(ig)en [bə'ɛnd(ig)ən] *vt* end, finish, terminate.

beengen [bə'ɛŋən] *vt* cramp; (*fig*) hamper, oppress.

beerben [bə'ɛrbən] *vt* inherit from.

beerdigen [bə'e:rdigən] *vt* bury.

Beerdigung *f* funeral, burial; **Beerdigungsunternehmer** *m* undertaker.

Beere ['be:rə] *f* **-, -n** berry; (*Trauben~*) grape.

Beet [be:t] *nt* **-(e)s, -e** bed.

befähigen [bə'fɛ:igən] *vt* enable.

befähigt *a* (*begabt*) talented; (*fähig*) capable (*für* of).

Befähigung *f* capability; (*Begabung*) talent, aptitude.

befahrbar [bə'fa:rba:r] *a* passable; (*NAUT*) navigable.

befahren [bə'fa:rən] *vt unreg* use, drive over; (*NAUT*) navigate // *a* used.

befallen [bə'falən] *vt unreg* come over.

befangen [bə'faŋən] *a* (*schüchtern*) shy, self-conscious; (*voreingenommen*) biased; **B~heit** *f* shyness; bias.

befassen [bə'fasən] *vr* concern o.s.

Befehl [bə'fe:l] *m* **-(e)s, -e** command, order; **b~en** *unreg vt* order; **jdm etw b~en** order sb to do sth // *vi* give orders; **Befehlshaber** *m* **-s, -** commanding officer; **Befehlsverweigerung** *f* insubordination.

befestigen [bə'fɛstigən] *vt* fasten (*an* +*dat* to); (*stärken*) strengthen; (*MIL*) fortify.

Befestigung *f* fastening; strengthening; (*MIL*) fortification.

befeuchten [bə'fɔʏçtən] *vt* damp(en), moisten.

befinden [bə'findən] *unreg vr* be; (*sich fühlen*) feel // *vt*: **jdn/etw für** *od* **als etw ~** deem sb/sth to be sth // *vi* decide (*über* +*akk* on), adjudicate; **B~** *nt* **-s** health, condition; (*Meinung*) view, opinion.

befolgen [bə'fɔlgən] *vt* comply with, follow.

befördern [bə'fœrdərn] *vt* (*senden*) transport, send; (*beruflich*) promote.

Beförderung *f* transport, conveyance; promotion.

befragen [bə'fra:gən] *vt* question.

befreien [bə'fraiən] *vt* set free; (*erlassen*) exempt.

Befreier *m* **-s, -** liberator.

Befreiung *f* liberation, release; (*Erlassen*) exemption.

befremden [bə'frɛmdən] *vt* surprise, disturb; **B~** *nt* **-s** surprise, astonishment.

befreunden [bə'frɔʏndən] *vr* make friends; (*mit Idee etc*) acquaint o.s.

befreundet *a* friendly.

befriedigen [bə'fri:digən] *vt* satisfy; **~d** *a* satisfactory.

Befriedigung *f* satisfaction, gratification.

befristet [bə'fristət] *a* limited.

befruchten [bə'fruxtən] *vt* fertilize; (*fig*) stimulate.

Befruchtung *f:* **künstliche ~** artificial insemination.

Befugnis [bə'fu:knis] *f* **-, -se** authorization, powers *pl*.

befugt *a* authorized, entitled.

Befund [bə'funt] *m* **-(e)s, -e** findings *pl*; (*MED*) diagnosis.

befürchten [bə'fʏrçtən] *vt* fear.

Befürchtung *f* fear, apprehension.

befürwort- [bə'fy:rvɔrt] *zW:* **~en** *vt* support, speak in favour of; **B~er** *m* **-s, -** supporter, advocate.

begabt [bə'ga:pt] *a* gifted.

Begabung [bə'ga:bʊŋ] *f* talent, gift.

begann *etc vt siehe* **beginnen**.

begeben [bə'ge:bən] *vr unreg* (*gehen*) proceed (*zu, nach* to); (*geschehen*) occur; **B~heit** *f* occurrence.

begegnen [bə'ge:gnən] *vi* meet (*jdm* sb); meet with (*etw* (*dat*)) sth); (*behandeln*) treat (*jdm* sb).

Begegnung f meeting.
begehen [bə'ge:ən] vt unreg (Straftat) commit; (abschreiten) cover; (Straße etc) use, negotiate; (Feier) celebrate.
begehren [bə'ge:rən] vt desire; **begehrenswert** a desirable.
begehrt a in demand; (Junggeselle) eligible.
begeistern [bə'gaistərn] vt fill with enthusiasm, inspire // vr: **sich für etw ~** get enthusiastic about sth.
begeistert a enthusiastic.
Begeisterung f enthusiasm.
Begierde [bə'gi:rdə] f -, -n desire, passion.
begierig [bə'gi:rɪç] a eager, keen.
begießen [bə'gi:sən] vt unreg water; (mit Alkohol) drink to.
Beginn [bə'gɪn] m -(e)s beginning; **zu ~** at the beginning; **b~en** vti unreg start, begin.
beglaubigen [bə'glaubɪgən] vt countersign.
Beglaubigung f countersignature.
begleichen [bə'glaiçən] vt unreg settle, pay.
Begleit- [bə'glait] zW: **b~en** vt accompany; (MIL) escort; **~er** m -s, - companion; (Freund) escort; (MUS) accompanist; **~erscheinung** f concomitant (occurrence); **~schreiben** nt covering letter; **~umstände** pl concomitant circumstances pl; **~ung** f company; (MIL) escort; (MUS) accompaniment.
beglücken [bə'glykən] vt make happy, delight.
beglückwünschen [bə'glykvynʃən] vt congratulate (zu on).
begnadigen [bə'gna:dɪgən] vt pardon.
Begnadigung f pardon, amnesty.
begnügen [bə'gny:gən] vr be satisfied, content o.s.
Begonie [bə'go:niə] f begonia.
begonnen v siehe **beginnen**.
begraben [bə'gra:bən] vt unreg bury.
Begräbnis [bə'grɛ:pnɪs] nt -ses, -se burial, funeral.
begreifen [bə'graifən] vt unreg understand, comprehend.
begreiflich [bə'graiflɪç] a understandable.
Begrenztheit [bə'grɛntsthait] f limitation, restriction; (fig) narrowness.
Begriff [bə'grɪf] m -(e)s, -e concept, idea; **im ~ sein, etw zu tun** be about to do sth; **schwer von ~** (umg) slow, dense; **begriffsstutzig** a dense, slow.
begründ- [bə'grynd] zW: **~en** vt (Gründe geben) justify; **begründet** a well-founded, justified; **B~ung** f justification, reason.
begrüßen [bə'gry:sən] vt greet, welcome.

Begrüßung f greeting, welcome.
begünstigen [bə'gynstɪgən] vt (Person) favour; (Sache) further, promote.
begutachten [bə'gu:t'axtən] vt assess.
begütert [bə'gy:tərt] a wealthy, well-to-do.
behaart [bə'ha:rt] a hairy.
behäbig [bə'hɛ:bɪç] a (dick) portly, stout; (geruhsam) comfortable.
behagen [bə'ha:gən] vi: **das behagt ihm nicht** he does not like it; **B~** nt -s comfort, ease.
behaglich [bə'ha:klɪç] a comfortable, cosy; **B~keit** f comfort, cosiness.
behalten [bə'haltən] vt unreg keep, retain; (im Gedächtnis) remember.
Behälter [bə'hɛltər] m -s, - container, receptacle.
behandeln [bə'handəln] vt treat; (Thema) deal with; (Maschine) handle.
Behandlung f treatment; (von Maschine) handling.
beharren [bə'harən] vi: **auf etw (dat) ~** stick od keep to sth.
beharrlich [bə'harlɪç] a (ausdauernd) steadfast, unwavering; (hartnäckig) tenacious, dogged; **B~keit** f steadfastness; tenacity.
behaupten [bə'hauptən] vt claim, assert, maintain; (sein Recht) defend // vr assert o.s.
Behauptung f claim, assertion.
beheizen [bə'haitsən] vt heat.
behelfen [bə'hɛlfən] vr unreg: **sich mit etw ~** make do with sth; **behelfsmäßig** a improvised, makeshift; (vorübergehend) temporary.
behelligen [bə'hɛlɪgən] vt trouble, bother.
beherbergen [bə'hɛrbɛrgən] vt put up, house.
beherrschen [bə'hɛrʃən] vt (Volk) rule, govern; (Situation) control; (Sprache, Gefühle) master // vr control o.s.
beherrscht a controlled.
Beherrschung f rule; control; mastery.
beherzigen [bə'hɛrtsɪgən] vt take to heart.
beherzt a spirited, brave.
behilflich [bə'hɪlflɪç] a helpful; **jdm ~ sein** help sb (bei with).
behindern [bə'hɪndərn] vt hinder, impede.
Behinderte(r) mf disabled person.
Behinderung f hindrance; (Körper~) handicap.
Behörde [bə'hø:rdə] f -, -n authorities pl.
behördlich [bə'hø:rtlɪç] a official.
behüten [bə'hy:tən] vt guard; **jdn vor etw (dat) ~** preserve sb from sth.

behutsam [bə'hu:tza:m] *a* cautious, careful; **B~keit** *f* caution, carefulness.

bei [baɪ] *präp auf* **dt 1** (*nahe ~*) near; (*zum Aufenthalt*) at, with; (*unter, zwischen*) among; **~ München** near Munich; ~ uns at our place; ~m Friseur at the hairdresser's; ~ seinen Eltern wohnen live with one's parents; ~ einer Firma arbeiten work for a firm; etw ~ sich haben have sth on one; jdn ~ sich haben have sb with one; ~ Goethe in Goethe; ~m Militär in the army **2** (*zeitlich*) at, on; (*während*) during; (*Zustand, Umstand*) in; ~ Nacht at night; ~ Nebel in fog; ~ Regen if it rains; ~ solcher Hitze in such heat; ~ meiner Ankuft on my arrival; ~ der Arbeit when I'm *etc* working; ~m Fahren while driving.

beibehalten ['baɪbəhaltən] *vt unreg* keep, retain.

beibringen ['baɪbrɪŋən] *vt unreg* (*Beweis, Zeugen*) bring forward; (*Gründe*) adduce; jdm etw ~ (*zufügen*) inflict sth on sb; (*zu verstehen geben*) make sb understand sth; (*lehren*) teach sb sth.

Beichte ['baɪçtə] *f* -, -n confession; **b~n** *vt* confess // *vi* go to confession.

Beichtstuhl *m* confessional.

beide(s) ['baɪdə(s)] *pron, a* both; meine ~n Brüder my two brothers, both my brothers; die ersten ~n the first two; wir ~ we two; einer von ~n one of the two; alles ~s both (of them).

beider- ['baɪdər] *zW:* ~lei *a inv* of both; ~seitig *a* mutual, reciprocal; ~seits *ad* mutually // *präp +gen* on both sides of.

beieinander [baɪʔaɪ'nandər] *ad* together.

Beifahrer ['baɪfa:rər] *m* passenger; ~sitz *m* passenger seat.

Beifall ['baɪfal] *m* -(e)s applause; (*Zustimmung*) approval.

beifällig ['baɪfɛlɪç] *a* approving; (*Kommentar*) favourable.

beifügen ['baɪfy:gən] *vt* enclose.

beige ['be:ʒ] *a* beige, fawn.

beigeben ['baɪge:bən] *unreg vt* (*zufügen*) add; (*mitgeben*) give // *vi* (*nachgeben*) give in (*dat* to).

Beigeschmack ['baɪgəʃmak] *m* aftertaste.

Beihilfe ['baɪhɪlfə] *f* aid, assistance; (*Studien~*) grant; (*JUR*) aiding and abetting.

beikommen ['baɪkɔmən] *vi unreg* (*+dat*) get at; (*einem Problem*) deal with.

Beil [baɪl] *nt* -(e)s, -e axe, hatchet.

Beilage [baɪla:gə] *f* (*Buch~ etc*) supplement; (*KOCH*) vegetables and potatoes *pl*.

beiläufig ['baɪlɔyfɪç] *a* casual, incidental // *ad* casually, by the way.

beilegen ['baɪle:gən] *vt* (*hinzufügen*) enclose, add; (*beimessen*) attribute, ascribe; (*Streit*) settle.

Beileid ['baɪlaɪt] *nt* condolence, sympathy; herzliches ~ deepest sympathy.

beiliegend ['baɪli:gənt] *a* (*COMM*) enclosed.

beim [baɪm] = **bei dem**.

beimessen ['baɪmɛsən] *vt unreg* attribute, ascribe (*dat* to).

Bein [baɪn] *nt* -(e)s, -e leg; ~bruch *m* fracture of the leg.

beinah(e) ['baɪna:(ə)] *ad* almost, nearly.

beinhalten [bə'ʔɪnhaltən] *vt* contain.

beipflichten ['baɪpflɪçtən] *vi:* jdm/etw ~ agree with sb/sth.

beirren [bə'ʔɪrən] *vt* confuse, muddle; sich nicht ~ lassen not let o.s. be confused.

beisammen [baɪ'zamən] *ad* together; **B~sein** *nt* -s get-together.

Beischlaf ['baɪʃla:f] *m* sexual intercourse.

Beisein ['baɪzaɪn] *nt* -s presence.

beiseite [baɪ'zaɪtə] *ad* to one side, aside; (*stehen*) on one side, aside; etw ~ legen (*sparen*) put sth by; jdn/etw ~ schaffen put sb/get sth out of the way.

beisetzen ['baɪzɛtsən] *vt* bury.

Beisetzung *f* funeral.

Beisitzer ['baɪzɪtsər] *m* -s, - (*bei Prüfung*) assessor.

Beispiel ['baɪʃpi:l] *nt* -(e)s, -e example; sich an jdm ein ~ nehmen take sb as an example; zum ~ for example; **b~haft** *a* exemplary; **b~los** *a* unprecedented, unexampled; **beispielsweise** *ad* for instance *od* example.

beißen ['baɪsən] *unreg vti* bite; (*stechen: Rauch, Säure*) burn // *vr* (*Farben*) clash; ~d *a* biting, caustic; (*fig auch*) sarcastic.

Beistand ['baɪʃtant] *m* -(e)s, -̈e support, help; (*JUR*) adviser.

beistehen ['baɪʃte:ən] *vi unreg:* jdm ~ stand by sb.

beisteuern ['baɪʃtɔyərn] *vt* contribute.

beistimmen ['baɪʃtɪmən] *vi* (*+dat*) agree with.

Beitrag ['baɪtra:k] *m* -(e)s, -̈e contribution; (*Zahlung*) fee, subscription; (*Versicherungs~*) premium; **b~en** ['baɪtra:gən] *vt unreg* contribute (*zu* to); (*mithelfen*) help (*zu* with).

beitreten ['baɪtre:tən] *vi unreg* join (*einem Verein* a club).

Beitritt ['baɪtrɪt] *m* joining, membership.

beiwohnen ['baivo:nən] *vi: einer Sache (dat)* ~ attend *od* be present at sth.

Beize ['baitsə] *f* -, -n *(Holz~)* stain; *(KOCH)* marinade.

beizeiten [bai'tsaitən] *ad* in time.

bejahen [bə'ja:ən] *vt (Frage)* say yes to, answer in the affirmative; *(gutheißen)* agree with.

bejahrt [bə'ja:rt] *a* aged, elderly.

bekämpfen [bə'kɛmpfən] *vt (Gegner)* fight; *(Seuche)* combat // *vr* fight.

Bekämpfung *f* fight *od* struggle against.

bekannt [bə'kant] *a* (well-) known; *(nicht fremd)* familiar; mit jdm ~ sein know sb; jdn mit jdm ~ machen introduce sb to sb; das ist mir ~ I know that; es/sie kommt mir ~ vor it/she seems familiar; **B~e(r)** *mf* friend, acquaintance; **B~enkreis** *m* circle of friends; **B~gabe** *f* announcement; ~**geben** *vt unreg* announce publicly; ~**lich** *ad* as is well known, as you know; ~**machen** *vt* announce; **B~machung** *f* publication; announcement; **B~schaft** *f* acquaintance.

bekehren [bə'ke:rən] *vt* convert // *vr* become converted.

bekennen [bə'kɛnən] *vt unreg* confess; *(Glauben)* profess; Farbe ~ *(umg)* show where one stands.

Bekenntnis [bə'kɛntnɪs] *nt* -ses, -se admission, confession; *(Religion)* confession, denomination.

beklagen [bə'kla:gən] *vt* deplore, lament // *vr* complain; **beklagenswert** *a* lamentable, pathetic.

bekleiden [bə'klaidən] *vt* clothe; *(Amt)* occupy, fill.

Bekleidung *f* clothing.

beklemmen [bə'klɛmən] *vt* oppress.

beklommen [bə'klɔmən] *a* anxious, uneasy; **B~heit** *f* anxiety, uneasiness.

bekommen [bə'kɔmən] *unreg vt* get, receive; *(Kind)* have; *(Zug)* catch, get // *vi:* jdm ~ agree with sb.

bekömmlich [bə'kœmlɪç] *a* wholesome, easily digestible.

bekräftigen [bə'krɛftɪgən] *vt* confirm, corroborate.

Bekräftigung *f* corroboration.

bekreuzigen [bə'krɔytsɪgən] *vr* cross o.s.

bekümmern [bə'kʏmərn] *vt* worry, trouble.

bekunden [bə'kʊndən] *vt (sagen)* state; *(zeigen)* show.

belächeln [bə'lɛçəln] *vt* laugh at.

beladen [bə'la:dən] *vt unreg* load.

Belag [bə'la:k] *m* -(e)s, -̈e covering, coating; *(Brot~)* spread; *(Zahn~)* tartar; *(auf Zunge)* fur; *(Brems~)*

belagern [bə'la:gərn] *vt* besiege.

Belagerung *f* siege.

Belang [bə'laŋ] *m* -(e)s importance; ~**e** *pl* interests *pl*, concerns *pl*; **b~en** *vt (JUR)* take to court; **b~los** *a* trivial, unimportant; ~**losigkeit** *f* triviality.

belassen [bə'lasən] *vt unreg (in Zustand, Glauben)* leave; *(in Stellung)* retain.

belasten [bə'lastən] *vt (lit)* burden; *(fig: bedrücken)* trouble, worry; *(COMM: Konto)* debit; *(JUR)* incriminate // *vr* weigh o.s. down; *(JUR)* incriminate o.s.; ~**d** *a (JUR)* incriminating.

belästigen [bə'lɛstɪgən] *vt* annoy, pester.

Belästigung *f* annoyance, pestering.

Belastung [bə'lastʊŋ] *f (lit)* load; *(fig: Sorge etc)* weight; *(COMM)* charge, debit(ing); *(JUR)* incriminatory evidence; **Belastungsprobe** *f* capacity test; *(fig)* test; **Belastungszeuge** *m* witness for prosecution.

belaufen [bə'laufən] *vr unreg* amount *(auf +akk* to*)*.

belebt [bə'le:pt] *a (Straße)* crowded.

Beleg [bə'le:k] *m* -(e)s, -e *(COMM)* receipt; *(Beweis)* documentary evidence, proof; *(Beispiel)* example; **b~en** [bə'le:gən] *vt* cover; *(Kuchen, Brot)* spread; *(Platz)* reserve, book; *(Kurs, Vorlesung)* register for; *(beweisen)* verify, prove; *(MIL: mit Bomben)* bomb; ~**schaft** *f* personnel, staff; **belegt** *a:* belegtes Brot open sandwich.

belehren [bə'le:rən] *vt* instruct, teach.

Belehrung *f* instruction.

beleibt [bə'laipt] *a* stout, corpulent.

beleidigen [bə'laidɪgən] *vt* insult, offend.

Beleidigung *f* insult; *(JUR)* slander, libel.

belesen [bə'le:zən] *a* well-read.

beleuchten [bə'lɔʏçtən] *vt* light, illuminate; *(fig)* throw light on.

Beleuchtung *f* lighting, illumination.

Belg- ['bɛlg] *zW:* ~**ien** [-iən] *nt* Belgium; ~**ier(in** *f)* *m* Belgian; **b~isch** *a* Belgian.

belichten [bə'lɪçtən] *vt* expose.

Belichtung *f* exposure; **Belichtungsmesser** *m* exposure meter.

Belieben [bə'li:bən] *nt:* (ganz) nach ~ (just) as you wish.

beliebig [bə'li:bɪç] *a* any you like, as you like; ~ viel as many as you like; ein ~es Thema any subject you like *od* want.

beliebt [bə'li:pt] *a* popular; sich bei jdm ~ machen make o.s. popular with sb; **B~heit** *f* popularity.

beliefern [bə'li:fərn] *vt* supply.
bellen ['belən] *vi* bark.
Belletristik [bele'trɪstɪk] *f* fiction and poetry.
belohnen [bə'lo:nən] *vt* reward.
Belohnung *f* reward.
belügen [bə'ly:gən] *vt unreg* lie to, deceive.
belustigen [bə'lʊstɪgən] *vt* amuse.
Belustigung *f* amusement.
bemalen [bə'ma:lən] *vt* paint.
bemängeln [bə'mɛŋəln] *vt* criticize.
bemannen [bə'manən] *vt* man.
bemerk- [bə'mɛrk] *zW:* **~bar** *a* perceptible, noticeable; **sich ~bar machen** (*Person*) make *od* get o.s. noticed; (*Unruhe*) become noticeable; **~en** *vt* (*wahrnehmen*) notice, observe; (*sagen*) say, mention; **~enswert** *a* remarkable, noteworthy; **B~ung** *f* remark; (*schriftlich auch*) note.
bemitleiden [bə'mɪtlaɪdən] *vt* pity.
bemühen [bə'my:ən] *vr* take trouble *od* pains.
Bemühung *f* trouble, pains *pl*, effort.
benachbart [bə'naxba:rt] *a* neighbouring.
benachrichtigen [bə'na:xrɪçtɪgən] *vt* inform.
Benachrichtigung *f* notification, information.
benachteiligen [bə'na:xtaɪlɪgən] *vt* disadvantage, victimize.
benehmen [bə'ne:mən] *vr unreg* behave; **B~** *nt* **-s** behaviour.
beneiden [bə'naɪdən] *vt* envy; **beneidenswert** *a* enviable.
benennen [bə'nɛnən] *vt unreg* name.
Bengel ['bɛŋəl] *m* **-s, -** (little) rascal *od* rogue.
benommen [bə'nɔmən] *a* dazed.
benötigen [bə'nø:tɪgən] *vt* need.
benutzen [bə'nʊtsən], **benützen** [bə'nʏtsən] *vt* use.
Benutzer *m* **-s, -** user; **b~freundlich** *a* user-friendly.
Benutzung *f* utilization, use.
Benzin [bɛnt'si:n] *nt* **-s, -e** (*AUT*) petrol (*Brit*), gas(oline) (*US*); **~kanister** *m* petrol can (*Brit*), gas can (*US*); **~tank** *m* petrol tank (*Brit*), gas tank (*US*); **~uhr** *f* petrol gauge (*Brit*), gas gauge (*US*).
beobacht- [bə'o:baxt] *zW:* **~en** *vt* observe; **B~er** *m* **-s, -** observer; (*eines Unfalls*) witness; (*PRESSE, TV*) correspondent; **B~ung** *f* observation.
bepacken [bə'pakən] *vt* load, pack.
bequem [bə'kve:m] *a* comfortable; (*Ausrede*) convenient; (*Person*) lazy, indolent; **~en** *vr* condescend (*zu* to); **B~lichkeit** *f* convenience, comfort; (*Faulheit*) laziness, indolence.
beraten [bə'ra:tən] *unreg vt* advise;

(*besprechen*) discuss, debate // *vr* consult; **gut/schlecht ~ sein** be well/ill advised; **sich ~ lassen** get advice.
Berater *m* **-s, -** adviser.
Beratung *f* advice, consultation; (*Besprechung*) consultation; **Beratungsstelle** *f* advice centre.
berauben [bə'raubən] *vt* rob.
berechenbar [bə'rɛçənba:r] *a* calculable.
berechnen [bə'rɛçnən] *vt* calculate; (*COMM: anrechnen*) charge; **~d** *a* (*Mensch*) calculating, scheming.
Berechnung *f* calculation; (*COMM*) charge.
berechtig- [bə'rɛçtɪg] *zW:* **~en** *vt* entitle, authorize; (*fig*) justify; **~t** [bə'rɛçtɪçt] *a* justifiable, justified; **B~ung** *f* authorization; (*fig*) justification.
bereden [bə're:dən] *vtr* (*besprechen*) discuss; (*überreden*) persuade.
Bereich [bə'raɪç] *m* **-(e)s, -e** (*Bezirk*) area; (*PHYS*) range; (*Ressort, Gebiet*) sphere.
bereichern [bə'raɪçərn] *vt* enrich // *vr* get rich.
bereinigen [bə'raɪnɪgən] *vt* settle.
bereit [bə'raɪt] *a* ready, prepared; **zu etw ~ sein** be ready for sth; **sich ~ erklären** declare o.s. willing; **~en** *vt* prepare, make ready; (*Kummer, Freude*) cause; **~halten** *vt unreg* keep in readiness; **~legen** *vt* lay out; **~machen** *vtr* prepare, get ready; **~s** *ad* already; **B~schaft** *f* readiness; (*Polizei*) alert; **B~schaftsdienst** *m* emergency service; **~stehen** *vi unreg* (*Person*) be prepared; (*Ding*) be ready; **~stellen** *vt* (*Kisten, Pakete etc*) put ready; (*Geld etc*) make available; (*Truppen, Maschinen*) put at the ready; **~willig** *a* willing, ready; **B~willigkeit** *f* willingness, readiness.
bereuen [bə'rɔyən] *vt* regret.
Berg [bɛrk] *m* **-(e)s, -e** mountain, hill; **b~ab** *ad* downhill; **b~auf** *ad* uphill; **~arbeiter** *m* miner; **~bahn** *f* mountain railway; **~bau** *m* mining; **b~en** ['bɛrgən] *vt unreg* (*retten*) rescue; (*Ladung*) salvage; (*enthalten*) contain; **~führer** *m* mountain guide; **b~ig** ['bɛrgɪç] *a* mountainous, hilly; **~kette** *f* mountain range; **~mann** *m, pl* **~leute** miner; **~rutsch** *m* landslide; **~steigen** *nt* mountaineering; **~steiger(in** *f*) *m* **-s, -** mountaineer, climber; **~ung** ['bɛrgʊŋ] *f* (*von Menschen*) rescue; (*von Material*) recovery; (*NAUT*) salvage; **~wacht** *f* mountain rescue service; **~werk** *nt* mine.
Bericht [bə'rɪçt] *m* **-(e)s, -e** report, account; **b~en** *vti* report; **~erstatter**

m -s, - reporter, (newspaper) correspondent.

berichtigen [bə'rɪçtɪgən] *vt* correct.

Berichtigung *f* correction.

Bernstein ['bɛrnʃtaɪn] *m* amber.

bersten ['bɛrstən] *vi unreg* burst, split.

berüchtigt [bə'rʏçtɪçt] *a* notorious, infamous.

berücksichtigen [bə'rʏkzɪçtɪgən] *vt* consider, bear in mind.

Berücksichtigung *f* consideration.

Beruf [bə'ruːf] *m* -(e)s, -e occupation, profession; (*Gewerbe*) trade; **b~en** *unreg vt* (*in Amt*) appoint (*in +akk* to; *zu* as) // *vr*: **sich auf jdn/etw b~en** refer *od* appeal to sb/sth; **b~en** *a* competent, qualified; **b~lich** *a* professional.

Berufs- *zW:* **~berater** *m* careers adviser; **~beratung** *f* vocational guidance; **~geheimnis** *nt* professional secret; **~leben** *nt* professional life; **b~mäßig** *a* professional; **~schule** *f* vocational *od* trade school; **~sportler** *m* professional (sportsman); **b~tätig** *a* employed; **~verkehr** *m* commuter traffic.

Berufung *f* vocation, calling; (*Ernennung*) appointment; (*JUR*) appeal; **~ einlegen** appeal.

beruhen [bə'ruːən] *vi*: **auf etw** (*dat*) **~** be based on sth; **etw auf sich ~ lassen** leave sth at that.

beruhigen [bə'ruːɪgən] *vt* calm, pacify, soothe // *vr* (*Mensch*) calm (o.s.) down; (*Situation*) calm down.

Beruhigung *f* reassurance; (*der Nerven*) calming; **zu jds ~** to reassure sb; **Beruhigungsmittel** *nt* sedative.

berühmt [bə'ryːmt] *a* famous; **B~heit** *f* (*Ruf*) fame; (*Mensch*) celebrity.

berühren [bə'ryːrən] *vt* touch; (*gefühlsmäßig bewegen*) affect; (*flüchtig erwähnen*) mention, touch on // *vr* meet, touch.

Berührung *f* contact.

besagen [bə'zaːgən] *vt* mean.

besagt *a* (*Tag etc*) in question.

besänftig- [bə'zɛnftɪg] *zW:* **~en** *vt* soothe, calm; **~end** *a* soothing; **B~ung** *f* soothing, calming.

Besatz [bə'zats] *m* -es, -e trimming, edging; **~ung** *f* garrison; (*NAUT, AVIAT*) crew; **~ungsmacht** *f* occupying power.

beschädig- [bə'ʃɛːdɪg] *zW:* **~en** *vt* damage; **B~ung** *f* damage; (*Stelle*) damaged spot.

beschaffen [bə'ʃafən] *vt* get, acquire // *a* constituted; **B~heit** *f* constitution, nature.

Beschaffung *f* acquisition.

beschäftigen [bə'ʃɛftɪgən] *vt* occupy; (*beruflich*) employ // *vr* occupy *od* concern o.s.

beschäftigt *a* busy, occupied.

Beschäftigung *f* (*Beruf*) employment; (*Tätigkeit*) occupation; (*Befassen*) concern.

beschämen [bə'ʃɛːmən] *vt* put to shame; **~d** *a* shameful; (*Hilfsbereitschaft*) shaming.

beschämt *a* ashamed.

beschatten [bə'ʃatən] *vt* shade; (*Verdächtige*) shadow.

Bescheid [bə'ʃaɪt] *m* -(e)s, -e information; (*Weisung*) directions *pl*; **~ wissen** be well-informed (*über +akk* about); **ich weiß ~** I know; **jdm ~ geben** *od* **sagen** let sb know.

bescheiden [bə'ʃaɪdən] *vr unreg* content o.s. // *a* modest; **B~heit** *f* modesty.

bescheinen [bə'ʃaɪnən] *vt unreg* shine on.

bescheinigen [bə'ʃaɪnɪgən] *vt* certify; (*bestätigen*) acknowledge.

Bescheinigung *f* certificate; (*Quittung*) receipt.

bescheren [bə'ʃeːrən] *vt*: **jdm etw ~** give sb sth as a present; **jdn ~** give presents to sb.

Bescherung *f* giving of presents; (*umg*) mess.

beschildern [bə'ʃɪldərn] *vt* signpost.

beschimpfen [bə'ʃɪmpfən] *vt* abuse.

Beschimpfung *f* abuse, insult.

Beschlag [bə'ʃlaːk] *m* -(e)s, -e (*Metallband*) fitting; (*auf Fenster*) condensation; (*auf Metall*) tarnish; finish; (*Hufeisen*) horseshoe; **jdn/etw in ~ nehmen** *od* **mit ~ belegen** monopolize sb/sth; **b~en** [bə'ʃlaːgən] *unreg vt* cover; (*Pferd*) shoe; (*Fenster, Metall*) cover; **b~en sein** be well versed (*in od auf +dat in*) // *vir* (*Fenster etc*) mist over; **b~nahmen** *vt* seize, confiscate; requisition; **~nahmung** *f* confiscation, sequestration.

beschleunigen [bə'ʃlɔynɪgən] *vt* accelerate, speed up // *vi* (*AUT*) accelerate.

Beschleunigung *f* acceleration.

beschließen [bə'ʃliːsən] *vt unreg* decide on; (*beenden*) end, close.

Beschluß [bə'ʃlus] *m* -sses, -schlüsse decision, conclusion; (*Ende*) close, end.

beschmutzen [bə'ʃmutsən] *vt* dirty, soil.

beschönigen [bə'ʃøːnɪgən] *vt* gloss over.

beschränken [bə'ʃrɛŋkən] *vt* limit, restrict (*auf +akk* to) // *vr* restrict o.s.

beschränk- *zW:* **~t** *a* confined, narrow; (*Mensch*) limited, narrow-minded; **Beschränktheit** *f* narrowness; **B~ung** *f* limitation.

beschreiben [bə'ʃraɪbən] *vt unreg* de-

scribe; (*Papier*) write on.
Beschreibung *f* description.
beschriften [bə'ʃrɪftən] *vt* mark, label.
Beschriftung *f* lettering.
beschuldigen [bə'ʃʊldɪgən] *vt* accuse.
Beschuldigung *f* accusation.
beschütz- [bə'ʃʏts] *zW:* ~**en** *vt* protect (*vor* +*dat* from); **B**~**er** *m* -**s**, - protector.
Beschwerde [bə'ʃveːrdə] *f* -, -**n** complaint; (*Mühe*) hardship; (*pl: Leiden*) pain.
beschweren [bə'ʃveːrən] *vt* weight down; (*fig*) burden // *vr* complain.
beschwerlich *a* tiring, exhausting.
beschwichtigen [bə'ʃvɪçtɪgən] *vt* soothe, pacify.
beschwindeln [bə'ʃvɪndəln] *vt* (*betrügen*) cheat; (*belügen*) fib to.
beschwingt [bə'ʃvɪŋt] *a* cheery, in high spirits.
beschwören [bə'ʃvøːrən] *vt unreg* (*Aussage*) swear to; (*anflehen*) implore; (*Geister*) conjure up.
beseitigen [bə'zaɪtɪgən] *vt* remove.
Beseitigung *f* removal.
Besen ['beːzən] *m* -**s**, - broom; ~**stiel** *m* broomstick.
besessen [bə'zɛsən] *a* possessed.
besetz- [bə'zɛts] *zW:* ~**en** *vt* (*Haus, Land*) occupy; (*Platz*) take, fill; (*Posten*) fill; (*Rolle*) cast; (*mit Edelsteinen*) set; ~**t** *a* full; (*TEL*) engaged, busy; (*Platz*) taken; (*WC*) engaged; **Besetztzeichen** *nt* engaged tone; **B**~**ung** *f* occupation; filling; (*von Rolle*) casting; (*die Schauspieler*) cast.
besichtigen [bə'zɪçtɪgən] *vt* visit, look at.
Besichtigung *f* visit.
Besied(e)lung [bə'ziːd(ə)lʊŋ] *f* population.
besiegen [bə'ziːgən] *vt* defeat, overcome.
besinnen [bə'zɪnən] *vr unreg* (*nachdenken*) think, reflect; (*erinnern*) remember; sich anders ~ change one's mind.
besinnlich *a* contemplative.
Besinnung *f* consciousness; zur ~ kommen recover consciousness; (*fig*) come to one's senses; **besinnungslos** *a* unconscious.
Besitz [bə'zɪts] *m* -**es** possession; (*Eigentum*) property; **b**~**en** *vt unreg* possess, own; (*Eigenschaft*) have; ~**er(in** *f*) *m* -**s**, - owner, proprietor; ~**ergreifung** *f* occupation, seizure.
besoffen [bə'zɔfən] *a* (*umg*) drunk.
besohlen [bə'zoːlən] *vt* sole.
Besoldung [bə'zɔldʊŋ] *f* salary, pay.
besondere(r, s) [bə'zɔndərə(r,z)] *a* special; (*eigen*) particular; (*gesondert*) separate; (*eigentümlich*) pecu-

liar.
Besonderheit [bə'zɔndərhaɪt] *f* peculiarity.
besonders [bə'zɔndərs] *ad* especially, particularly; (*getrennt*) separately.
besonnen [bə'zɔnən] *a* sensible, level-headed; **B**~**heit** *f* prudence.
besorg- [bə'zɔrg] *zW:* ~**en** *vt* (*beschaffen*) acquire; (*kaufen auch*) purchase; (*erledigen: Geschäfte*) deal with; (*sich kümmern um*) take care of; **B**~**nis** *f* -, -**se** anxiety, concern; ~**t** [bə'zɔrçt] *a* anxious, worried; **Besorgtheit** *f* anxiety, worry; **B**~**ung** *f* acquisition; (*Kauf*) purchase.
bespielen [bə'ʃpiːlən] *vt* record.
bespitzeln [bə'ʃpɪtsəln] *vt* spy on.
besprechen [bə'ʃprɛçən] *unreg vt* discuss; (*Tonband etc*) record, speak onto; (*Buch*) review // *vr* discuss, consult.
Besprechung *f* meeting, discussion; (*von Buch*) review.
besser ['bɛsər] *a* better; ~**n** *vt* make better, improve // *vr* improve; (*Menschen*) reform; **B**~**ung** *f* improvement; gute **B**~**ung!** get well soon; **B**~**wisser** *m* -**s**, - know-all.
Bestand [bə'ʃtant] *m* -**(e)s**, -̈**e** (*Fortbestehen*) duration, stability; (*Kassen*~) amount, balance; (*Vorrat*) stock; ~ haben, von ~ sein last long, endure.
beständig [bə'ʃtɛndɪç] *a* (*ausdauernd*) constant (*auch fig*); (*Wetter*) settled; (*Stoffe*) resistant; (*Klagen etc*) continual.
Bestandsaufnahme *f* stocktaking.
Bestandteil *m* part, component; (*Zutat*) ingredient.
bestärken [bə'ʃtɛrkən] *vt:* jdn in etw (*dat*) ~ strengthen *od* confirm sb in sth.
bestätigen [bə'ʃtɛːtɪgən] *vt* confirm; (*anerkennen, COMM*) acknowledge.
Bestätigung *f* confirmation; acknowledgement.
bestatt- [bə'ʃtat] *zW:* ~**en** *vt* bury; **B**~**er** *m* -**s**, - undertaker; **B**~**ung** *f* funeral.
beste(r, s) ['bɛstə(r, s)] *a* best; so ist es am ~**n** it's best that way; am ~**n** gehst du gleich you'd better go at once; jdn zum ~**n** haben pull sb's leg; etw zum ~**n** geben tell a joke/ story *etc*; aufs ~ in the best possible way; zu jds **B**~**n** for the benefit of sb.
bestechen [bə'ʃtɛçən] *vt unreg* bribe.
bestechlich *a* corruptible.
Bestechung *f* bribery, corruption.
Besteck [bə'ʃtɛk] *nt* -**(e)s**, -**e** knife, fork and spoon, cutlery; (*MED*) set of instruments.
bestehen [bə'ʃteːən] *unreg vi* be; ex-

ist; (andauern) last // vt (Kampf, Probe, Prüfung) pass; ~ **auf** (+dat) insist on; ~ **aus** consist of.

bestehlen [bə'ʃteːlən] vt unreg rob.

besteigen [bə'ʃtaɪgən] vt unreg climb, ascend; (Pferd) mount; (Thron) ascend.

Bestell- [bə'ʃtɛl] zW: ~**buch** nt order book; **b~en** vt order; (kommen lassen) arrange to see; (nominieren) name; (Acker) cultivate; (Grüße, Auftrag) pass on; ~**schein** m order coupon; ~**ung** f (COMM) order; (Bestellen) ordering.

bestenfalls ['bɛstən'fals] ad at best.

bestens ['bɛstəns] ad very well.

Bestie ['bɛstiə] f (lit, fig) beast.

bestimm- [bə'ʃtɪm] zW: ~**en** vt (Regeln) lay down; (Tag, Ort) fix; (beherrschen) characterize; (ausersehen) mean; (ernennen) appoint; (definieren) define; (veranlassen) induce; ~**t** a (entschlossen) firm; (gewiß) certain, definite; (Artikel) definite; **suchen Sie etwas B~tes?** are you looking for something in particular? // ad (gewiß) definitely, for sure; **Bestimmtheit** f certainty; **B~ung** f (Verordnung) regulation; (Festsetzen) determining; (Verwendungszweck) purpose; (Schicksal) fate; (Definition) definition; **B~ungsort** m destination.

Bestleistung f best performance.

bestmöglich a best possible.

bestrafen [bə'ʃtraːfən] vt punish.

Bestrafung f punishment.

bestrahlen [bə'ʃtraːlən] vt shine on; (MED) treat with X-rays.

Bestrahlung f (MED) X-ray treatment, radiotherapy.

Bestreben [bə'ʃtreːbən] nt -s endeavour, effort.

bestreichen [bə'ʃtraɪçən] vt unreg (Brot) spread.

bestreiten [bə'ʃtraɪtən] vt unreg (abstreiten) dispute; (finanzieren) pay for, finance.

bestreuen [bə'ʃtrɔyən] vt sprinkle, dust; (Straße) grit.

bestürmen [bə'ʃtʏrmən] vt (mit Fragen, Bitten etc) overwhelm, swamp.

bestürzt [bə'ʃtʏrtst] a dismayed.

Bestürzung f consternation.

Besuch [bə'zuːx] m -(e)s, -e visit; (Person) visitor; **einen ~ machen bei jdm** pay sb a visit od call; ~ **haben** have visitors; **bei jdm auf** or **zu ~ sein** be visiting sb; **b~en** vt visit; (SCH etc) attend; **gut ~t** well-attended; ~**er(in** f) m -s, - visitor, guest; **Besuchszeit** f visiting hours pl.

betagt [bə'taːkt] a aged.

betätigen [bə'tɛːtɪgən] vt (bedienen) work, operate // vr involve o.s.; **sich als etw ~** work as sth.

Betätigung f activity; (beruflich) occupation; (TECH) operation.

betäuben [bə'tɔybən] vt stun; (fig: Gewissen) still; (MED) anaesthetize.

Betäubungsmittel nt anaesthetic.

Bete ['beːtə] f -, -n: **rote** ~ beetroot (Brit), beet (US).

beteiligen [bə'taɪlɪgən] vr (an +dat in) take part, participate, share; (an Geschäft: finanziell) have a share // vt: **jdn ~** give sb a share od interest (an +dat in).

Beteiligung f participation; (Anteil) share, interest; (Besucherzahl) attendance.

beten ['beːtən] vti pray.

beteuern [bə'tɔyərn] vt assert; (Unschuld) protest.

Beteuerung f assertion, protest(ation), assurance.

Beton [be'tõː] m -s, -s concrete.

betonen [bə'toːnən] vt stress.

betonieren [beto'niːrən] vt concrete.

Betonung f stress, emphasis.

betören [bə'tøːrən] vt beguile.

Betr. abk (= Betreff; betrifft) re.

Betracht [bə'traxt] m: **in ~ kommen** be concerned od relevant; **etw in ~ ziehen** consider sth; **außer ~ bleiben** not be considered; **b~en** vt look at; (fig auch) consider; ~**er(in** f) m -s, -onlooker.

beträchtlich [bə'trɛçtlɪç] a considerable.

Betrachtung f (Ansehen) examination; (Erwägung) consideration.

Betrag [bə'traːk] m -(e)s, -̈e amount; **b~en** [bə'traːgən] unreg vt amount to // vr behave; ~**en** nt -s behaviour.

betreffen [bə'trɛfən] vt unreg concern, affect; **was mich betrifft** as for me; ~**d** a relevant, in question.

betreffs [bə'trɛfs] präp +gen concerning, regarding.

betreiben [bə'traɪbən] vt unreg (ausüben) practise; (Politik) follow; (Studien) pursue; (vorantreiben) push ahead; (TECH: antreiben) drive.

betreten [bə'treːtən] vt unreg enter; (Bühne etc) step onto; **B~ verboten** keep off/out // a embarrassed.

Betrieb [bə'triːp] m -(e)s, -e (Firma) firm, concern; (Anlage) plant; (Tätigkeit) operation; (Treiben) traffic; **außer ~ sein** be out of order; **in ~ sein** be in operation.

Betriebs- zW: **b~fähig** a in working order; ~**ferien** pl company holidays pl (Brit), company vacation (US); ~**klima** nt (working) atmosphere; ~**kosten** pl running costs pl; ~**rat** m workers' council; **b~sicher** a safe, reliable; **~störung** *f* breakdown; **~unfall** *m* industrial accident; **~wirtschaft** *f* economics.

betrinken [bə'trɪŋkən] *vr unreg* get drunk.

betroffen [bə'trɔfən] *a* (*bestürzt*) amazed, perplexed; **von etw ~ werden** *od* **sein** be affected by sth.

betrüben [bə'try:bən] *vt* grieve.

betrübt [bə'try:pt] *a* sorrowful, grieved.

Betrug [bə'tru:k] *m* **-(e)s** deception; (*JUR*) fraud.

betrügen [bə'try:gən] *unreg vt* cheat; (*JUR*) defraud; (*Ehepartner*) be unfaithful to // *vr* deceive o.s.

Betrüger *m* **-s**, **-** cheat, deceiver; **b~isch** *a* deceitful; (*JUR*) fraudulent.

betrunken [bə'trʊŋkən] *a* drunk.

Bett [bɛt] *nt* **-(e)s**, **-en** bed; **ins** *od* **zu ~ gehen** go to bed; **~bezug** *m* duvet cover; **~decke** *f* blanket; (*Daunen~*) quilt; (*Überwurf*) bedspread.

Bettel- ['bɛtəl] *zW:* **b~arm** *a* very poor, destitute; **~ei** [bɛtə'laɪ] *f* begging; **b~n** *vi* beg.

bettlägerig ['bɛtlɛːgərɪç] *a* bedridden.

Bettlaken *nt* sheet.

Bettler(in *f*) ['bɛtlər(ɪn)] *m* **-s**, **-** beggar.

Bett- *zW:* **~vorleger** *m* bedside rug; **~(t)uch** *nt*, **~wäsche** *f*, **~zeug** *nt* bedclothes *pl*, bedding.

beugen ['bɔygən] *vt* bend; (*GRAM*) inflect // *vr* (*sich fügen*) bow (*dat* to).

Beule ['bɔylə] *f* **-**, **-n** bump, swelling.

beunruhigen [bə''unru:ɪgən] *vt* disturb, alarm // *vr* become worried.

Beunruhigung *f* worry, alarm.

beurlauben [bə''u:rlaʊbən] *vt* give leave of absence to (*Brit*), grant vacation time to (*US*).

beurteilen [bə''urtaɪlən] *vt* judge; (*Buch etc*) review.

Beurteilung *f* judgement; review; (*Note*) mark.

Beute ['bɔytə] *f* **-**, booty, loot; **~!** *m* **-s**, **-** bag; (*Geld~*) purse; (*Tabak~*) pouch.

Bevölkerung [bə'fœlkərʊŋ] *f* population.

bevollmächtigen [bə'fɔlmɛçtɪgən] *vt* authorize.

Bevollmächtigte(r) *mf* authorized agent.

bevor [bə'fo:r] *kj* before; **~munden** *vt insep* dominate; **~stehen** *vi unreg* be in store (*dat* for); **~stehend** *a* imminent, approaching; **~zugen** *vt insep* prefer; **B~zugung** *f* preference.

bewachen [bə'vaxən] *vt* watch, guard.

Bewachung *f* (*Bewachen*) guarding; (*Leute*) guard, watch.

bewaffnen [bə'vafnən] *vt* arm.

Bewaffnung *f* (*Vorgang*) arming;

(*Ausrüstung*) armament, arms *pl*.

bewahren [bə'va:rən] *vt* keep; **jdn vor jdm/etw ~** save sb from sb/sth.

bewähren [bə've:rən] *vr* prove o.s.; (*Maschine*) prove its worth.

bewahrheiten [bə'va:rhaɪtən] *vr* come true.

bewährt *a* reliable.

Bewährung *f* (*JUR*) probation; **Bewährungsfrist** *f* (period of) probation.

bewältigen [bə'vɛltɪgən] *vt* overcome; (*Arbeit*) finish; (*Portion*) manage.

bewandert [bə'vandərt] *a* expert, knowledgeable.

bewässern [bə'vɛsərn] *vt* irrigate.

Bewässerung *f* irrigation.

Beweg- [bə've:g] *zW:* **b~en** *vtr* move; **jdn zu etw b~en** induce sb to (do) sth; **~grund** [bə've:k-] *m* motive; **b~lich** *a* movable, mobile; (*flink*) quick; **b~t** *a* (*Leben*) eventful; (*Meer*) rough; (*ergriffen*) touched; **~ung** *f* movement, motion; (*innere*) emotion; (*körperlich*) exercise; **~ungsfreiheit** *f* freedom of movement *od* action; **b~ungslos** *a* motionless.

Beweis [bə'vaɪs] *m* **-es**, **-e** proof; (*Zeichen*) sign; **b~bar** [bə'vaɪz-] *a* provable; **b~en** *vt unreg* prove; (*zeigen*) show; **~mittel** *nt* evidence.

Bewerb- [bə'vɛrb] *zW:* **b~en** *vr unreg* apply (*um* for); **~er(in** *f*) *m* **-s**, **-** applicant; **~ung** *f* application.

bewerkstelligen [bə'vɛrkʃtɛlɪgən] *vt* manage, accomplish.

bewerten [bə've:rtən] *vt* assess.

bewilligen [bə'vɪlɪgən] *vt* grant, allow.

Bewilligung *f* granting.

bewirken [bə'vɪrkən] *vt* cause; bring about.

bewirten [bə'vɪrtən] *vt* entertain.

bewirtschaften [bə'vɪrtʃaftən] *vt* manage.

Bewirtung *f* hospitality.

bewog *etc v siehe* **bewegen**.

bewohn- [bə'vo:n] *zW:* **~bar** *a* inhabitable; **~en** *vt* inhabit, live in; **B~er(in** *f*) *m* **-s**, **-** inhabitant; (*von Haus*) resident.

bewölkt [bə'vœlkt] *a* cloudy, overcast.

Bewölkung *f* clouds *pl*.

Bewunder- [bə'vundər] *zW:* **~er** *m* **-s**, **-** admirer; **b~n** *vt* admire; **b~nswert** *a* admirable, wonderful; **~ung** *f* admiration.

bewußt [bə'vust] *a* conscious; (*absichtlich*) deliberate; **sich** (*dat*) **einer Sache** **~ sein** be aware of sth; **~los** *a* unconscious; **B~losigkeit** *f* unconsciousness; **B~sein** *nt* consciousness; **bei B~sein** conscious.

bezahlen [bə'tsa:lən] *vt* pay (for).

Bezahlung *f* payment.

bezaubern [bə'tsaubərn] *vt* enchant, charm.

bezeichnen [bə'tsaiçnən] *vt* (*kennzeichnen*) mark; (*nennen*) call; (*beschreiben*) describe; (*zeigen*) show, indicate; **~d** a characteristic, typical (*für* of).

Bezeichnung *f* (*Zeichen*) mark, sign; (*Beschreibung*) description.

Bezichtigung [bə'tsiçtiguŋ] *f* accusation.

beziehen [bə'tsi:ən] *unreg vt* (*mit Überzug*) cover; (*Bett*) make; (*Haus, Position*) move into; (*Standpunkt*) take up; (*erhalten*) receive; (*Zeitung*) subscribe to, take; **etw auf jdn/etw ~** relate sth to sb/sth // *vr* refer (*auf* +*akk* to); (*Himmel*) cloud over.

Beziehung *f* (*Verbindung*) connection; (*Zusammenhang*) relation; (*Verhältnis*) relationship; (*Hinsicht*) respect; **~en haben** (*vorteilhaft*) have connections *od* contacts; **b~sweise** *ad* or; (*genauer gesagt auch*) that is, or rather.

Bezirk [bə'tsɪrk] *m* **-(e)s, -e** district.

Bezug [bə'tsu:k] *m* **-(e)s, -e** (*Hülle*) covering; (*COMM*) ordering; (*Gehalt*) income, salary; (*Beziehung*) relationship (*zu* to); **in b~ auf** (+*akk*) with reference to; **~ nehmen auf** (+*akk*) refer to.

bezüglich [bə'tsy:klɪç] *präp* +*gen* concerning, referring to // *a* concerning; (*GRAM*) relative.

bezwecken [bə'tsvɛkən] *vt* aim at.

bezweifeln [bə'tsvaɪfəln] *vt* doubt, query.

Bhf. *abk* (= *Bahnhof*) station.

Bibel ['bi:bəl] *f* **-, -n** Bible.

Biber ['bi:bər] *m* **-s, -** beaver.

Biblio- *zW:* **~graphie** [bibliogra'fi:] *f* bibliography; **~thek** [biblio'te:k] *f* **-, -en** library; **~thekar(in** *f*) [bibliote'ka:r(ɪn)] *m* **-s, -e** librarian.

biblisch ['bi:blɪʃ] *a* biblical.

bieder ['bi:dər] *a* upright, worthy; (*Kleid etc*) plain.

bieg- [bi:g] *zW:* **~en** *unreg vtr* bend // *vi* turn; **~sam** ['bi:k-] *a* supple; **B~ung** *f* bend, curve.

Biene ['bi:nə] *f* **-, -n** bee.

Bienenhonig *m* honey.

Bier [bi:r] *nt* **-(e)s, -e** beer; **~deckel** *m* beer mat; **~krug** *m* beer mug.

bieten ['bi:tən] *unreg vt* offer; (*bei Versteigerung*) bid // *vr* (*Gelegenheit*) be open (*dat* to); **sich** (*dat*) **etw ~** lassen put up with sth.

Bikini [bi'ki:ni] *m* **-s, -s** bikini.

Bilanz [bi'lants] *f* balance; (*fig*) outcome; **~ ziehen** take stock (*aus* of).

Bild [bɪlt] *nt* **-(e)s, -er** (*lit, fig*) picture; photo; (*Spiegel~*) reflection; **~bericht** *m* pictorial report.

bilden ['bɪldən] *vt* form; (*erziehen*) educate; (*ausmachen*) constitute // *vr* arise; (*erziehen*) educate o.s.

Bilder- ['bɪldər] *zW:* **~buch** *nt* picture book; **~rahmen** *m* picture frame.

Bild- *zW:* **~fläche** *f* screen; (*fig*) scene; **~hauer** *m* **-s, -** sculptor; **b~hübsch** *a* lovely, pretty as a picture; **b~lich** *a* figurative; pictorial; **~schirm** *m* television screen; (*COMPUT*) monitor; **b~schön** *a* lovely; **~sichtgerät** *nt* visual display unit, VDU; **~ung** ['bɪlduŋ] *f* formation; (*Wissen, Benehmen*) education; **~ungslücke** *f* gap in one's education; **~ungspolitik** *f* educational policy.

Billard ['bɪljart] *nt* **-s, -e** billiards; **~kugel** *f* billiard ball.

billig ['bɪlɪç] *a* cheap; (*gerecht*) fair, reasonable; **~en** ['bɪlɪgən] *vt* approve of; **B~laden** *m* (*umg*) discount store; **B~ung** *f* approval.

Billion [bɪli'o:n] *f* billion, trillion (*US*).

Binde ['bɪndə] *f* **-, -n** bandage; (*Arm~*) band; (*MED*) sanitary towel; **~glied** *nt* connecting link; **b~n** *vt unreg* bind, tie; **~strich** *m* hyphen; **~wort** *nt* conjunction.

Bind- *zW:* **~faden** *m* string; **~ung** *f* bond, tie; (*Ski~*) binding.

binnen ['bɪnən] *präp* +*dat od gen* within; **B~hafen** *m* inland harbour; **B~handel** *m* internal trade.

Binse ['bɪnzə] *f* **-, -n** rush, reed; **Binsenwahrheit** *f* truism.

Bio- [bio] *zW* bio-; **~graphie** [-gra'fi:] *f* biography; **~loge** [-'lo:gə] *m* **-n, -n** biologist; **~logie** [-lo'gi:] *f* biology; **b~logisch** [-'lo:gɪʃ] *a* biological.

Birke ['bɪrkə] *f* **-, -n** birch.

Birma ['bɪrma] *nt* Burma.

Birnbaum *m* pear tree.

Birne ['bɪrnə] *f* **-, -n** pear; (*ELEK*) (light) bulb.

bis [bɪs] ♦*präp* +*akk, ad* **1** (*zeitlich*) till, until; (*~ spätestens*) by; **Sie haben ~ Dienstag Zeit** you have until *od* till Tuesday; **~ Dienstag muß es fertig sein** it must be ready by Tuesday; **~ auf weiteres** until further notice; **~ in die Nacht** into the night; **~ bald/gleich** see you later/soon

2 (*räumlich*) (up) to; **ich fahre ~ Köln** I'm going to *od* I'm going as far as Cologne; **~ an unser Grundstück** (right *od* up) to our plot; **~ hierher** this far

3 (*bei Zahlen*) up to; **~ zu** up to

4: **~ auf etw** (*akk*) (*außer*) except sth; (*einschließlich*) including sth.

♦*kj* **1** (*mit Zahlen*) to); **10 ~ 20** 10 to 20

2 (*zeitlich*) till, until; **~ es dunkel wird** till *od* until it gets dark; **von ...**

Bischof ['bɪʃɔf] m -s, -̈e bishop.
bischöflich ['bɪʃøːflɪç] a episcopal.
bisher [bɪs'heːr] ad, ~ig a till now, hitherto.
Biskuit [bɪs'kviːt] m od nt -(e)s, -s od -e biscuit; ~teig m sponge mixture.
biß etc v siehe **beißen**.
Biß [bɪs] m -sses, -sse bite.
bißchen ['bɪsçən] a, ad bit.
Bissen ['bɪsən] m -s, - bite, morsel.
bissig ['bɪsɪç] a (Hund) snappy; (Bemerkung) cutting, biting.
bist v siehe **sein**.
bisweilen [bɪs'vaɪlən] ad at times, occasionally.
Bit [bɪt] nt (COMPUT) bit.
Bitte ['bɪtə] f -, -n request; b~ interj please; (wie b~?) (I beg your) pardon; (als Antwort auf Dank) you're welcome; darf ich? — aber ~! may I? — please do; b~ schön! it was a pleasure; b~n vti unreg ask (um for); b~nd a pleading, imploring.
bitter ['bɪtər] a bitter; ~böse a very angry; B~keit f bitterness; ~lich a bitter.
Blähungen ['blɛːʊŋən] pl (MED) wind.
blamabel [bla'maːbəl] a disgraceful.
Blamage [bla'maːʒə] f -, -n disgrace.
blamieren [bla'miːrən] vr make a fool of o.s., disgrace o.s. // vt let down, disgrace.
blank [blaŋk] a bright; (unbedeckt) bare; (sauber) clean, polished; (umg: ohne Geld) broke; (offensichtlich) blatant.
blanko ['blaŋko] ad blank; B~scheck m blank cheque.
Bläschen ['blɛːsçən] nt bubble; (MED) spot, blister.
Blase ['blaːzə] f -, -n bubble; (MED) blister; (ANAT) bladder; ~balg m -(e)s, -bälge bellows pl; b~n vti unreg blow.
Blas- ['blaːs] zW: ~instrument nt wind instrument; ~kapelle f brass band; ~musik f brass band music.
blaß [blas] a pale.
Blässe ['blɛsə] f - paleness, pallor.
Blatt [blat] nt -(e)s, -̈er leaf; newspaper; (von Papier) sheet; (KARTEN) hand.
blättern ['blɛtərn] vi: in etw (dat) ~ leaf through sth.
Blätterteig m flaky od puff pastry.
blau [blaʊ] a blue; (umg) drunk, stoned; (KOCH) boiled; (Auge) black; ~er Fleck bruise; Fahrt ins B~e mystery tour; ~äugig a blue-eyed; B~licht nt flashing blue light; ~machen vi (umg) skive off work.
Blech [blɛç] nt -(e)s, -e tin, sheet metal; (Back~) baking tray; ~büchse f, ~dose f tin, can; b~en vti (umg)

pay; ~schaden m (AUT) damage to bodywork.
Blei [blaɪ] nt -(e)s, -e lead.
Bleibe ['blaɪbə] f -, -n roof over one's head; b~n vi unreg stay, remain; **bleibenlassen** vt unreg leave (alone).
bleich [blaɪç] a faded, pale; ~en vt bleach.
Blei- zW: b~ern a leaden; b~frei a (Benzin) lead-free; ~stift m pencil; ~stiftspitzer m pencil sharpener.
Blende ['blɛndə] f -, -n (PHOT) aperture; b~n vt blind, dazzle; (fig) hoodwink; b~nd a (umg) grand; b~nd aussehen look smashing.
Blick [blɪk] m -(e)s, -e (kurz) glance, glimpse; (Anschauen) look, gaze; (Aussicht) view; b~en vi look; sich b~en lassen put in an appearance; ~fang m eye-catching object; ~feld nt range of vision (auch fig).
blieb etc v siehe **bleiben**.
blind [blɪnt] a blind; (Glas etc) dull; ~er Passagier stowaway; B~darm m appendix; B~darmentzündung f appendicitis; B~enschrift ['blɪndən-] f braille; B~heit f blindness; ~lings ad blindly; B~schleiche f slow worm.
blink- [blɪŋk] zW: ~en vi twinkle, sparkle; (Licht) flash, signal; (AUT) indicate // vt flash, signal; B~er m -s, - (AUT) indicator.
blinzeln ['blɪntsəln] vi blink, wink.
Blitz [blɪts] m -es, -e (flash of) lightning; ~ableiter m lightning conductor; b~en vi (aufleuchten) glint, shine; es blitzt (MET) there's a flash of lightning; ~licht nt flashlight; b~schnell a, ad as quick as a flash.
Block [blɔk] m -(e)s, -̈e (lit, fig) block; (von Papier) pad; **Blockade** [blɔ'kaːdə] f -, -n blockade; ~flöte f recorder; b~frei a (POL) unaligned; b~ieren [blɔ'kiːrən] vt block // vi (Räder) jam; ~schrift f block letters pl.
blöd [bløːt] a silly, stupid; B~sinn m nonsense; ~sinnig a silly, idiotic.
blond [blɔnt] a blond, fair-haired.
bloß [bloːs] a 1 (unbedeckt) bare; (nackt) naked; mit der ~en Hand with one's bare hand; mit ~em Auge with the naked eye
2 (alleinig, nur) mere; der ~e Gedanke the very thought; ~er Neid sheer envy
♦ ad only, merely; laß das ~! just don't do that!; wie ist das ~ passiert? how on earth did that happen?
Blöße ['bløːsə] f -, -n bareness; nakedness; (fig) weakness.
bloß- zW: ~legen vt expose; ~stellen vt show up.
blühen ['blyːən] vi (lit) bloom, be in

bloom; (fig) flourish.

Blume ['blu:mə] f -, -n flower; (von Wein) bouquet; **Blumenkohl** m cauliflower; **Blumentopf** m flowerpot; **Blumenzwiebel** f bulb.

Bluse ['blu:zə] f -, -n blouse.

Blut [blu:t] nt -(e)s blood; **b~arm** a anaemic; (fig) penniless; **b~befleckt** a bloodstained; **~druck** m blood pressure.

Blüte ['bly:tə] f -, -n blossom; (fig) prime; **~zeit** f flowering period; (fig) prime.

Blutegel m leech.

bluten vi bleed.

Blütenstaub m pollen.

Blut- zW: **~er** m -s, - (MED) haemophiliac; **~erguß** m haemorrhage; (auf Haut) bruise; **~gruppe** f blood group; **b~ig** a bloody; **b~jung** a very young; **~probe** f blood test; **~spender** m blood donor; **~übertragung** f blood transfusion; **~ung** f bleeding, haemorrhage; **~vergiftung** f blood poisoning; **~wurst** f black pudding.

Bö(e) ['bø:(ə)] f -, -en squall.

Bock [bɔk] m -(e)s, ⸚e buck, ram; (Gestell) trestle, support; (SPORT) buck; **~wurst** f type of pork sausage.

Boden ['bo:dən] m -s, ⸚ ground; (Fuß~) floor; (Meeres~, Faß~) bottom; (Speicher) attic; **~see** m: der **~see** Lake Constance; **b~los** a bottomless; (umg) incredible; **~schätze** pl mineral wealth; **~turnen** nt floor exercises pl.

Bogen ['bo:gən] m -s, - (Biegung) curve; (ARCHIT) arch; (Waffe, MUS) bow; (Papier) sheet; **~gang** m arcade.

Bohle ['bo:lə] f -, -n plank.

Bohne ['bo:nə] f -, -n bean; **Bohnenkaffee** m pure coffee; **bohnern** vt wax, polish; **Bohnerwachs** nt floor polish.

Bohr- ['bo:r] zW: **b~en** vt bore; **~er** m -s, - drill; **~insel** f oil rig; **~maschine** f drill; **~turm** m derrick.

Boje ['bo:jə] f -, -n buoy.

Bolivien [bo'li:viən] nt Bolivia.

Bolzen ['bɔltsən] m -s, - bolt.

bombardieren [bɔmbar'di:rən] vt bombard; (aus der Luft) bomb.

Bombe ['bɔmbə] f -, -n bomb.

Bombenangriff m bombing raid.

Bombenerfolg m (umg) huge success.

Bonbon [bõ'bõ:] m od nt -s, -s sweet.

Boot [bo:t] nt -(e)s, -e boat.

Bord [bɔrt] m -(e)s, -e (AVIAT, NAUT) board; an ~ on board // nt (Brett) shelf; **Bordell** [bɔr'dɛl] nt -s, -e brothel; **~stein** m kerb(stone).

borgen ['bɔrgən] vt borrow; jdm etw

~ lend sb sth.

borniert [bɔr'ni:rt] a narrow-minded.

Börse ['bœrzə] f -, -n stock exchange; (Geld~) purse.

Borste ['bɔrstə] f -, -n bristle.

Borte ['bɔrtə] f -, -n edging; (Band) trimming.

bös(e) [bø:s, 'bø:zə] a bad, evil; (zornig) angry.

bösartig ['bø:s-] a malicious.

Böschung ['bœʃuŋ] f slope; (Ufer~ etc) embankment.

bos- ['bo:s] zW: **~haft** a malicious, spiteful; **B~heit** f malice, spite.

böswillig ['bø:svɪlɪç] a malicious.

bot etc v siehe **bieten**.

Botanik [bo'ta:nɪk] f botany.

botanisch [bo'ta:nɪʃ] a botanical.

Bot- ['bo:t] zW: **~e** m -n, -n messenger; **~schaft** f message, news; (POL) embassy; **~schafter** m -s, - ambassador.

Bottich ['bɔtɪç] m -(e)s, -e vat, tub.

Bouillon [bʊ'ljõ:] f -, -s consommé.

Bowle ['bo:lə] f -, -n punch.

Box- ['bɔks] zW: **b~en** vi box; **~er** m -s, - boxer; **~handschuh** m boxing glove; **~kampf** m boxing match.

boykottieren [bɔykɔ'ti:rən] vt boycott.

brach etc v siehe **brechen**.

brachte etc v siehe **bringen**.

Branche ['brã:ʃə] f -, -n line of business; **Branchenverzeichnis** nt yellow pages pl.

Brand [brant] m -(e)s, ⸚e fire; (MED) gangrene; **b~en** [brandən] vi surge; (Meer) break; **b~marken** vt brand; (fig) stigmatize; **~salbe** f ointment for burns; **~stifter** m arsonist, fire-raiser; **~stiftung** f arson; **~ung** f surf; **~wunde** f burn.

Branntwein ['brantvaɪn] m brandy.

Brasil- [bra'zi:l] zW: **~ien** [-iən] nt Brazil; **~ianer(in f)** [-i'a:nər(ɪn)] m Brazilian; **b~ianisch** a Brazilian.

Brat- [bra:t] zW: **~apfel** m baked apple; **b~en** vt unreg roast, fry; **~en** m -s, - roast, joint; **~hähnchen** nt, **~huhn** nt roast chicken; **~kartoffeln** pl fried od roast potatoes pl; **~pfanne** f frying pan.

Bratsche ['bra:tʃə] f -, -n viola.

Brat- zW: **~spieß** m spit; **~wurst** f grilled sausage.

Brauch [braux] m -(e)s, Bräuche custom; **b~bar** a usable, serviceable; (Person) capable; **b~en** vt (bedürfen) need; (müssen) have to; (verwenden) use.

Braue ['brauə] f -, -n brow; **b~n** vt brew; **Brauerei** f brewery.

braun [braun] a brown; (von Sonne auch) tanned.

Bräune ['brɔynə] f - brownness; (Sonnen~) tan; **b~n** vt make brown;

(*Sonne*) tan.
braungebrannt *a* tanned.
Brause ['brauzə] *f* -, -n shower bath; (*von Gießkanne*) rose; (*Getränk*) lemonade; **b~n** *vi* roar; (*auch vr: duschen*) take a shower.
Braut [braut] *f* -, **Bräute** bride; (*Verlobte*) fiancée.
Bräutigam ['brɔytıgam] *m* -s, -e bridegroom; fiancé.
Brautpaar *nt* bride and bridegroom, bridal pair.
brav [bra:f] *a* (*artig*) good; (*ehrenhaft*) worthy, honest.
bravo ['bra:vo] *interj* well done.
BRD ['be:'ɛr'de:] *f abk von* **Bundesrepublik Deutschland**.
Brech- ['brɛç] *zW:* **~eisen** *nt* crowbar; **b~en** *vti unreg* break; (*Licht*) refract; (*fig: Mensch*) crush; (*speien*) vomit; **~reiz** *m* nausea, retching.
Brei [brai] *m* -(e)s, -e (*Masse*) pulp; (*KOCH*) gruel; (*Hafer~*) porridge (*Brit*), oat meal (*US*).
breit [brait] *a* wide, broad; **B~e** *f* -, -n width; breadth; (*GEOG*) latitude; **~en** *vt:* etw über etw (*akk*) **~en** spread sth over sth; **B~engrad** *m* degree of latitude; **~machen** *vr* spread o.s. out; **~treten** *vt unreg* (*umg*) enlarge upon.
Brems- ['brɛms] *zW:* **~belag** *m* brake lining; **~e** [-zə] *f* -, -n brake; (*ZOOL*) horsefly; **b~en** [-zən] *vi* brake, apply the brakes // *vt* (*Auto*) brake; (*fig*) slow down; **~licht** *nt* brake light; **~pedal** *nt* brake pedal; **~spur** *f* tyre (*Brit*) *od* tire (*US*) marks *pl*; **~weg** *m* braking distance.
Brenn- ['brɛn] *zW:* **b~bar** *a* inflammable; **b~en** *unreg vi* burn, be on fire; (*Licht, Kerze etc*) burn // *vt* (*Holz etc*) burn; (*Ziegel, Ton*) fire; (*Kaffee*) roast; darauf **b~en**, etw zu tun be dying to do sth; **~(n)essel** *f* nettle; **~spiritus** *m* methylated spirits; **~stoff** *m* liquid fuel.
brenzlig ['brɛnslıç] *a* (*fig*) precarious.
Brett [brɛt] *nt* -(e)s, -er board, plank; (*Bord*) shelf; (*Spiel~*) board; **Schwarze(s)** *nt* notice board; **~er** *pl* (*SKI*) skis *pl*; (*THEAT*) boards *pl*; **~erzaun** *m* wooden fence.
Brezel ['bre:tsəl] *f* -, -n pretzel.
brichst *etc v siehe* **brechen**.
Brief [bri:f] *m* -(e)s, -e letter; **~freund** *m* penfriend; **~kasten** *m* letterbox; **~kopf** *m* letterhead; **b~lich** *a,ad* by letter; **~marke** *f* postage stamp; **~öffner** *m* letter opener; **~papier** *nt* notepaper; **~tasche** *f* wallet; **~träger** *m* postman; **~umschlag** *m* envelope; **~wechsel** *m* correspondence.
briet *etc v siehe* **braten**.

Brikett [bri'kɛt] *nt* -s, -s briquette.
brillant [brıl'jant] *a* (*fig*) sparkling, brilliant; **B~** *m* -en, -en brilliant, diamond.
Brille ['brılə] *f* -, -n spectacles *pl*; (*Schutz~*) goggles *pl*; (*Toiletten~*) (toilet) seat.
bringen ['brıŋən] *vt unreg* bring; (*mitnehmen, begleiten*) take; (*einbringen: Profit*) bring in; (*veröffentlichen*) publish; (*THEAT, CINE*) show; (*RAD, TV*) broadcast; (*in einen Zustand versetzen*) get; (*umg: tun können*) manage; **jdn dazu ~** make sb do sth; **etw zu tun ~** make sb do sth; **jdn nach Hause ~** take sb home; **jdn um etw ~** make sb lose sth; **jdn auf eine Idee ~** give sb an idea.
Brise ['bri:zə] *f* -, -n breeze.
Brit- ['brıt] *zW:* **~e** *m*, **~in** *f* Briton; **b~isch** *a* British.
bröckelig ['brœkəlıç] *a* crumbly.
Brocken ['brɔkən] *m* -s, - piece, bit; (*Fels~*) lump of rock.
brodeln ['bro:dəln] *vi* bubble.
Brokat [bro'ka:t] *m* -(e)s, -e brocade.
Brombeere ['brɔmbe:rə] *f* blackberry, bramble (*Brit*).
Bronchien ['brɔnçiən] *pl* bronchia(l tubes) *pl*.
Bronze ['brõ:sə] *f* -, -n bronze.
Brosche ['brɔʃə] *f* -, -n brooch.
Broschüre [brɔ'ʃy:rə] *f* -, -n pamphlet.
Brot [bro:t] *nt* -(e)s, -e bread; (*~laib*) loaf.
Brötchen ['brø:tçən] *nt* roll.
Bruch [brux] *m* -(e)s, **-e** breakage; (*zerbrochene Stelle*) break; (*fig*) split, breach; (*MED: Eingeweide~*) rupture, hernia; (*Bein~ etc*) fracture; (*MATH*) fraction.
brüchig ['bryçıç] *a* brittle, fragile; (*Haus*) dilapidated.
Bruch- *zW:* **~landung** *f* crash landing; **~strich** *m* (*MATH*) line; **~stück** *nt* fragment; **~teil** *m* fraction.
Brücke ['brykə] *f* -, -n bridge; (*Teppich*) rug.
Bruder ['bru:dər] *m* -s, **-** brother.
brüderlich ['bry:dərlıç] *a* brotherly.
Brühe ['bry:ə] *f* -, -n broth, stock; (*pej*) muck.
brüllen ['brylən] *vi* bellow, scream.
brummen ['brumən] *vi* (*Bär, Mensch etc*) growl; (*Insekt, Radio*) buzz; (*Motoren*) roar; (*murren*) grumble // *vt* grumble.
brünett [bry'nɛt] *a* brunette, dark-haired.
Brunnen ['brunən] *m* -s, - fountain; (*tief*) well; (*natürlich*) spring.
brüsk [brysk] *a* abrupt, brusque.
Brüssel ['brysəl] *nt* Brussels.
Brust [brust] *f* -, **-e** breast; (*Männer~*) chest.

brüsten ['brʏstən] *vr* boast.

Brust- *zW:* **~fellentzündung** *f* pleurisy; **~kasten** *m* chest; **~schwimmen** *nt* breast-stroke; **~warze** *f* nipple.

Brüstung ['brʏstuŋ] *f* parapet.

Brut [bru:t] *f* -, **-en** brood; (*Brüten*) hatching; **brutal** [bru'ta:l] *a* brutal; **Brutali'tät** *f* brutality; **~kasten** *m* incubator.

brüten ['bry:tən] *vi* hatch, brood (*auch fig*).

brutto ['bruto] *ad* gross; **B~einkommen** *nt*, **B~gehalt** *nt* gross salary; **B~gewicht** *nt* gross weight; **B~lohn** *m* gross wages *pl*.

Bube ['bu:bə] *m* -n, **-n** (*Schurke*) rogue; (*KARTEN*) jack.

Buch [bu:x] *nt* -(e)s, ⁼er book; (*COMM*) account book; **~binder** *m* bookbinder; **~drucker** *m* printer; **~e** *f* -, **-n** beech tree; **b~en** *vt* book; (*Betrag*) enter.

Bücher- ['by:çər] *zW:* **~brett** *nt* bookshelf; **~ei** [-'raɪ] *f* library; **~regal** *nt* bookshelves *pl*, bookcase; **~schrank** *m* bookcase.

Buch- *zW:* **~fink** *m* chaffinch; **~führung** *f* book-keeping, accounting; **~halter(in** *f*) *m* -s, - bookkeeper; **~handel** *m* book trade; **~händler(in** *f*) *m* bookseller; **~handlung** *f* bookshop.

Büchse ['bʏksə] *f* -, **-n** tin, can; (*Holz~*) box; (*Gewehr*) rifle; **Büchsenfleisch** *nt* tinned meat; **Büchsenöffner** *m* tin od can opener.

Buch- *zW:* **~stabe** *m* -ns, **-n** letter (of the alphabet); **b~stabieren** [bu:xʃta'bi:rən] *vt* spell; **b~stäblich** ['bu:xʃtɛ:plɪç] *a* literal.

Bucht ['bʊxt] *f* -, **-en** bay.

Buchung ['bu:xuŋ] *f* booking; (*COMM*) entry.

Buckel ['bʊkəl] *m* -s, - hump.

bücken ['bʏkən] *vr* bend.

Bückling ['bʏklɪŋ] *m* (*Fisch*) kipper; (*Verbeugung*) bow.

Bude ['bu:də] *f* -, **-n** booth, stall; (*umg*) digs *pl* (*Brit*).

Büfett [by'fe:] *nt* -s, **-s** (*Anrichte*) sideboard; (*Geschirrschrank*) dresser; **kaltes ~** cold buffet.

Büffel ['bʏfəl] *m* -s, - buffalo.

Bug [bu:k] *m* -(e)s, **-e** (*NAUT*) bow; (*AVIAT*) nose.

Bügel ['by:gəl] *m* -s, - (*Kleider~*) hanger; (*Steig~*) stirrup; (*Brillen~*) arm; **~brett** *nt* ironing board; **~eisen** *nt* iron; **~falte** *f* crease; **b~n** *vti* iron.

Bühne ['by:nə] *f* -, **-n** stage; **Bühnenbild** *nt* set, scenery.

Buhruf ['bu:ru:f] *m* boo.

buk *etc v siehe* **backen**.

Bulgarien [bul'ga:riən] *nt* Bulgaria.

Bull- ['bul] *zW:* **~dogge** *f* bulldog; **~dozer** ['buldo:zər] *m* -s, - bulldozer; **~e** *m* -n, **-n** bull.

Bummel ['bʊməl] *m* -s, - stroll; (*Schaufenster~*) window-shopping; **~ant** [-'lant] *m* slowcoach; **~ei** [-'laɪ] *f* wandering; dawdling; skiving; **b~n** *vi* wander, stroll; (*trödeln*) dawdle; (*faulenzen*) skive, loaf around; **~streik** *m* go-slow; **~zug** *m* slow train.

Bund [bunt] *m* -(e)s, ⁼e (*Freundschafts~ etc*) bond; (*Organisation*) union; (*POL*) confederacy; (*Hosen~, Rock~*) waistband // *nt* -(e)s, **-e** bunch; (*Stroh~*) bundle.

Bündel ['byndəl] *nt* -s, - bundle, bale; **b~n** *vt* bundle.

Bundes- ['bundəs] *in zW* Federal (*bes* West German); **~bahn** *f* Federal Railways *pl*; **~hauptstadt** *f* Federal capital; **~kanzler** *m* Federal Chancellor; **~land** *nt* Land; **~liga** *f* football league; **~präsident** *m* Federal President; **~rat** *m* upper house of West German Parliament; **~republik** *f* Federal Republic (of West Germany); **~staat** *m* Federal state; **~tag** *m* West German Parliament; **~verfassungsgericht** *nt* Federal Constitutional Court; **~wehr** *f* West German Armed Forces *pl*.

Bünd- *zW:* **b~ig** *a* (*kurz*) concise; **~nis** *nt* -ses, **-se** alliance.

Bunker ['buŋkər] *m* -s, - bunker.

bunt [bunt] *a* coloured; (*gemischt*) mixed; **jdm wird es zu ~** it's getting too much for sb; **B~stift** *m* coloured pencil, crayon.

Burg [bʊrk] *f* -, **-en** castle, fort.

Bürge ['bʏrgə] *m* -n, **-n** guarantor; **b~n** *vi* vouch (*für* for).

Bürger(in *f*) ['bʏrgər(ɪn)] *m* -s, - citizen; member of the middle class; **~krieg** *m* civil war; **b~lich** *a* (*Rechte*) civil; (*Klasse*) middleclass; (*pej*) bourgeois; **~meister** *m* mayor; **~recht** *nt* civil rights *pl*; **~schaft** *f* population, citizens *pl*; **~steig** *m* pavement; **~tum** *nt* citizens *pl*.

Bürgschaft *f* surety; **~ leisten** give security.

Büro [by'ro:] *nt* -s, **-s** office; **~angestellte(r)** *mf* office worker; **~automatisierung** *f* office automation, OA; **~klammer** *f* paper clip; **~krat** [byro'kra:t] *m* -en, **-en** bureaucrat; **~kra'tie** *f* bureaucracy; **b~'kratisch** *a* bureaucratic; **~schluß** *m* office closing time.

Bursch(e) [burʃ(ə)] *m* -en, **-en** lad, fellow; (*Diener*) servant.

Bürste ['bʏrstə] *f* -, **-n** brush; **b~n** *vt* brush.

Bus [bus] *m* **-ses, -se** bus.
Busch [buʃ] *m* **-(e)s,** ⁓e bush, shrub.
Büschel ['byʃəl] *nt* **-s,** - tuft.
buschig *a* bushy.
Busen ['bu:zən] *m* **-s,** - bosom; (*Meer~*) inlet, bay.
Buße ['bu:sə] *f* **-, -n** atonement, penance; (*Geld*) fine.
büßen ['by:sən] *vti* do penance (for), atone (for).
Bußgeld ['bu:sgɛlt] *nt* fine.
Büste ['bystə] *f* **-, -n** bust; **Büstenhalter** *m* bra.
Butter ['butər] *f* - butter; **~blume** *f* buttercup; **~brot** *nt* (piece of) bread and butter; **~brotpapier** *nt* greaseproof paper; **~dose** *f* butter dish; **b~weich** *a* soft as butter; (*fig, umg*) soft.
b.w. *abk* (= *bitte wenden*) p.t.o.
Byte [baɪt] *nt* **-s** byte.
bzgl. *abk* (= *bezüglich*) re.
bzw. *abk von* **beziehungsweise**.

C

(*siehe auch* **K, Z;**
für **CH** *siehe auch* **SCH**)

C, c [tse:] *nt* C, c.
ca. *abk* (= *circa*) approx.
Café [ka'fe:] *nt* **-s, -s** café.
Cafeteria [kafete'ri:a] *f* **-,** ⁓s cafeteria.
Camp- [kɛmp] *zW:* **c~en** *vi* camp; **~er(in** *f*) *m* **-s,** - camper; **~ing** *nt* **-s** camping; **~ingkocher** *m* camping stove; **~ingplatz** *m* camp(ing) site.
CDU [tse:de:'u:] *f abk* (= *Christlich-Demokratische Union*) Christian Democratic Union.
Cellist [tʃɛ'lɪst] *m* cellist.
Cello ['tʃɛlo] *nt* **-s, -s** *od* **Celli** cello.
Chamäleon [ka'mɛ:leɔn] *nt* **-s, -s** chameleon.
Champagner [ʃam'panjər] *m* **-s,** - champagne.
Champignon ['ʃampɪnjɔ] *m* **-s, -s** button mushroom.
Chance ['ʃã:s(ə)] *f* **-, -n** chance, opportunity.
Chaos ['ka:ɔs] *nt* **-,** - chaos.
chaotisch [ka'o:tɪʃ] *a* chaotic.
Charakter [ka'raktər] *m* **-s, -e** [karak'te:rə] character; **c~fest** *a* of firm character, strong; **c~i'sieren** *vt* characterize; **c~istisch** [karakte'rɪstɪʃ] *a* characteristic, typical (*für* of); **c~los** *a* unprincipled; **~losigkeit** *f* lack of principle; **~schwäche** *f* weakness of character; **~stärke** *f* strength of character; **~zug** *m* characteristic, trait.
charmant [ʃar'mant] *a* charming.
Charme [ʃarm] *m* **-s** charm.
Charterflug ['(t)ʃa:rtərflu:k] *m* charter flight.

Chassis [ʃa'si:] *nt* **-,** - chassis.
Chauffeur [ʃo'fø:r] *m* chauffeur.
Chauvinist [ʃovi'nɪst] *m* chauvinist, jingoist.
Chef [ʃɛf] *m* **-s, -s** head; (*umg*) boss; **~arzt** *m* head physician; **~in** *f* (*umg*) boss.
Chemie [çe'mi:] *f* - chemistry; **~faser** *f* man-made fibre.
Chemikalie [çemi'ka:liə] *f* **-, -n** chemical.
Chemiker(in *f*) ['çe:mikər(ɪn)] *m* **-s,** - (industrial) chemist.
chemisch ['çe:mɪʃ] *a* chemical; **~e Reinigung** dry cleaning.
Chiffre ['ʃɪfrə] *f* **-, -n** (*Geheimzeichen*) cipher; (*in Zeitung*) box number.
Chile ['çi:le, 'tʃi:le] *nt* Chile; **~ne** [-'le:nə] *m*, **~nin** *f* Chilean; **c~nisch** *a* Chilean.
Chin- ['çi:n] *zW:* **~a** *nt* China; **~ese** [-'ne:zə] *m*, **~esin** *f* Chinese; **c~esisch** *a* Chinese.
Chips [tʃɪps] *pl* crisps *pl*, chips *pl* (*US*).
Chirurg [çi'rʊrk] *m* **-en, -en** surgeon; **~ie** [-'gi:] *f* surgery; **c~isch** *a* surgical.
Chlor [klo:r] *nt* **-s** chlorine; **Chloro'form** *nt* **-s** chloroform.
Cholera ['ko:lera] *f* - cholera.
cholerisch [ko'le:rɪʃ] *a* choleric.
Chor [ko:r] *m* **-(e)s,** ⁓e choir; (*Musikstück, THEAT*) chorus; **~al** [ko'ra:l] *m* **-s, -äle** chorale.
Choreograph [koreo'gra:f] *m* **-en, -en** choreographer; **~ie** [-'fi:] *f* choreography.
Chorknabe *m* choirboy.
Christ ['krɪst] *m* **-en, -en** Christian; **~baum** *m* Christmas tree; **~entum** *nt* Christianity; **~in** *f* Christian; **~kind** *nt* ≈ Father Christmas; (*Jesus*) baby Jesus; **c~lich** *a* Christian; **Christus** *m* - Christ.
Chrom [kro:m] *nt* **-s** (*CHEM*) chromium; chrome.
Chron- ['kro:n] *zW:* **~ik** *f* chronicle; **c~isch** *a* chronic; **c~ologisch** [-'lo:gɪʃ] *a* chronological.
Chrysantheme [kryzan'te:mə] *f* **-, -n** chrysanthemum.
circa ['tsɪrka] *ad* about, approximately.
Clown [klaun] *m* **-s, -s** clown.
cm *abk von* **Zentimeter**.
COBOL ['ko:bɔl] (*COMPUT*) COBOL.
Cola ['ko:la] *f* **-, -s** Coke ®.
Computer [kɔm'pju:tər] *m* **-s,** - computer.
Conférencier [kõferãsi'e:] *m* **-s, -s** compère.
Coupé [ku'pe:] *nt* **-s, -s** (*AUT*) coupé, sports version.
Coupon [ku'põ:] *m* **-s, -s** coupon;

(Stoff~) length of cloth.

Cousin [ku'zɛ:] m -s, -s cousin; ~**e** [ku'zi:nə] f -, -n cousin.

Creme [krɛ:m] f -, -s (lit, fig) cream; (Schuh~) polish; (Zahn~) paste; (KOCH) mousse; **c~farben** a cream(-coloured).

CSU [tse:'ɛs''u:] f abk (= Christlich-Soziale Union) Christian Social Union.

Curry(pulver nt) ['kœri(pulfər)] m od nt -s curry powder.

Cursor ['kœrsər] m cursor.

Cutter(in f) ['katər(ɪn)] m -s, - (CINE) editor.

D

D, d [de:] nt D, d.

da [da:] ◆ad 1 (örtlich) there; (hier) here; ~ **draußen** out there; ~ **bin ich** here I am; ~, **wo** where; **ist noch Milch** ~? is there any milk left? 2 (zeitlich) then; (folglich) so 3: ~ **haben wir Glück gehabt** we were lucky there; ~ **kann man nichts machen** nothing can be done about it ◆kj (weil) as, since.

dabehalten vt unreg keep.

dabei [da'baɪ] ad (räumlich) close to it; (noch dazu) besides; (zusammen mit) with them; (zeitlich) during this; (obwohl doch) but, however; **was ist schon** ~? what of it?; **es ist doch nichts** ~, **wenn** ... it doesn't matter if ...; **bleiben wir** ~ let's leave it at that; **es bleibt** ~ that's settled; **das Dumme/Schwierige** ~ the stupid/difficult part of it; **er war gerade** ~, **zu gehen** he was just leaving; ~**sein** vi unreg (anwesend) be present; (beteiligt) be involved; ~**stehen** vi unreg stand around.

Dach [dax] nt -(e)s, ¨er roof; ~**boden** m attic, loft; ~**decker** m -s, - slater, tiler; ~**fenster** nt, ~**luke** f skylight; ~**pappe** f roofing felt; ~**rinne** f gutter; ~**ziegel** m roof tile.

Dachs [daks] m -es, -e badger.

dachte etc v siehe **denken**.

Dackel ['dakəl] m -s, - dachshund.

dadurch [da'dʊrç] ad (räumlich) through it; (durch diesen Umstand) thereby, in that way; (deshalb) because of that, for that reason // kj: ~, **daß** because.

dafür [da'fy:r] ad for it; (anstatt) instead; **er kann nichts** ~ he can't help it; **er ist bekannt** ~ he is well-known for that; **was bekomme ich** ~? what will I get for it?

dagegen [da'ge:gən] ad against it; (im Vergleich damit) in comparison with it; (bei Tausch) to it; **ich habe**

nichts ~ I don't mind; **ich war** ~ I was against it; ~ **kann man nichts tun** one can't do anything about it // kj however; ~**halten** vt unreg (vergleichen) compare with it; (entgegnen) object to it.

daheim [da'haɪm] ad at home; **D~** nt -s home.

daher [da'he:r] ad (räumlich) from there; (Ursache) from that // kj (deshalb) that's why.

dahin [da'hɪn] ad (räumlich) there; (zeitlich) then; (vergangen) gone; ~**gegen** kj on the other hand; ~**gehend** ad on this matter; ~**gestellt** ad: ~**gestellt bleiben** remain to be seen; ~**gestellt sein lassen** leave sth open od undecided.

dahinten [da'hɪntən] ad over there.

dahinter [da'hɪntər] ad behind it; ~**kommen** vi unreg get to the bottom of sth.

Dahlie ['da:liə] f -, -n dahlia.

dalli ['dali] adv (umg) chop chop.

damalig ['da:ma:lɪç] a of that time, then.

damals ['da:ma:ls] ad at that time, then.

Damast [da'mast] m -(e)s, -e damask.

Dame ['da:mə] f -, -n lady; (SCHACH, KARTEN) queen; (Spiel) draughts; **damenhaft** a ladylike; **Damenwahl** f ladies' excuse-me.

damit [da'mɪt] ad with it; (begründend) by that; **was meint er** ~? what does he mean by that?; **genug** ~! that's enough; ~ **eilt es nicht** there's no hurry // kj in order that od to.

dämlich ['dɛ:mlɪç] a (umg) silly, stupid.

Damm [dam] m -(e)s, ¨e dyke; (Stau~) dam; (Hafen~) mole; (Bahn~, Straßen~) embankment.

Dämm- ['dɛm] zW: **d~en** vt (Wasser) dam up; (Schmerzen) keep back; **d~erig** a dim, faint; **d~ern** vi (Tag) dawn; (Abend) fall; ~**erung** f twilight; (Morgen~) dawn; (Abend~) dusk.

dämonisch [dɛ'mo:nɪʃ] a demoniacal.

Dampf [dampf] m -(e)s, ¨e steam; (Dunst) vapour; **d~en** vi steam.

dämpfen ['dɛmpfən] vt (KOCH) steam; (bügeln auch) iron with a damp cloth; (fig) dampen, subdue.

Dampf- zW: ~**er** m -s, - steamer; ~**kochtopf** m pressure cooker; ~**schiff** nt steamship; ~**walze** f steamroller.

danach [da'na:x] ad after that; (zeitlich auch) afterwards; (gemäß) accordingly; according to which od that; **er sieht** ~ he looks it.

daneben [da'ne:bən] ad beside it; (im Vergleich) in comparison;

~benehmen *vr unreg* misbehave; **~gehen** *vi unreg* miss; (*Plan*) fail.

Dän- ['dɛːn] *zW:* **~e** *m*, **~in** *f* Dane; **~emark** *nt* Denmark; **d~isch** *a* Danish.

Dank [daŋk] *m* **-(e)s** thanks *pl*; **vielen** *od* **schönen ~** many thanks; **jdm ~ sagen** thank sb; **d~** *präp +dat od gen* thanks to; **d~bar** *a* grateful; (*Aufgabe*) rewarding; **~barkeit** *f* gratitude; **d~e** *interj* thank you, thanks; **d~en** *vi* (+*dat*) thank; **d~enswert** *a* (*Arbeit*) worthwhile; rewarding; (*Bemühung*) kind; **d~sagen** *vi* express one's thanks.

dann [dan] *ad* then; **~ und wann** now and then.

daran [da'ran] *ad* on it; (*stoßen*) against it; **es liegt ~, daß ...** the cause of it is that ...; **gut/schlecht ~ sein** be well-/badly off; **das Beste/ Dümmste ~** the best/stupidest thing about it; **ich war nahe ~, zu ...** I was on the point of ...; **er ist ~ gestorben** he died from *od* of it; **~gehen** *vi unreg* start; **~setzen** *vt* stake; **er hat alles ~gesetzt, von Glasgow wegzukommen** he has done his utmost to get away from Glasgow.

darauf [da'rauf] *ad* (*räumlich*) on it; (*zielgerichtet*) towards it; (*danach*) afterwards; **es kommt ganz ~ an, ob ...** it depends whether ...; **die Tage ~** the days following *od* thereafter; **am Tag ~** the next day; **~folgend** *a* (*Tag, Jahr*) next, following; **~legen** *vt* lay *od* put on top.

daraus [da'raus] *ad* from it; **was ist ~ geworden?** what became of it?; **~ geht hervor, daß ...** this means that ...

Darbietung ['daːrbiːtuŋ] *f* performance.

darf *etc v siehe* **dürfen**.

darin [da'rin] *ad* in (there), in it.

Dar- ['daːr] *zW:* **d~legen** *vt* explain, expound, set forth; **~legung** *f* explanation; **~leh(e)n** *nt* **-s, -** loan.

Darm [darm] *m* **-(e)s, ̈e** intestine; (*Wurst~*) skin; **~saite** *f* gut string.

Darstell- ['daːrʃtɛl] *zW:* **d~en** *vt* (*abbilden, bedeuten*) represent; (*THEAT*) act; (*beschreiben*) describe // *vr* appear to be; **~er(in** *f*) *m* **-s, -** actor/actress; **~ung** *f* portrayal, depiction.

darüber [da'ryːbər] *ad* (*räumlich*) over/above it; (*fahren*) over it; (*mehr*) more; (*währenddessen*) meanwhile; (*sprechen, streiten*) about it; **~ geht nichts** there's nothing like it.

darum [da'rum] *ad* (*räumlich*) round it; **er bittet ~** he is pleading for it; **es geht ~, daß ...** the thing is that ...;

er würde viel ~ geben, wenn ... he would give a lot to ... // *kj* that's why; **ich tue es ~, weil ...** I am doing it because ...

darunter [da'runtər] *ad* (*räumlich*) under it; (*dazwischen*) among them; (*weniger*) less; **ein Stockwerk ~** one floor below (it); **was verstehen Sie ~?** what do you understand by that?.

das [das] *def art* the // *pron* that.

Dasein ['daːzain] *nt* **-s** (*Leben*) life; (*Anwesenheit*) presence; (*Bestehen*) existence; **d~** *vi unreg* be there.

daß [das] *kj* that.

dasselbe [das'zɛlbə] *art, pron* the same.

dastehen ['daːʃteːən] *vi unreg* stand there.

Datei [da'tai] *f* file.

Daten- ['daːtən] *zW:* **~bank** *f* data base; **~sichtgerät** *nt* visual display unit, VDU.

datieren [da'tiːrən] *vt* date.

Dattel ['datəl] *f* **-, -n** date.

Datum ['daːtum] *nt* **-s, Daten** date; (*pl:* **Daten**) data *pl*.

Dauer ['dauər] *f* **-, -n** duration; (*gewisse Zeitspanne*) length; (*Bestand, Fortbestehen*) permanence; **es war nur von kurzer ~** it didn't last long; **auf die ~** in the long run; (*auf längere Zeit*) indefinitely; **~auftrag** *m* standing order; **d~haft** *a* lasting, durable; **~karte** *f* season ticket; **~lauf** *m* long-distance run; **d~n** *vi* last; **es hat sehr lang gedauert, bis er ...** it took him a long time to ...;

dauernd *a* constant; **~welle** *f* perm(anent wave); **~wurst** *f* German salami; **~zustand** *m* permanent condition.

Daumen ['daumən] *m* **-s, -** thumb.

Daune ['daunə] *f* **-, -n** down; **Daunendecke** *f* down duvet *od* quilt.

davon [da'fɔn] *ad* of it; (*räumlich*) away; (*weg von*) from it; (*Grund*) because of it; **das kommt ~!** that's what you get; **~ abgesehen** apart from that; **~ sprechen/wissen** talk/ know of *od* about it; **was habe ich ~?** what's the point?; **~gehen** *vi unreg* leave, go away; **~laufen** *vi unreg* run away.

davor [da'foːr] *ad* (*räumlich*) in front of it; (*zeitlich*) before (that); **~ warnen** warn about it.

dazu [da'tsuː] *ad* (*legen, stellen*) by it; (*essen, singen*) with it; **und ~ noch** and in addition; **ein Beispiel/seine Gedanken ~** one example for/his thoughts on this; **wie komme ich denn ~?** why should I?; **~ fähig sein** be capable of it; **sich ~ äußern** say sth on it; **~gehören** *vi* belong to it; **~kommen** *vi unreg* (*Ereignisse*) happen too; (an einen Ort) come along.

dazwischen [da'tsvɪʃən] ad in between; (räumlich auch) between (them); (zusammen mit) among them; **der Unterschied ~** the difference between them; **~kommen** vi unreg (hineingeraten) get caught in it; **es ist etwas ~gekommen** something cropped up; **~reden** vi (unterbrechen) interrupt; (sich einmischen) interfere; **~treten** vi unreg intervene.

DB abk (= Deutsche Bundesbahn) Federal Railways.

DDR [de:de:'ɛr] f abk (= Deutsche Demokratische Republik) GDR.

Debatte [de'batə] f -, -n debate.

Deck [dɛk] nt -(e)s, -s od -e deck; **an ~ gehen** go on deck; **~e** f -, -n cover; (Bett~) blanket; (Tisch~) tablecloth; (Zimmer~) ceiling; **unter einer ~e stecken** be hand in glove; **~el** m -s, - lid; **d~en** vt cover // vr coincide; **~ung** f (Schützen) covering; (Schutz) cover; (SPORT) defence; (Übereinstimmen) agreement; **d~ungsgleich** a congruent.

Defekt [de'fɛkt] m -(e)s, -e fault, defect; **d~** a faulty.

defensiv [defɛn'si:f] a defensive.

definieren [defi'ni:rən] vt define.

Definition [definitsi'o:n] f definition.

Defizit [de:fitsit] nt -s, -e deficit.

deftig ['dɛftɪç] a (Essen) large; (Witz) coarse.

Degen ['de:gən] m -s, - sword.

degenerieren [degene'ri:rən] vi degenerate.

Dehn- ['de:n] zW: **d~bar** a elastic; (fig: Begriff) loose; **~barkeit** f elasticity; looseness; **d~en** vtr stretch.

Deich [daɪç] m -(e)s, -e dyke, dike.

Deichsel ['daɪksəl] f -, -n shaft; **d~n** vt (fig, umg) wangle.

dein [daɪn] pron (**D~** in Briefen) your; **~e(r, s)** yours; **~er** pron gen of **du** of you; **~erseits** ad on your part; **~esgleichen** pron people like you; **~etwegen, ~etwillen** ad (für dich) for your sake; (wegen dir) on your account; **~ige** pron: **der/die/das ~ige** yours.

dekadent [deka'dɛnt] a decadent.

Dekadenz f decadence.

Deklination [deklinatsi'o:n] f declension.

deklinieren [dekli'ni:rən] vt decline.

Dekolleté [dekɔl'te:] nt -s, -s low neckline.

Deko- [deko] zW: **~rateur** [-ra'tø:r] m window dresser; **~ration** [-ratsi'o:n] f decoration; (in Laden) window dressing; **d~rativ** [-ra'ti:f] a decorative; **d~rieren** [-'ri:rən] vt decorate.

(Schaufenster) dress.

Delegation [delegatsi'o:n] f delegation.

delikat [deli'ka:t] a (zart, heikel) delicate; (köstlich) delicious.

Delikatesse [delika'tɛsə] f -, -n delicacy; (pl: Feinkost) delicatessen food; **Delikatessengeschäft** nt delicatessen.

Delikt [de'lɪkt] nt -(e)s, -e (JUR) offence.

Delle ['dɛlə] f -, -n (umg) dent.

Delphin [dɛl'fi:n] m -s, -e dolphin.

dem [de(:)m] art dat von **der**.

Demagoge [dema'go:gə] m -n, -n demagogue.

dementieren [demɛn'ti:rən] vt deny.

dem- zW: **~gemäß, ~nach** ad accordingly; **~nächst** ad shortly.

Demokrat [demo'kra:t] m -en, -en democrat; **~ie** [-'ti:] f democracy; **d~isch** a democratic; **d~isieren** [-i'zi:rən] vt democratize.

demolieren [demo'li:rən] vt demolish.

Demon- [demən] zW: **~strant(in** f) [-'strant(in)] m demonstrator; **~stration** [-stratsi'o:n] f demonstration; **d~strativ** [-stra'ti:f] a demonstrative; (Protest) pointed; **d~strieren** [-'stri:rən] vti demonstrate.

Demoskopie [demosko'pi:] f public opinion research.

Demut ['de:mu:t] f - humility.

demütig ['de:my:tɪç] a humble; **~en** ['de:my:tɪgən] vt humiliate; **D~ung** f humiliation.

demzufolge ['de:mtsu'fɔlgə] ad accordingly.

den [de(:)n] art akk von **der**.

denen ['de:nən] pron dat pl von **der**, **die**, **das**.

Denk- ['dɛnk] zW: **d~bar** a conceivable; **d~en** vti unreg think; **~en** nt -s thinking; **~fähigkeit** f intelligence; **d~faul** a lazy; **~fehler** m logical error; **~mal** nt -s, -̈er monument; **d~würdig** a memorable; **~zettel** m: **jdm einen ~zettel verpassen** teach sb a lesson.

denn [dɛn] kj for // ad then; (nach Komparativ) than; **warum ~?** why?

dennoch ['dɛnɔx] kj nevertheless.

Denunziant [denuntsi'ant] m informer.

deponieren [depo'ni:rən] vt (COMM) deposit.

Depot [de'po:] nt -s, -s warehouse; (Bus~, EISENB) depot; (Bank~) strongroom, safe (US).

Depression [depresi'o:n] f depression.

deprimieren [depri'mi:rən] vt depress.

der, die, das [de:r, di:, das] ♦ def art gen **des, der, des**, dat **dem, der, dem** akk **den, die, das**, pl **die** the; **der Rhein** the Rhine; **der Klaus** (umg) Klaus; **die Frau** (im allgemeinen) women; **der Tod/das Leben** death/ life; **der Fuß des Berges** the foot of the hill; **gib es der Frau** give it to the woman; **er hat sich die Hand verletzt** he has hurt his hand

◆ *rel pron* (*bei Menschen*) who, that; (*bei Tieren, Sachen*) which, that; **der Mann, den ich gesehen habe** the man who *od* whom *od* that I saw

◆ *dem pron* he/she/it; (*jener, dieser*) that; *pl* those; **der/die war es** it was him/her; **der mit der Brille** the one with glasses; **ich will den (da)** I want that one.

derart ['de:r'a:rt] *ad* so; (*solcher Art*) such; **~ig** a such, this sort of.

derb [derp] a sturdy; (*Kost*) solid; (*grob*) coarse; **D~heit** f sturdiness; solidity; coarseness.

der- *zW*: '~**gleichen** *pron* such; '~**jenige** *pron* he; she; it; (*rel*) the one (who); that (which); '~**maßen** *ad* to such an extent, so; **~'selbe** *art*, *pron* the same; '~**weil(en)** *ad* in the meantime; '~**zeitig** a present, current; (*damalig*) then.

des [des] *art gen von* **der**.

desertieren [dezɛr'ti:rən] *vi* desert.

desgleichen ['des'glaiçən] *pron* the same.

deshalb ['des'halp] *ad* therefore, that's why.

Desinfektion [dezinfɛktsi'o:n] f disinfection; **Desinfektionsmittel** nt disinfectant.

desinfizieren [dezinfi'tsi:rən] *vt* disinfect.

dessen ['desən] *pron gen von* **der**, **das**; **~'ungeachtet** *ad* nevertheless, regardless.

Dessert [de'se:r] nt **-s, -s** dessert.

destillieren [dɛstɪ'li:rən] *vt* distil.

desto ['desto] *ad* all *od* so much the; **~ besser** all the better.

deswegen ['dɛs've:gən] *kj* therefore, hence.

Detail [de'tai] nt **-s, -s** detail.

Detektiv [detɛk'ti:f] m **-s, -e** detective.

deut- ['dɔyt] *zW*: **~en** *vt* interpret, explain // *vi* point (*auf +akk* to *od* at); **~lich** a clear; (*Unterschied*) distinct; **D~lichkeit** f clarity; distinctness.

deutsch [dɔytʃ] a German; **auf ~ in** German; **D~e Demokratische Republik** German Democratic Republic, East Germany; **~es Beefsteak** nt ≈ hamburger; **D~** nt German; **D~e** f, **D~er** m German; **ich bin D~er** I am German; **D~land** nt Germany.

Devise [de'vi:zə] f **-, -n** motto, device; (*pl: FIN*) foreign currency *od* exchange.

Dezember [de'tsɛmbər] m **-(s), -** December.

dezent [de'tsɛnt] a discreet.

dezimal [detsi'ma:l] a decimal; **D~bruch** m decimal (fraction); **D~system** nt decimal system.

d.h. *abk* (= *das heißt*) i.e.

Dia ['di:a] nt **-s, -s** (*PHOT*) slide, transparency.

Diabetes [dia'be:tɛs] m **-, -** (*MED*) diabetes.

Diagnose [dia'gno:zə] f **-, -n** diagnosis.

diagonal [diago'na:l] a diagonal; **D~e** f **-, -n** diagonal.

Dialekt [dia'lɛkt] m **-(e)s, -e** dialect; **d~isch** a dialectal; (*Logik*) dialectical.

Dialog [dia'lo:k] m **-(e)s, -e** dialogue.

Diamant [dia'mant] m diamond.

Diät [di'ɛ:t] f **-** diet; **~en** *pl* (*POL*) allowance.

dich [dɪç] *pron akk von* **du** you; yourself.

dicht [dɪçt] a dense; (*Nebel*) thick; (*Gewebe*) close; (*undurchlässig*) (water)tight; (*fig*) concise // *ad*: **~ an/bei** close to; **~bevölkert** a densely *od* heavily populated; **D~e** f **-, -** density; thickness; closeness; (water)tightness; (*fig*) conciseness; **~en** *vt* (*dicht machen*) make watertight; seal; (*NAUT*) caulk // *vti* (*LITER*) compose, write; **D~er(in** f) m **-s, -** poet; (*Autor*) writer; **~erisch** a poetical; **~halten** *vi unreg* (*umg*) keep one's mouth shut; **D~ung** f (*TECH*) washer; (*AUT*) gasket; (*Gedichte*) poetry; (*Prosa*) (piece of) writing.

dick [dɪk] a thick; (*fett*) fat; **durch ~ und dünn** through thick and thin; **D~e** f **-, -** thickness; fatness; **~flüssig** a viscous; **D~icht** nt **-s, -e** thicket; **D~kopf** m mule; **D~milch** f soured milk.

die [di:] *def art siehe* **der**.

Dieb(in f) [di:p/di:bɪn] m **-(e)s, -e** thief; **d~isch** a thieving; (*umg*) immense; **~stahl** m **-(e)s, -e** theft.

Diele ['di:lə] f **-, -n** (*Brett*) board; (*Flur*) hall, lobby.

dienen ['di:nən] *vi* serve (*jdm* sb).

Diener m **-s, -** servant; **~in** f (maid)servant; **~schaft** f servants *pl*.

Dienst [di:nst] m **-(e)s, -e** service; **außer ~** retired; **~ haben** be on duty.

Dienstag ['di:nsta:k] m Tuesday; **d~s** *ad* on Tuesdays.

Dienst- *zW*: **~geheimnis** nt professional secret; **~gespräch** nt business call; **d~habend** (*Arzt*) on duty; **~leistungsgewerbe** nt service industries *pl*; **d~lich** a official; **~mädchen** nt domestic servant; **~reise** f business trip; **~stelle** f office; **~vorschrift** f service regulations *pl*; **~weg** m official channels *pl;* ~**zeit** *f* office hours *pl;* (*MIL*) period of service.

dies- [di:s] *zW:* ~**bezüglich** *a* (*Frage*) on this matter; ~**e(r, s)** [di:zə(r,z)] *pron* this (one); **dieselbe** [di:'zɛlbə] *pron, art* the same.

Dieselöl ['di:zəl'ø:l] *nt* diesel oil.

diesig ['di:zɪç] *a* drizzly.

dies- *zW:* ~**jährig** *a* this year's; ~**mal** *ad* this time; ~**seits** *präp* +*gen* on this side; **D**~**seits** *nt* - this life.

Dietrich ['di:trɪç] *m* -s, -e picklock.

differential [dɪfɛrɛnˈtsiˈa:l] *a* a differential; **D**~**getriebe** *nt* differential gear; **D**~**rechnung** *f* differential calculus.

differenzieren [dɪferɛnˈtsi:rən] *vt* make differences in; **differenziert** complex.

Dikt- [dɪkt] *zW:* ~**aphon** [-aˈfo:n] *nt* dictaphone; ~**at** [-ˈta:t] *nt* -(e)s, -e dictation; ~**ator** [-ˈta:tɔr] *m* dictator; **d**~**atorisch** [-aˈto:rɪʃ] *a* dictatorial; ~**atur** [-aˈtu:r] *f* dictatorship; **d**~**ieren** [-ˈti:rən] *vt* dictate.

Dilemma [diˈlɛma] *nt* -s, -s *od* -ta dilemma.

Dilettant [dɪlɛˈtant] *m* dilettante, amateur; **d**~**isch** *a* amateurish, dilettante.

Dimension [dimɛnˈzi:o:n] *f* dimension.

Ding [dɪŋ] *nt* -(e)s, -e thing, object; **d**~**lich** *a* real, concrete; **Dings, Dingsbums** ['dɪŋksbʊms] *nt* - (*umg*) thingummybob.

Diözese [diøˈtse:zə] *f* -, *n* diocese.

Diphtherie [dɪfteˈri:] *f* diphtheria.

Diplom [diˈplo:m] *nt* -(e)s, -e diploma, certificate; ~**at** [-ˈma:t] *m* -en, -en diplomat; ~**atie** [-aˈti:] *f* diplomacy; **d**~**atisch** [-ˈma:tɪʃ] *a* diplomatic; ~**ingenieur** *m* qualified engineer.

dir [di:r] *pron dat von* **du** (to) you.

direkt [diˈrɛkt] *a* direct; **D**~**or** *m* director; (*SCH*) principal, headmaster; **D**~**übertragung** *f* live broadcast.

Dirigent [diriˈgɛnt] *m* conductor.

dirigieren [diriˈgi:rən] *vt* direct; (*MUS*) conduct.

Dirne ['dɪrnə] *f* -, -n prostitute.

Diskette [dɪsˈkɛtə] *f* diskette, floppy disk.

Diskont [dɪsˈkɔnt] *m* -s, -e discount; ~**satz** *m* rate of discount.

Diskothek [dɪskoˈte:k] *f* -, -en disco(theque).

diskret [dɪsˈkre:t] *a* discreet; **D**~**ion** [-tsiˈo:n] *f* discretion.

Diskussion [dɪskʊsiˈo:n] *f* discussion; debate; **zur** ~ **stehen** be under discussion.

diskutabel [dɪskuˈta:bəl] *a* debatable.

diskutieren [dɪskuˈti:rən] *vti* discuss; debate.

Distanz [dɪsˈtants] *f* distance.

Distel ['dɪstəl] *f* -, -n thistle.

Disziplin [dɪstsiˈpli:n] *f* discipline.

Dividende [diviˈdɛndə] *f* -, -n dividend.

dividieren [diviˈdi:rən] *vt* divide (*durch* by).

DM [de:ˈɛm] *abk* (= *Deutsche Mark*) German Mark.

D-Mark ['de:mark] *f* D Mark, German Mark.

doch [dɔx] ◆*ad* **1** (*dennoch*) after all; (*sowieso*) anyway; **er kam** ~ **noch** he came after all; **du weißt es ja** ~ **besser** you know better than I do anyway; **und** ~ ... **and yet** ...

2 (*als bejahende Antwort*) yes I do/it does *etc*; **das ist nicht wahr** — ~! that's not true — yes it is!

3 (*auffordernd*): **komm** ~ do come; **laß ihn** ~ just leave him; **nicht** ~! oh no!

4: **sie ist** ~ **noch so jung** but she's still so young; **Sie wissen** ~, **wie das ist** you know how it is(, don't you?); **wenn** ~ if only

◆*kj* (*aber*) but; (*trotzdem*) all the same; **und** ~ **hat er es getan** but he did it.

Docht [dɔxt] *m* -(e)s, -e wick.

Dogge ['dɔgə] *f* -, -n bulldog.

Dogma ['dɔgma] *nt* -s, -men dogma; **d**~**tisch** [dɔˈgma:tɪʃ] *a* dogmatic.

Doktor ['dɔktɔr] *m* -s, -en [-ˈto:rən] doctor; **Doktorand** [-ˈrant] *m* -en, -en candidate for a doctorate; ~**arbeit** *f* doctoral thesis.

Dokument [dokuˈmɛnt] *nt* document.

Dokumentar- [dokumɛnˈta:r] *zW:* ~**bericht** [-ˈta:rbərɪçt] *m* documentary; ~**film** *m* documentary (film); **d**~**isch** *a* documentary.

Dolch [dɔlç] *m* -(e)s, -e dagger.

dolmetschen ['dɔlmɛtʃən] *vti* interpret.

Dolmetscher(in *f*) *m* -s, - interpreter.

Dom [do:m] *m* -(e)s, -e cathedral.

dominieren [domiˈni:rən] *vt* dominate // *vi* predominate.

Dompfaff ['dɔmpfaf] *m* bullfinch.

Donau ['do:nau] *f* Danube.

Donner ['dɔnər] *m* -s, - thunder; **d**~**n** *vi unpers* thunder.

Donnerstag ['dɔnərsta:k] *m* Thursday.

doof [do:f] *a* (*umg*) daft, stupid.

Doppel ['dɔpəl] *nt* -s, - duplicate; (*SPORT*) doubles; ~~ *in zW* double; ~**bett** *nt* double bed; ~**fenster** *nt* double glazing; ~**gänger** *m* -s, - double; ~**haus** *nt* semi-detached house; ~**punkt** *m* colon; ~**stecker** *m* two-way adaptor; **d**~**t** *a* double; **in d**~**ter Ausführung** in duplicate; ~**zentner** *m* 100 kilograms; ~**zimmer** *nt* double room.

Dorf [dɔrf] *nt* -(e)s, ¨-er village; ~**bewohner** *m* villager.

Dorn [dɔrn] *m* -(e)s, -en (*BOT*) thorn;

pl **-e** (*Schnallen~*) tongue, pin; **d~ig** *a* thorny.

dörren ['dœrən] *vt* dry.

Dörrobst ['dœr'o:pst] *nt* dried fruit.

Dorsch [dɔrʃ] *m* **-(e)s, -e** cod.

dort [dɔrt] *ad* there; **~ drüben** over there; **~her** from there; **~hin** (to) there; **~ig** *a* of that place; in that town.

Dose ['do:zə] *f* **-, -n** box; (*Blech~*) tin, can; **Dosenöffner** *m* tin *od* can opener.

Dosis ['do:zɪs] *f* **-, Dosen** dose.

Dotter ['dɔtər] *m* **-s, -** egg yolk.

Dozent [do'tsɛnt] *m* university lecturer.

Drache ['draxə] *m* **-n, -n** (*Tier*) dragon; **~n** *m* **-s, -** kite.

Draht [dra:t] *m* **-(e)s, -̈e** wire; **auf ~ sein** be on the ball; **~gitter** *nt* wire grating; **~seil** *nt* cable; **~seilbahn** *f* cable railway, funicular; **~zange** *f* pliers *pl*.

Drama ['dra:ma] *nt* **-s, Dramen** drama, play; **~tiker** [-'ma:tikər] *m* **-s, -** dramatist; **d~tisch** [-'ma:tɪʃ] *a* dramatic.

dran [dran] *ad* (*umg*) **jetzt bin ich ~!** it's my turn now; *siehe* **daran.**

Drang [draŋ] *m* **-(e)s, -̈e** (*Trieb*) impulse, urge, desire (*nach* for); (*Druck*) pressure.

drängeln ['drɛŋəln] *vti* push, jostle.

drängen ['drɛŋən] *vt* (*schieben*) push, press; (*antreiben*) urge // *vi* (*eilig sein*) be urgent; (*Zeit*) press; **auf etw** (*akk*) **~** press for sth.

drastisch ['drastɪʃ] *a* drastic.

drauf [drauf] *ad* (*umg*) *siehe* **darauf; D~gänger** *m* **-s, -** daredevil.

draußen ['drausən] *ad* outside, out-of-doors.

Dreck [drɛk] *m* **-(e)s, -e** mud, dirt; **d~ig** *a* dirty, filthy.

Dreh- ['dre:] *zW:* **~arbeiten** *pl* (*CINE*) shooting; **~bank** *f* lathe; **d~bar** *a* revolving; **~buch** *nt* (*CINE*) script; **d~en** *vti* turn, rotate; (*Zigaretten*) roll; (*Film*) shoot // *vr* turn; (*handeln von*) be (*um* about); **~orgel** *f* barrel organ; **~tür** *f* revolving door; **~ung** *f* (*Rotation*) rotation; (*Um~, Wendung*) turn; **~zahl** *f* rate of revolutions; **~zahlmesser** *m* rev(olution) counter.

drei [drai] *num* three; **D~eck** *nt* triangle; **~eckig** *a* triangular; **~einhalb** *num* three and a half; **~erlei** *a inv* of three kinds; **~fach** *a,ad* triple, treble; **~hundert** *num* three hundred; **D~'königsfest** *nt* Epiphany; **~mal** *ad* three times; **~malig** *a* three times.

dreinreden ['drainre:dən] *vi:* **jdm ~** (*dazwischenreden*) interrupt sb; (*sich einmischen*) interfere with sb.

dreißig ['draisɪç] *num* thirty.

dreist [draist] *a* bold, audacious; **D~igkeit** *f* boldness, audacity.

drei- *zW:* **~viertel** *num* three-quarters; **D~viertelstunde** *f* three-quarters of an hour; **~zehn** *num* thirteen.

dressieren [drɛ'si:rən] *vt* train.

Drill- ['drɪl] *zW:* **~bohrer** *m* light drill; **d~en** *vt* (*bohren*) drill, bore; (*MIL*) drill; (*fig*) train; **Drilling** *m* triplet.

drin [drɪn] *ad* (*umg*) *siehe* **darin.**

dringen ['drɪŋən] *vi unreg* (*Wasser, Licht, Kälte*) penetrate (*durch* through; *in* +*akk* into); **auf etw** (*akk*) **~** insist on sth.

dringend ['drɪŋənt], **dringlich** ['drɪŋlɪç] *a* urgent.

Dringlichkeit *f* urgency.

drinnen ['drɪnən] *ad* inside, indoors.

dritte(r, s) ['drɪtə(r, s)] *a* third; **~ Welt** Third World; **D~s Reich** Third Reich; **Drittel** *nt* **-s, -** third; **drittens** *ad* thirdly.

droben ['dro:bən] *ad* above, up there.

Droge ['dro:gə] *f* **-, -n** drug; **drogenabhängig** *a* addicted to drugs; **Drogenhändler** *m* drug pedlar, pusher; **Drogerie** [dro:gə-'ri:] *f* chemist's shop.

Drogist [dro'gɪst] *m* pharmacist, chemist.

drohen ['dro:ən] *vi* threaten (*jdm* sb).

dröhnen ['drø:nən] *vi* (*Motor*) roar; (*Stimme, Musik*) ring, resound.

Drohung ['dro:ʊŋ] *f* threat.

drollig ['drɔlɪç] *a* droll.

Drossel ['drɔsəl] *f* **-, -n** thrush.

drüben ['dry:bən] *ad* over there, on the other side.

drüber ['dry:bər] *ad* (*umg*) *siehe* **darüber.**

Druck [drʊk] *m* **-(e)s, -e** (*PHYS, Zwang*) pressure; (*TYP: Vorgang*) printing; (: *Produkt*) print; (*fig: Belastung*) burden, weight; **~buchstabe** *m* block letter; **~er** *m* printer.

Drück- ['drʏk] *zW:* **d~en** *vti* (*Knopf, Hand*) press; (*zu eng sein*) pinch; (*fig: Preise*) keep down; (*fig: belasten*) oppress, weigh down // *vr:* **sich vor etw** (*dat*) **d~en** get out of (doing) sth; **d~end** *a* oppressive; **~er** *m* **-s, -** button; (*Tür~*) handle; (*Gewehr~*) trigger.

Druck- *zW:* **~er** *m* **-s, -** printer; **Drucke'rei** *f* printing works, press; **~erschwärze** *f* printer's ink; **~fehler** *m* misprint; **~knopf** *m* press stud, snap fastener; **~sache** *f* printed matter; **~schrift** *f* block *od* printed letters *pl*.

drum [drʊm] *ad* (*umg*) *siehe* **darum.**

drunten ['drʊntən] *ad* below, down there.

Drüse ['dry:zə] *f* -, -n gland.
Dschungel ['dʒʊŋəl] *m* -s, - jungle.
du [du:] *pron* (**D~** *in Briefen*) you; **D~ sagen** *siehe* **duzen.**
ducken ['dʊkən] *vt* (*Kopf, Person*) duck; (*fig*) take down a peg or two // *vr* duck.
Duckmäuser ['dʊkmɔʏzər] *m* -s, - yes-man.
Dudelsack ['du:dəlzak] *m* bagpipes *pl.*
Duell [du'ɛl] *nt* -s, -e duel.
Duett [du'ɛt] *nt* -(e)s, -e duet.
Duft [dʊft] *m* -(e)s, -e scent, odour; **d~en** *vi* smell, be fragrant; **d~ig** *a* (*Stoff, Kleid*) delicate, diaphanous.
duld- [dʊld] *zW:* ~en *vti* suffer; (*zulassen*) tolerate; ~sam *a* tolerant.
dumm [dʊm] *a* stupid; (*ärgerlich*) annoying; **der D~e** sein be the loser; ~erweise *ad* stupidly; **D~heit** *f* stupidity; (*Tat*) blunder, stupid mistake; **D~kopf** *m* blockhead.
dumpf [dʊmpf] *a* (*Ton*) hollow, dull; (*Luft*) close; (*Erinnerung, Schmerz*) vague; ~ig *a* musty.
Düne ['dy:nə] *f* -, -n dune.
düngen ['dyŋən] *vt* manure.
Dünger *m* -s, - dung, manure; (*künstlich*) fertilizer.
dunkel ['dʊŋkəl] *a* dark; (*Stimme*) deep; (*Ahnung*) vague; (*rätselhaft*) obscure; (*verdächtig*) dubious, shady; **im ~n tappen** (*fig*) grope in the dark.
Dunkel- *zW:* ~heit *f* darkness; (*fig*) obscurity; ~kammer *f* (*PHOT*) dark room; **d~n** *vi unpers* grow dark; ~ziffer *f* estimated number of unreported cases.
dünn [dyn] *a* thin; ~flüssig *a* watery, thin.
Dunst [dʊnst] *m* -es, -e vapour; (*Wetter*) haze.
dünsten ['dynstən] *vt* steam.
dunstig ['dʊnstɪç] *a* vaporous; (*Wetter*) hazy, misty.
Duplikat [dupli'ka:t] *nt* -(e)s, -e duplicate.
Dur [du:r] *nt* -, - (*MUS*) major.
durch [dʊrç] ◆*präp* +*akk* **1** (*hin~*) through; ~ **den Urwald** through the jungle; ~ **die ganze Welt reisen** travel all over the world
2 (*mittels*) through, by (means of); (*aufgrund*) due to, owing to; **Tod ~ Herzschlag/den Strang** death from a heart attack/by hanging; ~ **die Post** by post; ~ **seine Bemühungen** through his efforts
◆*ad* **1** (*hin~*) through; **die ganze Nacht** ~ all through the night; **den Sommer** ~ during the summer; **8 Uhr** ~ past 8 o'clock; ~ **und** ~ completely
2 (*~gebraten etc*): (**gut**) ~ well-done.

durch- *zW:* ~arbeiten *vti* work through // *vr* work one's way through; ~'aus *ad* completely; (*unbedingt*) definitely; ~aus nicht absolutely not; ~blättern *vt* leaf through.
Durchblick ['dʊrçblɪk] *m* view; (*fig*) comprehension; **d~en** *vi* look through; (*umg: verstehen*) understand (*bei etw* sth); **etw d~en lassen** (*fig*) hint at sth.
durchbrechen ['dʊrçbrɛçən] *vti unreg* break; [dʊrç'brɛçən] *vt unreg insep* (*Schranken*) break through; (*Schallmauer*) break; (*Gewohnheit*) break free from.
durchbrennen ['dʊrçbrɛnən] *vi unreg* (*Draht, Sicherung*) burn through; (*umg*) run away.
Durchbruch ['dʊrçbrʊx] *m* (*Öffnung*) opening; (*MIL*) breach; (*von Gefühlen etc*) eruption; (*der Zähne*) cutting; (*fig*) breakthrough; **zum ~ kommen** break through.
durch- *zW:* ~dacht [dʊrç'daxt] *a* well thought-out; ~denken *vt unreg insep* think out; ~drehen *vt* (*Fleisch*) mince // *vi* (*umg*) crack up.
durcheinander [dʊrç'aɪ'nandər] *ad* in a mess, in confusion; (*umg: verwirrt*) confused; ~ **trinken** mix one's drinks; **D~** *nt* -s (*Verwirrung*) confusion; (*Unordnung*) mess; ~bringen *vt unreg* mess up; (*verwirren*) confuse; ~reden *vi* talk at the same time.
durch- *zW:* **D~fahrt** *f* transit; (*Verkehr*) thoroughfare; **D~fall** *m* (*MED*) diarrhoea; ~fallen *vi unreg* fall through; (*in Prüfung*) fail; ~finden *vr unreg* find one's way through; ~'forschen *vt insep* explore; ~fragen *vr* find one's way by asking.
durchführ- ['dʊrçfy:r] *zW:* ~bar *a* feasible, practicable; ~en *vt* carry out; **D~ung** *f* execution, performance.
Durchgang ['dʊrçgaŋ] *m* passage(way); (*bei Produktion, Versuch*) run; (*SPORT*) round; (*bei Wahl*) ballot; ~ **verboten** no thoroughfare.
Durchgangs- *zW:* ~handel *m* transit trade; ~lager *nt* transit camp; ~verkehr *m* through traffic.
durchgefroren ['dʊrçgefro:rən] *a* (*Mensch*) frozen stiff.
durchgehen ['dʊrçge:ən] *unreg vt* (*behandeln*) go over // *vi* go through; (*ausreißen: Pferd*) break loose; (*Mensch*) run away; **mein Temperament ging mit mir durch** my temper got the better of me; **jdm etw ~ lassen** let sb get away with sth; ~d *a* (*Zug*) through; (*Öffnungszeiten*) continuous.
durch- *zW:* ~greifen *vi unreg* take

strong action; ~**halten** *unreg vi* last out // *vt* keep up; ~**kommen** *vi unreg* get through; (*überleben*) pull through.

durch'kreuzen *vt insep* thwart, frustrate.

durch- *zW:* ~**lassen** *vt unreg* (*Person*) let through; (*Wasser*) let in; ~**lässig** *a* leaky; **D~lauferhitzer** *m -s*, - (hot water) geyser.

durch- *zW:* ~'**leben** *vt insep* live *od* go through, experience; '~**lesen** *vt unreg* read through; ~'**leuchten** *vt insep* X-ray; '~**machen** *vt* go through; die Nacht ~**machen** make a night of it.

Durch- *zW:* ~**marsch** *m* march through; ~**messer** *m -s*, - diameter.

durch'nässen *vt insep* soak (through).

durch- *zW:* ~**nehmen** *vt unreg* go over; ~**numerieren** *vt* number consecutively.

durchqueren [durç'kve:rən] *vt insep* cross.

durch- *zW:* **D~reiche** *f -*, -**n** (serving) hatch; **D~reise** *f* transit; auf der **D~reise** passing through; (*Güter*) in transit; ~**ringen** *vr unreg* reach after a long struggle; ~**rosten** *vi* rust through.

durchs [durçs] = **durch das.**

Durchsage ['durçza:gə] *f -*, -**n** intercom *od* radio announcement.

Durchsatz ['durçzats] *m* throughput.

durchschauen ['durç'ʃauən] *vi* (*lit*) look *od* see through // [durç'ʃauən] *vt insep* (*Person*, *Lüge*) see through.

durchscheinen ['durç'ʃaınən] *vi unreg* shine through; ~**d** *a* translucent.

Durchschlag ['durçʃlaːk] *m* (*Doppel*) carbon copy; (*Sieb*) strainer; **d~en** *unreg vt* (*entzweischlagen*) split (in two); (*sieben*) sieve // *vi* (*zum Vorschein kommen*) emerge, come out // *vr* get by; **d~end** *a* resounding.

durchschneiden ['durçʃnaıdən] *vt unreg* cut through.

Durchschnitt ['durçʃnıt] *m* (*Mittelwert*) average; über/unter dem ~ above/below average; im ~ on average; **d~lich** *a* average // *ad* on average.

Durchschnitts- *zW:* ~**geschwindigkeit** *f* average speed; ~**mensch** *m* average man, man in the street; ~**wert** *m* average.

durch- *zW:* **D~schrift** *f* copy; ~**sehen** *vt unreg* look through; ~**setzen** *vt* enforce; seinen Kopf ~**setzen** get one's own way // *vr* (*Erfolg haben*) succeed; (*sich behaupten*) get one's way // [durç'zetsən] *vt insep* mix.

Durchsicht ['durçzıçt] *f* looking through, checking; **d~ig** *a* transparent; ~**igkeit** *f* transparence.

durch- *zW:* '~**sprechen** *vt unreg* talk over; '~**stehen** *vt unreg* live through; '~**streichen** *vt unreg* cross out; ~'**suchen** *vt insep* search; **D~'suchung** *f* search; ~**trieben** [-'tri:bən] *a* cunning, wily; ~'**wachsen** *a* (*lit: Speck*) streaky; (*fig: mittelmäßig*) so-so.

durch- *zW:* ~**weg** *ad* throughout, completely; ~**ziehen** *unreg vt* (*Faden*) draw through // *vi* pass through; **D~zug** *m* (*Luft*) draught; (*von Truppen, Vögeln*) passage.

dürfen ['dyrfən] *vi unreg* **1** (*Erlaubnis haben*) be allowed to; ich darf das I'm allowed to (do that); darf ich? may I?; darf ich ins Kino? can *od* may I go to the cinema?; es darf geraucht werden you may smoke

2 (*in Verneinungen*): er darf das nicht he's not allowed to (do that); das darf nicht geschehen that must not happen; da darf sie sich nicht wundern that shouldn't surprise her

3 (*in Höflichkeitsformeln*): darf ich Sie bitten, das zu tun? may *od* could I ask you to do that?; was darf es sein? what can I do for you?

4 (*können*): das ~ Sie mir glauben you can believe me

5 (*Möglichkeit*): das dürfte genug sein that should be enough; es dürfte Ihnen bekannt sein, daß ... as you will probably know ...

dürftig ['dyrftıç] *a* (*ärmlich*) needy, poor; (*unzulänglich*) inadequate.

dürr [dyr] *a* dried-up; (*Land*) arid; (*mager*) skinny, gaunt; **D~e** *f -*, -**n** aridity; (*Zeit*) drought; (*Magerkeit*) skinniness.

Durst [durst] *m -(e)s* thirst; ~ haben be thirsty; **d~ig** *a* thirsty.

Dusche ['duʃə] *f -*, -**n** shower; **d~n** *vir* have a shower.

Düse ['dy:zə] *f -*, -**n** nozzle; (*Flugzeug~*) jet.

Düsen- *zW:* ~**antrieb** *m* jet propulsion; ~**flugzeug** *nt* jet (plane); ~**jäger** *m* jet fighter.

Dussel ['dusəl] *m -s*, - (*umg*) twit.

düster ['dy:stər] *a* dark; (*Gedanken, Zukunft*) gloomy.

Dutzend ['dutsənt] *nt -s*, -**e** dozen; **d~(e)mal** *ad* a dozen times; **d~weise** *ad* by the dozen.

duzen ['du:tsən] *vtr* use the familiar form of address *od* 'du' (*jdn* to *od* with sb).

Dynamik [dy'na:mık] *f* (*PHYS*) dynamics; (*fig: Schwung*) momentum; (*von Mensch*) dynamism.

dynamisch [dy'na:mıʃ] *a* (*lit, fig*) dynamic.

Dynamit [dyna'mi:t] *nt -s* dynamite.

Dynamo [dy'na:mo] *m* -s, -s dynamo.
D-Zug ['de:tsu:k] *m* through train.

E

E, e [e:] *nt* E, e.
Ebbe ['ɛbə] *f* -, -n low tide.
eben ['e:bən] *a* level; *(glatt)* smooth // *ad* just; *(bestätigend)* exactly; ~ **deswegen** just because of that; **ebenbürtig** *a*: jdm ebenbürtig sein be sb's peer; **E~e** *f* -, -n plain; ~**falls** *ad* likewise; ~**so** *ad* just as; ~**sogut** *ad* just as well; ~**sooft** *ad* just as often; ~**soweit** *ad* just as far; ~**sowenig** *ad* just as little.
Eber ['e:bər] *m* -s, - boar; ~**esche** *f* mountain ash, rowan.
ebnen ['e:bnən] *vt* level.
Echo ['ɛço] *nt* -s, -s echo.
echt [ɛçt] *a* genuine; *(typisch)* typical; **E~heit** *f* genuineness.
Eck- ['ɛk] *zW*: ~**ball** *m* corner (kick); ~**e** *f* -, -n corner; *(MATH)* angle; **e~ig** *a* angular; ~**zahn** *m* eye tooth.
edel ['e:dəl] *a* noble; **E~metall** *nt* rare metal; **E~stein** *m* precious stone.
EDV [e:de:'fau] *abk* (= *elektronische Datenverarbeitung*) electronic data processing.
Efeu ['e:fɔy] *m* -s ivy.
Effekten [ɛ'fɛktən] *pl* stocks *pl*.
effektiv [ɛfɛk'ti:f] *a* effective, actual.
EG [e:'ge:] *abk* (= *Europäische Gemeinschaft*) European Community.
egal [e'ga:l] *a* all the same.
Ego- [e:go] *zW*: ~**ismus** [-'ısmus] *m* selfishness, egoism; ~**ist** [-'ıst] *m* egoist; **e~istisch** *a* selfish, egoistic.
Ehe ['e:ə] *f* -, -n marriage; ~ *kj* before; ~**bruch** *m* adultery; ~**frau** *f* married woman; wife; ~**leute** *pl* married people *pl*; ~**lich** *a* matrimonial; *(Kind)* legitimate; **e~malig** *a* former; **e~mals** *ad* formerly; ~**mann** *m* married man; husband; ~**paar** *nt* married couple.
eher ['e:ər] *ad (früher)* sooner; *(lieber)* rather, sooner; *(mehr)* more.
eheste(r, s) ['e:əstə(r, s)] *a (früheste)* first, earliest; am ~n *(liebsten)* soonest; *(meist)* most; *(wahrscheinlichst)* most probably.
Ehr- ['e:r] *zW*: **e~bar** *a* honourable, respectable; ~**e** *f* -, -n honour; **e~en** *vt* honour.
Ehren- ['e:rən] *zW*: ~**gast** *m* guest of honour; **e~haft** *a* honourable; ~**runde** *f* lap of honour; ~**sache** *f* point of honour; **e~voll** *a* honourable; ~**wort** *nt* word of honour.
Ehr- ['e:r] *zW*: ~**furcht** *f* awe, deep respect; ~**gefühl** *nt* sense of honour; ~**geiz** *m* ambition; **e~geizig** *a* ambitious;

e~lich *a* honest; ~**lichkeit** *f* honesty; **e~los** *a* dishonourable; ~**ung** *f* honour(ing); **e~würdig** *a* venerable.
Ei [aɪ] *nt* -(e)s, -er egg; **e~** *interj* well, well.
Eich- ['aɪç] *zW*: ~**amt** *nt* Office of Weights and Measures; ~**e** *f* -, -n oak (tree); ~**el** *f* -, -n acorn; **e~en** *vt* standardize; ~**hörnchen** *nt* squirrel; ~**maß** *nt* standard.
Eid ['aɪt] *m* -(e)s, -e oath; ~**echse** ['aɪdɛksə] *f* -, -n lizard; **e~esstattlich** *a*: ~**esstattliche Erklärung** affidavit; ~**genosse** *m* Swiss.
Eidotter ['aɪdɔtər] *nt* egg yolk.
Eier- *zW*: ~**becher** *m* eggcup; ~**kuchen** *m* omelette; pancake; ~**likör** *m* advocaat; ~**schale** *f* eggshell; ~**stock** *m* ovary; ~**uhr** *f* egg timer.
Eifer ['aɪfər] *m* -s zeal, enthusiasm; ~**sucht** *f* jealousy; **e~süchtig** *a* jealous *(auf +akk* of).
eifrig ['aɪfrɪç] *a* zealous, enthusiastic.
Eigelb ['aɪgɛlp] *nt* -(e)s, - egg yolk.
eigen ['aɪgən] *a* own; *(~artig)* peculiar; mit der/dem ihm ~en ... with that ... peculiar to him; sich *(dat)* etw zu ~ machen make sth one's own; **E~art** *f* peculiarity; characteristic; ~**artig** *a* peculiar; ~**händig** *a* with one's own hand; **E~heim** *nt* owner-occupied house; **E~heit** *f* peculiarity; ~**mächtig** *a* high-handed; **E~name** *m* proper name; ~**s** *ad* expressly, on purpose; **E~schaft** *f* quality, property, attribute; **E~schaftswort** *nt* adjective; **E~sinn** *m* obstinacy; **e~sinnig** *a* obstinate; **eigentlich** *a* actual, real // *ad* actually, really; **E~tor** *nt* own goal; **E~tum** *nt* property; **E~tümer(in** *f) m* -s, - owner, proprietor; ~**tümlich** *a* peculiar; **E~tümlichkeit** *f* peculiarity; **E~tumswohnung** *f* freehold flat.
eignen ['aɪgnən] *vr* be suited.
Eignung *f* suitability.
Eil- ['aɪl] *zW*: ~**bote** *m* courier; ~**brief** *m* express letter; ~**e** *f* - haste; es hat keine ~e there's no hurry; **e~en** *vi (Mensch)* hurry; *(dringend sein)* be urgent; **e~ends** *ad* hastily; ~**gut** *nt* express goods *pl*, fast freight *(US)*; **e~ig** *a* hasty, hurried; *(dringlich)* urgent; es e~ig haben be in a hurry; ~**zug** *m* semi-fast train, limited stop train.
Eimer ['aɪmər] *m* -s, - bucket, pail.
ein(e) [aɪn(ə)] *num* one // *indef art* a, an // *ad*: nicht ~ noch aus wissen not know what to do; ~**e(r, s)** *pron* one; *(jemand)* someone.
einander [aɪ'nandər] *pron* one another, each other.
einarbeiten ['aɪnarbaɪtən] *vr* familiar-

ize o.s. (in +akk with).

einatmen ['aina:tmən] vti inhale, breathe in.

Einbahnstraße ['ainba:nʃtra:sə] f one-way street.

Einband ['ainbant] m binding, cover.

einbau- ['ainbau] zW: ~en vt build in; (Motor) install, fit; E~möbel pl built-in furniture.

einberufen ['ainbəru:fən] vt unreg convene; (MIL) call up.

einbeziehen ['ainbətsi:ən] vt unreg include.

einbiegen ['ainbi:gən] vi unreg turn.

einbilden ['ainbildən] vt: sich (dat) etw ~ imagine sth.

Einbildung f imagination; (Dünkel) conceit; **Einbildungskraft** f imagination.

Einblick ['ainblik] m insight.

einbrechen ['ainbreçən] vi unreg (in Haus) break in; (in Land etc) invade; (Nacht) fall; (Winter) set in; (durchbrechen) break.

Einbrecher m -s, - burglar.

einbringen ['ainbrinən] vt unreg bring in; (Geld, Vorteil) yield; (mitbringen) contribute.

Einbruch ['ainbrux] m (Haus~) break-in, burglary; (Eindringen) invasion; (des Winters) onset; (Durchbrechen) break; (MET) approach; (MIL) penetration; ~ der Nacht nightfall; **einbruchssicher** a burglarproof.

einbürgern ['ainbyrgərn] vt naturalize // vr become adopted.

Einbürgerung f naturalization.

Einbuße ['ainbu:sə] f loss, forfeiture.

einbüßen ['ainby:sən] vt lose, forfeit.

einchecken ['aintʃekən] vti check in.

eindecken ['aindεkən] vr lay in stocks (mit of).

eindeutig ['aindɔytiç] a unequivocal.

eindring- ['aindrin] zW: ~en vi unreg (in +akk) force one's way in(to); (in Haus) break in(to); (in Land) invade; (Gas, Wasser) penetrate; (mit Bitten) pester (auf jdn sb); ~lich a forcible, urgent; E~ling m intruder.

Eindruck ['aindruk] m impression; **eindrucksvoll** a impressive.

eindrücken ['aindrykən] vt press in.

eineiig ['ain'aiiç] a (Zwillinge) identical.

eineinhalb ['ain'ain'halp] num one and a half.

einengen ['ain'εnən] vt confine, restrict.

einer- ['ainər] zW: 'E~lei nt -s sameness; '~lei a (gleichartig) the same kind of; es ist mir ~lei it is all the same to me; ~seits ad on the one hand.

einfach ['ainfax] a simple; (nicht

mehrfach) single // ad simply; E~heit f simplicity.

einfahren ['ainfa:rən] unreg vt bring in; (Barriere) knock down; (Auto) run in // vi drive in; (Zug) pull in; (MIN) go down.

Einfahrt f (Vorgang) driving in; pulling in; (MIN) descent; (Ort) entrance.

Einfall ['ainfal] m (Idee) idea, notion; (Licht~) incidence; (MIL) raid; e~en vi unreg (Licht) fall; (MIL) raid; (einstimmen) join in (in +akk with); (einstürzen) fall in, collapse; etw fällt jdm ein sth occurs to sb; das fällt mir gar nicht ein I wouldn't dream of it; sich (dat) etwas e~en lassen have a good idea.

einfältig ['ainfεltiç] a simple(-minded).

Einfamilienhaus [ainfa'mi:liənhaus] nt detached house.

einfarbig ['ainfarbiç] a all one colour; (Stoff etc) self-coloured.

einfetten ['ainfεtən] vt grease.

einfinden ['ainfindən] vr unreg come, turn up.

einfließen ['ainfli:sən] vi unreg flow in.

einflößen ['ainflø:sən] vt: jdm etw ~ (lit) give sb sth; (fig) instil sth in sb.

Einfluß ['ainflus] m influence; ~bereich m sphere of influence; e~reich a influential.

einförmig ['ainfœrmiç] a uniform; E~keit f uniformity.

einfrieren ['ainfri:rən] unreg vi freeze (in) // vt freeze.

einfügen ['ainfy:gən] vt fit in; (zusätzlich) add.

Einfuhr ['ainfu:r] f - import; ~artikel m imported article.

einführ- ['ainfy:r] zW: ~en vt bring in; (Mensch, Sitten) introduce; (Ware) import; E~ung f introduction.

Eingabe ['ainga:bə] f petition; (COMPUT) input.

Eingang ['aingan] m entrance; (COMM: Ankunft) arrival; (Sendung) post; e~s ad, präp +gen at the outset (of).

eingeben ['ainge:bən] vt unreg (Arznei) give; (Daten etc) enter; (Gedanken) inspire.

eingebildet ['aingəbildət] a imaginary; (eitel) conceited.

Eingeborene(r) ['aingəbo:rənə(r)] mf native.

Eingebung f inspiration.

eingedenk ['aingədenk] präp +gen bearing in mind.

eingefroren ['aingəfro:rən] a frozen.

eingehen ['ainge:ən] unreg vi (Aufnahme finden) come in; (verständlich sein) be comprehensible (jdm to sb); (Sendung, Geld) be received;

(*Tier, Pflanze*) die; (*Firma*) fold; (*schrumpfen*) shrink; **auf etw** (*akk*) ~ go into sth; **auf jdn** ~ respond to sb // *vt* enter into; (*Wette*) make; **~d** *a* exhaustive, thorough.

Eingemachte(s) ['aɪŋəmaxtə(s)] *nt* preserves *pl*.

eingenommen ['aɪŋənɔmən] *a* (*von*) fond (of), partial (to); (*gegen*) prejudiced.

eingeschrieben ['aɪŋəʃriːbən] *a* registered.

eingespielt ['aɪŋəʃpiːlt] *a*: aufeinander ~ sein be in tune with each other.

Eingeständnis ['aɪŋəʃtɛntnɪs] *nt* **-ses, -se** admission, confession.

eingestehen ['aɪŋəʃteːən] *vt unreg* confess.

Eingeweide ['aɪŋəwaɪdə] *nt* **-s, -** innards *pl*, intestines *pl*.

Eingeweihte(r) ['aɪŋəwaɪtə(r)] *mf* initiate.

eingleisig ['aɪŋlaɪzɪç] *a* single-track.

eingreifen ['aɪŋraɪfən] *vi unreg* intervene, interfere; (*Zahnrad*) mesh.

Eingriff ['aɪŋrɪf] *m* intervention, interference; (*Operation*) operation.

einhaken ['aɪnhaːkən] *vt* hook in // *vr*: **sich bei jdm** ~ link arms with sb // *vi* (*sich einmischen*) intervene.

Einhalt ['aɪnhalt] *m*: ~ **gebieten** (+*dat*) put a stop to; **e~en** *unreg vt* (*Regel*) keep // *vi* stop.

einhändigen ['aɪnhɛndɪgən] *vt* hand in.

einhängen ['aɪnhɛŋən] *vt* hang; (*Telefon: auch vi*) hang up; **sich bei jdm** ~ link arms with sb.

einheimisch ['aɪnhaɪmɪʃ] *a* native.

Einheit ['aɪnhaɪt] *f* unity; (*Maß, MIL*) unit; **e~lich** *a* uniform; **Einheitspreis** *m* uniform price.

einholen ['aɪnhoːlən] *vt* (*Tau*) haul in; (*Fahne, Segel*) lower; (*Vorsprung aufholen*) catch up with; (*Verspätung*) make up; (*Rat, Erlaubnis*) ask // *vi* (*einkaufen*) buy, shop.

Einhorn ['aɪnhɔrn] *nt* unicorn.

einhüllen ['aɪnhʏlən] *vt* wrap up.

einig ['aɪnɪç] *a* (*vereint*) united; **sich** (*dat*) ~ **sein** be in agreement; ~ **werden** agree; **~e** ['aɪnɪgə] *pl* some; (*mehrere*) several; **~e(r, s)** *a* some; **einigemal** *ad* a few times; **~en** *vt* unite // *vr* agree (*auf* +*akk* on); **~ermaßen** *ad* somewhat; (*leidlich*) reasonably; **~es** *pron* something; **~gehen** *vi unreg* agree; **E~keit** *f* unity; (*Übereinstimmung*) agreement; **E~ung** *f* agreement; (*Vereinigung*) unification.

einkalkulieren ['aɪnkalkuliːrən] *vt* take

into account, allow for.

Einkauf ['aɪnkaʊf] *m* purchase; **e~en** *vt* buy // *vi* go shopping.

Einkaufs- *zW*: **~bummel** *m* shopping spree; **~korb** *m* shopping basket; **~netz** *nt* string bag; **~wagen** *m* shopping trolley; **~preis** *m* cost price; **~zentrum** *nt* shopping centre.

einklammern ['aɪnklamərn] *vt* put in brackets, bracket.

Einklang ['aɪnklaŋ] *m* harmony.

einklemmen ['aɪnklɛmən] *vt* jam.

einkochen ['aɪnkɔxən] *vt* boil down; (*Obst*) preserve, bottle.

Einkommen ['aɪnkɔmən] *nt* **-s, -** income; **~(s)steuer** *f* income tax.

Einkünfte ['aɪnkʏnftə] *pl* income, revenue.

einlad- ['aɪnlaːd] *zW*: **~en** *vt unreg* (*Person*) invite; (*Gegenstände*) load; **jdn ins Kino ~en** take sb to the cinema; **E~ung** *f* invitation.

Einlage ['aɪnlaːgə] *f* (*Programm~*) interlude; (*Spar~*) deposit; (*Schuh~*) insole; (*Fußstütze*) support; (*Zahn~*) temporary filling; (*KOCH*) noodles *pl*, vegetables *pl etc* in soup.

einlagern *vt* store.

einlassen ['aɪnlasən] *unreg vt* let in; (*einsetzen*) set in // *vr*: **sich mit jdm/auf etw** (*akk*) ~ get involved with sb/sth.

Einlauf ['aɪnlaʊf] *m* arrival; (*von Pferden*) finish; (*MED*) enema; **e~en** *unreg vi* arrive, come in; (*in Hafen*) enter; (*SPORT*) finish; (*Wasser*) run in; (*Stoff*) shrink // *vt* (*Schuhe*) break in; **jdm das Haus e~en** invade sb's house // *vr* (*SPORT*) warm up; (*Motor, Maschine*) run in.

einleben ['aɪnleːbən] *vr* settle down.

einlegen ['aɪnleːgən] *vt* (*einfügen*: *Blatt, Sohle*) insert; (*KOCH*) pickle; (*Pause*) have; (*Protest*) make; (*Veto*) use; (*Berufung*) lodge.

einleiten ['aɪnlaɪtən] *vt* introduce, start; (*Geburt*) induce.

Einleitung *f* introduction; induction.

einleuchten ['aɪnlɔʏçtən] *vi* be clear *od* evident (*jdm* to sb); **~d** *a* clear.

einliefern ['aɪnliːfərn] *vt* take (*in* +*akk* into).

einlösen ['aɪnløːzən] *vt* (*Scheck*) cash; (*Schuldschein, Pfand*) redeem; (*Versprechen*) keep.

einmachen ['aɪnmaxən] *vt* preserve.

einmal ['aɪnmaːl] *ad* once; (*erstens*) first; (*zukünftig*) sometime; **nehmen wir ~ an** just let's suppose; **noch ~** once more; **nicht ~** not even; **auf ~** all at once; **es war ~** once upon a time there was/were; **E~eins** *nt* multiplication tables *pl*; **~ig** *a* unique; (*einmal geschehend*) single; (*prima*) fantastic.

Einmannbetrieb [aɪn'manbətriːp] *m* one-man business.

Einmarsch ['aɪnmarʃ] *m* entry; (MIL) invasion; **e~ieren** *vi* march in.

einmischen ['aɪnmɪʃən] *vr* interfere (*in + akk* with).

einmütig ['aɪnmyːtɪç] *a* unanimous.

Einnahme ['aɪnnaːmə] *f* -, -n (Geld) takings *pl*, revenue; (von Medizin) taking; (MIL) capture, taking; **~quelle** *f* source of income.

einnehmen ['aɪnneːmən] *vt unreg* take; (Stellung, Raum) take up; (~ für/gegen) persuade in favour of/against; **~d** *a* charming.

Einöde ['aɪn'øːdə] *f* desert, wilderness.

einordnen ['aɪn'ɔrdnən] *vt* arrange, fit in // *vr* adapt; (AUT) get into lane.

einpacken ['aɪnpakən] *vt* pack (up).

einparken ['aɪnparkən] *vt* park.

einpendeln ['aɪnpɛndəln] *vr* even out.

einpflanzen ['aɪnpflantsən] *vt* plant; (MED) implant.

einplanen ['aɪnplaːnən] *vt* plan for.

einprägen ['aɪnprɛːgən] *vt* impress, imprint; (beibringen) impress (jdm on sb); **sich** (dat) **etw ~** memorize sth.

einrahmen ['aɪnraːmən] *vt* frame.

einräumen ['aɪnrɔymən] *vt* (ordnend) put away; (überlassen: Platz) give up; (zugestehen) admit, concede.

einreden ['aɪnreːdən] *vt*: **jdm/sich etw ~** talk sb/o.s. into believing sth.

einreiben ['aɪnraɪbən] *vt unreg* rub in.

einreichen ['aɪnraɪçən] *vt* hand in; (Antrag) submit.

Einreise ['aɪnraɪzə] *f* entry; **~bestimmungen** *pl* entry regulations *pl*; **~erlaubnis** *f*, **~genehmigung** *f* entry permit; **e~n** *vi* enter (in ein Land a country).

einrichten ['aɪnrɪçtən] *vt* (Haus) furnish; (schaffen) establish, set up; (arrangieren) arrange; (möglich machen) manage // *vr* (in Haus) furnish one's house; (sich vorbereiten) prepare o.s. (auf +akk for); (sich anpassen) adapt (auf +akk to).

Einrichtung *f* (Wohnungs~) furnishings *pl*; (öffentliche Anstalt) organization; (Dienste) service.

einrosten ['aɪnrɔstən] *vi* get rusty.

Eins [aɪns] *f* -, -en one; **e~** *num* one; **es ist mir alles e~** it's all one to me.

einsam ['aɪnzaːm] *a* lonely, solitary; **E~keit** *f* loneliness, solitude.

einsammeln ['aɪnzaməln] *vt* collect.

Einsatz ['aɪnzats] *m* (Teil) inset; (an Kleid) insertion; (Verwendung) use, employment; (Spiel~) stake; (Risiko) risk; (MIL) operation; (MUS) entry; **im ~** in action; **e~bereit** *a* ready for action.

einschalten ['aɪnʃaltən] *vt* (einfügen) insert; (Pause) make; (ELEK) switch on; (AUT: Gang) engage; (Anwalt) bring in // *vr* (dazwischentreten) intervene.

einschätzen ['aɪnʃɛtsən] *vt* estimate, assess // *vr* rate o.s.

einschenken ['aɪnʃɛŋkən] *vt* pour out.

einschicken ['aɪnʃɪkən] *vt* send in.

einschl. *abk* (= einschließlich) incl.

einschlafen ['aɪnʃlaːfən] *vi unreg* fall asleep, go to sleep.

einschläfernd ['aɪnʃlɛːfərnt] *a* (MED) soporific; (langweilig) boring; (Stimme) lulling.

Einschlag ['aɪnʃlaːk] *m* impact; (fig: Beimischung) touch, hint; **e~en** *unreg vt* knock in; (Fenster) smash, break; (Zähne, Schädel) smash in; (Steuer) turn; (kürzer machen) take up; (Ware) pack, wrap up; (Weg, Richtung) take // *vi* hit (in etw (akk) sth, auf jdn sb); (sich einigen) agree; (Anklang finden) work, succeed.

einschlägig ['aɪnʃlɛːgɪç] *a* relevant.

einschließen ['aɪnʃliːsən] *unreg vt* (Kind) lock in; (Häftling) lock up; (Gegenstand) lock away; (Bergleute) cut off; (umgeben) surround; (MIL) encircle; (fig) include, comprise // *vr* lock o.s. in.

einschließlich *ad* inclusive // *präp* +gen inclusive of, including.

einschmeicheln ['aɪnʃmaɪçəln] *vr* ingratiate o.s. (bei with).

einschnappen ['aɪnʃnapən] *vi* (Tür) click to; (fig) be touchy; **eingeschnappt sein** be in a huff.

einschneidend ['aɪnʃnaɪdənt] *a* incisive.

Einschnitt ['aɪnʃnɪt] *m* cutting; (MED) incision; (Ereignis) incident.

einschränken ['aɪnʃrɛŋkən] *vt* limit, restrict; (Kosten) cut down, reduce // *vr* cut down (on expenditure); **~d** *a* restrictive.

Einschränkung *f* restriction, limitation; reduction; (von Behauptung) qualification.

Einschreib- ['aɪnʃraɪb] *zW*: **~(e)brief** *m* recorded delivery letter; **e~en** *unreg vt* write in; (Post) send recorded delivery // *vr* register; (UNIV) enrol; **~en** *nt* recorded delivery letter.

einschreiten ['aɪnʃraɪtən] *vi unreg* step in, intervene; **~ gegen** take action against.

einschüchtern ['aɪnʃyçtərn] *vt* intimidate.

einschweißen ['aɪnʃvaɪsən] *vt* shrink-wrap.

einsehen ['aɪnzeːən] *vt unreg* (hineinsehen in) realize; (Akten) have a look at; (verstehen) see; **E~** *nt* **-s**

understanding; **ein E~ haben** show understanding.

einseitig ['aɪnzaɪtɪç] a one-sided.

Einsend- ['aɪnzɛnd] zW: **e~en** vt unreg send in; **~er** m **-s, -** sender, contributor; **~ung** f sending in.

einsetzen ['aɪnzɛtsən] vt put (in); (in Amt) appoint, install; (Geld) stake; (verwenden) use; (MIL) employ // vi (beginnen) set in; (MUS) enter, come in // vr work hard; **sich für jdn/etw ~** support sb/sth.

Einsicht ['aɪnzɪçt] f insight; (in Akten) look, inspection; **zu der ~ kommen, daß** ... come to the conclusion that ...; **e~ig** a (Mensch) judicious; **~nahme** f -, - examination; **einsichtslos** a unreasonable; **einsichtsvoll** a understanding.

Einsiedler ['aɪnziːdlər] m hermit.

einsilbig ['aɪnzɪlbɪç] a (lit, fig) monosyllabic.

einsperren ['aɪnʃpɛrən] vt lock up.

einspielen ['aɪnʃpiːlən] vr (SPORT) warm up; **sich aufeinander ~** become attuned to each other // vt (Film: Geld) bring in; (Instrument) play in; **gut eingespielt** smoothly running.

einspringen ['aɪnʃprɪŋən] vi unreg (aushelfen) help out, step into the breach.

Einspritzmotor ['aɪnʃprɪtsmoːtɔr] m fuel injection engine.

Einspruch ['aɪnʃprʊx] m protest, objection; **Einspruchsrecht** nt veto.

einspurig ['aɪnʃpuːrɪç] a single-lane.

einst [aɪnst] ad once; (zukünftig) one od some day.

Einstand ['aɪnʃtant] m (TENNIS) deuce; (Antritt) entrance (to office).

einstecken ['aɪnʃtɛkən] vt stick in, insert; (Brief) post; (ELEK: Stecker) plug in; (Geld) pocket; (mitnehmen) take; (überlegen sein) put in the shade; (hinnehmen) swallow.

einstehen ['aɪnʃteːən] vi unreg guarantee (für jdn/etw sb/sth); (verantworten) answer (für for).

einsteigen ['aɪnʃtaɪgən] vi unreg get in od on; (in Schiff) go on board; (sich beteiligen) come in; (hineinklettern) climb in.

einstell- ['aɪnʃtɛl] zW: **~en** vti (aufhören) stop; (Geräte) adjust; (Kamera etc) focus; (Sender, Radio) tune in; (unterstellen) put; (in Firma) employ, take on // vr (anfangen) set in; (kommen) arrive; **sich auf jdn/etw ~en** adapt to sb/prepare o.s. for sth; **E~ung** f (Aufhören) suspension, cessation; adjustment; focusing; (von Arbeiter etc) appointment; (Haltung) attitude.

Einstieg ['aɪnʃtiːk] m **-(e)s, -e** entry; (fig) approach.

einstig ['aɪnstɪç] a former.

einstimmig ['aɪnʃtɪmɪç] a unanimous; (MUS) for one voice.

einst- ['aɪnst] zW: **~malig** a former; **~mals** ad once, formerly.

einstöckig ['aɪnʃtœkɪç] a single-storeyed.

Einsturz ['aɪnʃtʊrts] m collapse; **~gefahr** f danger of collapse.

einstürzen ['aɪnʃtʏrtsən] vi fall in, collapse.

einst- ['aɪnst] zW: **~weilen** ad meanwhile; (vorläufig) temporarily, for the time being; **~weilig** a temporary.

eintägig ['aɪntɛːgɪç] a one-day.

eintasten ['aɪntastən] vt key (in).

eintauschen ['aɪntaʊʃən] vt exchange.

eintausend ['aɪn'taʊzənt] num one thousand.

einteil- ['aɪntaɪl] zW: **~en** vt (in Teile) divide (up); (Menschen) assign; **~ig** a one-piece.

eintönig ['aɪntøːnɪç] a monotonous; **E~keit** f monotony.

Eintopf(gericht nt) ['aɪntɔpf(gərɪçt)] m stew.

Eintracht ['aɪntraxt] f - concord, harmony.

einträchtig ['aɪntrɛçtɪç] a harmonious.

Eintrag ['aɪntraːk] m **-(e)s, -̈e** entry; **amtlicher ~** entry in the register; **e~en** unreg vt (in Buch) enter; (Profit) yield; **jdm etw e~en** bring sb sth // vr put one's name down.

einträglich ['aɪntrɛːklɪç] a profitable.

eintreffen ['aɪntrɛfən] vi unreg happen; (ankommen) arrive.

eintreten ['aɪntreːtən] unreg vi occur; (hineingehen) enter (in etw (akk) sth); (sich einsetzen) intercede; (in Club, Partei) join (in etw (akk) sth); (in Stadium etc) enter // vt (Tür) kick open.

Eintritt ['aɪntrɪt] m (Betreten) entrance; (Anfang) commencement; (in Club etc) joining.

Eintritts- zW: **~geld** nt, **~preis** m charge for admission; **~karte** f (admission) ticket.

einüben ['aɪn'yːbən] vt practise, drill.

Einvernehmen ['aɪnfɛrneːmən] nt -s, - agreement, understanding.

einverstanden ['aɪnfɛrʃtandən] interj agreed // a: **~ sein** agree, be agreed.

Einverständnis ['aɪnfɛrʃtɛntnɪs] nt understanding; (gleiche Meinung) agreement.

Einwand ['aɪnvant] m **-(e)s, -̈e** objection.

Einwanderer ['aɪnvandərər] m immigrant.

einwandern vi immigrate.

Einwanderung f immigration.

einwandfrei a perfect // ad absolutely.

Einwegflasche ['aınveːgflaʃə] *f* no-deposit bottle.

einweichen ['aınvaıçən] *vt* soak.

einweih- ['aınvaı] *zW:* **~en** *vt* (*Kirche*) consecrate; (*Brücke*) open; (*Gebäude*) inaugurate; (*Person*) initiate (*in +akk* in); **E~ung** *f* consecration; opening; inauguration; initiation.

einweisen ['aınvaızən] *vt unreg* (*in Amt*) install; (*in Arbeit*) introduce; (*in Anstalt*) send.

einwenden ['aınvɛndən] *vt unreg* object, oppose (*gegen* to).

einwerfen ['aınvɛrfən] *vt unreg* throw in; (*Brief*) post; (*Geld*) put in, insert; (*Fenster*) smash; (*äußern*) interpose.

einwickeln ['aınvıkəln] *vt* wrap up; (*fig umg*) outsmart.

einwillig- ['aınvılıg] *zW:* **~en** *vi* consent, agree (*in +akk* to); **E~ung** *f* consent.

einwirken ['aınvırkən] *vi:* **auf jdn/etw ~en** influence sb/sth.

Einwohner ['aınvoːnər] *m* **-s,** - inhabitant; **~'meldeamt** *nt* registration office; **~schaft** *f* population, inhabitants *pl.*

Einwurf ['aınvurf] *m* (*Öffnung*) slot; (*Einwand*) objection; (*SPORT*) throw-in.

Einzahl ['aıntsaːl] *f* singular; **e~en** *vt* pay in; **~ung** *f* paying in.

einzäunen ['aıntsɔynən] *vt* fence in.

Einzel ['aıntsəl] *nt* **-s,** - (*TENNIS*) singles // *in zW* individual; single; **~fall** *m* single instance, individual case; **~handel** *m* retail trade; **~handelspreis** *m* retail price; **~haft** *f* solitary confinement; **~heit** *f* particular, detail; **~karte** *f* single ticket; **e~n** *a* single; (*vereinzelt*) the odd // *ad* singly; **e~n angeben** specify; **der/die ~ne** the individual; **das e~ne** the particular; **ins e~ne gehen** go into detail(s); **~teil** *nt* component (part); **~zimmer** *nt* single room.

einziehen ['aıntsiːən] *unreg vt* draw in, take in; (*Kopf*) duck; (*Fühler, Antenne, Fahrgestell*) retract; (*Steuern, Erkundigungen*) collect; (*MIL*) draft, call up; (*aus dem Verkehr ziehen*) withdraw; (*konfiszieren*) confiscate // *vi* move in(to); (*Friede, Ruhe*) come; (*Flüssigkeit*) penetrate.

einzig ['aıntsıg] *a* only; (*ohnegleichen*) unique; **das ~e** the only thing; **der/die ~e** the only one; **~artig** *a* unique.

Einzug ['aıntsuːk] *m* entry, moving in.

Eis [aıs] **-es,** - *nt*, *es* (*Speise~*) ice cream; **~bahn** *f* ice *od* skating rink; **~bär** *m* polar bear; **~becher** *m* sundae; **~bein** *nt* pig's trotters *pl*;

~berg *m* iceberg; **~decke** *f* sheet of ice; **~diele** *f* ice-cream parlour.

Eisen ['aızən] *nt* **-s,** - iron; **~bahn** *f* railway, railroad (*US*); **~bahner** *m* **-s,** - railwayman, railway employee, railroader (*US*); **~bahnschaffner** *m* railway guard; **~bahnübergang** *m* level crossing, grade crossing (*US*); **~bahnwagen** *m* railway carriage; **~erz** *nt* iron ore; **e~haltig** *a* containing iron.

eisern ['aızərn] *a* iron; (*Gesundheit*) robust; (*Energie*) unrelenting; (*Reserve*) emergency.

Eis- *zW:* **e~frei** *a* clear of ice; **~hockey** *nt* ice hockey; **e~ig** ['aızıç] *a* icy; **e~kalt** *a* icy cold; **~kunstlauf** *m* figure skating; **~laufen** *nt* ice skating; **~läufer(in** *f) m* ice-skater; **~pickel** *m* ice-axe; **~schießen** *nt* ≈ curling; **~schrank** *m* fridge, ice-box (*US*); **~zapfen** *m* icicle; **~zeit** *f* ice age.

eitel ['aıtəl] *a* vain; **E~keit** *f* vanity.

Eiter ['aıtər] *m* **-s,** pus; **e~ig** *a* suppurating; **e~n** *vi* suppurate.

Ei- [aı] *zW:* **~weiß** *nt* **-es,** -e white of an egg; **~zelle** *f* ovum.

Ekel ['eːkəl] *m* **-s,** nausea, disgust // *nt* **-s,** - (*umg: Mensch*) nauseating person; **e~erregend, e~haft, ek(e)lig** *a* nauseating, disgusting; **e~n** *vt* disgust; **es ekelt jdn** *od* **jdm sb** is disgusted // *vr* loathe, be disgusted (*vor +dat* at).

Ekstase [ɛk'staːzə] *f* **-,** **-n** ecstasy.

Ekzem [ɛk'tseːm] *nt* **-s,** -e (*MED*) eczema.

Elan [e'laːn] *m* **-s** elan.

elastisch [e'lastıʃ] *a* elastic.

Elastizität [elastitsi'tɛːt] *f* elasticity.

Elch [ɛlç] *m* **-(e)s,** -e elk.

Elefant [ele'fant] *m* elephant.

elegant [ele'gant] *a* elegant.

Eleganz [ele'gants] *f* elegance.

Elek- [e'lek] *zW:* **~triker** [-trikər] *m* **-s,** - electrician; **e~trisch** [-trıʃ] *a* electric; **e~trisieren** [-tri'ziːrən] *vt* (*lit, fig*) electrify; (*Mensch*) give an electric shock to // *vr* get an electric shock; **~trizität** [-tritsi'tɛːt] *f* electricity; **~trizitätswerk** *nt* electricity works, power plant.

Elektro- [e'lektro] *zW:* **~de** [elɛk'troːdə] *f* **-,** **-n** electrode; **~herd** *m* electric cooker; **~n** [-ɔn] *nt* **-s,** -en electron; **~nen(ge)hirn** [elɛk'troːnən-] *nt* electronic brain; **~nenrechner** *m* computer; **e~nisch** *a* electronic; **e~nische Post** electronic mail; **e~nischer Briefkasten** electronic mailbox; **~rasierer** *m* electric razor.

Element [ele'mɛnt] *nt* **-s,** -e element; (*ELEK*) cell, battery; **e~ar** [-'taːr] *a* elementary; (*naturhaft*) elemental.

Elend ['e:lɛnt] nt -(e)s misery; e~ a miserable; **Elendsviertel** nt slum.

elf [ɛlf] num eleven; **E~** f -, -en (SPORT) eleven; **E~e** f -, -n elf; **E~enbein** nt ivory; **E~meter** m (SPORT) penalty (kick).

Elite [e'li:tə] f -, -n elite.

Elixier [eli'ksi:r] nt -s, -e elixir.

Ell- zW: ~e ['ɛlə] f -, -n ell; (Maß) yard; ~(en)bogen m elbow; **Ellipse** [ɛ'lɪpsə] f -, -n ellipse.

Elsaß ['ɛlzas] nt: das ~ Alsace.

Elster ['ɛlstər] f -, -n magpie.

elterlich ['ɛltərlɪç] a parental.

Eltern ['ɛltərn] pl parents pl; ~haus nt home; ~los a parentless.

Email [e'ma:j] nt -s, -s enamel; e~lieren [ema'ji:rən] vt enamel.

Emanzipation [emantsipatsi'o:n] f emancipation.

emanzi'pieren vt emancipate.

Embryo ['ɛmbryo] m -s, -s od -nen embryo.

Emi- [emi] zW: ~gration [-gratsi'o:n] f emigration; e~grieren [-'gri:rən] vi emigrate.

empfahl etc v siehe **empfehlen**.

Empfang [ɛm'pfaŋ] m -(e)s, ⁀e reception; (Erhalten) receipt; in ~ nehmen receive; e~en unreg vt receive // vi (schwanger werden) conceive.

Empfäng- [ɛm'pfɛŋ] zW: ~er m -s, - receiver; (COMM) addressee, consignee; e~lich a receptive, susceptible; ~nis f -, -se conception; ~nisverhütung f contraception.

Empfangs- zW: ~bestätigung f acknowledgement; ~dame f receptionist; ~schein m receipt; ~zimmer nt reception room.

empfehlen [ɛm'pfe:lən] unreg vt recommend // vr take one's leave; ~swert a recommendable.

Empfehlung f recommendation.

empfiehlst etc v siehe **empfehlen**.

empfind- [ɛm'pfɪnt] zW: ~en [ɛm'pfɪndən] vt unreg feel; ~lich a sensitive; (Stelle) sore; (reizbar) touchy; ~sam a sentimental; **E~ung** f feeling, sentiment.

empfohlen v siehe **empfehlen**.

empor [ɛm'po:r] ad up, upwards.

empören [ɛm'pø:rən] vt make indignant; shock // vr become indignant; ~d a outrageous.

Emporkömmling [ɛm'po:rkœmlɪŋ] m upstart, parvenu.

Empörung f indignation.

emsig ['ɛmzɪç] a diligent, busy.

End- [ɛnt] in zW final; ~e nt -s, -n end; am ~e at the end; (schließlich) in the end; am ~e sein be at the end of one's tether; ~e Dezember at the end of December; zu ~e sein be

finished; e~en vi end; e~gültig a final, definite; **Endivie** [ɛn'di:viə] f endive; e~lich a final; (MATH) finite // ad finally; e~lich! at last!; komm e~lich! come on!; e~los a endless, infinite; ~lospapier nt continuous stationery; ~spiel nt final(s); ~spurt m (SPORT) final spurt; ~station f terminus; ~ung f ending.

Energie [enɛr'gi:] f energy; ~einsparung f energy saving; e~los a lacking in energy, weak; ~wirtschaft f energy industry.

energisch [e'nɛrgɪʃ] a energetic.

eng [ɛŋ] a narrow; (Kleidung) tight; (fig: Horizont auch) limited; (Freundschaft, Verhältnis) close; ~ an etw (dat) close to sth.

Engagement [ãgaʒə'mã:] nt -s, -s engagement; (Verpflichtung) commitment.

engagieren [ãga'ʒi:rən] vt engage; ein engagierter Schriftsteller a committed writer // vr commit o.s.

Enge ['ɛŋə] f -, -n (lit,fig) narrowness; (Land~) defile; (Meer~) straits pl; jdn in die ~ treiben drive sb into a corner.

Engel ['ɛŋəl] m -s, - angel; e~haft a angelic; ~macher(in f) m -s, - (umg) backstreet abortionist.

eng- zW: ~herzig a petty; **E~land** nt England; **E~länder** m Englishman; **E~länderin** f Englishwoman; ~lisch a English; **E~paß** m defile, pass; (fig, Verkehr) bottleneck.

en gros [ã'gro:] ad wholesale.

engstirnig ['ɛŋʃtɪrnɪç] a narrow-minded.

Enkel ['ɛŋkəl] m -s, - grandson; ~in f granddaughter.

enorm [e'nɔrm] a enormous.

Ensemble [ã'sãbəl] nt -s, -s company, ensemble.

entbehr- [ɛnt'be:r] zW: ~en vt do without, dispense with; ~lich a superfluous.

entbinden [ɛnt'bɪndən] unreg vt release (gen from); (MED) deliver // vi (MED) give birth.

Entbindung f release; (MED) confinement; **Entbindungsheim** nt maternity hospital.

entdeck- [ɛnt'dɛk] zW: ~en vt discover. **E~er** m -s, - discoverer; **E~ung** f discovery.

Ente ['ɛntə] f -, -n duck; (fig) canard, false report.

enteignen [ɛnt'aignən] vt expropriate; (Besitzer) dispossess.

enteisen [ɛnt'aizən] vt de-ice, defrost.

enterben [ɛnt'ɛrbən] vt disinherit.

entfallen [ɛnt'falən] vi unreg drop, fall; (wegfallen) be dropped; jdm ~ (vergessen) slip sb's memory; auf jdn ~ be allotted to sb.

entfalten [ɛnt'faltən] *vt* unfold; (*Talente*) develop // *vr* open; (*Mensch*) develop one's potential.

Entfaltung *f* unfolding; (*von Talenten*) development.

entfern- [ɛnt'fɛrn] *zW:* ~**en** *vt* remove; (*hinauswerfen*) expel // *vr* go away, withdraw; ~**t** *a* distant; weit davon ~t sein, etw zu tun be far from doing sth; **E~ung** *f* distance; (*Wegschaffen*) removal; **E~ungsmesser** *m* -s, - (*PHOT*) rangefinder.

entfremd- [ɛnt'frɛmd] *zW:* ~**en** *vt* estrange, alienate; **E~ung** *f* alienation, estrangement.

entfrost- [ɛnt'frɔst] *zW:* ~**en** *vt* defrost; **E~er** *m* -s, - (*AUT*) defroster.

entführ- [ɛnt'fyːr] *zW:* ~**en** *vt* carry off, abduct; kidnap; **E~er** *m* kidnapper; **E~ung** *f* abduction; kidnapping.

entgegen [ɛnt'geːgən] *präp +dat* contrary to, against // *ad* towards; ~**bringen** *vt unreg* bring; (*fig*) show (*jdm etw* sb sth); ~**gehen** *vi unreg* (+*dat*) go to meet, go towards; ~**gesetzt** *a* opposite; (*widersprechend*) opposed; ~**halten** *vt unreg* (*fig*) object; ~**kommen** *vi unreg* approach; meet (*jdm* sb); (*fig*) accommodate (*jdm* sb); **E~kommen** *nt* obligingness; ~**kommend** *a* obliging; ~**nehmen** *vt unreg* receive, accept; ~**sehen** *vi unreg* (+*dat*) await; ~**setzen** *vt* oppose (*dat* to); ~**treten** *vi unreg* (+*dat*: *lit*) step up to; (*fig*) oppose, counter; ~**wirken** *vi* (+*dat*) counteract.

entgegnen [ɛnt'geːgnən] *vt* reply, retort.

entgehen [ɛnt'geːən] *vi unreg* (*fig*) jdm ~ escape sb's notice; sich (*dat*) etw ~ lassen miss sth.

entgeistert [ɛnt'gaistərt] *a* thunderstruck.

Entgelt [ɛnt'gɛlt] *nt* -(e)s, -e compensation, remuneration.

entgleisen [ɛnt'glaizən] *vi* (*EISENB*) be derailed; (*fig: Person*) misbehave; ~ lassen derail.

entgräten [ɛnt'grɛːtən] *vt* fillet, bone.

Enthaarungsmittel [ɛnt'haːrʊŋsmɪtəl] *nt* depilatory.

enthalten [ɛnt'haltən] *unreg vt* contain // *vr* abstain, refrain (*gen* from).

enthaltsam [ɛnt'haltzaːm] *a* abstinent, abstemious; **E~keit** *f* abstinence.

enthemmen [ɛnt'hɛmən] *vt:* jdn ~ free sb from his inhibitions.

enthüllen [ɛnt'hʏlən] *vt* reveal, unveil.

Enthusiasmus [ɛntuzi'asmʊs] *m* enthusiasm.

entkommen [ɛnt'kɔmən] *vi unreg* get away, escape (*dat, aus* from).

entkräften [ɛnt'krɛftən] *vt* weaken, exhaust; (*Argument*) refute.

entladen [ɛnt'laːdən] *unreg vt* unload; (*ELEK*) discharge // *vr* (*ELEK, Gewehr*) discharge; (*Ärger etc*) vent itself.

entlang [ɛnt'laŋ] *präp +akk od dat*, ad along; ~ dem Fluß, den Fluß ~ along the river; ~**gehen** *vi unreg* walk along.

entlarven [ɛnt'larfən] *vt* unmask, expose.

entlassen [ɛnt'lasən] *vt unreg* discharge; (*Arbeiter*) dismiss.

Entlassung *f* discharge; dismissal; **Entlassungsabfindung** *f* redundancy payment.

entlasten [ɛnt'lastən] *vt* relieve; (*Achse*) relieve the load on; (*Angeklagten*) exonerate; (*Konto*) clear.

Entlastung *f* relief; (*COMM*) crediting.

entlegen [ɛnt'leːgən] *a* remote.

entlocken [ɛnt'lɔkən] *vt* elicit (*jdm etw* sth from sb).

entmachten [ɛnt'maxtən] *vt* deprive of power.

entmilitarisiert [ɛntmilitari'ziːrt] *a* demilitarized.

entmündigen [ɛnt'mʏndɪgən] *vt* certify.

entmutigen [ɛnt'muːtɪgən] *vt* discourage.

entnehmen [ɛnt'neːmən] *vt unreg* (+*dat*) take out (of), take (from); (*folgern*) infer (from).

entrahmen [ɛnt'raːmən] *vt* skim.

entreißen [ɛnt'raisən] *vt unreg* snatch (away) (*jdm etw* sth from sb).

entrichten [ɛnt'rɪçtən] *vt* pay.

entrosten [ɛnt'rɔstən] *vt* derust.

entrüst- [ɛnt'rʏst] *zW:* ~**en** *vt* incense, outrage // *vr* be filled with indignation; ~**et** *a* indignant, outraged; **E~ung** *f* indignation.

entschädigen [ɛnt'ʃɛːdɪgən] *vt* compensate.

Entschädigung *f* compensation.

entschärfen [ɛnt'ʃɛrfən] *vt* defuse; (*Kritik*) tone down.

Entscheid [ɛnt'ʃait] *m* -(e)s, -e decision; e~**en** *vtir unreg* decide; e~**end** *a* decisive; (*Stimme*) casting; ~**ung** *f* decision.

entschieden [ɛnt'ʃiːdən] *a* decided; (*entschlossen*) resolute; **E~heit** *f* firmness, determination.

entschließen [ɛnt'ʃliːsən] *vr unreg* decide.

entschlossen [ɛnt'ʃlɔsən] *a* determined, resolute; **E~heit** *f* determination.

Entschluß [ɛnt'flus] *m* decision; e~**freudig** *a* decisive; ~**kraft** *f* determination, decisiveness.

entschuld- [ɛnt'ʃʊld] zW: ~**igen** vt excuse // vr apologize; **E~igung** f apology; (Grund) excuse; **jdn um E~igung bitten** apologize to sb; **E~igung!** excuse me; (Verzeihung) sorry.

entsetz- [ɛnt'zɛts] zW: ~**en** vt horrify; (MIL) relieve // vr be horrified od appalled; **E~en** nt **-s** horror, dismay; ~**lich** a dreadful, appalling; ~**t** a horrified.

entsinnen [ɛnt'zɪnən] vr unreg remember (gen sth).

entspannen [ɛnt'ʃpanən] vtr (Körper) relax; (POL: Lage) ease.

Entspannung f relaxation, rest; (POL) détente; **Entspannungspolitik** f policy of détente.

entsprechen [ɛnt'ʃprɛçən] vi unreg (+dat) correspond to; (Anforderungen, Wünschen) meet, comply with; ~**d** a appropriate // ad accordingly.

entspringen [ɛnt'ʃprɪŋən] vi unreg spring (from).

entstehen [ɛnt'ʃteːən] vi unreg arise, result.

Entstehung f genesis, origin.

entstellen [ɛnt'ʃtɛlən] vt disfigure; (Wahrheit) distort.

entstören [ɛnt'ʃtøːrən] vt (RAD) eliminate interference from; (AUT) suppress.

enttäuschen [ɛnt'tɔyʃən] vt disappoint.

Enttäuschung f disappointment.

Entwarnung [ɛnt'varnʊŋ] f all clear (signal).

entwässern [ɛnt'vɛsərn] vt drain.

entweder ['ɛntveːdər] kj either.

entwenden [ɛnt'vɛndən] vt unreg purloin, steal.

entwerfen [ɛnt'vɛrfən] vt unreg (Zeichnung) sketch; (Modell) design; (Vortrag, Gesetz etc) draft.

entwerten [ɛnt'veːrtən] vt devalue; (stempeln) cancel.

Entwerter m **-s**, - ticket punching machine.

entwickeln [ɛnt'vɪkəln] vtr develop (auch PHOT); (Mut, Energie) show, display.

Entwickler m **-s**, - developer.

Entwicklung [ɛnt'vɪklʊŋ] f development; (PHOT) developing.

Entwicklungs- zW: ~**hilfe** f aid for developing countries; ~**jahre** pl adolescence sing; ~**land** nt developing country.

entwöhnen [ɛnt'vøːnən] vt wean; (Süchtige) cure (dat, von of).

Entwöhnung f weaning; cure, curing.

entwürdigend [ɛnt'vʏrdɪgənt] a degrading.

Entwurf [ɛnt'vʊrf] m outline, design;

(Vertrags~, Konzept) draft.

entziehen [ɛnt'tsiːən] unreg vt withdraw, take away (dat from); (Flüssigkeit) draw, extract // vr escape (dat from); (jds Kenntnis) be outside; (der Pflicht) shirk.

Entziehung f withdrawal.

Entziehungs- zW: ~**anstalt** f drug addiction/alcoholism treatment centre; ~**kur** f treatment for drug addiction/alcoholism.

entziffern [ɛnt'tsɪfərn] vt decipher; decode.

entzücken [ɛnt'tsʏkən] vt delight; **E~** nt **-s** delight; ~**d** a delightful, charming.

entzünden [ɛnt'tsyndən] vt light, set light to; (fig, MED) inflame; (Streit) spark off // vr (lit, fig) catch fire; (Streit) start; (MED) become inflamed.

Entzündung f (MED) inflammation.

entzwei [ɛnt'tsvaɪ] ad broken; in two; ~**brechen** vti unreg break in two; ~**en** vt set at odds // vr fall out; ~**gehen** vi unreg break (in two).

Enzian ['ɛntsiaːn] m **-s**, **-e** gentian.

Enzym [ɛn'tsyːm] nt **-s**, **-e** enzyme.

Epidemie [epide'miː] f epidemic.

Epilepsie [epile'psiː] f epilepsy.

Episode [epi'zoːdə] f **-**, **-n** episode.

Epoche [e'pɔxə] f **-**, **-n** epoch; **e~machend** a epoch-making.

Epos ['eːpɔs] nt **-**, **Epen** epic (poem).

er [eːr] pron he; it.

erachten [ɛr''axtən] vt: ~ **für** od **als** consider (to be); **meines E~s** in my opinion.

erarbeiten [ɛr''arbaɪtən] vt (auch sich (dat) ~) work for, acquire; (Theorie) work out.

erbarmen [ɛr'barmən] vr have pity od mercy (gen on); **E~** nt **-s** pity.

erbärmlich [ɛr'bɛrmlɪç] a wretched, pitiful; **E~keit** f wretchedness.

erbarmungslos [ɛr'barmʊŋsloːs] a pitiless, merciless.

erbau- [ɛr'bau] zW: ~**en** vt build, erect; (fig) edify; **E~er** m **-s**, - builder; ~**lich** a edifying; **E~ung** f construction; (fig) edification.

Erbe ['ɛrbə] m **-n**, **-n** heir // nt **-s** inheritance; (fig) heritage; **e~n** vt inherit.

erbeuten [ɛr'bɔytən] vt carry off; (MIL) capture.

Erb- [ɛrb] zW: ~**faktor** m gene; ~**folge** f (line of) succession; ~**in** f heiress.

erbittern [ɛr'bɪtərn] vt embitter; (erzürnen) incense.

erbittert [ɛr'bɪtərt] a (Kampf) fierce, bitter.

erblassen [ɛr'blasən] vi, **erbleichen** [ɛr'blaɪçən] vi unreg (turn) pale.

erblich ['ɛrplɪç] a hereditary.

erbosen [ɛr'boːzən] vt anger // vr grow angry.

erbrechen [ɛr'brɛçən] vtr unreg vomit.

Erbschaft f inheritance, legacy.

Erbse ['ɛrpsə] f -, -n pea.

Erd- ['eːrd] zW: ~**achse** f earth's axis; ~**atmosphäre** f earth's atmosphere; ~**beben** nt earthquake; ~**beere** f strawberry; ~**boden** m ground; ~**e** f -, -n earth; **zu ebener** ~**e** at ground level; **e~en** vt (ELEK) earth.

erdenklich [ɛr'dɛŋklɪç] a conceivable.

Erd- zW: ~**gas** nt natural gas; ~**geschoß** nt ground floor; ~**kunde** f geography; ~**nuß** f peanut; ~**oberfläche** f surface of the earth; ~**öl** nt (mineral) oil.

erdrosseln [ɛr'drɔsəln] vt strangle, throttle.

erdrücken [ɛr'drykən] vt crush.

Erd- zW: ~**rutsch** m landslide; ~**teil** m continent.

erdulden [ɛr'duldən] vt endure, suffer.

ereifern [ɛr'aifərn] vr get excited.

ereignen [ɛr'aignən] vr happen.

Ereignis [ɛr'aignɪs] nt -ses, -se event; **e~reich** a eventful.

erfahren [ɛr'faːrən] vt unreg learn, find out; (erleben) experience // a experienced.

Erfahrung f experience; **erfahrungsgemäß** ad according to experience.

erfassen [ɛr'fasən] vt seize; (fig: einbeziehen) include, register; (verstehen) grasp.

erfind- [ɛr'find] zW: ~**en** vt unreg invent; **E~er** m -s, - inventor; ~**erisch** a inventive; **E~ung** f invention.

Erfolg [ɛr'fɔlk] m -(e)s, -e success; (Folge) result; **e~en** vi follow; (sich ergeben) result; (stattfinden) take place; (Zahlung) be effected; **e~los** a unsuccessful; ~**losigkeit** f lack of success; **e~reich** a successful; **e~versprechend** a promising.

erforder- [ɛr'fɔrdər] zW: ~**lich** a requisite, necessary; ~**n** vt require, demand.

erforsch- [ɛr'fɔrʃ] zW: ~**en** vi (Land) explore; (Problem) investigate; (Gewissen) search; **E~ung** f exploration; investigation; searching.

erfreuen [ɛr'frɔyən] vr: **sich ~ an** (+dat) enjoy; **sich einer Sache** (gen) ~ enjoy sth // vt delight.

erfreulich [ɛr'frɔylɪç] a pleasing, gratifying; ~**erweise** ad happily, luckily.

erfrieren [ɛr'friːrən] vi unreg freeze (to death); (Glieder) get frostbitten; (Pflanzen) be killed by frost.

erfrischen [ɛr'frɪʃən] vt refresh.

Erfrischung f refreshment; **Erfrischungsraum** m snack bar, cafeteria.

erfüllen [ɛr'fylən] vt (Raum etc) fill; (fig: Bitte etc) fulfil // vr come true.

ergänzen [ɛr'gɛntsən] vt supplement, complete // vr complement one another.

Ergänzung f completion; (Zusatz) supplement.

ergeben [ɛr'geːbən] unreg vt yield, produce // vr surrender; (sich hingeben) give o.s. up, yield (dat to); (folgen) result // a devoted, humble; (dem Trunk) addicted (to); **E~heit** f devotion, humility.

Ergebnis [ɛr'geːpnɪs] nt -ses, -se result; **e~los** a without result, fruitless.

ergehen [ɛr'geːən] unreg vi be issued, go out; **etw über sich ~ lassen** put up with sth // vi unpers: **es ergeht ihm gut/schlecht** he's faring od getting on well/badly // vr: **sich in etw** (dat) ~ indulge in sth.

ergiebig [ɛr'giːbɪç] a productive.

ergreifen [ɛr'graifən] vt unreg (lit, fig) seize; (Beruf) take up; (Maßnahmen) resort to; (rühren) move.

ergriffen [ɛr'grɪfən] a deeply moved.

Erguß [ɛr'gus] m discharge; (fig) outpouring, effusion.

erhaben [ɛr'haːbən] a (lit) raised, embossed; (fig) exalted, lofty; **über etw** (akk) ~ **sein** be above sth.

erhalten [ɛr'haltən] vt unreg receive; (bewahren) preserve, maintain; **gut** ~ in good condition.

erhältlich [ɛr'hɛltlɪç] a obtainable, available.

Erhaltung f maintenance, preservation.

erhärten [ɛr'hɛrtən] vt harden; (These) substantiate, corroborate.

erheben [ɛr'heːbən] unreg vt raise; (Protest, Forderungen) make; (Fakten) ascertain, establish // vr rise (up); **sich über etw** (akk) ~ rise above sth.

erheblich [ɛr'heːplɪç] a considerable.

erheitern [ɛr'haitərn] vt amuse, cheer (up).

Erheiterung f exhilaration; **zur allgemeinen** ~ to everybody's amusement.

erhitzen [ɛr'hitsən] vt heat // vr heat up; (fig) become heated.

erhoffen [ɛr'hɔfən] vt hope for.

erhöhen [ɛr'høːən] vt raise; (verstärken) increase.

erhol- [ɛr'hoːl] zW: ~**en** vr recover; (entspannen) have a rest; ~**sam** a restful; **E~ung** f recovery; relaxation, rest; ~**ungsbedürftig** a in need of a rest, run-down; **E~ungsheim** nt convalescent/rest home.

erhören [ɛr'høːrən] vt (Gebet etc) hear; (Bitte etc) yield to.

erinnern [ɛr'ɪnərn] vt remind (an +akk of) // vr remember (an etw (akk)) sth).

Erinnerung f memory; (Andenken) reminder.

erkält- [ɛr'kɛlt] zW: ~en vr catch cold; ~et a with a cold; ~et sein have a cold; E~ung f cold.

erkenn- [ɛr'kɛn] zW: ~bar a recognizable; ~en vt unreg recognize; (sehen, verstehen) see.

erkennt- zW: ~lich a: sich ~lich zeigen show one's appreciation; E~lichkeit f gratitude; (Geschenk) token of one's gratitude; E~nis f -, -se knowledge; (das Erkennen) recognition; (Einsicht) insight; zur E~t-nis kommen realize.

Erkennung f recognition.

Erker ['ɛrkər] m -s, - bay; ~fenster nt bay window.

erklär- [ɛr'klɛːr] zW: ~bar a explicable; ~en vt explain; ~lich a explicable; (verständlich) understandable; E~ung f explanation; (Aussage) declaration.

erkranken [ɛr'kraŋkən] vi fall ill.

Erkrankung f illness.

erkund- [ɛr'kʊnd] zW: ~en vt find out, ascertain; (bes MIL) reconnoitre, scout; ~igen vr inquire (nach about); E~igung f inquiry; E~ung f reconnaissance, scouting.

erlahmen [ɛr'laːmən] vi tire; (nachlassen) flag, wane.

erlangen [ɛr'laŋən] vt attain, achieve.

Erlaß [ɛr'las] m -sses, -lässe decree; (Aufhebung) remission.

erlassen vt unreg (Verfügung) issue; (Gesetz) enact; (Strafe) remit; jdm etw ~ release sb from sth.

erlauben [ɛr'laubən] vt allow, permit (jdm etw sb to do sth) // vr permit o.s., venture.

Erlaubnis [ɛr'laupnɪs] f -, -se permission; (Schriftstück) permit.

erläutern [ɛr'lɔytərn] vt explain.

Erläuterung f explanation.

Erle ['ɛrlə] f -, -n alder.

erleben [ɛr'leːbən] vt experience; (Zeit) live through; (mit~) witness; (noch mit~) live to see.

Erlebnis [ɛr'leːpnɪs] nt -ses, -se experience.

erledigen [ɛr'leːdɪgən] vt take care of, deal with; (Antrag etc) process; (umg: erschöpfen) wear out; (umg: ruinieren) finish; (umg: umbringen) do in.

erleichter- [ɛr'laɪçtər] zW: ~n vt make easier; (fig: Last) lighten; (lindern, beruhigen) relieve; ~t a relieved; E~ung f facilitation; lightening; relief.

erleiden [ɛr'laɪdən] vt unreg suffer, endure.

erlernen [ɛr'lɛrnən] vt learn, acquire.

erlesen [ɛr'leːzən] a select, choice.

erleuchten [ɛr'lɔyçtən] vt illuminate; (fig) inspire.

Erleuchtung f (Einfall) inspiration.

Erlös [ɛr'løːs] m -es, -e proceeds pl.

erlösen [ɛr'løːzən] vt redeem, save.

Erlösung f release; (REL) redemption.

ermächtigen [ɛr'mɛçtɪgən] vt authorize, empower.

Ermächtigung f authorization; authority.

ermahnen [ɛr'maːnən] vt exhort, admonish.

Ermahnung f admonition, exhortation.

ermäßigen [ɛr'mɛːsɪgən] vt reduce.

Ermäßigung f reduction.

ermessen [ɛr'mɛsən] vt unreg estimate, gauge; E~ nt -s estimation; discretion; in jds E~ liegen lie within sb's discretion.

ermitteln [ɛr'mɪtəln] vt determine; (Täter) trace // vi: gegen jdn ~ investigate sb.

Ermittlung [ɛr'mɪtlʊŋ] f determination; (Polizei~) investigation.

ermöglichen [ɛr'møːklɪçən] vt make possible (dat for).

ermorden [ɛr'mɔrdən] vt murder.

Ermordung f murder.

ermüden [ɛr'myːdən] vti tire; (TECH) fatigue; ~d a tiring; (fig) wearisome.

Ermüdung f fatigue; **Ermüdungserscheinung** f sign of fatigue.

ermutigen [ɛr'muːtɪgən] vt encourage.

ernähr- [ɛr'nɛːr] zW: ~en vt feed, nourish; (Familie) support // vr support o.s., earn a living; sich ~en von live on; E~er m -s, - breadwinner; E~ung f nourishment; nutrition; (Unterhalt) maintenance.

ernennen [ɛr'nɛnən] vt unreg appoint.

Ernennung f appointment.

erneu- [ɛr'nɔy] zW: ~ern vt renew; restore; renovate; E~erung f renewal; restoration; renovation; ~t a renewed, fresh // ad once more.

Ernst [ɛrnst] m -es seriousness; das ist mein ~ I'm quite serious; im ~ in earnest; ~ machen mit etw put sth into practice; e~ a serious; ~fall m emergency; e~gemeint a meant in earnest, serious; e~haft a serious; ~haftigkeit f seriousness; e~lich a serious.

Ernte ['ɛrntə] f -, -n harvest; e~n vt harvest; (Lob etc) earn.

ernüchtern [ɛr'nʏçtərn] vt sober up; (fig) bring down to earth.

Erober- [ɛr'oːbər] zW: ~er m -s, - conqueror; e~n vt conquer; ~ung f conquest.

eröffnen [ɛr''œfnən] *vt* open; **jdm etw ~** disclose sth to sb // *vr* present itself.

Eröffnung *f* opening.

erörtern [ɛr''œrtərn] *vt* discuss.

Erörterung *f* discussion.

Erotik [e'ro:tik] *f* eroticism.

erotisch *a* erotic.

erpress- [ɛr'prɛs] *zW:* **~en** *vt* (*Geld etc*) extort; (*Mensch*) blackmail; **E~er** *m* **-s,** - blackmailer; **E~ung** *f* blackmail; extortion.

erraten [ɛr'ra:tən] *vt unreg* guess.

erreg- [ɛr're:g] *zW:* **~en** *vt* excite; (*ärgern*) infuriate; (*hervorrufen*) arouse, provoke // *vr* get excited *od* worked up; **E~er** *m* **-s,** - causative agent; **E~ung** *f* excitement.

erreichbar *a* accessible, within reach.

erreichen [ɛr'raiçən] *vt* reach; (*Zweck*) achieve; (*Zug*) catch.

errichten [ɛr'riçtən] *vt* erect, put up; (*gründen*) establish, set up.

erringen [ɛr'rɪŋən] *vt unreg* gain, win.

erröten [ɛr'rø:tən] *vi* blush, flush.

Errungenschaft [ɛr'rʊŋənʃaft] *f* achievement; (*umg: Anschaffung*) acquisition.

Ersatz [ɛr'zats] *m* **-es** substitute; replacement; (*Schaden~*) compensation; (*MIL*) reinforcements *pl*; **~dienst** *m* (*MIL*) alternative service; **~reifen** *m* (*AUT*) spare tyre; **~teil** *nt* spare (part).

erschaffen [ɛr'ʃafən] *vt unreg* create.

erscheinen [ɛr'ʃainən] *vi unreg* appear.

Erscheinung *f* appearance; (*Geist*) apparition; (*Gegebenheit*) phenomenon; (*Gestalt*) figure.

erschießen [ɛr'ʃi:sən] *vt unreg* shoot (dead).

erschlagen [ɛr'ʃla:gən] *vt unreg* strike dead.

erschöpf- [ɛr'ʃœpf] *zW:* **~en** *vt* exhaust; **~end** *a* exhaustive, thorough; **~t** *a* exhausted; **E~ung** *f* exhaustion.

erschrecken [ɛr'ʃrɛkən] *vt* startle, frighten // *vi unreg* be frightened *od* startled; **~d** *a* alarming, frightening.

erschrocken [ɛr'ʃrɔkən] *a* frightened, startled.

erschüttern [ɛr'ʃʏtərn] *vt* shake; (*ergreifen*) move deeply.

Erschütterung *f* shaking; shock.

erschweren [ɛr'ʃve:rən] *vt* complicate.

erschwingen [ɛr'ʃvɪŋən] *vt unreg* afford.

erschwinglich *a* within one's means.

ersehen [ɛr'ze:ən] *vt unreg:* **aus etw ~, daß** gather from sth that.

ersetzen [ɛr'zɛtsən] *vt* replace; **jdm Unkosten** *etc* **~** pay sb's expenses *etc*.

ersichtlich [ɛr'zɪçtlɪç] *a* evident, obvious.

ersparen [ɛr'ʃpa:rən] *vt* (*Ärger etc*) spare; (*Geld*) save.

Ersparnis *f* **-, -se** saving.

erst [e:rst] *ad* **1** first; **mach ~ mal die Arbeit fertig** finish your work first; **wenn du das ~ mal hinter dir hast** once you've got that behind you

2 (*nicht früher als, nur*) only; (*nicht bis*) not till; **~ gestern** only yesterday; **~ morgen** not until tomorrow; **~ als** only when, not until; **wir fahren ~ später** we're not going until later; **er ist (gerade) ~ angekommen** he's only just arrived

3: **~ wäre er doch ~ zurück!** if only he were back!

erstatten [ɛr'ʃtatən] *vt* (*Kosten*) (re)pay; **Anzeige** *etc* **~** report sb; **Bericht ~** make a report.

Erstaufführung ['e:rst'aʊffy:rʊŋ] *f* first performance.

erstaunen [ɛr'ʃtaʊnən] *vt* astonish // *vi* be astonished; **E~** *nt* **-s** astonishment.

erstaunlich *a* astonishing.

erst- ['e:rst] *zW:* **E~ausgabe** *f* first edition; **~beste(r, s)** *a* first that comes along; **~e(r, s)** *a* first.

erstechen [ɛr'ʃtɛçən] *vt unreg* stab (to death).

erstehen [ɛr'ʃte:ən] *vt unreg* buy // *vi* (a)rise.

erstens ['e:rstəns] *ad* firstly, in the first place.

ersticken [ɛr'ʃtɪkən] *vt* (*lit, fig*) stifle; (*Mensch*) suffocate; (*Flammen*) smother // *vi* (*Mensch*) suffocate; (*Feuer*) be smothered; **in Arbeit ~** be snowed under with work.

erst- *zW:* **~klassig** *a* first-class; **E~kommunion** *f* first communion; **~malig** *a* first; **~mals** *ad* for the first time.

erstrebenswert [ɛr'ʃtre:bənsve:rt] *a* desirable, worthwhile.

erstrecken [ɛr'ʃtrɛkən] *vr* extend, stretch.

ersuchen [ɛr'zu:xən] *vt* request.

ertappen [ɛr'tapən] *vt* catch, detect.

erteilen [ɛr'tailən] *vt* give.

Ertrag [ɛr'tra:k] *m* **-(e)s, -̈e** yield; (*Gewinn*) proceeds *pl*; **e~en** *vt unreg* bear, stand.

erträglich [ɛr'tre:klɪç] *a* tolerable, bearable.

ertrinken [ɛr'trɪŋkən] *vi unreg* drown; **E~** *nt* **-s** drowning.

erübrigen [ɛr'y:brɪgən] *vt* spare // *vr* be unnecessary.

erwachen [ɛr'vaxən] *vi* awake.

erwachsen [ɛr'vaksən] *a* grown-up; **E~e(r)** *mf* adult; **E~enbildung** *f* adult education.

erwägen [ɛr'vɛːgən] vt unreg consider.

Erwägung f consideration.

erwähn- [ɛr'vɛːn] zW: ~**en** vt mention; ~**enswert** a worth mentioning; **E~ung** f mention.

erwärmen [ɛr'vɛrmən] vt warm, heat // vr get warm, warm up; **sich** ~ **für** warm to.

erwarten [ɛr'vartən] vt expect; (warten auf) wait for; **etw kaum** ~ **können** hardly be able to wait for sth.

Erwartung f expectation; **erwartungsgemäß** ad as expected; **erwartungsvoll** a expectant.

erwecken [ɛr'vɛkən] vt rouse, awake; **den Anschein** ~ give the impression.

Erweis [ɛr'vais] m -es, -e proof; **e~en** unreg vt prove; (Ehre, Dienst) do (jdm sb) // vr prove (als to be).

Erwerb [ɛr'vɛrp] m -(e)s, -e acquisition; (Beruf) trade; **e~en** vt unreg acquire.

erwerbs- zW: ~**los** a unemployed; **E~quelle** f source of income; ~**tätig** a (gainfully) employed; ~**unfähig** a unemployable.

erwidern [ɛr'viːdərn] vt reply; (vergelten) return.

erwiesen [ɛr'viːzən] a proven.

erwischen [ɛr'vɪʃən] vt (umg) catch, get.

erwünscht [ɛr'vynʃt] a desired.

erwürgen [ɛr'vyrgən] vt strangle.

Erz [eːrts] nt -es, -e ore.

erzähl- [ɛr'tsɛːl] zW: ~**en** vt tell // vi: **sie kann gut** ~**en** she's a good storyteller; **E~er** m -s, - narrator; **E~ung** f story, tale.

Erz- zW: ~**bischof** m archbishop; ~**engel** m archangel.

erzeug- [ɛr'tsɔyg] zW: ~**en** vt produce; (Strom) generate; **E~nis** nt -ses, -se product, produce; **E~ung** f production; generate.

erziehen [ɛr'tsiːən] vt unreg bring up; (bilden) educate, train.

Erziehung f bringing up; (Bildung) education.

Erziehungs- zW: ~**beihilfe** f educational grant; ~**berechtigte(r)** mf parent; guardian; ~**heim** nt approved school.

erzielen [ɛr'tsiːlən] vt achieve, obtain; (Tor) score.

erzwingen [ɛr'tsvɪŋən] vt unreg force, obtain by force.

es [ɛs] pron nom, akk it.

Esche ['ɛʃə] f -, -n ash.

Esel ['eːzəl] m -s, - donkey, ass.

Eskalation [ɛskalatsi'oːn] f escalation.

eßbar ['ɛsbaːr] a eatable, edible.

essen ['ɛsən] vti unreg eat; **E~** nt -s, - meal; food; **Essenszeit** f mealtime; dinner time.

Essig ['ɛsɪç] m -s, -e vinegar; ~**gurke** f gherkin.

Eß- ['ɛs] zW: ~**kastanie** f sweet chestnut; ~**löffel** m tablespoon; ~**tisch** m dining table; ~**waren** pl food stuffs pl, provisions pl; ~**zimmer** nt dining room.

etablieren [eta'bliːrən] vr become established; set up in business.

Etage [e'taːʒə] f -, -n floor, storey; **Etagenbetten** pl bunk beds pl; **Etagenwohnung** f flat.

Etappe [e'tapə] f -, -n stage.

Etat [e'ta] m -s, -s budget.

etepetete [eːtəpe'teːtə] a (umg) fussy.

Ethik ['eːtɪk] f ethics sing.

ethisch ['eːtɪʃ] a ethical.

Etikett [eti'kɛt] nt -(e)s, -e label; tag; ~**e** f etiquette, manners pl; **e~ieren** [-'tiːrən] vt label; tag.

etliche ['ɛtlɪçə] pron pl some, quite a few; ~**s** a thing or two.

Etui [ɛt'viː] nt -s, -s case.

etwa ['ɛtva] ad (ungefähr) about; (vielleicht) perhaps; (beispielsweise) for instance; **nicht** ~ by no means; ~**ig** ['ɛtvaɪç] a possible; **etwas** pron something; anything; (ein wenig) a little // ad a little.

euch [ɔyç] pron akk von **ihr** you; yourselves // dat von **ihr** (to) you.

euer ['ɔyər] pron gen von **ihr** of you // pron your; ~**e(r, s)** yours.

Eule ['ɔylə] f -, -n owl.

eure(r, s) ['ɔyrə(r, s)] pron your; yours; **eurerseits** ad on your part; **euresgleichen** pron people like you; **euretwegen, euretwillen** ad (für euch) for your sakes; (wegen euch) on your account.

eurige ['ɔyrɪgə] pron: **der/die/das** ~ yours.

Euro- zW: ~**pa** [ɔy'roːpa] nt Europe; ~**päer(in)** [ɔyro'pɛːər(ɪn)] mf European; **e~päisch** a European; ~**pameister** [ɔy'roːpa-] m European champion.

Euter ['ɔytər] nt -s, - udder.

ev. abk von **evangelisch**.

evakuieren [evaku'iːrən] vt evacuate.

evangelisch [evaŋ'geːlɪʃ] a Protestant.

Evangelium [evaŋ'geːlium] nt gospel.

eventuell [eventu'ɛl] a possible // ad possibly, perhaps.

evtl. abk von **eventuell**.

EWG [eːveː'geː] f - abk (= Europäische Wirtschaftsgemeinschaft) EEC, Common Market.

ewig ['eːvɪç] a eternal; **E~keit** f eternity.

Ex- [ɛks] in zW ex-.

exakt [ɛ'ksakt] a exact.

Examen [ɛ'ksaːmən] nt -s, - od **Examina** examination.

Exemplar [ɛksɛm'plaːr] nt -s, -e specimen; (Buch~) copy; e~isch a exemplary.

exerzieren [ɛksɛr'tsiːrən] vi drill.

Exil [ɛ'ksiːl] nt -s, -e exile.

Existenz [ɛksɪs'tɛnts] f existence; (Unterhalt) livelihood, living; (pej: Mensch) character; ~kampf m struggle for existence; ~minimum nt -s subsistence level.

existieren [ɛksɪs'tiːrən] vi exist.

exklusiv [ɛksklu'ziːf] a exclusive; ~e [-'ziːvə] ad, präp +gen exclusive of, not including.

exotisch [ɛ'ksoːtɪʃ] a exotic.

Expedition [ɛkspeditsi'oːn] f expedition.

Experiment [ɛksperi'mɛnt] nt experiment; e~ell [-'tɛl] a experimental; e~ieren [-'tiːrən] vi experiment.

Experte [ɛks'pɛrtə] m -n, -n, **Expertin** f expert, specialist.

explo- [ɛksploː] zW: ~dieren [-'diːrən] vi explode; E~sion [-sploziˈoːn] f explosion; ~siv [-'ziːf] a explosive.

Export [ɛks'pɔrt] m -(e)s, -e export; **Exporteur** [-'tøːr] m exporter; ~handel m export trade; e~ieren [-'tiːrən] vt export; ~land nt exporting country.

Expreß- [ɛks'prɛs] zW: ~gut nt express goods pl od freight; ~zug m express (train).

extra ['ɛkstra] a inv (umg: gesondert) separate; (besonders) extra // ad (gesondert) separately; (speziell) specially; (absichtlich) on purpose; (vor Adjektiven, zusätzlich) extra; E~ nt -s, -s extra; E~ausgabe f, E~blatt nt special edition.

Extrakt [ɛks'trakt] m -(e)s, -e extract.

extrem [ɛks'treːm] a extreme; ~istisch [-'mɪstɪʃ] a (POL) extremist; E~itäten [-'tɛːtən] pl extremities pl.

exzentrisch [ɛks'tsɛntrɪʃ] a eccentric.

Exzeß [ɛks'tsɛs] m -sses, -sse excess.

F

F, f [ɛf] nt F, f.

Fa. abk (= Firma) firm; (in Briefen) Messrs.

Fabel ['faːbəl] f -, -n fable; f~haft a fabulous, marvellous.

Fabrik [fa'briːk] f factory; ~ant [-'kant] m (Hersteller) manufacturer; (Besitzer) industrialist; ~arbeiter m factory worker; ~at [-'kaːt] nt -(e)s, -e manufacture, product; ~ation [-atsi'oːn] f manufacture, production; ~gelände nt factory premises pl.

Fach [fax] nt -(e)s, -er compartment; (Sachgebiet) subject; ein Mann vom ~ an expert; ~arbeiter m skilled worker; ~arzt m (medical) special-

ist; ~ausdruck m technical term.

Fächer ['fɛçər] m -s, - fan.

Fach- zW: ~hochschule f ≈ technical college; f~kundig a expert, specialist; f~lich a professional; expert; ~mann, m, pl -leute specialist; f~männisch a professional; ~schule f technical college; f~simpeln vi talk shop; ~werk nt timber frame.

Fackel ['fakəl] f -, -n torch.

fad(e) ['faːt, faːdə] a insipid; (langweilig) dull.

Faden ['faːdən] m -s, - thread; f~scheinig a (lit, fig) threadbare.

fähig ['fɛːɪç] a capable (zu, gen of); able; F~keit f ability.

fahnden ['faːndən] vi: ~ nach search for.

Fahndung f search; **Fahndungsliste** f list of wanted criminals, wanted list.

Fahne ['faːnə] f -, -n flag, standard; eine ~ haben (umg) smell of drink; **Fahnenflucht** f desertion.

Fahr- ['faːr] zW: ~ausweis m ticket; ~bahn f carriageway (Brit), roadway.

Fähre ['fɛːrə] f -, -n ferry.

fahren ['faːrən] unreg vt drive (Rad) ride; (befördern) drive, take; (Rennen) drive in // vi (sich bewegen) go; (Schiff) sail; (abfahren) leave; mit dem Auto/Zug ~ go od travel by car/train; mit der Hand ~ über (+akk) pass one's hand over.

Fahr- zW: ~er(in f) m -s, - driver; ~erflucht f hit-and-run; ~gast m passenger; ~geld nt fare; ~gestell nt chassis; (AVIAT) undercarriage; ~karte f ticket; ~kartenausgabe f, ~kartenschalter m ticket office; f~lässig a negligent; f~lässige Tötung manslaughter; ~lässigkeit f negligence; ~lehrer m driving instructor; ~plan m timetable; f~planmäßig a (EISENB) scheduled; ~preis m fare; ~prüfung f driving test; ~rad nt bicycle; ~schein m ticket; ~schule f driving school; ~stuhl m lift (Brit), elevator (US).

Fahrt [faːrt] f -, -en journey; (kurz) trip; (AUT) drive; (Geschwindigkeit) speed; gute ~! have a good journey.

Fährte ['fɛːrtə] f -, -n track, trail.

Fahrkosten pl travelling expenses pl.

Fahrtrichtung f course, direction.

Fahrzeug nt vehicle; ~halter m -s, - owner of a vehicle.

Faksimile [fak'ziːmile] nt facsimile.

Faktor ['faktɔr] m factor.

Faktum ['faktum] nt -s, -ten fact.

Fakultät [fakul'tɛːt] f faculty.

Falke ['falkə] m -n, -n falcon.

Fall [fal] m -(e)s, -e (Sturz) fall; (Sachverhalt, JUR, GRAM) case; auf jeden ~, auf alle -e in any case; (be-

stimmt) definitely; **auf keinen ~!** no way!; **~e** f -, **-n** trap; **f~en** vi unreg fall; **etw f~en lassen** drop sth.

fällen ['fɛlən] vt (*Baum*) fell; (*Urteil*) pass.

fallenlassen vt unreg (*Bemerkung*) make; (*Plan*) abandon, drop.

fällig ['fɛlɪç] a due.

falls [fals] ad in case, if.

Fall- zW: **~schirm** m parachute; **~schirmjäger** pl paratroops pl; **~schirmspringer** m parachutist.

falsch [falʃ] a false; (*unrichtig*) wrong.

fälschen ['fɛlʃən] vt forge.

Falschgeld nt counterfeit money.

fälsch- zW: **~lich** a false; **~licherweise** ad mistakenly; **F~ung** f forgery.

Falte ['faltə] f -, **-n** (*Knick*) fold, crease; (*Haut~*) wrinkle; (*Rock~*) pleat; **f~n** vt fold; (*Stirn*) wrinkle.

familiär [famili'ɛːr] a familiar.

Familie [fa'miːliə] f family.

Familien- zW: **~kreis** m family circle; **~name** m surname; **~stand** m marital status.

Fanatiker [fa'naːtikər] m -s, - fanatic.

fanatisch a fanatical.

Fanatismus [fana'tɪsmʊs] m fanaticism.

fand etc v siehe **finden**.

Fang [faŋ] m -(e)s, **ᴂe** catch; (*Jagen*) hunting; (*Kralle*) talon, claw; **f~en** unreg vt catch // vr get caught; (*Flugzeug*) level out; (*Mensch: nicht fallen*) steady o.s.; (*fig*) compose o.s.; (*in Leistung*) get back on form.

Farb- ['farb] zW: **~aufnahme** f colour photograph; **~band** m typewriter ribbon; **~e** f -, **-n** colour; (*zum Malen etc*) paint; (*Stoff~*) dye; **f~echt** a colourfast.

färben ['fɛrbən] vt colour; (*Stoff, Haar*) dye.

farben- ['farbən] zW: **~blind** a colourblind; **~froh** a colourful, gay.

Farb- zW: **~fernsehen** nt colour television; **~film** m colour film; **~foto** nt colour photograph; **f~ig** a coloured; **~ige(r)** mf coloured; **~kasten** m paint-box; **f~los** a colourless; **~stift** m coloured pencil; **~stoff** m dye; **~ton** m hue, tone.

Färbung ['fɛrbʊŋ] f colouring; (*Tendenz*) bias.

Farn [farn] m -(e)s, **-e**, **~kraut** nt fern; bracken.

Fasan [fa'zaːn] m -(e)s, **-e(n)** pheasant.

Fasching ['faʃɪŋ] m -s, **-e** od **-s** carnival.

Faschismus [fa'ʃɪsmʊs] m fascism.

Faschist m fascist.

Faser ['faːzər] f -, **-n** fibre; **f~n** vi fray.

Faß [fas] nt **-sses**, **Fässer** vat, barrel; (*für Öl*) drum; **Bier vom ~** draught beer.

Fassade [fa'saːdə] f facade.

faßbar ['fasbaːr] a comprehensible.

fassen ['fasən] vt (*ergreifen*) grasp, take; (*inhaltlich*) hold; (*Entschluß etc*) take; (*verstehen*) understand; (*Ring etc*) set; (*formulieren*) formulate, phrase; **nicht zu ~** unbelievable // vr calm down.

Fassung ['fasʊŋ] f (*Umrahmung*) mounting; (*Lampen~*) socket; (*Wortlaut*) version; (*Beherrschung*) composure; **jdn aus der ~ bringen** upset sb; **fassungslos** a speechless.

fast [fast] ad almost, nearly.

fasten ['fastən] vi fast; **F~zeit** f Lent.

Fastnacht f Shrove Tuesday; carnival.

fatal [fa'taːl] a fatal; (*peinlich*) embarrassing.

faul [faʊl] a rotten; (*Person*) lazy; (*Ausreden*) lame; **daran ist etwas ~** there's sth fishy about it; **~en** vi rot; **faulenzen** vi idle; **Faulenzer** m -s, - idler, loafer; **F~heit** f laziness; **~ig** a putrid.

Fäulnis ['fɔylnɪs] f - decay, putrefaction.

Faust [faʊst] f -, **Fäuste** fist; **auf eigene ~** off one's own bat; **~handschuh** m mitten.

Favorit [favo'riːt] m -en, **-en** favourite.

FDP [ɛfdeː'peː] f abk (= *Freie Demokratische Partei*) Free Democratic Party.

Februar ['feːbruaːr] m -(s), **-e** February.

fechten ['fɛçtən] vi unreg fence.

Feder ['feːdər] f -, **-n** feather; (*Schreib~*) pen nib; (*TECH*) spring; **~ball** m shuttlecock. **~bett** nt continental quilt; **~halter** m penholder, pen; **f~leicht** a light as a feather; **f~n** vi (*nachgeben*) be springy; (*sich bewegen*) bounce // vt spring; **~ung** f suspension.

Fege- ['feːgə] zW: **~feuer** nt purgatory; **f~n** vt sweep.

fehl [feːl] a: **~ am Platz** od **Ort** out of place; **~en** vi be wanting od missing; (*abwesend sein*) be absent; **etw fehlt jdm** sb lacks sth; **du fehlst mir** I miss you; **was fehlt ihm?** what's wrong with him? **F~er** m -s, - mistake, error; (*Mangel, Schwäche*) fault; **~erfrei** a faultless; without any mistakes; **~erhaft** a incorrect; faulty; **F~geburt** f miscarriage; **~gehen** vi unreg go astray; **F~griff** m blunder; **F~konstruktion** f badly designed thing; **F~schlag** m failure; **~schlagen** vi unreg fail; **F~start** m

(*SPORT*) false start; **F~zündung** *f*
(*AUT*) misfire, backfire.
Feier ['faɪər] *f* -, -n celebration;
~abend *m* time to stop work;
~abend machen stop, knock off; jetzt
ist **~abend!** that's enough!; **f~lich** *a*
solemn; **~lichkeit** *f* solemnity;
~lichkeiten *pl* festivities *pl*; **f~n** *vti*
celebrate; **~tag** *m* holiday.
feig(e) ['faɪg(ə)] *a* cowardly; **F~e** *f* -,
-n fig; **F~heit** *f* cowardice; **F~ling** *m*
coward.
Feil- [faɪl] *zW*: **~e** *f* -, -n file; **f~schen**
vi haggle.
fein [faɪn] *a* fine; (*vornehm*) refined;
(*Gehör etc*) keen; **~!** great!
Feind [faɪnt] *m* -(e)s, -e enemy; **f~lich**
a hostile; **~schaft** *f* enmity; **f~selig**
a hostile; **~seligkeit** *f* hostility.
Fein- *zW*: **f~fühlend, f~fühlig** *a* sensitive; **~gefühl** *nt* delicacy, tact;
~heit *f* fineness; refinement; keen-
ness; **~kostgeschäft** *nt* delicatessen
(shop); **~schmecker** *m* -s, - gourmet.
Feld [fɛlt] *nt* -(e)s, -er field; (*SCHACH*)
square; (*SPORT*) pitch; **~herr** *m*
commander; **~stecher** *m* -s, - binoculars *pl*; **~webel** *m* -s, - sergeant;
~weg *m* path.
Felge ['fɛlgə] *f* -, -n (wheel) rim.
Fell [fɛl] *nt* -(e)s, -e fur; coat; (*von
Schaf*) fleece; (*von toten Tieren*)
skin.
Fels [fɛls] *m* -en, -en, **Felsen** ['fɛlzən]
m -s, - rock; (*Klippe*) cliff; **f~enfest**
a firm; **~envorsprung** *m* ledge; **f~ig**
a rocky; **~spalte** *f* crevice.
feminin [femi'niːn] *a* feminine; (*pej*)
effeminate.
Fenster ['fɛnstər] *nt* -s, - window;
~brett *nt* windowsill; **~ platz** *m* window seat; **~putzer** *m* -s, - window
cleaner; **~scheibe** *f* windowpane;
~sims *m* windowsill.
Ferien ['feːriən] *pl* holidays *pl*, vacation (*US*); **~ haben** be on holiday;
~kurs *m* holiday course; **~reise** *f*
holiday; **~zeit** *f* holiday period.
Ferkel ['fɛrkəl] *nt* -s, - piglet.
fern [fɛrn] *a,ad* far-off, distant; **~ von
hier** a long way (away) from here;
der **F~e Osten** the Far East; **F~amt**
nt (*TEL*) exchange; **F~bedienung** *f*
remote control; **F~e** *f* -, -n distance;
~er *a,ad* further; (*weiterhin*) in future; **F~gespräch** *nt* trunk call;
F~glas *nt* binoculars *pl*; **~halten** *vtr*
unreg keep away; **F~lenkung** *f* remote control; **F~meldeamt** *nt* international exchange; **F~rohr** *nt* telescope; **F~schreiben** *nt* telex;
F~sehapparat *m* television set;
~sehen *vi unreg* watch television;
F~sehen *nt* -s television; im

F~sehen on television; **F~seher** *m*
television; **F~sehüberwachungsan-
lage** *f* closed-circuit television; **F~-
sprecher** *m* telephone; **F~sprechzelle**
f telephone box *od* booth (*US*).
Ferse ['fɛrzə] *f* -, -n heel.
fertig ['fɛrtɪç] *a* (*bereit*) ready; (*been-
det*) finished; (*gebrauchs~*) ready-
made; **F~bau** *m* prefab(ricated
house); **F~keit** *f* skill; **~machen** *vt*
(*beenden*) finish; (*umg: Person*)
finish; (: *körperlich*) exhaust; (:
moralisch) get down // *vr* get ready;
~stellen *vt* complete.
Fessel ['fɛsəl] *f* -, -n fetter; **f~n** *vt*
bind; (*mit Fesseln*) fetter; (*fig*) spell-
bind; **f~nd** *a* fascinating, captivat-
ing.
fest [fɛst] *a* firm; (*Nahrung*) solid;
(*Gehalt*) regular; **f~e Kosten** fixed
cost // *ad* (*schlafen*) soundly; **F~** *nt*
-(e)s, -e party; festival; **frohes ~!**
Happy Christmas!; **~angestellt** *a*
permanently employed; **~binden** *vt
unreg* tie, fasten; **~bleiben** *vi unreg*
stand firm; **F~essen** *nt* banquet;
~halten *unreg vt* seize, hold fast;
(*Ereignis*) record // *vr* hold on (*an
+dat* to); **~igen** *vt* strengthen;
F~igkeit *f* strength; **Festival**
['fɛstival] *nt* -s, -s festival; **F~land** *nt*
mainland; **~legen** *vt* fix // *vr* commit
o.s.; **~lich** *a* festive; **~machen** *vt*
fasten; (*Termin etc*) fix; **F~nahme** *f*
-, -n capture; **~nehmen** *vt unreg*
capture, arrest; **F~rede** *f* address;
~setzen *vt* fix, settle; **F~spiel** *nt*,
F~spiele *pl* festival; **~stehen** *vi
unreg* be certain; **~stellen** *vt* establish; (*sagen*) remark; **F~ung** *f* fortress; **F~wochen** *pl* festival.
Fett [fɛt] *nt* -(e)s, -e fat, grease; **f~** *a*
fat; (*Essen etc*) greasy; **f~arm** *a* low
fat; **f~en** *vt* grease; **f~ig** *a* greasy,
fatty; **~näpfchen** *nt*: **ins ~näpfchen
treten** put one's foot in it.
Fetzen ['fɛtsən] *m* -s, - scrap.
feucht [fɔʏçt] *a* damp; (*Luft*) humid;
F~igkeit *f* dampness; humidity.
Feuer ['fɔʏər] *nt* -s, - fire; (*zum
Rauchen*) a light; (*fig: Schwung*)
spirit; **~alarm** *m* fire alarm; **~eifer**
m zeal; **f~fest** *a* fireproof; **~gefahr** *f*
danger of fire; **f~gefährlich** *a* inflammable; **~leiter** *f* fire escape ladder;
~löscher *m* -s, - fire extinguisher;
~melder *m* -s, - fire alarm; **f~n** *vti*
(*lit, fig*) fire; **~stein** *m* flint; **~wehr**
f -, -en fire brigade; **~wehrwagen** *m*
fire engine; **~werk** *nt* fireworks *pl*;
~zeug *nt* (cigarette) lighter.
Fichte ['fɪçtə] *f* -, -n spruce, pine.
Fieber ['fiːbər] *nt* -s, - fever, temperature; **f~haft** *a* feverish; **~messer** *m*,
~thermometer *nt* thermometer.

fiel etc v siehe **fallen**.
fies [fi:s] a (umg) nasty.
Figur [fi'gu:r] f -, -en figure; (Schach~) chessman, chess piece.
Filiale [fili'a:lə] f -, -n (COMM) branch.
Film [fɪlm] m -(e)s, -e film; ~**aufnahme** f shooting; f~**en** vti film; ~**kamera** f cine-camera.
Filter ['fɪltər] m -s, - filter; f~**n** vt filter; ~**papier** nt filter paper; ~**zigarette** f tipped cigarette.
Filz [fɪlts] m -es, -e felt; f~**en** vt (umg) frisk // vi (Wolle) mat; ~**stift** m felt-tip pen.
Finale [fi'na:lə] nt -s, -(s) finale; (SPORT) final(s).
Finanz [fi'nants] f finance; ~**amt** nt Inland Revenue Office; ~**beamte(r)** m revenue officer; f~**iell** [-tsi'ɛl] a financial; f~**ieren** [-'tsi:rən] vt finance; ~**minister** m Chancellor of the Exchequer (Brit), Minister of Finance.
Find- ['fɪnd] zW: f~**en** unreg vt find; (meinen) think // vr be (found); (sich fassen) compose o.s.; **ich finde nichts dabei, wenn** ... I don't see what's wrong if ...; **das wird sich f~en** things will work out; ~**er** m -s, -finder; f~**ig** a resourceful.
fing etc v siehe **fangen**.
Finger ['fɪŋər] m -s, - finger; ~**abdruck** m fingerprint; ~**hut** m thimble; (BOT) foxglove; ~**nagel** m fingernail; ~**spitze** f fingertip.
fingieren [fɪŋ'gi:rən] vt feign.
fingiert a made-up, fictitious.
Fink [fɪŋk] m -en, -en finch.
Finn- [fɪn] zW: ~**e** m, ~**in** f Finn; f~**isch** a Finnish; ~**land** nt Finland.
finster ['fɪnstər] a dark, gloomy; (verdächtig) dubious; (verdrossen) grim; (Gedanke) dark; F~**nis** f - darkness, gloom.
Finte ['fɪntə] f -, -n feint, trick.
Firma ['fɪrma] f -, -men firm.
Firmen- ['fɪrmən] zW: ~**inhaber** m owner of firm; ~**schild** nt (shop) sign; ~**zeichen** nt registered trademark.
Firnis ['fɪrnɪs] m -ses, -se varnish.
Fisch [fɪʃ] m -(e)s, -e fish // pl (ASTROL) Pisces; f~**en** vti fish; ~**er** m -s, - fisherman; ~**e'rei** f fishing, fishery; ~**fang** m fishing; ~**geschäft** nt fishmonger's (shop); ~**gräte** f fishbone.
fix [fɪks] a fixed; (Person) alert, smart; ~ **und fertig** finished; (erschöpft) done in; ~**ieren** [fi'ksi:rən] vt fix; (anstarren) stare at.
flach [flax] a flat; (Gefäß) shallow.
Fläche ['flɛçə] f -, -n area; (Ober~) surface; ~**ninhalt** m surface area.
Flachland nt lowland.
flackern ['flakərn] vi flare, flicker.

Flagge ['flagə] f -, -n flag.
Flamme ['flamə] f -, -n flame.
Flanell [fla'nɛl] m -s, -e flannel.
Flanke ['flaŋkə] f -, -n flank; (SPORT: Seite) wing.
Flasche ['flaʃə] f -, -n bottle; (umg: Versager) wash-out.
Flaschen- zW: ~**bier** nt bottled beer; ~**öffner** m bottle opener; ~**zug** m pulley.
flatterhaft a flighty, fickle.
flattern ['flatərn] vi flutter.
flau [flau] a weak, listless; (Nachfrage) slack; **jdm ist** ~ sb feels queasy.
Flaum [flaum] m -(e)s (Feder) down; (Haare) fluff.
flauschig ['flauʃɪç] a fluffy.
Flausen ['flauzən] pl silly ideas pl; (Ausflüchte) weak excuses pl.
Flaute ['flautə] f -, -n calm; (COMM) recession.
Flechte ['flɛçtə] f -, -n plait; (MED) dry scab; (BOT) lichen; f~**n** vt unreg plait; (Kranz) twine.
Fleck [flɛk] m -(e)s, -e, **Flecken** m -s, -spot; (Schmutz~) stain; (Stoff~) patch; (Makel) blemish; **nicht vom** ~ **kommen** (lit, fig) not get any further; **vom** ~ **weg** straight away; f~**enlos** a spotless; ~**enmittel** nt, ~**enwasser** nt stain remover; f~**ig** a spotted; stained.
Fledermaus ['fle:dərmaus] f bat.
Flegel ['fle:gəl] m -s, - (Mensch) lout; f~**haft** a loutish, unmannerly; ~**jahre** pl adolescence.
flehen ['fle:ən] vi implore; **flehentlich** a imploring.
Fleisch [flaɪʃ] nt -(e)s flesh; (Essen) meat; ~**brühe** f beef tea, stock; ~**er** m -s, - butcher; ~**e'rei** f butcher's (shop); ~**wolf** m mincer; ~**wunde** f flesh wound.
Fleiß [flaɪs] m -es diligence, industry; f~**ig** a diligent, industrious.
fletschen ['flɛtʃən] vt (Zähne) show.
flexibel [flɛ'ksi:bəl] a flexible.
Flicken ['flɪkən] m -s, - patch; f~ vt mend.
Flieder ['fli:dər] m -s, - lilac.
Fliege ['fli:gə] f -, -n fly; (Kleidung) bow tie; f~**n** vti unreg fly; **auf jdn/etw f~en** (umg) be mad about sb/sth; **Fliegenpilz** m toadstool; ~**r** m -s, -flier, airman.
fliehen ['fli:ən] vi unreg flee.
Fliese ['fli:zə] f -, -n tile.
Fließ- ['fli:s] zW: ~**band** nt production od assembly line; f~**en** vi unreg flow; f~**end** a flowing; (Rede, Deutsch) fluent; (Übergänge) smooth.
flimmern ['flɪmərn] vi glimmer.
flink [flɪŋk] a nimble, lively.

Flinte ['flɪntə] f -, -n rifle; shotgun.

Flitter ['flɪtər] m -s, - spangle, tinsel; **~wochen** pl honeymoon.

flitzen ['flɪtsən] vi flit.

Flocke ['flɔkə] f -, -n flake.

flog etc v siehe **fliegen**.

Floh ['floː] m -(e)s, ⸚e flea; **~markt** m flea market.

florieren [flo'riːrən] vi flourish.

Floskel ['flɔskəl] f -, -n empty phrase.

floß etc v siehe **fließen**.

Floß [floːs] nt -es, ⸚e raft, float.

Flosse ['flɔsə] f -, -n fin.

Flöte ['fløːtə] f -, -n flute; (Block~) recorder.

Flötist(in f) [flø'tɪst(ɪn)] m flautist.

flott [flɔt] a lively; (elegant) smart; (NAUT) afloat; **F~e f** -, -n fleet, navy.

Fluch [fluːx] m -(e)s, ⸚e curse; **f~en** vi curse, swear.

Flucht [fluxt] f -, -en flight; (Fenster~) row; (Reihe) range; (Zimmer~) suite; **f~artig** a hasty.

flücht- ['flʏçt] zW: **~en** vir flee, escape; **~ig** a fugitive; (vergänglich) transitory; (oberflächlich) superficial; (eilig) fleeting; **F~igkeit f** transitoriness; superficiality; **F~igkeitsfehler** m careless slip; **F~ling m** fugitive, refugee.

Flug [fluːk] m -(e)s, ⸚e flight; **im ~** airborne, in flight; **~blatt** nt pamphlet.

Flügel ['flyːgəl] m -s, - wing; (MUS) grand piano.

Fluggast m airline passenger.

flügge ['flʏgə] a (fully-)fledged.

Flug- zW: **~geschwindigkeit f** flying od air speed; **~gesellschaft f** airline (company); **~hafen m** airport; **~höhe f** altitude (of flight); **~plan m** flight schedule; **~platz m** airport; (klein) airfield; **~schein m** plane ticket; **~verkehr m** air traffic; **~zeug** nt (aero)plane, airplane (US); **~zeugentführung f** hijacking of a plane; **~zeughalle f** hangar; **~zeugträger m** aircraft carrier.

Flunder ['flʊndər] f -, -n flounder.

flunkern ['flʊŋkərn] vi fib, tell stories.

Fluor ['fluːɔr] nt -s fluorine.

Flur [fluːr] m -(e)s, -e hall; (Treppen~) staircase.

Fluß [flʊs] m -sses, ⸚sse river; (Fließen) flow; **im ~ sein** (fig) be in a state of flux.

flüssig ['flʏsɪç] a liquid; **F~keit f** liquid; (Zustand) liquidity; **~machen** vt (Geld) make available.

flüstern ['flʏstərn] vti whisper.

Flut [fluːt] f -, -en (lit, fig) flood; (Gezeiten) high tide; **f~en** vi flood; **~licht** nt floodlight.

Fohlen ['foːlən] nt -s, - foal.

Föhre ['føːrə] f -, -n Scots pine.

Folge ['fɔlgə] f -, -n series, sequence;

(Fortsetzung) instalment; (Auswirkung) result; **in rascher ~** in quick succession; **etw zur ~ haben** result in sth; **~n haben** have consequences; **einer Sache ~ leisten** comply with sth; **f~n** vi follow (jdm sb); (gehorchen) obey (jdm sb); **jdm f~n können** (fig) follow od understand sb; **f~nd** a following; **f~nde(r, s)** a following; **f~ndermaßen** ad as follows, in the following way; **f~nschwer** a momentous; **~rn** vt conclude (aus +dat from); **~rung f** conclusion.

folglich ad consequently.

folgsam a obedient.

Folie ['foːliə] f -, -n foil.

Folter ['fɔltər] f -, -n torture; (Gerät) rack; **f~n** vt torture.

Fön ® [føːn] m -(e)s, -e hair-dryer; **f~en** vt (blow) dry.

Fontäne [fɔn'tɛːnə] f -, -n fountain.

Förder- ['fœrdər] zW: **~band** nt conveyor belt; **~gebiet** nt development area; **~korb m** pit cage; **f~lich** a beneficial.

fordern ['fɔrdərn] vt demand.

Förder- zW: **f~n** vt promote; (unterstützen) help; (Kohle) extract; **~ung f** promotion; help; extraction.

Forderung ['fɔrdərʊŋ] f demand.

Forelle [fo'rɛlə] f -, -n trout.

Form [fɔrm] f -, -en shape; (Gestaltung) form; (Guß~) mould; (Back~) baking tin; **in ~ sein** be in good form od shape; **in ~ von** in the shape of; **~alität** [-'maːt] nt -(e)s, -e format; (fig) distinction; **f~atieren** vt format; **~ati'on f** formation; **f~bar** a malleable; **~el f** -, -n formula; **f~ell** [-'mɛl] a formal; **f~en** vt form, shape; **~fehler m** faux-pas, gaffe; (JUR) irregularity; **f~ieren** [-'miːrən] vt form // vr form up.

förmlich ['fœrmlɪç] a formal; (umg) real; **F~keit f** formality.

Form- zW: **f~los** a shapeless; (Benehmen etc) informal; **~u'lar** nt -s, -e form; **f~u'lieren** vt formulate.

forsch [fɔrʃ] a energetic, vigorous; **~en** vt search (nach for) // vi (wissenschaftlich) (do) research; **~end** a searching; **F~er m** -s, - research scientist; (Natur~) explorer.

Forschung ['fɔrʃʊŋ] f research; **Forschungsreise f** scientific expedition.

Forst [fɔrst] m -(e)s, -e forest.

Förster ['fœrstər] m -s, - forester; (für Wild) gamekeeper.

fort [fɔrt] ad away; (verschwunden) gone; (vorwärts) on; **und so ~** and so on; **in einem ~** on and on; **~bestehen** vi survive; **~bewegen** vtr move away; **~bilden** vr continue one's education;

~bleiben *vi unreg* stay away; **F~dauer** *f* continuance; **~fahren** *vi unreg* depart; (*fortsetzen*) go on, continue; **~führen** *vt* continue, carry on; **~gehen** *vi unreg* go away; **~geschritten** *a* advanced; **~müssen** *vi unreg* have to go; **~pflanzen** *vr* reproduce; **F~pflanzung** *f* reproduction; **~schaffen** *vt* remove; **~schreiten** *vi unreg* advance.

Forts. *abk* (= *Fortsetzung*) cont(d).

Fortschritt ['fɔrtʃrɪt] *m* advance; **~e machen** make progress; **f~lich** *a* progressive.

fort- *zW:* **~setzen** *vt* continue; **F~setzung** *f* continuation; (*folgender Teil*) instalment; **F~setzung folgt** to be continued; **~während** *a* incessant, continual.

Foto ['fo:to] *nt* **-s, -s** photo(graph); **~apparat** *m* camera; **~'graf** *m* photographer; **~gra'fie** *f* photography; (*Bild*) photograph; **f~gra'fieren** *vt* photograph // *vi* take photographs; **~kopie** *f* photocopy; **f~kopieren** *vt* photocopy.

Foul [faʊl] *nt* **-s, -s** foul.

Fr. *abk* (= *Frau*) Mrs, Ms.

Fracht [fraxt] *f* **-, -en** freight; (*NAUT*) cargo; (*Preis*) carriage; **~ zahlt Empfänger** (*COMM*) carriage forward; **~er** *m* **-s, -** freighter, cargo boat; **~gut** *nt* freight.

Frack [frak] *m* **-(e)s, ⁻e** tails *pl*.

Frage ['fra:gə] *f* **-, -n** question; **etw in ~ stellen** question sth; **jdm eine ~ stellen** ask sb a question, put a question to sb; **nicht in ~ kommen** be out of the question; **~bogen** *m* questionnaire; **f~n** *vti* ask; **~zeichen** *nt* question mark.

fraglich *a* questionable, doubtful.

fraglos *ad* unquestionably.

Fragment [fra'gmɛnt] *nt* fragment.

fragwürdig ['fra:kvʏrdɪç] *a* questionable, dubious.

Fraktion [fraktsi'o:n] *f* parliamentary party.

frankieren [fraŋ'ki:rən] *vt* stamp, frank.

Frankiermaschine *f* franking machine.

franko ['fraŋko] *ad* post-paid; carriage paid.

Frankreich ['fraŋkraiç] *nt* **-s** France.

Franse ['franzə] *f* **-, -n** fringe.

Franzose [fran'tso:zə] *m* Frenchman.

Französ- [fran'tsø:z] *zW:* **~in** *f* Frenchwoman; **f~isch** *a* French.

fraß *etc v siehe* **fressen**.

Fratze ['fratsə] *f* **-, -n** grimace.

Frau [frau] *f* **-, -en** woman; (*Ehe~*) wife; (*Anrede*) Mrs, Ms.; **~ Doktor** Doctor; **~enarzt** *m* gynaecologist; **~enbewegung** *f* feminist movement;

f~enfeindlich *a* anti-women; **~enzimmer** *nt* female, broad (*US*).

Fräulein ['frɔylain] *nt* young lady; (*Anrede*) Miss, Ms.

fraulich ['frauliç] *a* womanly.

frech [frɛç] *a* cheeky, impudent; **F~dachs** *m* cheeky monkey; **F~heit** *f* cheek, impudence.

Fregatte [fre'gatə] *f* frigate.

frei [frai] *a* free; (*Stelle, Sitzplatz auch*) vacant; (*Mitarbeiter*) freelance; (*unbekleidet*) bare; **sich** (*dat*) **einen Tag ~ nehmen** take a day off; **von etw ~ sein** be free of sth; **im F~en** in the open air; **~ sprechen** talk without notes; **~ Haus** (*COMM*) carriage paid; **~er Wettbewerb** (*COMM*) fair/open competition; **F~bad** *nt* open-air swimming pool; **~bekommen** *vt unreg*: **jdm/einen Tag ~bekommen** get sb freed/get a day off; **~gebig** *a* generous; **~halten** *vt unreg* keep free; **~händig** *ad* (*fahren*) with no hands; **F~heit** *f* freedom; **~heitlich** *a* liberal; **F~heitsstrafe** *f* prison sentence; **F~karte** *f* free ticket; **~lassen** *vt unreg* (set) free; **~legen** *vt* expose; **~lich** *ad* certainly, admittedly; **ja ~lich** yes of course; **F~lichtbühne** *f* open-air theatre; **~machen** *vt* (*Post*) frank; **Tage ~machen** take days off // *vr* arrange to be free; (*entkleiden*) undress; **~sprechen** *vt unreg* acquit (*von* of); **F~spruch** *m* acquittal; **~stellen** *vt*: **jdm etw ~stellen** leave sth (up) to sb; **F~stoß** *m* free kick; **F~tag** *m* Friday; **~tags** *ad* on Fridays; **~willig** *a* voluntary; **F~zeit** *f* spare od free time; **~zeitbeschäftigung** *f* leisure pursuit; **~zügig** *a* liberal, broad-minded; (*mit Geld*) generous.

fremd [frɛmt] *a* (*unvertraut*) strange; (*ausländisch*) foreign; (*nicht eigen*) someone else's; **etw ist jdm ~** sth is foreign to sb; **~artig** *a* strange; **F~e(r)** *f(m)* stranger; (*Ausländer*) foreigner; **F~enführer** *m* (tourist) guide; **F~enlegion** *f* foreign legion; **F~enverkehr** *m* tourism; **F~enzimmer** *nt* guest room; **F~körper** *m* foreign body; **~ländisch** *a* foreign; **F~ling** *m* stranger; **F~sprache** *f* foreign language; **F~wort** *nt* foreign od loan word.

Frequenz [fre'kvɛnts] *f* (*RAD*) frequency.

fressen ['frɛsən] *vti unreg* eat.

Freude ['frɔydə] *f* **-, -n** joy, delight.

freudig *a* joyful, happy.

freuen ['frɔyən] *vt unpers* make happy od pleased; **freut mich!** pleased to meet you // *vr* be glad od happy; **sich auf etw** (*akk*) **~** look forward to sth;

sich über etw (akk) ~ be pleased about sth.

Freund [frɔynt] m -(e)s, -e friend; boyfriend; ~in [-dɪn] f friend; girlfriend; f~lich a kind, friendly; f~licherweise ad kindly; ~lichkeit f friendliness, kindness; ~schaft f friendship; f~schaftlich a friendly.

Frieden [ˈfriːdən] m -s, - peace; im ~ in peacetime.

Friedens- zW: ~schluß m peace agreement; ~vertrag m peace treaty; ~zeit f peacetime.

fried- [ˈfriːt] zW: ~fertig a peaceable; F~hof m cemetery; ~lich a peaceful.

frieren [ˈfriːrən] vti unreg freeze; ich friere, es friert mich I am freezing, I'm cold.

Fries [friːs] m -es, -e frieze.

frigid(e) [friˈɡiːt, friˈɡiːdə] a frigid.

Frikadelle [frikaˈdɛlə] f meatball.

frisch [frɪʃ] a fresh; (lebhaft) lively; ~ gestrichen! wet paint!; sich ~ machen freshen (o.s.) up; F~e f - freshness; liveliness.

Friseur [friˈzøːr] m, **Friseuse** [friˈzøːzə] f hairdresser.

Frisier- [friˈziːr] zW: f~en vtr do (one's hair); (fig: Abrechnung) fiddle, doctor; ~salon m hairdressing salon; ~tisch m dressing table.

frißt etc v siehe **fressen.**

Frist [frɪst] f -, -en period; (Termin) deadline; f~los a (Entlassung) instant.

Frisur [friˈzuːr] f hairdo, hairstyle.

frivol [friˈvoːl] a frivolous.

froh [froː] a happy, cheerful; ich bin ~, daß ... I'm glad that ...

fröhlich [ˈfrøːlɪç] a merry, happy; F~keit f merriness, gaiety.

Frohsinn m cheerfulness.

fromm [frɔm] a pious, good; (Wunsch) idle.

Frömmigkeit [ˈfrœmɪçkaɪt] f piety.

Fronleichnam [froːnˈlaɪçnaːm] m -(e)s Corpus Christi.

Front [frɔnt] f -, -en front; f~al [frɔnˈtaːl] a frontal.

fror etc v siehe **frieren.**

Frosch [frɔʃ] m -(e)s, -e frog; (Feuerwerk) squib; ~mann m frogman; ~schenkel m frog's leg.

Frost [frɔst] m -(e)s, -e frost; ~beule f chilblain.

frösteln [ˈfrœstəln] vi shiver.

Frost- zW: ~gefahr f icy conditions; f~ig a frosty; ~schutzmittel nt antifreeze.

Frottee [frɔˈteː] nt od m -(s), -s towelling.

Frottier(hand)tuch [frɔˈtiːr(hant)tuːx] nt towel.

Frucht [fruxt] f -, -e (lit, fig) fruit; (Getreide) corn; f~bar a fruitful,

fertile; ~barkeit f fertility; f~en vi be of use; f~los a fruitless; ~saft m fruit juice.

früh [fryː] a, ad early; heute ~ this morning; F~aufsteher m -s, - early riser; F~e f - early morning; ~er a earlier; (ehemalig) former // ad formerly; ~er war das anders that used to be different; ~estens ad at the earliest; F~geburt f premature birth/baby; F~jahr nt, F~ling m spring; ~reif a precocious; F~stück nt breakfast; ~stücken vi (have) breakfast; ~zeitig a early; (pej) untimely.

frustrieren [frusˈtriːrən] vt frustrate.

Fuchs [fuks] m -es, -e fox; f~en (umg) vt rile, annoy; f~teufelswild a hopping mad.

Füchsin [ˈfʏksɪn] f vixen.

fuchteln [ˈfuxtəln] vi gesticulate wildly.

Fuge [ˈfuːɡə] f -, -n joint; (MUS) fugue.

fügen [ˈfyːɡən] vt place, join // vr be obedient (in +akk to); (anpassen) adapt oneself (in +akk to) // vr unpers happen.

fügsam [ˈfyːkzaːm] a obedient.

fühl- [fyːl] zW: ~bar a perceptible, noticeable; ~en vtir feel; F~er m -s, - feeler.

fuhr etc v siehe **fahren.**

führen [ˈfyːrən] vt lead; (Geschäft) run; (Name) bear; (Buch) keep // vi lead // vr behave.

Führer [ˈfyːrər] m -s, - leader; (Fremden~) guide; ~schein m driving licence.

Führung [ˈfyːruŋ] f leadership; (eines Unternehmens) management; (MIL) command; (Benehmen) conduct; (Museums~) conducted tour; Führungskraft f executive; Führungszeugnis nt certificate of good conduct.

Fülle [ˈfʏlə] f - wealth, abundance; f~n vtr fill; (KOCH) stuff; ~n nt -s, - foal; ~r m -s, -, **Füllfederhalter** m fountain pen.

Füllung f filling; (Holz~) panel.

fummeln [ˈfuməln] vi (umg) fumble.

Fund [funt] m -(e)s, -e find; ~ament [-daˈmɛnt] nt foundation; f~amental a fundamental; ~büro nt lost property office, lost and found; ~grube f (fig) treasure trove; f~ieren [-ˈdiːrən] vt back up; f~iert a sound.

fünf [fynf] num five; ~hundert num five hundred; F~kampf m pentathlon; ~te(r, s) a fifth; F~tel nt -s, - fifth; ~zehn num fifteen; ~zig num fifty.

Funk [fuŋk] m -s radio, wireless; ~e(n) m -ns, -n (lit, fig) spark;

f~eln vi sparkle; **~er** m -s, - radio operator; **~gerät** nt radio set; **~spruch** m radio signal; **~station** f radio station; **~streife** f police radio patrol.

Funktion [fʊŋktsi'o:n] f function; **f~ieren** [-'ni:rən] vi work, function.

für [fy:r] präp +akk for; **was ~** what kind od sort of; **das F~ und Wider** the pros and cons pl; **Schritt ~ Schritt** step by step; **F~bitte** f intercession.

Furche ['fʊrçə] f -, -n furrow.

Furcht [fʊrçt] f - fear; **f~bar** a terrible, frightful.

fürcht- ['fʊrçt] zW: **~en** vt be afraid of, fear // vr be afraid (vor +dat of); **~erlich** a awful.

furchtlos a fearless.

furchtsam a timid.

füreinander [fy:r'aɪ'nandər] ad for each other.

Furnier [fʊr'ni:r] nt -s, -e veneer.

fürs [fy:rs] = **für das**.

Fürsorge f ['fy:rzɔrgə] f care; (Sozial~) welfare; **~r(in** f) m -s, - welfare worker; **~unterstützung** f social security, welfare benefit (US).

Fürsprache f recommendation; (um Gnade) intercession.

Fürsprecher m advocate.

Fürst [fʏrst] m -en, -en prince; **~entum** nt principality; **~in** f princess; **f~lich** a princely.

Fusion [fuzi'o:n] f merger.

Fuß [fu:s] m -es, -e foot; (von Glas, Säule etc) base; (von Möbel) leg; **zu ~ on** foot; **~ball** m football; **~ballplatz** m football pitch; **~ballspiel** nt football match; **~ballspieler** m footballer; **~boden** m floor; **~bremse** f (AUT) footbrake; **~ende** nt foot; **~gänger(in** f) m -s, - pedestrian; **~gängerzone** f pedestrian precinct; **~note** f footnote; **~spur** f footprint; **~tritt** m kick; (Spur) footstep; **~weg** m footpath.

Futter [fʊtər] nt -s, - fodder, feed; (Stoff) lining; **~al** [-'ra:l] nt -s, -e case.

füttern ['fʏtərn] vt feed; (Kleidung) line.

Futur [fu'tu:r] nt -s, -e future.

G

G, g [ge:] nt G, g.

g abk von **Gramm**.

gab etc v siehe **geben**.

Gabe ['ga:bə] f -, -n gift.

Gabel ['ga:bəl] f -, -n fork; **~ung** f fork.

gackern ['gakərn] vi cackle.

gaffen ['gafən] vi gape.

Gage ['ga:ʒə] f, -n fee; salary.

gähnen ['gɛːnən] vi yawn.

galant [ga'lant] a gallant, courteous.

Galerie [galə'ri:] f gallery.

Galgen ['galgən] m -s, - gallows pl; **~frist** f respite; **~humor** m macabre humour.

Galle ['galə] f -, -n gall; (Organ) gallbladder.

Galopp [ga'lɔp] m -s, -s od -e gallop; **g~ieren** [-'pi:rən] vi gallop.

Gamasche [ga'maʃə] f -, -n gaiter; (kurz) spat.

gammeln ['gaməln] vi (umg) bum around.

Gang [gaŋ] m -(e)s, -e walk; (Boten~) errand; (~art) gait; (Abschnitt eines Vorgangs) operation; (Essens~, Ablauf) course; (Flur etc) corridor; (Durch~) passage; (TECH) gear; **in ~ bringen** start up; (fig) get off the ground; **in ~ sein** be in operation; (fig) be underway; **g~ a: g~ und gäbe** usual, normal.

gängig ['gɛŋɪç] a common, current; (Ware) in demand, selling well.

Ganove [ga'no:və] m -n, -n (umg) crook.

Gans [gans] f -, -e goose.

Gänse- ['gɛnzə] zW: **~blümchen** nt daisy; **~braten** m roast goose; **~haut** f goose pimples pl; **~marsch** m: **im ~marsch** in single file; **Gänserich** m -s, -e gander.

ganz [gants] a whole; (vollständig) complete; **~ Europa** all Europe; **sein ~es Geld** all his money // ad quite; (völlig) completely; **~ und gar nicht** not at all; **es sieht ~ so aus** it really looks like it; **aufs G~e gehen** go for the lot.

gänzlich ['gɛntslɪç] a,ad complete(ly), entire(ly).

gar [ga:r] a cooked, done // ad quite; **~ nicht/nichts/keiner** not/nothing/nobody at all; **~ nicht schlecht** not bad at all.

Garage [ga'ra:ʒə] f -, -n garage.

Garantie [garan'ti:] f guarantee; **g~ren** vt guarantee; **er kommt garantiert** he's guaranteed to come.

Garbe ['garbə] f -, -n sheaf; (MIL) burst of fire.

Garderobe [gardə'ro:bə] f -, -n wardrobe; (Abgabe) cloakroom; **Garderobenfrau** f cloakroom attendant; **Garderobenständer** m hallstand.

Gardine [gar'di:nə] f curtain.

gären ['gɛːrən] vi unreg ferment.

Garn [garn] nt -(e)s, -e thread; yarn (auch fig).

Garnele [gar'ne:lə] f -, -n shrimp, prawn.

garnieren [gar'ni:rən] vt decorate; (Speisen) garnish.

Garnitur [garni'tu:r] f (Satz) set; (Unterwäsche) set of (matching) underwear; (fig) erste ~ top rank; zweite ~ second rate.

garstig ['garstıç] a nasty, horrid.

Garten ['gartən] m -s, ¨: garden; ~arbeit f gardening; ~gerät nt gardening tool; ~schere f pruning shears pl; ~tür f garden gate.

Gärtner(in f) ['gɛrtnər(ın)] m -s, - gardener; ~ei [-'raı] f nursery; (Gemüse~) market garden (Brit), truck farm (US).

Gärung ['gɛːrʊŋ] f fermentation.

Gas [ga:s] nt -es, -e gas; ~ geben (AUT) accelerate, step on the gas; ~herd m, ~kocher m gas cooker; ~leitung f gas pipeline; ~maske f gasmask; ~pedal nt accelerator, gas pedal.

Gasse ['gasə] f -, -n lane, alley; **Gassenjunge** m street urchin.

Gast [gast] m -es, ¨e guest; (in Lokal) patron; bei jdm zu ~ sein be a guest at sb's place; ~arbeiter(in f) m foreign worker.

Gästebuch ['gɛstəbu:x] nt visitors' book, guest book.

Gast- zW: g~freundlich a hospitable; ~geber m -s, - host; ~geberin f hostess; ~haus nt, ~hof m hotel, inn; g~ieren [-'ti:rən] vi (THEAT) (appear as a) guest; g~lich a hospitable; ~rolle f guest role.

gastronomisch [gastro'no:mıʃ] a gastronomic(al).

Gast- zW: ~spiel nt (THEAT) guest performance; ~stätte f restaurant; pub; ~wirt m innkeeper; ~wirtschaft f hotel, inn; ~zimmer nt (guest) room.

Gas- zW: ~vergiftung f gas poisoning; ~werk nt gasworks sing od pl; ~zähler m gas meter.

Gatte ['gatə] m -n, -n husband, spouse.

Gatter ['gatər] nt -s, - railing, grating; (Eingang) gate.

Gattin f wife, spouse.

Gattung ['gatʊŋ] f genus; kind.

Gaul [gaul] m -(e)s, Gäule horse; nag.

Gaumen ['gaumən] m -s, - palate.

Gauner ['gaunər] m -s, - rogue; ~ei [-'raı] f swindle.

Gaze ['ga:zə] f -, -n gauze.

geb. abk von geboren.

Gebäck [gə'bɛk] nt -(e)s, -e pastry.

gebacken [gə'bakən] a baked; (gebraten) fried.

Gebälk [gə'bɛlk] nt -(e)s timberwork.

Gebärde [gə'bɛːrdə] f -, -n gesture; g~n vr behave.

gebären [gə'bɛːrən] vt unreg give birth to, bear.

Gebärmutter f uterus, womb.

Gebäude [gə'bɔydə] nt -s, - building; ~komplex m (building) complex.

Gebell [gə'bɛl] nt -(e)s barking.

geben ['ge:bən] unreg vti (jdm etw) give (sb sth od sth to sb); (Karten) deal; ein Wort gab das andere one angry word led to another // v unpers es gibt there is/are; there will be; was gibt's? what's up?; was gibt es im Kino? what's on at the cinema?; gegeben given; zu gegebener Zeit in good time // vr (sich verhalten) behave, act; (aufhören) abate; sich geschlagen ~ admit defeat; das wird sich schon ~ that'll soon sort itself out.

Gebet [gə'be:t] nt -(e)s, -e prayer.

gebeten v siehe **bitten**.

Gebiet [gə'bi:t] nt -(e)s, -e area; (Hoheits~) territory; (fig) field; g~en vt unreg command, demand; g~erisch a imperious.

Gebilde [gə'bıldə] nt -s, - object, structure; g~t a cultured, educated.

Gebirge [gə'bırgə] nt -s, - mountain chain.

Gebiß [gə'bıs] nt -sses, -sse teeth pl; (künstlich) dentures pl.

gebissen v siehe **beißen**.

geblieben v siehe **bleiben**.

geboren [gə'bo:rən] a born; (Frau) née.

geborgen [gə'bɔrgən] a secure, safe.

Gebot [gə'bo:t] nt -(e)s, -e command(ment REL); (bei Auktion) bid.

geboten v siehe **bieten**.

Gebr. abk (= Gebrüder) Bros.

gebracht v siehe **bringen**.

gebraten [gə'bra:tən] a fried.

Gebrauch [gə'braux] m -(e)s, Gebräuche use; (Sitte) custom; g~en vt use.

gebräuchlich [gə'brɔyçlıç] a usual, customary.

Gebrauchs- zW: ~anweisung f directions pl for use; ~artikel m article of everyday use; g~fertig a ready for use; ~gegenstand m commodity.

gebraucht [gə'brauxt] a used; **G~wagen** m secondhand od used car.

gebrechlich [gə'brɛçlıç] a frail.

gebrochen [gə'brɔxən] a broken.

Gebrüder [gə'bry:dər] pl brothers pl.

Gebrüll [gə'brʏl] nt -(e)s roaring.

Gebühr [gə'by:r] f -, -en charge, fee; nach ~ fittingly; über ~ unduly; g~en vi: jdm g~en be sb's due od due to sb // vr be fitting; g~end a, ad fitting(ly), appropriate(ly).

Gebühren- zW: ~erlaß m remission of fees; ~ermäßigung f reduction of fees; g~frei a free of charge; g~pflichtig a subject to charges.

gebunden v siehe **binden**.

Geburt [gə'buːrt] *f* -, -en birth.

Geburten- *zW*: **~beschränkung** *f*, **~kontrolle** *f*, **~regelung** *f* birth control; **~ziffer** *f* birth-rate.

gebürtig [gə'byrtɪç] *a* born in, native of; **~e** Schweizerin native of Switzerland.

Geburts- *zW*: **~anzeige** *f* birth notice; **~datum** *nt* date of birth; **~jahr** *nt* year of birth; **~ort** *m* birthplace; **~tag** *m* birthday; **~urkunde** *f* birth certificate.

Gebüsch [gə'byʃ] *nt* -(e)s, -e bushes *pl*.

gedacht *v siehe* **denken**.

Gedächtnis [gə'dɛçtnɪs] *nt* -ses, -se memory; **~feier** *f* commemoration.

Gedanke [gə'daŋkə] *m* -ns, -n thought; sich über etw (*akk*) **~n** machen think about sth.

Gedanken- *zW*: **~austausch** *m* exchange of ideas; **g~los** *a* thoughtless; **~losigkeit** *f* thoughtlessness; **~strich** *m* dash; **~übertragung** *f* thought transference, telepathy; **g~voll** *a* thoughtful.

Gedeck [gə'dɛk] *nt* -(e)s, -e cover(ing); (*Speisenfolge*) menu; ein **~** auflegen lay a place.

gedeihen [gə'daɪən] *vi unreg* thrive, prosper.

gedenken [gə'dɛŋkən] *vi unreg* (*sich erinnern*: +*gen*) remember; (*beabsichtigen*) intend.

Gedenk- *zW*: **~feier** *f* commemoration; **~minute** *f* minute's silence; **~tag** *m* remembrance day.

Gedicht [gə'dɪçt] *nt* -(e)s, -e poem.

gediegen [gə'diːgən] *a* (good) quality; (*Mensch*) reliable, honest.

Gedränge [gə'drɛŋə] *nt* -s crush, crowd; ins **~** kommen (*fig*) get into difficulties.

gedrängt *a* compressed; **~** voll packed.

gedrungen [gə'drʊŋən] *a* thickset, stocky.

Geduld [gə'dʊlt] *f* - patience; **g~en** [gə'dʊldən] *vr* be patient; **g~ig** *a* patient, forbearing; **Geduldsprobe** *f* trial of (one's) patience.

gedurft *v siehe* **dürfen**.

geehrt [gə'eːrt] *a*: sehr **~e** Frau X dear Mrs X.

geeignet [gə'aɪgnət] *a* suitable.

Gefahr [gə'faːr] *f* -, -en danger; **~** laufen, etw zu tun run the risk of doing sth; auf eigene **~** at one's own risk.

gefährden [gə'fɛːrdən] *vt* endanger.

Gefahrenquelle *f* source of danger.

Gefahrenzulage *f* danger money.

gefährlich [gə'fɛːrlɪç] *a* dangerous.

Gefälle [gə'fɛlə] *nt* -s, - gradient, incline.

Gefallen [gə'falən] *m* -s, - favour // *nt* -s pleasure; an etw (*dat*) **~** finden derive pleasure from sth; **g~** *vi unreg*: jdm g**~** please sb; er/es gefällt mir I like him/it; das gefällt mir an ihm that's one thing I like about him; sich (*dat*) etw g**~** lassen put up with sth // *ptp von* **fallen**.

gefällig [gə'fɛlɪç] *a* (*hilfsbereit*) obliging; (*erfreulich*) pleasant; **G~keit** *f* favour; helpfulness; etw aus **G~keit** tun do sth as a favour.

gefälligst *ad* kindly.

gefangen [gə'faŋən] *a* captured; (*fig*) captivated; **G~e(r)** *m* prisoner, captive; **~halten** *vt unreg* keep prisoner; **G~nahme** *f* -, -n capture; **~nehmen** *vt unreg* take prisoner; **G~schaft** *f* captivity.

Gefängnis [gə'fɛŋnɪs] *nt* -ses, -se prison; **~strafe** *f* prison sentence; **~wärter** *m* prison warder.

Gefäß [gə'fɛːs] *nt* -es, -e vessel (*auch ANAT*), container.

gefaßt [gə'fast] *a* composed, calm; auf etw (*akk*) **~** sein be prepared *od* ready for sth.

Gefecht [gə'fɛçt] *nt* -(e)s, -e fight; (*MIL*) engagement.

Gefieder [gə'fiːdər] *nt* -s, - plumage, feathers *pl*.

gefleckt [gə'flɛkt] *a* spotted, mottled.

geflogen *v siehe* **fliegen**.

geflossen *v siehe* **fließen**.

Geflügel [gə'flyːgəl] *nt* -s poultry.

Gefolge [gə'fɔlgə] *nt* -s, - retinue.

Gefolgschaft *f* following.

gefragt [gə'fraːkt] *a* in demand.

gefräßig [gə'frɛːsɪç] *a* voracious.

Gefreite(r) [gə'fraɪtə(r)] *m* -n, -n lance corporal; (*NAUT*) able seaman; (*AVIAT*) aircraftman.

gefrieren [gə'friːrən] *vi unreg* freeze.

Gefrier- *zW*: **~fach** *nt* icebox; **~fleisch** *nt* frozen meat; **g~getrocknet** *a* freeze-dried; **~punkt** *m* freezing point; **~schutzmittel** *nt* antifreeze; **~truhe** *f* deep-freeze.

gefroren *v siehe* **frieren**.

gefügig [gə'fyːgɪç] *a* pliant; (*Mensch*) obedient.

Gefühl [gə'fyːl] *nt* -(e)s, -e feeling; etw im **~** haben have a feel for sth; **g~los** *a* unfeeling.

gefühls- *zW*: **~betont** *a* emotional; **G~duselei** [-duːzə'laɪ] *f* emotionalism; **~mäßig** *a* instinctive.

gefunden *v siehe* **finden**.

gegangen *v siehe* **gehen**.

gegebenenfalls [gə'geːbənənfals] *ad* if need be.

gegen ['geːgən] *präp* +*akk* **1** against; nichts **~** jdn haben have nothing against sb; X **~** Y (*SPORT, JUR*) X

versus Y; ein Mittel ~ Schnupfen something for colds
2 (in Richtung auf) towards; ~ Osten to(wards) the east; ~ Abend towards evening; ~ einen Baum fahren drive into a tree
3 (ungefähr) round about, around; ~ 3 Uhr around 3 o'clock
4 (gegenüber) towards; gerecht ~ alle fair to all
5 (im Austausch für) for; ~ bar for cash; ~ Quittung against a receipt
6 (verglichen mit) compared with.

Gegenangriff m counter-attack.
Gegenbeweis m counter-evidence.
Gegend ['ge:gənt] f -, -en area, district.
Gegen- zW: **g~ei'nander** ad against one another; **~fahrbahn** f oncoming carriageway; **~frage** f counter-question; **~gewicht** nt counterbalance; **~gift** nt antidote; **~leistung** f service in return; **~satz** m contrast; **~sätze überbrücken** overcome differences; **g~sätzlich** a contrary, opposite; (widersprüchlich) contradictory; **g~seitig** a mutual, reciprocal; sich g~seitig helfen help each other; **~seitigkeit** f reciprocity; **~spieler** m opponent; **~stand** m object; **g~ständlich** a objective, concrete; **~stimme** f vote against; **~stoß** m counterblow; **~stück** nt counterpart; **~teil** nt opposite; im **~teil** on the contrary; **g~teilig** a opposite, contrary.
gegenüber [ge:gn''y:bər] präp +dat opposite; (zu) to(wards); (angesichts) in the face of // ad opposite; **G~** nt -s, - person opposite; **~liegen** vr unreg face each other; **~stehen** vr unreg be opposed (to each other); **~stellen** vt confront; (fig) contrast; **G~stellung** f confrontation; (fig) contrast; **~treten** vi unreg (+dat) face.
Gegen- zW: **~verkehr** m oncoming traffic; **~vorschlag** m counterproposal; **~wart** f present; **g~wärtig** a present; das ist mir nicht mehr g~wärtig that has slipped my mind // ad at present; **~wert** m equivalent; **~wind** m headwind; **g~zeichnen** vti countersign.
gegessen v siehe essen.
Gegner ['ge:gnər] m -s, - opponent; **g~isch** a opposing; **~schaft** f opposition.
gegrillt [gə'grɪlt] a grilled.
Gehackte(s) [gə'haktə(s)] nt mince(d meat).
Gehalt [gə'halt] m -(e)s, -e content // nt -(e)s, -er salary.
Gehalts- zW: **~empfänger** m salary earner; **~erhöhung** f salary increase; **~zulage** f salary increment.

gehaltvoll a (nahrhaft) nutritious.
gehässig [gə'hɛsɪç] a spiteful, nasty; **G~keit** f spite(fulness).
Gehäuse [gə'hɔyzə] nt -s, - case; casing; (von Apfel etc) core.
geheim [gə'haɪm] a secret; **G~dienst** m secret service, intelligence service; **~halten** vt unreg keep secret; **G~nis** nt -ses, -se secret; mystery; **~nisvoll** a mysterious; **G~nummer** f (TEL) ex-directory (Brit) or unlisted (US) number; **G~polizei** f secret police.
gehen ['ge:ən] unreg vti go; (zu Fuß ~) walk; ~ nach (Fenster) face // v unpers: wie geht es (dir)? how are you od things?; mir/ihm geht es gut I'm/he's (doing) fine; geht das? is that possible?; geht's noch? can you manage?; es geht not too bad, O.K.; das geht nicht that's not on; es geht um etw sth is concerned, it's about sth.
geheuer [gə'hɔyər] a: nicht ~ eerie; (fragwürdig) dubious.
Gehilfe [gə'hɪlfə] m -n, -n, **Gehilfin** f assistant.
Gehirn [gə'hɪrn] nt -(e)s, -e brain; **~erschütterung** f concussion; **~wäsche** f brainwashing.
geholfen v siehe helfen.
Gehör [gə'hø:r] nt -(e)s hearing; musikalisches ~ ear; ~ finden gain a hearing; jdm ~ schenken give sb a hearing.
gehorchen [gə'hɔrçən] vi obey (jdm sb).
gehören [gə'hø:rən] vi belong // vr unpers be right od proper.
gehörig a proper; ~ zu od +dat belonging to; part of.
gehorsam [gə'ho:rza:m] a obedient; **G~** m -s obedience.
Gehsteig ['ge:ʃtaɪk] m, **Gehweg** m ['ge:ve:k] pavement, sidewalk (US).
Geier ['gaɪər] m -s, - vulture.
Geige ['gaɪgə] f -, -n violin.
Geiger m -s, - violinist; **~zähler** m geiger counter.
geil [gaɪl] a randy (Brit), horny (US).
Geisel ['gaɪzəl] f -, -n hostage.
Geist [gaɪst] m -(e)s, -er spirit; (Gespenst) ghost; (Verstand) mind.
geisterhaft a ghostly.
Geistes- zW: **g~abwesend** a absentminded; **~blitz** m brainwave; **~gegenwart** f presence of mind; **g~krank** a mentally ill; **~kranke(r)** mf mentally ill person; **~krankheit** f mental illness; **~zustand** m state of mind.
geist- zW: **~ig** a intellectual; mental; (Getränke) alcoholic; **~ig behindert** mentally handicapped; **~lich** a spiritual, religious; clerical; **G~liche(r)**

m clergyman; **G~lichkeit** *f* clergy; **~los** *a* uninspired, dull; **~reich** *a* clever; witty; **~voll** *a* intellectual; (*weise*) wise.

Geiz [gaɪts] *m* **-es** miserliness, meanness; **g~en** *vi* be miserly; **~hals** *m*, **~kragen** *m* miser; **g~ig** *a* miserly, mean.

gekannt *v siehe* **kennen**.

geknickt [gə'knɪkt] *a* (*fig*) dejected.

gekocht [gə'kɔxt] *a* boiled.

gekonnt [gə'kɔnt] *a* skilful // *v siehe* **können**.

Gekritzel [gə'krɪtsəl] *nt* **-s** scrawl, scribble.

gekünstelt [ge'kʏnstəlt] *a* artificial, affected.

Gelächter [gə'lɛçtər] *nt* **-s**, **-** laughter.

geladen [ge'la:dən] *a* loaded; (*ELEK*) live; (*fig*) furious.

gelähmt [gə'lɛ:mt] *a* paralysed.

Gelände [gə'lɛndə] *nt* **-s**, **-** land, terrain; (*von Fabrik, Sport~*) grounds *pl*; (*Bau~*) site; **~lauf** *m* crosscountry race.

Geländer [gə'lɛndər] *nt* **-s**, **-** railing; (*Treppen~*) banister(s).

gelangen [gə'laŋən] *vi* (*an +akk od zu*) reach; (*erwerben*) attain; **in jds Besitz ~** come into sb's possession.

gelassen [gə'lasən] *a* calm, composed; **G~heit** *f* calmness, composure.

Gelatine [ʒela'ti:nə] *f* gelatine.

geläufig [gə'lɔyfɪç] *a* (*üblich*) common; **das ist mir nicht ~** I'm not familiar with that.

gelaunt [gə'launt] *a*: **schlecht/gut ~** in a bad/good mood; **wie ist er ~?** what sort of mood is he in?

gelb [gɛlp] *a* yellow; (*Ampellicht*) amber; **~lich** *a* yellowish; **G~sucht** *f* jaundice.

Geld [gɛlt] *nt* **-(e)s, -er** money; **etw zu ~ machen** sell sth off; **~anlage** *f* investment; **~automat** *m* cash dispenser; **~beutel** *m*, **~börse** *f* purse; **~geber** *m* **-s**, **-** financial backer; **g~gierig** *a* avaricious; **~schein** *m* banknote; **~schrank** *m* safe, strongbox; **~strafe** *f* fine; **~stück** *nt* coin; **~wechsel** *m* exchange (of money).

Gelee [ʒe'le:] *nt od m* **-s**, **-s** jelly.

gelegen [gə'le:gən] *a* situated; (*passend*) convenient, opportune; **etw kommt jdm ~** sth is convenient for sb // *v siehe* **liegen**.

Gelegenheit [gə'le:gənhaɪt] *f* opportunity; (*Anlaß*) occasion; **bei jeder ~** at every opportunity.

Gelegenheits- *zW*: **~arbeit** *f* casual work; **~arbeiter** *m* casual worker; **~kauf** *m* bargain.

gelegentlich [gə'le:gəntlɪç] *a* occasional // *ad* occasionally; (*bei Gelegenheit*) some time (or other) // *präp*

+gen on the occasion of.

gelehrt [gə'le:rt] *a* learned; **G~e(r)** *f* scholar; **G~heit** *f* scholarliness.

Geleise [gə'laɪzə] *nt* **-s**, **-** *siehe* **Gleis**.

Geleit [gə'laɪt] *nt* **-(e)s**, **-e** escort; **g~en** *vt* escort; **~schutz** *m* escort.

Gelenk [gə'lɛŋk] *nt* **-(e)s**, **-e** joint; **g~ig** *a* supple.

gelernt [gə'lɛrnt] *a* skilled.

Geliebte(r) [gə'li:ptə(r)] *mf* sweetheart, beloved.

geliehen *v siehe* **leihen**.

gelind(e) [gə'lɪnt, gə'lɪndə] *a* mild, light; (*fig: Wut*) fierce; **~e gesagt** to put it mildly.

gelingen [gə'lɪŋən] *vi unreg* succeed; **es ist mir gelungen, etw zu tun** I succeeded in doing sth.

gell [gɛl] *interj* isn't it?; aren't you? *etc*.

geloben [gə'lo:bən] *vt* vow, swear.

gelten ['gɛltən] *unreg vt* (*wert sein*) be worth; **jdm viel/wenig ~** mean a lot/not mean much to sb; **was gilt die Wette?** do you want to bet? // *vi* (*gültig sein*) be valid; (*erlaubt sein*) be allowed; **jdm ~** (*gemünzt sein auf*) be meant for *od* aimed at sb; **etw ~ lassen** accept sth; **als** *od* **für etw ~** be considered to be sth; **jdm** *od* **für jdn ~** (*betreffen*) apply to *od* for sb // *v unpers*: **es gilt, etw zu tun** it is necessary to do sth; **~d** *a* prevailing; **etw ~d machen** to assert sth; **sich ~d machen** make itself/o.s. felt.

Geltung ['gɛltʊŋ] *f*: **~ haben** have validity; **sich/etw** (*dat*) **verschaffen** establish oneself/sth; **etw zur ~ bringen** show sth to its best advantage; **zur ~ kommen** be seen/heard *etc* to its best advantage.

Geltungsbedürfnis *nt* desire for admiration.

Gelübde [gə'lʏpdə] *nt* **-s**, **-** vow.

gelungen [gə'lʊŋən] *a* successful.

gem. *abk von* **gemischt**.

gemächlich [gə'mɛ:çlɪç] *a* leisurely.

Gemahl [gə'ma:l] *m* **-(e)s**, **-e** husband; **~in** *f* wife.

Gemälde [gə'mɛ:ldə] *nt* **-s**, **-** picture, painting.

gemäß [gə'mɛ:s] *präp +dat* in accordance with // *a* appropriate (*dat* to).

gemäßigt [gə'mɛ:sɪçt] *a* moderate; (*Klima*) temperate.

gemein [gə'maɪn] *a* common; (*niederträchtig*) mean; **etw ~ haben** (*mit*) have sth in common (with).

Gemeinde [gə'maɪndə] *f* **-, -n** district, community; (*Pfarr~*) parish; (*Kirchen~*) congregation; **~steuer** *f* local rates *pl*; **~verwaltung** *f* local administration; **~wahl** *f* local election.

Gemein- zW: **g~gefährlich** a danger-ous to the public; **~heit** f common-ness; mean thing to do/to say; **~platz** m commonplace, platitude; **g~sam** a joint, common (auch MATH); **g~same Sache mit jdm machen** be in cahoots with sb // ad together, jointly; **etw g~sam haben** have sth in common; **~samkeit** f community, having in common; **g~schaft** f com-munity; **in ~schaft mit** jointly od to-gether with; **g~schaftlich** a siehe **g~sam**; **~schaftsarbeit** f teamwork; team effort; **~sinn** m public spirit; **~wohl** nt common good.

Gemenge [gə'mɛŋə] nt -s, - mixture; (Hand~) scuffle.

gemessen [gə'mɛsən] a measured.

Gemetzel [gə'mɛtsəl] nt -s, - slaugh-ter, carnage, butchery.

Gemisch [gə'mɪʃ] nt -es, -e mixture; **g~t** a mixed.

gemocht v siehe **mögen**.

Gemse ['gɛmzə] f -, -n chamois.

Gemunkel [gə'mʊŋkəl] nt -s gossip.

Gemurmel [gə'mʊrməl] nt -s mur-mur(ing).

Gemüse [gə'my:zə] nt -s, - vegetables pl; **~garten** m vegetable garden; **~händler** m greengrocer.

gemußt v siehe **müssen**.

Gemüt [gə'my:t] nt -(e)s, -er disposi-tion, nature; person; **sich** (dat) **etw zu ~e führen** (umg) indulge in sth; **die ~er erregen** arouse strong feel-ings; **g~lich** a comfortable, cosy; (Person) good-natured; **~lichkeit** f comfortableness, cosiness; amiabil-ity.

Gemüts- zW: **~mensch** m senti-mental person; **~ruhe** f composure; **~zustand** m state of mind.

gemütvoll a warm, tender.

genannt v siehe **nennen**.

genau [gə'nau] a,ad exact(ly), pre-cise(ly); **etw ~ nehmen** take sth seriously; **~genommen** ad strictly speaking; **~igkeit** f exactness, ac-curacy; **~so** ad just the same; **~so gut** just as good.

genehm [gə'ne:m] a agreeable, ac-ceptable; **~igen** vt approve, author-ize; **sich** (dat) **etw ~igen** indulge in sth; **G~igung** f approval, authoriza-tion; (Schriftstück) permit.

General [gene'ra:l] m -s, -e od -e gen-eral; **~direktor** m director general; **~konsulat** nt consulate general; **~probe** f dress rehearsal; **~streik** m general strike; **g~überholen** vt thor-oughly overhaul.

Generation [generatsi'o:n] f genera-tion.

Generator [gene'ra:tɔr] m generator, dynamo.

generell [gene'rɛl] a general.

genesen [ge'ne:zən] vi unreg conva-lesce, recover, get well.

Genesung f recovery, convalescence.

genetisch [ge'ne:tɪʃ] a genetic.

Genf [gɛnf] nt Geneva; **~er See** Lake Geneva.

genial [geni'a:l] a brilliant; **G~ität** f brilliance, genius.

Genick [gə'nɪk] nt -(e)s, -e (back of the) neck; **~starre** f stiff neck.

Genie [ʒe'ni:] nt -s, -s genius.

genieren [ʒe'ni:rən] vt bother; **geniert es Sie, wenn ...?** do you mind if ...? // vr feel awkward od self-conscious.

genießbar a edible; drinkable.

genießen [gə'ni:sən] vt unreg enjoy; eat; drink.

Genießer m -s, - epicure; pleasure lover; **g~isch** a appreciative // ad with relish.

genommen v siehe **nehmen**.

Genosse [gə'nɔsə] m -n, -n, **Genossin** f comrade (bes POL), companion; **Genossenschaft** f cooperative (asso-ciation).

genug [gə'nu:k] ad enough.

Genüge [gə'ny:gə] f -: **jdm/etw ~ tun** od **leisten** satisfy sb/sth; **g~n** vi be enough (+dat for); **g~nd** a sufficient.

genügsam [gə'ny:kza:m] a modest, easi-ly satisfied; **G~keit** f moderation.

Genugtuung [gə'nu:ktu:ʊŋ] f satisfac-tion.

Genuß [gə'nʊs] m -sses, -sse pleas-ure; (Zusichnehmen) consumption; **in den ~ von etw kommen** receive the benefit of sth; **~mittel** pl (semi-)luxury items pl.

genüßlich [gə'nʏslɪç] ad with relish.

geöffnet [gə'œfnət] a open.

Geograph [geo'gra:f] m -en, -en ge-ographer; **~ie** [-'fi:] f geography; **g~isch** a geographical.

Geologe [geo'lo:gə] m -n, -n geolo-gist; **Geolo'gie** f geology.

Geometrie [geome'tri:] f geometry.

Gepäck [gə'pɛk] nt -(e)s luggage, bag-gage; **~abfertigung** f, **~annahme** f, **~aufgabe** f, **~ausgabe** f luggage office; **~aufbewahrung** f left-luggage office (Brit), baggage check (US); **~netz** nt luggage-rack; **~rückgabe** f luggage office; **~träger** m porter; (Fahrrad) carrier; **~wagen** m lug-gage van (Brit), baggage car (US).

gepflegt [gə'pfle:kt] a well-groomed; (Park etc) well looked after.

gerade [gə'ra:də] ◆a straight; (auf-recht) upright; **eine ~ Zahl** an even number
◆ad 1 (genau) just, exactly; (spe-ziell) especially; **~ deshalb** that's just od exactly why; **das ist es ja ~!** that's just it!; **~ du** you especially;

warum ~ ich? why me (of all people)?; jetzt ~ nicht! not now!; ~ neben right next to

2 (*eben, soeben*) just; er wollte ~ aufstehen he was just about to get up; ~ erst only just; ~ noch (only) just.

Gerade *f* -n, -n straight line; **g~aus** *ad* straight ahead; **g~heraus** *ad* straight out, bluntly; **g~zu** *ad* (*beinahe*) virtually, almost.

gerannt *v siehe* **rennen**.

Gerät [gə'rɛ:t] *nt* -(e)s, -e device; (*Werkzeug*) tool; (*SPORT*) apparatus; (*Zubehör*) equipment *no pl.*

geraten [gə'ra:tən] *vi unreg* (*gelingen*) turn out well (*jdm* for sb); (*gedeihen*) thrive; gut/schlecht ~ turn out well/badly; an jdn ~ come across sb; in etw (*akk*) ~ get into sth; in Angst ~ get frightened; nach jdm ~ take after sb.

Geratewohl [gəra:tə'vo:l] *nt*: aufs ~ on the off chance; (*bei Wahl*) at random.

geräumig [gə'rɔymiç] *a* roomy.

Geräusch [gə'rɔyʃ] *nt* -(e)s, -e sound, noise; **g~los** *a* silent.

gerben ['gɛrbən] *vt* tan.

gerecht [gə'rɛçt] *a* just, fair; **jdm/etw** ~ werden do justice to sb/sth; **G~igkeit** *f* justice, fairness.

Gerede [gə're:də] *nt* -s talk, gossip.

gereizt [gə'raɪtst] *a* irritable; **G~heit** *f* irritation.

Gericht [gə'rɪçt] *nt* -(e)s, -e court; (*Essen*) dish; mit jdm ins ~ gehen (*fig*) judge sb harshly; das Jüngste ~ the Last Judgement; **g~lich** *a,ad* judicial(ly), legal(ly).

Gerichts- *zW*: **~barkeit** *f* jurisdiction; **~hof** *m* court (of law); **~kosten** *pl* (legal) costs *pl*; **~saal** *m* courtroom; **~verfahren** *nt* legal proceedings *pl*; **~verhandlung** *f* court proceedings *pl*; **~svollzieher** *m* bailiff.

gerieben [gə'ri:bən] *a* grated; (*umg: schlau*) smart, wily // *v siehe* **reiben**.

gering [gə'rɪŋ] *a* slight, small; (*niedrig*) low; (*Zeit*) short; **~fügig** *a* slight, trivial; **~schätzig** *a* disparaging.

geringste(r, -s) *a* slightest, least; **~nfalls** *ad* at the very least.

gerinnen [gə'rɪnən] *vi unreg* congeal; (*Blut*) clot; (*Milch*) curdle.

Gerippe [gə'rɪpə] *nt* -s, - skeleton.

gerissen [gə'rɪsən] *a* wily, smart.

geritten *v siehe* **reiten**.

gern(e) ['gɛrn(ə)] *ad* willingly, gladly; ~ haben, ~ mögen like; etwas ~ tun like doing something; ich möchte ~ ... I'd like ...; ja, ~ yes, please; yes, I'd like to; ~ geschehen it's a pleasure.

gerochen *v siehe* **riechen**.

Geröll [gə'rœl] *nt* -(e)s, -e scree.

Gerste ['gɛrstə] *f* -, -n barley; **Gerstenkorn** *nt* (*im Auge*) stye.

Geruch [gə'rux] *m* -(e)s, ⁻e smell, odour; **g~los** *a* odourless; **g~tilgend** *a* deodorant.

Gerücht [gə'rʏçt] *nt* -(e)s, -e rumour.

geruhen [gə'ru:ən] *vi* deign.

Gerümpel [gə'rʏmpəl] *nt* -s junk.

Gerüst [gə'rʏst] *nt* -(e)s, -e (*Bau~*) scaffold(ing); frame.

gesamt [gə'zamt] *a* whole, entire; (*Kosten*) total; (*Werke*) complete; im ~ en all in all; **~deutsch** *a* all-German; **G~eindruck** *m* general impression; **G~heit** *f* totality, whole; **G~schule** *f* ≈ comprehensive school.

gesandt *v siehe* **senden**.

Gesandte(r) [gə'zantə(r)] *m* envoy.

Gesandtschaft [gə'zantʃaft] *f* legation.

Gesang [gə'zaŋ] *m* -(e)s, ⁻e song; (*Singen*) singing; **~buch** *nt* (*REL*) hymn book.

Gesäß [gə'zɛ:s] *nt* -es, -e seat, bottom.

Geschäft [gə'ʃɛft] *nt* -(e)s, -e business; (*Laden*) shop; (*~sabschluß*) deal; **~emacher** *m* -s, wheeler-dealer; **g~ig** *a* active, busy; (*pej*) officious; **g~lich** *a* commercial // *ad* on business.

Geschäfts- *zW*: **~bericht** *m* financial report; **~essen** *nt* business lunch; **~führer** *m* manager; (*Klub*) secretary; **~geheimnis** *nt* trade secret; **~jahr** *nt* financial year; **~lage** *f* business conditions *pl*; **~mann** *m* businessman; **g~mäßig** *a* businesslike; **~reise** *f* business trip; **~schluß** *m* closing time; **~stelle** *f* office, place of business; **g~tüchtig** *a* efficient; **~viertel** *nt* business quarter; shopping centre; **~wagen** *m* company car; **~zeiten** *pl* business hours.

geschehen [gə'ʃe:ən] *vi unreg* happen; es war um ihn ~ that was the end of him.

gescheit [gə'ʃaɪt] *a* clever.

Geschenk [gə'ʃɛŋk] *nt* -(e)s, -e present, gift.

Geschichte [gə'ʃɪçtə] *f* -, -n story; (*Sache*) affair; (*Historie*) history.

geschichtlich *a* historical.

Geschick [gə'ʃɪk] *nt* -(e)s, -e aptitude; (*Schicksal*) fate; **~lichkeit** *f* skill, dexterity; **g~t** *a* skilful.

geschieden [gə'ʃi:dən] *a* divorced.

geschienen *v siehe* **scheinen**.

Geschirr [gə'ʃɪr] *nt* -(e)s, -e crockery; pots and pans *pl*; (*Pferd*) harness; **~spülmaschine** *f* dishwashing machine; **~tuch** *nt* dish cloth.

Geschlecht [gə'ʃlɛçt] *nt* -(e)s, -er sex; (*GRAM*) gender; (*KUNST*) species; family; **g~lich** *a* sexual.

Geschlechts- *zW:* **~krankheit** *f* venereal disease; **~teil** *nt* genitals *pl;* **~verkehr** *m* sexual intercourse.

geschlossen [gə'ʃlɔsən] *a* shut // *v siehe* **schließen**.

Geschmack [gə'ʃmak] *m* -(e)s, ⁻e taste; **nach jds ~** to sb's taste; **~ finden an etw** (*dat*) (come to) like sth; **g~los** *a* tasteless; (*fig*) in bad taste; **~(s)sache** *f* matter of taste; **~sinn** *m* sense of taste; **g~voll** *a* tasteful.

geschmeidig [gə'ʃmaɪdɪç] *a* supple; (*formbar*) malleable.

geschnitten *v siehe* **schneiden**.

Geschöpf [gə'ʃœpf] *nt* -(e)s, -e creature.

Geschoß [gə'ʃɔs] *nt* -sses, -sse (*MIL*) projectile, missile; (*Stockwerk*) floor.

geschossen *v siehe* **schießen**.

geschraubt [gə'ʃraʊpt] *a* stilted, artificial.

Geschrei [gə'ʃraɪ] *nt* -s cries *pl,* shouting; (*fig: Aufheben*) noise, fuss.

geschrieben *v siehe* **schreiben**.

Geschütz [gə'ʃʏts] *nt* -es, -e gun, cannon; **ein schweres ~ auffahren** (*fig*) bring out the big guns; **~feuer** *nt* artillery fire, gunfire; **g~t** *a* protected.

Geschwader [gə'ʃvaːdər] *nt* -s, - (*NAUT*) squadron; (*AVIAT*) group.

Geschwafel [gə'ʃvaːfəl] *nt* -s silly talk.

Geschwätz [gə'ʃvɛts] *nt* -es chatter, gossip; **g~ig** *a* talkative.

geschweige [gə'ʃvaɪgə] *ad:* **~ (denn)** let alone, not to mention.

geschwind [gə'ʃvɪnt] *a* quick, swift; **G~igkeit** [-dɪçkaɪt] *f* speed, velocity; **G~igkeitsbegrenzung** *f* speed limit; **G~igkeitsüberschreitung** *f* exceeding the speed limit.

Geschwister [gə'ʃvɪstər] *pl* brothers and sisters *pl.*

geschwollen [gə'ʃvɔlən] *a* pompous.

geschwommen *v siehe* **schwimmen**.

Geschworene(r) [gə'ʃvoːrənə(r)] *mf* juror // *pl* jury.

Geschwulst [gə'ʃvʊlst] *f* -, ⁻e swelling; growth, tumour.

Geschwür [gə'ʃvyːr] *nt* -(e)s, -e ulcer.

Gesell- [gə'zɛl] *zW:* **~e** *m* -n, -n fellow; (*Handwerk~*) journeyman; **g~ig** *a* sociable; **~igkeit** *f* sociability; **~schaft** *f* society; (*Begleitung, COMM*) company; (*Abend~schaft etc*) party; **g~schaftlich** *a* social; **~schaftsordnung** *f* social structure; **~schaftsschicht** *f* social stratum.

gesessen *v siehe* **sitzen**.

Gesetz [gə'zɛts] *nt* -es, -e law; **~buch** *nt* statute book; **~entwurf** *m,* **~esvorlage** *f* bill; **g~gebend** *a* legislative; **~gebung** *f* legislation; **g~lich** *a* legal, lawful; **~lichkeit** *f* legality,

lawfulness; **g~los** *a* lawless; **g~mäßig** *a* lawful; **g~t** *a* (*Mensch*) sedate; **g~widrig** *a* illegal, unlawful.

ges. gesch. *abk* (= *gesetzlich geschützt*) registered.

Gesicht [gə'zɪçt] *nt* -(e)s, -er face; **das zweite ~** second sight; **das ist mir nie zu ~ gekommen** I've never laid eyes on that.

Gesichts- *zW:* **~ausdruck** *m* (facial) expression; **~farbe** *f* complexion; **~punkt** *m* point of view; **~züge** *pl* features *pl.*

Gesindel [gə'zɪndəl] *nt* -s rabble.

gesinnt [gə'zɪnt] *a* disposed, minded.

Gesinnung [gə'zɪnʊŋ] *f* disposition; (*Ansicht*) views *pl;* **Gesinnungswandel** *m* change of opinion, volteface.

gesittet [gə'zɪtət] *a* well-mannered.

Gespann [gə'ʃpan] *nt* -(e)s, -e team; (*umg*) couple; **g~t** *a* tense, strained; (*begierig*) eager; **ich bin g~t, ob I** wonder if *od* whether; **auf etw/jdn g~t sein** look forward to sth/meeting sb.

Gespenst [gə'ʃpɛnst] *nt* -(e)s, -er ghost, spectre; **g~erhaft** *a* ghostly.

gesperrt [gə'ʃpɛrt] *a* closed off.

Gespött [gə'ʃpœt] *nt* -(e)s mockery; **zum ~ werden** become a laughing stock.

Gespräch [gə'ʃprɛːç] *nt* -(e)s, -e conversation; discussion(s); (*Anruf*) call; **g~ig** *a* talkative; **~igkeit** *f* talkativeness; **Gesprächsthema** *nt* subject *od* topic (of conversation).

gesprochen *v siehe* **sprechen**.

gesprungen *v siehe* **springen**.

Gespür [gə'ʃpyːr] *nt* -s feeling.

Gestalt [gə'ʃtalt] *f* -, -en form, shape; (*Person*) figure; **in ~ von** in the form of; **~ annehmen** take shape; **g~en** *vt* (*formen*) shape, form; (*organisieren*) arrange, organize // *vr* turn out (*zu* to be); **~ung** *f* formation; organization.

gestanden *v siehe* **stehen**.

Geständnis [gə'ʃtɛntnɪs] *nt* -ses, -se confession.

Gestank [gə'ʃtaŋk] *m* -(e)s stench.

gestatten [gə'ʃtatən] *vt* permit, allow; **~ Sie?** may I?; **sich** (*dat*) **~, etw zu tun** take the liberty of doing sth.

Geste ['gɛstə] *f* -, -n gesture.

gestehen [gə'ʃteːən] *vt unreg* confess.

Gestein [gə'ʃtaɪn] *nt* -(e)s, -e rock.

Gestell [gə'ʃtɛl] *nt* -(e)s, -e frame; (*Regal*) rack, stand.

gestern ['gɛstərn] *ad* yesterday; **~ abend/morgen** yesterday evening/ morning.

Gestirn [gə'ʃtɪrn] *nt* -(e)s, -e star; (*Sternbild*) constellation.

gestohlen *v siehe* **stehlen**.

gestorben *v siehe* **sterben**.

gestreift [gə'ʃtraift] a striped.
gestrichen [gə'ʃtriçən] a cancelled.
gestrig ['gestriç] a yesterday's.
Gestrüpp [gə'ʃtryp] nt -(e)s, -e undergrowth.
Gestüt [gə'ʃty:t] nt -(e)s, -e stud farm.
Gesuch [gə'zu:x] nt -(e)s, -e petition; (Antrag) application; **g~t** a (COMM) in demand; wanted; (fig) contrived.
gesund [gə'zunt] a healthy; **wieder ~ werden** get better; **G~heit** f health(iness); **G~heit!** bless you!; **~heitlich** a,ad health attr, physical; **wie geht es Ihnen ~heitlich?** how's your health?; **~heitsschädlich** a unhealthy; **G~heitswesen** nt health service; **G~heitszustand** m state of health.
gesungen v siehe **singen**.
getan v siehe **tun**.
Getöse [gə'tø:zə] nt -s din, racket.
Getränk [gə'trɛŋk] nt -(e)s, -e drink; **Getränkekarte** f wine list.
getrauen [gə'trauən] vr dare, venture.
Getreide [gə'traidə] nt -s, - cereals pl, grain; **~speicher** m granary.
getrennt [gə'trɛnt] a separate.
Getriebe [gə'tri:bə] nt -s, - (Leute) bustle; (AUT) gearbox.
getrieben v siehe **treiben**.
getroffen v siehe **treffen**.
getrost [gə'tro:st] ad without any bother.
getrunken v siehe **trinken**.
Getue [gə'tu:ə] nt -s fuss.
geübt [gə'y:pt] a experienced.
Gewächs [gə'vɛks] nt -es, -e growth; (Pflanze) plant.
gewachsen [gə'vaksən] a: **jdm/etw ~ sein** be sb's equal/equal to sth.
Gewächshaus nt greenhouse.
gewagt [gə'va:kt] a daring, risky.
gewählt [gə'vɛ:lt] a (Sprache) refined, elegant.
Gewähr [gə'vɛ:r] f - guarantee; **keine ~ übernehmen für** accept no responsibility for; **g~en** vt grant; (geben) provide; **g~leisten** vt guarantee.
Gewahrsam [gə'va:rza:m] m -s, -e safekeeping; (Polizei~) custody.
Gewährsmann m informant, source.
Gewährung f granting.
Gewalt [gə'valt] f -, -en power; (große Kraft) force; (~taten) violence; **mit aller ~** with all one's might; **~anwendung** f use of force; **g~ig** a tremendous, (Irrtum) huge; **~marsch** m forced march; **g~sam** a forcible; **g~tätig** a violent.
gewandt [gə'vant] a deft, skilful; (erfahren) experienced; **G~heit** f dexterity, skill.
gewann etc v siehe **gewinnen**.
Gewässer [gə'vɛsər] nt -s, - waters pl.
Gewebe [gə've:bə] nt -s, - (Stoff) fab-

ric; (BIOL) tissue.
Gewehr [gə've:r] nt -(e)s, -e gun; rifle; **~lauf** m rifle barrel.
Geweih [gə'vai] nt -(e)s, -e antlers pl.
Gewerb- [gə'vɛrb] zW: **~e** nt -s, - trade, occupation; **Handel und ~e** trade and industry; **~eschule** f technical school; **g~lich** a industrial; trade attr; **gewerbsmäßig** a professional; **Gewerbszweig** m line of trade.
Gewerkschaft [gə'vɛrkʃaft] f trade union; **~ler** m -s, - trade unionist; **Gewerkschaftsbund** m trade unions federation.
Gewicht [gə'viçt] nt -(e)s, -e weight; (fig) importance; **g~ig** a weighty.
gewieft [gə'vi:ft] a, **gewiegt** [gə'vi:kt] a shrewd, cunning.
gewillt [gə'vilt] a willing, prepared.
Gewimmel [gə'viməl] nt -s swarm.
Gewinde [gə'vində] nt -s, - (Kranz) wreath; (von Schraube) thread.
Gewinn [gə'vin] m -(e)s, -e profit; (bei Spiel) winnings pl; **etw mit ~ verkaufen** sell sth at a profit; **~- und Verlustrechnung** (COMM) profit and loss account; **~beteiligung** f profit-sharing; **g~bringend** a profitable; **g~en** unreg vt win; (erwerben) gain; (Kohle, Öl) extract // vi win; (profitieren) gain; **an etw** (dat) **g~en** gain in sth; **~er(in** f) m -s, - winner; **~spanne** f profit margin; **~(n)ummer** f winning number; **~ung** f winning; gaining; (von Kohle etc) extraction.
Gewirr [gə'vir] nt -(e)s, -e tangle; (von Straßen) maze.
gewiß [gə'vis] a,ad certain(ly).
Gewissen [gə'visən] nt -s, - conscience; **g~haft** a conscientious; **~haftigkeit** f conscientiousness; **g~los** a unscrupulous.
Gewissens- zW: **~bisse** pl pangs of conscience pl, qualms pl; **~frage** f matter of conscience; **~freiheit** f freedom of conscience; **~konflikt** m moral conflict.
gewissermaßen [gəvisər'ma:sən] ad more or less, in a way.
Gewißheit [gə'vishait] f certainty.
Gewitter [gə'vitər] nt -s, - thunderstorm; **g~n** vi unpers: **es gewittert** there's a thunderstorm.
gewitzt [gə'vitst] a shrewd, cunning.
gewogen [gə'vo:gən] a well-disposed (+dat towards).
gewöhnen [gə'vø:nən] vt: **jdn an etw** (akk) **~ accustom** sb to sth; (erziehen zu) teach sb sth // vr: **sich an etw** (akk) **~ get used to/ad** accustomed to sth.
Gewohnheit [gə'vo:nhait] f habit; (Brauch) custom; **aus ~** from habit;

zur ~ werden become a habit.
Gewohnheits- *in zW* habitual;
~**mensch** *m* creature of habit;
~**recht** *nt* common law.
gewöhnlich [gə'vø:nlıç] *a* usual; ordinary; (*pej*) common; **wie** ~ as usual.
gewohnt [gə'vo:nt] *a* usual; **etw** ~
sein be used to sth.
Gewöhnung *f* getting accustomed
(*an* +*akk* to).
Gewölbe [gə'vœlbə] *nt* -s, - vault.
gewonnen *v siehe* **gewinnen.**
geworden *v siehe* **werden.**
geworfen *v siehe* **werfen.**
Gewühl [gə'vy:l] *nt* -(e)s throng.
Gewürz [gə'vyrts] *nt* -es, -e spice, seasoning; ~**nelke** *f* clove; ~**t** *a* spiced.
gewußt *v siehe* **wissen.**
Gezeiten [gə'tsaɪtən] *pl* tides *pl.*
gezielt [gə'tsi:lt] *a* with a particular
aim in mind, purposeful; (*Kritik*)
pointed.
geziert [gə'tsi:rt] *a* affected.
gezogen *v siehe* **ziehen.**
Gezwitscher [gə'tsvɪtʃər] *nt* -s twitter(ing), chirping.
gezwungen [gə'tsvʊŋən] *a* forced;
~**ermaßen** *ad* of necessity.
gibst *etc v siehe* **geben.**
Gicht [gıçt] *f* - gout; **g~isch** *a* gouty.
Giebel [gi:bəl] *m* -s, - gable; ~**dach**
nt gable(d) roof; ~**fenster** *nt* gable
window.
Gier [gi:r] *f* - greed; **g~ig** *a* greedy.
Gieß- [gi:s] *zW:* **g~en** *vt unreg* pour;
(*Blumen*) water; (*Metall*) cast;
(*Wachs*) mould; ~**kanne** *f* watering
can.
Gift [gıft] *nt* -(e)s, -e poison; **g~ig** *a*
poisonous; (*fig: boshaft*) venomous;
~**zahn** *m* fang.
ging *etc v siehe* **gehen.**
Ginster ['gınstər] *m* -s, - broom.
Gipfel ['gıpfəl] *m* -s, - summit, peak;
(*fig*) height; **g~n** *vi* culminate;
~**treffen** *nt* summit (meeting).
Gips [gıps] *m* -es, -e plaster; (*MED*)
plaster (of Paris); ~**abdruck** *m* plaster cast; **g~en** *vt* plaster; ~**verband**
m plaster (cast).
Giraffe [gi'rafə] *f* -, -n giraffe.
Girlande [gır'landə] *f* -, -n garland.
Giro ['ʒi:ro] *nt* -s, -s giro; ~**konto** *nt*
current account.
Gischt [gıʃt] *m* -(e)s, -e spray, foam.
Gitarre [gi'tarə] *f* -, -n guitar.
Gitter ['gıtər] *nt* -s, - grating, bars *pl;*
(*für Pflanzen*) trellis; (*Zaun*) railing(s); ~**bett** *nt* cot; ~**fenster** *nt*
barred window; ~**zaun** *m* railing(s).
Glacéhandschuh [gla'se:hantʃu:] *m*
kid glove.
Gladiole [gladi'o:lə] *f* -, -n gladiolus.
Glanz [glants] *m* -es shine, lustre;
(*fig*) splendour.

glänzen ['glɛntsən] *vi* shine (*also fig*),
gleam // *vt* polish; ~**d** *a* shining;
(*fig*) brilliant.
Glanz- *zW:* ~**leistung** *f* brilliant
achievement; **g~los** *a* dull; ~**zeit** *f*
heyday.
Glas [gla:s] *nt* -es, -̈er glass; ~**bläser**
m -s, - glass blower; ~**er** *m* -s, -
glazier; ~**faser** *f* fibreglass; **g~ieren**
[gla'zi:rən] *vt* glaze; **g~ig** *a* glassy;
~**scheibe** *f* pane; (*KOCH*) icing.
glatt [glat] *a* smooth; (*rutschig*) slippery; (*Absage*) flat; (*Lüge*) downright; **G~eis** *nt* (black) ice; **jdn aufs**
G~eis führen (*fig*) take sb for a ride.
Glätte ['glɛtə] *f* -, -n smoothness; slipperiness; **g~n** *vt* smooth out.
Glatze ['glatsə] *f* -, -n bald head; **eine**
~ **bekommen** go bald.
Glaube ['glaubə] *m* -ns, -n faith (*an*
+*akk* in); belief (*an* +*akk* in); **g~n**
vti believe (*an* +*akk* in, **jdm** sb);
think; **daran g~n müssen** (*umg*) be
for it; **Glaubensbekenntnis** *nt* creed.
glaubhaft ['glaubhaft] *a* credible.
gläubig ['glɔybıç] *a* (*REL*) devout;
(*vertrauensvoll*) trustful; **G~e(r)** *mf*
believer; **die G~en** the faithful; **G~er**
m -s, - creditor.
glaubwürdig ['glaubvyrdıç] *a* credible; (*Mensch*) trustworthy; **G~keit** *f*
credibility; trustworthiness.
gleich [glaıç] *a* equal; (*identisch*)
(the) same, identical; **es ist mir** ~
it's all the same to me; **2 mal 2** ~ **4** 2
times 2 is *od* equals 4 // *ad* equally;
(*sofort*) straight away; (*bald*) in a
minute; ~ **groß** the same size; ~
nach/an right after/at; ~**altrig** *a* of
the same age; ~**artig** *a* similar;
~**bedeutend** *a* synonymous; ~**be-**
rechtigt *a* having equal rights;
G~berechtigung *f* equal rights *pl;*
~**bleibend** *a* constant; ~**en** *unreg vi:*
jdm/etw ~**en** be like sb/sth // *vr* be
alike; ~**falls** *ad* likewise; **danke**
~**falls** the same to you; **G~**-
förmigkeit *f* uniformity; ~**gesinnt**
a like-minded; **G~gewicht** *nt* equilibrium, balance; ~**gültig** *a* indifferent; (*unbedeutend*) unimportant;
G~gültigkeit *f* indifference; **G~heit** *f*
equality; ~**kommen** *vi unreg* +*dat*
be equal to; ~**mäßig** *a* even, equal;
G~mut *m* equanimity; **G~nis** *nt*
-ses, -se parable; ~**sam** *ad* as it
were; **G~strom** *m* (*ELEK*) direct
current; ~**tun** *vi unreg:* **es jdm** ~**tun**
match sb; **G~ung** *f* equation; ~**viel**
ad no matter; ~**zeitig** *a* simultaneous.
Gleis [glaıs] *nt* -es, -e track, rails *pl;*
(*Bahnsteig*) platform.
gleiten ['glaıtən] *vi unreg* glide;

(*rutschen*) slide.
Gletscher ['glɛtʃər] *m* **-s,** - glacier; **~spalte** *f* crevasse.
Glied [gliːt] *nt* **-(e)s, -er** member; (*Arm, Bein*) limb; (*von Kette*) link; (MIL) rank(s); **g~ern** *vt* organize, structure; **~erung** *f* structure, organization; **~maßen** *pl* limbs *pl*.
glimmen ['glɪmən] *vi unreg* glow, gleam.
glimpflich ['glɪmpflɪç] *a* mild, lenient; ~ davonkommen get off lightly.
glitzern ['glɪtsərn] *vi* glitter, twinkle.
Globus ['gloːbus] *m* - *od* **-ses, Globen** *od* **-se** globe.
Glocke ['glɔkə] *f* **-, -n** bell; etw an die große ~ hängen (*fig*) shout sth from the rooftops.
Glocken- *zW:* **~geläut** *nt* peal of bells; **~spiel** *nt* chime(s); (MUS) glockenspiel; **~turm** *m* bell tower.
Glosse ['glɔsə] *f* **-, -n** comment.
glotzen ['glɔtsən] *vi* (*umg*) stare.
Glück [glʏk] *nt* **-(e)s** luck, fortune; (*Freude*) happiness; ~ haben be lucky; **viel ~** good luck; **zum ~** fortunately; **g~en** *vi* succeed; es glückte ihm, es zu bekommen he succeeded in getting it.
gluckern ['glʊkərn] *vi* glug.
Glück- *zW:* **g~lich** *a* fortunate; (*froh*) happy; **g~licherweise** *ad* fortunately; **Glücksbringer** *m* **-s,** - lucky charm; **g~selig** *a* blissful.
Glücks- *zW:* **~fall** *m* stroke of luck; **~kind** *nt* lucky person; **~sache** *f* matter of luck; **~spiel** *nt* game of chance.
Glückwunsch *m* congratulations *pl,* best wishes *pl.*
Glüh- ['glyː] *zW:* **~birne** *f* light bulb; **g~en** *vi* glow; **~wein** *m* mulled wine; **~würmchen** *nt* glow-worm.
Glut [gluːt] *f* **-, -en** (*Röte*) glow; (*Feuers~*) fire; (*Hitze*) heat; (*fig*) ardour.
GmbH ['geːʔɛmbeːˈhaː] *f abk* (= *Gesellschaft mit beschränkter Haftung*) (private) limited company, Ltd. (*Brit*); corporation, inc. (*US*).
Gnade ['gnaːdə] *f* **-, -n** (*Gunst*) favour; (*Erbarmen*) mercy; (*Milde*) clemency.
Gnaden- *zW:* **~frist** *f* reprieve, respite; **g~los** *a* merciless; **~stoß** *m* coup de grâce.
gnädig ['gnɛːdɪç] *a* gracious; (*voll Erbarmen*) merciful.
Gold [gɔlt] *nt* **-(e)s** gold; **g~en** *a* golden; **~fisch** *m* goldfish; **~grube** *f* goldmine; **~regen** *m* laburnum.
Golf [gɔlf] *m* **-(e)s, -e** gulf // *nt* **-s** golf; **~platz** *m* golf course; **~schläger** *m* golf club; **~spieler** *m* golfer; **~strom** *m* Gulf Stream.

Gondel ['gɔndəl] *f* **-, -n** gondola; (*Seilbahn*) cable-car.
gönnen ['gœnən] *vt:* jdm etw ~ not begrudge sb sth; sich (*dat*) etw ~ allow oneself sth.
Gönner *m* **-s,** - patron; **g~haft** *a* patronizing.
Gosse ['gɔsə] *f* **-, -n** gutter.
Gott [gɔt] *m* **-es, -er** god; mein ~, um ~es Willen! for heaven's sake!; grüß ~! hello; ~ sei Dank! thank God!; **~esdienst** *m* service; **~eslästerung** *f* blasphemy; **~heit** *f* deity.
Gött- [gœt] *zW:* **~in** *f* goddess; **g~lich** *a* divine.
gottlos *a* godless.
Götze ['gœtsə] *m* **-n, -n** idol.
Grab [graːp] *nt* **-(e)s, -er** grave; **g~en** ['graːbən] *vt unreg* dig; **~en** *m* **-s, -** ditch; (MIL) trench; **~stein** *m* gravestone.
Grad [graːt] *m* **-(e)s, -e** degree; **~einteilung** *f* graduation.
Graf [graːf] *m* **-en, -en** count, earl; **~schaft** *f* county.
Gräfin ['grɛːfɪn] *f* countess.
Gram [graːm] *m* **-(e)s** grief, sorrow.
grämen ['grɛːmən] *vr* grieve.
Gramm [gram] *nt* **-s, -e** gram(me).
Grammatik [graˈmatɪk] *f* grammar.
grammatisch *a* grammatical.
Grammophon [gramoˈfoːn] *nt* **-s, -e** gramophone.
Granat [graˈnaːt] *m* **-(e)s, -e** (*Stein*) garnet; **~e** *f* **-, -n** (MIL) shell; (*Hand~*) grenade.
Granit [graˈniːt] *m* **-s, -e** granite.
graphisch ['graːfɪʃ] *a* graphic.
Gras [graːs] *nt* **-es, -er** grass; **g~en** *vi* graze; **~halm** *m* blade of grass.
grassieren [graˈsiːrən] *vi* be rampant, rage.
gräßlich ['grɛslɪç] *a* horrible.
Grat [graːt] *m* **-(e)s, -e** ridge.
Gräte ['grɛːtə] *f* **-, -n** fishbone.
gratis ['graːtɪs] *a,ad* free (of charge); **G~probe** *f* free sample.
Gratulation [gratulatsiˈoːn] *f* congratulation(s).
gratulieren [gratuˈliːrən] *vi:* jdm ~ (zu etw) congratulate sb (on sth); (ich) gratuliere! congratulations!
grau [grau] *a* grey; **~en** *vi unpers:* es graut jdm vor etw sb dreads sth, sb is afraid of sth // *vr:* sich ~en vor dread, have a horror of; **G~en** *nt* **-s** horror; **~enhaft** *a* horrible; **~haarig** *a* grey-haired.
grausam ['grauzaːm] *a* cruel; **G~keit** *f* cruelty.
Grausen ['grauzən] *nt* **-s** horror; **g~** *vi* unpers, vr siehe **grauen**.
gravieren [graˈviːrən] *vt* engrave; **~d** *a* grave.
Grazie ['graːtsiə] *f* **-, -n** grace.

graziös [gratsi'ø:s] a graceful.

greif- [graif] zW: ~**bar** a tangible, concrete; in ~**barer Nähe** within reach; ~**en** vt unreg seize; grip; **nach etw ~en** reach for sth; **um sich ~en** (fig) spread; **zu etw ~en** (fig) turn to sth.

Greis [grais] m -es, -e old man; ~**enalter** nt old age; **g~enhaft** a senile; ~**in** f old woman.

grell [grɛl] a harsh.

Grenz- ['grɛnts] zW: ~**beamte(r)** m frontier official; ~**e** f -, -n boundary; (Staats~) frontier; (Schranke) limit; **g~en** vi border (an +akk on); **g~enlos** a boundless; ~**fall** m borderline case; ~**übergang** m frontier crossing.

Greuel ['grɔyəl] m -s, - horror, revulsion; **etw ist jdm ein ~** sb loathes sth; ~**tat** f atrocity.

greulich ['grɔylɪç] a horrible.

Griech- [gri:ç] zW: ~**e** m, ~**in** f Greek; ~**enland** nt Greece; **g~isch** a Greek.

griesgrämig ['gri:sgrɛ:mɪç] a grumpy.

Grieß [gri:s] m -es, -e (KOCH) semolina.

Griff [grɪf] m -(e)s, -e grip; (Vorrichtung) handle; **g~bereit** a handy.

Grill [grɪl] m grill; ~**e** f -, -n cricket; **g~en** vt grill.

Grimasse [gri'masə] f -, -n grimace.

grimmig ['grɪmɪç] a furious; (heftig) fierce, severe.

grinsen ['grɪnzən] vi grin.

Grippe ['grɪpə] f -, -n influenza, flu.

grob [gro:p] a coarse, gross; (Fehler, Verstoß) gross; **G~heit** f coarseness; coarse expression.

Groll [grɔl] m -(e)s resentment; **g~en** vi bear ill will (+dat od mit towards); (Donner) rumble.

Groschen ['grɔʃən] m 10 pfennig piece.

groß [gro:s] a big, large; (hoch) tall; (fig) great; **im ~en und ganzen** on the whole // ad greatly; ~**artig** a great, splendid; **G~aufnahme** f (CINE) close-up; **G~britannien** nt Great Britain.

Größe ['grø:sə] f -, -n size; (fig) greatness; (Länge) height.

Groß- zW: ~**einkauf** m bulk purchase; ~**eltern** pl grandparents pl; **g~enteils** ad mostly.

Größenwahn ['grø:sənva:n] m megalomania.

Groß- zW: ~**format** nt large size; ~**handel** m wholesale trade; ~**händler** m wholesaler; ~**macht** f great power; ~**maul** m braggart; **g~mütig** a magnanimous; ~**mutter** f grandmother; ~**rechner** m mainframe (computer); **g~spurig** a pompous; ~**stadt** f city, large town.

größte(r, s) [grø:stə(r, s)] a superl von **groß**; **größtenteils** ad for the most part.

Groß- zW: **g~tun** vi unreg boast; ~**vater** m grandfather; **g~ziehen** vt unreg raise; **g~zügig** a generous; (Planung) on a large scale.

grotesk [gro'tɛsk] a grotesque.

Grotte ['grɔtə] f -, -n grotto.

Grübchen ['gry:pçən] nt dimple.

Grube ['gru:bə] f -, -n pit; mine; **Grubenarbeiter** m miner.

grübeln ['gry:bəln] vi brood.

Gruft [gruft] f -, -e tomb, vault.

grün [gry:n] a green; **die G~en** (POL) the Greens; **G~anlage** f park.

Grund [grunt] m -(e)s, -e ground; (von See, Gefäß) bottom; (fig) reason; **im ~e genommen** basically; ~**ausbildung** f basic training; ~**besitz** m land(ed property), real estate; ~**buch** nt land register.

gründ- [grynd] zW: ~**en** vt found; ~**en auf** (+akk) base on // vr be based (auf +dat on); **G~er** m -s, - founder.

Grund- zW: ~**gebühr** f basic charge; ~**gesetz** nt constitution; ~**lage** f foundation; **g~legend** a fundamental.

gründlich a thorough.

Grund- zW: **g~los** a groundless; ~**regel** f basic rule; ~**riß** m plan; (fig) outline; ~**satz** m principle; **g~sätzlich** a,ad fundamental(ly); (Frage) of principle; (prinzipiell) on principle; ~**schule** f elementary school; ~**stein** m foundation stone; ~**stück** nt estate; plot.

Gründung f foundation.

Grundzug m characteristic.

Grün- zW: ~**kohl** m kale; ~**schnabel** m greenhorn; ~**span** m verdigris; ~**streifen** m central reservation.

grunzen ['gruntsən] vi grunt.

Gruppe ['grupə] f -, -n group; **g~nweise** ad in groups.

gruppieren [gru'pi:rən] vtr group.

gruselig a creepy.

gruseln ['gru:zəln] vi unpers: **es gruselt jdm vor etw** sth gives sb the creeps // vr have the creeps.

Gruß [gru:s] m -es, -e greeting; (MIL) salute; **viele ~e** best wishes; **mit freundlichen ~en** yours sincerely; ~**e an** (+akk) regards to.

grüßen ['gry:sən] vt greet; (MIL) salute; **jdn von jdm ~** give sb sb's regards; **jdn ~ lassen** send sb one's regards.

gucken ['gukən] vi look.

Gulasch ['gu:laʃ] m -(e)s, -e goulash.

gültig ['gyltɪç] a valid; **G~keit** f validity.

Gummi ['gumi] nt od m -s, -s rubber; (~harze) gum; ~**band** nt rubber od

elastic band; (Hosen~) elastic;
~baum m rubber plant; gummieren
[gʊ'miːrən] vt gum; ~knüppel m rubber truncheon; ~strumpf m elastic
stocking.

günstig ['gʏnstɪç] a convenient; (Gelegenheit) favourable; das habe ich ~
bekommen it was a bargain.

Gurgel ['gʊrgəl] f -, -n throat; g~n vi
gurgle; (im Mund) gargle.

Gurke ['gʊrkə] f -, -n cucumber; saure
~ pickled cucumber, gherkin.

Gurt [gʊrt] m -(e)s, -e belt.

Gürtel ['gʏrtəl] m -s, - belt; (GEOG)
zone; ~reifen m radial tyre.

Guß [gʊs] m -sses, Güsse casting;
(Regen~) downpour; (KOCH) glazing; ~eisen nt cast iron.

gut [guːt] ◆a good; alles G~e all the
best; also ~ all right then
◆ad well; ~ schmecken taste good;
~, aber ... ok, but ...; (na) ~, ich
komme all right, I'll come; ~ drei
Stunden a good three hours; das kann
~ sein that may well be; laß es ~
sein that'll do.

Gut [guːt] nt -(e)s, -er (Besitz) possession; (pl: Waren) goods pl; laß es g~
sein that'll do; ~achten nt -s, - (expert) opinion; ~achter m -s, - expert; g~artig a good-natured; (MED)
benign; g~bürgerlich a (Küche)
(good) plain; ~dünken nt: nach
~dünken at one's discretion.

Güte ['gyːtə] f - goodness, kindness;
(Qualität) quality.

Güter- zW: ~abfertigung f (EISENB)
goods office; ~bahnhof m goods station; ~wagen m goods waggon
(Brit), freight car (US); ~zug m
goods train (Brit), freight train (US).

Gut- zW: g~gehen v unpers unreg
work, come off; es geht jdm g~ sb's
doing fine; g~gemeint a well meant;
g~gläubig a trusting; ~haben nt -s
credit; g~heißen vt unreg approve
(of).

gütig ['gyːtɪç] a kind.

Gut- zW: g~mütig a good-natured;
~mütigkeit f good nature; ~schein
m voucher; g~schreiben vt unreg
credit; ~schrift f credit; g~tun vi
unreg: jdm g~tun do sb good;
g~willig a willing.

Gymnasium [gʏm'naːziʊm] nt grammar school (Brit), high school (US).

Gymnastik [gʏm'nastɪk] f exercises pl,
keep fit.

H

H, h [haː] nt H, h.

Haag [haːg] m: Den ~ the Hague.

Haar [haːr] nt -(e)s, -e hair; um ein ~

nearly; an den ~en herbeigezogen
(umg: Vergleich) very far-fetched;
~bürste f hairbrush; h~en vir lose
hair; ~esbreite f: um ~esbreite by a
hair's-breadth; h~genau ad precisely; h~ig a hairy; (fig) nasty;
~klemme f hair grip; ~nadel f hair-
pin; h~scharf ad (beobachten) very
sharply; (daneben) by a hair's
breadth; ~schnitt m haircut;
~shampoo nt shampoo; ~spange f
hair slide; h~sträubend a hair-
raising; ~teil nt hairpiece;
~waschmittel nt shampoo.

Habe ['haːbə] f - property.

haben ['haːbən] vt, v aux unreg have;
Hunger/Angst ~ be hungry/afraid;
woher hast du das? where did you
get that from?; was hast du denn?
what's the matter (with you)?; du
hast zu schweigen you're to be quiet;
ich hätte gern I would like; H~ nt -s,
- credit.

Habgier f avarice; h~ig a avaricious.

Habicht ['haːbɪçt] m -s, -e hawk.

Habseligkeiten pl belongings pl.

Hachse ['haksə] f -, -n (KOCH)
knuckle.

Hacke ['hakə] f -, -n hoe; (Ferse)
heel; h~n vt hack, chop; (Erde) hoe.

Hackfleisch nt mince, minced meat.

Hafen ['haːfən] m -s, ⁻ harbour, port;
~arbeiter m docker; ~damm m jetty, mole; ~stadt f port.

Hafer ['haːfər] m -s, - oats pl;
~flocken pl rolled oats pl; ~schleim
m gruel.

Haft [haft] f - custody; h~bar a liable,
responsible; ~befehl m warrant (of
arrest); h~en vi stick, cling; h~en
für be liable od responsible for;
h~enbleiben vi unreg stick (an
+dat to); ~pflicht f liability;
~pflichtversicherung f third party insurance; ~schalen pl contact lenses
pl; ~ung f liability.

Hage- ['haːgə] zW: ~butte f -, -n rose
hip; ~dorn m hawthorn.

Hagel ['haːgəl] m -s hail; h~n vi
unpers hail.

hager ['haːgər] a gaunt.

Hahn [haːn] m -(e)s, ⁻e cock; (Was-
ser~) tap, faucet (US).

Hähnchen ['hɛːnçən] nt cockerel;
(KOCH) chicken.

Hai(fisch) ['haɪ(fɪʃ)] m -(e)s, -e shark.

Häkchen ['hɛːkçən] nt small hook.

Häkel- ['hɛːkəl] zW: ~arbeit f crochet
work; h~n vt crochet; ~nadel f
crochet hook.

Haken ['haːkən] m -s, - hook; (fig)
catch; ~kreuz nt swastika; ~nase f
hooked nose.

halb [halp] a half; ~ eins half past
twelve; ein ~es Dutzend half a doz-

en; **H~dunkel** nt semi-darkness.

halber ['halbər] präp +gen (wegen) on account of; (für) for the sake of.

Halb- zW: **~heit** f half-measure; **h~ieren** vt halve; **~insel** f peninsula; **h~jährlich** a half-yearly; **~kreis** m semicircle; **~kugel** f hemisphere; **~leiter** m semiconductor; **h~links** a (SPORT) inside left; **~mond** m half-moon; (fig) crescent; **h~offen** a half-open; **~pension** f half-board; **h~rechts** a (SPORT) inside right; **~schuh** m shoe; **~tagsarbeit** f part-time work; **h~wegs** ad half-way; **h~wegs besser** more or less better; **~wertzeit** f half-life; **~wüchsige(r)** mf adolescent; **~zeit** f (SPORT) half; (Pause) half-time.

half etc v siehe **helfen**.

Hälfte ['hɛlftə] -, -n f half.

Halfter ['halftər] f -, -n, od nt -s, - halter; (Pistolen~) holster.

Halle ['halə] f -, -n hall; (AVIAT) hangar; **h~n** vi echo, resound; **Hallenbad** nt indoor swimming pool.

hallo [ha'lo:] interj hello.

Halluzination [halutsinatsi'o:n] f hallucination.

Halm [halm] m -(e)s, -e blade, stalk.

Hals [hals] m -es, ⁻e neck; (Kehle) throat; **~ über Kopf** in a rush; **~kette** f necklace; **~-Nasen-Ohren-Arzt** m ear nose and throat specialist; **~schlagader** f carotid artery; **~schmerzen** pl sore throat; **~tuch** nt scarf; **~wirbel** m cervical vertebra.

Halt [halt] m -(e)s, -e stop; (fester ~) hold; (innerer ~) stability; **h~** interj stop!, halt! // ad just; **h~bar** a durable; (Lebensmittel) non-perishable; (MIL, fig) tenable; **~barkeit** f durability; (non-)perishability.

halten ['haltən] unreg vt keep; (fest~) hold; **~ für** regard as; **~ von** think of // vi hold; (frisch bleiben) keep; (stoppen) stop; **an sich ~** restrain oneself // vr (frisch bleiben) keep; (sich behaupten) hold out; **sich rechts/links ~** keep to the right/left.

Haltestelle f stop.

Halteverbot nt: **hier ist ~** it's no waiting here.

Halt- zW: **h~los** a unstable; **h~machen** vi stop; **~ung** f posture; (fig) attitude; (Selbstbeherrschung) composure.

Halunke [ha'luŋkə] m -n, -n rascal.

hämisch ['hɛ:mɪʃ] a malicious.

Hammel ['haməl] m -s, ⁻ od - wether; **~fleisch** nt mutton.

Hammer ['hamər] m -s, ⁻ hammer.

hämmern ['hɛmərn] vti hammer.

Hämorrhoiden [hɛmɔro'i:dən] pl haemorrhoids.

Hampelmann ['hampəlman] m (lit,

fig) puppet.

Hamster ['hamstər] m -s, - hamster; **~ei** [-'rai] f hoarding; **h~n** vi hoard.

Hand [hant] f -, ⁻e hand; **~arbeit** f manual work; (Nadelarbeit) needlework; **~arbeiter** m manual worker; **~bremse** f handbrake; **~buch** nt handbook, manual.

Händedruck ['hɛndədruk] m handshake.

Handel ['handəl] m -s trade; (Geschäft) transaction.

handeln ['handəln] vi trade; act; **~ von** be about // vr unpers: **sich ~ um** be a question of, be about; **H~** nt -s action.

Handels- zW: **~bilanz** f balance of trade; **~kammer** f chamber of commerce; **~name** m trade name; **~reisende(r)** m commercial traveller; **~schule** f business school; **h~üblich** a customary; (Preis) going attr; **~vertreter** m sales representative.

Hand- zW: **~feger** m -s, - brush; **h~fest** a hefty; **h~gearbeitet** a handmade; **~gelenk** nt wrist; **~gemenge** nt scuffle; **~gepäck** nt hand-luggage; **h~greiflich** a palpable; **h~greiflich werden** become violent; **~griff** m flick of the wrist; **h~haben** vt insep handle.

Händler ['hɛndlər] m -s, - trader, dealer.

handlich ['hantlɪç] a handy.

Handlung ['handluŋ] f -, -en act(ion); (in Buch) plot; (Geschäft) shop; **Handlungsweise** f manner of dealing.

Hand- zW: **~pflege** f manicure; **~schelle** f handcuff; **~schlag** m handshake; **~schrift** f handwriting; (Text) manuscript; **~schuh** m glove; **~tasche** f handbag; **~tuch** nt towel; **~werk** nt trade, craft; **~werker** m -s, - craftsman, artisan; **~werkzeug** nt tools pl.

Hanf [hanf] m -(e)s hemp.

Hang [haŋ] m -(e)s, ⁻e inclination; (Ab~) slope.

Hänge- ['hɛŋə] in zW hanging; **~brücke** f suspension bridge; **~matte** f hammock.

hängen ['hɛŋən] vi unreg hang; **~ an** (fig) be attached to // vi hang (an +akk on(to)); **sich ~ an** (+akk) hang on to, cling to; **~bleiben** vi unreg be caught (an +dat on); (fig) remain, stick; **~lassen** vt unreg (vergessen) leave; **den Kopf ~lassen** get downhearted.

Hannover [ha'no:fər] nt -s Hanover.

hänseln ['hɛnzəln] vt tease.

hantieren [han'ti:rən] vi work, be busy; **mit etw ~** handle sth.

hapern ['haːpərn] *vi unpers*: es hapert an etw (*dat*) there is a lack of sth.
Happen ['hapən] *m* -s, - mouthful.
Hardware ['haːdwɛə] *f* hardware.
Harfe ['harfə] *f* -, -n harp.
Harke ['harkə] *f* -, -n rake; **h~n** *vti* rake.
harmlos ['harmloːs] *a* harmless; **H~igkeit** *f* harmlessness.
Harmonie [harmoˈniː] *f* harmony; **h~ren** *vi* harmonize.
Harmonika [harˈmoːnika] *f* -, -s (*Zieh~*) concertina.
harmonisch [harˈmoːniʃ] *a* harmonious.
Harmonium [harˈmoːniʊm] *nt* -s, -nien *od* -s harmonium.
Harn [harn] *m* -(e)s, -e urine; **~blase** *f* bladder.
Harpune [harˈpuːnə] *f* -, -n harpoon.
harren ['harən] *vi* wait (*auf* +*akk* for).
hart [hart] *a* hard; (*fig*) harsh.
Härte ['hɛrtə] *f* -, -n hardness; (*fig*) harshness.
hart- *zW*: **~gekocht** *a* hard-boiled; **~herzig** *a* hard-hearted; **~näckig** *a* stubborn; **H~näckigkeit** *f* stubbornness; **H~platte** *f* hard disk.
Harz [haːrts] *nt* -es, -e resin.
Haschee [haˈʃeː] *nt* -s, -s hash.
Haschisch ['haʃɪʃ] *nt* - hashish.
Hase ['haːzə] *m* -n, -n hare.
Haselnuß ['haːzəlnʊs] *f* hazelnut.
Hasenfuß *m* coward.
Hasenscharte *f* harelip.
Haß [has] *m* -sses hate, hatred.
hassen ['hasən] *vt* hate.
häßlich ['hɛslɪç] *a* ugly; (*gemein*) nasty; **H~keit** *f* ugliness; nastiness.
hast *v siehe* **haben**.
Hast [hast] *f* - haste; **h~en** *vi* rush; **h~ig** *a* hasty.
hat, hatte *etc v siehe* **haben**.
Haube ['haubə] *f* -, -n hood; (*Mütze*) cap; (*AUT*) bonnet, hood (*US*).
Hauch [haux] *m* -(e)s, -e breath; (*Luft~*) breeze; (*fig*) trace; **h~dünn** *a* very thin; **h~en** *vi* breathe.
Haue ['hauə] *f* -, -n hoe, pick; (*umg*) hiding; **h~n** *vt unreg* hew, cut; (*umg*) thrash.
Haufen ['haufən] *m* -s, - heap; (*Leute*) crowd; **ein ~ (x)** (*umg*) loads *od* a lot (of x); **auf einem ~** in one heap.
häufen ['hɔyfən] *vt* pile up // *vr* accumulate.
haufenweise *ad* in heaps; in droves; **etw ~ haben** have piles of sth.
häufig ['hɔyfɪç] *a,ad* frequent(ly); **H~keit** *f* frequency.
Haupt [haupt] *nt* -(e)s, **Häupter** head; (*Ober~*) chief; (*in zW*) main; **~bahnhof** *m* central station; **h~beruflich** *ad* as one's main occupation; **~darsteller(in** *f*) *m* leading

actor/actress; **~eingang** *m* main entrance; **~film** *m* main film.
Häuptling ['hɔyptlɪŋ] *m* chief, chieftain.
Haupt- *zW*: **~mann** *m*, *pl* **-leute** (*MIL*) captain; **~person** *f* central figure; **~quartier** *nt* headquarters *pl*; **~rolle** *f* leading part; **~sache** *f* main thing; **h~sächlich** *a,ad* chief(ly); **~satz** *m* main clause; **~schlagader** *f* aorta; **~schule** *f* ≈ secondary school; **~sendezeit** *f* (*TV*) prime time; **~stadt** *f* capital; **~straße** *f* main street; **~wort** *nt* noun.
Haus [haus] *nt* -es, **Häuser** house; **nach ~e** home; **zu ~e** at home; **~angestellte** *f* domestic servant; **~arbeit** *f* housework; (*SCH*) homework; **~arzt** *m* family doctor; **~aufgabe** *f* (*SCH*) homework; **~besitzer(in** *f*) *m*, **~eigentümer(in** *f*) *m* house-owner.
Häuser- ['hɔyzər] *zW*: **~block** *m* block (of houses); **~makler** *m* estate agent (*Brit*), real estate agent (*US*).
Haus- *zW*: **~frau** *f* housewife; **h~gemacht** *a* home-made; **~halt** *m* household; (*POL*) budget; **h~halten** *vi unreg* (*sparen*) economize; **~hälterin** *f* housekeeper; **~haltsgeld** *nt* housekeeping (money); **~haltsgerät** *nt* domestic appliance; **~herr** *m* host; (*Vermieter*) landlord; **h~hoch** *ad*: **h~hoch verlieren** lose by a mile.
hausieren [hauˈziːrən] *vi* peddle.
Hausierer *m* -s, - peddlar.
häuslich ['hɔyslɪç] *a* domestic.
Haus- *zW*: **~meister** *m* caretaker, janitor; **~nummer** *f* street number; **~ordnung** *f* house rules *pl*; **~putz** *m* house cleaning; **~schlüssel** *m* front-door key; **~schuh** *m* slipper; **~suchung** *f* police raid; **~tier** *nt* domestic animal; **~wirt** *m* landlord; **~wirtschaft** *f* domestic science.
Haut [haut] *f* -, **Häute** skin; (*Tier~*) hide.
Haut- *zW*: **h~eng** *a* skin-tight; **~farbe** *f* complexion.
Haxe ['haksə] *f* -, -n *siehe* **Hachse**.
Hbf *abk von* **Hauptbahnhof**.
he [heː] *interj* hey.
Hebamme ['heːpˌʔamə] *f* -, -n midwife.
Hebel ['heːbəl] *m* -s, - lever.
heben ['heːbən] *vt unreg* raise, lift.
Hecht [hɛçt] *m* -(e)s, -e pike.
Heck [hɛk] *nt* -(e)s, -e stern; (*von Auto*) rear.
Hecke ['hɛkə] *f* -, -n hedge.
Heckenrose *f* dog rose.
Heckenschütze *m* sniper.
Heer [heːr] *nt* -(e)s, -e army.
Hefe ['heːfə] *f* -, -n yeast.
Heft [hɛft] *nt* -(e)s, -e exercise book; (*Zeitschrift*) number; (*von Messer*)

haft; **h~en** vt fasten (an +akk to); (nähen) tack; ~er m -s, - folder.

heftig a fierce, violent; **H~keit** f fierceness, violence.

Heft- zW: **~klammer** f paper clip; **~maschine** f stapling machine; **~pflaster** nt sticking plaster; **~zwecke** f drawing pin.

Hehl [he:l] m od nt: **kein(en) ~ aus etw** (dat) **machen** make no secret of sth; **~er** m -s, - receiver (of stolen goods), fence.

Heide ['haɪdə] f -, -n heath, moor; (~kraut) heather // m -n, -n, **Heidin** f heathen, pagan; **~kraut** nt heather; **Heidelbeere** f bilberry; **Heidentum** nt paganism.

heikel ['haɪkəl] a awkward, thorny; (wählerisch) fussy.

Heil [haɪl] nt -(e)s well-being; (Seelen~) salvation; **h~** a in one piece, intact; **~and** m -(e)s, -e saviour; **h~bar** a curable; **h~en** vt cure // vi heal; **h~froh** a very relieved.

heilig ['haɪlɪç] a holy; **H~abend** m Christmas Eve; **H~e(r)** mf saint; **~en** vt sanctify, hallow; **H~enschein** m halo; **H~keit** f holiness; **~sprechen** vt unreg canonize; **H~tum** nt shrine; (Gegenstand) relic.

Heil- zW: **h~los** a unholy; **~mittel** nt remedy; **h~sam** a (fig) salutary; **Heilsarmee** f Salvation Army; **~ung** f cure.

Heim [haɪm] nt -(e)s, -e home; **h~** ad home.

Heimat ['haɪmaːt] f -, -en home (town/country etc); **~land** nt homeland; **h~lich** a native, home attr; (Gefühle) nostalgic; **h~los** a homeless; **~ort** m home town/area; **~vertriebene(r)** mf displaced person.

Heim- zW: **~computer** m home computer; **h~fahren** vi unreg drive/go home; **~fahrt** f journey home; **h~gehen** vi unreg go home; (sterben) pass away; **h~isch** a (gebürtig) native; **sich h~isch fühlen** feel at home; **~kehr** f -, -en homecoming; **h~kehren** vi return home; **h~lich** a secret; **~lichkeit** f secrecy; **~reise** f journey home; **h~suchen** vt afflict; (Geist) haunt; **h~tückisch** a malicious; **~weg** m way home; **~weh** nt homesickness; **~weh haben** be homesick; **h~zahlen** vt: **jdm etw h~zahlen** pay back sb for sth.

Heirat ['haɪraːt] f -, -en marriage; **h~en** vti marry.

Heiratsantrag m proposal.

heiser ['haɪzər] a hoarse; **H~keit** f hoarseness.

heiß [haɪs] a hot; **~e(r) Draht** hot line; **~es Eisen** (umg) hot potato; **~blütig** a hot-blooded.

heißen ['haɪsən] unreg vi be called; (bedeuten) mean; **das heißt** that is to say // vt command; (nennen) name // vi unpers it says; it is said.

Heißhunger m ravenous hunger.

heißlaufen vir unreg overheat.

heiter ['haɪtər] a cheerful; (Wetter) bright; **H~keit** f cheerfulness; (Belustigung) amusement.

Heiz- ['haɪts] zW: **h~bar** a heated; (Raum) with heating; **~decke** f electric blanket; **h~en** vt heat; **~er** m -s, - stoker; **~körper** m radiator; **~öl** nt fuel oil; **~sonne** f electric fire; **~ung** f heating; **~ungsanlage** f heating system.

hektisch ['hɛktɪʃ] a hectic.

Held [hɛlt] m -en, -en hero; **~in** f heroine.

helfen ['hɛlfən] unreg vi help (jdm sb, bei with); (nützen) be of use; **sich** (dat) **zu ~ wissen** be resourceful // v unpers: **es hilft nichts, du mußt ...** it's no use, you have to ...

Helfer m -s, - helper, assistant; **Helfershelfer** m accomplice.

hell [hɛl] a clear, bright; (Farbe, Bier) light; **~blau** a light blue; **~blond** a ash-blond; **H~e** f - clearness, brightness; **H~seher** m clairvoyant; **~wach** a wide-awake.

Helm [hɛlm] m -(e)s, -e (auf Kopf) helmet.

Hemd [hɛmt] nt -(e)s, -en shirt; (Unter~) vest; **~bluse** f blouse.

hemmen ['hɛmən] vt check, hold up; **gehemmt sein** be inhibited.

Hemmung f check; (PSYCH) inhibition; **hemmungslos** a unrestrained, without restraint.

Hengst [hɛŋst] m -es, -e stallion.

Henkel ['hɛŋkəl] m -s, - handle.

Henker m -s, - hangman.

Henne ['hɛnə] f -, -n hen.

her [heːr] ad **1** (Richtung) **komm ~ zu mir** come here (to me); **von England ~** from England; **von weit ~** from a long way away; **~ damit!** hand it over!; **wo hat er das ~?** where did he get that from?
2 (Blickpunkt): **von der Form ~** as far as the form is concerned
3 (zeitlich): **das ist 5 Jahre ~** that was 5 years ago; **wo bist du ~?** where do you come from? **ich kenne ihn von früher ~** I know him from before.

herab [hɛˈrap] ad down(ward(s)); **~hängen** vi unreg hang down; **~lassen** unreg vt let down // vr condescend; **~lassend** a condescending; **~setzen** vt lower, reduce; (fig) belittle, disparage; **~würdigen** vt belittle, disparage.

heran [hɛˈran] *ad:* näher ~! come up closer!; ~ **zu mir!** come up to me!; ~**bringen** *vt unreg* bring up (*an* +*akk* to); ~**fahren** *vt unreg* drive up (*an* +*akk* to); ~**kommen** *vi unreg* (*an* +*akk*) approach, come near; ~**machen** *vr:* sich an jdn ~**machen** make up to sb; ~**wachsen** *vi unreg* grow up; ~**ziehen** *vt unreg* pull nearer; (*aufziehen*) raise; (*ausbilden*) train; jdn zu etw ~ziehen call upon sb to help in sth.

herauf [hɛˈrauf] *ad* up(ward(s)), up here; ~**beschwören** *vt unreg* conjure up, evoke; ~**bringen** *vt unreg* bring up.

heraus [hɛˈraus] *ad* out; outside; from; ~**bekommen** *vt unreg* get out; (*fig*) find *od* figure out; ~**bringen** *vt unreg* bring out; (*Geheimnis*) elicit; ~**finden** *vt unreg* find out; ~**fordern** *vt* challenge; **H**~**forderung** *f* challenge; provocation; ~**geben** *vt unreg* give up, surrender; (*Geld*) give back; (*Buch*) edit; (*veröffentlichen*) publish; ~**geber** *m* -s, - editor; (*Verleger*) publisher; ~**halten** *vr unreg:* sich aus etw ~**halten** keep out of sth; ~**hängen** *vti unreg* hang out; ~**holen** *vt* get out (*aus* of); ~**kommen** *vi unreg* come out; dabei kommt nichts ~ nothing will come of it; ~**reißen** *vt unreg* tear out; pull out; ~**rücken** *vt* (*Geld*) fork out, hand over; mit etw ~**rücken** (*fig*) come out with sth; ~**stellen** *vr* turn out (*als* to be); ~**ziehen** *vt unreg* pull out, extract.

herb [hɛrp] *a* (slightly) bitter, acid; (*Wein*) dry; (*fig: schmerzlich*) bitter; (: *streng*) stern, austere.

herbei [hɛrˈbai] *ad* (over) here; ~**führen** *vt* bring about; ~**schaffen** *vt* procure.

herbemühen [ˈhɛːrbəmyːən] *vr* take the trouble to come.

Herberge [ˈhɛrbɛrgə] *f* -, -n shelter; hostel, inn.

Herbergsmutter *f,* **Herbergsvater** *m* warden.

her- *zW:* ~**bitten** *vt unreg* ask to come (here); ~**bringen** *vt unreg* bring here.

Herbst [hɛrpst] *m* -(e)s, -e autumn, fall (*US*); **h**~**lich** *a* autumnal.

Herd [hɛːrt] *m* -(e)s, -e cooker; (*fig, MED*) focus, centre.

Herde [ˈhɛːrdə] *f* -, -n herd; (*Schaf*~) flock.

herein [hɛˈrain] *ad* in (here), here; ~! come in!; ~**bitten** *vt unreg* ask in; ~**brechen** *vi unreg* set in; ~**bringen** *vt unreg* bring in; ~**dürfen** *vi unreg* have permission to enter; ~**fallen** *vi unreg* be caught, taken in; ~**fallen auf** (+*akk*) fall for; ~**kommen** *vi*

unreg come in; ~**lassen** *vt unreg* admit; ~**legen** *vt:* jdn ~legen take sb in.

Her- *zW:* ~**fahrt** *f* journey here; **h**~**fallen** *vi unreg:* **h**~**fallen über** fall upon; ~**gang** *m* course of events, circumstances *pl;* **h**~**geben** *vt unreg* give, hand (over); sich zu etw **h**~**geben** lend one's name to sth; **h**~**gehen** *vi unreg:* hinter jdm **h**~**gehen** follow sb; es geht hoch **h**~ there are a lot of goings-on; **h**~**halten** *vt unreg* hold out; **h**~**halten müssen** (*umg*) have to suffer; **h**~**hören** *vi* listen.

Hering [ˈheːrɪŋ] *m* -s, -e herring.

her- *zW:* ~**kommen** *vi unreg* come; **komm mal** ~! come here!; ~**kömmlich** *a* traditional; **H**~**kunft** *f* -, -künfte origin; ~**laufen** *vi unreg:* ~**laufen hinter** (+*dat*) run after.

Hermelin [hɛrməˈliːn] *m od nt* -s, -e ermine.

hermetisch [hɛrˈmeːtɪʃ] *a,ad* hermetic(ally).

her- [hɛr] *zW:* ~'**nach** *ad* afterwards; ~'**nieder** *ad* down.

Herr [hɛr] *m* -(e)n, -en master; (*Mann*) gentleman; (*REL*) Lord; (*vor Namen*) Mr.; mein ~! sir!; meine ~en! gentlemen!; ~**endoppel** *nt* men's doubles; ~**eneinzel** *nt* men's singles; ~**enhaus** *nt* mansion; ~**enkonfektion** *f* menswear; **h**~**enlos** *a* ownerless.

herrichten [ˈheːrrɪçtən] *vt* prepare.

Herr- *zW:* ~**in** *f* mistress; **h**~**isch** *a* domineering; **h**~**lich** *a* marvellous, splendid; ~**lichkeit** *f* splendour, magnificence; ~**schaft** *f* power, rule; (*Herr und Herrin*) master and mistress; meine ~**schaften!** ladies and gentlemen!

herrschen [ˈhɛrʃən] *vi* rule; (*bestehen*) prevail, be.

Herrscher(in *f*) *m* -s, - ruler.

her- *zW:* ~**rühren** *vi* arise, originate; ~**sagen** *vt* recite; ~**stellen** *vt* make, manufacture; **H**~**steller** *m* -s, - manufacturer; **H**~**stellung** *f* manufacture.

herüber [hɛˈryːbər] *ad* over (here), across.

herum [hɛˈrum] *ad* about, (a)round; um etw ~ around sth; ~**führen** *vt* show around; ~**gehen** *vi unreg* walk *od* go round (um etw sth); walk about; ~**irren** *vi* wander about; ~**kriegen** *vt* (*umg*) bring *od* talk around; ~**sprechen** *vr unreg* get around, be spread; ~**treiben** *vir unreg* drift about; ~**ziehen** *vir unreg* wander about.

herunter [hɛˈruntər] *ad* downward(s), down (there); ~**gekommen** *a* run-

down; ~**hängen** *vi unreg* hang down;
~**holen** *vt* bring down; ~**kommen** *vi
unreg* come down; (*fig*) come down
in the world; ~**machen** *vt* take
down; (*schimpfen*) have a go at.

hervor [hɛr'fo:r] *ad* out, forth;
~**bringen** *vt unreg* produce; (*Wort*)
utter; ~**gehen** *vi unreg* emerge, result; ~**heben** *vt unreg* stress; (*als
Kontrast*) set off; ~**ragend** *a* (*fig*)
excellent; ~**rufen** *vt unreg* cause,
give rise to.

Herz [hɛrts] *nt* -ens, -en heart; (*KAR-
TEN*) hearts; ~**anfall** *m* heart attack;
~**enslust** *f*: nach ~enslust to one's
heart's content; ~**fehler** *m* heart defect; **h~haft** *a* hearty; ~**infarkt** *m*
heart attack; ~**klopfen** *nt* palpitation; **h~lich** *a* cordial; **h~lichen**
Glückwunsch congratulations *pl*;
h~liche Grüße best wishes; **h~los** *a*
heartless.

Herzog ['hɛrtso:k] *m* -(e)s, ̈e duke;
~**in** *f* duchess; **h~lich** *a* ducal; ~**tum**
nt duchy.

Herzschlag *m* heartbeat; (*MED*) heart
attack.

herzzerreißend *a* heartrending.

heterogen [hetero'ge:n] *a* hetero-
geneous.

Hetze ['hɛtsə] *f* -, -n (*Eile*) rush; **h~n**
vt hunt; (*verfolgen*) chase; jdn/etw
auf jdn/etw **h~n** set sb/sth on sb/sth //
vi (*eilen*) rush; **h~n** gegen stir up
feeling against; **h~n** zu agitate for;
Hetze'rei *f* agitation; (*Eile*) rush.

Heu [hɔy] *nt* -(e)s hay; **Geld wie ~**
stacks of money; ~**boden** *m* hayloft.

Heuchelei [hɔyçə'laɪ] *f* hypocrisy.

heucheln ['hɔyçəln] *vt* pretend, feign //
vi be hypocritical.

Heuchler(in *f*) [hɔyçlər(ɪn)] *m* -s, -
hypocrite; **h~isch** *a* hypocritical.

heulen ['hɔylən] *vi* howl; cry; das ~de
Elend bekommen get the blues.

Heuschnupfen *m* hay fever.

Heuschrecke ['hɔyʃrɛkə] *f* grass-
hopper, locust.

heute ['hɔytə] *ad* today; ~ abend/früh
this evening/morning.

heutig ['hɔytɪç] *a* today's.

heutzutage ['hɔyttsuta:gə] *ad* nowa-
days.

Hexe ['hɛksə] *f* -, -n witch; **h~n** *vi*
practise witchcraft; **ich kann doch
nicht h~n** I can't work miracles;
Hexenkessel *m* (*lit, fig*) cauldron;
Hexenschuß *m* lumbago; **Hexe'rei** *f*
witchcraft.

Hieb [hi:p] *m* -(e)s, -e blow; (*Wunde*)
cut, gash; (*Stichelei*) cutting remark;
~**e bekommen** get a thrashing.

hielt *etc v siehe* **halten.**

hier [hi:r] *ad* here; ~**auf** *ad* there-
upon; (*danach*) after that; ~**be-**

halten *vt unreg* keep here; ~**bei** *ad*
herewith, enclosed; ~**bleiben** *vi
unreg* stay here; ~**durch** *ad* by this
means; (*örtlich*) through here; ~**her**
ad this way, here; ~**hin** *ad* here;
~**lassen** *vt unreg* leave here; ~**mit**
ad hereby; ~**nach** *ad* hereafter;
~**von** *ad* about this, hereof;
~**zulande** *ad* in this country.

hiesig ['hi:zɪç] *a* of this place, local.

hieß *etc v siehe* **heißen.**

Hilfe ['hɪlfə] *f* -, -n help; aid; **Erste ~**
first aid; ~! help!.

Hilf- *zW*: **h~los** *a* helpless; ~**losigkeit**
f helplessness; **h~reich** *a* helpful.

Hilfs- *zW*: ~**arbeiter** *m* labourer;
h~bedürftig *a* needy; **h~bereit** *a*
ready to help; ~**kraft** *f* assistant,
helper; ~**schule** *f* school for backward children.

hilfst *etc v siehe* **helfen.**

Himbeere ['hɪmbe:rə] *f* -, -n raspberry.

Himmel ['hɪməl] *m* -s, - sky; (*REL, liter*) heaven; **h~blau** *a* sky-blue;
~**fahrt** *f* Ascension; **h~schreiend** *a*
outrageous; **Himmelsrichtung** *f* direction.

himmlisch ['hɪmlɪʃ] *a* heavenly.

hin [hɪn] *ad* 1 (*Richtung*) ~ **und zurück** there and back; ~ **und her** to and
fro; **bis zur Mauer ~** up to the wall;
wo ist er ~? where has he gone?;
Geld ~, Geld her money or no money
2 (*auf ... ~*): **auf meine Bitte ~** at
my request; **auf seinen Rat ~** on the
basis of his advice
3: **mein Glück ist ~** my happiness
has gone.

hinab [hɪ'nap] *ad* down; ~**gehen** *vi
unreg* go down; ~**sehen** *vi unreg*
look down.

hinauf [hɪ'nauf] *ad* up; ~**arbeiten** *vr*
work one's way up; ~**steigen** *vi
unreg* climb.

hinaus [hɪ'naus] *ad* out; ~**gehen** *vi
unreg* go out; ~**gehen über** (+*akk*)
exceed; ~**laufen** *vi unreg* run out;
~**laufen auf** (+*akk*) come to, amount
to; ~**lehnen** *vr* lean out; ~**schieben**
vt unreg put off, postpone; ~**wollen**
vi want to go out; ~**wollen auf**
(+*akk*) drive at, get at.

Hinblick ['hɪnblɪk] *m*: **in** *od* **im ~ auf**
(+*akk*) in view of.

hinder- ['hɪndər] *zW*: ~**lich** *a* awkward; ~**n** *vt* hinder, hamper; **jdn an
etw** (*dat*) ~**n** prevent sb from doing
sth; ~**nis** *nt* -ses, -se obstacle;
H~nissrennen *nt* steeple chase.

hindeuten ['hɪndɔytən] *vi* point (*auf
+akk* to).

hindurch [hɪn'dʊrç] *ad* through;
across; (*zeitlich*) over.

hinein [hɪ'naɪn] *ad* in; ~**fallen** *vi*

unreg fall in; **~fallen in** (+*akk*) fall into; **~gehen** *vi unreg* go in; **~gehen in** (+*akk*) go into, enter; **~geraten** *vi unreg*: **~geraten in** (+*akk*) get into; **~passen** *vi* fit in; **~passen in** (+*akk*) fit into; **~steigern** *vr* get worked up; **~versetzen** *vr*: sich **~versetzen in** (+*akk*) put oneself in the position of.

hin- ['hɪn] *zW*: **~fahren** *unreg vi* go; drive // *vt* take; drive; **H~fahrt** *f* journey there; **~fallen** *vi unreg* fall down; **~fällig** *a* frail, decrepit; (*Regel etc*) unnecessary, otiose; **H~gabe** *f* devotion; **~geben** *vr unreg* +*dat* give oneself up to, devote oneself to; **~gehen** *vi unreg* go; (*Zeit*) pass; **~halten** *vt unreg* hold out; (*warten lassen*) put off, stall.

hinken ['hɪŋkən] *vi* limp; (*Vergleich*) be unconvincing.

hin- ['hɪn] *zW*: **~legen** *vt* put down // *vr* lie down; **~nehmen** *vt unreg* (*fig*) put up with, take; **H~reise** *f* journey out; **~reißen** *vt unreg* carry away, enrapture; sich **~reißen lassen**, etw zu tun get carried away and do sth; **~richten** *vt* execute; **H~richtung** *f* execution; **~setzen** *vt* put down // *vr* sit down; **~sichtlich** *präp* +*gen* with regard to; **H~spiel** *nt* (*SPORT*) first leg; **~stellen** *vt* put (down) // *vr* place o.s.

hintanstellen [hɪnt''anʃtɛlən] *vt* (*fig*) ignore.

hinten ['hɪntən] *ad* at the back; behind; **~herum** *ad* round the back; (*fig*) secretly.

hinter ['hɪntər] *präp* +*dat od akk* behind; (*nach*) after; **~** jdm hersein be after sb; **H~achse** *f* rear axle; **H~bliebene(r)** *mf* surviving relative; **~e(r, s)** *a* rear, back; **~einander** *ad* one after the other; **H~gedanke** *m* ulterior motive; **~gehen** *vt unreg* deceive; **H~grund** *m* background; **H~halt** *m* ambush; **~hältig** *a* underhand, sneaky; **~her** *ad* afterwards, after; **H~hof** *m* backyard; **H~kopf** *m* back of one's head; **~'lassen** *vt unreg* leave; **~'legen** *vt* deposit; **H~list** *f* cunning, trickery; (*Handlung*) trick, dodge; **~listig** *a* cunning, crafty; **H~mann** *m*, *pl* **~männer** person behind; **H~rad** *nt* back wheel; **H~radantrieb** *m* (*AUT*) rear wheel drive; **~rücks** *ad* from behind; **H~tür** *f* back door; (*fig: Ausweg*) escape, loophole; **~'ziehen** *vt unreg* (*Steuern*) evade (paying).

hinüber [hɪ'ny:bər] *ad* across, over; **~gehen** *vi unreg* go over *od* across.

hinunter [hɪ'nʊntər] *ad* down; **~bringen** *vt unreg* take down; **~schlucken** *vt* (*lit*, *fig*) swallow; **~steigen** *vi unreg* descend.

Hinweg ['hɪnveːk] *m* journey out.

hinweg- [hɪn'vɛk] *zW*: **~helfen** *vi unreg*: jdm über etw (*akk*) **~helfen** help sb to get over sth; **~setzen** *vr*: sich **~setzen über** (+*akk*) disregard.

hin- ['hɪn] *zW*: **H~weis** *m* **-es, -e** (*Andeutung*) hint; (*Anweisung*) instruction; (*Verweis*) reference; **~weisen** *vi unreg* (*auf* +*akk*: *anzeigen*) point to; (*sagen*) point out, refer to; **~werfen** *vt unreg* throw down; **~ziehen** *vr unreg* (*fig*) drag on.

hinzu [hɪn'tsuː] *ad* in addition; **~fügen** *vt* add.

Hirn [hɪrn] *nt* **-(e)s, -e** brain(s); **~gespinst** *nt* **-(e)s, -e** fantasy; **h~verbrannt** *a* half-baked, crazy.

Hirsch [hɪrʃ] *m* **-(e)s, -e** stag.

Hirse ['hɪrzə] *f* **-, -n** millet.

Hirt ['hɪrt] *m* **-en, -en** herdsman; (*Schaf~*, *fig*) shepherd.

hissen ['hɪsən] *vt* hoist.

Historiker [hɪs'toːrikər] *m* **-s, -** historian.

historisch [hɪs'toːrɪʃ] *a* historical.

Hitze ['hɪtsə] *f* **-** heat; **h~beständig** *a* heat-resistant; **h~frei** *a*: **h~frei haben** have time off from school on account of excessively hot weather; **~welle** *f* heatwave.

hitzig ['hɪtsɪç] *a* hot-tempered; (*Debatte*) heated.

Hitz- *zW*: **~kopf** *m* hothead; **h~köpfig** *a* fiery, hotheaded; **~schlag** *m* heatstroke.

hm [(h)m] *interj* hm.

Hobby ['hɔbɪ] *nt* hobby.

Hobel ['hoːbəl] *m* **-s, -** plane; **~bank** *f* carpenter's bench; **h~n** *vti* plane; **~späne** *pl* wood shavings *pl*.

hoch [hoːx] *a* high; **H~** *nt* **-s, -s** (*Ruf*) cheer; (*MET*) anticyclone; **~achten** *vt* respect; **H~achtung** *f* respect, esteem; **~achtungsvoll** *ad* yours faithfully; **H~amt** *nt* high mass; **~begabt** *a* extremely gifted; **H~betrieb** *m* intense activity; (*COMM*) peak time; **H~burg** *f* stronghold; **H~deutsch** *nt* High German; **~dotiert** *a* highly paid; **H~druck** *m* high pressure; **H~ebene** *f* plateau; **~erfreut** *a* highly delighted; **H~form** *f* top form; **~halten** *vt unreg* hold up; (*fig*) uphold, cherish; **H~haus** *nt* multistorey building; **~heben** *vt unreg* lift (up); **H~konjunktur** *f* boom; **H~land** *nt* highlands *pl*; **~leben** *vi*: jdn **~leben lassen** give sb three cheers; **H~mut** *m* pride; **~mütig** *a* proud, haughty; **~näsig** *a* stuck-up, snooty; **H~ofen** *m* blast furnace; **~prozentig** *a* (*Alkohol*) strong; **H~rechnung** *f* projected result; **H~saison** *f* high season; **H~schätzung** *f* high esteem; **H~schule** *f* college; university;

H~sommer *m* middle of summer;
H~spannung *f* high tension; **H~**
sprung *m* high jump.
höchst [hø:çst] *ad* highly, extremely;
~e(r, s) *a* highest; (*äußerste*) extreme.
Hochstapler ['ho:xsta:plər] *m* -s, - swindler.
Höchst- *zW*: **h~ens** *ad* at the most;
~geschwindigkeit *f* maximum
speed; **h~persönlich** *ad* in person;
~preis *m* maximum price;
h~wahrscheinlich *ad* most probably.
Hoch- *zW*: **~verrat** *m* high treason;
~wasser *nt* high water; (*Überschwemmung*) floods *pl*; **~würden** *m*
Reverend; **~zahl** *f* (*MATH*) exponent.
Hochzeit ['hɔxtsaɪt] *f* -, -en wedding;
Hochzeitsreise *f* honeymoon.
hocken ['hɔkən] *vir* squat, crouch.
Hocker *m* -s, - stool.
Höcker ['hœkər] *m* -s, - hump.
Hoden ['ho:dən] *m* -s, - testicle.
Hof [ho:f] *m* -(e)s, ̈e (*Hinter~*) yard;
(*Bauern~*) farm; (*Königs~*) court.
hoffen ['hɔfən] *vi* hope (*auf* +*akk* for).
hoffentlich ['hɔfəntlɪç] *ad* I hope,
hopefully.
Hoffnung ['hɔfnʊŋ] *f* hope.
Hoffnungs- *zW*: **h~los** *a* hopeless;
~losigkeit *f* hopelessness; **~schimmer** *m* glimmer of hope; **h~voll** *a*
hopeful.
höflich ['hø:flɪç] *a* polite, courteous;
H~keit *f* courtesy, politeness.
hohe(r, s) ['ho:ə(r, s)] *a siehe* **hoch**.
Höhe ['hø:ə] *f* -, -n height; (*An~*) hill.
Hoheit ['ho:haɪt] *f* (*POL*) sovereignty;
(*Titel*) Highness.
Hoheitsgebiet *nt* sovereign territory.
Hoheitsgewässer *nt* territorial waters *pl*.
Höhen- ['hø:ən] *zW*: **~angabe** *f* altitude reading; (*auf Karte*) height
marking; **~messer** *m* -s, - altimeter;
~sonne *f* sun lamp; **~unterschied** *m*
difference in altitude.
Höhepunkt *m* climax.
höher *a*,*ad* higher.
hohl [ho:l] *a* hollow.
Höhle ['hø:lə] *f* -, -n cave, hole;
(*Mund~*) cavity; (*fig, ZOOL*) den.
Hohlheit *f* hollowness.
Hohlmaß *nt* measure of volume.
Hohn [ho:n] *m* -(e)s scorn.
höhnisch *a* scornful, taunting.
holen ['ho:lən] *vt* get, fetch; (*Atem*)
take; **jdn/etw ~ lassen** send for sb/
sth.
Holl- ['hɔl] *zW*: **~and** *nt* Holland;
~änder *m* Dutchman; **~änderin** *f*
Dutchwoman; **h~ändisch** *a* Dutch.
Hölle ['hœlə] *f* -, -n hell.
höllisch ['hœlɪʃ] *a* hellish, infernal.
holperig ['hɔlpərɪç] *a* rough, bumpy.

Holz [hɔlts] *nt* -es, ̈er wood.
hölzern ['hœltsərn] *a* (*lit, fig*) wooden.
Holz- *zW*: **~fäller** *m* -s, - lumberjack,
woodcutter; **h~ig** *a* woody; **~kohle** *f*
charcoal; **~scheit** *nt* log; **~schuh** *m*
clog; **~weg** *m* (*fig*) wrong track;
~wolle *f* fine wood shavings *pl*.
homosexuell [homozɛksu'ɛl] *a* homosexual.
Honig ['ho:nɪç] *m* -s, -e honey;
~wabe *f* honeycomb.
Honorar [hono'ra:r] *nt* -s, -e fee.
honorieren [hono'ri:rən] *vt* remunerate; (*Scheck*) honour.
Hopfen ['hɔpfən] *m* -s, - hops *pl*.
hopsen ['hɔpsən] *vi* hop.
Hör- ['hø:r] *zW*: **~apparat** *m* hearing
aid; **h~bar** *a* audible.
horch [hɔrç] *interj* listen; **~en** *vi* listen; (*pej*) eavesdrop.
Horde ['hɔrdə] *f* -, -n horde.
hören ['hø:rən] *vti* hear; **Musik/Radio**
~ listen to music/the radio.
Hörer *m* -s, - hearer; (*RAD*) listener;
(*UNIV*) student; (*Telefon~*) receiver.
Horizont [hori'tsɔnt] *m* -(e)s, -e horizon; **h~al** [-'ta:l] *a* horizontal.
Hormon [hɔr'mo:n] *nt* -s, -e hormone.
Hörmuschel *f* (*TEL*) earpiece.
Horn [hɔrn] *nt* -(e)s, ̈er horn; **~haut** *f*
horny skin.
Hornisse [hɔr'nɪsə] *f* -, -n hornet.
Horoskop [horo'sko:p] *nt* -s, -e horoscope.
Hörsaal *m* lecture room.
horten ['hɔrtən] *vt* hoard.
Hose ['ho:zə] *f* -, -n trousers *pl*, pants
(*US*) *pl*.
Hosen- *zW*: **~anzug** *m* trouser suit;
~rock *m* culottes *pl*; **~tasche** *f*
(trouser) pocket; **~träger** *m* braces
pl (*Brit*), suspenders (*US*) *pl*.
Hostie ['hɔstiə] *f* (*REL*) host.
Hotel [ho'tɛl] *nt* -s, -s hotel.
Hotelier [hoteli'e:] *m* -s, -s hotelkeeper, hotelier.
Hubraum *m* (*AUT*) cubic capacity.
hübsch [hʏpʃ] *a* pretty, nice.
Hubschrauber ['hu:bʃraubər] *m* -s, -
helicopter.
Huf ['hu:f] *m* -(e)s, -e hoof; **~eisen** *nt*
horseshoe; **~nagel** *m* horseshoe nail.
Hüft- ['hʏft] *zW*: **~e** *f* -, -n hip;
~gürtel *m*, **~halter** *m* -s, - girdle.
Hügel ['hy:gəl] *m* -s, - hill; **h~ig** *a*
hilly.
Huhn [hu:n] *nt* -(e)s, ̈er hen; (*KOCH*)
chicken.
Hühner- ['hy:nər] *zW*: **~auge** *nt* corn;
~brühe *f* chicken broth.
Hülle ['hʏlə] *f* -, -n cover(ing); wrapping; **in ~ und Fülle** galore; **h~n** *vt*
cover, wrap (*in* +*akk* with).
Hülse ['hʏlzə] *f* -, -n husk, shell;
Hülsenfrucht *f* pulse.

human [hu'ma:n] *a* humane; ~i'tär *a* humanitarian; **H~i'tät** *f* humanity.

Hummel ['hʊməl] *f* -, -n bumblebee.

Hummer ['hʊmər] *m* -s, - lobster.

Humor [hu'mo:r] *m* -s, -e humour; ~ haben have a sense of humour; ~ist [-'rɪst] *m* humorist; **h~istisch** *a*, **h~voll** *a* humorous.

humpeln ['hʊmpəln] *vi* hobble.

Humpen ['hʊmpən] *m* -s, - tankard.

Hund [hʊnt] *m* -(e)s, -e dog.

Hunde- ['hʊndə] *zW:* ~**hütte** *f* (dog) kennel; ~**kuchen** *m* dog biscuit; **h~müde** *a* (*umg*) dog-tired.

hundert ['hʊndərt] *num* hundred; **H~'jahrfeier** *f* centenary; ~**prozentig** *a,ad* one hundred per cent.

Hündin ['hʏndɪn] *f* bitch.

Hunger ['hʊŋər] *m* -s hunger; ~ haben be hungry; **h~n** *vi* starve; **Hungersnot** *f* famine; ~**streik** *m* hunger strike.

hungrig ['hʊŋrɪç] *a* hungry.

Hupe ['hu:pə] *f* -, -n horn; **h~n** *vi* hoot, sound one's horn.

hüpfen ['hʏpfən] *vi* hop, jump.

Hürde ['hʏrdə] *f* -, -n hurdle; (*für Schafe*) pen; **Hürdenlauf** *m* hurdling.

Hure ['hu:rə] *f* -, -n whore.

hurra [hu'ra:] *inter* hooray.

hurtig ['hʊrtɪç] *a,ad* brisk(ly), quick-(ly).

huschen ['hʊʃən] *vi* flit, scurry.

Husten ['hu:stən] *m* -s cough; **h~** *vi* cough; ~**anfall** *m* coughing fit; ~**bonbon** *m od nt* cough drop; ~**saft** *m* cough mixture.

Hut [hu:t] *m* -(e)s, -e hat // *f* - care; auf der ~ sein be on one's guard.

hüten ['hy:tən] *vt* guard // *vr* watch out; sich ~, zu take care not to; sich ~ vor beware of.

Hütte ['hʏtə] *f* -, -n hut, cottage; (*Eisen~*) forge.

Hyäne [hy'ɛ:nə] *f* -, -n hyena.

Hyazinthe [hya'tsɪntə] *f* -, -n hyacinth.

Hydrant [hy'drant] *m* hydrant.

hydraulisch [hy'draʊlɪʃ] *a* hydraulic.

Hygiene [hygi'e:nə] *f* - hygiene.

hygienisch [hygi'e:nɪʃ] *a* hygienic.

Hymne ['hʏmnə] *f* -, -n hymn, anthem.

hyper- ['hypɛr] *präf* hyper-.

Hypno- [hʏp'no:] *zW:* ~**se** *f* -, -n hypnosis; **h~tisch** *a* hypnotic; ~**tiseur** [-ti'zø:r] hypnotist; **h~ti'sieren** *vt* hypnotize.

Hypothek [hypo'te:k] *f* -, -en mortgage.

Hypothese [hypo'te:zə] *f* -, -n hypothesis.

hypothetisch [hypo'te:tɪʃ] *a* hypothetical.

Hysterie [hyste'ri:] *f* hysteria.

hysterisch [hɪs'te:rɪʃ] *a* hysterical.

I

I, i [i:] *nt* I, i.

i.A. *abk* (= *im Auftrag*) for; (*in Briefen auch*) pp.

ich [ɪç] *pron* I; ~ bin's! it's me!; **I~** *nt* -(s), -(s) self; (*PSYCH*) ego.

Ideal [ide'a:l] *nt* -s, -e ideal; **i~** *a* ideal; ~**ist** [-'lɪst] *m* idealist; **i~istisch** [-'lɪstɪʃ] *a* idealistic.

Idee [i'de:] *f* -, -n [i'de:ən] idea.

identifizieren [i'dɛntifi'tsi:rən] *vt* identify.

identisch [i'dɛntɪʃ] *a* identical.

Identität [idɛnti'tɛ:t] *f* identity.

Ideo- [ideo] *zW:* ~**loge** [-'lo:gə] *m* -n, -n ideologist; ~**logie** [-'lo'gi:] *f* ideology; **i~logisch** [-'lo:gɪʃ] *a* ideological.

Idiot [idi'o:t] *m* -en, -en idiot; **i~isch** *a* idiotic.

idyllisch [i'dʏlɪʃ] *a* idyllic.

Igel ['i:gəl] *m* -s, - hedgehog.

ignorieren [ɪgno'ri:rən] *vt* ignore.

ihm [i:m] *pron dat von* **er, es** (to) him, (to) it.

ihn [i:n] *pron akk von* **er** him; it; ~**en** *pron dat von* **sie** *pl* (to) them; **I~en** *pron dat von* **Sie** (to) you.

ihr [i:r] ◆*pron* **1** *nom pl* you; ~ seid es it's you

2 *dat von* **sie** sing to her; gib es ~ give it to her; er steht neben ~ he is standing beside her

◆*poss pron* **1** *sing* her; (*bei Tieren, Dingen*) its; ~ Mann her husband

2 *pl* their; die Bäume und ~e Blätter the trees and their leaves

ihr(e) [i:r(ə)] *poss pron* your; ~**e(r, s)** *poss pron sing* hers; its // *pl* theirs; **I~e(r, s)** *poss pron yours*; ~**er** *pron gen von* **sie** *sing/pl* of her/them; **I~er** *pron gen von* **Sie** of you; ~**erseits** *ad* for her/their part; ~**esgleichen** *pron* people like her/them; (*von Dingen*) others like it; ~**etwegen**, ~**etwillen** *ad* (*für sie*) for her/its/their sake; (*wegen ihr*) on her/its/their account; ~**ige** *pron*: **der/die/das** ~**ige** hers; its; theirs.

illegal ['ɪlegaːl] *a* illegal.

Illusion [ɪluzi'o:n] *f* illusion.

illusorisch [ɪlu'zo:rɪʃ] *a* illusory.

illustrieren [ɪlus'tri:rən] *vt* illustrate.

Illustrierte *f* -n, -n picture magazine.

Iltis ['ɪltɪs] *m* -ses, -se polecat.

im [ɪm] = in dem.

Imbiß ['ɪmbɪs] *m* -sses, -sse snack; ~**halle** *f*, ~**stube** *f* snack bar.

imitieren [ɪmi'ti:rən] *vt* imitate.

immatrikulieren [ɪmatriku'li:rən] *vir* register.

immer ['ɪmər] *ad* always; ~ wieder again and again; ~ noch still; ~ noch nicht still not; **für ~** forever; **~ wenn ich ... everytime I ...; ~ schöner/ trauriger** more and more beautiful/ sadder and sadder; **was/wer (auch) ~** whatever/whoever; **~hin** ad all the same; **~zu** all the time.

Immobilien [ımo'bi:liən] pl real estate.

immun [ı'mu:n] a immune; **I~ität** [-i'tɛ:t] f immunity.

Imperfekt ['ımpɛrfɛkt] nt -s, -e imperfect (tense).

Impf- ['ımpf] zW: **i~en** vt vaccinate; **~stoff** m vaccine, serum; **~ung** f vaccination; **~zwang** m compulsory vaccination.

imponieren [ımpo'ni:rən] vi impress (jdm sb).

Import [ım'pɔrt] m -(e)s, -e import; **i~ieren** [-'ti:rən] vt import.

impotent ['ımpotɛnt] a impotent.

imprägnieren [ımprɛ'gni:rən] vt (water)proof.

improvisieren [ımprovi'zi:rən] vti improvize.

Impuls [ım'pʊls] m -es, -e impulse; **i~iv** [-'zi:f] a impulsive.

imstande [ım'ʃtandə] a: **~ sein** be in a position; (fähig) be able.

in [ın] ◆präp +akk 1 (räumlich: wohin?) in, into; **~ die Stadt** into town; **~ die Schule gehen** go to school 2 (zeitlich): **bis ~s 20. Jahrhundert** into od up to the 20th century ◆präp +dat 1 (räumlich: wo) in; **~ der Stadt** in town; **~ der Schule sein** be at school 2 (zeitlich: wann): **~ diesem Jahr** this year; (~ jenem Jahr) in that year; **heute ~ zwei Wochen** two weeks today.

Inanspruchnahme [ın''anʃpruxna:mə] f -, **-n** demands pl (gen on).

Inbegriff ['ınbəgrıf] m embodiment, personification; **i~en** ad included.

indem [ın'de:m] kj while; **~ man etw macht** (dadurch) by doing sth.

Inder(in f) ['ındər(ın)] m Indian.

Indianer(in f) [ındi'a:nər(ın)] m -s, - Red Indian.

indianisch a Red Indian.

Indien ['ındiən] nt India.

indirekt ['ındirɛkt] a indirect.

indisch ['ındıʃ] a Indian.

indiskret ['ındıskre:t] a indiscreet.

indiskutabel ['ındısku'ta:bəl] a out of the question.

Individu- [ındividu] zW: **~alist** [-a'lıst] m individualist; **~alität** [-ali'tɛ:t] f individuality; **i~ell** [-'ɛl] a individual; **~um** [ındi'vi:duʊm] nt -s, **-en** individual.

Indiz [ın'di:ts] nt -es, **-ien** sign (für of); (JUR) clue.

Indonesien [ındo'ne:ziən] nt Indonesia.

industrialisieren [ındustriali'zi:rən] vt industrialize.

Industrie [ındʊs'tri:] f industry; **in** zW industrial; **~gebiet** nt industrial area; **~gelände** nt industrial od trading estate; **industriell** [ındustri'ɛl] a industrial; **~zweig** m branch of industry.

ineinander [ın'aı'nandər] ad in(to) one another od each other.

Infarkt [ın'farkt] m -(e)s, -e coronary (thrombosis).

Infektion [ınfɛktsi'o:n] f infection; **Infektionskrankheit** f infectious disease.

Infinitiv ['ınfiniti:f] m -s, -e infinitive.

infizieren [ınfi'tsi:rən] vt infect // vr be infected (bei by).

Inflation [ınflatsi'o:n] f inflation.

inflationär [ınflatsio'nɛ:r] a inflationary.

infolge [ın'fɔlgə] präp +gen as a result of, owing to; **~dessen** [-'dɛsən] ad consequently.

Informatik [ınfɔr'ma:tık] f information studies pl.

Information [ınfɔrmatsi'o:n] f information no pl.

informieren [ınfɔr'mi:rən] vt inform // vr find out (über +akk about).

Infusion [ınfuzi'o:n] f infusion.

Ingenieur [ınʒeni'ø:r] m engineer; **~schule** f school of engineering.

Ingwer ['ıŋvər] m -s ginger.

Inh. abk (= Inhaber) prop.; (= Inhalt) contents.

Inhaber(in f) ['ınha:bər(ın)] m -s, - owner; (Haus~) occupier; (Lizenz~) licensee, holder; (FIN) bearer.

inhalieren [ınha'li:rən] vti inhale.

Inhalt ['ınhalt] m -(e)s, -e contents pl; (eines Buchs etc) content; (MATH) area; volume; **i~lich** a as regards content.

Inhalts- zW: **~angabe** f summary; **i~los** a empty; **~sverzeichnis** nt table of contents.

inhuman ['ınhuma:n] a inhuman.

Initiative [initsia'ti:və] f initiative.

injektion [ınjɛktsi'o:n] f injection.

inklusive [ınklu'zi:və] präp, ad inclusive (gen of).

inkognito [ın'kɔgnito] ad incognito.

Inkrafttreten [ın'kraftre:tən] nt -s coming into force.

Inland ['ınlant] nt -(e)s (GEOG) inland; (POL, COMM) home (country).

inmitten [ın'mıtən] präp +gen in the middle of; **~ von** amongst.

innehaben ['ınəha:bən] vt unreg hold.

innen ['ınən] ad inside; **I~architekt** m interior designer; **I~einrichtung** f (interior) furnishings pl; **I~minister** m minister of the interior, Home Sec-

retary (Brit); I~politik f domestic policy; I~stadt f town/city centre.
inner- ['ɪnər] zW: ~e(r, s) a inner; (im Körper, inländisch) internal; I~e(s) nt inside; (Mitte) centre; (fig) heart; **Innereien** [-'raɪən] pl innards pl; ~halb ad, präp +gen within; (räumlich) inside; ~lich a internal; (geistig) inward; ~ste(s) nt heart; ~ste(r, s) a innermost.
inoffiziell ['ɪn'ɔfitsiɛl] a unofficial.
ins [ɪns] = **in das.**
Insasse ['ɪnzasə] m -n, -n (Anstalt) inmate; (AUT) passenger.
insbesondere [ɪnsbə'zɔndərə] ad (e)specially.
Inschrift ['ɪnʃrɪft] f inscription.
Insekt [ɪn'zɛkt] nt -(e)s, -en insect.
Insel ['ɪnzəl] f -, -n island.
Inser- zW: ~at [ɪnzə'ra:t] nt -(e)s, -e advertisement; ~ent [ɪnze'rɛnt] m advertiser; i~ieren [ɪnze'ri:rən] vti advertise.
insgeheim [ɪnsgə'haɪm] ad secretly.
insgesamt [ɪnsgə'zamt] ad altogether, all in all.
insofern ['ɪnzo'fɛrn], **insoweit** ['ɪnzo'vaɪt] ad in this respect; ~ als in so far as // kj (deshalb) (and) so.
Installateur [ɪnstala'tø:r] m electrician; plumber.
Instand- [ɪn'ʃtant] zW: ~haltung f maintenance; ~setzung f overhaul; (eines Gebäudes) restoration.
Instanz [ɪn'stants] f authority; (JUR) court; ~enweg m official channels pl.
Instinkt [ɪn'stɪŋkt] m -(e)s, -e instinct; i~iv [-'ti:f] a instinctive.
Institut [ɪnsti'tu:t] nt -(e)s, -e institute.
Instrument [ɪnstru'mɛnt] nt instrument.
Intell- [ɪntɛl] zW: i~ektuell [-ɛktu'ɛl] a intellectual; i~igent [-i'gɛnt] a intelligent; ~igenz [-i'gɛnts] f intelligence; (Leute) intelligentsia pl.
Intendant [ɪntɛn'dant] m director.
intensiv [ɪntɛn'zi:f] a intensive.
Interess- zW: i~ant [ɪntɛrɛ'sant] a interesting; i~anterweise ad interestingly enough; ~e [ɪntɛ'rɛsə] nt -s, -n interest; ~e haben be interested (an +dat in); ~ent [ɪntɛrɛ'sɛnt] m interested party; i~ieren [ɪntɛrɛ'si:rən] vt interest // vr be interested (für in).
Inter- [ɪntɛr] zW: ~nat [-'na:t] nt -(e)s, -e boarding school; i~national [-natsio'na:l] a international; i~pretieren [-pre'ti:rən] vt interpret; ~vall [-'val] nt -s, -e interval; ~view ['-vju:] nt -s, -s interview; i~viewen [-'vju:ən] vt interview.
intim [ɪn'ti:m] a intimate; I~ität [ɪntimi'tɛ:t] f intimacy.
intolerant ['ɪntolerant] a intolerant.

intransitiv ['ɪntranziti:f] a (GRAM) intransitive.
Intrige [ɪn'tri:gə] f -, -n intrigue, plot.
Invasion [ɪnvazi'o:n] f invasion.
Inventar [ɪnvɛn'ta:r] nt -s, -e inventory.
Inventur [ɪnvɛn'tu:r] f stocktaking; ~ machen stocktake.
investieren [ɪnvɛs'ti:rən] vt invest.
Investition [ɪnvɛstɪtsi'o:n] f investment.
Investmentgesellschaft [ɪn'vɛstmɛntgəzɛlʃaft] f unit trust.
inwiefern [ɪnvi'fɛrn], **inwieweit** [ɪnvi'vaɪt] ad how far, to what extent.
inzwischen [ɪn'tsvɪʃən] ad meanwhile.
Irak [i'ra:k] m -s: der ~ Iraq; i~sch a Iraqi.
Iran [i'ra:n] n -s: der ~ Iran; i~isch a Iranian.
irdisch ['ɪrdɪʃ] a earthly.
Ire ['i:rə] m -n, -n Irishman.
irgend ['ɪrgənt] ad at all; **wann/was/wer** ~ whenever/whatever/whoever; ~ jemand/etwas somebody/something; ~einer somebody/something; anybody/anything; ~ein(e,s) a some, any; ~einmal ad sometime or other; (fragend) ever; ~wann ad sometime; ~wer ad (umg) somebody; anybody; ~wie ad somehow; ~wo ad somewhere; anywhere; ~wohin ad somewhere (or other).
Irin ['i:rɪn] f Irishwoman.
Irland ['ɪrlant] nt -s Ireland.
Ironie [iro'ni:] f irony.
ironisch [i'ro:nɪʃ] a ironic(al).
irre ['ɪrə] a crazy, mad; I~(r) mf lunatic; ~führen vt mislead; ~machen vt confuse; ~n vir be mistaken; (umher~) wander, stray; **Irrenanstalt** f lunatic asylum.
irrig ['ɪrɪç] a incorrect, wrong.
Irr- zW: i~sinnig a mad, crazy; (umg) terrific; ~tum m -s, -tümer mistake, error; i~tümlich a mistaken.
Island ['i:slant] nt -s Iceland.
Isolation [izolatsi'o:n] f isolation; (ELEK) insulation.
Isolator [izo'la:tor] m insulator.
Isolier- [izo'li:r] zW: ~band nt insulating tape; i~en vt isolate; (ELEK) insulate; ~station f (MED) isolation ward; ~ung f isolation; (ELEK) insulation.
Israel ['ɪsrael] nt -s Israel; ~i [-'e:li] m -s, -s Israeli; ~isch a Israeli.
ißt v siehe **essen.**
ist v siehe **sein.**
Italien [i'ta:liən] nt -s Italy; ~er(in f) [-li'e:nər(ɪn)] m -s Italian; i~isch a Italian.
i.V. abk von **in Vertretung.**

J

J, j [jɔt] *nt* J, j.

ja [ja:] *adv* **1** yes; **haben Sie das gesehen?** — ~ **did you see it?** — yes(, I did); **ich glaube** ~ (yes) I think so
2 (*fragend*) really?; **ich habe gekündigt** — ~? I've quit — have you?; **du kommst,** ~? you're coming, aren't you?
3 sei ~ **vorsichtig** do be careful; **Sie wissen** ~, **daß ...** as you know, ...; **tu das** ~ **nicht!** don't do that!; **ich habe es** ~ **gewußt** I just knew it; ~, **also,** ... well you see ...

Jacht [jaxt] *f* -, **-en** yacht.

Jacke ['jakə] *f* -, **-n** jacket; (*Woll~*) cardigan.

Jackett [ʒa'kɛt] *nt* **-s, -s** od **-e** jacket.

Jagd [ja:kt] *f* -, **-en** hunt; (*Jagen*) hunting; **~beute** *f* kill; **~flugzeug** *nt* fighter; **~gewehr** *nt* sporting gun.

jagen ['ja:gən] *vi* hunt; (*eilen*) race // *vt* hunt; (*weg~*) drive (off); (*verfolgen*) chase.

Jäger ['jɛ:gər] *m* -s, - hunter.

jäh [jɛ:] *a* sudden, abrupt; (*steil*) steep, precipitous.

Jahr [ja:r] *nt* -(e)s, -e year; **j~elang** *ad* for years.

Jahres- *zW*: **~abonnement** *nt* annual subscription; **~abschluß** *m* end of the year; (*COMM*) annual statement of account; **~bericht** *m* annual report; **~hauptversammlung** *f* annual general meeting, AGM; **~wechsel** *m* turn of the year; **~zahl** *f* date, year; **~zeit** *f* season.

Jahr- *zW*: **~gang** *m* age group; (*von Wein*) vintage; **~'hundert** *nt* -s, -e century; **~'hundertfeier** *f* centenary.

jährlich ['jɛ:rlɪç] *a,ad* yearly.

Jahrmarkt *m* fair.

Jahr'zehnt *nt* decade.

Jähzorn ['jɛ:tsɔrn] *m* sudden anger; hot temper; **j~ig** *a* hot-tempered.

Jalousie [ʒalu'zi:] *f* venetian blind.

Jammer ['jamər] *m* -s misery; **es ist ein** ~, **daß ...** it is a crying shame that ...

jämmerlich ['jɛmərlɪç] *a* wretched, pathetic.

jammern *vi* wail // *vt* unpers: **es jammert jdn** it makes sb feel sorry.

jammerschade *a*: **es ist** ~ it is a crying shame.

Januar ['janua:r] *m* -s, -e January.

Japan ['ja:pan] *nt* -s Japan; **~er(in** *f*) [-'pa:nər(ɪn)] *m* -s Japanese; **j~isch** *a* Japanese.

Jargon [ʒar'gõ:] *m* -s, -s jargon.

jäten ['jɛ:tən] *vt*: **Unkraut** ~ weed.

jauchzen ['jauxtsən] *vi* rejoice, shout (with joy).

jaulen ['jaulən] *vi* howl.

jawohl [ja'vo:l] *ad* yes (of course).

Jawort ['ja:vɔrt] *nt* consent.

Jazz [dʒɛs] *m* - Jazz.

je [je:] ◆*ad* **1** (*jemals*) ever; **hast du so was** ~ **gesehen?** did you ever see anything like it?
2 (*jeweils*) every, each; **sie zahlten** ~ **3 Mark** they paid 3 marks each
◆*kj* **1:** ~ **nach** depending on; ~ **nachdem** it depends; ~ **nachdem, ob** ... depending on whether ...
2: ~ **eher, desto** od **um so besser** the sooner the better.

Jeans [dʒi:nz] *pl* jeans.

jede(r, s) ['je:də(r, s)] *a* every, each // *pron* everybody; (~ *einzelne*) each; **ohne** ~ **x** without any x.

jedenfalls *ad* in any case.

jedermann *pron* everyone.

jederzeit *ad* at any time.

jedesmal *ad* every time, each time.

jedoch [je'dɔx] *ad* however.

jemals ['je:ma:ls] *ad* ever.

jemand ['je:mant] *pron* somebody; anybody.

Jemen ['je:mən] *m* -s: **der** ~ the Yemen.

jene(r, s) ['je:nə(r, s)] *a* that // *pron* that one.

jenseits ['je:nzaits] *ad* on the other side // *präp* +*gen* on the other side of, beyond; **das J~** the hereafter, the beyond.

jetzig ['jɛtsɪç] *a* present.

jetzt [jɛtst] *ad* now.

je- *zW*: **~weilig** *a* respective; **~weils** *ad*: **~weils zwei zusammen** two at a time; **zu ~weils 5 DM** at 5 marks each; **~weils das erste** the first each time.

Jh. *abk von* Jahrhundert.

Jockei ['dʒɔkɛ] *m* -s, -s jockey.

Jod [jo:t] *nt* -(e)s iodine.

jodeln ['jo:dəln] *vi* yodel.

joggen ['dʒɔgən] *vi* jog.

Joghurt ['jo:gurt] *m* od *nt* -s, -s yogurt.

johlen ['jo:lən] *vi* yell.

Jolle ['jɔlə] *f* -, **-n** dinghy.

jonglieren [ʒõ'gli:rən] *vi* juggle.

Jordanien [jɔr'da:niən] *nt* -s Jordan.

Journal- [ʒurnal] *zW*: **~ismus** [-'lɪsmus] *m* journalism; **~ist(in** *f*) [-'lɪst] *m* journalist; **j~istisch** *a* journalistic.

Jubel ['ju:bəl] *m* -s rejoicing; **j~n** *vi* rejoice.

Jubiläum [jubi'lɛ:um] *nt* -s, **Jubiläen** anniversary, jubilee.

jucken ['jukən] *vi* itch // *vt* **es juckt**

mich am Arm my arm is itching; das juckt mich that's itchy.

Juckreiz ['jʊkraɪts] *m* itch.

Jude ['juːdə] *m* -n, -n Jew.

Judentum *nt* - Judaism; Jewry.

Judenverfolgung *f* persecution of the Jews.

Jüd- ['jyːd] *zW*: ~**in** *f* Jewess; **j~isch** *a* Jewish.

Judo ['juːdo] *nt* -(s) judo.

Jugend ['juːgənt] *f* - youth; ~**club** *m* youth club; ~**herberge** *f* youth hostel; ~**kriminalität** *f* juvenile crime; **j~lich** *a* youthful; ~**liche(r)** *mf* teenager, young person.

Jugoslaw- [jugɔ'slaːv] *zW*: ~**e** *m*, ~**in** *f* Yugoslavian; ~**ien** *nt* Yugoslavia; **j~isch** *a* Yugoslavian.

Juli ['juːli] *m* -(s), -s July.

jun. *abk* (= *junior*) jr.

jung [jʊŋ] *a* young; **J~e** *m* -n, -n boy, lad; **J~e(s)** *nt* young animal; (*pl*) young *pl*.

Jünger ['jʏŋər] *m* -s, - disciple; **j~** *a* younger.

Jungfer ['jʊŋfər] *f* -, -n: alte ~ old maid.

Jungfernfahrt *f* maiden voyage.

Jung- *zW*: ~**frau** *f* virgin; (*ASTROL*) Virgo; ~**geselle** *m* bachelor; ~**gesellin** *f* unmarried woman.

jüngst ['jʏŋst] *ad* lately, recently; ~**e(r, s)** *a* youngest; (*neueste*) latest.

Juni ['juːni] *m* -(s), -s June.

Junior ['juːniɔr] *m* -s, -en [-'oːrən] junior.

Jurist [ju'rɪst] *m* jurist, lawyer; **j~isch** *a* legal.

Justiz [jus'tiːts] *f* - justice; ~**beamte(r)** *m* judicial officer; ~**irrtum** *m* miscarriage of justice.

Juwel [ju've:l] *nt od m* -s, -en jewel.

Juwelier [juve'liːr] *m* -s, -e jeweller; ~**geschäft** *nt* jeweller's (shop).

Jux [jʊks] *m* -es, -e joke, lark.

K

K, k [kaː] *nt* K, k.

Kabarett [kaba'rɛt] *nt* -s, -e *od* -s cabaret; ~**ist** [-'tɪst] *m* cabaret artiste.

Kabel ['kaːbəl] *nt* -s, - (*ELEK*) wire; (*stark*) cable; ~**fernsehen** *nt* cable television.

Kabeljau ['kaːbəljaʊ] *m* -s, -e *od* -s cod.

kabeln *vti* cable.

Kabine [ka'biːnə] *f* cabin; (*Zelle*) cubicle.

Kabinett [kabi'nɛt] *nt* -s, -e (*POL*) cabinet.

Kachel ['kaxəl] *f* -, -n tile; **k~n** *vt* tile; ~**ofen** *m* tiled stove.

Käfer ['kɛːfər] *m* -s, - beetle.

Kaffee ['kafe] *m* -s, -s coffee; ~**kanne** *f* coffeepot; ~**klatsch** *m*, ~**kränzchen** *nt* hen party; coffee morning; ~**löffel** *m* coffee spoon; ~**satz** *m* coffee grounds *pl*.

Käfig ['kɛːfɪç] *m* -s, -e cage.

kahl [kaːl] *a* bald; ~**geschoren** *a* shaven, shorn; **K~heit** *f* baldness; ~**köpfig** *a* bald-headed.

Kahn [kaːn] *m* -(e)s, ⁼e boat, barge.

Kai [kaɪ] *m* -s, -e *od* -s quay.

Kaiser ['kaɪzər] *m* -s, - emperor; ~**in** *f* empress; **k~lich** *a* imperial; ~**reich** *nt* empire; ~**schnitt** *m* (*MED*) Caesarian (section).

Kakao [ka'kao] *m* -s, -s cocoa.

Kaktee [kak'teː(ə)] *f* -, -n, **Kaktus** ['kaktus] *m* -, -se cactus.

Kalb [kalp] *nt* -(e)s, ⁼er calf; **k~en** ['kalbən] *vi* calve; ~**fleisch** *nt* veal; **Kalbsleder** *nt* calf(skin).

Kalender [ka'lɛndər] *m* -s, - calendar; (*Taschen~*) diary.

Kaliber [ka'liːbər] *nt* -s, - (*lit, fig*) calibre.

Kalk [kalk] *m* -(e)s, -e lime; (*BIOL*) calcium; ~**stein** *m* limestone.

kalkulieren [kalku'liːrən] *vt* calculate.

Kalorie [kalo'riː] *f* calorie.

kalt [kalt] *a* cold; mir ist (es) ~ I am cold; ~**bleiben** *vi unreg* be unmoved; ~**blütig** *a* cold-blooded; (*ruhig*) cool.

Kälte ['kɛltə] *f* - cold; coldness; ~**grad** *m* degree of frost *od* below zero; ~**welle** *f* cold spell.

kalt- *zW*: ~**herzig** *a* cold-hearted; ~**schnäuzig** *a* cold, unfeeling; ~**stellen** *vt* chill; (*fig*) leave out in the cold.

kam *etc v siehe* kommen.

Kamel [ka'meːl] *nt* -(e)s, -e camel.

Kamera ['kamera] *f* -, -s camera.

Kamerad [kama'raːt] *m* -en, -en comrade, friend; ~**schaft** *f* comradeship; **k~schaftlich** *a* comradely.

Kamille [ka'mɪlə] *f* -, -n camomile.

Kamillentee *m* camomile tea.

Kamin [ka'miːn] *m* -s, -e (*außen*) chimney; (*innen*) fireside, fireplace; ~**feger**, ~**kehrer** *m* -s, - chimney sweep.

Kamm [kam] *m* -(e)s, ⁼e comb; (*Berg~*) ridge; (*Hahnen~*) crest.

kämmen ['kɛmən] *vt* comb // *vr* comb one's hair.

Kammer ['kamər] *f* -, -n chamber; small bedroom; ~**diener** *m* valet.

Kampagne [kam'panjə] *f* -, -n campaign.

Kampf [kampf] *m* -(e)s, ⁼e fight, battle; (*Wettbewerb*) contest; (*fig: Anstrengung*) struggle; **k~bereit** *a* ready for action.

kämpfen ['kɛmpfən] *vi* fight.

Kämpfer *m* -s, - fighter, combatant.

Kampf- zW: **~handlung** f action;
k~los a without a fight; **~richter** m
(SPORT) referee; (Tennis) umpire.

Kanada ['kanada] nt -s Canada.

Kanadier(in f) [ka'na:diər(in)] m -s, -
Canadian.

kanadisch [ka'na:dɪʃ] a Canadian.

Kanal [ka'na:l] m -s, **Kanäle** (Fluß)
canal; (Rinne, Ärmel~) channel;
(für Abfluß) drain; **~inseln** pl Channel Islands; **~isation** [-izatsi'o:n] f
sewage system.

Kanarienvogel [ka'na:riənfo:gəl] m canary.

kanarisch [ka'na:rɪʃ] a: K~e Inseln
Canary Islands, Canaries.

Kandi- [kandi] zW: **~dat** [-'da:t] m
-en, -en candidate; **~datur** [-da'tu:r] f
candidature, candidacy; **k~dieren**
[-'di:rən] vi stand, run.

Kandis(zucker) ['kandis(tsukər] m -
candy.

Känguruh ['kɛŋguru] nt -s, -s kangaroo.

Kaninchen [ka'ni:nçən] nt rabbit.

Kanister [ka'nɪstər] m -s, - can, canister.

Kännchen ['kɛnçən] nt pot.

Kanne ['kanə] f -, -n (Krug) jug;
(Kaffee~) pot; (Milch~) churn;
(Gieß~) can.

kannst etc v siehe **können**.

Kanon ['ka:nɔn] m -s, -s canon.

Kanone [ka'no:nə] f -, -n gun; (HIST)
cannon; (fig: Mensch) ace.

Kantate [kan'ta:tə] f -, -n cantata.

Kante ['kantə] f -, -n edge.

Kantine [kan'ti:nə] f canteen.

Kanu ['ka:nu] nt -s, -s canoe.

Kanzel ['kantsəl] f -, -n pulpit.

Kanzler ['kantslər] m -s, - chancellor.

Kap [kap] nt -s, -s cape; ~ der Guten
Hoffnung Cape of Good Hope.

Kapazität [kapatsi'tɛ:t] f capacity;
(Fachmann) authority.

Kapelle [ka'pɛlə] f (Gebäude) chapel;
(MUS) band.

kapieren [ka'pi:rən] vti (umg) understand.

Kapital [kapi'ta:l] nt -s, -e od -ien capital; **~anlage** f investment; **~ismus**
[-'lɪsmus] m capitalism; **~ist** [-'lɪst] m
capitalist; **k~istisch** a capitalist.

Kapitän [kapi'tɛ:n] m -s, -e captain.

Kapitel [ka'pɪtəl] nt -s, - chapter.

Kapitulation [kapitulatsi'o:n] f capitu-
lation.

kapitulieren [kapitu'li:rən] vi capitulate.

Kaplan [ka'pla:n] m -s, **Kapläne** chaplain.

Kappe ['kapə] f -, -n cap; (Kapuze)
hood; **k~n** vt cut.

Kapsel ['kapsəl] f -, -n capsule.

Kapstadt ['kapʃtat] nt -s Cape Town.

kaputt [ka'put] a (umg) kaput, broken; (Person) exhausted, finished;
am Auto ist etwas ~ there's something wrong with the car; **~gehen** vi
unreg break; (Schuhe) fall apart;
(Firma) go bust; (Stoff) wear out;
(sterben) cop it; **~machen** vt break;
(Mensch) exhaust, wear out.

Kapuze [ka'pu:tsə] f -, -n hood.

Karaffe [ka'rafə] f -, -n carafe; (ge-
schliffen) decanter.

Karamel [kara'mɛl] m -s caramel;
~bonbon m od nt toffee.

Karat [ka'ra:t] nt -(e)s, -e carat.

Karate [ka'ra:tə] nt -s karate.

Karawane [kara'va:nə] f -, -n caravan.

Kardinal [kardi'na:l] m -s, **Kardinäle**
cardinal; **~zahl** f cardinal number.

Karfreitag [ka:r'fraita:k] m Good Friday.

kärglich ['kɛrklɪç] a poor, scanty.

karibisch [ka'ri:bɪʃ] a: K~e Inseln
Caribbean Islands.

kariert [ka'ri:rt] a (Stoff) checked;
(Papier) squared.

Karies ['ka:ries] f - caries.

Karikatur [karika'tu:r] f caricature;
~ist [-'rɪst] m cartoonist.

Karneval ['karnəval] m -s, -e od -s
carnival.

Karo ['ka:ro] nt -s, -s square; (KAR-
TEN) diamonds; **~-As** nt ace of diamonds.

Karosserie [karɔsə'ri:] f (AUT)
body(work).

Karotte [ka'rɔtə] f -, -n carrot.

Karpaten [kar'pa:tən] pl Carpathians.

Karpfen ['karpfən] m -s, - carp.

Karre ['karə] f -, -n, **~n** m -s, - cart,
barrow.

Karriere [kari'ɛ:rə] f -, -n career; **~**
machen get on, get to the top;
~macher m -s, - careerist.

Karte ['kartə] f -, -n card; (Land~)
map; (Speise~) menu; (Eintritts~,
Fahr~) ticket; alles auf eine ~
setzen put all one's eggs in one basket.

Kartei [kar'tai] f card index; **~karte** f
index card.

Kartell [kar'tɛl] nt -s, -e cartel.

Kartenspiel nt card game; pack of
cards.

Kartoffel [kar'tɔfəl] f -, -n potato;
~brei m, **~mus** nt, **~püree** nt
mashed potatoes pl; **~salat** m potato
salad.

Karton [kar'tɔ̃:] m -s, -s cardboard;
(Schachtel) cardboard box; **k~iert**
[karto'ni:rt] a hardback.

Karussell [karu'sɛl] nt -s, -s
roundabout (Brit), merry-go-round.

Karwoche [ka:rvɔxə] f Holy Week.

Käse ['kɛ:zə] m -s, - cheese; **~blatt**
nt (umg) (local) rag; **~kuchen** m

cheesecake.

Kaserne [ka'zɛrnə] *f* -, **-n** barracks *pl*; **Kasernenhof** *m* parade ground.

Kasino [ka'zi:no] *nt* -s, -s club; (*MIL*) officers' mess; (*Spiel~*) casino.

kaspisch ['kaspiʃ] *a*: **K~es Meer** Caspian Sea.

Kasse ['kasə] *f* -, **-n** (*Geldkasten*) cashbox; (*in Geschäft*) till, cash register; (*Kino~, Theater~* etc) box office; ticket office; (*Kranken~*) health insurance; (*Spar~*) savings bank; ~ **machen** count the money; **getrennte** ~ **führen** pay separately; **an der** ~ (*in Geschäft*) at the desk; **gut bei** ~ **sein** be in the money.

Kassen- *zW*: **~arzt** *m* panel doctor (*Brit*); **~bestand** *m* cash balance; **~patient** *m* panel patient (*Brit*); **~prüfung** *f* audit; **~sturz** *m*: **~sturz machen** check one's money; **~zettel** *m* receipt.

Kassette [ka'sɛtə] *f* small box; (*Tonband, PHOT*) cassette; (*Bücher~*) case.

Kassettengerät *nt*, **Kassettenrecorder** *m* -s, - cassette recorder.

kassieren [ka'si:rən] *vt* take // *vi*: **darf ich ~?** would you like to pay now?

Kassierer [ka'si:rər] *m* -s, - cashier; (*von Klub*) treasurer.

Kastanie [kas'ta:niə] *f* chestnut; (*Baum*) chestnut tree.

Kasten ['kastən] *m* -s, ⁼ box (*Sport auch*), case; (*Truhe*) chest; **~wagen** *m* van.

kastrieren [kas'tri:rən] *vt* castrate.

Katalog [kata'lo:k] *m* -(e)s, -e catalogue.

Katalysator [kataly'za:tɔr] *m* catalyst.

Katarrh [ka'tar] *m* -s, -e catarrh.

katastrophal [katastro'fa:l] *a* catastrophic.

Katastrophe [kata'stro:fə] *f* -, **-n** catastrophe, disaster.

Kat-Auto ['kat'auto] *n* car fitted with a device for purifying exhaust fumes.

Kategorie [katego'ri:] *f* category.

kategorisch [kate'go:rɪʃ] *a* categorical.

Kater ['ka:tər] *m* -s, - tomcat; (*umg*) hangover.

kath. *abk* (= *katholisch*) Cath.

Kathedrale [kate'dra:lə] *f* -, **-n** cathedral.

Kathode [ka'to:də] *f* -, **-n** cathode.

Katholik [kato'li:k] *m* -en, -en Catholic.

katholisch [ka'to:lɪʃ] *a* Catholic.

Kätzchen ['kɛtsçən] *nt* kitten.

Katze ['katsə] *f* -, **-n** cat; **für die Katz** (*umg*) in vain, for nothing.

Katzen- *zW*: **~auge** *nt* cat's eye; (*Fahrrad*) rear light; **~jammer** *m* (*umg*) hangover; **~sprung** *m* (*umg*)

stone's throw; short journey.

Kauderwelsch ['kaudərvɛlʃ] *nt* -(s) jargon; (*umg*) double Dutch.

kauen ['kauən] *vti* chew.

Kauf [kauf] *m* -(e)s, **Käufe** purchase, buy; (*Kaufen*) buying; **ein guter** ~ a bargain; **etw in** ~ **nehmen** put up with sth; **k~en** *vt* buy.

Käufer(in *f*) ['kɔyfər(ın)] *m* -s, - buyer.

Kaufhaus *nt* department store.

Kaufkraft *f* purchasing power.

käuflich ['kɔyflıç] *a,ad* purchasable, for sale; (*pej*) venal; ~ **erwerben** purchase.

Kauf- *zW*: **k~lustig** *a* interested in buying; **~mann** *m*, *pl* **~leute** businessman; shopkeeper; **k~männisch** *a* commercial; **~männischer Angestellter** office worker.

Kaugummi ['kaugumi] *m* chewing gum.

Kaulquappe ['kaulkvapə] *f* -, **-n** tadpole.

kaum [kaum] *ad* hardly, scarcely.

Kaution [kautsi'o:n] *f* deposit; (*JUR*) bail.

Kauz [kauts] *m* -es, **Käuze** owl; (*fig*) queer fellow.

Kavalier [kava'li:r] *m* -s, -e gentleman, cavalier; **Kavaliersdelikt** *nt* peccadillo.

Kaviar ['ka:viar] *m* caviar.

keck [kɛk] *a* daring, bold; **K~heit** *f* daring, boldness.

Kegel ['ke:gəl] *m* -s, - skittle; (*MATH*) cone; **~bahn** *f* skittle alley; bowling alley; **k~n** *vi* play skittles.

Kehle ['ke:lə] *f* -, **-n** throat.

Kehlkopf *m* larynx.

Kehre ['ke:rə] *f* -, **-n** turn(ing), bend; **k~n** *vti* (*wenden*) turn; (*mit Besen*) sweep; **sich an etw** (*dat*) **nicht k~n** not heed sth.

Kehricht ['ke:rıçt] *m* -s sweepings *pl*.

Kehrmaschine *f* sweeper.

Kehrseite *f* reverse, other side; wrong side; bad side.

kehrtmachen *vi* turn about, about-turn.

keifen ['kaifən] *vi* scold, nag.

Keil [kail] *m* -(e)s, -e wedge; (*MIL*) arrowhead; **~riemen** *m* (*AUT*) fan belt.

Keim [kaim] *m* -(e)s, -e bud; (*MED, fig*) germ; **k~en** *vi* germinate; **k~frei** *a* sterile; **~zelle** *f* (*fig*) nucleus.

kein [kain] *a* no, not ... any; **~e(r, s)** *pron* no one, nobody; none.

keinesfalls *ad* on no account.

keineswegs *ad* by no means.

keinmal *ad* not once.

Keks [ke:ks] *m od nt* -es, -e biscuit.

Kelch [kɛlç] *m* -(e)s, -e cup, goblet, chalice.

Kelle ['kɛlə] f -, -n ladle; (Maurer~) trowel.

Keller ['kɛlər] m -s, - cellar; ~assel f -, -n woodlouse.

Kellner ['kɛlnər] m -s, - waiter; ~in f waitress.

keltern ['kɛltərn] vt press.

kennen ['kɛnən] vt unreg know; ~lernen vt get to know; sich ~lernen get to know each other; (zum ersten-mal) meet.

Kenner m -s, - connoisseur.

kenntlich a distinguishable, discern-ible; etw ~ machen mark sth.

Kenntnis f -, -se knowledge no pl; etw zur ~ nehmen note sth; von etw ~ nehmen take notice of sth; jdn in ~ setzen inform sb.

Kenn- zW: ~zeichen nt mark, charac-teristic; k~zeichnen vt insep charac-terize; ~ziffer f reference number.

kentern ['kɛntərn] vi capsize.

Keramik [ke'ra:mɪk] f -, -en ceramics pl, pottery.

Kerb- ['kɛrb] zW: ~e f -, -n notch, groove; k~en vt notch; ~holz nt: etw auf dem ~holz haben have done sth wrong.

Kerker ['kɛrkər] m -s, - prison.

Kerl [kɛrl] m -s, -e chap, bloke (Brit), guy; sie ist ein netter ~ she's a good sort.

Kern [kɛrn] m -(e)s, -e pip, stone; (Nuß~) kernel; (Atom~) nu-cleus; (fig) heart, core; ~energie f nuclear energy; ~forschung f nu-clear research; ~frage f central is-sue; k~gesund a thoroughly healthy, fit as a fiddle; k~ig a robust; (Aus-spruch) pithy; ~kraftwerk nt nuclear power station; k~los a seedless, pip-less; ~physik f nuclear physics; ~reaktion f nuclear reaction; ~schmelze f meltdown; ~spaltung f nuclear fission; ~waffen pl nuclear weapons pl.

Kerze ['kɛrtsə] f -, -n candle; (Zünd~) plug; **kerzengerade** a straight as a die; **Kerzenständer** m candle holder.

keß [kɛs] a saucy.

Kessel ['kɛsəl] m -s, - kettle; (von Lokomotive etc) boiler; (GEOG) de-pression; (MIL) encirclement.

Kette ['kɛtə] f -, -n chain; k~n vt chain.

Ketten- zW: ~laden m chain store; ~rauchen nt chain smoking; ~reaktion f chain reaction.

Ketzer ['kɛtsər] m -s, - heretic.

keuchen ['kɔʏçən] vi pant, gasp.

Keuchhusten m whooping cough.

Keule ['kɔʏlə] f -, -n club; (KOCH) leg.

keusch [kɔʏʃ] a chaste; K~heit f chastity.

kfm. abk von **kaufmännisch**.

Kfz [ka:'ɛf'tsɛt] abk von **Kraftfahrzeug**.

KG [ka:'ge:] abk (= Kommandit-gesellschaft) limited partnership.

kg abk von **Kilogramm**.

kichern ['kɪçərn] vi giggle.

kidnappen ['kɪdnɛpən] vt kidnap.

Kiefer ['ki:fər] m -s, - jaw // f -, -n pine; **Kiefernzapfen** m pine cone.

Kiel [ki:l] m -(e)s, -e (Feder~) quill; (NAUT) keel.

Kieme ['ki:mə] f -, -n gill.

Kies [ki:s] m -es, -e gravel; **Kiesel-stein** ['ki:zəlʃtaɪn] m pebble.

Kilo ['ki:lo] kilo; ~gramm [kilo'gram] nt -s, -e kilogram; ~meter [kilo-'me:tər] m kilometre; ~meterzähler m ≈ milometer.

Kind [kɪnt] nt -(e)s, -er child; von ~ auf from childhood.

Kinder- ['kɪndər] zW: ~ei f childish-ness; ~garten m nursery school, playgroup; ~geld nt family allow-ance; ~lähmung f poliomyelitis; k~leicht a childishly easy; k~los a childless; ~mädchen nt nursemaid; k~reich a with a lot of children; ~spiel nt child's play; ~tagesstätte f day-nursery; ~wagen m pram, baby carriage (US).

Kind- zW: ~heit f childhood; k~isch a childish; k~lich a childlike.

Kinn [kɪn] nt -(e)s, -e chin; ~haken m (Boxen) uppercut; ~lade f jaw.

Kino ['ki:no] nt -s, -s cinema; ~besucher m cinema-goer; ~pro-gramm nt film programme.

Kiosk ['ki:ɔsk] m -(e)s, -e kiosk.

Kipp- ['kɪp] zW: ~e f -, -n cigarette end; (umg) fag; auf der ~e stehen (fig) be touch and go; k~en vi topple over, overturn // vt tilt.

Kirch- ['kɪrç] zW: ~e f -, -n church; ~enlied nt hymn; ~gänger m -s, - churchgoer; ~hof m churchyard; k~lich a ecclesiastical; ~turm m church tower, steeple.

Kirmes ['kɪrmɛs] f -, -sen fair.

Kirsche ['kɪrʃə] f -, -n cherry.

Kissen ['kɪsən] nt -s, - cushion; (Kopf~) pillow; ~bezug m pillow-slip.

Kiste ['kɪstə] f -, -n box; chest.

Kitsch [kɪtʃ] m -(e)s trash; k~ig a trashy.

Kitt [kɪt] m -(e)s, -e putty; **Kittel** m -s, - overall, smock; **kitten** vt putty; (fig: Ehe etc) cement.

Kitz [kɪts] nt -es, -e kid; (Reh~) fawn.

kitzel- ['kɪtsəl] zW: ~ig a (lit, fig) ticklish; ~n vi tickle.

KKW [ka:ka:'ve:] nt abk von **Kern-kraftwerk**.

kläffen ['klɛfən] vi yelp.

Klage ['kla:gə] f -, -n complaint; (JUR) action; k~n vi (weh~) lament, wail;

(*sich beschweren*) complain; (*JUR*) take legal action.

Kläger(in *f*) ['klɛːgər(ɪn)] *m* -s, - plaintiff.

kläglich ['klɛːklɪç] *a* wretched.

klamm [klam] *a* (*Finger*) numb; (*feucht*) damp.

Klammer ['klamər] *f* -, -n clamp; (*in Text*) bracket; (*Büro~*) clip; (*Wäsche~*) peg; (*Zahn~*) brace; **k~n** *vr* cling (*an* +*akk* to).

Klang [klaŋ] *m* -(e)s, ⁻e sound; **k~voll** *a* sonorous.

Klappe ['klapə] *f* -, -n valve; (*Ofen~*) damper; (*umg: Mund*) trap; **k~n** *vi* (*Geräusch*) click // *vti* (*Sitz etc*) tip // *v unpers* work; **Klappentext** *m* blurb.

Klapper ['klapər] *f* -, -n rattle; **k~ig** *a* run-down, worn-out; **k~n** *vi* clatter, rattle; **~schlange** *f* rattlesnake; **~storch** *m* stork.

Klapp- *zW:* **~messer** *nt* jack-knife; **~rad** *nt* collapsible bicycle; **~stuhl** *m* folding chair; **~tisch** *m* folding table.

klar [klaːr] *a* clear; (*NAUT*) ready for sea; (*MIL*) ready for action; sich (*dat*) im **~en** sein über (+*akk*) be clear about; ins **~e** kommen get clear; (na) **~!** of course.

Klär- ['klɛːr] *zW:* **~anlage** *f* purification plant; **k~en** *vt* (*Flüssigkeit*) purify; (*Probleme*) clarify // *vr* clear (itself) up.

Klarheit *f* clarity.

Klarinette [klari'nɛtə] *f* clarinet.

klar- *zW:* **~legen** *vt* clear up, explain; **~machen** *vt* (*Schiff*) get ready for sea; jdm etw **~machen** make sth clear to sb; **~sehen** *vi unreg* see clearly; **K~sichtfolie** *f* transparent film; **~stellen** *vt* clarify.

Klärung ['klɛːrʊŋ] *f* purification; clarification.

Klasse ['klasə] *f* -, -n class; (*SCH auch*) form; **k~** *a* (*umg*) smashing.

Klassen- *zW:* **~arbeit** *f* test; **~bewußtsein** *nt* class consciousness; **~gesellschaft** *f* class society; **~kampf** *m* class conflict; **~lehrer** *m* form master; **~los** *a* classless; **~sprecher(in** *f*) *m* form prefect; **~zimmer** *nt* classroom.

klassifizieren [klasifi'tsiːrən] *vt* classify.

Klassik ['klasɪk] *f* (*Zeit*) classical period; (*Stil*) classicism; **~er** *m* -s, - classic.

klassisch *a* (*lit, fig*) classical.

Klatsch [klatʃ] *m* -(e)s, -e smack, crack; (*Gerede*) gossip; **~base** *f* gossip, scandalmonger; **~e** *f* -, -n (*umg*) crib; **k~en** *vi* (*Geräusch*) clash; (*reden*) gossip; (*Beifall*) applaud, clap; **~mohn** *m* (corn) poppy; **k~naß** *a*

soaking wet.

Klaue ['klauə] *f* -, -n claw; (*umg: Schrift*) scrawl; **k~n** *vt* claw; (*umg*) pinch.

Klausel ['klauzəl] *f* -, -n clause.

Klausur [klau'zuːr] *f* seclusion; **~arbeit** *f* examination paper.

Klaviatur [klavia'tuːr] *f* keyboard.

Klavier [kla'viːr] *nt* -s, -e piano.

Kleb- ['kleːb] *zW:* **k~en** *vt* stick (*an* +*akk* to); **k~rig** *a* sticky; **~stoff** *m* glue; **~streifen** *m* adhesive tape.

Klecks [klɛks] *m* -es, -e blot, stain; **k~en** *vi* blot; (*pej*) daub.

Klee [kleː] *m* -s clover; **~blatt** *nt* cloverleaf; (*fig*) trio.

Kleid [klait] *nt* -(e)s, -er garment; (*Frauen~*) dress // *pl* clothes *pl*; **k~en** ['klaidən] *vt* clothe, dress; (*auch vi*) suit // *vr* dress.

Kleider- ['klaidər] *zW:* **~bügel** *m* coat hanger; **~bürste** *f* clothes brush; **~schrank** *m* wardrobe.

Kleid- *zW:* **k~sam** *a* becoming; **~ung** *f* clothing; **~ungsstück** *nt* garment.

Kleie ['klaiə] *f* -, -n bran.

klein [klain] *a* little, small; **K~asien** *nt* Asia Minor; **K~e(r, s)** little one; **K~format** *nt* small size; im **K~format** small-scale; **K~geld** *nt* small change; **~hacken** *vt* chop up, mince; **K~igkeit** *f* trifle; **K~kind** *nt* infant; **K~kram** *m* details *pl*; **~laut** *a* dejected, quiet; **~lich** *a* petty, paltry; **Kleinod** ['klainoːt] *nt* -s, -odien gem, jewel; treasure; **~schneiden** *vt unreg* chop up; **~städtisch** *a* provincial; **kleinstmöglich** *a* smallest possible.

Kleister ['klaistər] *m* -s, - paste; **k~n** *vt* paste.

Klemme ['klɛmə] *f* -, -n clip; (*MED*) clamp; (*fig*) jam; **k~n** *vt* (*festhalten*) jam; (*quetschen*) pinch, nip // *vr* catch o.s.; (*sich hineinzwängen*) squeeze o.s.; sich hinter jdn/etw **k~n** get on to sb/get down to sth // *vi* (*Tür*) stick, jam.

Klempner ['klɛmpnər] *m* -s, - plumber.

Kleptomanie [klɛptoma'niː] *f* kleptomania.

Klerus ['kleːrʊs] *m* - clergy.

Klette ['klɛtə] *f* -, -n burr.

Kletter- ['klɛtər] *zW:* **~er** *m* -s, - climber; **k~n** *vi* climb; **~pflanze** *f* creeper.

Klient(in *f*) [kli'ɛnt(ɪn)] *m* client.

Klima ['kliːma] *nt* -s, -s *od* -te [kli'maːtə] climate; **~anlage** *f* air conditioning; **~wechsel** *m* change of air.

Klinge ['klɪŋə] *f* -, -n blade, sword.

Klingel ['klɪŋəl] *f* -, -n bell; **~beutel** *m* collection bag; **k~n** *vi* ring.

klingen ['klɪŋən] *vi unreg* sound; (*Gläser*) clink.

Klinik ['kliːnɪk] *f* hospital, clinic.

Klinke ['klɪŋkə] *f* -, -n handle.

Klippe ['klɪpə] *f* -, -n cliff; (*im Meer*) reef; (*fig*) hurdle.

klipp und klar ['klɪp'ʊntklaːr] *a* clear and concise.

Klips [klɪps] *m* -es, -e clip; (*Ohr~*) earring.

klirren ['klɪrən] *vi* clank, jangle; (*Gläser*) clink; **~de Kälte** biting cold.

Klischee [klɪ'ʃeː] *nt* -s, -s (*Druckplatte*) plate, block; (*fig*) cliché; **~vorstellung** *f* stereotyped idea.

Klo [kloː] *nt* -s, -s (*umg*) loo (*Brit*), john (*US*).

Kloake [klo'aːkə] *f* -, -n sewer.

klobig ['kloːbɪç] *a* clumsy.

klopfen ['klɔpfən] *vti* knock; (*Herz*) thump; **es klopft** somebody's knocking; **jdm auf die Schulter ~** tap sb on the shoulder // *vt* beat.

Klopfer *m* -s, - (*Teppich~*) beater; (*Tür~*) knocker.

Klops [klɔps] *m* -es, -e meatball.

Klosett [klo'zɛt] *nt* -s, -e *od* -s lavatory, toilet; **~papier** *nt* toilet paper.

Kloß [kloːs] *m* -es, ⁻e (*Erd~*) clod; (*im Hals*) lump; (*KOCH*) dumpling.

Kloster ['kloːstər] *nt* -s, ⁻ (*Männer~*) monastery; (*Frauen~*) convent.

klösterlich ['klø:stərlɪç] *a* monastic; convent.

Klotz [klɔts] *m* -es, ⁻e log; (*Hack~*) block; **ein ~ am Bein** (*fig*) drag, millstone round (sb's) neck.

Klub [klʊp] *m* -s, -s club; **~sessel** *m* easy chair.

Kluft [klʊft] *f* -, ⁻e cleft, gap; (*GEOL*) gorge, chasm.

klug [kluːk] *a* clever, intelligent; **K~heit** *f* cleverness, intelligence.

Klumpen ['klʊmpən] *m* -s, - (*Erd~*) clod; (*Blut~*) lump, clot; (*Gold~*) nugget; (*KOCH*) lump; **k~** *vi* go lumpy, clot.

km *abk von* **Kilometer**.

km/h *abk* (= *Kilometer je Stunde*) kph, ≈ mph.

knabbern ['knabərn] *vti* nibble.

Knabe ['knaːbə] *m* -n, -n boy; **knabenhaft** *a* boyish.

Knäckebrot ['knɛkəbroːt] *nt* crispbread.

knacken ['knakən] *vti* (*lit, fig*) crack.

Knall [knal] *m* -(e)s, -e bang; (*Peitschen~*) crack; **~ und Fall** (*umg*) unexpectedly; **~bonbon** *nt* cracker; **k~en** *vi* bang; crack; **k~rot** *a* bright red.

knapp [knap] *a* tight; (*Geld*) scarce; (*Sprache*) concise; **eine ~e Stunde** just under an hour; **~ unter/neben** just under/by; **~halten** *vt* unreg

stint; **K~heit** *f* tightness; scarcity; conciseness.

knarren ['knarən] *vi* creak.

knattern ['knatərn] *vi* rattle; (*MG*) chatter.

Knäuel ['knɔʏəl] *m od nt* -s, - (*Woll~*) ball; (*Menschen~*) knot.

Knauf [knaʊf] *m* -(e)s, **Knäufe** knob; (*Schwert~*) pommel.

knautschen ['knaʊtʃən] *vti* crumple.

Knebel ['kneːbəl] *m* -s, - gag; **k~n** *vt* gag; (*NAUT*) fasten.

kneifen ['knaɪfən] *vti unreg* pinch; (*sich drücken*) back out; **vor etw ~** dodge sth.

Kneipe ['knaɪpə] *f* -, -n (*umg*) pub.

kneten ['kneːtən] *vt* knead; (*Wachs*) mould.

Knick [knɪk] *m* -(e)s, -e (*Sprung*) crack; (*Kurve*) bend; (*Falte*) fold; **k~en** *vti* (*springen*) crack; (*brechen*) break; (*Papier*) fold; **geknickt sein** be downcast.

Knicks [knɪks] *m* -es, -e curtsey; **k~en** *vi* curtsey.

Knie [kniː] *nt* -s, - knee; **~beuge** *f* -, -n knee bend; **~fall** *m* genuflection; **~gelenk** *nt* knee joint; **~kehle** *f* back of the knee; **k~n** *vi* kneel; **~scheibe** *f* kneecap; **~strumpf** *m* knee-length sock.

Kniff [knɪf] *m* -(e)s, -e (*fig*) trick, knack; **kniffelig** *a* tricky.

knipsen ['knɪpsən] *vti* (*Fahrkarte*) punch; (*PHOT*) take a snap (of), snap.

Knirps [knɪrps] *m* -es, -e little chap; ® (*Schirm*) telescopic umbrella.

knirschen ['knɪrʃən] *vi* crunch; **mit den Zähnen ~** grind one's teeth.

knistern ['knɪstərn] *vi* crackle.

Knitter- ['knɪtər] *zW*: **~falte** *f* crease; **k~frei** *a* non-crease; **k~n** *vi* crease.

Knoblauch ['knoːplaʊx] *m* -(e)s garlic.

Knöchel ['knœçəl] *m* -s, - knuckle; (*Fuß~*) ankle.

Knochen ['knɔxən] *m* -s, - bone; **~bau** *m* bone structure; **~bruch** *m* fracture; **~gerüst** *nt* skeleton.

knöchern ['knœçərn] *a* bone.

knochig ['knɔxɪç] *a* bony.

Knödel ['knøːdəl] *m* -s, - dumpling.

Knolle ['knɔlə] *f* -, -n bulb.

Knopf [knɔpf] *m* -(e)s, ⁻e button; (*Kragen~*) stud; **~loch** *nt* buttonhole.

knöpfen ['knœpfən] *vt* button.

Knorpel ['knɔrpəl] *m* -s, - cartilage, gristle; **k~ig** *a* gristly.

Knospe ['knɔspə] *f* -, -n bud.

Knoten ['knoːtən] *m* -s, - knot; (*BOT*) node; (*MED*) lump; **k~** *vt* knot; **~punkt** *m* junction.

Knüller ['knʏlər] *m* -s, - (*umg*) hit; (*Reportage*) scoop.

knüpfen ['knʏpfən] *vt* tie; (*Teppich*) knot; (*Freundschaft*) form.

Knüppel ['knʏpəl] *m* -s, - cudgel; (*Polizei~*) baton, truncheon; (*AVIAT*) (joy)stick; **~schaltung** *f* (*AUT*) floor-mounted gear change.

knurren ['knʊrən] *vi* (*Hund*) snarl, growl; (*Magen*) rumble; (*Mensch*) mutter.

knusperig ['knʊspəriç] *a* crisp; (*Keks*) crunchy.

k.o. [ka:'o:] *a* (*lit*) knocked out; (*fig*) done in.

Koalition [koalitsi'o:n] *f* coalition.

Kobalt ['ko:balt] *nt* -s cobalt.

Kobold ['ko:bɔlt] *m* -(e)s, -e goblin, imp.

Kobra ['ko:bra] *f* -, -s cobra.

Koch [kɔx] *m* -(e)s, -̈e cook; **~buch** *nt* cook(ery) book; **k~en** *vti* cook; (*Wasser*) boil; **~er** *m* -s, - stove, cooker.

Köcher ['kœçər] *m* -s, - quiver.

Kochgelegenheit ['kɔxgəle:gənhaɪt] *f* cooking facilities *pl*.

Köchin ['kœçɪn] *f* cook.

Koch- *zW*: **~löffel** *m* kitchen spoon; **~nische** *f* kitchenette; **~platte** *f* boiling ring, hotplate; **~salz** *nt* cooking salt; **~topf** *m* saucepan, pot.

Köder ['kø:dər] *m* -s, - bait, lure.

Koexistenz [kɔɛksɪs'tɛnts] *f* coexistence.

Koffein [kɔfe'i:n] *nt* -s caffeine; **k~frei** *a* decaffeinated.

Koffer ['kɔfər] *m* -s, - suitcase; (*Schrank~*) trunk; **~radio** *nt* portable radio; **~raum** *m* (*AUT*) boot (*Brit*), trunk (*US*).

Kognak ['kɔnjak] *m* -s, -s brandy, cognac.

Kohl [ko:l] *m* -(e̱)s, -e cabbage.

Kohle ['ko:lə] *f* -, -n coal; (*Holz~*) charcoal; (*CHEM*) carbon; **~hydrat** *nt* -(e)s, -e carbohydrate.

Kohlen- *zW*: **~dioxyd** *nt* -(e)s, -e carbon dioxide; **~händler** *m* coal merchant, coalman; **~säure** *f* carbon dioxide; **~stoff** *m* carbon.

Kohlepapier *nt* carbon paper.

kohlrübe *f* turnip.

Koje ['ko:jə] *f* -, -n cabin; (*Bett*) bunk.

Kokain [koka'i:n] *nt* -s cocaine.

kokett [ko'kɛt] *a* coquettish, flirtatious.

Kokosnuß ['ko:kɔsnʊs] *f* coconut.

Koks [ko:ks] *m* -es, -e coke.

Kolben ['kɔlbən] *m* -s, - (*Gewehr~*) rifle butt; (*Keule*) club; (*CHEM*) flask; (*TECH*) piston; (*Mais~*) cob.

Kolchose [kɔl'ço:zə] *f* -, -n collective farm.

Kolik ['ko:lɪk] *f* colic, gripe.

Kollaps [ko'laps] *m* -es, -e collapse.

Kolleg [kɔl'e:k] *nt* -s, -s *od* -ien lecture course; **~e** [kɔ'le:gə] *m* -n, -n, **~in** *f* colleague; **~ium** *nt* board; (*SCH*) staff.

Kollekte [kɔ'lɛktə] *f* -, -n (*REL*) collection.

kollektiv [kɔlɛk'ti:f] *a* collective.

Kollision [kɔlizi'o:n] *f* collision; (*zeitlich*) clash.

Köln [kœln] *nt* -s Cologne.

Kolonie [kolo'ni:] *f* colony.

kolonisieren [koloni'zi:rən] *vt* colonize.

Kolonne [ko'lɔnə] *f* -, -n column; (*von Fahrzeugen*) convoy.

Koloß [ko'lɔs] *m* -sses, -sse colossus.

kolossal [kolɔ'sa:l] *a* colossal.

Kombi- ['kɔmbi] *zW*: **~nation** [-natsi'o:n] *f* combination; (*Vermutung*) conjecture; (*Hemdhose*) combinations *pl*; **~nationsschloß** *nt* combination lock; **k~nieren** [-'ni:rən] *vt* combine // *vi* deduce, work out; (*vermuten*) guess; **~wagen** *m* station wagon; **~zange** *f* (pair of) pliers.

Komet [ko'me:t] *m* -en, -en comet.

Komfort [kɔm'fo:r] *m* -s luxury.

Komik ['ko:mɪk] *f* humour, comedy; **~er** *m* -s, - comedian.

komisch ['ko:mɪʃ] *a* funny.

Komitee [komi'te:] *nt* -s, -s committee.

Komma ['kɔma] *nt* -s, -s *od* -ta comma; 2 ~ 3 2 point 3.

Kommand- [kɔ'mand] *zW*: **~ant** [-'dant] *m* commander, commanding officer; **~eur** [-'dø:r] *m* commanding officer; **k~ieren** [-'di:rən] *vti* command; **Kommando** *nt* -s, -s command, order; (*Truppe*) detachment, squad; **auf Kommando** to order.

kommen ['kɔmən] *vi unreg* come; (*näher~*) approach; (*passieren*) happen; (*gelangen, geraten*) get; (*Blumen, Zähne, Tränen etc*) appear; (*in die Schule, das Zuchthaus etc*) go; ~ **lassen** send for; **das kommt in den Schrank** that goes in the cupboard; **zu sich** ~ come round *od* to; **zu etw** ~ acquire sth; **um etw** ~ lose sth; **nichts auf jdn/etw** ~ **lassen** have nothing said against sb/sth; **jdm frech** ~ get cheeky with sb; **auf jeden vierten kommt ein Platz** there's one place for every fourth person; **wer kommt zuerst?** who's first?; **unter ein Auto** ~ be run over by a car; **wie hoch kommt das?** what does that cost?; **komm gut nach Hause!** safe journey (home); **~den Sonntag** next Sunday; **K~** *nt* -s coming.

Kommentar [kɔmɛn'ta:r] *m* commentary; **kein** ~ no comment; **k~los** *a* without comment.

Kommentator [kɔmɛn'ta:tor] *m* (*TV*) commentator.

kommentieren [kɔmɛn'tiːrən] *vt* comment on.

kommerziell [kɔmɛrtsi'ɛl] *a* commercial.

kommilitone [kɔmili'toːnə] *m* -n, -n fellow student.

Kommissar [kɔmɪ'saːr] *m* police inspector.

Kommission [kɔmɪsi'oːn] *f* (*COMM*) commission; (*Ausschuß*) committee.

Kommode [kɔ'moːdə] *f* -, -n (chest of) drawers.

Kommunalsteuer [kɔmu'naːlʃtɔyər] *f* rates *pl*.

Kommune [kɔ'muːnə] *f* -, -n commune.

Kommunikation [kɔmunɪkatsi'oːn] *f* communication.

Kommunion [kɔmuni'oːn] *f* communion.

Kommuniqué [kɔmyni'keː] *nt* -s, -s communiqué.

Kommunismus [kɔmu'nɪsmus] *m* communism.

Kommunist(in *f*) [kɔmu'nɪst(ɪn)] *m* communist; **k~isch** *a* communist.

kommunizieren [kɔmuni'tsiːrən] *vi* communicate; (*ECCL*) receive communion.

Komödie [ko'møːdiə] *f* comedy.

Kompagnon [kɔmpan'jõ] *m* -s, -s (*COMM*) partner.

kompakt [kɔm'pakt] *a* compact.

Kompanie [kɔmpa'niː] *f* company.

Kompaß ['kɔmpas] *m* -sses, -sse compass.

kompatibel [kɔmpa'tiːbəl] *a* compatible.

kompetent [kɔmpe'tɛnt] *a* competent.

Kompetenz *f* competence, authority.

komplett [kɔm'plɛt] *a* complete.

Komplikation [kɔmplikatsi'oːn] *f* complication.

Kompliment [kɔmpli'mɛnt] *nt* compliment.

Komplize [kɔm'pliːtsə] *m* -n, -n accomplice.

kompliziert [kɔmpli'tsiːrt] *a* complicated.

komponieren [kɔmpo'niːrən] *vt* compose.

Komponist [kɔmpo'nɪst] *m* composer.

Komposition [kɔmpozitsi'oːn] *f* composition.

Kompost [kɔm'pɔst] *m* -(e)s, -e compost.

Kompott [kɔm'pɔt] *nt* -(e)s, -e stewed fruit.

Kompromiß [kɔmpro'mɪs] *m* -sses, -sse compromise; **k~bereit** *a* willing to compromise; **~lösung** *f* compromise solution.

Kondens- [kɔn'dɛns] *zW*: **~ation** [kɔndɛnzatsi'oːn] *f* condensation; **~ator** [kɔndɛn'zaːtɔr] *m* condenser;

k~ieren [kɔndɛn'ziːrən] *vt* condense; **~milch** *f* condensed milk.

Konditionstraining [kɔnditsi'oːnstrɛːnɪŋ] *nt* fitness training.

Konditor [kɔn'diːtɔr] *m* pastrycook; **Konditorei** [kɔndito'raɪ] *f* café; cake shop.

Kondom [kɔn'doːm] *nt* -s, -e condom.

Konferenz [kɔnfe'rɛnts] *f* conference, meeting.

Konfession [kɔnfɛsi'oːn] *f* religion; (*christlich*) denomination; **k~ell** [-'nɛl] *a* denominational; **konfessionslos** *a* non-denominational.

Konfetti [kɔn'fɛti] *nt* -(s) confetti.

Konfirmand [kɔnfɪr'mant] *m* candidate for confirmation.

Konfirmation [kɔnfɪrmatsi'oːn] *f* (*ECCL*) confirmation.

konfirmieren [kɔnfɪr'miːrən] *vt* confirm.

konfiszieren [kɔnfɪs'tsiːrən] *vt* confiscate.

Konfitüre [kɔnfi'tyːrə] *f* -, -n jam.

Konflikt [kɔn'flɪkt] *m* -(e)s, -e conflict.

konfrontieren [kɔnfrɔn'tiːrən] *vt* confront.

konfus [kɔn'fuːs] *a* confused.

Kongreß [kɔn'grɛs] *m* -sses, -sse congress.

Kongruenz [kɔngru'ɛnts] *f* agreement, congruence.

König ['køːnɪç] *m* -(e)s, -e king; **~in** ['køːnɪgɪn] *f* queen; **k~lich** *a* royal; **~reich** *nt* kingdom; **~tum** *nt* -(e)s, -tümer kingship.

Konjugation [kɔnjugatsi'oːn] *f* conjugation.

konjugieren [kɔnju'giːrən] *vt* conjugate.

Konjunktion [kɔnjuŋktsi'oːn] *f* conjunction.

Konjunktiv ['kɔnjuŋktiːf] *m* -s, -e subjunctive.

Konjunktur [kɔnjuŋk'tuːr] *f* economic situation; (*Hoch~*) boom.

konkav [kɔn'kaːf] *a* concave.

konkret [kɔn'kreːt] *a* concrete.

Konkurrent(in *f*) [kɔnku'rɛnt(ɪn)] *m* competitor.

Konkurrenz [kɔnku'rɛnts] *f* competition; **k~fähig** *a* competitive; **~kampf** *m* competition; (*umg*) rat race.

konkurrieren [kɔnku'riːrən] *vi* compete.

Konkurs [kɔn'kurs] *m* -es, -e bankruptcy.

können ['kœnən] *vti pt* **konnte**, *ptp* **gekonnt** *od* (*als Hilfsverb*) **können 1** be able to; **ich kann es machen** I can do it, I am able to do it; **ich kann es nicht machen** I can't do it, I'm not able to do it; **ich kann nicht ...** I can't ..., I cannot ...; **ich kann nicht**

mehr I can't go on
2 (*wissen, beherrschen*) know; ~ **Sie Deutsch?** can you speak German?; **er kann gut Englisch** he speaks English well; **sie kann keine Mathematik** she can't do mathematics
3 (*dürfen*) to be allowed to; **kann ich gehen?** can I go?; **könnte ich ...? could I ...?; kann ich mit?** (*umg*) can I come with you?
4 (*möglich sein*): **Sie könnten recht haben** you may be right; **das kann sein** that's possible; **kann sein** maybe.
Können ['kœnən] *nt* **-s** ability.
konnte *etc v siehe* **können.**
konsequent [kɔnze'kvɛnt] *a* consistent.
Konsequenz [kɔnze'kvɛnts] *f* consistency; (*Folgerung*) conclusion.
Konserv- [kɔn'zɛrv] *zW:* **k~ativ** [-a'ti:f] *a* conservative; **~ative(r)** [-a'ti:və(r)] *mf* (*POL*) conservative; **~e** *f -, -n* tinned food; **~enbüchse** *f* tin, can; **k~ieren** [-'vi:rən] *vt* preserve; **~ierung** *f* preservation; **~ierungsmittel** *nt* preservative.
Konsonant [kɔnzo'nant] *m* consonant.
konstant [kɔn'stant] *a* constant.
konstruieren [kɔnstru'i:rən] *vt* construct.
Konstrukteur [kɔnstruk'tø:r] *m* engineer, designer.
Konstruktion [kɔnstruktsi'o:n] *f* construction.
konstruktiv [kɔnstruk'ti:f] *a* constructive.
Konsul ['kɔnzʊl] *m* **-s, -n** consul; **~at** [-'la:t] *nt* consulate.
konsultieren [kɔnzʊl'ti:rən] *vt* consult.
Konsum [kɔn'zu:m] *m* **-s** consumption; **~artikel** *m* consumer article; **~ent** [-'mɛnt] *m* consumer; **k~ieren** [-'mi:rən] *vt* consume.
Kontakt [kɔn'takt] *m* **-(e)s, -e** contact; **k~arm** *a* unsociable; **k~freudig** *a* sociable; **~linsen** *pl* contact lenses *pl.*
kontern ['kɔntərn] *vti* counter.
Kontinent ['kɔntinɛnt] *m* continent.
Kontingent [kɔntɪŋ'gɛnt] *nt* **-(e)s, -e** quota; (*Truppen~*) contingent.
kontinuierlich [kɔntinu'i:rlɪç] *a* continuous.
Konto ['kɔnto] *nt* **-s, Konten** account; **~auszug** *m* statement (of account); **~inhaber(in** *f*) *m* account holder; **~stand** *m* balance.
Kontra ['kɔntra] *nt* **-s, -s** (*KARTEN*) double; **jdm ~ geben** (*fig*) contradict sb; **~baß** *m* double bass; **Kontrahent** [-'hɛnt] *m* contracting party; **~punkt** *m* counterpoint.
Kontrast [kɔn'trast] *m* **-(e)s, -e** contrast.
Kontroll- [kɔn'trɔl] *zW:* **~e** *f -, -n* con-

trol, supervision; (*Paß~*) passport control; **~eur** [-'lo:r] *m* inspector; **k~ieren** [-'li:rən] *vt* control, supervise; (*nachprüfen*) check.
Kontur [kɔn'tu:r] *f* contour.
Konvention [kɔnvɛntsi'o:n] *f* convention; **k~ell** [-'nɛl] *a* conventional.
Konversation [kɔnvɛrzatsi'o:n] *f* conversation; **Konversationslexikon** *nt* encyclopaedia.
konvex [kɔn'vɛks] *a* convex.
Konvoi ['kɔnvɔy] *m* **-s, -s** convoy.
Konzentration [kɔntsɛntratsi'o:n] *f* concentration.
konzentrieren [kɔntsɛn'tri:rən] *vtr* concentrate.
konzentriert *a* concentrated // *ad* (*zuhören, arbeiten*) intently.
Konzept [kɔn'tsɛpt] *nt* **-(e)s, -e** rough draft; **jdn aus dem ~ bringen** confuse sb.
Konzern [kɔn'tsɛrn] *m* **-s, -e** combine.
Konzert [kɔn'tsɛrt] *nt* **-(e)s, -e** concert; (*Stück*) concerto; **~saal** *m* concert hall.
Konzession [kɔntsɛsi'o:n] *f* licence; (*Zugeständnis*) concession.
Konzil [kɔn'tsi:l] *nt* **-s, -e** *od* **-ien** council.
kooperativ [ko'opera'ti:f] *a* cooperative.
koordinieren [ko'ɔrdi'ni:rən] *vt* coordinate.
Kopf [kɔpf] *m* **-(e)s, ̈-e** head; **~bedeckung** *f* headgear; **~ haut** *f* scalp; **~hörer** *m* headphones *pl*; **~kissen** *nt* pillow; **k~los** *a* panicstricken; **k~rechnen** *vi* do mental arithmetic; **~salat** *m* lettuce; **~schmerzen** *pl* headache; **~sprung** *m* header, dive; **~tuch** *nt* headscarf; **~weh** *nt* headache; **~zerbrechen** *nt*: **jdm ~zerbrechen machen** give sb a lot of headaches.
Kopie [ko'pi:] *f* copy; **k~ren** *vt* copy.
Koppel ['kɔpəl] *f -, -n* (*Weide*) enclosure // *nt* **-s, -** (*Gürtel*) belt; **k~n** *vt* couple; **~ung** *f* coupling.
Koralle [ko'ralə] *f -, -n* coral; **Korallenriff** *nt* coral reef.
Korb [kɔrp] *m* **-(e)s, ̈-e** basket; **jdm einen ~ geben** (*fig*) turn sb down; **~ball** *m* basketball; **~stuhl** *m* wicker chair.
Kord [kɔrt] *m* **-(e)s, -e** corduroy.
Kordel ['kɔrdəl] *f -, -n* cord, string.
Kork [kɔrk] *m* **-(e)s, -e** cork; **~en** *m* **-s, -** stopper, cork; **~enzieher** *m* **-s, -** corkscrew.
Korn [kɔrn] *nt* **-(e)s, ̈-er** corn, grain; (*Gewehr*) sight; **~blume** *f* cornflower.
Körper ['kœrper] *m* **-s, -** body; **~bau** *m* build; **k~behindert** *a* disabled; **~gewicht** *nt* weight; **~größe** *f*

height; **k~lich** a physical; **~pflege** f personal hygiene; **~schaft** f corporation; **~schaftssteuer** f corporation tax; **~teil** m part of the body.

korpulent [kɔrpu'lɛnt] a corpulent.

korrekt [kɔ'rɛkt] a correct; **K~or** m proofreader; **K~ur** [-'tuːr] f (*eines Textes*) proofreading; (*Text*) proof; (*SCH*) marking, correction.

Korrespond- [kɔrɛspɔnd] zW: **~ent(in** f) [-'dɛnt(ɪn)] m correspondent; **~enz** [-'dɛnts] f correspondence; **k~ieren** [-'diːrən] vi correspond.

Korridor ['kɔridoːr] m **-s, -e** corridor.

korrigieren [kɔri'giːrən] vt correct.

Korruption [kɔruptsi'oːn] f corruption.

Korsett [kɔr'zɛt] nt **-(e)s, -s** corset.

Kose- ['koːzə] zW: **~form** f pet form; **~name** m pet name; **~wort** nt term of endearment.

Kosmetik [kɔs'meːtik] f cosmetics pl; **~erin** f beautician.

kosmetisch a cosmetic; (*Chirurgie*) plastic.

kosmisch ['kɔsmiʃ] a cosmic.

Kosmo- ['kɔsmo] zW: **~naut** [-'naut] m **-en, -en** cosmonaut; **~polit** [-po'liːt] m **-en, -en** cosmopolitan; **k~politisch** [-po'liːtiʃ] a cosmopolitan; **Kosmos** ['kɔsmɔs] m - cosmos.

Kost [kɔst] f - (*Nahrung*) food; (*Verpflegung*) board; **k~bar** a precious; (*teuer*) costly, expensive; **~barkeit** f preciousness; costliness, expensiveness; (*Wertstück*) valuable.

Kosten pl cost(s); (*Ausgaben*) expenses pl; **auf ~** von at the expense of; **k~** vt cost was kostet ...? what does ... cost?, how much is ...? // (*versuchen*) taste; **~anschlag** m estimate; **k~los** a free (of charge).

köstlich ['kœstliç] a precious; (*Einfall*) delightful; (*Essen*) delicious; **sich ~ amüsieren** have a marvellous time.

Kost- zW: **~probe** f taste; (*fig*) sample; **k~spielig** a expensive.

Kostüm [kɔs'tyːm] nt **-s, -e** costume; (*Damen~*) suit; **~fest** nt fancy-dress party; **k~ieren** [kɔsty'miːrən] vtr dress up; **~verleih** m costume agency.

Kot [koːt] m **-(e)s** excrement.

Kotelett [kɔtə'lɛt] nt **-(e)s, -e** od **-s** cutlet, chop; **~en** pl sideboards pl.

Köter ['køːtər] m **-s, -** cur.

Kotflügel m (*AUT*) wing.

Krabbe ['krabə] f -, **-n** shrimp; **krabbeln** vi crawl.

Krach [krax] m **-(e)s, -s** od **-e** crash; (*andauernd*) noise; (*umg: Streit*) quarrel, argument; **k~en** vi crash; (*beim Brechen*) crack // vr (*umg*) argue, quarrel.

krächzen ['krɛçtsən] vi croak.

Kraft [kraft] f -, **-e** strength, power, force; (*Arbeits~*) worker; **in ~ treten** come into effect; **k~** präp +gen by virtue of; **~fahrer** m motor driver; **~fahrzeug** nt motor vehicle; **~fahrzeugbrief** m logbook; **~fahrzeugsteuer** f ≈ road tax.

kräftig ['krɛftiç] a strong; **~en** [krɛftigən] vt strengthen.

Kraft- zW: **k~los** a weak; powerless; (*JUR*) invalid; **~probe** f trial of strength; **k~voll** a vigorous; **~wagen** m motor vehicle; **~werk** nt power station.

Kragen ['kraːgən] m **-s, -** collar; **~weite** f collar size.

Krähe ['krɛːə] f -, **-n** crow; **k~n** vi crow.

Kralle ['kralə] f -, **-n** claw; (*Vogel~*) talon; **k~n** vt clutch; (*krampfhaft*) claw.

Kram [kraːm] m **-(e)s** stuff, rubbish; **k~en** vi rummage; **~laden** m (*pej*) small shop.

Krampf [krampf] m **-(e)s, -e** cramp; (*zuckend*) spasm; **~ader** f varicose vein; **k~haft** a convulsive; (*fig: Versuche*) desperate.

Kran [kraːn] m **-(e)s, -e** crane; (*Wasser~*) tap.

Kranich ['kraːniç] m **-s, -e** (*ZOOL*) crane.

krank [kraŋk] a ill, sick; **K~e(r)** mf sick person; invalid, patient.

kranken ['kraŋkən] vi: **an etw** (*dat*) **~** (*fig*) suffer from sth.

kränken ['krɛŋkən] vt hurt.

Kranken- zW: **~bericht** m medical report; **~geld** nt sick pay; **~haus** nt hospital; **~kasse** f health insurance; **~pfleger** m nursing orderly; **~schwester** f nurse; **~schein** m health insurance card; **~versicherung** f health insurance; **~wagen** m ambulance.

Krank- zW: **k~haft** a diseased; (*Angst etc*) morbid; **~heit** f illness, disease; **~heitserreger** m disease-carrying agent.

kränk- ['krɛŋk] zW: **~lich** a sickly; **K~ung** f insult, offence.

Kranz [krants] m **-es, -e** wreath, garland.

kraß [kras] a crass.

Krater ['kraːtər] m **-s, -** crater.

Kratz- ['krats] zW: **~bürste** f (*fig*) crosspatch; **k~en** vti scratch; **~er** m **-s, -** scratch; (*Werkzeug*) scraper.

Kraul ['kraul] nt **-s** crawl; **~ schwimmen** do the crawl; **k~en** vi (*schwimmen*) do the crawl // vt (*streicheln*) tickle.

kraus [kraus] a crinkly; (*Haar*) frizzy; (*Stirn*) wrinkled; **K~e** ['krauzə] f -, **-n** frill, ruffle.

Kraut [kraʊt] *nt* -(e)s, **Kräuter** plant; (*Gewürz*) herb; (*Gemüse*) cabbage.

Krawall [kra'val] *m* -s, -e row, uproar.

Krawatte [kra'vatə] *f* -, -n tie.

Krebs [kre:ps] *m* -es, -e crab; (MED, ASTROL) cancer.

Kredit [kre'di:t] *m* -(e)s, -e credit; ~**karte** *f* credit card.

Kreide [kraɪdə] *f* -, -n chalk; **k~bleich** *a* as white as a sheet.

Kreis [kraɪs] *m* -es, -e circle; (*Stadt~ etc*) district; **im ~ gehen** (*lit, fig*) go round in circles.

kreischen ['kraɪʃən] *vi* shriek, screech.

Kreis- *zW*: ~**el** ['kraɪzəl] *m* -s, - top; (*Verkehrs~*) roundabout; **k~en** ['kraɪzən] *vi* spin; ~**lauf** *m* (MED) circulation; (*fig: der Natur etc*) cycle; ~**säge** *f* circular saw; ~**stadt** *f* county town; ~**verkehr** *m* roundabout traffic.

Kreißsaal ['kraɪs-za:l] *m* delivery room.

Krematorium [krema'to:rɪʊm] *nt* crematorium.

Kreml ['krɛm(ə)l] *m* -s Kremlin.

krepieren [kre'pi:rən] *vi* (*umg: sterben*) die, kick the bucket.

Krepp [krɛp] *m* -s, -s *od* -e crepe; ~**(p)apier** *nt* crepe paper; ~**sohle** *f* crepe sole.

Kresse ['krɛsə] *f* -, -n cress.

Kreta ['kre:ta] *nt* -s Crete.

Kreuz [krɔʏts] *nt* -es, -e cross; (ANAT) small of the back; (KARTEN) clubs; **k~en** *vtr* cross // *vi* (NAUT) cruise; ~**er** *m* -s, - (*Schiff*) cruiser; ~**fahrt** *f* cruise; ~**gang** *m* cloisters *pl*; **k~igen** *vt* crucify; ~**igung** *f* crucifixion; ~**otter** *f* adder; ~**ung** *f* (*Verkehrs~*) crossing, junction; (*Züchten*) cross; ~**verhör** *nt* cross-examination; ~**weg** *m* crossroads; (REL) Way of the Cross; ~**worträtsel** *nt* crossword puzzle; ~**zug** *m* crusade.

Kriech- ['kri:ç] *zW*: **k~en** *vi unreg* crawl, creep; (*pej*) grovel, crawl; ~**er** *m* -s, - crawler; ~**spur** *f* crawler lane; ~**tier** *nt* reptile.

Krieg [kri:k] *m* -(e)s, -e war.

kriegen ['kri:gən] *vt* (*umg*) get.

Kriegs- *zW*: ~**dienstverweigerer** *m* conscientious objector; ~**erklärung** *f* declaration of war; ~**fuß** *m*: mit jdm/etw auf ~fuß stehen be at loggerheads with sb/not get on with sth; ~**gefangene(r)** *m* prisoner of war; ~**gefangenschaft** *f* captivity; ~**gericht** *nt* court-martial; ~**schiff** *nt* warship; ~**verbrecher** *m* war criminal; ~**versehrte(r)** *m* person disabled in the war; ~**zustand** *m* state of war.

Krim [krɪm] *f* - Crimea.

Krimi ['kri:mi] *m* -s, -s (*umg*) thriller.

Kriminal- [krimi'na:l] *zW*: ~**beamte(r)** *m* detective; ~**i'tät** *f* criminality; ~**'polizei** *f* ≈ Criminal Investigation Department, CID (*Brit*), Federal Bureau of Investigation, FBI (*US*); ~**'roman** *m* detective story.

kriminell [krimi'nɛl] *a* criminal; **K~e(r)** *m* criminal.

Krippe ['krɪpə] *f* -, -n manger, crib; (*Kinder~*) crèche.

Krise ['kri:zə] *f* -, -n crisis; **k~ln** *vi*: es kriselt there's a crisis.

Kristall [krɪs'tal] *m* -s, -e crystal // *nt* -s (*Glas*) crystal.

Kriterium [kri'te:rɪʊm] *nt* criterion.

Kritik [kri'ti:k] *f* criticism; (*Zeitungs~*) review, write-up; ~**er** ['kri:tikər] *m* -s, - critic; **k~los** *a* uncritical.

kritisch ['kri:tɪʃ] *a* critical.

kritisieren [kriti'zi:rən] *vti* criticize.

kritzeln ['krɪtsəln] *vti* scribble, scrawl.

Krokodil [kroko'di:l] *nt* -s, -e crocodile.

Krokus ['kro:kʊs] *m* -, - *od* -se crocus.

Krone ['kro:nə] *f* -, -n crown; (*Baum~*) top.

krönen ['krø:nən] *vt* crown.

Kron- *zW*: ~**korken** *m* bottle top; ~**leuchter** *m* chandelier; ~**prinz** *m* crown prince.

Krönung ['krø:nʊŋ] *f* coronation.

Kropf [krɔpf] *m* -(e)s, ̈-e (MED) goitre; (*von Vogel*) crop.

Kröte ['krø:tə] *f* -, -n toad.

Krücke ['krʏkə] *f* -, -n crutch.

Krug [kru:k] *m* -(e)s, ̈-e jug; (*Bier~*) mug.

Krümel ['kry:məl] *m* -s, - crumb; **k~n** *vti* crumble.

krumm [krʊm] *a* (*lit, fig*) crooked; (*kurvig*) curved; ~**beinig** *a* bandylegged; ~**lachen** *vr* (*umg*) laugh o.s. silly; ~**nehmen** *vt unreg* (*umg*): jdm etw ~nehmen take sth amiss.

Krümmung ['krʏmʊŋ] *f* bend, curve.

Krüppel ['krʏpəl] *m* -s, - cripple.

Kruste ['krʊstə] *f* -, -n crust.

Kruzifix [krutsi'fɪks] *nt* -es, -e crucifix.

Kübel ['ky:bəl] *m* -s, - tub; (*Eimer*) pail.

Kubikmeter [ku'bi:kme:tər] *m* cubic metre.

Küche ['kʏçə] *f* -, -n kitchen; (*Kochen*) cooking, cuisine.

Kuchen ['ku:xən] *m* -s, - cake; ~**form** *f* baking tin; ~**gabel** *f* pastry fork.

Küchen- *zW*: ~**herd** *m* range; (*Gas, ELEK*) cooker, stove; ~**schabe** *f* cockroach; ~**schrank** *m* kitchen cabinet.

Kuckuck ['kʊkʊk] *m* -s, -e cuckoo; **Kuckucksuhr** *f* cuckoo clock.

Kufe ['ku:fə] *f* -, -n (*Faß*) vat; (*Schlit-*

ten~) runner; (*AVIAT*) skid.

Kugel ['ku:gəl] *f* -, -n ball; (*MATH*) sphere; (*MIL*) bullet; (*Erd~*) globe; (*SPORT*) shot; **k~förmig** *a* spherical; **~kopf** *m* golf ball; **~lager** *nt* ball bearing; **k~rund** *a* (*Gegenstand*) round; (*umg: Person*) tubby; **~schreiber** *m* ball-point (pen), biro ®; **k~sicher** *a* bulletproof; **~stoßen** *nt* -s shot-put.

Kuh [ku:] *f* -, -e cow.

kühl [ky:l] *a* (*lit, fig*) cool; **K~anlage** *f* refrigerating plant; **K~e** *f* - coolness; **~en** *vt* cool; **K~er** *m* -s, - (*AUT*) radiator; **K~erhaube** *f* (*AUT*) bonnet (*Brit*), hood (*US*); **K~raum** *m* cold-storage chamber; **K~schrank** *m* refrigerator; **K~truhe** *f* freezer; **K~ung** *f* cooling; **K~wasser** *nt* cooling water.

kühn [ky:n] *a* bold, daring; **K~heit** *f* boldness.

Küken ['ky:kən] *nt* -s, - chicken.

kulant [ku'lant] *a* obliging.

Kuli ['ku:li] *m* -s, -s coolie; (*umg: Kugelschreiber*) biro ®.

Kulisse [ku'lɪsə] *f* -, -n scene.

kullern ['kʊlərn] *vi* roll.

Kult [kʊlt] *m* -(e)s, -e worship, cult; **mit etw einen ~ treiben** make a cult out of sth; **k~ivieren** [-i'vi:rən] *vt* cultivate; **k~iviert** *a* cultivated, refined.

Kultur [kʊl'tu:r] *f* culture; civilization; (*des Bodens*) cultivation; **~banause** *m* (*umg*) philistine, low-brow; **k~ell** [-u'rɛl] *a* cultural.

Kümmel ['kʏməl] *m* -s, - caraway seed; (*Branntwein*) kümmel.

Kummer ['kʊmər] *m* -s grief, sorrow.

kümmer- ['kʏmər] *zW:* **~lich** *a* miserable, wretched; **~n** *vr:* **sich um jdn ~n** look after sb; **sich um etw ~n** see to sth // *vt* concern; **das kümmert mich nicht** that doesn't worry me.

Kumpel ['kʊmpəl] *m* -s, - (*umg*) mate.

kündbar ['kʏntba:r] *a* redeemable, recallable; (*Vertrag*) terminable.

Kunde ['kʊndə] *m* -n, -n, **Kundin** *f* customer // *f* -, -n (*Botschaft*) news; **Kundendienst** *m* after-sales service; **Kundenkonto** *nt* charge account.

Kund- *zW:* **~gabe** *f* announcement; **k~geben** *vt* *unreg* announce; **~gebung** *f* announcement; (*Versammlung*) rally.

Künd- *zW:* **k~igen** *vi* give in one's notice; **jdm k~igen** give sb his notice // *vt* cancel; (*jdm*) **die Stellung/Wohnung k~igen** give (sb) notice; **~igung** *f* notice; **~igungsfrist** *f* period of notice.

Kundschaft *f* customers *pl*, clientele.

künftig ['kʏnftɪç] *a* future // *ad* in future.

Kunst [kʊnst] *f* -, -e art; (*Können*) skill; **das ist doch keine ~** it's easy; **~dünger** *m* artificial manure; **~faser** *f* synthetic fibre; **~fertigkeit** *f* skilfulness; **~geschichte** *f* history of art; **~gewerbe** *nt* arts and crafts *pl*; **~griff** *m* trick, knack; **~händler** *m* art dealer.

Künstler(in *f*) ['kʏnstlər(ɪn)] *m* -s, - artist; **k~isch** *a* artistic; **~name** *m* stagename; pseudonym.

künstlich ['kʏnstlɪç] *a* artificial.

Kunst- *zW:* **~sammler** *m* -s, - art collector; **~seide** *f* artificial silk; **~stoff** *m* synthetic material; **~stück** *nt* trick; **~turnen** *nt* gymnastics; **k~voll** *a* ingenious, artistic; **~werk** *nt* work of art.

kunterbunt ['kʊntərbʊnt] *a* higgledy-piggledy.

Kupfer ['kʊpfər] *nt* -s, - copper; **~geld** *nt* coppers *pl*; **k~n** *a* copper.

Kuppe ['kʊpə] *f* -, -n (*Berg~*) top; (*Finger~*) tip.

Kupp- ['kʊp] *zW:* **Kuppe'lei** *f* (*JUR*) procuring; **kuppeln** *vi* (*JUR*) procure; (*AUT*) declutch // *vt* join; **~lung** *f* coupling; (*AUT*) clutch.

Kur [ku:r] *f* -, -en cure, treatment.

Kür [ky:r] *f* -, -en (*SPORT*) free skating/exercises *pl*.

Kurbel ['kʊrbəl] *f* -, -n crank, winch; (*AUT*) starting handle; **~welle** *f* crankshaft.

Kürbis ['kʏrbɪs] *m* -ses, -se pumpkin; (*exotisch*) gourd.

Kur- ['ku:r] *zW:* **~gast** *m* visitor (to a health resort); **k~ieren** [ku'ri:rən] *vt* cure; **k~ios** [kuri'o:s] *a* curious, odd; **~iosi'tät** *f* curiosity; **~ort** *m* health resort; **~pfuscher** *m* quack.

Kurs [kʊrs] *m* -es, -e course; (*FIN*) rate; **~buch** *nt* timetable; **k~ieren** [kʊr'zi:rən] *vi* circulate; **k~iv** *ad* in italics; **~us** ['kʊrzʊs] *m* -, **Kurse** course; **~wagen** *m* (*EISENB*) through carriage.

Kurve ['kʊrvə] *f* -, -n curve; (*Straßen~ auch*) bend; **kurvenreich, kurvig** *a* (*Straße*) bendy.

kurz [kʊrts] *a* short; **~ gesagt** in short; **zu ~ kommen** come off badly; **den ~eren ziehen** get the worst of it; **K~arbeit** *f* short-time work; **~ärm(e)lig** *a* short-sleeved.

Kürze ['kʏrtsə] *f* -, -n shortness, brevity; **k~n** *vt* cut short; (*in der Länge*) shorten; (*Gehalt*) reduce.

kurz- *zW:* **~erhand** *ad* on the spot; **~fristig** *a* short-term; **K~geschichte** *f* short story; **~halten** *vt* *unreg* keep short; **~lebig** *a* short-lived.

kürzlich ['kʏrtslɪç] *ad* lately, recently.

Kurz- *zW:* **~schluß** *m* (*ELEK*) short circuit; **~schrift** *f* shorthand; **k~sichtig** *a* short-sighted; **~welle** *f* shortwave.

kuscheln ['kuʃəln] vr snuggle up.

Kusine [ku'zi:nə] f cousin.

Kuß [kus] m **-sses, ⁻sse** kiss.

küssen ['kysən] vtr kiss.

Küste ['kystə] f -, -n coast, shore; **Küstenwache** f coastguard (station).

Küster ['kystər] m -s, - sexton, verger.

Kutsche ['kutʃə] f -, -n coach, carriage; ~r m -s, - coachman.

Kutte ['kutə] f -, -n cowl.

Kuvert [ku've:r] nt -s, -e od -s envelope; cover.

Kybernetik [kybɛr'ne:tɪk] f cybernetics.

L

L, l [ɛl] nt L, l // l. abk von **Liter.**

Labor [la'bo:r] nt -s, -e od -s lab; ~ant(in f) [labo'rant(ɪn)] m lab(oratory) assistant; ~atorium [labora'to:rium] nt laboratory.

Labyrinth [laby'rɪnt] nt -s, -e labyrinth.

lächeln ['lɛçəln] vi smile; **L~** nt -s smile.

lachen ['laxən] vi laugh.

lächerlich ['lɛçərlɪç] a ridiculous.

Lachgas nt laughing gas.

lachhaft a laughable.

Lachs [laks] m -es, -e salmon.

Lack [lak] m -(e)s, -e lacquer, varnish; (von Auto) paint; l~ieren [la'ki:rən] vt varnish; (Auto) spray; ~ierer [la'ki:rər] m -s, - varnisher.

Lackmus ['lakmus] m od nt - litmus.

laden ['la:dən] vt unreg (Lasten) load; (JUR) summon; (einladen) invite.

Laden ['la:dən] m -s, ⁻ shop; (Fenster~) shutter; ~dieb m shoplifter; ~diebstahl m shoplifting; ~schluß m closing time; ~tisch m counter.

Ladung ['la:duŋ] f (Last) cargo, load; (Beladen) loading; (JUR) summons; (Einladung) invitation; (Spreng~) charge.

lag etc v siehe **liegen.**

Lage ['la:gə] f -, -n position, situation; (Schicht) layer; in der ~ sein be in a position.

Lager ['la:gər] nt -s, - camp; (COMM) warehouse; (Schlaf~) bed; (von Tier) lair; (TECH) bearing; ~bestand m stocks pl; ~haus nt warehouse, store.

lagern ['la:gərn] vi (Dinge) be stored; (Menschen) camp // vt store; (betten) lay down; (Maschine) bed.

Lagune [la'gu:nə] f -, -n lagoon.

lahm [la:m] a lame; ~en vi be lame, limp.

lähmen ['lɛ:mən] vt paralyse.

lahmlegen vt paralyse.

Lähmung f paralysis.

Laib [laip] m -s, -e loaf.

Laie ['laiə] m -n, -n layman; **laienhaft** a amateurish.

Laken ['la:kən] nt -s, - sheet.

Lakritze [la'krɪtsə] f -, -n liquorice.

lallen ['lalən] vti slur; (Baby) babble.

Lamelle [la'mɛlə] f lamella; (ELEK) lamina; (TECH) plate.

Lametta [la'mɛta] nt -s tinsel.

Lamm [lam] nt -(e)s, ⁻er lamb; ~fell nt lambskin.

Lampe ['lampə] f -, -n lamp; **Lampenfieber** nt stage fright; **Lampenschirm** m lampshade.

Lampion [lampi'õ:] m -s, -s Chinese lantern.

Land [lant] nt -(e)s, ⁻er land; (Nation, nicht Stadt) country; (Bundes~) state; auf dem ~(e) in the country; ~besitz m landed property; **Landebahn** f runway; l~en ['landən] vti land.

Landes- ['landəs] zW: ~farben pl national colours pl; ~innere(s) nt inland region; ~sprache f national language; l~üblich a customary; ~verrat m high treason; ~währung f national currency.

Land- zW: ~haus nt country house; ~karte f map; ~kreis m administrative region; l~läufig a customary.

ländlich ['lɛntlɪç] a rural.

Land- zW: ~schaft f countryside; (KUNST) landscape; l~schaftlich a scenic; regional; ~straße f country road; ~streicher m -s, - tramp; ~strich m region; ~tag m (POL) regional parliament.

Landung ['landuŋ] f landing.

Landungs- zW: ~boot nt landing craft; ~brücke f jetty, pier; ~stelle f landing place.

Land- zW: ~wirt m farmer; ~wirtschaft f agriculture; ~zunge f spit.

lang [laŋ] a long; (Mensch) tall; ~atmig a long-winded; ~e ad for a long time; (dauern, brauchen) a long time.

Länge ['lɛŋə] f -, -n length; (GEOG) longitude.

langen ['laŋən] vi (ausreichen) do, suffice; (fassen) reach (nach for); es langt mir I've had enough.

Längen- zW: **Längengrad** m longitude; **Längenmaß** nt linear measure.

lang- zW: **L~eweile** f boredom; ~fristig a long-term; ~lebig a long-lived.

länglich a longish.

längs [lɛŋs] präp +gen od dat along // ad lengthwise.

lang- zW: ~sam a slow; **L~samkeit** f

slowness; **L~schläfer(in** f) m late riser; **L~spielplatte** f long-playing record.

längst ['lɛŋst] ad: das ist ~ fertig that was finished a long time ago, that has been finished for a long time; **~e(r, s)** a longest.

lang- zW: **~weilen** vt bore // vr be bored; **~weilig** a boring, tedious; **L~welle** f long wave; **~wierig** a lengthy, long-drawn-out.

Lanze ['lantsə] f -, -n lance.

Lappalie [la'pa:liə] f trifle.

Lappen ['lapən] m -s, - cloth, rag; (ANAT) lobe.

läppisch ['lɛpɪʃ] a foolish.

Lappland ['laplant] nt -s Lapland.

Lapsus ['lapsʊs] m -, - slip.

Lärche ['lɛrçə] f -, -n larch.

Lärm [lɛrm] m -(e)s noise; **l~en** vi be noisy, make a noise.

Larve ['larfə] f -, -n (BIOL) larva.

las etc v siehe **lesen**.

lasch [laʃ] a slack.

Lasche ['laʃə] f -, -n (Schuh~) tongue.

Laser ['leɪzə] m -s, - laser.

lassen ['lasən] ♦vt pt **ließ**, ptp **gelassen 1** (unterlassen) stop; (momentan) leave; laß das (sein)! don't (do it)!; (hör auf) stop it!; laß mich! leave me alone; ~ wir das! let's leave it; er kann das Trinken nicht ~ he can't stop drinking

2 (zurücklassen) leave; etw ~, wie es ist leave sth (just) as it is

3 (überlassen): jdm etw ~ let sb have sth

4 (zulassen): jdn ins Haus ~ let sb into the house

♦vi: laß mal, ich mache das schon leave it, I'll do it

♦ (als Hilfsverb) pt **ließ**, ptp **lassen 1** (veranlassen): etw machen ~ have od get sth done; sich dat etw schicken ~ have sth sent (to one)

2 (zulassen): jdn etw wissen ~ let sb know sth; das Licht brennen ~ leave the light on; jdn warten ~ keep sb waiting; das läßt sich machen that can be done

3: laß uns gehen let's go.

lässig ['lɛsɪç] a casual; **L~keit** f casualness.

Last [last] f -, -en load, burden; (NAUT, AVIAT) cargo; (meist pl: Gebühr) charge; jdm zur ~ fallen be a burden to sb; **~auto** nt lorry, truck; **l~en** vi (auf +dat) weigh on.

Laster ['lastər] nt -s, - vice.

lästern ['lɛstərn] vti (Gott) blaspheme; (schlecht sprechen) mock.

Lästerung ['lɛstərʊŋ] f jibe; (Gottes~) blasphemy.

lästig ['lɛstɪç] a troublesome, tiresome.

Last- zW: **~kahn** m barge; **~**

kraftwagen m heavy goods vehicle; **~schrift** f debit; **~wagen** m lorry, truck.

Latein [la'taɪn] nt -s Latin; **~amerika** nt Latin America.

latent [la'tɛnt] a latent.

Laterne [la'tɛrnə] f -, -n lantern; (Straßen~) lamp, light; **Laternenpfahl** m lamppost.

latschen ['la:tʃən] vi (umg: gehen) wander, go; (lässig) slouch.

Latte ['latə] f -, -n lath; (SPORT) goalpost; (quer) crossbar.

Latzhose ['latsho:zə] f dungarees pl.

lau [lau] a (Nacht) balmy; (Wasser) lukewarm.

Laub [laup] nt -(e)s foliage; **~baum** m deciduous tree; **~frosch** m tree frog; **~säge** f fretsaw.

Lauch [laux] m -(e)s, -e leek.

Lauer ['lauər] f: auf der ~ sein od liegen, **l~n** vi lie in wait; (Gefahr) lurk.

Lauf [lauf] m -(e)s, **Läufe** run; (Wett~) race; (Entwicklung, ASTRON) course; (Gewehr) barrel; einer Sache ihren ~ lassen let sth take its course; **~bahn** f career.

laufen ['laufən] vti unreg run; (umg: gehen) walk; **~d** a running; (Monat, Ausgaben) current; auf dem **~den** sein/halten be/keep up to date; am **~den Band** (fig) continuously.

Läufer ['lɔyfər] m -s, - (Teppich, SPORT) runner; (Fußball) half-back; (Schach) bishop.

Lauf- zW: **~masche** f run, ladder (Brit); **~stall** m playpen; **~steg** m catwalk; **~werk** nt (COMPUT) disk drive; **~zettel** m circular.

Lauge ['laugə] f -, -n soapy water; (CHEM) alkaline solution.

Laune ['launə] f -, -n mood, humour; (Einfall) caprice; (schlechte) temper; **l~nhaft** a capricious, changeable.

launisch a moody; bad-tempered.

Laus [laus] f -, **Läuse** louse; **~bub** m rascal, imp.

lauschen ['lauʃən] vi eavesdrop, listen in.

lauschig ['lauʃɪç] a snug.

laut [laut] a loud // ad loudly; (lesen) aloud // präp +gen od dat according to; **L~** m -(e)s, -e sound.

Laute ['lautə] f -, -n lute.

lauten ['lautən] vi say; (Urteil) be.

läuten ['lɔytən] vti ring, sound.

lauter ['lautər] a (Wasser) clear, pure; (Wahrheit, Charakter) honest; inv (Freude, Dummheit etc) sheer; (mit pl) nothing but, only.

läutern ['lɔytərn] vt purify.

Läuterung f purification.

laut- zW: **~hals** ad at the top of one's

voice; ~**los** a noiseless, silent; **L~schrift** f phonetics pl; **L~sprecher** m loudspeaker; **L~sprecherwagen** m loudspeaker van; ~**stark** a vociferous; **L~stärke** f (RAD) volume.

lauwarm ['lauvarm] a (lit, fig) lukewarm.

Lava ['la:va] f -, **Laven** lava.

Lavendel [la'vɛndəl] m -s, - lavender.

Lawine [la'vi:nə] f avalanche; **Lawinengefahr** f danger of avalanches.

lax [laks] a lax.

Lazarett [latsa'rɛt] nt -(e)s, -e (MIL) hospital, infirmary.

leben ['le:bən] vti live; **L~** nt -s, - life; ~**d** a living; **lebendig** [le'bɛndɪç] a able to live; (lebhaft) lively; **Lebendigkeit** f liveliness.

Lebens- zW: ~**alter** nt age; ~**art** f way of life; ~**erwartung** f life expectancy; **l~fähig** a able to live; ~**gefahr** f: ~**gefahr!** danger!; in ~**gefahr** dangerously ill; **l~gefährlich** a dangerous; (Verletzung) critical; ~**haltungskosten** pl cost of living sing; ~**jahr** nt year of life; ~**lauf** m curriculum vitae; **l~lustig** a cheerful, lively; ~**mittel** pl food sing; ~**mittelgeschäft** nt grocer's; **l~müde** a tired of life; ~**retter** m lifesaver; ~**standard** m standard of living; ~**unterhalt** m livelihood; ~**versicherung** f life insurance; ~**wandel** m way of life; ~**zeichen** nt sign of life.

Leber ['le:bər] f -, -n liver; ~**fleck** m mole; ~**tran** m cod-liver oil; ~**wurst** f liver sausage.

Lebewesen nt creature.

Lebewohl nt farewell, goodbye.

leb- ['le:p] zW: ~**haft** a lively, vivacious; **L~kuchen** m gingerbread; ~**los** a lifeless.

leck [lɛk] a leaky, leaking; **L~** nt -(e)s, -e leak; ~**en** vi (Loch haben) leak // vti (schlecken) lick.

lecker ['lɛkər] a delicious, tasty; **L~bissen** m dainty morsel.

led. abk von **ledig**.

Leder ['le:dər] nt -s, - leather; **l~n** a leather; ~**waren** pl leather goods pl.

ledig ['le:dɪç] a single; einer Sache ~ sein be free of sth; ~**lich** ad merely, solely.

leer [le:r] a empty; vacant; ~ **machen** empty; **L~e** f - emptiness; ~**en** vt empty // vr empty; **L~gewicht** nt weight when empty; ~**lauf** m neutral; ~**stehend** a empty; **L~ung** f emptying; (Post) collection.

legal [le'ga:l] a legal, lawful; ~**i'sieren** vt legalize; **L~i'tät** f legality.

legen ['le:gən] vt lay, put, place; (Ei) lay // vr lie down; (fig) subside.

Legende [le'gɛndə] f -, -n legend.

leger [le'ʒɛːr] a casual.

legieren [le'gi:rən] vt alloy.

Legierung f alloy.

Legislative [legɪsla'ti:və] f legislature.

legitim [legi'ti:m] a legitimate; **L~ation** [-atsi'o:n] f legitimation; ~**ieren** [-'mi:rən] vt legitimate // vr prove one's identity.

Lehm [le:m] m -(e)s, -e loam; **l~ig** a loamy.

Lehne ['le:nə] f -, -n arm; back; **l~n** vtr lean.

Lehnstuhl m armchair.

Lehr- zW: ~**amt** nt teaching profession; ~**brief** m indentures pl; ~**buch** nt textbook.

Lehre ['le:rə] f -, -n teaching, doctrine; (beruflich) apprenticeship; (moralisch) lesson; (TECH) gauge; **l~n** vt teach; ~**r(in** f) m -s, - teacher; **Lehrerzimmer** nt staff room.

Lehr- zW: ~**gang** m course; ~**jahre** pl apprenticeship; ~**ling** m apprentice; **l~reich** a instructive; ~**stelle** f apprenticeship; ~**stuhl** m chair; ~**zeit** f apprenticeship.

Leib [laɪp] m -(e)s, -er body; halt ihn mir vom ~! keep him away from me; **l~haftig** a personified; (Teufel) incarnate; **l~lich** a bodily; (Vater etc) own; ~**wache** f bodyguard.

Leiche ['laɪçə] f -, -n corpse.

Leichen- zW: ~ **haus** nt mortuary; ~**träger** m bearer; ~**wagen** m hearse.

Leichnam ['laɪçna:m] m -(e)s, -e corpse.

leicht [laɪçt] a light; (einfach) easy; **L~athletik** f athletics sing; ~**fallen** vi unreg: jdm ~**fallen** be easy for sb; ~**fertig** a frivolous; ~**gläubig** a gullible, credulous; **L~gläubigkeit** f gullibility, credulity; ~**hin** ad lightly; **L~igkeit** f easiness; mit **L~igkeit** with ease; ~**machen** vt: es sich (dat) ~**machen** make things easy for oneself; **L~sinn** m carelessness; ~**sinnig** a careless.

Leid [laɪt] nt -(e)s grief, sorrow; **l~** a: etw **l~** haben od sein be tired of sth; es tut mir/ihm **l~** I am/he is sorry; er/das tut mir **l~** I am sorry for him/ it; **l~en** ['laɪdən] unreg vt suffer; (erlauben) permit; jdn/etw nicht **l~en** können not be able to stand sb/sth // vi suffer; ~**en** nt -s, - suffering; (Krankheit) complaint; ~**enschaft** f passion; **l~enschaftlich** a passionate.

leider ['laɪdər] ad unfortunately; ja, ~ yes, I'm afraid so; ~ **nicht** I'm afraid not.

Leidtragende(r) mf bereaved; (Benachteiligter) one who suffers.

Leidwesen nt: zu jds ~ to sb's dismay.

Leier ['laɪər] f -, -n lyre; (fig) old story; **~kasten** m barrel organ.

Leihbibliothek f lending library.

leihen ['laɪən] vt unreg lend; **sich** (dat) etw ~ borrow sth.

Leih- zW: **~gebühr** f hire charge; **~haus** nt pawnshop; **~schein** m pawn ticket; (Buch~ etc) borrowing slip; **~wagen** m hired car.

Leim [laɪm] m -(e)s, -e glue; **l~en** vt glue.

Leine ['laɪnə] f -, -n line, cord; (Hunde~) leash, lead; **~n** nt -s, - linen; **l~n** a linen.

Leintuch nt (Bett~) sheet; linen cloth.

Leinwand f (KUNST) canvas; (CINE) screen.

leise ['laɪzə] a quiet; (sanft) soft, gentle.

Leiste ['laɪstə] f -, -n ledge; (Zier~) strip; (ANAT) groin.

leisten ['laɪstən] vt (Arbeit) do; (Gesellschaft) keep; (Ersatz) supply; (vollbringen) achieve; **sich** (dat) etw ~ können be able to afford sth.

Leistung f performance; (gute) achievement.

Leistungs- zW: **~druck** m pressure; **l~fähig** a efficient; **~fähigkeit** f efficiency; **~sport** m competitive sport; **~zulage** f productivity bonus.

Leitartikel m leading article.

Leitbild nt model.

leiten ['laɪtən] vt lead; (Firma) manage; (in eine Richtung) direct; (ELEK) conduct.

Leiter ['laɪtər] m -s, - leader, head; (ELEK) conductor // f -, -n ladder.

Leit- zW: **~faden** m guide; **~motiv** nt leitmotiv; **~planke** f crash barrier.

Leitung f (Führung) direction; (CINE, THEAT etc) production; (von Firma) management; directors pl; (Wasser~) pipe; (Kabel) cable; **eine lange ~ haben** be slow on the uptake.

Leitungs- zW: **~draht** m wire; **~rohr** nt pipe; **~wasser** nt tap water.

Lektion [lɛktsiˈoːn] f lesson.

Lektüre [lɛkˈtyːrə] f -, -n (Lesen) reading; (Lesestoff) reading matter.

Lende ['lɛndə] f -, -n loin; **Lendenstück** nt fillet.

lenk- ['lɛŋk] zW: **~bar** a (Fahrzeug) steerable; (Kind) manageable; **~en** vt steer; (Kind) guide; (Blick, Aufmerksamkeit) direct (auf +akk at); **L~rad** nt steering wheel; **L~stange** f handlebars pl.

Leopard [leoˈpart] m -en, -en leopard.

Lepra ['leːpra] f - leprosy.

Lerche ['lɛrçə] f -, -n lark.

lern- ['lɛrn] zW: **~begierig** a eager to learn; **~en** vt learn.

lesbar ['leːsbaːr] a legible.

Lesbierin ['lɛsbiərɪn] f lesbian.

lesbisch ['lɛsbɪʃ] a lesbian.

Lese ['leːzə] f -, -n (Wein) harvest; **~buch** nt reading book, reader; **l~n** vti unreg read; (ernten) gather, pick.

Leser(in f) m -s, - reader; **~brief** m reader's letter; **l~lich** a legible.

Lesung ['leːzʊŋ] f (PARL) reading.

letzte(r, s) ['lɛtstə(r, s)] a last; (neueste) latest; **zum ~nmal** ad for the last time; **~ns** ad lately; **~re(r, s)** a latter.

Leuchte ['lɔʏçtə] f -, -n lamp, light; **l~n** vi shine, gleam; **~r** m -s, - candlestick.

Leucht- zW: **~farbe** f fluorescent colour; **~kugel** f, **~rakete** f flare; **~reklame** f neon sign; **~röhre** f strip light; **~turm** m lighthouse; **~zifferblatt** nt luminous dial.

leugnen ['lɔʏɡnən] vti deny.

Leugnung f denial.

Leukämie [lɔʏkɛˈmiː] f leukaemia.

Leukoplast ® [lɔʏkoˈplast] nt -(e)s, -e elastoplast ®.

Leumund ['lɔʏmʊnt] m -(e)s, -e reputation.

Leumundszeugnis nt character reference.

Leute ['lɔʏtə] pl people pl.

Leutnant ['lɔʏtnant] m -s, -s od -e lieutenant.

Lexikon ['lɛksikɔn] nt -s, **Lexiken** od **Lexika** encyclopaedia.

libanesisch [libaˈneːzɪʃ] a Lebanese.

Libanon ['liːbanɔn] n -s: (der) ~ the Lebanon.

Libelle [liˈbɛlə] f -, -n dragonfly; (TECH) spirit level.

liberal [libeˈraːl] a liberal; **L~e(r)** mf liberal; **L~ismus** [liberaˈlɪsmʊs] m liberalism.

Libero ['liːbero] m -s, -s (Fußball) sweeper.

Libyen ['liːbiən] nt -s Libya.

libysch ['liːbɪʃ] a Libyan.

Licht [lɪçt] nt -(e)s, -er light; **~bild** nt photograph; (Dia) slide; **~blick** m cheering prospect; **l~empfindlich** a sensitive to light; **l~en** vt clear; (Anker) weigh // vr clear up; (Haar) thin; **~hupe** f flashing of headlights; **~jahr** nt light year; **~maschine** f dynamo; **~schalter** m light switch.

Lichtung f clearing, glade.

Lid [liːt] nt -(e)s, -er eyelid; **~schatten** m eyeshadow.

lieb [liːp] a dear; **das ist ~ von dir** that's kind of you; **~äugeln** vi insep ogle (mit jdm/etw sb/sth).

Liebe ['liːbə] f -, -n love; **l~bedürftig** a: **l~bedürftig sein** need love; **~'lei** f flirtation; **l~n** vt love; like.

liebens- zW: **~wert** a loveable; **~würdig** a kind; **~würdigerweise** ad kindly; **L~würdigkeit** f kindness.

lieber ['li:bər] ad rather, preferably; ich gehe ~ nicht I'd rather not go // siehe **gern, lieb.**

Liebes- zW: **~brief** m love letter; **~kummer** m: **~kummer** haben be lovesick; **~paar** nt courting couple, lovers pl.

liebevoll a loving.

lieb- ['li:p] zW: **~gewinnen** vt unreg get fond of; **~haben** vt unreg be fond of; **L~haber** m -s, - lover; **L~habe'rei** f hobby; **~kosen** [li:p'ko:zən] vt insep caress; **~lich** a lovely, charming; **L~ling** m darling; **L~lings-** in zW favourite; **~los** a unloving; **L~schaft** f love affair; **~ste(r, s)** a favourite; etw am ~sten mögen like sth best.

Lied [li:t] nt -(e)s, -er song; (ECCL) hymn; **~erbuch** nt songbook; hymn book.

liederlich ['li:dərlıç] a slovenly; (Lebenswandel) loose, immoral; **L~keit** f slovenliness; immorality.

lief etc v siehe **laufen.**

Lieferant [lifə'rant] m supplier.

liefern ['li:fərn] vt deliver; (versorgen mit) supply; (Beweis) produce.

Liefer- zW: **~schein** m delivery note; **~termin** m delivery date; **~ung** f delivery; supply; **~wagen** m van.

Liege ['li:gə] f -, -n bed.

liegen ['li:gən] vi unreg lie; (sich befinden) be; mir liegt nichts/viel daran it doesn't matter to me/it matters a lot to me; es liegt bei Ihnen, ob ... it's up to you whether ...; Sprachen ~ mir nicht languages are not my line; woran liegt es? what's the cause?; **~bleiben** vi unreg (Person) stay in bed; stay lying down; (Ding) be left (behind); **~lassen** vt unreg (vergessen) leave behind.

Liege- zW: **~sitz** m (AUT) reclining seat; **~stuhl** m deck chair; **~wagen** m (EISENB) couchette.

lieh etc v siehe **leihen.**

ließ etc v siehe **lassen.**

liest etc v siehe **lesen.**

Lift [lıft] m -(e)s, -e od -s lift.

Likör [li'kø:r] m -s, -e liqueur.

lila ['li:la] a inv purple, lilac; **L~** nt -s, -s (Farbe) purple, lilac.

Lilie ['li:liə] f lily.

Limonade [limo'na:də] f lemonade.

Linde ['lındə] f -, -n lime tree, linden.

lindern ['lındərn] vt alleviate, soothe.

Linderung f alleviation.

Lineal [line'a:l] nt -s, -e ruler.

Linie ['li:niə] f line.

Linien- zW: **~blatt** nt ruled sheet; **~flug** m scheduled flight; **~richter** m linesman; **l~treu** a (POL) loyal to the party line.

linieren [lini'i:rən] vt line.

Linke ['lıŋkə] f -, -n left side; left hand; (POL) left; **l~(r, s)** a left; ein **L~r** (POL) a left-winger; **l~ Masche** purl.

linkisch a awkward, gauche.

links [lıŋks] ad left; to od on the left; **~** von mir on od to my left; **L~außen** [lıŋks"ausən] m -s, - (SPORT) outside left; **L~händer(in** f) m -s, - left-handed person; **L~kurve** f left-hand bend; **L~verkehr** m traffic on the left.

Linoleum [li'no:leum] nt -s lino(leum).

Linse ['lınzə] f -, -n lentil; (optisch) lens.

Lippe ['lıpə] f -, -n lip; **Lippenstift** m lipstick.

lispeln ['lıspəln] vi lisp.

Lissabon ['lısabon] nt -s Lisbon.

List [lıst] f -, -en cunning; trick, ruse.

Liste ['lıstə] f -, -n list.

listig ['lıstıç] a cunning, sly.

Litanei [lita'nai] f litany.

Liter ['li:tər] nt od m -s, - litre.

literarisch [lıte'ra:rıʃ] a literary.

Literatur [lıtera'tu:r] f literature.

Litfaßsäule ['lıtfaszoylə] f advertising pillar.

Lithographie [litogra'fi:] f lithography.

Liturgie [litur'gi:] f liturgy.

liturgisch [li'turgıʃ] a liturgical.

Litze ['lıtsə] f -, -n braid; (ELEK) flex.

live [laıf] ad (RAD, TV) live.

Livree [li'vre:] f -, -n livery.

Lizenz [li'tsents] f licence.

Lkw [elka:ve:] m abk von **Lastkraftwagen.**

Lob [lo:p] nt -(e)s praise.

Lobby ['lobı] f lobby.

loben ['lo:bən] vt praise; **lobenswert** a praiseworthy.

löblich ['lø:plıç] a praiseworthy, laudable.

Loch [lox] nt -(e)s, ̈-er hole; **l~en** vt punch holes in; **~er** m -s, - punch.

löcherig ['lœçərıç] a full of holes.

Lochkarte f punch card.

Lochstreifen m punch tape.

Locke ['lokə] f -, -n lock, curl; **l~n** vt entice; (Haare) curl; **Lockenwickler** m -s, - curler.

locker ['lokər] a loose; **~lassen** vi unreg: nicht **~lassen** not let up; **~n** vt loosen.

lockig ['lokıç] a curly.

Lodenmantel ['lo:dənmantəl] m thick woollen coat.

lodern ['lo:dərn] vi blaze.

Löffel ['lœfəl] m -s, - spoon.

Logarithmus [loga'rıtmus] m logarithm.

Loge ['lo:ʒə] f -, -n (THEAT) box; (Freimaurer) (masonic) lodge; (Pförtner~) office.

Logik ['lo:gɪk] f logic.
logisch ['lo:gɪʃ] a logical.
Lohn [lo:n] m -(e)s, ⁻e reward; (*Arbeits~*) pay, wages pl; ~**büro** nt wages office; ~**empfänger** m wage earner.
lohnen ['lo:nən] vt (*liter*) reward (*jdm etw* sb for sth) // vr unpers be worth it; ~**d** a worthwhile.
Lohn- zW: ~**steuer** f income tax; ~**streifen** m pay slip; ~**tüte** f pay packet.
lokal [lo'ka:l] a local; **L**~ nt -(e)s, -e pub(lic house); ~**isieren** vt localize.
Lokomotive [lokomo'ti:və] f -, -n locomotive.
Lokomotivführer m engine driver.
Lorbeer ['lɔrbe:r] m -s, -en (*lit, fig*) laurel; ~**blatt** nt (*KOCH*) bay leaf.
Lore ['lo:rə] f -, -n (*MIN*) truck.
Los [lo:s] nt -es, -e (*Schicksal*) lot, fate; (*Lotterie~*) lottery ticket.
los [lo:s] a (*locker*) loose; ~! go on!; etw ~ sein be rid of sth; was ist ~? what's the matter?; dort ist nichts/viel ~ there's nothing/a lot going on there; etw ~ haben (*umg*) be clever; ~**binden** vt unreg untie.
löschen ['lœʃən] vt (*Feuer, Licht*) put out, extinguish; (*Durst*) quench; (*COMM*) cancel; (*COMPUT*) delete; (*Tonband*) erase; (*Fracht*) unload // vi (*Feuerwehr*) put out a fire; (*Papier*) blot.
Lösch- zW: ~**fahrzeug** nt fire engine; fire boat; ~**gerät** nt fire extinguisher; ~**papier** nt blotting paper.
lose ['lo:zə] a loose.
Lösegeld nt ransom.
losen ['lo:zən] vi draw lots.
lösen ['lø:zən] vt loosen; (*Rätsel etc*) solve; (*Verlobung*) call off; (*CHEM*) dissolve; (*Partnerschaft*) break up; (*Fahrkarte*) buy // vr (*aufgehen*) come loose; (*Zucker etc*) dissolve; (*Problem, Schwierigkeit*) (re)solve itself.
los- zW: ~**fahren** vi unreg leave; ~**gehen** vi unreg set out; (*anfangen*) start; (*Bombe*) go off; **auf jdn** ~**gehen** go for sb; ~**kaufen** vt (*Gefangene, Geiseln*) pay ransom for; ~**kommen** vi unreg: **von etw** ~**kommen** get away from sth; ~**lassen** vt unreg (*Seil*) let go of; (*Schimpfe*) let loose; ~**laufen** vi unreg run off.
löslich ['lø:slɪç] a soluble; **L**~**keit** f solubility.
los- zW: ~**lösen** vtr free; ~**machen** vt loosen; (*Boot*) unmoor // vr get free; ~**schrauben** vt unscrew; ~**sprechen** vt unreg absolve.
Losung ['lo:zʊŋ] f watchword, slogan.
Lösung ['lø:zʊŋ] f (*Lockermachen*)

loosening; (*eines Rätsels, CHEM*) solution; **Lösungsmittel** nt solvent.
loswerden vt unreg get rid of.
Lot [lo:t] nt -(e)s, -e plummet; **im** ~ vertical; (*fig*) on an even keel.
löten [lø:tən] vt solder.
Lothringen ['lo:trɪŋən] nt -s Lorraine.
Lötkolben m soldering iron.
Lotse ['lo:tsə] m -n, -n pilot; (*AVIAT*) air traffic controller; **l**~**n** vt pilot; (*umg*) lure.
Lotterie [lɔtə'ri:] f lottery.
Löwe ['lø:və] m -n, -n lion; (*ASTROL*) Leo; **Löwenanteil** m lion's share; **Löwenzahn** m dandelion.
loyal [loa'ja:l] a loyal.
lt. abk (= *laut*) according to.
Luchs ['luks] m -es, -e lynx.
Lücke ['lʏkə] f -, -n gap; **Lückenbüßer** m -s, - stopgap; **lückenlos** a complete.
Luder ['lu:dər] nt -s, - (*pej: Frau*) hussy; (*bedauernswert*) poor wretch.
Luft [luft] f -, ⁻e air; (*Atem*) breath; **in der** ~ **liegen** be in the air; **jdn wie** ~ **behandeln** ignore sb; ~**angriff** m air raid; ~**ballon** m balloon; ~**blase** f air bubble; **l**~**dicht** a airtight; ~**druck** m atmospheric pressure.
lüften ['lʏftən] vti air; (*Hut*) lift, raise.
Luft- zW: ~**fahrt** f aviation; **l**~**gekühlt** a air-cooled; **l**~**ig** a (*Ort*) breezy; (*Raum*) airy; (*Kleider*) summery; ~**kissenfahrzeug** nt hovercraft; ~**kurort** m health resort; **l**~**leer** a: ~**leerer Raum** vacuum; ~**linie** f: **in der** ~**linie** as the crow flies; ~**loch** nt air-hole; (*AVIAT*) airpocket; ~**matratze** f lilo ® (*Brit*), air mattress; ~**pirat** m hijacker; ~**post** f airmail; ~**röhre** f (*ANAT*) wind pipe; ~**schlange** f streamer; ~**schutzkeller** m air-raid shelter.
Lüftung ['lʏftʊŋ] f ventilation.
Luft- zW: ~**verkehr** m air traffic; ~**waffe** f air force; ~**zug** m draught.
Lüge ['ly:gə] f -, -n lie; **jdn/etw** ~**n strafen** give the lie to sb/sth; **l**~**n** vi unreg lie.
Lügner(in f) m -s, - liar.
Luke ['lu:kə] f -, -n dormer window, hatch.
Lümmel ['lʏməl] m -s, - lout; **l**~**n** vr lounge (about).
Lump [lump] m -en, -en scamp, rascal.
Lumpen ['lumpən] m -s, - rag; **sich nicht l**~ **lassen** not be mean.
lumpig ['lumpɪç] a shabby.
Lunge ['luŋə] f -, -n lung; **Lungenentzündung** f pneumonia; **lungenkrank** a consumptive.
lungern ['luŋərn] vi hang about.
Lupe ['lu:pə] f -, -n magnifying glass;

unter die ~ **nehmen** (*fig*) scrutinize.
Lupine [lu'pi:nə] *f* lupin.
Lust [lust] *f* -, ⁻e joy, delight; (*Neigung*) desire; ~ **haben zu** *od* **auf etw** (*akk*)/**etw zu tun** feel like sth/doing sth.
lüstern ['lystərn] *a* lustful, lecherous.
lustig ['lustiç] *a* (*komisch*) amusing, funny; (*fröhlich*) cheerful.
Lüstling *m* lecher.
Lust- *zW*: **l~los** *a* unenthusiastic; **~mord** *m* sex(ual) murder; **~spiel** *nt* comedy.
lutschen ['lutʃən] *vti* suck; **am Daumen ~** suck one's thumb.
Lutscher *m* -s, - lollipop.
Luxemburg ['luksəmburk] *nt* -s Luxembourg.
luxuriös [luksuri'ø:s] *a* luxurious.
Luxus ['luksus] *m* - luxury; **~artikel** *pl* luxury goods *pl*; **~hotel** *nt* luxury hotel.
Lymphe ['lymfə] *f* -, -n lymph.
lynchen ['lynçən] *vt* lynch.
Lyrik ['ly:rik] *f* lyric poetry; **~er** *m* -s, - lyric poet.
lyrisch ['ly:rıʃ] *a* lyrical.

M

M, m [ɛm] *nt* M, m // **m** *abk von* **Meter.**
Maas [ma:s] *f* - Meuse.
Mach- [max] *zW*: **~art** *f* make; **m~bar** *a* feasible; **~e** *f* - (*umg*) show, sham.
machen ['maxən] ◆*vt* **1** do; (*herstellen, zubereiten*) make; **was machst du da?** what are you doing (there)?; **das ist nicht zu ~** that can't be done; **das Radio leiser ~** turn the radio down; **aus Holz gemacht** made of wood
2 (*verursachen, bewirken*) make; **jdm Angst ~** make sb afraid; **das macht die Kälte** it's the cold that does that
3 (*ausmachen*) matter; **das macht nichts** that doesn't matter; **die Kälte macht mir nichts** I don't mind the cold
4 (*kosten, ergeben*) be; **3 und 5 macht 8** 3 and 5 is *od* are 8; **was** *od* **wieviel macht das?** how much does that make?
5: **was macht die Arbeit?** how's the work going?; **was macht dein Bruder?** how is your brother doing?; **das Auto ~ lassen** have the car done; **mach's gut!** take care! (*viel Glück*) good luck!
◆*vi*: **mach schnell** hurry up!; **Schluß ~** finish (off); **mach schon!** come on!; **das macht müde** it makes you

tired; **in etw** (*dat*) ~ be *od* deal in sth
◆*vr* come along (nicely); **sich an etw** (*akk*) ~ set about sth; **sich verständlich ~** make oneself understood; **sich** (*dat*) **viel aus jdm/etw ~** like sb/sth.
Macht [maxt] *f* -, ⁻e power; **~haber** *m* -s, - ruler.
mächtig ['meçtiç] *a* powerful, mighty; (*umg: ungeheuer*) enormous.
Macht- *zW*: **m~los** *a* powerless; **~probe** *f* trial of strength; **~stellung** *f* position of power; **~wort** *nt*: **ein ~wort sprechen** lay down the law.
Machwerk *nt* work; (*schlechte Arbeit*) botched-up job.
Mädchen ['mɛːtçən] *nt* girl; **m~haft** *a* girlish; **~name** *m* maiden name.
Made ['maːdə] *f* -, -n maggot.
madig ['maːdiç] *a* maggoty; **jdm etw ~ machen** spoil sth for sb.
mag *etc v siehe* **mögen.**
Magazin [maga'tsi:n] *nt* -s, -e magazine.
Magen ['maːgən] *m* -s, - *od* ⁻ stomach; **~schmerzen** *pl* stomachache.
mager ['maːgər] *a* lean; (*dünn*) thin; **M~keit** *f* leanness; thinness.
Magie [ma'gi:] *f* magic.
Magier ['maːgiər] *m* -s, - magician.
magisch ['maːgıʃ] *a* magical.
Magnet [ma'gne:t] *m* -s *od* -en, -en magnet; **~band** *nt* magnetic tape; **m~isch** *a* magnetic; **m~i'sieren** *vt* magnetize; **~nadel** *f* magnetic needle.
Mahagoni [maha'goːni] *nt* -s mahogany.
mähen ['mɛːən] *vti* mow.
Mahl [maːl] *nt* -(e)s, -e meal; **m~en** *vt unreg* grind; **~zeit** *f* meal // *interj* enjoy your meal.
Mahnbrief *m* reminder.
Mähne ['mɛːnə] *f* -, -n mane.
Mahn- ['maːn] *zW*: **m~en** *vt* remind; (*warnend*) warn; (*wegen Schuld*) demand payment from; **~ung** *f* reminder; admonition, warning.
Mähren ['mɛːrən] *nt* -s Moravia.
Mai [mai] *m* -(e)s, -e May; **~glöckchen** *nt* lily of the valley; **~käfer** *m* cockchafer; **~land** *nt* Milan; **m~ländisch** *a* Milanese.
Mais [mais] *m* -es, -e maize, corn (*US*); **~kolben** *m* corncob.
Majestät [majes'tɛːt] *f* majesty; **m~isch** *a* majestic.
Major [ma'joːr] *m* -s, -e (*MIL*) major; (*AVIAT*) squadron leader.
Majoran [majo'raːn] *m* -s, -e marjoram.
makaber [ma'kaːbər] *a* macabre.
Makel ['maːkəl] *m* -s, - blemish; (*moralisch*) stain; **m~los** *a* immaculate,

spotless.

mäkeln ['mɛːkəln] *vi* find fault.

Makkaroni [maka'roːni] *pl* macaroni *sing*.

Makler(in *f*) ['maːklər(ɪn)] *m* **-s,** - broker.

Makrele [ma'kreːlə] *f* -, **-n** mackerel.

Makrone [ma'kroːnə] *f* -, **-n** macaroon.

Mal [maːl] *nt* **-(e)s, -e** mark, sign; (*Zeitpunkt*) time; **m~** *ad* times; (*umg*) *siehe* **einmal**; **-m~** *suff* -times; **m~en** *vti* paint; **~er** *m* -s, - painter; **~e'rei** *f* painting; **m~erisch** *a* picturesque; **~kasten** *m* paintbox.

Mallorca [ma'lɔrka] *nt* -s Majorca.

malnehmen *vti unreg* multiply.

Malz [malts] *nt* **-es** malt; **~bonbon** *m* cough drop; **~kaffee** *m* malt coffee.

Mama ['mamaː] *f* -, **-s, Mami** ['mami] *f* -, **-s** (*umg*) mum(my).

Mammut ['mamʊt] *nt* **-s, -e** *od* **-s** mammoth.

man [man] *pron* one, you; **~** sagt, ... they *od* people say ...; **wie schreibt ~ das?** how do you write it? how is it written?

manche(r, s) ['mançə(r, s)] *a* many a; (*pl*) a number of // *pron* some.

mancherlei *a inv* various // *pron* a variety of things.

manchmal *ad* sometimes.

Mandant(in *f*) [man'dant(ɪn)] *m* (*JUR*) client.

Mandarine [manda'riːnə] *f* mandarin, tangerine.

Mandat [man'daːt] *nt* **-(e)s, -e** mandate.

Mandel ['mandəl] *f* -, **-n** almond; (*ANAT*) tonsil.

Manege [ma'nɛːʒə] *f* -, **-n** ring, arena.

Mangel ['maŋəl] *f* -, **-n** mangle // *m* **-s, ¨**- lack; (*Knappheit*) shortage (an +*dat* of); (*Fehler*) defect, fault; **~erscheinung** *f* deficiency symptom; **m~haft** *a* poor; (*fehlerhaft*) defective, faulty; **m~n** *vi unpers*: es mangelt jdm an etw (*dat*) sb lacks sth // *vt* (*Wäsche*) mangle; **m~s** *präp* +*gen* for lack of.

Manie [ma'niː] *f* mania.

Manier [ma'niːr] *f* - manner; style; (*pej*) mannerism; **~en** *pl* manners *pl*.

Manifest [mani'fɛst] *nt* **-es, -e** manifesto.

Maniküre [mani'kyːrə] *f* -, **-n** manicure; **m~n** *vt* manicure.

manipulieren [manipu'liːrən] *vt* manipulate.

Manko ['maŋko] *nt* **-s, -s** deficiency; (*COMM*) deficit.

Mann [man] *m* **-(e)s, ¨er** man; (*Ehe~*) husband; (*NAUT*) hand; **seinen ~ stehen** hold one's own.

Männchen ['mɛnçən] *nt* little man;

(*Tier*) male.

Mannequin [manə'kɛ̃ː] *nt* **-s, -s** fashion model.

männlich ['mɛnlɪç] *a* (*BIOL*) male; (*fig, GRAM*) masculine.

Mannschaft *f* (*SPORT, fig*) team; (*NAUT, AVIAT*) crew; (*MIL*) other ranks *pl*.

Manöver [ma'nøːvər] *nt* **-s, -** manoeuvre.

manövrieren [manøˈvriːrən] *vti* manoeuvre.

Mansarde [man'zardə] *f* -, **-n** attic.

Manschette [man'ʃɛtə] *f* cuff; (*TECH*) collar; sleeve; **Manschettenknopf** *m* cufflink.

Mantel ['mantəl] *m* **-s, ¨-** coat; (*TECH*) casing, jacket.

Manuskript [manu'skrɪpt] *nt* **-(e)s, -e** manuscript.

Mappe ['mapə] *f* -, **-n** briefcase; (*Akten~*) folder.

Märchen ['mɛːrçən] *nt* fairy tale; **m~haft** *a* fabulous; **~prinz** *m* Prince Charming.

Marder ['mardər] *m* **-s, -** marten.

Margarine [marga'riːnə] *f* margarine.

Marienkäfer [ma'riːənkɛːfər] *m* ladybird.

Marine [ma'riːnə] *f* navy; **m~blau** *a* navy-blue.

marinieren [mari'niːrən] *vt* marinate.

Marionette [mario'nɛtə] *f* puppet.

Mark [mark] *f* -, - (*Münze*) mark // *nt* **-(e)s** (*Knochen~*) marrow; **durch ~ und Bein gehen** go right through sb; **m~ant** [mar'kant] *a* striking.

Marke ['markə] *f* -, **-n** mark; (*Warensorte*) brand; (*Fabrikat*) make; (*Rabatt~, Brief~*) stamp; (*Essens~*) ticket; (*aus Metall etc*) token, disc.

Mark- *zW*: **m~ieren** [mar'kiːrən] *vti* (*umg*) act; **~ierung** *f* marking; **~ise** [mar'kiːzə] *f* -, **-n** awning; **~stück** *nt* one-mark piece.

Markt [markt] *m* **-(e)s, ¨e** market; **~forschung** *f* market research; **m~gängig** *a* marketable; **~platz** *m* market place; **~wirtschaft** *f* market economy.

Marmelade [marmə'laːdə] *f* -, **-n** jam.

Marmor ['marmɔr] *m* **-s, -e** marble; **m~ieren** [-'riːrən] *vt* marble; **m~n** *a* marble.

Marokk- [ma'rɔk] *zW*: **~o** *nt* **-s** Morocco; **~aner(in** *f*) [marɔ'kaːnər(ɪn)] *m* **-s, -** Moroccan; **m~'anisch** *a* Moroccan.

Marone [ma'roːnə] *f* -, **-n** *od* **Maroni** chestnut.

Marotte [ma'rɔtə] *f* -, **-n** fad, quirk.

Marsch [marʃ] *m* **-(e)s, ¨e** march; **m~** *interj* march // *f* -, **-en** marsh; **~befehl** *m* marching orders *pl*; **m~bereit** *a* ready to move; **m~ieren**

[mar'ʃiːrən] *vi* march.
Märtyrer(in *f*) ['mɛrtyrər(ɪn)] *m* **-s, -**
martyr.
März [mɛrts] *m* **-(es), -e** March.
Marzipan [martsi'paːn] *nt* **-s, -e** marzipan.
Masche ['maʃə] *f* **-, -n** mesh;
(*Strick~*) stitch; **das ist die neueste
~** that's the latest thing; **Maschen-
draht** *m* wire mesh; **maschenfest** *a*
runproof.
Maschine [ma'ʃiːnə] *f* machine; (*Motor*) engine; (*Schreib~*) typewriter;
maschinell [maʃi'nɛl] *a* machine(-);
mechanical.
Maschinen- *zW:* **~bauer** *m* mechanical engineer; **~gewehr** *nt* machine
gun; **~pistole** *f* submachine gun;
~schaden *m* mechanical fault;
~schlosser *m* fitter; **~schrift** *f* type-
script.
machineschreiben *vi unreg* type.
Maschinist [maʃi'nɪst] *m* engineer.
Maser ['maːzər] *f* **-, -n** grain; speckle;
~n *pl* (*MED*) measles *sing*; **~ung** *f*
grain(ing).
Maske ['maskə] *f* **-, -n** mask.
Maskenball *m* fancy-dress ball.
Maskerade [maskə'raːdə] *f* masquerade.
maskieren [mas'kiːrən] *vt* mask;
(*verkleiden*) dress up // *vr* disguise
o.s., dress up.
Maß [maːs] *nt* **-es, -e** measure;
(*Mäßigung*) moderation; (*Grad*) degree, extent // *f* **-, -(e)** litre of beer.
Massage [ma'saːʒə] *f* **-, -n** massage.
Maßanzug *m* made-to-measure suit.
Maßarbeit *f* (*fig*) neat piece of work.
Masse ['masə] *f* **-, -n** mass.
Massen- *zW:* **~artikel** *m* mass-
produced article; **~grab** *nt* mass
grave; **m~haft** *a* loads of; **~medien**
pl mass media *pl;* **~veranstaltung** *f*
mass meeting.
Masseur [ma'søːr] *m* masseur.
Masseuse [ma'søːzə] *f* masseuse.
maßgebend *a* authoritative.
maßhalten *vi unreg* exercise moderation.
massieren [ma'siːrən] *vt* massage;
(*MIL*) mass.
massig ['masɪç] *a* massive; (*umg*)
massive amount of.
mäßig ['mɛːsɪç] *a* moderate; **~en**
['mɛːsɪgən] *vt* restrain, moderate;
M~keit *f* moderation.
massiv [ma'siːf] *a* solid; (*fig*) heavy,
rough; **M~** *nt* **-s, -e** massif.
Maß- *zW:* **~krug** *m* tankard; **m~los**
a extreme; **~nahme** *f* **-, -n** measure,
step; **m~regeln** *vt insep* reprimand;
~stab *m* rule, measure; (*fig*) standard; (*GEOG*) scale; **m~voll** *a* moderate.

Mast ['mast] *m* **-(e)s, -e(n)** mast;
(*ELEK*) pylon.
mästen ['mɛstən] *vt* fatten.
Material [materi'aːl] *nt* **-s, -ien** ma-
terial(s); **~fehler** *m* material defect;
~ismus [-'lɪsmus] *m* materialism;
~ist [-'lɪst] *m* materialist; **m~istisch**
[-'lɪstɪʃ] *a* materialistic.
Materie [ma'teːriə] *f* matter, substance.
materiell [materi'el] *a* material.
Mathematik [matema'tiːk] *f* mathematics *sing*; **~er(in** *f*) [mate-
'maːtikər(ɪn)] *m* **-s, -** mathematician.
mathematisch [mate'maːtɪʃ] *a* math-
ematical.
Matratze [ma'tratsə] *f* **-, -n** mattress.
Matrixdrucker ['maːtriksdrʊkər] dot-
matrix printer.
Matrize [ma'tritsə] *f* **-, -n** matrix;
(*zum Abziehen*) stencil.
Matrose [ma'troːzə] *m* **-n, -n** sailor.
Matsch [matʃ] *m* **-(e)s** mud;
(*Schnee~*) slush; **m~ig** *a* muddy;
slushy.
matt [mat] *a* weak; (*glanzlos*) dull;
(*PHOT*) matt; (*Schach*) mate.
Matte ['matə] *f* **-, -n** mat.
Mattscheibe *f* (*TV*) screen; **~haben**
(*umg*) not be quite with it.
Mauer ['mauər] *f* **-, -n** wall; **m~n** *vti*
build; lay bricks.
Maul [maul] *nt* **-(e)s, Mäuler** mouth;
m~en *vi* (*umg*) grumble; **~esel** *m*
mule; **~korb** *m* muzzle; **~sperre** *f*
lockjaw; **~tier** *nt* mule; **~wurf** *m*
mole.
Maurer ['maurər] *m* **-s, -** bricklayer.
Maus [maus] *f* **-, Mäuse** (*auch COM-
PUT*) mouse.
Mause- ['mauzə] *zW:* **~falle** *f* mouse-
trap; **m~n** *vt* (*umg*) flinch // *vi* catch
mice; **m~tot** *a* stone dead.
maximal [maksi'maːl] *a* maximum.
Maximum ['maksimʊm] *nt* maximum.
Maxi-Single ['maksi'sɪŋgl] *f* **-, -s** 12-
inch single.
Mayonnaise [majo'nɛːzə] *f* **-, -n**
mayonnaise.
m.E. *abk* (*= meines Erachtens*) in
my opinion.
Mechan- [me'çaːn] *zW:* **~ik** *f* mechanics *sing*; (*Getriebe*) mechanics
pl; **~iker** *m* **-s, -** mechanic, engineer;
m~isch *a* mechanical; **~ismus**
[meça'nɪsmus] *m* mechanism.
meckern ['mɛkərn] *vi* bleat; (*umg*)
moan.
Medaille [me'daljə] *f* **-, -n** medal.
Medaillon [medal'jõː] *nt* **-s, -s**
(*Schmuck*) locket.
Medikament [medika'mɛnt] *nt* medicine.
meditieren [medi'tiːrən] *vi* meditate;
Medizin [medi'tsiːn] *f* **-, -en** medicine;

m~isch a medical.

Meer [me:r] nt -(e)s, -e sea; **~busen** m bay, gulf; **~enge** f straits pl; **Meeresspiegel** m sea level; **~rettich** m horseradish; **~schweinchen** nt guinea-pig.

Megaphon [mega'fo:n] nt -s, -e megaphone.

Mehl ['me:l] nt -(e)s, -e flour; **m~ig** a floury.

mehr [me:r] a,ad more; **~deutig** a ambiguous; **~ere** a several; **~eres** pron several things; **~fach** a multiple; (wiederholt) repeated; **M~heit** f majority; **~malig** a repeated; **~mals** ad repeatedly; **~stimmig** a for several voices; **~stimmig singen** harmonize; **M~wertsteuer** f value added tax, VAT; **M~zahl** f majority; (GRAM) plural.

meiden ['maɪdən] vt unreg avoid.

Meile ['maɪlə] f -, -n mile; **Meilenstein** m milestone; **meilenweit** a for miles.

mein [maɪn] pron my; **~e(r, s)** mine.

Meineid ['maɪn'aɪt] m perjury.

meinen ['maɪnən] vti think; (sagen) say; (sagen wollen) mean; das will ich ~ I should think so.

mein- zW: **~erseits** ad for my part; **~esgleichen** pron people like me; **~etwegen** ad (für mich) for my sake; (wegen mir) on my account; (von mir aus) as far as I'm concerned; I don't care od mind.

Meinung ['maɪnʊŋ] f opinion; ganz meine ~ I quite agree; jdm die ~ sagen give sb a piece of one's mind.

Meinungs- zW: **~austausch** m exchange of views; **~umfrage** f opinion poll; **~verschiedenheit** f difference of opinion.

Meise ['maɪzə] f -, -n tit(mouse).

Meißel ['maɪsəl] m -s, - chisel; **m~n** vt chisel.

meist ['maɪst] a,ad most(ly); am **~en** the most; **~ens** ad generally, usually.

Meister ['maɪstər] m -s, - master; (SPORT) champion; **m~haft** a masterly; **~schaft** f mastery; (SPORT) championship; **~stück** nt, **~werk** nt masterpiece.

Melancholie [melaŋko'li:] f melancholy.

melancholisch [melaŋ'ko:lɪʃ] a melancholy.

Melde- ['mɛldə] zW: **~frist** f registration period; **m~n** vt report // vr report (bei zu); (SCH) put one's hand up; (freiwillig) volunteer; (auf etw, am Telefon) answer; sich zu Wort **m~n** ask to speak; **~pflicht** f obligation to register with the police; **~stelle** f registration office.

Meldung ['mɛldʊŋ] f announcement; (Bericht) report.

meliert [me'li:rt] a mottled, speckled.

melken ['mɛlkən] vt unreg milk.

Melodie [melo'di:] f melody, tune.

melodisch [me'lo:dɪʃ] a melodious, tuneful.

Melone [me'lo:nə] f -, -n melon; (Hut) bowler (hat).

Membran(e) [mɛm'bra:n(ə)] f -, -en (TECH) diaphragm.

Memoiren [memo'a:rən] pl memoirs pl.

Menge ['mɛŋə] f -, -n quantity; (Menschen~) crowd; (große Anzahl) lot (of); **m~n** vt mix // vr sich **m~n** in (+akk) meddle with; **Mengenlehre** f (MATH) set theory; **Mengenrabatt** m bulk discount.

Mensch [mɛnʃ] m -en, -en human being, man; person; kein ~ nobody // interj hey.

Menschen- zW: **~feind** m misanthrope; **~freundlich** a philanthropical; **~kenner** m -s, - judge of human nature; **m~möglich** a humanly possible; **~recht** nt human rights pl; **m~unwürdig** a degrading; **~verstand** m: gesunder **~enverstand** common sense.

Mensch- zW: **~heit** f humanity, mankind; **m~lich** a human; (human) humane; **~lichkeit** f humanity.

Menstruation [mɛnstruatsi'o:n] f menstruation.

Mentalität [mɛntali'tɛ:t] f mentality.

Menü [me'ny:] nt -s, -s (auch COMPUT) menu.

Merk- [mɛrk] zW: **~blatt** nt instruction sheet od leaflet; **m~en** vt notice; sich (dat) etw **m~en** remember sth; **m~lich** a noticeable; **~mal** nt sign, characteristic; **m~würdig** a odd.

meßbar ['mɛsba:r] a measurable.

Messe ['mɛsə] f -, -n fair; (ECCL) mass; **m~n** unreg vt measure // vr compete.

Messer nt -s, - knife; **~spitze** f knife point; (in Rezept) pinch.

Meßgerät nt measuring device, gauge.

Messing ['mɛsɪŋ] nt -s brass.

Metall [me'tal] nt -s, -e metal; **m~en**, **m~isch** a metallic.

Meteor [me'teo:r] nt -s, -e meteor.

Meter ['me:tər] nt od m -s, - metre; **~maß** nt tape measure.

Methode [me'to:də] f -, -n method.

methodisch [me'to:dɪʃ] a methodical.

Metropole [metro'po:lə] f -, -n metropolis.

Metzger ['mɛtsgər] m -s, - butcher; **~ei** [-'raɪ] f butcher's (shop).

Meuchelmord ['mɔʏçəlmɔrt] m assassination.

Meute ['mɔytə] f -, -n pack; ~'rei f mutiny; ~rn vi mutiny.

miauen [mi'auən] vi miaow.

mich [mɪç] pron akk von **ich** me; myself.

Miene ['miːnə] f -, -n look, expression.

mies [miːs] a (umg) lousy.

Miet- ['miːt] zW: ~**auto** nt hired car; ~**e** f -, -n rent; zur ~**e** wohnen live in rented accommodation; **m~en** vt rent; (Auto) hire; ~**er(in** f) m -s, - tenant; **Mietshaus** nt tenement, block of flats; ~**vertrag** m tenancy agreement.

Migräne [mi'grɛːnə] f -, -n migraine.

Mikro- ['mikro] zW: ~**computer** m microcomputer; ~**fon**, ~**phon** [-'foːn] nt -s, -e microphone; ~**skop** [-'skoːp] nt -s, -e microscope; **m~skopisch** a microscopic; ~**wellenherd** m microwave (oven).

Milch [mɪlç] f - milk; ~**glas** nt frosted glass; **m~ig** a milky; ~**kaffee** m white coffee; ~**pulver** nt powdered milk; ~**straße** f Milky Way; ~**zahn** m milk tooth.

mild [mɪlt] a mild; (Richter) lenient; (freundlich) kind, charitable; **M~e** ['mɪldə] f -, -n mildness; leniency; ~**ern** vt mitigate, soften; (Schmerz) alleviate; ~**ernde Umstände** extenuating circumstances.

Milieu [mili'ø] nt -s, -s background, environment; **m~geschädigt** a maladjusted.

Mili- [mili] zW: **m~tant** [-'tant] a militant; ~**tär** [-'tɛːr] nt -s military, army; ~'**tärgericht** nt military court; **m~'tärisch** a military.

Milli- ['mɪli] zW: ~**ardär** [-ar'dɛːr] m multimillionaire; ~**arde** [-'ardə] f -, -n milliard; billion (bes US); ~**meter** m millimetre; ~**on** [-'oːn] f -, -en million; ~**onär** [-o'nɛːr] m millionaire.

Milz ['mɪlts] f -, -en spleen.

Mimik ['miːmɪk] f mime.

Mimose [mi'moːzə] f -, -n mimosa; (fig) sensitive person.

minder ['mɪndər] a inferior // ad less; **M~heit** f minority; ~**jährig** a minor; **M~jährigkeit** f minority; ~**n** vtr decrease, diminish; **M~ung** f decrease; ~**wertig** a inferior; **M~wertigkeitskomplex** m inferiority complex.

Mindest- ['mɪndəst] zW: ~**alter** nt minimum age; ~**betrag** m minimum amount; **m~e(r, s)** a least; **m~ens**, **zum m~en** ad at least; ~**lohn** m minimum wage; ~**maß** nt minimum.

Mine ['miːnə] f -, -n mine; (Bleistift~) lead; (Kugelschreiber~) refill; **Minenfeld** nt minefield.

Mineral [mine'raːl] nt -s, -e od -ien mineral; **m~isch** a mineral;

~**wasser** nt mineral water.

Miniatur [minia'tuːr] f miniature.

minimal [mini'maːl] a minimal.

Minimum ['minimʊm] nt minimum.

Minister [mi'nɪstər] m -s, - minister; **m~iell** [mɪnɪsteri'el] a ministerial; ~**ium** [mɪnɪs'teːrɪʊm] nt ministry; ~**präsident** m prime minister.

minus ['miːnʊs] ad minus; **M~** nt -, - deficit; **M~pol** m negative pole; **M~zeichen** nt minus sign.

Minute [mi'nuːtə] f -, -n minute; **Minutenzeiger** m minute hand.

Mio. abk (= Million(en)) million(s).

mir [miːr] pron dat von **ich** (to) me; ~ nichts, dir nichts just like that.

Misch- ['mɪʃ] zW: ~**ehe** f mixed marriage; **m~en** vt mix; ~**ling** m halfcaste; ~**ung** f mixture.

Miß- ['mɪs] zW: **m~achten** vt insep disregard; ~'**achtung** f disregard; ~**behagen** nt discomfort, uneasiness; ~**bildung** f deformity; **m~'billigen** vt insep disapprove of; ~**billigung** f disapproval; ~**brauch** m abuse; (falscher Gebrauch) misuse; **m~'brauchen** vt insep abuse; misuse (zu for); ~**erfolg** m failure; **m~fallen** vi unreg insep displease (jdm sb); ~**fallen** nt -s displeasure; ~**geburt** f freak; (fig) abortion; ~**geschick** nt misfortune; **m~glücken** [mɪs'glʏkən] vi insep fail; jdm m~glückt etw sb does not succeed with sth; ~**griff** m mistake; ~**gunst** f envy; **m~günstig** a envious; **m~'handeln** vt insep ill-treat; ~'**handlung** f ill-treatment.

Mission [misi'oːn] f mission; ~**ar** [misio'naːr] m missionary.

Miß- zW: ~**klang** m discord; ~**kredit** m discredit; **m~lingen** [mɪs'lɪŋən] vi unreg insep fail; ~**mut** m bad temper; **m~mutig** a cross; **m~'raten** vi (unreg insep) turn out badly // a illbred; ~**stand** m bad state of affairs; abuse; ~**stimmung** f ill-humour, discord; **m~'trauen** vi insep mistrust; ~**trauen** nt -s distrust, suspicion (of); ~**trauensantrag** m (POL) motion of no confidence; ~**trauensvotum** nt -s, -voten (POL) vote of no confidence; **m~trauisch** a distrustful, suspicious; ~**verhältnis** nt disproportion; ~**verständnis** nt misunderstanding; **m~verstehen** vt unreg insep misunderstand.

Mist [mɪst] m -(e)s dung; dirt; (umg) rubbish; ~**el** f -, -n mistletoe; ~**haufen** m dungheap.

mit [mɪt] präp +dat with; (mittels) by; ~ der Bahn by train; ~ 10 Jahren at the age of 10 // ad along, too; wollen Sie ~? do you want to come along?

Mitarbeit ['mit'arbait] f cooperation; **m~en** vi cooperate, collaborate; **~er(in** f) m collaborator; co-worker // pl staff.

Mit- zW: **~bestimmung** f participation in decision-making; **m~bringen** vt unreg bring along; **~bürger(in** f) m fellow citizen.

miteinander [mit'ai'nandər] ad together, with one another.

Mit- zW: **m~erleben** vt see, witness; **~esser** ['mit'esər] m -s, - blackhead; **m~geben** vt unreg give; **~gefühl** nt sympathy; **m~gehen** vi unreg go/ come along; (verstehen) keep up, follow; **~genommen** a done in, in a bad way; **~gift** f dowry.

Mitglied ['mitgliːt] nt member; **Mitgliederbeitrag** m membership fee; **~schaft** f membership.

Mit- zW: **m~halten** vi unreg keep up; **~hilfe** f help, assistance; **m~hören** vt listen along to; **m~kommen** vi unreg come along; (verstehen) keep up, follow; **~läufer** m hanger-on; (POL) fellow-traveller.

Mitleid nt sympathy; (Erbarmen) compassion; **~enschaft** f: in **~enschaft ziehen** affect; **m~ig** a sympathetic; **m~slos** a pitiless, merciless.

Mit- zW: **m~machen** vt join in, take part in; **~mensch** m fellow man; **m~nehmen** vt unreg take along/ away; (anstrengen) wear out, exhaust; **zum M~nehmen** to take away.

mitsamt [mit'zamt] präp +dat together with.

Mitschuld f complicity; **m~ig** a also guilty (an +dat of).

Mit- zW: **~schüler(in** f) m schoolmate; **m~spielen** vi join in, take part; **~spieler(in** f) m partner; **~spracherecht** ['mitʃpraːxərɛçt] nt voice, say.

Mittag ['mitaːk] m -(e)s, -e midday, lunchtime; (zu) ~ **essen** have lunch; **m~** ad at lunchtime od noon; **~essen** nt lunch, dinner.

mittags ad at lunchtime od noon; **M~pause** f lunch break; **M~schlaf** m early afternoon nap, siesta.

Mittäter(in f) ['mitːtɛːtər(in)] m accomplice.

Mitte ['mitə] f -, -n middle; (POL) centre; **aus unserer ~** from our midst.

mitteil- ['mitːtail] zW: **~en** vt: jdm etw ~en inform sb of sth, communicate sth to sb; **M~ung** f communication.

Mittel ['mitəl] nt -s - means; method; (MATH) average; (MED) medicine; **ein ~ zum Zweck** a means to an end; **~alter** nt Middle Ages pl; **m~alterlich** a mediaeval; **~amerika**

nt Central America; **m~bar** a indirect; **~ding** nt cross; **~europa** nt Central Europe; **m~los** a without means; **m~mäßig** a mediocre, middling; **~mäßigkeit** f mediocrity; **~meer** nt Mediterranean; **~punkt** m centre; **m~s** präp +gen by means of; **~stand** m middle class; **~streckenrakete** f medium-range missile; **~streifen** m central reservation; **~stürmer** m centre-forward; **~weg** m middle course; **~welle** f (RAD) medium wave.

mitten ['mitən] ad in the middle; ~ **auf der Straße/in der Nacht** in the middle of the street/night.

Mitternacht ['mitərnaxt] f midnight.

mittlere(r, s) ['mitlərə(r, s)] a middle; (durchschnittlich) medium, average.

mittlerweile ['mitlər'vailə] ad meanwhile.

Mittwoch ['mitvɔx] m -(e)s, -e Wednesday; **m~s** ad on Wednesdays.

mitunter [mit'untər] ad occasionally, sometimes.

Mit- zW: **m~verantwortlich** a also responsible; **m~wirken** vi contribute (bei to); (THEAT) take part (bei in); **~wirkung** f contribution; participation.

Möbel ['møːbəl] pl furniture; **~wagen** m furniture od removal van.

mobil [moˈbiːl] a mobile; (MIL) mobilized; **M~iar** [mobiliˈaːr] nt -s, -e movable assets pl; **M~machung** f mobilization.

möblieren [møˈbliːrən] vt furnish; **möbliert wohnen** live in furnished accommodation.

möchte(n) ['mœçtə(n)] v siehe mögen.

Mode ['moːdə] f -, -n fashion.

Modell [moˈdɛl] nt -s, -e model; **m~ieren** [-ˈliːrən] vt model.

Mode(n)schau f fashion show.

modern [moˈdɛrn] a modern; (modisch) fashionable; **modernisieren** vt modernize.

Mode- zW: **~schmuck** m fashion jewellery; **~schöpfer(in** f) m fashion designer; **~wort** nt fashionable word, buzz word.

modisch ['moːdiʃ] a fashionable.

Mofa ['moːfa] nt -s, -s small moped.

mogeln ['moːgəln] vi (umg) cheat.

mögen ['møːgən] ◆vti pt **mochte**, ptp **gemocht** like; **magst du/mögen Sie ihn?** do you like him?; **ich möchte ...** I would like ..., I'd like ...; **er möchte in die Stadt** he'd like to go into town; **ich möchte nicht, daß du ...** I wouldn't like you to ...; **ich mag nicht mehr** I've had enough

◆ (als Hilfsverb) pt **mochte**, ptp **mögen** like to; (wollen) want; **möchtest du etwas essen?** would you like something to eat?; **sie mag nicht bleiben** she doesn't want to stay; **das mag wohl sein** that may well be; **was mag das heißen?** what might that mean?; **Sie möchten zu Hause anrufen?** could you please call home?

möglich ['mø:klɪç] a possible; **~erweise** ad possibly; **M~keit** f possibility; **nach M~keit** if possible; **~st** ad as ... as possible.

Mohn [mo:n] m -(e)s, -e (~blume) poppy; (~samen) poppy seed.

Möhre ['mø:rə] f -, -n, **Mohrrübe** f carrot.

mokieren [mo'ki:rən] vr make fun (über +akk of).

Moldau ['mɔldau] f - Moldavia.

Mole ['mo:lə] f -, -n (harbour) mole.

Molekül [mole'ky:l] nt -s, -e molecule.

Molkerei [mɔlkə'rai] f dairy.

Moll [mɔl] nt -, - (MUS) minor (key); **m~ig** a cosy; (dicklich) plump.

Moment [mo'mɛnt] m -(e)s, -e moment; **im ~** at the moment; **~ (mal)!** just a moment // nt factor, element; **m~an** [-'ta:n] a momentary // ad at the moment.

Monarch [mo'narç] m -en, -en monarch; **~ie** [monar'çi:] f monarchy.

Monat ['mo:nat] m -(e)s, -e month; **m~elang** ad for months; **m~lich** a monthly; **~skarte** f monthly ticket.

Mönch ['mœnç] m -(e)s, -e monk.

Mond [mo:nt] m -(e)s, -e moon; **~finsternis** f eclipse of the moon; **m~hell** a moonlit; **~landung** f moon landing; **~schein** m moonlight; **~sonde** f moon probe.

Mono- [mono] in zW mono; **~log** [-'lo:k] m -s, -e monologue; **~pol** [-'po:l] nt -s, -e monopoly; **m~polisieren** [-poli'zi:rən] vt monopolize; **m~ton** [-'to:n] a monotonous; **~tonie** [-to'ni:] f monotony.

Monsun [mɔn'zu:n] m -s, -e monsoon.

Montag ['mo:nta:k] m -(e)s, -e Monday; **m~s** ad on Mondays.

Montage [mɔn'ta:ʒə] f -, -n (PHOT etc) montage; (TECH) assembly; (Einbauen) fitting.

Monteur [mɔn'tø:r] m fitter.

montieren [mɔn'ti:rən] vt assemble.

Monument [monu'mɛnt] nt monument; **m~al** [-'ta:l] a monumental.

Moor [mo:r] nt -(e)s, -e moor.

Moos [mo:s] nt -es, -e moss.

Moped ['mo:pɛt] nt -s, -e moped.

Mops [mɔps] m -es, ⁝e pug.

Moral [mo'ra:l] f -, -en morality; (einer Geschichte) moral; **m~isch** a moral.

Moräne [mo'rɛ:nə] f -, -n moraine.

Morast [mo'rast] m -(e)s, -e morass, mire; **m~ig** a boggy.

Mord [mɔrt] m -(e)s, -e murder; **~anschlag** m murder attempt.

Mörder ['mœrdər] m -s, - murderer; **~in** f murderess.

Mord- zW: **~kommission** f murder squad; **Mordsglück** nt (umg) amazing luck; **mordsmäßig** a (umg) terrific, enormous; **Mordsschreck** m (umg) terrible fright; **~verdacht** m suspicion of murder; **~waffe** f murder weapon.

morgen ['mɔrgən] ad, **M~** nt tomorrow; **~ früh** tomorrow morning; **M~** m -s, - morning; **M~mantel** m, **M~rock** m dressing gown; **M~röte** f dawn; **~s** ad in the morning.

morgig ['mɔrgɪç] a tomorrow's; **der ~e Tag** tomorrow.

Morphium ['mɔrfium] nt morphine.

morsch [mɔrʃ] a rotten.

Morse- ['mɔrzə] zW: **~alphabet** nt Morse code; **m~n** vi send a message by Morse code.

Mörtel ['mœrtəl] m -s, - mortar.

Mosaik [moza'i:k] nt -s, -en od -e mosaic.

Moschee [mɔ'ʃe:] f -, -n [mɔ'ʃe:ən] mosque.

Moskau ['mɔskau] nt -s Moscow; **~er** a Muscovite.

Moskito [mɔs'ki:to] m -s, -s mosquito.

Most [mɔst] m -(e)s, -e (unfermented) fruit juice; (Apfelwein) cider. ———

Motel [mo'tɛl] nt -s, -s motel.

Motiv [mo'ti:f] nt -s, -e motive; (MUS) theme; **~ieren** [moti'vi:rən] vt motivate; **~ierung** f motivation.

Motor ['mo:tɔr] m -s, -en [mo'to:rən] engine; (bes ELEK) motor; **~boot** nt motorboat; **~enöl** nt motor oil; **m~isieren** [motori'zi:rən] vt motorize; **~rad** nt motorcycle; **~schaden** m engine trouble od failure.

Motte ['mɔtə] f -, -n moth; **Mottenkugel** f mothball(s).

Motto ['mɔto] nt -s, -s motto.

Möwe ['mø:və] f -, -n seagull.

Mrd. abk (= Milliarde(n)) thousand millions, billion(s) (US).

Mücke ['mykə] f -, -n midge, gnat; **Mückenstich** m midge od gnat bite.

müde ['my:də] a tired.

Müdigkeit ['my:dɪçkait] f tiredness.

Muff [mʊf] m -(e)s, -e (Handwärmer) muff; **~el** m -s, - (umg) killjoy, sourpuss; **m~ig** a (Luft) musty.

Mühe ['my:ə] f -, -n trouble, pains pl; **mit Müh und Not** with great difficulty; **sich** (dat) **~ geben** go to a lot of trouble; **m~los** a without trouble, easy.

mühevoll a laborious, arduous.

Mühle ['myːlə] f -, -n mill; (Kaffee~) grinder.

Müh- zW: ~sal f -, -e hardship, tribulation; **m~sam** a arduous, troublesome; **m~selig** a arduous, laborious.

Mulde ['muldə] f -, -n hollow, depression.

Mull [mul] m -(e)s, -e thin muslin; ~binde f gauze bandage.

Müll [myl] m -(e)s refuse; ~abfuhr f rubbish disposal; (Leute) dustmen pl; ~abladeplatz m rubbish dump; ~eimer m dustbin, garbage can (US); ~haufen m rubbish heap; ~schlucker m -s, - garbage disposal unit; ~verbrennungsanlage f incinerator; ~wagen m dustcart, garbage truck (US).

mulmig ['mulmiç] a rotten; (umg) dodgy; **jdm ist** ~ sb feels funny.

multiplizieren [multipliˈtsiːrən] vt multiply.

Mumie ['muːmiə] f mummy.

Mumm [mum] m -s (umg) gumption, nerve.

München ['mynçən] nt -s Munich.

Mund [munt] m -(e)s, ˝er ['myndər] mouth; ~art f dialect.

Mündel ['myndəl] nt -s, - ward.

münden ['myndən] vi flow (in +akk into).

Mund- zW: **m~faul** a taciturn; ~geruch m bad breath; ~harmonika f mouth organ.

mündig ['myndiç] a of age; **M~keit** f majority.

mündlich ['myntliç] a oral.

Mundstück nt mouthpiece; (Zigaretten~) tip.

Mündung ['myndun] f mouth; (Gewehr) muzzle.

Mund- zW: ~wasser nt mouthwash; ~werk nt: **ein großes ~werk haben** have a big mouth; ~winkel m corner of the mouth.

Munition [munitsiˈoːn] f ammunition; **Munitionslager** nt ammunition dump.

munkeln ['munkəln] vi whisper, mutter.

Münster ['mynstər] nt -s, - minster.

munter ['muntər] a lively; **M~keit** f liveliness.

Münze ['myntsə] f -, -n coin; **m~n** vt coin, mint; **auf jdn gemünzt sein** be aimed at sb.

Münzfernsprecher ['myntsfɛrnʃprɛçər] m callbox (Brit), pay phone.

mürb(e) ['myrb(ə)] a (Gestein) crumbly; (Holz) rotten; (Gebäck) crisp; **jdn** ~ **machen** wear sb down; **M~(e)teig** m shortcrust pastry.

murmeln ['murməln] vti murmer, mutter.

Murmeltier ['murməltiːr] nt marmot.

murren ['murən] vi grumble, grouse.

mürrisch ['myriʃ] a sullen.

Mus [muːs] nt -es, -e purée.

Muschel ['muʃəl] f -, -n mussel; (~schale) shell; (Telefon~) receiver.

Muse ['muːzə] f -, -n muse.

Museum [muˈzeːum] nt -s, **Museen** museum.

Musik [muˈziːk] f music; (Kapelle) band; **m~alisch** [-ˈkaːliʃ] a musical; ~box f jukebox; ~er ['muːzikər] m -s, - musician; ~hochschule f music school; ~instrument nt musical instrument; ~truhe f radiogram.

musizieren [muziˈtsiːrən] vi make music.

Muskat [musˈkaːt] m -(e)s, -e nutmeg.

Muskel ['muskəl] m -s, -n muscle; ~kater m: **einen ~kater haben** be stiff.

Muskulatur [muskulaˈtuːr] f muscular system.

muskulös [muskuˈløːs] a muscular.

Muß [mus] nt - necessity, must.

Muße ['muːsə] f - leisure.

müssen ['mysən] vi pt **mußte**, ptp **gemußt** od (als Hilfsverb) **müssen 1** (Zwang) must (nur im Präsens), have to; **ich muß es tun** I must do it, I have to do it; **ich mußte es tun** I had to do it; **er muß es nicht tun** he doesn't have to do it; **muß ich?** must I?, do I have to?; **wann müßt ihr zur Schule?** when do you have to go to school?; **er hat gehen** ~ he (has) had to go; **muß das sein?** is that really necessary?; **ich muß mal** (umg) I need the toilet

2 (sollen): **das mußt du nicht tun!** you oughtn't to od shouldn't do that; **Sie hätten ihn fragen** ~ you should have asked him

3 (Vermutung): **es muß geregnet haben** it must have rained; **es muß nicht wahr sein** it need not be true.

müßig ['myːsiç] a idle; **M~gang** m idleness.

Muster ['mustər] nt -s, - model; (Dessin) pattern; (Probe) sample; **m~gültig** a exemplary; **m~n** vt (Tapete) pattern; (fig, MIL) examine; (Truppen) inspect; ~ung f (von Stoff) pattern; (MIL) inspection.

Mut [muːt] m courage; **nur** ~! cheer up!; **jdm** ~ **machen** encourage sb; **m~ig** a courageous; **m~los** a discouraged, despondent.

mutmaßlich ['muːtmaːsliç] a presumed // ad probably.

Mutter ['mutər] f -, ˝ mother; pl ~n (Schrauben~) nut; ~gesellschaft f parent company.

mütterlich ['mytərliç] a motherly; ~erseits ad on the mother's side.

Mutter- zW: ~liebe f motherly love; ~mal nt birthmark, mole; ~schaft f motherhood, maternity; **~schutz** *m* maternity regulations; **'m~'seelena'lein** *a* all alone; **~sprache** *f* native language; **~tag** *m* Mother's Day.

Mutti ['muti] *f* -, **-s** mum(my) (*Brit*), mom(my) (*US*).

mutwillig ['muːtvɪlɪç] *a* malicious, deliberate.

Mütze ['mʏtsə] *f* -, **-n** cap.

MwSt *abk* (= *Mehrwertsteuer*) VAT.

mysteriös [mʏsteri'øːs] *a* mysterious.

Mythos ['myːtɔs] *m* -, **Mythen** myth.

N

N, n [ɛn] *nt* N, n.

na [na] *interj* well; **~ gut** okay then.

Nabel ['naːbəl] *m* -**s**, - navel; **~schnur** *f* umbilical cord.

nach [naːx] ◆*präp* +*dat* **1** (*örtlich*) to; **~ Berlin** to Berlin; **~ links/rechts** (to the) left/right; **~ oben/hinten** up/back **2** (*zeitlich*) after; **einer ~ dem anderen** one after the other; **~ Ihnen!** after you!; **zehn (Minuten) ~ drei** ten (minutes) past three **3** (*gemäß*) according to; **~ dem Gesetz** according to the law; **dem Namen ~** judging by his/her name; **~ allem, was ich weiß** as far as I know ◆*adv*: **ihm ~!** after him!; **~ und ~** gradually, little by little; **~ wie vor** still.

nachahmen ['naːʔaːmən] *vt* imitate.

Nachahmung *f* imitation.

Nachbar(in *f)* ['naxbaːr(ɪn)] *m* -**s**, **-n** neighbour; **~haus** *nt*: **im ~haus** next door; **n~lich** *a* neighbourly; **~schaft** *f* neighbourhood; **~staat** *m* neighbouring state.

nach- *zW*: **~bestellen** *vt*: **50 Stück ~bestellen** order another 50; **N~bestellung** *f* (*COMM*) repeat order; **~bilden** *vt* copy; **N~bildung** *f* imitation, copy; **~blicken** *vi* gaze after; **~datieren** *vt* postdate.

nachdem [naːx'deːm] *kj* after; (*weil*) since; **je ~ (ob)** it depends (whether).

nach- *zW*: **~denken** *vi unreg* think (*über* +*akk* about); **N~denken** *nt* -**s** reflection, meditation; **~denklich** *a* thoughtful, pensive.

Nachdruck ['naːxdrʊk] *m* emphasis; (*TYP*) reprint, reproduction.

nachdrücklich ['naːxdrʏklɪç] *a* emphatic.

nacheinander [naːx'aɪ'nandər] *ad* one after the other.

nachempfinden ['naːx'ɛmpfɪndən] *vt unreg*: **jdm etw ~** feel sth with sb.

Nacherzählung ['naːx'ɛrtsɛːluŋ] *f* reproduction (of a story).

Nachfahr ['naːxfaːr] *m* -**s**, **-en** descendant.

Nachfolge ['naːxfɔlgə] *f* succession; **n~n** *vi* (*lit*) follow (*jdm/etw* sb/sth); **~r(in** *f)* *m* -**s**, - successor.

nachforschen *vti* investigate.

Nachforschung *f* investigation.

Nachfrage ['naːxfraːgə] *f* inquiry; (*COMM*) demand; **n~n** *vi* inquire.

nach- *zW*: **~fühlen** *vt* **siehe ~empfinden**; **~füllen** *vt* refill; **~geben** *vi unreg* give way, yield; **N~gebühr** *f* surcharge; (*Post*) excess postage; **N~geburt** *f* afterbirth.

nachgehen ['naːxgeːən] *vi unreg* follow (*jdm* sb); (*erforschen*) inquire (*einer Sache* into sth); (*Uhr*) be slow.

Nachgeschmack ['naːxgəʃmak] *m* aftertaste.

nachgiebig ['naːxgiːbɪç] *a* soft, accommodating; **N~keit** *f* softness.

nachhaltig ['naːxhaltɪç] *a* lasting; (*Widerstand*) persistent.

nachhelfen ['naːxhɛlfən] *vi unreg* assist, help (*jdm* sb).

nachher [naːx'heːr] *ad* afterwards.

Nachhilfeunterricht ['naːxhɪlfəʊntərrɪçt] *m* extra tuition.

nachholen ['naːxhoːlən] *vt* catch up with; (*Versäumtes*) make up for.

Nachkomme ['naːxkɔmə] *m* -, **-n** descendant.

nachkommen *vi unreg* follow; (*einer Verpflichtung*) fulfil; **N~schaft** *f* descendants *pl*.

Nachkriegs- ['naːxkriːks] *in zW* postwar; **~zeit** *f* postwar period.

Nach- *zW*: **~laß** *m* -*lasses*, -*lässe* (*COMM*) discount, rebate; (*Erbe*) estate; **n~lassen** *unreg vt* (*Strafe*) remit; (*Summe*) take off; (*Schulden*) cancel // *vi* decrease, ease off; (*Sturm auch*) die down; (*schlechter werden*) deteriorate; **er hat n~gelassen** he has got worse; **n~lässig** *a* negligent, careless; **~lässigkeit** *f* negligence, carelessness.

nachlaufen ['naːxlaufən] *vi unreg* run after, chase (*jdm* sb).

nachmachen ['naːxmaxən] *vt* imitate, copy (*jdm etw* sth from sb); (*fälschen*) counterfeit.

Nachmittag ['naːxmɪtaːk] *m* afternoon; **am ~, n~s** *ad* in the afternoon.

Nach- *zW*: **~nahme** *f* -, **-n** cash on delivery; **per ~nahme** C.O.D.; **~name** *m* surname; **~porto** *nt* excess postage.

nachprüfen ['naːxpryːfən] *vt* check, verify.

nachrechnen ['naːxrɛçnən] *vt* check.

Nachrede ['naːxreːdə] *f*: **üble ~** libel; slander.

Nachricht ['na:xrɪçt] *f* -, **-en** (piece of) news; (*Mitteilung*) message; **~en** *pl* news; **~enagentur** *f* news agency; **~endienst** *m* (*MIL*) intelligence service; **~ensprecher(in** *f*) *m* newsreader; **~entechnik** *f* telecommunications *sing*.

Nachruf ['na:xru:f] *m* obituary.

nachsagen ['na:xza:gən] *vt* repeat; jdm etw ~ say sth of sb.

nachschicken ['na:xʃɪkən] *vt* forward.

Nachschlag- ['na:xʃla:g] *zW:* **n~en** *vt unreg* look up; **Nachschlagewerk** *nt* reference book.

Nach- *zW:* **~schlüssel** *m* master key; **~schub** *m* supplies *pl*; (*Truppen*) reinforcements *pl*.

nachsehen ['na:xze:ən] *unreg vt* (*prüfen*) check; jdm etw ~ forgive sb sth // *vi* (*erforschen*) look and see; **das N~ haben** come off worst.

nachsenden ['na:xzɛndən] *vt unreg* send on, forward.

Nachsicht ['na:xzɪçt] *f* - indulgence, leniency; **n~ig** *a* indulgent, lenient.

nachsitzen ['na:xzɪtsən] *vi unreg:* ~(müssen) (*SCH*) be kept in.

Nachspeise ['na:xʃpaɪzə] *f* dessert, sweet, pudding.

Nachspiel ['na:xʃpi:l] *nt* epilogue; (*fig*) sequel.

nachsprechen ['na:xʃprɛçən] *vt unreg* repeat (*jdm* after sb).

nächst [nɛːçst] *präp +dat* (*räumlich*) next to; (*außer*) apart from; **~beste(r, s)** *a* first that comes along; (*zweitbeste*) next best; **N~e(r)** *mf* neighbour; **~e(r, s)** *a* next; (*nächstgelegen*) nearest; **N~enliebe** *f* love for one's fellow men; **~ens** *ad* shortly, soon; **~liegend** *a* (*lit*) nearest; (*fig*) obvious; **~möglich** *a* next possible.

nachsuchen ['na:xzu:xən] *vi:* **um etw** ~ ask *or* apply for sth.

Nacht [naxt] *f* -, ⁼e night.

Nachteil ['na:xtaɪl] *m* disadvantage; **n~ig** *a* disadvantageous.

Nachthemd *nt* nightshirt; nightdress.

Nachtigall ['naxtɪgal] *f* -, **-en** nightingale.

Nachtisch ['na:xtɪʃ] *m* siehe **Nachspeise.**

Nachtklub *m* night club.

nächtlich ['nɛçtlɪç] *a* nightly.

Nachtlokal *nt* night club.

Nach- *zW:* **~trag** *m* -(e)s, -träge supplement; **n~tragen** *vt unreg* carry (*jdm* after sb); (*zufügen*) add; jdm etw n~tragen hold sth against sb; **n~träglich** *a,ad* later, subsequent(ly); additional(ly); **n~trauern** *vi:* jdm/etw n~trauern mourn the loss of sb/sth.

Nacht- *zW:* **~ruhe** *f* sleep; **n~s** *ad* by

night; **~schicht** *f* nightshift; **nachtsüber** *ad* during the night; **~tarif** *m* off-peak tariff; **~tisch** *m* bedside table; **~wächter** *m* night watchman.

Nach- *zW:* **~untersuchung** *f* checkup; **n~wachsen** *vi unreg* grow again; **~wehen** *pl* afterpains *pl*; (*fig*) aftereffects *pl*.

Nachweis ['na:xvaɪs] *m* -es, -e proof; **n~bar** *a* provable, demonstrable; **n~en** ['na:xvaɪzən] *vt unreg* prove; jdm etw n~en point sth out to sb; **n~lich** *a* evident, demonstrable.

nach- *zW:* **~wirken** *vi* have aftereffects; **N~wirkung** *f* after-effect; **N~wort** *nt* appendix; **N~wuchs** *m* offspring; (*beruflich etc*) new recruits *pl*; **~zahlen** *vti* pay extra; **N~zahlung** *f* additional payment; (*zurückdatiert*) back pay; **~zählen** *vt* count again; **N~zügler** *m* -s, - straggler.

Nacken ['nakən] *m* -s, - nape of the neck.

nackt [nakt] *a* naked; (*Tatsachen*) plain, bare; **N~heit** *f* nakedness.

Nadel ['na:dəl] *f* -, **-n** needle; (*Steck~*) pin; **~kissen** *nt* pincushion; **~öhr** *nt* eye of a needle; **~wald** *m* coniferous forest.

Nagel ['na:gəl] *m* -s, ⁼ nail; **~feile** *f* nailfile; **~haut** *f* cuticle; **~lack** *m* nail varnish; **n~n** *vti* nail; **n~neu** *a* brand-new; **~schere** *f* nail scissors *pl*.

nagen ['na:gən] *vti* gnaw.

Nagetier ['na:gəti:r] *nt* rodent.

nah(e) ['na:(ə)] *a,ad* (*räumlich*) near(by); (*Verwandte*) near; (*Freunde*) close; (*zeitlich*) near, close; der N~e Osten the Near East // *präp +dat* near (to), close to; **N~aufnahme** *f* close-up.

Nähe ['nɛːə] *f* - nearness, proximity; (*Umgebung*) vicinity; **in der** ~ close by; at hand; **aus der** ~ from close to.

nahe- *zW:* **~bei** *ad* nearby; **~gehen** *vi unreg* grieve (*jdm* sb); **~kommen** *vi unreg* get close (*jdm* to sb); **~legen** *vt:* jdm etw ~legen suggest sth to sb; **~liegen** *vi unreg* be obvious; **~liegend** *a* obvious; **~n** *vir* approach, draw near.

Näh- ['nɛː] *zW:* **n~en** *vti* sew; **n~er** *a,ad* nearer; (*Erklärung, Erkundigung*) more detailed; **~ere(s)** *nt* details *pl*, particulars *pl*; **~erei** *f* sewing, needlework; **~erin** *f* seamstress; **n~erkommen** *vir unreg* get closer; **n~ern** *vr* approach.

nahe- *zW:* **~stehen** *vi unreg* be close (*jdm* to sb); **einer Sache ~stehen** sympathize with sth; **~stehend** *a* close; **~treten** *vi unreg:* jdm (zu) ~treten offend sb; **~zu** *ad* nearly.

Nähgarn nt thread.
nahm etc v siehe **nehmen**.
Näh- zW: **~maschine** f sewing machine; **~nadel** f needle.
nähren ['nɛ:rən] vtr feed.
nahrhaft ['na:rhaft] a nourishing, nutritious.
Nahrung [na:rʊŋ] f food; (fig auch) sustenance.
Nahrungs- zW: **~mittel** nt foodstuffs pl; **~mittelindustrie** f food industry; **~suche** f search for food.
Nährwert m nutritional value.
Naht [na:t] f -, ̃e seam; (MED) suture; (TECH) join; **n~los** a seamless; **n~los ineinander übergehen** follow without a gap.
Nah- zW: **~verkehr** m local traffic; **~verkehrszug** m local train; **~ziel** nt immediate objective.
naiv [na'i:f] a naive; **N~ität** [naivi'tɛ:t] f naivety.
Name ['na:mə] m -ns, -n name; **im ~n von** on behalf of; **n~ns** ad by the name of; **~nstag** m name day, saint's day; **n~ntlich** a by name // ad particularly, especially.
namhaft ['na:mhaft] a (berühmt) famed, renowned; (beträchtlich) considerable; **~ machen** name.
nämlich ['nɛ:mlɪç] ad that is to say, namely; (denn) since.
nannte etc v siehe **nennen**.
nanu [na'nu:] interj well, well!
Napf [napf] m -(e)s, ̃e bowl, dish.
Narbe ['narbə] f -, -n scar.
narbig ['narbɪç] a scarred.
Narkose [nar'ko:zə] f -, -n anaesthetic.
Narr [nar] m -en, -en fool; **n~en** vt fool; **~heit** f foolishness.
Närr- ['nɛr] zW: **~in** f fool; **n~isch** a foolish, crazy.
Narzisse [nar'tsɪsə] f -, -n narcissus; daffodil.
nasch- ['naʃ] zW: **~en** vti nibble; eat secretly; **~haft** a sweet-toothed.
Nase ['na:zə] f -, -n nose.
Nasen- zW: **~bluten** nt -s nosebleed; **~loch** nt nostril; **~tropfen** pl nose drops pl.
naseweis a pert, cheeky; (neugierig) nosey.
Nashorn ['na:shɔrn] nt rhinoceros.
naß [nas] a wet.
Nässe ['nɛsə] f - wetness; **n~n** vt wet.
naßkalt a wet and cold.
Naßrasur f wet shave.
Nation [natsi'o:n] f nation.
national [natsio'na:l] a national; **N~hymne** f national anthem; **~isieren** [-i'zi:rən] vt nationalize; **N~i'sierung** f nationalization; **N~ismus** [-'lɪsmʊs] m nationalism; **~istisch** [-'lɪstɪʃ] a nationalistic; **N~i'tät** f nationality; **N~mannschaft**

f national team; **N~sozialismus** m national socialism.
Natron ['na:trɔn] nt -s soda.
Natter ['natər] f -, -n adder.
Natur [na'tu:r] f nature; (körperlich) constitution; **~a'lismus** m naturalism; **~erscheinung** f natural phenomenon od event; **n~farben** a natural coloured; **n~gemäß** a natural; **~gesetz** nt law of nature; **~katastrophe** f natural disaster.
natürlich [na'ty:rlɪç] a natural // ad naturally; **ja, ~!** yes, of course; **N~keit** f naturalness.
Natur- zW: **~produkt** nt natural product; **n~rein** a natural, pure; **~schutzgebiet** nt nature reserve; **~wissenschaft** f natural science; **~wissenschaftler(in** f) m scientist; **~zustand** m natural state.
nautisch ['nautɪʃ] a nautical.
Nazi ['na:tsi] m -s, -s Nazi.
n.Chr. abk (= nach Christus) AD.
Neapel [ne'a:pəl] nt -s Naples.
Nebel ['ne:bəl] m -s, - fog, mist; **n~ig** a foggy, misty; **~scheinwerfer** m foglamp.
neben ['ne:bən] präp +akk od dat next to; (außer) apart from, besides; **~an** [ne:bən''an] ad next door; **N~anschluß** m (TEL) extension; **~bei** [ne:bən'bai] ad at the same time; (außerdem) additionally; (beiläufig) incidentally; **N~beschäftigung** f second job; **N~buhler(in** f) m -s, - rival; **~einander** [ne:bən'ai'nandər] ad side by side; **~einanderlegen** vt put next to each other; **N~eingang** m side entrance; **N~erscheinung** f side effect; **~fach** nt subsidiary subject; **N~fluß** m tributary; **N~geräusch** nt (RAD) atmospherics pl, interference; **~her** [ne:bən'he:r] ad (zusätzlich) besides; (gleichzeitig) at the same time; (daneben) alongside; **~herfahren** vi unreg drive alongside; **N~kosten** pl extra charges pl, extras pl; **N~produkt** nt by-product; **N~rolle** f minor part; **N~sache** f trifle, side issue; **~sächlich** a minor, peripheral; **N~straße** f side street.
neblig ['ne:blɪç] a = **nebelig**.
Necessaire [nesɛ'sɛ:r] nt -s, -s (Näh~) needlework box; (Nagel~) manicure case.
neck- ['nɛk] zW: **~en** vt tease; **N~e'rei** f teasing; **~isch** a coy; (Einfall, Lied) amusing.
Neffe ['nɛfə] m -n, -n nephew.
negativ [nega'ti:f] a negative; **N~** nt -s, -e (PHOT) negative.
Neger ['ne:gər] m -s, - negro; **~in** f negress.
nehmen ['ne:mən] vt unreg take; jdn

zu sich ~ take sb in; sich ernst ~ take o.s. seriously; **nimm dir noch einmal** help yourself.

Neid [naɪt] *m* -(e)s envy; **~er** *m* -s, - envier; **n~isch** *a* envious, jealous.

neigen ['naɪgən] *vt* incline, lean; (*Kopf*) bow // *vi*: **zu etw ~** tend to sth.

Neigung *f* (*des Geländes*) slope; (*Tendenz*) tendency, inclination; (*Vorliebe*) liking; (*Zuneigung*) affection.

nein [naɪn] *ad* no.

Nelke ['nɛlkə] *f* -, -n carnation, pink; (*Gewürz*) clove.

Nenn- ['nɛn] *zW*: **n~en** *vt unreg* name; (*mit Namen*) call; **wie ~t man ...?** what do you call ...?; **n~enswert** *a* worth mentioning; **~er** *m* -s, - denominator; **~wert** *m* nominal value; (*COMM*) par.

Neon ['neːɔn] *nt* -s neon; **~licht** *nt* neon light; **~röhre** *f* neon tube.

Nerv [nɛrf] *m* -s, -en nerve; **jdm auf die ~en gehen** get on sb's nerves; **n~enaufreibend** *a* nerve-racking; **~enbündel** *nt* bundle of nerves; **~enheilanstalt** *f* mental home; **n~enkrank** *a* mentally ill; **~enschwäche** *f* neurasthenia; **~ensystem** *nt* nervous system; **~enzusammenbruch** *m* nervous breakdown; **n~ös** [nɛr'vøːs] *a* nervous; **~osität** *f* nervousness; **n~tötend** *a* nerve-racking (*Arbeit*) soul-destroying.

Nerz [nɛrts] *m* -es, -e mink.

Nessel ['nɛsəl] *f* -, -n nettle.

Nest [nɛst] *nt* -(e)s, -er nest; (*umg: Ort*) dump.

nett [nɛt] *a* nice; (*freundlich auch*) kind; **~erweise** *ad* kindly.

netto ['nɛto] *ad* net.

Netz [nɛts] *nt* -es, -e net; (*Gepäck~*) rack; (*Einkaufs~*) string bag; (*Spinnen~*) web; (*System*) network; **jdm ins ~ gehen** (*fig*) fail into sb's trap; **~anschluß** *m* mains connection; **~haut** *f* retina.

neu [nɔy] *a* new; (*Sprache, Geschichte*) modern; **seit ~estem** (since) recently; **die ~esten Nachrichten** the latest news; **~ schreiben** rewrite, write again; **N~anschaffung** *f* new purchase *od* acquisition; **~artig** *a* new kind of; **N~auflage** *f* new edition; **N~bau** *m* new building; **~erdings** *ad* (*kürzlich*) (since) recently; (*von neuem*) again; **N~erung** *f* innovation, new departure; **N~fundland** *nt* Newfoundland; **N~gier** *f* curiosity; **~gierig** *a* curious; **N~guinea** *nt* New Guinea; **N~heit** *f* newness; novelty; **N~igkeit** *f* news; **N~jahr** *nt* New Year; **~lich**

ad recently, the other day; **N~ling** *m* novice; **N~mond** *m* new moon.

neun [nɔyn] *num* nine; **~zehn** *num* nineteen; **~zig** *num* ninety.

neureich *a* nouveau riche; **N~e(r)** *mf* nouveau riche.

Neur- *zW*: **~ose** [nɔy'roːzə] *f* -, -n neurosis; **~otiker** [nɔy'roːtikər] *m* -s, - neurotic; **n~otisch** *a* neurotic.

Neusee- [nɔy'zeː] *zW*: **~land** *nt* New Zealand; **~länder(in** *f*) *m* New Zealander; **n~ländisch** *a* New Zealand.

Neutr- *zW*: **n~al** [nɔy'traːl] *a* neutral; **n~alisieren** *vt* neutralize; **~alität** *f* neutrality; **~on** ['nɔytrɔn] *nt* -s, -en neutron; **~um** ['nɔytrum] *nt* -s, -a *od* -en neuter.

Neu- *zW*: **~wert** *m* purchase price; **~zeit** *f* modern age; **n~zeitlich** *a* modern, recent.

nicht [nɪçt] *ad* **1** (*Verneinung*) not; **er ist es ~** it's not him, it isn't him; **er raucht ~** (*gerade*) he isn't smoking; (*gewöhnlich*) he doesn't smoke; **ich kann das ~ — ich auch ~** neither — neither *od* nor can I; **es regnet ~ mehr** it's not raining any more **2** (*Bitte, Verbot*): **~! don't!, no!; ~ berühren!** do not touch!; **~ doch!** don't!

3 (*rhetorisch*): **du bist müde, ~ (wahr)?** you're tired, aren't you?; **das ist schön, ~ (wahr)?** it's nice, isn't it?

4: was du ~ sagst! the things you say!

Nichtangriffspakt [nɪçt''angrifspakt] *m* non-aggression pact.

Nichte ['nɪçtə] *f* -, -n niece.

nichtig ['nɪçtɪç] *a* (*ungültig*) null, void; (*wertlos*) futile; **N~keit** *f* nullity, invalidity; (*Sinnlosigkeit*) futility.

Nichtraucher(in *f*) *m* non-smoker.

nichtrostend *a* stainless.

nichts [nɪçts] *pron* nothing; **für ~ und wieder ~** for nothing at all; **N~** *nt* - nothingness; (*pej: Person*) nonentity; **~destoweniger** *ad* nevertheless; **N~nutz** *m* -es, -e good-for-nothing; **~nutzig** *a* worthless, useless; **~sagend** *a* meaningless; **N~tun** *nt* -s idleness.

Nickel ['nɪkəl] *nt* -s nickel.

nicken ['nɪkən] *vi* nod.

Nickerchen ['nɪkərçən] *nt* nap.

nie [niː] *ad* never; **~ wieder** *od* **mehr** never again; **~ und nimmer** never ever.

nieder ['niːdər] *a* low; (*gering*) inferior // *ad* down; **N~gang** *m* decline; **~gehen** *vi unreg* descend; (*AVIAT*) come down; (*Regen*) fall; (*Boxer*) go down; **~geschlagen** *a* depressed, dejected; **N~geschlagenheit** *f* depression, dejection; **N~lage** *f* defeat;

N~**lande** *pl* Netherlands; **N~-
länder(in** *f)* *m* Dutchman; Dutchwoman; ~**ländisch** *a* Dutch; ~**lassen**
vr unreg (sich setzen) sit down; *(an
Ort)* settle (down); *(Arzt, Rechtsanwalt)* set up a practice; **N~lassung** *f*
settlement; *(COMM)* branch; ~**legen**
vt lay down; *(Arbeit)* stop; *(Amt)* resign; **N~rhein** *nt* Lower Rhine;
N~sachsen *nt* Lower Saxony;
N~schlag *m (MET)* precipitation;
rainfall; ~**schlagen** *unreg vt (Gegner)* beat down; *(Gegenstand)* knock
down; *(Augen)* lower; *(Aufstand)* put
down // *vr (CHEM)* precipitate;
N~schrift *f* transcription; ~**trächtig** *a* base, mean; **N~trächtigkeit**
f meanness, baseness; outrage;
N~ung *f (GEOG)* depression; flats *pl*.
niedlich ['niːtlɪç] *a* sweet, cute.
niedrig ['niːdrɪç] *a* low; *(Stand)* lowly,
humble; *(Gesinnung)* mean.
niemals ['niːmaːls] *ad* never.
niemand ['niːmant] *pron* nobody, no
one; **Niemandsland** *nt* no-man's land.
Niere ['niːrə] *f -, -n* kidney;
Nierenentzündung *f* kidney infection.
nieseln ['niːzəln] *vi* drizzle.
niesen ['niːzən] *vi* sneeze.
Niete ['niːtə] *f -, -n (TECH)* rivet;
(Los) blank; *(Reinfall)* flop; *(Mensch)*
failure; **n~en** *vt* rivet.
Nikotin [niko'tiːn] *nt -s* nicotine.
Nil ['niːl] *m* Nile; ~**pferd** *nt* hippopotamus.
Nimmersatt ['nɪmərzat] *m -(e)s, -e*
glutton.
nimmst *etc v siehe* **nehmen**.
nippen ['nɪpən] *vti* sip.
nirgend- ['nɪrgənt] *zW:* ~**s**, ~**wo** *ad*
nowhere; ~**wohin** *ad* nowhere.
Nische ['niːʃə] *f -, -n* niche.
nisten ['nɪstən] *vi* nest.
Nitrat [ni'traːt] *nt -(e)s, -e* nitrate.
Niveau [ni'voː] *nt -s, -s* level.
Nixe ['nɪksə] *f -, -n* water nymph.
noch [nox] ◆*ad* **1** *(weiterhin)* still; ~
nicht not yet; ~ nie never (yet); ~
immer, immer ~ still; bleiben Sie
doch ~ stay a bit longer
2 *(in Zukunft)* still, yet; **das kann** ~
passieren that might still happen; **er
wird** ~ **kommen** he'll come (yet)
3 *(nicht später als)*: ~ **vor einer
Woche** only a week ago; ~ **am
selben Tag** the very same day; ~ **im
19. Jahrhundert** as late as the 19th
century; ~ **heute** today
4 *(zusätzlich)*: **wer war** ~ **da?** who
else was there?; ~ **einmal** once
more, again; ~ **dreimal** three more
times; ~ **einer** another one
5 *(bei Vergleichen)*: ~ **größer** even
bigger; **das ist** ~ **besser** that's better
still; **und wenn es** ~ **so schwer ist**

however hard it is
6: Geld ~ **und** ~ heaps (and heaps)
of money; **sie hat** ~ **und** ~ **versucht,**
... she tried again and again to ...
◆*kj* **weder A** ~ **B** neither A nor B.
nochmal(s) ['nɔxmaːl(s)] *ad* again,
once more.
nochmalig ['nɔxmaːlɪç] *a* repeated.
Nominativ ['noːminatiːf] *m -s, -e*
nominative.
nominell [nomi'nɛl] *a* nominal.
Nonne ['nɔnə] *f -, -n* nun.
Nord(en) ['nɔrd(ən)] *m -s* north;
N~'irland *nt* Northern Ireland;
n~isch *a* northern.
nördlich ['nœrtlɪç] *a* northerly, northern; ~ **von,** ~ **präp** +*gen* (to the)
north of.
Nord- *zW:* ~**pol** *m* North Pole;
~**rhein-Westfalen** *nt* North Rhine-
Westphalia; ~**see** *f* North Sea;
n~wärts *ad* northwards.
Nörg- ['nœrg] *zW:* ~**e'lei** *f* grumbling;
n~eln *vi* grumble; ~**ler** *m -s, -*
grumbler.
Norm [nɔrm] *f -, -en* norm;
(Größenvorschrift) standard; **n~al**
[nɔr'maːl] *a* normal; **n~alerweise** *ad*
normally; **n~ali'sieren** *vt* normalize
// *vr* return to normal; **n~en** *vt*
standardize.
Norweg- ['nɔrveːg] *zW:* ~**en** *nt* Norway; ~**er(in** *f)* *m -s, -* Norwegian;
n~isch *a* Norwegian.
Not [noːt] *f -, =e* need; *(Mangel)*
want; *(Mühe)* trouble; *(Zwang)* necessity; **zur** ~ if necessary; *(gerade
noch)* just about.
Notar [no'taːr] *m -s, -e* notary; **n~i'ell**
a notarial.
Not- *zW:* ~**ausgang** *m* emergency
exit; ~**behelf** *m -s, -e* makeshift;
~**bremse** *f* emergency brake;
n~dürftig *a* scanty; *(behelfsmäßig)*
makeshift.
Note ['noːtə] *f -, -n* note; *(SCH)* mark
(Brit), grade *(US)*.
Noten- *zW:* ~**blatt** *nt* sheet of music;
~**schlüssel** *m* clef; ~**ständer** *m* music stand.
Not- *zW:* ~**fall** *m* (case of) emergency; **n~falls** *ad* if need be;
n~gedrungen *a* necessary, unavoidable; **etw n~gedrungen machen** be
forced to do sth.
notieren [no'tiːrən] *vt* note; *(COMM)*
quote.
Notierung *f (COMM)* quotation.
nötig ['nøːtɪç] *a* necessary; **etw** ~
haben need sth; ~**en** *vt* compel,
force; ~**enfalls** *ad* if necessary.
Notiz [no'tiːts] *f -, -en* note; *(Zei-
tungs~)* item; ~ **nehmen** take notice;
~**buch** *nt* notebook.
Not- *zW:* ~**lage** *f* crisis, emergency;

n~landen vi make a forced od emergency landing; **n~leidend** a needy; **~lösung** f temporary solution; **~lüge** f white lie.

notorisch [no'to:rıʃ] a notorious.

Not- zW: **~ruf** m emergency call; **~stand** m state of emergency; **~unterkunft** f emergency accommodation; **~verband** m emergency dressing; **~wehr** f - self-defence; **n~wendig** a necessary; **~wendigkeit** f necessity; **~zucht** f rape.

Novelle [no'vɛlə] f -, -n short story; (JUR) amendment.

November [no'vɛmbər] m -(s), - November.

Nr. abk (= Nummer) no.

Nu [nu:] m: im ~ in an instant.

Nuance [ny'ã:sə] f -, -n nuance.

nüchtern ['nʏçtərn] a sober; (Magen) empty; (Urteil) prudent; **N~heit** f sobriety.

Nudel ['nu:dəl] f -, -n noodle; **~n** pasta; (in Suppe) noodles.

Null [nʊl] f -, -en nought, zero; (pej: Mensch) washout; **n~** num zero; (Fehler) no; **n~ Uhr** midnight; **n~ und nichtig** null and void; **~punkt** m zero; **auf dem ~punkt** at zero.

numerieren [nume'ri:rən] vt number.

numerisch [nu'me:rıʃ] a numerical.

Nummer ['nʊmər] f -, -n number; (Größe) size; **Nummernschild** nt (AUT) number od license (US) plate.

nun [nu:n] ad now; **das ist ~ mal so** that's the way it is // interj well.

nur [nu:r] ad just, only; **wo bleibt er ~?** (just) where is he?.

Nürnberg ['nʏrnbɛrk] nt -s Nuremberg.

Nuß [nʊs] f -, **Nüsse** nut; **~baum** m walnut tree; hazelnut tree; **~knacker** m -s, - nutcracker.

Nüster ['ny:stər] f -, -n nostril.

Nutte ['nʊtə] f -, -n tart.

nutz [nʊts], **nütze** ['nʏtsə] a: **zu nichts ~ sein** be useless; **~en**, **nützen** vt use (zu etw for sth) // vi be of use; **was nützt es?** what's the use?, what use is it?; **N~en** m -s usefulness; profit; **von N~en** useful.

nützlich ['nʏtslıç] a useful; **N~keit** f usefulness.

Nutz- zW: **n~los** a useless; **~losigkeit** f uselessness; **~nießer** m -s, - beneficiary.

Nylon ['naılɔn] nt nylon.

O

O, o [o:] nt O, o.

Oase [o'a:zə] f -, -n oasis.

ob [ɔp] kj if, whether; **~ das wohl wahr ist?** can that be true?; **und ~!** you bet!

Obdach ['ɔpdax] nt -(e)s shelter, lodging; **o~los** a homeless; **~lose(r)** mf homeless person.

Obduktion [ɔpdʊktsi'o:n] f postmortem.

obduzieren [ɔpdu'tsi:rən] vt do a post-mortem on.

O-Beine ['o:baınə] pl bow od bandy legs pl.

oben ['o:bən] ad above; (in Haus) upstairs; **nach ~** up; **von ~** down; **~ ohne** topless; **jdn von ~ bis unten ansehen** look sb up and down; **Befehl von ~** orders from above; **~an** ad at the top; **~auf** ad up above, on the top // a (munter) in form; **~drein** ad into the bargain; **~erwähnt**, **~genannt** a above-mentioned.

Ober ['o:bər] m -s, - waiter; **~arm** m upper arm; **~arzt** m senior physician; **~aufsicht** f supervision; **~bayern** nt Upper Bavaria; **~befehl** m supreme command; **~befehlshaber** m commander-in-chief; **~bekleidung** f outer clothing; **~'bürgermeister** m lord mayor; **~deck** nt upper od top deck; **o~e(r, s)** a upper; **die ~en** the bosses; (ECCL) the superiors; **~fläche** f surface; **o~flächlich** a superficial; **~geschoß** nt upper storey; **o~halb** ad, präp +gen above; **~haupt** nt head, chief; **~haus** nt upper house; House of Lords; **~hemd** nt shirt; **~herrschaft** f supremacy, sovereignty; **~in** f matron; (ECCL) Mother Superior; **~kellner** m head waiter; **~kiefer** m upper jaw; **~körper** m trunk, upper part of body; **~leitung** f direction; (ELEK) overhead cable; **~licht** nt skylight; **~lippe** f upper lip; **~schenkel** m thigh; **~schicht** f upper classes pl; **~schule** f grammar school (Brit), high school (US); **~schwester** f (MED) matron.

Oberst ['o:bərst] m -en od -s, -en od -e colonel; **o~e(r, s)** a very top, topmost.

Ober- zW: **~stufe** f upper school; **~teil** nt upper part; **~weite** f bust/ chest measurement.

obgleich [ɔp'glaıç] kj although.

Obhut ['ɔphu:t] f - care, protection; **in jds ~ sein** be in sb's care.

obig ['o:bıç] a above.

Objekt [ɔp'jɛkt] nt -(e)s, -e object; **~iv** [-'ti:f] nt -s, -e lens; **o~iv** a objective; **~ivität** f objectivity.

Oblate [o'bla:tə] f -, -n (Gebäck) wafer; (ECCL) host.

Obligation [ɔbligatsi'o:n] f bond.

obligatorisch [ɔbliga'to:rıʃ] a compulsory, obligatory.

Oboe [o'bo:ə] f -, -n oboe.

Obrigkeit ['oːbrıçkaıt] *f* (*Behörden*) authorities *pl*, administration; (*Regierung*) government.

obschon [ɔp'ʃoːn] *kj* although.

Observatorium [ɔpzɛrva'toːriʊm] *nt* observatory.

obskur [ɔps'kuːr] *a* obscure; (*verdächtig*) dubious.

Obst [oːpst] *nt* -(e)s fruit; ~**baum** *m* fruit tree; ~**garten** *m* orchard; ~**händler** *m* fruiterer, fruit merchant; ~**kuchen** *m* fruit tart.

obszön [ɔps'tsøːn] *a* obscene; **O~i'tät** *f* obscenity.

obwohl [ɔp'voːl] *kj* although.

Ochse ['ɔksə] *m* -n, -n ox; **o~n** *vti* (*umg*) cram, swot (*Brit*); **Ochsenschwanzsuppe** *f* oxtail soup; **Ochsenzunge** *f* oxtongue.

öd(e) ['øːd(ə)] *a* (*Land*) waste, barren; (*fig*) dull; **O~e** *f* -, -n desert, waste (land); (*fig*) tedium.

oder ['oːdər] *kj* or; das stimmt, ~? that's right, isn't it?

Ofen ['oːfən] *m* -s, ⸚ oven; (*Heiz*~) fire, heater; (*Kohlen*~) stove; (*Hoch*~) furnace; (*Herd*) cooker, stove; ~**rohr** *nt* stovepipe.

offen ['ɔfən] *a* open; (*aufrichtig*) frank; (*Stelle*) vacant; ~ gesagt to be honest; ~**bar** *a* obvious; ~**baren** [ɔfən'baːrən] *vt* reveal, manifest; **O~'barung** *f* (*REL*) revelation; ~**bleiben** *vi unreg* (*Fenster*) stay open; (*Frage, Entscheidung*) remain open; ~**halten** *vt unreg* keep open; **O~heit** *f* candour, frankness; ~**herzig** *a* candid, frank; (*Kleid*) revealing; ~**kundig** *a* well-known; (*klar*) evident; ~**lassen** *vt unreg* leave open; ~**sichtlich** *a* evident, obvious.

offensiv [ɔfɛn'ziːf] *a* offensive; **O~e** [-'ziːvə] *f* -, -n offensive.

offenstehen *vi unreg* be open; (*Rechnung*) be unpaid; es steht Ihnen offen, es zu tun you are at liberty to do it.

öffentlich ['œfəntlıç] *a* public; **Ö~keit** *f* (*Leute*) public; (*einer Versammlung etc*) public nature; in aller **Ö~keit** in public; an die **Ö~keit** dringen reach the public ear.

offiziell [ɔfitsi'ɛl] *a* official.

Offizier [ɔfi'tsiːr] *m* -s, -e officer; **Offizierskasino** *nt* officers' mess.

öffnen ['œfnən] *vtr* open; jdm die Tür ~ open the door for sb.

Öffner ['œfnər] *m* -s, - opener.

Öffnung ['œfnʊŋ] *f* opening; **Öffnungszeiten** *pl* opening times *pl*.

oft [ɔft] *ad* often.

öfter ['œftər] *ad* more often *od* frequently; ~s *ad* often, frequently.

oftmals *ad* often, frequently.

oh [oː] *interj* oh; ~ je! oh dear.

OHG [oːha'geː] *abk* (= *Offene Handelsgesellschaft*) general partnership.

ohne ['oːnə] *präp* +*akk*, *kj* without; das ist nicht ~ (*umg*) it's not bad; ~ weiteres without a second thought; ~ zu fragen without asking; ~ daß er es wußte without him knowing it; (*sofort*) immediately; ~**dies** [oːnə'diːs] *ad* anyway; ~**einander** [oːnəʔaı'nandər] *ad* without each other; ~**gleichen** [oːnə'glaıçən] *a* unsurpassed, without equal; ~**hin** [oːnə'hın] *ad* anyway, in any case.

Ohnmacht ['oːnmaxt] *f* faint; (*fig*) impotence; in ~ fallen faint.

ohnmächtig ['oːnmɛçtıç] *a* in a faint, unconscious; (*fig*) weak, impotent; sie ist ~ she has fainted.

Ohr [oːr] *nt* -(e)s, -en ear; (*Gehör*) hearing.

Öhr [øːr] *nt* -(e)s, -e eye.

Ohren- *zW*: ~**arzt** *m* ear specialist; **o~betäubend** *a* deafening; ~**schmalz** *nt* earwax; ~**schmerzen** *pl* earache; ~**schützer** *m* -s, - earmuff.

Ohr- *zW*: ~**feige** *f* slap on the face; box on the ears; **o~feigen** *vt* slap sb's face; box sb's ears; ~**läppchen** *nt* ear lobe; ~**ringe** *pl* earrings *pl*; ~**wurm** *m* earwig; (*MUS*) catchy tune.

ökonomisch [øko'noːmıʃ] *a* economical.

Oktave [ɔk'taːvə] *f* -, -n octave.

Oktober [ɔk'toːbər] *m* -(s), - October.

ökumenisch [øku'meːnıʃ] *a* ecumenical.

Öl [øːl] *nt* -(e)s, -e oil; ~**baum** *m* olive tree; **ö~en** *vt* oil; (*TECH*) lubricate; ~**farbe** *f* oil paint; ~**feld** *nt* oilfield; ~**film** *m* film of oil; ~**heizung** *f* oil-fired central heating; **ö~ig** *a* oily.

oliv [o'liːf] *a* olive-green; **O~e** [o'liːvə] *f* -, -n olive.

Öl- *zW*: ~**meßstab** *m* dipstick; ~**sardine** *f* sardine; ~**standanzeiger** *m* (*AUT*) oil gauge; ~**ung** *f* lubrication; oiling; (*ECCL*) anointment; die Letzte ~**ung** Extreme Unction; ~**wechsel** *m* oil change; ~**zeug** *nt* oilskins *pl*.

Olymp- [o'lymp] *zW*: ~**iade** [-i'aːdə] *f* Olympic Games *pl*; ~**iasieger(in** *f*) [-iaziːgər(ın)] *m* Olympic champion; ~**iateilnehmer(in** *f*) *m* Olympic competitor; **o~isch** *a* Olympic.

Oma [o'maː] *f* -, -s (*umg*) granny.

Omelett [ɔm(ə)'lɛt] *nt* -(e)s, -s omelet(te).

Omen ['oːmɛn] *nt* -s, - omen.

Omnibus ['ɔmnibʊs] *m* (omni)bus.

Onanie [ona'niː] *f* masturbation; **o~ren** *vi* masturbate.

Onkel ['ɔŋkəl] *m* -s, - uncle.

Opa ['o:pa] *m* -s, -s (*umg*) grandpa.

Opal [o'pa:l] *m* -s, -e opal.

Oper ['o:pər] *f* -, -n opera; opera house.

Operation [operatsi'o:n] *f* operation; **Operationssaal** *m* operating theatre.

Operette [ope'rɛtə] *f* operetta.

operieren [ope'ri:rən] *vti* operate.

Opern- *zW:* ~**glas** *nt* opera glasses *pl*; ~**haus** *nt* opera house; ~**sänger(in** *f*) *m* operatic singer.

Opfer ['ɔpfər] *nt* -s, - sacrifice; (*Mensch*) victim; **o~n** *vt* sacrifice; ~**stock** *m* (*ECCL*) offertory box; ~**ung** *f* sacrifice.

Opium ['o:piʊm] *nt* -s opium.

opponieren [ɔpo'ni:rən] *vi* oppose (*gegen jdn/etw* sb/sth).

opportun [ɔpɔr'tu:n] *a* opportune; **O~ist** [-'nɪst] *m* opportunist.

Opposition [ɔpozitsi'o:n] *f* opposition; **o~ell** [-'nɛl] *a* opposing.

Optik ['ɔptɪk] *f* optics *sing*; ~**er** *m* -s, - optician.

optimal [ɔpti'ma:l] *a* optimal, optimum.

Optimismus [ɔpti'mɪsmʊs] *m* optimism.

Optimist [ɔpti'mɪst] *m* optimist; **o~isch** *a* optimistic.

optisch ['ɔptɪʃ] *a* optical.

Orakel [o'ra:kəl] *nt* -s, - oracle.

Orange [o'rã:ʒə] *f* -, -n orange; **o~** *a* orange; **Orangeade** [orã'ʒa:də] *f* orangeade; **Orangeat** [orã'ʒa:t] *nt* -s, -e candied peel; **Orangensaft** *m* orange juice.

Orchester [ɔr'kɛstər] *nt* -s, - orchestra.

Orchidee [ɔrçi'de:ə] *f* -, -n orchid.

Orden ['ɔrdən] *m* -s, - (*ECCL*) order; (*MIL*) decoration; **Ordensschwester** *f* nun.

ordentlich ['ɔrdəntlıç] *a* (*anständig*) decent, respectable; (*geordnet*) tidy, neat; (*umg: annehmbar*) not bad; (*umg: tüchtig*) real, proper; ~**er** Professor (full) professor // *ad* properly; **O~keit** *f* respectability; tidiness, neatness.

ordinär [ɔrdi'nɛ:r] *a* common, vulgar.

ordnen ['ɔrdnən] *vt* order, put in order.

Ordner *m* -s, - steward; (*COMM*) file.

Ordnung *f* order; (*Ordnen*) ordering; (*Geordnetsein*) tidiness; ~ **machen** tidy up; **in** ~! okay.

Ordnungs- *zW:* **o~gemäß** *a* proper, according to the rules; **o~halber** *ad* as a matter of form; ~**strafe** *f* fine; **o~widrig** *a* contrary to the rules, irregular; ~**zahl** *f* ordinal number.

Organ [ɔr'ga:n] *nt* -s, -e organ; (*Stimme*) voice; ~**isation** [-izatsi'o:n] *f* organisation; ~**isator** [-i'za:tɔr] *m*

organizer; **o~isch** *a* organic; **o~isieren** [-i'zi:rən] *vt* organize, arrange; (*umg: beschaffen*) acquire // *vr* organize; ~**ismus** [-'nɪsmʊs] *m* organism; ~**ist** [-'nɪst] *m* organist.

Orgasmus [ɔr'gasmʊs] *m* orgasm.

Orgel ['ɔrgəl] *f* -, -n organ.

Orgie ['ɔrgiə] *f* orgy.

Orient ['o:riɛnt] *m* -s Orient, east; ~**ale** [-'ta:lə] *m* -n, -n Oriental; **o~alisch** [-'ta:lıʃ] *a* oriental; **o~ieren** [-'ti:rən] *vt* (*örtlich*) locate; (*fig*) inform // *vr* find one's way od bearings; inform oneself; ~**ierung** [-'ti:rʊŋ] *f* orientation; (*fig*) information; ~**ierungssinn** *m* sense of direction.

original [origi'na:l] *a* original; **O~** *nt* -s, -e original; **O~fassung** *f* original version; **O~i'tät** *f* originality.

originell [origi'nɛl] *a* original.

Orkan [ɔr'ka:n] *m* -(e)s, -e hurricane.

Ornament [ɔrna'mɛnt] *nt* decoration, ornament; **o~al** [-'ta:l] *a* decorative, ornamental.

Ort [ɔrt] *m* -(e)s, -e od -er place; an ~ und Stelle on the spot; **o~en** *vt* locate.

ortho- [ɔrto] *zW:* ~**dox** [-'dɔks] *a* orthodox; **O~graphie** [-gra'fi:] *f* spelling, orthography; **o~graphisch** *a* orthographic; **O~päde** [-'pɛ:də] *m* -n, -n orthopaedic specialist, orthopaedist; **O~pädie** [-pɛ'di:] *f* orthopaedics *sing*; **o~pädisch** *a* orthopaedic.

örtlich ['œrtlıç] *a* local; **Ö~keit** *f* locality.

Ortschaft *f* village, small town.

Orts- *zW:* **o~fremd** *a* non-local; ~**gespräch** *nt* local (phone) call; ~**name** *m* place-name; ~**netz** *nt* (*TEL*) local telephone exchange area; ~**zeit** *f* local time.

Ortung *f* locating.

Öse ['ø:zə] *f* -, -n loop, eye.

Ost- [ɔst] *zW:* ~'**asien** *nt* Eastern Asia; ~**block** *m* (*POL*) Eastern bloc; ~**en** *m* -s east; ~'**ende** *nt* Ostend.

Oster- ['o:stər] *zW:* ~**ei** *nt* Easter egg; ~**fest** *nt* Easter; ~**glocke** *f* daffodil; ~**hase** *m* Easter bunny; ~**montag** *m* Easter Monday; ~**n** *nt* -s, - Easter.

Österreich ['ø:stərraıç] *nt* -s Austria; ~**er(in** *f*) *m* -s, - Austrian; **ö~isch** *a* Austrian.

Ostersonntag *m* Easter Day od Sunday.

östlich ['œstlıç] *a* eastern, easterly.

Ost- *zW:* ~**see** *f* Baltic Sea; **o~wärts** *ad* eastwards; ~**wind** *m* east wind.

Otter ['ɔtər] *m* -s, - otter // *f* -, -n (*Schlange*) adder.

Ouvertüre [uver'ty:rə] *f* -, -n overture.

oval [o'va:l] *a* oval.

Ovation [ovatsi'o:n] *f* ovation.

Ovulation [ovulatsi'o:n] f ovulation.
Oxyd [ɔ'ksy:t] nt -(e)s, -e oxide;
o~**ieren** [ɔksy'di:rən] vti oxidize;
~**ierung** f oxidization.
Ozean ['o:tsea:n] m -s, -e ocean;
~**dampfer** m (ocean-going) liner.
Ozon [o'tso:n] nt -s ozone.

P

P, p [pe:] nt P, p.
Paar [pa:r] nt -(e)s, -e pair; (Ehe~)
couple; **ein p~ a few**; **p~en** vtr couple; (Tiere) mate; ~**lauf** m pair
skating; **p~mal** ad: **ein p~mal a few**
times; ~**ung** f combination; mating;
p~weise ad in pairs; in couples.
Pacht [paxt] f -, -en lease; **p~en** vt
lease.
Pächter ['pɛçtər] m -s, - leaseholder,
tenant.
Pack [pak] m -(e)s, -e od ̈-e bundle,
pack // nt -(e)s (pej) mob, rabble.
Päckchen ['pɛkçən] nt small package;
(Zigaretten) packet; (Post~) small
parcel.
Pack- zW: **p~en** vt pack; (fassen)
grasp, seize; (umg: schaffen) manage; (fig: fesseln) grip; ~**en** m -s, -
bundle; (fig: Menge) heaps of; ~**esel**
m (lit, fig) packhorse; ~**papier** nt
brown paper, wrapping paper; ~**ung**
f packet; (Pralinen~) box; (MED)
compress.
Pädagog- [pɛda'go:g] zW: ~**e** m -n, -n
teacher; ~**ik** f education; **p~isch** a
educational, pedagogical.
Paddel ['padəl] nt -s, - paddle; ~**boot**
nt canoe; **p~n** vi paddle.
Page ['pa:ʒə] m -n, -n page;
Pagenkopf m pageboy.
Paket [pa'ke:t] nt -(e)s, -e packet;
(Post~) parcel; ~**karte** f dispatch
note; ~**post** f parcel post; ~**schalter**
m parcels counter.
Pakt [pakt] m -(e)s, -e pact.
Palast [pa'last] m -es, **Paläste** palace.
Palästin- [palɛs'ti:n] zW: ~**a** nt -s
Palestine; ~**enser(in** f) [palɛsti-
'nɛnzər(ɪn)] m -s, - Palestinian;
p~'ensisch a Palestinian.
Palme ['palmə] f -, -n palm (tree).
Palmsonntag m Palm Sunday.
Pampelmuse ['pampəlmu:zə] f -, -n
grapefruit.
pampig ['pampɪç] a (umg: frech)
fresh.
panieren [pa'ni:rən] vt (KOCH) bread.
Paniermehl [pa'ni:rme:l] nt bread-
crumbs pl.
Panik ['pa:nɪk] f panic.
panisch ['pa:nɪʃ] a panic-stricken.
Panne ['panə] f -, -n (AUT etc) breakdown; (Mißgeschick) slip; **Pannen-**

hilfe f breakdown service.
panschen ['panʃən] vi splash about //
vt water down.
Panther ['pantər] m -s, - panther.
Pantoffel [pan'tɔfəl] m -s, -n slipper;
~**held** m (umg) henpecked husband.
Pantomime [panto'mi:mə] f -, -n
mime.
Panzer ['pantsər] m -s, - armour;
(Platte) armour plate; (Fahrzeug)
tank; ~**glas** nt bulletproof glass;
p~n vtr armour; (fig) arm o.s.
Papa [pa'pa:] m -s, -s (umg) dad, daddy.
Papagei [papa'gaɪ] m -s, -en parrot.
Papier [pa'pi:r] nt -s, -e paper;
(Wert~) share; ~**fabrik** f paper mill;
~**geld** nt paper money; ~**korb** m
wastepaper basket; ~**tüte** f paper
bag.
Papp- [pap] zW: ~**deckel** m, ~**e** f -,
-n cardboard; **Pappel** f -, -n poplar;
p~en vti (umg) stick; **p~ig** a sticky;
~**maché** [-ma'ʃe:] nt -s, -s papier-
mâché.
Paprika ['paprika] m -s, -s (Gewürz)
paprika; (~schote) pepper.
Papst [pa:pst] m -(e)s, ̈-e pope.
päpstlich ['pɛ:pstlɪç] a papal.
Parabel [pa'ra:bəl] f -, -n parable;
(MATH) parabola.
Parade [pa'ra:də] f (MIL) parade, review; (SPORT) parry; ~**marsch** m
march-past; ~**schritt** m goose-step.
Paradies [para'di:s] nt -es, -e paradise; **p~isch** a heavenly.
paradox [para'dɔks] a paradoxical;
P~ nt -es, -e paradox.
Paragraph [para'gra:f] m -en, -en
paragraph; (JUR) section.
parallel [para'le:l] a parallel; **P~e** f
parallel.
Paranuß ['pa:ranus] f Brazil nut.
Parasit [para'zi:t] m -en, -en (lit, fig)
parasite.
parat [pa'ra:t] a ready.
Pärchen ['pɛ:rçən] nt couple.
Parfüm [par'fy:m] nt -s, -s od -e perfume; ~**erie** [-ə'ri:] f perfumery;
~**flasche** f scent bottle; **p~ieren**
[-'mi:rən] vt scent, perfume.
parieren [pa'ri:rən] vt parry // vi
(umg) obey.
Paris [pa'ri:s] nt - Paris; ~**er(in** f) m
Parisian // a Parisian.
Park [park] m -s, -s park; ~**anlage** f
park; (um Gebäude) grounds pl;
p~en vti park; **Parkett** [par'ket] nt
-(e)s, -e parquet (floor); (THEAT)
stalls pl; ~**haus** nt multi-storey car
park; ~**lücke** f parking space;
~**platz** m parking place; car park,
parking lot (US); ~**scheibe** f parking
disc; ~**uhr** f parking meter; ~**verbot**
nt no parking.

Parlament [parla'mɛnt] nt parliament; **~arier** [-'ta:riər] m -s, - parliamentarian; **p~arisch** [-'ta:rɪʃ] a parliamentary.

Parlaments- zW: **~beschluß** m vote of parliament; **~mitglied** nt member of parliament; **~sitzung** f sitting (of parliament).

Parodie [paro'di:] f parody; **p~ren** vt parody.

Parole [pa'ro:lə] f -, -n password; (Wahlspruch) motto.

Partei [par'tai] f party; **~ ergreifen für jdn** take sb's side; **p~isch** a partial, biased; **~nahme** f -, -n support, taking the part of; **~tag** m party conference.

Parterre [par'tɛr(ə)] nt -s, -s ground floor; (THEAT) stalls pl.

Partie [par'ti:] f part; (Spiel) game; (Ausflug) outing; (Mann, Frau) catch; (COMM) lot; **mit von der ~ sein** join in.

Partisan [parti'za:n] m -s od -en, -en partisan.

Partitur [parti'tu:r] f (MUS) score.

Partizip [parti'tsi:p] nt -s, -ien participle.

Partner(in f) ['partnər(ɪn)] m -s, - partner; **p~schaftlich** a as partners.

Party ['pa:rti] f -, -s od Parties party.

Paß [pas] m -sses, -sse pass; (Ausweis) passport.

Pass- zW: **p~abel** [pa'sa:bəl] a passable, reasonable; **~age** [pa'sa:ʒə] f -, -n passage; **~agier** [pasa'ʒi:r] m -s, -e passenger; **~agierflugzeug** nt airliner; **~ant** [pa'sant] m passer-by.

Paßamt nt passport office.

Paßbild nt passport photograph.

passen ['pasən] vi fit; (Farbe) go (zu with); (auf Frage, KARTEN, SPORT) pass; **das paßt mir nicht** that doesn't suit me; **er paßt nicht zu dir** he's not right for you; **~d** a suitable; (zusammen~d) matching; (angebracht) fitting; (Zeit) convenient.

passier- [pa'si:r] zW: **~bar** a passable; **~en** vt pass; (durch Sieb) strain // vi happen; **P~schein** m pass, permit.

Passion [pasi'o:n] f passion; **p~iert** [-'ni:rt] a enthusiastic, passionate; **Passionsspiel** nt Passion Play.

passiv ['pasi:f] a passive; **P~** nt -s, -e passive; **Passiva** pl (COMM) liabilities pl; **P~i'tät** f passiveness.

Paß- zW: **~kontrolle** f passport control; **~stelle** f passport office; **~straße** f (mountain) pass.

Paste ['pastə] f -, -n paste.

Pastell [pas'tɛl] nt -(e)s, -e pastel.

Pastete [pas'te:tə] f -, -n pie.

pasteurisieren [pastøri'zi:rən] vt pasteurize.

Pastor ['pastor] m vicar; pastor, minister.

Pate ['pa:tə] m -n, -n godfather; **Patenkind** nt godchild.

Patent [pa'tɛnt] nt -(e)s, -e patent; (MIL) commission; **p~** a clever; **~amt** nt patent office; **p~ieren** [-'ti:rən] vt patent; **~inhaber** m patentee.

Pater ['pa:tər] m -s, - od **Patres** (ECCL) Father.

pathetisch [pa'te:tɪʃ] a emotional; bombastic.

Pathologe [pato'lo:gə] m -n, -n pathologist.

pathologisch a pathological.

Pathos ['pa:tɔs] nt - emotiveness, emotionalism.

Patient(in f) [patsi'ɛnt(ɪn)] m patient.

Patin ['pa:tɪn] f godmother.

Patina ['pa:tina] f - patina.

Patriot [patri'o:t] m -en, -en patriot; **p~isch** a patriotic; **~ismus** [-'tɪsmus] m patriotism.

Patrone [pa'tro:nə] f -, -n cartridge.

patrouillieren [patrul'ji:rən] vi patrol.

patsch [patʃ] interj splash; **P~e** f -, -n (umg: Bedrängnis) mess, jam; **~en** vti smack, slap; (im Wasser) splash; **~naß** a soaking wet.

patzig ['patsɪç] a (umg) cheeky, saucy.

Pauke ['pauka] f -, -n kettledrum; **auf die ~ hauen** live it up.

pausbäckig ['pausbɛkɪç] a chubby-cheeked.

pauschal [pau'ʃa:l] a (Kosten) inclusive; (Urteil) sweeping; **P~e** f -, -n, **P~gebühr** f flat rate; **P~preis** m all-in price; **P~reise** f package tour; **P~summe** f lump sum.

Pause ['pauzə] f -, -n break; (THEAT) interval; (Innehalten) pause; (Kopie) tracing.

pausen vt trace; **~los** a non-stop; **P~zeichen** nt call sign; (MUS) rest.

Pauspapier ['pauspapi:r] nt tracing paper.

Pavian ['pa:via:n] m -s, -e baboon.

Pazif- [pa'tsi:f] zW: **~ik** m -s Pacific; **p~isch** a: **~ischer Ozean** Pacific; **~ist** [patsi'fɪst] m pacifist; **p~istisch** a pacifist.

Pech [pɛç] nt -s, -e pitch; (fig) bad luck; **~ haben** be unlucky; **p~schwarz** a pitch-black; **~strähne** f (umg) unlucky patch; **~vogel** m (umg) unlucky person.

Pedal [pe'da:l] nt -s, -e pedal.

Pedant [pe'dant] m pedant; **~e'rie** f pedantry; **p~isch** a pedantic.

Pegel ['pe:gəl] m -s, - water gauge; **~stand** m water level.

peilen ['pailən] vt get a fix on.

Pein [pain] f - agony, pain; **p~igen** vt

torture; (*plagen*) torment; **p~lich** *a* (*unangenehm*) embarrassing, awkward, painful; (*genau*) painstaking; **P~lichkeit** *f* painfulness, awkwardness; scrupulousness.

Peitsche ['paɪtʃə] *f* -, -n whip; **p~n** *vt* whip; (*Regen*) lash.

Pelikan ['peːlikaːn] *m* -s, -e pelican.

Pelle ['pɛlə] *f* -, -n skin; **p~n** *vt* skin, peel.

Pellkartoffeln *pl* jacket potatoes *pl*.

Pelz [pɛlts] *m* -es, -e fur.

Pendel ['pɛndəl] *nt* -s, - pendulum; **~verkehr** *m* shuttle traffic; (*für Pendler*) commuter traffic.

Pendler ['pɛndlər] *m* -s, - commuter.

penetrant [pene'trant] *a* sharp; (*Person*) pushing.

Penis ['peːnɪs] *m* -, -se penis.

pennen ['pɛnən] *vi* (*umg*) kip.

Pension [pɛnzi'oːn] *f* (*Geld*) pension; (*Ruhestand*) retirement; (*für Gäste*) boarding od guest-house; **~är(in** *f*) [-'nɛr(ɪn)] *m* -s, -e pensioner; **~at** [-'naːt] *nt* -(e)s, -e boarding school; **p~ieren** [-'niːrən] *vt* pension (off); **p~iert** a retired; **~ierung** *f* retirement; **Pensionsgast** *m* boarder, paying guest.

Pensum ['pɛnzʊm] *nt* -s, **Pensen** quota; (*SCH*) curriculum.

per [pɛr] *präp* +*akk* by, per; (*pro*) per; (*bis*) by.

Perfekt ['pɛrfɛkt] *nt* -(e)s, -e perfect; **p~** [pɛr'fɛkt] *a* perfect; **~ionismus** [pɛrfɛktsio'nɪsmʊs] *m* perfectionism.

perforieren [pɛrfo'riːrən] *vt* perforate.

Pergament [pɛrga'mɛnt] *nt* parchment; **~papier** *nt* greaseproof paper.

Periode [peri'oːdə] *f* -, -n period.

periodisch [peri'oːdɪʃ] *a* periodic; (*dezimal*) recurring.

peripher [peri'feːr] *a* peripheral; **~es** Gerät peripheral.

Perle ['pɛrlə] *f* -, -n (*lit*, *fig*) pearl; **p~n** *vi* sparkle; (*Tropfen*) trickle.

Perlmutt ['pɛrlmʊt] *nt* -s mother-of-pearl.

perplex [pɛr'plɛks] *a* dumbfounded.

Pers- ['pɛrz] *zW*: **~er(in** *f*) *m* -s, - Persian; **~i'aner** *m* -s, - Persian lamb; **~ien** [-iən] *nt* -s Persia; **p~isch** *a* Persian.

Person [pɛr'zoːn] *f* -, -en person; ich für meine ~ personally I.

Personal [pɛrzo'naːl] *nt* -s personnel; (*Bedienung*) servants *pl*; **~ausweis** *m* identity card; **~computer** *m* personal computer, PC; **~ien** [-iən] *pl* particulars *pl*; **~i'tät** *f* personality; **~mangel** *m* undermanning; **~pronomen** *nt* personal pronoun.

Personen- *zW*: **~aufzug** *m* lift, elevator (*US*); **~gesellschaft** *f* partnership; **~kraftwagen** *m* private motor-

car; **~schaden** *m* injury to persons; **~zug** *m* stopping train; passenger train.

personifizieren [pɛrzonifi'tsiːrən] *vt* personify.

persönlich [pɛr'zøːnlɪç] *a* personal // *ad* in person; personally; **P~keit** *f* personality.

Perspektive [pɛrspɛk'tiːvə] *f* perspective.

Perücke [pe'rykə] *f* -, -n wig.

pervers [pɛr'vɛrs] *a* perverse; **P~i'tät** *f* perversity.

Pessimismus [pɛsi'mɪsmʊs] *m* pessimism.

Pessimist [pɛsi'mɪst] *m* pessimist; **p~isch** *a* pessimistic.

Pest [pɛst] *f* - plague.

Petersilie [petər'ziːliə] *f* parsley.

Petroleum [pe'troːleʊm] *nt* -s paraffin, kerosene (*US*).

Pfad [pfaːt] *m* -(e)s, -e path; **~finder** *m* -s, - boy scout; **~finderin** *f* girl guide.

Pfahl [pfaːl] *m* -(e)s, ̈-e post, stake.

Pfand [pfant] *nt* -(e)s, ̈-er pledge, security; (*Flaschen~*) deposit; (*im Spiel*) forfeit; **~brief** *m* bond.

pfänden ['pfɛndən] *vt* seize, distrain.

Pfänderspiel *nt* game of forfeits.

Pfandhaus *nt* pawnshop.

Pfandschein *m* pawn ticket.

Pfändung ['pfɛndʊŋ] *f* seizure, distraint.

Pfanne ['pfanə] *f* -, -n (frying) pan.

Pfannkuchen *m* pancake; (*Berliner*) doughnut.

Pfarr- ['pfar] *zW*: **~ei** [-'raɪ] *f* parish; **~er** *m* -s, - priest; (*evangelisch*) vicar; minister; **~haus** *nt* vicarage; manse.

Pfau [pfaʊ] *m* -(e)s, -en peacock; **~enauge** *nt* peacock butterfly.

Pfeffer ['pfɛfər] *m* -s, - pepper; **~korn** *nt* peppercorn; **~kuchen** *m* gingerbread; **~minz** *nt* -es, -e peppermint; **~mühle** *f* pepper-mill; **p~n** *vt* pepper; (*umg*: *werfen*) fling; gepfefferte Preise/Witze steep prices/spicy jokes.

Pfeife ['pfaɪfə] *f* -, -n whistle; (*Tabak~*, *Orgel~*) pipe; **p~n** *vti* unreg whistle; **~r** *m* -s, - piper.

Pfeil [pfaɪl] *m* -(e)s, -e arrow.

Pfeiler ['pfaɪlər] *m* -s, - pillar, prop; (*Brücken~*) pier.

Pfennig ['pfɛnɪç] *m* -(e)s, -e pfennig (*hundredth part of a mark*).

Pferd [pfeːrt] *nt* -(e)s, -e horse.

Pferde- ['pfeːrdə] *zW*: **~rennen** *nt* horse-race; horse-racing; **~schwanz** *m* (*Frisur*) ponytail; **~stall** *m* stable.

Pfiff [pfɪf] *m* -(e)s, -e whistle.

Pfifferling ['pfɪfərlɪŋ] *m* yellow chanterelle (*mushroom*); keinen ~ wert not worth a thing.

pfiffig *a* sly, sharp.

Pfingsten ['pfɪŋstən] *nt* -, - Whitsun.

Pfingstrose ['pfɪŋstroːzə] *f* peony.

Pfirsich ['pfɪrzɪç] *m* -s, -e peach.

Pflanz- ['pflants] *zW:* ~e *f* -, -n plant; **p~en** *vt* plant; **~enfett** *nt* vegetable fat; **p~lich** *a* vegetable; **~ung** *f* plantation.

Pflaster ['pflastər] *nt* -s, - plaster; *(Straße)* pavement; **p~n** *vt* pave; **~stein** *m* paving stone.

Pflaume ['pflaumə] *f* -, -n plum.

Pflege ['pfleːgə] *f* -, -n care; *(von Idee)* cultivation; *(Kranken~)* nursing; in ~ sein *(Kind)* be fostered out; **p~bedürftig** *a* needing care; **~eltern** *pl* foster parents *pl*; **~kind** *nt* foster child; **p~leicht** *a* easy-care; **~mutter** *f* foster mother; **p~n** *vt* look after; *(Kranke)* nurse; *(Beziehungen)* foster; **~r** *m* -s, - orderly; male nurse; **~rin** *f* nurse, attendant; **~vater** *m* foster father.

Pflicht [pflɪçt] *f* -, -en duty; *(SPORT)* compulsory section; **p~bewußt** *a* conscientious; **~fach** *nt* *(SCH)* compulsory subject; **~gefühl** *nt* sense of duty; **p~gemäß** *a* dutiful // *ad* as in duty bound; **~versicherung** *f* compulsory insurance.

pflücken ['pflʏkən] *vt* pick; *(Blumen auch)* pluck.

Pflug [pfluːk] *m* -(e)s, ¨e plough.

pflügen ['pflyːgən] *vt* plough.

Pforte ['pfɔrtə] *f* -, -n gate; door.

Pförtner ['pfœrtnər] *m* -s, - porter, doorkeeper, doorman.

Pfosten ['pfɔstən] *m* -s, - post.

Pfote ['pfoːtə] *f* -, -n paw; *(umg: Schrift)* scrawl.

Pfropfen ['pfrɔpfən] *m* -s, - *(Flaschen~)* stopper; *(Blut~)* clot; **p~** *vt* *(stopfen)* cram; *(Baum)* graft.

pfui [pfuɪ] *interj* ugh.

Pfund [pfʊnt] *nt* -(e)s, -e pound; **p~ig** *a* *(umg)* great.

pfuschen ['pfʊʃən] *vi* *(umg)* be sloppy; **jdm in etw** *(akk)* ~ interfere in sth.

Pfuscher ['pfʊʃər] *m* -s, - *(umg)* sloppy worker; *(Kur~)* quack; **~ei** [-'raɪ] *f* *(umg)* sloppy work; *(Kur~)* quackery.

Pfütze ['pfʏtsə] *f* -, -n puddle.

Phänomen [fɛnoˈmeːn] *nt* -s, -e phenomenon; **p~al** [-ˈnaːl] *a* phenomenal.

Phantasie [fantaˈziː] *f* imagination; **p~los** *a* unimaginative; **p~ren** *vi* fantasize; **p~voll** *a* imaginative.

phantastisch [fanˈtastɪʃ] *a* fantastic.

Pharmazeut(in *f)* [farmaˈtsɔɪt(ɪn)] *m* -en, -en pharmacist.

Phase ['faːzə] *f* -, -n phase.

Philippinen [filɪˈpiːnən] *pl* Philippines.

Philologe [filoˈloːgə] *m* -n, -n philologist.

Philologie [filoloˈgiː] *f* philology.

Philosoph [filoˈzoːf] *m* -en, -en philosopher; **~ie** [-ˈfiː] *f* philosophy; **p~isch** *a* philosophical.

Phlegma ['flɛgma] *nt* -s lethargy; **p~tisch** [flɛˈgmaːtɪʃ] *a* lethargic.

Phonet- [foˈneːt] *zW:* ~**ik** *f* phonetics *sing*; **p~isch** *a* phonetic.

Phosphor ['fɔsfɔr] *m* -s phosphorus.

Photo ['foːto] *nt* -s, -e *etc siehe* Foto.

Phrase ['fraːzə] *f* -, -n phrase; *(pej)* hollow phrase.

Physik [fyˈziːk] *f* physics *sing*; **p~alisch** [-ˈkaːlɪʃ] *a* of physics; **~er(in** *f)* ['fyːzikər(ɪn)] *m* -s, - physicist.

Physiologe [fyzioˈloːgə] *m* -n, -n physiologist.

Physiologie [fyzioloˈgiː] *f* physiology.

physisch ['fyːzɪʃ] *a* physical.

Pianist(in *f)* [piaˈnɪst(ɪn)] *m* pianist.

Pickel ['pɪkəl] *m* -s, - pimple; *(Werkzeug)* pickaxe; *(Berg~)* ice-axe; **p~ig** *a* pimply.

picken ['pɪkən] *vi* pick, peck.

Picknick ['pɪknɪk] *nt* -s, -e *od* -s picnic; ~ **machen** have a picnic.

piepen ['piːpən], **piepsen** ['piːpsən] *vi* chirp.

Pietät [pieˈtɛːt] *f* piety, reverence; **p~los** *a* impious, irreverent.

Pigment [pɪˈgmɛnt] *nt* pigment.

Pik [piːk] *nt* -s, -s *(KARTEN)* spades; **p~ant** [piˈkant] *a* spicy, piquant; *(anzüglich)* suggestive.

Pilger ['pɪlgər] *m* -s, - pilgrim; **~fahrt** *f* pilgrimage.

Pille ['pɪlə] *f* -, -n pill.

Pilot [piˈloːt] *m* -en, -en pilot.

Pils [pɪls] *nt* -, - lager.

Pilz [pɪlts] *m* -es, -e fungus; *(eßbar)* mushroom; *(giftig)* toadstool; **~krankheit** *f* fungal disease.

pingelig ['pɪŋəlɪç] *a* *(umg)* fussy.

Pinguin ['pɪŋguiːn] *m* -s, -e penguin.

Pinie ['piːniə] *f* pine.

pinkeln ['pɪŋkəln] *vi* *(umg)* pee.

Pinsel ['pɪnzəl] *m* -s, - paintbrush.

Pinzette [pɪnˈtsɛtə] *f* tweezers *pl*.

Pionier [pioˈniːr] *m* -s, -e pioneer; *(MIL)* sapper, engineer.

Pirat [piˈraːt] *m* -en, -en pirate; **~ensender** *m* pirate radio station.

Piste ['pɪstə] *f* -, -n *(SKI)* run, piste; *(AVIAT)* runway.

Pistole [pɪsˈtoːlə] *f* -, -n pistol.

Pizza ['pɪtsa] *f* -, -s pizza.

Pkw [peːkaːˈveː] *m* -(s), -(s) *abk von* Personenkraftwagen.

plädieren [plɛˈdiːrən] *vi* plead.

Plädoyer [plɛdoaˈjeː] *nt* -s, -s speech for the defence; *(fig)* plea.

Plage ['plaːgə] *f* -, -n plague; *(Mühe)*

nuisance; **~geist** *m* pest, nuisance; **p~n** *vt* torment // *vr* toil, slave.

Plakat [pla'ka:t] *nt* **-(e)s, -e** placard; poster.

Plan [pla:n] **-(e)s, ¨e** plan; (*Karte*) map; **~e** *f* -, **-n** tarpaulin; **p~en** *vt* plan; (*Mord etc*) plot; **~er** *m* **-s, -** planner; **Planet** [pla'ne:t] *m* **-en -en** planet; **p~gemäß** *ad* according to schedule *od* plan; (*EISENB*) on time; **p~ieren** [pla'ni:rən] *vt* plane, level.

Planke ['plaŋkə] *f* -, **-n** plank.

planlos *a* (*Vorgehen*) unsystematic; (*Umherlaufen*) aimless.

planmäßig *a* according to plan; systematic; (*EISENB*) scheduled.

Plansch- ['planʃ] *zW:* **~becken** *nt* paddling pool; **p~en** *vi* splash.

Plansoll *nt* **-s** output target.

Planstelle *f* post.

Plantage [plan'ta:ʒə] *f* -, **-n** plantation.

Planung *f* planning.

Planwirtschaft *f* planned economy.

plappern ['plapərn] *vi* chatter.

plärren ['plɛrən] *vi* (*Mensch*) cry, whine; (*Radio*) blare.

Plasma ['plasma] *nt* **-s, Plasmen** plasma.

Plastik ['plastɪk] *f* sculpture // *nt* **-s** (*Kunststoff*) plastic; **~folie** *f* plastic film.

plastisch ['plastɪʃ] *a* plastic; **stell dir das ~ vor!** just picture it!

Platane [pla'ta:nə] *f* -, **-n** plane (tree).

Platin ['pla:ti:n] *nt* **-s** platinum.

Platitüde [plati'ty:də] *f* -, **-n** platitude.

platonisch [pla'to:nɪʃ] *a* platonic.

platsch [platʃ] *interj* splash; **~en** *vi* splash; **~naß** *a* drenched.

plätschern ['plɛtʃərn] *vi* babble.

platt [plat] *a* flat; (*umg: überrascht*) flabbergasted; (*fig: geistlos*) flat, boring; **~deutsch** *a* low German; **P~e** *f* -, **-n** (*Speisen~*, *PHOT*, *TECH*) plate; (*Stein~*) flag; (*Kachel*) tile; (*Schall~*) record; **P~enspieler** *m* record player; **P~enteller** *m* turntable; **P~fuß** *m* flat foot.

Platz [plats] *m* **-es, ¨e** place; (*Sitz~*) seat; (*Raum*) space, room; (*in Stadt*) square; (*SPORT*) playing field; **~ nehmen** take a seat; **jdm ~ machen** make room for sb; **~angst** *f* (*MED*) agoraphobia; (*umg*) claustrophobia; **~anweiser(in** *f*) *m* **-s, -** usher(ette).

Plätzchen ['plɛtsçən] *nt* spot; (*Gebäck*) biscuit.

Platz- *zW:* **p~en** *vi* burst; (*Bombe*) explode; **vor Wut p~en** (*umg*) be bursting with anger; **~karte** *f* seat reservation; **~mangel** *m* lack of space; **~patrone** *f* blank cartridge; **~regen** *m* downpour; **~wunde** *f* cut.

Plauderei [plaudə'raɪ] *f* chat, conver-

sation; (*RAD*) talk.

plaudern ['plaudərn] *vi* chat, talk.

plausibel [plau'zi:bəl] *a* plausible.

plazieren [pla'tsi:rən] *vt* place // *vr* (*SPORT*) be placed; (*Tennis*) be seeded.

pleite ['plaɪtə] *a* (*umg*) broke; **P~** *f* -, **-n** bankruptcy; (*umg: Reinfall*) flop; **P~ machen** go bust.

Plenum ['ple:nʊm] *nt* **-s** plenum.

Plombe ['plɔmbə] *f* -, **-n** lead seal; (*Zahn~*) filling.

plombieren [plɔm'bi:rən] *vt* seal; (*Zahn*) fill.

plötzlich ['plœtslɪç] *a* sudden // *ad* suddenly.

plump [plʊmp] *a* clumsy; (*Hände*) coarse; (*Körper*) shapeless; **~sen** *vi* (*umg*) plump down, fall.

Plunder ['plʊndər] *m* **-s** rubbish.

plündern ['plʏndərn] *vti* plunder; (*Stadt*) sack.

Plünderung ['plʏndərʊŋ] *f* plundering, sack, pillage.

Plural ['plu:ra:l] *m* **-s, -e** plural; **p~istisch** [plura'lɪstɪʃ] *a* pluralistic.

Plus [plʊs] *nt* -, **-** plus; (*FIN*) profit; (*Vorteil*) advantage; **p~** *ad* plus.

Plüsch [ply:ʃ] *m* **-(e)s, -e** plush.

Plus- *zW:* **~pol** *m* (*ELEK*) positive pole; **~punkt** *m* point; (*fig*) point in sb's favour.

PLZ *abk von* **Postleitzahl.**

Po [po:] *m* **-s, -s** (*umg*) bottom, bum.

Pöbel ['pø:bəl] *m* **-s** mob, rabble; **~ei** [-'laɪ] *f* vulgarity; **p~haft** *a* low, vulgar.

pochen ['pɔxən] *vi* knock; (*Herz*) pound; **auf etw** (*akk*) **~** (*fig*) insist on sth.

Pocken ['pɔkən] *pl* smallpox.

Podium ['po:diʊm] *nt* podium; **Podiumsdiskussion** *f* panel discussion.

Poesie [poe'zi:] *f* poetry.

Poet [po'e:t] *m* **-en, -en** poet; **p~isch** *a* poetic.

Pointe [po'ɛ̃:tə] *f* -, **-n** point.

Pokal [po'ka:l] *m* **-s, -e** goblet; (*SPORT*) cup; **~spiel** *nt* cup-tie.

Pökel- ['pø:kəl] *zW:* **~fleisch** *nt* salt meat; **p~n** *vt* pickle, salt.

Pol [po:l] *m* **-s, -e** pole; **p~ar** [po'la:r] *a* polar; **~arkreis** *m* arctic circle; **~e** *m* **-n, -n, ~in** *f* Pole; **~en** *nt* **-s** Poland.

polemisch [po'le:mɪʃ] *a* polemical.

Police [po'li:s(ə)] *f* -, **-n** insurance policy.

Polier [po'li:r] *m* **-s, -e** foreman; **p~en** *vt* polish.

Poliklinik ['po:likli:nɪk] *f* outpatients.

Politik [poli'ti:k] *f* politics *sing*; (*eine bestimmte*) policy; **~er(in** *f*) [po'li:tikər(ɪn)] *m* **-s, -** politician.

politisch [po'li:tɪʃ] *a* political.
Politur [poli'tu:r] *f* polish.
Polizei [poli'tsai] *f* police; **~beamte(r)** *m* police officer; **p~lich** *a* police; **sich p~lich melden** register with the police; **~revier** *nt* police station; **~staat** *m* police state; **~streife** *f* police patrol; **~stunde** *f* closing time; **~wache** *f* ~revier.
Polizist [poli'tsɪst] *m* **-en, -en** policeman; **~in** *f* policewoman.
Pollen [polən] *m* **-s, -** pollen.
polnisch ['pɔlnɪʃ] *a* Polish.
Polster ['pɔlstər] *nt* **-s, -** cushion; (*Polsterung*) upholstery; (*in Kleidung*) padding; (*fig: Geld*) reserves *pl*; **~er** *m* **-s, -** upholsterer; **~möbel** *pl* upholstered furniture; **p~n** *vt* upholster; pad; **~ung** *f* upholstery.
Polter- ['pɔltər] *zW:* **~abend** *m* party on eve of wedding; **p~n** *vi* (*Krach machen*) crash; (*schimpfen*) rant.
Polyp [po'ly:p] *m* **-en -en** polyp; (*pl: MED*) adenoids *pl*; (*umg*) cop.
Pomade [po'ma:də] *f* pomade.
Pommes frites [pɔm'frɪt] *pl* chips *pl*, French fried potatoes *pl*.
Pomp [pɔmp] *m* **-(e)s** pomp.
Pony ['pɔni] *m* **-s, -s** (*Frisur*) fringe // *nt* **-s, -s** (*Pferd*) pony.
Popmusik ['pɔpmuzi:k] *f* pop music.
Popo [po'po:] *m* **-s, -s** bottom, bum.
populär [popu'lɛ:r] *a* popular.
Popularität [populari'tɛ:t] *f* popularity.
Pore ['po:rə] *f* **-, -n** pore.
Pornographie [pɔrnogra'fi:] *f* pornography.
porös [po'rø:s] *a* porous.
Porree ['pɔre] *m* **-s, -s** leek.
Portal [pɔr'ta:l] *nt* **-s, -e** portal.
Portefeuille [pɔrt'fø:j] *nt* (*POL, FIN*) portfolio.
Portemonnaie [pɔrtmo'ne:] *nt* **-s, -s** purse.
Portier [pɔrti'e:] *m* **-s, -s** porter.
Portion [pɔrtsi'o:n] *f* portion, helping; (*umg: Anteil*) amount.
Porto ['pɔrto] *ni* **-s, -s** postage; **p~frei** *a* post-free, (postage) prepaid.
Porträt [pɔr'trɛ:] *nt* **-s, -s** portrait; **p~ieren** [pɔrtrɛ'ti:rən] *vt* paint, portray.
Portug- ['pɔrtug] *zW:* **~al** *nt* **~s** Portugal; **~iese** [pɔrtu'gi:zə] *m* **-n, -n,** **~iesin** *f* Portuguese; **p~iesisch** *a* Portuguese.
Porzellan [pɔrtse'la:n] *nt* **-s, -e** china, porcelain; (*Geschirr*) china.
Posaune [po'zaunə] *f* **-, -n** trombone.
Pose ['po:zə] *f* **-, -n** pose.
posieren [po'zi:rən] *vi* pose.
Position [pozitsi'o:n] *f* position.
positiv ['po:ziti:f] *a* positive; **P~** *nt* **-s, -e** (*PHOT*) positive.
possessiv ['pɔsɛsi:f] *a* possessive;

P~pronomen *nt* **-s, -e** possessive pronoun.
possierlich [po'si:rlɪç] *a* funny.
Post [pɔst] *f* **-, -en** post (office); (*Briefe*) mail; **~amt** *nt* post office; **~anweisung** *f* postal order, money order; **~bote** *m* postman; **~en** *m* **-s, -** post, position; (*COMM*) item; (*auf Liste*) entry; (*MIL*) sentry; (*Streik~*) picket; **~er** *nt* **-s, -(s)** poster; **~fach** *nt* post-office box; **~karte** *f* postcard; **p~lagernd** *ad* poste restante; **~leitzahl** *f* postal code; **~scheckkonto** *nt* postal giro account; **~sparkasse** *f* post office savings bank; **~stempel** *m* postmark; **~wertzeichen** *nt* postage stamp.
potent [po'tɛnt] *a* potent.
Potential [potɛntsi'a:l] *nt* **-s, -e** potential.
potentiell [potɛntsi'ɛl] *a* potential.
Potenz [po'tɛnts] *f* power; (*eines Mannes*) potency.
Pracht [praxt] *f* **-** splendour, magnificence.
prächtig ['prɛçtɪç] *a* splendid.
Prachtstück *nt* showpiece.
prachtvoll *a* splendid, magnificent.
Prädikat [predi'ka:t] *nt* **-(e)s, -e** title; (*GRAM*) predicate; (*Zensur*) distinction.
Prag [pra:k] *nt* **-s** Prague.
prägen ['prɛ:gən] *vt* stamp; (*Münze*) mint; (*Ausdruck*) coin; (*Charakter*) form.
prägnant [prɛ'gnant] *a* precise, terse.
Prägung ['prɛ:gʊŋ] *f* minting; forming; (*Eigenart*) character, stamp.
prahlen ['pra:lən] *vi* boast, brag.
Prahlerei [pra:lə'rai] *f* boasting.
Praktik ['praktɪk] *f* practice; **p~abel** [-'ka:bəl] *a* practicable; **~ant(in** *f)* [-'kant(ɪn)] *m* trainee; **~um** *nt* **-s,** **Praktika** *od* **Praktiken** practical training.
praktisch ['praktɪʃ] *a* practical, handy; **~er Arzt** general practitioner.
praktizieren [prakti'tsi:rən] *vti* practise.
Praline [pra'li:nə] *f* chocolate.
prall [pral] *a* firmly rounded; (*Segel*) taut; (*Arme*) plump; (*Sonne*) blazing; **~en** *vi* bounce, rebound; (*Sonne*) blaze.
Prämie ['prɛ:miə] *f* premium; (*Belohnung*) award, prize; **p~ren** [prɛ'mi:rən] *vt* give an award to.
Pranger ['praŋər] *m* **-s, -** (*HIST*) pillory; **jdn an den ~ stellen** (*fig*) pillory sb.
Präparat [prepa'ra:t] *nt* **-(e)s, -e** (*BIOL*) preparation; (*MED*) medicine.
Präposition [prepozitsi'o:n] *f* preposition.

Präsens ['prɛːzɛns] *nt* - present tense.

präsentieren [prɛzɛn'tiːrən] *vt* present.

Präservativ [prɛzɛrva'tiːf] *nt* **-s, -e** contraceptive.

Präsident(in *f)* [prɛzi'dɛnt(ɪn)] *m* president; **~schaft** *f* presidency.

Präsidium [prɛ'ziːdiʊm] *nt* presidency, chair(manship); (*Polizei~*) police headquarters *pl*.

prasseln ['prasəln] *vi* (*Feuer*) crackle; (*Hagel*) drum; (*Wörter*) rain down.

Praxis ['praksɪs] *f* **-, Praxen** practice; (*Behandlungsraum*) surgery; (*von Anwalt*) office.

präzis [prɛ'tsiːs] *a* precise; **P~ion** [prɛtsizi'oːn] *f* precision.

predigen ['preːdɪgən] *vti* preach.

Prediger *m* **-s,** - preacher.

Predigt ['preːdɪçt] *f* **-, -en** sermon.

Preis [praɪs] *m* **-es, -e** price; (*Sieges~*) prize; **um keinen** ~ not at any price; **Preiselbeere** *f* cranberry; **p~en** [praɪzən] *vi unreg* praise; **p~geben** *vt unreg* abandon; (*opfern*) sacrifice; (*zeigen*) expose; **p~gekrönt** *a* prize-winning; **~gericht** *nt* jury; **p~günstig** *a* inexpensive; **~lage** *f* price range; **~träger(in** *f) m* prizewinner; **p~wert** *a* inexpensive.

prekär [pre'kɛːr] *a* precarious.

Prell- [prɛl] *zW:* **~bock** *m* buffers *pl*; **p~en** *vt* bump; (*fig*) cheat, swindle; **~ung** *f* bruise.

Premiere [prəmi'ɛːrə] *f* **-, -n** premiere.

Premierminister [prəmi'eːmɪnɪstər] *m* prime minister, premier.

Presse ['prɛsə] *f* **-, -n** press; **~freiheit** *f* freedom of the press; **p~n** *vt* press; **~verlautbarung** *f* press release.

pressieren [prɛ'siːrən] *vi* (be in a) hurry.

Preßluft ['prɛslʊft] *f* compressed air; **~bohrer** *m* pneumatic drill.

Prestige [prɛs'tiːʒə] *nt* **-s** prestige.

Preuß- [prɔʏs] *zW:* **~e** *m* **-n, -n, -n** *f* Prussian; **~en** *nt* **-s** Prussia; **p~isch** *a* Prussian.

prickeln ['prɪkəln] *vti* tingle, tickle.

Priester ['priːstər] *m* **-s,** - priest.

prima ['priːma] *a inv* first-class, excellent; **P~** *f* **-, Primen** sixth form, top class.

primär [pri'mɛːr] *a* primary.

Primel ['priːməl] *f* **-, -n** primrose.

primitiv [primi'tiːf] *a* primitive.

Prinz [prɪnts] *m* **-en, -en** prince; **Prinzessin** [prɪn'tsɛsɪn] *f* princess.

Prinzip [prɪn'tsiːp] *nt* **-s, -ien** principle; **p~iell** [-i'ɛl] *a,ad* on principle; **p~ienlos** *a* unprincipled.

Priorität [priori'tɛːt] *f* priority.

Prise ['priːzə] *f* **-, -n** pinch.

Prisma ['prɪsma] *nt* **-s, Prismen** prism.

privat [pri'vaːt] *a* private.

pro [proː] *präp +akk* per; **P~** *nt* - pro.

Probe ['proːbə] *f* **-, -n** test; (*Teststück*) sample; (*THEAT*) rehearsal; **jdn auf die** ~ **stellen** put sb to the test; **~exemplar** *nt* specimen copy; **~fahrt** *f* test drive; **p~n** *vt* try; (*THEAT*) rehearse; **p~weise** *ad* on approval; **~zeit** *f* probation period.

probieren [pro'biːrən] *vti* try; (*Wein, Speise*) taste, sample.

Problem [pro'bleːm] *nt* **-s, -e** problem; **~atik** [-'maːtɪk] *f* problem; **p~atisch** [-'maːtɪʃ] *a* problematic; **p~los** *a* problem-free.

Produkt [pro'dʊkt] *nt* **-(e)s, -e** product; (*AGR*) produce *no pl*; **~ion** [prodʊktsi'oːn] *f* production; output; **p~iv** [-'tiːf] *a* productive; **~ivität** *f* productivity.

Produzent [produ'tsɛnt] *m* manufacturer; (*Film*) producer.

produzieren [produ'tsiːrən] *vt* produce.

Professor [pro'fɛsɔr] *m* professor.

Profi ['proːfi] *m* **-s, -s** (*umg, SPORT*) pro.

Profil [pro'fiːl] *nt* **-s, -e** profile; (*fig*) image; **p~ieren** [profi'liːrən] *vr* create an image for o.s.

Profit [pro'fiːt] *m* **-(e)s, -e** profit; **p~ieren** [profi'tiːrən] *vi* profit (*von* from).

Prognose [pro'gnoːzə] *f* **-, -n** prediction, prognosis.

Programm [pro'gram] *nt* **-s, -e** programme; (*COMPUT*) program; **p~ieren** [-'miːrən] *vt* programme; (*COMPUT*) program; **~ierer(in** *f) m* **-s,** - programmer.

progressiv [progrɛ'siːf] *a* progressive.

Projekt [pro'jɛkt] *nt* **-(e)s, -e** project; **~or** [pro'jɛktɔr] *m* projector.

proklamieren [prokla'miːrən] *vt* proclaim.

Prolet [pro'leːt] *m* **-en, -en** prole, pleb; **~ariat** [-ari'aːt] *nt* **-(e)s, -e** proletariat; **~arier** [-'taːriər] *m* **-s,** - proletarian.

Prolog [pro'loːk] *m* **-(e)s, -e** prologue.

Promenade [promə'naːdə] *f* promenade.

Promille [pro'mɪlə] *nt* **-(s),** - alcohol level.

prominent [promi'nɛnt] *a* prominent.

Prominenz [promi'nɛnts] *f* VIPs *pl*.

Promotion [promotsi'oːn] *f* doctorate, Ph.D.

promovieren [promo'viːrən] *vi* do a doctorate *od* Ph.D.

prompt [prɔmpt] *a* prompt.

Pronomen [pro'noːmɛn] *nt* **-s,** - pronoun.

Propaganda [propa'ganda] *f* - propaganda.

Propeller [pro'pɛlər] *m* -s, - propeller.
Prophet [pro'fe:t] *m* -en, -en prophet.
prophezeien [profe'tsaɪən] *vt* prophesy.
Prophezeiung *f* prophecy.
Proportion [proportsi'o:n] *f* proportion; **p~al** [-'na:l] *a* proportional.
Prosa ['pro:za] *f* - prose; **p~isch** [pro'za:ɪʃ] *a* prosaic.
prosit ['pro:zɪt] *interj* cheers.
Prospekt [pro'spɛkt] *m* -(e)s, -e leaflet, brochure.
prost [pro:st] *interj* cheers.
Prostituierte [prostitu'i:rtə] *f* -n, -n prostitute.
Prostitution [prostitutsi'o:n] *f* prostitution.
Protest [pro'tɛst] *m* -(e)s, -e protest; **~ant(in** *f*) [protes'tant] *m* Protestant; **p~antisch** [protes'tantɪʃ] *a* Protestant; **p~ieren** [protes'ti:rən] *vi* protest.
Prothese [pro'te:zə] *f* -, -n artificial limb; (*Zahn~*) dentures *pl*.
Protokoll [proto'kɔl] *nt* -s, -e register; (*von Sitzung*) minutes *pl*; (*diplomatisch*) protocol; (*Polizei~*) statement; **p~ieren** [-'li:rən] *vt* take down in the minutes.
protz- ['prots] *zW:* **~en** *vi* show off; **~ig** *a* ostentatious.
Proviant [provi'ant] *m* -s, -e provisions *pl*, supplies *pl*.
Provinz [pro'vɪnts] *f* -, -en province; **p~i'ell** *a* provincial.
Provision [provizi'o:n] *f* (*COMM*) commission.
provisorisch [provi'zo:rɪʃ] *a* provisional.
Provokation [provokatsi'o:n] *f* provocation.
provozieren [provo'tsi:rən] *vt* provoke.
Prozedur [protse'du:r] *f* procedure; (*pej*) carry-on.
Prozent [pro'tsɛnt] *nt* -(e)s, -e per cent, percentage; **~satz** *m* percentage; **p~ual** [-u'a:l] *a* percentage; as a percentage.
Prozeß [pro'tsɛs] *m* -sses, -sse trial, case.
Prozession [protsɛsi'o:n] *f* procession.
prüde ['pry:də] *a* prudish; **P~rie** [-'ri:] *f* prudery.
Prüf- ['pry:f] *zW:* **p~en** *vt* examine, test; (*nach~*) check; **~er** *m* -s, - examiner; **~ling** *m* examinee; **~ung** *f* examination; checking; **~ungsausschuß** *m* examining board.
Prügel ['pry:gəl] *m* -s, - cudgel // *pl* beating; **~ei** [-'laɪ] *f* fight; **~knabe** *m* scapegoat; **p~n** *vt* beat // *vr* fight; **~strafe** *f* corporal punishment.
Prunk [prʊŋk] *m* -(e)s pomp, show; **p~voll** *a* splendid, magnificent.
PS [pe:'ɛs] *abk* (= *Pferdestärke*) horsepower, HP.

Psalm [psalm] *m* -s, -en psalm.
pseudo- ['psɔydo] *in zW* pseudo.
pst [pst] *interj* psst.
Psych- ['psyç] *zW:* **~iater** [-i'a:tər] *m* -s, - psychiatrist; **p~isch** *a* psychological; **~oanalyse** [-o'ana'ly:zə] *f* psychoanalysis; **~ologe** [-o'lo:gə] *m* -n, -n psychologist; **~olo'gie** *f* psychology; **p~ologisch** *a* psychological.
Pubertät [puber'tɛ:t] *f* puberty.
Publikum ['pu:blikʊm] *nt* -s audience; (*SPORT*) crowd.
publizieren [publi'tsi:rən] *vt* publish, publicize.
Pudding ['pʊdɪŋ] *m* -s, -e *od* -s blancmange.
Pudel ['pu:dəl] *m* -s poodle.
Puder ['pu:dər] *m* -s, - powder; **~dose** *f* powder compact; **p~n** *vt* powder; **~zucker** *m* icing sugar.
Puff [pʊf] *m* -s, -e (*Wäsche~*) linen basket; (*Sitz~*) pouf; *pl* -e (*umg: Stoß*) push; *pl* -s (*umg: Bordell*) brothel; **~er** *m* -s, - buffer; **~erspeicher** *m* (*COMPUT*) buffer.
Pullover [pʊ'lo:vər] *m* -s, - pullover, jumper.
Puls [pʊls] *m* -es, -e pulse; **~ader** *f* artery; **p~ieren** [pʊl'zi:rən] *vi* throb, pulsate.
Pult [pʊlt] *nt* -(e)s, -e desk.
Pulver ['pʊlfər] *nt* -s, - powder; **p~ig** *a* powdery; **~schnee** *m* powdery snow.
pummelig ['pʊməlɪç] *a* chubby.
Pumpe ['pʊmpə] *f* -, -n pump; **p~n** *vt* pump; (*umg*) lend; borrow.
Punkt [pʊŋkt] *m* -(e)s, -e point; (*bei Muster*) dot; (*Satzzeichen*) full stop; **p~ieren** [-'ti:rən] *vt* dot; (*MED*) aspirate.
pünktlich ['pyŋktlɪç] *a* punctual; **P~keit** *f* punctuality.
Punktsieg *m* victory on points.
Punktzahl *f* score.
Punsch [pʊnʃ] *m* -(e)s, -e punch.
Pupille [pu'pɪlə] *f* -, -n pupil.
Puppe ['pʊpə] *f* -, -n doll; (*Marionette*) puppet; (*Insekten~*) pupa, chrysalis; **~nspieler** *m* puppeteer.
pur [pu:r] *a* pure; (*völlig*) sheer; (*Whisky*) neat.
Püree [py're:] *nt* -s, -s mashed potatoes *pl*.
Purzel- ['pʊrtsəl] *zW:* **~baum** *m* somersault; **p~n** *vi* tumble.
Puste ['pu:stə] *f* - (*umg*) puff; (*fig*) steam; **p~n** *vi* puff, blow.
Pute ['pu:tə] *f* -, -n turkey-hen; **~r** *m* -s, - turkey-cock.
Putsch [pʊtʃ] *m* -(e)s, -e revolt, putsch.
Putz [pʊts] *m* -es (*Mörtel*) plaster, roughcast; **p~en** *vt* clean; (*Nase*)

wipe, blow // *vr* clean oneself; dress oneself up; **~frau** *f* charwoman; **p~ig** *a* quaint, funny; **~lappen** *m* cloth.

Puzzle ['pasəl] *nt* -s, -s jigsaw.

Pyjama [py'dʒa:ma] *m* -s, -s pyjamas *pl.*

Pyramide [pyra'mi:də] *f* -, -n pyramid.

Pyrenäen [pyre'nɛ:ən] *pl* Pyrenees *pl.*

Q

Q, q [ku:] *nt* Q, q.

Quacksalber ['kvakzalbər] *m* -s, - quack (doctor).

Quader ['kva:dər] *m* -s, - square stone; (*MATH*) cuboid.

Quadrat [kva'dra:t] *nt* -(e)s, -e square; **q~isch** *a* square; **~meter** *m* square metre.

quaken ['kva:kən] *vi* croak; (*Ente*) quack.

quäken ['kvɛ:kən] *vi* screech.

Qual [kva:l] *f* -, -en pain, agony; (*seelisch*) anguish.

Quäl- [kvɛ:l] *zW:* **q~en** *vt* torment // *vr* struggle; (*geistig*) torment oneself; **~erei** [-ə'raɪ] *f* torture, torment; **~geist** *m* pest.

qualifizieren [kvalifi'tsi:rən] *vtr* qualify; (*einstufen*) label.

Qualität [kvali'tɛ:t] *f* quality; **Qualitätsware** *f* article of high quality.

Qualle ['kvalə] *f* -, -n jellyfish.

Qualm [kvalm] *m* -(e)s thick smoke; **q~en** *vti* smoke.

qualvoll ['kva:lfɔl] *a* excruciating, painful, agonizing.

Quant- ['kvant] *zW:* **~entheorie** *f* quantum theory; **~ität** [-i'tɛ:t] *f* quantity; **q~itativ** [-ita'ti:f] *a* quantitative; **~um** *nt* -s, **Quanten** quantity, amount.

Quarantäne [karan'tɛ:nə] *f* -, -n quarantine.

Quark [kvark] *m* -s curd cheese; (*umg*) rubbish.

Quarta ['kvarta] *f* -, **Quarten** third year of secondary school; **Quartal** [kvar'ta:l] *nt* -s, -e quarter (year).

Quartier [kvar'ti:r] *nt* -s, -e accommodation; (*MIL*) quarters *pl*; (*Stadt~*) district.

Quarz [kva:rts] *m* -es, -e quartz.

quasseln ['kvasəln] *vi* (*umg*) natter.

Quatsch [kvatʃ] *m* -es rubbish; **q~en** *vi* chat, natter.

Quecksilber ['kvɛkzılbər] *nt* mercury.

Quelle ['kvɛlə] *f* -, -n spring; (*eines Flusses*) source; **q~n** *vi* (*hervor~*) pour *od* gush forth; (*schwellen*) swell.

quer [kve:r] *ad* crossways, diagonally; (*rechtwinklig*) at right angles; **~ auf**

dem Bett across the bed; **Q~balken** *m* crossbeam; **~feldein** *ad* across country; **Q~flöte** *f* flute; **Q~schnitt** *m* cross-section; **~schnittsgelähmt** *a* paralysed below the waist; **Q~straße** *f* intersecting road.

quetschen ['kvɛtʃən] *vt* squash, crush; (*MED*) bruise.

Quetschung *f* bruise, contusion.

quieken ['kvi:kən] *vi* squeak.

quietschen ['kvi:tʃən] *vi* squeak.

Quint- ['kvɪnt] *zW:* **~a** *f* -, -en second form in secondary school; **~essenz** [-'ɛsɛnts] *f* quintessence; **~ett** [-'tɛt] *nt* -(e)s, -e quintet.

Quirl [kvɪrl] *m* -(e)s, -e whisk.

quitt [kvɪt] *a* quits, even; **Q~e** *f* -, -n quince; **~ieren** [-'ti:rən] *vt* give a receipt for; (*Dienst*) leave; **Q~ung** *f* receipt.

Quiz [kvɪs] *nt* -, - quiz.

Quote ['kvo:tə] *f* -, -n number, rate.

R

R, r [ɛr] *nt* R, r.

Rabatt [ra'bat] *m* -(e)s, -e discount; **~e** *f* -, -n flowerbed, border; **~marke** *f* trading stamp.

Rabe ['ra:bə] *m* -n, -n raven.

rabiat [rabi'a:t] *a* furious.

Rache ['raxə] *f* - revenge, vengeance; **~n** *m* -s, - throat.

rächen ['rɛçən] *vt* avenge, revenge // *vr* take (one's) revenge; **das wird sich ~** you'll pay for that.

Rachitis [ra'xi:tɪs] *f* - rickets *sing.*

Rad [ra:t] *nt* -(e)s, -er wheel; (*Fahr~*) bike; **Radar** ['ra:da:r] *m od nt* -s radar; **Radarfalle** *f* speed trap; **Radarkontrolle** *f* radar-controlled speed trap; **Radau** [ra'dau] *m* -s (*umg*) row; **~dampfer** *m* paddle steamer; **radebrechen** *vi insep:* deutsch *etc* radebrechen speak broken German *etc*; **r~fahren** *vi unreg* cycle; **~fahrer(in** *f*) *m* cyclist; **~fahrweg** *m* cycle track *od* path.

Radier- [ra'di:r] *zW:* **r~en** *vt* rub out, erase; (*ART*) etch; **~gummi** *m* rubber, eraser; **~ung** *f* etching.

Radieschen [ra'di:sçən] *nt* radish.

radikal [radi'ka:l] *a*, **R~e(r)** *mf* radical.

Radio ['ra:dio] *nt* -s, -s radio, wireless; **r~ak'tiv** *a* radioactive; **~aktivi'tät** *f* radioactivity; **~apparat** *m* radio, wireless set.

Radius ['ra:dius] *m* -, **Radien** radius.

Rad- *zW:* **~kappe** *f* (*AUT*) hub cap; **~rennen** *nt* cycle race; cycle racing; **~sport** *m* cycling.

raff- [raf] *zW:* **~en** *vt* snatch, pick up; (*Stoff*) gather (up); (*Geld*) pile up, rake in; **R~inade** [-i'na:də] *f* refined sugar; **~i'niert** *a* crafty, cunning.

ragen ['ra:gən] *vi* tower, rise.

Rahm [ra:m] *m* **-s** cream; **~en** *m* **-s**, - frame(work); im **~en** des Möglichen within the bounds of possibility; **r~en** *vt* frame; **~enplan** *m* outline plan; **r~ig** *a* creamy.

Rakete [ra'ke:tə] *f* **-**, **-n** rocket; **Raketenstützpunkt** *m* missile base.

rammen ['ramən] *vt* ram.

Rampe ['rampə] *f* **-**, **-n** ramp; **Rampenlicht** *vt* (THEAT) footlights *pl*.

ramponieren [rampo'ni:rən] *vt* (umg) damage.

Ramsch [ramʃ] *m* **-(e)s**, **-e** junk.

ran [ran] *ad* (umg) = **heran.**

Rand [rant] *m* **-(e)s**, **-e** rim; edge; (von Brille, Tasse etc) rim; (Hut~) brim; (auf Papier) margin; (Schmutz~, unter Augen) ring; (fig) verge, brink; außer ~ und Band wild; am ~e bemerkt mentioned in passing; **r~alieren** [randa'li:rən] *vi* (go on the) rampage.

Rang [raŋ] *m* **-(e)s**, **-e** rank; (Stand) standing; (Wert) quality; (THEAT) circle.

Rangier- [rãʒi:r] zW: **~bahnhof** *m* marshalling yard; **r~en** *vt* (EISENB) shunt, switch (US) // *vi* rank, be classed; **~gleis** *nt* siding.

Ranke ['raŋkə] *f* **-**, **-n** tendril, shoot.

rannte etc *v siehe* **rennen.**

ranzig ['rantsıç] *a* rancid.

Rappe ['rapə] *m* **-n**, **-n** black horse.

Rappen ['rapən] *m* (FIN) rappen, centime.

rar [ra:r] *a* rare; sich ~ machen (umg) keep oneself to oneself; **R~i'tät** *f* rarity; (Sammelobjekt) curio.

rasant [ra'zant] *a* quick, rapid.

rasch [raʃ] *a* quick; **~eln** *vi* rustle.

Rasen ['ra:zən] *m* **-s**, - lawn; grass; **r~** *vi* rave; (schnell) race; **r~d** *a* furious; **r~de Kopfschmerzen** a splitting headache; **~mäher** *m* **-s**, - *f* lawnmower; **~platz** *m* lawn.

Rasier- [ra'zi:r] zW: **~apparat** *m* shaver; **~creme** *f* shaving cream; **r~en** *vtr* shave; **~klinge** *f* razor blade; **~messer** *nt* razor; **~pinsel** *m* shaving brush; **~seife** *f* shaving soap od stick; **~wasser** *nt* shaving lotion.

Rasse ['rasə] *f* **-**, **-n** race; (Tier~) breed; **~hund** *m* thoroughbred dog; **Rassenhaß** *m* race od racial hatred; **Rassentrennung** *f* racial segregation.

Rassismus [ra'sısmus] *m* racism.

Rast [rast] *f* **-**, **-en** rest; **r~en** *vi* rest; **~haus** *nt*, **~hof** *m* (AUT) service station; **r~los** *a* tireless; (unruhig) restless; **~platz** *m* (AUT) layby; **~stätte**

f (AUT) service station.

Rasur [ra'zu:r] *f* shaving.

Rat [ra:t] *m* **-(e)s**, **-schläge** advice *no pl*; ein ~ a piece of advice; jdn zu **~e** ziehen consult sb; keinen ~ wissen not know what to do; **~e** *f* **-**, **-n** instalment; **r~en** *vti unreg* guess; (empfehlen) advise (jdm sb); **~enzahlung** *f* hire purchase; **~geber** *m* **-s**, - adviser; **~haus** *nt* town hall.

ratifizieren [ratifi:tsi:rən] *vt* ratify.

Ration [ratsi'o:n] *f* ration; **r~al** [-'na:l] *a* rational; **r~ali'sieren** *vt* rationalize; **r~ell** [-'nɛl] *a* efficient; **r~ieren** [-'ni:rən] *vt* ration.

Rat- zW: **r~los** *a* at a loss, helpless; **r~sam** *a* advisable; **~schlag** *m* (piece of) advice.

Rätsel ['rɛ:tsəl] *nt* **-s**, - puzzle; (Wort~) riddle; **r~haft** *a* mysterious; es ist mir r~haft it's a mystery to me.

Ratte ['ratə] *f* **-**, **-n** rat; **Rattenfänger** *m* **-s**, - ratcatcher.

rattern ['ratərn] *vi* rattle, clatter.

Raub [raup] *m* **-(e)s** robbery; (Beute) loot, booty; **~bau** *m* ruthless exploitation; **r~en** [raubən] *vt* rob; (Mensch) kidnap, abduct.

Räuber ['rɔybər] *m* **-s**, - robber.

Raub- zW: **~mord** *m* robbery with murder; **~tier** *nt* predator; **~überfall** *m* robbery with violence; **~vogel** *m* bird of prey.

Rauch ['raux] *m* **-(e)s** smoke; **r~en** *vti* smoke; **~er** *m* **-s**, - smoker; **~erabteil** *nt* (EISENB) smoker.

räuchern [rɔyçərn] *vt* smoke, cure.

Rauchfleisch *nt* smoked meat.

rauchig *a* smoky.

rauf [rauf] *ad* (umg) = **herauf, hinauf;** **~en** *vt* (Haare) pull out // *vir* fight; **R~e'rei** *f* brawl, fight.

rauh [rau] *a* rough, coarse; (Wetter) harsh; **R~reif** *m* hoarfrost.

Raum [raum] *m* **-(e)s**, **Räume** space; (Zimmer, Platz) room; (Gebiet) area.

räumen ['rɔymən] *vt* clear; (Wohnung, Platz) vacate; (wegbringen) shift, move; (in Schrank etc) put away.

Raum- zW: **~fähre** *f* space shuttle; **~fahrt** *f* space travel; **~inhalt** *m* cubic capacity, volume.

räumlich ['rɔymlıç] *a* spatial; **R~keiten** *pl* premises *pl*.

Raum- zW: **~mangel** *m* lack of space; **~pflegerin** *f* cleaner; **~schiff** *nt* spaceship; **~schiffahrt** *f* space travel.

Räumung ['rɔymuŋ] *f* vacating, evacuation; clearing (away); **Räumungsverkauf** *m* clearance sale; (bei Geschäftsaufgabe) closing down sale.

Raupe ['raʊpə] *f* -, -n caterpillar; (~*nkette*) (caterpillar) track; **Raupenschlepper** *m* caterpillar tractor.

raus [raʊs] *ad* (*umg*) = heraus, hinaus.

Rausch [raʊʃ] *m* -(e)s, Räusche intoxication; r~en *vi* (*Wasser*) rush; (*Baum*) rustle; (*Radio etc*) hiss; (*Mensch*) sweep, sail; r~end *a* (*Beifall*) thunderous; (*Fest*) sumptuous; ~gift *nt* drug; ~gifthandel *m* drug traffic; ~giftsüchtige(r) *mf* drug addict.

räuspern ['rɔʏspərn] *vr* clear one's throat.

Razzia ['ratsia] *f* -, Razzien raid.

Reagenzglas [rea'gɛntsglaːs] *nt* test tube.

reagieren [rea'giːrən] *vi* react (*auf* +*akk* to).

Reakt- *zW:* ~ion [reaktsi'oːn] *f* reaction; r~ionär *a* reactionary; ~or [re'aktɔr] *m* reactor.

real [re'aːl] *a* real, material; R~ismus [-'lɪsmʊs] *m* realism; ~istisch *a* realistic; R~schule *f* secondary school.

Rebe ['reːbə] *f* -, -n vine.

Rebell [re'bɛl] *m* -en, -en rebel; ~i'on *f* rebellion; r~isch *a* rebellious.

Rechen ['rɛçən] *m* -s, - rake; r~ *vti* rake; ~fehler *m* miscalculation; ~maschine *f* calculating machine; ~schaft *f* account; für etw ~schaft ablegen account for sth; ~schieber *m* slide rule.

Rech- ['rɛç] *zW:* r~nen *vti* calculate; jdn/etw r~nen zu count sb/sth among; r~nen mit reckon with; r~nen auf (+*akk*) count on; ~nen *nt* arithmetic; ~ner *m* -s, - calculator; (*COMPUT*) computer; ~nung *f* calculation(s); (*COMM*) bill, check (*US*); jdm/etw ~nung tragen take sb/sth into account; ~nungsjahr *nt* financial year; ~nungsprüfer *m* auditor.

recht [rɛçt] *a, ad* right; (*vor Adjektiv*) really, quite; das ist mir ~ that suits me; jetzt erst ~ now more than ever; ~ haben be right; jdm ~ geben agree with sb; R~ *nt* -(e)s, -e right; (*JUR*) law; mit R~ rightly, justly; von R~s wegen by rights; R~e *f* -n, -n right (hand); (*POL*) Right; ~e(r, s) *a* right; (*POL*) right-wing; ein R~r a right-winger; R~e(s) *nt* right thing; etwas/nichts R~es something/nothing proper; R~eck *nt* -s, -e rectangle; ~eckig *a* rectangular; ~fertigen *vtr insep* justify (o.s.); R~fertigung *f* justification; ~mäßig *a* legal, lawful.

rechts [rɛçts] *ad* on/to the right; R~anwalt *m*, R~anwältin *f* lawyer, barrister; R~'außen *m* -, - (*SPORT*) outside right.

rechtschaffen *a* upright.

Rechtschreibung *f* spelling.

Rechts- *zW:* ~fall *m* (law) case; ~händer *m* -s, - right-handed person; r~kräftig *a* valid, legal; ~kurve *f* right-hand bend; ~streit *m* law-suit; r~verbindlich *a* legally binding; ~verkehr *m* driving on the right; r~widrig *a* illegal; ~wissenschaft *f* jurisprudence.

rechtwinklig *a* right-angled.

rechtzeitig *a* timely // *ad* in time.

Reck [rɛk] *nt* -(e)s, -e horizontal bar; r~en *vtr* stretch.

Redakteur [redak'tøːr] *m* editor.

Redaktion [redaktsi'oːn] *f* editing; (*Leute*) editorial staff; (*Büro*) editorial office(s).

Rede ['reːdə] *f* -, -n speech; (*Gespräch*) talk; jdn zur ~ stellen take sb to task; ~freiheit *f* freedom of speech; r~gewandt *a* eloquent; r~n *vi* talk, speak // *vt* say; (*Unsinn etc*) talk; **Redensart** *f* set phrase; ~wendung *f* expression, idiom.

red- ['reːd] *zW:* ~lich *a* honest; R~ner *m* -s, - speaker, orator; ~selig *a* talkative, loquacious.

reduzieren [redu'tsiːrən] *vt* reduce.

Reede ['reːdə] *f* -, -n protected anchorage; ~r *m* -s, - shipowner; ~'rei *f* shipping line *od* firm.

reell [re'ɛl] *a* fair, honest; (*MATH*) real.

Refer- *zW:* ~at [refe'raːt] *nt* -(e)s, -e report; (*Vortrag*) paper; (*Gebiet*) section; ~ent [refe'rɛnt] *m* speaker; (*Berichterstatter*) reporter; (*Sachbearbeiter*) expert; ~enz [refe'rɛnts] *f* reference; r~ieren [refe'riːrən] *vi*: r~ieren über (+*akk*) speak *od* talk on.

Reflex [re'flɛks] *m* -es, -e reflex; ~bewegung *f* reflex action; r~iv [-'ksiːf] *a* (*GRAM*) reflexive.

Reform [re'fɔrm] *f* -, -en reform; ~ati'on *f* reformation; ~haus *nt* health food shop; r~ieren [-'miːrən] *vt* reform.

Regal [re'gaːl] *nt* -s, -e (book)shelves *pl*, bookcase; stand, rack.

Regel ['reːgəl] *f* -, -n rule; (*MED*) period; r~mäßig *a* regular; ~mäßigkeit *f* regularity; r~n *vt* regulate, control; (*Angelegenheit*) settle // *vr*: sich von selbst r~n take care of itself; r~recht *a* regular, proper, thorough; ~ung *f* regulation; settlement; r~widrig *a* irregular, against the rules.

Regen ['reːgən] *m* -s, - rain; R~bogen *m* rainbow; R~bogenpresse *f* tabloids *pl*; R~mantel *m* raincoat, mac(kintosh); R~schauer *m* shower (of rain); R~schirm *m* umbrella; ~wurm *m* earthworm.

Regie [re'ʒiː] f (Film etc) direction; (THEAT) production.

Regier- [re'giːr] zW: **r~en** vti govern, rule; **~ung** f government; (Monarchie) reign; **~ungswechsel** m change of government; **~ungszeit** f period in government; (von König) reign.

Regiment [regi'mɛnt] nt -s, -er regiment.

Region [regi'oːn] f region.

Regisseur [reʒi'søːr] m director; (THEAT) (stage) producer.

Register [re'gɪstər] nt -s, - register; (in Buch) table of contents, index.

registrieren [regɪs'triːrən] vt register.

reg- ['reːg] zW: **R~ler** m -s, - regulator, governor; **~los** ['reːkloːs] a motionless; **regnen** vi unpers rain; **regnerisch** a rainy.

regulär [regu'lɛːr] a regular.

regulieren [regu'liːrən] vt regulate; (COMM) settle.

Regung ['reːgʊŋ] f motion; (Gefühl) feeling, impulse; **regungslos** a motionless.

Reh [reː] nt -(e)s, -e deer, roe; **~bock** m roebuck; **~kalb** nt, **~kitz** nt fawn.

Reib- ['raɪb] zW: **~e** f -, -n, **~eisen** nt grater; **r~en** vt unreg rub; (KOCH) grate; **~e'rei** f friction no pl; (fig) **~fläche** f rough surface; **~ung** f friction; **r~ungslos** a smooth.

reich [raɪç] a rich; **R~** nt -(e)s, -e empire, kingdom; (fig) realm; das Dritte R~ the Third Reich; **~en** vi reach; (genügen) be enough od sufficient (jdm for sb) // vt hold out; (geben) pass, hand; (anbieten) offer; **~haltig** a ample, rich; **~lich** a ample, plenty of; **R~tum** m -s, -tümer wealth; **R~weite** f range.

reif [raɪf] a ripe; (Mensch, Urteil) mature; **R~** m -(e)s hoarfrost // -(e)s, -e (Ring) ring, hoop; **R~e** f - ripeness; maturity; **~en** vi mature; ripen; **R~en** m -s, - ring, hoop; (Fahrzeug~) tyre; **R~endruck** m tyre pressure; **R~enpanne** f puncture.

Reihe ['raɪə] f -, -n row; (von Tagen etc, umg: Anzahl) series sing; der ~ nach in turn; er ist an der ~ it's his turn; an die ~ kommen have one's turn; **Reihenfolge** f sequence; alphabetische Reihenfolge alphabetical order; **~nhaus** nt terraced house.

Reim [raɪm] m -(e)s, -e rhyme; **r~en** vt rhyme.

rein [raɪn] ad (umg) = **herein**, **hinein** // a, ad pure(ly); (sauber) clean; etw ins ~e schreiben make a fair copy of sth; etw ins ~e bringen clear up sth; **R~fall** m (umg) let-down; **R~gewinn** m net profit; **R~heit** f purity; cleanness; **~igen** vt clean; (Wasser) puri-

fy; **R~igung** f cleaning; purification; (Geschäft) cleaners; **chemische R~igung** dry cleaning; dry cleaners; **~lich** a clean; **~rassig** a pedigree; **R~schrift** f fair copy.

Reis [raɪs] m -es, -e rice.

Reise ['raɪzə] f -, -n journey; (Schiffs~) voyage; gute ~! have a good journey; **~n** pl travels pl; **~andenken** nt souvenir; **~büro** nt travel agency; **r~fertig** a ready to start; **~führer** m guide(book); (Mensch) travel guide; **~gepäck** nt luggage; **~gesellschaft** f party of travellers; **~kosten** pl travelling expenses pl; **~leiter** m courier; **~lektüre** f reading matter for the journey; **r~n** vi travel; go (nach to); **Reisende(r)** mf traveller; **~paß** m passport; **~proviant** m food and drink for the journey; **~scheck** m traveller's cheque; **~ziel** nt destination.

Reiß- ['raɪs] zW: **r~en** vti unreg tear; (ziehen) pull, drag; (Witz) crack; etw an sich r~en snatch sth up; (fig) take over sth; sich um etw r~en scramble for sth; **~nagel** m drawing pin (Brit), thumbtack (US); **~verschluß** m zip(per), zip fastener; **~wolf** m shredder; **~zwecke** f = **~nagel**.

Reit- ['raɪt] zW: **r~en** vti unreg ride; **~er(in** f) m -s, - rider; (MIL) cavalryman, trooper; **~hose** f riding breeches pl; **~pferd** nt saddle horse; **~stiefel** m riding boot; **~zeug** nt riding outfit.

Reiz [raɪts] m -es, -e stimulus; (angenehm) charm; (Verlockung) attraction; **r~bar** a irritable; **~barkeit** f irritability; **r~en** vt stimulate; (unangenehm) irritate; (verlocken) appeal to, attract; **r~end** a charming; **r~voll** a attractive.

rekeln ['reːkəln] vr stretch out; (lümmeln) lounge od loll about.

Reklamation [reklamatsi'oːn] f complaint.

Reklame [re'klaːmə] f -, -n advertising; advertisement; ~ machen für etw advertise sth.

rekonstruieren [rekɔnstru'iːrən] vt reconstruct.

Rekord [re'kɔrt] m -(e)s, -e record; **~leistung** f record performance.

Rektor ['rɛktɔr] m (UNIV) rector, vice-chancellor; (SCH) headteacher (Brit), principal (US); **~at** [-'raːt] nt -(e)s, -e rectorate, vice-chancellorship; headship; (Zimmer) rector's etc office.

Relais [rə'lɛː] nt -, - relay.

relativ [rela'tiːf] a relative; **R~ität** [relativi'tɛːt] f relativity.

relevant [rele'vant] *a* relevant.
Relief [reli'ef] *nt* **-s, -s** relief.
Religion [religi'o:n] *f* religion.
religiös [religi'ø:s] *a* religious.
Reling ['re:lɪŋ] *f* **-, -s** (*NAUT*) rail.
Remoulade [remu'la:də] *f* remoulade.
Rendezvous [rãde'vu:] *nt* **-, -** rendez-vous.
Renn- ['rɛn] *zW*: **~bahn** *f* racecourse; (*AUT*) circuit, race track; **r~en** *vti unreg* run, race; **~en** *nt* **-s, -** running; (*Wettbewerb*) race; **~fahrer** *m* racing driver; **~pferd** *nt* racehorse; **~wagen** *m* racing car.
renovier- [reno'vi:r] *zW*: **~en** *vt* renovate; **R~ung** *f* renovation.
rentabel [rɛn'ta:bəl] *a* profitable, lucrative.
Rentabilität [rɛntabili'tɛ:t] *f* profitability.
Rente ['rɛntə] *f* **-, -n** pension; **rentendynamisch** *a* index-linked; **Rentenversicherung** *f* pension scheme.
Rentier ['rɛnti:r] *nt* reindeer.
rentieren [rɛn'ti:rən] *vr* pay, be profitable.
Rentner(in *f*) ['rɛntnər(ɪn)] *m* **-s, -** pensioner.
Reparatur [repara'tu:r] *f* repairing; repair; **~werkstatt** *f* repair shop; (*AUT*) garage.
reparieren [repa'ri:rən] *vt* repair.
Reportage [repɔr'ta:ʒə] *f* **-, -n** (on-the-spot) report; (*TV, RAD*) live commentary *od* coverage.
Reporter [re'pɔrtər] *m* **-s, -** reporter, commentator.
Repressalien [repre'sa:liən] *pl* reprisals *pl*.
Reprivatisierung [reprivati'zi:rʊŋ] *f* denationalisation.
Reproduktion [reprodʊktsi'o:n] *f* reproduction.
reproduzieren [reprodu'tsi:rən] *vt* reproduce.
Reptil [rɛp'ti:l] *nt* **-s, -ien** reptile.
Republik [repu'bli:k] *f* republic; **r~anisch** [-'ka:nɪʃ] *a* republican.
Reservat [rezɛr'va:t] *nt* **-(e)s, -e** reservation.
Reserve [re'zɛrvə] *f* **-, -n** reserve; **~rad** *nt* (*AUT*) spare wheel; **~spieler** *m* reserve; **~tank** *m* reserve tank.
reservieren [rezɛr'vi:rən] *vt* reserve.
Reservoir [rezɛrvo'a:r] *nt* **-s, -e** reservoir.
Residenz [rezi'dɛnts] *f* residence, seat.
resignieren [rezi'gni:rən] *vi* resign.
resolut [rezo'lu:t] *a* resolute.
Resonanz [rezo'nants] *f* (*lit*) resonance; (*fig*) response.
Resopal ® [rezo'pa:l] *nt* **-s** Formica ®.
Resozialisierung [rezotsiali'zi:rʊŋ] *f* rehabilitation.
Respekt [rɛ'spɛkt] *m* **-(e)s** respect; **r~ieren** [-'ti:rən] *vt* respect; **r~los** *a* disrespectful; **r~voll** *a* respectful.
Ressort [rɛ'so:r] *nt* **-s, -s** department.
Rest [rɛst] *m* **-(e)s, -e** remainder, rest; (*Über~*) remains *pl*.
Restaurant [rɛsto'rã:] *nt* **-s, -s** restaurant.
restaurieren [rɛstaʊ'ri:rən] *vt* restore.
Rest- *zW*: **~betrag** *m* remainder, outstanding sum; **r~lich** *a* remaining; **r~los** *a* complete.
Resultat [rezʊl'ta:t] *nt* **-(e)s, -e** result.
Retorte [re'tɔrtə] *f* **-, -n** retort.
Retouren [re'tu:rən] *pl* (*COMM*) returns *pl*.
retten ['rɛtən] *vt* save, rescue.
Rettich ['rɛtɪç] *m* **-s, -e** radish.
Rettung *f* rescue; (*Hilfe*) help; **seine letzte ~** his last hope.
Rettungs- *zW*: **~boot** *nt* lifeboat; **r~los** *a* hopeless; **~ring** *m* lifebelt, life preserver (*US*).
retuschieren [retʊ'ʃi:rən] *vt* (*PHOT*) retouch.
Reue ['rɔʏə] *f* **-** remorse; (*Bedauern*) regret; **r~n** *vt*: **es reut ihn** he regrets (it) *od* is sorry (about it).
reuig ['rɔʏɪç] *a* penitent.
Revanche [re'vã:ʃə] *f* **-, -n** revenge; (*SPORT*) return match.
revanchieren [revã'ʃi:rən] *vr* (*sich rächen*) get one's own back, have one's revenge; (*erwidern*) reciprocate, return the compliment.
Revier [re'vi:r] *nt* **-s, -e** district; (*Jagd~*) preserve; police station/beat.
Revolte [re'vɔltə] *f* **-, -n** revolt.
Revolution [revolutsi'o:n] *f* revolution; **~är** [-'nɛ:r] *m* **-s, -e** revolutionary; **r~ieren** [-'ni:rən] *vt* revolutionize.
Rezept [re'tsɛpt] *nt* **-(e)s, -e** recipe; (*MED*) prescription; **~ion** [retseptsi'o:n] *f* reception; **r~pflichtig** *a* available only on prescription.
rezitieren [retsi'ti:rən] *vt* recite.
R-Gespräch ['ɛrgəʃprɛːç] *nt* reverse charge call (*Brit*), collect call (*US*).
Rhabarber [ra'barbər] *m* **-s** rhubarb.
Rhein [raɪn] *m* **-s** Rhine; **r~isch** *a* Rhenish.
Rhesusfaktor ['re:zusfaktɔr] *m* rhesus factor.
rhetorisch [re'to:rɪʃ] *a* rhetorical.
Rheuma ['rɔʏma] *nt* **-s, Rheumatismus** [rɔʏma'tɪsmʊs] *m* rheumatism.
Rhinozeros [ri'no:tserɔs] *nt* **-** *od* **-ses, -se** rhinoceros.
rhyth- ['rʏt] *zW*: **~misch** *a* rhythmical; **R~mus** *m* rhythm.
Richt- ['rɪçt] *zW*: **r~en** *vt* direct (*an* +*akk* at; (*fig*) to); (*Waffe*) aim (*auf* +*akk* at); (*einstellen*) adjust;

(*instandsetzen*) repair; (*zurecht-machen*) prepare; (*bestrafen*) pass judgement on // *vr:* sich r~en nach go by; ~er(in *f*) *m* -s, - judge; r~erlich *a* judicial; r~ig *a* right, correct; (*echt*) proper; bin ich hier r~ig? am I in the right place? // *ad* (*umg: sehr*) really; der/die ~ige the right one/person; das ~ige the right thing; ~igkeit *f* correctness; ~igstellung *f* correction, rectification; ~preis *m* recommended price; ~ung *f* direction; tendency, orientation.

rieb *etc v siehe* **reiben.**

riechen ['riːçən] *vti unreg* smell (*an etw* (*dat*) sth; *nach* of); ich kann das/ihn nicht ~ (*umg*) I can't stand it/him.

rief *etc v siehe* **rufen.**

Riegel ['riːgəl] *m* -s, - bolt, bar.

Riemen ['riːmən] *m* -s, - strap; (*Gürtel, TECH*) belt; (*NAUT*) oar.

Riese ['riːzə] *m* -n, -n giant; **rieseln** *vi* trickle; (*Schnee*) fall gently; **Riesenerfolg** *m* enormous success; r~ngroß *a* colossal, gigantic, huge.

riesig ['riːzɪç] *a* enormous, huge, vast.

riet *etc v siehe* **raten.**

Riff [rɪf] *nt* -(e)s, -e reef.

Rille ['rɪlə] *f* -, -n groove.

Rind [rɪnt] *nt* -(e)s, -er ox; cow; cattle *pl*; (*KOCH*) beef; ~e *f* ['rɪndə] -, -n rind; (*Baum~*) bark; (*Brot~*) crust; ~fleisch *nt* beef; ~vieh *nt* cattle *pl*; (*umg*) blockhead, stupid oaf.

Ring [rɪŋ] *m* -(e)s, -e ring; ~buch *nt* ring binder; **Ringelnatter** *f* grass snake; r~en *vi unreg* wrestle; ~en *nt* -s wrestling; ~finger *m* ring finger; ~kampf *m* wrestling bout; ~richter *m* referee; **rings um** *ad* round; **ringsherum** *ad* round about; ~straße *f* ring road; **ringsum(her)** *ad* (*rundherum*) round about; (*überall*) all round.

Rinn- ['rɪn] *zW:* ~e *f* -, -n gutter, drain; r~en *vi unreg* run, trickle; ~stein *m* gutter.

Rippchen ['rɪpçən] *nt* small rib; cutlet.

Rippe ['rɪpə] *f* -, -n rib; **Rippenfellentzündung** *f* pleurisy.

Risiko ['riːziko] *nt* -s, -s *od* **Risiken** risk.

riskant [rɪs'kant] *a* risky, hazardous.

riskieren [rɪs'kiːrən] *vt* risk.

Riß [rɪs] *m* -sses, -sse tear; (*in Mauer, Tasse etc*) crack; (*in Haut*) scratch; (*TECH*) design.

rissig ['rɪsɪç] *a* torn; cracked; scratched.

ritt *etc v siehe* **reiten.**

Ritt [rɪt] *m* -(e)s, -e ride; ~er *m* -s, - knight; r~erlich *a* chivalrous.

Ritze ['rɪtsə] *f* -, -n crack, chink.

Rivale [ri'vaːlə] *m* -n, -n rival.

Rivalität [rivali'tɛːt] *f* rivalry.

Rizinusöl ['riːtsinusøːl] *nt* castor oil.

Robbe ['rɔbə] *f* -, -n seal.

Roboter ['rɔbɔtər] *m* -s, - robot.

roch *etc v siehe* **riechen.**

Rock [rɔk] *m* -(e)s, ⸚e skirt; (*Jackett*) jacket; (*Uniform~*) tunic.

Rodel ['roːdəl] *m* -s, - toboggan; ~bahn *f* toboggan run; r~n *vi* toboggan.

roden ['roːdən] *vti* clear.

Rogen ['roːgən] *m* -s, - roe, spawn.

Roggen ['rɔgən] *m* -s, - rye.

roh [roː] *a* raw; (*Mensch*) coarse, crude; **R~bau** *m* shell of a building; **R~material** *nt* raw material; **R~öl** *nt* crude oil.

Rohr ['roːr] *nt* -(e)s, -e pipe, tube; (*BOT*) cane; (*Schilf*) reed; (*Gewehr~*) barrel; ~bruch *m* burst pipe.

Röhre ['røːrə] *f* -, -n tube, pipe; (*RAD etc*) valve; (*Back~*) oven.

Rohr- *zW:* ~leitung *f* pipeline; ~post *f* pneumatic post; ~zucker *m* cane sugar.

Rohstoff *m* raw material.

Rokoko ['rɔkoko] *nt* -s rococo.

Roll- ['rɔl] *zW:* ~(l)aden *m* shutter; ~bahn *f*, ~feld *nt* (*AVIAT*) runway.

Rolle ['rɔlə] *f* -, -n roll; (*THEAT, soziologisch*) role; (*Garn~ etc*) reel, spool; (*Walze*) roller; (*Wäsche~*) mangle; keine ~ spielen not matter; eine (wichtige) ~ spielen bei play a (major) part *od* role in; r~n *vti* roll; (*AVIAT*) taxi; ~r *m* -s, - scooter; (*Welle*) roller.

Roll- *zW:* ~mops *m* pickled herring; ~schuh *m* roller skate; ~stuhl *m* wheelchair; ~treppe *f* escalator.

Rom [roːm] *nt* -s Romeo.

Roman [ro'maːn] *m* -s, -e novel; ~tik [ro'mantik] *f* romanticism; ~tiker [ro'mantikər] *m* -s, - romanticist; r~tisch [ro'mantiʃ] *a* romantic; **Romanze** [ro'mantsə] *f* -, -n romance.

Röm- ['røːm] *zW:* ~er *m* -s, - wineglass; (*Mensch*) Roman; r~isch *a* Roman.

röntgen ['rœntgən] *vt* X-ray; **R~aufnahme** *f*, **R~bild** *nt* X-ray; **R~strahlen** *pl* X-rays *pl*.

rosa ['roːza] *a inv* pink, rose(-coloured).

Rose ['roːzə] *f* -, -n rose; **Rosenkohl** *m* Brussels sprouts *pl*; **Rosenkranz** *m* rosary.

rosig ['roːzɪç] *a* rosy.

Rosine [ro'ziːnə] *f* raisin, currant.

Roß [rɔs] *nt* -sses, -sse horse, steed; ~kastanie *f* horse chestnut.

Rost [rɔst] *m* -(e)s, -e rust; (*Gitter*) grill, gridiron; (*Bett~*) springs *pl*;

~braten *m* roast(ed) meat, joint; **r~en** *vi* rust.

rösten ['rø:stən] *vt* roast; toast; grill.

Rost- *zW:* **r~frei** *a* rust-free; rustproof; stainless; **r~ig** *a* rusty; **~schutz** *m* rust-proofing.

rot [ro:t] *a* red; in den **~en** Zahlen in the red; das **R~e** Meer the Red Sea.

Röte ['rø:tə] *f* - redness; **Röteln** *pl* German measles *sing*; **r~n** *vtr* redden.

rot- *zW:* **~haarig** *a* red-haired; **~ieren** [ro'ti:rən] *vi* rotate; **R~kehlchen** *nt* robin; **R~stift** *m* red pencil; **R~wein** *m* red wine.

Rouge [ru:ʒ] *nt* blusher.

Roulade [ru'la:də] *f* (KOCH) beef olive.

Route ['ru:tə] *f* -, **-n** route.

Routine [ru'ti:nə] *f* experience; routine.

Rübe ['ry:bə] *f* -, **-n** turnip; gelbe **~** carrot; rote **~** beetroot (Brit), beet (US).

rüber ['ry:bər] *ad* (umg) = **herüber, hinüber.**

Rubin [ru'bi:n] *m* -s, **-e** ruby.

Rubrik [ru'bri:k] *f* heading; (Spalte) column.

Ruck [rʊk] *m* -(e)s, **-e** jerk, jolt.

Rück- ['rʏk] *zW:* **~antwort** *f* reply, answer; **r~bezüglich** *a* reflexive; **r~blickend** *a* retrospective.

rücken ['rʏkən] *vti* move; **R~** *m* -s, **-** back; (Berg~) ridge; **R~mark** *nt* spinal cord; **R~schwimmen** *nt* backstroke; **R~wind** *m* following wind.

Rück- *zW:* **~erstattung** *f* return, restitution; **~fahrkarte** *f* return; **~fahrt** *f* return journey; **~fall** *m* relapse; **r~fällig** *a* relapsing; **r~fällig werden** relapse; **~flug** *m* return flight; **~frage** *f* question; **~gabe** *f* return; **~gang** *m* decline, fall; **r~gängig** *a:* etw **r~gängig machen** cancel sth; **~grat** *nt* -(e)s, **-e** spine, backbone; **~kehr** *f* -, **-en** return; **~licht** *nt* back light; **r~lings** *ad* from behind; backwards; **~nahme** *f* -, **-n** taking back; **~porto** *nt* return postage; **~reise** *f* return journey; (NAUT) home voyage; **~ruf** *m* recall.

Rucksack ['rʊkzak] *m* rucksack.

Rück- *zW:* **~schau** *f* reflection; **~schluß** *m* conclusion; **~schritt** *m* retrogression; **r~schrittlich** *a* reactionary; retrograde; **~seite** *f* back; (von Münze etc) reverse; **~sicht** *f* consideration; **~sicht nehmen auf** (+akk) show consideration for; **r~sichtslos** *a* inconsiderate; (Fahren) reckless; (unbarmherzig) ruthless; **r~sichtsvoll** *a* considerate; **~sitz** *m* back seat; **~spiegel** *m* (AUT) rear-view mirror; **~spiel** *nt*

return match; **~sprache** *f* further discussion *od* talk; **~stand** *m* arrears *pl*; **r~ständig** *a* backward, out-of-date; (Zahlungen) in arrears; **~stoß** *m* recoil; **~strahler** *m* -s, **-** rear reflector; **~tritt** *m* resignation; **~trittbremse** *f* pedal brake; **~vergütung** *f* repayment; (COMM) refund; **~versicherung** *f* reinsurance; **r~wärtig** *a* rear; **r~wärts** *ad* backward(s), back; **~wärtsgang** *m* (AUT) reverse gear; **~weg** *m* return journey, way back; **r~wirkend** *a* retroactive; **~wirkung** *f* reaction; retrospective effect; **~zahlung** *f* repayment; **~zug** *m* retreat.

Rudel ['ru:dəl] *nt* -s, **-** pack; herd.

Ruder ['ru:dər] *nt* -s, **-** oar; (Steuer) rudder; **~boot** *nt* rowing boat; **r~n** *vti* row.

Ruf [ru:f] *m* -(e)s, **-e** call, cry; (Ansehen) reputation; **r~en** *vti unreg* call; cry; **~name** *m* usual (first) name; **~nummer** *f* (tele)phone number; **~zeichen** *nt* (RAD) call sign; (TEL) ringing tone.

Rüge ['ry:gə] *f* -, **-n** reprimand, rebuke.

Ruhe ['ru:ə] *f* - rest; (Ungestörtheit) peace, quiet; (Gelassenheit, Stille) calm; (Schweigen) silence; jdn in **~** lassen leave sb alone; sich zur **~** setzen retire; **~!** be quiet!, silence!; **r~n** *vi* rest; **~pause** *f* break; **~platz** *m* resting place; **~stand** *m* retirement; letzte **~stätte** *f* final resting place; **~störung** *f* breach of the peace; **~tag** *m* closing day.

ruhig ['ru:ɪç] *a* quiet; (bewegungslos) still; (Hand) steady; (gelassen, friedlich) calm; (Gewissen) clear; kommen Sie **~** herein just come on in; tu das **~** feel free to do that.

Ruhm [ru:m] *m* -(e)s fame, glory.

rühmen ['ry:mən] *vt* praise // *vr* boast.

Ruhr ['ru:r] *f* - dysentery.

Rühr- ['ry:r] *zW:* **~ei** *nt* scrambled egg; **r~en** *vtr* (lit, fig) move, stir (auch KOCH) // *vi:* **r~en von** come *od* stem from; **r~en an** (+akk) touch; (fig) touch on; **r~end** *a* touching, moving; **r~ig** *a* active, lively; **r~selig** *a* sentimental, emotional; **~ung** *f* emotion.

Ruin [ru'i:n] *m* -s, **-e**, *f* -, **-n** ruin; **r~ieren** [rui'ni:rən] *vt* ruin.

rülpsen ['rʏlpsən] *vi* burp, belch.

rum [rʊm] *ad* (umg) = **herum.**

Rum [rʊm] *m* -s, **-s** rum.

Rumän- [ru'mɛ:n] *zW:* **~e** *m* -n, **-n, ~in** *f* Ro(u)manian; **~ien** *nt* -s Ro(u)mania; **r~isch** *a* Ro(u)manian.

Rummel ['rʊməl] *m* -s (umg) hubbub; (Jahrmarkt) fair; **~platz** *m* fairground, fair.

Rumpf [rʊmpf] *m* -(e)s, ⁻e trunk, torso; (*AVIAT*) fuselage; (*NAUT*) hull.

rümpfen ['rʏmpfən] *vt* (*Nase*) turn up.

rund [rʊnt] *a* round // *ad* (*etwa*) around; ~ **um etw** round sth; **R~brief** *m* circular; **R~e** ['rʊndə] *f* -, -n round; (*in Rennen*) lap; (*Gesellschaft*) circle; **R~fahrt** *f* (round) trip.

Rundfunk ['rʊntfʊŋk] *m* -(e)s broadcasting; **im ~ on the radio**; ~**gerät** *nt* wireless set; ~**sendung** *f* broadcast, radio programme.

Rund- *zW:* **r~heraus** *ad* straight out, bluntly; **r~herum** *ad* round about; all round; **r~lich** *a* plump, rounded; ~**reise** *f* round trip; ~**schreiben** *nt* (*COMM*) circular.

runter ['rʊntər] *ad* (*umg*) = **herunter, hinunter.**

Runzel ['rʊntsəl] *f* -, -n wrinkle; **r~ig** *a* wrinkled; **r~n** *vt* wrinkle; **die Stirn r~n** frown.

rupfen ['rʊpfən] *vt* pluck; **R~** *m* -s, - sackcloth.

ruppig ['rʊpɪç] *a* rough, gruff.

Rüsche ['ryːʃə] *f* -, -n frill.

Ruß [ruːs] *m* -es soot.

Russe ['rʊsə] *m* -n, -n Russian.

Rüssel ['rʏsəl] *m* -s, - snout; (*Elefanten~*) trunk.

rußig ['ruːsɪç] *a* sooty.

Russ- [rʊs] *zW:* ~**in** *f* Russian; **r~isch** *a* Russian.

Rußland ['rʊslant] *nt* -s Russia.

rüsten ['rʏstən] *vtri* prepare; (*MIL*) arm.

rüstig ['rʏstɪç] *a* sprightly, vigorous.

Rüstung ['rʏstʊŋ] *f* preparation; arming; (*Ritter~*) armour; (*Waffen etc*) armaments *pl*; **Rüstungskontrolle** *f* arms control.

Rute ['ruːtə] *f* -, -n rod.

Rutsch [rʊtʃ] *m* -(e)s, -e slide; (*Erd~*) landslide; ~**bahn** *f* slide; **r~en** *vi* slide; (*ausr~en*) slip; **r~ig** *a* slippery.

rütteln ['rʏtəln] *vti* shake, jolt.

S

S, s [ɛs] *nt* S, s.

S. *abk* (= *Seite*) p. // *abk von* **Schilling.**

s. *abk* (= *siehe*) see.

Saal [zaːl] *m* -(e)s, **Säle** hall; room.

Saarland ['zaːrlant] *nt:* **das ~** the Saar (land).

Saat [zaːt] *f* -, -en seed; (*Pflanzen*) crop; (*Säen*) sowing.

Säbel ['zɛːbəl] *m* -s, - sabre, sword.

Sabotage [zaboˈtaːʒə] *f* -, -n sabotage.

sabotieren [zaboˈtiːrən] *vt* sabotage.

Sach- [zax] *zW:* ~**bearbeiter** *m* specialist; **s~dienlich** *a* relevant, helpful; ~**e** *f* -, -n thing; (*Angelegenheit*) affair, business; (*Frage*) matter; (*Pflicht*) task; **zur ~e** to the point; **s~kundig** *a* expert; **s~lich** *a* matter-of-fact, objective; (*Irrtum, Angabe*) factual.

sächlich ['zɛçlɪç] *a* neuter.

Sachschaden *m* material damage.

Sachsen ['zaksən] *nt* -s Saxony.

sächsisch ['zɛksɪʃ] *a* Saxon.

sacht(e) ['zaxt(ə)] *ad* softly, gently.

Sachverständige(r) *mf* expert.

Sack [zak] *m* -(e)s, ⁻e sack; ~**gasse** *f* cul-de-sac, dead-end street (*US*).

Sadismus [zaˈdɪsmʊs] *m* sadism.

Sadist [zaˈdɪst] *m* sadist; **s~isch** *a* sadistic.

säen ['zɛːən] *vti* sow.

Saft [zaft] *m* -(e)s, ⁻e juice; (*BOT*) sap; **s~ig** *a* juicy; **s~los** *a* dry.

Sage ['zaːgə] *f* -, -n saga.

Säge ['zɛːgə] *f* -, -n saw; ~**mehl** *nt* sawdust; **s~n** *vti* saw.

sagen ['zaːgən] *vti* say (*jdm* to sb); (*mitteilen*), tell (*jdm* sb); ~ **Sie ihm, daß ...** tell him ...; ~**haft** *a* legendary; (*umg*) great, smashing.

sah *etc v siehe* **sehen.**

Sahne ['zaːnə] *f* - cream.

Saison [zɛˈzõ] *f* -, -s season; ~**arbeiter** *m* seasonal worker.

Saite ['zaɪtə] *f* -, -n string; **Saiteninstrument** *nt* string instrument.

Sakko ['zako] *m od nt* -s, -s jacket.

Sakrament [zakraˈmɛnt] *nt* sacrament.

Sakristei [zakrɪsˈtaɪ] *f* sacristy.

Salat [zaˈlaːt] *m* -(e)s, -e salad; (*Kopfsalat*) lettuce; ~**soße** *f* salad dressing.

Salb- ['zalb] *zW:* ~**e** *f* -, -n ointment; ~**ei** [zalˈbaɪ] *m od f* -s *od* - sage; **s~en** *vt* anoint.

Saldo ['zaldo] *m* -s, **Salden** balance.

Salmiak [zalmiˈak] *m* -s sal ammoniac; ~**geist** *m* liquid ammonia.

salopp [zaˈlɔp] *a* casual.

Salpeter [zalˈpeːtər] *m* -s saltpetre; ~**säure** *f* nitric acid.

Salve ['zalvə] *f* -, -n salvo.

Salz [zalts] *nt* -es, -e salt; **s~en** *vt* unreg salt; **s~ig** *a* salty; ~**kartoffeln** *pl* boiled potatoes *pl*; ~**säure** *f* hydrochloric acid.

Samen ['zaːmən] *m* -s, - seed; (*ANAT*) sperm.

Sammel- ['zaməl] *zW:* ~**band** *m* anthology; **s~n** *vt* collect // *vr* assemble, gather; (*konzentrieren*) concentrate.

Sammlung ['zamlʊŋ] *f* collection; assembly, gathering; concentration.

Samstag ['zamstaːk] *m* Saturday; **s~s** *ad* (on) Saturdays.

Samt [zamt] *m* -(e)s, -e velvet; **s~**

präp +*dat* (along) with, together with; s~ und sonders each and every one (of them).

sämtlich ['zɛmtlɪç] *a* all (the), entire.

Sand [zant] *m* -(e)s, -e sand; **Sandale** [zan'da:lə] *f* -, -n sandal; ~**bank** *f* sandbank; s~**ig** ['zandɪç] *a* sandy; ~**kasten** *m* sandpit; ~**kuchen** *m* Madeira cake; ~**papier** *nt* sandpaper; ~**stein** *m* sandstone; s~**strahlen** *vti insep* sandblast.

sandte *etc v siehe* **senden**.

Sanduhr *f* hourglass.

sanft [zanft] *a* soft, gentle; ~**mütig** *a* gentle, meek.

sang *etc v siehe* **singen**.

Sänger(in *f*) ['zɛŋər(ɪn)] *m* -s, - singer.

Sani- *zW*: s~**eren** [za'ni:rən] *vt* redevelop; (*Betrieb*) make financially sound // *vr* line one's pockets; become financially sound; s~**tär** [zani'tɛ:r] *a* sanitary; s~**täre Anlagen** sanitation; ~**täter** [zani'tɛ:tər] *m* -s, - first-aid attendant; (*MIL*) (medical) orderly.

sanktionieren [zaŋktsio'ni:rən] *vt* sanction.

Saphir ['za:fi:r] *m* -s, -e sapphire.

Sardelle [zar'dɛlə] *f* anchovy.

Sardin- [zar'di:n] *zW*: ~**e** *f* sardine; ~**ien** [-iən] *nt* -s Sardinia.

Sarg [zark] *m* -(e)s, ̈e coffin.

Sarkasmus [zar'kasmus] *m* sarcasm.

sarkastisch [zar'kastɪʃ] *a* sarcastic.

saß *etc v siehe* **sitzen**.

Satan ['za:tan] *m* -s, -e Satan; devil.

Satellit [zatɛ'li:t] *m* -en, -en satellite; ~**enfoto** *nt* satellite picture.

Satire [za'ti:rə] *f* -, -n satire.

satirisch [za'ti:rɪʃ] *a* satirical.

satt [zat] *a* full; (*Farbe*) rich, deep; **jdn/etw** ~ **sein** *od* **haben** be fed up with sb/sth; **sich** ~ **hören/sehen an** (+*dat*) see/hear enough of; **sich** ~ **essen** eat one's fill; ~ **machen** be filling.

Sattel ['zatəl] *m* -s, ̈ saddle; (*Berg*) ridge; s~**n** *vt* saddle; ~**schlepper** *m* articulated lorry.

sättigen ['zɛtɪgən] *vt* satisfy; (*CHEM*) saturate.

Satz [zats] *m* -es, ̈e (*GRAM*) sentence; (*Neben~, Adverbial~*) clause; (*Theorem*) theorem; (*MUS*) movement; (*TENNIS, Briefmarken etc*) set; (*Kaffee*) grounds *pl*; (*COMM*) rate; (*Sprung*) jump; ~**teil** *m* part of a sentence; ~**zeichen** *nt* punctuation mark.

Sau [zau] *f* -, **Säue** sow; (*umg*) dirty pig.

sauber ['zaubər] *a* clean; (*ironisch*) fine; ~**halten** *vt unreg* keep clean; S~**keit** *f* cleanness; (*einer Person*) cleanliness.

säuberlich ['zɔybərlɪç] *ad* neatly.

saubermachen *vti* clean.

säubern *vt* clean; (*POL etc*) purge.

Säuberung *f* cleaning; purge.

Sauce ['zo:sə] *f* -, -n sauce, gravy.

sauer ['zauər] *a* sour; (*CHEM*) acid; (*umg*) cross; **Saurer Regen** acid rain.

Sauerei [zauə'rai] *f* (*umg*) rotten state of affairs, scandal; (*Schmutz etc*) mess; (*Unanständigkeit*) obscenity.

Sauer- *zW*: ~**milch** *f* sour milk; ~**stoff** *m* oxygen; ~**teig** *m* leaven.

saufen ['zaufən] *vti unreg* (*umg*) drink, booze.

Säufer ['zɔyfər] *m* -s, - (*umg*) boozer.

saugen ['zaugən] *vti unreg* suck.

Sauger [zaugər] *m* -s, - dummy, comforter (*US*); (*auf Flasche*) teat; (*Staub~*) vacuum cleaner, hoover ®.

Säug- ['zɔyg] *zW*: **Säugetier** *nt* mammal; ~**ling** *m* infant, baby.

Säule ['zɔylə] *f* -, -n column, pillar.

Saum [zaum] *m* -(e)s, **Säume** hem; (*Naht*) seam.

säumen ['zɔymən] *vt* hem; seam // *vi* delay, hesitate.

Sauna ['zauna] *f* -, -s sauna.

Säure ['zɔyrə] *f* -, -n acid; (*Geschmack*) sourness, acidity.

sausen ['zauzən] *vi* blow; (*umg*: *eilen*) rush; (*Ohren*) buzz; **etw** ~ **lassen** (*umg*) not bother with sth.

Saustall ['zauʃtal] *m* (*umg*) pigsty.

Saxophon [zakso'fo:n] *nt* -s, -e saxophone.

SB *abk von* **Selbstbedienung**.

S-Bahn *abk* (= *Schnellbahn*) high speed railway; (= *Stadtbahn*) suburban railway.

schaben ['ʃa:bən] *vt* scrape.

schäbig ['ʃe:bɪç] *a* shabby.

Schablone [ʃa'blo:nə] *f* -, -n stencil; (*Muster*) pattern; (*fig*) convention.

Schach [ʃax] *nt* -s, -e chess; (*Stellung*) check; ~**brett** *nt* chessboard; ~**figur** *f* chessman; **'s~'matt** *a* checkmate; ~**spiel** *nt* game of chess.

Schacht [ʃaxt] *m* -(e)s, ̈e shaft; **Schachtel** *f* -, -n box; (*pej*: *Frau*) bag, cow.

schade ['ʃa:də] *a* a pity *od* shame; **sich** (*dat*) **zu** ~ **sein für etw** consider oneself too good for sth // *interj*: (*wie*) ~! (what a) pity *od* shame.

Schädel ['ʃe:dəl] *m* -s, - skull; ~**bruch** *m* fractured skull.

Schaden ['ʃa:dən] *m* -s, ̈ damage; (*Verletzung*) injury; (*Nachteil*) disadvantage; s~ *vi* (+*dat*) hurt; **einer Sache** s~ damage sth; ~**ersatz** *m* compensation, damages *pl*; ~**freude** *f* malicious glee.

schadhaft ['ʃa:thaft] *a* faulty, damaged.

schäd- [ˈʃɛːt] zW: **~igen** [ˈʃɛdɪgən] vt damage; (Person) do harm to, harm; **~lich** a harmful (für to); **S~lichkeit** f harmfulness; **S~ling** m pest.

Schadstoff [ˈʃaːtʃtɔf] m harmful substance.

Schaf [ʃaːf] nt -(e)s, -e sheep; **~bock** m ram.

Schäfer [ˈʃɛːfər] m -s, -e shepherd; **~hund** m Alsatian.

schaffen [ˈʃafən] vt unreg create; (Platz) make; **sich** (dat) etw ~ get o.s. sth // vt (erreichen) manage, do; (erledigen) finish; (Prüfung) pass; (transportieren) take // vi (umg: arbeiten) work; **sich an etw** (dat) **zu ~ machen** busy oneself with sth; **S~** nt -s (creative) activity.

Schaffner(in f) [ˈʃafnər(ɪn)] m -s, - (Bus~) conductor/conductress; (EISENB) guard.

Schaft [ʃaft] m -(e)s, ̈e shaft; (von Gewehr) stock; (von Stiefel) leg; (BOT) stalk; tree trunk; **~stiefel** m high boot.

Schakal [ʃaˈkaːl] m -s, -e jackal.

schal [ʃaːl] a flat; (fig) insipid; **S~** m -s, -e od -s scarf.

Schälchen [ˈʃɛːlçən] nt cup, bowl.

Schale [ˈʃaːlə] f -, -n skin; (abgeschält) peel; (Nuß~, Muschel~, Ei~) shell; (Geschirr) dish, bowl.

schälen [ˈʃɛːlən] vt peel; shell // vr peel.

Schall [ʃal] m -(e)s, -e sound; **~dämpfer** m -s, - (AUT) silencer; **s~dicht** a soundproof; **s~en** vi (re)sound; **s~end** a resounding, loud; **~mauer** f sound barrier; **~platte** f (gramophone) record.

Schalt- [ˈʃalt] zW: **~bild** nt circuit diagram; **~brett** nt switchboard; **s~en** vt switch, turn // vi (AUT) change (gear); (umg: begreifen) catch on; **~er** m -s, - counter; (an Gerät) switch; **~erbeamte(r)** m counter clerk; **~hebel** m switch; (AUT) gear-lever; **~jahr** nt leap year; **~ung** f switching; (ELEK) circuit; (AUT) gear change.

Scham [ʃaːm] f - shame; (~gefühl) modesty; (Organe) private parts pl.

schämen [ˈʃɛːmən] vr be ashamed.

schamlos a shameless.

Schande [ˈʃandə] f - disgrace.

schändlich [ˈʃɛntlɪç] a disgraceful, shameful.

Schändung [ˈʃɛndʊŋ] f violation, defilement.

Schank- [ˈʃaŋk] zW: **~erlaubnis** f (publican's) licence; **~tisch** m bar.

Schanze [ˈʃantsə] f -, -n (Sprung~) skijump.

Schar [ʃaːr] f -, -en band, company; (Vögel) flock; (Menge) crowd; **in**

~en in droves; **s~en** vr assemble, rally.

scharf [ʃarf] a sharp; (Essen) hot; (Munition) live; ~ **nachdenken** think hard; **auf etw** (acc) ~ **sein** (umg) be keen on sth.

Schärf- [ˈʃɛrf] zW: **~e** f -, -n sharpness; (Strenge) rigour; **s~en** vt sharpen.

Scharf- zW: **s~machen** vt (umg) stir up; **~richter** m executioner; **~schütze** m marksman, sharpshooter; **~sinn** m penetration, astuteness; **s~sinnig** a astute, shrewd.

Scharnier [ʃarˈniːr] nt -s, -e hinge.

Schärpe [ˈʃɛrpə] f -, -n sash.

scharren [ˈʃarən] vti scrape, scratch.

Schaschlik [ˈʃaʃlɪk] m od nt -s, -s (shish) kebab.

Schatten [ˈʃatən] m -s, - shadow; **~bild** nt, **~riß** m silhouette; **~seite** f shady side, dark side; **~wirtschaft** f black economy.

schattieren [ʃaˈtiːrən] vti shade.

schattig [ˈʃatɪç] a shady.

Schatulle [ʃaˈtʊlə] f -, -n casket; (Geld~) coffer.

Schatz [ʃats] m -es, ̈e treasure; (Person) darling.

schätz- [ˈʃɛts] zW: **~bar** a assessable; **S~chen** nt darling, love; **~en** vt (abschätzen) estimate; (Gegenstand) value; (würdigen) value, esteem; (vermuten) reckon; **S~ung** f estimate; estimation; valuation; **nach meiner S~ung...** I reckon that...; **~ungsweise** ad approximately; it is thought.

Schau [ʃau] f - show; (Ausstellung) display, exhibition; **etw zur ~ stellen** make a show of sth, show sth off; **~bild** nt diagram.

Schauder [ˈʃaudər] m -s, -s shudder; (wegen Kälte) shiver; **s~haft** a horrible; **s~n** vi shudder; shiver.

schauen [ˈʃauən] vi look.

Schauer [ˈʃauər] m -s, - (Regen~) shower; (Schreck) shudder; **~geschichte** f horror story; **s~lich** a horrific, spine-chilling.

Schaufel [ˈʃaufəl] f -, -n shovel; (NAUT) paddle; (TECH) scoop; **s~n** vt shovel, scoop.

Schau- zW: **~fenster** nt shop window; **~fensterbummel** m window shopping (expedition); **~kasten** m showcase.

Schaukel [ˈʃaukəl] f -, -n swing; **s~n** vi swing, rock; **~pferd** nt rocking horse; **~stuhl** m rocking chair.

Schaum [ʃaum] m -(e)s, **Schäume** foam; (Seifen~) lather.

schäumen [ˈʃɔʏmən] vi foam.

Schaum- zW: **~gummi** m foam (rubber); **s~ig** a frothy, foamy; **~wein** m sparkling wine.

Schau- *zW:* **~platz** *m* scene; **s~rig** *a* horrific, dreadful; **~spiel** *nt* spectacle; *(THEAT)* play; **~spieler** *m* actor; **~spielerin** *f* actress; **s~spielern** *vi insep* act; **~spielhaus** *nt* theatre.

Scheck [ʃɛk] *m* **-s, -s** cheque; **~heft** *m* cheque book; **~karte** *f* cheque card.

scheffeln ['ʃɛfəln] *vt* amass.

Scheibe ['ʃaɪbə] *f* **-, -n** disc; *(Brot etc)* slice; *(Glas~)* pane; *(MIL)* target.

Scheiben- *zW:* **~bremse** *f* *(AUT)* disc brake; **~waschanlage** *f* *(AUT)* windscreen washers *pl;* **~wischer** *m* *(AUT)* windscreen wiper.

Scheich [ʃaɪç] *m* **-s, -e** *od* **-s** sheik(h).

Scheide ['ʃaɪdə] *f* **-, -n** sheath; *(Grenze)* boundary; *(ANAT)* vagina; **s~n** *unreg vt* separate; *(Ehe)* dissolve; **sich s~n lassen** get a divorce // *vi* (de)part.

Scheidung *f* *(Ehe~)* divorce.

Schein [ʃaɪn] *m* **-(e)s, -e** light; *(An~)* appearance; *(Geld)* (bank)note; *(Bescheinigung)* certificate; **zum ~** in pretence; **s~bar** *a* apparent; **s~en** *vi unreg* shine; *(Anschein haben)* seem; **s~heilig** *a* hypocritical; **~werfer** *m* **-s, -** floodlight; spotlight; *(Such~)* searchlight; *(AUT)* headlamp.

Scheiß- ['ʃaɪs] *in zW (umg)* bloody; **~e** *f* - *(umg)* shit.

Scheit [ʃaɪt] *nt* **-(e)s, -e** *od* **-er** log, billet.

Scheitel ['ʃaɪtəl] *m* **-s, -** top; *(Haar)* parting; **s~n** *vt* part.

scheitern ['ʃaɪtərn] *vi* fail.

Schelle ['ʃɛlə] *f* **-, -n** small bell; **s~n** *vi* ring.

Schellfisch ['ʃɛlfɪʃ] *m* haddock.

Schelm [ʃɛlm] *m* **-(e)s, -e** rogue; **s~isch** *a* mischievous, roguish.

Schelte ['ʃɛltə] *f* **-, -n** scolding; **s~n** *vt unreg* scold.

Schema ['ʃeːma] *nt* **-s, -s** *od* **-ta** scheme, plan; *(Darstellung)* schema; **nach ~** quite mechanically; **s~tisch** [ʃeˈmaːtɪʃ] *a* schematic; *(pej)* mechanical.

Schemel ['ʃeːməl] *m* **-s, -** (foot)stool.

Schenkel ['ʃɛŋkəl] *m* **-s, -** thigh.

schenken ['ʃɛŋkən] *vt* (lit, fig) give; *(Getränk)* pour; **sich** *(dat)* **etw ~** *(umg)* skip sth; **das ist geschenkt!** *(billig)* that's a giveaway!; *(nichts wert)* that's worthless!

Scherbe ['ʃɛrbə] *f* **-, -n** broken piece, fragment; *(archäologisch)* potsherd.

Schere ['ʃeːrə] *f* **-, -n** scissors *pl;* *(groß)* shears *pl;* **s~n** *vt unreg* cut; *(Schaf)* shear; *(kümmern)* bother // *vr* care; **scher dich zum Teufel!** get lost!; **~'rei** *f (umg)* bother, trouble.

Scherz [ʃɛrts] *m* **-es, -e** joke; fun;

~frage *f* conundrum; **s~haft** *a* joking, jocular.

scheu [ʃɔy] *a* shy; **S~** *f* - shyness; *(Angst)* fear *(vor +dat* of); *(Ehrfurcht)* awe; **~en** *vr:* **sich ~en vor** *(+dat)* be afraid of, shrink from // *vt* shun // *vi (Pferd)* shy.

scheuern ['ʃɔyərn] *vt* scour, scrub.

Scheuklappe *f* blinker.

Scheune ['ʃɔynə] *f* **-, -n** barn.

Scheusal ['ʃɔyzaːl] *nt* **-s, -e** monster.

scheußlich ['ʃɔyslɪç] *a* dreadful, frightful; **S~keit** *f* dreadfulness.

Schi [ʃiː] *m siehe* **Ski**.

Schicht [ʃɪçt] *f* **-, -en** layer; *(Klasse)* class, level; *(in Fabrik etc)* shift; **~arbeit** *f* shift work; **s~en** *vt* layer, stack.

schick [ʃɪk] *a* stylish, chic; **~en** *vt* send // *vr* resign oneself *(in +akk* to) // *v unpers (anständig sein)* be fitting; **~lich** *a* proper, fitting; **S~sal** *nt* **-s, -e** fate; **S~salsschlag** *m* great misfortune, blow.

Schieb- ['ʃiːb] *zW:* **Schiebedach** *nt* *(AUT)* sun roof; **s~en** *vti unreg* *(auch Drogen)* push; *(Schuld)* put *(auf jdn on* sb); **Schiebetür** *f* sliding door; **~ung** *f* fiddle.

Schieds- ['ʃiːts] *zW:* **~gericht** *nt* court of arbitration; **~richter** *m* referee, umpire; *(Schlichter)* arbitrator; **~verfahren** *nt* arbitration.

schief [ʃiːf] *a* crooked; *(Ebene)* sloping; *(Turm)* leaning; *(Winkel)* oblique; *(Blick)* funny; *(Vergleich)* distorted // *ad* crooked(ly); *(ansehen)* askance; **etw ~ stellen** slope sth.

Schiefer ['ʃiːfər] *m* **-s, -** slate; **~dach** *nt* slate roof; **~tafel** *f* (child's) slate.

schiefgehen *vi unreg (umg)* go wrong.

schielen ['ʃiːlən] *vi* squint; **nach etw ~** *(fig)* eye sth.

schien *etc v siehe* **scheinen**.

Schienbein *nt* shinbone.

Schiene ['ʃiːnə] *f* **-, -n** rail; *(MED)* splint; **s~n** *vt* put in splints.

schier [ʃiːr] *a (fig)* sheer // *ad* nearly, almost.

Schieß- ['ʃiːs] *zW:* **~bude** *f* shooting gallery; **s~en** *vti unreg* shoot *(auf +akk* at); *(Salat etc)* run to seed; *(Ball)* kick; *(Geschoß)* fire; **~e'rei** *f* shooting incident, shoot-up; **~pulver** *nt* gunpowder; **~scharte** *f* embrasure.

Schiff [ʃɪf] *nt* **-(e)s, -e** ship, vessel; *(Kirchen~)* nave; **~bau** *m* shipbuilding; **~bruch** *m* shipwreck; **s~brüchig** *a* shipwrecked; **~chen** *nt* small boat; *(Weben)* shuttle; *(Mütze)* forage cap; **~er** *m* **-s, -** bargeman, boatman; **~(f)ahrt** *f* shipping;

(*Reise*) voyage; ~**(f)ahrtslinie** *f* shipping route.

Schikane [ʃiˈkaːnə] *f* -, -**n** harassment; dirty trick; **mit allen** ~**n** with all the trimmings.

schikanieren [ʃikaˈniːrən] *vt* harass, torment.

Schild [ʃɪlt] *m* -(e)s, -e shield; **etw im** ~**e führen** be up to sth // *nt* -(e)s, -er sign; nameplate; (*Etikett*) label; ~**drüse** *f* thyroid gland; **s~ern** [ˈʃɪldərn] *vt* depict, portray; ~**erung** *f* description, portrayal; ~**kröte** *f* tortoise; (*Wasser~*) turtle.

Schilf [ʃɪlf] *nt* -(e)s, -e, ~**rohr** *nt* (*Pflanze*) reed; (*Material*) reeds *pl*, rushes *pl*.

schillern [ˈʃɪlərn] *vi* shimmer; ~**d** *a* iridescent.

Schilling [ˈʃɪlɪŋ] *m* schilling.

Schimmel [ˈʃɪməl] *m* -s, - mould; (*Pferd*) white horse; **s~ig** *a* mouldy; **s~n** *vi* get mouldy.

schimmern [ˈʃɪmərn] *vi* glimmer, shimmer.

Schimpanse [ʃɪmˈpanzə] *m* -n, -n chimpanzee.

Schimpf- [ʃɪmpf] *zW*: **s~en** *vti* scold // *vi* curse, complain; ~**wort** *nt* term of abuse.

Schind- [ˈʃɪnd] *zW*: **s~en** *unreg vt* maltreat, drive too hard; **Eindruck s~en** (*umg*) create an impression // *vr* sweat and strain, toil away (*mit at*); ~**e'rei** *f* grind, drudgery.

Schinken [ˈʃɪŋkən] *m* -s, - ham.

Schippe [ˈʃɪpə] *f* -, -**n** shovel; **s~n** *vt* shovel.

Schirm [ʃɪrm] *m* -(e)s, -e (*Regen~*) umbrella; (*Sonnen~*) parasol, sunshade; (*Wand~*, *Bild~*) screen; (*Lampen~*) (lamp)shade; (*Mützen~*) peak; (*Pilz~*) cap; ~**mütze** *f* peaked cap; ~**ständer** *m* umbrella stand.

schizophren [ʃitsoˈfreːn] *a* schizophrenic.

Schlacht [ʃlaxt] *f* -, -**en** battle; **s~en** *vt* slaughter, kill; ~**enbummler** *m* football supporter; ~**er** *m* -s, - butcher; ~**feld** *nt* battlefield; ~**haus** *nt*, ~**hof** *m* slaughterhouse, abattoir; ~**schiff** *nt* battleship; ~**vieh** *nt* animals kept for meat; beef cattle.

Schlacke [ˈʃlakə] *f* -, -**n** slag.

Schlaf [ʃlaːf] *m* -(e)s sleep; ~**anzug** *m* pyjamas *pl*.

Schläfe [ˈʃlɛːfə] *f* -, -**n** temple.

schlafen [ˈʃlaːfən] *vi unreg* sleep; ~ **gehen** go to bed; **S~gehen** *nt* -s going to bed; **Schlafenszeit** *f* bedtime.

schlaff [ʃlaf] *a* slack; (*energielos*) limp; (*erschöpft*) exhausted.

Schlaf- *zW*: ~**gelegenheit** *f* sleeping accommodation; ~**lied** *nt* lullaby;

s~los *a* sleepless; ~**losigkeit** *f* sleeplessness, insomnia; ~**mittel** *nt* sleeping pill.

schläfrig [ˈʃlɛːfrɪç] *a* sleepy.

Schlaf- *zW*: ~**saal** *m* dormitory; ~**sack** *m* sleeping bag; ~**tablette** *f* sleeping pill; ~**wagen** *m* sleeping car, sleeper; **s~wandeln** *vi insep* sleepwalk; ~**zimmer** *nt* bedroom.

Schlag [ʃlaːk] *m* -(e)s, ⸚e (*lit, fig*) blow; stroke (*auch MED*); (*Puls~*, *Herz~*) beat; (*pl*: *Tracht Prügel*) beating; (*ELEK*) shock; (*Blitz~*) bolt, stroke; (*Autotür*) car door; (*umg*: *Portion*) helping; (*Art*) kind, type; **mit einem** ~ all at once; ~ **auf** ~ in rapid succession; ~**ader** *f* artery; ~**anfall** *m* stroke; **s~artig** *a* sudden, without warning; ~**baum** *m* barrier; **s~en** [ˈʃlaːgən] *unreg vti* strike, hit; (*wiederholt s~en, besiegen*) beat; (*Glocke*) ring; (*Stunde*) strike; (*Sahne*) whip; (*Schlacht*) fight; **nach jdm s~en** (*fig*) take after sb // *vr* fight; **sich gut s~en** (*fig*) do well; ~**er** [ˈʃlaːgər] *m* -s, - (*lit, fig*) hit; ~**ersänger(in** *f*) *m* pop singer.

Schläg- [ˈʃlɛːg] *zW*: ~**er** *m* -s, - brawler; (*SPORT*) bat; (*TENNIS etc*) racket; (*Golf*) club; hockey stick; (*Waffe*) rapier; ~**e'rei** *f* fight, punch-up.

Schlag- *zW*: **s~fertig** *a* quick-witted; ~**fertigkeit** *f* ready wit, quickness of repartee; ~**loch** *nt* pothole; ~**sahne** *f* (whipped) cream; ~**seite** *f* (*NAUT*) list; ~**wort** *nt* slogan, catch phrase; ~**zeile** *f* headline; ~**zeug** *nt* percussion; drums *pl*; ~**zeuger** *m* -s, - drummer.

Schlamassel [ʃlaˈmasəl] *m* -s, - (*umg*) mess.

Schlamm [ʃlam] *m* -(e)s, -e mud; **s~ig** *a* muddy.

Schlamp- [ˈʃlamp] *zW*: ~**e** *f* -, -**n** (*umg*) slut; **s~en** *vi* (*umg*) be sloppy; ~**e'rei** *f* (*umg*) disorder, untidiness; sloppy work.

Schlange [ˈʃlaŋə] *f* -, -**n** snake; (*Menschen~*) queue (*Brit*), line-up (*US*); ~ **stehen** (form a) queue, line up.

Schlangen- *zW*: ~**biß** *m* snake bite; ~**gift** *nt* snake venom; ~**linie** *f* wavy line.

schlank [ʃlaŋk] *a* slim, slender; **S~heit** *f* slimness, slenderness; **S~heitskur** *f* diet.

schlapp [ʃlap] *a* limp; (*locker*) slack; **S~e** *f* -, -**n** (*umg*) setback.

Schlaraffenland [ʃlaˈrafənlant] *nt* land of milk and honey.

schlau [ʃlau] *a* crafty, cunning.

Schlauch [ʃlaux] *m* -(e)s, **Schläuche** hose; (*in Reifen*) inner tube; (*umg*:

Anstrengung) grind; **~boot** nt rubber dinghy; **s~en** vt (*umg*) tell on, exhaust; **s~los** a (*Reifen*) tubeless.

Schlau- zW: **~heit** f, **Schläue** ['flɔyə] f - cunning; **~kopf** m clever dick.

schlecht [flɛçt] a bad; es geht ihr ~ she's in a bad way; ~ gelaunt in a bad mood; **~ und recht** after a fashion; jdm ist ~ sb feels sick od bad; **~gehen** vi unpers unreg: jdm geht es ~ sb is in a bad way; **S~igkeit** f badness; bad deed; **~machen** vt run down; etw ~ machen do sth badly.

schlecken ['flɛkən] vti lick.

Schlegel ['fle:gəl] m **-s,** - (drum)stick; (*Hammer*) mallet, hammer; (*KOCH*) leg.

schleichen ['flaɪçən] vi unreg creep, crawl; **~d** a gradual; creeping.

Schleier ['flaɪər] m **-s,** - veil; **s~haft** a (*umg*): jdm s~haft sein be a mystery to sb.

Schleif- ['flaɪf] zW: **~e** f -, **-n** loop; (*Band*) bow; **s~en** vti drag // vt unreg grind; (*Edelstein*) cut; (*MIL: Soldaten*) drill; **~stein** m grindstone.

Schleim [flaɪm] m **-(e)s, -e** slime; (*MED*) mucus; (*KOCH*) gruel; **s~ig** a slimy.

Schlemm- [flɛm] zW: **s~en** vi feast; **~er** m **-s,** - gourmet; **~e'rei** f gluttony, feasting.

schlendern ['flɛndərn] vi stroll.

schlenkern ['flɛŋkərn] vti swing, dangle.

Schlepp- [flɛp] zW: **~e** f -, **-n** train; **s~en** vt drag; (*Auto, Schiff*) tow; (*tragen*) lug; **s~end** a dragging, slow; **~er** m **-s,** - tractor; (*Schiff*) tug.

Schleuder ['flɔydər] f -, **-n** catapult; (*Wäsche~*) spin-drier; (*Butter~ etc*) centrifuge; **s~n** vt hurl; (*Wäsche*) spin-dry // vi (*AUT*) skid; **~preis** m give-away price; **~sitz** m (*AVIAT*) ejector seat; (*fig*) hot seat; **~ware** f cheap od cut-price goods pl.

schleunigst ['flɔynɪçst] ad straight away.

Schleuse ['flɔyzə] f -, **-n** lock; (*Schleusentor*) sluice.

schlicht [flɪçt] a simple, plain; **~en** vt smooth; dress; (*Streit*) settle; **S~er** m **-s,** - mediator, arbitrator; **S~ung** f settlement; arbitration.

Schlick [flɪk] m **-(e)s, -e** mud; (*Öl~*) slick.

schlief etc v siehe **schlafen**.

Schließ- ['fli:s] zW: **~e** f -, **-n** fastener; **s~en** vtir unreg close, shut; (*beenden*) close; (*Freundschaft, Bündnis, Ehe*) enter into; (*folgern*) infer (*aus +dat* from); etw in sich s~en include sth; **~fach** nt locker; **s~lich** ad finally; (*s~lich doch*) after all.

Schliff [flɪf] m **-(e)s, -e** cut(ting); (*fig*) polish.

schlimm [flɪm] a bad; **~er** a worse; **~ste(r, s)** a worst; **~stenfalls** ad at (the) worst.

Schling- ['flɪŋ] zW: **~e** f -, **-n** loop; (*des Henkers*) noose; (*Falle*) snare; (*MED*) sling; **~el** m **-s,** - rascal; **s~en** unreg vt wind; vti (*essen*) bolt (one's food), gobble; **s~ern** vi roll.

Schlips [flɪps] m **-es, -e** tie.

Schlitten ['flɪtən] m **-s,** - sledge, sleigh; **~bahn** f toboggan run; **~fahren** nt -s tobogganing.

schlittern ['flɪtərn] vi slide.

Schlittschuh ['flɪt-fu:] m skate; ~ **laufen** skate; **~bahn** f skating rink; **~läufer(in** f) m skater.

Schlitz [flɪts] m **-es, -e** slit; (*für Münze*) slot; (*Hosen~*) flies pl; **s~äugig** a slant-eyed; **s~en** vt slit.

schloß etc v siehe **schließen**.

Schloß [flɔs] nt **-sses, -sser** lock; (*an Schmuck etc*) clasp; (*Bau*) castle; château.

Schlosser ['flɔsər] m **-s,** - (*Auto~*) fitter; (*für Schlüssel etc*) locksmith; **~ei** [-'raɪ] f metal (working) shop.

Schlot [flo:t] m **-(e)s, -e** chimney; (*NAUT*) funnel.

schlottern ['flɔtərn] vi shake, tremble; (*Kleidung*) be baggy.

Schlucht [fluxt] f -, **-en** gorge, ravine.

schluchzen ['fluxtsən] vi sob.

Schluck [fluk] m **-(e)s, -e** swallow; (*Menge*) drop; **~auf** m **-s, -s** hiccups pl; **s~en** vti swallow.

schludern ['flu:dərn] vi skimp, do sloppy work.

schlug etc v siehe **schlagen**.

Schlummer ['flumər] m **-s** slumber; **s~n** vi slumber.

Schlund [flunt] m **-(e)s, -̈e** gullet; (*fig*) jaw.

schlüpfen ['flypfən] vi slip; (*Vogel etc*) hatch (out).

Schlüpfer ['flypfər] m **-s,** - panties pl, knickers pl.

schlüpfrig ['flypfrɪç] a slippery; (*fig*) lewd; **S~keit** f slipperiness; (*fig*) lewdness.

schlurfen ['flurfən] vi shuffle.

schlürfen ['flyrfən] vti slurp.

Schluß [flus] m **-sses, -̈sse** end; (*~folgerung*) conclusion; am ~ at the end; ~ machen mit finish with.

Schlüssel ['flysəl] m **-s,** - (lit, fig) key; (*Schraub~*) spanner, wrench; (*MUS*) clef; **~bein** nt collarbone; **~blume** f cowslip, primrose; **~bund** m bunch of keys; **~loch** nt keyhole; **~position** f key position; **~wort** nt keyword.

schlüssig ['ʃlʏsɪç] *a* conclusive.

Schluß- *zW:* **~licht** *nt* taillight; *(fig)* tailender; **~strich** *m* *(fig)* final stroke; **~verkauf** *m* clearance sale.

schmächtig ['ʃmɛçtɪç] *a* slight.

schmackhaft ['ʃmakhaft] *a* tasty.

schmal [ʃmaːl] *a* narrow; *(Person, Buch etc)* slender, slim; *(karg)* meagre.

schmälern ['ʃmɛːlərn] *vt* diminish; *(fig)* belittle.

Schmalfilm *m* cine film.

Schmalz [ʃmalts] *nt* -es, -e dripping, lard; *(fig)* sentiment, schmaltz; **s~ig** *a* *(fig)* schmaltzy.

schmarotzen [ʃma'rɔtsən] *vi* sponge; *(BOT)* be parasitic.

Schmarotzer *m* -s, - parasite; sponger.

Schmarren ['ʃmarən] *m* -s, - *(Aus)* small piece of pancake; *(fig)* rubbish, tripe.

schmatzen ['ʃmatsən] *vi* smack one's lips; eat noisily.

schmecken ['ʃmɛkən] *vti* taste; es schmeckt ihm he likes it.

Schmeichel- ['ʃmaɪçəl] *zW:* **~ei** [-'laɪ] *f* flattery; **s~haft** *a* flattering; **s~n** *vi* flatter.

schmeißen ['ʃmaɪsən] *vt unreg (umg)* throw, chuck.

Schmeißfliege *f* bluebottle.

Schmelz [ʃmɛlts] *m* -es, -e enamel; *(Glasur)* glaze; *(von Stimme)* melodiousness; **s~bar** *a* fusible; **s~en** *vti unreg* melt; *(Erz)* smelt; **~punkt** *m* melting point; **~wasser** *nt* melted snow.

Schmerz [ʃmɛrts] *m* -es, -en pain; *(Trauer)* grief; **s~empfindlich** *a* sensitive to pain; **s~en** *vti* hurt; **Schmerzensgeld** *nt* compensation; **s~haft**, **s~lich** *a* painful; **s~los** *a* painless; **s~stillend** *a* soothing; **~tablette** *f* painkiller.

Schmetterling ['ʃmɛtərlɪŋ] *m* butterfly.

Schmied [ʃmiːt] *m* -(e)s, -e blacksmith; **~e** ['ʃmiːdə] *f* -, -n smithy, forge; **Schmiedeeisen** *nt* wrought iron; **s~en** *vt* forge; *(Pläne)* devise, concoct.

schmiegen ['ʃmiːgən] *vt* press, nestle // *vr* cling, nestle (up) *(an +akk* to).

Schmier- ['ʃmiːr] *zW:* **~e** *f* -, -n grease; *(THEAT)* greasepaint, make-up; **s~en** *vt* smear; *(ölen)* lubricate, grease; *(bestechen)* bribe // *vti (schreiben)* scrawl; **~fett** *nt* grease; **~fink** *m* messy person; **~geld** *nt* bribe; **s~ig** *a* greasy; **~seife** *f* soft soap.

Schminke ['ʃmɪŋkə] *f* -, -n make-up; **s~n** *vtr* make up.

schmirgel- ['ʃmɪrgəl] *zW:* **~n** *vt* sand

(down); **S~papier** *nt* emery paper.

schmollen ['ʃmɔlən] *vi* sulk, pout.

Schmor- ['ʃmoːr] *zW:* **~braten** *m* stewed *od* braised meat; **s~en** *vt* stew, braise.

Schmuck [ʃmʊk] *m* -(e)s, -e jewellery; *(Verzierung)* decoration.

schmücken ['ʃmʏkən] *vt* decorate.

Schmuck- *zW:* **s~los** *a* unadorned, plain; **~losigkeit** *f* simplicity; **~sachen** *pl* jewels *pl*, jewellery.

Schmuggel ['ʃmʊgəl] *m* -s smuggling; **s~n** *vti* smuggle.

Schmuggler *m* -s, - smuggler.

schmunzeln ['ʃmʊntsəln] *vi* smile benignly.

Schmutz [ʃmʊts] *m* -es dirt, filth; **~fink** *m* filthy creature; **~fleck** *m* stain; **s~ig** *a* dirty.

Schnabel ['ʃnaːbəl] *m* -s, ⁻ beak, bill; *(Ausguß)* spout.

Schnake ['ʃnaːkə] *f* -, -n cranefly; *(Stechmücke)* gnat.

Schnalle ['ʃnalə] *f* -, -n buckle, clasp; **s~n** *vt* buckle.

Schnapp- ['ʃnap] *zW:* **s~en** *vt* grab, catch // *vi* snap; **~schloß** *nt* spring lock; **~schuß** *m* *(PHOT)* snapshot.

Schnaps [ʃnaps] *m* -es, ⁻e spirits *pl*; schnapps.

schnarchen ['ʃnarçən] *vi* snore.

schnauben ['ʃnaʊbən] *vi* snort // *vr* blow one's nose.

schnaufen ['ʃnaʊfən] *vi* puff, pant.

Schnauz- ['ʃnaʊts] *zW:* **~bart** *m* moustache; **~e** *f* -, -n snout, muzzle; *(Ausguß)* spout; *(umg)* gob.

Schnecke ['ʃnɛkə] *f* -, -n snail; **Schneckenhaus** *nt* snail's shell.

Schnee [ʃneː] *m* -s snow; *(Ei~)* beaten egg white; **~ball** *m* snowball; **~flocke** *f* snowflake; **~gestöber** *nt* snowstorm; **~glöckchen** *nt* snowdrop; **~kette** *f* *(AUT)* snow chain; **~pflug** *m* snowplough; **~schmelze** *f* -, -n thaw; **~wehe** *f* snowdrift.

schneien ['ʃnaɪən] *vi unpers* snow.

Schneise ['ʃnaɪzə] *f* -, -n clearing.

schnell [ʃnɛl] *a, ad* quick(ly), fast; **S~hefter** *m* -s, - loose-leaf binder; **S~igkeit** *f* speed; **S~imbiß** *m* *(Lokal)* snack bar; **S~kochtopf** *m* *(Dampfkochtopf)* pressure cooker; **S~reinigung** *f* dry cleaner's; **~stens** *ad* as quickly as possible; **S~straße** *f* expressway; **S~zug** *m* fast *od* express train.

schneuzen ['ʃnɔʏtsən] *vr* blow one's

nose.

schnippisch ['ʃnɪpɪʃ] *a* sharp-tongued.

schnitt *etc v siehe* schneiden.

Schnitt [ʃnɪt] *m* **-(e)s, -e** cut(ting); (~*punkt*) intersection; (*Quer*~) (cross) section; (*Durch*~) average; (~*muster*) pattern; (*an Buch*) edge; (*umg: Gewinn*) profit; ~**blumen** *pl* cut flowers *pl*; ~**e** *f* **-, -n** slice; (*belegt*) sandwich; ~**fläche** *f* section; ~**lauch** *m* chive; ~**muster** *nt* pattern; ~**punkt** *m* (point of) intersection; ~**stelle** *f* (*COMPUT*) interface; ~**wunde** *f* cut.

Schnitz- ['ʃnɪts] *zW:* ~**arbeit** *f* wood carving; ~**el** *nt* **-s, -** chip; (*KOCH*) escalope; **s~en** *vt* carve; ~**er** *m* **-s, -** carver; (*umg*) blunder; ~**e'rei** *f* carving; carved woodwork.

schnodderig ['ʃnɔdərɪç] *a* (*umg*) snotty.

Schnorchel ['ʃnɔrçəl] *m* **-s, -** snorkel.

Schnörkel ['ʃnœrkəl] *m* **-s, -** flourish; (*ARCHIT*) scroll.

schnorren ['ʃnɔrən] *vti* cadge.

schnüffeln ['ʃnʏfəln] *vi* sniff; **S~** *nt* (*umg: von Klebstoff etc*) glue-sniffing.

Schnüffler *m* **-s, -** snooper.

Schnuller ['ʃnʊlər] *m* **-s, -** dummy, comforter (*US*).

Schnupfen ['ʃnʊpfən] *m* **-s, -** cold.

schnuppern ['ʃnʊpərn] *vi* sniff.

Schnur [ʃnuːr] *f* **-, -e** string, cord; (*ELEK*) flex; **s~gerade** *a* straight (as a die).

schnüren ['ʃnyːrən] *vt* tie.

Schnurr- ['ʃnʊr] *zW:* ~**bart** *m* moustache; **s~en** *vi* purr; (*Kreisel*) hum.

Schnür- ['ʃnyːr] *zW:* ~**schuh** *m* lace-up (shoe); ~**senkel** *m* shoelace.

schnurstracks *ad* straight (away).

Schock [ʃɔk] *m* **-(e)s, -e** shock; **s~ieren** [ʃɔ'kiːrən] *vt* shock, outrage.

Schöffe ['ʃœfə] *m* **-n, -n** lay magistrate.

Schokolade [ʃoko'laːdə] *f* **-, -n** chocolate.

Scholle ['ʃɔlə] *f* **-, -n** clod; (*Eis*~) ice floe; (*Fisch*) plaice.

schon [ʃoːn] *ad* **1** (*bereits*) already; **er ist ~ da** he's there already, he's already there; **ist er ~ da?** is he there yet?; **warst du ~ einmal da?** have you ever been there?; **ich war ~ einmal da** I've been there before; **das war ~ immer so** that has always been the case; **~ oft** often; **hast du ~ gehört?** have you heard?

2 (*bestimmt*) all right; **du wirst ~ sehen** you'll see (all right); **das wird ~ noch gut** that'll be OK

3 (*bloß*) just; **allein ~ das Gefühl ...** just the very feeling ...; **~ der Gedanke** the very thought; **wenn ich**

das **~ höre** I only have to hear that

4 (*einschränkend*): **ja ~, aber ...** yes (well), but ...

5: **~ möglich** possible; **~ gut!** OK!; **du weißt ~** you know; **komm ~!** come on!

schön [ʃøːn] *a* beautiful; (*nett*) nice; ~**e Grüße** best wishes; ~**e Ferien** have a nice holiday; ~**en Dank** (many) thanks.

schonen ['ʃoːnən] *vt* look after // *vr* take it easy; ~**d** *a* careful, gentle.

Schön- *zW:* ~**heit** *f* beauty; ~**heitsfehler** *m* blemish, flaw; ~**heitsoperation** *f* cosmetic plastic surgery; **s~machen** *vr* make oneself look nice.

Schon- *zW:* ~**ung** *f* good care; (*Nachsicht*) consideration; (*Forst*) plantation of young trees; **s~ungslos** *a* unsparing, harsh; ~**zeit** *f* close season.

Schöpf- ['ʃœpf] *zW:* **s~en** *vt* scoop, ladle; (*Mut*) summon up; (*Luft*) breathe in; ~**er** *m* **-s, -** creator; **s~erisch** *a* creative; ~**kelle** *f* ladle; ~**löffel** *m* skimmer; scoop; ~**ung** *f* creation.

Schorf [ʃɔrf] *m* **-(e)s, -e** scab.

Schornstein ['ʃɔrnʃtaɪn] *m* chimney; (*NAUT*) funnel; ~**feger** *m* **-s, -** chimney sweep.

schoß *etc v siehe* schießen.

Schoß [ʃoːs] *m* **-es, -e** lap; (*Rock*~) coat tail; ~**hund** *m* pet dog, lapdog.

Schote ['ʃoːtə] *f* **-, -n** pod.

Schotte ['ʃɔtə] *m* Scot, Scotsman.

Schotter ['ʃɔtər] *m* **-s, -** broken stone, road metal; (*EISENB*) ballast.

Schott- ['ʃɔt] *zW:* ~**in** *f* Scotswoman; **s~isch** *a* Scottish, Scots; ~**land** *nt* Scotland.

schraffieren [ʃra'fiːrən] *vt* hatch.

schräg [ʃrɛːk] *a* slanting, not straight; **etw ~ stellen** put sth at an angle; ~ **gegenüber** diagonally opposite; **S~e** *f* **-, -n** slant; **S~strich** *m* oblique stroke.

Schramme ['ʃramə] *f* **-, -n** scratch; **s~n** *vt* scratch.

Schrank [ʃraŋk] *m* **-(e)s, -e** cupboard; (*Kleider*~) wardrobe; ~**e** *f* **-, -n** barrier; ~**enwärter** *m* (*EISENB*) level crossing attendant; ~**koffer** *m* trunk.

Schraube ['ʃraubə] *f* **-, -n** screw.

schrauben *vt* screw; **S~schlüssel** *m* spanner; **S~zieher** *m* **-s, -** screwdriver.

Schraubstock ['ʃraubʃtɔk] *m* (*TECH*) vice.

Schreck [ʃrɛk] *m* **-(e)s, -e**, ~**en** *m* **-s, -** terror; fright; **s~en** *vt* frighten, scare; ~**gespenst** *nt* spectre, nightmare; **s~haft** *a* jumpy, easily frightened; **s~lich** *a* terrible, dreadful.

Schrei [ʃraɪ] m -(e)s, -e scream; (Ruf) shout.

Schreib- ['ʃraɪb] zW: **~block** m writing pad; **~dichte** f: einfache/ doppelte **~dichte** (Diskette) single/ double density; **s~en** vti unreg write; (buchstabieren) spell; **~en** nt -s, - letter, communication; **s~faul** a bad about writing letters; **~fehler** m spelling mistake; **~maschine** f typewriter; **~papier** nt notepaper; **~tisch** m desk; **~ung** f spelling; **~waren** pl stationery; **~warenhandlung** f stationer's; **~weise** f spelling; way of writing; **~zentrale** f typing pool; **~zeug** nt writing materials pl.

schreien ['ʃraɪən] vti unreg scream; (rufen) shout; **~d** a (fig) glaring; (Farbe) loud.

Schreiner ['ʃraɪnər] m -s, - joiner; (Zimmermann) carpenter; (Möbel~) cabinetmaker; **~ei** [-'raɪ] f joiner's workshop.

schreiten ['ʃraɪtən] vi unreg stride.

schrieb etc v siehe **schreiben**.

Schrift [ʃrɪft] f -, -en writing; handwriting; (~art) script; (Gedrucktes) pamphlet, work; **~deutsch** nt written German; **~führer** m secretary; **s~lich** a written // ad in writing; **~setzer** m compositor; **~sprache** f written language; **~steller(in** f) m -s, - writer; **~stück** nt document.

schrill [ʃrɪl] a shrill.

Schritt [ʃrɪt] m -(e)s, -e step; (Gangart) walk; (Tempo) pace; (von Hose) crutch; **~ fahren** drive at walking pace; **~macher** m -s, - pacemaker; **~(t)empo** nt: im **~(t)empo** at a walking pace.

schroff [ʃrɔf] a steep; (zackig) jagged; (fig) brusque; (ungeduldig) abrupt.

schröpfen ['ʃrœpfən] vt (fig) fleece.

Schrot [ʃroːt] m od nt -(e)s, -e (Blei) (small) shot; (Getreide) coarsely ground grain, groats pl; **~flinte** f shotgun.

Schrott [ʃrɔt] m -(e)s, -e scrap metal; **~haufen** m scrap heap; **s~reif** a ready for the scrap heap.

schrubben ['ʃrʊbən] vt scrub.

Schrubber m -s, - scrubbing brush.

schrumpfen ['ʃrʊmpfən] vi shrink; (Apfel) shrivel.

Schub- ['ʃuːb] zW: **~fach** nt drawer; **~karren** m wheelbarrow; **~lade** f drawer.

schüchtern ['ʃʏçtərn] a shy; **S~heit** f shyness.

Schuft [ʃʊft] m -(e)s, -e scoundrel; **s~en** vi (umg) graft, slave away.

Schuh [ʃuː] m -(e)s, -e shoe; **~band** nt shoelace; **~creme** f shoe polish; **~löffel** m shoehorn; **~macher** m -s, -

shoemaker.

Schul- ['ʃuːl] zW: **~aufgaben** pl homework; **~besuch** m school attendance; **~buch** nt school book.

Schuld [ʃʊlt] f -, -en guilt; (FIN) debt; (Verschulden) fault; **s~** a: **s~ sein** od haben be to blame (an +dat for); er ist od hat **s~** it's his fault; jdm **s~** geben blame sb; **s~en** ['ʃʊldən] vt owe; **s~enfrei** a free from debt; **~gefühl** nt feeling of guilt; **s~ig** a guilty (an +dat of); (gebührend) due; jdm etw **s~ig sein** owe sb sth; jdm etw **s~ig bleiben** not provide sb with sth; **s~los** a innocent, without guilt; **~ner** m -s, - debtor; **~schein** m promissory note, IOU; **~spruch** m verdict of guilty.

Schule ['ʃuːlə] f -, -n school; **s~n** vt train, school.

Schüler(in f) ['ʃyːlər(ɪn)] m -s, - pupil; **~lotse** m pupil acting as road crossing warden.

Schul- ['ʃuːl] zW: **~ferien** pl school holidays pl; **s~frei** a: **s~freier Tag** holiday; **s~frei sein** be a holiday; **~hof** m playground; **~jahr** nt school year; **~junge** m schoolboy; **~mädchen** nt schoolgirl; **s~pflichtig** a of school age; **~schiff** nt (NAUT) training ship; **~stunde** f period, lesson; **~tasche** f school bag.

Schulter ['ʃʊltər] f -, -n shoulder; **~blatt** nt shoulder blade; **s~n** vt shoulder.

Schul- zW: **~ung** f education, schooling; **~zeugnis** nt school report.

Schund [ʃʊnt] m -(e)s trash, garbage; **~roman** m trashy novel.

Schuppe ['ʃʊpə] f -, -n scale; **~n** pl (Haar~) dandruff; **s~n** vt scale // vr peel; **~n** m -s, - shed.

schuppig ['ʃʊpɪç] a scaly.

Schur [ʃuːr] f -, -en shearing.

Schür- ['ʃyːr] zW: **s~en** vt rake; (fig) stir up; **schürfen** ['ʃʏrfən] vti scrape, scratch; (MIN) prospect, dig.

Schurke ['ʃʊrkə] m -n, -n rogue.

Schürze ['ʃʏrtsə] f -, -n apron.

Schuß [ʃʊs] m -sses, -sse shot; (WEBEN) woof; **~bereich** m effective range.

Schüssel ['ʃʏsəl] f -, -n bowl.

Schuß- zW: **~linie** f line of fire; **~verletzung** f bullet wound; **~waffe** f firearm; **~weite** f range (of fire).

Schuster ['ʃuːstər] m -s, - cobbler, shoemaker.

Schutt [ʃʊt] m -(e)s rubbish; (Bau~) rubble; **~abladeplatz** m refuse dump.

Schütt- ['ʃʏt] zW: **Schüttelfrost** m shivering; **s~eln** vtr shake; **s~en** vt pour; (Zucker, Kies etc) tip; (ver~en) spill // vi unpers pour (down).

Schutthalde f dump.

Schutthaufen m heap of rubble.

Schutz [ʃʊts] m -es protection; (*Unterschlupf*) shelter; jdn in ~ nehmen stand up for sb; ~**anzug** m overalls pl; ~**blech** nt mudguard; ~**brille** f goggles pl.

Schütze [ˈʃʏtsə] m -n, -n gunman; (*Gewehr*~) rifleman; (*Scharf-, Sport*~) marksman; (ASTROL) Sagittarius; s~n vt protect (vor +dat, gegen from); **Schützenfest** nt fair featuring shooting matches.

Schutz- zW: ~**engel** m guardian angel; ~**gebiet** nt protectorate; (*Natur*~) reserve; ~**impfung** f immunisation; s~**los** a defenceless; ~**mann** m, pl -**leute** od -**männer** policeman; ~**patron** m patron saint.

Schwaben [ˈʃvaːbən] nt Swabia.

schwäbisch [ˈʃvɛːbɪʃ] a Swabian.

schwach [ʃvax] a weak, feeble.

Schwäche [ˈʃvɛçə] f -, -n weakness; s~n vt weaken.

Schwachheit f weakness.

schwächlich a weakly, delicate.

Schwächling m weakling.

Schwach- zW: ~**sinn** m imbecility; s~**sinnig** a mentally deficient; (*Idee*) idiotic; ~**strom** m weak current.

Schwächung [ˈʃvɛçʊŋ] f weakening.

schwafeln [ˈʃvaːfəln] vti drivel.

Schwager [ˈʃvaːgər] m -s, ⁼ brother-in-law.

Schwägerin [ˈʃvɛːgərɪn] f sister-in-law.

Schwalbe [ˈʃvalbə] f -, -n swallow.

Schwall [ʃval] m -(e)s, -e surge; (*Worte*) flood, torrent.

schwamm etc v siehe **schwimmen**.

Schwamm [ʃvam] m -(e)s, -e sponge; (*Pilz*) fungus; s~**ig** a spongy; (*Gesicht*) puffy.

Schwan [ʃvaːn] m -(e)s, ⁼e swan; s~**en** vi unpers: jdm schwant etw sb has a foreboding of sth.

schwanger [ˈʃvaŋər] a pregnant.

schwängern [ˈʃvɛŋərn] vt make pregnant.

Schwangerschaft f pregnancy.

Schwank [ʃvaŋk] m -(e)s, ⁼e funny story; s~**en** vi sway; (*taumeln*) stagger, reel; (*Preise, Zahlen*) fluctuate; (*zögern*) hesitate, vacillate; ~**ung** f fluctuation.

Schwanz [ʃvants] m -es, ⁼e tail.

schwänzen [ˈʃvɛntsən] (umg) vt skip, cut // vi play truant.

Schwarm [ʃvarm] m -(e)s, ⁼e swarm; (umg) heart-throb, idol.

schwärm- [ˈʃvɛrm] zW: ~**en** vi swarm; ~**en für** be mad od wild about; S~**erei** f [-ɔˈraɪ] f enthusiasm; ~**erisch** a impassioned, effusive.

Schwarte [ˈʃvartə] f -, -n hard skin; (*Speck*~) rind.

schwarz [ʃvarts] a black; ~**es Brett** notice board; ins S~**e treffen** (lit, fig) hit the bull's eye; in den ~**en Zahlen** in the black; S~**arbeit** f illicit work, moonlighting; S~**brot** nt black bread.

Schwärze [ˈʃvɛrtsə] f -, -n blackness; (*Farbe*) blacking; (*Drucker*~) printer's ink; s~n vt blacken.

Schwarz- zW: s~**fahren** vi unreg travel without paying; drive without a licence; ~**handel** m black-market (trade); s~**hören** vi listen to the radio without a licence; ~**markt** m black market; s~**sehen** vi unreg (umg) see the gloomy side of things; (*TV*) watch TV without a licence; ~**seher** m pessimist; (*TV*) viewer without a licence; ~**wald** m Black Forest; s~**weiß** a black and white.

schwatzen [ˈʃvatsən], **schwätzen** [ˈʃvɛtsən] vi chatter.

Schwätzer [ˈʃvɛtsər] m -s, - gasbag; ~**in** f chatterbox, gossip.

schwatzhaft a talkative, gossipy.

Schwebe [ˈʃveːbə] f: in der ~ (fig) in abeyance; ~**bahn** f overhead railway; ~**balken** m (SPORT) beam; s~n vi drift, float; (hoch) soar.

Schwed- [ˈʃveːd] zW: ~**e** m Swede; ~**en** nt Sweden; ~**in** f Swede; s~**isch** a Swedish.

Schwefel [ˈʃveːfəl] m -s sulphur; s~**ig** a sulphurous; ~**säure** f sulphuric acid.

Schweig- [ˈʃvaɪg] zW: **Schweigegeld** nt hush money; s~**en** vi unreg be silent; stop talking; ~**en** nt -s silence; s~**sam** [ˈʃvaɪkzaːm] a silent, taciturn; ~**samkeit** f taciturnity, quietness.

Schwein [ʃvaɪn] nt -(e)s, -e pig; (umg) (good) luck.

Schweine- zW: ~**fleisch** nt pork; ~**rei** f mess; (*Gemeinheit*) dirty trick; ~**stall** m pigsty.

schweinisch a filthy.

Schweinsleder nt pigskin.

Schweiß [ʃvaɪs] m -es sweat, perspiration; s~**en** vti weld; ~**er** m -s, - welder; ~**füße** pl sweaty feet pl; ~**naht** f weld.

Schweiz [ʃvaɪts] f Switzerland; ~**er(in** f) m Swiss; s~**erisch** a Swiss.

schwelgen [ˈʃvɛlgən] vi indulge.

Schwelle [ˈʃvɛlə] f -, -n threshold (auch fig); doorstep; (EISENB) sleeper; s~n vi unreg swell.

Schwellung f swelling.

Schwenk- [ˈʃvɛŋk] zW: s~**bar** a swivel-mounted; s~**en** vt swing; (*Fahne*) wave; (abspülen) rinse // vi turn, swivel; (MIL) wheel; ~**ung** f turn; wheel.

schwer [ʃveːr] *a* heavy; *(schwierig)* difficult, hard; *(schlimm)* serious, bad // *ad (sehr)* very (much) // *(verletzt etc)* seriously, badly; **S~arbeiter** *m* manual worker, labourer; **S~e** *f* -, **-n** weight, heaviness; *(PHYS)* gravity; **schwerlos** *a* weightless; *(Kammer)* zero-G; **~erziehbar** *a* difficult (to bring up); **~fallen** *vi unreg:* jdm ~fallen be difficult for sb; **~fällig** *a* ponderous; **S~gewicht** *nt* heavyweight; *(fig)* emphasis; **~hörig** *a* hard of hearing; **S~industrie** *f* heavy industry; **S~kraft** *f* gravity; **S~kranke(r)** *mf* person who is seriously ill; **~lich** *ad* hardly; **~machen** *vt:* jdm/sich etw ~machen make sth difficult for sb/o.s.; **~mütig** *a* melancholy; **~nehmen** *vt unreg* take to heart; **S~punkt** *m* centre of gravity; *(fig)* emphasis, crucial point.

Schwert [ʃveːrt] *nt* **-(e)s, -er** sword; **~lilie** *f* iris.

schwer- *zW:* **~tun** *vi unreg:* sich *(dat od akk)* ~tun have difficulties; **S~verbrecher(in** *f)* *m* criminal, serious offender; **~verdaulich** *a* indigestible, heavy; **~verletzt** *a* badly injured; **~wiegend** *a* weighty, important.

Schwester [ʃvɛstər] *f* -, **-n** sister; *(MED)* nurse; **s~lich** *a* sisterly.

Schwieger- [ʃviːgər] *zW:* **~eltern** *pl* parents-in-law *pl;* **~mutter** *f* mother-in-law; **~sohn** *m* son-in-law; **~tochter** *f* daughter-in-law; **~vater** *m* father-in-law.

Schwiele [ʃviːlə] *f* -, **-n** callus.

schwierig [ʃviːrɪç] *a* difficult, hard; **S~keit** *f* difficulty.

Schwimm- [ʃvɪm] *zW:* **~bad** *nt* swimming baths *pl;* **~becken** *nt* swimming pool; **s~en** *vi unreg* swim; *(treiben, nicht sinken)* float; *(fig: unsicher sein)* be all at sea; **~er** *m* **-s, -** swimmer; *(Angeln)* float; **~lehrer** *m* swimming instructor; **~weste** *f* life jacket.

Schwindel [ʃvɪndəl] *m* **-s** giddiness; dizzy spell; *(Betrug)* swindle, fraud; *(Zeug)* stuff; **s~frei** *a;* s~frei sein have a good head for heights; **s~n** *vi* *(umg: lügen)* fib; jdm schwindelt es sb feels dizzy.

schwinden [ʃvɪndən] *vi unreg* disappear; *(sich verringern)* decrease; *(Kräfte)* decline.

Schwind- [ʃvɪnd] *zW:* **~ler** *m* **-s, -** swindler; *(Lügner)* liar; **s~lig** *a* dizzy; mir ist s~lig I feel dizzy.

Schwung [ʃvʊŋ] *zW:* **s~en** *vti unreg* swing; *(Waffe etc)* brandish; *(vibrieren)* vibrate; *(klingen)* sound; **~tür** *f* swing door(s); **~ung** *f* vibra-

tion; *(PHYS)* oscillation.

Schwips [ʃvɪps] *m* **-es, -e:** einen ~ haben be tipsy.

schwirren [ʃvɪrən] *vi* buzz.

schwitzen [ʃvɪtsən] *vi* sweat, perspire.

schwören [ʃvøːrən] *vti unreg* swear.

schwul [ʃvuːl] *a (umg)* gay, queer.

schwül [ʃvyːl] *a* sultry, close; **S~e** *f* - sultriness, closeness.

schwülstig [ʃvʏlstɪç] *a* pompous.

Schwung [ʃvʊŋ] *m* **-(e)s, ²e** swing; *(Triebkraft)* momentum; *(fig: Energie)* verve, energy; *(umg: Menge)* batch; **s~haft** *a* brisk, lively; **s~voll** *a* vigorous.

Schwur [ʃvuːr] *m* **-(e)s, ²e** oath; **~gericht** *nt* court with a jury.

sechs [zɛks] *num* six; **~hundert** *num* six hundred; **~te(r, s)** *a* sixth; **S~tel** *nt* **-s -** sixth.

sechzehn [ʃzɛçtseːn] *num* sixteen.

sechzig [ʃzɛçtsɪç] *num* sixty.

See [zeː] *f* -, **-n** sea // *m* **-s, -n** lake; **~bad** *nt* seaside resort; **~fahrt** *f* seafaring; *(Reise)* voyage; **~gang** *m* (motion of the sea); **~hund** *m* seal; **~igel** [zeːˈʔiːgəl] *m* sea urchin; **s~krank** *a* seasick; **~krankheit** *f* seasickness; **~lachs** *m* rock salmon.

Seele [zeːlə] *f* -, **-n** soul; **seelenruhig** *ad* calmly.

Seeleute [zeːlɔʏtə] *pl* seamen *pl.*

Seel- *zW:* **s~isch** *a* mental; **~sorge** *f* pastoral duties *pl;* **~sorger** *m* **-s, -** clergyman.

See- *zW:* **~macht** *f* naval power; **~mann** *m, pl* **-leute** seaman, sailor; **~meile** *f* nautical mile; **~not** *f* distress; **~pferd(chen)** *nt* sea horse; **~räuber** *m* pirate; **~rose** *f* water lily; **~stern** *m* starfish; **s~tüchtig** *a* seaworthy; **~weg** *m* sea route; auf dem ~weg by sea; **~zunge** *f* sole.

Segel [zeːgəl] *nt* **-s, -** sail; **~boot** *nt* yacht; **~fliegen** *nt* **-s** gliding; **~flieger** *m* glider pilot; **~flugzeug** *nt* glider; **s~n** *vti* sail; **~schiff** *nt* sailing vessel; **~sport** *m* sailing; **~tuch** *nt* canvas.

Segen [zeːgən] *m* **-s, -** blessing; **segensreich** *a* beneficial.

Segler [zeːglər] *m* **-s, -** sailor, yachtsman.

segnen [zeːgnən] *vt* bless.

Seh- [zeː] *zW:* **s~en** *vti unreg* see; mal s~en(, ob ...) let's see (if ...); *(in bestimmte Richtung)* look; **s~enswert** *a* worth seeing; **~enswürdigkeiten** *pl* sights *pl* (of a town); **~er** *m* **-s, -** seer; **~fehler** *m* sight defect.

Sehn- [zeːn] *zW:* **~e** *f* -, **-n** sinew; *(an Bogen)* string; **s~en** *vr* long, yearn *(nach* for); **s~ig** *a* sinewy;

s~lich *a* ardent; ~sucht *f* longing; s~süchtig *a* longing.

sehr [ze:r] *ad* very; (*mit Verben*) a lot, (very) much; zu ~ too much; ~ geehrte(r) ... dear ....

seicht [zaɪçt] *a* (*lit, fig*) shallow.

Seide ['zaɪdə] *f* -, -n silk; s~n *a* silk; Seidenpapier *nt* tissue paper.

seidig ['zaɪdɪç] *a* silky.

Seife ['zaɪfə] *f* -, -n soap.

Seifen- *zW*: ~lauge *f* soapsuds *pl*; ~schale *f* soap dish; ~schaum *m* lather.

seihen ['zaɪən] *vt* strain, filter.

Seil [zaɪl] *nt* -(e)s, -e rope; cable; ~bahn *f* cable railway; ~hüpfen *nt* -s, ~springen *nt* -s skipping; ~tänzer(in *f*) *m* tightrope walker.

sein [zaɪn] *vi pt* war, *ptp* gewesen **1** be; ich bin I am; du bist you are; er/sie/es ist he/she/it is; wir sind/ihr seid/sie sind we/you/they are; wir waren we were; wir sind gewesen we have been
2: seien Sie nicht böse don't be angry; sei so gut und ... be so kind as to ...; das wäre gut that would *od* that'd be a good thing; wenn ich Sie wäre if I were *od* was you; das wär's that's all, that's it; morgen bin ich in Rom tomorrow I'll *od* I will *od* I shall be in Rome; waren Sie mal in Rom? have you ever been to Rome?
3: wie ist das zu verstehen? how is that to be understood?; er ist nicht zu ersetzen he cannot be replaced; mit ihr ist nicht zu reden you can't talk to her
4: mir ist kalt I'm cold; was ist? what's the matter?, what is it?; ist was? is something the matter?; es sei denn, daß ... unless ...; wie dem auch sei be that as it may; wie wäre es mit ...? how *od* what about ...?; laß das ~! stop that!

sein [zaɪn] *pron* his; its; ~e(r, s) his; its; ~er *pron gen von* er of him; ~erseits *ad* for his part; ~erzeit *ad* in those days, formerly; ~esgleichen *pron* people like him; ~etwegen, ~etwillen *ad* (*für ihn*) for his sake; (*wegen ihm*) on his account; (*von ihm aus*) as far as he is concerned; ~ige *pron*: der/die/das ~ige his.

Seismograph [zaɪsmo'graːf] *m* -en, -en seismograph.

seit [zaɪt] *präp, kj* since; er ist ~ einer Woche hier he has been here for a week; ~ langem for a long time; ~dem [zaɪt'de:m] *ad, kj* since.

Seite ['zaɪtə] *f* -, -n side; (*Buch~*) page; (*MIL*) flank.

Seiten- *zW*: ~ansicht *f* side view; ~hieb *m* (*fig*) passing shot, dig; seitens *präp* (+*gen*) on the part of;

~schiff *nt* aisle; ~sprung *m* extra-marital escapade; ~stechen *nt* (a) stitch; ~straße *f* side road.

seit- *zW*: ~her [zaɪt'he:r] *ad, kj* since (then); ~lich *a* on one *od* the side; side; ~wärts *ad* sideways.

Sekretär [zekre'tɛ:r] *m* secretary; (*Möbel*) bureau; ~in *f* secretary.

Sekretariat [zekretari'a:t] *nt* -(e)s, -e secretary's office, secretariat.

Sekt [zɛkt] *m* -(e)s, -e champagne.

Sekte ['zɛktə] *f* -, -n sect.

Sekunde [ze'kʊndə] *f* -, -n second.

selber ['zɛlbər] = selbst.

selbst [zɛlpst] ◆*pron* **1**: ich/er/wir ~ I myself/he himself/we ourselves; sie ist die Tugend ~ she's virtue itself; er braut sein Bier ~ he brews his own beer; wie geht's? — gut, und ~? how are things? — fine, and yourself? **2** (*ohne Hilfe*) alone, on my/his/one's *etc* own; von ~ by itself; er kam von ~ he came of his own accord
◆*ad* even; ~ wenn even if; ~ Gott even God (himself).

Selbst [zɛlpst] *nt* - self; ~achtung *f* self-respect; selbständig ['zɛlpʃtɛndɪç] *a* independent; Selbständigkeit *f* independence; ~auslöser *m* (*PHOT*) delayed-action shutter release; ~bedienung *f* self-service; ~befriedigung *f* masturbation; ~beherrschung *f* self-control; s~bewußt *a* (self-)confident; ~bewußtsein *nt* self-confidence; ~erhaltung *f* self-preservation; ~erkenntnis *f* self-knowledge; s~gefällig *a* smug, self-satisfied; s~gemacht *a* home-made; ~gespräch *nt* conversation with oneself; ~kostenpreis *m* cost price; s~los *a* unselfish, selfless; ~mord *m* suicide; ~mörder(in *f*) *m* suicide; s~mörderisch *a* suicidal; s~sicher *a* self-assured; s~tätig *a* automatic; s~verständlich *a* obvious // *ad* naturally; ich halte das für s~verständlich I take that for granted; ~vertrauen *nt* self-confidence; ~verwaltung *f* autonomy, self-government.

selig ['ze:lɪç] *a* happy, blissful; (*REL*) blessed; (*tot*) late; S~keit *f* bliss.

Sellerie ['zɛləri:] *m* -s, (-s) *od f* -, - celery.

selten ['zɛltən] *a* rare // *ad* seldom, rarely; S~heit *f* rarity.

Selterswasser ['zɛltərsvasər] *nt* soda water.

seltsam ['zɛltza:m] *a* strange, curious; ~erweise *ad* curiously, strangely; S~keit *f* strangeness.

Semester [ze'mɛstər] *nt* -s, - semester.

Semi- [zemi] *in zW* semi-; ~kolon [-'ko:lɔn] *nt* -s, -s semicolon; ~nar

[-'naːr] *nt* -s, -e seminary; (*Kurs*) seminar; (*UNIV: Ort*) department building.

Semmel ['zɛməl] *f* -, -n roll.

sen. *abk* (= *senior*) sen.

Senat [ze'naːt] *m* -(e)s, -e senate, council.

Sende- ['zɛndə] *zW:* **~bereich** *m* transmission range; **~folge** *f* (*Serie*) series; **s~n** *vt unreg* send // *vti* (*RAD, TV*) transmit, broadcast; **~r** *m* -s, - station; (*Anlage*) transmitter; **~reihe** *f* series (of broadcasts).

Sendung ['zɛnduŋ] *f* consignment; (*Aufgabe*) mission; (*RAD, TV*) transmission; (*Programm*) programme.

Senf [zɛnf] *m* -(e)s, -e mustard.

Senk- ['zɛŋk] *zW:* **~blei** *n* plumb; **~e** *f* -, -n depression; **s~en** *vt* lower // *vr* sink, drop gradually; **s~recht** *a* vertical, perpendicular; **~rechte** *f* -n, -n perpendicular; **~rechtstarter** *m* (*AVIAT*) vertical take-off plane; (*fig*) high-flyer.

Sensation [zɛnzatsi'oːn] *f* sensation; **s~ell** [-'nɛl] *a* sensational.

Sense ['zɛnzə] *f* -, -n scythe.

sensibel [zɛn'ziːbəl] *a* sensitive.

sentimental [zɛntimɛn'taːl] *a* sentimental; **S~i'tät** *f* sentimentality.

separat [zepa'raːt] *a* separate.

September [zɛp'tɛmbər] *m* -(s), - September.

Serie ['zeːriə] *f* series; **serienweise** *ad* in series.

seriös [zeri'øːs] *a* serious, bona fide.

Serum ['zeːrʊm] *nt* -s, Seren serum.

Service [zɛr'viːs] *nt* -(s), - set, service // ['zœrvɪs] *m* -s, - service.

servieren [zɛr'viːrən] *vti* serve.

Serviette [zɛrvi'ɛtə] *f* napkin, serviette.

Sessel ['zɛsəl] *m* -s, - armchair; **~lift** *m* chairlift.

seßhaft ['zɛshaft] *a* settled; (*ansässig*) resident.

setzen ['zɛtsən] *vt* put, set; (*Baum etc*) plant; (*Segel, TYP*) set // *vr* settle; (*Person*) sit down // *vi* (*springen*) leap; (*wetten*) bet.

Setz- [zɛts] *zW:* **~er** *m* -s, - (*TYP*) compositor; **~e'rei** *f* caseroom; **~ling** *m* young plant.

Seuche ['zɔyçə] *f* -, -n epidemic; **Seuchengebiet** *nt* infected area.

seufzen ['zɔyftsən] *vti* sigh.

Seufzer ['zɔyftsər] *m* -s, - sigh.

Sex [zɛks] *m* -(es) sex; **~ualität** [-uali'tɛt] *f* sex, sexuality; **s~uell** [-u'ɛl] *a* sexual.

sezieren [ze'tsiːrən] *vt* dissect.

Shampoo ['ʃampuː] *nt* shampoo.

Sibirien [zi'biːriən] *nt* Siberia.

sibirisch [zi'biːrɪʃ] *a* Siberian.

sich [zɪç] *pron* (*mit Infinitiv*) **1** (*akk*):

er/sie/es ... ~ he/she/it ... himself/herself/itself; sie (*pl*)/man ... ~ they/one ... themselves/oneself; Sie ... ~ you ... yourself/(*pl*) yourselves; ~ wiederholen repeat oneself/itself

2 (*dat*): er/sie/es ... ~ he/she/it ... to himself/herself/itself; sie (*pl*)/man ... ~ they/one ... to themselves/oneself; Sie ... ~ you ... to yourself/(*pl*) yourselves; sie hat ~ einen Pullover gekauft she bought herself a jumper; ~ die Haare waschen wash one's hair

3 (*mit Präposition*): haben Sie Ihren Ausweis bei ~? do you have your pass on you?; er hat nichts bei ~ he's got nothing on him; sie bleiben gern unter ~ they keep themselves to themselves

4 (*einander*) each other, one another; sie bekämpfen ~ they fight each other *od* one another

5: dieses Auto fährt ~ gut this car drives well; hier sitzt es ~ gut it's good to sit here.

Sichel ['zɪçəl] *f* -, -n sickle; (*Mond~*) crescent.

sicher ['zɪçər] *a* safe (*vor* +*dat* from); (*gewiß*) certain (+*gen* of); (*zuverlässig*) secure, reliable; (*selbst~*) confident; ich bin nicht ~ I'm not sure *od* certain; ~ nicht surely not; aber ~! of course; **~gehen** *vi unreg* make sure.

Sicherheit ['zɪçərhaɪt] *f* safety; security (*auch FIN*); (*Gewißheit*) certainty; (*Selbst~*) confidence.

Sicherheits- *zW:* **~abstand** *m* safe distance; **~glas** *nt* safety glass; **~gurt** *m* safety belt; **s~halber** *ad* for safety; to be on the safe side; **~nadel** *f* safety pin; **~vorkehrung** *f* safety precaution.

sicher- *zW:* **~lich** *ad* certainly, surely; **~n** *vt* secure; (*schützen*) protect; (*Waffe*) put the safety catch on; jdm/sich etw **~n** secure sth for sb/for o.s.; **~stellen** *vt* impound; (*COMPUT*) save; **S~ung** *f* (*Sichern*) securing; (*Vorrichtung*) safety device; (*an Waffen*) safety catch; (*ELEK*) fuse; **S~ungskopie** *f* back-up copy.

Sicht [zɪçt] *f* - sight; (*Aus~*) view; auf *od* nach ~ (*FIN*) at sight; auf lange ~ on a long-term basis; **s~bar** *a* visible; **s~en** *vt* sight; (*auswählen*) sort out; **s~lich** *a* evident, obvious; **~verhältnisse** *pl* visibility; **~vermerk** *m* visa.

sickern ['zɪkərn] *vi* trickle, seep.

Sie [ziː] *pron sing, pl, nom, akk* you.

sie [ziː] *pron sing nom* she // *akk* her // *pl nom* they // *akk* them.

Sieb [ziːp] *nt* -(e)s, -e sieve; (*KOCH*) strainer; **s~en** ['ziːbən] *vt* sift; (*Flüssigkeit*) strain.

sieben ['ziːbən] *num* seven; **~hundert** *num* seven hundred; **S~sachen** *pl* belongings *pl*.

siebte(r, s) ['ziːptə(r,s)] *a* seventh; **Siebtel** *nt* -s, - seventh.

siebzehn ['ziːptseːn] *num* seventeen.

siebzig ['ziːptsɪç] *num* seventy.

sied- [ziːd] *zW:* **~en** *vti* boil, simmer; **Siedepunkt** *m* boiling point; **S~lung** *f* settlement; (*Häuser~lung*) housing estate.

Sieg [ziːk] *m* -(e)s, -e victory.

Siegel ['ziːɡəl] *nt* -s, - seal; **~lack** *m* sealing wax; **~ring** *m* signet ring.

Sieg- *zW:* **S~en** *vi* be victorious; (*SPORT*) win; **~er** *m* -s, - victor; (*SPORT etc*) winner; **siegessicher** *a* sure of victory; **s~reich** *a* victorious.

siehe [ziːə] (*Imperativ*) see.

siehst *etc v siehe* **sehen**.

siezen ['ziːtsən] *vt* address as 'Sie'.

Signal [zɪ'ɡnaːl] *nt* -s, -e signal.

Silbe ['zɪlbə] *f* -, -n syllable.

Silber ['zɪlbər] *nt* -s silver; **s~n** *a* silver; **~papier** *nt* silver paper.

Silhouette [zilu'ɛtə] *f* silhouette.

Silo ['ziːlo] *nt od m* -s, -s silo.

Silvester(abend) *m* [zɪl'vɛstər(aːbənt)] *nt* -s, - New Year's Eve, Hogmanay (*Scot*).

simpel ['zɪmpəl] *a* simple.

Sims [zɪms] *nt od m* -es, -e (*Kamin~*) mantelpiece; (*Fenster~*) (window)-sill.

simulieren [zimu'liːrən] *vti* simulate; (*vortäuschen*) feign.

simultan [zimul'taːn] *a* simultaneous.

Sinfonie [zɪnfo'niː] *f* symphony.

singen ['zɪŋən] *vti unreg* sing.

Singular ['zɪŋgulaːr] *m* singular.

Singvogel ['zɪŋfoːɡəl] *m* songbird.

sinken ['zɪŋkən] *vi unreg* sink; (*Preise etc*) fall, go down.

Sinn [zɪn] *m* -(e)s, -e mind; (*Wahrnehmungs~*) sense; (*Bedeutung*) sense, meaning; **~ für etw** sense of sth; **von ~en** sein be out of one's mind; **es hat keinen ~** there's no point; **~bild** *nt* symbol; **s~en** *vi unreg* ponder; **auf etw** (*akk*) **s~en** contemplate sth; **Sinnestäuschung** *f* illusion; **s~gemäß** *a* faithful; (*Wiedergabe*) in one's own words; **s~ig** *a* clever; **s~lich** *a* sensual, sensuous; (*Wahrnehmung*) sensory; **~lichkeit** *f* sensuality; **s~los** *a* senseless; meaningless; **~losigkeit** *f* senselessness; meaninglessness; **s~voll** *a* meaningful; (*vernünftig*) sensible.

Sintflut ['zɪntfluːt] *f* Flood.

Siphon [zi'fõː] *m* -s, -s siphon.

Sippe ['zɪpə] *f* -, -n clan, kin.

Sippschaft ['zɪpʃaft] *f* (*pej*) relations *pl*, tribe; (*Bande*) gang.

Sirene [zi'reːnə] *f* -, -n siren.

Sirup ['ziːrʊp] *m* -s, -e syrup.

Sitt- [zɪt] *zW:* **~e** *f* -, -n custom // *pl* morals *pl*; **Sittenpolizei** *f* vice squad; **s~lich** *a* moral; **~lichkeit** *f* morality; **~lichkeitsverbrechen** *nt* sex offence; **s~sam** *a* modest, demure.

Situation [zituatsi'oːn] *f* situation.

Sitz [zɪts] *m* -es, -e seat; der Anzug hat einen guten ~ the suit is a good fit; **s~en** *vi unreg* sit; (*Bemerkung, Schlag*) strike home, tell; (*Gelerntes*) have sunk in; **s~en bleiben** remain seated; **s~enbleiben** *vi unreg* (*SCH*) have to repeat a year; **auf etw** (*dat*) **s~enbleiben** be lumbered with sth; **s~end** *a* (*Tätigkeit*) sedentary; **s~enlassen** *vt unreg* (*SCH*) make (sb) repeat a year; (*Mädchen*) jilt; (*Wartenden*) stand up; **etw auf sich** (*dat*) **s~enlassen** take sth lying down; **~gelegenheit** *f* place to sit down; **~platz** *m* seat; **~streik** *m* sit-down strike; **~ung** *f* meeting.

Sizilien [zi'tsiːliən] *nt* Sicily.

Skala ['skaːla] *f* -, **Skalen** scale.

Skalpell [skal'pɛl] *nt* -s, -e scalpel.

Skandal [skan'daːl] *m* -s, -e scandal; **s~ös** [skanda'løːs] *a* scandalous.

Skandinav- [skandi'naːv] *zW:* **~ien** [-iən] *nt* Scandinavia; **~ier(in** *f*) *m* Scandinavian; **s~isch** *a* Scandinavian.

Skelett [ske'lɛt] *nt* -(e)s, -e skeleton.

Skepsis ['skɛpsɪs] *f* - scepticism.

skeptisch ['skɛptɪʃ] *a* sceptical.

Ski, Schi [ʃiː] *m* -s, -er ski; **~ laufen** *od* **fahren** ski; **~fahrer** *m*, **~läufer** *m* skier; **~lehrer** *m* ski instructor; **~lift** *m* ski-lift; **~springen** *nt* ski-jumping; **~stock** *m* ski-pole.

Skizze ['skɪtsə] *f* -, -n sketch.

skizzieren [skɪ'tsiːrən] *vti* sketch.

Sklave ['sklaːvə] *m* -n, -n, **Sklavin** *f* slave; **~'rei** *f* slavery.

Skonto ['skɔnto] *m od nt* -s, -s discount.

Skorpion [skɔrpi'oːn] *m* -s, -e scorpion; (*ASTROL*) Scorpio.

Skrupel ['skruːpəl] *m* -s, - scruple; **s~los** *a* unscrupulous.

Slalom ['slaːlɔm] *m* -s, -s slalom.

Smaragd [sma'rakt] *m* -(e)s, -e emerald.

Smoking ['smoːkɪŋ] *m* -s, -s dinner jacket.

s.o. *abk = siehe oben.*

so [zoː] ◆ *ad* 1 (*~sehr*) so; ~ **groß/schön** *etc* so big/nice *etc*; ~ **groß/schön wie ...** as big/nice as ...; das hat ihn ~ **geärgert, daß ...** that annoyed him so much that ...; ~ **einer wie ich** somebody like me; **na** ~ **was!** well, well!

2 (*auf diese Weise*) like this; **mach es nicht** ~ don't do it like that; ~

oder ~ in one way or the other; und ~ weiter and so on; ... oder ~ was ... or something like that; das ist gut ~ that's fine
3 (umg: umsonst): ich habe es ~ bekommen I got it for nothing
◆kj: ~ daß so that; ~ wie es jetzt ist as things are at the moment
◆interj: ~? really?; ~, das wär's so, that's it then.

sobald [zo'balt] kj as soon as.
Socke ['zɔkə] f -, -n sock.
Sockel ['zɔkəl] m -s, - pedestal, base.
Sodawasser ['zo:davasər] nt soda water.
Sodbrennen ['zo:tbrɛnən] nt -s, - heartburn.
soeben [zo'e:bən] ad just (now).
Sofa ['zo:fa] nt -s, -s sofa.
sofern [zo'fɛrn] kj if, provided (that).
sofort [zo'fɔrt] ad immediately, at once; ~ig a immediate.
Software ['sɔftwɛər] f software.
so- zW: ~**gar** [zo'ga:r] ad even; ~**genannt** ['zo:gənant] a so-called; ~**gleich** [zo'glaiç] ad straight away, at once.
Sohle ['zo:lə] f -, -n sole; (Tal~ etc) bottom; (MIN) level.
Sohn [zo:n] m -(e)s, ⁻e son.
solang(e) [zo'laŋ(ə)] kj as od so long as.
solch [zɔlç] pron such; ein ~e(r, s)... such a...
Sold [zɔlt] m -(e)s, -e pay; **Soldat** [zɔl'da:t] m -en, -en soldier.
Söldner ['zœldnər] m -s, - mercenary.
solid(e) [zo'li:d(ə)] a solid; (Leben, Person) respectable; ~**arisch** [zoli'da:rɪʃ] a in/with solidarity; sich ~**arisch erklären** declare one's solidarity.
Solist(in f) [zo'lɪst(ɪn)] m soloist.
Soll [zɔl] nt -(s), -(s) (FIN) debit (side); (Arbeitsmenge) quota, target.
sollen ['zɔlən] ◆ (als Hilfsverb) pt **sollte**, ptp **sollen 1** (Pflicht, Befehl) be supposed to; du hättest nicht gehen ~ you shouldn't have gone, you oughtn't to have gone; soll ich? shall I?; soll ich dir helfen? shall I help you?; sag ihm, er soll warten tell him he's to wait; was soll ich machen? what should I do?
2 (Vermutung): sie soll verheiratet sein she's said to be married; was soll das heißen? what's that supposed to mean?; man sollte glauben, daß ... you would think that ...; sollte das passieren, ... if that should happen ...
◆vti pt **sollte**, ptp **gesollt: was soll das?** what's all this?; das sollst du nicht you shouldn't do that; was soll's? what the hell!

Solo ['zo:lo] nt -s, -s od **Soli** solo.
somit [zo'mɪt] kj and so, therefore.
Sommer ['zɔmər] m -s, - summer; s~**lich** a summery; summer; ~**schlußverkauf** m summer sale; ~**sprossen** pl freckles pl.
Sonate [zo'na:tə] f -, -n sonata.
Sonde ['zɔndə] f -, -n probe.
Sonder- ['zɔndər] in zW special; ~**angebot** nt special offer; s~**bar** a strange, odd; ~**fahrt** f special trip; ~**fall** m special case; s~**gleichen** inv without parallel, unparalleled; s~**lich** a particular; (außergewöhnlich) remarkable; (eigenartig) peculiar; s~**n** kj but; nicht nur ..., s~**n** auch not only..., but also // vt separate; ~**preis** m special price; ~**zug** m special train.
Sonett [zo'nɛt] nt -(e)s, -e sonnet.
Sonnabend ['zɔn'a:bənt] m Saturday.
Sonne ['zɔnə] f -, -n sun; s~**n** vr sun oneself.
Sonnen- zW: ~**aufgang** m sunrise; s~**baden** vi sunbathe; ~**brand** m sunburn; ~**brille** f sunglasses pl; ~**creme** f suntan lotion; ~**energie** f solar energy; ~**finsternis** f solar eclipse; ~**schein** m sunshine; ~**schirm** m parasol, sunshade; ~**stich** m sunstroke; ~**uhr** f sundial; ~**untergang** m sunset; ~**wende** f solstice.
sonnig ['zɔnɪç] a sunny.
Sonntag ['zɔnta:k] m Sunday; s~s ad (on) Sundays.
sonst [zɔnst] ad otherwise (auch kj); (mit pron, in Fragen) else; (zu anderer Zeit) at other times, normally; ~ noch etwas? anything else?; ~ nichts nothing else; ~**ig** a other; ~**jemand** pron anybody (at all); ~**wo(hin)** ad somewhere else; ~**woher** ad from somewhere else.
sooft [zo'ɔft] kj whenever.
Sopran [zo'pra:n] m -s, -e soprano.
Sorge ['zɔrgə] f -, -n care, worry.
sorgen vi: für jdn ~ look after sb; für etw ~ take care of od see to sth // vr worry (um about); ~**frei** a carefree; **S~kind** nt problem child; ~**voll** a troubled, worried.
Sorgerecht nt custody (of a child).
Sorg- [zɔrk] zW: ~**falt** f - care(fulness); s~**fältig** a careful; s~**los** a careless; (ohne Sorgen) carefree; s~**sam** a careful.
Sorte ['zɔrtə] f -, -n sort; (Waren~) brand; ~**n** pl (FIN) foreign currency.
sortieren [zɔr'ti:rən] vt sort (out).
Sortiment [zɔrti'mɛnt] nt assortment.
sosehr [zo'ze:r] kj as much as.
Soße ['zo:sə] f -, -n sauce; (Braten~) gravy.
Souffleur [zu'flø:r] m, **Souffleuse**

[zu'flø:zə] f prompter.
soufflieren [zu'fli:rən] vti prompt.
souverän [zuvə're:n] a sovereign; (überlegen) superior.
so- zW: **~viel** [zo'fi:l] kj: ~viel ich weiß as far as I know // pron as much (wie as); rede nicht ~viel don't talk so much; **~weit** [zo'vait] kj as far as // a: ~weit sein be ready; ~weit wie od als möglich as far as possible; ich bin ~weit zufrieden by and large I'm quite satisfied; **~wenig** [zo've:nɪç] kj little as // pron as little (wie as); **~wie** [zo'vi:] kj (sobald) as soon as; (ebenso) as well as; **~wieso** [zovi'zo:] ad anyway.
Sowjet- [zɔ'vjet] zW: **s~isch** a Soviet; **~union** f Soviet Union.
sowohl [zo'vo:l] kj: ~ ... als od wie auch both ... and.
sozial [zotsi'a:l] a social; **S~abgaben** pl national insurance contributions pl; **S~demokrat** m social democrat; **~demokratisch** a social democratic; **~i'sieren** vt socialize; **~ismus** [-'lɪsmus] m socialism; **S~ist** [-'lɪst] m socialist; **~istisch** a socialist; **S~politik** f social welfare policy; **S~produkt** nt (gross/net) national product; **S~staat** m welfare state.
Sozio- [zotsio] zW: **~loge** [-'lo:gə] m -n, -n sociologist; **~logie** [-lo'gi:] f sociology; **s~logisch** [-'lo:gɪʃ] a sociological.
sozusagen [zotsu'za:gən] ad so to speak.
Spachtel ['ʃpaxtəl] m -s, - spatula.
spähen ['ʃpe:ən] vi peep, peek.
Spalier [ʃpa'li:r] nt -s, -e (Gerüst) trellis; (Leute) guard of honour.
Spalt [ʃpalt] m -(e)s, -e crack; (Tür~) chink; (fig: Kluft) split; **~e** f -, -n crack, fissure; (Gletscher~e) crevasse; (in Text) column; **s~en** vtr (lit, fig) split; **~ung** f splitting.
Span [ʃpa:n] m -(e)s, -e shaving; **~ferkel** nt sucking-pig; **~ien** nt Spain; **~ier(in** f) m Spaniard; **s~isch** a Spanish.
Spange ['ʃpaŋə] f -, -n clasp; (Haar~) hair slide; (Schnalle) buckle; (Armreif) bangle.
Spann- ['ʃpan] zW: **~beton** m prestressed concrete; **~e** f -, -n (Zeit~e) space; (Differenz) gap; **s~en** vt (straffen) tighten, tauten; (befestigen) brace // vi be tight; **s~end** a exciting, gripping; **~ung** f tension; (ELEK) voltage; (fig) suspense; (unangenehm) tension.
Spar- ['ʃpa:r] zW: **~buch** nt savings book; **~büchse** f moneybox; **s~en** vti save; sich (dat) etw s~en save oneself sth; (Bemerkung) keep sth to oneself; mit etw (dat) s~en be spar-

ing with sth; an etw (dat) s~en economize on sth; **~er** m -s, - saver.
Spargel ['ʃpargəl] m -s, - asparagus.
Spar- zW: **~kasse** f savings bank; **~konto** nt savings account.
spärlich ['ʃpɛ:rlɪç] a meagre; (Bekleidung) scanty.
Spar- zW: **~maßnahme** f economy measure, cut; **s~sam** a economical, thrifty; **~samkeit** f thrift, economizing; **~schwein** nt piggy bank.
Sparte ['ʃpartə] f -, -n field; line of business; (PRESSE) column.
Spaß [ʃpa:s] m -es, ¨-e joke; (Freude) fun; jdm ~ machen be fun (for sb); viel ~! have fun!; s~en vi joke; mit ihm ist nicht zu s~en you can't take liberties with him; **s~haft, s~ig** a funny, droll; **~verderber** m -s, - spoilsport.
spät [ʃpe:t] a, ad late; wie ~ ist es? what's the time?
Spaten ['ʃpa:tən] m -s, - spade.
spät- zW: **~er** a, ad later; **~estens** ad at the latest.
Spatz [ʃpats] m -en, -en sparrow.
spazier- [ʃpa'tsi:r] zW: **~en** vi stroll, walk; **~enfahren** vi unreg go for a drive; **~engehen** vi unreg go for a walk; **S~gang** m walk; **S~stock** m walking stick; **S~weg** m path, walk.
SPD [espe:'de:] f abk (= Sozialdemokratische Partei Deutschlands) Social Democratic Party.
Specht [ʃpeçt] m -(e)s, -e woodpecker.
Speck [ʃpek] m -(e)s, -e bacon.
Spediteur [ʃpedi'tø:r] m carrier; (Möbel~) furniture remover.
Spedition [ʃpeditsi'o:n] f carriage; (~sfirma) road haulage contractor; removal firm.
Speer [ʃpe:r] m -(e)s, -e spear; (SPORT) javelin.
Speiche ['ʃpaiçə] f -, -n spoke.
Speichel ['ʃpaiçəl] m -s saliva, spit(tle).
Speicher ['ʃpaiçər] m -s, - storehouse; (Dach~) attic, loft; (Korn~) granary; (Wasser~) tank; (TECH) store; (COMPUT) memory; **s~n** vt store; (COMPUT) save.
speien ['ʃpaiən] vti unreg spit; (erbrechen) vomit; (Vulkan) spew.
Speise ['ʃpaizə] f -, -n food; **~eis** ['-ais] nt ice-cream; **~kammer** f larder, pantry; **~karte** f menu; **s~n** vt feed; eat // vi dine; **~röhre** f gullet, oesophagus; **~saal** m dining room; **~wagen** m dining car.
Speku- [ʃpeku] zW: **~lant** [-'lant] m speculator; **~lation** [-latsi'o:n] f speculation; **s~lieren** [-'li:rən] vi (fig) speculate; auf etw (akk) s~lieren have hopes of sth.
Spelunke [ʃpe'luŋkə] f -, -n dive.

Spende [ˈʃpɛndə] f -, -n donation; **s~n** vt donate, give; **~r** m -s, - donor, donator.

spendieren [ʃpɛnˈdiːrən] vt pay for, buy; jdm etw ~ treat sb to sth, stand sb sth.

Sperling [ˈʃpɛrlɪŋ] m sparrow.

Sperma [ˈʃpɛrma] nt -s, Spermen sperm.

Sperr- [ˈʃpɛr] zW: **~e** f -, -n barrier; (Verbot) ban; **s~en** vt block; (SPORT) suspend, bar; (vom Ball) obstruct; (einschließen) lock; (verbieten) ban // vr baulk, jib(e); **~gebiet** nt prohibited area; **~holz** nt plywood; **s~ig** a bulky; **~sitz** m (THEAT) stalls pl; **~stunde** f closing time.

Spesen [ˈʃpeːzən] pl expenses pl; **~abrechnung** f expense account.

Spezial- [ʃpetsiˈaːl] in zW special; **s~angefertigt** a custom-built; (Kleidung) tailor-made; **s~i'sieren** vr specialize; **~i'sierung** f specialization; **~ist** [-ˈlɪst] m specialist; **~i'tät** f speciality.

speziell [ʃpetsiˈɛl] a special.

spezifisch [ʃpeˈtsiːfɪʃ] a specific.

Sphäre [ˈsfɛːrə] f -, -n sphere.

Spiegel [ˈʃpiːgəl] m -s, - mirror; (Wasser~) level; (MIL) tab; **~bild** nt reflection; **s~bildlich** a reversed; **~ei** [ˈ-ˈaɪ] nt fried egg; **s~n** vt mirror, reflect // vr be reflected // vi gleam; (wider~n) be reflective; **~schrift** f mirror-writing; **~ung** f reflection.

Spiel [ʃpiːl] nt -(e)s, -e game; (Schau~) play; (Tätigkeit) play(ing); (KARTEN) deck; (TECH) (free) play; **s~en** vti play; (um Geld) gamble; (THEAT) perform, act; **s~end** ad easily; **~er** m -s, - player; (um Geld) gambler; **~e'rei** f trifling pastime; **~feld** nt pitch, field; **~film** m feature film; **~plan** m (THEAT) programme; **~platz** m playground; **~raum** m room to manoeuvre, scope; **~regel** f rule; **~sachen** pl toys pl; **~verderber** m -s, - spoilsport; **~waren** pl, **~zeug** nt toys pl.

Spieß [ʃpiːs] m -es, -e spear; (Brat~) spit; **~bürger** m, **~er** m -s, - bourgeois; **~rutenlaufen** nt running the gauntlet.

Spikes [spaɪks] pl spikes pl; (AUT) studs pl.

Spinat [ʃpiˈnaːt] m -(e)s, -e spinach.

Spind [ʃpɪnt] m od nt -(e)s, -e locker.

Spinn- [ˈʃpɪn] zW: **~e** f -, -n spider; **s~en** vti unreg spin; (umg) talk rubbish; (verrückt) be crazy od mad; **~e'rei** f spinning mill; **~rad** nt spinning-wheel; **~webe** f cobweb.

Spion [ʃpiˈoːn] m -s, -e spy; (in Tür)

spyhole; **~age** [ʃpioˈnaːʒə] f -, -n espionage; **s~ieren** [ʃpioˈniːrən] vi spy.

Spirale [ʃpiˈraːlə] f -, -n spiral.

Spirituosen [ʃpirituˈoːzən] pl spirits pl.

Spiritus [ˈʃpiːritʊs] m -, -se (methylated) spirit.

Spital [ʃpiˈtaːl] nt -s, ⁀er hospital.

spitz [ʃpɪts] a pointed; (Winkel) acute; (fig: Zunge) sharp; (: Bemerkung) caustic; **S~bogen** m pointed arch; **S~bube** m rogue; **S~e** f -, -n point, tip; (Berg~) peak; (Bemerkung) taunt, dig; (erster Platz) lead, top; (meist pl: Gewebe) lace; **S~el** m -s, - police informer; **~en** vt sharpen.

Spitzen- zW: **~leistung** f top performance; **~lohn** m top wages pl; **~marke** f brand leader; **~sportler** m top-class sportsman.

spitzfindig a (over)subtle.

Spitzname m nickname.

Splitter [ˈʃplɪtər] m -s, - splinter; **s~nackt** a stark naked.

sponsern [ˈspɔnzərn, ˈʃpɔnzərn] vt sponsor.

spontan [ʃpɔnˈtaːn] a spontaneous.

Sport [ʃpɔrt] m -(e)s, -e sport; (fig) hobby; **~lehrer(in** f) m games od P.E. teacher; **~ler(in** f) m -s, - sportsman/woman; **s~lich** a sporting; (Mensch) sporty; **~platz** m playing od sports field; **~verein** m sports club; **~wagen** m sports car.

Spott [ʃpɔt] m -(e)s mockery, ridicule; **s~billig** a dirt-cheap; **s~en** vi mock (über +akk at), ridicule.

spöttisch [ˈʃpɶtɪʃ] a mocking.

sprach etc v siehe **sprechen**.

Sprach- [ˈʃpraːx] zW: **s~begabt** a good at languages; **~e** f -, -n language; **~fehler** m speech defect; **~führer** m phrasebook; **~gefühl** nt feeling for language; **~labor** nt language laboratory; **s~lich** a linguistic; **s~los** a speechless.

sprang etc v siehe **springen**.

Spray [spreː] m od nt -s, -s spray.

Sprech- [ˈʃprɛç] zW: **~anlage** f intercom; **s~en** unreg vi speak, talk (mit to); das spricht für ihn that's a point in his favour // vt say; (Sprache) speak; (Person) speak to; **~er(in** f) m -s, - speaker; (für Gruppe) spokesman; (RAD, TV) announcer; **~stunde** f consultation (hour); (doctor's) surgery; **~stundenhilfe** f (doctor's) receptionist; **~zimmer** nt consulting room, surgery.

Spreng- [ˈʃprɛŋ] zW: **~arbeiten** pl blasting operations pl; **s~en** vt sprinkle; (mit Sprengstoff) blow up; (Gestein) blast; (Versammlung) break up; ~**kopf** m warhead; ~**ladung** f explosive charge; ~**stoff** m explosive(s).

Spreu [ʃprɔy] f - chaff.

sprichst etc v siehe **sprechen**.

Sprich- ['ʃpriç] zW: ~**wort** nt proverb; **s~wörtlich** a proverbial.

Spring- ['ʃpriŋ] zW: ~**brunnen** m fountain; **s~en** vi unreg jump; (Glas) crack; (mit Kopfsprung) dive; ~**er** m -s, - jumper; (Schach) knight.

Spritz- ['ʃprits] zW: ~**e** f -, -n syringe; injection; (an Schlauch) nozzle; **s~en** vt spray; (heraus~en) spurt; (MED) give injections; ~**pistole** f spray gun.

spröde ['ʃprøːdə] a brittle; (Person) reserved, coy.

Sprosse ['ʃprɔsə] f -, -n rung.

Spruch [ʃprux] m -(e)s, ⁼e saying, maxim; (JUR) judgement.

Sprudel ['ʃpruːdəl] m -s, - mineral water; lemonade; **s~n** vi bubble.

Sprüh- ['ʃpryː] zW: ~**dose** f aerosol (can); **s~en** vti spray; (fig) sparkle; ~**regen** m drizzle.

Sprung [ʃpruŋ] m -(e)s, ⁼e jump; (Riß) crack; ~**brett** nt springboard; **s~haft** a erratic; (Aufstieg) rapid; ~**schanze** f skijump.

Spucke ['ʃpukə] f - spit; **s~n** vti spit.

Spuk [ʃpuːk] m -(e)s, -e haunting; (fig) nightmare; **s~en** vi (Geist) walk; **hier spukt es** this place is haunted.

Spule ['ʃpuːlə] f -, -n spool; (ELEK) coil.

Spül- ['ʃpyːl] zW: ~**e** f -, -n (kitchen) sink; **s~en** vti rinse; (Geschirr) wash up; (Toilette) flush; ~**maschine** f dishwasher; ~**mittel** nt washing-up liquid; ~**stein** m sink; ~**ung** f rinsing; flush; (MED) irrigation.

Spur [ʃpuːr] f -, -en trace; (Fuß~, Rad~, Tonband~) track; (Fährte) trail; (Fahr~) lane.

spür- ['ʃpyːr] zW: ~**bar** a noticeable, perceptible; ~**en** vt feel.

spurlos ad without (a) trace.

Spurt [ʃpurt] m -(e)s, -s od -e spurt.

sputen ['ʃpuːtən] vr make haste.

St. abk von **Stück** // abk (= Sankt) St.

Staat [ʃtaːt] m -(e)s, -en state; (Prunk) show; (Kleidung) finery; **mit etw ~ machen** show off od parade sth; **s~enlos** a stateless; **s~lich** a state(-); state-run.

Staats- zW: ~**angehörigkeit** f nationality; ~**anwalt** m public prosecutor; ~**bürger** m citizen; ~**dienst** m civil service; **s~feindlich** a subversive; ~**mann** m, pl -**männer** statesman; ~**sekretär** m secretary of state.

Stab [ʃtaːp] m -(e)s, ⁼e rod; (Gitter~) bar; (Menschen) staff; ~**hochsprung** m pole vault; **stabil** [ʃtaˈbiːl] a stable; (Möbel) sturdy; **stabili'sieren** vt stabilize.

Stachel ['ʃtaxəl] m -s, -n spike; (von Tier) spine; (von Insekten) sting; ~**beere** f gooseberry; ~**draht** m barbed wire; **s~ig** a prickly; ~**schwein** nt porcupine.

Stadion ['ʃtaːdiɔn] nt -s, **Stadien** stadium.

Stadium ['ʃtaːdiʊm] nt stage, phase.

Stadt [ʃtat] f ⁼e town.

Städt- ['ʃtɛːt] zW: ~**chen** nt small town; **Städtebau** m town planning; ~**er(in** f) m -s, - town dweller; **s~isch** a municipal; (nicht ländlich) urban.

Stadt- zW: ~**mauer** f city wall(s); ~**mitte** f town centre; ~**plan** m street map; ~**rand** m outskirts pl; ~**rundfahrt** f tour of a/the city; ~**teil** m district, part of town; ~**zentrum** nt town centre.

Staffel ['ʃtafəl] f -, -n rung; (SPORT) relay (team); (AVIAT) squadron; **s~n** vt graduate.

stahl etc v siehe **stehlen**.

Stahl [ʃtaːl] m -s, ⁼e steel.

stak etc v siehe **stecken**.

Stall [ʃtal] m -(e)s, ⁼e stable; (Kaninchen~) hutch; (Schweine~) sty; (Hühner~) henhouse.

Stamm [ʃtam] m -(e)s, ⁼e (Baum~) trunk; (Menschen~) tribe; (GRAM) stem; ~**baum** m family tree; (von Tier) pedigree; **s~eln** vti stammer; **s~en** vi: **s~en von** od **aus** come from; ~**gast** m regular (customer).

stämmig ['ʃtɛmiç] a sturdy; (Mensch) stocky.

Stammtisch ['ʃtamtiʃ] m table for the regulars.

stampfen ['ʃtampfən] vti stamp; (stapfen) tramp; (mit Werkzeug) pound.

stand etc v siehe **stehen**.

Stand [ʃtant] m -(e)s, ⁼e position; (Wasser~, Benzin~ etc) level; (Stehen) standing position; (Zustand) state; (Spiel~) score; (Messe~ etc) stand; (Klasse) class; (Beruf) profession.

Standard ['ʃtandart] m -s, -s standard.

Ständer ['ʃtɛndər] m -s, - stand.

Standes- ['ʃtandəs] zW: ~**amt** nt registry office; ~**beamte(r)** m registrar; **s~gemäß** a, ad according to one's social position; ~**unterschied** m social difference.

Stand- zW: **s~haft** a steadfast; ~**haftigkeit** f steadfastness; **s~halten** vi unreg stand firm (jdm/etw against sb/sth), resist (jdm/etw sb/sth).

ständig ['ʃtɛndɪç] a permanent; (*ununterbrochen*) constant, continual.

Stand- zW: **~licht** nt sidelights pl, parking lights pl (US); **~ort** m location; (MIL) garrison; **~punkt** m standpoint.

Stange ['ʃtaŋə] f -, -n stick; (*Stab*) pole, bar; rod; (*Zigaretten*) carton; von der ~ (COMM) off the peg; eine ~ Geld quite a packet.

Stanniol [ʃtani'oːl] nt -s, -e tinfoil.

Stapel ['ʃtaːpəl] m -s, - pile; (NAUT) stocks pl; **~lauf** m launch; **s~n** vt pile (up).

Star [ʃtaːr] m -(e)s, -e starling; (MED) cataract // m -s, -s (*Film etc*) star.

starb etc v siehe **sterben**.

stark [ʃtark] a strong; (*heftig*, *groß*) heavy; (*Maßangabe*) thick.

Stärke ['ʃtɛrkə] f -, -n strength; heaviness; thickness; (KOCH, *Wäsche~*) starch; **s~n** vt strengthen; (*Wäsche*) starch.

Starkstrom m heavy current.

Stärkung ['ʃtɛrkʊŋ] f strengthening; (*Essen*) refreshment.

starr [ʃtar] a stiff; (*unnachgiebig*) rigid; (*Blick*) staring; **~en** vi stare; **~en vor** od **von** be covered in; (*Waffen*) be bristling with; **S~heit** f rigidity; **~köpfig** a stubborn; **S~sinn** m obstinacy.

Start [ʃtart] m -(e)s, -e start; (AVIAT) takeoff; **~automatik** f (AUT) automatic choke; **~bahn** f runway; **s~en** vti start; take off; **~er** m -s, - starter; **~erlaubnis** f takeoff clearance.

Station [ʃtatsi'oːn] f station; hospital ward; **s~ieren** [-'niːrən] vt station.

Statist [ʃta'tɪst] m extra, supernumerary; **~ik** f statistics; **~iker** m -s, - statistician; **s~isch** a statistical.

Stativ [ʃta'tiːf] nt -s, -e tripod.

statt [ʃtat] kj, präp +gen od dat instead of.

Stätte ['ʃtɛtə] f -, -n place.

statt- zW: **~finden** vi unreg take place; **~haft** a admissible; **~lich** a imposing, handsome.

Statue ['ʃtaːtuə] f -, -n statue.

Status ['ʃtaːtʊs] m -, - status; **~symbol** nt status symbol.

Statuten [ʃta'tuːtən] pl rules pl.

Stau [ʃtau] m -(e)s, -e blockage; (*Verkehrs~*) (traffic) jam.

Staub [ʃtaup] m -(e)s dust; **s~en** ['ʃtaubən] vi be dusty; **s~ig** a dusty; **~sauger** m vacuum cleaner; **~tuch** nt duster.

Staudamm m dam.

Staude ['ʃtaudə] f -, -n shrub.

stauen ['ʃtauən] vt (*Wasser*) dam up; (*Blut*) stop the flow of // vr (*Wasser*) become dammed up; (MED, *Verkehr*)

become congested; (*Menschen*) collect together; (*Gefühle*) build up.

staunen ['ʃtaunən] vi be astonished; **S~** nt -s amazement.

Stauung ['ʃtauʊŋ] f (von *Wasser*) damming-up; (von *Blut*, *Verkehr*) congestion.

Std. abk (= *Stunde*) hr.

Steak [steːk] nt steak.

Stech- ['ʃtɛç] zW: **s~en** vt unreg (*mit Nadel etc*) prick; (*mit Messer*) stab; (*mit Finger*) poke; (*Biene etc*) sting; (*Mücke*) bite; (*Sonne*) burn; (KARTEN) take; (ART) engrave; (*Torf*, *Spargel*) cut; **in See s~en** put to sea; **~en** nt -s, - (SPORT) play-off; jumpoff; **s~end** a piercing, stabbing; (*Geruch*) pungent; **~palme** f holly; **~uhr** f time clock.

Steck- ['ʃtɛk] zW: **~brief** m 'wanted' poster; **~dose** f (wall) socket; **s~en** vt put, insert; (*Nadel*) stick; (*Pflanzen*) plant; (*beim Nähen*) pin // vi (*auch unreg*) be; (*festsitzen*) be stuck; (*Nadeln*) stick; **s~enbleiben** vi unreg get stuck; **s~enlassen** vt unreg leave in; **~enpferd** nt hobbyhorse; **~er** m -s, - plug; **~nadel** f pin; **~rübe** f turnip.

Steg [ʃteːk] m -(e)s, -e small bridge; (*Anlege~*) landing stage; **~reif** m: aus dem **~reif** just like that.

stehen ['ʃteːən] unreg vi stand (zu by); (*sich befinden*) be; (in *Zeitung*) say; (*still~*) have stopped; **jdm ~** suit sb // vi unpers: es steht schlecht um things are bad for; wie steht's? how are things?; (SPORT) what's the score?; **~ bleiben** remain standing; **~bleiben** vi unreg (*Uhr*) stop; (*Fehler*) stay as it is; **~lassen** vt unreg leave; (*Bart*) grow.

Stehlampe ['ʃteːlampə] f standard lamp.

stehlen ['ʃteːlən] vt unreg steal.

Stehplatz ['ʃteːplats] m standing place.

steif [ʃtaif] a stiff; **S~heit** f stiffness.

Steig- [ʃtaik] zW: **~bügel** m stirrup; **~eisen** nt crampon; **s~en** vi unreg rise; (*klettern*) climb; **s~en in** (+*akk*)/**auf** (+*akk*) get in/on; **s~ern** vt raise; (GRAM) compare // vi (*Auktion*) bid // vr increase; **~erung** f raising; (GRAM) comparison; **~ung** f incline, gradient, rise.

steil [ʃtail] a steep.

Stein [ʃtain] m -(e)s, -e stone; (in *Uhr*) jewel; **~bock** m (ASTROL) Capricorn; **~bruch** m quarry; **~butt** m -s, -e turbot; **s~ern** a (made of) stone; (*fig*) stony; **~gut** nt stoneware; **s~hart** a hard as stone; **s~ig** a stony; **s~igen** vt stone; **~kohle** f mineral coal.

Stelle ['ʃtɛlə] *f* -, **-n** place; (*Arbeit*) post, job; (*Amt*) office; **an Ihrer/ meiner ~** in your/my place.

stellen *vt* put; (*Uhr etc*) set; (*zur Verfügung ~*) supply; (*fassen: Dieb*) apprehend // *vr* (*sich aufstellen*) stand; (*sich einfinden*) present oneself; (*bei Polizei*) give oneself up; (*vorgeben*) pretend (to be); **sich zu etw ~** have an opinion of sth; **S~angebot** *nt* offer of a post; (*Zeitung*) vacancies; **S~gesuch** *nt* application for a post; **S~vermittlung** *f* employment agency.

Stell- *zW*: **~ung** *f* position; (*MIL*) line; **~ung nehmen zu** comment on; **~ungnahme** *f* -, **-n** comment; **s~vertretend** *a* deputy, acting; **~vertreter** *m* deputy; **~werk** *nt* (*EISENB*) signal box.

Stelze ['ʃtɛltsə] *f* -, **-n** stilt.

Stemm- ['ʃtɛm] *zW*: **~bogen** *m* (*SKI*) stem turn; **s~en** *vt* lift (up); (*drükken*) press; **sich s~en gegen** (*fig*) resist, oppose.

Stempel ['ʃtɛmpəl] *m* -s, - stamp; (*BOT*) pistil; **~kissen** *nt* inkpad; **s~n** *vt* stamp; (*Briefmarke*) cancel; **s~n gehen** (*umg*) be/go on the dole.

Stengel ['ʃtɛŋəl] *m* -s, - stalk.

Steno- [ʃteno] *zW*: **~gramm** [-'gram] *nt* shorthand report; **~graphie** [-gra'fiː] *f* shorthand; **s~graphieren** [-gra'fiːrən] *vti* write (in) shorthand; **~typist(in** *f*) [-ty'pɪst(ɪn)] *m* shorthand typist.

Stepp- ['ʃtɛp] *zW*: **~decke** *f* quilt; **~e** *f* -, **-n** prairie; steppe; **s~en** *vt* stitch // *vi* tap-dance.

Sterb- ['ʃtɛrb] *zW*: **Sterbefall** *m* death; **s~en** *vi unreg* die; **s~lich** ['ʃtɛrplɪç] *a* mortal; **~lichkeit** *f* mortality; **~lichkeitsziffer** *f* death rate.

stereo- ['steːreo] *in zW* stereo(-); **S~anlage** *f* stereo (system); **~typ** [ʃtereo'tyːp] *a* stereotype.

steril [ʃte'riːl] *a* sterile; **~isieren** *vt* sterilize; **S~isierung** *f* sterilization.

Stern [ʃtɛrn] *m* -(e)s, **-e** star; **~bild** *nt* constellation; **~schnuppe** *f* -, **-n** meteor, falling star; **~stunde** *f* historic moment.

stet [ʃteːt] *a* steady; **~ig** *a* constant, continual; **~s** *ad* continually, always.

Steuer ['ʃtɔyər] *nt* -s, - (*NAUT*) helm; (*~ruder*) rudder; (*AUT*) steering wheel // *f* -, **-n** tax; **~erklärung** *f* tax return; **~freibetrag** *m* tax allowance; **~klasse** *f* tax group; **~knüppel** *m* control column; (*AVIAT*, *COMPUT*) joystick; **~mann** *m, pl* **-männer** *od* **-leute** helmsman; **s~n** *vti* steer; (*Flugzeug*) pilot; (*Entwicklung, Tonstärke*) control; **~paradies** *nt* tax haven; **~rad** *nt* steering wheel; **~ung** *f*

steering (*auch AUT*); piloting; control; (*Vorrichtung*) controls *pl*; **~vergünstigung** *f* tax relief; **~zahler** *m* -s, - taxpayer.

Steward ['stjuːərt] *m* -s, **-s** steward; **Stewardeß** ['stjuːərdɛs] *f* -, **-essen** stewardess; air hostess.

Stich [ʃtɪç] *m* -(e)s, **-e** (*Insekten~*) sting; (*Messer~*) stab; (*beim Nähen*) stitch; (*Färbung*) tinge; (*KARTEN*) trick; (*ART*) engraving; **jdn im ~ lassen** leave sb in the lurch; **s~eln** *vi* (*fig*) jibe; **s~haltig** *a* sound, tenable; **~probe** *f* spot check; **~wahl** *f* final ballot; **~wort** *nt* cue; (*in Wörterbuch*) headword; (*für Vortrag*) note.

Stick- [ʃtɪk] *zW*: **s~en** *vti* embroider; **~e'rei** *f* embroidery; **s~ig** *a* stuffy, close; **~stoff** *m* nitrogen.

Stiefel ['ʃtiːfəl] *m* -s, - boot.

Stief- ['ʃtiːf] *in zW* step; **~kind** *nt* stepchild; (*fig*) Cinderella; **~mutter** *f* stepmother; **~mütterchen** *nt* pansy.

Stiege ['ʃtiːgə] *f* -, **-n** staircase.

stiehlst *etc v siehe* **stehlen**.

Stiel [ʃtiːl] *m* -(e)s, **-e** handle; (*BOT*) stalk.

stier [ʃtiːr] *a* staring, fixed; **S~** *m* -(e)s, **-e** bull; (*ASTROL*) Taurus; **~en** *vi* stare.

Stift [ʃtɪft] *m* -(e)s, **-e** peg; (*Nagel*) tack; (*Farb~*) crayon; (*Blei~*) pencil // *nt* -(e)s, **-e** (*charitable*) foundation; (*ECCL*) religious institution; **s~en** *vt* found; (*Unruhe*) cause; (*spenden*) contribute; **~er(in** *f*) *m* -s, - founder; **~ung** *f* donation; (*Organisation*) foundation; **~zahn** *m* crown tooth.

Stil [ʃtiːl] *m* -(e)s, **-e** style.

still [ʃtɪl] *a* quiet; (*unbewegt*) still; (*heimlich*) secret; **S~er Ozean** Pacific; **S~e** *f* -, **-n** stillness, quietness; **in aller S~e** quietly; **~en** *vt* stop; (*befriedigen*) satisfy; (*Säugling*) breast-feed; **~halten** *vi unreg* keep still; **~(l)egen** *vt* close down; **S~(l)egung** *f* shut-down; **~schweigen** *vi unreg* be silent; **S~schweigen** *nt* silence; **~schweigend** *a, ad* silent(ly); (*Einverständnis*) tacit(ly); **S~stand** *m* standstill; **~stehen** *vi unreg* stand still.

Stimm- ['ʃtɪm] *zW*: **~bänder** *pl* vocal chords *pl*; **s~berechtigt** *a* entitled to vote; **~e** *f* -, **-n** voice; (*Wahl~e*) vote; **s~en** *vt* (*MUS*) tune; **das stimmte ihn traurig** that made him feel sad // *vi* be right; **s~en für/gegen** vote for/against; **stimmt so!** that's right; **~enmehrheit** *f* majority (of votes); **~enthaltung** *f* abstention; **~gabel** *f* tuning fork; **~recht** *nt* right to vote; **~ung** *f* mood; atmosphere;

s~ungsvoll a enjoyable; full of atmosphere; **~zettel** m ballot paper.
tinken [ˈʃtɪŋkən] vi unreg stink.
Stipendium [ʃtiˈpɛndiʊm] nt grant.
tirbst etc v siehe **sterben**.
Stirn [ʃtɪrn] f -, -en forehead, brow; (Frechheit) impudence; **~höhle** f sinus; **~runzeln** nt -s frown(ing).
töbern [ˈʃtøːbərn] vi rummage.
tochern [ˈʃtɔxərn] vi poke (about).
Stock [ʃtɔk] m -(e)s, ¨e stick; (BOT) stock // pl **-werke** storey; **s~en** vi stop, pause; **s~end** a halting; **~ung** f stoppage; **~werk** nt storey, floor.
Stoff [ʃtɔf] m -(e)s, -e (Gewebe) material, cloth; (Materie) matter; (von Buch etc) subject (matter); **s~lich** a material; **~wechsel** m metabolism.
töhnen [ˈʃtøːnən] vi groan.
stoisch [ˈʃtoːɪʃ] a stoical.
Stollen [ˈʃtɔlən] m -s, - (MIN) gallery; (KOCH) cake eaten at Christmas; (von Schuhen) stud.
stolpern [ˈʃtɔlpərn] vi stumble, trip.
Stolz [ʃtɔlts] m -es pride; **s~** a proud; **s~ieren** [ʃtɔlˈtsiːrən] vi strut.
Stopf- [ˈʃtɔpf] zW: **s~en** vt (hinein~en) stuff; (voll~en) fill (up); (nähen) darn // vi (MED) cause constipation; **~garn** nt darning thread.
Stoppel [ˈʃtɔpəl] f -, -n stubble.
Stopp- [ˈʃtɔp] zW: **s~en** vti stop; (mit Uhr) time; **~schild** nt stop sign; **~uhr** f stopwatch.
Stöpsel [ˈʃtœpsəl] m -s, - plug; (für Flaschen) stopper.
Storch [ʃtɔrç] m -(e)s, ¨e stork.
Stör- [ˈʃtøːr] zW: **s~en** vt disturb; (behindern, RAD) interfere with // vr sich an etw (dat) **s~en** let sth bother one; **s~end** a disturbing, annoying; **~enfried** m -(e)s, -e troublemaker.
störrisch [ˈʃtœrɪʃ] a stubborn, perverse.
Störsender m jammer.
Störung f disturbance; interference.
Stoß [ʃtoːs] m -es, ¨e (Schub) push; (Schlag) blow; knock; (mit Schwert) thrust; (mit Fuß) kick; (Erd~) shock; (Haufen) pile; **~dämpfer** m -s, - shock absorber; **s~en** unreg vt (mit Druck) shove, push; (mit Schlag) knock, bump; (mit Fuß) kick; (Schwert etc) thrust; (an~en: Kopf etc) bump; // vr get a knock; sich **s~en** an (+dat) (fig) take exception to // vi: **s~en** an od auf (+akk) bump into; (finden) come across; (angrenzen) be next to; **~stange** f (AUT) bumper.
stottern [ˈʃtɔtərn] vti stutter.
Str. abk (= Straße) St.
Straf- [ˈʃtraːf] zW: **~anstalt** f penal institution; **~arbeit** f (SCH) punishment; lines pl; **s~bar** a punishable;

~barkeit f criminal nature; **~e** f -, -n punishment; (JUR) penalty; (Gefängnis~e) sentence; (Geld~e) fine; **s~en** vt punish.
straff [ʃtraf] a tight; (streng) strict; (Stil etc) concise; (Haltung) erect; **~en** vt tighten, tauten.
Straf- zW: **~gefangene(r)** mf prisoner, convict; **~gesetzbuch** nt penal code.
Sträf- [ˈʃtrɛːf] zW: **s~lich** a criminal; **~ling** m convict.
Straf- zW: **~porto** nt excess postage (charge); **~predigt** f telling-off; **~raum** m (SPORT) penalty area; **~recht** nt criminal law; **~stoß** m (SPORT) penalty (kick); **~tat** f punishable act; **~zettel** m ticket.
Strahl [ʃtraːl] m -s, -en ray, beam; (Wasser~) jet; **s~en** vi radiate; (fig) beam; **~entherapie** f radiotherapy; **~ung** f radiation.
Strähne [ˈʃtrɛːnə] f -, -n strand.
stramm [ʃtram] a tight; (Haltung) erect; (Mensch) robust.
strampeln [ˈʃtrampəln] vi kick (about), fidget.
Strand [ʃtrant] m -(e)s, ¨e shore; (mit Sand) beach; **~bad** nt open-air swimming pool, lido; **s~en** [ˈʃtrandən] vi run aground; (fig: Mensch) fail; **~gut** nt flotsam; **~korb** m beach chair.
Strang [ʃtraŋ] m -(e)s, ¨e cord, rope; (Bündel) skein.
Strapaz- zW: **~e** [ʃtraˈpaːtsə] f -, -n strain, exertion; **s~ieren** [ʃtrapaˈtsiːrən] vt (Material) treat roughly, punish; (Mensch, Kräfte) wear out, exhaust; **s~ierfähig** a hard-wearing; **s~iös** [ʃtrapatsiˈøːs] a exhausting, tough.
Straße [ˈʃtraːsə] f -, -n street, road.
Straßen- zW: **~bahn** f tram, streetcar (US); **~beleuchtung** f street lighting; **~feger, ~kehrer** m -s, - roadsweeper; **~sperre** f roadblock; **~verkehrsordnung** f highway code.
Strateg- [ʃtraˈteːg] zW: **~e** m -n, -n strategist; **~ie** [ʃtrateˈgiː] f strategy; **s~isch** a strategic.
sträuben [ˈʃtrɔybən] vt ruffle // vr bristle; (Mensch) resist (gegen etw sth).
Strauch [ʃtraʊx] m -(e)s, Sträucher bush, shrub.
Strauß [ʃtraʊs] m -es, Sträuße bunch; bouquet // pl -e ostrich.
Streb- [ˈʃtreːb] zW: **s~en** vi strive (nach for), endeavour; **~er** m -s, - (pej) pusher, climber; (SCH) swot (Brit), bootlicker (US); **s~sam** a industrious.
Strecke [ˈʃtrɛkə] f -, -n stretch; (Entfernung) distance; (EISENB)

line; (MATH) line; **s~n** vt stretch; (Waffen) lay down; (KOCH) eke out // vr stretch (oneself).

Streich [ʃtraɪç] m -(e)s, -e trick, prank; (Hieb) blow; **s~eln** vt stroke; **s~en** unreg vt (berühren) stroke; (auftragen) spread; (anmalen) paint; (durch~en) delete; (nicht genehmigen) cancel // vi (berühren) brush; (schleichen) prowl; **~holz** nt match; **~instrument** nt string instrument.

Streif- [ʃtraɪf] zW: **~e** f -, -n patrol; **s~en** vt (leicht berühren) brush against, graze; (Blick) skim over; (Thema, Problem) touch on; (ab~en) take off // vi (gehen) roam; **~en** m -s, - (Linie) stripe; (Stück) strip; (Film) film; **~endienst** m patrol duty; **~enwagen** m patrol car; **~schuß** m graze, grazing shot; **~zug** m scouting trip.

Streik [ʃtraɪk] m -(e)s, -s strike; **~brecher** m -s, - blackleg, strikebreaker; **s~en** vi strike; **~kasse** f strike fund; **~posten** m (strike) picket.

Streit [ʃtraɪt] m -(e)s, -e argument; dispute; **s~en** vir unreg argue; dispute; **~frage** f point at issue; **s~ig** a: jdm etw s~ig machen dispute sb's right to sth; **~igkeiten** pl quarrel, dispute; **~kräfte** pl (MIL) armed forces pl.

streng [ʃtrɛŋ] a severe; (Lehrer, Maßnahme) strict; (Geruch etc) sharp; **S~e** f -, severity; strictness; sharpness; **~genommen** ad strictly speaking; **~gläubig** a orthodox, strict; **~stens** ad strictly.

Streu [ʃtrɔʏ] f -, -en litter, bed of straw; **s~en** vt strew, scatter, spread; **~ung** f dispersion.

Strich [ʃtrɪç] m -(e)s, -e (Linie) line; (Feder~, Pinsel~) stroke; (von Geweben) nap; (von Fell) pile; auf den ~ gehen (umg) walk the streets; jdm gegen den ~ gehen rub sb up the wrong way; einen ~ machen durch (lit) cross out; (fig) foil; **~mädchen** nt streetwalker; **~punkt** m semicolon; **s~weise** ad here and there.

Strick [ʃtrɪk] m -(e)s, -e rope; **s~en** vti knit; **~jacke** f cardigan; **~leiter** f rope ladder; **~nadel** f knitting needle; **~waren** pl knitwear.

strikt [strɪkt] a strict.

strittig [ʃtrɪtɪç] a disputed, in dispute.

Stroh [ʃtroː] nt -(e)s straw; **~blume** f everlasting flower; **~dach** nt thatched roof; **~halm** m (drinking) straw.

Strom [ʃtroːm] m -(e)s, -̈e river; (fig) stream; (ELEK) current; **s~abwärts** [-ˈʔapvɛrts] ad downstream; **s~aufwärts** [-ˈʔaʊfvɛrts] ad upstream.

strömen [ˈʃtrøːmən] vi stream, pour.

Strom- zW: **~kreis** m circuit; **s~linienförmig** a streamlined; **~rechnung** f electricity bill; **~sperre** f power cut.

Strömung [ˈʃtrøːmʊŋ] f current.

Strophe [ˈʃtroːfə] f -, -n verse.

strotzen [ˈʃtrɔtsən] vi: ~ vor od von abound in, be full of.

Strudel [ˈʃtruːdəl] m -s, - whirlpool, vortex; (KOCH) strudel.

Struktur [ʃtrʊkˈtuːr] f structure.

Strumpf [ʃtrʊmpf] m -(e)s, -̈e stocking; **~band** nt garter; **~hose** f (pair of) tights.

Stube [ˈʃtuːbə] f -, -n room.

Stuben- zW: **~arrest** m confinement to one's room; (MIL) confinement to quarters; **~hocker** m (umg) stay-at-home; **s~rein** a house-trained.

Stuck [ʃtʊk] m -(e)s stucco.

Stück [ʃtʏk] nt -(e)s, -e piece; (etwas) bit; (THEAT) play; **~chen** nt little piece; **~lohn** m piecework wages pl; **s~weise** ad bit by bit, piecemeal; (COMM) individually; **~werk** nt bits and pieces pl.

Student(in f) [ʃtuˈdɛnt(ɪn)] m student; **s~isch** a student, academic.

Studie [ˈʃtuːdiə] f study.

studieren [ʃtuˈdiːrən] vti study.

Studio [ˈʃtuːdio] nt -s, -s studio.

Studium [ˈʃtuːdiʊm] nt studies pl.

Stufe [ˈʃtuːfə] f -, -n step; (Entwicklungs~) stage; **stufenweise** ad gradually.

Stuhl [ʃtuːl] m -(e)s, -̈e chair; **~gang** m bowel movement.

stülpen [ˈʃtʏlpən] vt (umdrehen) turn upside down; (bedecken) put.

stumm [ʃtʊm] a silent; (MED) dumb; **Stummel** m -s, - stump; (Zigaretten~) stub; **S~film** m silent film; **S~heit** f silence; dumbness.

Stümper [ˈʃtʏmpər] m -s, - incompetent, duffer; **s~haft** a bungling, incompetent; **s~n** vi (umg) bungle.

stumpf [ʃtʊmpf] a blunt; (teilnahmslos, glanzlos) dull; (Winkel) obtuse; **S~** m -(e)s, -̈e stump; **S~sinn** m tediousness; **~sinnig** a dull.

Stunde [ˈʃtʊndə] f -, -n hour; (SCH) lesson.

stunden vt: jdm etw ~ give sb time to pay sth; **S~geschwindigkeit** f average speed per hour; **S~kilometer** pl kilometres per hour; **~lang** a for hours; **S~lohn** m hourly wage; **S~plan** m timetable; **~weise** a by the hour; every hour.

stündlich [ˈʃtʏntlɪç] a hourly.

Stups [ʃtʊps] m -es, -e (umg) push; **~nase** f snub nose.

stur [ʃtuːr] a obstinate, pigheaded.

Sturm [ʃturm] *m* -(e)s, ⸚e storm, gale; (*MIL etc*) attack, assault.

stürm- [ʃtyrm] *zW*: ~**en** *vi* (*Wind*) blow hard, rage; (*rennen*) storm // *vt* (*MIL, fig*) storm // *v unpers* es ~t there's a gale blowing; **S~er** *m* -s, - (*SPORT*) forward, striker; ~**isch** *a* stormy.

Sturmwarnung *f* gale warning.

Sturz [ʃturts] *m* -es, ⸚e fall; (*POL*) overthrow.

stürzen [ʃtyrtsən] *vt* (*werfen*) hurl; (*POL*) overthrow; (*umkehren*) overturn // *vr* rush; (*hinein~*) plunge // *vi* fall; (*AVIAT*) dive; (*rennen*) dash.

Sturz- *zW*: ~**flug** *m* nose-dive; ~**helm** *m* crash helmet.

Stute [ʃtuːtə] *f* -, -n mare.

Stütz- [ʃtyts] *zW*: ~**balken** *m* brace, joist; ~**e** *f* -, -n support; help; **s~en** *vt* (*lit, fig*) support; (*Ellbogen etc*) prop up.

stutz- [ʃtuts] *zW*: ~**en** *vt* trim; (*Ohr, Schwanz*) dock; (*Flügel*) clip // *vi* hesitate; become suspicious; ~**ig** *a* perplexed, puzzled; (*mißtrauisch*) suspicious.

Stützpunkt *m* point of support; (*von Hebel*) fulcrum; (*MIL, fig*) base.

Styropor ® [ʃtyroˈpoːr] *nt* -s polystyrene.

s.u. *abk* = *siehe unten*.

Subjekt [zupˈjɛkt] *nt* -(e)s, -e subject; **s~iv** [-ˈtiːf] *a* subjective; ~**ivi'tät** *f* subjectivity.

Substantiv [ˈzupstantiːf] *nt* -s, -e noun.

Substanz [zupˈstants] *f* substance.

subtil [zupˈtiːl] *a* subtle.

subtrahieren [zuptraˈhiːrən] *vt* subtract.

Subvention [zupvɛntsiˈoːn] *f* subsidy; **s~ieren** [-ˈniːrən] *vt* subsidize.

Such- [zuːx] *zW*: ~**aktion** *f* search; ~**e** *f* -, -n search; **s~en** *vti* look (for), seek; (*ver~en*) try; ~**er** *m* -s, - seeker, searcher; (*PHOT*) viewfinder.

Sucht [zuxt] *f* -, ⸚e mania; (*MED*) addiction, craving.

süchtig [ˈzʏçtıç] *a* addicted; **S~e(r)** *mf* addict.

Süd- [zyːt] *zW*: ~**en** [ˈzyːdən] *m* -s south; ~**früchte** *pl* Mediterranean fruit; **s~lich** *a* southern; **s~lich von** (to the) south of; ~**pol** *m* South Pole; **s~wärts** *ad* southwards.

süffig [ˈzʏfıç] *a* (*Wein*) pleasant to the taste.

süffisant [zʏfiˈzant] *a* smug.

suggerieren [zugeˈriːrən] *vt* suggest (*jdm etw* sth to sb).

Sühne [ˈzyːnə] *f* -, -n atonement, expiation; **s~n** *vt* atone for, expiate.

Sultan [ˈzʊltan] *m* -s, -e sultan; ~**ine** [zʊltaˈniːnə] *f* sultana.

Sülze [ˈzʏltsə] *f* -, -n brawn.

Summ- [ˈzʊm] *zW*: ~**e** *f* -, -n sum, total; **s~en** *vti* buzz; (*Lied*) hum.

Sumpf [zʊmpf] *m* -(e)s, ⸚e swamp, marsh; **s~ig** *a* marshy.

Sünde [ˈzʏndə] *f* -, -n sin; **Sündenbock** *m* (*umg*) scapegoat; **Sündenfall** *m* Fall (of man); ~**r(in** *f*) *m* -s, - sinner.

Super [ˈzuːpər] *nt* -s (*Benzin*) four star (petrol); **Superlativ** [-latiːf] *m* -s, -e superlative; ~**markt** *m* supermarket.

Suppe [ˈzupə] *f* -, -n soup.

süß [zyːs] *a* sweet; **S~e** *f* - sweetness; ~**en** *vt* sweeten; **S~igkeit** *f* sweetness; (*Bonbon etc*) sweet (*Brit*), candy (*US*); ~**lich** *a* sweetish; (*fig*) sugary; **S~speise** *f* pudding, sweet; **S~stoff** *m* sweetener; **S~wasser** *nt* fresh water.

Sylvester [zylˈvɛstər] *nt* -s, - *siehe* **Silvester**.

Symbol [zymˈboːl] *nt* -s, -e symbol; **s~isch** *a* symbolic(al).

Symmetrie [zymeˈtriː] *f* symmetry.

symmetrisch [zyˈmeːtrıʃ] *a* symmetrical.

Sympath- *zW*: ~**ie** [zympaˈtiː] *f* liking, sympathy; **s~isch** [zymˈpaːtıʃ] *a* likeable; **er ist mir s~isch** I like him; **s~i'sieren** *vi* sympathize.

Symptom [zympˈtoːm] *nt* -s, -e symptom; **s~atisch** [zymptoˈmaːtıʃ] *a* symptomatic.

Synagoge [zynaˈgoːgə] *f* -, -n synagogue.

synchron [zynˈkroːn] *a* synchronous; **S~getriebe** *nt* synchromesh (gears *pl*); ~**i'sieren** *vt* synchronize; (*Film*) dub.

Synonym [zynoˈnyːm] *nt* -s, -e synonym; **s~** *a* synonymous.

Synthese [zynˈteːzə] *f* -, -n synthesis.

synthetisch [zynˈteːtıʃ] *a* synthetic.

Syphilis [ˈzyfilıs] *f* - syphilis.

Syr- [ˈzyːr] *zW*: ~**er(in** *f*) *m* Syrian; ~**ien** *nt* Syria; **s~isch** *a* Syrian.

System [zysˈteːm] *nt* -s, -e system; **s~atisch** [zystɛˈmaːtıʃ] *a* systematic; **s~ati'sieren** *vt* systematize; ~**platte** *f* system disk.

Szene [ˈstsseːnə] *f* -, -n scene; **Szenerie** [stsenəˈriː] *f* scenery.

T

T, t [teː] T, t.

t *abk* (= *Tonne*) t.

Tabak [ˈtaːbak] *m* -s, -e tobacco.

Tabell- [taˈbɛl] *zW*: **t~arisch** [tabɛˈlaːrıʃ] *a* tabular; ~**e** *f* table; **Tabellenführer** *m* top of the table, league leader.

Tablett [ta'blɛt] *nt* tray; **~e** *f* tablet, pill.

Tabu [ta'buː] *nt* taboo; **t~** *a* taboo.

Tachometer [taxo'meːtər] *m* **-s**, - (*AUT*) speedometer.

Tadel ['taːdəl] *m* **-s**, - censure, scolding; (*Fehler*) fault, blemish; **t~los** *a* faultless, irreproachable; **t~n** *vt* scold; **t~nswert** *a* blameworthy.

Tafel ['taːfəl] *f* -, **-n** table (*auch MATH*); (*Anschlag~*) board; (*Wand~*) blackboard; (*Schiefer~*) slate; (*Gedenk~*) plaque; (*Illustration*) plate; (*Schalt~*) panel; (*Schokolade etc*) bar.

Taft [taft] *m* **-(e)s**, **-e** taffeta.

Tag [taːk] *m* **-(e)s**, **-e** day; daylight; **unter/über ~e** (*MIN*) underground/on the surface; **an den ~ kommen** come to light; **guten ~!** good morning/afternoon!; **t~aus**, **t~ein** *ad* day in, day out; **~dienst** *m* day duty.

Tage- ['taːgə] *zW*: **~buch** ['taːgəbuːx] *nt* diary, journal; **~geld** *nt* daily allowance; **t~lang** *ad* for days; **t~n** *vi* sit, meet // *v unpers*: **es tagt** dawn is breaking.

Tages- *zW*: **~ablauf** *m* course of the day; **~anbruch** *m* dawn; **~karte** *f* menu of the day; (*Fahrkarte*) day ticket; **~licht** *nt* daylight; **~ordnung** *f* agenda; **~zeit** *f* time of day; **~zeitung** *f* daily (paper).

täglich ['tɛːklɪç] *a*, *ad* daily.

tagsüber ['taːksˈyːbər] *ad* during the day.

Tagung *f* conference.

Taille ['taljə] *f* -, **-n** waist.

Takt [takt] *m* **-(e)s**, **-e** tact; (*MUS*) time; **~gefühl** *nt* tact; **~ik** *f* tactics *pl*; **t~isch** *a* tactical; **t~los** *a* tactless; **~losigkeit** *f* tactlessness; **~stock** *m* (conductor's) baton; **t~voll** *a* tactful.

Tal [taːl] *nt* **-(e)s**, **-er** valley.

Talent [ta'lɛnt] *nt* **-(e)s**, **-e** talent; **t~iert** [talɛn'tiːrt] *a* talented, gifted.

Talisman ['taːlɪsman] *m* **-s**, **-e** talisman.

Tal- *zW*: **~sohle** *f* bottom of a valley; **~sperre** *f* dam.

Tamburin [tambu'riːn] *nt* **-s**, **-e** tambourine.

Tampon ['tampɔn] *m* **-s**, **-s** tampon.

Tang [taŋ] *m* **-(e)s**, **-e** seaweed.

Tangente [taŋ'gɛntə] *f* -, **-n** tangent.

tangieren [taŋ'giːrən] *vt* (*lit*) touch; (*fig*) affect.

Tank [taŋk] *m* **-s**, **-e** tank; **t~en** *vi* fill up with petrol (*Brit*) *od* gas (*US*); (*AVIAT*) (re)fuel; **~er** *m* **-s**, -, **~schiff** *nt* tanker; **~stelle** *f* petrol (*Brit*) *od* gas (*US*) station; **~wart** *m* petrol pump (*Brit*) *od* gas station (*US*) attendant.

Tanne ['tanə] *f* -, **-n** fir; **Tannenbaum** *m* fir tree; **Tannenzapfen** *m* fir cone.

Tante ['tantə] *f* -, **-n** aunt.

Tanz [tants] *m* **-es**, **-e** dance; **t~en** *vti* dance.

Tänzer(in *f*) ['tɛntsər(ɪn)] *m* **-s**, - dancer.

Tanz- *zW*: **~fläche** *f* (dance) floor; **~schule** *f* dancing school.

Tapete [ta'peːtə] *f* -, **-n** wallpaper; **Tapetenwechsel** *m* (*fig*) change of scenery.

tapezieren [tape'tsiːrən] *vt* (wall)-paper.

Tapezierer [tape'tsiːrər] *m* **-s**, - (interior) decorator.

tapfer ['tapfər] *a* brave; **T~keit** *f* courage, bravery.

Tarif [ta'riːf] *m* **-s**, **-e** tariff, (scale of) fares/charges; **~lohn** *m* standard wage rate; **~verhandlungen** *pl* wage negotiations *pl*.

Tarn- ['tarn] *zW*: **t~en** *vt* camouflage; (*Person, Absicht*) disguise; **~farbe** *f* camouflage paint; **~ung** *f* camouflaging; disguising.

Tasche ['taʃə] *f* -, **-n** pocket; handbag.

Taschen- *in zW* pocket; **~buch** *nt* paperback; **~dieb** *m* pickpocket; **~geld** *nt* pocket money; **~lampe** *f* (electric) torch, flashlight (*US*); **~messer** *nt* penknife; **~tuch** *nt* handkerchief.

Tasse ['tasə] *f* -, **-n** cup.

Tastatur [tasta'tuːr] *f* keyboard.

Taste ['tastə] *f* -, **-n** push-button control; (*an Schreibmaschine*) key; **t~n** *vt* feel, touch // *vi* feel, grope // *vr* feel one's way.

tat *etc v siehe* **tun.**

Tat [taːt] *f* -, **-en** act, deed, action; **in der ~** indeed, as a matter of fact; **~bestand** *m* facts *pl* of the case; **t~enlos** *a* inactive.

Tät- ['tɛːt] *zW*: **~er(in** *f*) *m* **-s**, - perpetrator, culprit; **t~ig** *a* active; **in einer Firma t~ig sein** work for a firm; **~igkeit** *f* activity; (*Beruf*) occupation; **t~lich** *a* violent; **~lichkeit** *f* violence // *pl* blows *pl*.

tätowieren [tɛto'viːrən] *vt* tattoo.

Tat- *zW*: **~sache** *f* fact; **t~sächlich** *a* actual // *ad* really.

Tau [tau] *nt* **-(e)s**, **-e** rope // *m* **-(e)s** dew.

taub [taup] *a* deaf; (*Nuß*) hollow; **T~heit** *f* deafness; **~stumm** *a* deaf-and-dumb.

Taube ['taubə] *f* -, **-n** dove; pigeon; **Taubenschlag** *m* dovecote; **hier geht es zu wie in einem Taubenschlag** it's a hive of activity here.

Tauch- ['taux] *zW*: **t~en** *vt* dip // *vi* dive; (*NAUT*) submerge; **~er** *m* **-s**, - diver; **~eranzug** *m* diving suit; **~sieder** *m* **-s**, - immersion coil (*for* boiling water).

tauen ['tauən] vti, v unpers thaw.

Tauf- ['tauf] zW: ~**becken** nt font; ~**e** f -, -n baptism; **t~en** vt christen, baptize; ~**name** m Christian name; ~**pate** m godfather; ~**patin** f godmother; ~**schein** m certificate of baptism.

Taug- ['taug] zW: **t~en** vi be of use; **t~en für** do od be good for; **nicht t~en** be no good od useless; **Taugenichts** m -es, -e good-fornothing; **t~lich** ['tauklɪç] a suitable; (MIL) fit (for service).

Taumel ['tauməl] m -s dizziness; (fig) frenzy; **t~n** vi reel, stagger.

Tausch [tauʃ] m -(e)s, -e exchange; **t~en** vt exchange, swap; ~**handel** m barter.

täuschen ['tɔyʃən] vt deceive // vi be deceptive // vr be wrong; ~**d** a deceptive.

Täuschung f deception; (optisch) illusion.

tausend ['tauzənt] num (a) thousand; **T~füßler** m -s, - centipede; millipede.

Tauwetter nt thaw.

Taxi ['taksi] nt -(s), -(s) taxi; ~**fahrer** m taxi driver; ~**stand** m taxi rank.

Tech- [tɛç] zW: ~**nik** f technology; (Methode, Kunstfertigkeit) technique; ~**niker** m -s, - technician; **t~nisch** a technical; ~**nolo'gie** f technology; **t~no'logisch** a technological.

TEE [te:'e:'e:] m abk (= Trans-Europ-Express) Trans-European Express.

Tee [te:] m -s, -s tea; ~**kanne** f teapot; ~**löffel** m teaspoon.

Teer [te:r] m -(e)s, -e tar; **t~en** vt tar.

Teesieb nt tea strainer.

Teich [taiç] m -(e)s, -e pond.

Teig [taik] m -(e)s, -e dough; **t~ig** a doughy; ~**waren** pl pasta sing.

Teil [tail] m od nt -(e)s, -e part; (An~) share; (Bestand~) component; **zum ~** partly; **t~bar** a divisible; ~**betrag** m instalment; ~**chen** nt (atomic) particle; **t~en** vtr divide; (mit jdm) share; **t~haben** vi unreg share (an +dat in); ~**haber** m -s, - partner; ~**kaskoversicherung** f third party, fire and theft insurance; ~**nahme** f -, -n participation; (Mitleid) sympathy; **t~nahmslos** a disinterested, apathetic; **t~nehmen** vi unreg take part (an +dat in); ~**nehmer** m -s, - participant; **t~s** ad partly; ~**ung** f division; **t~weise** ad partially, in part; ~**zahlung** f payment by instalments.

Teint [tɛ̃] m -s, -s complexion.

Telefax ['telefaks] nt fax.

Telefon [tele'fo:n] nt -s, -e telephone; ~**amt** nt telephone exchange; ~**anruf** m, ~**at** [telefo'na:t] nt -(e)s, -e (tele)phone call; ~**buch** nt telephone directory; **t~ieren** [telefo'ni:rən] vi telephone; **t~isch** [-ɪʃ] a telephone; (Benachrichtigung) by telephone; ~**ist(in** f) [telefo'nɪst(ɪn)] m telephonist; ~**nummer** f (tele)phone number; ~**verbindung** f telephone connection; ~**zelle** f telephone kiosk, callbox; ~**zentrale** f telephone exchange.

Telegraf [tele'gra:f] m -en, -en telegraph; ~**enleitung** f telegraph line; ~**enmast** m telegraph pole; ~**ie** [-'fi:] f telegraphy; **t~ieren** [-'fi:rən] vti telegraph, wire; **t~isch** a telegraphic.

Telegramm [tele'gram] nt -s, -e telegram, cable; ~**adresse** f telegraphic address.

Tele- zW: ~**objektiv** ['te:le'ɔpjɛkti:f] nt telephoto lens; ~**pathie** [telepa'ti:] f telepathy; **t~pathisch** [tele'pa:tɪʃ] a telepathic; ~**skop** [tele'sko:p] nt -s, -e telescope.

Telex ['teleks] nt -es, -e telex.

Teller ['tɛlər] m -s, - plate.

Tempel ['tɛmpəl] m -s, - temple.

Temperament [tɛmpəra'mɛnt] nt temperament; (Schwung) vivacity, liveliness; **t~los** a spiritless; **t~voll** a high-spirited, lively.

Temperatur [tɛmpəra'tu:r] f temperature.

Tempo ['tɛmpo] nt -s, -s speed, pace // pl **Tempi** (MUS) tempo; ~**!** get a move on!

Tendenz [tɛn'dɛnts] f tendency; (Absicht) intention; **t~iös** [-i'ø:s] a biased, tendentious.

tendieren [tɛn'di:rən] vi show a tendency, incline (zu to(wards)).

Tennis ['tɛnɪs] nt - tennis; ~**platz** m tennis court; ~**schläger** m tennis racket; ~**spieler(in** f) m tennis player.

Tenor [te'no:r] m -s, -̈e tenor.

Teppich ['tɛpɪç] m -s, -e carpet; ~**boden** m wall-to-wall carpeting.

Termin [tɛr'mi:n] m -s, -e (Zeitpunkt) date; (Frist) time limit, deadline; (Arzt~ etc) appointment; ~**kalender** m diary, appointments book.

Termite [tɛr'mi:tə] f -, -n termite.

Terpentin [tɛrpɛn'ti:n] nt -s, -e turpentine, turps sing.

Terrasse [tɛ'rasə] f -, -n terrace.

Terrine [tɛ'ri:nə] f tureen.

territorial [tɛritori'a:l] a territorial.

Territorium [tɛri'to:riʊm] nt territory.

Terror ['tɛrɔr] m -s terror; reign of terror; **t~isieren** [tɛrori'zi:rən] vt terrorize; ~**ismus** [-'rɪsmʊs] m terrorism; ~**ist** [-'rɪst] *m* terrorist.

Terz [tɛrts] *f* -, -en (*MUS*) third; ~**ett** [tɛr'tsɛt] *nt* -(e)s, -e trio.

Tesafilm ® ['te:zafɪlm] *m* sellotape (*Brit*), Scotch tape ® (*US*).

Test [tɛst] *m* -s, -s test.

Testament [tɛsta'mɛnt] *nt* will, testament; (*REL*) Testament; **t~arisch** [-'ta:rɪʃ] *a* testamentary; **Testamentsvollstrecker** *m* executor (of a will).

Testbild *nt* (*TV*) test card.

testen *vt* test.

Tetanus ['te:tanʊs] *m* - tetanus; ~**impfung** *f* (anti-)tetanus injection.

teuer ['tɔyər] *a* dear, expensive; **T~ung** *f* increase in prices; **T~ungszulage** *f* cost of living bonus.

Teufel ['tɔyfəl] *m* -s, - devil.

teuflisch ['tɔyflɪʃ] *a* fiendish, diabolical.

Text [tɛkst] *m* -(e)s, -e text; (*Lieder~*) words *pl*; **t~en** *vi* write the words.

textil [tɛks'ti:l] *a* textile; **T~ien** *pl* textiles *pl*; **T~industrie** *f* textile industry; **T~waren** *pl* textiles *pl*.

Theater [te'a:tər] *nt* -s, - theatre; (*umg*) fuss; ~ **spielen** (*lit, fig*) play-act; ~**besucher** *m* playgoer; ~**kasse** *f* box office; ~**stück** *nt* (stage-)play.

Theke ['te:kə] *f* -, -n (*Schanktisch*) bar; (*Ladentisch*) counter.

Thema ['te:ma] *nt* -s, **Themen** *od* -**ta** theme, topic, subject.

Themse ['tɛmzə] *f* Thames.

Theo- [teo] *zW:* ~**loge** [-'lo:gə] *m* -**n**, -**n** theologian; ~**logie** [-lo'gi:] *f* theology; **t~logisch** [-'lo:gɪʃ] *a* theological; ~**retiker** [-'re:tikər] *m* -s, - theorist; **t~retisch** [-'re:tɪʃ] *a* theoretical; ~**rie** [-'ri:] *f* theory.

Thera- [tera] *zW:* ~**peut** [-'pɔyt] *m* -**en**, -**en** therapist; **t~peutisch** [-'pɔytɪʃ] *a* therapeutic; ~**pie** [-'pi:] *f* therapy.

Therm- *zW:* ~**albad** [tɛrm'a:lba:t] *nt* thermal bath; thermal spa; ~**odrucker** ['tɛrmo-] *m* thermal printer; ~**ometer** [tɛrmo'me:tər] *nt* -s, - thermometer; ~**osflasche** ['tɛrmɔsflaʃə] *f* Thermos ® flask; ~**ostat** [tɛrmo'sta:t] *m* -(e)s *od* -en, -e(n) thermostat.

These ['te:zə] *f* -, -n thesis.

Thrombose [trɔm'bo:zə] *f* -, -n thrombosis.

Thron [tro:n] *m* -(e)s, -e throne; ~**folge** *f* succession (to the throne).

Thunfisch ['tu:nfɪʃ] *m* tuna.

Thymian ['ty:mia:n] *m* -s, -e thyme.

Tick [tɪk] *m* -(e)s, -s tic; (*Eigenart*) quirk; (*Fimmel*) craze; **t~en** *vi* tick.

tief [ti:f] *a* deep; (*tiefsinnig*) profound; (*Ausschnitt, Preis, Ton*) low; **T~** *nt* -s, -s (*MET*) depression; **T~druck** *m*

low pressure; **T~e** *f* -, -n depth; **T~ebene** *f* plain; **Tiefenpsychologie** *f* depth psychology; **Tiefenschärfe** (*PHOT*) depth of focus; **T~garage** *f* underground garage; ~**gekühlt** *a* frozen; ~**greifend** *a* far-reaching; **T~kühlfach** *nt* deep-freeze compartment; **T~kühltruhe** *f* deep-freeze, freezer; **T~land** *nt* lowlands *pl*; **T~punkt** *m* low point; (*fig*) low ebb; **T~schlag** *m* (*Boxen, fig*) blow below the belt; ~**schürfend** *a* profound; **T~see** *f* deep sea; ~**sinnig** *a* profound; melancholy; **T~stand** *m* low level; **Tiefstwert** *m* minimum *od* lowest value.

Tier [ti:r] *nt* -(e)s, -e animal; ~**arzt** *m* vet(erinary surgeon); ~**garten** *m* zoo(logical gardens *pl*); **t~isch** *a* animal; (*lit, fig*) brutish; (*fig: Ernst etc*) deadly; ~**kreis** *m* zodiac; ~**kunde** *f* zoology; **t~liebend** *a* fond of animals; ~**quälerei** [-kvɛ:lə'raɪ] *f* cruelty to animals; ~**schutzverein** *m* society for the prevention of cruelty to animals.

Tiger ['ti:gər] *m* -s, - tiger; ~**in** *f* tigress.

tilgen ['tɪlgən] *vt* erase; (*Sünden*) expiate; (*Schulden*) pay off.

Tinte ['tɪntə] *f* -, -n ink.

Tinten- *zW:* ~**fisch** *m* cuttlefish; ~**stift** *m* copying *od* indelible pencil.

Tip [tɪp] *m* tip; **tippen** *vti* tap, touch; (*umg: schreiben*) type; (*umg: raten*) tip (*auf jdn* sb); (*im Lotto etc*) bet (on).

Tipp- [tɪp] *zW:* ~**fehler** *m* (*umg*) typing error; **t~topp** *a* (*umg*) tip-top; ~**zettel** *m* (pools) coupon.

Tirol [ti'ro:l] *nt* the Tyrol; ~**er(in** *f*) *m* Tyrolean; **t~isch** *a* Tyrolean.

Tisch [tɪʃ] *m* -(e)s, -e table; **bei ~** at table; **vor/nach ~** before/after eating; **unter den ~ fallen** (*fig*) be dropped; ~**decke** *f* tablecloth; ~**ler** *m* -s, - carpenter, joiner; ~**le'rei** *f* joiner's workshop; (*Arbeit*) carpentry, joinery; **t~lern** *vi* do carpentry *etc*; ~**rede** *f* after-dinner speech; ~**tennis** *nt* table tennis.

Titel ['ti:təl] *m* -s, - title; ~**anwärter** *m* (*SPORT*) challenger; ~**bild** *nt* cover (picture); (*von Buch*) frontispiece; ~**geschichte** *f* main story; ~**rolle** *f* title role; ~**seite** *f* cover; (*Buch~*) title page; ~**verteidiger** *m* defending champion, title holder.

Toast [to:st] *m* -(e)s, -s *od* -e toast; ~**er** *m* -s, - toaster.

tob- [to:b] *zW:* ~**en** *vi* rage; (*Kinder*) romp about; **T~sucht** *f* raving madness; ~**süchtig** *a* maniacal.

Tochter ['tɔxtər] *f* -, - daughter; ~**gesellschaft** *f* subsidiary (company).

Tod [to:t] *m* **-(e)s, -e** death; **t~ernst** *a* deadly serious // *ad* in dead earnest.

Todes- ['to:dəs] *zW:* **~angst** [-aŋst] *f* mortal fear; **~anzeige** *f* obituary (notice); **~fall** *m* death; **~strafe** *f* death penalty; **~ursache** *f* cause of death; **~urteil** *nt* death sentence; **~verachtung** *f* utter disgust.

todkrank *a* dangerously ill.

tödlich ['tø:tlıç] *a* deadly, fatal.

tod- *zW:* **~müde** *a* dead tired; **~schick** *a* (*umg*) smart, classy; **~sicher** *a* (*umg*) absolutely *od* dead certain; **T~sünde** *f* deadly sin.

Toilette [toa'lɛtə] *f* toilet, lavatory; (*Frisiertisch*) dressing table; (*Kleidung*) outfit.

Toiletten- *zW:* **~artikel** *pl* toiletries *pl*, toilet articles *pl*; **~papier** *nt* toilet paper; **~tisch** *m* dressing table.

toi, toi, toi ['tɔy, 'tɔy, 'tɔy] *interj* touch wood.

tolerant [tole'rant] *a* tolerant.

Toleranz [tole'rants] *f* tolerance.

tolerieren [tole'ri:rən] *vt* tolerate.

toll [tɔl] *a* mad; (*Treiben*) wild; (*umg*) terrific; **~en** *vi* romp; **T~kirsche** *f* deadly nightshade; **~kühn** *a* daring; **T~wut** *f* rabies.

Tomate [to'ma:tə] *f* **-, -n** tomato; **Tomatenmark** *nt* tomato puree.

Ton [to:n] *m* **-(e)s, -e** (*Erde*) clay // *pl* **-e** (*Laut*) sound; (*MUS*) note; (*Redeweise*) tone; (*Farb~, Nuance*) shade; (*Betonung*) stress; **~abnehmer** *m* pick-up; **t~angebend** *a* leading; **~art** *f* (*musical*) key; **~band** *nt* tape; **~bandgerät** *nt* tape recorder.

tönen ['tø:nən] *vi* sound // *vt* shade; (*Haare*) tint.

tönern ['tø:nərn] *a* clay.

Ton- *zW:* **~fall** *m* intonation; **~film** *m* sound film; **~leiter** *f* (*MUS*) scale; **t~los** *a* soundless.

Tonne ['tɔnə] *f* **-, -n** barrel; (*Maß*) ton.

Ton- *zW:* **~spur** *f* soundtrack; **~taube** *f* clay pigeon; **~waren** *pl* pottery, earthenware.

Topf [tɔpf] *m* **-(e)s, -̈e** pot; **~blume** *f* pot plant.

Töpfer ['tœpfər] *m* **-s, -** potter; **~ei** [-'raɪ] *f* piece of pottery; potter's workshop; **~scheibe** *f* potter's wheel.

topographisch [topo'gra:fɪʃ] *a* topographic.

Tor [to:r] *m* **-en, -en** fool // *nt* **-(e)s, -e** gate; (*SPORT*) goal; **~bogen** *m* archway.

Torf [tɔrf] *m* **-(e)s** peat.

Tor- *zW:* **~heit** *f* foolishness; foolish deed; **~hüter** *m* **-s, -** goalkeeper.

töricht ['tø:rɪçt] *a* foolish.

torkeln ['tɔrkəln] *vi* stagger, reel.

Torpedo [tɔr'pe:do] *m* **-s, -s** torpedo.

Torte ['tɔrtə] *f* **-, -n** cake; (*Obst~*) flan, tart.

Tortur [tɔr'tu:r] *f* ordeal.

Torwart *m* **-(e)s, -e** goalkeeper.

tosen ['to:zən] *vi* roar.

tot [to:t] *a* dead.

total [to'ta:l] *a* total; **~itär** [totali'tɛ:r] *a* totalitarian; **T~schaden** *m* (*AUT*) complete write-off.

töten ['tø:tən] *vti* kill.

Toten- ['to:tən] *zW:* **~bett** *nt* death bed; **t~blaß** *a* deathly pale, white as a sheet; **~kopf** *m* skull; **~schein** *m* death certificate; **~stille** *f* deathly silence.

Tot- *zW:* **~e(r)** *mf* dead person; **t~fahren** *vt unreg* run over; **t~geboren** *a* stillborn; **t~lachen** *vr* (*umg*) laugh one's head off.

Toto ['to:to] *m od nt* **-s, -s** pools *pl*; **~schein** *m* pools coupon.

tot- *zW:* **~sagen** *vt:* jdn **~sagen** say that sb is dead; **T~schlag** *m* manslaughter; **~schlagen** *vt unreg* (*lit, fig*) kill; **~schweigen** *vt unreg* hush up; **~stellen** *vr* pretend to be dead.

Tötung ['tø:tuŋ] *f* killing.

Toupet [tu'pe:] *nt* **-s, -s** toupee.

toupieren [tu'pi:rən] *vt* back-comb.

Tour [tu:r] *f* **-, -en** tour, trip; (*Umdrehung*) revolution; (*Verhaltensart*) way; **in einer ~** incessantly; **Tourenzähler** *m* rev counter; **~ismus** [tu'rɪsmʊs] *m* tourism; **~ist** [tu'rɪst] *m* tourist; **~istenklasse** *f* tourist class; **Tournee** [tʊr'ne:] *f* **-, -n** (*THEAT etc*) tour; **auf Tournee gehen** go on tour.

Trab [tra:p] *m* **-(e)s** trot; **~ant** [tra'bant] *m* satellite; **~antenstadt** *f* satellite town; **t~en** *vi* trot.

Tracht [traxt] *f* **-, -en** (*Kleidung*) costume, dress; **eine ~ Prügel** a sound thrashing; **t~en** *vi* strive (*nach for*), endeavour; **jdm nach dem Leben t~en** seek to kill sb.

trächtig ['trɛçtɪç] *a* (*Tier*) pregnant.

Tradition [traditsi'o:n] *f* tradition; **t~ell** [-'nɛl] *a* traditional.

traf *etc v siehe* **treffen**.

Trag- ['tra:g] *zW:* **~bahre** *f* stretcher; **t~bar** *a* (*Gerät*) portable; (*Kleidung*) wearable; (*erträglich*) bearable.

träge ['trɛːgə] *a* sluggish, slow; (*PHYS*) inert.

tragen ['tra:gən] *unreg vt* carry; (*Kleidung, Brille*) wear; (*Namen, Früchte*) bear; (*erdulden*) endure; **sich mit einem Gedanken ~** have an idea in mind // *vi* (*schwanger sein*) be pregnant; (*Eis*) hold; **zum T~ kommen** have an effect.

Träger ['trɛːgər] *m* **-s, -** carrier; wearer; bearer; (*Ordens~*) holder; (*an*

Kleidung) (shoulder) strap; (*Körperschaft etc*) sponsor; **~rakete** *f* launch vehicle; **~rock** *m* skirt with shoulder straps.

Trag- ['tra:k] *zW:* **~fläche** *f* (AVIAT) wing; **~flügelboot** *nt* hydrofoil.

Trägheit ['trɛːkhaɪt] *f* laziness; (PHYS) inertia.

Tragik ['tra:gɪk] *f* tragedy.

tragisch ['tra:gɪʃ] *a* tragic.

Tragödie [tra'gøːdiə] *f* tragedy.

Tragweite *f* range; (*fig*) scope.

Train- [trɛːn] *zW:* **~er** *m* -s, - (SPORT) trainer, coach; (*Fußball*) manager; **t~ieren** [trɛ'niːrən] *vti* train; (*Mensch auch*) coach; (*Übung*) practise; **~ing** *nt* -s, -s training; **~ingsanzug** *m* track suit.

Traktor ['traktɔr] *m* -s, -en tractor; (*von Drucker*) tractor feed.

trällern ['trɛlərn] *vti* trill, sing.

trampeln ['trampəln] *vti* trample, stamp.

trampen ['trɛmpən] *vi* hitch-hike.

Tran [tra:n] *m* -(e)s, -e train oil, blubber.

Tranchierbesteck [trã'ʃiːrbəʃtɛk] *nt* (pair of) carvers.

tranchieren [trã'ʃiːrən] *vt* carve.

Träne ['trɛːnə] *f* -, -n tear; **t~n** *vi* water; **Tränengas** *nt* teargas.

trank *etc v siehe* **trinken.**

tränken ['trɛŋkən] *vt* (*Tiere*) water.

Trans- *zW:* **~formator** [transfɔr'ma:tɔr] *m* transformer; **~istor** [tran'zistɔr] *m* transistor; **t~itiv** ['tranzitiːf] *a* transitive; **Transitverkehr** *m* transit traffic; **Transitvisum** *nt* transit visa; **t~parent** [transpa'rɛnt] *a* transparent; **~parent** *nt* -(e)s, -e (*Bild*) transparency; (*Spruchband*) banner; **t~pirieren** [transpi'riːrən] *vi* perspire; **~plantation** [transplantatsi'oːn] *f* transplantation; (*Haut~plantation*) graft(ing).

Transport [trans'pɔrt] *m* -(e)s, -e transport; **t~ieren** [transpɔr'tiːrən] *vt* transport; **~kosten** *pl* transport charges *pl*, carriage; **~mittel** *nt* means of transportation; **~unternehmen** *nt* carrier.

Trapez [tra'pe:ts] *nt* -es, -e trapeze; (MATH) trapezium.

Traube ['traubə] *f* -, -n grape; bunch (of grapes); **Traubenzucker** *m* glucose.

trauen ['trauən] *vi:* jdm/etw ~ trust sb/sth // *vr* dare // *vt* marry.

Trauer ['trauər] *f* - sorrow; (*für Verstorbenen*) mourning; **~fall** *m* death, bereavement; **~kleidung** *f* mourning; **t~n** *vi* mourn (*um* for); **~rand** *m* black border; **~spiel** *nt* tragedy.

traulich ['traulɪç] *a* cosy, intimate.

Traum [traum] *m* -(e)s, **Träume** dream; **Trauma** *nt* -s, -men trauma.

träum- ['trɔym] *zW:* **~en** *vti* dream; **T~er** *m* -s, - dreamer; **T~e'rei** *f* dreaming; **~erisch** *a* dreamy.

traumhaft *a* dreamlike; (*fig*) wonderful.

traurig ['trauriç] *a* sad; **T~keit** *f* sadness.

Trau- ['trau] *zW:* **~ring** *m* wedding ring; **~schein** *m* marriage certificate; **~ung** *f* wedding ceremony; **~zeuge** *m* witness (to a marriage).

treffen ['trɛfən] *unreg vti* strike, hit; (*Bemerkung*) hurt; (*begegnen*) meet; (*Entscheidung etc*) make; (*Maßnahmen*) take; er hat es gut getroffen he did well; ~ auf (+*akk*) come across, meet with // *vr* meet; es traf sich, daß... so it so happened that...; es trifft sich gut it's convenient; wie es so trifft as these things happen; **T~** *nt* -s, - meeting; **~d** *a* pertinent, apposite.

Treffer *m* -s, - hit; (*Tor*) goal; (*Los*) winner.

Treffpunkt *m* meeting place.

Treib- ['traɪp] *zW:* **~eis** *nt* drift ice; **t~en** *unreg vt* drive; (*Studien etc*) pursue; (*Sport*) do, go in for; Unsinn **t~en** fool around // *vi* (*Schiff etc*) drift; (*Pflanzen*) sprout; (KOCH: *aufgehen*) rise; (*Tee, Kaffee*) be diuretic; **~haus** *nt* greenhouse; **~stoff** *m* fuel.

Trend [trɛnt] *m* -s, -s trend; **~wende** *f* trend away (from sth).

trenn- ['trɛn] *zW:* **~bar** *a* separable; **~en** *vt* separate; (*teilen*) divide // *vr* separate; sich **~en** von part with; **T~schärfe** *f* (RAD) selectivity; **T~ung** *f* separation; **T~wand** *f* partition (wall).

Trepp- [trɛp] *zW:* **t~ab** *ad* downstairs; **t~auf** *ad* upstairs; **~e** *f* -, -n stair(case); **Treppengeländer** *nt* banister; **Treppenhaus** *nt* staircase.

Tresor [tre'zo:r] *m* -s, -e safe.

treten ['tre:tən] *unreg vi* step; (*Tränen, Schweiß*) appear; ~ nach kick at; ~ in (+*akk*) step in(to); in Verbindung ~ get in contact; in Erscheinung ~ appear // *vt* (*mit Fußtritt*) kick; (*nieder~*) tread, trample.

treu [trɔy] *a* faithful, true; **T~e** *f* - loyalty, faithfulness; **T~händer** *m* -s, - trustee; **T~handgesellschaft** *f* trust company; **~herzig** *a* innocent; **~los** *a* faithless.

Tribüne [tri'byːnə] *f* -, -n grandstand; (*Redner~*) platform.

Trichter ['trɪçtər] *m* -s, - funnel; (*in Boden*) crater.

Trick [trɪk] *m* -s, -e *od* -s trick; **~film**

m cartoon.

trieb *etc v siehe* **trieben.**

Trieb [tri:p] *m* **-(e)s, -e** urge, drive; (*Neigung*) inclination; (*an Baum etc*) shoot; **~feder** *f* (*fig*) motivating force; **~kraft** *f* (*fig*) drive; **~täter** *m* sex offender; **~werk** *nt* engine.

triefen ['tri:fən] *vi* drip.

triffst *etc v siehe* **treffen.**

triftig ['trɪftɪç] *a* good, convincing.

Trikot [tri'ko:] *nt* **-s, -s** vest; (*SPORT*) shirt.

Trimester [tri'mɛstər] *nt* **-s, -** term.

trimmen ['trɪmən] *vr* do keep fit exercises.

trink- ['trɪŋk] *zW:* **~bar** *a* drinkable; **~en** *vti unreg* drink; **T~er** *m* **-s, -** drinker; **T~geld** *nt* tip; **T~spruch** *m* toast; **T~wasser** *nt* drinking water.

Tripper ['trɪpər] *m* **-s, -** gonorrhoea.

Tritt [trɪt] *m* **-(e)s, -e** step; (*Fuß~*) kick; **~brett** *nt* (*EISENB*) step; (*AUT*) running-board.

Triumph [tri'ʊmf] *m* **-(e)s, -e** triumph; **~bogen** *m* triumphal arch; **t~ieren** [-'fi:rən] *vi* triumph; (*jubeln*) exult.

trocken ['trɔkən] *a* dry; **T~element** *nt* dry cell; **T~haube** *f* hair-dryer; **T~heit** *f* dryness; **~legen** *vt* (*Sumpf*) drain; (*Kind*) put a clean nappy on; **T~milch** *f* dried milk.

trocknen ['trɔknən] *vti* dry.

Trödel ['trø:dəl] *m* **-s** (*umg*) junk; **~markt** *m* flea market; **t~n** *vi* (*umg*) dawdle.

Trog [tro:k] *m* **-(e)s, ⁻e** trough.

Trommel ['trɔməl] *f* **-, -n** drum; **~fell** *nt* eardrum; **t~n** *vti* drum.

Trommler ['trɔmlər] *m* **-s, -** drummer.

Trompete [trɔm'pe:tə] *f* **-, -n** trumpet; **~r** *m* **-s, -** trumpeter.

Tropen ['tro:pən] *pl* tropics *pl*; **~helm** *m* sun helmet.

tröpfeln ['trœpfəln] *vi* drop, trickle.

Tropfen ['trɔpfən] *m* **-s, -** drop; **t~** *vti* drip // *v unpers*: es tropft a few raindrops are falling; **t~weise** *ad* in drops.

Tropfsteinhöhle *f* stalactite cave.

tropisch ['tro:pɪʃ] *a* tropical.

Trost [tro:st] *m* **-es** consolation, comfort; **t~bedürftig** *a* in need of consolation.

tröst- ['trø:st] *zW:* **~en** *vt* console, comfort; **T~er(in** *f*) *m* **-s, -** comfort(er); **~lich** *a* comforting.

trost- *zW:* **~los** *a* bleak; (*Verhältnisse*) wretched; **T~preis** *m* consolation prize; **~reich** *a* comforting.

Trott [trɔt] *m* **-(e)s, -e** trot; (*Routine*) routine; **Trottel** *m* **-s, -** (*umg*) fool, dope; **t~en** *vi* trot; **Trottoir** [trɔto'a:r] *nt* **-s, -s** *od* **-e** pavement, sidewalk (*US*).

Trotz [trɔts] *m* **-es** pigheadedness; etw aus ~ tun do sth just to show them; jdm zum ~ in defiance of sb; **t~** *präp* +*gen od dat* in spite of; **t~dem** *ad* nevertheless, all the same // *kj* although; **t~ig** *a* defiant, pig-headed; **~kopf** *m* obstinate child; **~reaktion** *f* fit of pique.

trüb [try:p] *a* dull; (*Flüssigkeit, Glas*) cloudy; (*fig*) gloomy.

Trubel ['tru:bəl] *m* **-s, -** hurly-burly.

trüb- *zW:* **~en** ['try:bən] *vt* cloud // *vr* become clouded; **T~heit** *f* dullness; cloudiness; gloom; **T~sal** *f* **-, -e** distress; **~selig** *a* sad, melancholy; **T~sinn** *m* depression; **~sinnig** *a* depressed, gloomy.

Trüffel ['tryfəl] *f* **-, -n** truffle.

trug *etc v siehe* **tragen.**

trüg- ['try:g] *zW:* **~en** *unreg vt* deceive // *vi* be deceptive; **~erisch** *a* deceptive.

Trugschluß ['tru:gʃlʊs] *m* false conclusion.

Truhe ['tru:ə] *f* **-, -n** chest.

Trümmer ['trymər] *pl* wreckage; (*Bau~*) ruins *pl*; **~haufen** *m* heap of rubble.

Trumpf [trʊmpf] *m* **-(e)s, ⁻e** (*lit, fig*) trump; **t~en** *vti* trump.

Trunk [trʊŋk] *m* **-(e)s, ⁻e** drink; **t~en** *a* intoxicated; **~enheit** *f* intoxication; **~enheit am Steuer** drunken driving; **~sucht** *f* alcoholism.

Trupp [trʊp] *m* **-s, -s** troop; **~e** *f* **-, -n** troop; (*Waffengattung*) force; (*Schauspiel~*) troupe; **~en** *pl* troops *pl*; **~enübungsplatz** *m* training area.

Truthahn ['tru:tha:n] *m* turkey.

Tschech- [tʃɛç] *zW:* **~e** *m*, **~in** *f*, **~oslowake** [-oslo'va:kə] *m*, **~oslowakin** *f* Czech, Czechoslovak(ian); **t~isch**, **t~oslowakisch** [-oslo'va:kɪʃ] *a* Czech, Czechoslovak(ian).

tschüs [tʃy:s] *interj* cheerio.

T-Shirt ['ti:ʃœrt] *nt* T-shirt.

Tube ['tu:bə] *f* **-, -n** tube.

Tuberkulose [tuberku'lo:zə] *f* **-, -n** tuberculosis.

Tuch [tu:x] *nt* **-(e)s, ⁻er** cloth; (*Hals~*) scarf; (*Kopf~*) headscarf; (*Hand~*) towel.

tüchtig ['tʏçtɪç] *a* efficient, (cap)able; (*umg: kräftig*) good, sound; **T~keit** *f* efficiency, ability.

Tücke ['tʏkə] *f* **-, -n** (*Arglist*) malice; (*Trick*) trick; (*Schwierigkeit*) difficulty, problem; seine ~n haben be temperamental.

tückisch ['tʏkɪʃ] *a* treacherous; (*böswillig*) malicious.

Tugend ['tu:gənt] *f* **-, -en** virtue; **t~haft** *a* virtuous.

Tüll [tʏl] *m* **-s, -e** tulle; **~e** *f* **-, -n**

spout.

Tulpe ['tʊlpə] *f* -, -n tulip.

Tumor ['tuːmɔr] *m* -s, -e tumour.

Tümpel ['tʏmpəl] *m* -s, - pool, pond.

Tumult [tu'mʊlt] *m* -(e)s, -e tumult.

tun [tuːn] *unreg vt (machen)* do; *(legen)* put; jdm etw ~ *(antun)* do sth to sb; etw tut es auch sth will do; das tut nichts that doesn't matter; das tut nichts zur Sache that's neither here nor there // *vi* act; so ~, als ob act as if // *vr*: es tut sich etwas/viel something/a lot is happening.

tünchen ['tʏnçən] *vt* whitewash.

Tunesien [tu'neːziən] *nt* Tunisia.

Tunke ['tʊŋkə] *f* -, -n sauce; **t~n** *vt* dip, dunk.

tunlichst ['tuːnlɪçst] *ad* if at all possible; ~ bald as soon as possible.

Tunnel ['tʊnəl] *m* -s, -s *od* - tunnel.

tupfen ['tʊpfən] *vti* dab; *(mit Farbe)* dot; **T~** *m* -s, - dot, spot.

Tür [tyːr] *f* -, -en door.

Turban ['tʊrban] *m* -s, -e turban.

Turbine [tʊr'biːnə] *f* turbine.

Türk- [tʏrk] *zW*: **~e** *m* Turk; **~ei** [tʏr'kaɪ] *f*: die ~ei Turkey.

Türkis [tʏr'kiːs] *m* -es, -e turquoise; **t~** *a* turquoise.

türkisch ['tʏrkɪʃ] *a* Turkish.

Turm [tʊrm] *m* -(e)s, ̈-e tower; *(Kirch~)* steeple; *(Sprung~)* diving platform; *(SCHACH)* castle, rook.

türmen ['tʏrmən] *vr* tower up // *vt* heap up // *vi (umg)* scarper, bolt.

Turn- ['tʊrn] *zW*: **t~en** *vi* do gymnastic exercises // *vt* perform; **~en** *nt* -s gymnastics; *(SCH)* physical education, P.E.; **~er(in *f*)** *m* -s, - gymnast; **~halle** *f* gym(nasium); **~hose** *f* gym shorts *pl*.

Turnier [tʊr'niːr] *nt* -s, -e tournament.

Turn- *zW*: **~verein** *m* gymnastics club; **~schuh** *m* gym shoe; **~zeug** *nt* gym things *pl*.

Tusche ['tʊʃə] *f* -, -n Indian ink.

tuscheln ['tʊʃəln] *vti* whisper.

Tuschkasten *m* paintbox.

Tüte ['tyːtə] *f* -, -n bag.

tuten ['tuːtən] *vi (AUT)* hoot *(Brit)*, honk *(US)*.

TÜV [tʏf] *m abk* (= Technischer Überwachungsverein) MOT.

Typ [tyːp] *m* -s, -en type; **~e** *f* -, -n *(TYP)* type; **Typenraddrucker** *m* daisy-wheel printer.

Typhus ['tyːfʊs] *m* - typhoid (fever).

typisch ['tyːpɪʃ] *a* typical *(für* of*)*.

Tyrann [ty'ran] *m* -en, -en tyrant; **~ei** [-'naɪ] *f* tyranny; **t~isch** *a* tyrannical; **t~i'sieren** *vt* tyrannize.

U

U, u [uː] *nt* U, u.

u. *abk von* und.

u.a. *abk von* unter anderem.

U-Bahn ['uːbaːn] *f* underground, tube.

übel ['yːbəl] *a* bad; *(moralisch auch)* wicked; jdm ist ~ sb feels sick; **Ü~nt** -s, - evil; *(Krankheit)* disease; **~gelaunt** *a* bad-tempered; **Ü~keit** *f* nausea; **~nehmen** *vt unreg*: jdm eine Bemerkung etc **~nehmen** be offended at sb's remark *etc*.

üben ['yːbən] *vti* exercise, practise.

über ['yːbər] ♦*präp* +dat **1** *(räumlich)* over, above; zwei Grad ~ Null two degrees above zero.

2 *(zeitlich)* over; ~ der Arbeit einschlafen fall asleep over one's work ♦*präp* +akk **1** *(räumlich)* over; *(hoch ~ auch)* above; *(quer ~ auch)* across.

2 *(zeitlich)* over; ~ Weihnachten over Christmas; ~ kurz oder lang sooner or later

3 *(mit Zahlen)*: Kinder ~ 12 Jahren children over *od* above 12 years of age; ein Scheck ~ 200 Mark a cheque for 200 marks

4 *(auf dem Wege)* via; nach Köln ~ Aachen to Cologne via Aachen; ich habe es ~ die Auskunft erfahren I found out from information

5 *(betreffend)* about; ein Buch ~ ... a book about *od* on ...; ~ jdn/etw lachen laugh about *od* at sb/sth

6: Macht ~ jdn haben have power over sb; sie liebt ihn ~ alles she loves him more than everything ♦*ad* over; ~ und ~ over and over; den ganzen Tag ~ all day long; jdm in etw *(dat)* ~ sein be superior to sb in sth.

überall [yːbər''al] *ad* everywhere; **~'hin** *ad* everywhere.

überanstrengen [yːbər''anʃtrɛŋən] *vtr insep* overexert (o.s.).

überarbeiten [yːbər''arbaɪtən] *vt insep* revise, rework // *vr* overwork (o.s.).

überaus ['yːbər'aus] *ad* exceedingly.

überbelichten ['yːbərbəlɪçtən] *vt (PHOT)* overexpose.

über'bieten *vt unreg insep* outbid; *(übertreffen)* surpass; *(Rekord)* break.

Überbleibsel ['yːbərblaɪpsəl] *nt* -s, - residue, remainder.

Überblick ['yːbərblɪk] *m* view; *(fig: Darstellung)* survey, overview; *(Fähigkeit)* overall view, grasp *(über* +akk of*)*; **ü~en** [-'blɪkən] *vt insep* survey.

überbring- [yːbər'brɪŋ] *zW*: **~en**

überbrücken *vt unreg insep* deliver, hand over; **Ü~er** *m* **-s, -** bearer; **Ü~ung** *f* delivery.

überbrücken [y:bər'brʏkən] *vt insep* bridge (over).

über'dauern *vt insep* outlast.

über'denken *vt unreg insep* think over.

überdies [y:bər'di:s] *ad* besides.

überdimensional ['y:bərdimenziona:l] *a* oversize.

Überdruß ['y:bərdrus] *m* **-sses** weariness; **bis zum ~** *ad* nauseam.

überdrüssig ['y:bərdrʏsiç] *a* tired, sick (*gen* of).

übereifrig ['y:bəraifriç] *a* overkeen.

übereilt [y:bər''ailt] *a* (over)hasty, premature.

überein- [y:bər''ain] *zW*: **~ander** [y:bər'ai'nandər] *ad* one upon the other; (*sprechen*) about each other; **~kommen** *vi unreg* agree; **Ü~kunft** *f* **-, -künfte** agreement; **~stimmen** *vi* agree; **Ü~stimmung** *f* agreement.

überempfindlich ['y:bərempfintliç] *a* hypersensitive.

überfahren [y:bər'fa:rən] *vt unreg insep* (AUT) run over; (*fig*) walk all over.

Überfahrt ['y:bərfa:rt] *f* crossing.

Überfall ['y:bərfal] *m* (Bank~, MIL) raid; (*auf jdn*) assault; **ü~en** [-'falən] *vt unreg insep* attack; (*Bank*) raid; (*besuchen*) surprise.

überfällig ['y:bərfeliç] *a* overdue.

über'fliegen *vt unreg insep* fly over, overfly; (*Buch*) skim through.

Überfluß ['y:bərflus] *m* (super)-abundance, excess (*an* +dat of).

überflüssig ['y:bərflʏsiç] *a* superfluous.

über'fordern *vt insep* demand too much of; (*Kräfte etc*) overtax.

über'führen *vt insep* (Leiche etc) transport; (*Täter*) have convicted (*gen* of).

Über'führung *f* transport; conviction; (*Brücke*) bridge, overpass.

Übergabe ['y:bərga:bə] *f* handing over; (MIL) surrender.

Übergang ['y:bərgaŋ] *m* crossing; (Wandel, Überleitung) transition.

Übergangs- *zW*: **~erscheinung** *f* transitory phenomenon; **~lösung** *f* provisional solution, stopgap; **~stadium** *ni* transitional stage; **~zeit** *f* transitional period.

über'geben *unreg insep vt* hand over; (MIL) surrender; **dem Verkehr ~** open to traffic // *vr* be sick.

übergehen ['y:bərge:ən] *unreg vi* (Besitz) pass; (zum Feind etc) go over, defect; (*überleiten*) go on (zu to); (*sich verwandeln*) turn (in +akk into) // [-'ge:ən] *vt insep* pass over, omit.

Übergewicht ['y:bərgəviçt] *nt* excess weight; (*fig*) preponderance.

überglücklich ['y:bərglʏkliç] *a* overjoyed.

übergroß ['y:bərgro:s] *a* outsize, huge.

überhandnehmen [y:bər'hantne:mən] *vi unreg* gain the ascendancy.

überhaupt [y:bər'haupt] *ad* at all; (*im allgemeinen*) in general; (*besonders*) especially; **~ nicht/keine** not/none at all.

überheblich [y:bər'he:pliç] *a* arrogant; **Ü~keit** *f* arrogance.

über'holen *vt insep* overtake; (TECH) overhaul.

überholt *a* out-of-date, obsolete.

über'hören *vt insep* not hear; (*absichtlich*) ignore.

überirdisch ['y:bər'irdiʃ] *a* supernatural, unearthly.

über'laden *vt unreg insep* overload // *a* (*fig*) cluttered.

über'lassen *unreg insep vt*: **jdm etw ~** leave sth to sb // *vr*: **sich etw** (*dat*) **~** give o.s. over to sth.

über'lasten *vt insep* overload; (*Mensch*) overtax.

überlaufen ['y:bərlaufən] *unreg vi* (*Flüssigkeit*) flow over; (*zum Feind etc*) go over, defect // [-'laufən] *vt insep* (Schauer etc) come over; **~ sein** be inundated *od* besieged.

Überläufer ['y:bərloyfər] *m* deserter.

über'leben *vt insep* survive; **Ü~de(r)** *mf* survivor.

über'legen *vt insep* consider; **ich muß es mir ~** I'll have to think about it // *a* superior; **Ü~heit** *f* superiority.

Überlegung *f* consideration, deliberation.

über'liefern *vt insep* hand down, transmit.

Überlieferung *f* tradition.

überlisten [y:bər'listən] *vt insep* outwit.

überm ['y:bərm] = **über dem**.

Übermacht ['y:bərmaxt] *f* superior force, superiority.

übermächtig ['y:bərmeçtiç] *a* superior (in strength); (*Gefühl etc*) overwhelming.

übermannen [y:bər'manən] *vt insep* overcome.

Übermaß ['y:bərma:s] *nt* excess (*an* +dat of).

übermäßig ['y:bərme:siç] *a* excessive.

Übermensch ['y:bərmenʃ] *m* superman; **ü~lich** *a* superhuman.

übermitteln [y:bər'mitəln] *vt insep* convey.

übermorgen ['y:bərmorgən] *ad* the day after tomorrow.

Übermüdung [y:bər'my:duŋ] *f* fatigue, overtiredness.

Übermut ['y:bərmu:t] *m* exuberance.

übermütig ['y:bərmy:tıç] *a* exuberant, high-spirited; ~ **werden** get overconfident.

übernachten [y:bər'naxtən] *vi insep* spend the night (*bei jdm* at sb's place).

Übernachtung [y:bər'naxtʊŋ] *f* overnight stay.

Übernahme ['y:bərna:mə] *f* -, -**n** taking over *od* on, acceptance.

über'nehmen *unreg insep vt* take on, accept; (*Amt, Geschäft*) take over // *vr* take on too much.

über'prüfen *vt insep* examine, check.

Überprüfung *f* examination.

überqueren [y:bər'kve:rən] *vt insep* cross.

überragen [y:bər'ra:gən] *vt insep* tower above; (*fig*) surpass.

überraschen [y:bər'raʃən] *vt insep* surprise.

Überraschung *f* surprise.

überreden [y:bər're:dən] *vt insep* persuade.

überreichen [y:bər'raıçən] *vt insep* present, hand over.

Überreste ['y:bərrɛstə] *pl* remains *pl*, remnants *pl*.

überrumpeln [y:bər'rʊmpəln] *vt insep* take by surprise.

überrunden [y:bər'rʊndən] *vt insep* lap.

übers ['y:bərs] = **über das.**

Überschall- ['y:bərʃal] *zW:* ~**flugzeug** *nt* supersonic jet; ~**geschwindigkeit** *f* supersonic speed.

über'schätzen *vtr insep* overestimate.

Überschlag ['y:bərʃla:k] *m* (*FIN*) estimate; (*SPORT*) somersault; **ü~en** [-'ʃla:gən] *unreg insep vt* (*berechnen*) estimate; (*auslassen: Seite*) omit // *vr* somersault; (*Stimme*) crack; (*AVIAT*) loop the loop // ['y:bərʃla:gən] *unreg vt* (*Beine*) cross // *vi* (*Wellen*) break over; (*Funken*) flash over.

überschnappen ['y:bərʃnapən] *vi* (*Stimme*) crack; (*umg: Mensch*) flip one's lid.

über'schneiden *vr unreg insep* (*lit, fig*) overlap; (*Linien*) intersect.

über'schreiben *vt unreg insep* provide with a heading; **jdm etw** ~ transfer *od* make over sth to sb.

über'schreiten *vt unreg insep* cross over; (*fig*) exceed; (*verletzen*) transgress.

Überschrift ['y:bərʃrıft] *f* heading, title.

Überschuß ['y:bərʃus] *m* surplus (*an* +*dat* of).

überschüssig ['y:bərʃysıç] *a* surplus, excess.

über'schütten *vt insep:* **jdn/etw mit** etw ~ (*lit*) pour sth over sb/sth; **jdn mit etw** ~ (*fig*) shower sb with sth.

überschwemmen [y:bər'ʃvɛmən] *vt insep* flood.

Überschwemmung *f* flood.

überschwenglich ['y:bərʃvɛŋlıç] *a* effusive.

Übersee ['y:bərze:] *f:* **nach/in** ~ overseas; **ü~isch** *a* overseas.

über'sehen *vt unreg insep* look (out) over; (*fig: Folgen*) see, get an overall view of; (: *nicht beachten*) overlook.

über'senden *vt unreg insep* send, forward.

übersetz- *zW:* ~**en** [y:bər'zɛtsən] *vt insep* translate // ['y:bərzɛtsən] *vi* cross; **Ü~er(in** *f*) [-'zɛtsər(ın)] *m* -**s,** - translator; **Ü~ung** [-zɛtsʊŋ] *f* translation; (*TECH*) gear ratio.

Übersicht ['y:bərzıçt] *f* overall view; (*Darstellung*) survey; **ü~lich** *a* clear; (*Gelände*) open; ~**lichkeit** *f* clarity, lucidity.

übersiedeln ['y:bərzi:dəln] *od* [y:bər'zi:dəln] *vi sep od insep* move.

über'spannen *vt insep* (*zu sehr spannen*) overstretch; (*überdecken*) cover.

über'spannt *a* eccentric; (*Idee*) wild, crazy; **Ü~heit** *f* eccentricity.

überspitzt [y:bər'ʃpıtst] *a* exaggerated.

über'springen *vt unreg insep* jump over; (*fig*) skip.

überstehen [y:bər'ʃte:ən] *unreg vt insep* overcome, get over; (*Winter etc*) survive, get through // ['y:bərʃte:ən] *vi* project.

über'steigen *vt unreg insep* climb over; (*fig*) exceed.

über'stimmen *vt insep* outvote.

Überstunden ['y:bərʃtʊndən] *pl* overtime.

über'stürzen *insep vt* rush // *vr* follow (one another) in rapid succession.

überstürzt *a* (*over*)hasty.

über'tönen *vt insep* drown (out).

Übertrag ['y:bərtra:k] *m* -**(e)s, -träge** (*COMM*) amount brought forward; **ü~bar** [-'tra:kba:r] *a* transferable; (*MED*) infectious; **ü~en** [-'tra:gən] *unreg insep vt* transfer (*auf* +*akk* to); (*RAD*) broadcast; (*übersetzen*) render; (*Krankheit*) transmit; **jdm etw ü~en** assign sth to sb // *vr* spread (*auf* +*akk* to) // *a* figurative; ~**ung** [-'tra:gʊŋ] *f* transfer(ence); (*RAD*) broadcast; rendering; transmission.

über'treffen *vt unreg insep* surpass.

über'treiben *vt unreg insep* exaggerate.

Übertreibung *f* exaggeration.

übertreten [y:bər'tre:tən] *unreg vt*

insep cross; (*Gebot etc*) break //
['y:bərtre:tən] *vi* (*über Linie, Gebiet*)
step (over); (*SPORT*) overstep; (*in
andere Partei*) go over (*in* +*akk* to);
(*zu anderem Glauben*) be converted.

Über'tretung *f* violation, transgression.

übertrieben [y:bər'tri:bən] *a* exaggerated, excessive.

übervölkert [y:bər'fœlkərt] *a* overpopulated.

übervoll ['y:bərfɔl] *a* overfull.

übervorteilen [y:bər'fɔrtailən] *vt insep*
dupe, cheat.

über'wachen *vt insep* supervise;
(*Verdächtigen*) keep under surveillance.

Überwachung *f* supervision; surveillance.

überwältigen [y:bər'vɛltigən] *vt insep*
overpower; **~d** *a* overwhelming.

überweisen [y:bər'vaizən] *vt unreg
insep* transfer.

Überweisung *f* transfer.

über'wiegen *vi unreg insep* predominate; **~d** *a* predominant.

über'winden *unreg insep vt* overcome // (*vr*) make an effort, bring oneself (*to* do sth).

Überwindung *f* effort, strength of
mind.

Überzahl ['y:bərtsa:l] *f* superiority,
superior numbers *pl*; **in der ~ sein**
outnumber sb, be numerically superior.

überzählig ['y:bərtsɛ:liç] *a* surplus.

über'zeugen *vt insep* convince (*von
etw* of sth) ; **~d** *a* convincing.

Überzeugung *f* conviction; **Überzeugungskraft** *f* power of persuasion.

überziehen ['y:bərtsi:ən] *unreg vt* put
on // [-'tsi:ən] *vt insep* cover; (*Konto*)
overdraw.

Überzug ['y:bərtsu:k] *m* cover; (*Belag*) coating.

üblich ['y:pliç] *a* usual.

U-Boot ['u:bo:t] *nt* submarine.

übrig ['y:briç] *a* remaining; **für jdn
etwas ~ haben** (*umg*) be fond of sb;
die ~en ['y:brigən] the others; **das
~e** the rest; **im ~en** besides;
~bleiben *vi unreg* remain, be left
(over); **übrigens** *ad* besides;
(*nebenbei bemerkt*) by the way;
~lassen *vt unreg* leave (over).

Übung ['y:buŋ] *f* practice; (*Turn-,
Aufgabe etc*) exercise; **~ macht den
Meister** practice makes perfect.

UdSSR [u:de:'ɛs'ɛs''ɛr] *f abk* (=
Union der Sozialistischen Sowjetrepubliken) USSR.

Ufer ['u:fər] *nt* **-s,** - bank; (*Meeres~*)
shore.

Uhr [u:r] *f* **-,** **-en** clock; (*Armband~*)
watch; **wieviel ~ ist es?** what time is

it?; **1 ~ 1 o'clock; 20 ~ 8 o'clock,
20.00** (twenty hundred) hours; **~band**
nt watch strap; **~kette** *f* watch
chain; **~macher** *m* **-s,** - watchmaker; **~werk** *nt* clockwork; works
of a watch; **~zeiger** *m* hand;
~zeigersinn *m*: **im ~zeigersinn**
clockwise; **entgegen dem ~zeigersinn**
anticlockwise; **~zeit** *f* time (of day).

Uhu ['u:hu] *m* **-s,** **-s** eagle owl.

UKW [u:ka:'ve:] *abk* (= *Ultrakurzwelle*) VHF.

Ulk [ʊlk] *m* **-s,** **-e** lark; **u~ig** *a* funny.

Ulme ['ʊlmə] *f* **-,** **-n** elm.

Ultimatum [ʊlti'ma:tʊm] *nt* **-s,**
Ultimaten ultimatum.

ultraviolett ['ʊltravio'lɛt] *a* ultraviolet.

um [ʊm] **♦***präp* +*akk* **1** (**~ herum**)
(a) round; **~ Weihnachten** around
Christmas; **er schlug ~ sich** he hit
about him

2 (*mit Zeitangabe*) at; **~ acht (Uhr)**
at eight (o'clock)

3 (*mit Größenangabe*) by; **etw ~ 4
cm kürzen** shorten sth by 4 cm; **~
10% teurer** 10% more expensive; **~
vieles besser** better by far; **~ nichts
besser** not in the least bit better; **~
so besser** so much the better

4: **der Kampf ~ den Titel** the battle
for the title; **~ Geld spielen** play for
money; **Stunde ~ Stunde** hour after
hour; **Auge ~ Auge** an eye for an eye
♦*präp* +*gen*: **~ ... willen** for the
sake of ...; **~ Gottes willen** for goodness *od* (*stärker*) God's sake

♦*kj*: **~ ... zu** (in order) to; **zu klug,
~ zu ...** too clever to ...; **~ so
besser/schlimmer** so much the
better/worse

♦*ad* **1** (*ungefähr*) about; **~ (die) 30
Leute** about *od* around 30 people

2 (*vorbei*): **die 2 Stunden sind ~** the
two hours are up

umänder- ['ʊm'ɛndər] *zW*: **~n** *vt* alter; **U~ung** *f* alteration.

umarbeiten ['ʊm'arbaitən] *vt* remodel; (*Buch etc*) revise, rework.

umarmen [ʊm''armən] *vt insep* embrace.

Umbau ['ʊmbau] *m* **-(e)s,** **-e** *od* **-ten**
reconstruction, alteration(s); **u~en**
vt rebuild, reconstruct.

umbenennen ['ʊmbənɛnən] *vt unreg*
rename.

umbilden ['ʊmbildən] *vt* reorganize;
(*POL: Kabinett*) reshuffle.

umbinden ['ʊmbindən] *vt unreg*
(*Krawatte etc*) put on.

umblättern ['ʊmblɛtərn] *vt* turn over.

umblicken ['ʊmblikən] *vr* look around.

umbringen ['ʊmbriŋən] *vt unreg* kill.

Umbruch ['ʊmbrʊx] *m* radical
change; (*TYP*) make-up.

umbuchen ['ʊmbu:xən] *vti* change

one's reservation/flight *etc*.

umdenken ['ʊmdɛŋkən] *vi unreg* adjust one's views.

umdrehen ['ʊmdre:ən] *vtr* turn (round); (*Hals*) wring.

Um'drehung *f* revolution; rotation.

umeinander [ʊm'ʔaɪ'nandər] *ad* round one another; (*füreinander*) for one another.

umfahren ['ʊmfa:rən] *vt unreg* run over // [-'fa:rən] *insep* drive/sail round.

umfallen ['ʊmfalən] *vi unreg* fall down *od* over.

Umfang ['ʊmfaŋ] *m* extent; (*von Buch*) size; (*Reichweite*) range; (*Fläche*) area; (*MATH*) circumference; **u~reich** *a* extensive; (*Buch etc*) voluminous.

um'fassen *vt insep* embrace; (*umgeben*) surround; (*enthalten*) include; **~d** *a* comprehensive, extensive.

umform- ['ʊmfɔrm] *zW*: **~en** *vi* transform; **U~er** *m* **-s, -** (*ELEK*) transformer, converter.

Umfrage ['ʊmfra:gə] *f* poll.

umfüllen ['ʊmfʏlən] *vt* transfer; (*Wein*) decant.

umfunktionieren ['ʊmfʊŋktsioni:rən] *vt* convert, transform.

Umgang ['ʊmgaŋ] *m* company; (*mit jdm*) dealings *pl*; (*Behandlung*) way of behaving.

umgänglich ['ʊmgɛŋlɪç] *a* sociable.

Umgangs- *zW*: **~formen** *pl* manners *pl*; **~sprache** *f* colloquial language.

umgeb- [ʊm'ge:b] *zW*: **~en** *vt unreg insep* surround; **U~ung** *f* surroundings *pl*; (*Milieu*) environment; (*Personen*) people in one's circle.

umgehen ['ʊmge:ən] *unreg vi* go (a)round; **im Schlosse ~** haunt the castle; **mit jdm grob** *etc* **~** treat sb roughly *etc*; **mit Geld sparsam ~** be careful with one's money // [-'ge:ən] *vt insep* bypass; (*MIL*) outflank; (*Gesetz etc*) circumvent; (*vermeiden*) avoid; **~d** *a* immediate.

Um'gehung *f* bypassing; outflanking; circumvention; avoidance; **Umgehungsstraße** *f* bypass.

umgekehrt ['ʊmgəke:rt] *a* reverse(d); (*gegenteilig*) opposite // *ad* the other way around; **und ~** and vice versa.

umgraben ['ʊmgra:bən] *vt unreg* dig up.

Umhang ['ʊmhaŋ] *m* wrap, cape.

umhauen ['ʊmhaʊən] *vt* fell; (*fig*) bowl over.

umher [ʊm'he:r] *ad* about, around; **~gehen** *vi unreg* walk about; **~ziehen** *vi unreg* wander from place to place.

umhinkönnen [ʊm'hɪnkœnən] *vi unreg*: **ich kann nicht umhin, das zu tun** I can't help doing it.

umhören ['ʊmhø:rən] *vr* ask around.

Umkehr ['ʊmke:r] *f* - turning back; (*Änderung*) change; **u~en** *vi* turn back // *vt* turn round, reverse; (*Tasche etc*) turn inside out; (*Gefäß etc*) turn upside down.

umkippen ['ʊmkɪpən] *vt* tip over // *vi* overturn; (*fig: Meinung ändern*) change one's mind; (*umg: Mensch*) keel over.

Umkleideraum ['ʊmklaɪdəraʊm] *m* changing- *od* dressing room.

umkommen ['ʊmkɔmən] *vi unreg* die, perish; (*Lebensmittel*) go bad.

Umkreis ['ʊmkraɪs] *m* neighbourhood; **im ~ von** within a radius of.

Umlage ['ʊmla:gə] *f* share of the costs.

Umlauf ['ʊmlaʊf] *m* (*Geld~*) circulation; (*von Gestirn*) revolution; **~bahn** *f* orbit.

Umlaut ['ʊmlaʊt] *m* umlaut.

umlegen ['ʊmle:gən] *vt* put on; (*verlegen*) move, shift; (*Kosten*) share out; (*umkippen*) tip over; (*umg: töten*) bump off.

umleiten ['ʊmlaɪtən] *vt* divert.

Umleitung *f* diversion.

umliegend ['ʊmli:gənt] *a* surrounding.

um'rahmen *vt insep* frame.

um'randen *vt insep* border, edge.

umrechnen ['ʊmrɛçnən] *vt* convert.

Umrechnung *f* conversion; **Umrechnungskurs** *m* rate of exchange.

um'reißen *vt unreg insep* outline, sketch.

um'ringen *vt insep* surround.

Umriß ['ʊmrɪs] *m* outline.

umrühren ['ʊmry:rən] *vti* stir.

ums [ʊms] **= um das.**

Umsatz ['ʊmzats] *m* turnover.

umschalten ['ʊmʃaltən] *vt* switch.

Umschau ['ʊmʃaʊ] *f* look(ing) round; **~ halten nach** look around for; **u~en** *vr* look round.

Umschlag ['ʊmʃla:k] *m* cover; (*Buch~ auch*) jacket; (*MED*) compress; (*Brief~*) envelope; (*Wechsel*) change; (*von Hose*) turn-up; **u~en** ['ʊmʃla:gən] *unreg vi* change; (*NAUT*) capsize // *vt* knock over; (*Ärmel*) turn up; (*Seite*) turn over; (*Waren*) transfer; **~platz** *m* (*COMM*) distribution centre.

umschreiben *vt unreg* ['ʊmʃraɪbən] (*neu~*) rewrite; (*übertragen*) transfer (*auf* +*akk* to) // [-'ʃraɪbən] *insep* paraphrase; (*abgrenzen*) define.

umschulen ['ʊmʃu:lən] *vt* retrain; (*Kind*) send to another school.

Umschweife ['ʊmʃvaɪfə] *pl*: **ohne ~** without beating about the bush, straight out.

Umschwung ['ʊmʃvʊŋ] *m* change

(around), revolution.

umsehen ['umze:ən] vr unreg look around or about; (suchen) look out (nach for).

umseitig ['umzaıtıç] ad overleaf.

Umsicht ['umzıçt] f prudence, caution; **u~ig** a cautious, prudent.

umsonst [um'zɔnst] ad in vain; (gratis) for nothing.

umspringen ['umʃprıŋən] vi unreg change; (Wind auch) veer; mit jdm ~ treat sb badly.

Umstand ['umʃtant] m circumstance; **Umstände** pl (fig: Schwierigkeiten) fuss; in anderen Umständen sein to be pregnant; Umstände machen go to a lot of trouble; unter Umständen possibly.

umständlich ['umʃtɛntlıç] a, ad (Methode) cumbersome, complicated; (Ausdrucksweise, Erklärung auch) long-winded; (Mensch) ponderous.

Umstandskleid nt maternity dress.

Umstehende(n) ['umʃte:əndə(n)] pl bystanders pl.

umsteigen ['umʃtaıgən] vi unreg (EISENB) change.

umstellen ['umʃtɛlən] vt (an anderen Ort) change round, rearrange; (TECH) convert // vr adapt o.s. (auf +akk to) // ['um'ʃtɛlən] vt insep surround.

Umstellung ['umʃtɛluŋ] f change; (Umgewöhnung) adjustment; (TECH) conversion.

umstimmen ['umʃtımən] vt (MUS) retune; jdn ~ make sb change his mind.

umstoßen ['umʃto:sən] vt unreg (lit) overturn; (Plan etc) change, upset.

umstritten ['umʃtrıtən] a disputed.

Umsturz ['umʃturts] m overthrow.

umstürzen ['umʃtyrtsən] vt (umwerfen) overturn // vi collapse, fall down; (Wagen) overturn.

Umtausch ['umtauʃ] m exchange; **u~en** vt exchange.

umwandeln ['umvandəln] vt change, convert; (ELEK) transform.

~~umwechseln ['umvɛksəln] vt change.~~

Umweg ['umve:k] m detour, roundabout way.

Umwelt ['umvɛlt] f environment; **u~freundlich** a not harmful to the environment; **u~feindlich** a ecologically harmful; **~schutz** m conservation; **~schützer** m environmentalist; **~verschmutzung** f environmental pollution.

umwenden ['umvɛndən] vtr unreg turn (round).

um'werben vt unreg insep court, woo.

umwerfen ['umvɛrfən] vt unreg (lit)

upset, overturn; (Mantel) throw on; (fig: erschüttern) upset, throw.

umziehen ['umtsi:ən] unreg vtr change // vi move.

umzingeln [um'tsıŋəln] vt insep surround, encircle.

Umzug ['umtsu:k] m procession; (Wohnungs~) move, removal.

unab- ['un'ap] zW: **~änderlich** a irreversible, unalterable; **~hängig** a independent; **U~hängigkeit** f independence; **~kömmlich** a indispensable; zur Zeit ~kömmlich not free at the moment; **~lässig** a incessant, constant; **~sehbar** a immeasurable; (Folgen) unforeseeable; (Kosten) incalculable; **~sichtlich** a unintentional; **~'wendbar** a inevitable.

unachtsam ['un'axtza:m] a careless; **U~keit** f carelessness.

unan- ['un'an] zW: **~'fechtbar** a indisputable; **~gebracht** a uncalled-for; **~gemessen** a inadequate; **~genehm** a unpleasant; **~gepaßt** a nonconformist; **U~nehmlichkeit** f inconvenience // pl trouble; **~sehnlich** a unsightly; **~ständig** a indecent, improper.

unappetitlich ['un'apeti:tlıç] a unsavoury.

Unart ['un'a:rt] f bad manners pl; (Angewohnheit) bad habit; **u~ig** a naughty, badly behaved.

unauf- ['un'auf] zW: **~fällig** a unobtrusive; (Kleidung) inconspicuous; **~'findbar** a not to be found; **~gefordert** a unasked // ad spontaneously; **~haltsam** a irresistible; **~'hörlich** a incessant, continuous; **~merksam** a inattentive; **~richtig** a insincere.

unaus- ['un'aus] zW: **~'bleiblich** a inevitable, unavoidable; **~geglichen** a unbalanced; **~'sprechlich** a inexpressible; **~'stehlich** a intolerable.

unbarmherzig ['unbarmhɛrtsıç] a pitiless, merciless.

unbeabsichtigt ['unbə'apzıçtıçt] a unintentional.

unbeachtet ['unbə'axtət] a unnoticed, ignored.

unbedenklich ['unbədɛŋklıç] a (Plan) unobjectionable // ad without hesitation.

unbedeutend ['unbədɔytənt] a insignificant, unimportant; (Fehler) slight.

unbedingt ['unbədıŋt] a unconditional // ad absolutely; mußt du ~ gehen? do you really have to go?

unbefangen ['unbəfaŋən] a impartial, unprejudiced; (ohne Hemmungen) uninhibited; **U~heit** f impartiality; uninhibitedness.

unbefriedig- ['unbəfri:dıg] zW: **~end**

a unsatisfactory; **~t** [-dıçt] *a* unsatisfied, dissatisfied.

unbefugt ['ʊnbəfuːkt] *a* unauthorized.

unbegreiflich [ʊnbə'graıflıç] *a* inconceivable.

unbegrenzt ['ʊnbəgrɛntst] *a* unlimited.

unbegründet ['ʊnbəgrʏndət] *a* unfounded.

Unbehag- ['ʊnbəhaːg] *zW:* **~en** *nt* discomfort; **u~lich** [-klıç] *a* uncomfortable; (*Gefühl*) uneasy.

unbeholfen ['ʊnbəhɔlfən] *a* awkward, clumsy; **U~heit** *f* awkwardness, clumsiness.

unbeirrt ['ʊnbə'ırt] *a* imperturbable.

unbekannt ['ʊnbəkant] *a* unknown.

unbekümmert ['ʊnbəkʏmərt] *a* unconcerned.

unbeliebt ['ʊnbəliːpt] *a* unpopular.

unbequem ['ʊnbəkveːm] *a* (*Stuhl*) uncomfortable; (*Mensch*) bothersome; (*Regelung*) inconvenient.

unberech- *zW:* **~enbar** [ʊnbə'rɛçənbaːr] *a* incalculable; (*Mensch, Verhalten*) unpredictable; **~tigt** ['ʊnbərɛçtıçt] *a* unjustified; (*nicht erlaubt*) unauthorized.

unberührt ['ʊnbəryːrt] *a* untouched, intact; sie ist noch ~ she is still a virgin.

unbescheiden ['ʊnbəʃaıdən] *a* presumptuous.

unbeschreiblich [ʊnbə'ʃraıplıç] *a* indescribable.

unbesonnen ['ʊnbəzɔnən] *a* unwise, rash, imprudent.

unbeständig ['ʊnbəʃtɛndıç] *a* (*Mensch*) inconstant; (*Wetter*) unsettled; (*Lage*) unstable.

unbestechlich [ʊnbə'ʃtɛçlıç] *a* incorruptible.

unbestimmt ['ʊnbəʃtımt] *a* indefinite; (*Zukunft auch*) uncertain.

unbeteiligt ['ʊnbətaılıçt] *a* unconcerned, indifferent.

unbewacht ['ʊnbəvaxt] *a* unguarded, unwatched.

unbeweglich ['ʊnbəveːklıç] *a* immovable.

unbewußt ['ʊnbəvʊst] *a* unconscious.

unbrauchbar ['ʊnbrauxbaːr] *a* (*Arbeit*) useless; (*Gerät auch*) unusable.

und [ʊnt] *kj* and; ~ so weiter and so on.

Undank ['ʊndaŋk] *m* ingratitude; **u~bar** *a* ungrateful; **~barkeit** *f* ingratitude.

undefinierbar [ʊndefi'niːrbaːr] *a* indefinable.

undenkbar [ʊn'dɛŋkbaːr] *a* inconceivable.

undeutlich ['ʊndɔʏtlıç] *a* indistinct.

undicht ['ʊndıçt] *a* leaky.

Unding ['ʊndıŋ] *nt* absurdity.

undurch- ['ʊndʊrç] *zW:* **~führbar**

[-'fyːrbaːr] *a* impracticable; **~lässig** [-lɛsıç] *a* waterproof, impermeable; **~sichtig** [-zıçtıç] *a* opaque; (*fig*) obscure.

uneben ['ʊn'eːbən] *a* uneven.

unehelich ['ʊn'eːəlıç] *a* illegitimate.

uneigennützig ['ʊn'aıgənnʏtsıç] *a* unselfish.

uneinig ['ʊn'aınıç] *a* divided; ~ sein disagree; **U~keit** *f* discord, dissension.

uneins ['ʊn'aıns] *a* at variance, at odds.

unempfindlich ['ʊn'ɛmpfıntlıç] *a* insensitive; (*Stoff*) practical.

unendlich [ʊn'ɛntlıç] *a* infinite; **U~keit** *f* infinity.

unent- ['ʊn'ɛnt] *zW:* **~behrlich** [-'beːrlıç] *a* indispensable; **~geltlich** [-gɛltlıç] *a* free (of charge); **~schieden** [-'ʃiːdən] *a* undecided; **~schieden enden** (*SPORT*) end in a draw; **~schlossen** [-ʃlɔsən] *a* undecided; irresolute; **~wegt** [-'veːkt] *a* unswerving; (*unaufhörlich*) incessant.

uner- ['ʊn'er] *zW:* **~bittlich** ['bıtlıç] *a* unyielding, inexorable; **~fahren** [-'faːrən] *a* inexperienced; **~freulich** [-frɔʏlıç] *a* unpleasant; **~gründlich** [-'grʏntlıç] *a* unfathomable; **~heblich** [-heːplıç] *a* unimportant; **~hört** [-høːrt] *a* unheard-of; (*Bitte*) outrageous; **~läßlich** [-'lɛslıç] *a* indispensable; **~laubt** [-laupt] *a* unauthorized; **~meßlich** [-'mɛslıç] *a* immeasurable, immense; **~müdlich** [-'myːtlıç] *a* indefatigable; **~sättlich** [-'zɛtlıç] *a* insatiable; **~schöpflich** [-'ʃœpflıç] *a* inexhaustible; **~schütterlich** [-'ʃʏtərlıç] *a* unshakeable; **~schwinglich** [-'ʃvıŋlıç] *a* (*Preis*) exorbitant; too expensive; **~träglich** [-'treːklıç] *a* unbearable; (*Frechheit*) insufferable; **~wartet** [-vartət] *a* unexpected; **~wünscht** [-vʏnʃt] *a* undesirable, unwelcome.

unfähig ['ʊnfɛːıç] *a* incapable (*zu* of); incompetent; **U~keit** *f* incapacity; incompetence.

unfair ['ʊnfɛːr] *a* unfair.

Unfall ['ʊnfal] *m* accident; **~flucht** *f* hit-and-run (driving); **~stelle** *f* scene of the accident; **~versicherung** *f* accident insurance.

unfaßbar [ʊn'fasbaːr] *a* inconceivable.

unfehlbar [ʊn'feːlbaːr] *a* infallible // *ad* inevitably; **U~keit** *f* infallibility.

unfit ['ʊnfıt] *a* unfit.

unfrei ['ʊnfraı] *a* not free, unfree; (*Paket*) unfranked; **~willig** *a* involuntary, against one's will.

unfreundlich ['ʊnfrɔʏntlıç] *a* unfriendly; **U~keit** *f* unfriendliness.

Unfriede(n) ['ʊnfriːdə(n)] *m* dissension, strife.

unfruchtbar ['ʊnfrʊxtbaːr] *a* infertile;

(*Gespräche*) unfruitful; **U~keit** *f* infertility; unfruitfulness.

Unfug ['unfuːk] *m* -s (*Benehmen*) mischief; (*Unsinn*) nonsense; grober ~ (*JUR*) gross misconduct; malicious damage.

Ungar(in *f*) ['ungar(ɪn)] *m* Hungarian; **~n** *nt* Hungary; **u~isch** *a* Hungarian.

ungeachtet ['ungə'axtət] *präp* +*gen* notwithstanding.

ungeahnt ['ungə'aːnt] *a* unsuspected, undreamt-of.

ungebeten ['ungəbeːtən] *a* uninvited.

ungebildet ['ungəbɪldət] *a* uneducated; uncultured.

ungedeckt ['ungədɛkt] *a* (*Scheck*) uncovered.

Ungeduld ['ungədult] *f* impatience; **u~ig** [-dɪç] *a* impatient.

ungeeignet ['ungə'aɪɡnət] *a* unsuitable.

ungefähr ['ungəfɛːr] *a* rough, approximate; **das kommt nicht von ~** that's hardly surprising; **~lich** *a* not dangerous, harmless.

ungehalten ['ungəhaltən] *a* indignant.

ungeheuer ['ungəhɔyər] *a* huge // *ad* (*umg*) enormously; **U~** *nt* -s, - monster; **~lich** [-'hɔyərlɪç] *a* monstrous.

ungehobelt ['ungəhoːbəlt] *a* (*fig*) uncouth.

ungehörig ['ungəhøːrɪç] *a* impertinent, improper; **U~keit** *f* impertinence.

ungehorsam ['ungəhoːrzaːm] *a* disobedient; **U~** *m* disobedience.

ungeklärt ['ungəklɛːrt] *a* not cleared up; (*Rätsel*) unsolved.

ungeladen ['ungəlaːdən] *a* not loaded; (*Gast*) uninvited.

ungelegen ['ungəleːɡən] *a* inconvenient.

ungelernt ['ungəlɛrnt] *a* unskilled.

ungelogen ['ungəloːɡən] *ad* really, honestly.

ungemein ['ungəmaɪn] *a* uncommon.

ungemütlich ['ungəmyːtlɪç] *a* uncomfortable; (*Person*) disagreeable.

ungenau ['ungənaʊ] *a* inaccurate; **U~igkeit** *f* inaccuracy.

ungeniert ['unʒeniːrt] *a* free and easy, unceremonious // *ad* without embarrassment, freely.

ungenießbar ['ungəniːsbaːr] *a* inedible; undrinkable; (*umg*) unbearable.

ungenügend ['ungənyːɡənt] *a* insufficient, inadequate.

ungepflegt ['ungəpfleːkt] *a* (*Garten etc*) untended; (*Person*) unkempt; (*Hände*) neglected.

ungerade ['ungəraːdə] *a* uneven, odd.

ungerecht ['ungərɛçt] *a* unjust; **~fertigt** *a* unjustified; **U~igkeit** *f* injustice, unfairness.

ungern ['ungɛrn] *ad* unwillingly, reluctantly.

ungeschehen ['ungəʃeːən] *a*: ~ machen undo.

Ungeschick- ['ungəʃɪk] *zW*: **~lichkeit** *f* clumsiness; **u~t** *a* awkward, clumsy.

ungeschminkt ['ungəʃmɪŋkt] *a* without make-up; (*fig*) unvarnished.

ungesetzlich ['ungəzɛtslɪç] *a* illegal.

ungestört ['ungəʃtøːrt] *a* undisturbed.

ungestraft ['ungəʃtraːft] *ad* with impunity.

ungestüm ['ungəʃtyːm] *a* impetuous; tempestuous; **U~** *nt* -(e)s impetuosity; passion.

ungesund ['ungəzunt] *a* unhealthy.

ungetrübt ['ungətryːpt] *a* clear; (*fig*) untroubled; (*Freude*) unalloyed.

Ungetüm ['ungətyːm] *nt* -(e)s, -e monster.

ungewiß ['ungəvɪs] *a* uncertain; **U~heit** *f* uncertainty.

ungewöhnlich ['ungəvøːnlɪç] *a* unusual.

ungewohnt ['ungəvoːnt] *a* unaccustomed.

Ungeziefer ['ungətsiːfər] *nt* -s vermin.

ungezogen ['ungətsoːɡən] *a* rude, impertinent; **U~heit** *f* rudeness, impertinence.

ungezwungen ['ungətsvuŋən] *a* natural, unconstrained.

ungläubig ['unglɔybɪç] *a* unbelieving; **die U~en** the infidel(s).

unglaublich [un'glaʊplɪç] *a* incredible.

ungleich ['unglaɪç] *a* dissimilar; unequal // *ad* incomparably; **~artig** *a* different; **U~heit** *f* dissimilarity; inequality.

Unglück ['unglyk] *nt* -(e)s, -e misfortune; (*Pech*) bad luck; (*~sfall*) calamity, disaster; (*Verkehrs~*) accident; **u~lich** *a* unhappy; (*erfolglos*) unlucky; (*unerfreulich*) unfortunate; **u~licherweise** [-'vaɪzə] *ad* unfortunately; **u~selig** *a* calamitous; (*Person*) unfortunate; **Unglücksfall** *m* accident, calamity.

ungültig ['ungyltɪç] *a* invalid; **U~keit** *f* invalidity.

ungünstig ['ungynstɪç] *a* unfavourable.

ungut ['unguːt] *a* (*Gefühl*) uneasy; **nichts für ~** no offence.

unhaltbar ['unhaltbaːr] *a* untenable.

Unheil ['unhaɪl] *nt* evil; (*Unglück*) misfortune; ~ anrichten cause mischief; **u~bar** *a* incurable; **u~bringend** *a* fatal, fateful; **u~voll** *a* disastrous.

unheimlich ['unhaɪmlɪç] *a* weird, uncanny // *ad* (*umg*) tremendously.

unhöflich ['unhøːflɪç] *a* impolite; **U~keit** *f* impoliteness.

unhygienisch ['unhygiˈeːnɪʃ] *a* unhygienic.

Uni ['uni] f -, -s (umg) university; **u~** [y'ni:] a self-coloured.

Uniform [uni'fɔrm] f uniform; **u~iert** [-'mi:rt] a uniformed.

uninteressant ['unɪntɛrɛsant] a uninteresting.

Universität [univɛrzi'tɛ:t] f university.

unkenntlich ['unkɛntlɪç] a unrecognizable.

Unkenntnis ['unkɛntnɪs] f ignorance.

unklar ['unkla:r] a unclear; **im ~en sein über** (+akk) be in the dark about; **U~heit** f unclarity; (Unentschiedenheit) uncertainty.

unklug ['unklu:k] a unwise.

Unkosten ['unkɔstən] pl expense(s).

Unkraut ['unkraut] nt weed; weeds pl.

unlängst ['unlɛŋst] ad not long ago.

unlauter ['unlautər] a unfair.

unleserlich ['unle:zərlɪç] a illegible.

unlogisch ['unlo:gɪʃ] a illogical.

unlösbar [un'lø:sbar], **unlöslich** [un'lø:slɪç] a insoluble.

Unlust ['unlust] f lack of enthusiasm; **u~ig** a unenthusiastic.

unmäßig ['unmɛ:sɪç] a immoderate.

Unmenge ['unmɛŋə] f tremendous number, hundreds pl.

Unmensch ['unmɛnʃ] m ogre, brute; **u~lich** a inhuman, brutal; (ungeheuer) awful.

unmerklich [un'mɛrklɪç] a imperceptible.

unmißverständlich ['unmɪsfɛrʃtɛntlɪç] a unmistakable.

unmittelbar ['unmɪtəlba:r] a immediate.

unmöbliert ['unmøbli:rt] a unfurnished.

unmöglich ['unmø:klɪç] a impossible; **U~keit** f impossibility.

unmoralisch ['unmora:lɪʃ] a immoral.

Unmut ['unmu:t] m ill humour.

unnachgiebig ['unna:xgi:bɪç] a unyielding.

unnahbar [un'na:ba:r] a unapproachable.

unnötig ['unnø:tɪç] a unnecessary.

unnütz ['unnʏts] a useless.

unordentlich ['un'ɔrdəntlɪç] a untidy.

Unordnung ['un'ɔrdnuŋ] f disorder.

unparteiisch ['unpartaɪʃ] a impartial; **U~e(r)** m umpire; (Fußball) referee.

unpassend ['unpasənt] a inappropriate; (Zeit) inopportune.

unpäßlich ['unpɛslɪç] a unwell.

unpersönlich ['unpɛrzø:nlɪç] a impersonal.

unpolitisch ['unpoli:tɪʃ] a apolitical.

unpraktisch ['unpraktɪʃ] a unpractical.

unpünktlich ['unpʏnktlɪç] a unpunctual.

unrationell ['unratsionɛl] a inefficient.

unrecht ['unrɛçt] a wrong; **U~** nt

wrong; **zu U~** wrongly; **U~ haben** be wrong; **~mäßig** a unlawful, illegal.

unregelmäßig ['unre:gəlmɛsɪç] a irregular; **U~keit** f irregularity.

unreif ['unraɪf] a (Obst) unripe; (fig) immature.

unrentabel ['unrɛnta:bəl] a unprofitable.

unrichtig ['unrɪçtɪç] a incorrect, wrong.

Unruhe ['unru:ə] f -, **-n** unrest; **~stifter** m troublemaker.

unruhig ['unru:ɪç] a restless.

uns [uns] pron akk, dat von **wir** us; ourselves.

unsachlich ['unzaxlɪç] a not to the point, irrelevant.

unsagbar [un'za:kba:r] a indescribable.

unsanft ['unzanft] a rough.

unsauber ['unzaubər] a unclean, dirty; (fig) crooked; (MUS) fuzzy.

unschädlich ['unʃɛ:tlɪç] a harmless; **jdn/etw ~ machen** render sb/sth harmless.

unscharf ['unʃarf] a indistinct; (Bild etc) out of focus, blurred.

unscheinbar [un'ʃaɪnba:r] a insignificant; (Aussehen, Haus etc) unprepossessing.

unschlagbar [un'ʃla:kba:r] a invincible.

unschlüssig ['unʃlʏsɪç] a undecided.

Unschuld ['unʃult] f innocence; **u~ig** [-dɪç] a innocent.

unselbständig ['unzɛlpʃtɛndɪç] a dependent, over-reliant on others.

unser ['unzər] pron our; **~e(r, s)** ours; **~einer**, **~eins** pron people like us; **unsererseits** ad on our part; **unsertwegen**, **um unsertwillen** ad (für uns) for our sake; (wegen uns) on our account.

unsicher ['unzɪçər] a uncertain; (Mensch) insecure; **U~heit** f uncertainty; insecurity.

unsichtbar ['unzɪçtba:r] a invisible.

Unsinn ['unzɪn] m nonsense; **u~ig** a nonsensical.

Unsitte ['unzɪtə] f deplorable habit.

unsittlich ['unzɪtlɪç] a indecent.

unsportlich ['unʃpɔrtlɪç] a not sporty; unfit; (Verhalten) unsporting.

unsre ['unzrə] = **unsere.**

unsterblich ['unʃtɛrplɪç] a immortal; **U~keit** f immortality.

Unstimmigkeit ['unʃtɪmɪçkaɪt] f inconsistency; (Streit) disagreement.

unsympathisch ['unzʏmpa:tɪʃ] a unpleasant; **er ist mir ~** I don't like him.

untätig ['untɛ:tɪç] a idle.

untauglich ['untauklɪç] a unsuitable; (MIL) unfit.

unteilbar [un'taɪlba:r] a indivisible.

unten ['ʊntən] *ad* below; (*im Haus*) downstairs; (*an der Treppe etc*) at the bottom; **nach ~** down; **~ am Berg** *etc* at the bottom of the mountain *etc*; **ich bin bei ihm ~ durch** (*umg*) he's through with me.

unter [ʊntər] ◆*präp +dat* 1 (*räumlich, mit Zahlen*) under; (*drunter*) underneath, below; **~ 18 Jahren** under 18 years

2 (*zwischen*) among(st); **sie waren ~ sich** they were by themselves; **einer ~ ihnen** one of them; **~ anderem** among other things

◆*präp +akk* under, below.

Unterarm ['ʊntər'arm] *m* forearm.

unter *zW:* **~belichten** *vt* (*PHOT*) underexpose; **U~bewußtsein** *nt* subconscious; **~bezahlt** *a* underpaid.

unterbieten [ʊntər'biːtən] *vt unreg insep* (*COMM*) undercut; (*Rekord*) lower.

unterbinden [ʊntər'bɪndən] *vt unreg insep* stop, call a halt to.

unterbrech- [ʊntər'brɛç] *zW:* **~en** *vt unreg insep* interrupt; **U~ung** *f* interruption.

unterbringen ['ʊntərbrɪŋən] *vt* unreg (*in Koffer*) stow; (*in Zeitung*) place; (*Person: in Hotel etc*) accommodate, put up; (*: beruflich*) fix up (*auf, in* with).

unterdessen [ʊntər'dɛsən] *ad* meanwhile.

Unterdruck ['ʊntərdrʊk] *m* low pressure.

unterdrücken [ʊntər'drʏkən] *vt insep* suppress; (*Leute*) oppress.

untere(r, s) ['ʊntərə(r, s)] *a* lower.

untereinander [ʊntər'ai'nandər] *ad* with each other; among themselves *etc*.

unterentwickelt ['ʊntər'entvɪkəlt] *a* underdeveloped.

unterernährt ['ʊntər'ɛrnɛːrt] *a* undernourished, underfed.

Unterernährung *f* malnutrition.

Unter'führung *f* subway, underpass.

Untergang ['ʊntərgaŋ] *m* (down)fall, decline; (*NAUT*) sinking; (*von Gestirn*) setting.

unter'geben *a* subordinate.

untergehen ['ʊntərgeːən] *vi unreg* go down; (*Sonne auch*) set; (*Staat*) fall; (*Volk*) perish; (*Welt*) come to an end; (*im Lärm*) be drowned.

Untergeschoß ['ʊntərgəʃos] *nt* basement.

unter'gliedern *vt insep* subdivide.

Untergrund ['ʊntərgrʊnt] *m* foundation; (*POL*) underground; **~bahn** *f* underground, tube, subway (*US*); **~bewegung** *f* underground (movement).

unterhalb ['ʊntərhalp] *präp +gen, ad*

below; **~ von** below.

Unterhalt ['ʊntərhalt] *m* maintenance; **u~en** [ʊntər'haltən] *unreg insep vt* maintain; (*belustigen*) entertain // *vr* talk; (*sich belustigen*) enjoy o.s.; **~ung** *f* maintenance; (*Belustigung*) entertainment, amusement; (*Gespräch*) talk.

Unterhemd ['ʊntərhemt] *nt* vest, undershirt (*US*).

Unterhose ['ʊntərhoːzə] *f* underpants *pl*.

unterirdisch ['ʊntər'ɪrdɪʃ] *a* underground.

Unterkiefer ['ʊntərkiːfər] *m* lower jaw.

unterkommen ['ʊntərkəmən] *vi unreg* find shelter; find work; **das ist mir noch nie untergekommen** I've never met with that.

Unterkunft ['ʊntərkʊnft] *f* -, **-künfte** accommodation.

Unterlage ['ʊntərlaːgə] *f* foundation; (*Beleg*) document; (*Schreib~ etc*) pad.

unter'lassen *vt unreg insep* (*versäumen*) fail (to do); (*sich enthalten*) refrain from.

unterlaufen [ʊntər'laufən] *vi unreg insep* happen // *a:* **mit Blut ~** suffused with blood; (*Augen*) bloodshot.

unterlegen ['ʊntərleːgən] *vt lay od put under* // [ʊntər'leːgən] *a* inferior (*dat* to); (*besiegt*) defeated.

Unterleib ['ʊntərlaip] *m* abdomen.

unter'liegen *vi unreg insep* be defeated *od* overcome (*jdm* by *sb*); (*unterworfen sein*) be subject to.

Untermiete ['ʊntərmiːtə] *f:* **zur ~ wohnen** be a subtenant *od* lodger; **~r(in** *f*) *m* subtenant, lodger.

unter'nehmen *vt unreg insep* undertake; **U~** *nt* -s, - undertaking, enterprise (*auch COMM*).

Unternehmer [ʊntər'neːmər] *m* -s, - entrepreneur, businessman.

Unterredung [ʊntər'reːdʊŋ] *f* discussion, talk.

Unterricht ['ʊntərrɪçt] *m* -(e)s, -e instruction, lessons *pl*; **u~en** [ʊntər'rɪçtən] *insep vt* instruct; (*SCH*) teach // *vr* inform o.s. (*über +akk* about).

Unterrock ['ʊntərrɔk] *m* petticoat, slip.

unter'sagen *vt insep* forbid (*jdm etw* sb to do sth).

unter'schätzen *vt insep* underestimate.

unter'scheiden *unreg insep vt* distinguish // *vr* differ.

Unter'scheidung *f* (*Unterschied*) distinction; (*Unterscheiden*) differentiation.

Unterschied ['ʊntərʃiːt] *m* -(e)s, -e difference, distinction; **im ~ zu** as dis-

tinct from; **u~lich** *a* varying, differing; *(diskriminierend)* discrimina-
tory; **unterschiedslos** *ad* indiscrimi-
nately.

unter'schlagen *vt unreg insep* embezzle; *(verheimlichen)* suppress.

Unter'schlagung *f* embezzlement.

Unterschlupf ['ʊntərʃlʊpf] *m* **-(e)s,
-schlüpfe** refuge.

unter'schreiben *vt unreg insep* sign.

Unterschrift ['ʊntərʃrɪft] *f* signature.

Unterseeboot ['ʊntərzeːboːt] *nt* submarine.

Untersetzer ['ʊntərzɛtsər] *m* tablemat; *(für Gläser)* coaster.

untersetzt [ʊntər'zɛtst] *a* stocky.

unterste(r, s) ['ʊntərstə(r, s)] *a* lowest,
bottom.

unterstehen [ʊntər'ʃteːən] *unreg vi
insep* be under *(jdm sb)* // *vr* dare //
['ʊntərʃteːən] *vi* shelter.

unterstellen [ʊntər'ʃtələn] *vt insep*
subordinate *(dat* to); *(fig)* impute
(jdm etw sth to sb) // ['ʊntərʃtələn] *vt*
(Auto) garage, park // *vr* take shelter.

unter'streichen *vt unreg insep* *(lit,
fig)* underline.

Unterstufe ['ʊntərʃtuːfə] *f* lower
grade.

unter'stützen *vt insep* support.

Unter'stützung *f* support, assistance.

unter'suchen *vt insep* *(MED)* examine; *(Polizei)* investigate.

Unter'suchung *f* examination; investigation, inquiry; **Untersuchungsausschuß** *m* committee of inquiry;
Untersuchungshaft *f* imprisonment
on remand.

Untertan ['ʊntərtaːn] *m* **-s, -en** subject.

untertänig ['ʊntərtɛːnɪç] *a* submissive,
humble.

Untertasse ['ʊntərtasə] *f* saucer.

untertauchen ['ʊntərtaʊxən] *vi* dive;
(fig) disappear, go underground.

Unterteil ['ʊntərtaɪl] *nt od m* lower
part, bottom; **u~en** [ʊntər'taɪlən] *vt
insep* divide up.

Unterwäsche ['ʊntərvɛʃə] *f* underwear.

unterwegs [ʊntər'veːks] *ad* on the
way.

unter'weisen *vt unreg insep* instruct.

unter'werfen *unreg insep vt* subject;
(Volk) subjugate // *vr* submit *(dat*
to).

unterwürfig ['ʊntərvʏrfɪç] *a* obsequious, servile.

unter'zeichnen *vt insep* sign.

unter'ziehen *unreg insep vt* subject
(dat to) // *vr* undergo *(etw (dat)*
sth); *(einer Prüfung)* take.

untreu ['ʊntrɔy] *a* unfaithful; **U~e** *f*
unfaithfulness.

untröstlich [ʊn'trøːstlɪç] *a* inconsol-
able.

unüber- ['ʊn'yːbər] *zW:* **~legt** [-leːkt]
a ill-considered // *ad* without thinking; **~sehbar** [-'zeːbaːr] *a* incalculable.

unum- [ʊn'ʊm] *zW:* **~gänglich**
[-'gɛŋlɪç] *a* indispensable, vital; absolutely necessary; **~wunden** [-'vʊn-
dən] *a* candid // *ad* straight out.

ununterbrochen ['ʊn'ʊntərbrɔxən] *a*
uninterrupted.

unver- [ʊnfɛr] *zW:* **~änderlich**
[-'ɛndərlɪç] *a* unchangeable; **~
antwortlich** [-'antvɔrtlɪç] *a* irresponsible; *(unentschuldbar)* inexcusable;
~besserlich [-'bɛsərlɪç] *a* incorrigible;
~bindlich [-'bɪntlɪç] *a* not binding;
(Antwort) curt // *ad* *(COMM)* without
obligation; **~blümt** [-'blyːmt] *a, ad*
plain(ly), blunt(ly); **~daulich**
[-'daʊlɪç] *a* indigestible; **~dorben**
[-'dɔrbən] *a* unspoilt; **~einbar**
[-'aɪnbaːr] *a* incompatible; **~fänglich**
[-'fɛŋlɪç] *a* harmless; **~froren**
[-'froːrən] *a* impudent; **~hofft** [-'hɔft]
a unexpected; **~kennbar** [-'kɛnbaːr] *a*
unmistakable; **~meidlich** [-'maɪtlɪç] *a*
unavoidable; **~mutet** [-'muːtət] *a* unexpected; **~nünftig** [-'nʏnftɪç] *a* foolish; **~schämt** [-'ʃɛːmt] *a* impudent;
U~schämtheit *f* impudence, insolence; **~sehens** [-'zeːəns] *ad* all of a
sudden; **~sehrt** [-'zeːrt] *a* uninjured;
~söhnlich [-'zøːnlɪç] *a* irrecocilable;
~ständlich [-'ʃtɛntlɪç] *a* unintelligible;
~träglich [-'trɛːklɪç] *a* quarrelsome;
(Meinungen, MED) incompatible;
~wüstlich [-'vyːstlɪç] *a* indestructible;
(Mensch) irrepressible; **~zeihlich**
[-'tsaɪlɪç] *a* unpardonable; **~züglich**
[-'tsyːklɪç] *a* immediate.

unvoll- ['ʊnfɔl] *zW:* **~kommen** *a* imperfect; **~ständig** *a* incomplete.

unvor- ['ʊnfoːr] *zW:* **~bereitet** *a* un-
prepared; **~eingenommen** *a* unbiased; **~hergesehen** [-heːrgəzeːən] *a*
unforeseen; **~sichtig** [-zɪçtɪç] *a* careless, imprudent; **~stellbar** [-'ʃtɛlbaːr]
a inconceivable; **~teilhaft** [-taɪlhaft] *a*
disadvantageous.

unwahr ['ʊnvaːr] *a* untrue;
~scheinlich *a* improbable, unlikely //
ad (umg) incredibly.

unweigerlich [ʊn'vaɪgərlɪç] *a* un-
questioning // *ad* without fail.

Unwesen ['ʊnveːzən] *nt* nuisance;
(Unfug) mischief; **sein ~ treiben**
wreak havoc; **unwesentlich** *a* ines-
sential, unimportant; **unwesentlich
besser** marginally better.

Unwetter ['ʊnvɛtər] *nt* thunderstorm.

unwichtig ['ʊnvɪçtɪç] *a* unimportant.

unwider- [ʊnviːdər] *zW:* **~legbar**
[-'leːkbaːr] *a* irrefutable; **~ruflich**

[-'ru:fliç] *a* irrevocable; **~stehlich** [-'ʃte:liç] *a* irresistible.

unwill- ['unvil] *zW:* **U~e(n)** *m* indignation; **~ig** *a* indignant; *(widerwillig)* reluctant; **~kürlich** [-ky:rliç] *a* involuntary // *ad* instinctively; *(lachen)* involuntarily.

unwirklich ['unvirkliç] *a* unreal.

unwirsch ['unvirʃ] *a* cross, surly.

unwirtschaftlich ['unvirtʃaftliç] *a* uneconomical.

unwissen- ['unvisən] *zW:* **~d** *a* ignorant; **U~heit** *f* ignorance; **~schaftlich** *a* unscientific.

unwohl ['unvo:l] *a* unwell, ill; **U~sein** *nt* -s indisposition.

unwürdig ['unvyrdiç] *a* unworthy *(jds of sb)*.

unzählig [un'tsɛ:liç] *a* innumerable, countless.

unzer- [untsɛr] *zW:* **~brechlich** [-'brɛçliç] *a* unbreakable; **~störbar** [-'ʃtø:rba:r] *a* indestructible; **~trennlich** [-'trɛnliç] *a* inseparable.

Unzucht ['untsuxt] *f* sexual offence.

unzüchtig ['untsyçtiç] *a* immoral; lewd.

unzu- ['untsu] *zW:* **~frieden** *a* dissatisfied; **U~friedenheit** *f* discontent; **~länglich** ['untsu:lɛŋliç] *a* inadequate; **~lässig** ['untsu:lɛsiç] *a* inadmissible; **~rechnungsfähig** ['untsu:rɛçnuŋsfɛ:iç] *a* irresponsible; **~treffend** ['untsu:-] *a* incorrect; **~verlässig** ['untsu:-] *a* unreliable.

unzweideutig ['untsvaidɔytiç] *a* unambiguous.

üppig ['ypiç] *a* *(Frau)* curvaceous; *(Busen)* full, ample; *(Essen)* sumptuous; *(Vegetation)* luxuriant, lush.

uralt ['u:r'alt] *a* ancient, very old.

Uran [u'ra:n] *nt* -s uranium.

Ur- ['u:r] *in zW* original; **~aufführung** *f* first performance; **~einwohner** *m* original inhabitant; **~eltern** *pl* ancestors *pl;* **~enkel(in** *f)* *m* great-grandchild; **~großmutter** *f* great-grandmother; **~großvater** *m* great-grandfather; **~heber** *m* -s, - originator; *(Autor)* author.

Urin [u'ri:n] *m* -s, -e urine.

Urkunde ['u:rkundə] *f* -, -n document, deed.

Urlaub ['u:rlaup] *m* -(e)s, -e holiday *(pl) (Brit),* vacation *(US); (MIL etc)* leave; **~er** [-laubər] *m* -s, - holiday-maker *(Brit),* vacationer *(US).*

Urne ['urnə] *f* -, -n urn.

Ursache ['u:rzaxə] *f* cause; **keine ~** that's all right.

Ursprung ['u:rʃpruŋ] *m* origin, source; *(von Fluß)* source.

ursprünglich [u:r'ʃpryŋliç] *a, ad* original(ly).

Urteil ['urtail] *nt* -s, -e opinion; *(JUR)*

sentence, judgement; **u~en** *vi* judge; **Urteilsspruch** *m* sentence, verdict.

Ur- *zW:* **~wald** *m* jungle; **~zeit** *f* prehistoric times *pl.*

USA [u:'ɛs''a:] *f* abk (= *Vereinigte Staaten von Amerika*) USA.

usw. [u:ɛsve:] abk (= *und so weiter*) etc.

Utensilien [utɛn'zi:liən] *pl* utensils *pl.*

Utopie [uto'pi:] *f* pipedream.

utopisch [u'to:piʃ] *a* utopian.

u.U. abk von **unter Umständen.**

V

V, v [faʊ] *nt* V, v.

vag(e) [va:k, 'va:gə] *a* vague.

Vagina [va'gi:na] *f* -, **Vaginen** vagina.

Vakuum ['va:kuʊm] *nt* -s, **Vakua** *od* **Vakuen** vacuum.

Vanille [va'niljə] *f* - vanilla.

Variation [variatsi'o:n] *f* variation.

variieren [vari'i:rən] *vti* vary.

Vase ['va:zə] *f* -, -n vase.

Vater ['fa:tər] *m* -s, ⸚ father; **~land** *nt* native country; Fatherland.

väterlich ['fɛ:tərliç] *a* fatherly; **väterlicherseits** *ad* on the father's side.

Vater- *zW:* **~schaft** *f* paternity; **~unser** *nt* -s, - Lord's prayer.

Vati ['fa:ti] *m* daddy.

v.Chr. abk (= *vor Christus*) BC.

Vegetarier(in *f)* [vege'ta:riər(in)] *m* -s, - vegetarian.

Veilchen ['failçən] *nt* violet.

Vene ['ve:nə] *f* -, -n vein.

Venedig [ve'ne:diç] *nt* Venice.

Ventil [vɛn'ti:l] *nt* -s, -e valve; **~ator** [vɛnti'la:tər] *m* ventilator.

verab- [fɛr''ap] *zW:* **~reden** *vt* agree, arrange; **mit jdm ~redet sein** have arranged to meet sb // *vr* arrange to meet *(mit jdm* sb); **V~redung** *f* arrangement; *(Treffen)* appointment; **~scheuen** *vt* detest, abhor; **~schieden** *vt (Gäste)* say goodbye to; *(entlassen)* discharge; *(Gesetz)* pass // *vr* take one's leave *(von* of); **V~schiedung** *f* leave-taking; discharge; passing.

ver- [fɛr] *zW:* **~achten** [-''axtən] *vt* despise; **~ächtlich** [-''ɛçtliç] *a* contemptuous; *(verachtenswert)* contemptible; **jdn ~ächtlich machen** run sb down; **V~achtung** *f* contempt.

verallgemein- [fɛr'algəmain] *zW:* **~ern** *vt* generalize; **V~erung** *f* generalization.

veralten [fɛr''altən] *vi* become obsolete *od* out-of-date.

Veranda [ve'randa] *f* -, **Veranden** veranda.

veränder- [fɛr''ɛndər] *zW:* **~lich** *a* changeable; **~n** *vtr* change, alter;

V~ung f change, alteration.

veran- [fɛr'ˈan] zW: **~lagt** a with a ... nature; **V~lagung** f disposition; **~lassen** vt cause; **Maßnahmen ~lassen** take measures; **sich ~laßt sehen** feel prompted; **~schaulichen** vt illustrate; **~schlagen** vt estimate; **~stalten** vt organize, arrange; **V~stalter** m -s, - organizer; **V~staltung** f (Veranstalten) organizing; (Konzert etc) event, function.

verantwort- [fɛr'ˈantvɔrt] zW: **~en** vt answer for // vr justify o.s.; **~lich** a responsible; **V~ung** f responsibility; **~ungsbewußt** a responsible; **~ungslos** a irresponsible.

verarbeiten [fɛr'ˈarbaɪtən] vt process; (geistig) assimilate; **etw zu etw ~** make sth into sth.

Verarbeitung f processing; assimilation.

verärgern [fɛr'ˈɛrgərn] vt annoy.

verausgaben [fɛr'ˈaʊsga:bən] vr run out of money; (fig) exhaust o.s.

veräußern [fɛr'ˈɔʏsərn] vt dispose of, sell.

Verb [vɛrp] nt -s, -en verb.

Verband [fɛr'bant] m -(e)s, ⁻e (MED) bandage, dressing; (Bund) association, society; (MIL) unit; **~kasten** m medicine chest, first-aid box; **~zeug** nt bandage.

verbannen [fɛr'banən] vt banish.

Verbannung f exile.

verbergen [fɛr'bɛrgən] vtr unreg hide (vor +dat from).

verbessern [fɛr'bɛsərn] vtr improve; (berichtigen) correct (o.s.).

Verbesserung f improvement; correction.

verbeugen [fɛr'bɔʏgən] vr bow.

Verbeugung f bow.

ver'biegen vi unreg bend.

ver'bieten vt unreg forbid (jdm etw sb to do sth).

verbilligt [fɛr'bɪlɪçt] a reduced.

ver'binden unreg vt connect; (kombinieren) combine; (MED) bandage; **jdm die Augen ~** blindfold sb // vr combine (auch CHEM), join.

verbindlich [fɛr'bɪntlɪç] a binding; (freundlich) friendly; **V~keit** f obligation; (Höflichkeit) civility.

Ver'bindung f connection; (Zusammensetzung) combination; (CHEM) compound; (UNIV) club.

ver'bitten vt unreg: **sich** (dat) **etw ~** not tolerate sth, not stand for sth.

verblassen [fɛr'blasən] vi fade.

Verbleib [fɛr'blaɪp] m -(e)s whereabouts; **v~en** [fɛr'blaɪbən] vi unreg remain.

verblüffen [fɛr'blʏfən] vt stagger, amaze.

Verblüffung f stupefaction.

ver'blühen vi wither, fade.

ver'bluten vi bleed to death.

verborgen [fɛr'bɔrgən] a hidden.

Verbot [fɛr'bo:t] nt -(e)s, -e prohibition, ban; **v~en** a forbidden; **Rauchen v~en!** no smoking; **Verbotsschild** nt prohibitory sign.

Verbrauch [fɛr'braʊx] m -(e)s consumption; **v~en** vt use up; **~er** m -s, - consumer; **v~t** a used up, finished; (Luft) stale; (Mensch) worn-out.

Verbrechen [fɛr'brɛçən] nt -s, - crime; **v~** vt unreg perpetrate.

Verbrecher [fɛr'brɛçər] m -s, - criminal; **v~isch** a criminal.

ver'breiten vtr spread; **sich über etw** (akk) **~** expound on sth.

verbreitern [fɛr'braɪtərn] vt broaden.

Verbreitung f spread(ing), propagation.

verbrenn- [fɛr'brɛn] zW: **~bar** a combustible; **~en** unreg vt burn; (Leiche) cremate; **V~ung** f burning; (in Motor) combustion; (von Leiche) cremation; **V~ungsmotor** m internal combustion engine.

ver'bringen vt unreg spend.

verbrühen [fɛr'bry:ən] vt scald.

verbuchen [fɛr'bu:xən] vt (FIN) register; (Erfolg) enjoy; (Mißerfolg) suffer.

verbunden [fɛr'bʊndən] a connected; **jdm ~ sein** be obliged od indebted to sb; **falsch ~** (TEL) wrong number; **V~heit** f bond, relationship.

verbünden [fɛr'bʏndən] vr ally o.s.

Verbündete(r) [fɛr'bʏndətə(r)] mf ally.

ver'bürgen vr: **sich ~ für** vouch for.

ver'büßen vt: **eine Strafe ~** serve a sentence.

Verdacht [fɛr'daxt] m -(e)s suspicion.

verdächtig [fɛr'dɛçtɪç] a suspicious, suspect; **~en** [fɛr'dɛçtɪgən] vt suspect.

verdammen [fɛr'damən] vt damn, condemn; **verdammt!** damn!

ver'dampfen vi vaporize, evaporate.

ver'danken vt: **jdm etw ~** owe sb sth.

verdauen [fɛr'daʊən] vt (lit, fig) digest.

verdaulich [fɛr'daʊlɪç] a digestible; **das ist schwer ~** that is hard to digest.

Verdauung f digestion.

Verdeck [fɛr'dɛk] nt -(e)s, -e (AUT) hood; (NAUT) deck; **v~en** vt cover (up); (verbergen) hide.

ver'denken vt unreg: **jdm etw ~** blame sb for sth, hold sth against sb.

Verderb- [fɛr'dɛrp] zW: **~en** [fɛr'dɛrbən] nt -s ruin; **v~en** unreg vt spoil; (schädigen) ruin; (moralisch) corrupt; **es mit jdm v~en** get into sb's bad books // vi (Essen) spoil, rot; (*Mensch*) go to the bad; **v~lich** *a* (*Einfluß*) pernicious; (*Lebensmittel*) perishable.

verdeutlichen [fɛr'dɔytlıçən] *vt* make clear.

ver'dichten *vtr* condense.

ver'dienen *vt* earn; (*moralisch*) deserve.

Ver'dienst *m* -(e)s, -e earnings *pl* // *nt* -(e)s, -e merit; (*Leistung*) service (*um* to).

verdient [fɛr'di:nt] *a* well-earned; (*Person*) deserving of esteem; **sich um etw ~ machen** do a lot for sth.

verdoppeln [fɛr'dɔpəln] *vt* double.

verdorben [fɛr'dɔrbən] *a* spoilt; (*geschädigt*) ruined; (*moralisch*) corrupt.

verdrängen [fɛr'drɛŋən] *vt* oust, displace (*auch PHYS*); (*PSYCH*) repress.

ver'drehen *vt* (*lit, fig*) twist; (*Augen*) roll; **jdm den Kopf ~** (*fig*) turn sb's head.

verdreifachen [fɛr'draɪfaxən] *vt* treble.

verdrießlich [fɛr'dri:slıç] *a* peevish, annoyed.

Verdruß [fɛr'drus] *m* -sses, -sse annoyance, worry.

verdummen [fɛr'dumən] *vt* make stupid // *vi* grow stupid.

verdunkeln [fɛr'duŋkəln] *vtr* darken; (*fig*) obscure.

Verdunk(e)lung *f* blackout; (*fig*) obscuring.

verdünnen [fɛr'dynən] *vt* dilute.

verdunsten [fɛr'dunstən] *vi* evaporate.

verdursten [fɛr'durstən] *vi* die of thirst.

verdutzt [fɛr'dutst] *a* nonplussed, taken aback.

verehr- [fɛr''e:r] *zW:* **~en** *vt* venerate, worship (*auch REL*); **jdm etw ~en** present sb with sth; **V~er(in f)** *m* -s, - admirer, worshipper (*auch REL*); **~t** *a* esteemed; **V~ung** *f* respect; (*REL*) worship.

Verein [fɛr'aɪn] *m* -(e)s, -e club, association; **v~bar** *a* compatible; **v~baren** [-ba:rən] *vt* agree upon; **~barung** *f* agreement; **v~fachen** [-faxən] *vt* simplify; **v~igen** [-ıgən] *vtr* unite; **V~igte Staaten** *pl* United States; **~igung** *f* union; (*Verein*) association; **v~t** *a* united; **vereinzelt** *a* isolated.

vereiteln [fɛr''aɪtəln] *vt* frustrate.

ver'eitern *vi* suppurate, fester.

verengen [fɛr''ɛŋən] *vr* narrow.

vererb- [fɛr''ɛrb] *zW:* **~en** *vt* bequeath; (*BIOL*) transmit // *vr* be hereditary; **~lich** [fɛr''ɛrplıç] *a* hereditary; **V~ung** *f* bequeathing; (*BIOL*) transmission; (*Lehre*) heredity.

verewigen [fɛr''e:vıgən] *vt* immortalize // *vr* leave one's name.

ver'fahren *unreg vi* act; **~ mit** deal with // *vr* get lost // *a* tangled; **V~** *nt* -s, - procedure; (*TECH*) process; (*JUR*) proceedings *pl*.

Verfall [fɛr'fal] *m* -(e)s (*von Haus*) dilapidation; (*FIN*) expiry; **v~en** *vi unreg* decline; (*Haus*) be falling down; (*FIN*) lapse; **v~en in** (+*acc*) lapse into; **v~en auf** (+*acc*) hit upon; **einem Laster v~en sein** be addicted to a vice.

ver'färben *vr* change colour.

Verfasser(in f) [fɛr'fasər(ın)] *m* -s, - author, writer.

Verfassung *f* constitution (*auch POL*).

Verfassungs- *zW:* **~gericht** *nt* constitutional court; **v~mäßig** *a* constitutional; **v~widrig** *a* unconstitutional.

ver'faulen *vi* rot.

ver'fehlen *vt* miss; **etw für verfehlt halten** regard sth as mistaken.

verfeinern [fɛr'faɪnərn] *vt* refine.

ver'filmen *vt* film.

ver'fluchen *vt* curse.

verfolg- [fɛr'fɔlg] *zW:* **~en** *vt* pursue; (*gerichtlich*) prosecute; (*grausam, bes POL*) persecute; **V~er** *m* -s, - pursuer; **V~ung** *f* pursuit; prosecution; persecution.

verfremden [fɛr'frɛmdən] *vt* alienate, distance.

verfrüht [fɛr'fry:t] *a* premature.

verfüg- [fɛr'fy:g] *zW:* **~bar** *a* available; **~en** *vt* direct, order // *vr* proceed // *vi:* **~en über** (+*akk*) have at one's disposal; **V~ung** *f* direction, order; **zur V~ung** at one's disposal; **jdm zur V~ung stehen** be available to sb.

verführ- [fɛr'fy:r] *zW:* **~en** *vt* tempt; (*sexuell*) seduce; **V~er** *m* tempter; seducer; **~erisch** *a* seductive; **V~ung** *f* seduction; (*Versuchung*) temptation.

ver'gammeln *vi* (*umg*) go to seed; (*Nahrung*) go off.

vergangen [fɛr'gaŋən] *a* past; **V~heit** *f* past.

vergänglich [fɛr'gɛŋlıç] *a* transitory; **V~keit** *f* transitoriness, impermanence.

vergasen [fɛr'ga:zən] *vt* (*töten*) gas.

Vergaser *m* -s, - (*AUT*) carburettor.

vergaß *etc v siehe* **vergessen**.

vergeb- [fɛr'ge:b] *zW:* **~en** *vt unreg* forgive (*jdm etw* sb for sth); (*weggeben*) give away; **~ens** *ad* in vain; **~lich** [fɛr'ge:plıç] *ad* in vain // *a* vain, futile; **V~ung** *f* forgiveness.

ver'gehen *unreg vi* pass by *od* away; **jdm vergeht etw** sb loses sth // *vr* commit an offence (*gegen etw* against sth); **sich an jdm ~** (*sexually*) assault sb; **V~** *nt* -s, - offence.

ver'gelten *vt unreg* pay back (*jdm*

etw sb for sth), repay.

Ver'geltung *f* retaliation, reprisal; **Vergeltungsschlag** *m* (MIL) reprisal.

vergessen [fɛr'gɛsən] *vt unreg* forget; **V~heit** *f* oblivion.

vergeßlich [fɛr'gɛslɪç] *a* forgetful; **V~keit** *f* forgetfulness.

vergeuden [fɛr'gɔʏdən] *vt* squander, waste.

vergewaltigen [fɛrgə'valtɪgən] *vt* rape; (*fig*) violate. **Vergewaltigung** *f* rape.

vergewissern [fɛrgə'vɪsərn] *vr* make sure.

ver'gießen *vt unreg* shed.

vergiften [fɛr'gɪftən] *vt* poison. **Vergiftung** *f* poisoning.

Vergißmeinnicht [fɛr'gɪsmaɪnnɪçt] *nt* -(e)s, -e forget-me-not.

vergißt *etc v siehe* **vergessen**.

Vergleich [fɛr'glaɪç] *m* -(e)s, -e comparison; (JUR) settlement; **im ~ mit** *od* **zu** compared with *od* to; **v~bar** *a* comparable; **v~en** *unreg vt* compare // *vr* reach a settlement.

vergnügen [fɛr'gny:gən] *vr* enjoy *od* amuse o.s.; **V~** *nt* -s, - pleasure; **viel V~!** enjoy yourself!

vergnügt [fɛr'gny:kt] *a* cheerful. **Vergnügung** *f* pleasure, amusement; **Vergnügungspark** *m* amusement park; **vergnügungssüchtig** *a* pleasure-loving.

vergolden [fɛr'gɔldən] *vt* gild.

vergöttern [fɛr'gœtərn] *vt* idolize.

ver'graben *vt* bury.

ver'greifen *vr unreg*: **sich an jdm ~** lay hands on sb; **sich an etw ~** misappropriate sth; **sich im Ton ~** say the wrong thing.

vergriffen [fɛr'grɪfən] *a* (*Buch*) out of print; (*Ware*) out of stock.

vergrößern [fɛr'grø:sərn] *vt* enlarge; (*mengenmäßig*) increase; (*Lupe*) magnify. **Vergrößerung** *f* enlargement; increase; magnification; **Vergrößerungsglas** *nt* magnifying glass.

Vergünstigung [fɛr'gʏnstɪgʊŋ] *f* concession, privilege.

vergüten [fɛr'gy:tən] *vt*: **jdm etw ~** compensate sb for sth. **Vergütung** *f* compensation.

verhaften [fɛr'haftən] *vt* arrest. **Verhaftung** *f* arrest.

ver'hallen *vi* die away.

ver'halten *unreg vr* be, stand; (*sich benehmen*) behave; (MATH) be in proportion to // *vt* hold *od* keep back; (*Schritt*) check; **V~** *nt* -s behaviour.

Verhältnis [fɛr'hɛltnɪs] *nt* -ses, -se relationship; (MATH) proportion, ratio // *pl* (*Umstände*) conditions *pl*; **über seine ~se leben** live beyond one's means; **v~mäßig** *a, ad* relative(ly),

comparative(ly).

verhandeln [fɛr'handəln] *vi* negotiate (*über etw* (akk) sth); (JUR) hold proceedings // *vt* discuss; (JUR) hear. **Verhandlung** *f* negotiation; (JUR) proceedings *pl*; **Verhandlungspaket** *nt* package (of proposals).

ver'hängen *vt* (*fig*) impose, inflict.

Verhängnis [fɛr'hɛŋnɪs] *nt* -ses, -se fate, doom; **jdm zum ~ werden** be sb's undoing; **v~voll** *a* fatal, disastrous.

verharmlosen [fɛr'harmlo:zən] *vt* make light of, play down.

verhärten [fɛr'hɛrtən] *vr* harden.

verhaßt [fɛr'hast] *a* odious, hateful.

verheerend [fɛr'he:rənt] *a* disastrous, devastating.

verheimlichen [fɛr'haɪmlɪçən] *vt* keep secret (*jdm* from sb).

verheiratet [fɛr'haɪra:tət] *a* married.

ver'helfen *vi unreg*: **jdm ~ zu** help sb to get.

verherrlichen [fɛr'hɛrlɪçən] *vt* glorify.

ver'hexen *vt* bewitch; **es ist wie verhext** it's jinxed.

ver'hindern *vt* prevent; **verhindert sein** be unable to make it.

verhöhnen [fɛr'hø:nən] *vt* mock, sneer at.

Verhör [fɛr'hø:r] *nt* -(e)s, -e interrogation; (*gerichtlich*) (cross-)examination; **v~en** *vt* interrogate; (cross-)examine // *vr* misunderstand, mishear.

ver'hungern *vi* starve, die of hunger.

ver'hüten *vt* prevent, avert. **Ver'hütung** *f* prevention; **Verhütungsmittel** *nt* contraceptive.

verirren [fɛr'ɪrən] *vr* go astray.

ver'jagen *vt* drive away *od* out.

verkalken [fɛr'kalkən] *vi* calcify; (*umg*) become senile.

verkannt [fɛr'kant] *a* unappreciated.

Verkauf [fɛr'kauf] *m* sale; **v~en** *vt* sell.

Verkäufer(in *f*) [fɛr'kɔʏfər(ɪn)] *m* -s, - seller; salesman; (*in Laden*) shop assistant.

verkäuflich [fɛr'kɔʏflɪç] *a* saleable.

Verkaufsbedingungen *pl* terms and conditions of sale.

Verkehr [fɛr'ke:r] *m* -s, -e traffic; (*Umgang, bes sexuell*) intercourse; (*Umlauf*) circulation; **v~en** *vi* (*Fahrzeug*) ply, run; (*besuchen*) visit regularly (*bei jdm* sb); **v~en mit** associate with // *vtr* turn, transform.

Verkehrs- *zW*: **~ampel** *f* traffic lights *pl*; **~amt** *nt* tourist office; **~delikt** *nt* traffic offence; **~stauung** *f*, **~stockung** *f* traffic jam, stoppage; **~teilnehmer** *m* road-user; **~unfall** *m* traffic accident; **~zeichen** *nt* traffic sign.

verkehrt a wrong; (umgekehrt) the wrong way round.

ver'kennen vt unreg misjudge, not appreciate.

ver'klagen vt take to court.

verkleiden [fɛr'klaɪdən] vtr disguise (o.s.), dress up.

Verkleidung f disguise; (ARCHIT) wainscoting.

verkleinern [fɛr'klaɪnərn] vt make smaller, reduce in size.

verklemmt [fɛr'klɛmt] a (fig) inhibited.

ver'klingen vi unreg die away.

ver'kneifen vt (umg): sich (dat) etw ~ (Lachen) stifle; (Schmerz) hide; (sich versagen) do without.

verknüpfen [fɛr'knypfən] vt tie (up), knot; (fig) connect.

ver'kommen vi unreg deteriorate, decay; (Mensch) go downhill, come down in the world // a (moralisch) dissolute, depraved.

verkörpern [fɛr'kœrpərn] vt embody, personify.

verkraften [fɛr'kraftən] vt cope with.

ver'kriechen vr unreg creep away, creep into a corner.

Verkrümmung f bend, warp; (ANAT) curvature.

verkrüppelt [fɛr'krypəlt] a crippled.

verkrustet [fɛr'krʊstət] a encrusted.

ver'kühlen vr get a chill.

ver'kümmern vi waste away.

ver'künden vt proclaim; (Urteil) pronounce.

verkürzen [fɛr'kyrtsən] vt shorten; (Wort) abbreviate; sich (dat) die Zeit ~ while away the time.

Verkürzung f shortening; abbreviation.

Verlag [fɛr'la:k] m -(e)s, -e publishing firm.

verlangen [fɛr'laŋən] vt demand; desire; ~ Sie Herrn X ask for Mr X // vi: ~ nach ask for, desire; **V~** nt -s, - desire (nach for); auf jds **V~** (hin) at sb's request.

verlängern [fɛr'lɛŋərn] vt extend; (länger machen) lengthen.

Verlängerung f extension; (SPORT) extra time; **Verlängerungsschnur** f extension cable.

verlangsamen [fɛr'laŋza:mən] vtr decelerate, slow down.

Verlaß [fɛr'las] m: auf ihn/das ist kein ~ he/it cannot be relied upon.

ver'lassen unreg vt leave // vr depend (auf +akk on) // a desolate; (Mensch) abandoned; **V~heit** f loneliness.

verläßlich [fɛr'lɛslɪç] a reliable.

Verlauf [fɛr'lauf] m course; **v~en** unreg vi (zeitlich) pass; (Farben) run // vr get lost; (Menschenmenge)

disperse.

ver'lauten vi: etw ~ lassen disclose sth; wie verlautet as reported.

ver'legen vt move; (verlieren) mislay; (Buch) publish // vr: sich auf etw (akk) ~ take up od to sth // a embarrassed; nicht ~ um never at a loss for; **V~heit** f embarrassment; (Situation) difficulty, scrape.

Verleger [fɛr'le:gər] m -s, - publisher.

Verleih [fɛr'laɪ] m -(e)s, -e hire service; **v~en** vt unreg lend; (Kraft, Anschein) confer, bestow; (Preis, Medaille) award; **~ung** f lending; bestowal; award.

ver'leiten vt lead astray; ~ zu talk into, tempt into.

ver'lernen vt forget, unlearn.

ver'lesen unreg vt read out; (aussondern) sort out // vr make a mistake in reading.

verletz- [fɛr'lɛts] zW: **~en** vt (lit, fig) injure, hurt; (Gesetz etc) violate; **~end** a (fig: Worte) hurtful; **~lich** a vulnerable, sensitive; **V~te(r)** mf injured person; **V~ung** f injury; (Verstoß) violation, infringement.

verleumd- [fɛr'lɔymd] zW: **~en** vt slander; **V~ung** f slander, libel.

ver'lieben vr fall in love (in jdn with sb).

verliebt [fɛr'li:pt] a in love; **V~heit** f being in love.

verlieren [fɛr'li:rən] unreg vti lose // vr get lost.

verlob- [fɛr'lo:b] zW: **~en** vr get engaged (mit to); **V~te(r)** [fɛr'lo:ptə(r)] mf fiancé(e); **V~ung** f engagement.

ver'locken vt entice, lure.

Ver'lockung f temptation, attraction.

verlogen [fɛr'lo:gən] a untruthful; **V~heit** f untruthfulness.

verlor etc v siehe **verlieren**.

verloren [fɛr'lo:rən] a lost; (Eier) poached; etw ~ geben give sth up for lost // v siehe **verlieren**; **~gehen** vi unreg get lost.

verlosen [fɛr'lo:zən] vt raffle, draw lots for.

Verlosung f raffle, lottery.

verlottern [fɛr'lɔtərn], **verludern** [fɛr'lu:dərn] vi (umg) go to the dogs.

Verlust [fɛr'lʊst] m -(e)s, -e loss; (MIL) casualty.

ver'machen vt bequeath, leave.

Vermächtnis [fɛr'mɛçtnɪs] nt -ses, -se legacy.

Vermählung f wedding, marriage.

vermehren [fɛr'me:rən] vtr multiply; (Menge) increase.

Vermehrung f multiplying; increase.

ver'meiden vt unreg avoid.

vermeintlich [fɛr'maɪntlɪç] a supposed.

Vermerk [fɛr'mɛrk] m -(e)s, -e note; (in Ausweis) endorsement; **v~en** vt note.

ver'messen *unreg vt* survey // *a* pre-sumptuous, bold; **V~heit** *f* presumpt-uousness; recklessness.

Ver'messung *f* survey(ing).

ver'mieten *vt* let, rent (out); (*Auto*) hire out, rent.

Ver'mieter(in *f)* *m* **-s,** - landlord/landlady.

Ver'mietung *f* letting, renting (out); (*von Autos*) hiring (out).

vermindern [fɛr'mɪndərn] *vtr* lessen, decrease; (*Preise*) reduce.

Verminderung *f* reduction.

ver'mischen *vtr* mix, blend.

vermissen [fɛr'mɪsən] *vt* miss.

vermißt [fɛr'mɪst] *a* missing.

vermitteln [fɛr'mɪtəln] *vi* mediate // *vt* (*Gespräch*) connect; **jdm etw ~** help sb to obtain sth.

Vermittler [fɛr'mɪtlər] *m* **-s,** - (*Schlichter*) agent, mediator.

Vermittlung *f* procurement; (*Stellen~*) agency; (*TEL*) exchange; (*Schlichtung*) mediation.

ver'mögen *vt unreg* be capable of; **~ zu** be able to; **V~** *nt* **-s,** - wealth; (*Fähigkeit*) ability; **ein V~ kosten** cost a fortune; **~d** *a* wealthy.

vermuten [fɛr'muːtən] *vt* suppose, guess; (*argwöhnen*) suspect.

vermutlich *a* supposed, presumed // *ad* probably.

Vermutung *f* supposition; suspicion.

vernachlässigen [fɛr'naːxlɛsɪgən] *vt* neglect.

ver'nehmen *vt unreg* perceive, hear; (*erfahren*) learn; (*JUR*) (cross)-examine; **dem V~ nach** from what I/we *etc* hear.

vernehmlich [fɛr'neːmlɪç] *a* audible.

Vernehmung *f* (cross-)examination.

verneigen [fɛr'naɪgən] *vr* bow.

verneinen [fɛr'naɪnən] *vt* (*Frage*) answer in the negative; (*ablehnen*) deny; (*GRAM*) negate; **~d** *a* negative.

Verneinung *f* negation.

vernichten [fɛr'nɪçtən] *vt* annihilate, destroy; **~d** *a* (*fig*) crushing; (*Blick*) withering; (*Kritik*) scathing.

Vernichtung *f* destruction, annihilation.

verniedlichen [fɛr'niːtlɪçən] *vt* play down.

Vernunft [fɛr'nʊnft] *f* - reason, understanding.

vernünftig [fɛr'nʏnftɪç] *a* sensible, reasonable.

veröffentlichen [fɛr''œfəntlɪçən] *vt* publish.

Veröffentlichung *f* publication.

verordnen [fɛr''ɔrdnən] *vt* (*MED*) prescribe.

Verordnung *f* order, decree; (*MED*)

prescription.

ver'pachten *vt* lease (out).

ver'packen *vt* pack.

Ver'packung *f,* **Verpackungsmaterial** *nt* packing, wrapping.

ver'passen *vt* miss; **jdm eine Ohrfeige ~** (*umg*) give sb a clip round the ear.

ver'pflanzen *vt* transplant.

Ver'pflanzung *f* transplant(ing).

ver'pflegen *vt* feed, cater for.

Ver'pflegung *f* feeding, catering; (*Kost*) food; (*in Hotel*) board.

verpflichten [fɛr'pflɪçtən] *vt* oblige, bind; (*anstellen*) engage // *vr* undertake; (*MIL*) sign on // *vi* carry obligations; **jdm zu Dank verpflichtet sein** be obliged to sb.

Verpflichtung *f* obligation, duty.

verpönt [fɛr'pøːnt] *a* disapproved (of), taboo.

ver'prügeln *vt* (*umg*) beat up, do over.

Verputz [fɛr'pʊts] *m* plaster, roughcast; **v~en** *vt* plaster; (*umg: Essen*) put away.

Verrat [fɛr'raːt] *m* **-(e)s** treachery; (*POL*) treason; **v~en** *unreg vt* betray; (*Geheimnis*) divulge // *vr* give o.s. away.

Verräter [fɛr'rɛːtər] *m* **-s,** - traitor; **~in** *f* traitress; **v~isch** *a* treacherous.

ver'rechnen *vt:* **~ mit** set off against // *vr* miscalculate.

Verrechnungsscheck [fɛr'rɛçnʊŋsʃɛk] *m* crossed cheque.

verregnet [fɛr'reːgnət] *a* spoilt by rain, rainy.

ver'reisen *vi* go away (on a journey).

verrenken [fɛr'rɛŋkən] *vt* contort; (*MED*) dislocate; **sich** (*dat*) **den Knöchel ~** sprain one's ankle.

ver'richten *vt* do, perform.

verriegeln [fɛr'riːgəln] *vt* bolt up, lock.

verringern [fɛr'rɪŋərn] *vt* reduce // *vr* diminish.

Verringerung *f* reduction; lessening.

ver'rinnen *vi unreg* run out *od* away; (*Zeit*) elapse.

ver'rosten *vi* rust.

verrotten [fɛr'rɔtən] *vi* rot.

ver'rücken *vt* move, shift.

verrückt [fɛr'rʏkt] *a* crazy, mad; **V~e(r)** *mf* lunatic; **V~heit** *f* madness, lunacy.

Verruf [fɛr'ruːf] *m:* **in ~ geraten/bringen** fall/bring into disrepute; **v~en** *a* notorious, disreputable.

Vers [fɛrs] *m* **-es, -e** verse.

ver'sagen *vt:* **jdm/sich** (*dat*) **etw ~** deny sb/o.s. sth // *vi* fail; **V~** *nt* **-s** failure.

Versager [fɛr'zaːgər] *m* **-s,** - failure.

ver'salzen *vt unreg* put too much salt

in; *(fig)* spoil.

ver'sammeln *vtr* assemble, gather.

Ver'sammlung *f* meeting, gathering.

Versand [fɛr'zant] *m* **-(e)s** forwarding; dispatch; *(~abteilung)* dispatch department; *(~haus)* mail-order firm.

versäumen [fɛr'zɔymən] *vt* miss; *(unterlassen)* neglect, fail.

ver'schaffen *vt*: jdm/sich etw ~ get *od* procure sth for sb/o.s.

verschämt [fɛr'ʃɛːmt] *a* bashful.

verschandeln [fɛr'ʃandəln] *vt (umg)* spoil.

verschärfen [fɛr'ʃɛrfən] *vtr* intensify; *(Lage)* aggravate.

ver'schätzen *vr* be out in one's reckoning.

ver'schenken *vt* give away.

ver'schicken *vt* send off.

ver'schieben *vt unreg* shift; *(EISENB)* shunt; *(Termin)* postpone.

verschieden [fɛr'ʃiːdən] *a* different; *(pl: mehrere)* various; **sie sind ~ groß** they are of different sizes; **~e** *pl* various people/things *pl*; **~es** *pron* various things *pl*; **etwas V~es** something different; **V~heit** *f* difference; **verschiedentlich** *ad* several times.

verschlafen [fɛr'ʃlaːfən] *unreg vt* sleep through; *(fig: versäumen)* miss // *vir* oversleep // *a* sleepy.

Verschlag [fɛr'ʃlaːk] *m* shed; **v~en** [fɛr'ʃlaːgən] *vt unreg* board up; **jdm den Atem v~en** take sb's breath away; **an einen Ort v~en werden** wind up in a place // *a* cunning.

verschlechtern [fɛr'ʃlɛçtərn] *vt* make worse // *vr* deteriorate, get worse.

Verschlechterung *f* deterioration.

Verschleiß [fɛr'ʃlaɪs] *m* **-es, -e** wear and tear; **v~en** *unreg vt* wear out.

ver'schleppen *vt* carry off, abduct; *(Krankheit)* protract; *(zeitlich)* drag out.

ver'schleudern *vt* squander; *(COMM)* sell dirt-cheap.

verschließ- [fɛr'ʃliːs] *zW*: **~bar** *a* lockable; **~en** *unreg vt* close; lock // *vr*: **sich einer Sache ~en** close one's mind to sth.

verschlimmern [fɛr'ʃlɪmərn] *vt* make worse, aggravate // *vr* get worse, deteriorate.

verschlingen [fɛr'ʃlɪŋən] *vt unreg* devour, swallow up; *(Fäden)* twist.

verschlossen [fɛr'ʃlɔsən] *a* locked; *(fig)* reserved; **V~heit** *f* reserve.

ver'schlucken *vt* swallow // *vr* choke.

Verschluß [fɛr'ʃlus] *m* lock; *(von Kleid etc)* fastener; *(PHOT)* shutter; *(Stöpsel)* plug; **unter ~ halten** keep under lock and key.

verschlüsseln [fɛr'ʃlʏsəln] *vt* encode.

verschmähen [fɛr'ʃmɛːən] *vt* disdain, scorn.

verschmerzen [fɛr'ʃmɛrtsən] *vt* get over.

verschmutzen [fɛr'ʃmʊtsən] *vt* soil; *(Umwelt)* pollute.

verschneit [fɛr'ʃnaɪt] *a* snowed up, covered in snow.

verschollen [fɛr'ʃɔlən] *a* lost, missing.

ver'schonen *vt* spare *(jdn mit etw* sb sth).

verschönern [fɛr'ʃøːnərn] *vt* decorate; *(verbessern)* improve.

ver'schreiben *unreg vt (MED)* prescribe // *vr* make a mistake (in writing); **sich einer Sache ~** devote oneself to sth.

verschroben [fɛr'ʃroːbən] *a* eccentric, odd.

verschrotten [fɛr'ʃrɔtən] *vt* scrap.

verschuld- [fɛr'ʃʊld] *zW*: **~en** *vt* be guilty of; **V~en** *nt* **-s** fault, guilt; **~et** *a* in debt; **V~ung** *f* fault; *(Geld)* debts *pl*.

ver'schütten *vt* spill; *(zuschütten)* fill; *(unter Trümmer)* bury.

ver'schweigen *vt unreg* keep secret; **jdm etw ~** keep sth from sb.

verschwend- [fɛr'ʃvɛnd] *zW*: **~en** *vt* squander; **V~er** *m* **-s, -** spendthrift; **~erisch** *a* wasteful, extravagant; **V~ung** *f* waste; extravagance.

verschwiegen [fɛr'ʃviːgən] *a* discreet; *(Ort)* secluded; **V~heit** *f* discretion; seclusion.

ver'schwimmen *vi unreg* grow hazy, become blurred.

ver'schwinden *vi unreg* disappear, vanish; **V~** *nt* **-s** disappearance.

verschwommen [fɛr'ʃvomən] *a* hazy, vague.

verschwör- [fɛr'ʃvøːr] *zW*: **~en** *vr unreg* plot, conspire; **V~er** *m* **-s, -** conspirator; **V~ung** *f* conspiracy, plot.

ver'sehen *unreg vt* supply, provide; *(Pflicht)* carry out; *(Amt)* fill; *(Haushalt)* keep // *vr (fig)* make a mistake; **ehe er (es) sich ~ hatte...** before he knew it...; **V~** *nt* **-s, -** oversight; **aus V~** by mistake; **versehentlich** *ad* by mistake.

Versehrte(r) [fɛr'zeːrtə(r)] *mf* disabled person.

ver'senden *vt unreg* forward, dispatch.

ver'senken *vt* sink // *vr* become engrossed *(in +akk* in).

versessen [fɛr'zɛsən] *a*: **~ auf** *(+akk)* mad about.

ver'setzen *vt* transfer; *(verpfänden)* pawn; *(umg)* stand up; **jdm einen Tritt/Schlag ~** kick/hit sb; **etw mit etw ~** mix sth with sth; **jdn in gute Laune ~** put sb in a good mood // *vr*: **sich in jdn** *od* **in jds Lage ~** put o.s. in sb's place.

Ver'setzung f transfer.

verseuchen [fɛr'zɔyçən] vt contaminate.

versichern [fɛr'zɪçərn] vt assure; (mit Geld) insure.

Versicherung f assurance; insurance; **Versicherungsgesellschaft** f insurance company; **Versicherungspolice** f insurance policy.

ver'siegen vi dry up.

ver'sinken vi unreg sink.

versöhnen [fɛr'zøːnən] vt reconcile // vr become reconciled.

Versöhnung f reconciliation.

ver'sorgen vt provide, supply (mit with); (Familie etc) look after.

Ver'sorgung f provision; (Unterhalt) maintenance; (Alters~ etc) benefit, assistance.

verspäten [fɛr'ʃpɛːtən] vr be late.

Verspätung f delay; ~ haben be late.

ver'sperren vt bar, obstruct.

ver'spotten vt ridicule, scoff at.

ver'sprechen vt unreg promise; sich (dat) etw von etw ~ expect sth from sth; **V~** nt -s, - promise.

verstaatlichen [fɛr'ʃtaːtlɪçən] vt nationalize.

Verstand [fɛr'ʃtant] m intelligence; mind; den ~ verlieren go out of one's mind; über jds ~ gehen go beyond sb.

verständig [fɛr'ʃtɛndɪç] a sensible; **~en** [fɛr'ʃtɛndɪgən] vt inform // vr communicate; (sich einigen) come to an understanding; **V~ung** f communication; (Benachrichtigung) informing; (Einigung) agreement.

verständ- [fɛr'ʃtɛnt] zW: **~lich** a understandable, comprehensible; **V~lichkeit** f clarity, intelligibility; **V~nis** nt -ses, -se understanding; **~nislos** a uncomprehending; **~nisvoll** a understanding, sympathetic.

verstärk- [fɛr'ʃtɛrk] zW: **~en** vt strengthen; (Ton) amplify; (erhöhen) intensify // vr intensify; **V~er** m -s, - amplifier; **V~ung** f strengthening; (Hilfe) reinforcements pl; (von Ton) amplification.

verstauchen [fɛr'ʃtauxən] vt sprain.

verstauen [fɛr'ʃtauən] vt stow away.

Versteck [fɛr'ʃtɛk] nt -(e)s, -e hiding (place); **v~en** vtr hide; **v~t** a hidden.

ver'stehen unreg vt understand // vr get on; das versteht sich (von selbst) that goes without saying.

versteigern [fɛr'ʃtaɪgərn] vt auction.

Versteigerung f auction.

verstell- [fɛr'ʃtɛl] zW: **~bar** a adjustable, variable; **~en** vt move, shift; (Uhr) adjust; (versperren) block; (fig) disguise // vr pretend, put

on an act; **V~ung** f pretence.

verstiegen [fɛr'ʃtiːgən] a exaggerated.

verstimmt [fɛr'ʃtɪmt] a out of tune; (fig) cross, put out; (Magen) upset.

verstohlen [fɛr'ʃtoːlən] a stealthy.

ver'stopfen vt block, stop up; (MED) constipate.

Ver'stopfung f obstruction; (MED) constipation.

verstorben [fɛr'ʃtɔrbən] a deceased, late.

verstört [fɛr'ʃtøːrt] a (Mensch) distraught.

Verstoß [fɛr'ʃtoːs] m infringement, violation (gegen of); **v~en** unreg vt disown, reject // vi: **v~en gegen** offend against.

ver'streichen unreg vt spread // vi elapse.

ver'streuen vt scatter (about).

verstümmeln [fɛr'ʃtʏməln] vt maim, mutilate (auch fig).

verstummen [fɛr'ʃtumən] vi go silent; (Lärm) die away.

Versuch [fɛr'zuːx] m -(e)s, -e attempt; (SCI) experiment; **v~en** vt try; (verlocken) tempt // vr: sich an etw (dat) **v~en** try one's hand at sth; **Versuchskaninchen** nt guinea-pig; **versuchsweise** ad tentatively; **~ung** f temptation.

versumpfen [fɛr'zumpfən] vi (fig umg) get into a booze-up.

versunken [fɛr'zuŋkən] a sunken; ~ sein in (+acc) be absorbed od engrossed in.

vertagen [fɛr'taːgən] vti adjourn.

ver'tauschen vt exchange; (versehentlich) mix up.

verteidig- [fɛr'taɪdɪç] zW: **~en** vt defend; **V~er** m -s, - defender; (JUR) defence counsel; **V~ung** f defence.

ver'teilen vt distribute; (Rollen) assign; (Salbe) spread.

Verteilung f distribution, allotment.

vertiefen [fɛr'tiːfən] vt deepen // vr: sich in etw (akk) ~ become engrossed od absorbed in sth.

Vertiefung f depression.

vertikal [vɛrti'kaːl] a vertical.

vertilgen [fɛr'tɪlgən] vt exterminate; (umg) eat up, consume.

vertonen [fɛr'toːnən] vt set to music.

Vertrag [fɛr'traːk] m -(e)s, -e contract, agreement; (POL) treaty; **v~en** [fɛr'traːgən] unreg vt tolerate, stand // vr get along; (sich aussöhnen) become reconciled; **v~lich** a contractual.

verträglich [fɛr'trɛːklɪç] a goodnatured, sociable; (Speisen) easily digested; (MED) easily tolerated; **V~keit** f sociability; good nature; digestibility.

Vertrags- zW: **~bruch** m breach of

contract; **~partner** *m* party to a contract; **v~widrig** *a* contrary to contract.

vertrauen [fɛr'trauən] *vi* trust (*jdm* sb); **~ auf** (+*akk*) rely on; **V~** *nt* -s confidence; **~erweckend** *a* inspiring trust; **vertrauensvoll** *a* trustful; **vertrauenswürdig** *a* trustworthy.

vertraulich [fɛr'traulɪç] *a* familiar; (*geheim*) confidential.

vertraut [fɛr'traut] *a* familiar; **V~heit** *f* familiarity.

ver'treiben *vt unreg* drive away; (*aus Land*) expel; (*COMM*) sell; (*Zeit*) pass.

vertret- [fɛr'treːt] *zW:* **~en** *vt unreg* represent; (*Ansicht*) hold, advocate; sich (*dat*) die Beine **~en** stretch one's legs; **V~er** *m* -s, - representative; (*Verfechter*) advocate; **V~ung** *f* representation; advocacy.

Vertrieb [fɛr'triːp] *m* -(e)s, -e marketing.

ver'trocknen *vi* dry up.

ver'trösten *vt* put off.

vertun [fɛr'tuːn] *unreg vt* (*umg*) waste // *vr* make a mistake.

vertuschen [fɛr'tuʃən] *vt* hush *od* cover up.

verübeln [fɛr'yːbəln] *vt:* jdm etw ~ be cross *od* offended with sb on account of sth.

verüben [fɛr'yːbən] *vt* commit.

verun- [fɛr'ʊn] *zW:* **~glimpfen** [-glɪmpfən] *vt* disparage; **~glücken** [-glʏkən] *vi* have an accident; tödlich **~glücken** be killed in an accident; **~reinigen** *vt* soil; (*Umwelt*) pollute; **~sichern** *vt* rattle; **~treuen** [-trɔyən] *vt* embezzle.

verur- [fɛr'uːr] *zW:* **~sachen** [-zaxən] *vt* cause; **~teilen** [-tailən] *vt* condemn; **V~teilung** *f* condemnation; (*JUR*) sentence.

verviel- [fɛr'fiːl] *zW:* **~fachen** [-faxən] *vt* multiply; **~fältigen** [-fɛltɪgən] *vt* duplicate, copy; **V~fältigung** *f* duplication, copying.

vervoll- [fɛr'fɔl] *zW:* **~kommnen** [-kɔmnən] *vt* perfect; **~ständigen** [-ʃtɛndɪgən] *vt* complete.

ver'wackeln *vt* (*PHOTO*) blur.

ver'wählen *vt* (*TEL*) dial the wrong number.

verwahr- [fɛr'vaːr] *zW:* **~en** *vi* keep, lock away // *vr* protest; **~losen** [-loːzən] *vi* become neglected; (*moralisch*) go to the bad; **~lost** [-loːst] *a* neglected; wayward.

verwalt- [fɛr'valt] *zW:* **~en** *vt* manage; administer; **V~er** *m* -s, - manager; (*Vermögens~er*) trustee; **V~ung** *f* administration; management; **V~ungsbezirk** *m* administrative district.

ver'wandeln *vtr* change, transform.

Ver'wandlung *f* change, transformation.

verwandt [fɛr'vant] *a* related (*mit* to); **V~e(r)** *mf* relative, relation; **V~schaft** *f* relationship; (*Menschen*) relations *pl.*

ver'warnen *vt* caution.

Ver'warnung *f* caution.

ver'wechseln *vt* confuse (*mit* with); mistake (*mit* for); zum **V~** ähnlich as like as two peas.

Ver'wechslung *f* confusion, mixing up.

verwegen [fɛr'veːgən] *a* daring, bold.

Verwehung [fɛr'veːʊŋ] *f* snow-/sanddrift.

verweichlicht [fɛr'vaiçlɪçt] *a* effeminate, soft.

ver'weigern *vt* refuse (*jdm etw* sb sth); den Gehorsam/die Aussage ~ refuse to obey/testify.

Ver'weigerung *f* refusal.

Verweis [fɛr'vais] *m* -es, -e reprimand, rebuke; (*Hinweis*) reference; **v~en** [fɛr'vaizən] *vt unreg* refer; jdn von der Schule **v~en** expel sb (from school); jdn des Landes **v~en** deport *od* expel sb.

ver'welken *vi* fade.

ver'wenden *unreg vt* use; (*Mühe, Zeit, Arbeit*) spend // *vr* intercede.

Ver'wendung *f* use.

ver'werfen *vt unreg* reject.

verwerflich [fɛr'vɛrflɪç] *a* reprehensible.

ver'werten *vt* utilize.

Ver'wertung *f* utilization.

verwesen [fɛr'veːzən] *vi* decay.

ver'wickeln *vt* tangle (up); (*fig*) involve (*in* +*akk* in) // *vr* get tangled (up); sich ~ in (+*acc*) (*fig*) get involved in.

verwildern [fɛr'vɪldərn] *vi* run wild.

ver'winden *vt unreg* get over.

verwirklichen [fɛr'vɪrklɪçən] *vt* realize, put into effect.

Verwirklichung *f* realization.

verwirren [fɛr'vɪrən] *vt* tangle (up); (*fig*) confuse.

Verwirrung *f* confusion.

verwittern [fɛr'vɪtərn] *vi* weather.

verwitwet [fɛr'vɪtvət] *a* widowed.

verwöhnen [fɛr'vøːnən] *vt* spoil.

verworfen [fɛr'vɔrfən] *a* depraved.

verworren [fɛr'vɔrən] *a* confused.

verwund- *zW:* **~bar** [fɛr'vʊntbaːr] *a* vulnerable; **~en** [fɛr'vʊndən] *vt* wound; **~erlich** [fɛr'vʊndərlɪç] *a* surprising; **V~erung** [fɛr'vʊndərʊŋ] *f* astonishment; **V~ete(r)** *mf* injured (person); **V~ung** *f* wound, injury.

ver'wünschen *vt* curse.

verwüsten [fɛr'vyːstən] *vt* devastate.

verzagen [fɛr'tsaːgən] *vi* despair.

ver'zählen *vr* miscount.

verzehren [fɛr'tseːrən] *vt* consume.

ver'zeichnen *vt* list; (*Niederlage, Verlust*) register.

Verzeichnis [fɛr'tsaɪçnɪs] *nt* **-ses, -se** list, catalogue; (*in Buch*) index.

verzeih- [fɛr'tsaɪ] *zW:* **~en** *vti unreg* forgive (*jdm etw* sb for sth); **~lich** *a* pardonable; **V~ung** *f* forgiveness, pardon; **V~ung!** sorry!, excuse me!

Verzicht [fɛr'tsɪçt] *m* **-(e)s** renunciation (*auf +akk* of); **v~en** *vi* forgo, give up (*auf etw* (*acc*) sth).

ver'ziehen *unreg vi* move // *vt* put out of shape; (*Kind*) spoil; (*Pflanzen*) thin out; **das Gesicht ~** pull a face // *vr* go out of shape; (*Gesicht*) contort; (*verschwinden*) disappear.

verzieren [fɛr'tsiːrən] *vt* decorate, ornament.

verzinsen [fɛr'tsɪnzən] *vt* pay interest on.

ver'zögern *vt* delay.

Ver'zögerung *f* delay, time-lag; **Verzögerungstaktik** *f* delaying tactics *pl*.

verzollen [fɛr'tsɔlən] *vt* declare, pay duty on.

verzück- [fɛr'tsʏk] *zW:* **~t** *a* enraptured; **V~ung** *f* ecstasy.

verzweif- [fɛr'tsvaɪf] *zW:* **~eln** *vi* despair; **~elt** *a* desperate; **V~lung** *f* despair.

verzwickt [fɛr'tsvɪkt] *a* (*umg*) awkward, complicated.

Vesuv [ve'zuːf] *m* Vesuvius.

Veto ['veːto] *nt* **-s, -s** veto.

Vetter ['fɛtər] *m* **-s, -n** cousin.

vgl. *abk* (= *vergleiche*) cf.

v.H. *abk* (= *vom Hundert*) pc.

vibrieren [vi'briːrən] *vi* vibrate.

Video ['viːdeo] *nt* video; **~gerät** *nt*, **~recorder** *m* video recorder.

Vieh [fiː] *nt* **-(e)s** cattle *pl*; **v~isch** *a* bestial.

viel [fiːl] *a* a lot of, much; **~e** *pl* a lot of, many // *ad* a lot, much; **~ zuwenig** much too little; **~erlei** *a* a great variety of; **~es** *a* a lot; **~fach** *a, ad* many times; **auf ~fachen Wunsch** at the request of many people; **V~falt** *f* variety; **~fältig** *a* varied, many-sided.

vielleicht [fiˈlaɪçt] *ad* perhaps.

viel- *zW:* **~mal(s)** *ad* many times; **danke ~mals** many thanks; **~mehr** *ad* rather, on the contrary; **~sagend** *a* significant; **~seitig** *a* many-sided; **~versprechend** *a* promising.

vier [fiːr] *num* four; **V~eck** *nt* **-(e)s, -e** four-sided figure; (*gleichseitig*) square; **~eckig** *a* four-sided; **V~taktmotor** *m* four-stroke engine; **~te(r, s)** ['fiːrtə(r,z)] *a* fourth; **V~tel** ['fɪrtəl] *nt* **-s, -** quarter; **~teljährlich** *a* quarterly; **V~telnote** *f* crotchet;

V~telstunde [fɪrtəl'ʃtundə] *f* quarter of an hour; **~zehn** ['fɪrtseːn] *num* fourteen; **in ~zehn Tagen** in a fortnight; **~zehntägig** *a* fortnightly; **~zig** ['fɪrtsɪç] *num* forty.

Villa ['vɪla] *f* **-, Villen** villa.

violett [vio'lɛt] *a* violet.

Violin- [vio'liːn] *zW:* **~e** *f* **-, -n** violin; **~konzert** *nt* violin concerto; **~schlüssel** *m* treble clef.

Virus ['viːrʊs] *m od nt* **-, Viren** virus.

vis-à-vis [viza'viː] *ad* opposite.

Visier [vi'ziːr] *nt* **-s, -e** gunsight; (*am Helm*) visor.

Visite [vi'ziːtə] *f* **-, -n** (*MED*) visit; **Visitenkarte** *f* visiting card.

Visum ['viːzʊm] *nt* **-s, Visa** *od* **Visen** visa.

vital [vi'taːl] *a* lively, full of life, vital.

Vitamin [vita'miːn] *nt* **-s, -e** vitamin.

Vogel ['foːgəl] *m* **-s, ⁝** bird; **einen ~ haben** (*umg*) have bats in the belfry; **jdm den ~ zeigen** (*umg*) tap one's forehead (*to indicate that one thinks sb stupid*); **~bauer** *nt* birdcage; **~scheuche** *f* **-, -n** scarecrow.

Vogesen [vo'geːzən] *pl* Vosges *pl*.

Vokabel [vo'kaːbəl] *f* **-, -n** word.

Vokabular [vokabu'laːr] *nt* **-s, -e** vocabulary.

Vokal [vo'kaːl] *m* **-s, -e** vowel.

Volk [fɔlk] *nt* **-(e)s, ⁝er** people; nation.

Völker- ['fœlkər] *zW:* **~recht** *nt* international law; **v~rechtlich** *a* according to international law; **~verständigung** *f* international understanding.

Volks- *zW:* **~abstimmung** *f* referendum; **v~eigen** *a* state-owned; **~fest** *nt* fair; **~hochschule** *f* adult education classes *pl*; **~lied** *nt* folksong; **~republik** *f* people's republic; **die ~republik China** the People's Republic of China; **~schule** *f* elementary school; **~tanz** *m* folk dance; **v~tümlich** ['fɔlksty:mlɪç] *a* popular; **~wirtschaft** *f* economics; **~zählung** *f* (national) census.

voll [fɔl] *a* full; **etw ~ machen** fill sth up; **~ und ganz** completely; **jdn für ~ nehmen** (*umg*) take sb seriously; **~auf** [fɔl'auf] *ad* amply; **V~bart** *m* full beard; **~'bringen** *vt unreg insep* accomplish; **~'enden** *vt insep* finish, complete; **vollends** ['fɔlɛnts] *ad* completely; **V~'endung** *f* completion; **~er** *a* fuller; (*+gen*) full of.

Volleyball ['vɔlibal] *m* volleyball.

Vollgas *nt:* **mit ~** at full throttle; **~ geben** step on it.

völlig ['fœlɪç] *a, ad* complete(ly).

voll- *zW:* **~jährig** *a* of age; **V~kaskoversicherung** *f* fully comprehensive insurance; **~'kommen** *a* perfect; **V~'kommenheit** *f* perfection; **V~kornbrot** *nt* wholemeal bread; **V~macht** f -, -en authority, full powers pl; **V~mond** m full moon; **V~pension** f full board; **~schlank** a: Kleidung für V~schlanke clothes for the fuller figure; **~ständig** a complete; **~'strecken** vt insep execute; **~tanken** vti fill up; **~zählig** a complete; in full number; **~'ziehen** vt unreg insep carry out // vr happen; **V~'zug** m execution.

Volt [vɔlt] nt - od -(e)s, - volt.

Volumen [vo'lu:mən] nt -s, - od Volumina volume.

vom [fɔm] = **von dem**.

von [fɔn] präp +dat **1** (Ausgangspunkt) from; ~ ... bis from ... to; ~ morgens bis abends from morning till night; ~ ... nach ... from ... to ...; ~ ... an from ...; ~ ... aus from ...; ~ dort aus from there; etw ~ sich aus tun do sth of one's own accord; ~ mir aus (umg) if you like, I don't mind; ~ wo/wann ...? where/when ... from? **2** (Ursache, im Passiv) by; ein Gedicht ~ Schiller a poem by Schiller; ~ etw müde tired from sth **3** (als Genitiv) of; ein Freund ~ mir a friend of mine; nett ~ dir nice of you; jeweils zwei ~ zehn two out of every ten **4** (über) about; er erzählte vom Urlaub he talked about his holiday **5**: ~ wegen! (umg) no way!

vonei'nander [fɔnaɪ'nandər] ad from each other.

vonstatten [fɔn'ʃtatən] ad: ~ gehen proceed, go.

vor [fo:r] ♦ präp +dat **1** (räumlich) in front of; ~ der Kirche links abbiegen turn left before the church **2** (zeitlich) before; ich war ~ ihm da I was there before him; ~ 2 Tagen 2 days ago; 5 (Minuten) ~ 4 5 (minutes) to 4; ~ kurzem a little while ago **3** (Ursache) with; ~ Wut/Liebe with rage/love; ~ Hunger sterben die of hunger; ~ lauter Arbeit because of work **4**: ~ allem, ~ allen Dingen most of all
♦ präp +akk (räumlich) in front of
♦ ad: ~ und zurück backwards and forwards.

Vorabend ['fo:r'a:bənt] m evening before, eve.

voran [fo'ran] ad before, ahead; mach ~! get on with it!; **~gehen** vi unreg go ahead; einer Sache (dat) ~gehen precede sth; **~gehend** a previous; **~kommen** vi unreg come along, make progress.

Vor- ['fo:r] zW: **~anschlag** m esti-

mate; **~arbeiter** m foreman.

voraus [fo'raus] ad ahead; (zeitlich) in advance; jdm ~ sein be ahead of sb; im ~ in advance; **~gehen** vi unreg go (on) ahead; (fig) precede; **~haben** vt unreg: jdm etw ~haben have the edge on sb in sth; **V~sage** f -, -n prediction; **~sagen** vt predict; **~sehen** vt unreg foresee; **~setzen** vt assume; **~gesetzt, daß** ... provided that ...; **V~setzung** f requirement, prerequisite; **V~sicht** f foresight; aller **V~sicht** nach in all probability; **~sichtlich** ad probably.

Vorbehalt ['fo:rbəhalt] m -(e)s, -e reservation, proviso; **v~en** vt unreg: sich/jdm etw v~en reserve sth (for o.s.)/for sb; **v~los** a, ad unconditional(ly).

vorbei [fo:r'baɪ] ad by, past; das ist ~ that's over; **~gehen** vi unreg pass by, go past.

vorbe- zW: **~lastet** ['fo:rbəlastət] a (fig) handicapped; **~reiten** ['fo:rbəraɪtən] vt prepare; **V~reitung** f preparation; **~straft** ['fo:rbəʃtraft] a previously convicted, with a record.

vorbeugen ['fo:rbɔygən] vtr lean forward // vi prevent (einer Sache (dat) sth); **~d** a preventive.

Vorbeugung f prevention; **zur ~ gegen** for the prevention of.

Vorbild ['fo:rbɪlt] nt model; sich (dat) jdn zum ~ nehmen model o.s. on sb; **v~lich** a model, ideal.

vorbringen ['fo:rbrɪŋən] vt unreg advance, state.

Vorder- ['fordər] zW: **~achse** f front axle; **~asien** nt the Near East; **v~e(r, s)** a front; **~grund** m foreground; **v~hand** ad for the present; **~mann** m, pl **~männer** man in front; jdn auf ~mann bringen (umg) get sb to shape up; **~seite** f front (side); **v~ste(r, s)** a front.

vordrängen ['fo:rdrɛŋən] vr push to the front.

voreilig ['fo:r'aɪlɪç] a hasty, rash.

voreingenommen ['fo:r'aɪngənɔmən] a biased; **V~heit** f bias.

vorenthalten ['fo:r'ɛnthaltən] vt unreg: jdm etw ~ withhold sth from sb.

vorerst ['fo:r'e:rst] ad for the moment od present.

Vorfahr ['fo:rfa:r] m -en, -en ancestor; **v~en** vi unreg drive (on) ahead; (vors Haus etc) drive up.

Vorfahrt f (AUT) right of way; ~ achten! give way!

Vorfahrts- zW: **~regel** f right of way; **~schild** nt give way sign; **~straße** f major road.

Vorfall ['fo:rfal] m incident; **v~en** vi unreg occur.

vorfinden ['fo:rfɪndən] vt unreg find.

vorführen ['foːrfyːrən] *vt* show, display; **dem Gericht ~** bring before the court.

Vorgabe ['foːrgaːbə] *f* (*SPORT*) start, handicap; **Vorgabe-** *in zW* (*COMPUT*) default.

Vorgang ['foːrgaŋ] *m* course of events; (*bes SCI*) process.

Vorgänger(in *f*) ['foːrgɛŋər(ɪn)] *m* **-s, -** predecessor.

vorgeben ['foːrgeːbən] *vt unreg* pretend, use as a pretext; (*SPORT*) give an advantage *od* a start of.

vorge- ['foːrgə] *zW*: **~faßt** [-fast] *a* preconceived; **~fertigt** [-fɛrtɪçt] *a* prefabricated.

vorgehen ['foːrgeːən] *vi unreg* (*voraus*) go (on) ahead; (*nach vorn*) go up front; (*handeln*) act, proceed; (*Uhr*) be fast; (*Vorrang haben*) take precedence; (*passieren*) go on; **V~** *nt* **-s** action.

Vorgeschmack ['foːrgəʃmak] *m* foretaste.

Vorgesetzte(r) ['foːrgəzɛtstə(r)] *mf* superior.

vorgestern ['foːrgɛstərn] *ad* the day before yesterday.

vorhaben ['foːrhaːbən] *vt unreg* intend; **hast du schon was vor?** have you got anything on?; **V~** *nt* **-s, -** intention.

vorhalten ['foːrhaltən] *unreg vt* hold *od* put up; (*fig*) reproach (*jdm etw* sb for sth) // *vi* last.

Vorhaltung *f* reproach.

vorhanden [foːr'handən] *a* existing; (*erhältlich*) available.

Vorhang ['foːrhaŋ] *m* curtain.

Vorhängeschloß ['foːrhɛŋəʃlɔs] *nt* padlock.

vorher [foːr'heːr] *ad* before(hand); **~bestimmen** *vt* (*Schicksal*) preordain; **~gehen** *vi unreg* precede; **~ig** [foːr'heːrɪç] *a* previous.

Vorherrschaft ['foːrhɛrʃaft] *f* predominance, supremacy.

vorherrschen ['foːrhɛrʃən] *vi* predominate.

vorher- [foːr'heːr] *zW*: **V~sage** *f* **-, -n** forecast; **~sagen** *vt* forecast, predict; **~sehbar** *a* predictable; **~sehen** *vt unreg* foresee.

vorhin [foːr'hɪn] *ad* not long ago, just now; **vorhinein** ['foːrhɪnaɪn] *ad*: **im vorhinein** beforehand.

vorig ['foːrɪç] *a* previous, last.

Vorkaufsrecht ['foːrkaufsrɛçt] *nt* option to buy.

Vorkehrung ['foːrkeːruŋ] *f* precaution.

vorkommen ['foːrkɔmən] *vi unreg* come forward; (*geschehen, sich finden*) occur; (*scheinen*) seem (to be); **sich** (*dat*) **dumm** *etc* **~** feel stupid *etc*; **V~** *nt* **-s, -** occurrence.

Vorkriegs- ['foːrkriːks] *in zW* prewar.

Vorladung ['foːrlaːduŋ] *f* summons.

Vorlage ['foːrlaːgə] *f* model, pattern; (*Gesetzes~*) bill; (*SPORT*) pass.

vorlassen ['foːrlasən] *vt unreg* admit; (*vorgehen lassen*) allow to go in front.

vorläufig ['foːrlɔyfɪç] *a* temporary, provisional.

vorlaut ['foːrlaut] *a* impertinent, cheeky.

vorlesen ['foːrleːzən] *vt unreg* read (out).

Vorlesung *f* (*UNIV*) lecture.

vorletzte(r, s) ['foːrlɛtstə(r, s)] *a* last but one.

Vorliebe ['foːrliːbə] *f* preference, partiality.

vorliebnehmen [foːr'liːpneːmən] *vi unreg*: **~ mit** make do with.

vorliegen ['foːrliːgən] *vi unreg* be (here); **etw liegt jdm vor** sb has sth; **~d** *a* present, at issue.

vormachen ['foːrmaxən] *vt*: **jdm etw ~** show sb how to do sth; (*fig*) fool sb; **have sb on.**

Vormachtstellung ['foːrmaxtʃtɛluŋ] *f* supremacy, hegemony.

Vormarsch ['foːrmarʃ] *m* advance.

vormerken ['foːrmɛrkən] *vt* book.

Vormittag ['foːrmɪtaːk] *m* morning; **v~s** *ad* in the morning, before noon.

Vormund ['foːrmʊnt] *m* **-(e)s, -e** *od* **-münder** guardian.

vorn(e) ['fɔrn(ə)] *ad* in front; **von ~ anfangen** start at the beginning; **nach ~** to the front.

Vorname ['foːrnaːmə] *m* first or Christian name.

vornehm ['foːrneːm] *a* distinguished; refined; elegant; **~en** *vt unreg* (*fig*) carry out; **sich** (*dat*) **etw ~en** start on sth; (*beschließen*) decide to do sth; **sich** (*dat*) **jdn ~en** tell sb off; **~lich** *ad* chiefly, specially.

vornherein ['fɔrnhɛraɪn] *ad*: **von ~** from the start.

Vorort ['foːrɔrt] *m* suburb.

Vorrang ['foːrraŋ] *m* precedence, priority; **v~ig** *a* of prime importance, primary.

Vorrat ['foːrraːt] *m* stock, supply; **Vorratskammer** *f* pantry.

vorrätig ['foːrrɛːtɪç] *a* in stock.

Vorrecht ['foːrrɛçt] *nt* privilege.

Vorrichtung ['foːrrɪçtuŋ] *f* device, contrivance.

vorrücken ['foːrrykən] *vi* advance // *vt* move forward.

Vorsatz ['foːrzats] *m* intention; (*JUR*) intent; **einen ~ fassen** make a resolution.

vorsätzlich ['foːrzɛtslɪç] *a, ad* intentional(ly); (*JUR*) premeditated.

Vorschau ['foːrʃau] *f* (*RAD, TV*) (programme) preview; (*Film*) trailer.

Vorschlag ['foːrʃlaːk] *m* suggestion, proposal; **v~en** *vt unreg* suggest, propose.

vorschnell ['foːrʃnɛl] *ad* hastily, too quickly.

vorschreiben ['foːrʃraɪbən] *vt unreg* prescribe, specify.

Vorschrift ['foːrʃrɪft] *f* regulation(s); rule(s); (*Anweisungen*) instruction(s); Dienst nach ~ work-to-rule; **vorschriftsmäßig** *a* as per regulations/instructions.

Vorschuß ['foːrʃʊs] *m* advance.

vorsehen ['foːrzeːən] *unreg vt* provide for, plan // *vr* take care, be careful // *vi* be visible.

Vorsehung *f* providence.

vorsetzen ['foːrzɛtsən] *vt* move forward; (*vor etw*) put in front; (*anbieten*) offer.

Vorsicht ['foːrzɪçt] *f* caution, care; ~! look out!, take care!; (*auf Schildern*) caution!, danger!; ~, Stufe! mind the step!; **v~ig** *a* cautious, careful; **vorsichtshalber** *ad* just in case.

Vorsilbe ['foːrzɪlbə] *f* prefix.

Vorsitz ['foːrzɪts] *m* chair(manship); **~ende(r)** *mf* chairman/-woman.

Vorsorge ['foːrzɔrgə] *f* precaution(s), provision(s); **v~n** *vi* für make provision(s) for; **~untersuchung** *f* check-up.

vorsorglich ['foːrzɔrklɪç] *ad* as a precaution.

Vorspeise ['foːrʃpaɪzə] *f* hors d'oeuvre, appetizer.

Vorspiel ['foːrʃpiːl] *nt* prelude.

vorsprechen ['foːrʃprɛçən] *unreg vt* say out loud, recite // *vi*: bei jdm ~ call on sb.

Vorsprung ['foːrʃprʊŋ] *m* projection, ledge; (*fig*) advantage, start.

Vorstadt ['foːrʃtat] *f* suburbs *pl*.

Vorstand ['foːrʃtant] *m* executive committee; (*COMM*) board (of directors); (*Person*) director, head.

vorstehen ['foːrʃteːən] *vi unreg* project; etw (*dat*) ~ (*fig*) be the head of sth.

vorstell- ['foːrʃtɛl] *zW*: **~bar** *a* conceivable; **~en** *vt* put forward; (*vor etw*) put in front; (*bekannt machen*) introduce; (*darstellen*) represent; sich (*dat*) etw **~en** imagine sth; **V~ung** *f* (*Bekanntmachen*) introduction; (*THEAT etc*) performance; (*Gedanke*) idea, thought.

Vorstrafe ['foːrʃtraːfə] *f* previous conviction.

Vortag ['foːrtak] *m* day before (*einer Sache* sth).

vortäuschen ['foːrtɔyʃən] *vt* feign, pretend.

Vorteil ['fɔrtaɪl] *m* **-s, -e** advantage

(*gegenüber* over); im ~ sein have the advantage; **v~haft** *a* advantageous.

Vortrag ['foːrtraːk] *m* **-(e)s, Vorträge** talk, lecture; **v~en** *vt unreg* carry forward; (*fig*) recite; (*Rede*) deliver; (*Lied*) perform; (*Meinung etc*) express.

vortrefflich [foːrtrɛflɪç] *a* excellent.

vortreten ['foːrtreːtən] *vi unreg* step forward; (*Augen etc*) protrude.

vorüber [foˈryːbər] *ad* past, over; **~gehen** *vi unreg* pass (by); **~gehen an** (+*dat*) (*fig*) pass over; **~gehend** *a* temporary, passing.

Vorurteil [ˈfoːrʊrtaɪl] *nt* prejudice.

Vorverkauf ['foːrfɛrkauf] *m* advance booking.

Vorwahl ['foːrvaːl] *f* preliminary election; (*TEL*) dialling code.

Vorwand ['foːrvant] *m* **-(e)s, Vorwände** pretext.

vorwärts ['foːrvɛrts] *ad* forward; **V~gang** *m* (*AUT etc*) forward gear; **~gehen** *vi unreg* progress; **~kommen** *vi unreg* get on, make progress.

vorweg [foˈrvɛk] *ad* in advance; **V~nahme** *f* **-, -n** anticipation; **~nehmen** *vt unreg* anticipate.

vorweisen ['foːrvaɪzən] *vt unreg* show, produce.

vorwerfen ['foːrvɛrfən] *vt unreg*: jdm etw ~ reproach sb for sth, accuse sb of sth; sich (*dat*) nichts vorzuwerfen haben have nothing to reproach o.s. with.

vorwiegend ['foːrviːgənt] *a*, *ad* predominant(ly).

Vorwort ['foːrvɔrt] *nt* **-(e)s, -e** preface.

Vorwurf ['foːrvʊrf] *m* reproach; jdm/ sich Vorwürfe machen reproach sb/ o.s.; **vorwurfsvoll** *a* reproachful.

vorzeigen ['foːrtsaɪgən] *vt* show, produce.

vorzeitig ['foːrtsaɪtɪç] *a* premature.

vorziehen ['foːrtsiːən] *vt unreg* pull forward; (*Gardinen*) draw; (*lieber haben*) prefer.

Vorzug ['foːrtsuːk] *m* preference; (*gute Eigenschaft*) merit, good quality; (*Vorteil*) advantage.

vorzüglich [foːrtsyːklɪç] *a* excellent.

vulgär [vʊlˈgɛːr] *a* vulgar.

Vulkan [vʊlˈkaːn] *m* **-s, -e** volcano.

W

W, w [veː] *nt* W, w.

Waage ['vaːgə] *f* **-, -n** scales *pl*; (*ASTROL*) Libra; **w~recht** *a* horizontal.

Wabe ['vaːbə] *f* **-, -n** honeycomb.

wach [vax] *a* awake; (*fig*) alert; **W~e**

f -, -n guard, watch; **W~e halten** keep watch; **W~e stehen** stand guard; **~en** *vi* be awake; *(W~e halten)* guard.

Wacholder [va'xɔldər] *m* -s, - juniper.

Wachs [vaks] *nt* -es, -e wax.

wachsam ['vaxzaːm] *a* watchful, vigilant, alert; **W~keit** *f* vigilance.

Wachs- *zW:* **w~en** *vi unreg* grow // *vt* *(Skier)* wax; **~tuch** *nt* oilcloth; **~tum** *nt* -s growth.

Wächter ['vɛçtər] *m* -s, - guard, warden, keeper; *(Parkplatz~)* attendant.

wackel- ['vakəl] *zW:* **~ig** *a* shaky, wobbly; **W~kontakt** *m* loose connection; **~n** *vi* shake; *(fig: Position)* be shaky.

wacker ['vakər] *a* valiant, stout // *ad* well, bravely.

Wade ['vaːdə] *f* -, -n *(ANAT)* calf.

Waffe ['vafə] *f* -, -n weapon.

Waffel *f* -, -n waffle; wafer.

Waffen- *zW:* **~schein** *m* gun licence; **~schieber** *m* gun-runner; **~stillstand** *m* armistice, truce.

Wagemut ['vaːgəmuːt] *m* daring.

wagen ['vaːgən] *vt* venture, dare.

Wagen ['vaːgən] *m* -s, - vehicle; *(Auto)* car; *(EISENB)* carriage; *(Pferde~)* cart; **~heber** *m* -s, - jack.

Waggon [va'gõː] *m* -s, -s carriage; *(Güter~)* goods van, freight truck (US).

waghalsig ['vaːkhalzɪç] *a* foolhardy.

Wagnis ['vaːknɪs] *nt* -ses, -se risk.

Wahl [vaːl] *f* -, -en choice; *(POL)* election; zweite ~ seconds *pl*.

wähl- ['vɛːl] *zW:* **~bar** *a* eligible; **~en** *vti* choose; *(POL)* elect, vote (for); *(TEL)* dial; **W~er(in** *f)* *m* -s, - voter; **~erisch** *a* fastidious, particular.

Wahl- *zW:* **~fach** *nt* optional subject; **~gang** *m* ballot; **~kabine** *f* polling booth; **~kampf** *m* election campaign; **~kreis** *m* constituency; **~lokal** *nt* polling station; **w~los** *ad* at random; **~recht** *nt* franchise; **~spruch** *m* motto; **~urne** *f* ballot box.

Wahn [vaːn] *m* -(e)s delusion; folly; **~sinn** *m* madness; **w~sinnig** *a* insane, mad // *ad* (*umg*) incredibly.

wahr [vaːr] *a* true; **~en** *vt* maintain, keep.

während ['vɛːrənd] *präp* +*gen* during // *kj* while; **~dessen** [vɛːrənt'dɛsən] *ad* meanwhile.

wahr- *zW:* **~haben** *vt unreg:* etw nicht ~haben wollen refuse to admit sth; **~haft** *ad* (*tatsächlich*) truly; **~haftig** [vaːr'haftɪç] *a* true, real // *ad* really; **W~heit** *f* truth; **~nehmen** *vt unreg* perceive, observe; **W~nehmung** *f* perception; **~sagen** *vi* prophesy, tell fortunes; **W~sager(in** *f)* *m* -s, - fortune teller;

~scheinlich [vaːr'ʃaɪnlɪç] *a* probable // *ad* probably; **W~'scheinlichkeit** *f* probability; aller **W~scheinlichkeit** nach in all probability; **W~zeichen** *nt* emblem.

Währung ['vɛːruŋ] *f* currency.

Waise ['vaɪzə] *f* -, -n orphan; **Waisenhaus** *nt* orphanage.

Wald [valt] *m* -(e)s, -̈er wood(s); *(groß)* forest; **~sterben** *nt* dying of trees due to pollution.

Wal(fisch) ['vaːl(fɪʃ)] *m* -(e)s, -e whale.

Wall [val] *m* -(e)s, -̈e embankment; *(Bollwerk)* rampart; **w~fahren** *vi unreg insep* go on a pilgrimage; **~fahrer(in** *f)* *m* pilgrim; **~fahrt** *f* pilgrimage.

Wal- ['val] *zW:* **~nuß** *f* walnut; **~roß** *nt* walrus.

Walze ['valtsə] *f* -, -n *(Gerät)* cylinder; *(Fahrzeug)* roller; **w~n** *vt* roll (out).

wälzen ['vɛltsən] *vt* roll (over); *(Bücher)* hunt through; *(Probleme)* deliberate on // *vr* wallow; *(vor Schmerzen)* roll about; *(im Bett)* toss and turn.

Walzer ['valtsər] *m* -s, - waltz.

Wand [vant] *f* -, -̈e wall; *(Trenn~)* partition; *(Berg~)* precipice.

Wandel ['vandəl] *m* -s change; **w~bar** *a* changeable, variable; **w~n** *vtr* change // *vi* (*gehen*) walk.

Wander- ['vandər] *zW:* **~er** *m* -s, - hiker, rambler; **w~n** *vi* hike; *(Blick)* wander; *(Gedanken)* stray; **~schaft** *f* travelling; **~ung** *f* walking tour, hike.

Wandlung *f* change, transformation.

Wange ['vaŋə] *f* -, -n cheek.

wankelmütig ['vaŋkəlmyːtɪç] *a* vacillating, inconstant.

wanken ['vankən] *vi* stagger; *(fig)* waver.

wann [van] *ad* when.

Wanne ['vanə] *f* -, -n tub.

Wanze ['vantsə] *f* -, -n bug.

Wappen ['vapən] *nt* -s, - coat of arms, crest; **~kunde** *f* heraldry.

war *etc* *v siehe* **sein.**

Ware ['vaːrə] *f* -, -n ware.

Waren- *zW:* **~haus** *nt:* department store; **~lager** *nt* stock, store; **~probe** *f* sample; **~zeichen** *nt:* (eingetragenes) **~zeichen** (registered) trademark.

warf *etc* *v siehe* **werfen.**

warm [varm] *a* warm; *(Essen)* hot.

Wärm- ['vɛrm] *zW:* **~e** *f* -, -n warmth; **w~en** *vtr* warm, heat; **~flasche** *f* hot-water bottle.

warnen ['varnən] *vt* warn.

Warnung *f* warning.

Warschau ['varʃaʊ] *nt* Warsaw; **~er**

Pakt Warsaw Pact.

warten ['vartən] *vi* wait (*auf* +*akk* for); **auf sich ~ lassen** take a long time.

Wärter(in *f*) ['vɛrtər(ɪn)] *m* **-s, -** attendant.

Warte- ['vartə] *zW:* **~raum, ~saal** *m* (*EISENB*), **~zimmer** *nt* waiting room.

Wartung *f* servicing; service; **~ und Instandhaltung** maintenance.

warum [va'rʊm] *ad* why.

Warze ['vartsə] *f* **-, -n** wart.

was [vas] *pron* what; (*umg: etwas*) something; **~ für (ein)** ... what sort of ....

Wasch- ['vaʃ] *zW:* **w~bar** *a* washable; **~becken** *nt* washbasin; **w~echt** *a* colourfast; (*fig*) genuine.

Wäsche ['vɛʃə] *f* **-, -n** wash(ing); (*Bett~*) linen; (*Unter~*) underclothing; **~klammer** *f* clothes peg (*Brit*), clothespin (*US*); **~leine** *f* washing line (*Brit*), clothesline (*US*).

waschen ['vaʃən] *unreg vti* wash // *vr* (have a) wash; **sich** (*dat*) **die Hände ~** wash one's hands.

Wäsche'rei *f* laundry.

Wasch- *zW:* **~küche** *f* laundry room; **~lappen** *m* face flannel, washcloth (*US*); (*umg*) sissy; **~maschine** *f* washing machine; **~mittel** *nt,* **~pulver** *nt* detergent, washing powder; **~raum** *m* washroom.

Wasser ['vasər] *nt* **-s, -** water; **~ball** *m* water polo; **w~dicht** *a* waterproof; **~fall** *m* waterfall; **~farbe** *f* watercolour; **w~gekühlt** *a* (*AUT*) water-cooled; **~hahn** *m* tap, faucet (*US*); **~kraftwerk** *nt* hydroelectric power station; **~leitung** *f* water pipe; **~mann** *m* (*ASTROL*) Aquarius.

wässern ['vɛsərn] *vti* water.

Wasser- *zW:* **w~scheu** *a* afraid of the water; **~ski** *nt* water-skiing; **~stoff** *m* hydrogen; **~stoffbombe** *f* hydrogen bomb; **~waage** *f* spirit level; **~zeichen** *nt* watermark.

wäßrig ['vɛsriç] *a* watery.

waten ['va:tən] *vi* wade.

watscheln ['va:tʃəln] *vi* waddle.

Watt [vat] *nt* **-(e)s, -en** mud flats *pl* // *nt* **-s, -** (*ELEK*) watt; **~e** *f* **-, -n** cotton wool, absorbent cotton (*US*).

WC ['ve:'tse:] *nt abk* (= water closet) WC.

Web- ['ve:b] *zW:* **w~en** *vt unreg* weave; **~er** *m* **-s, -** weaver; **~e'rei** *f* (*Betrieb*) weaving mill; **~stuhl** *m* loom.

Wechsel ['vɛksəl] *m* **-s, -** change; (*COMM*) bill of exchange; **~beziehung** *f* correlation; **~geld** *nt* change; **w~haft** *a* (*Wetter*) variable; **~jahre** *pl* change of life; **~kurs** *m* rate of exchange; **w~n** *vt* change;

(*Blicke*) exchange // *vi* change; vary; (*Geld* **w~n**) have change; **~sprechanlage** two-way intercom; **~strom** *m* alternating current; **~stube** *f* bureau de change; **~wirkung** *f* interaction.

wecken ['vɛkən] *vt* wake (up); call.

Wecker ['vɛkər] *m* **-s, -** alarm clock.

wedeln ['ve:dəln] *vi* (*mit Schwanz*) wag; (*mit Fächer etc*) wave.

weder ['ve:dər] *kj* neither; **~ ... noch** ... neither ... nor ...

weg [vɛk] *ad* away, off; **über etw** (*akk*) **~ sein** be over sth; **er war schon ~** he had already left; **Finger ~!** hands off!; **W~** [ve:k] *m* **-(e)s, -e** way; (*Pfad*) path; (*Route*) route; **sich auf den W~ machen** be on one's way; **jdm aus dem W~ gehen** keep out of sb's way; **W~bereiter** *m* **-s, -** pioneer; **~bleiben** *vi unreg* stay away.

wegen ['ve:gən] *präp* +*gen od* (*umg*) *dat* because of.

weg- ['vɛk] *zW:* **~fahren** *vi unreg* drive away; leave; **~fallen** *vi unreg* be left out; (*Ferien, Bezahlung*) be cancelled; (*aufhören*) cease; **~gehen** *vi unreg* go away; leave; **~lassen** *vt unreg* leave out; **~laufen** *vi unreg* run away *od od*; **~legen** *vt* put aside; **~machen** *vt* (*umg*) get rid of; **~müssen** *vi unreg* (*umg*) have to go; **~nehmen** *vt unreg* take away; **~tun** *vt unreg* put away; **W~weiser** ['ve:gvaɪzər] *m* **-s, -** road sign, signpost; **~werfen** *vt unreg* throw away; **~werfend** *a* disparaging; **W~werfgesellschaft** *f* throw-away society.

weh [ve:] *a* sore; **~ tun** hurt, be sore; **jdm/sich ~ tun** hurt sb/o.s.; **~(e)** *interj:* **~(e), wenn du...** woe betide you if...; **o ~!** oh dear!; **~e!** just you dare!; **~en** *vti* blow; (*Fahnen*) flutter; **W~en** *pl* (*MED*) labour pains *pl*; **~leidig** *a* whiny, whining; **W~mut** *f* - melancholy; **~mütig** *a* melancholy.

Wehr [ve:r] *nt* **-(e)s, -e** weir // *f:* **sich zur ~ setzen** defend o.s.; **~dienst** *m* military service; **w~en** *vr* defend o.s.; **w~los** *a* defenceless; **~pflicht** *f* compulsory military service; **w~pflichtig** *a* liable for military service.

Weib [vaɪp] *nt* **-(e)s, -er** woman, female; wife; **~chen** *nt* female; **w~lich** *a* feminine.

weich [vaɪç] *a* soft; **W~e** *f* **-, -n** (*EISENB*) points *pl*; **~en** *vi unreg* yield, give way; **W~heit** *f* softness; **~lich** *a* soft, namby-pamby; **W~ling** *m* weakling.

Weide ['vaɪdə] *f* **-, -n** (*Baum*) willow; (*Gras*) pasture; **w~n** *vi* graze // *vr:* **sich an etw** (*dat*) **w~n** delight in sth.

weidlich ['vaɪtlɪç] *ad* thoroughly.
weigern ['vaɪgərn] *vr* refuse.
Weigerung ['vaɪgəruŋ] *f* refusal.
Weih- ['vaɪ] *zW:* **~e** *f* -, **-n** consecration; (*Priester~*) ordination; **w~en** *vt* consecrate; ordain; **~er** *m* **-s,** - pond; **~nachten** *nt* -, - Christmas; **w~nachtlich** *a* Christmas; **~nachtsabend** *m* Christmas Eve; **~nachtslied** *nt* Christmas carol; **~nachtsmann** *m* Father Christmas, Santa Claus; **~nachtstag** *m* Christmas Day; **zweiter ~nachtstag** *m* Boxing Day; **~rauch** *m* incense; **~wasser** *nt* holy water.
weil [vaɪl] *kj* because.
Weile ['vaɪlə] *f* - while, short time.
Wein [vaɪn] *m* **-(e)s, -e** wine; (*Pflanze*) vine; **~bau** *m* cultivation of vines; **~beere** *f* grape; **~berg** *m* vineyard; **~bergschnecke** *f* snail; **~brand** *m* brandy; **w~en** *vti* cry; **das ist zum ~en** it's enough to make you cry *od* weep; **~karte** *f* wine list; **~lese** *f* vintage; **~rebe** *f* vine; **~stock** *m* vine; **~traube** *f* grape.
weise ['vaɪzə] *a* wise; **W~(r)** *mf* wise old man/woman, sage.
Weise ['vaɪzə] *f* -, **-n** manner, way; (*Lied*) tune; **auf diese ~** in this way; **w~n** *vt unreg* show.
Weisheit ['vaɪshaɪt] *f* wisdom; **Weisheitszahn** *m* wisdom tooth.
weiß [vaɪs] *a* white // *v siehe* **wissen**; **W~brot** *nt* white bread; **~en** *vt* whitewash; **W~glut** *f* (*TECH*) incandescence; **jdn bis zur W~glut bringen** (*fig*) make sb see red; **W~kohl** *m* (white) cabbage; **W~wein** *m* white wine.
weit [vaɪt] *a* wide; (*Begriff*) broad; (*Reise, Wurf*) long; **wie ~ ist es ...?** how far is it ...?; **in ~er Ferne** in the far distance; **das geht zu ~** that's going too far // *ad* far; **~aus** *ad* by far; **~blickend** a far-seeing; **W~e** *f* -, **-n** width; (*Raum*) space; (*von Entfernung*) distance; **~en** *vtr* widen.
weiter ['vaɪtər] *a* wider; broader; farther (away); (*zusätzlich*) further; **ohne ~es** without further ado; just like that // *ad* further; **~ nichts/niemand** nothing/nobody else; **~arbeiten** *vi* go on working; **~empfehlen** *vt unreg* recommend (to others); **W~fahrt** *f* continuation of the journey; **~gehen** *vi unreg* go on; **~hin** *ad:* **etw ~hin tun** go on doing sth; **~leiten** *vt* pass on; **~machen** *vti* continue.
weit- *zW:* **~gehend** *a* considerable // *ad* largely; **~läufig** *a* (*Gebäude*) spacious; (*Erklärung*) lengthy; (*Verwandter*) distant; **~schweifig** *a* longwinded; **~sichtig** *a* (*MED*) long-

sighted; (*fig*) far-sighted; **W~sprung** *m* long jump; **~verbreitet** *a* widespread; **W~winkelobjektiv** *nt* (*PHOT*) wide-angle lens.
Weizen ['vaɪtzən] *m* **-s,** - wheat.
welche(r, s) ['vɛlçə(r, s)] ◆*interrog pron* which; **~r von beiden?** which (one) of the two?; **~n hast du genommen?** which (one) did you take?; **welch eine ...** what a ...!; **~ Freude!** what joy!
◆*indef pron* some; (*in Fragen*) any; **ich habe ~** I have some; **haben Sie ~?** do you have any?
◆*rel pron* (*bei Menschen*) who; (*bei Sachen*) which, that; **~(r, s)** *auch immer* whoever/whichever/whatever.
welk [vɛlk] *a* withered; **~en** *vi* wither.
Well- [vɛl] *zW:* **~blech** *nt* corrugated iron; **~e** *f* -, **-n** wave; (*TECH*) shaft.
Wellen- *zW:* **~bereich** *m* waveband; **~länge** *f* (*lit, fig*) wavelength; **~sittich** *m* budgerigar.
Welt [vɛlt] *f* -, **-en** world; **~all** *nt* universe; **~anschauung** *f* philosophy of life; **w~berühmt** *a* world-famous; **w~fremd** *a* unworldly; **~krieg** *m* world war; **w~lich** *a* worldly; (*nicht kirchlich*) secular; **~macht** *f* world power; **~meister** *m* world champion; **~meisterschaft** *f* world championships *pl*; **~raum** *m* space; **~reise** *f* trip round the world; **~stadt** *f* metropolis; **w~weit** *a* world-wide.
wem [veːm] *pron* (*dat*) to whom.
wen [veːn] *pron* (*akk*) whom.
Wende ['vɛndə] *f* -, **-n** turn; (*Veränderung*) change; **~kreis** *m* (*GEOG*) tropic; (*AUT*) turning circle; **Wendeltreppe** *f* spiral staircase; **w~n** *vtir unreg* turn; **sich an jdn w~n** go/come to sb; **~punkt** *m* turning point.
Wendung *f* turn; (*Rede~*) idiom.
wenig ['veːnɪç] *a, ad* little; **~e** ['veːnɪgə] *pl* few *pl*; **~er** *a* less; (*mit pl*) fewer // *ad* less; **~ste(r, s)** *a* least; **am ~sten** least; **~stens** *ad* at least.
wenn [vɛn] *kj* **1** (*falls, bei Wünschen*) if; **~ auch ..., selbst ~ ...** even if ...; **~ ich doch ...** if only I ...
2 (*zeitlich*) when; **immer ~** whenever.
wennschon ['vɛnʃoːn] *ad:* **na ~** so what?; **~, dennschon!** in for a penny, in for a pound.
wer [veːr] *pron* who.
Werbe- ['vɛrbə] *zW:* **~fernsehen** *nt* commercial television; **w~n** *unreg* *vt* win; (*Mitglied*) recruit // *vi* advertise; **um jdn/etw w~n** try to win sb/sth; **für jdn/etw w~n** promote sb/sth; **~spot** *m* TV ad(vertisement).
Werbung *f* advertising; (*von Mitgliedern*) recruitment; (*um jdn/etw*) pro-

motion (*um* of).

werden ['vɛrdən] ◆*vi pt* **wurde**, *ptp* **geworden** become; **was ist aus ihm/ aus der Sache geworden?** what became of him/it?; **es ist nichts/gut geworden** it came to nothing/turned out well; **es wird Nacht/Tag** it's getting dark/light; **mir wird kalt** I'm getting cold; **mir wird schlecht** I feel ill; **Erster** ~ come *od* be first; **das muß anders** ~ that'll have to change; **rot/zu Eis** ~ turn red/to ice; **was willst du (mal)** ~? what do you want to be?; **die Fotos sind gut geworden** the photos have come out nicely

◆(*als Hilfsverb*) **1** (*bei Futur*): **er wird es tun he will** *od* he'll do it; **er wird das nicht tun** he will not *od* won't do it; **es wird gleich regnen** it's going to rain

2 (*bei Konjunktiv*): **ich würde ...** I would ...; **er würde gern ...** he would *od* he'd like to; **ich würde lieber ...** I would *od* I'd rather ...

3 (*bei Vermutung*): **sie wird in der Küche sein** she will be in the kitchen

4 (*bei Passiv*) *ptp* **worden**: **gebraucht** ~ be used; **er ist erschossen worden** he has *od* he's been shot; **mir wurde gesagt, daß ...** I was told that ...

werfen ['vɛrfən] *vt unreg* throw.

Werft [vɛrft] *f* -, **-en** shipyard, dockyard.

Werk [vɛrk] *nt* -(e)s, **-e** work; (*Tätigkeit*) job; (*Fabrik, Mechanismus*) works *pl*; **ans** ~ **gehen** set to work; **~statt** *f* -, **-stätten** workshop; (*AUT*) garage; **~tag** *m* working day; **w~tags** *ad* on working days; **w~tätig** *a* working; **~zeug** *nt* tool.

Wermut ['vɛrmuːt] *m* -(e)s wormwood; (*Wein*) vermouth.

Wert [vɛrt] *m* -(e)s, **-e** worth; (*FIN*) value; ~ **legen auf** (+*akk*) attach importance to; **es hat doch keinen** ~ it's useless; **w~** *a* worth; (*geschätzt*) dear; worthy; **das ist nichts/viel w~** it's not worth anything/it's worth a lot; **das ist es/er mir w~** it's/he's worth that to me; **w~en** *vt* rate; **w~los** *a* worthless; **~papier** *nt* security; **w~voll** *a* valuable.

Wesen ['veːzən] *nt* -s, - (*Geschöpf*) being; (*Natur, Character*) nature; **wesentlich** *a* significant; (*beträchtlich*) considerable.

weshalb [vɛs'halp] *ad* why.

Wespe ['vɛspə] *f* -, **-n** wasp.

wessen ['vɛsən] *pron* (*gen*) whose.

West- [vɛst] *zW*: **~deutschland** *nt* West Germany; **~e** *f* -, **-n** waistcoat, vest (*US*); (*Woll~e*) cardigan; **~en** *m* -s west; **~europa** *nt* Western Europe; **Westfalen** *nt* Westphalia;

~indien *nt* the West Indies; **w~lich** *a* western // *ad* to the west.

weswegen [vɛs'veːgən] *ad* why.

wett [vɛt] *a* even; **W~bewerb** *m* competition; **W~e** *f* -, **-n** bet, wager; **~en** *vti* bet.

Wetter ['vɛtɐr] *nt* -s, - weather; **~bericht** *m* weather report; **~dienst** *m* meteorological service; **~lage** *f* (weather) situation; **~vorhersage** *f* weather forecast; **~warte** *f* -, **-n** weather station.

Wett- *zW*: **~kampf** *m* contest; **~lauf** *m* race; **w~machen** *vt* make good; **~streit** *m* contest.

wichtig ['vɪçtɪç] *a* important; **W~keit** *f* importance.

wickeln ['vɪkəln] *vt* wind; (*Haare*) set; (*Kind*) change; **jdn/etw in etw** (*akk*) ~ wrap sb/sth in sth.

Widder ['vɪdɐr] *m* -s, - ram; (*ASTROL*) Aries.

wider ['viːdɐr] *präp* +*akk* against; **~fahren** *vi unreg* happen (*jdm* to sb); **~legen** *vt* refute.

widerlich ['viːdɐrlɪç] *a* disgusting, repulsive.

wider- ['viːdɐr] *zW*: **~rechtlich** *a* unlawful; **W~rede** *f* contradiction; **W~ruf** *m* retraction; countermanding; **w~'rufen** *vt unreg insep* retract; (*Anordnung*) revoke; (*Befehl*) countermand; **~setzen** *vr insep* oppose (*jdm/etw* sb/sth).

widerspenstig ['viːdɐrʃpɛnstɪç] *a* wilful.

wider'sprechen *vi unreg insep* contradict (*jdm* sb).

Widerspruch ['viːdɐrʃprʊx] *m* contradiction; **widerspruchslos** *ad* without arguing.

Widerstand ['viːdɐrʃtant] *m* resistance.

Widerstands- *zW*: **~bewegung** *f* resistance (movement); **w~fähig** *a* resistant, tough; **w~los** *a* unresisting.

wider'stehen *vi unreg insep* withstand (*jdm/etw* sb/sth).

Wider- ['viːdɐr] *zW*: **w~wärtig** *a* nasty, horrid; **~wille** *m* aversion (*gegen* to); **w~willig** *a* unwilling, reluctant.

widmen ['vɪtmən] *vt* dedicate // *vtr* devote (o.s.).

widrig ['viːdrɪç] *a* (*Umstände*) adverse.

wie [viː] ◆*ad* how; ~ **groß/schnell** how big/fast?; ~ **wär's?** how about it?; ~ **ist er?** what's he like?; ~ **gut du das kannst!** you're very good at it; ~ **bitte?** pardon?; (*entrüstet*) I beg your pardon!; **und** ~! and how!

◆*kj* **1** (*bei Vergleichen*): **so schön** ~ ... as beautiful as ...; ~ **ich schon sagte** as I said; ~ **du** like you; **singen**

~ ein ... sing like a ...; ~ (zum
Beispiel) such as (for example)
2 (zeitlich): ~ er das hörte, ging er
when he heard that he left; er hörte,
~ der Regen fiel he heard the rain
falling.

wieder ['vi:dər] ad again; ~ da sein
be back (again); gehst du schon ~?
are you off again?; ~ ein(e)... another...; **W~aufbau** [-'aʊfbaʊ] m re-
building; **~aufnehmen** vt unreg resume; **~bekommen** vt unreg get
back; **~bringen** vt unreg bring back;
~erkennen vt unreg recognize;
W~gabe f reproduction; **~geben** vt
unreg (zurückgeben) return; (Erzählung etc) repeat; (Gefühle etc) convey; **~gutmachen** [-'gu:tmaxən] vt
make up for; (Fehler) put right;
W~'gutmachung f reparation;
~'herstellen vt restore; **~'holen** vt
insep repeat; **W~'holung** f repetition; **W~hören** nt: auf **W~hören**
(TEL) goodbye; **W~kehr** f - return;
(von Vorfall) repetition, recurrence;
~sehen vt unreg see again; auf
W~sehen goodbye; **~um** ad again;
(andererseits) on the other hand;
W~wahl f re-election.
Wiege ['vi:gə] f -, -n cradle; **w~n** vt
(schaukeln) rock // vti unreg (Gewicht) weigh.
wiehern ['vi:ərn] vi neigh, whinny.
Wien [vi:n] nt Vienna; **~er** a Viennese; **~er(in** f) m Viennese; **~er**
Schnitzel Wiener schnitzel.
Wiese ['vi:zə] f -, -n meadow.
Wiesel ['vi:zəl] nt -s, - weasel.
wieso [vi:'zo:] ad why.
wieviel [vi:'fi:l] a how much; ~ Menschen how many people; **~mal** ad
how often; **~te(r, s)** a: zum **~ten**
Mal? how many times?; den **W~ten**
haben wir? what's the date?; an **~ter**
Stelle? in what place?; der **~te** Besucher war er? how many visitors were
there before him?
wieweit [vi:'vait] ad to what extent.
wild [vilt] a wild; **W~** nt -(e)s game;
~ern ['vildərn] vi poach; **~'fremd** a
(umg) quite strange od unknown;
W~heit f wildness; **W~leder** nt
suede; **W~nis** f -, -se wilderness;
W~schwein nt (wild) boar.
will etc v siehe **wollen**.
Wille ['vilə] m -ns, -n will; **w~n** präp
+gen: um... **w~n** for the sake of...;
willensstark a strong-willed.
will- zW: **~ig** a willing; **~kommen**
[vil'kɔmən] a welcome; jdn **~kommen**
heißen welcome sb; **W~kommen** nt
-s, - welcome; **~kürlich** a arbitrary;
(Bewegung) voluntary.
wimmeln ['vɪməln] vi swarm (von
with).

wimmern ['vɪmərn] vi whimper.
Wimper ['vɪmpər] f -, -n eyelash.
Wind [vɪnt] m -(e)s, -e wind; **~beutel**
m cream puff; (fig) windbag; **~e**
['vɪndə] f -, -n (TECH) winch, wind-
lass; (BOT) bindweed; **Windel**
['vɪndəl] f -, -n nappy, diaper (US);
w~en ['vɪndən] vi unpers be windy //
unreg vt wind; (Kranz) weave;
(ent~en) twist // vr wind; (Person)
writhe; **~hund** m greyhound;
(Mensch) fly-by-night; **w~ig** ['vɪndɪç]
a windy; (fig) dubious; **~mühle** f
windmill; **~pocken** pl chickenpox;
~schutzscheibe f (AUT) windscreen,
windshield (US); **~stille** f calm;
~stoß m gust of wind.
Wink [vɪŋk] m -(e)s, -e hint; (mit
Kopf) nod; (mit Hand) wave.
Winkel ['vɪŋkəl] m -s, - (MATH)
angle; (Gerät) set square; (in
Raum) corner.
winken ['vɪŋkən] vti wave.
winseln ['vɪnzəln] vi whine.
Winter ['vɪntər] m -s, - winter;
w~lich a wintry; **~sport** m winter
sports pl.
Winzer ['vɪntsər] m -s, - vine grower.
winzig ['vɪntsɪç] a tiny.
Wipfel ['vɪpfəl] m -s, - treetop.
wir [vi:r] pron we; ~ alle all of us, we
all.
Wirbel ['vɪrbəl] m -s, - whirl, swirl;
(Trubel) hurly-burly; (Aufsehen)
fuss; (ANAT) vertebra; **w~n** vi
whirl, swirl; **~säule** f spine.
wird v siehe **werden**.
wirfst etc v siehe **werfen**.
wirken ['vɪrkən] vi have an effect;
(erfolgreich sein) work; (scheinen)
seem // vt (Wunder) work.
wirklich ['vɪrklɪç] a real // ad really;
W~keit f reality.
wirksam ['vɪrkza:m] a effective;
W~keit f effectiveness, efficacy.
Wirkung ['vɪrkʊŋ] f effect;
wirkungslos a ineffective; **wirkungslos bleiben** have no effect; **wirkungs-
voll** a effective.
wirr [vɪr] a confused, wild; **W~warr**
[-ar] m -s disorder, chaos.
Wirsing ['vɪrzɪŋ] m -s savoy cabbage.
wirst v siehe **werden**.
Wirt [vɪrt] m -(e)s, -e landlord; **~in** f
landlady; **~schaft** f (Gaststätte)
pub; (Haushalt) housekeeping; (eines
Landes) economy; (umg: Durcheinander) mess; **w~schaftlich** a economical; (POL) economic.
Wirtschafts- zW: **~krise** f economic
crisis; **~prüfer** m chartered accountant; **~wunder** nt economic miracle.
Wirtshaus nt inn.
Wisch [vɪʃ] m -(e)s, -e scrap of paper;
w~en vt wipe; **~er** m -s, - (AUT)

wiper.

wispern ['vɪspərn] *vti* whisper.

Wißbegier(de) ['vɪsbəgiːr(də)] *f* thirst for knowledge; **w~ig** *a* inquisitive, eager for knowledge.

wissen ['vɪsən] *vt unreg* know; was weiß ich! I don't know!; **W~** *nt* **-s** knowledge; **W~schaft** *f* science; **W~schaftler(in** *f*) *m* **-s,** - scientist; **~schaftlich** *a* scientific; **wissenswert** *a* worth knowing; **wissentlich** *a* knowing.

wittern ['vɪtərn] *vt* scent; (*fig*) suspect.

Witterung *f* weather; (*Geruch*) scent.

Witwe ['vɪtvə] *f* **-, -n** widow; **~r** *m* **-s,** - widower.

Witz [vɪts] *m* **-(e)s, -e** joke; **~blatt** *nt* comic (paper); **~bold** *m* **-(e)s, -e** joker, wit; **w~ig** *a* funny.

wo [voː] *ad* where; (*umg: irgendwo*) somewhere; **im Augenblick,** ~ ... the moment (that) ...; **die Zeit,** ~ ... the time when ...; **~anders** [voː'andərs] *ad* elsewhere; **~andershin** *ad* somewhere else; **~bei** [voː'baɪ] *ad* (*rel*) by/with which; (*interrog*) what ... in/by/with.

Woche ['vɔxə] *f* **-, -n** week.

Wochen- *zW*: **~ende** *nt* weekend; **w~lang** *a, ad* for weeks; **~schau** *f* newsreel.

wöchentlich ['vœçəntlɪç] *a, ad* weekly.

wo- *zW*: **~durch** [voː'dʊrç] *ad* (*rel*) through which; (*interrog*) what ... through; **~für** [voː'fyːr] *ad* (*rel*) for which; (*interrog*) what ... for.

wog *etc v siehe* **wiegen**.

Woge ['voːgə] *f* **-, -n** wave.

wo- *zW*: **~gegen** [voː'geːgən] *ad* (*rel*) against which; (*interrog*) what ... against; **~her** [voː'heːr] *ad* where ... from; **~hin** [voː'hɪn] *ad* where ... to.

wohl [voːl] *ad* **1:** **sich** ~ **fühlen** (*zufrieden*) feel happy; (*gesundheitlich*) feel well; ~ **oder übel** whether one likes it or not

2 (*wahrscheinlich*) probably; (*gewiß*) certainly; (*vielleicht*) perhaps; **sie ist** ~ **zu Hause** she's probably at home; **das ist doch** ~ **nicht dein Ernst!** surely you're not serious! **das mag** ~ **sein** that may well be; **ob das** ~ **stimmt?** I wonder if that's true; **er weiß das sehr** ~ he knows that perfectly well.

Wohl [voːl] *nt* **-(e)s** welfare; **zum** ~! cheers!; **w~auf** [voːl'aʊf] *ad* well; **~behagen** *nt* comfort; **~fahrt** *f* welfare; **~fahrtsstaat** *m* welfare state; **w~habend** *a* wealthy; **w~ig** *a* contented, comfortable; **w~schmeckend** *a* delicious; **~stand** *m* prosperity; **~standsgesellschaft** *f* affluent society; **~tat** *f* relief; act of charity;

~täter(in *f*) *m* benefactor; **w~tätig** *a* charitable; **w~tun** *vi unreg* do good (*jdm* sb); **w~verdient** *a* well-earned, well-deserved; **w~weislich** *ad* prudently; **~wollen** *nt* **-s** good will; **w~wollend** *a* benevolent.

wohn- ['voːn] *zW*: **~en** *vi* live; **W~gemeinschaft** *f* (*Menschen*) people sharing a flat; **~haft** *a* resident; **~lich** *a* comfortable; **W~ort** *m* domicile; **W~sitz** *m* place of residence; **W~ung** *f* house; (*Etagen~ung*) flat, apartment (*US*); **W~wagen** *m* caravan; **W~zimmer** *nt* living room.

wölben ['vœlbən] *vtr* curve.

Wölbung *f* curve.

Wolf [vɔlf] *m* **-(e)s, ¨e** wolf.

Wolke ['vɔlkə] *f* **-, -n** cloud; **Wolkenkratzer** *m* skyscraper.

wolkig ['vɔlkɪç] *a* cloudy.

Wolle ['vɔlə] *f* **-, -n** wool; **w~n** *a* woollen.

wollen ['vɔlən] ◆*vti* want; **ich will nach Hause** I want to go home; **ich will nicht** he doesn't want to; **er wollte das nicht** he didn't want it; **wenn du willst** if you like; **ich will, daß du mir zuhörst** I want you to listen to me

◆ (*als Hilfsverb*) *ptp* **wollen: er will ein Haus kaufen** he wants to buy a house; **ich wollte, ich wäre ...** I wish I were ...; **etw gerade tun** ~ be going to do sth.

wollüstig ['vɔlʏstɪç] *a* lusty, sensual.

wo- *zW*: **~mit** [voː'mɪt] *ad* (*rel*) with which; (*interrog*) what ... with; **~möglich** [voː'møːklɪç] *ad* probably, I suppose; **~nach** [voː'naːx] *ad* (*rel*) after/for which; (*interrog*) what ... for/after; **~ran** [voː'ran] *ad* (*rel*) on/at which; (*interrog*) what ... on/at; **~rauf** [voː'raʊf] *ad* (*rel*) on which; (*interrog*) what ... on; **~raus** [voː'raʊs] *ad* (*rel*) from/out of which; (*interrog*) what ... from/out of; **~rin** [voː'rɪn] *ad* (*rel*) in which; (*interrog*) what ... in.

Wort [vɔrt] *nt* **-(e)s, ¨er** *od* **-e** word; **jdn beim** ~ **nehmen** take sb at his word; **mit anderen ~en** in other words; **w~brüchig** *a* not true to one's word.

Wörterbuch ['vœrtərbuːx] *nt* dictionary.

Wort- *zW*: **~führer** *m* spokesman; **w~karg** *a* taciturn; **~laut** *m* wording.

wörtlich ['vœrtlɪç] *a* literal.

Wort- *zW*: **w~los** *a* mute; **w~reich** *a* wordy, verbose; **~schatz** *m* vocabulary; **~spiel** *nt* play on words, pun.

wo- *zW*: **~rüber** [voː'ryːbər] *ad* (*rel*) over/about which; (*interrog*) what ...

over/about; ~**rum** [voːˈrʊm] *ad (rel)* about/round which; *(interrog)* what ... about/round; ~**runter** [voːˈrʊntər] *ad (rel)* under which; *(interrog)* what ... under; ~**von** [voːˈfɔn] *ad (rel)* from which; *(interrog)* what ... from; ~**vor** [voːˈfoːr] *ad (rel)* in front of/before which; *(interrog)* in front of/before what; of what; ~**zu** [voːˈtsuː] *ad (rel)* to/for which; *(interrog)* what ... for/to; *(warum)* why.

Wrack [vrak] *nt* -(e)s, -s wreck.

wringen [ˈvrɪŋən] *vt unreg* wring.

Wucher [ˈvuːxər] *m* -s profiteering; ~**er** *m* -s, - profiteer; **w~isch** *a* profiteering; **w~n** *vi (Pflanzen)* grow wild; ~**ung** *f (MED)* growth, tumour.

Wuchs [vuːks] *m* -es *(Wachstum)* growth; *(Statur)* build.

Wucht [vʊxt] *f* - force.

wühlen [ˈvyːlən] *vi* scrabble; *(Tier)* root; *(Maulwurf)* burrow; *(umg: arbeiten)* slave away // *vt* dig.

Wulst [vʊlst] *m* -es, ⸚e bulge; *(an Wunde)* swelling.

wund [vʊnt] *a* sore, raw; **W~e** [ˈvʊndə] *f* -, -n wound.

Wunder [ˈvʊndər] *nt* -s, - miracle; **es ist kein ~** it's no wonder; **w~bar** *a* wonderful, marvellous; ~**kind** *nt* infant prodigy; **w~lich** *a* odd, peculiar; **w~n** *vr* be surprised *(über +akk* at) // *vt* surprise; **w~schön** *a* beautiful; **w~voll** *a* wonderful.

Wundstarrkrampf [ˈvʊntʃtarkrampf] *m* tetanus, lockjaw.

Wunsch [vʊnʃ] *m* -(e)s, ⸚e wish.

wünschen [ˈvʏnʃən] *vt* wish; **sich** *(dat)* **etw ~** want sth, wish for sth; **wünschenswert** *a* desirable.

wurde *etc v siehe* **werden**.

Würde [ˈvyrdə] *f* -, -n dignity; *(Stellung)* honour; **w~voll** *a* dignified.

würdig [ˈvyrdɪç] *a* worthy; *(würdevoll)* dignified; ~**en** [ˈvyrdɪgən] *vt* appreciate; **jdn keines Blickes ~en** not so much as look at sb.

Wurf [vʊrf] *m* -s, ⸚e throw; *(Junge)* litter.

Würfel [ˈvyrfəl] *m* -s, - dice; *(MATH)* cube; ~**becher** *m* (dice) cup; **w~n** *vi* play dice // *vt* dice; ~**zucker** *m* lump sugar.

würgen [ˈvyrgən] *vti* choke.

Wurm [vʊrm] *m* -(e)s, ⸚er worm; **w~en** *vt (umg)* rile, nettle; ~**stichig** *a* worm-ridden.

Wurst [vʊrst] *f* -, ⸚e sausage; **das ist mir ~** *(umg)* I don't care, I don't give a damn.

Würstchen [ˈvʏrstçən] *nt* sausage.

Würze [ˈvyrtsə] *f* -, -n seasoning, spice.

Wurzel [ˈvʊrtsəl] *f* -, -n root.

würz- [ˈvyrts] *zW:* ~**en** *vt* season,

spice; ~**ig** *a* spicy.

wusch *etc v siehe* **waschen**.

wußte *etc v siehe* **wissen**.

wüst [vyːst] *a* untidy, messy; *(ausschweifend)* wild; *(öde)* waste; *(umg: heftig)* terrible; **W~e** *f* -, -n desert.

Wut [vuːt] *f* - rage, fury; ~**anfall** *m* fit of rage.

wüten [ˈvyːtən] *vi* rage; ~**d** *a* furious, mad.

X

X, x [ɪks] *nt* X, x.

X-Beine [ˈɪksbaɪnə] *pl* knock-knees *pl*.

x-beliebig [ɪksbəˈliːbɪç] *a* any (whatever).

xerokopieren [kseroko'piːrən] *vt* xerox, photocopy.

x-mal [ˈɪksmaːl] *ad* any number of times, n times.

Xylophon [ksyloˈfoːn] *nt* -s, -e xylophone.

Y

Y, y [ˈʏpsilɔn] *nt* Y, y.

Ypsilon *nt* -(s), -s the letter Y.

Z

Z, z [tsɛt] *nt* Z, z.

Zacke [ˈtsakə] *f* -, -n point; *(Berg~)* jagged peak; *(Gabel~)* prong; *(Kamm~)* tooth.

zackig [ˈtsakɪç] *a* jagged; *(umg)* smart; *(Tempo)* brisk.

zaghaft [ˈtsaːkhaft] *a* timid.

zäh [tsɛː] *a* tough; *(Mensch)* tenacious; *(Flüssigkeit)* thick; *(schleppend)* sluggish; **Z~igkeit** *f* toughness; tenacity.

Zahl [tsaːl] *f* -, -en number; **z~bar** *a* payable; **z~en** *vti* pay; **z~en bitte!** the bill please!

zählen [ˈtsɛːlən] *vti* count *(auf +akk* on); ~ **zu** be numbered among.

Zähler [ˈtsɛːlər] *m* -s, - *(TECH)* meter; *(MATH)* numerator.

Zahl- *zW:* **z~los** *a* countless; **z~reich** *a* numerous; ~**tag** *m* payday; ~**ung** *f* payment; **z~ungsfähig** *a* solvent; ~**ungsrückstände** *pl* arrears *pl*; ~**wort** *nt* numeral.

zahm [tsaːm] *a* tame.

zähmen [ˈtsɛːmən] *vt* tame; *(fig)* curb.

Zahn [tsaːn] *m* -(e)s, ⸚e tooth; ~**arzt** *m* dentist; ~**bürste** *f* toothbrush; ~**creme** *f* toothpaste; ~**fleisch** *nt* gums *pl*; ~**pasta** *f* toothpaste; ~**rad**

nt cog(wheel); **~schmerzen** *pl* toothache; **~stein** *m* tartar; **~stocher** *m* **-s, -** toothpick.

Zange ['tsaŋə] *f* **-, -n** pliers *pl*; (*Zucker~ etc*) tongs *pl*; (*Beiß~, ZOOL*) pincers *pl*; (*MED*) forceps *pl*.

zanken ['tsaŋkən] *vir* quarrel.

zänkisch ['tsɛŋkɪʃ] *a* quarrelsome.

Zäpfchen ['tsɛpfçən] *nt* (*ANAT*) uvula; (*MED*) suppository.

Zapfen ['tsapfən] *m* **-s, -** plug; (*BOT*) cone; (*Eis~*) icicle; **z~** *vt* tap; **~streich** *m* (*MIL*) tattoo.

zappeln ['tsapəln] *vi* wriggle; fidget.

zart [tsart] *a* (*weich, leise*) soft; (*Fleisch*) tender; (*fein, schwächlich*) delicate; **Z~gefühl** *nt* tact; **Z~heit** *f* softness; tenderness; delicacy.

zärtlich ['tsɛːrtlɪç] *a* tender, affectionate; **Z~keit** *f* tenderness; **Z~keiten** *pl* caresses *pl*.

Zauber ['tsaubər] *m* **-s, -** magic; (*~bann*) spell; **~ei** [-'raɪ] *f* magic; **~er** *m* **-s, -** magician; conjuror; **z~haft** *a* magical, enchanting; **~künstler** *m* conjuror; **z~n** *vi* conjure, practise magic.

zaudern ['tsaudərn] *vi* hesitate.

Zaum [tsaum] *m* **-(e)s, Zäume** bridle; etw im **~** halten keep sth in check.

Zaun [tsaun] *m* **-(e)s, Zäune** fence; **~könig** *m* wren.

z.B. *abk* (= *zum Beispiel*) e.g.

Zebra ['tse:bra] *nt* zebra; **~streifen** *m* zebra crossing.

Zeche ['tsɛçə] *f* **-, -n** bill; (*Bergbau*) mine.

Zehe ['tse:ə] *f* **-, -n** toe; (*Knoblauch~*) clove.

zehn [tse:n] *num* ten; **~te(r, s)** *a* tenth; **Z~tel** *nt* **-s, -** tenth (part).

Zeich- ['tsaɪç] *zW:* **~en** *nt* **-s, -** sign; **z~nen** *vti* draw; (*kenn~nen*) mark; (*unter~nen*) sign; **~ner** *m* **-s, -** artist; technischer **~ner** draughtsman; **~nung** *f* drawing; (*Markierung*) markings *pl*.

Zeige- ['tsaɪgə] *zW:* **~finger** *m* index finger; **z~n** *vt* show // *vi* point (*auf +akk* to, at) // *vr* show o.s.; es wird sich **z~n** time will tell; es zeigte sich, daß ... it turned out that ...; **~r** *m* **-s, -** pointer; (*Uhr~r*) hand.

Zeile ['tsaɪlə] *f* **-, -n** line; (*Häuser~*) row.

Zeit [tsaɪt] *f* **-, -en** time; (*GRAM*) tense; zur **~** at the moment; sich (*dat*) **~** lassen take one's time; von **~** zu **~** from time to time; **~alter** *nt* age; **z~gemäß** *a* in keeping with the times; **~genosse** *m* contemporary; **z~ig** *a* early; **z~lich** *a* temporal; **~lupe** *f* slow motion; **z~raubend** *a* time-consuming; **~raum** *m* period; **~rechnung** *f* time, era; **nach/vor** **unserer ~rechnung** A.D./B.C.; **~schrift** *f* periodical; **~ung** *f* newspaper; **~verschwendung** *f* waste of time; **~vertreib** *m* pastime, diversion; **z~weilig** *a* temporary; **z~weise** *ad* for a time; **~wort** *nt* verb; **~zünder** *m* time fuse.

Zell- ['tsɛl] *zW:* **~e** *f* **-, -n** cell; (*Telefon~e*) callbox; **~stoff** *m* cellulose.

Zelt [tsɛlt] *nt* **-(e)s, -e** tent; **z~en** *vi* camp.

Zement [tse'mɛnt] *m* **-(e)s, -e** cement; **z~ieren** [-'ti:rən] *vt* cement.

zensieren [tsɛn'zi:rən] *vt* censor; (*SCH*) mark.

Zensur [tsɛn'zuːr] *f* censorship; (*SCH*) mark.

Zentimeter [tsɛnti'me:tər] *m od nt* centimetre.

Zentner ['tsɛntnər] *m* **-s, -** hundredweight.

zentral [tsɛn'tra:l] *a* central; **Z~e** *f* **-, -n** central office; (*TEL*) exchange; **Z~einheit** *f* central processing unit, CPU; **Z~heizung** *f* central heating.

Zentrum ['tsɛntrum] *nt* **-s, Zentren** centre.

zerbrech- [tsɛr'brɛç] *zW:* **~en** *vti unreg* break; **~lich** *a* fragile.

zer'drücken *vt* squash, crush; (*Kartoffeln*) mash.

Zeremonie [tseremo'ni:] *f* ceremony.

Zerfall [tsɛr'fal] *m* decay; **z~en** *vi unreg* disintegrate, decay; (*sich gliedern*) fall (*in +akk* into).

zer'gehen *vi unreg* melt, dissolve.

zerkleinern [tsɛr'klaɪnərn] *vt* reduce to small pieces.

zerleg- [tsɛr'le:g] *zW:* **~bar** *a* able to be dismantled; **~en** *vt* take to pieces; (*Fleisch*) carve; (*Satz*) analyse.

zermürben [tsɛr'myrbən] *vt* wear down.

zerquetschen [tsɛr'kvɛtʃən] *vt* squash.

Zerrbild ['tsɛrbɪlt] *nt* caricature, distorted picture.

zer'reißen *unreg vt* tear to pieces // *vi* tear, rip.

zerren ['tsɛrən] *vt* drag // *vi* tug (*an +dat* at).

zer'rinnen *vi unreg* melt away.

zerrissen [tsɛr'rɪsən] *a* torn, tattered; **Z~heit** *f* tattered state; (*POL*) disunion, discord; (*innere Z~heit*) disintegration.

zerrütten [tsɛr'rytən] *vt* wreck, destroy.

zerrüttet *a* wrecked, shattered.

zer'schlagen *unreg vt* shatter, smash // *vr* fall through.

zer'schneiden *vt unreg* cut up.

zer'setzen *vtr* decompose, dissolve.

zer'springen *vi unreg* shatter, burst.

Zerstäuber [tsɛr'ʃtɔybər] *m* **-s, -** atomizer.

zerstör- [tsɛr'ʃtøːr] zW: **~en** vt destroy; **Z~ung** f destruction.

zerstreu- [tsɛr'ʃtrɔy] zW: **~en** vtr disperse, scatter; (*unterhalten*) divert; (*Zweifel etc*) dispel; **~t** a scattered; (*Mensch*) absent-minded; **Zerstreutheit** f absent-mindedness; **Z~ung** f dispersion; (*Ablenkung*) diversion.

zerstückeln [tsɛr'ʃtʏkəln] vt cut into pieces.

zer'teilen vt divide into parts.

Zertifikat [tsɛrtifi'kaːt] nt certificate.

zer'treten vt unreg crush underfoot.

zertrümmern [tsɛr'trʏmərn] vt shatter; (*Gebäude etc*) demolish.

zerzausen [tsɛr'tsauzən] vt (*Haare*) ruffle up, tousle.

zetern ['tseːtərn] vi shout, shriek.

Zettel ['tsɛtəl] m -s, - piece of paper, slip; (*Notiz~*) note; (*Formular*) form.

Zeug [tsɔyk] nt -(e)s, -e (*umg*) stuff; (*Ausrüstung*) gear; **dummes ~** (stupid) nonsense; **das ~ haben zu** have the makings of; **sich ins ~ legen** put one's shoulder to the wheel.

Zeuge ['tsɔygə] m -n, -n, **Zeugin** ['tsɔygɪn] f witness; **z~n** vi bear witness, testify; **es zeugt von ...** it testifies to ... // vt (*Kind*) father; **Zeugenaussage** f evidence.

Zeugnis ['tsɔygnɪs] nt -ses, -se certificate; (*SCH*) report; (*Referenz*) reference; (*Aussage*) evidence, testimony; **~ geben von** be evidence of, testify to.

z.H(d). abk (= zu Händen) attn.

Zickzack ['tsɪktsak] m -(e)s, -e zigzag.

Ziege ['tsiːgə] f -, -n goat; **Ziegenleder** nt kid.

Ziegel ['tsiːgəl] m -s, - brick; (*Dach~*) tile.

ziehen ['tsiːən] unreg vt draw; (*zerren*) pull; (*SCHACH etc*) move; (*züchten*) rear; **etw nach sich ~** lead to sth, entail sth // vi draw; (*um~, wandern*) move; (*Rauch, Wolke etc*) drift; (*reißen*) pull // v unpers: **es zieht** there is a draught, it's draughty // vr (*Gummi*) stretch; (*Grenze etc*) run; (*Gespräche*) be drawn out.

Ziehharmonika ['tsiːharmoːnika] f concertina; accordion.

Ziehung ['tsiːʊŋ] f (*Los~*) drawing.

Ziel [tsiːl] nt -(e)s, -e (*einer Reise*) destination; (*SPORT*) finish; (*MIL*) target; (*Absicht*) goal, aim; **z~en** vi aim (*auf +akk* at); **z~los** a aimless; **~scheibe** f target; **z~strebig** a purposeful.

ziemlich ['tsiːmlɪç] a quite a; fair // ad rather; quite a bit.

Zierde ['tsiːrdə] f ornament.

zieren ['tsiːrən] vr act coy.

zierlich ['tsiːrlɪç] a dainty; **Z~keit** f daintiness.

Ziffer ['tsɪfər] f -, -n figure, digit; **~blatt** nt dial, clock-face.

zig [tsɪç] a (*umg*) umpteen.

Zigarette [tsiga'rɛtə] f cigarette.

Zigaretten- zW: **~automat** m cigarette machine; **~schachtel** f cigarette packet; **~spitze** f cigarette holder.

Zigarillo [tsiga'rɪlo] nt od m -s, -s cigarillo.

Zigarre [tsi'garə] f -, -n cigar.

Zigeuner(in f) [tsi'gɔynər(ɪn)] m -s, - gipsy.

Zimmer ['tsɪmər] nt -s, - room; **~lautstärke** f reasonable volume; **~mädchen** nt chambermaid; **~mann** m carpenter; **z~n** vt make, carpenter; **~nachweis** m accommodation office; **~pflanze** f indoor plant.

zimperlich ['tsɪmpərlɪç] a squeamish; (*pingelig*) fussy, finicky.

Zimt [tsɪmt] m -(e)s, -e cinnamon.

Zink [tsɪŋk] nt -(e)s zinc.

Zinn [tsɪn] nt -(e)s (*Element*) tin; (*in ~waren*) pewter; **~soldat** m tin soldier.

Zins [tsɪns] m -es, -en interest; **Zinseszins** m compound interest; **~fuß** m, **~satz** m rate of interest; **z~los** a interest-free.

Zipfel ['tsɪpfəl] m -s, - corner; (*spitz*) tip; (*Hemd~*) tail; (*Wurst~*) end; **~mütze** f stocking cap; nightcap.

zirka ['tsɪrka] ad (round) about.

Zirkel ['tsɪrkəl] m -s, - circle; (*MATH*) pair of compasses.

Zirkus ['tsɪrkus] m -, -se circus.

zischen ['tsɪʃən] vi hiss.

Zitat [tsi'taːt] nt -(e)s, -e quotation, quote.

zitieren [tsi'tiːrən] vt quote.

Zitronat [tsitro'naːt] nt -(e)s, -e candied lemon peel.

Zitrone [tsi'troːnə] f -, -n lemon; **Zitronenlimonade** f lemonade; **Zitronensaft** m lemon juice.

zittern ['tsɪtərn] vi tremble.

zivil [tsi'viːl] a civil; (*Preis*) moderate; **Z~** nt -s plain clothes pl; (*MIL*) civilian clothing; **Z~bevölkerung** f civilian population; **Z~courage** f courage of one's convictions; **Z~dienstleistende(r)** f conscientious objector doing alternative service (in the community); **Z~isation** [tsivilizatsi'oːn] f civilization; **Z~isationskrankheit** f disease peculiar to civilization; **~i'sieren** vt civilize; **Z~ist** [tsivi'lɪst] m civilian.

zog etc v siehe **ziehen.**

zögern ['tsøːgərn] vi hesitate.

Zoll [tsɔl] m -(e)s, -e customs pl; (*Abgabe*) duty; **~abfertigung** f customs clearance; **~amt** nt customs office;

~**beamte(r)** *m* customs official; ~**erklärung** *f* customs declaration; **z~frei** *a* duty-free; ~**kontrolle** *f* customs check; **z~pflichtig** *a* liable to duty, dutiable.

Zone ['tso:nə] *f* -, -n zone.

Zoo [tso:] *m* -s, -s zoo; ~**loge** [tsoo'logə] *m* -n, -n zoologist; ~**lo'gie** *f* zoology; **z~'logisch** *a* zoological.

Zopf [tsɔpf] *m* -(e)s, ⁼e plait; pigtail; **alter ~** antiquated custom.

Zorn [tsɔrn] *m* -(e)s anger; **z~ig** *a* angry.

zottig ['tsɔtɪç] *a* shaggy.

z.T. *abk von* zum Teil.

zu [tsu:] ◆*präp* +*dat* **1** (*örtlich*) to; ~**m Bahnhof/Arzt gehen** go to the station/doctor; ~**r Schule/Kirche gehen** go to school/church; **sollen wir ~ euch gehen?** shall we go to your place?; **sie sah ~ ihm hin** she looked towards him; ~**m Fenster herein** through the window; ~ **meiner Linken** to *od* on my left

2 (*zeitlich*) at; ~ **Ostern** at Easter; **bis ~m 1. Mai** until May 1st; (*nicht später als*) by May 1st; ~ **meiner Zeit** in my time

3 (*Zusatz*) with; **Wein ~m Essen trinken** drink wine with one's meal; **sich ~ jdm setzen** sit down beside sb; **setz dich doch ~ uns** (come and) sit with us; **Anmerkungen ~ etw** notes on sth

4 (*Zweck*) for; **Wasser ~m Waschen** water for washing; **Papier ~m Schreiben** paper to write on; **etw ~m Geburtstag bekommen** get sth for one's birthday

5 (*Veränderung*) into; ~ **etw werden** turn into sth; **jdn ~ etw machen** make sb (into) sth; ~ **Asche verbrennen** burn to ashes

6 (*mit Zahlen*): **3 ~ 2** (*SPORT*) 3-2; **das Stück ~ 2 Mark** at 2 marks each; ~**m ersten Mal** for the first time

7: ~ **meiner Freude** *etc* to my joy *etc*; ~**m Glück** luckily; ~ **Fuß** on foot; **es ist ~m Weinen** it's enough to make you cry

◆*kj* to; **etw ~ essen** sth to eat; **um besser sehen ~ können** in order to see better; **ohne es ~ wissen** without knowing it; **noch ~ bezahlende Rechnungen** bills that are still to be paid

◆*ad* **1** (*allzu*) too; ~ **sehr** too much

2 (*örtlich*) toward(s); **er kam auf mich ~** he came up to me

3 (*geschlossen*) shut, closed; **die Geschäfte haben ~** the shops are closed; **'auf/~'** (*Wasserhahn etc*) 'on/off'

4 (*umg: los*): **nur ~!** just keep on!; **mach ~!** hurry up!

zualler- [tsu:'alər] *zW:* ~**erst** *ad* first of all; ~**letzt** *ad* last of all.

Zubehör ['tsu:bəhø:r] *nt* -(e)s, -e accessories *pl*.

zubereiten ['tsu:bəraɪtən] *vt* prepare.

zubilligen ['tsu:bɪlɪgən] *vt* grant.

zubinden ['tsu:bɪndən] *vt unreg* tie up.

zubringen ['tsu:brɪŋən] *vt unreg* (*Zeit*) spend.

Zubringer *m* -s, - (*Straße*) approach *od* slip road.

Zucht [tsuxt] *f* -, -en (*von Tieren*) breed(ing); (*von Pflanzen*) cultivation; (*Rasse*) breed; (*Erziehung*) raising; (*Disziplin*) discipline.

züchten ['tsyçtən] *vt* (*Tiere*) breed; (*Pflanzen*) cultivate, grow.

Züchter *m* -s, - breeder; grower.

Zuchthaus *nt* prison, penitentiary (*US*).

züchtigen ['tsyçtɪgən] *vt* chastise.

zucken ['tsʊkən] *vi* jerk, twitch; (*Strahl etc*) flicker // *vt* (*Schultern*) shrug.

Zucker ['tsʊkər] *m* -s, - sugar; (*MED*) diabetes; ~**dose** *f* sugar bowl; ~**guß** *m* icing; **z~krank** *a* diabetic; **z~n** *vt* sugar; ~**rohr** *nt* sugar cane; ~**rübe** *f* sugar beet.

Zuckung ['tsʊkʊŋ] *f* convulsion, spasm; (*leichte*) twitch.

zudecken ['tsu:dɛkən] *vt* cover (up).

zudem [tsu:'de:m] *ad* in addition (to this).

zudringlich ['tsu:drɪŋlɪç] *a* forward, pushing, obtrusive.

zudrücken ['tsu:drʏkən] *vt* close; **ein Auge ~** turn a blind eye.

zueinander [tsu:aɪ'nandər] *ad* to one other; (*in Verbverbindung*) together.

zuerkennen ['tsu:'ɛrkɛnən] *vt unreg* award (*jdm etw* to sb, sb sth).

zuerst [tsu:'e:rst] *ad* first; (*zu Anfang*) at first; ~ **einmal** first of all.

Zufahrt ['tsu:fa:rt] *f* approach; **Zufahrtsstraße** *f* approach road; (*von Autobahn etc*) slip road.

Zufall ['tsu:fal] *m* chance; (*Ereignis*) coincidence; **durch ~** by accident; **so ein ~** what a coincidence; **z~en** *vi unreg* close, shut itself; (*Anteil, Aufgabe*) fall (*jdm* to sb).

zufällig ['tsu:fɛlɪç] *a* chance // *ad* by chance; (*in Frage*) by any chance.

Zuflucht ['tsu:flʊxt] *f* recourse; (*Ort*) refuge.

zufolge [tsu:'fɔlgə] *präp* +*dat od gen* judging by; (*laut*) according to.

zufrieden [tsu:'fri:dən] *a* content(ed), satisfied; **Z~heit** *f* satisfaction, contentedness; ~**stellen** *vt* satisfy.

zufrieren ['tsu:fri:rən] *vi unreg* freeze up *od* over.

zufügen ['tsu:fy:gən] *vt* add (*dat* to); (*Leid etc*) cause (*jdm etw* sth to sb).

Zufuhr ['tsu:fu:r] *f* -, **-en** (*Herbeibringen*) supplying; (*MET*) influx.

Zug [tsu:k] *m* **-(e)s, ˜e** (*EISENB*) train; (*Luft˜*) draught; (*Ziehen*) pull(ing); (*Gesichts˜*) feature; (*SCHACH etc*) move; (*Klingel˜*) pull; (*Schrift˜*) stroke; (*Atem˜*) breath; (*Charakter˜*) trait; (*an Zigarette*) puff, pull, drag; (*Schluck*) gulp; (*Menschengruppe*) procession; (*von Vögeln*) flight; (*MIL*) platoon; **etw in vollen ˜en genießen** enjoy sth to the full.

Zu- ['tsu:] *zW*: **˜gabe** *f* extra; (*in Konzert etc*) encore; **˜gang** *m* access, approach; **z˜gänglich** *a* accessible; (*Mensch*) approachable.

zugeben ['tsu:ge:bən] *vt unreg* (*beifügen*) add, throw in; (*zugestehen*) admit; (*erlauben*) permit.

zugehen ['tsu:ge:ən] *vi unreg* (*schließen*) shut; **es geht dort seltsam zu** there are strange goingson there; **auf jdn/etw ˜** walk towards sb/sth; **dem Ende ˜** be finishing.

Zugehörigkeit ['tsu:gəhø:rɪçkaɪt] *f* membership (*zu* of), belonging (*zu* to).

Zügel ['tsy:gəl] *m* **-s, -** rein(s); (*fig auch*) curb; **z˜n** *vt* curb; (*Pferd auch*) rein in.

zuge- ['tsu:gə] *zW*: **Z˜ständnis** *nt* **-ses, -se** concession; **˜stehen** *vt unreg* admit; (*Rechte*) concede (*jdm* to sb); **˜stiegen** *a*: **noch jemand ˜stiegen?** tickets please.

zugig ['tsu:gɪç] *a* draughty.

zügig ['tsy:gɪç] *a* speedy, swift.

zugreifen ['tsu:graɪfən] *vi unreg* seize *od* grab at; (*helfen*) help; (*beim Essen*) help o.s.

Zugriff ['tsu:grɪf] *m* (*COMPUT*) access.

zugrunde [tsu:'grʊndə] *ad*: **˜ gehen** collapse; (*Mensch*) perish; **einer Sache etw ˜ legen** base sth on sth; **einer Sache ˜ liegen** be based on sth; **˜ richten** ruin, destroy.

zugunsten [tsu:'gʊnstən] *präp* +*gen od dat* in favour of.

zugute [tsu:'gu:tə] *ad*: **jdm etw ˜ halten** concede sth; **jdm ˜ kommen** be of assistance to sb.

Zugvogel *m* migratory bird.

Zuhälter ['tsu:hɛltər] *m* **-s, -** pimp.

Zuhause [tsu:'haʊzə] *nt* - home.

zuhören ['tsu:hø:rən] *vi* listen (*dat* to).

Zuhörer *m* **-s, -** listener; **˜schaft** *f* audience.

zukleben ['tsu:kle:bən] *vt* paste up.

zukommen ['tsu:kɔmən] *vi unreg* come up (*auf* +*akk* to); (*sich gehören*) be fitting (*jdm* for sb); (*Recht haben auf*) be entitled to; **jdm etw ˜ lassen** give sb sth; **etw auf sich ˜ lassen** wait and see.

Zukunft [tsu:kʊnft] *f* -, **Zukünfte** future.

zukünftig ['tsu:kynftɪç] *a* future; **mein ˜er Mann** my husband to be // *ad* in future.

Zulage ['tsu:la:gə] *f* bonus, allowance.

zulassen ['tsu:lasən] *vt unreg* (*hereinlassen*) admit; (*erlauben*) permit; (*Auto*) license; (*umg: nicht öffnen*) (keep) shut.

zulässig ['tsu:lɛsɪç] *a* permissible, permitted.

zuleide [tsu:'laɪdə] *a*: **jdm etw ˜ tun** hurt *od* harm sb.

zuletzt [tsu:'lɛtst] *ad* finally, at last.

zuliebe [tsu:'li:bə] *ad*: **jdm ˜** to please sb.

zum [tsum] = **zu dem**; **˜ dritten Mal** for the third time; **˜ Scherz** as a joke; **˜ Trinken** for drinking.

zumachen ['tsu:maxən] *vt* shut; (*Kleidung*) do up, fasten // *vi* shut; (*umg*) hurry up.

zumal [tsu:'ma:l] *kj* especially (as).

zumeist [tsu:'maɪst] *ad* mostly.

zumindest [tsu:'mɪndəst] *ad* at least.

zumut- *zW*: **˜bar** ['tsu:mu:tba:r] *a* reasonable; **˜e** *ad*: **wie ist ihm ˜e?** how does he feel?; **˜en** ['tsu:mu:tən] *vt* expect, ask (*jdm* of sb); **Z˜ung** ['tsu:mu:tʊŋ] *f* unreasonable expectation *od* demand, impertinence.

zunächst [tsu:'nɛ:çst] *ad* first of all; **˜ einmal** to start with.

Zunahme ['tsu:na:mə] *f* -, **-n** increase.

Zuname ['tsu:na:mə] *m* surname.

Zünd- [tsynd] *zW*: **z˜en** *vi* (*Feuer*) light, ignite; (*Motor*) fire; (*begeistern*) fire (with enthusiasm) (*bei jdm* sb); **z˜end** *a* fiery; **˜er** *m* **-s, -** fuse; (*MIL*) detonator; **˜holz** ['tsynt-] *nt* match; **˜kerze** *f* (*AUT*) spark(ing) plug; **˜schlüssel** *m* ignition key; **˜schnur** *f* fuse wire; **˜ung** *f* ignition.

zunehmen ['tsu:ne:mən] *vi unreg* increase, grow; (*Mensch*) put on weight.

Zuneigung *f* affection.

Zunft [tsʊnft] *f* -, **˜e** guild.

zünftig ['tsynftɪç] *a* proper, real; (*Handwerk*) decent.

Zunge ['tsʊŋə] *f* -, **-n** tongue.

zunichte [tsu:'nɪçtə] *ad*: **˜ machen** ruin, destroy; **˜ werden** come to nothing.

zunutze [tsu:'nʊtsə] *ad*: **sich** (*dat*) **etw ˜ machen** make use of sth.

zuoberst [tsu:'o:bərst] *ad* at the top.

zupfen ['tsʊpfən] *vt* pull, pick, pluck; (*Gitarre*) pluck.

zur [tsu:r] = **zu der**.

zurechnungsfähig ['tsu:rɛçnʊŋsfɛ:ɪç] *a* responsible, accountable; **Z˜keit** *f* responsibility, accountability.

zurecht- [tsu:'rɛçt] *zW*: **˜finden** *vr*

unreg find one's way (about); ~**kommen** *vi unreg* (be able to) deal (*mit* with), manage; ~**legen** *vt* get ready; (*Ausrede etc*) have ready; ~**machen** *vt* prepare // *vr* get ready; ~**weisen** *vt unreg* reprimand; **Z~weisung** *f* reprimand, rebuff.

zureden ['tsu:re:dən] *vi* persuade, urge (*jdm* sb).

zurück [tsu'ryk] *ad* back; ~**behalten** *vt unreg* keep back; ~**bekommen** *vt unreg* get back; ~**bleiben** *vi unreg* (*Mensch*) remain behind; (*nicht nachkommen*) fall behind, lag; (*Schaden*) remain; ~**bringen** *vt unreg* bring back; ~**fahren** *unreg vi* travel back; (*vor Schreck*) recoil, start // *vt* drive back; ~**finden** *vi unreg* find one's way back; ~**fordern** *vt* demand back; ~**führen** *vt* lead back; etw auf etw (*akk*) ~**führen** trace sth back to sth; ~**geben** *vt unreg* give back; (*antworten*) retort with; ~**geblieben** *a* retarded; ~**gehen** *vi unreg* go back; (*zeitlich*) date back (*auf* +*akk* to); (*fallen*) go down, fall; ~**gezogen** *a* retired, withdrawn; ~**halten** *unreg vt* hold back; (*Mensch*) restrain; (*hindern*) prevent // *vi* (*reserviert sein*) be reserved; (*im Essen*) hold back; ~**haltend** *a* reserved; **Z~haltung** *f* reserve; ~**kehren** *vi* return; ~**kommen** *vi unreg* come back; auf etw (*akk*) ~**kommen** return to sth; ~**lassen** *vt unreg* leave behind; ~**legen** *vt* put back; (*Geld*) put by; (*reservieren*) keep back; (*Strecke*) cover; ~**nehmen** *vt unreg* take back; ~**schrecken** *vi* shrink (*vor* +*dat* from); ~**stellen** *vt* put back, replace; (*aufschieben*) put off, postpone; (*MIL*) turn down; (*Interessen*) defer; (*Ware*) keep; ~**treten** *vi unreg* step back; (*vom Amt*) retire; **gegenüber** *od* **hinter etw** ~**treten** diminish in importance in view of sth; ~**weisen** *vt unreg* turn down; (*Mensch*) reject; ~**zahlen** *vt* repay, pay back; ~**ziehen** *unreg vt* pull back; (*Angebot*) withdraw // *vr* retire.

Zuruf ['tsu:ru:f] *m* shout, cry.

Zusage ['tsu:za:gə] *f* -, -**n** promise; (*Annahme*) consent; **z~n** *vt* promise // *vi* accept; **jdm z~n** (*gefallen*) agree with *od* please sb.

zusammen [tsu'zamən] *ad* together; **Z~arbeit** *f* cooperation; ~**arbeiten** *vi* cooperate; ~**beißen** *vt unreg* (*Zähne*) clench; ~**bleiben** *vi unreg* stay together; ~**brechen** *vi unreg* collapse; (*Mensch auch*) break down; ~**bringen** *vt unreg* bring *od* get together; (*Geld*) get; (*Sätze*) put together; **Z~bruch** *m* collapse;

~**fassen** *vt* summarize; (*vereinigen*) unite; **Z~fassung** *f* summary, résumé; ~**fügen** *vt* join (together), unite; ~**halten** *vi unreg* stick together; **Z~hang** *m* connection; im/ aus dem **Z~hang** in/out of context; ~**hängen** *vi unreg* be connected *od* linked; ~**kommen** *vi unreg* meet, assemble; (*sich ereignen*) occur at once *od* together; ~**legen** *vt* put together; (*stapeln*) pile up; (*falten*) fold; (*verbinden*) combine, unite; (*Termine, Fest*) amalgamate; (*Geld*) collect; ~**nehmen** *unreg vt* summon up; alles ~**genommen** all in all // *vr* pull o.s. together; ~**passen** *vi* go well together, match; ~**schließen** *vtr unreg* join (together); **Z~schluß** *m* amalgamation; ~**schreiben** *vt unreg* write as one word; (*Bericht*) put together; **Z~sein** *nt* -**s** get-together; ~**setzen** *vt* put together // *vr* (*Stoff*) be composed of; (*Menschen*) get together; **Z~setzung** *f* composition; ~**stellen** *vt* put together; compile; **Z~stoß** *m* collision; ~**stoßen** *vi unreg* collide; ~**treffen** *vi unreg* coincide; (*Menschen*) meet; **Z~treffen** *nt* meeting; coincidence; ~**zählen** *vt* add up; ~**ziehen** *unreg vt* (*verengern*) draw together; (*vereinigen*) bring together; (*addieren*) add up // *vr* shrink; (*sich bilden*) form, develop.

zusätzlich ['tsu:zɛtslɪç] *a* additional // *ad* in addition.

zuschauen ['tsu:ʃauən] *vi* watch, look on.

Zuschauer(in *f*) *m* -**s**, - spectator // *pl* (*THEAT*) audience.

zuschicken ['tsu:ʃɪkən] *vt* send, forward (*jdm etw* sth to sb).

Zuschlag ['tsu:ʃla:k] *m* extra charge, surcharge; **z~en** [-'tsu:ʃla:gən] *unreg vt* (*Tür*) slam; (*Ball*) hit (*jdm* to sb); (*bei Auktion*) knock down; (*Steine etc*) knock into shape // *vi* (*Fenster, Tür*) shut; (*Mensch*) hit, punch; ~**karte** *f* (*EISENB*) surcharge ticket; **z~pflichtig** *a* subject to surcharge.

zuschneiden ['tsu:ʃnaɪdən] *vt unreg* cut out *od* to size.

zuschrauben ['tsu:ʃraubən] *vt* screw down *od* up.

zuschreiben ['tsu:ʃraɪbən] *vt unreg* (*fig*) ascribe, attribute; (*COMM*) credit.

Zuschrift ['tsu:ʃrɪft] *f* letter, reply.

zuschulden ['tsu:ʃuldən] *ad*: sich (*dat*) etw ~ kommen lassen make o.s. guilty of sth.

Zuschuß ['tsu:ʃus] *m* subsidy, allowance.

zusehen ['tsu:ze:ən] *vi unreg* watch

(*jdm/etw* sb/sth); (*dafür sorgen*) take care; **zusehends** *ad* visibly.

zusenden ['tsuːzɛndən] *vt unreg* forward, send on (*jdm etw* sth to sb).

zusichern ['tsuːzɪçərn] *vt* assure (*jdm etw* sb of sth).

zuspielen ['tsuːʃpiːlən] *vti* pass (*jdm* to sb).

zuspitzen ['tsuːʃpɪtsən] *vt* sharpen // *vr* (*Lage*) become critical.

zusprechen ['tsuːʃprɛçən] *unreg vt* (*zuerkennen*) award (*jdm etw* sb sth, sth to sb); **jdm Trost** ~ comfort sb // *vi* speak (*jdm* to sb); **dem Essen/ Alkohol** ~ eat/drink a lot.

Zustand ['tsuːʃtant] *m* state, condition; **z~e** [tsuːʃtandə] *ad*: **z~e bringen** *vt unreg* bring about; **z~e kommen** *vi unreg* come about.

zuständig ['tsuːʃtɛndɪç] *a* responsible; **Z~keit** *f* competence, responsibility.

zustehen ['tsuːʃteːən] *vi unreg*: **jdm** ~ be sb's right.

zustellen ['tsuːʃtɛlən] *vt* (*verstellen*) block; (*Post etc*) send.

zustimmen ['tsuːʃtɪmən] *vi* agree (*dat* to).

Zustimmung *f* agreement, consent.

zustoßen ['tsuːʃtoːsən] *vi unreg* (*fig*) happen (*jdm* to sb).

zutage [tsuːˈtaːgə] *ad*: ~ **bringen** bring to light; ~ **treten** come to light.

Zutaten ['tsuːtaːtən] *pl* ingredients *pl*.

zutiefst [tsuːˈtiːfst] *ad* deeply.

zutragen ['tsuːtraːgən] *unreg vt* bring (*jdm etw* sth to sb); (*Klatsch*) tell // *vr* happen.

zutrau- ['tsuːtrau] *zW*: **~en** *vt* credit (*jdm etw* sb with sth); **Z~en** *nt* -s trust (*zu* in); **~lich** *a* trusting, friendly; **Z~lichkeit** *f* trust.

zutreffen ['tsuːtrɛfən] *vi unreg* be correct; apply; **Z~des bitte unterstreichen** please underline where applicable.

Zutritt ['tsuːtrɪt] *m* access, admittance.

Zutun ['tsuːtuːn] *nt* -s assistance.

zuverlässig ['tsuːfɛrlɛsɪç] *a* reliable; **Z~keit** *f* reliability.

Zuversicht ['tsuːfɛrzɪçt] *f* - confidence; **z~lich** *a* confident.

zuviel [tsuːˈfiːl] *ad* too much.

zuvor [tsuːˈfoːr] *ad* before, previously; **~kommen** *vi unreg* anticipate (*jdm* sb), beat (sb) to it; **~kommend** *a* obliging, courteous.

Zuwachs ['tsuːvaks] *m* -es increase, growth; (*umg*) addition; **z~en** *vi unreg* become overgrown; (*Wunde*) heal (up).

zuwege [tsuːˈveːgə] *ad*: **etw** ~ **bringen** accomplish sth.

zuweilen [tsuːˈvailən] *ad* at times, now and then.

zuweisen ['tsuːvaizən] *vt unreg* assign, allocate (*jdm* to sb).

zuwenden ['tsuːvɛndən] *unreg vt* turn (*dat* towards); **jdm seine Aufmerksamkeit** ~ give sb one's attention // *vr* devote o.s., turn (*dat* to).

zuwenig [tsuːˈveːnɪç] *ad* too little.

zuwider [tsuːˈviːdər] *ad*: **etw ist jdm** ~ sb loathes sth, sb finds sth repugnant // *präp* +*dat* contrary to; **~handeln** *vi* act contrary (*dat* to); **einem Gesetz ~handeln** contravene a law.

zuziehen ['tsuːtsiːən] *unreg vt* (*schließen: Vorhang*) draw, close; (*herbeirufen: Experten*) call in; **sich** (*dat*) **etw** ~ (*Krankheit*) catch; (*Zorn*) incur // *vi* move in, come.

zuzüglich ['tsuːtsyːklɪç] *präp* +*gen* plus, with the addition of.

Zwang [tsvaŋ] *m* -(e)s, -̈e compulsion, coercion.

zwängen ['tsvɛŋən] *vtr* squeeze.

zwanglos *a* informal.

Zwangs- *zW*: **~arbeit** *f* forced labour; (*Strafe*) hard labour; **~jacke** *f* straightjacket; **~lage** *f* predicament, tight corner; **z~läufig** *a* necessary, inevitable.

zwanzig ['tsvantsɪç] *num* twenty.

zwar [tsvaːr] *ad* to be sure, indeed; **das ist** ~ ..., **aber** ... that may be ... but ...; **und** ~ **am Sonntag** on Sunday to be precise; **und** ~ **so schnell, daß** ... in fact so quickly that ...

Zweck ['tsvɛk] *m* -(e)s, -e purpose, aim; **es hat keinen** ~ there's no point; **z~dienlich** *a* practical; expedient; **~e** *f* -, -n hobnail; (*Heft~e*) drawing pin, thumbtack (*US*); **z~los** *a* pointless; **z~mäßig** *a* suitable, appropriate; **zwecks** *präp* +*gen* for the purpose of.

zwei [tsvai] *num* two; **~deutig** *a* ambiguous; (*unanständig*) suggestive; **~erlei** *a*: **~erlei Stoff** two different kinds of material; **~erlei Meinung** of differing opinions; **~fach** *a* double.

Zweifel ['tsvaifəl] *m* -s, - doubt; **z~haft** *a* doubtful, dubious; **z~los** *a* doubtless; **z~n** *vi* doubt (*an etw* (*dat*) sth).

Zweig [tsvaik] *m* -(e)s, -e branch; **~stelle** *f* branch (office).

zwei- *zW*: **~hundert** *num* two hundred; **Z~kampf** *m* duel; **~mal** *ad* twice; **~sprachig** *a* bilingual; **~spurig** *a* (*AUT*) two-lane; **~stimmig** *a* for two voices; **Z~taktmotor** *m* two-stroke engine.

zweit- [tsvait] *ad*: **zu** ~ together; (*bei mehreren Paaren*) in twos; **~beste(r, s)** *a* second best; **~e(r, s)** *a* second; **~ens** *ad* secondly; **~größte(r, s)** *a* second largest; **~klassig** *a* second-class; **~letzte(r, s)** *a* last but one, pe-

nultimate; ~**rangig** *a* second-rate.
Zwerchfell ['tsvɛrçfɛl] *nt* diaphragm.
Zwerg [tsvɛrk] *m* -(e)s, -e dwarf.
Zwetsch(g)e ['tsvɛtʃ(g)ə] *f* -, -n plum.
Zwieback ['tsvi:bak] *m* -(e)s, -e rusk.
Zwiebel ['tsvi:bəl] *f* -, -n onion; (*Blumen*~) bulb.
Zwie- ['tsvi:] *zW:* **z**~**lichtig** *a* shady, dubious; **z**~**spältig** *a* (*Gefühle*) conflicting; (*Charakter*) contradictory; ~**tracht** *f* discord, dissension.
Zwilling ['tsvilin] *m* -s, -e twin; ~**e** *pl* (*ASTROL*) Gemini.
zwingen ['tsvinən] *vt unreg* force; ~**d** *a* (*Grund etc*) compelling.
zwinkern ['tsvinkərn] *vi* blink; (*absichtlich*) wink.
Zwirn [tsvirn] *m* -(e)s, -e thread.
zwischen ['tsvifən] *präp* +*akk od dat* between; **Z**~**bemerkung** *f* (incidental) remark; **Z**~**ding** *nt* cross; ~**durch** [-'durç] *ad* in between; (*räumlich*) here and there; **Z**~**ergebnis** *nt* intermediate result;

Z~**fall** *m* incident; **Z**~**frage** *f* question; **Z**~**handel** *m* middlemen *pl*; middleman's trade; **Z**~**landung** *f* stop, intermediate landing; ~**menschlich** *a* interpersonal; **Z**~**raum** *m* space; **Z**~**ruf** *m* interjection, **Z**~**station** *f* intermediate station; **Z**~**zeit** *f* interval; **in der Z**~**zeit** in the interim, meanwhile.
Zwist [tsvist] *m* -es, -e dispute, feud.
zwitschern ['tsvitʃərn] *vti* twitter, chirp.
zwo [tsvo:] *num* two.
zwölf [tsvœlf] *num* twelve.
Zyklus ['tsy:klus] *m* -, **Zyklen** cycle.
Zylinder [tsi'lindər] *m* -s, - cylinder; (*Hut*) top hat; **z**~**förmig** *a* cylindrical.
Zyniker ['tsy:nikər] *m* -s, - cynic.
zynisch ['tsy:niʃ] *a* cynical.
Zynismus [tsy'nismus] *m* cynicism.
Zypern ['tsy:pərn] *nt* Cyprus.
Zyste ['tsystə] *f* -, -n cyst.
z.Z(t). *abk von* **zur Zeit.**

ENGLISH - GERMAN
ENGLISCH - DEUTSCH

A

A [ei] *n* (*MUS*) A *nt*; ~ **road** Hauptverkehrsstraße *f.*

a [ei, ə] *indef art* (*before vowel or silent h:* **an**) **1** ein; eine; ~ **woman** eine Frau; ~ **book** ein Buch; **an apple** ein Apfel; **she's** ~ **doctor** sie ist Ärztin

2 (*instead of the number 'one'*) ein; eine; ~ **year ago** vor einem Jahr; ~ **hundred/thousand** *etc* **pounds** (ein)hundert/(ein)tausend *etc* Pfund

3 (*in expressing ratios, prices etc*) pro; **3** ~ **day/week** 3 pro Tag/Woche, 3 am Tag/in der Woche; **10 km an hour** 10 km pro Stunde/in der Stunde.

A.A. *n abbr* = **Automobile Association** (*Brit*); **Alcoholics Anonymous.**

A.A.A. *n abbr* (*US*) = **American Automobile Association.**

aback [ə'bæk] *ad:* **to be taken** ~ verblüfft sein.

abandon [ə'bændən] *vt* (*give up*) aufgeben; (*desert*) verlassen // *n* Hingabe *f.*

abashed [ə'bæʃt] *a* verlegen.

abate [ə'beit] *vi* nachlassen, sich legen.

abattoir ['æbætwɑ:*] *n* (*Brit*) Schlachthaus *nt.*

abbey ['æbi] *n* Abtei *f.*

abbot ['æbət] *n* Abt *m.*

abbreviate [ə'bri:vieit] *vt* abkürzen.

abbreviation [əbri:vi'eiʃən] *n* Abkürzung *f.*

abdicate ['æbdikeit] *vt* aufgeben // *vi* abdanken.

abdomen ['æbdəmən] *n* Unterleib *m.*

abduct [æb'dʌkt] *vt* entführen.

aberration [æbə'reiʃən] *n* (geistige) Verwirrung *f.*

abet [ə'bet] *vt see* **aid.**

abeyance [ə'beiəns] *n:* **in** ~ in der Schwebe; (*disuse*) außer Kraft.

abhor [əb'hɔ:*] *vt* verabscheuen.

abide [ə'baid] *vt* vertragen; leiden; ~ **by** *vt* sich halten an (+*acc*).

ability [ə'biliti] *n* (*power*) Fähigkeit *f*; (*skill*) Geschicklichkeit *f.*

abject ['æbdʒekt] *a* (*liar*) übel; (*poverty*) größte(r, s); (*apology*) zerknirscht.

ablaze [ə'bleiz] *a* in Flammen.

able ['eibl] *a* geschickt, fähig; **to be** ~ **to do sth** etw tun können; ~**-bodied** *a* kräftig; (*seaman*) Voll-.

ably ['eibli] *ad* geschickt.

abnormal [æb'nɔ:məl] *a* regelwidrig, abnorm.

aboard [ə'bɔ:d] *ad, prep* an Bord (+*gen*).

abode [ə'bəud] *n:* **of no fixed** ~ ohne festen Wohnsitz.

abolish [ə'bɒliʃ] *vt* abschaffen.

abolition [æbə'liʃən] *n* Abschaffung *f.*

abominable [ə'bɒminəbl] *a* scheußlich.

aborigine [æbə'ridʒini:] *n* Ureinwohner *m.*

abort [ə'bɔ:t] *vt* abtreiben; fehlgebären; ~**ion** [ə'bɔ:ʃən] *n* Abtreibung *f*; (*miscarriage*) Fehlgeburt *f*; ~**ive** *a* mißlungen.

abound [ə'baund] *vi* im Überfluß vorhanden sein; **to** ~ **in** Überfluß haben an (+*dat*).

about [ə'baut] ♦*ad* **1** (*approximately*) etwa, ungefähr; ~ **a hundred/thousand** *etc* etwa hundert/tausend *etc*; **at** ~ **2 o'clock** etwa um 2 Uhr; **I've just** ~ **finished** ich bin gerade fertig

2 (*referring to place*): herum, umher; **to leave things lying** ~ Sachen herumliegen lassen; **to run/walk** *etc* ~ herumrennen/gehen *etc*

3: **to be** ~ **to do sth** im Begriff sein, etw zu tun; **he was** ~ **to go to bed** er wollte gerade ins Bett gehen

♦*prep* **1** (*relating to*) über (+*acc*); **a book** ~ **London** ein Buch über London; **what is it** ~? worum geht es?; (*book etc*) wovon handelt es?; **we talked** ~ **it** wir haben darüber geredet; **what** *or* **how** ~ **doing this?** wollen wir das machen?

2 (*referring to place*) um (... herum); **to walk** ~ **the town** in der Stadt herumgehen; **her clothes were scattered** ~ **the room** ihre Kleider waren über das ganze Zimmer verstreut.

about-face [ə'baut'feis] *n*, **about-turn** [ə'baut'tɜ:n] *n* Kehrtwendung *f.*

above [ə'bʌv] *ad* oben // *prep* über; ~ **all** vor allem; ~ **board** *a* offen, ehrlich.

abrasive [ə'breiziv] *a* Abschleif-; (*personality*) zermürbend, aufreibend.

abreast [ə'brest] *ad* nebeneinander; **to keep** ~ **of** Schritt halten mit.

abridge [ə'bridʒ] *vt* (ab)kürzen.

abroad [ə'brɔ:d] *ad* (*be*) im Ausland; (*go*) ins Ausland.

abrupt [ə'brʌpt] *a* (*sudden*) abrupt, jäh; (*curt*) schroff.

abscess ['æbsis] *n* Geschwür *nt.*

abscond [əb'skɒnd] *vi* flüchten, sich davonmachen.

abseil ['æbsail] *vi* (*also:* ~ **down**) sich abseilen.

absence ['æbsəns] n Abwesenheit f.

absent ['æbsənt] a abwesend, nicht da; (lost in thought) geistesabwesend; **~ee** [æbsən'ti:] n Abwesende(r) m; **~eeism** [æbsən'ti:izəm] n Fehlen nt (am Arbeitsplatz/in der Schule); **~-minded** a zerstreut.

absolute ['æbsəlu:t] a absolut; (power) unumschränkt; (rubbish) vollkommen, rein; **~ly** [æbsə'lu:tlɪ] ad absolut, vollkommen; **~ly!** ganz bestimmt!

absolve [əb'zɒlv] vt entbinden; freisprechen.

absorb [əb'zɔ:b] vt aufsaugen, absorbieren; (fig) ganz in Anspruch nehmen, fesseln; to be **~ed** in a book in ein Buch vertieft sein; **~ent** a absorbierend; **~ent cotton** n (US) Verbandwatte f; **~ing** a aufsaugend; (fig) packend.

abstain [əb'steɪn] vi (in vote) sich enthalten; to **~ from** (keep from) sich enthalten (+gen).

abstemious [əb'sti:mɪəs] a enthaltsam.

abstention [əb'stenʃən] n (in vote) (Stimm)enthaltung f.

abstinence ['æbstɪnəns] n Enthaltsamkeit f.

abstract ['æbstrækt] a abstrakt.

absurd [əb'sɜ:d] a absurd.

abundance [ə'bʌndəns] n Überfluß m (of an +dat).

abundant [ə'bʌndənt] a reichlich.

abuse [ə'bju:s] n (rude language) Beschimpfung f; (ill usage) Mißbrauch m; (bad practice) (Amts)mißbrauch m // [ə'bju:z] vt (misuse) mißbrauchen.

abusive [ə'bju:sɪv] a beleidigend, Schimpf-.

abysmal [ə'bɪzməl] a scheußlich; (ignorance) bodenlos.

abyss [ə'bɪs] n Abgrund m.

AC abbr of alternating current.

academic [ækə'demɪk] a akademisch; (theoretical) theoretisch // n Akademiker(in f) m.

academy [ə'kædəmɪ] n (school) Hochschule f; (society) Akademie f.

accelerate [æk'seləreɪt] vi schneller werden; (AUT) Gas geben // vt beschleunigen.

acceleration [ækselə'reɪʃən] n Beschleunigung f.

accelerator [æk'seləreɪtə*] n Gas(pedal) nt.

accent ['æksənt] n Akzent m, Tonfall m; (mark) Akzent m; (stress) Betonung f.

accept [ək'sept] vt (take) annehmen; (agree to) akzeptieren; **~able** a annehmbar; **~ance** n Annahme f.

access ['ækses] n Zugang m; **~ible** [æk'sesɪbl] a (easy to approach) zugänglich; (within reach) (leicht) erreichbar.

accessory [æk'sesərɪ] n Zubehörteil nt; **accessories** pl Zubehör nt; **toilet ac-**

cessories pl Toilettenartikel pl.

accident ['æksɪdənt] n Unfall m; (coincidence) Zufall m; by **~** zufällig; **~al** [æksɪ'dentl] a unbeabsichtigt; **~ally** [æksɪ'dentəlɪ] ad zufällig; **~-prone** a: to be **~-prone** zu Unfällen neigen.

acclaim [ə'kleɪm] vt zujubeln (+dat) // n Beifall m.

acclimatize [ə'klaɪmətaɪz], (US) **acclimate** [ə'klaɪmət] vt: to become **~d** sich gewöhnen (to an +acc), sich akklimatisieren.

accolade ['ækəleɪd] n Auszeichnung f.

accommodate [ə'kɒmədeɪt] vt unterbringen; (hold) Platz haben für; (oblige) (aus)helfen (+dat).

accommodating [ə'kɒmədeɪtɪŋ] a entgegenkommend.

accommodation [ə'kɒmə'deɪʃən] n (US: **~s**) Unterkunft f.

accompaniment [ə'kʌmpənɪmənt] n Begleitung f.

accompany [ə'kʌmpənɪ] vt begleiten.

accomplice [ə'kʌmplɪs] n Helfershelfer m, Komplize m.

accomplish [ə'kʌmplɪʃ] vt (fulfil) durchführen; (finish) vollenden; (aim) erreichen; **~ed** a vollendet, ausgezeichnet; **~ment** n (skill) Fähigkeit f; (completion) Vollendung f; (feat) Leistung f.

accord [ə'kɔ:d] n Übereinstimmung f; of one's own **~** freiwillig // vt gewähren; **~ance** n: in **~ance with** in Übereinstimmung mit; **~ing to** prep nach, laut (+gen); **~ingly** ad danach, dementsprechend.

accordion [ə'kɔ:dɪən] n Akkordeon nt.

accost [ə'kɒst] vt ansprechen.

account [ə'kaunt] n (bill) Rechnung f; (narrative) Bericht m; (report) Rechenschaftsbericht m; (in bank) Konto nt; (importance) Geltung f; **~s** pl Bücher pl; on **~** auf Rechnung; of no **~** ohne Bedeutung; on no **~** keinesfalls; on **~** of wegen; to take into **~** berücksichtigen; **~ for** (expenditure) Rechenschaft ablegen für; how do you **~ for that?** wie erklären Sie (sich) das?; **~able** a verantwortlich; **~ancy** n Buchhaltung f; **~ant** n Wirtschaftsprüfer(in f) m; **~ number** n Kontonummer f.

accredited [ə'kredɪtɪd] a (offiziell) zugelassen.

accrue [ə'kru:] vi sich ansammeln.

accumulate [ə'kju:mjuleɪt] vt ansammeln // vi sich ansammeln.

accuracy ['ækjurəsɪ] n Genauigkeit f.

accurate ['ækjurɪt] a genau; **~ly** ad genau, richtig.

accusation [ækju:'zeɪʃən] n Anklage f, Beschuldigung f.

accuse [ə'kju:z] vt anklagen, beschuldigen; **~d** n Angeklagte(r) mf.

accustom [ə'kʌstəm] vt gewöhnen (to

an (+acc); **~ed** a gewohnt.

ace [eis] n As nt; (col) As nt, Kanone f.

ache [eik] n Schmerz m // vi (be sore) schmerzen, weh tun.

achieve [ə'tʃiːv] vt zustande bringen; (aim) erreichen; **~ment** n Leistung f; (act) Erreichen nt.

acid ['æsɪd] n Säure f // a sauer, scharf; **~ rain** n Saure(r) Regen m.

acknowledge [ək'nɒlɪdʒ] vt (receipt) bestätigen; (admit) zugeben; **~ment** n Anerkennung f; (letter) Empfangsbestätigung f.

acne ['æknɪ] n Akne f.

acorn ['eikɔːn] n Eichel f.

acoustic [ə'kuːstɪk] a akustisch; **~s** npl Akustik f.

acquaint [ə'kweint] vt vertraut machen; to be **~ed** with sb mit jdm bekannt sein; **~ance** n (person) Bekannte(r) mf; (knowledge) Kenntnis f.

acquiesce [ækwɪ'es] vi sich abfinden (in mit).

acquire [ə'kwaɪə*] vt erwerben.

acquisition [ækwɪ'zɪʃən] n Errungenschaft f; (act) Erwerb m.

acquisitive [ə'kwɪzɪtɪv] a gewinnsüchtig.

acquit [ə'kwɪt] vt (free) freisprechen; to **~ o.s. well** sich bewähren; **~tal** n Freispruch m.

acre ['eikə*] n Morgen m.

acrid ['ækrɪd] a (smell, taste) bitter; (smoke) beißend.

acrimonious [ækrɪ'məunɪəs] a bitter.

acrobat ['ækrəbæt] n Akrobat m.

across [ə'krɒs] prep über (+ acc); he lives **~** the river er wohnt auf der anderen Seite des Flusses // ad hinüber, herüber; ten metres **~** zehn Meter breit; he lives **~** from us er wohnt uns gegenüber.

act [ækt] n (deed) Tat f; (JUR) Gesetz nt; (THEAT) Akt m; (THEAT: turn) Nummer f // vi (take action) handeln; (behave) sich verhalten; (pretend) vorgeben; (THEAT) spielen // vt (in play) spielen; to **~** as fungieren als; **~ing** a stellvertretend // n Schauspielkunst f; (performance) Aufführung f.

action ['ækʃən] n (deed) Tat f; Handlung f; (motion) Bewegung f; (way of working) Funktionieren nt; (battle) Einsatz m, Gefecht nt; (lawsuit) Klage f, Prozeß m; out of **~** (person) nicht einsatzfähig; (thing) außer Betrieb; to take **~** etwas unternehmen; **~ replay** n (TV) Wiederholung f.

active ['æktɪv] a (brisk) rege, tatkräftig; (working) aktiv; (GRAM) aktiv, Tätigkeits-; **~ly** ad aktiv; (dislike) offen.

activity [æk'tɪvɪtɪ] n Aktivität f; (doings) Unternehmungen pl; (occupation) Tätigkeit f.

actor ['æktə*] n Schauspieler m.

actress ['æktrɪs] n Schauspielerin f.

actual ['æktjuəl] a wirklich; **~ly** ad tatsächlich; **~ly no** eigentlich nicht.

acumen ['ækjumen] n Scharfsinn m.

acute [ə'kjuːt] a (severe) heftig, akut; (keen) scharfsinnig.

ad [æd] n abbr of **advertisement**.

A.D. ad abbr (= Anno Domini) n. Chr.

Adam ['ædəm] n Adam m; **~'s apple** n Adamsapfel m.

adamant ['ædəmənt] a eisern; hartnäckig.

adapt [ə'dæpt] vt anpassen // vi sich anpassen (to an +acc); **~able** a anpassungsfähig; **~ation** [ædæp'teiʃən] f (THEAT etc) Bearbeitung f; (adjustment) Anpassung f; **~er** or **~or** n (ELEC) Zwischenstecker m.

add [æd] vt (join) hinzufügen; (numbers: also: **~ up**) addieren; **~ up** vi (make sense) stimmen; **~ up to** vt ausmachen.

adder ['ædə*] n Kreuzotter f, Natter f.

addict ['ædɪkt] n Süchtige(r) mf; **~ed** [ə'dɪktɪd] a: **~ed to** -süchtig; **~ion** [ə'dɪkʃən] n Sucht f; **~ive** a: to be **~ive** süchtig machen.

addition [ə'dɪʃən] n Anhang m, Addition f; (MATH) Addition f, Zusammenzählen nt; in **~** zusätzlich, außerdem; **~al** a zusätzlich, weiter.

additive ['ædɪtɪv] n Zusatz m.

address [ə'dres] n Adresse f; (speech) Ansprache f // vt (letter) adressieren; (speak to) ansprechen; (make speech to) eine Ansprache halten an (+acc).

adept ['ædept] a geschickt; to be **~** at gut sein in (+dat).

adequate ['ædɪkwɪt] a angemessen.

adhere [əd'hɪə*] vi: **~ to** (lit) haften an (+dat); (fig) festhalten an (+dat).

adhesive [əd'hiːzɪv] a klebend; Kleb(e)- // n Klebstoff m; **~ tape** n (Brit) Klebestreifen m; (US) Heftpflaster nt.

ad hoc [æd'hɒk] a (decision, committee) Ad-hoc- // ad (decide, appoint) ad hoc.

adjacent [ə'dʒeɪsənt] a benachbart; **~ to** angrenzend an (+acc).

adjective ['ædʒəktɪv] n Adjektiv nt, Eigenschaftswort nt.

adjoining [ə'dʒɔɪnɪŋ] a benachbart, Neben-.

adjourn [ə'dʒɜːn] vt vertagen // vi abbrechen.

adjudicate [ə'dʒuːdɪkeɪt] vi entscheiden, ein Urteil fällen.

adjust [ə'dʒʌst] vt (alter) anpassen; (put right) regulieren, richtig stellen // vi sich anpassen (to dat); **~able** a verstellbar.

ad-lib [æd'lɪb] vti improvisieren; **ad lib** ad aus dem Stegreif.

administer [æd'mɪnɪstə*] vt (manage) verwalten; (dispense) ausüben; (justice) sprechen; (medicine) geben.

administration [ədmɪnɪsˈtreɪʃən] *n* Verwaltung *f*; (*POL*) Regierung *f*.

administrative [ədˈmɪnɪstrətɪv] *a* Verwaltungs-.

administrator [ədˈmɪnɪstreɪtə*] *n* Verwaltungsbeamte(r) *m*.

admiral [ˈædmərəl] *n* Admiral *m*.

Admiralty [ˈædmərəltɪ] *n* (*Brit*) Admiralität *f*.

admiration [ædmɪˈreɪʃən] *n* Bewunderung *f*.

admire [ədˈmaɪə*] *vt* (*respect*) bewundern; (*love*) verehren; **~r** *n* Bewunderer *m*.

admission [ədˈmɪʃən] *n* (*entrance*) Einlaß; (*fee*) Eintritt(spreis) *m*; (*confession*) Geständnis *nt*.

admit [ədˈmɪt] *vt* (*let in*) einlassen; (*confess*) gestehen; (*accept*) anerkennen; **~tance** *n* Zulassung *f*; **~tedly** *ad* zugegebenermaßen.

admonish [ədˈmɒnɪʃ] *vt* ermahnen.

ad nauseam [ædˈnɔːsɪæm] *ad* (*repeat, talk*) endlos.

ado [əˈduː] *n*: without more ~ ohne weitere Umstände.

adolescence [ædəˈlɛsns] *n* Jugendalter *nt*.

adolescent [ædəˈlɛsnt] *a* jugendlich // *n* Jugendliche(r) *mf*.

adopt [əˈdɒpt] *vt* (*child*) adoptieren; (*idea*) übernehmen; **~ion** [əˈdɒpʃən] *n* (*of child*) Adoption *f*; (*of idea*) Übernahme *f*.

adore [əˈdɔː*] *vt* anbeten; verehren.

adorn [əˈdɔːn] *vt* schmücken.

Adriatic [eɪdrɪˈætɪk] *n*: the ~ (Sea) die Adria.

adrift [əˈdrɪft] *ad* Wind und Wellen preisgegeben.

adult [ˈædʌlt] *n* Erwachsene(r) *mf*.

adultery [əˈdʌltərɪ] *n* Ehebruch *m*.

advance [ədˈvɑːns] *n* (*progress*) Vorrücken *nt*; (*money*) Vorschuß *m* // *vt* (*move forward*) vorrücken; (*money*) vorschießen; (*argument*) vorbringen // *vi* vorwärtsgehen; in ~ im voraus; **~d** *a* (*ahead*) vorgerückt; (*modern*) fortgeschritten; (*study*) für Fortgeschrittene; **~ment** *n* Förderung *f*; (*promotion*) Beförderung *f*.

advantage [ədˈvɑːntɪdʒ] *n* Vorteil *m*; to have an ~ over sb jdm gegenüber im Vorteil sein; to take ~ of (*misuse*) ausnutzen; (*profit from*) Nutzen ziehen aus; **~ous** [ædvənˈteɪdʒəs] *a* vorteilhaft.

advent [ˈædvɛnt] *n* Ankunft *f*; A~ Advent *m*.

adventure [ədˈvɛntʃə*] *n* Abenteuer *nt*.

adventurous [ədˈvɛntʃərəs] *a* abenteuerlich, waghalsig.

adverb [ˈædvɜːb] *n* Adverb *nt*, Umstandswort *nt*.

adversary [ˈædvəsərɪ] *n* Gegner *m*.

adverse [ˈædvɜːs] *a* widrig.

adversity [ədˈvɜːsɪtɪ] *n* Widrigkeit *f*, Mißgeschick *nt*.

advert [ˈædvɜːt] *n* Anzeige *f*.

advertise [ˈædvətaɪz] *vt* werben für // *vi* annoncieren; to ~ for sth etw (per Anzeige) suchen.

advertisement [ədˈvɜːtɪsmənt] *n* Anzeige *f*, Inserat *nt*.

advertiser [ˈædvətaɪzə*] *n* (*in newspaper etc*) Inserent *m*.

advertising [ˈædvətaɪzɪŋ] *n* Werbung *f*.

advice [ədˈvaɪs] *n* Rat(schlag) *m*; (*notification*) Benachrichtigung *f*.

advisable [ədˈvaɪzəbl] *a* ratsam.

advise [ədˈvaɪz] *vt* raten (+*dat*); **~r** *n* Berater *m*.

advisedly [ədˈvaɪzədlɪ] *ad* (*deliberately*) bewußt.

advisory [ədˈvaɪzərɪ] *a* beratend, Beratungs-.

advocate [ˈædvəkeɪt] *vt* vertreten // *n* [ˈædvəkət] Befürworter(in *f*) *m*.

Aegean [iːˈdʒiːən] *n*: the ~ (Sea) die Ägäis.

aerial [ˈɛərɪəl] *n* Antenne *f* // *a* Luft-.

aerobics [ɛərˈəʊbɪks] *n* Aerobic *nt*.

aerodrome [ˈɛərədrəʊm] *n* (*Brit*) Flugplatz *m*.

aerodynamic [ˈɛərəʊdaɪˈnæmɪks] *a* aerodynamisch.

aeroplane [ˈɛərəpleɪn] *n* Flugzeug *nt*.

aerosol [ˈɛərəsɒl] *n* Aerosol *nt*; Sprühdose *f*.

aesthetic [ɪsˈθɛtɪk] *a* ästhetisch.

afar [əˈfɑː*] *ad*: from ~ aus der Ferne.

affable [ˈæfəbl] *a* umgänglich.

affair [əˈfɛə*] *n* (*concern*) Angelegenheit *f*; (*event*) Ereignis *nt*; (*love* ~) Verhältnis *nt*.

affect [əˈfɛkt] *vt* (*influence*) (ein-)wirken auf (+*acc*); (*move deeply*) bewegen; this change doesn't ~ us diese Änderung betrifft uns nicht; **~ed** *a* affektiert, gekünstelt.

affection [əˈfɛkʃən] *n* Zuneigung *f*; **~ate** [əˈfɛkʃənɪt] *a* liebevoll.

affiliated [əˈfɪlɪeɪtɪd] *a* angeschlossen (*to dat*).

affinity [əˈfɪnɪtɪ] *n* (*attraction*) gegenseitige Anziehung *f*; (*relationship*) Verwandtschaft *f*.

affirmation [æfəˈmeɪʃən] *n* Behauptung *f*.

affirmative [əˈfɜːmətɪv] *a* bestätigend.

affix [əˈfɪks] *vt* aufkleben, anheften.

afflict [əˈflɪkt] *vt* quälen, heimsuchen.

affluence [ˈæflʊəns] *n* (*wealth*) Wohlstand *m*.

affluent [ˈæflʊənt] *a* wohlhabend, Wohlstands-.

afford [əˈfɔːd] *vt* (sich) (*dat*) leisten; (*yield*) bieten, einbringen.

affront [əˈfrʌnt] *n* Beleidigung *f*.

Afghanistan [æfˈgænɪstɑːn] *n* Afghanistan *nt*.

afield [ə'fi:ld] ad: far ~ weit fort.
afloat [ə'fləʊt] a: to be ~ schwimmen.
afoot [ə'fʊt] ad im Gang.
afraid [ə'freɪd] a ängstlich; to be ~ of Angst haben vor (+dat); to be ~ to sich scheuen; I am ~ I have ... ich habe leider ...; I'm ~ so/not leider/leider nicht; I am ~ that ... ich fürchte, (daß) ...
afresh [ə'freʃ] ad von neuem.
Africa ['æfrɪkə] n Afrika nt; ~**n** a afrikanisch // n Afrikaner(in f) m.
aft [a:ft] ad achtern.
after ['a:ftə*] prep nach; (following, seeking) hinter ... (dat) ... her; (in imitation) nach, im Stil von // ad: soon ~ bald danach // cj nachdem; what are you ~? was wollen Sie?; ~ he left nachdem er gegangen war; ~ you! nach Ihnen!; ~ all letzten Endes; ~**-effects** npl Nachwirkungen pl; ~**life** n Leben nt nach dem Tode; ~**math** n Auswirkungen pl; ~**noon** n Nachmittag m; good ~**noon!** guten Tag!; ~**s** n (col: dessert) Nachtisch m; ~**sales service** n (Brit) Kundendienst m; ~**-shave (lotion)** n Rasierwasser nt; ~**thought** n nachträgliche(r) Einfall m; ~**wards** ad danach, nachher.
again [ə'gen] ad wieder, noch einmal; (besides) außerdem, ferner; ~ and ~ immer wieder.
against [ə'genst] prep gegen.
age [eɪdʒ] n (of person) Alter nt; (in history) Zeitalter nt // vi altern, alt werden // vt älter machen; to come of ~ mündig werden; **20 years of ~** 20 Jahre alt; it's been ~s since ... es ist ewig her, seit ...; ~**d** a ... Jahre alt, -jährig; ['eɪdʒɪd] (elderly) betagt; the ~**d** die Alten pl; ~ **group** n Altersgruppe f; ~ **limit** n Altersgrenze f.
agency ['eɪdʒənsɪ] n Agentur f; Vermittlung f; (CHEM) Wirkung f; **through** or **by the ~ of** ... mit Hilfe von ...
agenda [ə'dʒendə] n Tagesordnung f.
agent ['eɪdʒənt] n (COMM) Vertreter m; (spy) Agent m.
aggravate ['ægrəveɪt] vt (make worse) verschlimmern; (irritate) reizen.
aggregate ['ægrɪgɪt] n Summe f.
aggression [ə'greʃən] n Aggression f.
aggressive a [ə'gresɪv] aggressiv.
aggrieved [ə'gri:vd] a bedrückt, verletzt.
aghast [ə'ga:st] a entsetzt.
agile ['ædʒaɪl] a flink; agil; (mind) rege.
agitate ['ædʒɪteɪt] vt rütteln; to ~ **for** sich starkmachen für.
ago [ə'gəʊ] ad: two days ~ vor zwei Tagen; not long ~ vor kurzem; it's so long ~ es ist schon so lange her.
agog [ə'gog] a gespannt.
agonizing ['ægənaɪzɪŋ] a quälend.
agony ['ægənɪ] n Qual f; to be in ~ Qualen leiden.

agree [ə'gri:] vt (date) vereinbaren // vi (have same opinion, correspond) übereinstimmen (with mit); (consent) zustimmen; (be in harmony) sich vertragen; to ~ to sth einer Sache zustimmen; to ~ that ... (admit) zugeben, daß ...; to ~ to do sth sich bereit erklären, etw zu tun; garlic doesn't ~ with me Knoblauch vertrage ich nicht; I ~ einverstanden, ich stimme zu; to ~ **on** sth sich auf etw (acc) einigen; ~**able** a (pleasing) liebenswürdig; (willing to consent) einverstanden; ~**d** a vereinbart; ~**ment** n (agreeing) Übereinstimmung f; (contract) Vereinbarung f, Vertrag m; to be in ~**ment** übereinstimmen.
agricultural [ægrɪ'kʌltʃərəl] a landwirtschaftlich, Landwirtschafts-.
agriculture ['ægrɪkʌltʃə*] n Landwirtschaft f.
aground [ə'graʊnd] ad: to run ~ auf Grund laufen.
ahead [ə'hed] ad vorwärts; to be ~ voraus sein; ~ of time der Zeit voraus; go **right** or **straight** ~ gehen/fahren Sie geradeaus.
aid [eɪd] n (assistance) Hilfe f, Unterstützung f; (person) Hilfe f; (thing) Hilfsmittel nt; **in** ~ **of** zugunsten (+gen) // vt unterstützen, helfen (+dat); ~ **and abet** vti Beihilfe leisten (sb jdm).
aide [eɪd] n (person) Gehilfe m; (MIL) Adjutant m.
AIDS [eɪdz] n abbr (= acquired immune deficiency syndrome) Aids nt.
ailing ['eɪlɪŋ] a kränkelnd.
ailment ['eɪlmənt] n Leiden nt.
aim [eɪm] vt (gun, camera) richten auf (+acc) // vi (with gun: also: take ~) zielen; (intend) beabsichtigen // n (intention) Absicht f, Ziel nt; (pointing) Zielen nt, Richten nt; to ~ at sth etw anstreben; to ~ to do vorhaben, etw zu tun; ~**less** a, ~**lessly** ad ziellos.
ain't [eɪnt] (col) = am not; are not; is not; has not; have not.
air [eə*] n Luft f; (manner) Miene f, Anschein m; (MUS) Melodie f // vt lüften; (fig) an die Öffentlichkeit bringen // cpd Luft-; by ~ (travel) auf dem Luftweg; to be on the ~ (RADIO, TV: programme) gesendet werden; ~**bed** n (Brit) Luftmatratze f; ~**-borne** a in der Luft; ~**-conditioned** a mit Klimaanlage; ~**-conditioning** n Klimaanlage f; ~**craft** n Flugzeug nt, Maschine f; ~**craft carrier** n Flugzeugträger m; ~**field** n Flugplatz m; ~ **force** n Luftwaffe f; ~ **freshener** n Raumspray nt; ~**gun** n Luftgewehr nt; ~ **hostess** n (Brit) Stewardeß f; ~ **letter** n (Brit) Luftpostbrief m; ~**lift** n Luftbrücke f; ~**line** n Luftverkehrsgesellschaft f; ~**liner** n

Verkehrsflugzeug nt; ~lock n Luftblase f; ~mail n: by ~mail mit Luftpost; ~plane n (US) Flugzeug nt; ~port n Flughafen m, Flugplatz m; ~ raid n Luftangriff m; ~sick a luftkrank; ~strip n Landestreifen m; ~terminal n Terminal m; ~tight a luftdicht; ~ traffic controller n Fluglotse m; ~y a luftig; (manner) leichtfertig.

aisle [aɪl] n Gang m.

ajar [ə'dʒɑː*] ad angelehnt; einen Spalt offen.

akin [ə'kɪn] a: ~ to ähnlich (+dat).

alacrity [ə'lækrɪtɪ] n Bereitwilligkeit f.

alarm [ə'lɑːm] n (warning) Alarm m; (bell etc) Alarmanlage f; (anxiety) Sorge f // vt erschrecken; ~ clock n Wecker m.

alas [ə'læs] interj ach.

Albania [æl'beɪnɪə] n Albanien nt.

albeit [ɔːl'biːɪt] cj obgleich.

album [ælbəm] n Album nt.

alcohol ['ælkəhɒl] n Alkohol m; ~ic [ælkə'hɒlɪk] a (drink) alkoholisch // n Alkoholiker(in f) m; ~ism n Alkoholismus m.

alderman ['ɔːldəmən] n, pl -men Stadtrat m.

ale [eɪl] n Ale nt.

alert [ə'lɜːt] a wachsam // n Alarm m // vt alarmieren; to be on the ~ wachsam sein.

algebra ['ældʒɪbrə] n Algebra f.

Algeria [æl'dʒɪərɪə] n Algerien nt.

alias ['eɪlɪəs] ad alias // n Deckname m.

alibi ['ælɪbaɪ] n Alibi nt.

alien ['eɪlɪən] n Ausländer m // a (foreign) ausländisch; (strange) fremd; ~ to fremd (+dat); ~ate vt entfremden.

alight [ə'laɪt] a brennend; (of building) in Flammen // vi (descend) aussteigen; (bird) sich setzen.

align [ə'laɪn] vt ausrichten.

alike [ə'laɪk] a gleich, ähnlich // ad gleich, ebenso; to look ~ sich (dat) ähnlich sehen.

alimony ['ælɪmənɪ] n Unterhalt m, Alimente pl.

alive [ə'laɪv] a (living) lebend; (lively) lebendig, aufgeweckt; (full of) voll (with von), wimmelnd (with von).

all [ɔːl] a alle(r, s); ~ day/night den ganzen Tag/die ganze Nacht; ~ men are equal alle Menschen sind gleich; ~ five came alle fünf kamen; ~ the books/food die ganzen Bücher/das ganze Essen; ~ the time die ganze Zeit (über); ~ his life sein ganzes Leben (lang)
◆pron **1** alles; I ate it ~, I ate ~ of it ich habe alles gegessen; ~ of us/the boys went wir gingen alle/alle Jungen gingen; we ~ sat down wir setzten uns alle
2 (in phrases): above ~ vor allem; after ~ schließlich; at ~: not at ~ (in answer to question) überhaupt nicht; (in answer

to thanks) gern geschehen; I'm not at ~ tired ich bin überhaupt nicht müde; anything at ~ will do es ist egal, welche(r, s); ~ in ~ alles in allem
◆ad ganz; ~ alone ganz allein; it's not as hard as ~ that so schwer ist es nun auch wieder nicht; ~ the more/the better um so mehr/besser; ~ but fast; the score is 2 ~ es steht 2 zu 2.

allay [ə'leɪ] vt (fears) beschwichtigen.

all clear ['ɔːl'klɪə*] n Entwarnung f.

allegation [ælɪ'geɪʃən] n Behauptung f.

allege [ə'ledʒ] vt (declare) behaupten; (falsely) vorgeben; ~dly [ə'ledʒɪdlɪ] ad angeblich.

allegiance [ə'liːdʒəns] n Treue f.

allergic [ə'lɜːdʒɪk] a allergisch (to gegen).

allergy ['ælədʒɪ] n Allergie f.

alleviate [ə'liːvɪeɪt] vt lindern.

alley ['ælɪ] n Gasse f, Durchgang m.

alliance [ə'laɪəns] n Bund m, Allianz f.

allied ['ælaɪd] a vereinigt; (powers) alliiert; verwandt (to mit).

alligator ['ælɪgeɪtə*] n Alligator m.

all-in ['ɔːlɪn] a, ad (Brit: charge) alles inbegriffen, Gesamt-; ~ wrestling n Freistilringen nt.

all-night ['ɔːl'naɪt] a (café, cinema) die ganze Nacht geöffnet, Nacht-.

allocate ['æləkeɪt] vt zuteilen.

allot [ə'lɒt] vt zuteilen; ~ment n (share) Anteil m; (plot) Schrebergarten m.

all-out ['ɔːl'aʊt] a total; **all out** ad mit voller Kraft.

allow [ə'laʊ] vt (permit) erlauben, gestatten (sb jdm); (grant) bewilligen; (deduct) abziehen; (concede): to ~ that ... annehmen, daß ...; ~ for vt berücksichtigen, einplanen; ~ance n Beihilfe f; to make ~ances for berücksichtigen.

alloy ['ælɔɪ] n Metallegierung f.

all right ad (well) gut; (correct) richtig; (as answer) okay.

all-round ['ɔːl'raʊnd] a (sportsman) allseitig, Allround-; (view) Rundum-.

all-time ['ɔːl'taɪm] a (record, high) ... aller Zeiten, Höchst-.

allude [ə'luːd] vi hinweisen, anspielen (to auf +acc).

alluring [ə'ljʊərɪŋ] a verlockend.

allusion [ə'luːʒən] n Anspielung f.

ally ['ælaɪ] n Verbündete(r) m/f; (POL) Alliierte(r) m // vr [ə'laɪ]: to ~ o.s. with sich verbünden mit.

almighty [ɔːl'maɪtɪ] a allmächtig.

almond ['ɑːmənd] n Mandel f.

almost ['ɔːlməʊst] ad fast, beinahe.

alms [ɑːmz] npl Almosen nt.

aloft [ə'lɒft] ad (be) in der Luft; (throw) in die Luft.

alone [ə'ləʊn] a, ad allein; to leave sth ~ etw sein lassen; let alone ... geschweige denn ...

along [ə'lɒŋ] *prep* entlang, längs // *ad*
(*onward*) vorwärts, weiter; ~ **with**
zusammen mit; **he was limping** ~ er
humpelte einher; **all** ~ (*all the time*) die
ganze Zeit; ~**side** *ad* (*walk*) nebenher;
(*come*) nebendran; (*be*) daneben // *prep*
(*walk, compared with*) neben (+*dat*);
(*come*) neben (+*acc*); (*be*) entlang,
neben (+*dat*); (*of ship*) längsseits
(+*gen*).

aloof [ə'lu:f] *a* zurückhaltend // *ad* fern;
to stand ~ abseits stehen.

aloud [ə'laʊd] *ad* laut.

alphabet ['ælfəbet] *n* Alphabet *nt*; ~**ical**
[ælfə'betɪkl] *a* alphabetisch.

alpine ['ælpaɪn] *a* alpin, Alpen-.

Alps [ælps] *npl:* **the** ~ die Alpen.

already [ɔ:l'redɪ] *ad* schon, bereits.

alright ['ɔ:l'raɪt] *ad* (*Brit*) = **all right**.

Alsatian [æl'seɪʃən] *n* (*dog*) Schäferhund
m.

also ['ɔ:lsəʊ] *ad* auch, außerdem.

altar ['ɔ:ltə*] *n* Altar *m*.

alter ['ɔ:ltə*] *vt* ändern; (*dress*) um-
ändern; ~**ation** [ɒltə'reɪʃən] *n* Änderung *f*; Umänderung *f*; (*to building*)
Umbau *m*.

alternate [ɒl'tɜ:nɪt] *a* abwechselnd // *vi*
['ɒltɜ:neɪt] abwechseln (*with* mit); **on** ~
days jeden zweiten Tag.

alternating ['ɒltəneɪtɪŋ] *a:* ~ **current**
Wechselstrom *m*.

alternative [ɒl'tɜ:nətɪv] *a* andere(r, s) //
n Alternative *f*; ~**ly** *ad* im anderen
Falle; ~**ly** **one could** ... oder man könnte
...

alternator ['ɒltɜ:neɪtə*] *n* (*AUT*)
Lichtmaschine *f*.

although [ɔ:l'ðəʊ] *cj* obwohl.

altitude ['æltɪtju:d] *n* Höhe *f*.

alto ['æltəʊ] *n* Alt *m*.

altogether [ɔ:ltə'geðə*] *ad* (*on the
whole*) im ganzen genommen; (*entirely*)
ganz und gar.

aluminium [æljʊ'mɪnɪəm], (*US*) **aluminum** [ə'lu:mɪnəm] *n* Aluminium *nt*.

always ['ɔ:lweɪz] *ad* immer.

am [æm] *see* **be**.

a.m. *ad abbr* (= *ante meridiem*) vor-
mittags.

amalgamate [ə'mælgəmeɪt] *vi*
(*combine*) sich vereinigen // *vt* (*mix*)
amalgamieren.

amass [ə'mæs] *vt* anhäufen.

amateur ['æmətɜ:*] *n* Amateur *m*; (*pej*)
Amateur *m*, Stümper *m*; ~**ish** *a* (*pej*)
dilettantisch, stümperhaft.

amaze [ə'meɪz] *vt* erstaunen; **to be** ~**d**
(**at**) erstaunt sein (über); ~**ment** *n*
höchste(s) Erstaunen *nt*.

amazing [ə'meɪzɪŋ] *a* höchst erstaunlich.

Amazon ['æməzən] *n* (*GEOG*)
Amazonas *m*.

ambassador [æm'bæsədə*] *n* Bot-
schafter *m*.

amber ['æmbə*] *n* Bernstein *m*; **at** ~
(*Brit AUT*) (auf) gelb.

ambiguous [æm'bɪgjʊəs] *a* zweideutig;
(*not clear*) unklar.

ambition [æm'bɪʃən] *n* Ehrgeiz *m*.

ambitious [æm'bɪʃəs] *a* ehrgeizig.

ambivalent [æm'bɪvələnt] *n* (*attitude*)
zwiespältig.

amble ['æmbl] *vi* (*usu:* ~ **along**)
schlendern.

ambulance ['æmbjʊləns] *n* Kranken-
wagen *m*; ~**man** *n* Sanitäter *m*.

ambush ['æmbʊʃ] *n* Hinterhalt *m* // *vt*
(aus dem Hinterhalt) überfallen.

amenable [ə'mi:nəbl] *a* gefügig; (*to
reason*) zugänglich (*to dat*); (*to flattery*)
empfänglich (*to* für); (*to law*) unterworfen (*to dat*).

amend [ə'mend] *vt* (*law etc*) abändern,
ergänzen; **to make** ~**s** etw wiedergutmachen; ~**ment** *n* Abänderung *f*.

amenities [ə'mi:nɪtɪz] *npl* Einrichtungen
pl.

America [ə'merɪkə] *n* Amerika *nt*; ~**n** *a*
amerikanisch // *n* Amerikaner(in *f*) *m*.

amiable ['eɪmɪəbl] *a* liebenswürdig.

amicable ['æmɪkəbl] *a* freundschaftlich;
(*settlement*) gütlich.

amid(st) [ə'mɪd(st)] *prep* mitten in *or*
unter (+*dat*).

amiss [ə'mɪs] *ad:* **to take sth** ~ etw
übelnehmen; **there's something** ~ da
stimmt irgend etwas nicht.

ammunition [æmjʊ'nɪʃən] *n* Munition *f*.

amnesia   [æm'ni:zɪə]   *n*
Gedächtnisverlust *m*.

amnesty ['æmnɪstɪ] *n* Amnestie *f*.

among(st) [ə'mʌŋ(st)] *prep* unter.

amoral [æ'mɒrəl] *a* unmoralisch.

amorous ['æmərəs] *a* verliebt.

amount [ə'maʊnt] *n* (*of money*) Betrag
m; (*of time, energy*) Aufwand *m* (*of an*
+*dat*); (*of water, sand*) Menge *f* // *vi:* ~
to (*total*) sich belaufen auf (+*acc*); **this**
~**s to treachery** das kommt Verrat
gleich; **it** ~**s to the same** es läuft aufs
gleiche hinaus; **he won't** ~ **to much** aus
ihm wird nie was.

amp(ère) ['æmp(eə*)] *n* Ampere *nt*.

amphibian [æm'fɪbɪən] *n* Amphibie *f*.

amphibious [æm'fɪbɪəs] *a* amphibisch,
Amphibien-.

ample ['æmpl] *a* (*portion*) reichlich;
(*dress*) weit, groß; ~ **time** genügend
Zeit.

amplifier ['æmplɪfaɪə*] *n* Verstärker *m*.

amuse [ə'mju:z] *vt* (*entertain*) unterhalten; (*make smile*) belustigen;
~**ment** *n* (*feeling*) Unterhaltung *f*;
(*recreation*) Zeitvertreib *m*; ~**ment arcade** *n* Spielhalle *f*.

an [æn, ən] *see* **a**.

anaemia [ə'ni:mɪə] *n* Anämie *f*.

anaemic [ə'ni:mɪk] a blutarm.

anaesthetic [ænɪs'θetɪk] n Betäubungsmittel nt; under ~ unter Narkose.

anaesthetist [æ'ni:sθɪtɪst] n Anästhesist(in f) m.

analgesic [ænæl'dʒi:sɪk] n schmerzlindernde(s) Mittel nt.

analog(ue) ['ænəlɒg] a Analog-.

analogy [ə'nælədʒɪ] n Analogie f.

analyse ['ænəlaɪz] vt (Brit) analysieren.

analysis [ə'næləsɪs], pl **-ses** [-siːz] n Analyse f.

analyst ['ænəlɪst] n Analytiker(in f) m.

analytic(al) [ænə'lɪtɪk(əl)] a analytisch.

analyze ['ænəlaɪz] vt (US) = **analyse**.

anarchy ['ænəkɪ] n Anarchie f.

anathema [ə'næθɪmə] n (fig) Greuel nt.

anatomy [ə'nætəmɪ] n (structure) anatomische(r) Aufbau m; (study) Anatomie f.

ancestor ['ænsestə*] n Vorfahr m.

anchor ['æŋkə*] n Anker m // vi (also: to drop ~) ankern, vor Anker liegen // vt verankern; to weigh ~ den Anker lichten; ~age n Ankerplatz m.

anchovy ['æntʃəvɪ] n Sardelle f.

ancient ['eɪnʃənt] a alt; (car etc) uralt.

ancillary [æn'sɪlərɪ] a Hilfs-.

and [ænd] cj und; ~ so on und so weiter; try ~ come versuche zu kommen; better ~ better immer besser.

Andes ['ændiːz] npl: the ~ die Anden pl.

anemia [ə'niːmɪə] n (US) = **anaemia**.

anesthetic [ænɪs'θetɪk] n (US) = **anaesthetic**.

anew [ə'njuː] ad von neuem.

angel ['eɪndʒəl] n Engel m.

anger ['æŋgə*] n Zorn m // vt ärgern.

angle ['æŋgl] n Winkel m; (point of view) Standpunkt m; ~r n Angler m.

Anglican ['æŋglɪkən] a anglikanisch // n Anglikaner(in f) m.

angling ['æŋglɪŋ] n Angeln nt.

Anglo- ['æŋgləʊ] pref Anglo-.

angrily ['æŋgrɪlɪ] ad ärgerlich, böse.

angry ['æŋgrɪ] a ärgerlich, ungehalten, böse; (wound) entzündet; to be ~ with sb auf jdn böse sein; to be ~ at sth über etw (acc) verärgert sein.

anguish ['æŋgwɪʃ] n Qual f.

angular ['æŋgjʊlə*] a eckig, winkelförmig; (face) kantig.

animal ['ænɪməl] n Tier nt; (living creature) Lebewesen nt // a tierisch.

animate ['ænɪmeɪt] vt beleben // a ['ænɪmət] lebhaft; ~d a lebendig; (film) Zeichentrick-.

animosity [ænɪ'mɒsɪtɪ] n Feindseligkeit f, Abneigung f.

aniseed ['ænɪsiːd] n Anis m.

ankle ['æŋkl] n (Fuß)knöchel m; ~ sock n Söckchen n.

annex ['æneks] n (also: Brit: annexe) Anbau m // vt [ə'neks] anfügen; (POL) annektieren, angliedern.

annihilate [ə'naɪəleɪt] vt vernichten.

anniversary [ænɪ'vɜːsərɪ] n Jahrestag m.

annotate ['ænəteɪt] vt kommentieren.

announce [ə'naʊns] vt ankündigen, anzeigen; ~ment n Ankündigung f; (official) Bekanntmachung f; ~r n Ansager(in f) m.

annoy [ə'nɔɪ] vt ärgern; don't get ~ed! reg' dich nicht auf!; ~ance n Ärgernis nt, Störung f; ~ing a ärgerlich; (person) lästig.

annual ['ænjʊəl] a jährlich; (salary) Jahres- // n (plant) einjährige Pflanze f; (book) Jahrbuch nt; ~ly ad jährlich.

annul [ə'nʌl] vt aufheben, annullieren; ~ment n Aufhebung f, Annullierung f.

annum ['ænəm] n see **per**.

anomaly [ə'nɒməlɪ] n Abweichung f von der Regel.

anonymous [ə'nɒnɪməs] a anonym.

anorak ['ænəræk] n Anorak m, Windjacke f.

anorexia [ænə'reksɪə] n (MED) Magersucht f.

another [ə'nʌðə*] a, pron (different) ein(e) andere(r, s); (additional) noch eine(r, s); see also **one**.

answer ['ɑːnsə*] n Antwort f // vi antworten; (on phone) sich melden // vt (person) antworten (+dat); (letter, question) beantworten; (telephone) gehen an (+acc), abnehmen; (door) öffnen; to ~ the phone ans Telefon gehen; in ~ to your letter in Beantwortung Ihres Schreibens; to ~ the bell or the door aufmachen; ~ back vi frech sein; ~ for vt: to ~ for sth für etw verantwortlich sein; ~able a: to be ~ to sb for sth jdm gegenüber für etw verantwortlich sein; ~ing machine n Anrufbeantworter m.

ant [ænt] n Ameise f.

antagonism [æn'tægənɪzəm] n Antagonismus m.

antagonize [æn'tægənaɪz] vt reizen.

Antarctic [ænt'ɑːktɪk] a antarktisch // n: the ~ die Antarktis.

antelope ['æntɪləʊp] n Antilope f.

antenatal [æntɪ'neɪtl] a vor der Geburt; ~ clinic n Sprechstunde f für werdende Mütter.

antenna [æn'tenə], pl ~e [-niː] n (BIOL) Fühler m; (RAD) Antenne f.

anthem ['ænθəm] n Hymne f; national ~ Nationalhymne f.

anthology [æn'θɒlədʒɪ] n Gedichtsammlung f, Anthologie f.

anti- ['æntɪ] pref Gegen-, Anti-.

anti-aircraft ['æntɪ'eəkrɑːft] a Flugabwehr-.

antibiotic ['æntɪbaɪ'ɒtɪk] n Antibiotikum nt.

antibody ['æntɪbɒdɪ] n Antikörper m.

anticipate [æn'tɪsɪpeɪt] vt (expect: trouble, question) erwarten, rechnen mit;

(*look forward to*) sich freuen auf
(+*acc*); (*do first*) vorwegnehmen;
(*foresee*) ahnen, vorhersehen.
anticipation [æntɪsɪ'peɪʃən] *n* Erwartung *f*; (*foreshadowing*) Vorwegnahme *f*.
anticlimax ['æntɪ'klaɪmæks] *n* Ernüchte-
rung *f*.
anticlockwise ['æntɪ'klɒkwaɪz] *ad* entgegen dem Uhrzeigersinn.
antics ['æntɪks] *npl* Possen *pl*.
anticyclone ['æntɪ'saɪkləʊn] *n* Hoch *nt*,
Hochdruckgebiet *nt*.
antidote ['æntɪdəʊt] *n* Gegenmittel *nt*.
antifreeze ['æntɪfriːz] *n* Frost-
schutzmittel *nt*.
antihistamine [æntɪ'hɪstəmiːn] *n* An-
tihistamin *nt*.
antiquated ['æntɪkweɪtɪd] *a* antiquiert.
antique [æn'tiːk] *n* Antiquität *f* // *a* antik; (*old-fashioned*) altmodisch; ~ **shop**
n Antiquitätenladen *m*.
antiquity [æn'tɪkwɪtɪ] *n* Altertum *nt*.
antiseptic [æntɪ'septɪk] *n* Antiseptikum
nt // *a* antiseptisch.
antisocial [æntɪ'səʊʃl] *a* (*person*) unge-
sellig; (*law*) unsozial.
antlers ['æntləz] *npl* Geweih *nt*.
anus ['eɪnəs] *n* After *m*.
anvil ['ænvɪl] *n* Amboß *m*.
anxiety [æŋ'zaɪətɪ] *n* Angst *f*; (*worry*)
Sorge *f*.
anxious ['æŋkʃəs] *a* ängstlich; (*worried*)
besorgt; **to be ~ to do sth** etw unbedingt
tun wollen.
any ['enɪ] ◆ *a* 1 (*in questions etc*): **have
you ~ butter?** haben Sie (etwas)
Butter?; **have you ~ children?** haben Sie
Kinder?; **if there are ~ tickets left** falls
noch Karten da sind
2 (*with negative*): **I haven't ~ money/
books** ich habe kein Geld/keine Bücher
3 (*no matter which*) jede(r, s)
(beliebige); **~ colour (at all)** jede
beliebige Farbe; **choose ~ book you like**
nehmen Sie ein beliebiges Buch
4 (*in phrases*): **~ in case** in jedem Fall;
~ day now jeden Tag; **at ~ moment**
jeden Moment; **at ~ rate** auf jeden Fall
◆ *pron* 1 (*in questions etc*): **have you got
~?** haben Sie welche?; **can ~ of you
sing?** kann (irgend)einer von euch
singen?
2 (*with negative*): **I haven't ~ (of them)**
ich habe keinen/keines (davon)
3 (*no matter which one(s) you like*): **take ~ of
those books (you like)** nehmen Sie
irgendeines dieser Bücher
◆ *ad* 1 (*in questions etc*): **do you want ~
more soup/sandwiches?** möchten Sie
noch Suppe/Brote?; **are you feeling ~
better?** fühlen Sie sich etwas besser?
2 (*with negative*): **I can't hear him ~
more** ich kann ihn nicht mehr hören.
anybody ['enɪbɒdɪ] *pron* (*no matter
who*) jede(r); (*in questions etc*) (irgend)

jemand, (irgend) eine(r); (*with negative*): **I can't see ~** ich kann niemanden
sehen.
anyhow ['enɪhaʊ] *ad* (*at any rate*): **I
shall go ~** ich gehe sowieso; (*haphazard*): **do it ~** wie Sie wollen machen Sie es,
wie Sie wollen.
anyone ['enɪwʌn] *pron* = **anybody**.
anything ['enɪθɪŋ] *pron* 1 (*in questions
etc*) (irgend) etwas; **can you see ~?**
können Sie etwas sehen?
2 (*with negative*): **I can't see ~** ich
kann nichts sehen
3 (*no matter what*): **you can say ~** you
like Sie können sagen, was Sie wollen; **~
will do** irgend etwas, irgendeine(r, s);
he'll eat ~ er ißt alles.
anyway ['enɪweɪ] *ad* (*at any rate*) auf
jeden Fall; (*besides*): **~, I couldn't come
even if I wanted to** jedenfalls könnte ich
nicht kommen, selbst wenn ich wollte;
why are you phoning, ~? warum rufst
du überhaupt an?
anywhere ['enɪweə*] *ad* (*in questions
etc*) irgendwo; (: *with direction*)
irgendwohin; (*no matter where*) überall;
(: *with direction*) überallhin; (*with
negative*): **I can't see him ~** ich kann
ihn nirgendwo *or* nirgends sehen; **can
you see him ~?** siehst du ihn irgendwo?;
put the books down ~ leg die Bücher
irgendwohin.
apart [ə'pɑːt] *ad* (*parted*) auseinander;
(*away*) beiseite, abseits; **10 miles ~** 10
Meilen auseinander; **to take ~** auseinandernehmen; **~ from** *prep* außer.
apartheid [ə'pɑːteɪt] *n* Apartheid *f*.
apartment [ə'pɑːtmənt] *n* (*US*) Wohnung *f*; **~ building** *n* (*US*) Wohnhaus
nt.
apathy ['æpəθɪ] *n* Teilnahmslosigkeit *f*,
Apathie *f*.
ape [eɪp] *n* (Menschen)affe *m* // *vt* nachahmen.
aperture ['æpətjʊə*] *n* Öffnung *f*;
(*PHOT*) Blende *f*.
apex ['eɪpeks] *n* Spitze *f*.
apiece [ə'piːs] *ad* pro Stück; (*per
person*) pro Kopf.
apologetic [əpɒlə'dʒetɪk] *a* ent-
schuldigend; **to be ~** sich sehr entschuldigen.
apologize [ə'pɒlədʒaɪz] *vi* sich entschuldigen (*for sth to sb* für etw bei
jdm).
apology [ə'pɒlədʒɪ] *n* Entschuldigung *f*.
apostle [ə'pɒsl] *n* Apostel *m*.
apostrophe [ə'pɒstrəfɪ] *n* Apostroph *m*.
appal [ə'pɔːl] *vt* erschrecken; **~ling** *a*
schrecklich.
apparatus [æpə'reɪtəs] *n* Gerät *nt*.
apparel [ə'pærəl] *n* (*US*) Kleidung *f*.
apparent [ə'pærənt] *a* offenbar; **~ly** *ad*
anscheinend.
apparition [æpə'rɪʃən] *n* (*ghost*) Er-

scheinung *f*, Geist *m*; (*appearance*) Erscheinen *nt*.

appeal [ə'pi:l] *vi* dringend ersuchen; dringend bitten (*for* um); sich wenden (*to an* +*acc*); (*to public*) appellieren (*to an* +*acc*); (*JUR*) Berufung einlegen // *n* Aufruf *m*; (*JUR*) Berufung *f*; it doesn't ~ to me es gefällt mir nicht; ~**ing** *a* ansprechend.

appear [ə'pɪə*] *vi* (*come into sight*) erscheinen; (*be seen*) auftauchen; (*seem*) scheinen; ~**ance** *n* (*coming into sight*) Erscheinen *nt*; (*outward show*) Äußere(s) *nt*; it would ~ that ... anscheinend ...

appease [ə'pi:z] *vt* beschwichtigen.

appendicitis [əpendɪ'saɪtɪs] *n* Blinddarmentzündung *f*.

appendix [ə'pendɪks], *pl* **-dices** [-dɪsi:z] *n* (*in book*) Anhang *m*; (*MED*) Blinddarm *m*.

appetite ['æpɪtaɪt] *n* Appetit *m*; (*fig*) Lust *f*.

appetizer ['æpətaɪzə*] *n* Appetitanreger *m*.

appetizing ['æpɪtaɪzɪŋ] *a* appetitanregend.

applaud [ə'plɔ:d] *vti* Beifall klatschen (+*dat*), applaudieren.

applause [ə'plɔ:z] *n* Beifall *m*, Applaus *m*.

apple ['æpl] *n* Apfel *m*; ~ **tree** *n* Apfelbaum *m*.

appliance [ə'plaɪəns] *n* Gerät *nt*.

applicable [ə'plɪkəbl] *a* anwendbar; (*in forms*) zutreffend.

applicant ['æplɪkənt] *n* Bewerber(in *f*) *m*.

application [æplɪ'keɪʃən] *n* (*request*) Antrag *m*; (*for job*) Bewerbung *f*; (*putting into practice*) Anwendung *f*; (*hard work*) Fleiß *m*; ~ **form** *n* Bewerbungsformular *nt*.

applied [ə'plaɪd] *a* angewandt.

apply [ə'plaɪ] *vi* (*ask*) sich wenden (*to an* +*acc*), sich melden; (*be suitable*) zutreffen // *vt* (*place on*) auflegen; (*cream*) auftragen; (*put into practice*) anwenden; to ~ **for sth** sich um etw bewerben; to ~ **the brakes** die Bremsen betätigen; to ~ **o.s. to sth** sich bei etw anstrengen.

appoint [ə'pɔɪnt] *vt* (*to office*) ernennen, berufen; (*settle*) festsetzen; ~**ment** *n* (*meeting*) Verabredung *f*; (*at hairdresser etc*) Bestellung *f*; (*in business*) Termin *m*; (*choice for a position*) Ernennung *f*; (*UNIV*) Berufung *f*.

appraisal [ə'preɪzl] *n* Beurteilung *f*.

appreciable [ə'pri:ʃəbl] *a* (*perceptible*) merklich; (*able to be estimated*) abschätzbar.

appreciate [ə'pri:ʃɪeɪt] *vt* (*value*) zu schätzen wissen; (*understand*) einsehen // *vi* (*increase in value*) im Wert steigen.

appreciation [əpri:ʃɪ'eɪʃən] *n* Wert-

schätzung *f*; (*COMM*) Wertzuwachs *m*.

appreciative [ə'pri:ʃɪətɪv] *a* (*showing thanks*) dankbar; (*showing liking*) anerkennend.

apprehend [æprɪ'hend] *vt* (*arrest*) festnehmen; (*understand*) erfassen.

apprehension [æprɪ'henʃən] *n* Angst *f*.

apprehensive [æprɪ'hensɪv] *a* furchtsam.

apprentice [ə'prentɪs] *n* Lehrling *m*; ~**ship** *n* Lehrzeit *f*.

approach [ə'prəʊtʃ] *vi* sich nähern // *vt* herantreten an (+*acc*); (*problem*) herangehen an (+*acc*) // *n* Annäherung *f*; (*to problem*) Ansatz *m*; (*path*) Zugang *m*, Zufahrt *f*; ~**able** *a* zugänglich.

appropriate [ə'prəʊprɪət] *a* angemessen; (*remark*) angebracht // [ə'prəʊprɪeɪt] *vt* (*take for o.s.*) sich aneignen; (*set apart*) bereitstellen.

approval [ə'pru:vəl] *n* (*show of satisfaction*) Beifall *m*; (*permission*) Billigung *f*; (*COMM*) **on** ~ bei Gefallen.

approve [ə'pru:v] *vti* billigen; I don't ~ **of it/him** ich halte nichts davon/von ihm; ~**d school** *n* (*Brit*) Erziehungsheim *nt*.

approximate [ə'prɒksɪmɪt] *a* annähernd, ungefähr // *vt* [ə'prɒksɪmeɪt] nahekommen (+*dat*); ~**ly** *ad* rund, ungefähr.

apricot ['eɪprɪkɒt] *n* Aprikose *f*.

April ['eɪprəl] *n* April *m*; ~ **Fools' Day** *n* der erste April.

apron ['eɪprən] *n* Schürze *f*.

apt [æpt] *a* (*suitable*) passend; (*able*) begabt; (*likely*): **to be** ~ **to do sth** dazu neigen, etw zu tun.

aptitude ['æptɪtju:d] *n* Begabung *f*.

aqualung ['ækwəlʌŋ] *n* Unterwasseratmungsgerät *nt*.

aquarium [ə'kweərɪəm] *n* Aquarium *nt*.

Aquarius [ə'kweərɪəs] *n* Wassermann *m*.

aquatic [ə'kwætɪk] *a* Wasser-.

Arab ['ærəb] *n* Araber(in *f*) *m*.

Arabia [ə'reɪbɪə] *n* Arabien *nt*.

Arabian [ə'reɪbɪən] *a* arabisch.

Arabic ['ærəbɪk] *a* arabisch // *n* Arabisch *nt*; ~ **numerals** arabische Ziffern.

arable ['ærəbl] *a* bebaubar, Kultur-.

arbitrary ['ɑ:bɪtrərɪ] *a* willkürlich.

arbitration [ɑ:bɪ'treɪʃən] *n* Schlichtung *f*.

arc [ɑ:k] *n* Bogen *m*.

arcade [ɑ:'keɪd] *n* Säulengang *m*.

arch [ɑ:tʃ] *n* Bogen *m* // *vt* überwölben; (*back*) krumm machen.

archaeologist [ɑ:kɪ'ɒlədʒɪst] *n* Archäologe *m*.

archaeology [ɑ:kɪ'ɒlədʒɪ] *n* Archäologie *f*.

archaic [ɑ:'keɪɪk] *a* altertümlich.

archbishop ['ɑ:tʃ'bɪʃəp] *n* Erzbischof *m*.

arch-enemy ['ɑ:tʃ'enəmɪ] *n* Erzfeind *m*.

archeology etc (US) = **archaelogy** etc.

archer ['a:tʃə*] n Bogenschütze m; ~y n Bogenschießen nt.

archipelago [a:kɪ'pelɪgəʊ] n Archipel m; (sea) Inselmeer nt.

architect ['a:kɪtekt] n Architekt(in f) m; ~ural [a:kɪ'tektʃərəl] a architektonisch; ~ure n Architektur f.

archives ['a:kaɪvz] npl Archiv nt.

archway ['a:tʃweɪ] n Bogen m.

Arctic ['a:ktɪk] a arktisch // n: the ~ die Arktis.

ardent ['a:dənt] a glühend.

arduous ['a:djʊəs] a mühsam.

are [a:*] see be.

area ['eərɪə] n Fläche f; (of land) Gebiet nt; (part of sth) Teil m, Abschnitt m.

arena [ə'ri:nə] n Arena f.

aren't [a:nt] = are not.

Argentina [a:dʒən'ti:nə] n Argentinien nt; **Argentinian** [a:dʒən'tɪnɪən] a argentinisch // n Argentinier(in f) m.

arguably ['a:gjʊəblɪ] ad wohl.

argue ['a:gju:] vi diskutieren; (angrily) streiten.

argument ['a:gjʊmənt] n (theory) Argument nt; (reasoning) Argumentation f; (row) Auseinandersetzung f, Streit m; to have an ~ sich streiten; ~ative [a:gjʊ'mentətɪv] a streitlustig.

aria ['a:rɪə] n Arie f.

arid ['ærɪd] a trocken.

Aries ['eərɪːz] n Widder m.

arise, pt **arose**, pp **arisen** [ə'raɪz, ə'rəʊz, ə'rɪzn] vi aufsteigen; (get up) aufstehen; (difficulties etc) entstehen; (case) vorkommen; to ~ from sth herrühren von etw.

aristocracy [ærɪs'tɒkrəsɪ] n Adel m, Aristokratie f.

aristocrat ['ærɪstəkræt] n Adlige(r) mf, Aristokrat(in f) m.

arithmetic [ə'rɪθmətɪk] n Rechnen nt, Arithmetik f.

ark [a:k] n: Noah's A~ die Arche Noah.

arm [a:m] n Arm m; (branch of military service) Zweig m // vt bewaffnen.

armaments ['a:məmənts] npl Ausrüstung f.

arm: ~**chair** n Lehnstuhl m; ~**ed** a (forces) Streit-, bewaffnet; (robbery) bewaffnet.

armistice ['a:mɪstɪs] n Waffenstillstand m.

armour, (US) **armor** ['a:mə*] n (knight's) Rüstung f; (MIL) Panzerplatte f; ~**ed car** n Panzerwagen m; ~**y** n Waffenlager nt; (factory) Waffenfabrik f.

armpit ['a:mpɪt] n Achselhöhle f.

armrest ['a:mrest] n Armlehne f.

arms [a:mz] npl (weapons) Waffen pl; ~ **race** n Wettrüsten nt.

army ['a:mɪ] n Armee f, Heer nt; (host) Heer m.

aroma [ə'rəʊmə] n Duft m, Aroma nt; ~**tic** [ærə'mætɪk] a aromatisch, würzig.

arose [ə'rəʊz] pt of **arise**.

around [ə'raʊnd] ad ringsherum; (almost) ungefähr // prep um ... herum; is he ~? ist er hier?

arouse [ə'raʊz] vt wecken.

arrange [ə'reɪndʒ] vt (time, meeting) festsetzen; (holidays) festlegen; (flowers, hair, objects) anordnen; I ~**d** to meet him ich habe mit ihm ausgemacht, ihn zu treffen; it's all ~**d** es ist alles arrangiert; ~**ment** n (order) Reihenfolge f; (agreement) Vereinbarung f; ~**ments** pl Pläne pl.

array [ə'reɪ] n (collection) Ansammlung f.

arrears [ə'rɪəz] npl (of debts) Rückstand m; (of work) Unerledigte(s) nt; in ~ im Rückstand.

arrest [ə'rest] vt (person) verhaften; (stop) aufhalten // n Verhaftung f; under ~ in Haft.

arrival [ə'raɪvəl] n Ankunft f.

arrive [ə'raɪv] vi ankommen (at in +dat, bei).

arrogance ['ærəgəns] n Überheblichkeit f, Arroganz f.

arrow ['ærəʊ] n Pfeil m.

arse [a:s] n (col!) Arsch m (!).

arsenal ['a:sɪnl] n Waffenlager nt, Zeughaus nt.

arsenic ['a:snɪk] n Arsen nt.

arson ['a:sn] n Brandstiftung f.

art [a:t] n Kunst f; **A~s** pl Geisteswissenschaften pl.

artery ['a:tərɪ] n Schlagader f, Arterie f.

artful ['a:tfʊl] a verschlagen.

art gallery n Kunstgalerie f.

arthritis [a:'θraɪtɪs] n Arthritis f.

artichoke ['a:tɪtʃəʊk] n Artischocke f; Jerusalem ~ Erdartischocke f.

article ['a:tɪkl] n (PRESS, GRAM) Artikel m; (thing) Gegenstand m, Artikel m; (clause) Abschnitt m, Paragraph m; to do one's ~s (JUR) seine Referendarzeit ableisten; ~ **of clothing** Kleidungsstück nt.

articulate [a:'tɪkjʊlɪt] a (able to express o.s.) redegewandt; (speaking clearly) deutlich, verständlich; to be ~ sich gut ausdrücken können // vt [a:'tɪkjʊleɪt] (connect) zusammenfügen, gliedern; ~**d vehicle** n Sattelschlepper m.

artificial [a:tɪ'fɪʃəl] a künstlich, Kunst-; ~ **respiration** n künstliche Atmung f.

artisan ['a:tɪzæn] n gelernte(r) Handwerker m.

artist ['a:tɪst] n Künstler(in f) m; ~**ic** [a:'tɪstɪk] a künstlerisch; ~**ry** n künstlerische(s) Können nt.

artless ['a:tlɪs] a ungekünstelt; (character) arglos.

art school n Kunsthochschule f.

as [æz] ◆cj 1 (referring to time) als; ~

the years went by mit den Jahren; he came in ~ I was leaving als er hereinkam, ging ich gerade; ~ from tomorrow ab morgen **2** (*in comparisons*): ~ **big** ~ so groß wie; **twice** ~ **big** ~ zweimal so groß wie; ~ **much/many** ~ soviel/so viele wie; ~ **soon** ~ sobald **3** (*since, because*) da; he left early ~ he had to be home by 10 er ging früher, da er um 10 zu Hause sein mußte **4** (*referring to manner, way*) wie; do ~ you wish mach was du willst; ~ she said wie sie sagte **5** (*concerning*): ~ **for** or to **that** was das betrifft or angeht **6**: ~ **if** or **though** als ob.
◆ *prep* als; he works ~ a driver er arbeitet als Fahrer; he gave it to me ~ a present er hat es mir als Geschenk gegeben; *see also* **long, such, well**.

a.s.a.p. *abbr of* **as soon as possible.**

ascend [ə'send] *vi* aufsteigen // *vt* besteigen; **~ancy** *n* Oberhand *f*.

ascent [ə'sent] *n* Aufstieg *m*; Besteigung *f*.

ascertain [æsə'teɪn] *vt* feststellen.

ascribe [əs'kraɪb] *vt* zuschreiben (*to* dat).

ash [æʃ] *n* Asche *f*; (*tree*) Esche *f*.

ashamed [ə'ʃeɪmd] *a* beschämt; **to be** ~ **of sth** sich für etw schämen.

ashen [æʃən] *a* (*pale*) aschfahl.

ashore [ə'ʃɔː*] *ad* an Land.

ashtray [æʃtreɪ] *n* Aschenbecher *m*.

Ash Wednesday *n* Aschermittwoch *m*.

Asia [eɪʃə] *n* Asien *nt*; ~**n**, ~**tic** [eɪsɪ'ætɪk] *a* asiatisch // *n* Asiat(in *f*) *m*.

aside [ə'saɪd] *ad* beiseite // *n* beiseite gesprochene Worte *pl*.

ask [ɑːsk] *vt* fragen; (*permission*) bitten um; ~ **him his name** frage ihn nach seinem Namen; **he** ~**ed to see you** er wollte dich sehen; **to** ~ **sb to do sth** jdn bitten, etw zu tun; **to** ~ **sb about sth** jdn nach etw fragen; **to** ~ **(sb) a question** jdn etwas fragen; **to** ~ **sb out to dinner** jdn zum Essen einladen; **to** ~ **after sb** nach jdm fragen; **to** ~ **for sth** um etw (*acc*) bitten.

askance [əs'kɑːns] *ad*: **to look** ~ **at sb** jdn schief ansehen.

askew [əs'kjuː] *ad* schief.

asking price [ɑːskɪŋ-] *n* Verkaufspreis *m*.

asleep [ə'sliːp] *a*: **to be** ~ schlafen; **to fall** ~ einschlafen.

asparagus [əs'pærəgəs] *n* Spargel *m*.

aspect [æspekt] *n* Aspekt *m*.

aspersions [əs'pɜːʃənz] *npl*: **to cast** ~ **on sb/sth** sich abfällig über jdn/etw äußern.

asphyxiation [əsfɪksɪ'eɪʃən] *n* Erstickung *f*.

aspirations [æspə'reɪʃənz] *npl*: **to have**

~ **towards sth** etw anstreben.

aspire [əs'paɪə*] *vi* streben (*to* nach).

aspirin [æsprɪn] *n* Aspirin *nt*.

ass [æs] *n* (*lit, fig*) Esel *m*; (*US col!*) Arsch *m* (!).

assailant [ə'seɪlənt] *n* Angreifer *m*.

assassin [ə'sæsɪn] *n* Attentäter(in *f*) *m*; ~**ate** *vt* ermorden.

assault [ə'sɔːlt] *n* Angriff *m* // *vt* überfallen; (*woman*) herfallen über (+*acc*).

assemble [ə'sembl] *vt* versammeln; (*parts*) zusammensetzen // *vi* sich versammeln.

assembly [ə'semblɪ] *n* (*meeting*) Versammlung *f*; (*construction*) Zusammensetzung *f*, Montage *f*; ~ **line** *n* Fließband *nt*.

assent [ə'sent] *n* Zustimmung *f*.

assert [ə'sɜːt] *vt* erklären; ~**ion** [ə'sɜːʃən] *n* Behauptung *f*.

assess [ə'ses] *vt* schätzen; ~**ment** *n* Bewertung *f*, Einschätzung *f*; ~**or** *n* Steuerberater *m*.

asset [æset] *n* Vorteil *m*, Wert *m*; ~**s** *pl* Vermögen *nt*; (*estate*) Nachlaß *m*.

assiduous [ə'sɪdjuəs] *a* fleißig, aufmerksam.

assign [ə'saɪn] *vt* zuweisen.

assignment [ə'saɪnmənt] *n* Aufgabe *f*, Auftrag *m*.

assimilate [ə'sɪmɪleɪt] *vt* sich aneignen, aufnehmen.

assist [ə'sɪst] *vt* beistehen (+*dat*); ~**ance** *n* Unterstützung *f*, Hilfe *f*; ~**ant** *n* Assistent(in *f*) *m*, Mitarbeiter(in *f*) *m*; (*Brit: also*: **shop** ~**ant**) Verkäufer(in *f*) *m*.

assizes [ə'saɪzɪz] *npl* Landgericht *nt*.

associate [ə'səʊʃɪɪt] *n* (*partner*) Kollege *m*, Teilhaber *m*; (*member*) außerordentliche(s) Mitglied *nt* // [ə'səʊʃɪeɪt] verbinden (mit mit) // *vi* [ə'səʊʃɪeɪt] (*keep company*) verkehren (*with* mit).

association [əsəʊsɪ'eɪʃən] *n* Verband *m*, Verein *m*; (*PSYCH*) Assoziation *f*; (*link*) Verbindung *f*.

assorted [ə'sɔːtɪd] *a* gemischt.

assortment [ə'sɔːtmənt] *n* Sammlung *f*; (*COMM*) Sortiment *nt* (*of* von), Auswahl *f* (*of* an +*dat*).

assume [ə'sjuːm] *vt* (*take for granted*) annehmen; (*put on*) annehmen, sich geben; ~**d name** *n* Deckname *m*.

assumption [ə'sʌmpʃən] *n* Annahme *f*.

assurance [ə'ʃʊərəns] *n* (*firm statement*) Versicherung *f*; (*confidence*) Selbstsicherheit *f*; (*insurance*) (Lebens)versicherung *f*.

assure [ə'ʃʊə*] *vt* (*make sure*) sicherstellen; (*convince*) versichern (+*dat*); (*life*) versichern.

asterisk [æstərɪsk] *n* Sternchen *nt*.

astern [əs'tɜːn] *ad* achtern.

asthma [æsmə] *n* Asthma *nt*.

astonish [əsˈtɒnɪʃ] *vt* erstaunen; **~ment** *n* Erstaunen *nt*.

astound [əsˈtaund] *vt* verblüffen.

astray [əsˈtreɪ] *ad* in die Irre; auf Abwege; to go ~ (*go wrong*) sich vertun; to lead ~ irreführen.

astride [əsˈtraɪd] *ad* rittlings // *prep* rittlings auf.

astrologer [əsˈtrɒlədʒə*] *n* Astrologe *m*, Astrologin *f*.

astrology [əsˈtrɒlədʒɪ] *n* Astrologie *f*.

astronaut [ˈæstrənɔːt] *n* Astronaut(in *f*) *m*.

astronomer [əsˈtrɒnəmə*] *n* Astronom *m*.

astronomical [æstrəˈnɒmɪkəl] *a* astronomisch; (*success*) riesig.

astronomy [əsˈtrɒnəmɪ] *n* Astronomie *f*.

astute [əsˈtjuːt] *a* scharfsinnig; schlau, gerissen.

asylum [əˈsaɪləm] *n* (*home*) Heim *nt*; (*refuge*) Asyl *nt*.

at [æt, ət] *prep* **1** (*referring to position, direction*) an (+*dat*), bei (+*dat*); (*with place*) in (+*dat*); ~ **the top** an der Spitze; ~ **home/school** zu Hause/in der Schule; ~ **the baker's** beim Bäcker; to look ~ sth auf etw (*acc*) blicken; to throw sth ~ sb etw nach jdm werfen
2 (*referring to time*): ~ **4 o'clock** um 4 Uhr; ~ **night** bei Nacht; ~ **Christmas** zu Weihnachten; ~ **times** manchmal
3 (*referring to rates, speed etc*): ~ **£1** a kilo zu £1 pro Kilo; two ~ a time zwei auf einmal; ~ **50 km/h** mit 50 km/h
4 (*referring to manner*): ~ **a stroke** mit einem Schlag; ~ **peace** in Frieden
5 (*referring to activity*): to be ~ work bei der Arbeit sein; to play ~ cowboys Cowboy spielen; to be good ~ sth gut in etw (*dat*) sein
6 (*referring to cause*): **shocked/surprised/annoyed** ~ **sth** schockiert/überrascht/verärgert über etw (*acc*); I went ~ his suggestion ich ging auf seinen Vorschlag hin.

ate [et, eɪt] *pt of* **eat**.

atheist [ˈeɪθɪɪst] *n* Atheist(in *f*) *m*.

Athens [ˈæθɪnz] *n* Athen *nt*.

athlete [ˈæθliːt] *n* Athlet *m*, Sportler *m*.

athletic [æθˈletɪk] *a* sportlich, athletisch; **~s** *n* Leichtathletik *f*.

Atlantic [ətˈlæntɪk] *a* atlantisch // *n*: the ~ (*Ocean*) der Atlantik.

atlas [ˈætləs] *n* Atlas *m*.

atmosphere [ˈætməsfɪə*] *n* Atmosphäre *f*.

atom [ˈætəm] *n* Atom *nt*; (*fig*) bißchen *nt*; **~ic** [əˈtɒmɪk] *a* atomar, Atom-; **~(ic) bomb** *n* Atombombe *f*; **~izer** *n* Zerstäuber *m*.

atone [əˈtəun] *vi* sühnen (*for acc*).

atrocious [əˈtrəuʃəs] *a* gräßlich.

atrocity [əˈtrɒsɪtɪ] *n* Scheußlichkeit *f*; (*deed*) Greueltat *f*.

attach [əˈtætʃ] *vt* (*fasten*) befestigen; (*importance etc*) legen (*to* auf +*acc*), beimessen (*to dat*); to be ~ed to sb/sth an jdm/etw hängen.

attaché [əˈtæʃeɪ] *n* Attaché *m*; ~ **case** *n* Aktenkoffer *m*.

attachment [əˈtætʃmənt] *n* (*tool*) Zubehörteil *nt*; (*love*): ~ (*to* sb) Zuneigung *f* (zu jdm).

attack [əˈtæk] *vt* angreifen // *n* Angriff *m*; (*MED*) Anfall *m*; **~er** *n* Angreifer(in *f*) *m*.

attain [əˈteɪn] *vt* erreichen; **~ments** *npl* Kenntnisse *pl*.

attempt [əˈtempt] *n* Versuch *m* // *vt* versuchen; **~ed** murder Mordversuch *m*.

attend [əˈtend] *vt* (*go to*) teilnehmen (an +*dat*); (*lectures*) besuchen; to ~ to (*needs*) nachkommen (+*dat*); (*person*) sich kümmern um; **~ance** *n* (*presence*) Anwesenheit *f*; (*people present*) Besucherzahl *f*; good **~ance** gute Teilnahme; **~ant** *n* (*companion*) Begleiter(in *f*) *m*; Gesellschafter(in *f*) *m*; (*in car park etc*) Wächter(in *f*) *m*; (*servant*) Bedienstete(r) *mf* // *a* begleitend; (*fig*) damit verbunden.

attention [əˈtenʃən] *n* Aufmerksamkeit *f*; (*care*) Fürsorge *f*; (*for machine etc*) Pflege *f* // *interj* (*MIL*) Achtung!; **for the** ~ **of** ... zu Händen (von) ...

attentive *a* [əˈtentɪv] aufmerksam.

attest [əˈtest] *vi*: to ~ to sich verbürgen für.

attic [ˈætɪk] *n* Dachstube *f*, Mansarde *f*.

attitude [ˈætɪtjuːd] *n* (*mental*) Einstellung *f*.

attorney [əˈtɔːnɪ] *n* (*solicitor*) Rechtsanwalt *m*; A~ **General** *n* Justizminister *m*.

attract [əˈtrækt] *vt* anziehen; (*attention*) erregen; **~ion** [əˈtrækʃən] *n* Anziehungskraft *f*; (*thing*) Attraktion *f*; **~ive** *a* attraktiv.

attribute [ˈætrɪbjuːt] *n* Eigenschaft *f*, Attribut *nt* // *vt* [əˈtrɪbjuːt] zuschreiben (*to dat*).

attrition [əˈtrɪʃən] *n*: war of ~ Zermürbungskrieg *m*.

aubergine [ˈəubəʒiːn] *n* Aubergine *f*.

auburn [ˈɔːbən] *a* kastanienbraun.

auction [ˈɔːkʃən] *n* (*also*: sale by ~) Versteigerung *f*, Auktion *f* // *vt* versteigern; **~eer** [ɔːkʃəˈnɪə*] *n* Versteigerer *m*.

audacity [ɔːˈdæsɪtɪ] *n* (*boldness*) Wagemut *m*; (*impudence*) Unverfrorenheit *f*.

audible [ˈɔːdɪbl] *a* hörbar.

audience [ˈɔːdɪəns] *n* Zuhörer *pl*, Zuschauer *pl*; (*with king etc*) Audienz *f*.

audio-typist [ˈɔːdɪəuˈtaɪpɪst] *n* Phonotypistin *f*.

audio-visual [ˈɔːdɪəuˈvɪzjuəl] *a* audiovisuell.

audit [ˈɔːdɪt] vt prüfen.
audition [ɔːˈdɪʃən] n Probe f.
auditorium [ɔːdɪˈtɔːrɪəm] n Zuschauerraum m.
augment [ɔːgˈment] vt vermehren.
augur [ˈɔːgə*] vi bedeuten, voraussagen; this ~s well das ist ein gutes Omen.
August [ˈɔːgəst] n August m.
aunt [ɑːnt] n Tante f; ~y, ~ie n Tantchen n.
au pair [ˈəʊˈpɛə*] n (also: ~ girl) Au-pair-Mädchen n.
aura [ˈɔːrə] n Nimbus m.
auspices [ˈɔːspɪsɪz] npl: under the ~ of unter der Schirmherrschaft von.
auspicious [ɔːsˈpɪʃəs] a günstig; verheißungsvoll.
austere [ɒsˈtɪə*] a streng; (room) nüchtern.
austerity [ɒsˈterɪtɪ] n Strenge f; (POL) wirtschaftliche Einschränkung f.
Australia [ɒsˈtreɪlɪə] n Australien nt; ~n a australisch; // n Australier(in f) m.
Austria [ˈɒstrɪə] n Österreich nt; ~n a österreichisch // n Österreicher(in f) m.
authentic [ɔːˈθentɪk] a echt, authentisch.
author [ˈɔːθə*] n Autor m, Schriftsteller m; (beginner) Urheber m, Schöpfer m.
authoritarian [ɔːθɒrɪˈtɛərɪən] a autoritär.
authoritative [ɔːˈθɒrɪtətɪv] a (account) maßgeblich; (manner) herrisch.
authority [ɔːˈθɒrɪtɪ] n (power) Autorität f; (expert) Autorität f, Fachmann m; **the authorities** pl die Behörden pl.
authorize [ˈɔːθəraɪz] vt bevollmächtigen; (permit) genehmigen.
auto [ˈɔːtəʊ] n (US) Auto nt, Wagen m.
autobiography [ɔːtəʊbaɪˈɒgrəfɪ] n Autobiographie f.
autograph [ˈɔːtəgrɑːf] n (of celebrity) Autogramm nt // vt mit Autogramm versehen.
automatic [ɔːtəˈmætɪk] a automatisch // n (gun) Selbstladepistole f; (car) Automatik m; ~ally ad automatisch.
automobile [ˈɔːtəməbiːl] n (US) Auto(mobil) nt.
autonomous [ɔːˈtɒnəməs] a autonom.
autumn [ˈɔːtəm] n Herbst m.
auxiliary [ɔːgˈzɪlɪərɪ] a Hilfs-.
Av. abbr of **avenue**.
avail [əˈveɪl] vt: ~ o.s. of sth sich einer Sache bedienen // n: to no ~ nutzlos.
availability [əveɪləˈbɪlɪtɪ] n Erhältlichkeit f, Vorhandensein nt.
available [əˈveɪləbl] a erhältlich; zur Verfügung stehend; (person) erreichbar, abkömmlich.
avalanche [ˈævəlɑːnʃ] n Lawine f.
avarice [ˈævərɪs] n Habsucht f, Geiz m.
Ave. abbr of **avenue**.
avenge [əˈvendʒ] vt rächen, sühnen.

avenue [ˈævənjuː] n Allee f.
average [ˈævərɪdʒ] n Durchschnitt m // a durchschnittlich, Durchschnitts- // vt (figures) den Durchschnitt nehmen von; (perform) durchschnittlich leisten; (in car etc) im Schnitt fahren; **on** ~ durchschnittlich, im Durchschnitt; ~ **out** vi: to ~ out at im Durchschnitt betragen.
averse [əˈvɜːs] a: to be ~ to doing sth eine Abneigung dagegen haben, etw zu tun.
avert [əˈvɜːt] vt (turn away) abkehren; (prevent) abwehren.
aviary [ˈeɪvɪərɪ] n Vogelhaus nt.
aviation [eɪvɪˈeɪʃən] n Luftfahrt f, Flugwesen nt.
avid [ˈævɪd] a gierig (for auf +acc).
avocado [ævəˈkɑːdəʊ] n (also: Brit: ~ pear) Avocado(birne) f.
avoid [əˈvɔɪd] vt vermeiden; ~**ance** n Vermeidung f.
await [əˈweɪt] vt erwarten, entgegensehen (+dat).
awake [əˈweɪk] a wach // (v: pt **awoke**, pp **awoken** or **awaked**) vt (auf)wecken // vi aufwachen; to be ~ wach sein; ~**ning** n Erwachen nt.
award [əˈwɔːd] n (prize) Preis m // vt zuerkennen.
aware [əˈwɛə*] a bewußt; to be ~ sich bewußt sein (of gen); ~**ness** n Bewußtsein nt.
awash [əˈwɒʃ] a überflutet.
away [əˈweɪ] ad weg, fort; two hours ~ by car zwei Autostunden entfernt; the holiday was two weeks ~ es war noch zwei Wochen bis zum Urlaub; ~ **match** n (SPORT) Auswärtsspiel nt.
awe [ɔː] n Ehrfurcht f; ~-**inspiring**, ~**some** a ehrfurchtgebietend.
awful [ˈɔːful] a (very bad) furchtbar; ~**ly** ad furchtbar, sehr.
awkward [ˈɔːkwəd] a (clumsy) ungeschickt, linkisch; (embarrassing) peinlich.
awning [ˈɔːnɪŋ] n Markise f.
awoke [əˈwəʊk], **awoken** [əˈwəʊkən] pt, pp of **awake**.
awry [əˈraɪ] a,ad schief; to go ~ (person) fehlgehen; (plans) schiefgehen.
axe, (US) **ax** [æks] n Axt f, Beil nt // vt (end suddenly) streichen.
axis, pl **axes** [ˈæksɪs, -siːz] n Achse f.
axle [ˈæksl] n Achse f.
ay(e) [aɪ] interj (yes) ja; **the ayes** pl die Jastimmen pl.
azalea [əˈzeɪlɪə] n Azalee f.

B

B [biː] n (MUS) H nt.
B.A. n abbr of **Bachelor of Arts**.
babble [ˈbæbl] vi schwätzen; (stream)

murmeln.

baby ['beɪbɪ] n Baby nt, Säugling m; ~ **carriage** n (US) Kinderwagen m; ~-**sit** vi Kinder hüten, babysitten; ~-**sitter** n Babysitter m.

bachelor ['bætʃələ*] n Junggeselle m; **B~ of Arts/Science (B.A./B.Sc.)** Bakkalaureus m der philosophischen Fakultät/der Naturwissenschaften.

back [bæk] n (of person, horse) Rücken m; (of house) Rückseite f; (of train) Ende nt; (FOOTBALL) Verteidiger m // vt (support) unterstützen; (wager) wetten auf (+acc); (car) rückwärts fahren // vi (go backwards) rückwärts gehen or fahren // a hintere(r, s) // ad zurück; (to the rear) nach hinten; ~ **down** vi zurückstecken; ~ **out** vi sich zurückziehen; kneifen (col); ~ **up** vt (support) unterstützen; (car) zurücksetzen; (COMPUT) eine Sicherungskopie machen von; ~**bencher** n (Brit) Parlamentarier(in f) m; ~**bone** n Rückgrat nt; (support) Rückhalt m; ~**cloth** n Hintergrund m; ~**date** vt rückdatieren; ~**drop** n (THEAT) = ~**cloth**; (~ground) Hintergrund m; ~**fire** vi (plan) fehlschlagen; (TECH) fehlzünden; ~**ground** n Hintergrund m; (person's education) Vorbildung f, Family ~**ground** Familienverhältnisse pl; ~**hand** n (TENNIS: also: ~**hand stroke**) Rückhand f; ~**handed** a (shot) Rückhand-; (compliment) zweifelhaft; ~**hander** n (Brit: bribe) Schmiergeld nt; ~**ing** n (support) Unterstützung f; ~**lash** n (fig) Gegenschlag m; ~**log** n (of work) Rückstand m; ~ **number** n (PRESS) alte Nummer f; ~**pack** n Rucksack m; ~ **pay** n (Gehalts- or Lohn)nachzahlung f; ~ **payments** pl Zahlungsrückstände pl; ~ **seat** n (AUT) Rücksitz m; ~**side** n (col) Hintern m; ~**stage** ad hinter den Kulissen; ~**stroke** n Rückenschwimmen nt; ~**up** a (train) Zusatz-; (plane) Sonder-; (COMPUT) Sicherungs- // n (see a) Zusatzzug m; Sondermaschine f; Sicherungskopie f; ~**ward** a (less developed) zurückgeblieben; (primitive) rückständig; ~**wards** ad rückwärts; ~**water** n (fig) Kaff nt; ~**yard** n Hinterhof m.

bacon ['beɪkən] n Schinkenspeck m.

bacteria [bæk'tɪərɪə] npl Bakterien pl.

bad [bæd] a schlecht, schlimm; to go ~ schlecht werden.

bade [bæd] pt of **bid**.

badge [bædʒ] n Abzeichen nt.

badger ['bædʒə*] n Dachs m.

badly ['bædlɪ] ad schlecht, schlimm; ~ wounded schwerverwundet; he needs it ~ er braucht es dringend; to be ~ off (for money) dringend Geld nötig haben.

badminton ['bædmɪntən] n Federball m, Badminton nt.

bad-tempered ['bæd'tempəd] a schlecht gelaunt.

baffle ['bæfl] vt (puzzle) verblüffen.

bag [bæg] n (sack) Beutel m; (paper) Tüte f; (hand~) Tasche f; (suitcase) Koffer m; (booty) Jagdbeute f; (col: old woman) alte Schachtel f // vt (put in sack) in einen Sack stecken; (hunting) erlegen; ~**s of** (col: lots of) eine Menge (+acc).

baggage ['bægɪdʒ] n Gepäck nt.

baggy ['bægɪ] a bauschig, sackartig.

bagpipes ['bægpaɪps] npl Dudelsack m.

Bahamas [bə'hɑːməz] npl: the ~ die Bahamas pl.

bail [beɪl] n (money) Kaution f // vt (prisoner: gen: grant ~ to) gegen Kaution freilassen; (boat: also: ~ out) ausschöpfen; on ~ (prisoner) gegen Kaution freigelassen; to ~ **sb out** die Kaution für jdn stellen; see also **bale**.

bailiff ['beɪlɪf] n Gerichtsvollzieher(in f) m.

bait [beɪt] n Köder m // vt mit einem Köder versehen; (fig) ködern.

bake [beɪk] vti backen; ~**d beans** gebackene Bohnen pl; ~**r** n Bäcker m; ~**ry** n Bäckerei f.

baking ['beɪkɪŋ] n Backen nt; ~ **powder** n Backpulver nt.

balance ['bæləns] n (scales) Waage f; (equilibrium) Gleichgewicht nt; (FIN: state of account) Saldo m; (difference) Bilanz f; (amount remaining) Restbetrag m // vt (weigh) wägen; (make equal) ausgleichen; ~ **of trade/payments** Handels-/Zahlungsbilanz f; ~**d** a ausgeglichen; ~ **sheet** n Bilanz f, Rechnungsabschluß m.

balcony ['bælkənɪ] n Balkon m.

bald [bɔːld] a kahl; (statement) knapp.

bale [beɪl] n Ballen m; to ~ or bail out (from a plane) abspringen.

baleful ['beɪlful] a (sad) unglückselig; (evil) böse.

ball [bɔːl] n Ball m; ~ **bearing** n Kugellager nt.

ballet ['bæleɪ] n Ballett nt; ~ **dancer** n Ballettänzer(in f) m.

balloon [bə'luːn] n (Luft)ballon m.

ballot ['bælət] n (geheime) Abstimmung f.

ball-point (pen) ['bɔːlpɔɪnt('pen)] n Kugelschreiber m.

ballroom ['bɔːlrum] n Tanzsaal m.

balm [bɑːm] n Balsam m.

Baltic ['bɔːltɪk] n: the ~ (Sea) die Ostsee.

balustrade [bæləs'treɪd] n Brüstung f.

bamboo [bæm'buː] n Bambus m.

ban [bæn] n Verbot nt // vt verbieten.

banana [bə'nɑːnə] n Banane f.

band [bænd] n Band nt; (group) Gruppe f; (of criminals) Bande f; (MUS) Kapelle f, Band f // vi (+ together) sich zusammentun.

bandage ['bændɪdʒ] n Verband m; (elastic) Bandage f // vt (cut) verbinden; (broken limb) bandagieren.

bandaid ['bændeɪd] n (US) Heftpflaster nt.

bandwagon ['bændwægən] n: to jump on the ~ (fig) auf den fahrenden Zug aufspringen.

bandy ['bændɪ] vt wechseln; ~(-legged) a o-beinig.

bang [bæŋ] n (explosion) Knall m; (blow) Hieb m // vti knallen.

bangle ['bæŋgl] n Armspange f.

bangs [bæŋz] npl (US: fringe) Pony m.

banish ['bænɪʃ] vt verbannen.

banister(s) ['bænɪstə*(z)] n(pl) (Treppen)geländer nt.

bank [bæŋk] n (raised ground) Erdwall m; (of lake etc) Ufer nt; (FIN) Bank f // vt (tilt: AVIAT) in die Kurve bringen; (money) einzahlen; to ~ on sth mit etw rechnen; ~ account n Bankkonto nt; ~ card n Scheckkarte f; ~er n Bankier m; ~er's card n (Brit) = ~ card; B~ holiday n (Brit) gesetzliche(r) Feiertag m; ~ing n Bankwesen nt; ~note n Banknote f; ~ rate n Banksatz m.

bankrupt ['bæŋkrʌpt] a: to be ~ bankrott sein; to go ~ Pleite machen; ~cy n Bankrott m.

bank statement n Kontoauszug m.

banner ['bænə*] n Banner nt.

banns [bænz] npl Aufgebot nt.

baptism ['bæptɪzəm] n Taufe f.

baptize ['bæptaɪz] vt taufen.

bar [ba:*] n (rod) Stange f; (obstacle) Hindernis nt; (of chocolate) Tafel f; (of soap) Stück n; (for food, drink) Buffet nt, Bar f; (pub) Wirtschaft f; (MUS) Takt(strich) m // vt (fasten) verriegeln; (hinder) versperren; (exclude) ausschließen; behind ~s hinter Gittern; the B~: to be called to the B~ als Anwalt zugelassen werden; ~ none ohne Ausnahme.

barbaric [ba:'bærɪk] a primitiv, unkultiviert.

barbecue ['ba:bɪkju:] n Barbecue nt.

barbed wire ['ba:bd'waɪə*] n Stacheldraht m.

barber ['ba:bə*] n Herrenfriseur m.

bar code n (on goods) Registrierkode f.

bare [bɛə*] a nackt; (trees, country) kahl; (mere) bloß // vt entblößen; ~back ad ungesattelt; ~faced a unverfroren; ~foot a, ad barfuß; ~ly ad kaum, knapp.

bargain ['ba:gɪn] n (sth cheap) günstiger Kauf; (agreement: written) Kaufvertrag m; (: oral) Geschäft nt; into the ~ obendrein; ~ for vt: he got more than he ~ed for er erlebte sein blaues Wunder.

barge [ba:dʒ] n Lastkahn m; ~ in vi

hereinplatzen; ~ into vt rennen gegen.

bark [ba:k] n (of tree) Rinde f; (of dog) Bellen nt // vi (dog) bellen.

barley ['ba:lɪ] n Gerste f; ~ sugar n Malzbonbon nt.

barmaid ['ba:meɪd] n Bardame f.

barman ['ba:mən] n Barkellner m.

barn [ba:n] n Scheune f.

barometer [bə'rɒmɪtə*] n Barometer nt.

baron ['bærən] n Baron m; ~ess n Baronin f.

barracks ['bærəks] npl Kaserne f.

barrage ['bæra:ʒ] n (gunfire) Sperrfeuer nt; (dam) Staudamm m; Talsperre f.

barrel ['bærəl] n Faß nt; (of gun) Lauf m.

barren ['bærən] a unfruchtbar.

barricade [bærɪ'keɪd] n Barrikade f // vt verbarrikadieren.

barrier ['bærɪə*] n (obstruction) Hindernis nt; (fence) Schranke f.

barrister ['bærɪstə*] n (Brit) Rechtsanwalt m.

barrow ['bærəʊ] n (cart) Schubkarren m.

bartender ['ba:tendə*] n (US) Barmann or -kellner m.

barter ['ba:tə*] vt: to ~ sth for sth um etw handeln.

base [beɪs] n (bottom) Boden m, Basis f; (MIL) Stützpunkt m // vt gründen; (opinion, theory): to be ~d on basieren auf (+dat) // a (low) gemein; ~ball n Baseball m; ~ment n Kellergeschoß nt.

bases ['beɪsi:z] npl of **basis**; ['beɪsɪz] npl of **base**.

bash [bæʃ] vt (col) (heftig) schlagen.

bashful ['bæʃfʊl] a schüchtern.

basic ['beɪsɪk] a grundlegend; ~ally ad im Grunde.

basil ['bæzl] n Basilikum nt.

basin ['beɪsn] n (dish) Schüssel f; (for washing, also valley) Becken nt; (dock) (Trocken)becken nt.

basis ['beɪsɪs], pl -ses [-si:z] n Basis f, Grundlage f.

bask [ba:sk] vi: to ~ in the sun sich sonnen.

basket ['ba:skɪt] n Korb m; ~ball n Basketball m.

bass [beɪs] n (MUS, also instrument) Baß m; (voice) Baßstimme f.

bassoon [bə'su:n] n Fagott nt.

bastard ['ba:stəd] n Bastard m; (col!) Arschloch m (!).

bastion ['bæstɪən] n (lit, fig) Bollwerk nt.

bat [bæt] n (SPORT) Schlagholz nt; Schläger m; (ZOOL) Fledermaus f // vt: he didn't ~ an eyelid er hat nicht mit der Wimper gezuckt.

batch [bætʃ] n (of letters) Stoß m; (of samples) Satz m.

bated ['beɪtɪd] a: with ~ breath mit angehaltenem Atem.

bath [bɑ:θ] n Bad nt; (~ tub) Badewanne f; see also **baths** // vt baden; to have a ~ baden.

bathe [beɪð] vti baden; ~**r** n Badende(r) mf.

bathing ['beɪðɪŋ] n Baden nt; ~ **cap** n Badekappe f; ~ **costume**, (US) ~ **suit** n Badeanzug m; ~ **trunks** npl (Brit) Badehose f.

bathrobe ['bɑ:θrəʊb] n Bademantel m.

bathroom ['bɑ:θrʊm] n Bad(ezimmer) nt.

baths [bɑ:ðz] npl (Schwimm)bad nt.

bath towel n Badetuch nt.

batman ['bætmən] n (Offiziers)bursche m.

baton ['bætən] n (of police) Gummiknüppel m; (MUS) Taktstock m.

batter ['bætə*] vt verprügeln // n Schlagteig m; (for cake) Biskuitteig m; ~**ed** a (hat, pan) verbeult.

battery ['bætərɪ] n (ELEC) Batterie f; (MIL) Geschützbatterie f.

battle ['bætl] n Schlacht f; (small) Gefecht nt // vi kämpfen; ~**field** n Schlachtfeld nt; ~**ship** n Schlachtschiff nt.

bawdy ['bɔ:dɪ] a unflätig.

bawl [bɔ:l] vi brüllen.

bay [beɪ] n (of sea) Bucht f // vi bellen; to keep at ~ unter Kontrolle halten.

bay window n Erkerfenster nt.

bazaar [bə'zɑ:*] n Basar m.

b. & b., B. & B. abbr of **bed and breakfast**.

BBC n abbr (= British Broadcasting Corporation) BBC.

B.C. ad abbr (= before Christ) v. Chr.

be, pt **was**, **were**, pp **been** [bi:, wɒz, wɜ:*, bi:n] ◆aux v 1 (with present participle: forming continuous tenses): **what are you doing?** was machst du (gerade)?; **it is raining** es regnet; **I've been waiting for you for hours** ich warte schon seit Stunden auf dich
2 (with pp: forming passives): **to ~ killed** getötet werden; **the thief was no-where to ~ seen** der Dieb war nirgendwo zu sehen
3 (in tag questions): **it was fun, wasn't it?** es hat Spaß gemacht, nicht wahr?
4 (+ to +infinitive): **the house is to ~ sold** das Haus soll verkauft werden; **he's not to open it** er darf es nicht öffnen
◆v +complement **1** (gen) sein; **I'm tired** ich bin müde; **I'm hot/cold** mir ist heiß/kalt; **he's a doctor** er ist Arzt; **2 and 2 are 4** 2 und 2 ist or sind 4; **she's tall/pretty** sie ist groß/hübsch; ~ **careful/quiet** sei vorsichtig/ruhig
2 (of health): **how are you?** wie geht es dir?; **he's very ill** er ist sehr krank; **I'm better now** jetzt geht es mir besser
3 (of age): **how old are you?** wie alt bist

du? **I'm sixteen (years old)** ich bin sechzehn (Jahre alt)
4 (cost): **how much was the meal?** was or wieviel hat das Essen gekostet?; **that'll be £5.75, please** das macht £5.75, bitte
◆vi **1** (exist, occur etc) sein; **is there a God?** gibt es einen Gott?; ~ **that as it may** wie dem auch sei; **so** ~ **it** also gut
2 (referring to place) sein; **I won't** ~ **here tomorrow** ich werde morgen nicht hier sein
3 (referring to movement): **where have you been?** wo bist du gewesen?; **I've been in the garden** ich war im Garten
◆impers v **1** (referring to time, distance, weather) sein; **it's 5 o'clock** es ist 5 Uhr; **it's 10 km to the village** es sind 10 km bis zum Dorf; **it's too hot/cold** es ist zu heiß/kalt
2 (emphatic): **it's me** ich bin's; **it's the postman** es ist der Briefträger.

beach [bi:tʃ] n Strand m // vt (ship) auf den Strand setzen.

beacon ['bi:kən] n (signal) Leuchtfeuer nt; (traffic ~) Bake f.

bead [bi:d] n Perle f; (drop) Tropfen m.

beak [bi:k] n Schnabel m.

beaker ['bi:kə*] n Becher m.

beam [bi:m] n (of wood) Balken m; (of light) Strahl m; (smile) strahlende(s) Lächeln nt // vi strahlen.

bean [bi:n] n Bohne f; ~ **sprouts** npl Sojasprossen pl.

bear [beə*] n Bär m // v (pt **bore**, pp **borne**) vt (weight, crops) tragen; (tolerate) ertragen; (young) gebären // vi: **to** ~ **right/left** sich rechts/links halten; ~ **out** vt (suspicions etc) bestätigen; ~ **up** vi sich halten.

beard [bɪəd] n Bart m; ~**ed** a bärtig.

bearer ['beərə*] n Träger m.

bearing ['beərɪŋ] n (posture) Haltung f; (relevance) Relevanz f; (relation) Bedeutung f; (TECH) Kugellager nt; ~**s** pl (direction) Orientierung f; (ball) ~**s** pl (Kugel)lager nt.

beast [bi:st] n Tier nt, Vieh nt; (person) Bestie f; (nasty person) Biest nt; ~**ly** a viehisch; (col) scheußlich.

beat [bi:t] n (stroke) Schlag m; (pulsation) (Herz)schlag m; (police round) Runde f; Revier nt; (MUS) Takt m; Beat m // vti, pt **beat**, pp **beaten** schlagen; **to** ~ **it** abhauen; ~ **off** vt abschlagen; ~ **up** vt zusammenschlagen; ~**en** a: **off the** ~**en track** abgelegen; ~**ing** n Prügel pl.

beautiful ['bju:tɪful] a schön; ~**ly** ad ausgezeichnet.

beauty ['bju:tɪ] n Schönheit f; ~ **salon** n Schönheitssalon m; ~ **spot** n Schönheitsfleck m; (Brit: TOURISM) (besonders) schöne(r) Ort m.

beaver ['bi:və*] n Biber m.

became [bɪ'keɪm] pt of **become**.
because [bɪ'kɒz] cj weil // prep: ~ **of** wegen (+gen or (col) dat).
beck [bek] n: to be at the ~ and call of sb nach jds Pfeife tanzen.
beckon ['bekən] vt (also: ~ **to**) ein Zeichen geben (sb jdm).
become [bɪ'kʌm] (irreg: like **come**) vt werden; (clothes) stehen (+dat) // vi werden.
becoming [bɪ'kʌmɪŋ] a (suitable) schicklich; (clothes) kleidsam.
bed [bed] n Bett nt; (of river) Flußbett nt; (foundation) Schicht f; (in garden) Beet nt; to go to ~ zu Bett gehen; single/double ~ Einzel/Doppelbett nt; ~ **and breakfast** n Übernachtung f mit Frühstück; ~**clothes** npl Bettwäsche f; ~**ding** n Bettzeug nt.
bedlam ['bedləm] n (uproar) tolle(s) Durcheinander nt.
bedraggled [bɪ'drægld] a ramponiert.
bedridden ['bedrɪdn] a bettlägerig.
bedroom ['bedrʊm] n Schlafzimmer nt.
bedside ['bedsaɪd] n: at the ~ am Bett.
bed-sitter ['bed'sɪtə*] n (Brit) Einzimmerwohnung f, möblierte(s) Zimmer nt.
bedspread ['bedspred] n Tagesdecke f.
bedtime ['bedtaɪm] n Schlafenszeit f.
bee [biː] n Biene f.
beech [biːtʃ] n Buche f.
beef [biːf] n Rindfleisch nt; roast ~ Roastbeef nt; ~**burger** n Hamburger m.
beehive ['biːhaɪv] n Bienenstock m.
beeline ['biːlaɪn] n: to make a ~ for schnurstracks zugehen auf (+acc).
been [biːn] pp of **be**.
beer [bɪə*] n Bier nt.
beetle ['biːtl] n Käfer m.
beetroot ['biːtruːt] n (Brit) rote Bete f.
before [bɪ'fɔː*] prep vor // cj bevor // ad (of time) zuvor; früher; the week ~ die Woche zuvor or vorher; I've done it ~ das hab' ich schon mal getan; ~**hand** ad im voraus.
beg [beg] vti (implore) dringend bitten; (alms) betteln.
began [bɪ'gæn] pt of **begin**.
beggar ['begə*] n Bettler(in f) m.
begin [bɪ'gɪn], pt **began**, pp **begun** vti anfangen, beginnen; (found) gründen; to ~ **doing** or to do sth anfangen or beginnen, etw zu tun; to ~ **with** zunächst (einmal); ~**ner** n Anfänger m; ~**ning** n Anfang m.
begun [bɪ'gʌn] pp of **begin**.
behalf [bɪ'hɑːf] n: on ~ **of** im Namen (+gen); on my ~ für mich.
behave [bɪ'heɪv] vi sich benehmen.
behaviour, (US) **behavior** [bɪ'heɪvjə*] n Benehmen nt.
behead [bɪ'hed] vt enthaupten.
beheld [bɪ'held] pt, pp of **behold**.
behind [bɪ'haɪnd] prep hinter // ad (late)

im Rückstand; (in the rear) hinten // n (col) Hinterteil nt; ~ **the scenes** (fig) hinter den Kulissen.
behold [bɪ'həʊld] (irreg: like **hold**) vt (old) erblicken.
beige [beɪʒ] a beige.
being ['biːɪŋ] n (existence) (Da)sein nt; (person) Wesen nt; to come into ~ entstehen.
belated [bɪ'leɪtɪd] a verspätet.
belch [beltʃ] vi rülpsen // vt (smoke) ausspeien.
belfry ['belfrɪ] n Glockenturm m.
Belgian ['beldʒən] a belgisch // n Belgier(in f) m.
Belgium ['beldʒəm] n Belgien nt.
belie [bɪ'laɪ] vt Lügen strafen (+acc).
belief [bɪ'liːf] n Glaube m (in an +acc); (conviction) Überzeugung f.
believe [bɪ'liːv] vt glauben (+dat); (think) glauben, meinen, denken // vi (have faith) glauben; to ~ **in** sth an etw (acc) glauben; ~**r** n Gläubige(r) mf.
belittle [bɪ'lɪtl] vt herabsetzen.
bell [bel] n Glocke f.
belligerent [bɪ'lɪdʒərənt] a (person) streitsüchtig; (country) kriegsführend.
bellow ['beləʊ] vti brüllen.
bellows ['beləʊz] npl (TECH) Gebläse nt; (for fire) Blasebalg m.
belly ['belɪ] n Bauch m.
belong [bɪ'lɒŋ] vi gehören (to sb jdm); (to club) angehören (+dat); it does not ~ **here** es gehört nicht hierher; ~**ings** npl Habe f.
beloved [bɪ'lʌvɪd] a innig geliebt // n Geliebte(r) mf.
below [bɪ'ləʊ] prep unter // ad unten.
belt [belt] n (band) Riemen m; (round waist) Gürtel m // vt (fasten) mit Riemen befestigen; (col: beat) schlagen; ~**way** n (US AUT: ring road) Umgehungsstraße f.
bemused [bɪ'mjuːzd] a verwirrt.
bench [bentʃ] n (seat) Bank f; (workshop) Werkbank f; (judge's seat) Richterbank f; (judges) Richter pl.
bend [bend], pt, pp **bent** vt (curve) biegen; (stoop) beugen // vi sich biegen; sich beugen // n Biegung f; (Brit: in road) Kurve f; ~ **down** or **over** vi sich bücken.
beneath [bɪ'niːθ] prep unter // ad darunter.
benefactor ['benɪfæktə*] n Wohltäter(in f) m.
beneficial [benɪ'fɪʃl] a vorteilhaft; (to health) heilsam.
benefit ['benɪfɪt] n (advantage) Nutzen m // vt fördern // vi Nutzen ziehen (from aus).
Benelux ['benɪlʌks] n Beneluxstaaten pl.
benevolent [bɪ'nevələnt] a wohlwollend.
benign [bɪ'naɪn] a (person) gütig; (climate) mild.

bent [bent] *pt, pp of* **bend** // *n* (*inclination*) Neigung *f* // *a* (*col: dishonest*) unehrlich; **to be ~ on** versessen sein auf (+*acc*).

bequest [bɪ'kwest] *n* Vermächtnis *nt*.

bereaved [bɪ'riːvd] *npl:* **the ~** die Hinterbliebenen *pl*.

bereft [bɪ'reft] *a:* **~ of** bar (+*gen*).

beret ['berɪ] *n* Baskenmütze *f*.

Berlin [bɜː'lɪn] *n* Berlin *nt*.

berm [bɜːm] *n* (*US AUT*) Seitenstreifen *m*.

Bermuda [bɜː'mjuːdə] *n* Bermuda *nt*.

berry ['berɪ] *n* Beere *f*.

berserk [bə'sɜːk] *a:* **to go ~** wild werden.

berth [bɜːθ] *n* (*for ship*) Ankerplatz *m*; (*in ship*) Koje *f*; (*in train*) Bett *nt* // *vt* am Kai festmachen // *vi* anlegen.

beseech [bɪ'siːtʃ], *pt, pp* **besought** [-sɔːt] *vt* anflehen.

beset [bɪ'set], *pt, pp* **beset** *vt* bedrängen.

beside [bɪ'saɪd] *prep* neben, bei; (*except*) außer; **to be ~ o.s.** außer sich sein (*with* vor +*dat*); **that's ~ the point** das tut nichts zur Sache.

besides [bɪ'saɪdz] *prep* außer, neben // *ad* außerdem.

besiege [bɪ'siːdʒ] *vt* (*MIL*) belagern; (*surround*) umlagern, bedrängen.

best [best] *a* beste(r, s) // *ad* am besten; **the ~ part of** (*quantity*) das meiste (+*gen*); **at ~** höchstens; **to make the ~ of it** das Beste daraus machen; **to do one's ~** sein Bestes tun; **to the ~ of my knowledge** meines Wissens; **to the ~ of my ability** so gut ich kann; **for the ~** zum Besten; **~ man** *n* Trauzeuge *m*.

bestow [bɪ'stəu] *vt* verleihen.

bet [bet] *n* Wette *f* // *vti, pt, pp* **bet** *or* **betted** wetten.

betray [bɪ'treɪ] *vt* verraten.

better ['betə*] *a, ad* besser // *vt* verbessern // *n:* **to get the ~ of sb** jdn überwinden; **he thought ~ of it** er hat sich eines Besseren besonnen; **you had ~ leave** Sie gehen jetzt wohl besser; **to get ~** (*MED*) gesund werden; **~ off** *a* (*richer*) wohlhabender.

betting ['betɪŋ] *n* Wetten *nt*; **~ shop** *n* (*Brit*) Wettbüro *nt*.

between [bɪ'twiːn] *prep* zwischen; (*among*) unter // *ad* dazwischen.

beverage ['bevərɪdʒ] *n* Getränk *nt*.

bevy ['bevɪ] *n* Schar *f*.

beware [bɪ'weə*] *vti* sich hüten vor (+*dat*); **'~ of the dog'** 'Vorsicht, bissiger Hund!'

bewildered [bɪ'wɪldəd] *a* verwirrt.

bewitching [bɪ'wɪtʃɪŋ] *a* bestrickend.

beyond [bɪ'jɒnd] *prep* (*place*) jenseits (+*gen*); (*time*) über ... hinaus; (*out of reach*) außerhalb (+*gen*) // *ad* darüber hinaus; **~ doubt** ohne Zweifel; **~ repair** nicht mehr zu reparieren.

bias ['baɪəs] *n* (*slant*) Neigung *f*; (*prejudice*) Vorurteil *nt*; **~(s)ed** *a* voreingenommen.

bib [bɪb] *n* Latz *m*.

Bible ['baɪbl] *n* Bibel *f*.

bicarbonate of soda [baɪ'kɑːbəneɪt-əv'səudə] *n* Natron *nt*.

bicker ['bɪkə*] *vi* zanken.

bicycle ['baɪsɪkl] *n* Fahrrad *nt*.

bid [bɪd] *n* (*offer*) Gebot *nt*; (*attempt*) Versuch *m* // *vti, pt* **bade** [bæd] *or* **bid**, *pp* **bidden** ['bɪdn] *or* **bid** (*offer*) bieten; **to ~ farewell** Lebewohl sagen; **~der** *n* (*person*) Steigerer *m*; **the highest ~der** der Meistbietende; **~ding** *n* (*command*) Geheiß *nt*.

bide [baɪd] *vt:* **~ one's time** abwarten.

bifocals [baɪ'fəukəlz] *npl* Bifokalbrille *f*.

big [bɪg] *a* groß.

big dipper *n* Achterbahn *f*.

bigheaded ['bɪg'hedɪd] *a* eingebildet.

bigot ['bɪgət] *n* Frömmler *m*; **~ed** *a* bigott; **~ry** *n* Bigotterie *f*.

big top *n* Zirkuszelt *nt*.

bike [baɪk] *n* Rad *nt*.

bikini [bɪ'kiːnɪ] *n* Bikini *m*.

bile [baɪl] *n* (*BIOL*) Galle *f*.

bilingual [baɪ'lɪŋgwəl] *a* zweisprachig.

bill [bɪl] *n* (*account*) Rechnung *f*; (*POL*) Gesetzentwurf *m*; (*US FIN*) Geldschein *m*; **to fit** *or* **fill the ~** (*fig*) der/die/das richtige sein; **'post no ~s'** 'Plakate ankleben verboten'; **~board** *n* Reklameschild *nt*.

billet ['bɪlɪt] *n* Quartier *nt*.

billfold ['bɪlfəuld] *n* (*US*) Geldscheintasche *f*.

billion ['bɪlɪən] *n* Billion *f*; (*US*) Milliarde *f*.

bin [bɪn] *n* Kasten *m*; (*dust~*) (Abfall)eimer *m*; **litter ~** *n* Abfalleimer *m*.

bind [baɪnd], *pt, pp* **bound** *vt* (*tie*) binden; (*tie together*) zusammenbinden; (*oblige*) verpflichten; **~ing** *n* (Buch)einband *m* // *a* verbindlich.

binge [bɪndʒ] *n* (*col*) Sauferei *f*.

bingo ['bɪŋgəu] *n* Bingo *nt*.

binoculars [bɪ'nɒkjuləz] *npl* Fernglas *nt*.

biochemistry ['baɪəu'kemɪstrɪ] *n* Biochemie *f*.

biography [baɪ'ɒgrəfɪ] *n* Biographie *f*.

biological [baɪə'lɒdʒɪkəl] *a* biologisch.

biology [baɪ'ɒlədʒɪ] *n* Biologie *f*.

birch [bɜːtʃ] *n* Birke *f*.

bird [bɜːd] *n* Vogel *m*; (*Brit col: girl*) Mädchen *nt*; **~'s-eye view** *n* Vogelschau *f*; **~ watcher** *n* Vogelbeobachter(in *f*) *m*.

Biro ['baɪrəu] *n* ® Kugelschreiber *m*.

birth [bɜːθ] *n* Geburt *f*; **to give ~ to** zur Welt bringen; **~ certificate** *n*

Geburtsurkunde f; ~ **control** n Geburtenkontrolle f; ~**day** n Geburtstag m; ~**place** n Geburtsort m; ~ **rate** n Geburtenrate f.

biscuit ['bɪskɪt] n Keks m.

bisect [baɪ'sekt] vt halbieren.

bishop ['bɪʃəp] n Bischof m.

bit [bɪt] pt of **bite** // n bißchen, Stückchen nt; (horse's) Gebiß nt; (COMPUT) Bit nt; a ~ **tired** etwas müde.

bitch [bɪtʃ] n (dog) Hündin f; (unpleasant woman) Weibsstück nt.

bite [baɪt], pt **bit**, pp **bitten** vti beißen // n Biß m; (mouthful) Bissen m; let's have a ~ **to eat** laß uns etwas essen; **to** ~ **one's nails** Nägel kauen.

biting ['baɪtɪŋ] a beißend.

bitten ['bɪtn] pp of **bite**.

bitter ['bɪtə*] a bitter; (memory etc) schmerzlich; (person) verbittert // n (Brit: beer) dunkles Bier; ~**ness** n Bitterkeit f.

blab [blæb] vi klatschen // vt (also: ~ **out**) ausplaudern.

black [blæk] a schwarz; (night) finster // vt schwärzen; (shoes) wichsen; (eye) blau schlagen; (Brit INDUSTRY) boykottieren; **to give sb a** ~ **eye** jdm ein blaues Auge schlagen; **in the** ~ (bank account) in den schwarzen Zahlen; ~ **and blue** a grün und blau; ~**berry** n Brombeere f; ~**bird** n Amsel f; ~**board** n (Wand)tafel f; ~**currant** n schwarze Johannisbeere f; ~**en** vt schwärzen; (fig) verunglimpfen; ~**ice** n Glatteis nt; ~**jack** n (US) Siebzehn und Vier; ~**leg** n (Brit) Streikbrecher(in f) m; ~**list** n schwarze Liste f; ~**mail** n Erpressung f // vt erpressen; ~ **market** n Schwarzmarkt m; ~**out** n Verdunklung f; (MED): **to have a** ~**out** bewußtlos werden; **the B~ Sea** n das Schwarze Meer; ~ **sheep** n schwarze(s) Schaf nt; ~**smith** n Schmied m; ~ **spot** n (AUT) Gefahrenstelle f; (for unemployment etc) schwer betroffene(s) Gebiet nt.

bladder ['blædə*] n Blase f.

blade [bleɪd] n (of weapon) Klinge f; (of grass) Halm m; (of oar) Ruderblatt nt.

blame [bleɪm] n Tadel m, Schuld f // vt Vorwürfe machen (+dat); **to** ~ **sb for sth** jdm die Schuld an etw (dat) geben; **he is to** ~ **er** ist daran schuld.

bland [blænd] a mild.

blank [blæŋk] a leer, unbeschrieben; (look) verdutzt; (verse) Blank- // n (space) Lücke f; Zwischenraum m; (cartridge) Platzpatrone f; ~ **cheque** n Blankoscheck m; (fig) Freibrief m.

blanket ['blæŋkɪt] n (Woll)decke f.

blare [blɛə*] vi (radio) plärren; (horn) tuten; (MUS) schmettern.

blasé ['blɑːzeɪ] a blasiert.

blast [blɑːst] n Explosion f; (of wind) Windstoß m // vt (blow up) sprengen; ~!

(col) verflixt!; ~**-off** n (SPACE) (Raketen)abschuß m.

blatant ['bleɪtənt] a offenkundig.

blaze [bleɪz] n (fire) lodernde(s) Feuer nt // vi lodern // vt: ~ **a trail** Bahn brechen.

blazer ['bleɪzə*] n Blazer m.

bleach [bliːtʃ] n (also: **household** ~) Bleichmittel nt // vt bleichen.

bleachers ['bliːtʃəz] npl (US SPORT) unüberdachte Tribüne.

bleak [bliːk] a kahl, rauh; (future) trostlos.

bleary-eyed ['blɪəraɪd] a triefäugig; (on waking up) mit verschlafenen Augen.

bleat [bliːt] vi blöken; (fig: complain) meckern.

bleed [bliːd] v (pt, pp **bled** [bled]) vi bluten // vt (draw blood) zur Ader lassen; **to** ~ **to death** verbluten.

bleeper ['bliːpə*] n (of doctor etc) Funkrufempfänger m.

blemish ['blemɪʃ] n Makel m // vt verunstalten.

blend [blend] n Mischung f // vt mischen // vi sich mischen.

bless [bles], pt, pp **blessed** or **blest** [blest] vt segnen; (give thanks) preisen; (make happy) glücklich machen; ~ **you!** Gesundheit!; ~**ing** n Segen m; (at table) Tischgebet nt; (happiness) Wohltat f; Segen m; (good wish) Glück nt.

blew [bluː] pt of **blow**.

blight [blaɪt] vt zunichte machen.

blimey ['blaɪmɪ] interj (Brit col) verflucht.

blind [blaɪnd] a blind; (corner) unübersichtlich // n (for window) Rouleau nt // vt blenden; ~ **alley** n Sackgasse f; ~**fold** n Augenbinde f // a, ad mit verbundenen Augen // vt die Augen verbinden (sb jdm); ~**ly** ad blind; (fig) blindlings; ~**ness** n Blindheit f; ~ **spot** n (AUT) toter Winkel m; (fig) schwache(r) Punkt m.

blink [blɪŋk] vi blinzeln; ~**ers** npl Scheuklappen pl.

bliss [blɪs] n (Glück)seligkeit f.

blister ['blɪstə*] n Blase f // vi Blasen werfen.

blithe [blaɪð] a munter.

blitz [blɪts] n Luftkrieg m.

blizzard ['blɪzəd] n Schneesturm m.

bloated ['bləʊtɪd] a aufgedunsen; (col: full) nudelsatt.

blob [blɒb] n Klümpchen nt.

bloc [blɒk] n (POL) Block m.

block [blɒk] n (of wood) Block m, Klotz m; (of houses) Häuserblock m // vt hemmen; ~**ade** [blɒ'keɪd] n Blockade f // vt blockieren; ~**age** n Verstopfung f; ~**buster** n Knüller m; ~ **of flats** n (Brit) Häuserblock m; ~ **letters** pl Blockbuchstaben pl.

bloke [bləʊk] *n* (*Brit col*) Kerl *m*, Typ *m*.

blond(e) [blɒnd] *a* blond // *n* Blondine *f*.

blood [blʌd] *n* Blut *nt*; ~ **donor** *n* Blutspender *m*; ~ **group** *n* Blutgruppe *f*; ~ **pressure** *n* Blutdruck *m*; ~**shed** *n* Blutvergießen *nt*; ~**shot** *a* blutunterlaufen; ~**stained** *a* blutbefleckt; ~**stream** *n* Blut *nt*, Blutkreislauf *m*; ~ **test** *n* Blutprobe *f*; ~**thirsty** *a* blutdürstig; ~**y** *a* (*Brit col!*) verdammt; (*lit*) blutig; ~**y-minded** *a* (*Brit col*) stur.

bloom [bluːm] *n* Blüte *f*; (*freshness*) Glanz *m* // *vi* blühen.

blossom ['blɒsəm] *n* Blüte *f* // *vi* blühen.

blot [blɒt] *n* Klecks *m* // *vt* beklecksen; (*ink*) (ab)löschen; ~ **out** *vt* auslöschen.

blotchy ['blɒtʃɪ] *a* fleckig.

blotting paper ['blɒtɪŋpeɪpə*] *n* Löschpapier *nt*.

blouse [blaʊz] *n* Bluse *f*.

blow [bləʊ] *n* Schlag *m* // *v* (*pt* **blew**, *pp* **blown** [bləʊn]) *vt* blasen // *vi* (*wind*) wehen; to ~ **one's nose** sich (*dat*) die Nase putzen; ~ **away** *vt* wegblasen; ~ **down** *vt* unwehen; ~ **out** *vi* ausgehen; ~ **over** *vi* vorübergehen; ~ **up** *vi* explodieren // *vt* sprengen; ~~**dry** *n*: to have a ~~**dry** sich fönen lassen // *vt* fönen; ~**lamp** *n* (*Brit*) Lötlampe *f*; ~**out** *n* (*AUT*) geplatzte(r) Reifen *m*; ~**torch** *n* = ~**lamp**.

blue [bluː] *a* blau; (*col: unhappy*) niedergeschlagen; (*obscene*) pornographisch; (*joke*) anzüglich; **out of the** ~ (*fig*) aus heiterem Himmel; **to have the** ~**s** traurig sein; ~**bell** *n* Glockenblume *f*; ~**bottle** *n* Schmeißfliege *f*; ~ **film** *n* Pornofilm *m*; ~**print** *n* (*fig*) Entwurf *m*.

bluff [blʌf] *vi* bluffen, täuschen // *n* (*deception*) Bluff *m*; to call sb's ~ es darauf ankommen lassen.

blunder ['blʌndə*] *n* grobe(r) Fehler *m*, Schnitzer *m* // *vi* einen groben Fehler machen.

blunt [blʌnt] *a* (*knife*) stumpf; (*talk*) unverblümt // *vt* abstumpfen.

blur [blɜː*] *n* Fleck *m* // *vt* verschwommen machen.

blurb [blɜːb] *n* Waschzettel *m*.

blurt [blɜːt] *vt*: ~ **out** herausplatzen mit.

blush [blʌʃ] *vi* erröten // *n* (Scham)röte *f*.

blustery ['blʌstərɪ] *a* stürmisch.

boar [bɔː*] *n* Keiler *m*, Eber *m*.

board [bɔːd] *n* (*of wood*) Brett *nt*; (*of card*) Pappe *f*; (*committee*) Ausschuß *m*; (*of firm*) Aufsichtsrat *m*; (*SCH*) Direktorium *nt*; (*NAUT, AVIAT*): **on** ~ an Bord // *vt* (*train*) einsteigen in (+*acc*); (*ship*) an Bord gehen (+*gen*); ~ **and lodging** *n* Unterkunft *f* und Verpflegung; **full/half** ~ (*Brit*) Voll-/Halbpension *f*; **to go by the** ~ flachfallen, über Bord

gehen; ~ **up** *vt* mit Brettern vernageln; ~**er** *n* Kostgänger *m*; (*SCH*) Internatsschüler(in *f*) *m*; ~**ing card** *n* (*AVIAT, NAUT*) Bordkarte *f*; ~**ing house** *n* Pension *f*; ~**ing school** *n* Internat *nt*; ~ **room** *n* Sitzungszimmer *nt*.

boast [bəʊst] *vi* prahlen (*about, of* mit) // *vt* sich rühmen (+*gen*) // *n* Großtuerei *f*; Prahlerei *f*.

boat [bəʊt] *n* Boot *nt*; (*ship*) Schiff *nt*; ~**er** *n* (*hat*) Kreissäge *f*; ~**swain** ['bəʊsn] *n* = **bosun**.

bob [bɒb] *vi* sich auf und nieder bewegen; ~ **up** *vi* auftauchen // *n* (*Brit col*) = **shilling**.

bobbin ['bɒbɪn] *n* Spule *f*.

bobby ['bɒbɪ] *n* (*Brit col*) Bobby *m*.

bobsleigh ['bɒbsleɪ] *n* Bob *m*.

bode [bəʊd] *vi*: to ~ **well/ill** ein gutes/ schlechtes Zeichen sein.

bodily ['bɒdɪlɪ] *a, ad* körperlich.

body ['bɒdɪ] *n* Körper *m*; (*dead*) Leiche *f*; (*group*) Mannschaft *f*; (*AUT*) Karosserie *f*; (*trunk*) Rumpf *m*; ~**guard** *n* Leibwache *f*; ~**work** *n* Karosserie *f*.

bog [bɒg] *n* Sumpf *m* // *vt*: **to get** ~**ged down** sich festfahren.

boggle ['bɒgl] *vi* stutzen; **the mind** ~**s** es ist kaum auszumalen.

bogus ['bəʊgəs] *a* unecht, Schein-.

boil [bɔɪl] *vti* kochen // *n* (*MED*) Geschwür *nt*; **to come to the** (*Brit*) **or a** (*US*) ~ zu kochen anfangen; **to** ~ **down to** (*fig*) hinauslaufen auf (+*acc*); ~ **over** *vi* überkochen; ~**ed potatoes** *npl* Salzkartoffeln *pl*; ~**er** *n* Boiler *m*; ~**er suit** *n* (*Brit*) Arbeitsanzug *m*; ~**ing point** *n* Siedepunkt *m*.

boisterous ['bɔɪstərəs] *a* ungestüm.

bold [bəʊld] *a* (*fearless*) unerschrocken; (*handwriting*) fest und klar.

bollard ['bɒləd] *n* (*NAUT*) Poller *m*; (*Brit AUT*) Pfosten *m*.

bolster ['bəʊlstə*] *n* Polster *nt*; ~ **up** *vt* unterstützen.

bolt [bəʊlt] *n* Bolzen *m*; (*lock*) Riegel *m* // *ad*: ~ **upright** kerzengerade // *vt* verriegeln; (*swallow*) verschlingen // *vi* (*horse*) durchgehen.

bomb [bɒm] *n* Bombe *f* // *vt* bombardieren; ~**ard** [bɒm'bɑːd] *vt* bombardieren; ~**ardment** [bɒm'bɑːdmənt] *n* Beschießung *f*; ~**shell** *n* (*fig*) Bombe *f*.

bona fide ['bəʊnə'faɪdɪ] *a* echt.

bond [bɒnd] *n* (*link*) Band *nt*; (*FIN*) Schuldverschreibung *f*.

bondage ['bɒndɪdʒ] *n* Sklaverei *f*.

bone [bəʊn] *n* Knochen *m*; (*of fish*) Gräte *f*; (*piece of* ~) Knochensplitter *m* // *vt* die Knochen herausnehmen (+*dat*); (*fish*) entgräten; ~ **idle** *a* stinkfaul.

bonfire ['bɒnfaɪə*] *n* Feuer *nt* im Freien.

bonnet ['bɒnɪt] n Haube f; (for baby) Häubchen nt; (Brit AUT) Motorhaube f.

bonus ['bəʊnəs] n Bonus m; (annual ~) Prämie f.

bony ['bəʊnɪ] a knochig, knochendürr.

boo [buː] vt auspfeifen.

booby trap ['buːbɪ-] n Falle f.

book [bʊk] n Buch nt; (COMM): ~s Bücher pl // vt (ticket etc) vorbestellen; (person) verwarnen; ~**case** n Bücherregal nt, Bücherschrank m; ~**ing office** n (Brit RAIL) Fahrkartenschalter m; (Brit THEAT) Vorverkaufsstelle f; ~**keeping** n Buchhaltung f; ~**let** n Broschüre f; ~**maker** n Buchmacher m; ~**seller** n Buchhändler m; ~**shop**, ~**store** n Buchhandlung f.

boom [buːm] n (noise) Dröhnen nt; (busy period) Hochkonjunktur f // vi dröhnen.

boon [buːn] n Wohltat f, Segen m.

boost [buːst] n Auftrieb m; (fig) Reklame f // vt Auftrieb geben; ~**er** n (MED) Wiederholungsimpfung f.

boot [buːt] n Stiefel m; (Brit AUT) Kofferraum m // vt (kick) einen Fußtritt geben; (COMPUT) laden; to ~ (in addition) obendrein.

booth [buːð] n (at fair) Bude f; (telephone ~) Zelle f; (voting ~) Kabine f.

booty ['buːtɪ] n Beute f.

booze [buːz] n (col) Alkohol m, Schnaps m // vi saufen.

border ['bɔːdə*] n Grenze f; (edge) Kante f; (in garden) (Blumen)rabatte f // a Grenz-; (in garden) (Blumen)rabatte f // a Grenz-; the B~s Grenzregion f zwischen England und Schottland; ~ **on** vt grenzen an (+acc); ~**line** n Grenze f.

bore [bɔː*] pt of bear // vt bohren; (weary) langweilen // n (person) langweilige(r) Mensch m; (thing) langweilige Sache f; (of gun) Kaliber nt; I am ~d ich langweile mich; ~**dom** n Langeweile f.

boring ['bɔːrɪŋ] a langweilig.

born [bɔːn] a: to be ~ geboren werden.

borne [bɔːn] pp of bear.

borough ['bʌrə] n Stadt(gemeinde) f, Stadtbezirk m.

borrow ['bɒrəʊ] vt borgen.

bosom ['bʊzəm] n Busen m.

boss [bɒs] n Chef m, Boß m // vt: ~ around herumkommandieren; ~**y** a herrisch.

bosun ['bəʊsn] n Bootsmann m.

botany ['bɒtənɪ] n Botanik f.

botch [bɒtʃ] vt (also: ~ up) verpfuschen.

both [bəʊθ] a beide(s); ~ (of) the books beide Bücher // pron beide(s) // ad: ~ X and Y sowohl X wie or als auch Y.

bother ['bɒðə*] vt (pester) quälen // vi (fuss) sich aufregen // n Mühe f, Umstand m; to ~ doing sth sich (dat) die Mühe machen, etw zu tun; what a ~! wie ärgerlich!

bottle ['bɒtl] n Flasche f // vt (in Flaschen) abfüllen; ~ **up** vt aufstauen; ~**neck** n (lit, fig) Engpaß m; ~**opener** n Flaschenöffner m.

bottom ['bɒtəm] n Boden m; (of person) Hintern m; (riverbed) Flußbett nt // a unterste(r, s).

bough [baʊ] n Zweig m, Ast m.

bought [bɔːt] pt, pp of buy.

boulder ['bəʊldə*] n Felsbrocken m.

bounce [baʊns] vi (ball) hochspringen; (person) herumhüpfen; (cheque) platzen // vi (auf)springen lassen // n (rebound) Aufprall m; ~**r** n Rausschmeißer m.

bound [baʊnd] pt, pp of bind // n Grenze f; (leap) Sprung m // vi (spring, leap) (auf)springen // a (obliged) gebunden, verpflichtet; out of ~s Zutritt verboten; to be ~ to do sth verpflichtet sein, etw zu tun, etw tun müssen; it's ~ to happen es muß so kommen; to be ~ for ... nach ... fahren.

boundary ['baʊndərɪ] n Grenze f.

bouquet [bʊ'keɪ] n Strauß m; (of wine) Blume f.

bourgeois ['bʊəʒwɑː] a kleinbürgerlich, bourgeois // n Spießbürger(in f) m.

bout [baʊt] n (of illness) Anfall m; (of contest) Kampf m.

bow n [bəʊ] (ribbon) Schleife f; (weapon, MUS) Bogen m; [baʊ] (with head, body) Verbeugung f; (of ship) Bug m // vi [baʊ] sich verbeugen; (submit) sich beugen (+dat).

bowels ['baʊəlz] npl Darm m; (centre) Innere nt.

bowl [bəʊl] n (basin) Schüssel f; (of pipe) (Pfeifen)kopf m; (wooden ball) (Holz)kugel f // vti (die Kugel) rollen; ~**s** n (game) Bowls-Spiel nt.

bow-legged ['bəʊlegɪd] a o-beinig.

bowler ['bəʊlə*] n Werfer m; (Brit: also: ~ hat) Melone f.

bowling ['bəʊlɪŋ] n Kegeln nt; ~ **alley** n Kegelbahn f; ~ **green** n Rasen m zum Bowling-Spiel.

bow tie ['bəʊ'taɪ] n Fliege f.

box [bɒks] n (also: cardboard ~) Schachtel f; (bigger) Kasten m; (THEAT) Loge f // vt einpacken // vi boxen; ~**er** n Boxer m; ~**ing** n (SPORT) Boxen nt; B~**ing Day** n (Brit) zweiter Weihnachtsfeiertag; ~**ing gloves** npl Boxhandschuhe pl; ~**ing ring** n Boxring m; ~ **office** n (Theater)kasse f; ~**room** n Rumpelkammer f.

boy [bɔɪ] n Junge m.

boycott ['bɔɪkɒt] n Boykott m // vt boykottieren.

boyfriend ['bɔɪfrend] n Freund m.

boyish ['bɔɪɪʃ] a jungenhaft.

B.R. n abbr of British Rail.

bra [brɑː] n BH m.

brace [breɪs] n (TECH) Stütze f; (MED) Klammer f // vt stützen; **~s** pl (Brit) Hosenträger pl; **to ~ o.s. for sth** (fig) sich auf etw (acc) gefaßt machen.

bracelet ['breɪslɪt] n Armband nt.

bracing ['breɪsɪŋ] a kräftigend.

bracken ['brækən] n Farnkraut nt.

bracket ['brækɪt] n Halter m, Klammer f; (in punctuation) Klammer f; (group) Gruppe f // vt einklammern; (fig) in dieselbe Gruppe einordnen.

brag [bræg] vi sich rühmen.

braid [breɪd] n (hair) Flechte f; (trim) Borte f.

Braille [breɪl] n Blindenschrift f.

brain [breɪn] n (ANAT) Gehirn nt; (intellect) Intelligenz f, Verstand m; (person) kluge(r) Kopf m; **~s** pl Verstand m; **~child** n Erfindung f; **~wash** vt eine Gehirnwäsche vornehmen bei; **~wave** n Geistesblitz m; **~y** a gescheit.

braise [breɪz] vt schmoren.

brake [breɪk] n Bremse f // vti bremsen; **~ fluid** n Bremsflüssigkeit f; **~ light** n Bremslicht nt.

bramble ['bræmbl] n Brombeere f.

bran [bræn] n Kleie f; (food) Frühstückflocken pl.

branch [braːntʃ] n Ast m; (division) Zweig m // vi (also: **~ out**) (road) sich verzweigen.

brand [brænd] n (COMM) Marke f, Sorte f; (on cattle) Brandmal nt // vt brandmarken; (COMM) ein Warenzeichen geben (+dat).

brandish ['brændɪʃ] vt (drohend) schwingen.

brand-new ['brænd'njuː] a funkelnagelneu.

brandy ['brændɪ] n Weinbrand m, Kognak m.

brash [bræʃ] a unverschämt.

brass [braːs] n Messing nt; **the ~** (MUS) das Blech; **~ band** n Blaskapelle f.

brassière ['bræsɪə*] n Büstenhalter m.

brat [bræt] n ungezogene(s) Kind nt, Gör nt.

bravado [brə'vaːdəʊ] n Tollkühnheit f.

brave [breɪv] a tapfer // n indianische(r) Krieger m // vt die Stirn bieten (+dat).

bravery ['breɪvərɪ] n Tapferkeit f.

brawl [brɔːl] n Rauferei f.

brawn [brɔːn] n (ANAT) Muskeln pl; (strength) Muskelkraft f.

bray [breɪ] vi schreien.

brazen ['breɪzn] a (shameless) unverschämt // vt: **~ it out** sich mit Lügen und Betrügen durchsetzen.

brazier ['breɪzɪə*] n (of workmen) offene(r) Kohlenofen m.

Brazil [brə'zɪl] n Brasilien nt; **~ian** a brasilianisch // n Brasilianer(in f) m.

breach [briːtʃ] n (gap) Lücke f; (MIL) Durchbruch m; (of discipline) Verstoß m (gegen die Disziplin); (of faith) Vertrauensbruch m // vt durchbrechen; **~ of contract** Vertragsbruch m; **~ of the peace** öffentliche Ruhestörung f.

bread [bred] n Brot nt; **~ and butter** Butterbrot nt; **~bin**, (US) **~box** n Brotkasten m; **~crumbs** npl Brotkrumen pl; (COOK) Paniermehl nt; **~line** n: **to be on the ~line** sich gerade so durchschlagen.

breadth [bretθ] n Breite f.

breadwinner ['bredwɪnə*] n Ernährer m.

break [breɪk] v (pt **broke**, pp **broken**) vt (destroy) (ab- or zer)brechen; (promise) brechen, nicht einhalten // vi (fall apart) auseinanderbrechen; (collapse) zusammenbrechen; (of dawn) anbrechen // n (gap) Lücke f; (chance) Chance f, Gelegenheit f; (fracture) Bruch m; (rest) Pause f; **~ down** vt (figures, data) aufschlüsseln; (undermine) überwinden // vi (car) eine Panne haben; (person) zusammenbrechen; **~ even** vi die Kosten decken; **~ free** or **loose** vi sich losreißen; **~ in** vt (animal) abrichten; (horse) zureiten // vi (burglar) einbrechen; **~ into** vt (house) einbrechen in (+ acc); **~ off** vi abbrechen; **~ open** vt (door etc) aufbrechen; **~ out** vi ausbrechen; **to ~ out in spots** Pickel bekommen; **~ up** vi zerbrechen; (fig) sich zerstreuen; (SCH) in die Ferien gehen // vt zerbrechen; **~age** n Bruch m, Beschädigung f; **~down** n (TECH) Panne f; (MED: also: **nervous ~down**) Zusammenbruch m; **~down van** n (Brit) Abschleppwagen m; **~er** n Brecher m.

breakfast ['brekfəst] n Frühstück nt.

break-in ['breɪkɪn] n Einbruch m.

breaking ['breɪkɪŋ] n: **~ and entering** (JUR) Einbruch m.

breakthrough ['breɪkθruː] n Durchbruch m.

breakwater ['breɪkwɔːtə*] n Wellenbrecher m.

breast [brest] n Brust f; **~-feed** vti (irreg: like **feed**) stillen; **~-stroke** n Brustschwimmen nt.

breath [breθ] n Atem m; **out of ~** außer Atem; **under one's ~** flüsternd.

breathalyzer ['breθəlaɪzə*] n Röhrchen nt.

breathe [briːð] vti atmen; **~ in** vti einatmen; **~ out** vti ausatmen; **~r** n Verschnaufpause f.

breathing ['briːðɪŋ] n Atmung f.

breathless ['breθlɪs] a atemlos.

breath-taking ['breθteɪkɪŋ] a atemberaubend.

breed [briːd] v (pt, pp **bred** [bred]) vi sich vermehren // vt züchten // n (race) Rasse f, Zucht f; **~er** n (person) Züchter m; **~ing** n Züchtung f; (up-

bringing) Erziehung f; (*education*) Bildung f.

breeze [briːz] n Brise f.

breezy ['briːzɪ] a windig; (*manner*) munter.

brevity ['brevɪtɪ] n Kürze f.

brew [bruː] vt brauen; (*plot*) anzetteln // vi (*storm*) sich zusammenziehen; **~ery** n Brauerei f.

bribe [braɪb] n Bestechungsgeld nt or -geschenk nt // vt bestechen; **~ry** ['braɪbərɪ] n Bestechung f.

bric-a-brac ['brɪkəbræk] n Nippes pl.

brick [brɪk] n Backstein m; **~layer** n Maurer m; **~works** n Ziegelei f.

bridal ['braɪdl] a Braut-.

bride [braɪd] n Braut f; **~groom** n Bräutigam m; **bridesmaid** n Brautjungfer f.

bridge [brɪdʒ] n Brücke f; (NAUT) Kommandobrücke f; (CARDS) Bridge nt; (ANAT) Nasenrücken m // vt eine Brücke schlagen über (+acc); (*fig*) überbrücken.

bridle ['braɪdl] n Zaum m // vt (*fig*) zügeln; (*horse*) aufzäumen; **~ path** n Reitweg m.

brief [briːf] a kurz // n (JUR) Akten pl // vt instruieren; **~s** pl Schlüpfer m, Slip m; **~case** n Aktentasche f; **~ing** n (genaue) Anweisung f; **~ly** ad kurz.

brigadier [brɪgə'dɪə*] n Brigadegeneral m.

bright [braɪt] a hell; (*cheerful*) heiter; (*idea*) klug; **~en (up)** vt aufhellen; (*person*) aufheitern // vi sich aufheitern.

brilliance ['brɪljəns] n Glanz m; (of *person*) Scharfsinn m.

brilliant ['brɪljənt] a glänzend.

brim [brɪm] n Rand m.

brine [braɪn] n Salzwasser nt.

bring [brɪŋ], pt, pp **brought** vt bringen; **~ about** vt zustande bringen; **~ back** vt zurückbringen; **~ down** vt (*price*) senken; **~ forward** vt (*meeting*) vorverlegen; (COMM) übertragen; **~ in** vt hereinbringen; (*harvest*) einbringen; **~ off** vt davontragen; (*success*) erzielen; **~ out** vt (*object*) herausbringen; **~ round** or **to** vt wieder zu sich bringen; **~ up** vt aufziehen; (*question*) zur Sprache bringen.

brink [brɪŋk] n Rand m.

brisk [brɪsk] a lebhaft.

brisket ['brɪskɪt] n Bruststück nt.

bristle ['brɪsl] n Borste f // vi sich sträuben; **bristling with** strotzend vor (+dat).

Britain ['brɪtən] n (also: **Great ~**) Großbritannien nt.

British ['brɪtɪʃ] a britisch; **the ~** pl die Briten pl; **the ~ Isles** pl die Britischen Inseln pl; **~ Rail** n die Britischen Eisenbahnen pl.

Briton ['brɪtən] n Brite m, Britin f.

brittle ['brɪtl] a spröde.

broach [brəʊtʃ] vt (*subject*) anschneiden.

broad [brɔːd] a breit; (*hint*) deutlich; (*daylight*) hellicht; (*general*) allgemein; (*accent*) stark; **in ~ daylight** am hellichten Tag; **~cast** n Rundfunkübertragung f // vti, pt, pp **~cast** übertragen, senden; **~en** vt erweitern // vi sich erweitern; **~ly** ad allgemein gesagt; **~minded** a tolerant.

broccoli ['brɒkəlɪ] n Brokkoli pl.

brochure ['brəʊʃʊə*] n Broschüre f.

broil [brɔɪl] vt (*grill*) grillen.

broke [brəʊk] pt of **break** // a (col) pleite.

broken ['brəʊkən] pp of **break** // a: **~ leg** gebrochenes Bein; **in ~ English** in gebrochenen Englisch; **~-hearted** a untröstlich.

broker ['brəʊkə*] n Makler m.

brolly ['brɒlɪ] n (*Brit col*) Schirm m.

bronchitis [brɒŋ'kaɪtɪs] n Bronchitis f.

bronze [brɒnz] n Bronze f.

brooch [brəʊtʃ] n Brosche f.

brood [bruːd] n Brut f // vi brüten.

brook [brʊk] n Bach m.

broom [bruːm] n Besen m; **~stick** n Besenstiel m.

Bros. abbr of **Brothers.**

broth [brɒθ] n Suppe f, Fleischbrühe f.

brothel ['brɒθl] n Bordell nt.

brother ['brʌðə*] n Bruder m; **~-in-law** n Schwager m.

brought [brɔːt] pt, pp of **bring.**

brow [braʊ] n (*eyebrow*) (Augen)braue f; (*forehead*) Stirn f; (of hill) Bergkuppe f.

brown [braʊn] a braun // n Braun nt // vt bräunen; **~ bread** n Mischbrot nt; **~ie** n Wichtel m; **~ paper** n Packpapier nt; **~ sugar** n braune(r) Zucker m.

browse [braʊz] vi (in books) blättern; (in shop) schmökern, herumschauen.

bruise [bruːz] n Bluterguß m, blaue(r) Fleck m // vt einen blauen Fleck geben/bekommen.

brunt [brʌnt] n volle Wucht f.

brush [brʌʃ] n Bürste f; (for sweeping) Handbesen m; (for painting) Pinsel m; (*fight*) kurze(r) Kampf m; (MIL) Scharmützel nt; (*fig*) Auseinandersetzung f // vt (clean) bürsten; (sweep) fegen; (gen: **~ past**, **~ against**) streifen; **~ aside** vt abtun; **~ up** vt (knowledge) auffrischen; **~wood** n Gestrüpp nt.

brusque [bruːsk] a schroff.

Brussels sprouts ['brʌsɪz'spraʊts] npl Rosenkohl m.

brutal ['bruːtl] a brutal.

brute [bruːt] n (*person*) Scheusal nt // a: **by ~ force** mit roher Kraft.

B.Sc. n abbr of **Bachelor of Science.**

bubble ['bʌbl] n (Luft)blase f // vi sprudeln; (with joy) übersprudeln; **~**

bath n Schaumbad nt; **~gum** n Kaugummi m or nt.

buck [bʌk] n Bock m; (US col) Dollar m // vi bocken; **to pass the ~** (to sb) die Verantwortung (auf jdn) abschieben; **~ up** vi (col) sich zusammenreißen.

bucket ['bʌkɪt] n Eimer m.

buckle ['bʌkl] n Schnalle f // vt (an- or zusammen)schnallen // vi (bend) sich verziehen.

bud [bʌd] n Knospe f // vi knospen, keimen.

Buddhism ['budɪzəm] n Buddhismus m.

budding ['bʌdɪŋ] a angehend.

buddy ['bʌdɪ] n (col) Kumpel m.

budge [bʌdʒ] vti (sich) von der Stelle rühren.

budgerigar ['bʌdʒərɪgɑ:*] n Wellensittich m.

budget ['bʌdʒɪt] n Budget nt; (POL) Haushalt m // vi: **to ~ for sth** etw einplanen.

budgie ['bʌdʒɪ] n = budgerigar.

buff [bʌf] a (colour) lederfarben // n (enthusiast) Fan m.

buffalo ['bʌfələu], pl **~** or **~es** n (Brit) Büffel m; (US: bison) Bison m.

buffer ['bʌfə*] n Puffer m; (COMPUT) Pufferspeicher m.

buffet ['bʌfɪt] n (blow) Schlag m; ['bufeɪ] (Brit: bar) Imbißraum m, Erfrischungsraum m; (food) (kaltes) Büffet nt // vt ['bʌfɪt] (herum)stoßen; **~ car** n (Brit) Speisewagen m.

bug [bʌg] n (lit, fig) Wanze f // vt verwanzen.

bugle ['bju:gl] n Jagd- or Bügelhorn nt.

build [bɪld] vt, pt, pp **built** bauen // n Körperbau m; **~ up** vt aufbauen; **~er** n Bauunternehmer m; **~ing** n Gebäude nt; **~ing society** n (Brit) Bausparkasse f.

built [bɪlt] pt, pp of build // a: **~-in** a (cupboard) eingebaut; **~-up area** n Wohngebiet nt.

bulb [bʌlb] n (BOT) (Blumen)zwiebel f; (ELEC) Glühlampe f, Birne f.

Bulgaria [bʌl'gɛərɪə] n Bulgarien nt; **~n** a bulgarisch // n Bulgare m, Bulgarin f; (language) Bulgarisch nt.

bulge [bʌldʒ] n (Aus)bauchung f // vi sich (aus)bauchen.

bulk [bʌlk] n Größe f, Masse f; (greater part) Großteil m; **in ~** (COMM) en gros; **the ~ of** der größte Teil (+gen); **~head** n Schott nt; **~y** a (sehr) umfangreich; (goods) sperrig.

bull [bul] n (animal) Bulle m; (cattle) Stier m; (papal) Bulle f; **~dog** n Bulldogge f.

bulldozer ['buldəuzə*] n Planierraupe f.

bullet ['bulɪt] n Kugel f.

bulletin ['bulɪtɪn] n Bulletin nt, Bekanntmachung f.

bulletproof ['bulɪtpru:f] a kugelsicher.

bullfight ['bulfaɪt] n Stierkampf m; **~er** n Stierkämpfer m; **~ing** n Stierkampf m.

bullion ['buliən] n Barren m.

bullock ['bulək] n Ochse m.

bullring ['bulrɪŋ] n Stierkampfarena f.

bull's-eye ['bulzaɪ] n Zentrum nt.

bully ['bulɪ] n Raufbold m // vt einschüchtern.

bum [bʌm] n (col: backside) Hintern m; (tramp) Landstreicher m; (nasty person) fieser Kerl m.

bumblebee ['bʌmblbi:] n Hummel f.

bump [bʌmp] n (blow) Stoß m; (swelling) Beule f // vti stoßen, prallen; **~ into** vt stoßen gegen; (person) treffen; **~er** n (AUT) Stoßstange f // a (edition) dick; (harvest) Rekord-; **~er cars** npl (US: dodgems) Autoskooter pl.

bumptious ['bʌmpʃəs] a aufgeblasen.

bumpy ['bʌmpɪ] a holprig.

bun [bʌn] n Korinthenbrötchen nt.

bunch [bʌntʃ] n (of flowers) Strauß m; (of keys) Bund m; (of people) Haufen m.

bundle ['bʌndl] n Bündel nt // vt (also: **~ up**) bündeln.

bungalow ['bʌŋgələu] n einstöckige(s) Haus nt, Bungalow m.

bungle ['bʌŋgl] vt verpfuschen.

bunion ['bʌnjən] n entzündete(r) Fußballen m.

bunk [bʌŋk] n Schlafkoje f; **~ beds** npl Etagenbett nt.

bunker ['bʌŋkə*] n (coal store) Kohlenbunker m; (golf) Sandloch nt.

bunny ['bʌnɪ] n (also: **~ rabbit**) Häschen nt.

bunting ['bʌntɪŋ] n Fahnentuch nt.

buoy [bɔɪ] n Boje f; (lifebuoy) Rettungsboje f; **~ up** vt Auftrieb geben (+dat); **~ant** a (floating) schwimmend; (fig) heiter.

burden ['bɜ:dn] n (weight) Ladung f, Last f; (fig) Bürde f // vt belasten.

bureau ['bjuərəu], pl **~x** [-z] n (Brit: writing desk) Sekretär m; (US: chest of drawers) Kommode f; (for information etc) Büro n.

bureaucracy [bjuə'rɒkrəsɪ] n Bürokratie f.

bureaucrat ['bjuərəkræt] n Bürokrat(in f) m.

burglar ['bɜ:glə*] n Einbrecher m; **~ alarm** n Einbruchssicherung f; **~y** n Einbruch m.

burial ['berɪəl] n Beerdigung f.

burly ['bɜ:lɪ] a stämmig.

Burma ['bɜ:mə] n Birma nt.

burn [bɜ:n] v (pt, pp **burned** or **burnt**) vt verbrennen // vi brennen // n Brandwunde f; **~ down** vti abbrennen; **~er** n Brenner m; **~ing** a brennend.

burrow ['bʌrəu] n (of fox) Bau m; (of rabbit) Höhle f // vt eingraben.

bursar ['bɜːsəʳ] n Kassenverwalter m, Quästor m; **~y** n (Brit) Stipendium nt.

burst [bɜːst] v (pt, pp **burst**) vt zerbrechen // vi platzen; (into tears) ausbrechen // n Explosion f; (outbreak) Ausbruch m; (in pipe) Bruch(stelle f) m; to ~ into flames in Flammen aufgehen; to ~ into tears in Tränen ausbrechen; to ~ out laughing in Gelächter ausbrechen; ~ into vt (room etc) platzen in (+acc); ~ open vi aufbrechen.

bury ['berɪ] vt vergraben; (in grave) beerdigen.

bus [bʌs] n (Auto)bus m, Omnibus m.

bush [buʃ] n Busch m; to beat about the ~ wie die Katze um den heißen Brei herumgehen.

bushy ['buʃɪ] a buschig.

busily ['bɪzɪlɪ] ad geschäftig.

business ['bɪznɪs] n Geschäft nt; (concern) Angelegenheit f; it's none of your ~ es geht dich nichts an; to mean ~ es ernst meinen; to be away on ~ geschäftlich verreist sein; it's my ~ to ... es ist meine Sache, zu ...; ~like a geschäftsmäßig; ~man n Geschäftsmann m; ~ trip n Geschäftsreise f; ~woman n Geschäftsfrau f.

busker ['bʌskəʳ] n (Brit) Straßenmusikant m.

bus-stop ['bʌsstɔp] n Bushaltestelle f.

bust [bʌst] n Büste f // a (broken) kaputt(gegangen); (business) pleite; to go ~ pleite machen.

bustle ['bʌsl] n Getriebe nt // vi hasten.

bustling ['bʌslɪŋ] a geschäftig.

busy ['bɪzɪ] a beschäftigt; (road) belebt // vt: to ~ o.s. sich beschäftigen; ~body n Übereifrige(r) mf; ~ signal n (US TEL) Besetztzeichen n.

but [bʌt] ◆cj **1** (yet) aber; not X ~ Y nicht X sondern Y

2 (however): I'd love to come, ~ I'm busy ich würde gern kommen, bin aber beschäftigt

3 (showing disagreement, surprise etc): ~ that's fantastic! (aber) das ist ja fantastisch!

◆prep (apart from, except): nothing ~ trouble nichts als Ärger; no-one ~ him can do it niemand außer ihn kann es machen; ~ for you/your help ohne dich/deine Hilfe; anything ~ that alles, nur das nicht

◆ad (just, only): she's ~ a child sie ist noch ein Kind; had I ~ known wenn ich es nur gewußt hätte; I can ~ try ich kann es immerhin versuchen; all ~ finished so gut wie fertig.

butcher ['butʃəʳ] n Metzger m; (murderer) Schlächter m // vt schlachten; (kill) abschlachten; ~'s (shop) n Metzgerei f.

butler ['bʌtləʳ] n Butler m.

butt [bʌt] n (cask) große(s) Faß nt;

(Brit fig: target) Zielscheibe f; (thick end) dicke(s) Ende nt; (of gun) Kolben m; (of cigarette) Stummel m // vt (mit dem Kopf) stoßen; ~ in vi (interrupt) sich einmischen.

butter ['bʌtəʳ] n Butter f // vt buttern; ~ bean n Wachsbohne f; ~cup n Butterblume f.

butterfly ['bʌtəflaɪ] n Schmetterling m (SWIMMING: also: ~ stroke) Butterfly-stil m.

buttocks ['bʌtəks] npl Gesäß nt.

button ['bʌtn] n Knopf m // vti (also: ~ up) zuknöpfen.

buttress ['bʌtrɪs] n Strebepfeiler m; Stützbogen m.

buxom ['bʌksəm] a drall.

buy [baɪ], pt, pp **bought** vt kaufen // n Kauf m; to ~ sb a drink jdm einen Drink spendieren; ~er n Käufer(in f) m.

buzz [bʌz] n Summen nt // vi summen.

buzzer ['bʌzəʳ] n Summer m.

buzz word n Modewort nt.

by [baɪ] prep **1** (referring to cause, agent) von, durch; killed ~ lightning vom Blitz getötet; a painting ~ Picasso ein Gemälde von Picasso

2 (referring to method, manner, means): ~ bus/car/train mit dem Bus/Auto/Zug; to pay ~ cheque per Scheck bezahlen; ~ moonlight bei Mondschein; ~ saving hard, he ... indem er eisern sparte, ... er ...

3 (via, through) über (+acc); he came in ~ the back door er kam durch die Hintertür herein

4 (close to, past) bei, an (+dat); a holiday ~ the sea ein Urlaub am Meer; she rushed ~ me sie eilte an mir vorbei

5 (not later than): ~ 4 o'clock bis 4 Uhr; ~ this time tomorrow morgen um diese Zeit; ~ the time I got here it was too late als ich hier ankam, war es zu spät

6 (during): ~ day bei Tag

7 (amount): ~ the kilo/metre kiloweise/meterweise; paid ~ the hour stundenweise bezahlt

8 (MATH, measure): to divide ~ 3 durch 3 teilen; to multiply ~ 3 mit 3 malnehmen; a room 3 metres ~ 4 ein Zimmer 3 mal 4 Meter; it's broader ~ a metre es ist (um) einen Meter breiter

9 (according to) nach; it's all right ~ me von mir aus gern

10: (all) ~ oneself etc ganz allein

11: ~ the way übrigens

◆ad **1** see go, pass etc

2: ~ and ~ irgendwann; (with past tenses) nach einiger Zeit; ~ and large (on the whole) im großen und ganzen.

bye(-bye) ['baɪ('baɪ)] interj (auf) Wiedersehen.

by-election ['baɪɪˌlekʃən] n (Brit)

Nachwahl f.

bygone ['baɪgɒn] a vergangen // n: let ~s be ~s laß(t) das Vergangene vergangen sein.

by(e)-law ['baɪlɔ:] n Verordnung f.

bypass ['baɪpɑ:s] n Umgehungsstraße f // vt umgehen.

byproduct ['baɪprɒdʌkt] n Nebenprodukt nt.

bystander ['baɪstændə*] n Zuschauer m.

byte [baɪt] n (COMPUT) Byte nt.

byword ['baɪwɜ:d] n Inbegriff m.

C

C [si:] n (MUS): ~ sharp/flat Cis, cis nt/ Ces, ces nt.

C. abbr (= centigrade) C.

cab [kæb] n Taxi nt; (of train) Führerstand m; (of truck) Führersitz m.

cabaret ['kæbəreɪ] n Kabarett nt.

cabbage ['kæbɪdʒ] n Kohl(kopf) m.

cabin ['kæbɪn] n Hütte f; (NAUT) Kajüte f; (AVIAT) Kabine f; ~ cruiser n Motorjacht f.

cabinet ['kæbɪnɪt] n Schrank m; (for china) Vitrine f; (POL) Kabinett nt; ~maker n Kunsttischler m.

cable ['keɪbl] n Drahtseil nt, Tau nt; (TEL) (Leitungs)kabel nt; (telegram) Kabel nt // vt kabeln, telegraphieren; ~car n Seilbahn f; ~ television n Kabelfernsehen nt.

cache [kæʃ] n geheime(s) (Waffen-/ Proviant)lager nt.

cackle ['kækl] vi gacken.

cactus ['kæktəs], pl **cacti** [-taɪ] n Kaktus m, Kaktee f.

caddie, caddy ['kædɪ] n (GOLF) Golfjunge m.

cadet [kə'det] n Kadett m.

cadge [kædʒ] vt schmarotzen.

Caesarean [si:'zeərɪən] a: ~ (section) n Kaiserschnitt m.

café ['kæfɪ] n Café nt, Restaurant nt.

cafeteria [kæfɪ'tɪərɪə] n Selbstbedienungsrestaurant nt.

caffein(e) ['kæfi:n] n Koffein nt.

cage [keɪdʒ] n Käfig m // vt einsperren.

cagey ['keɪdʒɪ] a geheimnistuerisch, zurückhaltend.

cagoule [kə'gu:l] n Windhemd nt.

cajole [kə'dʒəʊl] vt überreden.

cake [keɪk] n Kuchen m; (of soap) Stück nt; ~d a verkrustet.

Cairo ['kaɪərəʊ] n Kairo nt.

calamity [kə'læmɪtɪ] n Unglück nt, (Schicksals)schlag m.

calcium ['kælsɪəm] n Kalzium nt.

calculate ['kælkjʊleɪt] vt berechnen, kalkulieren; **calculating** a berechnend; **calculation** [-'leɪʃən] n Berechnung f; **calculator** n Rechner m.

calculus ['kælkjʊləs] n Rechenart f.

calendar ['kælɪndə*] n Kalender m; ~ month n Kalendermonat m.

calf [kɑ:f], pl **calves** n Kalb nt; (also: ~skin) Kalbsleder nt; (ANAT) Wade f.

calibre, (US) caliber ['kælɪbə*] n Kaliber nt.

call [kɔ:l] vt rufen; (name) nennen; (meeting) einberufen; (awaken) wecken; (TEL) anrufen // vi (shout) rufen; (visit: also: ~ in, ~ round) vorbeikommen // n (shout) Ruf m; (TEL) Anruf m; to be ~ed heißen; on ~ in Bereitschaft; ~ back vi (return) wiederkommen; (TEL) zurückrufen; ~ for vt (demand) erfordern, verlangen; (fetch) abholen; ~ off vt (cancel) absagen; ~ on vt (visit) besuchen; (turn to) bitten; ~ out vi rufen; ~ up vt (MIL) einberufen; ~box n (Brit) Telefonzelle f; ~er n Besucher(in f) m; (TEL) Anrufer m; ~ girl n Call-Girl nt; ~-in n (US: phone-in) Phone-in nt; ~ing n (vocation) Berufung f; ~ing card n (US) Visitenkarte f.

callous ['kæləs] a herzlos.

calm [kɑ:m] n Ruhe f; (NAUT) Flaute f // vt beruhigen // a ruhig; (person) gelassen; ~ down vi sich beruhigen // vt beruhigen.

Calor gas ['kælə'gæs] n ® Propangas nt.

calorie ['kælərɪ] n Kalorie f.

calve [kɑ:v] vi kalben.

calves [kɑ:vz] pl of **calf**.

camber ['kæmbə*] n Wölbung f.

Cambodia [kæm'bəʊdjə] n Kambodscha nt.

came [keɪm] pt of **come**.

camel ['kæməl] n Kamel nt.

cameo ['kæmɪəʊ] n Kamee f.

camera ['kæmərə] n Fotoapparat m; (CINE, TV) Kamera f; in ~ unter Ausschluß der Öffentlichkeit; ~man n Kameramann m.

camouflage ['kæməflɑ:ʒ] n Tarnung f // vt tarnen.

camp [kæmp] n Lager nt // vi zelten, campen // a affektiert.

campaign [kæm'peɪn] n Kampagne f; (MIL) Feldzug m // vi ~ unter Ausführen; (fig) werben, Propaganda machen; (POL) den Wahlkampf führen.

campbed ['kæmp'bed] n (Brit) Campingbett nt.

camper ['kæmpə*] n Camper(in f) m; (vehicle) Camping-wagen m.

camping ['kæmpɪŋ] n: to go ~ zelten, Camping machen.

campsite ['kæmpsaɪt] n Campingplatz m.

campus ['kæmpəs] n Universitätsgelände nt, Campus m.

can [kæn] n Büchse f, Dose f; (for water) Kanne f // vt konservieren, in Büchsen einmachen.

can [kæn] *aux v* (*negative* **cannot**, **can't**; *conditional and pt* **could**) 1 (*be able to, know how to*) können; I ~ see you tomorrow, if you like ich könnte Sie morgen sehen, wenn Sie wollen; I ~ swim ich kann schwimmen; ~ you speak German? sprechen Sie Deutsch? 2 (*may*) können, dürfen; could I have a word with you? könnte ich Sie kurz sprechen?

Canada ['kænədə] *n* Kanada *nt*; **Canadian** [kə'neɪdɪən] *a* kanadisch // *n* Kanadier(in *f*) *m*.

canal [kə'næl] *n* Kanal *m*.

canary [kə'nɛərɪ] *n* Kanarienvogel *m*.

cancel ['kænsəl] *vt* absagen; (*delete*) durchstreichen; (*train*) streichen; **~lation** [kænsə'leɪʃən] *n* Absage *f*; Streichung *f*.

cancer ['kænsə*] *n* (*also ASTROL*: C~) Krebs *m*.

candid ['kændɪd] *a* offen, ehrlich.

candidate ['kændɪdeɪt] *n* Kandidat(in *f*) *m*.

candle ['kændl] *n* Kerze *f*; **~light** *n* Kerzenlicht *nt*; **~stick** *n* (*also*: ~ holder) Kerzenhalter *m*.

candour, (*US*) **candor** ['kændə*] *n* Offenheit *f*.

candy ['kændɪ] *n* Kandis(zucker) *m*; (*US*) Bonbons *pl*; **~-floss** *n* (*Brit*) Zuckerwatte *f*.

cane [keɪn] *n* (*BOT*) Rohr *nt*; (*stick*) Stock *m* // *vt* (*Brit SCH*) schlagen.

canine ['kænaɪn] *a* Hunde-.

canister ['kænɪstə*] *n* Blechdose *f*.

cannabis ['kænəbɪs] *n* Hanf *m*, Haschisch *nt*.

canned [kænd] *a* Büchsen-, eingemacht.

cannibal ['kænɪbəl] *n* Menschenfresser *m*.

cannon ['kænən] *n*, *pl* ~ *or* **~s** *n* Kanone *f*.

cannot ['kænɒt] = **can not**.

canny ['kænɪ] *a* schlau.

canoe [kə'nuː] *n* Kanu *nt*.

canon ['kænən] *n* (*clergyman*) Domherr *m*; (*standard*) Grundsatz *m*.

canonize ['kænənaɪz] *vt* heiligsprechen.

can opener *n* Büchsenöffner *m*.

canopy ['kænəpɪ] *n* Baldachin *m*.

can't [kɑːnt] = **can not**.

cantankerous [kæn'tæŋkərəs] *a* zänkisch, mürrisch.

canteen [kæn'tiːn] *n* Kantine *f*; (*Brit*: *of cutlery*) Besteckkasten *m*; (*bottle*) Feldflasche *f*.

canter ['kæntə*] *n* Kanter *m* // *vi* in kurzem Galopp reiten.

canvas ['kænvəs] *n* Segeltuch *nt*; (*sail*) Segel *nt*; (*for painting*) Leinwand *f*; **under ~** (*camping*) in Zelten.

canvass ['kænvəs] *vi* um Stimmen werben.

canyon ['kænjən] *n* Felsenschlucht *f*.

cap [kæp] *n* Mütze *f*; (*of pen*) Kappe *f*; (*of bottle*) Deckel *m* // *vt* (*surpass*) übertreffen; (*in sport*) aufstellen.

capability [keɪpə'bɪlɪtɪ] *n* Fähigkeit *f*.

capable ['keɪpəbl] *a* fähig.

capacity [kə'pæsɪtɪ] *n* Fassungsvermögen *nt*; (*ability*) Fähigkeit *f*; (*position*) Eigenschaft *f*.

cape [keɪp] *n* (*garment*) Cape *nt*, Umhang *m*; (*GEOG*) Kap *nt*.

caper ['keɪpə*] *n* (*CULIN*: *gen*: ~s) Kaper *f*; (*prank*) Kapriole *f*.

capital ['kæpɪtl] *n* (~ *city*) Hauptstadt *f*; (*FIN*) Kapital *nt*; (~ *letter*) Großbuchstabe *m*; **~ gains tax** *n* Kapitalertragssteuer *f*; **~ism** *n* Kapitalismus *m*; **~ist** *a* kapitalistisch // *n* Kapitalist(in *f*) *m*; **to ~ize on** *vt* Kapital schlagen aus; **~ punishment** *n* Todesstrafe *f*.

capitulate [kə'pɪtjʊleɪt] *vi* kapitulieren.

capricious [kə'prɪʃəs] *a* launisch.

Capricorn ['kæprɪkɔːn] *n* Steinbock *m*.

capsize [kæp'saɪz] *vti* kentern.

capsule ['kæpsjuːl] *n* Kapsel *f*.

captain ['kæptɪn] *n* Kapitän *m*; (*MIL*) Hauptmann *m* // *vt* anführen.

caption ['kæpʃən] *n* (*heading*) Überschrift *f*; (*to picture*) Unterschrift *f*.

captivate ['kæptɪveɪt] *vt* fesseln.

captive ['kæptɪv] *n* Gefangene(r) *mf* // *a* gefangen(gehalten).

captivity [kæp'tɪvɪtɪ] *n* Gefangenschaft *f*.

capture ['kæptʃə*] *vt* gefangennehmen; (*place*) erobern; (*attention*) erregen // *n* Gefangennahme *f*; (*data* ~) Erfassung *f*.

car [kɑː*] *n* Auto *nt*, Wagen *m*; (*RAIL*) Wagen *m*.

carafe [kə'ræf] *n* Karaffe *f*.

caramel ['kærəməl] *n* Karamelle *f*.

carat ['kærət] *n* Karat *nt*.

caravan ['kærəvæn] *n* (*Brit*) Wohnwagen *m*; (*in desert*) Karawane *f*; **~ site** *n* (*Brit*) Campingplatz *m* für Wohnwagen.

carbohydrate [kɑːbəʊ'haɪdreɪt] *n* Kohlenhydrat *nt*.

carbon ['kɑːbən] *n* Kohlenstoff *m*; **~ copy** *n* Durchschlag *m*; **~ paper** *n* Kohlepapier *nt*.

carburettor, (*US*) **carburetor** ['kɑːbjʊretə*] *n* Vergaser *m*.

carcass ['kɑːkəs] *n* Kadaver *m*.

card [kɑːd] *n* Karte *f*; **~board** *n* Pappe *f*; **~ game** *n* Kartenspiel *nt*.

cardiac ['kɑːdɪæk] *a* Herz-.

cardigan ['kɑːdɪgən] *n* Strickjacke *f*.

cardinal ['kɑːdɪnl] *a*: **~ number** Kardinalzahl *f* // *n* (*REL*) Kardinal *m*.

card index *n* Kartei *f*; (*in library*) Katalog *m*.

care [kɛə*] *n* (*of teeth, car etc*) Pflege *f*; (*of children*) Fürsorge *f*; (*carefulness*) Sorgfalt *f*; (*worry*) Sorge *f* // *vi*: **to ~ about** sich kümmern um; **~ of** (c/o) bei; **in sb's ~** in jds Obhut; **I don't ~** das ist mir egal; **I couldn't ~ less** es ist mir doch völlig egal; **to take ~ aufpassen; to take ~ of** sorgen für; **to take ~ to do sth** sich bemühen, etw zu tun; **~ for** *vt* sorgen für; (*like*) mögen.

career [kə'rɪə*] *n* Karriere *f*, Laufbahn *f* // *vi* (*also:* **~ along**) rasen.

carefree ['kɛəfriː] *a* sorgenfrei.

careful ['kɛəfʊl] *a* sorgfältig; (**be**) **~!** pass auf!

careless *a* ['kɛəlɪs] nachlässig; **~ness** *n* Nachlässigkeit *f*.

caress [kə'rɛs] *n* Liebkosung *f* // *vt* liebkosen.

caretaker ['kɛəteɪkə*] *n* Hausmeister *m*.

car-ferry ['kɑːferɪ] *n* Autofähre *f*.

cargo ['kɑːgəʊ], *pl* **~es** *n* Schiffsladung *f*.

car hire *n* Autovermietung *f*.

Caribbean [kærɪ'biːən] *n*: **the ~** (**Sea**) die Karibik.

caricature ['kærɪkətjʊə*] *n* Karikatur *f*.

caring ['kɛərɪŋ] *a* (*society, organization*) sozial eingestellt; (*person*) liebevoll.

carnage ['kɑːnɪdʒ] *n* Blutbad *nt*.

carnal ['kɑːnl] *a* fleischlich.

carnation [kɑː'neɪʃən] *n* Nelke *f*.

carnival ['kɑːnɪvəl] *n* Karneval *m*, Fasching *m*; (*US: fun fair*) Kirmes *f*.

carnivorous [kɑː'nɪvərəs] *a* fleischfressend.

carol ['kærl] *n*: (**Christmas**) **~** (Weihnachts)lied *nt*.

carp [kɑːp] *n* (*fish*) Karpfen *m*; **~ at** *vt* herumnörgeln an (+*dat*).

car park (*Brit*) Parkplatz *m*; (*covered*) Parkhaus *nt*.

carpenter ['kɑːpɪntə*] *n* Zimmermann *m*.

carpentry ['kɑːpɪntrɪ] *n* Zimmerei *f*.

carpet ['kɑːpɪt] *n* Teppich *m* // *vt* mit einem Teppich auslegen; **~ slippers** *npl* Pantoffeln *pl*; **~ sweeper** *n* Teppichkehrer *m*.

carriage ['kærɪdʒ] *n* Kutsche *f*; (*RAIL*, *of typewriter*) Wagen *m*; (*of goods*) Beförderung *f*; (*bearing*) Haltung *f*; **~ return** *n* (*on typewriter*) Rücklauftaste *f*; **~way** *n* (*Brit: part of road*) Fahrbahn *f*.

carrier ['kærɪə*] *n* Träger(in *f*) *m*; (*COMM*) Spediteur *m*; **~ bag** *n* (*Brit*) Tragetasche *f*.

carrot ['kærət] *n* Möhre *f*, Karotte *f*.

carry ['kærɪ] *vti* tragen; **to get carried away** (*fig*) sich nicht mehr bremsen können; **~ on** *vi* (*continue*) weitermachen; (*col: complain*) Theater machen; **~ out** *vt* (*orders*) ausführen; (*investigation*) durchführen; **~cot** *n* (*Brit*) Babytragetasche *f*; **~-on** *n* (*col: fuss*) Theater *nt*.

cart [kɑːt] *n* Wagen *m*, Karren *m* // *vt* schleppen.

cartilage ['kɑːtɪlɪdʒ] *n* Knorpel *m*.

carton ['kɑːtən] *n* Karton *m*; (*of milk*) Tüte *f*.

cartoon [kɑː'tuːn] *n* (*PRESS*) Karikatur *f*; (*comic strip*) Comics *pl*; (*CINE*) (Zeichen)trickfilm *m*.

cartridge ['kɑːtrɪdʒ] *n* Patrone *f*.

carve [kɑːv] *vt* (*wood*) schnitzen; (*stone*) meißeln; (*meat*) (vor)schneiden; **~ up** *vt* aufschneiden.

carving ['kɑːvɪŋ] *n* Schnitzerei *f*; **~ knife** *n* Tranchiermesser *nt*.

car wash *n* Autowäsche *f*.

cascade [kæs'keɪd] *n* Wasserfall *m* // *vi* kaskadenartig herabfallen.

case [keɪs] *n* (*box*) Kasten *m*; (*Brit: also:* **suit~**) Koffer *m*; (*JUR, matter*) Fall *m*; **in ~** falls, im Falle; **in any ~** jedenfalls, auf jeden Fall.

cash [kæʃ] *n* (Bar)geld *nt* // *vt* einlösen; **~ on delivery** (**C.O.D.**) per Nachnahme; **~ book** *n* Kassenbuch *nt*; **~ card** *n* Scheckkarte *f*; **~ desk** *n* (*Brit*) Kasse *f*; **~ dispenser** *n* Geldautomat *m*.

cashew [kæ'ʃuː] *n* (*also:* **~ nut**) Cashewnuß *f*.

cash flow *n* Cash-flow *m*.

cashier [kæ'ʃɪə*] *n* Kassierer(in *f*) *m*.

cashmere ['kæʃmɪə*] *n* Kaschmirwolle *f*.

cash register *n* Registrierkasse *f*.

casing ['keɪsɪŋ] *n* Gehäuse *f*.

casino [kə'siːnəʊ] *n* Kasino *nt*.

cask [kɑːsk] *n* Faß *nt*.

casket ['kɑːskɪt] *n* Kästchen *nt*; (*US: coffin*) Sarg *m*.

casserole ['kæsərəʊl] *n* Kasserole *f*; (*food*) Auflauf *m*.

cassette [kæ'set] *n* Kassette *f*; **~ player** *n* Kassettengerät *nt*.

cast [kɑːst], *pt, pp* **cast** *vt* werfen; (*horns*) verlieren; (*metal*) gießen; (*THEAT*) besetzen; (*vote*) abgeben // *n* (*THEAT*) Besetzung *f*; (*also:* **plaster ~**) Gipsverband *m*; **~ off** *vi* (*NAUT*) losmachen.

castaway ['kɑːstəweɪ] *n* Schiffbrüchige(r) *mf*.

caste [kɑːst] *n* Kaste *f*.

casting vote ['kɑːstɪŋ-] *n* (*Brit*) entscheidende Stimme *f*.

cast iron *n* Gußeisen *nt*.

castle ['kɑːsl] *n* Burg *f*; Schloß *nt*; (*chess*) Turm *m*.

castor ['kɑːstə*] *n* (*wheel*) Laufrolle *f*, **~ oil** *n* Rizinusöl *nt*; **~ sugar** *n* (*Brit*) Streuzucker *m*.

castrate [kæs'treɪt] *vt* kastrieren.

casual ['kæʒjʊl] *a* (*attitude*) nachlässig; (*dress*) leger; (*meeting*) zufällig; (*work*) Gelegenheits-; **~ly** *ad* (*dress*) zwanglos, leger; (*remark*) beiläufig.

casualty ['kæʒjʊltɪ] *n* Verletzte(r) *mf*; (*dead*) Tote(r) *mf*; (*also:* **~ department**) Unfallstation *f*.

cat [kæt] *n* Katze *f*.

catalogue, (US) **catalog** ['kætəlɒg] n Katalog m // vt katalogisieren.
catalyst ['kætəlɪst] n Katalysator m.
cataract ['kætərækt] n (MED) graue(r) Star m.
catarrh [kə'tɑː*] n Katarrh m.
catastrophe [kə'tæstrəfɪ] n Katastrophe f.
catch [kætʃ]- v (pt, pp **caught**) vt fangen; (arrest) fassen; (train) erreichen; (person: by surprise) ertappen; (also: ~ **up**) einholen // vi (fire) in Gang kommen; (in branches etc) hängenbleiben // n (fish etc) Fang m; (trick) Haken m; (of lock) Sperrhaken m; **to ~ an illness** sich (dat) eine Krankheit holen; **to ~ fire** Feuer fangen; **~ on** vi (understand) begreifen; (grow popular) ankommen; **~ up** vi (fig) aufholen.
catching ['kætʃɪŋ] a ansteckend.
catchment area ['kætʃmənt-] n (Brit) Einzugsgebiet nt.
catch phrase ['kætʃfreɪz] n Slogan m.
catchy ['kætʃɪ] a (tune) eingängig.
catechism ['kætɪkɪzəm] n Katechismus m.
categoric(al) a [kætə'gɒrɪk(l)] kategorisch.
category ['kætɪgərɪ] n Kategorie f.
cater ['keɪtə*] vi versorgen; **~ for** vt (Brit: party) ausrichten; (: needs) eingestellt sein auf (+acc); **~er** n Lieferant(in f) m von Speisen und Getränken; **~ing** n Gastronomie f.
caterpillar ['kætəpɪlə*] n Raupe f; **~ track** n Gleiskette f.
cathedral [kə'θiːdrəl] n Kathedrale f, Dom m.
Catholic ['kæθəlɪk] a (REL) katholisch; (tastes etc): **c~** vielseitig // n Katholik(in f) m.
cat's-eye ['kætsaɪ] n (Brit AUT) Katzenauge nt.
cattle ['kætl] npl Vieh nt.
catty ['kætɪ] a gehässig.
caucus ['kɔːkəs] n (POL) Gremium nt; (US: meeting) Sitzung f.
caught [kɔːt] pt, pp of **catch**.
cauliflower ['kɒlɪflaʊə*] n Blumenkohl m.
cause [kɔːz] n Ursache f; (purpose) Sache f // vt verursachen.
causeway ['kɔːzweɪ] n Damm m.
caustic ['kɔːstɪk] a ätzend; (fig) bissig.
caution ['kɔːʃən] n Vorsicht f; (warning) Verwarnung f // vt verwarnen.
cautious ['kɔːʃəs] a vorsichtig.
cavalier [kævə'lɪə*] a blasiert.
cavalry ['kævəlrɪ] n Kavallerie f.
cave [keɪv] n Höhle f; **~ in** vi einstürzen; **~man** n Höhlenmensch m.
cavern ['kævən] n Höhle f.
caviar(e) ['kævɪɑː*] n Kaviar m.
cavity ['kævɪtɪ] n Loch nt.
cavort [kə'vɔːt] vi umherspringen.

C.B. n abbr (= Citizens' Band (Radio)) CB.
C.B.I. n abbr (= Confederation of British Industry) ≈ BDI m.
cc n abbr (= cubic centimetres) cc; (= carbon copy) zk.
cease [siːs] vi aufhören // vt beenden; **~fire** n Feuereinstellung f; **~less** a unaufhörlich.
cedar ['siːdə*] n Zeder f.
cede [siːd] vt abtreten.
ceiling ['siːlɪŋ] n Decke f; (fig) Höchstgrenze f.
celebrate ['selɪbreɪt] vti feiern; **~d** a gefeiert.
celebration [selɪ'breɪʃən] n Feier f.
celebrity [sɪ'lebrɪtɪ] n gefeierte Persönlichkeit f.
celery ['selərɪ] n Sellerie m or f.
celestial [sɪ'lestɪəl] a himmlisch.
celibacy ['selɪbəsɪ] n Zölibat nt or m.
cell [sel] n Zelle f; (ELEC) Element nt.
cellar ['selə*] n Keller m.
'cello ['tʃeləʊ] n Cello nt.
cellophane ['seləfeɪn] n ® Cellophan nt ®.
cellular ['seljʊlə*] a zellular.
cellulose ['seljʊləʊs] n Zellulose f.
Celt [kelt, selt] n Kelte m, Keltin f; **~ic** a keltisch.
cement [sɪ'ment] n Zement m // vt zementieren; **~ mixer** n Betonmischmaschine f.
cemetery ['semɪtrɪ] n Friedhof m.
cenotaph ['senətɑːf] n Ehrenmal nt.
censor ['sensə*] n Zensor m // vt zensieren; **~ship** n Zensur f.
censure ['senʃə*] vt rügen.
census ['sensəs] n Volkszählung f.
cent [sent] n (US: coin) Cent m; see also **per cent**.
centenary [sen'tiːnərɪ] n Jahrhundertfeier f.
center ['sentə*] n (US) = **centre**.
centi... ['sentɪ] pref: **~grade** a Celsius; **~metre**, (US) **~meter** n Zentimeter nt; **~pede** n Tausendfüßler m.
central ['sentrəl] a zentral; **C~ America** n Mittelamerika nt; **~ heating** n Zentralheizung f; **~ize** vt zentralisieren.
centre ['sentə*] n Zentrum nt // vt zentrieren; **~-forward** n (SPORT) Mittelstürmer m; **~-half** n (SPORT) Stopper m.
century ['sentjʊrɪ] n Jahrhundert nt.
ceramic [sɪ'ræmɪk] a keramisch; **~s** npl Keramiken pl.
cereal ['sɪərɪəl] n (grain) Getreide nt; (at breakfast) Getreideflocken pl.
cerebral ['serɪbrəl] a zerebral; (intellectual) geistig.
ceremony ['serɪmənɪ] n; Zeremonie f; **to stand on ~** förmlich sein.
certain ['sɜːtən] a sicher; (particular) gewiß; **for ~** ganz bestimmt; **~ly** ad si-

cher, bestimmt; **~ty** n Gewißheit f.

certificate [sə'tıfıkıt] n Bescheinigung f; (SCH etc) Zeugnis nt.

certified ['sɜːtıfaıd] a: **~ mail** n (US) Einschreiben nt; **~ public accountant** n (US) geprüfter Buchhalter.

certify ['sɜːtıfaı] vt bescheinigen.

cervical ['sɜːvıkl] a (smear, cancer) Gebärmutterhals-.

cervix ['sɜːvıks] n Gebärmutterhals m.

cessation [se'seıʃən] n Einstellung f, Ende nt.

cesspit ['sespıt] n Senkgrube f.

c.f. abbr (= compare) vgl.

ch. abbr (= chapter) Kap.

chafe [tʃeıf] vt scheuern.

chaffinch ['tʃæfıntʃ] n Buchfink m.

chagrin ['ʃægrın] n Verdruß m.

chain [tʃeın] n Kette f // vt (also: ~ up) anketten; **~ reaction** n Kettenreaktion f; **~-smoke** vi kettenrauchen; **~ store** n Kettenladen m.

chair [tʃeə*] n Stuhl m; (arm~) Sessel m; (UNIV) Lehrstuhl m // vt (meeting) den Vorsitz führen bei; **~lift** n Sessellift m; **~man** n Vorsitzende(r) m.

chalet ['ʃæleı] n Chalet nt.

chalice ['tʃælıs] n Kelch m.

chalk [tʃɔːk] n Kreide f.

challenge ['tʃælındʒ] n Herausforderung f // vt herausfordern; (contest) bestreiten.

challenging ['tʃælındʒıŋ] a (tone) herausfordernd; (work) anspruchsvoll.

chamber ['tʃeımbə*] n Kammer f; **~ of commerce** n Handelskammer f; **~maid** n Zimmermädchen nt; **~ music** n Kammermusik f.

chamois ['ʃæmwɑː] n Gemse f.

champagne [ʃæm'peın] n Champagner m, Sekt m.

champion ['tʃæmpıən] n (SPORT) Meister(in f) m; (of cause) Verfechter(in f) m; **~ship** n Meisterschaft f.

chance [tʃɑːns] n (luck) Zufall m; (possibility) Möglichkeit f; (opportunity) Gelegenheit f, Chance f; (risk) Risiko nt // a zufällig // vt: to ~ it es darauf ankommen lassen; **by ~** zufällig; **to take a ~** ein Risiko eingehen.

chancellor ['tʃɑːnsələ*] n Kanzler m; **C~ of the Exchequer** n (Brit) Schatzkanzler m.

chandelier [ʃændı'lıə*] n Kronleuchter m.

change [tʃeındʒ] vt ändern; (replace, COMM: money) wechseln; (exchange) umtauschen; (transform) verwandeln // vi sich ändern; (~ trains) umsteigen; (~ clothes) sich umziehen; (be transformed): to ~ into sth sich in etw (acc) verwandeln // n Veränderung f; (money returned) Wechselgeld nt; (coins) Kleingeld nt; to ~ one's mind es sich (dat) anders überlegen; for a ~ zur

Abwechslung; **~able** a (weather) wechselhaft; **~ machine** n Geldwechselautomat m; **~over** n Umstellung f.

changing ['tʃeındʒıŋ] a veränderlich; **~ room** n (Brit) Umkleideraum m.

channel ['tʃænl] n (stream) Bachbett nt; (NAUT) Straße f; (TV) Kanal m; (fig) Weg m // vt (efforts) lenken; **the (English) C~** der Ärmelkanal; **the C~ Islands** npl die Kanalinseln pl.

chant [tʃɑːnt] n Gesang m; (of football fans etc) Sprechchor m // vt intonieren.

chaos ['keıɒs] n Chaos nt.

chap [tʃæp] n (col) Kerl m.

chapel ['tʃæpl] n Kapelle f.

chaperon ['ʃæpərəʊn] n Anstandsdame f.

chaplain ['tʃæplın] n Kaplan m.

chapped ['tʃæpt] a (skin, lips) spröde.

chapter ['tʃæptə*] n Kapitel nt.

char [tʃɑː*] vt (burn) verkohlen // n (Brit) = **charlady**.

character ['kærıktə*] n Charakter m, Wesen nt; (in novel, film) Figur f; (in writing) Schriftzeichen nt; **~istic** [kærıktə'rıstık] a charakteristisch (of für) // n Kennzeichen nt; **~ize** vt charakterisieren, kennzeichnen.

charade [ʃə'rɑːd] n Scharade f.

charcoal ['tʃɑːkəʊl] n Holzkohle f.

charge [tʃɑːdʒ] n (cost) Preis m; (JUR) Anklage f; (explosive) Ladung f; (attack) Angriff m // vt (gun, battery) laden; (price) verlangen; (JUR) anklagen; (MIL) angreifen // vi (rush) (an)stürmen; **bank ~s** pl Bankgebühren pl; **free of ~** kostenlos; **to reverse the ~s** (TEL) ein R-Gespräch führen; **to be in ~ of** verantwortlich sein für; **to take ~** (die Verantwortung) übernehmen; **to ~ sth (up) to sb's account** jdm etw in Rechnung stellen; **~ card** n Kundenkarte f.

charitable ['tʃærıtəbl] a wohltätig; (lenient) nachsichtig.

charity ['tʃærıtı] n (institution) Hilfswerk nt; (attitude) Nächstenliebe f.

charlady ['tʃɑːleıdı] n (Brit) Putzfrau f.

charlatan ['ʃɑːlətən] n Scharlatan m.

charm [tʃɑːm] n Charme m; (spell) Bann m; (object) Talisman m // vt bezaubern; **~ing** a reizend.

chart [tʃɑːt] n Tabelle f; (NAUT) Seekarte f // vt (course) abstecken.

charter ['tʃɑːtə*] vt chartern // n Schutzbrief m; **~ed accountant** n Wirtschaftsprüfer(in f) m; **~ flight** n Charterflug m.

charwoman ['tʃɑːwʊmən] n = **charlady**.

chase [tʃeıs] vt jagen, verfolgen // n Jagd f.

chasm ['kæzəm] n Kluft f.

chassis ['ʃæsı] n Fahrgestell nt.

chastity ['tʃæstıtı] n Keuschheit f.

chat [tʃæt] vi (also: have a ~) plaudern // n Plauderei f; ~ **show** n (Brit) Talkshow f.

chatter ['tʃætə*] vi schwatzen; (teeth) klappern // n Geschwätz nt; ~**box** n Quasselstrippe f.

chatty ['tʃætɪ] a geschwätzig.

chauffeur ['ʃəʊfə*] n Chauffeur m.

chauvinist ['ʃəʊvɪnɪst] n (male ~) Chauvi m (col); (nationalist) Chauvinist(in f) m.

cheap [tʃiːp] a, ad billig; ~**ly** ad billig.

cheat [tʃiːt] vti betrügen; (SCH) mogeln // n Betrüger(in f) m.

check [tʃek] vt (examine) prüfen; (make sure) nachsehen; (control) kontrollieren; (restrain) zügeln; (stop) anhalten // n (examination, restraint) Kontrolle f; (bill) Rechnung f; (pattern) Karo(muster) nt; (US) = **cheque**; // a (pattern, cloth) kariert; ~ **in** vi (in hotel, airport) einchecken // vt (luggage) abfertigen lassen; ~ **out** vi (of hotel) abreisen; ~ **up** vi nachschauen; ~ **up on** vt kontrollieren; ~**ered** a (US) = **chequered**; ~**ers** n (US: draughts) Damespiel nt; ~**-in (desk)** n Abfertigung f; ~**ing account** n (US: current account) Girokonto nt; ~**mate** n Schachmatt nt; ~**out** n Kasse f; ~**point** n Kontrollpunkt m; ~ **room** n (US: left-luggage office) Gepäckaufbewahrung f; ~**up** n (Nach)prüfung f; (MED) (ärztliche) Untersuchung f.

cheek [tʃiːk] n Backe f; (fig) Frechheit f; ~**bone** n Backenknochen m; ~**y** a frech.

cheep [tʃiːp] vi piepsen.

cheer [tʃɪə*] n Beifallsruf m; ~**s** Hurrarufe pl; ~**s!** Prost! // vt zujubeln; (encourage) aufmuntern // vi jauchzen; ~ **up** vi bessere Laune bekommen // vt aufmuntern; ~ **up!** nun lach doch mal!; ~**ful** a fröhlich.

cheerio ['tʃɪərɪ'əʊ] excl (Brit) tschüs!

cheese [tʃiːz] n Käse m; ~**board** n (gemischte) Käseplatte f.

cheetah ['tʃiːtə] n Gepard m.

chef [ʃef] n Küchenchef m.

chemical ['kemɪkəl] a chemisch // n Chemikalie f.

chemist ['kemɪst] n (Brit: pharmacist) Apotheker m, Drogist m; (scientist) Chemiker m; ~**ry** n Chemie f; ~'**s (shop)** n (Brit) Apotheke f, Drogerie f.

cheque [tʃek] n (Brit) Scheck m; ~**book** n Scheckbuch nt; ~ **card** n Scheckkarte f.

chequered ['tʃekəd] a (fig) bewegt.

cherish ['tʃerɪʃ] vt (person) lieben; (hope) hegen.

cherry ['tʃerɪ] n Kirsche f.

chess [tʃes] n Schach nt; ~**board** n Schachbrett nt; ~**man** n Schachfigur f.

chest [tʃest] n (ANAT) Brust f; (box) Ki-

ste f; ~ **of drawers** n Kommode f.

chestnut ['tʃesnʌt] n Kastanie f; ~ **(tree)** n Kastanienbaum m.

chew [tʃuː] vti kauen; ~**ing gum** n Kaugummi m.

chic [ʃiːk] a schick, elegant.

chick [tʃɪk] n Küken nt; (US col: girl) Biene f.

chicken ['tʃɪkɪn] n Huhn nt; (food) Hähnchen nt // ~ **out** vi (col) kneifen (col).

chickenpox ['tʃɪkɪnpɒks] n Windpocken pl.

chicory ['tʃɪkərɪ] n (in coffee) Zichorie f; (plant) Chicorée f.

chief [tʃiːf] n (of tribe) Häuptling m; (COMM) Chef m // a Haupt-; ~ **executive** n Geschäftsführer(in f) m; ~**ly** ad hauptsächlich.

chiffon ['ʃɪfɒn] n Chiffon m.

chilblain ['tʃɪlbleɪn] n Frostbeule f.

child [tʃaɪld], pl ~**ren** ['tʃɪldrən] n Kind nt; ~**birth** n Entbindung f; ~**hood** n Kindheit f; ~**ish** a kindisch; ~**like** a kindlich; ~ **minder** n (Brit) Tagesmutter f.

Chile ['tʃɪlɪ] n Chile nt; ~**an** a chilenisch.

chill [tʃɪl] n Kühle f; (MED) Erkältung f // vt (CULIN) kühlen.

chilli ['tʃɪlɪ] n Peperoni pl; (meal, spice) Chili m.

chilly ['tʃɪlɪ] a kühl, frostig.

chime [tʃaɪm] n Geläut nt // vi ertönen.

chimney ['tʃɪmnɪ] n Schornstein m; ~ **sweep** n Schornsteinfeger(in f) m.

chimpanzee [tʃɪmpæn'ziː] n Schimpanse m.

chin [tʃɪn] n Kinn nt.

china ['tʃaɪnə] n Porzellan nt.

China ['tʃaɪnə] n China nt; **Chinese** [tʃaɪ'niːz] a chinesisch // n, pl inv Chinese m, Chinesin f; (LING) Chinesisch.

chink [tʃɪŋk] n (opening) Ritze f; (noise) Klirren nt.

chip [tʃɪp] n (of wood etc) Splitter m; (gen pl: CULIN) Pommes frites pl; (in poker etc, US: crisp) Chip m // vt absplittern; ~ **in** vi Zwischenbemerkungen machen.

chiropodist [kɪ'rɒpədɪst] n (Brit) Fußpfleger(in f) m.

chirp [tʃɜːp] vi zwitschern.

chisel ['tʃɪzl] n Meißel m.

chit [tʃɪt] n Notiz f.

chitchat ['tʃɪttʃæt] n Plauderei f.

chivalrous ['ʃɪvəlrəs] a ritterlich.

chivalry ['ʃɪvəlrɪ] n Ritterlichkeit f.

chives [tʃaɪvz] npl Schnittlauch m.

chlorine ['klɔːriːn] n Chlor nt.

chock [tʃɒk]: ~**-a-block**, ~**-full** a vollgepfropft.

chocolate ['tʃɒklɪt] n Schokolade f.

choice [tʃɔɪs] n Wahl f; (of goods) Aus-

wahl f // a Qualitäts-.
choir [ˈkwaɪə*] n Chor m; **~boy** n
Chorknabe m.
choke [tʃəʊk] vi ersticken // vt erdrosseln; (block) (ab)drosseln // n (AUT)
Starterklappe f.
cholera [ˈkɒlərə] n Cholera f.
cholesterol [kəˈlestərəl] n Cholesterin
nt.
choose [tʃuːz], pt chose, pp chosen vt
wählen.
choosy [ˈtʃuːzɪ] a wählerisch.
chop [tʃɒp] vt (wood) spalten; (CULIN:
also: ~ up) (zer)hacken // n Hieb m;
(CULIN) Kotelett nt; **~s** pl (jaws)
Lefzen pl.
chopper [ˈtʃɒpə*] n (helicopter)
Hubschrauber m.
choppy [ˈtʃɒpɪ] a (sea) bewegt.
chopsticks [ˈtʃɒpstɪks] npl (Eß)stäb-
chen pl.
choral [ˈkɔːrəl] a Chor-.
chord [kɔːd] n Akkord m.
chore [tʃɔː*] n Pflicht f; **~s** pl
Hausarbeit f.
choreographer [kɒrɪˈɒgrəfə*] n Choreo-
graph(in f) m.
chorister [ˈkɒrɪstə*] n Chorsänger(in f)
m.
chortle [ˈtʃɔːtl] vi glucksen.
chorus [ˈkɔːrəs] n Chor m; (in song) Refrain m.
chose [tʃəʊz], **chosen** [ˈtʃəʊzn] pt, pp
of choose.
Christ [kraɪst] n Christus m.
christen [ˈkrɪsn] vt taufen.
Christian [ˈkrɪstɪən] a christlich // n
Christ(in f) m; **~ity** [krɪstɪˈænɪtɪ] n
Christentum nt; **~ name** n Vorname m.
Christmas [ˈkrɪsməs] n Weihnachten pl;
~ card n Weihnachtskarte f; **~ Day** n
der erste Weihnachtstag; **~ Eve** n
Heiligabend m; **~ tree** n
Weihnachtsbaum m.
chrome [krəʊm] n = chromium
plating.
chromium [ˈkrəʊmɪəm] n Chrom nt; **~
plating** n Verchromung f.
chronic [ˈkrɒnɪk] a chronisch.
chronicle [ˈkrɒnɪkl] n Chronik f.
chronological [krɒnəˈlɒdʒɪkəl] a
chronologisch.
chubby [ˈtʃʌbɪ] a rundlich.
chuck [tʃʌk] vt werfen; **~ out** vt
(person) rauswerfen; (old clothes etc)
wegwerfen; **~ (up)** vt (Brit) hinwerfen.
chuckle [ˈtʃʌkl] vi in sich hineinlachen.
chug [tʃʌg] vi tuckern.
chum [tʃʌm] n Kumpel m.
chunk [tʃʌŋk] n Klumpen m; (of food)
Brocken m.
church [tʃɜːtʃ] n Kirche f; **~yard** n
Kirchhof m.
churlish [ˈtʃɜːlɪʃ] a grob.
churn [tʃɜːn] n (for butter) Butterfaß nt;

(for milk) Milchkanne f; **~ out** vt (col)
produzieren.
chute [ʃuːt] n Rutsche f; (rubbish ~)
Müllschlucker m.
CIA n abbr (US: = Central Intelligence
Agency) CIA m.
CID n abbr (Brit: = Criminal Investigation Department) Kripo f.
cider [ˈsaɪdə*] n Apfelwein m.
cigar [sɪˈgɑː*] n Zigarre f.
cigarette [sɪgəˈret] n Zigarette f; **~
case** n Zigarettenetui nt; **~ end** n
Zigarettenstummel m; **~ holder** n
Zigarettenspitze f.
Cinderella [sɪndəˈrelə] n Aschenbrödel
nt.
cinders [ˈsɪndəz] npl Asche f.
cine [ˈsɪnɪ]: **~-camera** n (Brit)
Filmkamera f; **~-film** n (Brit)
Schmalfilm m.
cinema [ˈsɪnəmə] n Kino nt.
cinnamon [ˈsɪnəmən] n Zimt m.
cipher [ˈsaɪfə*] n (code) Chiffre f.
circle [ˈsɜːkl] n Kreis m; (in cinema)
Rang m // vi kreisen // vt (surround) umgeben; (move round) kreisen um.
circuit [ˈsɜːkɪt] n (track) Rennbahn f;
(lap) Runde f; (ELEC) Stromkreis m;
~ous [sɜːˈkjuːɪtəs] a weitschweifig.
circular [ˈsɜːkjʊlə*] a rund // n
Rundschreiben nt.
circulate [ˈsɜːkjʊleɪt] vi zirkulieren // vt
in Umlauf setzen; **circulation** [-ˈleɪʃən]
n (of blood) Kreislauf m; (of newspaper)
Auflage f; (of money) Umlauf m.
circumcise [ˈsɜːkəmsaɪz] vt be-
schneiden.
circumference [səˈkʌmfərəns] n
(Kreis)umfang m.
circumspect [ˈsɜːkəmspekt] a umsichtig.
circumstances [ˈsɜːkəmstənsəz] npl
Umstände pl; (financial condition) Verhältnisse pl.
circumvent [sɜːkəmˈvent] vt umgehen.
circus [ˈsɜːkəs] n Zirkus m.
cistern [ˈsɪstən] n Zisterne f; (of W.C.)
Spülkasten m.
cite [saɪt] vt zitieren, anführen.
citizen [ˈsɪtɪzn] n Bürger(in f) m; **~ship**
n Staatsbürgerschaft f.
citrus [ˈsɪtrəs] a: **~ fruit** n Zitrusfrucht
f.
city [ˈsɪtɪ] n Großstadt f; the C~ die City,
das Finanzzentrum Londons.
civic [ˈsɪvɪk] a (of town) städtisch; (of
citizen) Bürger-; **~ centre** n
Stadtverwaltung f.
civil [ˈsɪvɪl] a bürgerlich; (not military)
zivil; (polite) höflich; **~ engineer** n
Bauingenieur m; **~ian** [sɪˈvɪlɪən] n
Zivilperson f // a zivil, Zivil-.
civilization [sɪvɪlaɪˈzeɪʃən] n Zivilisation
f.
civilized a zivilisiert.

civil: ~ **law** n Zivilrecht nt; ~ **servant** n Staatsbeamte(r) m; **C~ Service** n Staatsdienst m; ~ **war** n Bürgerkrieg m.

clad [klæd] a: ~ **in** gehüllt in (+acc).

claim [kleɪm] vt beanspruchen; (have opinion) behaupten // vi (for insurance) Ansprüche geltend machen // n (demand) Forderung f; (right) Anspruch m; (pretension) Behauptung f; ~**ant** n Antragsteller(in f) m.

clairvoyant [kleə'vɔɪənt] n Hellseher(in f) m.

clam [klæm] n Venusmuschel f.

clamber ['klæmbə*] vi kraxeln.

clammy ['klæmɪ] a klamm.

clamour ['klæmə*] vi: to ~ **for** nach etw verlangen.

clamp [klæmp] n Schraubzwinge f // vt einspannen; ~ **down on** vt Maßnahmen ergreifen gegen.

clan [klæn] n Clan m.

clandestine [klæn'destɪn] a geheim.

clang [klæŋ] vi scheppern.

clap [klæp] vi Klatschen // vt Beifall klatschen (+dat) // n (of hands) Klatschen nt; (of thunder) Donnerschlag m; ~**ping** n Klatschen nt.

claret ['klærɪt] n rote(r) Bordeaux(wein) m.

clarify ['klærɪfaɪ] vt klären, erklären.

clarinet [klærɪ'net] n Klarinette f.

clarity ['klærɪtɪ] n Klarheit f.

clash [klæʃ] n (fig) Konflikt m // vi zusammenprallen; (colours) sich beißen; (argue) sich streiten.

clasp [klɑːsp] n Griff m; (on jewels, bag) Verschluß m // vt umklammern.

class [klɑːs] n Klasse f // vt einordnen; ~**conscious** a klassenbewußt.

classic ['klæsɪk] n Klassiker m // a klassisch; ~**al** a klassisch.

classified ['klæsɪfaɪd] a (information) Geheim-; ~ **advertisement** n Kleinanzeige f.

classify ['klæsɪfaɪ] vt klassifizieren.

class: ~**mate** n Klassenkamerad(in f) m; ~**room** n Klassenzimmer nt.

clatter ['klætə*] vi klappern; (feet) trappeln.

clause [klɔːz] n (JUR) Klausel f; (GRAM) Satz m.

claustrophobia [klɔstrə'fəʊbɪə] n Platzangst f.

claw [klɔː] n Kralle f // vt (zer)kratzen.

clay [kleɪ] n Lehm m; (for pots) Ton m.

clean [kliːn] a sauber // vt putzen; (clothes) reinigen; ~ **out** vt gründlich putzen; ~ **up** vt aufräumen; ~**cut** a (person) adrett; (clear) klar; ~**er** n (person) Putzfrau f; ~**ing** n Putzen nt; (clothes) Reinigung f; ~**liness** ['klenlɪnɪs] n Reinlichkeit f.

cleanse [klenz] vt reinigen; ~**r** n (for face) Reinigungsmilch f.

clean-shaven ['kliːn'ʃeɪvn] a glattrasiert.

cleansing department ['klenzɪŋ-] n (Brit) Stadtreinigung f.

clear ['klɪə*] a klar; (road) frei // vt (road etc) freimachen; (obstacle) beseitigen; (JUR: suspect) freisprechen // vi klarwerden; (fog) sich lichten // ad: ~ **of** von ... entfernt; ~ **up** vt aufräumen; (solve) aufklären; ~**ance** ['klɪərns] n (removal) Räumung f; (free space) Lichtung f; (permission) Freigabe f; ~**-cut** a (case) eindeutig; ~**ing** n Lichtung f; ~**ing bank** n (Brit) Clearingbank f; ~**ly** ad klar; (obviously) eindeutig; ~**way** n (Brit) (Straße f mit) Halteverbot nt.

cleaver ['kliːvə*] n Hackbeil f.

clef [klef] n Notenschlüssel m.

cleft [kleft] n (in rock) Spalte f.

clemency ['klemənsɪ] n Milde f.

clench [klentʃ] vt (teeth) zusammenbeißen; (fist) ballen.

clergy ['klɜːdʒɪ] n Geistliche(n) pl; ~**man** n Geistliche(r) m.

clerical ['klerɪkəl] a (office) Schreib-, Büro-; (ECCL) geistlich.

clerk [klɑːk, (US) klɜːk] n (in office) Büroangestellte(r) mf; (US: sales person) Verkäufer(in f) m.

clever a ['klevə*] klug; (crafty) schlau.

cliché ['kliːʃeɪ] n Klischee nt.

click [klɪk] vt (heels) zusammenklappen; (tongue) schnalzen mit.

client ['klaɪənt] n Klient(in f) m; ~**ele** [kliːɑ̃n'tel] n Kundschaft f.

cliff [klɪf] n Klippe f.

climate ['klaɪmɪt] n Klima nt.

climax ['klaɪmæks] n Höhepunkt m.

climb [klaɪm] vt besteigen // vi steigen, klettern // n Aufstieg m; ~**-down** n Abstieg m; ~**er** n Bergsteiger(in f) m; ~**ing** n Bergsteigen nt.

clinch [klɪntʃ] vt (decide) entscheiden; (deal) festmachen.

cling [klɪŋ], pt, pp **clung** [klʌŋ] vi (clothes) eng anliegen; to ~ **to** sich festklammern an (dat).

clinic ['klɪnɪk] n Klinik f; ~**al** a klinisch.

clink [klɪŋk] vi klimpern.

clip [klɪp] n Spange f; (also: paper ~) Klammer f // vt (papers) heften; (hair, hedge) stutzen; ~**pers** pl (for hedge) Heckenschere f; (for hair) Haarschneidemaschine f; ~**ping** n Ausschnitt m.

cloak [kləʊk] n Umhang m // vt hüllen; ~**room** n (for coats) Garderobe f; (Brit: W.C.) Toilette f.

clock [klɒk] n Uhr f; ~ **in** or **on** vi stempeln; ~ **off** or **out** vi stempeln; ~**wise** ad im Uhrzeigersinn; ~**work** n Uhrwerk nt // a zum Aufziehen.

clog [klɒg] n Holzschuh m // vt verstopfen.

cloister ['klɔɪstə*] n Kreuzgang m.

clone [kləʊn] n Klon m.

close a, ad and derivatives [kləʊs] a (near) in der Nähe; (friend, connection, print) eng; (relative) nahe; (result) knapp; (examination) eingehend; (weather) schwül; (room) stickig // ad nahe, dicht; **to have a ~ shave** (fig) mit knapper Not davorkommen; **~ by, ~ at hand** a, ad in der Nähe // v and derivatives [kləʊz] vt (shut) schließen; (end) beenden // vi (shop etc) schließen; (door etc) sich schließen // n Ende nt; **~ down** vi schließen; **~d** a (shop etc) geschlossen; **~d shop** n Gewerkschaftszwang m; **~-knit** a eng zusammengewachsen; **~ly** ad eng; (carefully) genau.

closet ['klɔzɪt] n Schrank m.

close-up ['kləʊsʌp] n Nahaufnahme f.

closure ['kləʊʒə*] n Schließung f.

clot [klɔt] n (of blood) Blutgerinnsel nt; (fool) Blödmann m // vi gerinnen.

cloth [klɔθ] n (material) Tuch nt; (rag) Lappen m.

clothe [kləʊð] vt kleiden; **~s** npl Kleider pl; **~s brush** n Kleiderbürste f; **~s line** n Wäscheleine f; **~s peg**, (US) **~s pin** n Wäscheklammer f.

clothing ['kləʊðɪŋ] n Kleidung f.

cloud [klaʊd] n Wolke f; **~burst** n Wolkenbruch m; **~y** a bewölkt; (liquid) trüb.

clout [klaʊt] vt hauen.

clove [kləʊv] n Gewürznelke f; **~ of garlic** n Knoblauchzehe f.

clover ['kləʊvə*] n Klee m.

clown [klaʊn] n Clown m // vi (also: **~ about, ~ around**) kaspern.

cloying ['klɔɪɪŋ] a (taste, smell) übersüß.

club [klʌb] n (weapon) Knüppel m; (society) Klub m; (also: golf **~**) Golfschläger m // vt prügeln // vi: **to ~ together** zusammenlegen; **~s** npl (CARDS) Kreuz nt; **~ car** n (US RAIL) Speisewagen m; **~house** n Klubhaus nt.

cluck [klʌk] vi glucken.

clue [kluː] n Anhaltspunkt m; (in crosswords) Frage f; **I haven't a ~** (ich hab) keine Ahnung.

clump [klʌmp] n Gruppe f.

clumsy ['klʌmzɪ] a (person) unbeholfen; (shape) unförmig.

clung [klʌŋ] pt, pp of **cling**.

cluster ['klʌstə*] n (of trees etc) Gruppe f // vi sich drängen, sich scharen.

clutch [klʌtʃ] n Griff m; (AUT) Kupplung f // vt sich festklammern an (+dat).

clutter ['klʌtə*] vt vollpropfen; (desk) übersäen.

CM abbr (= centimetre) cm.

CND n abbr = Campaign for Nuclear Disarmament.

Co. abbr of **county; company**.

c/o abbr (= care of) c/o.

coach [kəʊtʃ] n (bus) Reisebus m; (old) Kutsche f; (RAIL) (Personen)wagen m; (trainer) Trainer m // vt (SCH) Nachhilfeunterricht geben (+dat); (SPORT) trainieren; **~ trip** n Busfahrt f.

coagulate [kəʊ'ægjʊleɪt] vi gerinnen.

coal [kəʊl] n Kohle f; **~ face** n Streb m; **~ field** n Kohlengebiet nt.

coalition [kəʊə'lɪʃən] n Koalition f.

coal: ~man, ~merchant n Kohlenhändler m; **~ mine** n Kohlenbergwerk nt.

coarse [kɔːs] a (lit) grob; (fig) ordinär.

coast [kəʊst] n Küste f // vi dahinrollen; (AUT) im Leerlauf fahren; **~al** a Küsten-; **~guard** n Küstenwache f; **~line** n Küste(nlinie) f.

coat [kəʊt] n Mantel m; (on animals) Fell nt; (of paint) Schicht f // vt überstreichen; **~ of arms** n Wappen nt; **~hanger** n Kleiderbügel m; **~ing** n Überzug m; (of paint) Schicht f.

coax [kəʊks] vt beschwatzen.

cob [kɒb] n see **corn**.

cobbler ['kɒblə*] n Schuster m.

cobbles ['kɒblz], **cobblestones** ['kɒblstəʊnz] npl Pflastersteine pl.

cobweb ['kɒbweb] n Spinnennetz nt.

cocaine [kə'keɪn] n Kokain nt.

cock [kɒk] n Hahn m // vt (gun) entsichern; **~erel** n junge(r) Hahn m; **~-eyed** a (fig) verrückt.

cockle ['kɒkl] n Herzmuschel f.

cockney ['kɒknɪ] n echte(r) Londoner m.

cockpit ['kɒkpɪt] n (AVIAT) Pilotenkanzel f.

cockroach ['kɒkrəʊtʃ] n Küchenschabe f.

cocktail ['kɒkteɪl] n Cocktail m; **~ cabinet** n Hausbar f; **~ party** n Cocktailparty f.

cocoa ['kəʊkəʊ] n Kakao m.

coconut ['kəʊkənʌt] n Kokosnuß f.

cocoon [kə'kuːn] n Kokon m.

cod [kɒd] n Kabeljau m.

C.O.D. abbr of **cash on delivery**.

code [kəʊd] n Kode m; (JUR) Kodex m.

cod-liver oil ['kɒdlɪvər-] n Lebertran m.

coercion [kəʊ'ɜːʃən] n Zwang m.

coffee ['kɒfɪ] n Kaffee m; **~ bar** n (Brit) Café nt; **~ bean** n Kaffeebohne f; **~ break** n Kaffeepause f; **~ grounds** npl Kaffeesatz m; **~pot** n Kaffeekanne f; **~ table** n Couchtisch m.

coffin ['kɒfɪn] n Sarg m.

cog [kɒg] n (Rad)zahn m.

cogent ['kəʊdʒənt] a triftig, überzeugend, zwingend.

cognac ['kɒnjæk] n Kognak m.

coherent [kəʊ'hɪərənt] a zusammenhängend; (person) verständlich.

cohesion [kəʊ'hiːʒən] n Zusammenhang

m.

coil [kɔil] *n* Rolle *f*; (*ELEC*) Spule *f*; (*contraceptive*) Spirale *f* // *vt* aufwickeln.

coin [kɔin] *n* Münze *f* // *vt* prägen; **~age** *n* (*word*) Prägung *f*; **~-box** *n* (*Brit*) Münzfernsprecher *m*.

coincide [kəʊin'said] *vi* (*happen together*) zusammenfallen; (*agree*) übereinstimmen; **~nce** [kəʊ'insidəns] *n* Zufall *m*.

coke [kəʊk] *n* Koks *m*.

Coke *n* ® (*drink*) Coca-Cola *f* ®.

colander ['kʌləndə*] *n* Durchschlag *m*.

cold [kəʊld] *a* kalt // *n* Kälte *f*; (*MED*) Erkältung *f*; I'm ~ mir ist kalt; to catch ~ sich erkälten; in ~ blood kaltblütig; **~ly** *ad* kalt; **~-shoulder** *vt* (jdm) die kalte Schulter zeigen; **~ sore** *n* Erkältungsbläschen *nt*.

coleslaw ['kəʊlslɔː] *n* Krautsalat *m*.

colic ['kɒlik] *n* Kolik *f*.

collaborate [kə'læbəreit] *vi* zusammenarbeiten.

collaboration [kəlæbə'reiʃən] *n* Zusammenarbeit *f*; (*POL*) Kollaboration *f*.

collapse [kə'læps] *vi* (*people*) zusammenbrechen; (*things*) einstürzen // *n* Zusammenbruch *m*, Einsturz *m*.

collapsible [kə'læpsəbl] *a* zusammenklappbar, Klapp-.

collar ['kɒlə*] *n* Kragen *m*; **~bone** *n* Schlüsselbein *nt*.

collateral [kɒ'lætərəl] *n* (zusätzliche) Sicherheit.

colleague ['kɒliːg] *n* Kollege *m*, Kollegin *f*.

collect [kə'lekt] *vt* sammeln; (*Brit: call and pick up*) abholen // *vi* sich sammeln // *ad*: to call ~ (*US TEL*) ein R-Gespräch führen; **~ion** [kə'lekʃən] *n* Sammlung *f*; (*ECCL*) Kollekte *f*; (*of post*) Leerung *f*.

collective [kə'lektiv] *a* gemeinsam; (*POL*) kollektiv.

collector [kə'lektə*] *n* Sammler *m*; (*tax ~*) (Steuer)einnehmer *m*.

college ['kɒlidʒ] *n* (*UNIV*) College *nt*; (*TECH*) Fach-, Berufsschule *f*.

collide [kə'laid] *vi* zusammenstoßen.

colliery ['kɒliəri] *n* (*Brit*) Zeche *f*.

collision [kə'liʒən] *n* Zusammenstoß *m*.

colloquial [kə'ləʊkwiəl] *a* umgangssprachlich.

collusion [kə'luːʒən] *n* geheime(s) Einverständnis *nt*.

colon ['kəʊlən] *n* Doppelpunkt *m*; (*MED*) Dickdarm *m*.

colonel ['kɜːnl] *n* Oberst *m*.

colonial [kə'ləʊniəl] *a* Kolonial-.

colonize ['kɒlənaiz] *vt* kolonisieren.

colony ['kɒləni] *n* Kolonie *f*.

colour, (*US*) **color** ['kʌlə*] *n* Farbe *f* // *vt* (*lit, fig*) färben // *vi* sich verfärben; **~s** *pl* (*of club*) Fahne *f*; **~ bar** *n*

Rassenschranke *f*; **~-blind** *a* farbenblind; **~ed** *a* farbig; **~eds** *npl* Farbige *pl*; **~ film** *n* Farbfilm *m*; **~ful** *a* bunt; (*personality*) schillernd; **~ing** *n* (*complexion*) Gesichtsfarbe *f*; (*substance*) Farbstoff *m*; **~ scheme** *n* Farbgebung *f*; **~ television** *n* Farbfernsehen *nt*.

colt [kəʊlt] *n* Fohlen *nt*.

column ['kɒləm] *n* Säule *f*; (*MIL*) Kolonne *f*; (*of print*) Spalte *f*; **~ist** ['kɒləmnist] *n* Kolumnist *m*.

coma ['kəʊmə] *n* Koma *nt*.

comb [kəʊm] *n* Kamm *m* // *vt* kämmen; (*search*) durchkämmen.

combat ['kɒmbæt] *n* Kampf *m* // *vt* bekämpfen.

combination [kɒmbi'neiʃən] *n* Kombination *f*.

combine [kəm'bain] *vt* verbinden // *vi* sich vereinigen // *n* ['kɒmbain] (*COMM*) Konzern *m*; **~ (harvester)** *n* Mähdrescher *m*.

combustion [kəm'bʌstʃən] *n* Verbrennung *f*.

come [kʌm] *vi*, *pt* came, *pp* come kommen; to ~ undone aufgehen; ~ about *vi* geschehen; ~ across *vt* (*find*) stoßen auf (+*acc*); ~ away *vi* (*person*) weggehen; (*handle etc*) abgehen; ~ back *vi* zurückkommen; ~ by *vt* (*find*) zu etw kommen; ~ down *vi* (*price*) fallen; ~ forward *vi* (*volunteer*) sich melden; ~ from *vt* (*result*) kommen von; where do you ~ from? wo kommen Sie her?; I ~ from London ich komme aus London; ~ in *vi* hereinkommen; (*train*) einfahren; ~ in for *vt* abkriegen; ~ into *vt* (*inherit*) erben; ~ off *vi* (*handle*) abgehen; (*succeed*) klappen; ~ on *vi* (*progress*) vorankommen; ~ on! komm!; (*hurry*) beeil dich!; ~ out *vi* herauskommen; ~ round *vi* (*MED*) wieder zu sich kommen; ~ to *vi* (*MED*) wieder zu sich kommen; (*bill*) sich belaufen auf (+*acc*); ~ up *vi* hochkommen; (*sun*) aufgehen; (*problem*) auftauchen; ~ up against *vt* (*resistance, difficulties*) stoßen auf (+*acc*); ~ upon *vt* stoßen auf (+*acc*); ~ up with *vt* sich einfallen lassen.

comedian [kə'miːdiən] *n* Komiker *m*; **comedienne** [-'en] *n* Komikerin *f*.

comedown ['kʌmdaʊn] *n* Abstieg *m*.

comedy ['kɒmədi] *n* Komödie *f*.

comet ['kɒmit] *n* Komet *m*.

comeuppance [kʌm'ʌpəns] *n*: to get one's ~ seine Quittung bekommen.

comfort ['kʌmfət] *n* Komfort *m*; (*consolation*) Trost *m* // *vt* trösten; **~able** *a* bequem; **~ably** *ad* (*sit etc*) bequem; (*live*) angenehm; **~ station** *n* (*US*) öffentliche Toilette *f*.

comic ['kɒmik] *n* Comic(heft) *nt*; (*comedian*) Komiker *m* // *a* (*also:* **~al**) komisch.

coming ['kʌmɪŋ] n Kommen nt; ~(s) **and going(s)** n(pl) Kommen und Gehen nt.

comma ['kɔmə] n Komma nt.

command [kə'mɑ:nd] n Befehl m; (control) Führung f; (MIL) Kommando nt; (mastery) Beherrschung f // vt befehlen (+dat); (MIL) kommandieren; (be able to get) verfügen über (+acc); ~eer [kɔmən'dɪə*] vt requirieren; ~er n Kommandant m.

commandment [kə'mɑ:ndmənt] n (REL) Gebot nt.

commando [kə'mɑ:ndəʊ] n (Mitglied nt einer) Kommandotruppe f.

commemorate [kə'meməreɪt] vt gedenken (+gen).

commence [kə'mens] vti beginnen.

commend [kə'mend] vt (recommend) empfehlen; (praise) loben.

commensurate [kə'mensjʊrɪt] a entsprechend (with dat).

comment ['kɔment] n Bemerkung f // vi: to ~ (on) sich äußern (zu); ~ary ['kɔməntrɪ] n Kommentar m; ~ator ['kɔmənteɪtə*] n Kommentator m; (TV) Reporter(in f) m.

commerce ['kɔmɜ:s] n Handel m.

commercial [kə'mɜ:ʃəl] a kommerziell, geschäftlich; (training) kaufmännisch // n (TV) Fernsehwerbung f; ~ **break** n Werbespot m; ~ize vt kommerzialisieren.

commiserate [kə'mɪzəreɪt] vi: to ~ **with** Mitleid haben mit.

commission [kə'mɪʃən] n (act) Auftrag m; (fee) Provision f; (body) Kommission f // vt beauftragen; (MIL) zum Offizier ernennen; (work of art) in Auftrag geben; **out of** ~ außer Betrieb; ~aire [kəmɪʃə'neə*] n (Brit) Portier m; ~er n (POLICE) Polizeipräsident m.

commit [kə'mɪt] vt (crime) begehen; (entrust) anvertrauen; **to** ~ **o.s.** sich festlegen; ~ment n Verpflichtung f.

committee [kə'mɪtɪ] n Ausschuß m.

commodity [kə'mɔdɪtɪ] n Ware f.

common ['kɔmən] a (cause) gemeinsam; (pej) gewöhnlich; (widespread) üblich, häufig // n Gemeindeland nt; **the C~s** npl (Brit) das Unterhaus; ~er n Bürgerliche(r) mf; ~ **law** n Gewohnheitsrecht nt; ~ly ad gewöhnlich; **C~ Market** n Gemeinsame(r) Markt m; ~place a alltäglich; ~room n Gemeinschaftsraum m; ~ **sense** n gesunde(r) Menschenverstand m; **the C~wealth** n das Commonwealth.

commotion [kə'məʊʃən] n Aufsehen nt.

communal [kə'mju:nl] a Gemeinde-; Gemeinschafts-.

commune ['kɔmju:n] n Kommune f // vi sich mitteilen (with dat).

communicate [kə'mju:nɪkeɪt] vt

(transmit) übertragen // vi (be in touch) in Verbindung stehen; (make self understood) sich verständigen.

communication [kəmju:nɪ'keɪʃən] n (message) Mitteilung f; (making understood) Kommunikation f; ~s pl (transport etc) Verkehrswege pl; ~ **cord** n (Brit) Notbremse f.

communion [kə'mju:nɪən] n (also: Holy C~) Abendmahl nt, Kommunion f.

communism ['kɔmjʊnɪzəm] n Kommunismus m.

communist ['kɔmjʊnɪst] n Kommunist(in f) m // a kommunistisch.

community [kə'mju:nɪtɪ] n Gemeinschaft f; ~ **centre** n Gemeinschaftszentrum nt; ~ **chest** n (US) Wohltätigkeitsfonds m.

commutation ticket [kɔmjʊ'teɪʃən'tɪkɪt] n (US) Zeitkarte f.

commute [kə'mju:t] vi pendeln // vt umwandeln; ~r n Pendler m.

compact [kəm'pækt] a kompakt // n ['kɔmpækt] (for make-up) Puderdose f; ~ **disc** n Compact-disc f.

companion [kəm'pænɪən] n Begleiter(in f) m; ~ship n Gesellschaft f.

company ['kʌmpənɪ] n Gesellschaft f; (COMM also) Firma f; **to keep sb** ~ jdm Gesellschaft leisten; ~ **secretary** n (Brit) ≃ Prokurist(in f) m.

comparable ['kɔmpərəbl] a vergleichbar.

comparative [kəm'pærətɪv] a (relative) relativ; ~ly ad verhältnismäßig.

compare [kəm'peə*] vt vergleichen // vi sich vergleichen lassen.

comparison [kəm'pærɪsn] n Vergleich m; **in** ~ **(with)** im Vergleich (mit or zu).

compartment [kəm'pɑ:tmənt] n (RAIL) Abteil nt; (in drawer etc) Fach nt.

compass ['kʌmpəs] n Kompaß m; ~es pl Zirkel m.

compassion [kəm'pæʃən] n Mitleid nt; ~ate a mitfühlend.

compatible [kəm'pætɪbl] a vereinbar; (COMPUT) kompatibel.

compel [kəm'pel] vt zwingen.

compendium [kəm'pendɪəm] n Kompendium nt.

compensate ['kɔmpenseɪt] vt entschädigen // vi: to ~ **for** Ersatz leisten für.

compensation [kɔmpen'seɪʃən] n Entschädigung f.

compère ['kɔmpeə*] n Conférencier m.

compete [kəm'pi:t] vi (take part) teilnehmen; (vie with) konkurrieren.

competence ['kɔmpɪtəns] n Fähigkeit f.

competent ['kɔmpɪtənt] a kompetent.

competition [kɔmpɪ'tɪʃən] n (contest) Wettbewerb m; (COMM, rivalry) Konkurrenz f.

competitive [kəm'petɪtɪv] *a* Konkurrenz-; (*COMM*) konkurrenzfähig.

competitor [kəm'petɪtə*] *n* (*COMM*) Konkurrent(in *f*) *m*; (*participant*) Teilnehmer(in *f*) *m*.

compile [kəm'paɪl] *vt* zusammenstellen.

complacency [kəm'pleɪsnsɪ] *n* Selbstzufriedenheit *f*.

complacent [kəm'pleɪsnt] *a* selbstzufrieden.

complain [kəm'pleɪn] *vi* sich beklagen; (*formally*) sich beschweren; ~t *n* Klage *f*; (*formal* ~) Beschwerde *f*; (*MED*) Leiden *nt*.

complement ['komplɪmənt] *n* Ergänzung *f*; (*ship's crew etc*) Bemannung *f* // *vt* ['komplɪment] ergänzen; ~ary [komplɪ'mentərɪ] *a* (sich) ergänzend.

complete [kəm'pliːt] *a* (*full*) vollkommen, ganz; (*finished*) fertig // *vt* vervollständigen; (*finish*) beenden; (*fill in: form*) ausfüllen; ~ly *ad* ganz.

completion [kəm'pliːʃən] *n* Fertigstellung *f*; (*of contract etc*) Abschluß *m*.

complex ['kompleks] *a* kompliziert.

complexion [kəm'plekʃən] *n* Gesichtsfarbe *f*; (*fig*) Aspekt *m*.

complexity [kəm'pleksɪtɪ] *n* Kompliziertheit *f*.

compliance [kəm'plaɪəns] *n* Fügsamkeit *f*, Einwilligung *f*; in ~ with sth etw (*dat*) gemäß.

complicate ['komplɪkeɪt] *vt* komplizieren; ~d *a* kompliziert.

complication [komplɪ'keɪʃən] *n* Komplikation *f*.

complicity [kəm'plɪsɪtɪ] *n* Mittäterschaft *f* (*in* bei).

compliment ['komplɪmənt] *n* Kompliment *nt* // *vt* ['komplɪment] ein Kompliment machen (*sb* jdm); ~s *pl* Grüße *pl*; to pay sb a ~ jdm ein Kompliment machen; ~ary [komplɪ'mentərɪ] *a* schmeichelhaft; (*free*) Frei-, Gratis-.

comply [kəm'plaɪ] *vi*: to ~ with erfüllen (+*acc*); entsprechen (+*dat*).

component [kəm'pəunənt] *a* Teil- // *n* Bestandteil *m*.

compose [kəm'pəuz] *vt* (*music*) komponieren; (*poetry*) verfassen; to ~ o.s. sich sammeln; ~d *a* gefaßt; ~r *n* Komponist(in *f*) *m*.

composite ['kompəzɪt] *a* zusammengesetzt.

composition [kompə'zɪʃən] *n* (*MUS*) Komposition *f*; (*SCH*) Aufsatz *m*; (*structure*) Zusammensetzung *f*, Aufbau *m*.

compost ['kompost] *n* Kompost *m*.

composure [kəm'pəuʒə*] *n* Fassung *f*.

compound ['kompaund] *n* (*CHEM*) Verbindung *f*; (*enclosure*) Lager *nt*; (*LING*) Kompositum *nt* // *a* zusammengesetzt; (*fracture*) kompliziert; ~ **interest** *n* Zinseszins *m*.

comprehend [komprɪ'hend] *vt* begreifen.

comprehension [komprɪ'henʃən] *n* Verständnis *nt*.

comprehensive [komprɪ'hensɪv] *a* umfassend; ~ **insurance** *n* Vollkasko *nt*; ~ (**school**) *n* (*Brit*) Gesamtschule *f*.

compress [kəm'pres] *vt* komprimieren // *n* ['kompres] (*MED*) Kompresse *f*.

comprise [kəm'praɪz] *vt* (*also:* be ~d of) umfassen, bestehen aus.

compromise ['komprəmaɪz] *n* Kompromiß *m* // *vt* kompromittieren // *vi* einen Kompromiß schließen.

compulsion [kəm'pʌlʃən] *n* Zwang *m*.

compulsive [kəm'pʌlsɪv] *a* zwanghaft.

compulsory [kəm'pʌlsərɪ] *a* obligatorisch.

computer [kəm'pjuːtə*] *n* Computer *m*, Rechner *m*; ~**ize** *vt* (*information*) computerisieren; (*company, accounts*) auf Computer umstellen; ~ **programmer** *n* Programmierer(in *f*) *m*; ~ **programming** *n* Programmieren *nt*; ~ **science** *n* Informatik *f*; **computing** *n* (*science*) Informatik *f*; (*work*) Computerei *f*.

comrade ['komrɪd] *n* Kamerad *m*; (*POL*) Genosse *m*; ~**ship** *n* Kameradschaft *f*.

con [kon] *vt* hereinlegen // *n* Schwindel *nt*.

concave ['konkeɪv] *a* konkav.

conceal [kən'siːl] *vt* (*secret*) verschweigen; (*hide*) verbergen.

concede [kən'siːd] *vt* (*grant*) gewähren; (*point*) zugeben // *vi* (*admit*) zugeben.

conceit [kən'siːt] *n* Einbildung *f*; ~**ed** *a* eingebildet.

conceivable [kən'siːvəbl] *a* vorstellbar.

conceive [kən'siːv] *vt* (*idea*) ausdenken; (*imagine*) sich vorstellen // *vti* (*baby*) empfangen.

concentrate ['konsəntreɪt] *vi* sich konzentrieren (*on* auf +*acc*) // *vt* konzentrieren.

concentration [konsən'treɪʃən] *n* Konzentration *f*; ~ **camp** *n* Konzentrationslager *nt*, KZ *nt*.

concept ['konsept] *n* Begriff *m*.

conception [kən'sepʃən] *n* (*idea*) Vorstellung *f*; (*BIOL*) Empfängnis *f*.

concern [kən'sɜːn] *n* (*affair*) Angelegenheit *f*; (*COMM*) Unternehmen *nt*; (*worry*) Sorge *f* // *vt* (*interest*) angehen; (*be about*) handeln von; (*have connection with*) betreffen; to be ~ed (*about*) sich Sorgen machen (um); ~**ing** *prep* hinsichtlich (+*gen*).

concert ['konsət] *n* Konzert *nt*; ~**ed** [kən'sɜːtɪd] *a* gemeinsam; ~ **hall** *n* Konzerthalle *f*.

concertina [konsə'tiːnə] *n* Handharmonika *f*.

concerto [kən'tʃɜːtəu] *n* Konzert *nt*.

concession [kən'seʃən] n (*yielding*) Zugeständnis nt; tax ~ Steuer-Konzession f.

conciliation [kənsɪlɪ'eɪʃən] n Versöhnung f; (*official*) Schlichtung f.

concise [kən'saɪs] a präzis.

conclude [kən'kluːd] vt (*end*) beenden; (*treaty*) (ab)schließen; (*decide*) schließen, folgern.

conclusion [kən'kluːʒən] n (Ab)schluß m; (*deduction*) Schluß m.

conclusive [kən'kluːsɪv] a schlüssig.

concoct [kən'kɒkt] vt zusammenbrauen; ~**ion** n Gebräu nt.

concourse [kɒŋkɔːs] n (Bahnhofs)halle f, Vorplatz m.

concrete ['kɒŋkriːt] n Beton m // a konkret.

concur [kən'kɜː*] vi übereinstimmen.

concurrently [kən'kʌrəntlɪ] ad gleichzeitig.

concussion [kɒn'kʌʃən] n (Gehirn)erschütterung f.

condemn [kən'dem] vt (*JUR*) verurteilen; (*building*) abbruchreif erklären.

condensation [kɒnden'seɪʃən] n Kondensation f.

condense [kən'dens] vi (*CHEM*) kondensieren // vt (*fig*) zusammendrängen; ~**d milk** n Kondensmilch f.

condescending [kɒndɪ'sendɪŋ] a herablassend.

condition [kən'dɪʃən] n (*state*) Zustand m; (*presupposition*) Bedingung f // vt (*hair etc*) behandeln; (*accustom*) gewöhnen; **on** ~ **that** ... unter der Bedingung, daß ...; ~**al** a bedingt; (*GRAM*) Bedingungs-; ~**er** n (*for hair*) Spülung f; (*for fabrics*) Weichspüler m; ~**s** pl (*circumstances*) Verhältnisse pl.

condolences [kən'dəʊlənsɪz] npl Beileid nt.

condom ['kɒndəm] n Kondom nt or m.

condominium [kɒndə'mɪnɪəm] n (*US*) Eigentumswohnung f; (*block*) Eigentumsblock m.

condone [kən'dəʊn] vt gutheißen.

conducive [kən'djuːsɪv] a: ~ **to** dienlich (*dat*).

conduct ['kɒndʌkt] n (*behaviour*) Verhalten nt; (*management*) Führung f // vt [kən'dʌkt] führen; (*MUS*) dirigieren; ~**ed tour** n Führung f; ~**or** [kən'dʌktə*] n (*of orchestra*) Dirigent m; (*in bus, US: on train*) Schaffner m; (*ELEC*) Leiter m; ~**ress** [kən'dʌktrɪs] n (*in bus*) Schaffnerin f.

cone [kəʊn] n (*MATH*) Kegel m; (*for ice cream*) (Waffel)tüte f; (*fir*) Tannenzapfen m.

confectioner [kən'fekʃənə*] n Konditor m; ~**'s (shop)** n Konditorei f; ~**y** n Süßigkeiten pl.

confederation [kənfedə'reɪʃən] n Bund m.

confer [kən'fɜː*] vt (*degree*) verleihen // vi (*discuss*) konferieren, verhandeln; ~**ence** ['kɒnfərəns] n Konferenz f.

confess [kən'fes] vti gestehen; (*ECCL*) beichten; ~**ion** [kən'feʃən] n Geständnis nt; (*ECCL*) Beichte f; ~**ional** [kən'feʃənl] n Beichtstuhl m.

confetti [kən'fetɪ] n Konfetti nt.

confide [kən'faɪd] vi: **to** ~ **in** (sich) anvertrauen (+dat).

confidence ['kɒnfɪdəns] n Vertrauen nt; (*assurance*) Selbstvertrauen nt; (*secret*) Geheimnis nt; **in** ~ (*speak, write*) vertraulich; ~ **trick** n Schwindel m.

confident ['kɒnfɪdənt] a (*sure*) überzeugt; (*self-assured*) selbstsicher; ~**ial** [kɒnfɪ'denʃəl] a vertraulich.

confine [kən'faɪn] vt (*limit*) beschränken; (*lock up*) einsperren; ~**s** ['kɒnfaɪnz] npl Grenzen pl; ~**d** a (*space*) eng; ~**ment** n (*in prison*) Haft f; (*MED*) Wochenbett nt.

confirm [kən'fɜːm] vt bestätigen; ~**ation** [kɒnfə'meɪʃən] n Bestätigung f; (*REL*) Konfirmation f; ~**ed** a unverbesserlich; (*bachelor*) eingefleischt.

confiscate ['kɒnfɪskeɪt] vt beschlagnahmen.

conflict ['kɒnflɪkt] n Konflikt m // vi [kən'flɪkt] im Widerspruch stehen; ~**ing** [kən'flɪktɪŋ] a widersprüchlich.

conform [kən'fɔːm] vi (*things*) entsprechen (*to dat*); (*people*) sich anpassen (*to dat*); (*to rules*) sich richten (*to nach*); ~**ist** n Konformist(in f) m.

confound [kən'faʊnd] vt verblüffen; (*throw into confusion*) durcheinanderbringen.

confront [kən'frʌnt] vt (*enemy*) entgegentreten (+dat); (*problems*) sich stellen (+dat); **to** ~ **sb with sth** jdn mit etw konfrontieren; ~**ation** [kɒnfrən'teɪʃən] n Konfrontation f.

confuse [kən'fjuːz] vt verwirren; (*sth with sth*) verwechseln; ~**d** a verwirrt; **confusing** a verwirrend; **confusion** [kən'fjuːʒən] n (*perplexity*) Verwirrung f; (*mixing up*) Verwechslung f; (*tumult*) Aufruhr m.

congeal [kən'dʒiːl] vi (*freeze*) gefrieren; (*clot*) gerinnen.

congenial [kən'dʒiːnɪəl] a angenehm.

congenital [kən'dʒenɪtl] a angeboren.

congested [kən'dʒestɪd] a überfüllt.

congestion [kən'dʒestʃən] n Stau m.

conglomerate [kən'glɒmərət] n (*COMM, GEOL*) Konglomerat m.

conglomeration [kənglɒmə'reɪʃən] n Anhäufung f.

congratulate [kən'grætjʊleɪt] vt beglückwünschen (*on zu*).

congratulations [kəngrætjʊ'leɪʃənz] npl Glückwünsche pl; ~**!** gratuliere!, herzlichen Glückwunsch!

congregate ['kɒŋgrɪgeɪt] *vi* sich versammeln.

congregation [kɒŋgrɪ'geɪʃən] *n* Gemeinde *f*.

congress ['kɒŋgres] *n* Kongreß *m*; **~man** *n* (*US*) Mitglied *nt* des amerikanischen Repräsentantenhauses.

conical ['kɒnɪkəl] *a* kegelförmig.

conifer ['kɒnɪfə*] *n* Nadelbaum *m*.

conjecture [kən'dʒektʃə*] *n* Vermutung *f*.

conjugal ['kɒndʒʊgəl] *a* ehelich.

conjugate ['kɒndʒʊgeɪt] *vt* konjugieren.

conjunction [kən'dʒʌŋkʃən] *n* Verbindung *f*; (*GRAM*) Konjunktion *f*.

conjunctivitis [kəndʒʌŋktɪ'vaɪtɪs] *n* Bindehautentzündung *f*.

conjure ['kʌndʒə*] *vi* zaubern; **~ up** *vt* heraufbeschwören; **~r** *n* Zauberkünstler(in *f*) *m*.

conk [kɒŋk]: **~ out** *vi* (*col*) den Geist aufgeben.

connect [kə'nekt] *vt* verbinden; (*ELEC*) anschließen; **to be ~ed with** ein Beziehung haben zu; (*be related to*) verwandt sein mit; **~ion** [kə'nekʃən] *n* Verbindung *f*; (*relation*) Zusammenhang *m*; (*ELEC, TEL, RAIL*) Anschluß *m*.

connive [kə'naɪv] *vi*: **to ~ at** stillschweigend dulden.

connoisseur [kɒnɪ'sɜ:*] *n* Kenner *m*.

conquer ['kɒŋkə*] *vt* (*feelings*) überwinden; (*enemy*) besiegen; (*country*) erobern; **~or** *n* Eroberer *m*.

conquest ['kɒŋkwest] *n* Eroberung *f*.

cons [kɒnz] *npl see* **convenience, pro.**

conscience ['kɒnʃəns] *n* Gewissen *nt*.

conscientious [kɒnʃɪ'enʃəs] *a* gewissenhaft.

conscious ['kɒnʃəs] *a* bewußt; (*MED*) bei Bewußtsein; **~ness** *n* Bewußtsein *nt*.

conscript ['kɒnskrɪpt] *n* Wehrpflichtige(r) *m*; **~ion** [kən'skrɪpʃən] *n* Wehrpflicht *f*.

consecrate ['kɒnsɪkreɪt] *vt* weihen.

consecutive [kən'sekjʊtɪv] *a* aufeinanderfolgend.

consensus [kən'sensəs] *n* allgemeine Übereinstimmung *f*.

consent [kən'sent] *n* Zustimmung *f* // *vi* zustimmen (*to dat*).

consequence ['kɒnsɪkwəns] *n* (*importance*) Bedeutung *f*; (*effect*) Folge *f*.

consequently ['kɒnsɪkwəntlɪ] *ad* folglich.

conservation [kɒnsə'veɪʃən] *n* Erhaltung *f*; (*nature ~*) Umweltschutz *m*.

conservative [kən'sɜ:vətɪv] *a* konservativ; **C~** *a* (*Brit*) konservativ // *n* Konservative(r) *mf*.

conservatory [kən'sɜ:vətrɪ] *n* (*room*) Wintergarten *m*.

conserve [kən'sɜ:v] *vt* erhalten.

consider [kən'sɪdə*] *vt* überlegen; (*take into account*) in Betracht ziehen; (*regard as*) halten für; **to ~ doing sth** denken daran, etw zu tun.

considerable [kən'sɪdərəbl] *a* beträchtlich.

considerably *ad* beträchtlich.

considerate [kən'sɪdərɪt] *a* rücksichtsvoll.

consideration [kənsɪdə'reɪʃən] *n* Rücksicht(nahme) *f*; (*thought*) Erwägung *f*; (*reward*) Entgelt *nt*.

considering [kən'sɪdərɪŋ] *prep* in Anbetracht (+*gen*).

consign [kən'saɪn] *vt* übergeben; **~ment** *n* Sendung *f*.

consist [kən'sɪst] *vi*: **to ~ of** bestehen aus.

consistency [kən'sɪstənsɪ] *n* (*of material*) Konsistenz *f*; (*of argument, person*) Konsequenz *f*.

consistent [kən'sɪstənt] *a* (*person*) konsequent; (*argument*) folgerichtig.

consolation [kɒnsə'leɪʃən] *n* Trost *m*.

console [kən'səʊl] *vt* trösten // *n* ['kɒnsəʊl] Kontroll(pult) *nt*.

consolidate [kən'sɒlɪdeɪt] *vt* festigen.

consommé [kən'sɒmeɪ] *n* Fleischbrühe *f*.

consonant ['kɒnsənənt] *n* Konsonant *m*.

conspicuous [kən'spɪkjʊəs] *a* (*prominent*) auffällig; (*visible*) deutlich sichtbar.

conspiracy [kən'spɪrəsɪ] *n* Verschwörung *f*.

conspire [kən'spaɪə*] *vi* sich verschwören.

constable ['kʌnstəbl] *n* (*Brit*) Polizist(in *f*) *n*; **chief ~** Polizeipräsident *m*.

constabulary [kən'stæbjʊlərɪ] *n* Polizei *f*.

constant ['kɒnstənt] *a* (*continuous*) ständig; (*unchanging*) konstant; **~ly** *ad* ständig.

constellation [kɒnstə'leɪʃən] *n* Sternbild *nt*.

consternation [kɒnstə'neɪʃən] *n* Bestürzung *f*.

constipated ['kɒnstɪpeɪtəd] *a* verstopft.

constipation [kɒnstɪ'peɪʃən] *n* Verstopfung *f*.

constituency [kən'stɪtjʊənsɪ] *n* Wahlkreis *m*.

constituent [kən'stɪtjʊənt] *n* (*person*) Wähler *m*; (*part*) Bestandteil *m*.

constitute ['kɒnstɪtju:t] *vt* (*make up*) bilden; (*amount to*) darstellen.

constitution [kɒnstɪ'tju:ʃən] *n* Verfassung *f*; **~al** *a* Verfassungs-.

constraint [kən'streɪnt] *n* Zwang *m*; (*shyness*) Befangenheit *f*.

construct [kən'strʌkt] *vt* bauen; **~ion** [kən'strʌkʃən] *n* Konstruktion *f*; (*building*) Bau *m*; **~ive** *a* konstruktiv.

construe [kən'stru:] *vt* deuten.

consul ['kɒnsl] n Konsul m; **~ate** ['kɒnsjulət] n Konsulat nt.

consult [kən'sʌlt] vt um Rat fragen; (doctor) konsultieren; (book) nachschlagen in (+dat); **~ant** n (MED) Facharzt m; (other specialist) Gutachter m; **~ation** [kɒnsəl'teɪʃən] n Beratung f; (MED) Konsultation f; **~ing room** n Sprechzimmer nt.

consume [kən'sjuːm] vt verbrauchen; (food) konsumieren; **~r** n Verbraucher m; **~r goods** npl Konsumgüter pl; **consumerism** n Konsum m; **~r society** n Konsumgesellschaft f.

consummate ['kɒnsʌmeɪt] vt (marriage) vollziehen.

consumption [kən'sʌmpʃən] n Verbrauch m; (of food) Konsum m.

cont. abbr (= continued) Forts.

contact ['kɒntækt] n (touch) Berührung f; (connection) Verbindung f; (person) Kontakt m // vt sich in Verbindung setzen mit; **~ lenses** npl Kontaktlinsen pl.

contagious [kən'teɪdʒəs] a ansteckend.

contain [kən'teɪn] vt enthalten; **to ~ o.s.** sich zügeln; **~er** n Behälter m; (transport) Container m.

contamination [kəntæmɪ'neɪʃən] n Verunreinigung f.

cont'd abbr (= continued) Forts.

contemplate ['kɒntəmpleɪt] vt (look at) (nachdenklich) betrachten; (think about) überdenken; (plan) vorhaben.

contemporary [kən'tempərərɪ] a zeitgenössisch // n Zeitgenosse m.

contempt [kən'tempt] n Verachtung f; **~ of court** (JUR) Mißachtung f des Gerichts; **~ible** a verachtenswert; **~uous** a verächtlich.

contend [kən'tend] vt (argue) behaupten // vi kämpfen; **~er** n (for post) Bewerber(in f) m; (SPORT) Wettkämpfer(in f) m.

content [kən'tent] a zufrieden // vt befriedigen // n ['kɒntent] (also: **~s**) Inhalt m; **~ed** a zufrieden.

contention [kən'tenʃən] n (dispute) Streit m; (argument) Behauptung f.

contentment [kən'tentmənt] n Zufriedenheit f.

contest ['kɒntest] n (Wett)kampf m // vt [kən'test] (dispute) bestreiten; (JUR) anfechten; (POL) kandidieren in (+dat); **~ant** [kən'testənt] n Bewerber(in f) m.

context ['kɒntekst] n Zusammenhang m.

continent ['kɒntɪnənt] n Kontinent m; **the C~** (Brit) das europäische Festland; **~al** [kɒntɪ'nentl] a kontinental; **~al quilt** n (Brit) Federbett nt.

contingency [kən'tɪndʒənsɪ] n Möglichkeit f.

contingent [kən'tɪndʒənt] n Kontingent nt.

continual [kən'tɪnjuəl] a (endless)

fortwährend; (repeated) immer wiederkehrend; **~ly** ad immer wieder.

continuation [kəntɪnju'eɪʃən] n Fortsetzung f.

continue [kən'tɪnjuː] vi (person) weitermachen; (thing) weitergehen // vt fortsetzen.

continuity [kɒntɪ'njuːɪtɪ] n Kontinuität f.

continuous [kən'tɪnjuəs] a ununterbrochen; **~ stationery** n Endlospapier nt.

contort [kən'tɔːt] vt verdrehen; **~ion** [kən'tɔːʃən] n Verzerrung f.

contour ['kɒntuə*] n Umriß m; (also: **~ line**) Höhenlinie f.

contraband ['kɒntrəbænd] n Schmuggelware f.

contraception [kɒntrə'sepʃən] n Empfängnisverhütung f.

contraceptive [kɒntrə'septɪv] n empfängnisverhütende(s) Mittel nt // a empfängnisverhütend.

contract ['kɒntrækt] n Vertrag m // (vb: [kən'trækt]) vi (to do sth) sich vertraglich verpflichten; (muscle, metal) sich zusammenziehen // vt zusammenziehen; **~ion** [kən'trækʃən] n (shortening) Verkürzung f; **~or** [kən'træktə*] n Unternehmer m.

contradict [kɒntrə'dɪkt] vt widersprechen (+dat); **~ion** [kɒntrə'dɪkʃən] n Widerspruch m; **~ory** a widersprüchlich.

contraption [kən'træpʃən] n (col) Apparat m.

contrary ['kɒntrərɪ] a (opposite) entgegengesetzt; [kən'treərɪ] (obstinate) widerspenstig // n Gegenteil nt; **on the ~** im Gegenteil.

contrast ['kɒntrɑːst] n Kontrast m // vt [kən'trɑːst] entgegensetzen; **~ing** [kən'trɑːstɪŋ] a Kontrast-.

contravene [kɒntrə'viːn] vt verstoßen gegen.

contribute [kən'trɪbjuːt] vti: **to ~ to** beitragen zu.

contribution [kɒntrɪ'bjuːʃən] n Beitrag m.

contributor [kən'trɪbjutə*] n Beitragende(r) mf.

contrive [kən'traɪv] vt ersinnen // vi: **to ~ to do sth** es schaffen, etw zu tun.

control [kən'trəul] vt (direct, test) kontrollieren // n Kontrolle f; **~s** pl (of vehicle) Steuerung f; (of engine) Schalttafel f; **to be in ~ of** (business, office) leiten; (group of children) beaufsichtigen; **out of ~** außer Kontrolle; **under ~** unter Kontrolle; **~ panel** n Schalttafel f; **~ room** n Kontrollraum m; **~ tower** n (AVIAT) Kontrollturm m.

controversial [kɒntrə'vɜːʃəl] a umstritten.

controversy ['kɒntrəvɜːsɪ] n Kontroverse f.

conurbation [kɔnɜː'beɪʃən] n Ballungsgebiet nt.

convalesce [kɔnvə'les] vi genesen; **~nce** n Genesung f.

convector [kən'vektə*] n Heizlüfter m.

convene [kən'viːn] vt zusammenrufen // vi sich versammeln.

convenience [kən'viːnɪəns] n Annehmlichkeit f; all modern ~s, (Brit) all mod cons mit allem Komfort; at your ~ wann es Ihnen paßt.

convenient [kən'viːnɪənt] a günstig.

convent ['kɔnvənt] n Kloster nt.

convention [kən'venʃən] n Versammlung f; (custom) Konvention f; **~al** a konventionell.

converge [kən'vɜːdʒ] vi zusammenlaufen.

conversant [kən'vɜːsənt] a: to be ~ with bewandert sein in (+dat).

conversation [kɔnvə'seɪʃən] n Gespräch nt; **~al** a Unterhaltungs-.

converse [kən'vɜːs] vi sich unterhalten.

conversion [kən'vɜːʃən] n Umwandlung f; (esp REL) Bekehrung f.

convert [kən'vɜːt] vt (change) umwandeln; (REL) bekehren // n ['kɔnvɜːt] Bekehrte(r) mf; Konvertit(in f) m; **~ible** n (AUT) Kabriolett nt // a umwandelbar; (FIN) konvertierbar.

convex [kɔn'veks] a konvex.

convey [kən'veɪ] vt (carry) befördern; (feelings) vermitteln; **~or belt** n Fließband nt.

convict [kən'vɪkt] vt verurteilen // n ['kɔnvɪkt] Häftling m; **~ion** [kən'vɪkʃən] n (verdict) Verurteilung f; (belief) Überzeugung f.

convince [kən'vɪns] vt überzeugen; **~d** a: ~ that überzeugt davon, daß; **convincing** a überzeugend.

convoluted [kɔnvə'luːtɪd] a verwickelt; (style) gewunden.

convoy ['kɔnvɔɪ] n (of vehicles) Kolonne f; (protected) Konvoi m.

convulse [kən'vʌls] vt zusammenzucken lassen; to be ~d with laughter sich vor Lachen krümmen.

convulsion [kən'vʌlʃən] n (esp MED) Zuckung f, Krampf m.

coo [kuː] vi gurren.

cook [kʊk] vti kochen // n Koch m, Köchin f; ~ **book** n Kochbuch nt; **~er** n Herd m; **~ery** n Kochkunst f; **~ery book** (Brit) = ~ book; **~ie** n (US) Plätzchen nt; **~ing** n Kochen nt.

cool [kuːl] a kühl // vti (ab)kühlen; ~ **down** vti (fig) sich beruhigen; **~ness** n Kühle f; (of temperament) kühle(r) Kopf.

coop [kuːp] n Hühnerstall m // vt: ~ up (fig) einpferchen.

cooperate [kəʊ'ɔpəreɪt] vi zusammenarbeiten; **cooperation** [-'reɪʃən] n Zusammenarbeit f.

cooperative [kəʊ'ɔpərətɪv] a hilfsbereit; (COMM) genossenschaftlich // n (of farmers) Genossenschaft f; (~ store) Konsumladen m.

coordinate [kəʊ'ɔːdɪneɪt] vt koordinieren // n [kəʊ'ɔːdɪnət] (MATH) Koordinate f; **~s** pl (clothes) Kombinationen pl.

coordination [kəʊɔːdɪ'neɪʃən] n Koordination f.

cop [kɔp] n (col) Polyp m, Bulle m.

cope [kəʊp] vi: to ~ with fertig werden mit.

copious ['kəʊpɪəs] a reichhaltig.

copper ['kɔpə*] n (metal) Kupfer nt; (col: policeman) Polyp m, Bulle m; **~s** pl Kleingeld nt.

coppice ['kɔpɪs], **copse** [kɔps] n Unterholz nt.

copulate ['kɔpjʊleɪt] vi sich paaren.

copy ['kɔpɪ] n (imitation) Kopie f; (of book etc) Exemplar nt; (of newspaper) Nummer f // vt kopieren, abschreiben; **~right** n Copyright nt.

coral ['kɔrəl] n Koralle f; ~ **reef** n Korallenriff nt.

cord [kɔːd] n Schnur f; (ELEC) Kabel nt.

cordial ['kɔːdɪəl] a herzlich // n Fruchtsaft m.

cordon ['kɔːdn] n Absperrkette f; ~ **off** vt abriegeln.

corduroy ['kɔːdərɔɪ] n Kord(samt) m.

core [kɔː*] n Kern m // vt entkernen.

cork [kɔːk] n (bark) Korkrinde f; (stopper) Korken m; **~screw** n Korkenzieher m.

corn [kɔːn] n (Brit: wheat) Getreide nt, Korn nt; (US: maize) Mais m; (on foot) Hühnerauge nt; ~ **on the cob** Maiskolben m.

cornea ['kɔːnɪə] n Hornhaut f.

corned beef ['kɔːnd'biːf] n Corned Beef nt.

corner ['kɔːnə*] n Ecke f; (on road) Kurve f // vt in die Enge treiben; (market) monopolisieren // vi (AUT) in die Kurve gehen; **~stone** n Eckstein m.

cornet ['kɔːnɪt] n (MUS) Kornett nt; (Brit: of ice cream) Eistüte f.

cornflakes ['kɔːnfleɪks] npl Corn-flakes pl ®.

cornflour ['kɔːnflaʊə*] n (Brit), **cornstarch** ['kɔːnstaːtʃ] n (US) Maizena nt ®.

Cornwall ['kɔːnwəl] n Cornwall nt.

corny ['kɔːnɪ] a (joke) blöd(e).

corollary [kə'rɔlərɪ] n Folgesatz m.

coronary ['kɔrənərɪ] n: ~ **(thrombosis)** n Herzinfarkt m.

coronation [kɔrə'neɪʃən] n Krönung f.

coroner ['kɔrənə*] n Untersuchungsrichter m.

coronet ['kɔrənɪt] n Adelskrone f.

corporal ['kɔːpərəl] n Obergefreite(r) m // a: ~ **punishment** Prügelstrafe f.

corporate ['kɔ:pərɪt] *a* gemeinschaftlich, korporativ.

corporation [kɔ:pə'reɪʃən] *n (of town)* Gemeinde *f*; *(COMM)* Körperschaft *f*, Aktiengesellschaft *f*.

corps [kɔ:*], *pl* **corps** [kɔ:z] *n (Armee)korps nt*.

corpse [kɔ:ps] *n* Leiche *f*.

corpuscle ['kɔ:pʌsl] *n* Blutkörperchen *nt*.

corral [kə'ra:l] *n* Pferch *m*, Korral *m*.

correct [kə'rekt] *a (accurate)* richtig; *(proper)* korrekt // *vt* korrigieren; **~ion** [kə'rekʃən] *n* Berichtigung *f*.

correlation [kɒrɪ'leɪʃən] *n* Wechselbeziehung *f*.

correspond [kɒrɪs'pɒnd] *vi (agree)* übereinstimmen; *(exchange letters)* korrespondieren; **~ence** *n (similarity)* Entsprechung *f*; *(letters)* Briefwechsel *m*, Korrespondenz *f*; **~ence course** *n* Fernkurs *m*; **~ent** *n (PRESS)* Berichterstatter *m*.

corridor ['kɒrɪdɔ:*] *n* Gang *m*.

corroborate [kə'rɒbəreɪt] *vt* bestätigen.

corrode [kə'rəud] *vt* zerfressen // *vi* rosten; **corrosion** [kə'rəuʒən] *n* Korrosion *f*.

corrugated ['kɒrəgeɪtɪd] *a* gewellt; **~ iron** *n* Wellblech *nt*.

corrupt [kə'rʌpt] *a* korrupt // *vt* verderben; *(bribe)* bestechen; **~ion** [kə'rʌpʃən] *n (of society)* Verdorbenheit *f*; *(bribery)* Bestechung *f*.

corset ['kɔ:sɪt] *n* Korsett *nt*.

corsica ['kɔ:sɪkə] *n* Korsika *f*.

cortège [kɔ:'teɪʒ] *n* Zug *m*; *(of funeral)* Leichenzug *m*.

cosh [kɒʃ] *n (Brit)* Totschläger *m*.

cosmetic [kɒz'metɪk] *n* Kosmetikum *f*.

cosmic ['kɒzmɪk] *a* kosmisch.

cosmonaut ['kɒzmənɔ:t] *n* Kosmonaut(in *f*) *m*.

cosmopolitan [kɒzmə'pɒlɪtən] *a* international; *(city)* Welt-.

cosmos ['kɒzmɒs] *n* Kosmos *m*.

cosset ['kɒsɪt] *vt* verwöhnen.

cost [kɒst] *n* Kosten *pl*, Preis *m*; **~s** *pl* Kosten *pl* // *vti*, *pt*, *pp* **cost** kosten; **how much does it ~?** wieviel kostet das?; **at all ~s** um jeden Preis.

co-star ['kəustɔ:*] *n* eine(r) der Hauptdarsteller.

cost-effective ['kɒst'fektɪv] *a* rentabel.

costly ['kɒstlɪ] *a* kostspielig.

cost-of-living ['kɒstəv'lɪvɪŋ] *a (allowance, index)* Lebenshaltungskosten.

cost price ['kɒst'praɪs] *n (Brit)* Selbstkostenpreis *m*.

costume ['kɒstju:m] *n* Kostüm *nt*; *(fancy dress)* Maskenkostüm *nt*; *(Brit: also: swimming ~)* Badeanzug *m*; **~ jewellery** *n* Modeschmuck *m*.

cosy ['kəuzɪ] *a (Brit)* behaglich; (: *atmosphere*) gemütlich.

cot [kɒt] *n (Brit: child's)* Kinderbett(chen) *nt*; *(US: campbed)* Feldbett *nt*.

cottage ['kɒtɪdʒ] *n* kleine(s) Haus *nt*; **~ cheese** *n* Hüttenkäse *m*; **~ industry** *n* Heimindustrie *f*; **~ pie** *n* Auflauf mit Hackfleisch und Kartoffelbrei.

cotton ['kɒtn] *n* Baumwolle *f*; *(thread)* Garn *nt*; **~ on to** *vt (col)* kapieren; **~ candy** *n (US)* Zuckerwatte *f*; **~ wool** *n (Brit)* Watte *f*.

couch [kautʃ] *n* Couch *f*.

couchette [ku:'ʃet] *n (on train, boat)* Liegewagen(platz) *m*.

cough [kɒf] *vi* husten // *n* Husten *m*; **~ drop** *n* Hustenbonbon *nt*.

could [kud] *pt of* **can**; **~n't** = **could not**.

council ['kaunsl] *n (of town)* Stadtrat *m*; **~ estate/house** *n (Brit)* Siedlung *f*/Haus *nt* des sozialen Wohnungsbaus; **~lor** ['kaunslə*] *n* Stadtrat *m*/-rätin *f*.

counsel ['kaunsl] *n (barrister)* Anwalt *m*; *(advice)* Rat(schlag) *m* // *vt* beraten; **~lor** *n* Berater *m*.

count [kaunt] *vti* zählen // *n (reckoning)* Abrechnung *f*; *(nobleman)* Graf *m*; **~ on** *vt* zählen auf (+*acc*); **~down** *n* Countdown *m*.

countenance ['kauntɪnəns] *n (old)* Antlitz *nt* // *vt (tolerate)* gutheißen.

counter ['kauntə*] *n (in shop)* Ladentisch *m*; *(in café)* Theke *f*; *(in bank, post office)* Schalter *m* // *vt* entgegnen; **~act** [kauntə'rækt] *vt* entgegenwirken (+*dat*); **~espionage** *n* Spionageabwehr *f*.

counterfeit ['kauntəfɪt] *n* Fälschung *f* // *vt* fälschen // *a* gefälscht.

counterfoil ['kauntəfɔɪl] *n* (Kontroll)abschnitt *m*.

countermand ['kauntəma:nd] *vt* rückgängig machen.

counterpart ['kauntəpa:t] *n (object)* Gegenstück *nt*; *(person)* Gegenüber *nt*.

counterproductive ['kauntəprə'dʌktɪv] *a* destruktiv.

countersign ['kauntəsaɪn] *vt* gegenzeichnen.

countess ['kauntɪs] *n* Gräfin *f*.

countless ['kauntlɪs] *a* zahllos, unzählig.

country ['kʌntrɪ] *n* Land *nt*; **~ dancing** *n (Brit)* Volkstanz *m*; **~ house** *n* Landhaus *nt*; **~man** *n (national)* Landsmann *m*; *(rural)* Bauer *m*; **~side** *n* Landschaft *f*.

county ['kauntɪ] *n* Landkreis *m*; *(Brit)* Grafschaft *f*.

coup [ku:], *pl* **~s** [ku:z] *n* Coup *m*; *(also:* **~ d'état***)* *n* Staatsstreich *m*, Putsch *m*.

coupé [ku:'peɪ] *n (AUT)* Coupé *nt*.

couple ['kʌpl] *n* Paar *nt*; **a ~ of** ein paar // *vt* koppeln.

coupon ['ku:pɒn] *n* Gutschein *m*.

courage ['kʌrɪdʒ] n Mut m; **~ous** [kə'reɪdʒəs] a mutig.

courgette [kuə'ʒet] n (Brit) Zucchini f.

courier ['kurɪə*] n (for holiday) Reiseleiter m; (messenger) Kurier m.

course [kɔːs] n (race) Bahn f; (of stream) Lauf m; (golf ~) Platz m; (NAUT, SCH) Kurs m; (in meal) Gang m; **summer ~** n Sommerkurs m; **of ~** ad natürlich.

court [kɔːt] n (royal) Hof m; (JUR) Gericht nt // vt (woman) gehen mit; (danger) herausfordern; **to take to ~** vor Gericht bringen.

courteous ['kɜːtɪəs] a höflich.

courtesan [kɔːtɪ'zæn] n Kurtisane f.

courtesy ['kɜːtəsɪ] n Höflichkeit f.

court-house ['kɔːthaus] n (US) Gerichtsgebäude nt.

courtier ['kɔːtɪə*] n Höfling m.

court-martial ['kɔːt'mɑːʃəl], pl **courts-martial** ['kɔːts'mɑːʃəl] n Kriegsgericht nt // vt vor ein Kriegsgericht stellen.

courtroom ['kɔːtrum] n Gerichtssaal m.

courtyard ['kɔːtjɑːd] n Hof m.

cousin ['kʌzn] n Cousin m, Vetter m; Kusine f.

cove [kəuv] n kleine Bucht f.

covenant ['kʌvənənt] n (ECCL) Bund m; (JUR) Verpflichtung f.

cover ['kʌvə*] vt (spread over) bedecken; (shield) abschirmen; (include) sich erstrecken über (+acc); (protect) decken; (distance) zurücklegen; (report on) berichten über (+acc) // n (lid) Deckel m; (for bed) Decke f; (MIL) Bedeckung f; (of book) Einband m; (of magazine) Umschlag; (insurance) Versicherung f; **to take ~** (from rain) sich unterstellen; (MIL) in Deckung gehen; **under ~** (indoors) drinnen; **under ~ of** im Schutze (+ gen); **under separate ~** (COMM) mit getrennter Post; **to ~ up for sb** jdn decken; **~age** ['kʌvrɪdʒ] n (PRESS: reports) Berichterstattung f; (distribution) Verbreitung f; **~ charge** n Bedienungsgeld nt; **~ing** n Bedeckung f; **~ing letter**, (US) **~ letter** n Begleitbrief m; **~ note** n (INSURANCE) vorläufige(r) Versicherungsschein m.

covert ['kʌvət] a geheim.

cover-up ['kʌvərʌp] n Vertuschung f.

covet ['kʌvɪt] vt begehren.

cow [kau] n Kuh f // vt einschüchtern.

coward ['kauəd] n Feigling m; **~ice** ['kauədɪs] n Feigheit f; **~ly** a feige.

cowboy ['kaubɔɪ] n Cowboy m.

cower ['kauə*] vi kauern.

coxswain ['kɒksn] n (abbr: cox) Steuermann m.

coy [kɔɪ] a schüchtern.

coyote [kɔɪ'əutɪ] n Präriewolf m.

cozy ['kəuzɪ] a (US) = **cosy.**

CPA (US) abbr of **certified public accountant.**

crab [kræb] n Krebs m; **~ apple** n Holzapfel m.

crack [kræk] n Riß m, Sprung m; (noise) Knall m // vt (break) springen lassen; (joke) reißen; (nut, safe) knacken; (whip) knallen lassen // a erstklassig; (troops) Elite-; **~ down** vi: **to ~ down** (on) hart durchgreifen (bei); **~ up** vi (fig) zusammenbrechen; **~er** n (firework) Knallkörper m, Kracher m; (biscuit) Keks m; (Christmas ~) Knallbonbon nt.

crackle ['krækl] vi knistern; (fire) prasseln.

cradle ['kreɪdl] n Wiege f.

craft [krɑːft] n (skill) (Hand- und Kunst)fertigkeit f; (trade) Handwerk nt; (NAUT) Schiff nt; **~sman** n Handwerker m; **~smanship** n (quality) handwerkliche Ausführung f; (ability) handwerkliche(s) Können nt; **~y** a schlau.

crag [kræg] n Klippe f.

cram [kræm] vt vollstopfen (with mit) // vi (learn) pauken; **to ~ sth into** etw in (+acc) stopfen.

cramp [kræmp] n Krampf m // vt (limit) einengen; (hinder) hemmen; **~ed** a (position) verkrampft; (space) eng.

crampon ['kræmpən] n Steigeisen nt.

cranberry ['krænbərɪ] n Preiselbeere f.

crane [kreɪn] n (machine) Kran m; (bird) Kranich m.

crank [kræŋk] n (lever) Kurbel f; (person) Spinner m; **~shaft** n Kurbelwelle f.

cranny ['krænɪ] n see **nook.**

crash [kræʃ] n (noise) Krachen nt; (with cars) Zusammenstoß m; (with plane) Absturz m; (COMM) Zusammenbruch m // vt (plane) abstürzen mit // vi (cars) zusammenstoßen; (plane) abstürzen; (economy) zusammenbrechen; (noise) knallen; **~ course** n Schnellkurs m; **~ helmet** n Sturzhelm m; **~ landing** n Bruchlandung f.

crass [kræs] a kraß.

crate [kreɪt] n (lit, fig) Kiste f.

crater ['kreɪtə*] n Krater m.

cravat(e) [krə'væt] n Halstuch nt.

crave [kreɪv] vt verlangen nach.

crawl [krɔːl] vi kriechen; (baby) krabbeln // n Kriechen nt; (swim) Kraul nt.

crayfish ['kreɪfɪʃ] n, pl inv (freshwater) Krebs m; (saltwater) Languste f.

crayon ['kreɪən] n Buntstift m.

craze [kreɪz] n Fimmel m.

crazy ['kreɪzɪ] a verrückt; **~ paving** n Mosaikpflaster nt.

creak [kriːk] vi knarren.

cream [kriːm] n (from milk) Rahm m, Sahne f; (polish, cosmetic) Creme f;

(*fig: people*) Elite *f* // a cremfarbig; ~
cake *n* Sahnetorte *f*; ~ **cheese** *n*
Rahmquark *m*; ~**y** a sahnig.

crease [kriːs] *n* Falte *f* // *vt* falten;
(*untidy*) zerknittern // *vi* (*wrinkle up*)
knittern.

create [kriˈeɪt] *vt* erschaffen; (*cause*)
verursachen.

creation [kriˈeɪʃən] *n* Schöpfung *f*.

creative [kriˈeɪtɪv] *a* kreativ.

creator [kriˈeɪtə*] *n* Schöpfer *m*.

creature [ˈkriːtʃə*] *n* Geschöpf *nt*.

crèche, creche [kreʃ] *n* Krippe *f*.

credence [ˈkriːdəns] *n*: to lend *or* give ~
to sth etw (*dat*) Glauben schenken.

credentials [krɪˈdenʃəlz] *npl* Be-
glaubigungsschreiben *nt*.

credibility [kredɪˈbɪlɪtɪ] *n* Glaubwürdig-
keit *f*.

credible [ˈkredɪbl] a (*person*)
glaubwürdig; (*story*) glaubhaft.

credit [ˈkredɪt] *n* (COMM *also*) Kredit *m*
// vt Glauben geben (+*dat*); (COMM)
gutschreiben; ~**s** *pl* (*of film*) die Mit-
wirkenden; ~**able** a rühmlich; ~ **card**
n Kreditkarte *f*; ~**or** *n* Gläubiger *m*.

creed [kriːd] *n* Glaubensbekenntnis *nt*.

creek [kriːk] *n* (*inlet*) kleine Bucht *f*;
(US: *river*) kleine(r) Wasserlauf *m*.

creep [kriːp], *pt*, *pp* **crept** *vi* kriechen;
~**er** *n* Kletterpflanze *f*; ~**y** a
(*frightening*) gruselig.

cremation [krɪˈmeɪʃən] *n* Einäscherung
f.

crêpe [kreɪp] *n* Krepp *m*; ~ **bandage** *n*
(*Brit*) Elastikbinde *f*.

crept [krept] *pt*, *pp of* **creep**.

crescent [ˈkresnt] *n* (*of moon*)
Halbmond *m*.

cress [kres] *n* Kresse *f*.

crest [krest] *n* (*of cock*) Kamm *m*; (*of
wave*) Wellenkamm *m*; (*coat of arms*)
Wappen *nt*; ~**fallen** a niedergeschlagen.

Crete [kriːt] *n* Kreta *nt*.

crevasse [krɪˈvæs] *n* Gletscherspalte *f*.

crevice [ˈkrevɪs] *n* Riß *m*.

crew [kruː] *n* Besatzung *f*, Mannschaft *f*;
~**-cut** *n* Bürstenschnitt *m*; ~**-neck** *n*
runde(r) Ausschnitt *m*.

crib [krɪb] *n* (*bed*) Krippe *f* // *vt* spicken
(*col*).

crick [krɪk] *n* Muskelkrampf *m*.

cricket [ˈkrɪkɪt] *n* (*insect*) Grille *f*;
(*game*) Kricket *nt*.

crime [kraɪm] *n* Verbrechen *nt*.

criminal [ˈkrɪmɪnl] *n* Verbrecher *m* // a
kriminell; (*act*) strafbar.

crimson [ˈkrɪmzn] a leuchtend rot.

cringe [krɪndʒ] *vi* sich ducken.

crinkle [ˈkrɪŋkl] *vt* zerknittern.

cripple [ˈkrɪpl] *n* Krüppel *m* // *vt*
lahmlegen; (MED) verkrüppeln.

crisis [ˈkraɪsɪs], *pl* **-ses** [ˈkraɪsiːz] *n*
Krise *f*.

crisp [krɪsp] a knusprig; ~**s** *npl* (*Brit*)

Chips *pl*.

criss-cross [ˈkrɪskrɒs] a gekreuzt,
Kreuz-.

criterion [kraɪˈtɪərɪən], *pl* **-ria**
[kraɪˈtɪərɪə] *n* Kriterium *nt*.

critic [ˈkrɪtɪk] *n* Kritiker(in *f*) *m*; ~**al** a
kritisch; ~**ally** ad kritisch; (*ill*) gefährlich; ~**ism** [ˈkrɪtɪsɪzəm] *n* Kritik *f*;
~**ize** [ˈkrɪtɪsaɪz] *vt* kritisieren.

croak [krəʊk] *vi* krächzen; (*frog*)
quaken.

crochet [ˈkrəʊʃeɪ] *n* Häkelei *f*.

crockery [ˈkrɒkərɪ] *n* Geschirr *nt*.

crocodile [ˈkrɒkədaɪl] *n* Krokodil *nt*.

crocus [ˈkrəʊkəs] *n* Krokus *m*.

croft [krɒft] *n* (*Brit*) kleine(s) Pachtgut
nt.

crony [ˈkrəʊnɪ] *n* (*col*) Kumpel *m*.

crook [krʊk] *n* (*criminal*) Gauner *m*;
(*stick*) Hirtenstab *m*; ~**ed** [ˈkrʊkɪd] a
krumm.

crop [krɒp] *n* (*harvest*) Ernte *f*; (*riding
~*) Reitpeitsche *f* // *vt* ernten; ~ **up** *vi*
passieren.

croquet [ˈkrəʊkeɪ] *n* Krocket *nt*.

croquette [krəˈket] *n* Krokette *f*.

cross [krɒs] *n* Kreuz *nt* // *vt* (*road*) überqueren; (*legs*) übereinander legen;
kreuzen // a (*annoyed*) böse; ~ **out** *vt*
streichen; ~ **over** *vi* hinübergehen;
~**bar** *n* Querstange *f*; ~**breed** *n* Kreuzung *f*; ~**country** (*race*) *n* Geländelauf
m; ~**-examine** *vt* ins Kreuzverhör
nehmen; ~**-eyed** a: to be ~**-eyed**
schielen; ~**fire** *n* Kreuzfeuer *nt*; ~**ing** *n*
(*crossroads*) (Straßen)kreuzung *f*; (*of
ship*) Überfahrt *f*; (*for pedestrians*)
Fußgängerübergang *m*; ~**ing guard** *n*
(US) Schülerlotse *m*; ~ **purposes** *npl*:
to be at ~ purposes aneinander vor-
beireden; ~**-reference** *n* Querverweis
m; ~**roads** *n* Straßenkreuzung *f*; (*fig*)
Scheideweg *m*; ~ **section** *n* Querschnitt
m; ~**walk** *n* (US) Fußgängerübergang
m; ~**wind** *n* Seitenwind *m*; ~**word
(puzzle)** *n* Kreuzworträtsel *nt*.

crotch [krɒtʃ] *n* Zwickel *m*; (ANAT)
Unterleib *nt*.

crotchet [ˈkrɒtʃɪt] *n* Viertelnote *f*.

crotchety [ˈkrɒtʃɪtɪ] a launenhaft.

crouch [kraʊtʃ] *vi* hocken.

croupier [ˈkruːpɪeɪ] *n* Croupier *m*.

crow [krəʊ] *n* (*bird*) Krähe *f*; (*of cock*)
Krähen *nt* // *vi* krähen.

crowbar [ˈkrəʊbaː*] *n* Stemmeisen *nt*.

crowd [kraʊd] *n* Menge *f* // *vt* (*fill*) über-
füllen // *vi* drängen; ~**ed** a überfüllt.

crown [kraʊn] *n* Krone *f*; (*of head, hat*)
Kopf *m* // *vt* krönen; ~ **jewels** *pl*
Kronjuwelen *pl*; ~ **prince** *n* Kronprinz
m.

crow's-feet [ˈkrəʊzfiːt] *npl* Krähenfüße
pl.

crucial [ˈkruːʃəl] a entscheidend.

crucifix [ˈkruːsɪfɪks] *n* Kruzifix *nt*; ~**ion**

[kruːsɪˈfɪkʃən] n Kreuzigung f.
crucify ['kruːsɪfaɪ] vt kreuzigen.
crude [kruːd] a (raw) roh; (humour, behaviour) grob; (basic) primitiv; ~ (oil) n Rohöl nt.
cruel ['kruəl] a grausam; ~ty n Grausamkeit f.
cruet ['kruːɪt] n Gewürzständer m.
cruise [kruːz] n Kreuzfahrt f // vi kreuzen; ~r n (MIL) Kreuzer m.
crumb [krʌm] n Krume f.
crumble ['krʌmbl] vti zerbröckeln.
crumbly ['krʌmblɪ] a krümelig.
crumpet ['krʌmpɪt] n Tee(pfann)kuchen m.
crumple ['krʌmpl] vt zerknittern.
crunch [krʌntʃ] n: the ~ (fig) der Knackpunkt // vt knirschen; ~y a knusprig.
crusade [kruːˈseɪd] n Kreuzzug m.
crush [krʌʃ] n Gedränge nt; (drink) lemon ~ Zitronensaft m // vt zerdrücken; (rebellion) unterdrücken.
crust [krʌst] n Kruste f.
crutch [krʌtʃ] n Krücke f.
crux [krʌks] n der springende Punkt.
cry [kraɪ] vi (shout) schreien; (weep) weinen // n (call) Schrei m; ~ off vi (plötzlich) absagen.
crypt [krɪpt] n Krypta f.
cryptic ['krɪptɪk] a hintergründig.
crystal ['krɪstl] n Kristall m; (glass) Kristallglas nt; (mineral) Bergkristall m; ~-clear a kristallklar; ~lize vti (lit) kristallisieren; (fig) klären.
cub [kʌb] n Junge(s) nt; (also: ~ scout) Wölfling m.
Cuba ['kjuːbə] n Kuba nt; ~n a kubanisch // n Kubaner(in f) m.
cubbyhole ['kʌbɪhəul] n Eckchen nt.
cube [kjuːb] n Würfel m // vt (MATH) hoch drei nehmen; ~ root n Kubikwurzel f.
cubic ['kjuːbɪk] a würfelförmig; (centimetre etc) Kubik-; ~ capacity n Fassungsvermögen nt.
cubicle ['kjuːbɪkl] n Kabine f.
cuckoo ['kuku:] n Kuckuck m; ~ clock n Kuckucksuhr f.
cucumber ['kjuːkʌmbə*] n Gurke f.
cuddle ['kʌdl] vti herzen, drücken (col).
cue [kjuː] n (THEAT) Stichwort nt; (snooker ~) Billardstock m.
cuff [kʌf] n (Brit: of shirt, coat etc) Manschette f; Aufschlag m; (US) = turn-up; off the ~ ad aus dem Handgelenk; ~link n Manschettenknopf m.
cuisine [kwɪˈziːn] n Kochkunst f, Küche f.
cul-de-sac ['kʌldəsæk] n Sackgasse f.
culinary ['kʌlɪnərɪ] a Koch-.
cull [kʌl] vt (flowers) pflücken; (select) auswählen.
culminate ['kʌlmɪneɪt] vi gipfeln.

culmination [kʌlmɪˈneɪʃən] n Höhepunkt m.
culottes [kjuˈlɔts] npl Hosenrock m.
culpable ['kʌlpəbl] a schuldig.
culprit ['kʌlprɪt] n Täter m.
cult [kʌlt] n Kult m.
cultivate ['kʌltɪveɪt] vt (AGR) bebauen; (mind) bilden.
cultivation [kʌltɪˈveɪʃən] n (AGR) Bebauung f; (of person) Bildung f.
cultural ['kʌltʃərəl] a kulturell, Kultur-.
culture ['kʌltʃə*] n Kultur f; ~d a gebildet.
cumbersome ['kʌmbəsəm] a (object) sperrig.
cummerbund ['kʌməbʌnd] n Kummerbund m.
cumulative ['kjuːmjʊlətɪv] a gehäuft.
cunning ['kʌnɪŋ] n Verschlagenheit f // a schlau.
cup [kʌp] n Tasse f; (prize) Pokal m.
cupboard ['kʌbəd] n Schrank m.
Cupid ['kjuːpɪd] n Amor m.
cup-tie ['kʌptaɪ] n (Brit) Pokalspiel nt.
curate ['kjuərɪt] n (Catholic) Kurat m; (Protestant) Vikar m.
curator [kjuˈreɪtə*] n Kustos m.
curb [kɜːb] vt zügeln // n (on spending etc) Einschränkung f; (US) Bordstein m.
curdle ['kɜːdl] vi gerinnen.
cure [kjuə*] n Heilmittel nt; (process) Heilverfahren nt // vt heilen.
curfew ['kɜːfjuː] n Ausgangssperre f; Sperrstunde f.
curiosity [kjuərɪˈɒsɪtɪ] n Neugier f.
curious ['kjuərɪəs] a neugierig; (strange) seltsam.
curl [kɜːl] n Locke f // vt locken // vi sich locken; ~ up vi sich zusammenrollen; (person) sich ankuscheln; ~er n Lockenwickler m; ~y a lockig.
currant ['kʌrənt] n Korinthe f.
currency ['kʌrənsɪ] n Währung f; to gain ~ an Popularität gewinnen.
current ['kʌrənt] n Strömung f // a (expression) gängig, üblich; (issue) neueste; ~ account n (Brit) Girokonto nt; ~ affairs npl Zeitgeschehen nt; ~ly ad zur Zeit.
curriculum [kəˈrɪkjuləm], pl ~s or curricula [kəˈrɪkjulə] n Lehrplan m; ~ vitae (CV) n Lebenslauf m.
curry ['kʌrɪ] n Currygericht nt // vt: to ~ favour with sich einschmeicheln bei; ~ powder n Curry(pulver) nt.
curse [kɜːs] vi (swear) fluchen (at auf +acc) // vt (insult) verwünschen // n Fluch m.
cursor ['kɜːsə*] n (COMPUT) Cursor m.
cursory ['kɜːsərɪ] a flüchtig.
curt [kɜːt] a schroff.
curtail [kɜːˈteɪl] vt abkürzen; (rights) einschränken.
curtain ['kɜːtn] n Vorhang m.
curtsey ['kɜːtsɪ] n Knicks m // vi

knicksen.

curve [kɜ:v] *n* Kurve *f*; (*of body, vase etc*) Rundung *f* // *vi* sich biegen; (*hips, breasts*) sich runden; (*road*) einen Bogen machen.

cushion ['kuʃən] *n* Kissen *nt* // *vt* dämpfen.

custard ['kʌstəd] *n* Vanillesoße *f*.

custodian [kʌs'təudɪən] *n* Kustos *m*, Verwalter(in *f*) *m*.

custody ['kʌstədɪ] *n* Aufsicht *f*; (*police*) Haft *f*; **to take into** ~ verhaften.

custom ['kʌstəm] *n* (*tradition*) Brauch *m*; (*COMM*) Kundschaft *f*; ~**ary** *a* üblich.

customer ['kʌstəmə*] *n* Kunde *m*, Kundin *f*.

customized ['kʌstəmaɪzd] *a* (*car etc*) mit Spezialausrüstung.

custom-made ['kʌstəm'meɪd] *a* speziell angefertigt.

customs ['kʌstəmz] *npl* Zoll *m*; ~ **officer** *n* Zollbeamte(r) *mf*.

cut [kʌt], *pt, pp* **cut** *vt* schneiden; (*wages*) kürzen; (*prices*) heruntersetzen; // *vi* schneiden; (*intersect*) sich schneiden // *n* Schnitt *m*; (*wound*) Schnittwunde *f*; (*in book, income etc*) Kürzung *f*; (*share*) Anteil *m*; **to** ~ **a tooth** zahnen; ~ **down** *vt* (*tree*) fällen; (*reduce*) einschränken; ~ **off** *vt* (*lit, fig*) abschneiden; (*allowance*) sperren; ~ **out** *vt* (*shape*) ausschneiden; (*delete*) streichen; ~ **up** *vt* (*meat*) aufschneiden; ~**back** *n* Kürzung; (*CINE*) Rückblende.

cute [kju:t] *a* niedlich.

cuticle ['kju:tɪkl] *n* Nagelhaut *f*.

cutlery ['kʌtlərɪ] *n* Besteck *nt*.

cutlet ['kʌtlɪt] *n* (*pork*) Kotelett *nt*; (*veal*) Schnitzel *nt*.

cutout ['kʌtaut] *n* (*cardboard* ~) Ausschneidemodell *nt*.

cut-price ['kʌtpraɪs], (*US*) **cut-rate** ['kʌtreɪt] *a* verbilligt.

cut throat ['kʌtθrəut] *n* Verbrechertyp *m* // *a* mörderisch.

cutting ['kʌtɪŋ] *a* schneidend // *n* (*Brit: PRESS*) Ausschnitt *m*; (: *RAIL*) Durchstich *m*.

CV *n abbr of* **curriculum vitae**.

cwt *abbr of* **hundredweight(s)**.

cyanide ['saɪənaɪd] *n* Zyankali *nt*.

cycle ['saɪkl] *n* Fahrrad *nt*; (*series*) Reihe *f* // *vi* radfahren; **cycling** ['saɪklɪŋ] *n* Radfahren *nt*; **cyclist** ['saɪklɪst] *n* Radfahrer(in *f*) *m*.

cyclone ['saɪkləun] *n* Zyklon *m*.

cygnet ['sɪgnɪt] *n* junge(r) Schwan *m*.

cylinder ['sɪlɪndə*] *n* Zylinder *m*; (*TECH*) Walze *f*; ~**-head gasket** *n* Zylinderkopfdichtung *f*.

cymbals ['sɪmbəlz] *npl* Becken *nt*.

cynic ['sɪnɪk] *n* Zyniker(in *f*) *m*; ~**al** *a* zynisch; ~**ism** ['sɪnɪsɪzəm] *n* Zynismus

m.

cypress ['saɪprɪs] *n* Zypresse *f*.

Cypriot ['sɪprɪət] *a* zypriotisch // *n* Zypriot(in *f*) *m*.

Cyprus ['saɪprəs] *n* Zypern *nt*.

cyst [sɪst] *n* Zyste *f*; ~**itis** *n* Blasenentzündung *f*.

czar [zɑ:*] *n* Zar *m*.

Czech [tʃek] *a* tschechisch // *n* Tscheche *m*, Tschechin *f*.

Czechoslovakia [tʃekəslə'vækɪə] *n* die Tschechoslowakei; ~**n** *a* tschechoslowakisch // *n* Tschechoslowake *m*, Tchechoslowakin *f*.

D

D [di:] *n* (*MUS*): ~ **sharp/flat** Dis, dis *nt*/ Des, des *nt*.

dab [dæb] *vt* (*wound, paint*) betupfen // *n* (*little bit*) bißchen *nt*; (*of paint*) Tupfer *m*.

dabble ['dæbl] *vi*: **to** ~ **in sth** in etw (*dat*) machen.

dad [dæd], **daddy** ['dædɪ] *n* Papa *m*, Vati *m*; **daddy-long-legs** *n* Weberknecht *m*.

daffodil ['dæfədɪl] *n* Osterglocke *f*.

daft [dɑ:ft] *a* (*col*) blöd(e), doof.

dagger ['dægə*] *n* Dolch *m*.

daily ['deɪlɪ] *a* täglich // *n* (*PRESS*) Tageszeitung *f*; (*woman*) Haushaltshilfe *f* // *ad* täglich.

dainty ['deɪntɪ] *a* zierlich.

dairy ['dɛərɪ] *n* (*Brit: shop*) Milchgeschäft *nt*; (*on farm*) Molkerei *f* // *a* Milch-; ~ **farm** *n* Hof *m* mit Milchwirtschaft; ~ **produce** *n* Molkereiprodukte *pl*; ~ **store** *n* (*US*) Milchgeschäft *nt*.

dais ['deɪɪs] *n* Podium *nt*.

daisy ['deɪzɪ] *n* Gänseblümchen *nt*; ~ **wheel** *n* (*on printer*) Typenrad *nt*.

dale [deɪl] *n* Tal *nt*.

dam [dæm] *n* (Stau)damm *m* // *vt* stauen.

damage ['dæmɪdʒ] *n* Schaden *m* // *vt* beschädigen; ~**s** *pl* (*JUR*) Schaden(s)ersatz *m*.

damn [dæm] *vt* verdammen // *n* (*col*): I don't give a ~ das ist mir total egal // *a* (*col: also:* ~ed) verdammt; ~ **it!** verflucht!; ~**ing** *a* vernichtend.

damp [dæmp] *a* feucht // *n* Feuchtigkeit *f* // *vt* (*also:* ~**en**) befeuchten; (*discourage*) dämpfen.

damson ['dæmzən] *n* Damaszenerpflaume *f*.

dance [dɑ:ns] *n* Tanz *m* // *vi* tanzen; ~ **hall** *n* Tanzlokal *nt*; ~**r** *n* Tänzer *m*.

dancing ['dɑ:nsɪŋ] *n* Tanzen *nt*.

dandelion ['dændɪlaɪən] *n* Löwenzahn *m*.

dandruff ['dændrəf] *n* (Kopf)schuppen *pl*.

Dane [deɪn] n Däne m, Dänin f.

danger ['deɪndʒə*] n Gefahr f; ~! (sign) Achtung!; to be in ~ of doing sth Gefahr laufen, etw zu tun; ~ous a, ~ously ad gefährlich.

dangle ['dæŋgl] vi baumeln // vt herabhängen lassen.

Danish ['deɪnɪʃ] a dänisch // n Dänisch nt.

dapper ['dæpə*] a elegant.

dare [dɛə*] vt herausfordern // vi: to ~ (to) do sth es wagen, etw zu tun; I ~ say ich würde sagen; ~-devil n Draufgänger(in f) m.

daring ['dɛərɪŋ] a (audacious) verwegen; (bold) wagemutig; (dress) gewagt // n Mut m.

dark [dɑːk] a dunkel; (fig) düster, trübe; (deep colour) dunkel- // n Dunkelheit f; to be left in the ~ about im dunkeln sein über (+ acc); after ~ nach Anbruch der Dunkelheit; ~en vti verdunkeln; ~ glasses npl Sonnenbrille f; ~ness n Finsternis nt; ~room n Dunkelkammer f.

darling ['dɑːlɪŋ] n Liebling m // a lieb.

darn [dɑːn] vt stopfen.

dart [dɑːt] n (weapon) Pfeil m; (in sewing) Abnäher m // vi sausen; ~s pl (game) Pfeilwerfen nt; ~board n Zielscheibe f.

dash [dæʃ] n Sprung m; (mark) (Gedanken)strich m; (small amount) bißchen nt // vt (hopes) zunichte machen // vi stürzen; ~ away or off vi davonstürzen.

dashboard ['dæʃbɔːd] n Armaturenbrett nt.

dashing ['dæʃɪŋ] a schneidig.

data ['deɪtə] npl Einzelheiten pl, Daten pl; ~ base n Datenbank f; ~ processing n Datenverarbeitung f.

date [deɪt] n Datum nt; (for meeting etc) Termin m; (with person) Verabredung f; (fruit) Dattel f // vt (letter etc) datieren; (person) gehen mit; ~ of birth Geburtsdatum nt; to ~ ad bis heute; out of ~ überholt; up to ~ (clothes) modisch; (report) up-to-date; (with news) auf dem laufenden; ~d a altmodisch.

daub [dɔːb] vt beschmieren; (paint) schmieren.

daughter ['dɔːtə*] n Tochter f; ~-in-law n Schwiegertochter f.

daunting ['dɔːntɪŋ] a entmutigend.

dawdle ['dɔːdl] vi trödeln.

dawn [dɔːn] n Morgendämmerung f // vi dämmern; (fig): it ~ed on him that ... es dämmerte ihm, daß ...

day [deɪ] n Tag m; the ~ before/after am Tag zuvor/danach; the ~ after tomorrow übermorgen; the ~ before yesterday vorgestern; by ~ am Tage; ~break n Tagesanbruch m; ~dream vi mit

offenen Augen träumen; ~light n Tageslicht nt; ~ return n (Brit) Tagesrückfahrkarte f; ~time n Tageszeit f; ~-to-~ a alltäglich.

daze [deɪz] vt betäuben // n Betäubung f; in a ~ benommen.

dazzle ['dæzl] vt blenden.

DC abbr (= direct current) Gleichstrom m.

D-day ['diːdeɪ] n (HIST) Tag der Invasion durch die Alliierten (6.6.44); (fig) der Tag X.

deacon ['diːkən] n Diakon m.

dead [ded] a tot; (without feeling) gefühllos; // ad ganz; (exactly) genau; to shoot sb ~ jdn erschießen; ~ tired todmüde; to stop ~ abrupt stehenbleiben; the ~ pl die Toten pl; ~en vt (pain) abtöten; (sound) ersticken; ~ end n Sackgasse f; ~ heat n tote(s) Rennen nt; ~line n Stichtag m; ~lock n Stillstand m; ~ly a tödlich; ~pan a undurchdringlich; the D~ Sea n das Tote Meer.

deaf [def] a taub; ~en vt taub machen; ~ness n Taubheit f; ~-mute n Taubstumme(r) m.

deal [diːl] n Geschäft nt // vt, pt, pp dealt [delt] austeilen; (CARDS) geben; a great ~ of sehr viel; ~ in vt handeln mit; ~ with vt (person) behandeln; (subject) sich befassen mit; (problem) in Angriff nehmen; ~er n (COMM) Händler m; (CARDS) Kartengeber m; ~ings npl (FIN) Geschäfte pl; (relations) Beziehungen pl.

dean [diːn] n (Protestant) Superintendent m; (Catholic) Dechant m; (UNIV) Dekan m.

dear [dɪə*] a lieb; (expensive) teuer // n Liebling m // interj: ~ me! du liebe Zeit!; D~ Sir Sehr geehrter Herr!; D~ John Lieber John!; ~ly ad (love) herzlich; (pay) teuer.

death [deθ] n Tod m; (statistic) Todesfall m; ~ certificate n Totenschein m; ~ duties npl (Brit) Erbschaftssteuer f; ~ly a totenähnlich, Toten-; ~ penalty n Todesstrafe f; ~ rate n Sterblichkeitsziffer f.

debar [dɪ'bɑː*] vt ausschließen.

debase [dɪ'beɪs] vt entwerten.

debatable [dɪ'beɪtəbl] a anfechtbar.

debate [dɪ'beɪt] n Debatte f // vt debattieren, diskutieren; (consider) überlegen.

debauchery [dɪ'bɔːtʃərɪ] n Ausschweifungen pl.

debilitating [dɪ'bɪlɪteɪtɪŋ] a schwächend.

debit ['debɪt] n Schuldposten m // vt belasten.

debris ['debriː] n Trümmer pl.

debt [det] n Schuld f; to be in ~ verschuldet sein; ~or n Schuldner m.

debunk [diː'bʌŋk] vt entlarven.
decade ['dekeɪd] n Jahrzehnt nt.
decaffeinated [diː'kæfɪneɪtɪd] a koffein-frei.
decanter [dɪ'kæntə*] n Karaffe f.
decay [dɪ'keɪ] n Verfall m; (tooth ~) Karies m // vi verfallen; (teeth, meat etc) faulen; (leaves etc) verrotten.
deceased [dɪ'siːst] a verstorben.
deceit [dɪ'siːt] n Betrug m; ~ful a falsch.
deceive [dɪ'siːv] vt täuschen.
December [dɪ'sembə*] n Dezember m.
decency ['diːsənsɪ] n Anstand m.
decent [diːsənt] a (respectable) an-ständig; (pleasant) annehmbar.
deception [dɪ'sepʃən] n Betrug m.
deceptive [dɪ'septɪv] a irreführend.
decibel ['desɪbel] n Dezibel n.
decide [dɪ'saɪd] vt entscheiden // vi sich entscheiden; to ~ on sth etw be-schließen; ~d a entschieden; ~dly [-dɪdlɪ] ad entschieden.
deciduous [dɪ'sɪdjʊəs] a Laub-.
decimal ['desɪməl] a dezimal // n Dezimalzahl f; ~ point n Komma nt.
decimate ['desɪmeɪt] vt dezimieren.
decipher [dɪ'saɪfə*] vt entziffern.
decision [dɪ'sɪʒən] n Entscheidung f, Entschluß m.
decisive [dɪ'saɪsɪv] a entscheidend; (person) entschlossen.
deck [dek] n (NAUT) Deck nt; (of cards) Pack m; ~chair n Liegestuhl m.
declaration [deklə'reɪʃən] n Erklärung f.
declare [dɪ'klɛə*] vt erklären; (CUS-TOMS) verzollen.
decline [dɪ'klaɪn] n (decay) Verfall m; (lessening) Rückgang m // vt (invitation) ablehnen // vi (of strength) nachlassen; (say no) ablehnen.
declutch ['diː'klʌtʃ] vi auskuppeln.
decode ['diː'kəʊd] vt entschlüsseln.
decompose [diːkəm'pəʊz] vi (sich) zersetzen.
décor ['deɪkɔː*] n Ausstattung f.
decorate ['dekəreɪt] vt (room: paper) tapezieren; (: paint) streichen; (adorn) (aus)schmücken; (cake) verzieren; (honour) auszeichnen.
decoration [dekə'reɪʃən] n (of house) (Wand)dekoration f; (medal) Orden m.
decorator ['dekəreɪtə*] n Maler m, An-streicher m.
decorum [dɪ'kɔːrəm] n Anstand m.
decoy ['diːkɔɪ] n Lockvogel m.
decrease ['diːkriːs] n Abnahme f // v [diː'kriːs] vt vermindern // vi abnehmen.
decree [dɪ'kriː] n Erlaß m; ~ nisi n vorläufiges Scheidungsurteil nt.
decrepit [dɪ'krepɪt] a hinfällig.
dedicate ['dedɪkeɪt] vt widmen.
dedication [dedɪ'keɪʃən] n (devotion) Ergebenheit; (in book) Widmung f.

deduce [dɪ'djuːs] vt ableiten, schließen (from aus).
deduct [dɪ'dʌkt] vt abziehen; ~ion [dɪ'dʌkʃən] n (of money) Abzug m; (conclusion) (Schluß)folgerung f.
deed [diːd] n Tat f; (document) Urkunde f.
deem [diːm] vt: to ~ sb/sth (to be) sth jdn/etw für etw halten.
deep [diːp] a tief // ad: the spectators stood 20 ~ die Zuschauer standen in 20 Reihen hintereinander; ~en vt vertiefen // vi (darkness) tiefer werden; ~-freeze n Tiefkühlung f; ~-fry vt fritieren; ~ly ad tief; ~-sea diving n Tiefseetauchen nt; ~-seated a tiefsitzend.
deer [dɪə*] n Reh nt; ~skin n Hirsch-/Rehleder nt.
deface [dɪ'feɪs] vt entstellen.
defamation [defə'meɪʃən] n Verleum-dung f.
default [dɪ'fɔːlt] n Versäumnis nt // vi versäumen // n (COMPUT) Standardwert m; by ~ durch Nichterscheinen nt.
defeat [dɪ'fiːt] n Niederlage f // vt schlagen; ~ist a defätistisch // n Defätist m.
defect ['diːfekt] n Fehler m // vi [dɪ'fekt] überlaufen; ~ive [dɪ'fektɪv] a fehlerhaft.
defence [dɪ'fens] n Verteidigung f; ~less a wehrlos.
defend [dɪ'fend] vt verteidigen; ~ant n Angeklagte(r) m; ~er n Verteidiger m.
defense [dɪ'fens] n (US) = **defence**.
defensive [dɪ'fensɪv] a defensiv // n: on the ~ in der Defensive.
defer [dɪ'fɜː*] vt verschieben.
deference ['defərəns] n Rücksichtnahme f.
defiance [dɪ'faɪəns] n Trotz m, Unnachgiebigkeit f; in ~ of sth etw (dat) zum Trotz.
defiant [dɪ'faɪənt] a trotzig, unnachgiebig.
deficiency [dɪ'fɪʃənsɪ] n (lack) Mangel m; (weakness) Schwäche f.
deficient [dɪ'fɪʃənt] a mangelhaft.
deficit ['defɪsɪt] n Defizit nt.
defile [dɪ'faɪl] vt beschmutzen.
define [dɪ'faɪn] vt bestimmen; (explain) definieren.
definite ['defɪnɪt] a (fixed) definitiv; (clear) eindeutig; ~ly ad bestimmt.
definition [defɪ'nɪʃən] n Definition f; (PHOT) Schärfe f.
deflate [diː'fleɪt] vt die Luft ablassen aus.
deflect [dɪ'flekt] vt ablenken.
deform [dɪ'fɔːm] vt deformieren; ~ity n Mißbildung f.
defraud [dɪ'frɔːd] vt betrügen.
defray [dɪ'freɪ] vt (costs) übernehmen.
defrost [diː'frɒst] vt (fridge) abtauen; (food) auftauen; ~er n (US: demister)

Gebläse *nt.*

deft [deft] *a* geschickt.

defunct [dɪ'fʌŋkt] *a* verstorben.

defuse [diː'fjuːz] *vt* entschärfen.

defy [dɪ'faɪ] *vt* (*disobey*) sich widersetzen (+*dat*); (*orders, death*) trotzen (+*dat*); (*challenge*) herausfordern.

degenerate [dɪ'dʒenəreɪt] *vi* degenerieren // *a* [dɪ'dʒenərɪt] degeneriert.

degrading [dɪ'greɪdɪŋ] *a* erniedrigend.

degree [dɪ'griː] *n* Grad *m*; (*UNIV*) Universitätsabschluß *m*; by ~s allmählich; to some ~ zu einem gewissen Grad.

dehydrated [diːhaɪ'dreɪtɪd] *a* (*person*) ausgetrocknet; (*food*) Trocken-.

de-ice [diː'aɪs] *vt* enteisen.

deign [deɪn] *vi* sich herablassen.

deity ['diːɪtɪ] *n* Gottheit *f.*

dejected [dɪ'dʒektɪd] *a* niedergeschlagen.

delay [dɪ'leɪ] *vt* (*hold back*) aufschieben // *vi* (*linger*) sich aufhalten // *n* Aufschub *m*, Verzögerung *f*; (*of train etc*) Verspätung *f*; to be ~ed (*train*) Verspätung haben; without ~ unverzüglich.

delectable [dɪ'lektəbl] *a* köstlich; (*fig*) reizend.

delegate ['delɪgɪt] *n* Delegierte(r) *mf* // *vt* ['delɪgeɪt] delegieren.

delete [dɪ'liːt] *vt* (*aus*)streichen.

deliberate [dɪ'lɪbərɪt] *a* (*intentional*) absichtlich; (*slow*) bedächtig // *vi* [dɪ'lɪbəreɪt] (*consider*) überlegen; (*debate*) sich beraten; ~ly *ad* absichtlich.

delicacy ['delɪkəsɪ] *n* Zartheit *f*; (*weakness*) Anfälligkeit *f*; (*food*) Delikatesse *f.*

delicate ['delɪkɪt] *a* (*fine*) fein; (*fragile*) zart; (*situation*) heikel; (*MED*) empfindlich.

delicatessen [delɪkə'tesn] *n* Feinkostgeschäft *nt.*

delicious [dɪ'lɪʃəs] *a* lecker.

delight [dɪ'laɪt] *n* Wonne *f* // *vt* entzücken; to take ~ in sth Freude an etw (*dat*) haben; ~ed *a*: ~ed (at or with/to do) entzückt (über +*acc*/etw zu tun); ~ful *a* entzückend, herrlich.

delinquency [dɪ'lɪŋkwənsɪ] *n* Kriminalität *f.*

delinquent [dɪ'lɪŋkwənt] *n* Straffällige(r) *mf* // *a* straffällig.

delirious [dɪ'lɪrɪəs] *a* im Fieberwahn.

deliver [dɪ'lɪvə*] *vt* (*goods*) (ab)liefern; (*letter*) zustellen; (*speech*) halten; ~y *n* (Ab)lieferung *f*; (*of letter*) Zustellung *f*; (*of speech*) Vortragsweise *f*; (*MED*) Entbindung *f*; to take ~y of in Empfang nehmen.

delude [dɪ'luːd] *vt* täuschen.

deluge ['deljuːdʒ] *n* Überschwemmung *f*; (*fig*) Flut *f* // *vt* (*fig*) überfluten.

delusion [dɪ'luːʒən] *n* (Selbst)täuschung

f.

de luxe [dɪ'lʌks] *a* Luxus-.

delve [delv] *vi*: to ~ into sich vertiefen in (+*acc*).

demand [dɪ'mɑːnd] *vt* verlangen // *n* (*request*) Verlangen *nt*; (*COMM*) Nachfrage *f*; in ~ gefragt; on ~ auf Verlangen; ~ing *a* anspruchsvoll.

demarcation [diːmɑː'keɪʃən] *n* Abgrenzung *f.*

demean [dɪ'miːn] *vt*: to ~ o.s. sich erniedrigen.

demeanour, (*US*) **demeanor** [dɪ'miːnə*] *n* Benehmen *nt.*

demented [dɪ'mentɪd] *a* wahnsinnig.

demise [dɪ'maɪz] *n* Ableben *nt.*

demister [diː'mɪstə*] *n* (*AUT*) Gebläse *nt.*

demo ['deməʊ] *n abbr* (*col*: = *demonstration*) Demo *f.*

democracy [dɪ'mɒkrəsɪ] *n* Demokratie *f.*

democrat ['deməkræt] *n* Demokrat *m*; ~ic *a* [demə'krætɪk] demokratisch.

demolish [dɪ'mɒlɪʃ] *vt* (*lit*) abreißen; (*fig*) vernichten.

demolition [demə'lɪʃən] *n* Abbruch *m.*

demon ['diːmən] *n* Dämon *m.*

demonstrate ['demənstreɪt] *vti* demonstrieren.

demonstration [demən'streɪʃən] *n* Demonstration *f.*

demonstrator ['demənstreɪtə*] *n* (*POL*) Demonstrant(in *f*) *m.*

demote [dɪ'məʊt] *vt* degradieren.

demure [dɪ'mjʊə*] *a* ernst.

den [den] *n* (*of animal*) Höhle *f*; (*study*) Bude *f.*

denatured alcohol [diː'neɪtʃəd-] (*US*) *n* ungenießbar gemachte(r) Alkohol *m.*

denial [dɪ'naɪəl] *n* Leugnung *f*; **official** ~ Dementi *nt.*

denim ['denɪm] *a* Denim-; ~s *npl* Denim-Jeans *pl.*

Denmark ['denmɑːk] *n* Dänemark *nt.*

denomination [dɪnɒmɪ'neɪʃən] *n* (*ECCL*) Bekenntnis *nt*; (*type*) Klasse *f*; (*FIN*) Wert *m.*

denominator [dɪ'nɒmɪneɪtə*] *n* Nenner *m.*

denote [dɪ'nəʊt] *vt* bedeuten.

denounce [dɪ'naʊns] *vt* brandmarken.

dense [dens] *a* dicht; (*stupid*) schwer von Begriff; ~ly *ad* dicht.

density ['densɪtɪ] *n* Dichte *f*; **single-/ double-~ disk** *n* Diskette *f* mit einfacher/doppelter Dichte.

dent [dent] *n* Delle *f* // *vt* (*also*: make a ~ in) einbeulen.

dental ['dentl] *a* Zahn-; ~ **surgeon** *n* = **dentist**.

dentist ['dentɪst] *n* Zahnarzt *m*/-ärztin *f*; ~ry *n* Zahnmedizin *f.*

dentures ['dentʃəz] *npl* Gebiß *nt.*

deny [dɪ'naɪ] vt leugnen; (officially) dementieren; (help) abschlagen.

deodorant [di:'əudərənt] n Deodorant nt.

depart [dɪ'pɑːt] vi abfahren; to ~ from (fig: differ from) abweichen von.

department [dɪ'pɑːtmənt] n (COMM) Abteilung f; (UNIV) Seminar nt; (POL) Ministerium nt; ~ **store** n Warenhaus nt.

departure [dɪ'pɑːtʃə*] n (of person) Abreise f; (of train) Abfahrt f; (of plane) Abflug m; new ~ Neuerung f; ~ **lounge** n (at airport) Abflughalle f.

depend [dɪ'pend] vi: to ~ on abhängen von; (rely on) angewiesen sein auf (+acc); it ~s es kommt darauf an; ~ing on the result ... abhängend vom Resultat ...; ~**able** a zuverlässig; ~**ant** n Angehörige(r) mf; ~**ence** n Abhängigkeit f; ~**ent** a abhängig (on von) // n = ~**ant**.

depict [dɪ'pɪkt] vt schildern.

depleted [dɪ'pliːtɪd] a aufgebraucht.

deplorable [dɪ'plɔːrəbl] a bedauerlich.

deplore [dɪ'plɔː*] vt mißbilligen.

deploy [dɪ'plɔɪ] vt einsetzen.

depopulation ['diːpɔpjʊ'leɪʃən] n Entvölkerung f.

deport [dɪ'pɔːt] vt deportieren; ~**ation** [diːpɔː'teɪʃən] n Abschiebung f.

deportment [dɪ'pɔːtmənt] n Betragen nt.

depose [dɪ'pəuz] vt absetzen.

deposit [dɪ'pɔzɪt] n (in bank) Guthaben nt; (down payment) Anzahlung f; (security) Kaution f; (CHEM) Niederschlag m // vt (in bank) deponieren; (put down) niederlegen; ~ **account** n Sparkonto nt.

depot ['depəu] n Depot nt.

depraved [dɪ'preɪvd] a verkommen.

depreciate [dɪ'priːʃɪeɪt] vi im Wert sinken; **depreciation** [-'eɪʃən] n Wertminderung f.

depress [dɪ'pres] vt (press down) niederdrücken; (in mood) deprimieren; ~**ed** a deprimiert; ~**ing** a deprimierend; ~**ion** [dɪ'preʃən] n (mood) Depression f; (in trade) Wirtschaftskrise f; (hollow) Vertiefung f; (MET) Tief(druckgebiet) nt.

deprivation [deprɪ'veɪʃən] n Not f.

deprive [dɪ'praɪv] vt: to ~ sb of sth jdn etw (gen) berauben; ~**d** a (child) sozial benachteiligt; (area) unterentwickelt.

depth [depθ] n Tiefe f; in the ~s of despair in tiefster Verzweiflung.

deputation [depjʊ'teɪʃən] n Abordnung f.

deputize ['depjʊtaɪz] vi vertreten (for acc).

deputy ['depjʊtɪ] a stellvertretend // n (Stell)vertreter m.

derail [dɪ'reɪl] vt: to be ~ed entgleisen;

~**ment** n Entgleisung f.

deranged [dɪ'reɪndʒd] a verrückt.

derby ['dɑːbɪ] n (US: bowler hat) Melone f.

derelict ['derɪlɪkt] a verlassen.

deride [dɪ'raɪd] vt auslachen.

derisory [dɪ'raɪsərɪ] a spöttisch.

derivative [dɪ'rɪvətɪv] n Derivat nt // a abgeleitet.

derive [dɪ'raɪv] vt (get) gewinnen; (deduce) ableiten // vi (come from) abstammen.

dermatitis [dɜːmə'taɪtɪs] n Hautentzündung f.

derogatory [dɪ'rɔgətərɪ] a geringschätzig.

derrick ['derɪk] n Drehkran m.

derv [dɜːv] n (Brit) Dieselkraftstoff m.

descend [dɪ'send] vti hinuntersteigen; to ~ from abstammen von; ~**ant** n Nachkomme m.

descent [dɪ'sent] n (coming down) Abstieg m; (origin) Abstammung f.

describe [dɪs'kraɪb] vt beschreiben.

description [dɪs'krɪpʃən] n Beschreibung f; (sort) Art f.

descriptive [dɪs'krɪptɪv] a beschreibend; (word) anschaulich.

desecrate ['desɪkreɪt] vt schänden.

desert ['dezət] n Wüste f // v [dɪ'zɜːt] vt verlassen; (temporarily) im Stich lassen // vi (MIL) desertieren; ~**er** n Deserteur m; ~**ion** [dɪ'zɜːfən] n (of wife) Verlassen nt; (MIL) Fahnenflucht f; ~ **island** n einsame Insel f; ~**s** [dɪ'zɜːts] pl: to get one's just ~s seinen gerechten Lohn bekommen.

deserve [dɪ'zɜːv] vt verdienen.

deserving [dɪ'zɜːvɪŋ] a verdienstvoll.

design [dɪ'zaɪn] n (plan) Entwurf m; (planning) Design nt // vt entwerfen.

designate ['dezɪgneɪt] vt bestimmen // a ['dezɪgnɪt] designiert.

designer [dɪ'zaɪnə*] n Designer(in f) m; (TECH) Konstrukteur(in f) m; (fashion ~) Modeschöpfer(in f) m.

desirable [dɪ'zaɪərəbl] a wünschenswert.

desire [dɪ'zaɪə*] n Wunsch m, Verlangen nt // vt (lust) begehren; (ask for) wollen.

desk [desk] n Schreibtisch m; (Brit: in shop, restaurant) Kasse f.

desolate ['desəlɪt] a öde; (sad) trostlos.

desolation [desə'leɪʃən] n Trostlosigkeit f.

despair [dɪs'peə*] n Verzweiflung f // vi verzweifeln (of an +dat).

despatch [dɪs'pætʃ] n, vt = **dispatch**.

desperate a, ~**ly** ad ['despərɪt, -ɪtlɪ] verzweifelt.

desperation [despə'reɪʃən] n Verzweiflung f.

despicable [dɪs'pɪkəbl] a abscheulich.

despise [dɪs'paɪz] vt verachten.

despite [dɪs'paɪt] prep trotz (+gen).

despondent [dɪs'pɔndənt] a mutlos.

dessert [dɪ'zɜːt] *n* Nachtisch *m*; **~spoon** *n* Dessertlöffel *m*.

destination [destɪ'neɪʃən] *n* (*of person*) (Reise)ziel *nt*; (*of goods*) Bestimmungsort *m*.

destine ['destɪn] *vt* (*set apart*) bestimmen.

destiny ['destɪnɪ] *n* Schicksal *nt*.

destitute ['destɪtjuːt] *a* notleidend.

destroy [dɪs'trɔɪ] *vt* zerstören; **~er** *n* (*NAUT*) Zerstörer *m*.

destruction [dɪs'trʌkʃən] *n* Zerstörung *f*.

destructive [dɪs'trʌktɪv] *a* zerstörend.

detach [dɪ'tætʃ] *vt* loslösen; **~able** *a* abtrennbar; **~ed** *a* (*attitude*) distanziert; (*house*) Einzel-; **~ment** *n* (*MIL*) Sonderkommando *nt*; (*fig*) Abstand *m*.

detail ['diːteɪl] *n* Einzelheit *f*, Detail *nt* // *vt* (*relate*) ausführlich berichten; (*appoint*) abkommandieren; **in ~** im Detail; **~ed** *a* detailliert.

detain [dɪ'teɪn] *vt* aufhalten; (*imprison*) in Haft halten.

detect [dɪ'tekt] *vt* entdecken; **~ion** [dɪ'tekʃən] *n* Aufdeckung *f*; **~ive** *n* Detektiv *m*; **~ive story** *n* Krimi(nalgeschichte *f*) *m*; **~or** *n* Detektor *m*.

détente ['deɪtɑːnt] *n* Entspannung *f*.

detention [dɪ'tenʃən] *n* Haft *f*; (*SCH*) Nachsitzen *nt*.

deter [dɪ'tɜː*] *vt* abschrecken.

detergent [dɪ'tɜːdʒənt] *n* Waschmittel *nt*.

deteriorate [dɪ'tɪərɪəreɪt] *vi* sich verschlechtern; **deterioration** [-'reɪʃən] *n* Verschlechterung *f*.

determination [dɪtɜːmɪ'neɪʃən] *n* Entschlossenheit *f*.

determine [dɪ'tɜːmɪn] *vt* bestimmen; **~d** *a* entschlossen.

deterrent [dɪ'terənt] *n* Abschreckungsmittel *nt*.

detest [dɪ'test] *vt* verabscheuen.

detonate ['detəneɪt] *vt* explodieren lassen // *vi* detonieren.

detour ['diːtuə*] *n* Umweg *m*; (*US AUT: diversion*) Umleitung *f* // *vt* (*US: traffic*) umleiten.

detract [dɪ'trækt] *vi* schmälern (*from acc.*)

detriment ['detrɪmənt] *n*: **to the ~ of** zum Schaden (+*gen*); **~al** [detrɪ'mentl] *a* schädlich.

devaluation [dɪvæljʊ'eɪʃən] *n* Abwertung *f*.

devalue ['diː'væljuː] *vt* abwerten.

devastate ['devəsteɪt] *vt* verwüsten.

devastating ['devəsteɪtɪŋ] *a* verheerend.

develop [dɪ'veləp] *vt* entwickeln; (*resources*) erschließen // *vi* sich entwickeln; **~ing country** *n* Entwick-

lungsland *nt*; **~ment** *n* Entwicklung *f*.

deviate ['diːvɪeɪt] *vi* abweichen; **deviation** [-'eɪʃən] *n* Abweichung *f*.

device [dɪ'vaɪs] *n* Gerät *nt*.

devil ['devl] *n* Teufel *m*; **~ish** *a* teuflisch.

devious ['diːvɪəs] *a* (*means*) krumm; (*person*) verschlagen.

devise [dɪ'vaɪz] *vt* entwickeln.

devoid [dɪ'vɔɪd] *a*: **~ of** ohne.

devolution [diːvə'luːʃən] *n* (*POL*) Dezentralisierung *f*.

devote [dɪ'vəʊt] *vt* widmen (*to dat*); **~d** *a* ergeben; **devotee** [devəʊ'tiː] *n* Anhänger(in *f*) *m*, Verehrer(in *f*) *m*.

devotion [dɪ'vəʊʃən] *n* (*piety*) Andacht *f*; (*loyalty*) Ergebenheit *f*, Hingabe *f*.

devour [dɪ'vaʊə*] *vt* verschlingen.

devout [dɪ'vaʊt] *a* andächtig.

dew [djuː] *n* Tau *m*.

dexterity [deks'terɪtɪ] *n* Geschicklichkeit *f*.

DHSS *n abbr* (*Brit*) = *Department of Health and Society Security*.

diabetes [daɪə'biːtiːz] *n* Zuckerkrankheit *f*.

diabetic [daɪə'betɪk] *a* zuckerkrank; (*food*) Diabetiker-; // *n* Diabetiker *m*.

diabolical [daɪə'bɒlɪkl] *a* (*col: weather, behaviour*) saumäßig.

diagnose ['daɪəgnəʊz] *vt* diagnostizieren.

diagnosis [daɪəg'nəʊsɪs], *pl* **-ses** [-'nəʊsiːz] *n* Diagnose *f*.

diagonal [daɪ'ægənl] *a* diagonal // *n* Diagonale *f*.

diagram ['daɪəgræm] *n* Diagramm *nt*, Schaubild *nt*.

dial ['daɪəl] *n* (*TEL*) Wählscheibe *f*; (*of clock*) Zifferblatt *nt* // *vt* wählen; **~ code** *n* (*US*) = **dialling code**; **~ tone** *n* (*US*) = **dialling tone**.

dialect ['daɪəlekt] *n* Dialekt *m*.

dialling ['daɪəlɪŋ]: **~ code** *n* Vorwahl *f*; **~ tone** *n* Amtszeichen *nt*.

dialogue ['daɪəlɒg] *n* Dialog *m*.

diameter [daɪ'æmɪtə*] *n* Durchmesser *m*.

diamond ['daɪəmənd] *n* Diamant *m*; **~s** *pl* (*CARDS*) Karo *nt*.

diaper ['daɪəpə*] *n* (*US*) Windel *f*.

diaphragm ['daɪəfræm] *n* Zwerchfell *nt*.

diarrhoea, (*US*) **diarrhea** [daɪə'riːə] *n* Durchfall *m*.

diary ['daɪərɪ] *n* Taschenkalender *m*; (*account*) Tagebuch *nt*.

dice [daɪs] *n* Würfel *pl* // *vt* in Würfel schneiden.

dichotomy [dɪ'kɒtəmɪ] *n* Kluft *f*.

dictate [dɪk'teɪt] *vt* diktieren; **~s** ['dɪkteɪts] *pl* Gebote *pl*.

dictation [dɪk'teɪʃən] *n* Diktat *nt*.

dictator [dɪk'teɪtə*] *n* Diktator *m*.

dictatorship [dɪk'teɪtəʃɪp] *n* Diktatur *f*.

diction ['dɪkʃən] *n* Ausdrucksweise *f*.

dictionary ['dɪkʃənrɪ] n Wörterbuch nt.

did [dɪd] pt of **do**.

didn't ['dɪdənt] = **did not**.

die [daɪ] vi sterben; to be dying for sth/to do sth etw unbedingt haben wollen/ darauf brennen, etw zu tun; ~ **away** vi schwächer werden; ~ **down** vi nachlassen; ~ **out** vi aussterben.

diehard ['daɪhɑːd] n Dickkopf m; (POL) Reaktionär m.

diesel ['diːzəl]: ~ **engine** n Dieselmotor m; ~ **(oil)** n Diesel(kraftstoff) m.

diet ['daɪət] n Nahrung f; (special food) Diät f; (slimming) Abmagerungskur f // vi (also: be on a ~) eine Abmagerungskur machen.

differ ['dɪfə*] vi sich unterscheiden; (disagree) anderer Meinung sein; ~**ence** n Unterschied m; ~**ent** a anders; (two things) verschieden; ~**ential** [dɪfə'renʃəl] n (in wages) Lohnstufe f; ~**entiate** [dɪfə'renʃɪeɪt] vti unterscheiden; ~**ently** ad anders; (from one another) unterschiedlich.

difficult ['dɪfɪkəlt] a schwierig; ~**y** n Schwierigkeit f.

diffident ['dɪfɪdənt] a schüchtern.

diffuse [dɪ'fjuːs] a langatmig // vt [dɪ'fjuːz] vt verbreiten.

dig [dɪg] v (pt, pp **dug**) vt graben // n (prod) Stoß m; (remark) Spitze f; (archaeological) Ausgrabung f; ~ **in** vi (MIL) sich eingraben; ~ **into** vt (sb's past) wühlen in (+dat); (savings) angreifen; ~ **up** vt ausgraben; (fig) aufgabeln.

digest [daɪ'dʒest] vt verdauen // n ['daɪdʒest] Auslese f; ~**ion** n Verdauung f; ~**ive** a (juices, system) Verdauungs-.

digit ['dɪdʒɪt] n Ziffer f; (ANAT) Finger m; ~**al** a digital, Digital-.

dignified ['dɪgnɪfaɪd] a würdevoll.

dignity ['dɪgnɪtɪ] n Würde f.

digress [daɪ'gres] vi abschweifen.

digs [dɪgz] npl (Brit col) Bude f.

dilapidated [dɪ'læpɪdeɪtɪd] a baufällig.

dilate [daɪ'leɪt] vti (sich) weiten.

dilemma [daɪ'lemə] n Dilemma nt.

diligent ['dɪlɪdʒənt] a fleißig.

dilute [daɪ'luːt] vt verdünnen.

dim [dɪm] a trübe; (stupid) schwer von Begriff // vt verdunkeln; to ~ one's headlights (esp US) abblenden.

dime [daɪm] n (US) Zehncentstück nt.

dimension [dɪ'menʃən] n Dimension f.

diminish [dɪ'mɪnɪʃ] vti verringern.

diminutive [dɪ'mɪnjutɪv] a winzig // n Verkleinerungsform f.

dimmer ['dɪmə*] n (US AUT) Abblendschalter m.

dimple ['dɪmpl] n Grübchen nt.

din [dɪn] n Getöse nt.

dine [daɪn] vi speisen; ~**r** n Tischgast m; (RAIL) Speisewagen m.

dinghy ['dɪŋgɪ] n Dinghy nt; **rubber** ~ Schlauchboot nt.

dingy ['dɪndʒɪ] a armselig.

dining car ['daɪnɪŋkɑː*] n (Brit) Speisewagen m.

dining room ['daɪnɪŋrum] n Eßzimmer nt; (in hotel) Speisezimmer nt.

dinner ['dɪnə*] n (lunch) Mittagessen nt; (evening) Abendessen nt; (public) Festessen nt; ~ **jacket** n Smoking m; ~ **party** n Tischgesellschaft f; ~ **time** n Tischzeit f.

dinosaur ['daɪnəsɔː*] n Dinosaurier m.

dint [dɪnt] n: **by** ~ **of** durch.

diocese ['daɪəsɪs] n Diözese f.

dip [dɪp] n (hollow) Senkung f; (bathe) kurze(s) Bad(en) nt // vt eintauchen; (Brit AUT: lights) abblenden // vi (slope) sich senken, abfallen.

diploma [dɪ'pləumə] n Diplom nt.

diplomacy [dɪ'pləuməsɪ] n Diplomatie f.

diplomat ['dɪpləmæt] n Diplomat(in f) m; ~**ic** [dɪplə'mætɪk] a diplomatisch.

dipstick ['dɪpstɪk] n Ölmeßstab m.

dipswitch ['dɪpswɪtʃ] n (Brit AUT) Abblendschalter n.

dire [daɪə*] a schrecklich.

direct [daɪ'rekt] a direkt // vt leiten; (film) die Regie führen (+gen); (aim) richten; (order) anweisen; **can you** ~ **me to ...?** können Sie mir sagen, wie ich zu ... komme?

direction [dɪ'rekʃən] n Richtung f; (CINE) Regie f; Leitung f; ~**s** (for use) Gebrauchsanleitung f; (orders) Anweisungen pl; ~ **sense of** ~ Orientierungssinn m.

directly [dɪ'rektlɪ] ad direkt; (at once) sofort.

director [dɪ'rektə*] n Direktor m; (of film) Regisseur m.

directory [dɪ'rektərɪ] n (TEL) Telefonbuch nt.

dirt [dɜːt] n Schmutz m, Dreck m; ~-**cheap** a spottbillig; ~**y** a schmutzig // vt beschmutzen; ~**y trick** n gemeiner Trick.

disability [dɪsə'bɪlɪtɪ] n Körperbehinderung f.

disabled [dɪs'eɪbld] a körperbehindert.

disadvantage [dɪsəd'vɑːntɪdʒ] n Nachteil m.

disaffection [dɪsə'fekʃən] n Entfremdung f.

disagree [dɪsə'griː] vi nicht übereinstimmen; (quarrel) (sich) streiten; (food) nicht bekommen (with dat); ~**able** a unangenehm; ~**ment** n (between persons) Streit m; (between things) Widerspruch m.

disallow [dɪsə'lau] vt nicht zulassen.

disappear [dɪsə'pɪə*] vi verschwinden; ~**ance** n Verschwinden nt.

disappoint [dɪsə'pɔɪnt] vt enttäuschen; ~**ed** a enttäuscht; ~**ing** a enttäuschend; ~**ment** n Enttäuschung f.

disapproval [dɪsə'pruːvəl] n Mißbilligung f.

disapprove [dɪsə'pruːv] vi mißbilligen (of acc).

disarm [dɪs'aːm] vt entwaffnen; (POL) abrüsten; ~**ament** n Abrüstung f.

disarray ['dɪsə'reɪ] n: to be in ~ (army) in Auflösung (begriffen) sein; (clothes) in unordentlichen Zustand sein.

disaster [dɪ'zaːstə*] n Katastrophe f.

disastrous [dɪ'zaːstrəs] a verhängnisvoll.

disband [dɪs'bænd] vt auflösen // vi auseinandergehen.

disbelief ['dɪsbə'liːf] n Ungläubigkeit f.

disc [dɪsk] n Scheibe f; (record) (Schall)platte f; (COMPUT) = disk.

discard ['dɪskaːd] vt ablegen.

discern [dɪ'sɜːn] vt erkennen; ~**ing** a scharfsinnig.

discharge [dɪs'tʃaːdʒ] vt (ship) entladen; (duties) nachkommen (+dat); (dismiss) entlassen; (gun) abschießen; (JUR) freisprechen // n ['dɪstʃaːdʒ] (of ship, ELEC) Entladung f; (dismissal) Entlassung f; (MED) Ausfluß m.

disciple [dɪ'saɪpl] n Jünger m.

discipline ['dɪsɪplɪn] n Disziplin f // vt (train) schulen; (punish) bestrafen.

disc jockey ['dɪskdʒɒkɪ] n Diskjockey m.

disclaim [dɪs'kleɪm] vt nicht anerkennen.

disclose [dɪs'kləʊz] vt enthüllen.

disclosure [dɪs'kləʊʒə*] n Enthüllung f.

disco ['dɪskəʊ] n abbr of discothèque.

discoloured, (US) **discolored** [dɪs'kʌləd] a verfärbt.

discomfort [dɪs'kʌmfət] n Unbehagen nt.

disconcert [dɪskən'sɜːt] vt aus der Fassung bringen.

disconnect ['dɪskə'nekt] vt abtrennen.

discontent ['dɪskən'tent] n Unzufriedenheit f; ~**ed** a unzufrieden.

discontinue ['dɪskən'tɪnjuː] vt einstellen.

discord ['dɪskɔːd] n Zwietracht f; (noise) Dissonanz f; ~**ant** [dɪs'kɔːdənt] a uneinig.

discothèque ['dɪskəʊtek] n Diskothek f.

discount ['dɪskaʊnt] n Rabatt m // vt [dɪs'kaʊnt] außer acht lassen.

discourage [dɪs'kʌrɪdʒ] vt entmutigen; (prevent) abraten.

discouraging [dɪs'kʌrɪdʒɪŋ] a entmutigend.

discourteous [dɪs'kɜːtɪəs] a unhöflich.

discover [dɪs'kʌvə*] vt entdecken; ~**y** n Entdeckung f.

discredit [dɪs'kredɪt] vt in Verruf bringen.

discreet a [dɪs'kriːt] diskret.

discrepancy [dɪs'krepənsɪ] n Diskrepanz f.

discriminate [dɪs'krɪmɪneɪt] vi unterscheiden; to ~ against diskriminieren.

discriminating [dɪs'krɪmɪneɪtɪŋ] a anspruchsvoll.

discrimination [dɪskrɪmɪ'neɪʃən] n Urteilsvermögen nt; (pej) Diskriminierung f.

discuss [dɪs'kʌs] vt diskutieren, besprechen; ~**ion** [dɪs'kʌʃən] n Diskussion f, Besprechung f.

disdain [dɪs'deɪn] vt verachten // n Verachtung f.

disease [dɪ'ziːz] n Krankheit f.

disembark [dɪsɪm'baːk] vt aussteigen lassen // vi von Bord gehen.

disenchanted ['dɪsɪn'tʃaːntɪd] a desillusioniert.

disengage [dɪsɪn'geɪdʒ] vt (AUT) auskuppeln.

disentangle ['dɪsɪn'tæŋgl] vt entwirren.

disfigure [dɪs'fɪgə*] vt entstellen.

disgrace [dɪs'greɪs] n Schande f // vt Schande bringen über (+acc); ~**ful** a unerhört.

disgruntled [dɪs'grʌntld] a verärgert.

disguise [dɪs'gaɪz] vt verkleiden; (feelings) verhehlen // n Verkleidung f; in ~ verkleidet, maskiert.

disgust [dɪs'gʌst] n Abscheu f // vt anwidern; ~**ing** a widerlich.

dish [dɪʃ] n Schüssel f; (food) Gericht nt; to do or wash the ~es abwaschen; ~ **up** vt auftischen; ~ **cloth** n Spüllappen m.

dishearten [dɪs'haːtn] vt entmutigen.

dishevelled [dɪ'ʃevəld] a (hair) zerzaust; (clothing) ungepflegt.

dishonest [dɪs'ɒnɪst] a unehrlich; ~**y** n Unehrlichkeit f.

dishonour, (US) **dishonor** [dɪs'ɒnə*] n Unehre f; ~**able** a unehrenhaft.

dish towel n (US: tea towel) Geschirrtuch nt.

dishwasher ['dɪʃwɒʃə*] n Geschirrspülmaschine f.

disillusion [dɪsɪ'luːʒən] vt enttäuschen, desillusionieren.

disincentive ['dɪsɪn'sentɪv] n Entmutigung f.

disinfect [dɪsɪn'fekt] vt desinfizieren; ~**ant** n Desinfektionsmittel nt.

disintegrate [dɪs'ɪntɪgreɪt] vi sich auflösen.

disinterested [dɪs'ɪntrɪstɪd] a uneigennützig; (col) uninteressiert.

disjointed [dɪs'dʒɔɪntɪd] a unzusammenhängend.

disk [dɪsk] n (COMPUT) Diskette f; **single-/double-sided** ~ einseitige/beidseitige Diskette f; ~ **drive** n Diskettenlaufwerk nt; ~**ette** n (US) = disk.

dislike [dɪs'laɪk] n Abneigung f // vt nicht leiden können.

dislocate ['dɪsləʊkeɪt] *vt* auskugeln.

dislodge [dɪs'lɒdʒ] *vt* verschieben; (*MIL*) aus der Stellung werfen.

disloyal ['dɪs'lɔɪəl] *a* treulos.

dismal ['dɪzməl] *a* trostlos, trübe.

dismantle [dɪs'mæntl] *vt* demontieren.

dismay [dɪs'meɪ] *n* Bestürzung *f* // *vt* bestürzen.

dismiss [dɪs'mɪs] *vt* (*employee*) entlassen; (*idea*) von sich weisen; (*send away*) wegschicken; (*JUR*) abweisen; ~**al** *n* Entlassung *f*.

dismount [dɪs'maʊnt] *vi* absteigen.

disobedience [dɪsə'biːdɪəns] *n* Ungehorsam *m*.

disobedient [dɪsə'biːdɪənt] *a* ungehorsam.

disobey ['dɪsə'beɪ] *vt* nicht gehorchen (+*dat*).

disorder [dɪs'ɔːdə*] *n* (*confusion*) Verwirrung *f*; (*commotion*) Aufruhr *m*; (*MED*) Erkrankung *f*.

disorderly [dɪs'ɔːdəlɪ] *a* (*untidy*) unordentlich; (*unruly*) ordnungswidrig.

disorganized [dɪs'ɔːgənaɪzd] *a* unordentlich.

disown [dɪs'əʊn] *vt* (*son*) verstoßen.

disparaging [dɪs'pærɪdʒɪŋ] *a* geringschätzig.

disparity [dɪs'pærɪtɪ] *n* Verschiedenheit *f*.

dispassionate [dɪs'pæʃnɪt] *a* objektiv.

dispatch [dɪs'pætʃ] *vt* (*goods*) abschicken, abfertigen // *n* Absendung *f*; (*esp MIL*) Meldung *f*.

dispel [dɪs'pel] *vt* zerstreuen.

dispensary [dɪs'pensərɪ] *n* Apotheke *f*.

dispense [dɪs'pens]: ~ **with** *vt* verzichten auf (+*acc*); ~**r** *n* (*container*) Spender *m*.

dispensing [dɪs'pensɪŋ] *a*: ~ **chemist** (*Brit*) Apotheker *m*.

dispersal [dɪs'pɜːsəl] *n* Zerstreuung *f*.

disperse [dɪs'pɜːs] *vt* zerstreuen // *vi* sich verteilen.

dispirited [dɪs'pɪrɪtɪd] *a* niedergeschlagen.

displace [dɪs'pleɪs] *vt* verschieben; ~**d person** *n* Verschleppte(r) *mf*.

display [dɪs'pleɪ] *n* (*of goods*) Auslage *f*; (*of feeling*) Zurschaustellung *f* // *vt* zeigen; (*ostentatiously*) vorführen; (*goods*) ausstellen.

displease [dɪs'pliːz] *vt* mißfallen (+*dat*).

displeasure [dɪs'pleʒə*] *n* Mißfallen *nt*.

disposable [dɪs'pəʊzəbl] *a* Wegwerf-; ~ **nappy** *n* Papierwindel *f*.

disposal [dɪs'pəʊzəl] *n* (*of property*) Verkauf *m*; (*throwing away*) Beseitigung *f*; **to be at one's** ~ einem zur Verfügung stehen.

dispose [dɪs'pəʊz]: ~ **of** *vt* loswerden.

disposed [dɪs'pəʊzd] *a* geneigt.

disposition [dɪspə'zɪʃən] *n* Wesen *nt*.

disproportionate [dɪsprə'pɔːʃnɪt] *a* unverhältnismäßig.

disprove [dɪs'pruːv] *vt* widerlegen.

dispute [dɪs'pjuːt] *n* Streit *m*; (*also:* **industrial** ~) Arbeitskampf *m* // *vt* bestreiten.

disqualify [dɪs'kwɒlɪfaɪ] *vt* disqualifizieren.

disquiet [dɪs'kwaɪət] *n* Unruhe *f*.

disregard [dɪsrɪ'gɑːd] *vt* nicht (be)achten.

disrepair ['dɪsrɪ'pɛə*] *n*: **to fall into** ~ verfallen.

disreputable [dɪs'repjʊtəbl] *a* verrufen.

disrespectful [dɪsrɪs'pektfʊl] *a* respektlos.

disrupt [dɪs'rʌpt] *vt* stören; (*service*) unterbrechen; ~**ion** [dɪs'rʌpʃən] *n* Störung *f*, Unterbrechung *f*.

dissatisfaction ['dɪssætɪs'fækʃən] *n* Unzufriedenheit *f*.

dissatisfied ['dɪs'sætɪsfaɪd] *a* unzufrieden.

dissect [dɪ'sekt] *vt* zerlegen, sezieren.

disseminate [dɪ'semɪneɪt] *vt* verbreiten.

dissent [dɪ'sent] *n* abweichende Meinung *f*.

dissertation [dɪsə'teɪʃən] *n* wissenschaftliche Arbeit *f*; (*PhD*) Doktorarbeit *f*.

disservice [dɪs'sɜːvɪs] *n*: **to do sb a** ~ jdm einen schlechten Dienst erweisen.

dissident ['dɪsɪdənt] *a* andersdenkend // *n* Dissident *m*.

dissimilar [dɪ'sɪmɪlə*] *a* unähnlich (*to dat*).

dissipate ['dɪsɪpeɪt] *vt* (*waste*) verschwenden; (*scatter*) zerstreuen.

dissociate [dɪ'səʊʃɪeɪt] *vt* trennen.

dissolute ['dɪsəluːt] *a* liederlich.

dissolution [dɪsə'luːʃən] *n* Auflösung *f*.

dissolve [dɪ'zɒlv] *vt* auflösen // *vi* sich auflösen.

dissuade [dɪs'weɪd] *vt*: **to** ~ **sb from doing sth** jdn davon abbringen, etw zu tun.

distance ['dɪstəns] *n* Entfernung *f*; **in the** ~ in der Ferne.

distant ['dɪstənt] *a* entfernt, fern; (*with time*) fern; (*formal*) distanziert.

distaste [dɪs'teɪst] *n* Abneigung *f*; ~**ful** *a* widerlich.

distended [dɪs'tendɪd] *a* (*stomach*) aufgebläht.

distil [dɪs'tɪl] *vt* destillieren; ~**lery** *n* Brennerei *f*.

distinct [dɪs'tɪŋkt] *a* (*separate*) getrennt; (*clear*) klar, deutlich; **as** ~ **from** im Unterschied zu; ~**ion** [dɪs'tɪŋkʃən] *n* Unterscheidung *f*; (*eminence*) Auszeichnung *f*; ~**ive** *a* bezeichnend.

distinguish [dɪs'tɪŋgwɪʃ] *vt* unterscheiden; ~**ed** *a* (*eminent*) berühmt; ~**ing** *a* bezeichnend.

distort [dɪs'tɔːt] *vt* verdrehen; (*mis-*

represent) entstellen; **~ion** [dɪs'tɔ:ʃən] *n* Verzerrung *f*.

distract [dɪs'trækt] *vt* ablenken; **~ing** *a* verwirrend; **~ion** [dɪs'trækʃən] *n* (*distress*) Raserei *f*; (*diversion*) Zerstreuung *f*.

distraught [dɪs'trɔ:t] *a* bestürzt.

distress [dɪs'tres] *n* Not *f*; (*suffering*) Qual *f* // *vt* quälen; **~ing** *a* erschütternd; **~ signal** *n* Notsignal *nt*.

distribute [dɪs'trɪbju:t] *vt* verteilen.

distribution [dɪstrɪ'bju:ʃən] *n* Verteilung *f*.

distributor [dɪs'trɪbjʊtə*] *n* Verteiler *m*.

district ['dɪstrɪkt] *n* (*of country*) Kreis *m*; (*of town*) Bezirk *m*; **~ attorney** *n* (*US*) Oberstaatsanwalt *m*; **~ nurse** *n* (*Brit*) Kreiskrankenschwester *f*.

distrust [dɪs'trʌst] *n* Mißtrauen *nt* // *vt* mißtrauen (*+dat*).

disturb [dɪs'tɜ:b] *vt* stören; (*agitate*) erregen; **~ance** *n* Störung *f*; **~ed** *a* beunruhigt; **emotionally ~ed** emotional gestört; **~ing** *a* beunruhigend.

disuse ['dɪs'ju:s] *n*: **to fall into ~** außer Gebrauch kommen.

disused ['dɪs'ju:zd] *a* außer Gebrauch.

ditch [dɪtʃ] *n* Graben *m* // *vt* (*person*) loswerden; (*plan*) fallenlassen.

dither ['dɪðə*] *vi* verdattert sein.

ditto ['dɪtəʊ] *ad* dito, ebenfalls.

divan [dɪ'væn] *n* Liegesofa *nt*.

dive [daɪv] *n* (*into water*) Kopfsprung *m*; (*AVIAT*) Sturzflug *m* // *vi* tauchen; **~r** *n* Taucher *m*.

diverge [daɪ'vɜ:dʒ] *vi* auseinandergehen.

diverse [daɪ'vɜ:s] *a* verschieden.

diversion [daɪ'vɜ:ʃən] *n* Ablenkung *f*; (*Brit AUT*) Umleitung *f*.

diversity [daɪ'vɜ:sɪtɪ] *n* Vielfalt *f*.

divert [daɪ'vɜ:t] *vt* ablenken; (*traffic*) umleiten.

divide [dɪ'vaɪd] *vt* teilen // *vi* sich teilen; **~d highway** *n* (*US*) Schnellstraße *f*.

dividend ['dɪvɪdend] *n* Dividende *f*.

divine [dɪ'vaɪn] *a* göttlich.

diving ['daɪvɪŋ] *n* (*SPORT*) Turmspringen *nt*; (*underwater ~*) Tauchen *nt*; **~ board** *n* Sprungbrett *nt*.

divinity [dɪ'vɪnɪtɪ] *n* Gottheit *f*; (*subject*) Religion *f*.

division [dɪ'vɪʒən] *n* Teilung *f*; (*MIL*) Division *f*; (*part*) Abteilung *f*; (*in opinion*) Uneinigkeit *f*; (*Brit POL*) Abstimmung *f* durch Hammelsprung.

divorce [dɪ'vɔ:s] *n* (*Ehe*)scheidung *f* // *vt* scheiden; **~d** *a* geschieden; **~e** [dɪvɔ:'si:] *n* Geschiedene(r) *mf*.

divulge [daɪ'vʌldʒ] *vt* preisgeben.

D.I.Y. *n abbr* (*Brit*) of **do-it-yourself.**

dizzy ['dɪzɪ] *a* schwindlig.

DJ *n abbr* of **disc jockey.**

do [du:] ♦ *n* (*col: party etc*) Fete *f* ♦ *v* (*pt* **did,** *pp* **done**) *aux v* 1 (*in negative constructions and questions*): **I don't**

understand ich verstehe nicht; **didn't you know?** wußtest du das nicht?; **what ~ you think?** was meinen Sie?

2 (*for emphasis, in polite expressions*): **she does seem rather tired** sie scheint wirklich sehr müde zu sein; **~ sit down/help yourself** setzen Sie sich doch hin/greifen Sie doch zu

3 (*used to avoid repeating v*): **she swims better than I ~** sie schwimmt besser als ich; **she lives in Glasgow — so ~ I** sie wohnt in Glasgow — ich auch

4 (*in question tags*): **you like him, don't you?** du magst ihn doch, oder?

♦*vt* **1** (*carry out, perform etc*) tun, machen; **what are you ~ing tonight?** was machst du heute abend?; **I've got nothing to ~** ich habe nichts zu tun; **to ~ one's hair/nails** sich die Haare/Nägel machen

2 (*AUT etc*) fahren

♦*vi* **1** (*act, behave*): **~ as I ~** mach es wie ich

2 (*get on, fare*): **he's ~ing well/badly at school** er ist gut/schlecht in der Schule; **how ~ you ~?** guten Tag

3 (*be suitable*) gehen; (*be sufficient*) reichen; **to make ~ (with)** auskommen mit

do away with *vt* (*kill*) umbringen; (*abolish: law etc*) abschaffen

do up *vt* (*laces, dress, buttons*) zumachen; (*renovate: room, house*) renovieren

do with *vt* (*need*) brauchen; (*be connected*) zu tun haben mit

do without *vti* auskommen ohne.

docile ['dəʊsaɪl] *a* gefügig.

dock [dɒk] *n* Dock *nt*; (*JUR*) Anklagebank *f* // *vi* ins Dock gehen; **~s** *pl* Hafen *m*; **~er** *n* Hafenarbeiter *m*; **~yard** *n* Werft *f*.

doctor ['dɒktə*] *n* Arzt *m*, Ärztin *f*; (*UNIV*) Doktor *m* // *vt* (*fig*) fälschen; (*drink etc*) etw beimischen (*+dat*); **D~ of Philosophy (Ph. D.)** *n* Doktor *m* der Philosophie (Dr. Phil.).

doctrine ['dɒktrɪn] *n* Doktrin *f*.

document ['dɒkjʊmənt] *n* Dokument *nt*; **~ary** [dɒkjʊ'mentərɪ] *n* Dokumentarbericht *m*; (*film*) Dokumentarfilm *m* // *a* dokumentarisch; **~ation** [dɒkjʊmen'teɪʃən] *n* dokumentarische(r) Nachweis *m*.

dodge [dɒdʒ] *n* Kniff *m* // *vt* ausweichen (*+dat*); **~ms** *npl* (*Brit*) Autoskooter *m*.

doe [dəʊ] *n* (*roe deer*) Ricke *f*; (*red deer*) Hirschkuh *f*; (*rabbit*) Weibchen *nt*.

does [dʌz] *v see* **do**; **~n't = ~ not.**

dog [dɒg] *n* Hund *m*; **~ collar** *n* Hundehalsband *nt*; (*ECCL*) Kragen *m* des Geistlichen; **~-eared** *a* mit Eselsohren.

dogged ['dɒgɪd] *a* hartnäckig.

dogsbody ['dɒgsbɒdɪ] *n* Mädchen *nt* für

alles.

doings ['duːɪŋz] npl (activities) Treiben nt.

do-it-yourself ['duːɪtjə'self] n Do-it-yourself nt.

doldrums ['dɔldrəmz] npl: to be in the ~ (business) Flaute haben; (person) deprimiert sein.

dole [dəʊl] n (Brit) Stempelgeld nt; to be on the ~ stempeln gehen; ~ **out** vt ausgeben, austeilen.

doleful ['dəʊlful] a traurig.

doll [dɔl] n Puppe f // vt: ~ o.s. up sich aufdonnern.

dollar ['dɔlə*] n Dollar m.

dolphin ['dɔlfɪn] n Delphin m.

domain [də'meɪn] n Domäne f.

dome [dəʊm] n Kuppel f.

domestic [də'mestɪk] a häuslich; (within country) Innen-, Binnen-; (animal) Haus-; ~**ated** a (person) häuslich; (animal) zahm.

dominant ['dɔmɪnənt] a vorherrschend.

dominate ['dɔmɪneɪt] vt beherrschen.

domineering [dɔmɪ'nɪərɪŋ] a herrisch.

dominion [də'mɪnɪən] n (rule) Regierungsgewalt f; (land) Staatsgebiet nt mit Selbstverwaltung.

domino ['dɔmɪnəʊ] n, pl ~**es** Dominostein m; ~**es** n (game) Domino(spiel) nt.

don [dɔn] n (Brit) akademische(r) Lehrer m.

donate [də'neɪt] vt (blood, little money) spenden; (lot of money) stiften.

donation [də'neɪʃən] n Spende f.

done [dʌn] pp of do.

donkey ['dɔŋkɪ] n Esel m.

donor ['dəʊnə*] n Spender m.

don't [dəʊnt] = do not.

doodle ['duːdl] vi kritzeln.

doom [duːm] n böse(s) Geschick nt; (downfall) Verderben nt // vt: to be ~ed zum Untergang verurteilt sein; ~**sday** n der Jüngste Tag.

door [dɔː*] n Tür f; ~**bell** n Türklingel f; ~**handle** n Türklinke f; ~**man** n Türsteher m; ~**mat** n Fußmatte f; ~**step** n Türstufe f; ~**way** n Türöffnung f.

dope [dəʊp] n (drug) Aufputschmittel nt // vt (horse etc) dopen.

dopey ['dəʊpɪ] a (col) bekloppt.

dormant ['dɔːmənt] a latent.

dormitory ['dɔːmɪtrɪ] n Schlafsaal m.

dormouse ['dɔːmaʊs], pl -**mice** [-maɪs] n Haselmaus f.

DOS [dɔs] n abbr (= disk operating system) DOS nt.

dosage ['dəʊsɪdʒ] n Dosierung f.

dose [dəʊs] n Dosis f.

doss house ['dɔs-] n (Brit) Bleibe f.

dot [dɔt] n Punkt m; ~**ted with** übersät mit; on the ~ pünktlich.

dote [dəʊt]: ~ **on** vt vernarrt sein in

(+acc).

dot-matrix printer [dɔt'meɪtrɪks-] n Matrixdrucker m.

double ['dʌbl] a, ad doppelt // n Doppelgänger m // vt verdoppeln // vi sich verdoppeln; on the ~, at the ~ (Brit) im Laufschritt; ~**s** n (TENNIS) Doppel nt; ~ **bass** n Kontrabaß m; ~ **bed** n Doppelbett nt; ~ **bend** n (Brit) S-Kurve f; ~**breasted** a zweireihig; ~**cross** vt hintergehen; ~**decker** n Doppeldecker m; ~ **glazing** n (Brit) Doppelverglasung f; ~ **room** n Doppelzimmer nt.

doubly ['dʌblɪ] ad doppelt.

doubt [daʊt] n Zweifel m // vt bezweifeln; ~**ful** a zweifelhaft; ~**less** ad ohne Zweifel.

dough [dəʊ] n Teig m; ~**nut** n Berliner m.

douse [daʊz] vt (drench) mit Wasser begießen, durchtränken; (extinguish) ausmachen.

dove [dʌv] n Taube f; ~**tail** vi (plans) übereinstimmen.

dowdy ['daʊdɪ] a unmodern.

down [daʊn] n (fluff) Flaum m; (hill) Hügel m // ad unten; (motion) herunter; hinunter // prep: to go ~ the street die Straße hinuntergehen // vt niederschlagen; ~ with X! nieder mit X!; ~ **under** (Brit col) Australien nt; ~**and-out** n Tramp m; ~**at-heel** a schäbig; ~**cast** a niedergeschlagen; ~**fall** n Sturz m; ~**hearted** a niedergeschlagen; ~**hill** ad bergab; ~ **payment** n Anzahlung f; ~**pour** n Platzregen m; ~**right** a ausgesprochen; ~**stairs** ad unten; (motion) nach unten; ~**stream** ad flußabwärts; ~**to-earth** a praktisch; ~**town** ad in die/der Innenstadt; ~**ward** a, ad, ~**wards** ad abwärts, nach unten.

dowry ['daʊrɪ] n Mitgift f.

doz. abbr (= dozen) Dtzd.

doze [dəʊz] vi dösen; ~ **off** vi einnicken.

dozen ['dʌzn] n Dutzend nt.

Dr. abbr of doctor; drive.

drab [dræb] a düster, eintönig.

draft [drɑːft] n Entwurf m; (FIN) Wechsel m; (US MIL) Einberufung f // vt skizzieren.

draftsman ['drɑːftsmən] n (US) = **draughtsman**.

drag [dræg] vt schleppen; (river) mit einem Schleppnetz absuchen // vi sich (dahin)schleppen // n (bore) etwas Blödes; in ~ als Tunte; ~ **on** vi sich in die Länge ziehen.

dragon ['drægən] n Drache m; ~**fly** n Libelle f.

drain [dreɪn] n (lit) Abfluß m; (fig: burden) Belastung f // vt ableiten; (exhaust) erschöpfen // vi (of water) abfließen; **~age** n Kanalisation f; **~ing board**, (US) **~board** n Ablaufbrett nt; **~pipe** n Abflußrohr nt.

drama ['drɑːmə] n Drama nt; **~tic** [drə'mætɪk] a dramatisch; **~tist** n Dramatiker m; **~tize** vt (events) dramatisieren; (adapt: for TV, cinema) bearbeiten.

drank [dræŋk] pt of **drink**.

drape [dreɪp] vt drapieren // npl: **~s** (US) Vorhänge pl; **~r** n (Brit) Tuchhändler m.

drastic ['dræstɪk] a drastisch.

draught, (US) **draft** [drɑːft] n Zug m; (NAUT) Tiefgang m; **~s** n (Brit) Damespiel nt; (beer): **on ~** vom Faß; **~board** n (Brit) Zeichenbrett nt.

draughtsman ['drɑːftsmən] n technische(r) Zeichner m.

draw [drɔː], pt **drew**, pp **drawn** vt ziehen; (crowd) anlocken; (picture) zeichnen; (money) abheben; (water) schöpfen // vi (SPORT) unentschieden spielen // n (SPORT) Unentschieden nt; (lottery) Ziehung f; **~ near** vi näherrücken; **~ out** vi (train) ausfahren; (lengthen) sich hinziehen; **~ up** vi (stop) halten // vt (document) aufsetzen; **~back** n Nachteil m; **~bridge** n Zugbrücke f.

drawer [drɔː*] n Schublade f.

drawing ['drɔːɪŋ] n Zeichnung f; Zeichnen nt; **~ board** n Reißbrett nt; **~ pin** n (Brit) Reißzwecke f; **~ room** n Salon m.

drawl [drɔːl] n schleppende Sprechweise f.

drawn [drɔːn] pp of **draw**.

dread [dred] n Furcht f // vt fürchten; **~ful** a furchtbar.

dream [driːm] n Traum m // vti, pt, pp **dreamed** or **dreamt** [dremt] träumen (about von); **~er** n Träumer m; **~y** a verträumt.

dreary ['drɪərɪ] a trostlos, öde.

dredge [dredʒ] vt ausbaggern.

dregs [dregz] npl Bodensatz m; (fig) Abschaum m.

drench [drentʃ] vt durchnässen.

dress [dres] n Kleidung f; (garment) Kleid nt // vt anziehen; (MED) verbinden; **to get ~ed** sich anziehen; **~ up** vi sich fein machen; **~ circle** n (Brit) erste(r) Rang m; **~er** n (furniture) Anrichte f; **~ing** n (MED) Verband m; (COOK) Soße f; **~ing gown** n (Brit) Morgenrock m; **~ing room** n (THEAT) Garderobe f; (SPORT) Umkleideraum m; **~ing table** n Toilettentisch m; **~maker** n Schneiderin f; **~making** n Schneidern nt; **~ rehearsal** n Generalprobe f; **~ shirt** n Frackhemd nt; **~y** a (col) schick.

dribble ['drɪbl] vi sabbern // vt (ball) dribbeln.

drew [druː] pt of **draw**.

dried [draɪd] a getrocknet; (fruit also) Dörr-; **~ milk** n Milchpulver nt.

drier ['draɪə*] n = **dryer**.

drift [drɪft] n Strömung f; (snow~) Schneewehe f; (fig) Richtung f // vi sich treiben lassen; **~wood** n Treibholz nt.

drill [drɪl] n Bohrer m; (MIL) Drill m // vt bohren; (MIL) ausbilden // vi bohren (for nach).

drink [drɪŋk] n Getränk nt; (spirits) Drink m // vti, pt **drank**, pp **drunk** trinken; **~er** n Trinker m; **~ing water** n Trinkwasser nt.

drip [drɪp] n Tropfen m // vi tropfen; **~-dry** a bügelfrei; **~ping** n Bratenfett nt.

drive [draɪv] n Fahrt f; (road) Einfahrt f; (campaign) Aktion f; (energy) Schwung m; (SPORT) Schlag m; (also: disk **~**) Diskettenlaufwerk nt // v (pt **drove**, pp **driven** ['drɪvn]) vt (car) fahren; (animals) treiben; (power) antreiben; (force) treiben // vi fahren; **to ~ sb mad** jdn verrückt machen; **left-/right-hand ~** Links-/Rechtssteuerung f.

drivel ['drɪvl] n Faselei f.

driver ['draɪvə*] n Fahrer m; **~'s license** n (US) Führerschein m.

driveway ['draɪvweɪ] n Auffahrt f; (longer) Zufahrtsstraße f.

driving ['draɪvɪŋ] a (rain) stürmisch; **~ instructor** n Fahrlehrer m; **~ lesson** n Fahrstunde f; **~ licence** n (Brit) Führerschein m; **~ mirror** n Rückspiegel m; **~ school** n Fahrschule f; **~ test** n Fahrprüfung f.

drizzle ['drɪzl] n Nieselregen m // vi nieseln.

drone [drəun] n (sound) Brummen nt; (bee) Drohne f.

drool [druːl] vi sabbern.

droop [druːp] vi (schlaff) herabhängen.

drop [drɒp] n (of liquid) Tropfen m; (fall) Fall m // vt fallen lassen; (lower) senken; (abandon) fallenlassen // vi (fall) herunterfallen; **~s** pl (MED) Tropfen pl; **~ off** vi (sleep) einschlafen // vt (passenger) absetzen; **~ out** vi (withdraw) ausscheiden; **~-out** n Aussteiger m; **~per** n Pipette f; **~pings** npl Kot m.

drought [draut] n Dürre f.

drove [drəuv] pt of **drive**.

drown [draun] vt ertränken; (sound) übertönen // vi ertrinken.

drowsy ['drauzɪ] a schläfrig.

drudgery ['drʌdʒərɪ] n Plackerei f.

drug [drʌg] n (MED) Arznei f; (narcotic) Rauschgift nt // vt betäuben; **~ addict** n Rauschgiftsüchtige(r) mf; **~gist** n (US) Drogist(in f) m; **~store** n (US) Drogerie f.

drum [drʌm] n Trommel f // vi trommeln; **~s** pl Schlagzeug nt; **~mer** n Trommler m.

drunk [drʌŋk] *pp* of **drink** // *a* betrunken // *n* (*also:* ~ard) Trinker(in *f*) *m*; ~**en** *a* betrunken.

dry [draɪ] *a* trocken // *vt* (ab)trocknen // *vi* trocknen; ~ **up** *vi* austrocknen // *vt* (*dishes*) abtrocknen; ~**-cleaning** *n* chemische Reinigung *f*; ~**er** *n* Trockner *m*; (*US: spin-drier*) (Wäsche)schleuder *f*; ~ **goods store** *n* (*US*) Kurzwarengeschäft *nt*; ~**ness** *n* Trockenheit *f*; ~ **rot** *n* Hausschwamm *m*.

dual ['djʊəl] *a* doppelt; ~ **carriageway** *n* (*Brit*) zweispurige Fahrbahn *f*; ~**-control** *a* mit Doppelsteuerung; ~ **nationality** *n* doppelte Staatsangehörigkeit *f*; ~**-purpose** *a* Mehrzweck-.

dubbed [dʌbd] *a* (*film*) synchronisiert.

dubious ['djuːbɪəs] *a* zweifelhaft.

duchess ['dʌtʃɪs] *n* Herzogin *f*.

duck [dʌk] *n* Ente *f* // *vi* sich ducken; ~**ling** *n* Entchen *nt*.

duct [dʌkt] *n* Röhre *f*.

dud [dʌd] *n* Niete *f* // *a* (*cheque*) ungedeckt.

due [djuː] *a* fällig; (*fitting*) angemessen // *n* Gebühr *f*; (*right*) Recht *nt* // *ad* (*south etc*) genau; ~**s** *pl* (*for club, union*) Beitrag *m*; (*in harbour*) Gebühren *pl*; ~ **to** wegen (+*gen*).

duel ['djʊəl] *n* Duell *nt*.

duet [djuː'et] *n* Duett *nt*.

duffel ['dʌfl] *a*: ~ **bag** *n* Matchbeutel *m*, Matchsack *m*; ~ **coat** *n* Dufflecoat *m*.

dug [dʌg] *pt, pp* of **dig**.

duke [djuːk] *n* Herzog *m*.

dull [dʌl] *a* (*colour, weather*) trübe; (*stupid*) schwer von Begriff; (*boring*) langweilig // *vt* abstumpfen.

duly ['djuːlɪ] *ad* ordnungsgemäß.

dumb [dʌm] *a* (*lit*) stumm; (*col: stupid*) doof, blöde; ~**founded** [dʌm'faʊndɪd] *a* verblüfft.

dummy ['dʌmɪ] *n* Schneiderpuppe *f*; (*substitute*) Attrappe *f*; (*Brit: for baby*) Schnuller *m* // *a* Schein-.

dump [dʌmp] *n* Abfallhaufen *m*; (*MIL*) Stapelplatz *m*; (*col: place*) Nest *nt* // *vt* abladen, auskippen; ~**ing** *n* (*COMM*) Schleuderexport *m*; (*of rubbish*) Schuttabladen *nt*.

dumpling ['dʌmplɪŋ] *n* Kloß *m*, Knödel *m*.

dumpy ['dʌmpɪ] *a* pummelig.

dunce [dʌns] *n* Dummkopf *m*.

dune [djuːn] *n* Düne *f*.

dung [dʌŋ] *n* Dünger *m*.

dungarees [dʌŋgə'riːz] *npl* Latzhose *f*.

dungeon ['dʌndʒən] *n* Kerker *m*.

dupe [djuːp] *n* Gefoppte(r) *m* // *vt* hintergehen, anführen.

duplex ['djuːpleks] *n* (*US*) zweistöckige Wohnung *f*.

duplicate ['djuːplɪkɪt] *n* Duplikat *nt* // *vt* ['djuːplɪkeɪt] verdoppeln; (*make copies*)

kopieren; **in** ~ in doppelter Ausführung.

duplicity [djuː'plɪsɪtɪ] *n* Doppelspiel *nt*.

durable ['djʊərəbl] *a* haltbar.

duration [djʊə'reɪʃən] *n* Dauer *f*.

duress [djʊə'res] *n*: **under** ~ unter Zwang.

during ['djʊərɪŋ] *prep* während (+*gen*).

dusk [dʌsk] *n* Abenddämmerung *f*.

dust [dʌst] *n* Staub *m* // *vt* abstauben; (*sprinkle*) bestäuben; ~**bin** *n* (*Brit*) Mülleimer *m*; ~**er** *n* Staubtuch *nt*; ~ **jacket** *n* Schutzumschlag *m*; ~**man** *n* (*Brit*) Müllmann *m*; ~**y** *a* staubig.

Dutch [dʌtʃ] *a* holländisch, niederländisch // *n* (*LING*) Holländisch *nt*, Niederländisch *nt*; **the** ~ *pl* die Holländer, die Niederländer; **to go** ~ getrennte Kasse machen; ~**man/woman** *n* Holländer *m*, Niederländer *m*/ Holländerin *f*, Niederländerin *f*.

dutiful ['djuːtɪfʊl] *a* pflichtbewußt.

duty ['djuːtɪ] *n* Pflicht *f*; (*job*) Aufgabe *f*; (*tax*) Einfuhrzoll *m*; **on** ~ im Dienst; ~**-free** *a* zollfrei.

duvet ['duːveɪ] *n* (*Brit*) Daunendecke *nt*.

dwarf [dwɔːf], *pl* **dwarves** [dwɔːvz] *n* Zwerg *m* // *vt* überragen.

dwell [dwel], *pt, pp* **dwelt** [dwelt] *vi* wohnen; ~ **on** *vt* verweilen bei; ~**ing** *n* Wohnung *f*.

dwindle ['dwɪndl] *vi* schwinden.

dye [daɪ] *n* Farbstoff *m* // *vt* färben.

dying ['daɪɪŋ] *a* (*person*) sterbend; (*moments*) letzt.

dyke [daɪk] *n* (*Brit: channel*) Kanal *m*; (: *barrier*) Deich *m*, Damm *m*.

dynamic [daɪ'næmɪk] *a* dynamisch.

dynamite ['daɪnəmaɪt] *n* Dynamit *nt*.

dynamo ['daɪnəməʊ] *n* Dynamo *m*.

E

E [iː] *n* (*MUS*) E *nt*.

each [iːtʃ] *a* jeder/jede/jedes // *pron* (ein) jeder/(eine) jede/(ein) jedes; ~ **other** einander, sich.

eager *a* ['iːgə*] eifrig.

eagle ['iːgl] *n* Adler *m*.

ear [ɪə*] *n* Ohr *nt*; (*of corn*) Ähre *f*; ~**ache** *n* Ohrenschmerzen *pl*; ~**drum** *n* Trommelfell *nt*.

earl [ɜːl] *n* Graf *m*.

early ['ɜːlɪ] *a, ad* früh; ~ **retirement** *n* vorzeitige Pensionierung.

earmark ['ɪəmɑːk] *vt* vorsehen.

earn [ɜːn] *vt* verdienen.

earnest ['ɜːnɪst] *a* ernst; **in** ~ *ad* im Ernst.

earnings ['ɜːnɪŋz] *npl* Verdienst *m*.

earphones ['ɪəfəʊnz] *npl* Kopfhörer *pl*.

earring ['ɪərɪŋ] *n* Ohrring *m*.

earshot ['ɪəʃɒt] *n* Hörweite *f*.

earth [ɜːθ] *n* Erde *f*; (*Brit ELEC*) Erdung *f* // *vt* erden; ~**enware** *n* Steingut *nt*; ~**quake** *n* Erdbeben *nt*.

earthy ['ɜ:θɪ] *a* roh; (*sensual*) sinnlich.

earwig ['ɪəwɪg] *n* Ohrwurm *m*.

ease [i:z] *n* (*simplicity*) Leichtigkeit *f*; (*social*) Ungezwungenheit *f* // *vt* (*pain*) lindern; (*burden*) erleichtern; at ~ ungezwungen; (*MIL*) rührt euch!; ~ **off** *or* **up** *vi* nachlassen.

easel ['i:zl] *n* Staffelei *f*.

easily ['i:zɪlɪ] *ad* leicht.

east [i:st] *n* Osten *m* // *a* östlich // *ad* nach Osten.

Easter ['i:stə*] *n* Ostern *nt*; ~ **egg** *n* Osterei *nt*.

easterly ['i:stəlɪ] *a* östlich, Ost-.

eastern ['i:stən] *a* östlich.

East Germany *n* die DDR.

eastward(s) ['i:stwəd(z)] *ad* ostwärts.

easy ['i:zɪ] *a* (*task*) einfach; (*life*) bequem; (*manner*) ungezwungen, natürlich // *ad* leicht; ~ **chair** *n* Sessel *m*; ~-**going** *a* gelassen; (*lax*) lässig.

eat [i:t], *pt* **ate**, *pp* **eaten** ['i:tn] *vt* essen; (*animals*) fressen; (*destroy*) (zer)fressen; ~ **into**, ~ **away** *vt* zerfressen.

eau de Cologne [əʊdəkə'ləʊn] *n* Kölnisch Wasser *nt*.

eaves [i:vz] *npl* Dachrand *m*.

eavesdrop ['i:vzdrɒp] *vi* lauschen; to ~ **on sb** jdn belauschen.

ebb [eb] *n* Ebbe *f* // *vi* (*fig*: *also*: ~ **away**) (ab)ebben; ~ **tide** *n* Ebbe *f*.

ebony ['ebənɪ] *n* Ebenholz *nt*.

ebullient [ɪ'bʌlɪənt] *a* sprudelnd, temperamentvoll.

eccentric [ɪk'sentrɪk] *a* exzentrisch // *n* Exzentriker(in *f*) *m*.

ecclesiastical [ɪkli:zɪ'æstɪkəl] *a* kirchlich.

echo ['ekəʊ], *pl* ~**es** *n* Echo *nt* // *vt* zurückwerfen; (*fig*) nachbeten // *vi* widerhallen.

eclipse [ɪ'klɪps] *n* Finsternis *f* // *vt* verfinstern.

ecology [ɪ'kɒlədʒɪ] *n* Ökologie *f*.

economic [i:kə'nɒmɪk] *a* wirtschaftlich; ~**al** *a* wirtschaftlich; (*person*) sparsam; ~**s** *n* Volkswirtschaft *f*.

economist [ɪ'kɒnəmɪst] *n* Volkswirt(schaftler) *m*.

economize [ɪ'kɒnəmaɪz] *vi* sparen.

economy [ɪ'kɒnəmɪ] *n* (*thrift*) Sparsamkeit *f*; (*of country*) Wirtschaft *f*.

ecstasy ['ekstəsɪ] *n* Ekstase *f*.

ecstatic [eks'tætɪk] *a* hingerissen.

ecumenical [i:kjʊ'menɪkəl] *a* ökumenisch.

eczema ['eksɪmə] *n* Ekzem *nt*.

edge [edʒ] *n* Rand *m*; (*of knife*) Schneide *f* // *vt* (*SEWING*) einfassen; on ~ (*fig*) = **edgy**; to ~ **away from** langsam abrücken von; ~**ways** *ad*: he couldn't get a word in ~**ways** er kam überhaupt nicht zu Wort.

edgy ['edʒɪ] *a* nervös.

edible ['edɪbl] *a* eßbar.

edict ['i:dɪkt] *n* Erlaß *m*.

edifice ['edɪfɪs] *n* Gebäude *nt*.

edit ['edɪt] *vt* redigieren; ~**ion** [ɪ'dɪʃən] *n* Ausgabe *f*; ~**or** *n* (*of newspaper*) Redakteur *m*; (*of book*) Lektor *m*; ~**orial** [edɪ'tɔ:rɪəl] *a* Redaktions- // *n* Leitartikel *m*.

educate ['edjʊkeɪt] *vt* erziehen, (aus)bilden.

education [edjʊ'keɪʃən] *n* (*teaching*) Unterricht *m*; (*system*) Schulwesen *nt*; (*schooling*) Erziehung *f*; Bildung *f*; ~**al** *a* pädagogisch.

EEC *n abbr* (= *European Economic Community*) EG *f*.

eel [i:l] *n* Aal *m*.

eerie ['ɪərɪ] *a* unheimlich.

effect [ɪ'fekt] *n* Wirkung *f* // *vt* bewirken; ~**s** *pl* (*sound, visual*) Effekte *pl*; **in** ~ in der Tat; **to take** ~ (*law*) in Kraft treten; (*drug*) wirken; ~**ive** *a*, ~**ly** *ad* wirksam, effektiv.

effeminate [ɪ'femɪnɪt] *a* weibisch.

effervescent [efə'vesnt] *a* (*lit, fig*) sprudelnd.

efficacy ['efɪkəsɪ] *n* Wirksamkeit *f*.

efficiency [ɪ'fɪʃənsɪ] *n* Leistungsfähigkeit *f*.

efficient [ɪ'fɪʃənt] *a* tüchtig; (*TECH*) leistungsfähig; (*method*) wirksam.

effigy ['efɪdʒɪ] *n* Abbild *nt*.

effort ['efət] *n* Anstrengung *f*; ~**less** *a* mühelos.

effrontery [ɪ'frʌntərɪ] *n* Unverfrorenheit *f*.

effusive [ɪ'fju:sɪv] *a* überschwenglich.

e.g. *ad abbr* (= *exempli gratia*) z.B.

egalitarian [ɪgælɪ'tɛərɪən] *a* Gleichheits-, egalitär.

egg [eg] *n* Ei *nt*; ~ **on** *vt* anstacheln; ~**cup** *n* Eierbecher *m*; ~**plant** *n* (*esp US*) Aubergine *f*; ~**shell** *n* Eierschale *f*.

ego ['i:gəʊ] *n* Ich *nt*, Selbst *nt*.

egotism ['egəʊtɪzəm] *n* Ichbezogenheit *f*.

egotist ['egəʊtɪst] *n* Egozentriker *m*.

Egypt ['i:dʒɪpt] *n* Ägypten *nt*; ~**ian** [ɪ'dʒɪpʃən] *a* ägyptisch // *n* Ägypter(in *f*) *m*.

eiderdown ['aɪdədaʊn] *n* Daunendecke *f*.

eight [eɪt] *num* acht; ~**een** *num* achtzehn; **eighth** [eɪtθ] *a* achte(r, s) // *n* Achtel *nt*; ~**y** *num* achtzig.

Eire ['ɛərə] *n* Irland *nt*.

either ['aɪðə*] *cj*: ~ ... **or** entweder ... oder // *pron*: ~ **of the two** eine(r, s) von beiden; I don't want ~ ich will keins von beiden // *a*: on ~ **side** auf beiden Seiten // *ad*: I don't ~ ich auch nicht.

eject [ɪ'dʒekt] *vt* ausstoßen, vertreiben.

eke [i:k]: ~ **out** *vt* strecken.

elaborate [ɪ'læbərɪt] *a* sorgfältig ausgearbeitet, ausführlich // *v* [ɪ'læbəreɪt] *vt* sorgfältig ausarbeiten // *vi* ausführlich darstellen; **~ly** *ad* genau, ausführlich.

elapse [ɪ'læps] *vi* vergehen.

elastic [ɪ'læstɪk] *n* Gummiband *nt* // *a* elastisch; **~ band** *n* (*Brit*) Gummiband *nt*.

elated [ɪ'leɪtɪd] *a* froh.

elation [ɪ'leɪʃən] *n* gehobene Stimmung *f*.

elbow ['elbəʊ] *n* Ellbogen *m*.

elder ['eldə*] *a* älter // *n* Ältere(r) *mf*; **~ly** *a* ältere(r, s) // *n*: the **~ly** die Älteren.

eldest ['eldɪst] *a* älteste(r, s) // *n* Älteste(r) *mf*.

elect [ɪ'lekt] *vt* wählen // *a* zukünftig; **~ion** *n* Wahl *f*; **~ioneering** [ɪlekʃə'nɪərɪŋ] *n* Wahlpropaganda *f*; **~or** *n* Wähler *m*; **~oral** *a* Wahl-; **~orate** *n* Wähler *pl*, Wählerschaft *f*.

electric [ɪ'lektrɪk] *a* elektrisch, Elektro-; **~al** *a* elektrisch; **~ blanket** *n* Heizdecke *f*; **~ chair** *n* elektrische(r) Stuhl *m*; **~ fire** *n* elektrische(r) Heizofen *m*.

electrician [ɪlek'trɪʃən] *n* Elektriker *m*.

electricity [ɪlek'trɪsɪtɪ] *n* Elektrizität *f*.

electrify [ɪ'lektrɪfaɪ] *vt* elektrifizieren; (*fig*) elektrisieren.

electrocute [ɪ'lektrəʊkjuːt] *vt* durch elektrischen Strom töten.

electronic [ɪlek'trɒnɪk] *a* elektronisch, Elektronen-; **~ mail** *n* elektronische(r) Briefkasten *m*; **~s** *n* Elektronik *f*.

elegance ['elɪgəns] *n* Eleganz *f*.

elegant ['elɪgənt] *a* elegant.

element ['elɪmənt] *n* Element *nt*; **~ary** [elɪ'mentərɪ] *a* einfach; (*primary*) Grund-.

elephant ['elɪfənt] *n* Elefant *m*.

elevate ['elɪveɪt] *vt* emporheben.

elevation [elɪ'veɪʃən] *n* (*height*) Erhebung *f*; (*ARCHIT*) (Quer)schnitt *m*.

elevator ['elɪveɪtə*] *n* (*US*) Fahrstuhl *m*, Aufzug *m*.

eleven [ɪ'levn] *num* elf; **~ses** *npl* (*Brit*) zweite(s) Frühstück *nt*; **~th** *a* elfte(r, s).

elf [elf], *pl* **elves** [elvz] *n* Elfe *f*.

elicit [ɪ'lɪsɪt] *vt* herausbekommen.

eligible ['elɪdʒəbl] *a* wählbar; to be ~ for a pension pensionsberechtigt sein.

eliminate [ɪ'lɪmɪneɪt] *vt* ausschalten.

elimination [ɪlɪmɪ'neɪʃən] *n* Ausschaltung *f*.

elite [eɪ'liːt] *n* Elite *f*.

elm [elm] *n* Ulme *f*.

elocution [elə'kjuːʃən] *n* Sprecherziehung *f*.

elongated ['iːlɒŋgeɪtɪd] *a* verlängert.

elope [ɪ'ləʊp] *vi* entlaufen; **~ment** *n* Entlaufen *m*.

eloquence ['eləkwəns] *n* Beredsamkeit *f*.

eloquent ['eləkwənt] *a* redegewandt.

else [els] *ad* sonst; who ~? wer sonst?; sb ~ jd anders; or ~ sonst; **~where** *ad* anderswo, woanders.

elucidate [ɪ'luːsɪdeɪt] *vt* erläutern.

elude [ɪ'luːd] *vt* entgehen (+*dat*).

elusive [ɪ'luːsɪv] *a* schwer faßbar.

elves [elvz] *npl* of **elf**.

emaciated [ɪ'meɪsɪeɪtɪd] *a* abgezehrt.

emanate ['eməneɪt] *vi* ausströmen (*from* aus).

emancipate [ɪ'mænsɪpeɪt] *vt* emanzipieren; (*slave*) freilassen.

emancipation [ɪmænsɪ'peɪʃən] *n* Emanzipation *f*; Freilassung *f*.

embankment [ɪm'bæŋkmənt] *n* (*of river*) Uferböschung *f*; (*of road*) Straßendamm *m*.

embargo [ɪm'baːgəʊ], *pl* **~es** *n* Embargo *nt*.

embark [ɪm'baːk] *vi* sich einschiffen; **~ on** *vt* unternehmen; **~ation** [embaː'keɪʃən] *n* Einschiffung *f*.

embarrass [ɪm'bærəs] *vt* in Verlegenheit bringen; **~ed** *a* verlegen; **~ing** *a* peinlich; **~ment** *n* Verlegenheit *f*.

embassy ['embəsɪ] *n* Botschaft *f*.

embed [ɪm'bed] *vt* einbetten.

embellish [ɪm'belɪʃ] *vt* verschönern.

embers ['embəz] *npl* Glut(asche) *f*.

embezzle [ɪm'bezl] *vt* unterschlagen; **~ment** *n* Unterschlagung *f*.

embitter [ɪm'bɪtə*] *vt* verbittern.

embody [ɪm'bɒdɪ] *vt* (*ideas*) verkörpern; (*new features*) (in sich) vereinigen.

embossed [ɪm'bɒst] *a* geprägt.

embrace [ɪm'breɪs] *vt* umarmen; (*include*) einschließen // *vi* sich umarmen // *n* Umarmung *f*.

embroider [ɪm'brɔɪdə*] *vt* (be)sticken; (*story*) ausschmücken; **~y** *n* Stickerei *f*.

emerald ['emərəld] *n* Smaragd *m*.

emerge [ɪ'mɜːdʒ] *vi* auftauchen; (*truth*) herauskommen.

emergence [ɪ'mɜːdʒəns] *n* Erscheinen *nt*.

emergency [ɪ'mɜːdʒənsɪ] *n* Notfall *m*; **~ cord** *n* (*US*) Notbremse *f*; **~ exit** *n* Notausgang *m*; **~ landing** *n* Notlandung *f*; **the ~ services** *npl* die Notdienste *pl*.

emery board ['emərɪ-] *n* Papiernagelfeile *f*.

emetic [ɪ'metɪk] *n* Brechmittel *nt*.

emigrant ['emɪgrənt] *n* Auswanderer *m*.

emigrate ['emɪgreɪt] *vi* auswandern.

emigration [emɪ'greɪʃən] *n* Auswanderung *f*.

eminence ['emɪnəns] *n* hohe(r) Rang *m*.

eminent ['emɪnənt] *a* bedeutend.

emission [ɪ'mɪʃən] *n* Ausströmen *nt*.

emit [ɪ'mɪt] *vt* von sich (*dat*) geben.

emotion [ɪ'məʊʃən] *n* Emotion *f*, Gefühl *nt*; **~al** *a* (*person*) emotional; (*scene*)

ergreifend.
emotive [ɪ'məʊtɪv] a gefühlsbetont.
emperor ['empərə*] n Kaiser m.
emphasis ['emfəsɪs], pl **-ses** [-siːz] n
(LING) Betonung f; (fig) Nachdruck m.
emphasize ['emfəsaɪz] vt betonen.
emphatic a, **~ally** ad [ɪm'fætɪk, -əlɪ]
nachdrücklich.
empire ['empaɪə*] n Reich nt.
empirical [em'pɪrɪkl] a empirisch.
employ [ɪm'plɔɪ] vt (hire) anstellen;
(use) verwenden; **~ee** [emplɔɪ'iː] n An-
gestellte(r) mf; **~er** n Arbeitgeber(in f)
m; **~ment** n Beschäftigung f; **~ment
agency** n Stellenvermittlung f.
empower [ɪm'paʊə*] vt: to ~ sb to do
sth jdn ermächtigen, etw zu tun.
empress ['emprɪs] n Kaiserin f.
emptiness ['emptɪnɪs] n Leere f.
empty ['emptɪ] a leer // n (bottle)
Leergut nt // vt (contents) leeren;
(container) ausleeren // vi (water)
abfließen; (river) münden; (house) sich
leeren; **~-handed** a mit leeren Händen.
emulate ['emjʊleɪt] vt nacheifern
(+dat).
emulsion [ɪ'mʌlʃən] n Emulsion f.
enable [ɪ'neɪbl] vt: to ~ sb to do sth es
jdm ermöglichen, etw zu tun.
enamel [ɪ'næməl] n Email nt; (of teeth)
(Zahn)schmelz m.
enact [ɪn'ækt] vt (law) erlassen; (play)
aufführen; (role) spielen.
encased [ɪn'keɪst] a: ~ in (enclosed)
eingeschlossen in (+dat); (covered) verkleidet mit.
enchant [ɪn'tʃɑːnt] vt bezaubern; **~ing**
a entzückend.
encircle [ɪn'sɜːkl] vt umringen.
encl. abbr (= enclosed) Anl.
enclose [ɪn'kləʊz] vt einschließen; (in
letter) beilegen (in, with dat); **~d** (in
letter) beiliegend, anbei.
enclosure [ɪn'kləʊʒə*] n Einfriedung f;
(in letter) Anlage f.
encompass [ɪn'kʌmpəs] vt (include)
umfassen.
encore ['ɒŋkɔː*] n Zugabe f.
encounter [ɪn'kaʊntə*] n Begegnung f;
(MIL) Zusammenstoß m // vt treffen;
(resistance) stoßen auf (+acc).
encourage [ɪn'kʌrɪdʒ] vt ermutigen;
~ment n Ermutigung f, Förderung f.
encouraging [ɪn'kʌrɪdʒɪŋ] a
ermutigend, vielversprechend.
encroach [ɪn'krəʊtʃ] vi: to ~ (up)on
eindringen in (+acc); (time) in Anspruch nehmen.
encrusted [ɪn'krʌstəd] a: ~ with besetzt
mit.
encumber [ɪn'kʌmbə*] vt: to be **~ed**
with (parcels) beladen sein mit; (debts)
belastet sein mit.
encyclop(a)edia [ensaɪkləʊ'piːdɪə] n
Konversationslexikon nt.

end [end] n Ende nt, Schluß m;
(purpose) Zweck m // vt (also: **bring to
an ~**, **put an ~ to**) beenden // vi zu Ende
gehen; **in the ~** zum Schluß; **on ~**
(object) hochkant; **to stand on ~** (hair)
zu Berge stehen; **for hours on ~**
stundenlang; **~ up** vi landen.
endanger [ɪn'deɪndʒə*] vt gefährden.
endearing [ɪn'dɪərɪŋ] a gewinnend.
endeavour, (US) **endeavor** [ɪn'devə*]
n Bestrebung f // vi sich bemühen.
ending ['endɪŋ] n Ende nt.
endless ['endlɪs] a endlos.
endorse [ɪn'dɔːs] vt unterzeichnen; (approve) unterstützen; **~ment** n (on
licence) Eintrag m.
endow [ɪn'daʊ] vt: ~ sb with sth jdm
etw verleihen; (with money) jdm etw
stiften.
endurance [ɪn'djʊərəns] n Ausdauer f.
endure [ɪn'djʊə*] vt ertragen // vi (last)
(fort)dauern.
enemy ['enɪmɪ] n Feind m // a feindlich.
energetic [enə'dʒetɪk] a tatkräftig.
energy ['enədʒɪ] n Energie f.
enforce [ɪn'fɔːs] vt durchsetzen.
engage [ɪn'geɪdʒ] vt (employ) einstellen; (in conversation) verwickeln;
(TECH) einschalten // vi (TECH)
ineinandergreifen; (clutch) fassen; **to ~
in** sich beteiligen an (+dat); **~d** a ver-
lobt; (Brit: TEL, toilet) besetzt; (: busy)
beschäftigt; **to get ~d** sich verloben; **~d
tone** n (Brit TEL) Besetztzeichen nt;
~ment n (appointment) Verabredung f;
(to marry) Verlobung f; (MIL) Gefecht
nt; **~ment ring** n Verlobungsring m.
engaging [ɪn'geɪdʒɪŋ] a gewinnend.
engender [ɪn'dʒendə*] vt hervorrufen.
engine ['endʒɪn] n (AUT) Motor m;
(RAIL) Lokomotive f; ~ **driver** n
Lokführer(in f) m.
engineer [endʒɪ'nɪə*] n Ingenieur m;
(US RAIL) Lokomotivführer m.
engineering [endʒɪ'nɪərɪŋ] n Technik f.
England ['ɪŋglənd] n England nt.
English ['ɪŋglɪʃ] a englisch // n (LING)
Englisch nt; **the ~** pl die Engländer;
the ~ Channel n der Ärmelkanal m;
~man/woman n Engländer m/
Engländerin f.
engraving [ɪn'greɪvɪŋ] n Stich m.
engrossed [ɪn'grəʊst] a vertieft.
engulf [ɪn'gʌlf] vt verschlingen.
enhance [ɪn'hɑːns] vt steigern, heben.
enigma [ɪ'nɪgmə] n Rätsel nt; **~tic**
[enɪg'mætɪk] a rätselhaft.
enjoy [ɪn'dʒɔɪ] vt genießen; (privilege)
besitzen; **to ~ o.s.** sich amüsieren;
~able a erfreulich; **~ment** n Genuß m,
Freude f.
enlarge [ɪn'lɑːdʒ] vt erweitern; (PHOT)
vergrößern // vi: **to ~ on** sth etw weiter
ausführen; **~ment** n Vergrößerung f.
enlighten [ɪn'laɪtn] vt aufklären; **the**

E~ment n (HIST) die Aufklärung.
enlist [ɪnˈlɪst] vt gewinnen // vi (MIL) sich melden.
enmity [ˈenmɪtɪ] n Feindschaft f.
enormity [ɪˈnɔːmɪtɪ] n Ungeheuerlichkeit f.
enormous [ɪˈnɔːməs] a ungeheuer.
enough [ɪˈnʌf] a, ad genug; **funnily ~** komischerweise.
enquire [ɪnˈkwaɪə*] vti = **inquire**.
enrage [ɪnˈreɪdʒ] vt wütend machen.
enrich [ɪnˈrɪtʃ] vt bereichern.
enrol [ɪnˈrəʊl] vt einschreiben // vi (register) sich anmelden; **~ment** n (for course) Anmeldung f.
en route [ɑ̃ːnˈruːt] ad unterwegs.
ensign [ˈensaɪn] n (NAUT) Flagge f; (MIL) Fähnrich m.
enslave [ɪnˈsleɪv] vt versklaven.
ensue [ɪnˈsjuː] vi folgen, sich ergeben.
ensure [ɪnˈʃʊə*] vt garantieren.
entail [ɪnˈteɪl] vt mit sich bringen.
entangle [ɪnˈtæŋgl] vt verwirren, verstricken.
enter [ˈentə*] vt eintreten in (+dat), betreten; (club) beitreten (+dat); (in book) eintragen // vi hereinkommen, hineingehen; **~ for** vt sich beteiligen an (+dat); **~ into** vt (agreement) eingehen; (plans) eine Rolle spielen bei; **~ (up)on** vt beginnen.
enteritis [entəˈraɪtɪs] n Dünndarmentzündung f.
enterprise [ˈentəpraɪz] n (in person) Initiative f; (COMM) Unternehmen nt.
enterprising [ˈentəpraɪzɪŋ] a unternehmungslustig.
entertain [entəˈteɪn] vt (guest) bewirten; (amuse) unterhalten; **~er** n Unterhaltungskünstler(in f) m; **~ing** a unterhaltsam; **~ment** n Unterhaltung f.
enthralled [ɪnˈθrɔːld] a gefesselt.
enthusiasm [ɪnˈθuːzɪæzəm] n Begeisterung f.
enthusiast [ɪnˈθuːzɪæst] n Enthusiast m; **~ic** [ɪnθuːzɪˈæstɪk] a begeistert.
entice [ɪnˈtaɪs] vt verleiten, locken.
entire [ɪnˈtaɪə*] a ganz; **~ly** ad ganz, völlig; **~ty** [ɪnˈtaɪərətɪ] n: in its **~ty** in seiner Gesamtheit.
entitle [ɪnˈtaɪtl] vt (allow) berechtigen; (name) betiteln; **~d** a (book) mit dem Titel.
entity [ˈentɪtɪ] n Ding nt, Wesen nt.
entourage [ɒntuːˈrɑːʒ] n Gefolge nt.
entrails [ˈentreɪlz] npl Eingeweide pl.
entrance [ˈentrəns] n Eingang m; (entering) Eintritt m // vt [ɪnˈtrɑːns] hinreißen; **~ examination** n Aufnahmeprüfung f; **~ fee** n Eintrittsgeld nt; **~ ramp** n (US AUT) Einfahrt f.
entrant [ˈentrənt] n (for exam) Kandidat m; (in race) Teilnehmer m.
entreat [ɪnˈtriːt] vt anflehen.
entrenched [ɪnˈtrentʃt] a (fig) verwurzelt.

entrepreneur [ɒntrəprəˈnɜː*] n Unternehmer(in f) m.
entrust [ɪnˈtrʌst] vt anvertrauen (sb with sth jdm etw).
entry [ˈentrɪ] n Eingang m; (THEAT) Auftritt m; (in account) Eintragung f; (in dictionary) Eintrag m; **'no ~'** 'Eintritt verboten'; (for cars) 'Einfahrt verboten'; **~ form** n Anmeldeformular nt; **~ phone** n Sprechanlage f.
enumerate [ɪˈnjuːməreɪt] vt aufzählen.
enunciate [ɪˈnʌnsɪeɪt] vt aussprechen.
envelop [ɪnˈveləp] vt einhüllen.
envelope [ˈenvələʊp] n Umschlag m.
enviable [ˈenvɪəbl] a beneidenswert.
envious [ˈenvɪəs] a neidisch.
environment [ɪnˈvaɪərənmənt] n Umgebung f; (ecology) Umwelt f; **~al** [ɪnvaɪərənˈmentl] a Umwelt-.
envisage [ɪnˈvɪzɪdʒ] vt sich (dat) vorstellen.
envoy [ˈenvɔɪ] n Gesandte(r) mf.
envy [ˈenvɪ] n Neid m // vt: to **~** sb sth jdn um etw beneiden.
enzyme [ˈenzaɪm] n Enzym nt.
ephemeral [ɪˈfemərəl] a flüchtig.
epic [ˈepɪk] n Epos nt // a episch.
epidemic [epɪˈdemɪk] n Epidemie f.
epilepsy [ˈepɪlepsɪ] n Epilepsie f.
epileptic [epɪˈleptɪk] a epileptisch // n Epileptiker(in f) m.
episode [ˈepɪsəʊd] n (incident) Vorfall m; (story) Episode f.
epistle [ɪˈpɪsl] n Brief m.
epitaph [ˈepɪtɑːf] n Grab(in)schrift f.
epithet [ˈepɪθət] n Beiname m.
epitome [ɪˈpɪtəmɪ] n Inbegriff m.
epitomize [ɪˈpɪtəmaɪz] vt verkörpern.
equable [ˈekwəbl] a ausgeglichen.
equal [ˈiːkwl] a gleich // n Gleichgestellte(r) mf // vt gleichkommen (+dat); **~ to the task** der Aufgabe gewachsen; **~ity** [ɪˈkwɒlɪtɪ] n Gleichheit f; (equal rights) Gleichberechtigung f; **~ize** vt gleichmachen // vi (SPORT) ausgleichen; **~izer** n (SPORT) Ausgleich(streffer) m; **~ly** ad gleich.
equanimity [ekwəˈnɪmɪtɪ] n Gleichmut m.
equate [ɪˈkweɪt] vt gleichsetzen.
equation [ɪˈkweɪʒən] n Gleichung f.
equator [ɪˈkweɪtə*] n Äquator m.
equestrian [ɪˈkwestrɪən] a Reit-.
equilibrium [iːkwɪˈlɪbrɪəm] n Gleichgewicht nt.
equinox [ˈiːkwɪnɒks] n Tag- und Nachtgleiche f.
equip [ɪˈkwɪp] vt ausrüsten; **~ment** n Ausrüstung f; (TECH) Gerät nt.
equitable [ˈekwɪtəbl] a gerecht, billig.
equities [ˈekwɪtɪz] npl (Brit COMM) Stammaktien pl.
equivalent [ɪˈkwɪvələnt] a gleichwertig (to dat), entsprechend (to dat) // n

Äquivalent nt; (in money) Gegenwert m.
equivocal [ɪ'kwɪvəkəl] a zweideutig.
era ['ɪərə] n Epoche f, Ära f.
eradicate [ɪ'rædɪkeɪt] vt ausrotten.
erase [ɪ'reɪz] vt ausradieren; (tape) löschen; **~r** n Radiergummi m.
erect [ɪ'rekt] a aufrecht // vt errichten.
erection [ɪ'rekʃən] n Errichtung f; (ANAT) Erektion f.
ermine ['ɜ:mɪn] n Hermelin(pelz) m.
erode [ɪ'rəʊd] vt zerfressen; (land) auswaschen.
erotic [ɪ'rɒtɪk] a erotisch; **~ism** [ɪ'rɒtɪsɪzəm] n Erotik f.
err [ɜ:*] vi sich irren.
errand ['erənd] n Besorgung f; **~ boy** n Laufbursche m.
erratic [ɪ'rætɪk] a unberechenbar.
erroneous [ɪ'rəʊnɪəs] a irrig.
error ['erə*] n Fehler m.
erudite ['erʊdaɪt] a gelehrt.
erupt [ɪ'rʌpt] vi ausbrechen; **~ion** n Ausbruch m.
escalate ['eskəleɪt] vi sich steigern.
escalator ['eskəleɪtə*] n Rolltreppe f.
escape [ɪs'keɪp] n Flucht f; (of gas) Entweichen nt // vti entkommen (+dat); (prisoners) fliehen; (leak) entweichen.
escapism [ɪs'keɪpɪzəm] n Flucht f (vor der Wirklichkeit).
escort ['eskɔ:t] n (person accompanying) Begleiter m; (guard) Eskorte f // vt [ɪs'kɔ:t] (lady) begleiten; (MIL) eskortieren.
Eskimo ['eskɪməʊ] n Eskimo m.
especially [ɪs'peʃəlɪ] ad besonders.
espionage ['espɪənɑ:ʒ] n Spionage f.
esplanade ['espləneɪd] n Promenade f.
espouse [ɪ'spaʊz] vt Partei ergreifen für.
Esquire [ɪs'kwaɪə*] n (abbr Esq.) J. Brown **~** Herrn J. Brown.
essay ['eseɪ] n Aufsatz m; (LITER) Essay m.
essence ['esəns] n (quality) Wesen nt; (extract) Essenz f.
essential [ɪ'senʃəl] a (necessary) unentbehrlich; (basic) wesentlich // n Allernötigste(s) nt; **~ly** ad eigentlich.
establish [ɪs'tæblɪʃ] vt (set up) gründen; (prove) nachweisen; **~ed** a anerkannt; (belief, laws etc) herrschend; **~ment** n (setting up) Einrichtung f; the E**~ment** das Establishment.
estate [ɪs'teɪt] n Gut nt; (Brit: housing **~**) Siedlung f; (will) Nachlaß m; **~ agent** n (Brit) Grundstücksmakler m; **~ car** n (Brit) Kombiwagen m.
esteem [ɪs'ti:m] n Wertschätzung f.
esthetic [es'θetɪk] a (US) = **aesthetic**.
estimate ['estɪmət] n Schätzung f; (of price) (Kosten)voranschlag m // vt ['estɪmeɪt] schätzen.
estimation [estɪ'meɪʃən] n Einschätzung f; (esteem) Achtung f.

estranged [ɪ'streɪndʒd] a entfremdet.
estuary ['estjʊərɪ] n Mündung f.
etc abbr (= et cetera) etc.
etching ['etʃɪŋ] n Kupferstich m.
eternal [ɪ'tɜ:nl] a ewig.
eternity [ɪ'tɜ:nɪtɪ] n Ewigkeit f.
ether ['i:θə*] n (MED) Äther m.
ethical ['eθɪkəl] a ethisch.
ethics ['eθɪks] n Ethik f // npl Moral f.
Ethiopia [i:θɪ'əʊpɪə] n Äthiopien nt.
ethnic ['eθnɪk] a Volks-, ethnisch.
etiquette ['etɪket] n Etikette f.
euphemism ['ju:fɪmɪzəm] n Euphemismus m.
Eurocheque ['jʊərəʊ'tʃek] n Euroscheck m.
Europe ['jʊərəp] n Europa nt; **~an** [-'pi:ən] a europäisch // n Europäer(in f) m.
evacuate [ɪ'vækjʊeɪt] vt (place) räumen; (people) evakuieren.
evacuation [ɪvækjʊ'eɪʃən] n Räumung f; Evakuierung f.
evade [ɪ'veɪd] vt (escape) entkommen (+dat); (avoid) meiden; (duty) sich entziehen (+dat).
evaluate [ɪ'væljʊeɪt] vt bewerten; (information) auswerten.
evaporate [ɪ'væpəreɪt] vi verdampfen // vt verdampfen lassen; **~d milk** n Kondensmilch f.
evasion [ɪ'veɪʒən] n Umgehung f.
evasive [ɪ'veɪzɪv] a ausweichend.
eve [i:v] n: **on the ~ of** am Vorabend (+gen).
even ['i:vən] a eben; gleichmäßig; (score etc) unentschieden; (number) gerade // ad: **~ you** sogar du; **~ if** selbst wenn; **~ so** dennoch; **to get ~ with** sb jdm heimzahlen; **~ out** vi sich ausgleichen.
evening ['i:vnɪŋ] n Abend m; **in the ~** abends, am Abend; **~ class** n Abendschule f; **~ dress** n (man's) Gesellschaftsanzug m; (woman's) Abendkleid nt.
event [ɪ'vent] n (happening) Ereignis nt; (SPORT) Disziplin f; **in the ~ of** im Falle (+gen); **~ful** a ereignisreich.
eventual [ɪ'ventʃʊəl] a (final) schließlich; **~ity** [ɪventʃʊ'ælɪtɪ] n Möglichkeit f; **~ly** ad (at last) am Ende; (given time) schließlich.
ever ['evə*] ad (always) immer; (at any time) je(mals); **~ since** ad seitdem // cj seit; **~green** n Immergrün nt; **~lasting** a immerwährend.
every ['evrɪ] a jede(r, s); **~ other/third day** jeden zweiten/dritten Tag; **~ one of them** alle; **I have ~ confidence in him** ich habe uneingeschränktes Vertrauen in ihn; **we wish you ~ success** wir wünschen Ihnen viel Erfolg; **he's ~ bit as clever as his brother** er ist genauso klug wie sein Bruder; **~ now and then** ab und

zu; **~body** pron = **~one**; **~day** a (daily) täglich; (commonplace) alltäglich, Alltags-; **~one** pron jeder, alle pl; **~thing** pron alles; **~where** ad überall(hin); (wherever) wohin; **~where you go** wohin du auch gehst.

evict [ɪ'vɪkt] vt ausweisen; **~ion** n Ausweisung f.

evidence ['evɪdəns] n (sign) Spur f; (proof) Beweis m; (testimony) Aussage f.

evident ['evɪdənt] a augenscheinlich; **~ly** ad offensichtlich.

evil ['iːvl] a böse // n Böse nt.

evocative [ɪ'vokɪtɪv] a: to be ~ of sth an etw (acc) erinnern.

evoke [ɪ'vəʊk] vt hervorrufen.

evolution [iːvə'luːʃən] n Entwicklung f; (of life) Evolution f.

evolve [ɪ'vɒlv] vt entwickeln // vi sich entwickeln.

ewe [juː] n Mutterschaf nt.

ex- [eks] pref Ex-, Alt-, ehemalig.

exacerbate [ek'sæsəbeɪt] vt verschlimmern.

exact [ɪg'zækt] a genau // vt (demand) verlangen; **~ing** a anspruchsvoll; **~itude** n Genauigkeit f.

exaggerate [ɪg'zædʒəreɪt] vti übertreiben.

exaggeration [ɪgzædʒə'reɪʃən] n Übertreibung f.

exalted [ɪg'zɔːltɪd] a (position, style) hoch; (person) exaltiert.

exam [ɪg'zæm] n abbr of examination.

examination [ɪgzæmɪ'neɪʃən] n Untersuchung f; (SCH) Prüfung f, Examen nt; (customs) Kontrolle f.

examine [ɪg'zæmɪn] vt untersuchen; (SCH) prüfen; (consider) erwägen; **~r** n Prüfer m.

example [ɪg'zɑːmpl] n Beispiel nt; for ~ zum Beispiel.

exasperate [ɪg'zɑːspəreɪt] vt zum Verzweifeln bringen.

exasperating [ɪg'zɑːspəreɪtɪŋ] a ärgerlich, zum Verzweifeln bringend.

exasperation [ɪgzɑːspə'reɪʃən] n Verzweiflung f.

excavate ['ekskəveɪt] vt ausgraben.

excavation [ekskə'veɪʃən] n Ausgrabung f.

exceed [ɪk'siːd] vt überschreiten; (hopes) übertreffen.

excel [ɪk'sel] vi sich auszeichnen.

excellence ['eksələns] n Vortrefflichkeit f.

excellency ['eksələnsɪ] n: His E~ Seine Exzellenz f.

excellent ['eksələnt] a ausgezeichnet.

except [ɪk'sept] prep (also: ~ for, ~ing) außer (+dat) // vt ausnehmen; **~ion** [ɪk'sepʃən] n Ausnahme f; to take ~ion to Anstoß nehmen an (+dat); **~ional** [ɪk'sepʃənl] a außergewöhnlich.

excerpt ['eksɜːpt] n Auszug m.

excess [ek'ses] n Übermaß nt (of an +dat); Exzeß m; ~ **baggage** n Mehrgepäck nt; ~ **fare** n Nachlösegebühr f; **~ive** a übermäßig.

exchange [ɪks'tʃeɪndʒ] n Austausch m; (also: telephone ~) Zentrale f // vt (goods) tauschen; (greetings) austauschen; (money, blows) wechseln; ~ **rate** n Wechselkurs m.

Exchequer [ɪks'tʃekə*] n: the ~ (Brit) das Schatzamt.

excise ['eksaɪz] n Verbrauchssteuer f // vt [ek'saɪz] (MED) herausschneiden.

excite [ɪk'saɪt] vt erregen; to get **~d** sich aufregen; **~ment** n Aufregung f.

exciting [ɪk'saɪtɪŋ] a spannend.

exclaim [ɪks'kleɪm] vi ausrufen.

exclamation [eksklə'meɪʃən] n Ausruf m; ~ **mark** n Ausrufezeichen nt.

exclude [ɪks'kluːd] vt ausschließen.

exclusion [ɪks'kluːʒən] n Ausschluß m.

exclusive [ɪks'kluːsɪv] a (select) exklusiv; (sole) ausschließlich, Allein-; ~ **of exklusive** (+gen); **~ly** ad nur, ausschließlich.

excommunicate [ekskə'mjuːnɪkeɪt] vt exkommunizieren.

excrement ['ekskrɪmənt] n Kot m.

excruciating [ɪks'kruːʃɪeɪtɪŋ] a qualvoll.

excursion [ɪks'kɜːʃən] n Ausflug m.

excusable [ɪks'kjuːzəbl] a entschuldbar.

excuse [ɪks'kjuːs] n Entschuldigung f // vt [ɪks'kjuːz] entschuldigen; ~ **me!** entschuldigen Sie!

ex-directory ['eksdaɪ'rektərɪ] a (Brit): to be ~ nicht im Telefonbuch stehen.

execute ['eksɪkjuːt] vt (carry out) ausführen; (kill) hinrichten.

execution [eksɪ'kjuːʃən] n Ausführung f; (killing) Hinrichtung f; **~er** n Scharfrichter m.

executive [ɪg'zekjʊtɪv] n (COMM) Geschäftsführer m; (POL) Exekutive f // a Exekutiv-, ausführend.

executor [ɪg'zekjʊtə*] n Testamentsvollstrecker m.

exemplary [ɪg'zemplərɪ] a musterhaft.

exemplify [ɪg'zemplɪfaɪ] vt veranschaulichen.

exempt [ɪg'zempt] a befreit // vt befreien; **~ion** [ɪg'zempʃən] n Befreiung f.

exercise ['eksəsaɪz] n Übung f // vt (power) ausüben; (muscle, patience) üben; (dog) ausführen // vi Sport treiben; ~ **book** n (Schul)heft nt.

exert [ɪg'zɜːt] vt (influence) ausüben; ~ **o.s.** sich anstrengen; **~ion** [-ʃən] n Anstrengung f.

exhale [eks'heɪl] vti ausatmen.

exhaust [ɪg'zɔːst] n (fumes) Abgase pl; (pipe) Auspuffrohr nt // vt erschöpfen; **~ed** a erschöpft; **~ion** n Erschöpfung f; **~ive** a erschöpfend.

exhibit 66 **extinguish**

exhibit [ɪgˈzɪbɪt] n (ART) Ausstellungsstück nt; (JUR) Beweisstück nt // vt ausstellen; **~ion** [eksɪˈbɪʃən] n (ART) Ausstellung f; (of temper etc) Zurschaustellung f; **~ionist** [eksɪˈbɪʃənɪst] n Exhibitionist m.

exhilarating [ɪgˈzɪləreɪtɪŋ] a erhebend.

exhort [ɪgˈzɔːt] vt ermahnen.

exile [ˈeksaɪl] n Exil nt; (person) Verbannte(r) mf // vt verbannen.

exist [ɪgˈzɪst] vi existieren; **~ence** n Existenz f; **~ing** a bestehend.

exit [ˈeksɪt] n Ausgang m; (THEAT) Abgang m // vi (THEAT) abtreten; (COMPUT) aus einem Programm herausgehen; **~ ramp** n (US AUT) Ausfahrt f.

exonerate [ɪgˈzɒnəreɪt] vt entlasten.

exorbitant [ɪgˈzɔːbɪtənt] a übermäßig; (price) Phantasie-.

exotic [ɪgˈzɒtɪk] a exotisch.

expand [ɪksˈpænd] vt ausdehnen // vi sich ausdehnen.

expanse [ɪksˈpæns] n Fläche f.

expansion [ɪksˈpænʃən] n Erweiterung f.

expatriate [eksˈpætrɪɪt] n Ausländer(in f) m.

expect [ɪksˈpekt] vt erwarten; (suppose) annehmen // vi: to be **~ing** ein Kind erwarten; **~ancy** n Erwartung f; **~ant mother** n werdende Mutter f; **~ation** [ekspekˈteɪʃən] n Hoffnung f.

expedience [ɪksˈpiːdɪəns], **expediency** [ɪksˈpiːdɪənsɪ] n Zweckdienlichkeit f.

expedient [ɪksˈpiːdɪənt] a zweckdienlich // n (Hilfs)mittel nt.

expedition [ekspɪˈdɪʃən] n Expedition f.

expel [ɪksˈpel] vt ausweisen; (student) (ver)weisen.

expend [ɪksˈpend] vt (effort) aufwenden; **~iture** n Ausgaben pl.

expense [ɪksˈpens] n Kosten pl; **~s** pl Spesen pl; at the **~** of auf Kosten von; **~ account** n Spesenkonto nt.

expensive [ɪksˈpensɪv] a teuer.

experience [ɪksˈpɪərɪəns] n (incident) Erlebnis nt; (practice) Erfahrung f // vt erleben; **~d** a erfahren.

experiment [ɪksˈperɪmənt] n Versuch m, Experiment nt // vi [ɪksˈperɪment] experimentieren; **~al** [ɪksperɪˈmentl] a experimentell.

expert [ˈekspɜːt] n Fachmann m; (official) Sachverständige(r) m // a erfahren; **~ise** [ekspəˈtiːz] n Sachkenntnis f.

expire [ɪksˈpaɪə*] vi (end) ablaufen; (die) sterben; (ticket) verfallen.

expiry [ɪksˈpaɪərɪ] n Ablauf m.

explain [ɪksˈpleɪn] vt erklären.

explanation [ekspləˈneɪʃən] n Erklärung f.

explanatory [ɪksˈplænətərɪ] a erklärend.

explicit [ɪksˈplɪsɪt] a ausdrücklich.

explode [ɪksˈpləʊd] vi explodieren // vt (bomb) sprengen; (theory) platzen lassen.

exploit [ˈeksplɔɪt] n (Helden)tat f // vt [ɪksˈplɔɪt] ausbeuten; **~ation** [eksplɔɪˈteɪʃən] n Ausbeutung f.

exploration [eksplɔːˈreɪʃən] n Erforschung f.

exploratory [eksˈplɔrətərɪ] a Probe-.

explore [ɪksˈplɔː*] vt (travel) erforschen; (search) untersuchen; **~r** n Erforscher(in f) m.

explosion [ɪksˈpləʊʒən] n (lit) Explosion f; (fig) Ausbruch m.

explosive [ɪksˈpləʊzɪv] a explosiv, Spreng- // n Sprengstoff m.

exponent [eksˈpəʊnənt] n Exponent m.

export [eksˈpɔːt] vt exportieren // n [ˈekspɔːt] Export m // cpd (trade) Export-; **~er** n Exporteur m.

expose [ɪksˈpəʊz] vt (to danger etc) aussetzen (to dat); (imposter) entlarven.

exposed [ɪksˈpəʊzd] a (position) exponiert.

exposure [ɪksˈpəʊʒə*] n (MED) Unterkühlung f; (PHOT) Belichtung f; **~ meter** n Belichtungsmesser m.

expound [ɪksˈpaʊnd] vt entwickeln.

express [ɪksˈpres] a (definite) ausdrücklich; (speedy) Expreß-, Eil- // n (RAIL) Zug m // ad (send) per Expreß // vt ausdrücken; to **~** o.s. sich ausdrücken; **~ion** [ɪksˈpreʃən] n Ausdruck m; **~ive** a ausdrucksvoll; **~ly** ad ausdrücklich; **~way** n (US: urban motorway) Schnellstraße f.

expulsion [ɪksˈpʌlʃən] n Ausweisung f.

expurgate [ˈekspɜːgeɪt] vt zensieren.

exquisite [eksˈkwɪzɪt] a erlesen.

extend [ɪksˈtend] vt (visit etc) verlängern; (building) ausbauen; (hand) ausstrecken; (welcome) bieten // vi (land) sich erstrecken.

extension [ɪksˈtenʃən] n Erweiterung f; (of building) Anbau m; (TEL) Apparat m.

extensive [ɪksˈtensɪv] a (knowledge) umfassend; (use) weitgehend.

extent [ɪksˈtent] n Ausdehnung f; Ausmaß nt; to a certain **~** bis zu einem gewissen Grade; to such an **~** that ... dermaßen, daß ...; to what **~**? inwieweit?

extenuating [eksˈtenjʊeɪtɪŋ] a mildernd.

exterior [eksˈtɪərɪə*] a äußere(r, s), Außen- // n Äußere(s) nt.

exterminate [eksˈtɜːmɪneɪt] vt ausrotten.

extermination [ekstɜːmɪˈneɪʃən] n Ausrottung f.

external [eksˈtɜːnl] a äußere(r, s), Außen-.

extinct [ɪksˈtɪŋkt] a ausgestorben; **~ion** [ɪksˈtɪŋkʃən] n Aussterben nt.

extinguish [ɪksˈtɪŋgwɪʃ] vt

(aus)löschen; **~er** n Löschgerät nt.

extort [ɪks'tɔ:t] vt erpressen (sth from sb jdn um etw); **~ion** [ɪks'tɔ:ʃən] n Erpressung f; **~ionate** [ɪks'tɔ:ʃənɪt] a überhöht, erpresserisch.

extra [ekstrə] a zusätzlich // ad besonders // n (for car etc) Extra nt; (charge) Zuschlag m; (THEAT) Statist m.

extra... [ekstrə] pref außer...

extract [ɪks'trækt] vt (heraus)ziehen // n ['ekstrækt] (from book etc) Auszug m; (COOK) Extrakt m.

extracurricular ['ekstrəkə'rɪkjulə*] a außerhalb des Stundenplans.

extradite ['ekstrədaɪt] vt ausliefern.

extramarital [ekstrə'mærɪtl] a außerehelich.

extramural [ekstrə'mjuərl] a (course) Volkshochschul-.

extraordinary [ɪks'trɔ:dnrɪ] a außerordentlich; (amazing) erstaunlich.

extravagance [ɪks'trævəgəns] n Verschwendung f; (lack of restraint) Zügellosigkeit f; (an ~) Extravaganz f.

extravagant [ɪks'trævəgənt] a extravagant.

extreme [ɪks'tri:m] a (edge) äußerste(r, s), hinterste(r, s); (cold) äußerste(r, s); (behaviour) außergewöhnlich, übertrieben // n Extrem nt; **~ly** ad äußerst, höchst.

extremity [ɪks'tremɪtɪ] n (end) Spitze f, äußerste(s) Ende nt; (hardship) bitterste Not f; (ANAT) Hand f; Fuß m.

extricate ['ekstrɪkeɪt] vt losmachen, befreien.

extrovert ['ekstrəuvɜ:t] n extrovertierte(r) Mensch m.

exuberant [ɪg'zu:bərənt] a ausgelassen.

exude [ɪg'zju:d] vt absondern.

exult [ɪg'zʌlt] vi frohlocken.

eye [aɪ] n Auge nt; (of needle) Öhr nt // vt betrachten; (up and down) mustern; to keep an ~ on aufpassen auf (+acc); **~ball** n Augapfel m; **~bath** n Augenbad nt; **~brow** n Augenbraue f; **~brow pencil** n Augenbrauenstift m; **~drops** npl Augentropfen pl; **~lash** n Augenwimper f; **~lid** n Augenlid nt; **~liner** n Eyeliner nt; **~opener** n: that was an ~opener das hat mir die Augen geöffnet; **~shadow** n Lidschatten m; **~sight** n Sehkraft f; **~sore** n Schandfleck m; ~ **witness** n Augenzeuge m.

F

F [ef] n (MUS) F nt.
F. abbr (= Fahrenheit) F.
fable ['feɪbl] n Fabel f.
fabric ['fæbrɪk] n Stoff m; (fig) Gefüge nt.

fabrication [fæbrɪ'keɪʃən] n Erfindung f.
fabulous ['fæbjuləs] a sagenhaft.

face [feɪs] n Gesicht nt; (surface) Oberfläche f; (of clock) Zifferblatt nt // vt (point towards) liegen nach; (situation, difficulty) sich stellen (+dat); ~ **down** (person) mit dem Gesicht nach unten; (card) mit der Vorderseite nach unten; **to make or pull a** ~ das Gesicht verziehen; **in the** ~ **of** angesichts (+gen); **on the** ~ **of it** so, wie es aussieht; **to** ~ **to** ~ Auge in Auge; **to** ~ **up to** sth einer Sache ins Auge sehen; ~ **cloth** n (Brit) Waschlappen m; ~ **cream** n Gesichtscreme f; ~ **lift** n Facelifting nt; ~ **powder** n (Gesichts)puder m.

facet ['fæsɪt] n Aspekt m; (of gem) Facette f.

facetious [fə'si:ʃəs] a witzig.

face value n Nennwert m; (fig) to take sth at its ~ etw für bare Münze nehmen.

facial ['feɪʃəl] a Gesichts-.

facile ['fæsaɪl] a oberflächlich; (US: easy) leicht.

facilitate [fə'sɪlɪteɪt] vt erleichtern.

facilities [fə'sɪlɪtɪz] npl Einrichtungen pl; credit ~ Kreditmöglichkeiten pl.

facing ['feɪsɪŋ] a zugekehrt // prep gegenüber.

fact [fækt] n Tatsache f; in ~ in der Tat.

faction ['fækʃən] n Splittergruppe f.

factor ['fæktə*] n Faktor m.

factory ['fæktərɪ] n Fabrik f.

factual ['fæktjuəl] a sachlich.

faculty ['fækəltɪ] n Fähigkeit f; (UNIV) Fakultät f; (US: teaching staff) Lehrpersonal nt.

fad [fæd] n Tick m; (fashion) Masche f.

fade [feɪd] vi (lose colour) verblassen; (grow dim) nachlassen; (sound, memory) schwächer werden; (wither) verwelken.

fag [fæg] n (col: cigarette) Kippe f.

fail [feɪl] vt (exam) nicht bestehen; (student) durchfallen lassen; (courage) verlassen; (memory) im Stich lassen // vi (supplies) zu Ende gehen; (student) durchfallen; (eyesight) nachlassen; (light) schwächer werden; (crop) fehlschlagen; (remedy) nicht wirken; **to do sth** (neglect) es unterlassen, etw zu tun; (be unable) es nicht schaffen, etw zu tun; **without** ~ unbedingt; **~ing** n Schwäche f // prep mangels (+gen); **~ure** n (person) Versager m; (act) Versagen nt; (TECH) Defekt m.

faint [feɪnt] a schwach // n Ohnmacht f // vi ohnmächtig werden.

fair [feə*] a (just) schön; (hair) blond; (skin) hell; (just) gerecht, fair; (not very good) mittelmäßig; (sizeable) ansehnlich // ad (play) fair // n (COMM) Messe f; (Brit: fun~) Jahrmarkt m; **~ly** ad (honestly) gerecht, fair; (rather) ziemlich; **~ness** n Fairneß f.

fairy ['fɛərɪ] n Fee f; ~ **tale** n Märchen nt.

faith [feɪθ] n Glaube m; (trust) Vertrauen nt; (sect) Bekenntnis nt; ~**ful** a, ~**fully** ad treu; yours ~**fully** (Brit) hochachtungsvoll.

fake [feɪk] n (thing) Fälschung f; (person) Schwindler m // a vorgetäuscht // vt fälschen.

falcon ['fɔːlkən] n Falke m.

fall [fɔːl] n Fall m, Sturz m; (decrease) Fallen nt; (of snow) (Schnee)fall m; (US: autumn) Herbst m // vi, pt **fell**, pp **fallen** ['fɔːlən] (lit, fig) fallen; (night) hereinbrechen; ~**s** pl (waterfall) Fälle pl; ~ **back** vi zurückweichen; ~ **back on** vt zurückgreifen auf (+ acc); ~ **behind** vi zurückbleiben; ~ **down** vi (person) hinfallen; (building) einstürzen; ~ **flat** vi (lit) platt hinfallen; (joke) nicht ankommen; ~ **for** vt (trick) hereinfallen auf (+acc); (person) sich verknallen in (+acc); ~ **in** vi (roof) einstürzen; ~ **off** vi herunterfallen (von); (diminish) sich vermindern; ~ **out** vi sich streiten; (MIL) wegtreten; ~ **through** vi (plan) ins Wasser fallen.

fallacy ['fæləsɪ] n Trugschluß m.

fallen ['fɔːlən] pp of **fall**.

fallible ['fæləbl] a fehlbar.

fallout ['fɔːlaʊt] n radioaktive(r) Niederschlag m; ~ **shelter** n Atombunker m.

fallow ['fæləʊ] a brach(liegend).

false [fɔːls] a falsch; (artificial) künstlich; **under** ~ **pretences** unter Vorspiegelung falscher Tatsachen; ~ **alarm** n Fehlalarm m; ~ **teeth** npl (Brit) Gebiß nt.

falter ['fɔːltə*] vi schwanken; (in speech) stocken.

fame [feɪm] n Ruhm m.

familiar [fə'mɪlɪə*] a bekannt; (intimate) familiär; to be ~ with vertraut sein mit; ~**ize** vt vertraut machen.

family ['fæmɪlɪ] n Familie f; (relations) Verwandtschaft f; ~ **business** n Familienunternehmen nt; ~ **doctor** n Hausarzt m.

famine ['fæmɪn] n Hungersnot f.

famished ['fæmɪʃt] a ausgehungert.

famous ['feɪməs] a berühmt; ~**ly** ad (get on) prächtig.

fan [fæn] n (folding) Fächer m; (ELEC) Ventilator m; (admirer) Fan m // vt fächeln; ~ **out** vi sich (fächerförmig) ausbreiten.

fanatic [fə'nætɪk] n Fanatiker(in f) m.

fan belt n Keilriemen m.

fanciful ['fænsɪful] a (odd) seltsam; (imaginative) phantasievoll.

fancy ['fænsɪ] n (liking) Neigung f; (imagination) Einbildung f // a schick // vt (like) gern haben; wollen; (imagine) sich einbilden; **he fancies her** er mag

sie; ~ **dress** n Maskenkostüm nt; ~- **dress ball** n Maskenball m.

fang [fæŋ] n Fangzahn m; (snake's) Giftzahn m.

fantastic [fæn'tæstɪk] a phantastisch.

fantasy ['fæntəzɪ] n Phantasie f.

far [fɑː*] a weit // ad weit entfernt; (very much) weitaus, by ~ bei weitem; so ~ soweit; bis jetzt; go as ~ as the farm gehen Sie bis zum Bauernhof; as ~ as I know soweit or soviel ich weiß; ~**away** a weit entfernt.

farce [fɑːs] n Farce f.

farcical ['fɑːsɪkəl] a lächerlich.

fare [fɛə*] n Fahrpreis m; Fahrgeld nt; (food) Kost f.

Far East n: the ~ der Ferne Osten.

farewell [fɛə'wel] n Abschied(sgruß m) m // interj lebe wohl!

farm [fɑːm] n Bauernhof m, Farm f // vt bewirtschaften; ~**er** n Bauer m, Landwirt m; ~**hand** n Landarbeiter m; ~**house** n Bauernhaus nt; ~**ing** n Landwirtschaft f; ~**land** n Ackerland nt; ~**yard** n Hof m.

fart [fɑːt] (col!) n Furz m // vi furzen.

farther ['fɑːðə*] ad weiter.

farthest ['fɑːðɪst] a fernste(r, s) // ad am weitesten.

fascinate ['fæsɪneɪt] vt faszinieren.

fascination [fæsɪ'neɪʃən] n Faszination f.

fascist ['fæʃɪst] n Faschist m // a faschistisch.

fashion ['fæʃən] n (of clothes) Mode f; (manner) Art f (und Weise f) // vt machen; in ~ in Mode; out of ~ unmodisch; ~**able** a (clothes) modisch; (place) elegant; ~ **show** n Mode(n)schau f.

fast [fɑːst] a schnell; (firm) fest // ad schnell; (firmly) fest // n Fasten nt // vi fasten; to be ~ (clock) vorgehen.

fasten ['fɑːsn] vt (attach) befestigen; (seat belt) festmachen; (with rope) zusschnüren // vi sich schließen lassen; ~**er**, ~**ing** n Verschluß m.

fastidious [fæs'tɪdɪəs] a wählerisch.

fat [fæt] a dick // n Fett nt.

fatal ['feɪtl] a tödlich; (disastrous) verhängnisvoll; ~**ity** [fə'tælɪtɪ] n (road death etc) Todesopfer nt; ~**ly** ad tödlich.

fate [feɪt] n Schicksal nt; ~**ful** a (prophetic) schicksalsschwer; (important) schicksalhaft.

father ['fɑːðə*] n Vater m; (REL) Pater m; ~-**in-law** n Schwiegervater m; ~**ly** a väterlich.

fathom ['fæðəm] n Klafter m // vt ausloten; (fig) ergründen.

fatigue [fə'tiːg] n Ermüdung f.

fatten ['fætn] vt dick machen; (animals) mästen // vi dick werden.

fatty ['fætɪ] a fettig // n (col) Dickerchen nt.

fatuous ['fætjʊəs] a albern, affig.

faucet ['fɔːsɪt] n (US) Wasserhahn m.

fault [fɔːlt] n (defect) Defekt m; (ELEC) Störung f; (blame) Schuld f; (GEOG) Verwerfung f; it's your ~ du bist daran schuld; at ~ im Unrecht // vt: to ~ sth etwas an etw (dat) auszusetzen haben; **~less** a tadellos; **~y** a fehlerhaft, defekt.

favour, (US) **favor** ['feɪvə*] n (approval) Wohlwollen nt; (kindness) Gefallen m // vt (prefer) vorziehen; in ~ of für; zugunsten (+gen); to find ~ with sb bei jdm Anklang finden; **~able** a günstig; **~ite** ['feɪvərɪt] a Lieblings- // n (child) Liebling m; (SPORT) Favorit m; **~itism** n (SCH) Bevorzugung f.

fawn [fɔːn] a rehbraun // n (colour) Rehbraun nt; (animal) (Reh)kitz nt // vi: to ~ (up)on (fig) katzbuckeln vor (+dat).

fax [fæks] n (document) Fax nt; (machine) Telefax nt // vt per Fax schicken.

FBI ['efbiː'aɪ] n abbr (US: = Federal Bureau of Investigation) FBI nt.

fear [fɪə*] n Furcht f // vt fürchten; **~ful** a (timid) furchtsam; (terrible) fürchterlich; **~less** a furchtlos.

feasible ['fiːzəbl] a durchführbar.

feast [fiːst] n Festmahl nt; (REL: also: ~ day) Feiertag m // vi sich gütlich tun (on an +dat).

feat [fiːt] n Leistung f.

feather ['feðə*] n Feder f.

feature ['fiːtʃə*] n (Gesichts)zug m; (important part) Grundzug m; (CINE, PRESS) Feature nt // vt darstellen; (advertising etc) groß herausbringen // vi vorkommen; featuring X mit X; **~ film** n Spielfilm m.

February ['februərɪ] n Februar m.

fed [fed] pt, pp of **feed**.

federal ['fedərəl] a Bundes-.

federation [fedə'reɪʃən] n (society) Verband m; (of states) Staatenbund m.

fed-up [fed'ʌp] a: to be ~ with sth etw satt haben; **I'm ~** ich habe die Nase voll.

fee [fiː] n Gebühr f.

feeble ['fiːbl] a (person) schwach; (excuse) lahm.

feed [fiːd] n (for baby) Essen nt; (for animals) Futter nt // vt, pt, pp, fed füttern; (support) ernähren; (data) eingeben; to ~ on fressen; **~back** n (information) Feedback nt; **~ing bottle** n (Brit) Flasche f.

feel [fiːl] n: it has a soft ~ es fühlt sich weich an; to get the ~ of sth sich an etw (acc) gewöhnen // v (pt, pp felt) vt (sense) fühlen; (touch) anfassen; (think) meinen // vi (person) sich fühlen; (thing) sich anfühlen; I ~ cold mir ist kalt; I ~ like a cup of tea ich habe Lust auf eine Tasse Tee; **~ about** or **around** vi herumsuchen; **~er** n Fühler m; **~ing** n Gefühl nt; (opinion) Meinung f.

feet [fiːt] pl of **foot**.

feign [feɪn] vt vortäuschen.

feline ['fiːlaɪn] a katzenartig.

fell [fel] pt of **fall** // vt (tree) fällen.

fellow ['feləʊ] n (man) Kerl m; **~ citizen** n Mitbürger(in f) m; **~ countryman** n Landsmann m; **~ men** npl Mitmenschen pl; **~ship** n (group) Körperschaft f; (friendliness) Kameradschaft f; (scholarship) Forschungsstipendium nt; **~ student** n Kommilitone m, Kommilitonin f.

felony ['felənɪ] n schwere(s) Verbrechen nt.

felt [felt] pt, pp of **feel** // n Filz m; **~-tip pen** n Filzstift m.

female ['fiːmeɪl] n (of animals) Weibchen nt // a weiblich.

feminine ['femɪnɪn] a (GRAM) weiblich; (qualities) fraulich.

feminist ['femɪnɪst] n Feminist(in f) m.

fence [fens] n Zaun m // vt (also: ~ in) einzäunen // vi fechten.

fencing ['fensɪŋ] n Zaun m; (SPORT) Fechten nt.

fend [fend] vi: ~ for o.s. sich (allein) durchschlagen; ~ off vt abwehren.

fender ['fendə*] n Kaminvorsetzer m; (US AUT) Kotflügel m.

ferment [fə'ment] vi (CHEM) gären // ['fɜːment] n (excitement) Unruhe f.

fern [fɜːn] n Farn m.

ferocious [fə'rəʊʃəs] a wild, grausam.

ferret ['ferɪt] n Frettchen nt // vt: to ~ out aufspüren.

ferry ['ferɪ] n Fähre f // vt übersetzen.

fertile ['fɜːtaɪl] a fruchtbar.

fertilize ['fɜːtɪlaɪz] vt (AGR) düngen; (BIOL) befruchten; **~r** n (Kunst)dünger m.

fervent ['fɜːvənt] a (admirer) glühend; (hope) innig.

fervour, (US) **fervor** [fɜːvə*] n Leidenschaft f.

fester ['festə*] vi eitern.

festival ['festɪvəl] n (REL etc) Fest nt; (ART, MUS) Festspiele pl.

festive ['festɪv] a festlich; **the ~ season** (Christmas) die Festzeit f.

festivity [fes'tɪvɪtɪ] n Festlichkeit f.

festoon [fes'tuːn] vt: to ~ with schmücken mit.

fetch [fetʃ] vt holen; (in sale) einbringen.

fetching ['fetʃɪŋ] a reizend.

fête [feɪt] n Fest nt.

fetus ['fiːtəs] n (US) = **foetus**.

feud [fjuːd] n Fehde f; **~al** a Feudal-.

fever ['fiːvə*] n Fieber nt; **~ish** a (MED) fiebrig; (fig) fieberhaft.

few [fjuː] a wenig; **a ~** a, pron einige; **~er** a weniger; **~est** a wenigste(r, s).

fiancé [fɪ'ɑːnseɪ] n Verlobte(r) m; **~e** n Verlobte f.

fib [fɪb] n Flunkerei f // vi flunkern.
fibre, (US) **fiber** ['faɪbə*] n Faser f; ~-**glass** n Glaswolle f.
fickle ['fɪkl] a unbeständig.
fiction ['fɪkʃən] n (novels) Romanliteratur f; (story) Erdichtung f; ~**al** a erfunden.
fictitious [fɪk'tɪʃəs] a erfunden, fingiert.
fiddle ['fɪdl] n Geige f; (trick) Schwindelei f // vt (Brit: accounts) frisieren; ~ **with** vi herumfummeln an (+dat).
fidelity [fɪ'delɪtɪ] n Treue f.
fidget ['fɪdʒɪt] vi zappeln.
field [fi:ld] n Feld nt; (range) Gebiet nt; ~ **marshal** n Feldmarschall m; ~**work** n (UNIV) Feldforschung f.
fiend [fi:nd] n Teufel m; ~**ish** a teuflisch.
fierce [fɪəs] a wild.
fiery ['faɪərɪ] a (hot-tempered) hitzig.
fifteen [fɪf'ti:n] num fünfzehn.
fifth [fɪfθ] a fünfte(r, s) // n Fünftel nt.
fifty ['fɪftɪ] num fünfzig; ~-~ a halbe halbe, fifty fifty (col).
fig [fɪg] n Feige f.
fight [faɪt] n Kampf m; (brawl) Schlägerei f; (argument) Streit m // v (pt, pp **fought**) vt kämpfen gegen; sich schlagen mit; (fig) bekämpfen // vi kämpfen; sich schlagen; streiten; ~**er** n Kämpfer(in f) m; (plane) Jagdflugzeug nt; ~**ing** n Kämpfen nt; (war) Kampfhandlungen pl.
figment ['fɪgmənt] n: ~ of the imagination Einbildung f.
figurative ['fɪgərətɪv] a bildlich.
figure ['fɪgə*] n (of person) Figur f; (person) Gestalt f; (number) Zahl f // vt (US: imagine) glauben // vi (appear) erscheinen; ~ **out** vt herausbekommen; ~**head** n (NAUT, fig) Galionsfigur f; ~ **of speech** n Redensart f.
filament ['fɪləmənt] n Faden m; (ELEC) Glühfaden m.
filch [fɪltʃ] vt (col) filzen.
file [faɪl] n (tool) Feile f; (dossier) Akte f; (folder) Aktenordner m; (COMPUT) Datei f; (row) Reihe f // vt (metal, nails) feilen; (papers) abheften; (claim) einreichen // vi: to ~ in/out hintereinander hereinkommen/hinausgehen; to ~ past vorbeimarschieren.
filing ['faɪlɪŋ] n Ablage f; ~ **cabinet** n Aktenschrank m.
fill [fɪl] vt füllen; (occupy) ausfüllen; (satisfy) sättigen // n: to eat one's ~ sich richtig satt essen; ~ **in** vt (hole) (auf)füllen; (form) ausfüllen; ~ **up** vt (container) auffüllen; (form) ausfüllen // vi (AUT) tanken.
fillet ['fɪlɪt] n Filet nt; ~ **steak** n Filetsteak nt.
filling ['fɪlɪŋ] n (COOK) Füllung f; (for tooth) (Zahn)plombe f; ~ **station** n

Tankstelle f.
film [fɪlm] n Film m // vt (scene) filmen; ~ **star** n Filmstar m; ~**strip** n Filmstreifen m.
filter ['fɪltə*] n Filter m // vt filtern; ~ **lane** n (Brit) Abbiegespur f; ~-**tipped** a Filter-.
filth [fɪlθ] n Dreck m; ~**y** a dreckig; (weather) scheußlich.
fin [fɪn] n Flosse f.
final ['faɪnl] a letzte(r, s); End-; (conclusive) endgültig // n (FOOTBALL etc) Endspiel nt; ~**s** pl (UNIV) Abschlußexamen nt; (SPORT) Schlußrunde f; ~**e** [fɪ'nɑːlɪ] n (MUS) Finale nt; ~**ist** n (SPORT) Schlußrundenteilnehmer m; ~**ize** vt endgültige Form geben (+dat); abschließen; ~**ly** ad (lastly) zuletzt; (eventually) endlich; (irrevocably) endgültig.
finance [faɪ'næns] n Finanzwesen nt; ~**s** pl Finanzen pl // vt finanzieren.
financial [faɪ'nænʃəl] a Finanz-; finanziell.
find [faɪnd], pt, pp **found** vt finden // n Fund m; to ~ sb guilty jdn für schuldig erklären; ~ **out** vt herausfinden; ~**ings** npl (JUR) Ermittlungsergebnis nt; (of report) Befund m.
fine [faɪn] a fein; (good) gut; (weather) schön // ad (well) gut; (small) klein // n (JUR) Geldstrafe f // vt (JUR) mit einer Geldstrafe belegen; ~ **arts** npl die schönen Künste pl.
finery ['faɪnərɪ] n Putz m.
finger ['fɪŋgə*] n Finger m // vt befühlen; ~**nail** n Fingernagel m; ~**print** n Fingerabdruck m; ~**tip** n Fingerspitze f.
finicky ['fɪnɪkɪ] a pingelig.
finish ['fɪnɪʃ] n Ende nt; (SPORT) Ziel nt; (of object) Verarbeitung f; (of paint) Oberflächenwirkung f // vt beenden; (book) zu Ende lesen // vi aufhören; (SPORT) am Ziel kommen; to be ~**ed** with sth fertig sein mit etw; ~**ing line** n Ziellinie f; ~**ing school** n Mädchenpensionat nt.
finite ['faɪnaɪt] a endlich, begrenzt.
Finland ['fɪnlənd] n Finnland nt.
Finn [fɪn] n Finne m, Finnin f; ~**ish** a finnisch // n (LING) Finnisch nt.
fir [fɜː*] n Tanne f.
fire [faɪə*] n Feuer nt; (in house etc) Brand m // vt (gun) abfeuern; (imagination) entzünden; (dismiss) hinauswerfen // vi (AUT) zünden; to be on ~ brennen; ~ **alarm** n Feueralarm m; ~**arm** n Schußwaffe f; ~ **brigade** (Brit), ~ **department** (US) n Feuerwehr f; ~ **engine** n Feuerwehrauto nt; ~ **escape** n Feuerleiter f; ~ **extinguisher** n Löschgerät nt; ~**man** n Feuerwehrmann m; ~**place** n Kamin

m; ~**side** n Kamin m; ~**station** n Feuerwehrwache f; ~**works** npl Feuerwerk nt.

firing ['faɪərɪŋ] n Schießen nt; ~ **squad** n Exekutionskommando nt.

firm [fɜːm] a fest // n Firma f.

first [fɜːst] a erste(r, s) // ad zuerst; (arrive) als erste(r); (happen) zum ersten mal // n (person: in race) Erste(r) mf; (UNIV) Eins f; (AUT) erste(r) Gang m; at ~ zuerst; ~ of all zu allererst; ~ **aid** n Erste Hilfe f; ~-**aid kit** n Verbandskasten m; ~-**class** a erstklassig; (travel) erster Klasse; ~-**hand** a aus erster Hand; ~**ly** ad erstens; ~ **name** n Vorname m; ~-**rate** a erstklassig.

fiscal ['fɪskəl] a Finanz-.

fish [fɪʃ] n, pl inv Fisch m // vi fischen; angeln; to go ~**ing** angeln gehen; (in sea) fischen gehen; ~**erman** n Fischer m; ~ **farm** n Fischzucht f; ~ **fingers** npl (Brit) Fischstäbchen; ~**ing boat** n Fischerboot nt; ~**ing line** n Angelschnur f; ~**ing rod** n Angel(rute) f; ~**monger's (shop)** n Fischhändler m; ~ **slice** n Fischvorleger m; ~ **sticks** npl (US) = ~ **fingers**; ~**y** a (col: suspicious) faul.

fission ['fɪʃən] n Spaltung f.

fissure ['fɪʃə*] n Riß m.

fist [fɪst] n Faust f.

fit [fɪt] a (MED) gesund; (SPORT) in Form, fit; (suitable) geeignet // vt passen (+dat); (insert, attach) einsetzen // vi (correspond) passen (zu); (clothes) passen; (in space, gap) hineinpassen // n (of clothes) Sitz m; (MED, of anger) Anfall m; (of laughter) Krampf m; by ~s **and starts** (move) ruckweise; (work) unregelmäßig; ~ **in** vi hineinpassen; (fig: person) passen; ~ **out** vt (also: ~ up) ausstatten; ~**ful** a (sleep) unruhig; ~**ment** n Einrichtungsgegenstand m; ~**ness** n (suitability) Eignung f; (MED) Gesundheit f; (SPORT) Fitneß f; ~**ted carpet** n Teppichboden m; ~**ted kitchen** n Einbauküche f; ~**ter** n (TECH) Monteur m; ~**ting** a passend // n (of dress) Anprobe f; (piece of equipment) (Ersatz)teil nt; ~**ting room** n Anproberaum m; ~**tings** npl Zubehör nt.

five [faɪv] num fünf; ~**r** n (col: Brit) Fünf-Pfund-Note f; (: US) Fünf-Dollar-Note f.

fix [fɪks] vt befestigen; (settle) festsetzen; (repair) reparieren // n: in a ~ in der Klemme; ~ **up** vt (meeting) arrangieren; to ~ sb up with sth jdm etw (acc) verschaffen; ~**ation** n Fixierung f; ~**ed** a fest; ~**ture** ['fɪkstʃə*] n Installationsteil m; (SPORT) Spiel nt.

fizz [fɪz] vi sprudeln.

fizzle ['fɪzl] vi: to ~ **out** verpuffen.

fizzy ['fɪzɪ] a Sprudel-, sprudelnd.

flabbergasted ['flæbəgɑːstɪd] a (col) platt.

flabby ['flæbɪ] a wabbelig.

flag [flæg] n Fahne f // vi (strength) nachlassen; (spirit) erlahmen; ~ **down** vt anhalten.

flagpole ['flægpəʊl] n Fahnenstange f.

flagrant ['fleɪgrənt] a kraß.

flair [flɛə*] n Talent nt.

flak [flæk] n Flakfeuer nt.

flake [fleɪk] n (of snow) Flocke f; (of rust) Schuppe f // vi (also: ~ off) abblättern.

flamboyant [flæm'bɔɪənt] a extravagant.

flame [fleɪm] n Flamme f.

flamingo [flə'mɪŋgəʊ] n Flamingo m.

flammable ['flæməbl] a brennbar.

flan [flæn] n (Brit) Obsttorte f.

flank [flæŋk] n Flanke f // vt flankieren.

flannel ['flænl] n Flanell m; (Brit: also: face ~) Waschlappen m; (Brit col) Geschwafel nt; ~**s** pl Flanellhose f.

flap [flæp] n Klappe f; (col: crisis) (helle) Aufregung f // vt (wings) schlagen mit // vi flattern.

flare [flɛə*] n (signal) Leuchtsignal nt; (in skirt etc) Weite f; ~ **up** vi aufflammen; (fig) aufbrausen; (revolt) (plötzlich) ausbrechen.

flash [flæʃ] n Blitz m; (also: news ~) Kurzmeldung f; (PHOT) Blitzlicht nt // vt aufleuchten lassen // vi aufleuchten; **in a** ~ im Nu; ~ **by** or **past** vi vorbeirasen; ~**back** n Rückblende f; ~**bulb** n Blitzlichtbirne f; ~ **cube** n Blitzwürfel m; ~**light** n Blitzlicht nt.

flashy ['flæʃɪ] a (pej) knallig.

flask [flɑːsk] n (CHEM) Kolben m; (also: vacuum ~) Thermosflasche f.

flat [flæt] a flach; (dull) matt; (MUS) erniedrigt; (beer) schal; (tyre) platt // n (Brit: rooms) Wohnung f; (MUS) b nt; (AUT) Platte(r) m; to **work** ~ **out** auf Hochtouren arbeiten; ~**ly** ad glatt; ~**ten** vt (also: ~**ten out**) ebnen.

flatter ['flætə*] vt schmeicheln (+dat); ~**ing** a schmeichelhaft; ~**y** n Schmeichelei f.

flatulence ['flætjʊləns] n Blähungen pl.

flaunt [flɔːnt] vt prunken mit.

flavour, (US) **flavor** ['fleɪvə*] n Geschmack m // vt würzen; ~~strawberry-~ed~~ a mit Erdbeergeschmack; ~**ing** n Würze f.

flaw [flɔː] n Fehler m; ~**less** a einwandfrei.

flax [flæks] n Flachs m; ~**en** a flachsfarben.

flea [fliː] n Floh m.

fleck [flek] n (mark) Fleck m; (pattern) Tupfen m.

flee [fliː], pt, pp **fled** [fled] vi fliehen // vt fliehen vor (+dat); (country) fliehen aus.

fleece [fliːs] n Vlies nt // vt (col)

schröpfen.

fleet [fli:t] *n* Flotte *f*.

fleeting ['fli:tɪŋ] *a* flüchtig.

Flemish ['flemɪʃ] *a* flämisch.

flesh [fleʃ] *n* Fleisch *nt*; ~ **wound** *n* Fleischwunde *f*.

flew [flu:] *pt of* **fly**.

flex [fleks] *n* Kabel *nt* // *vt* beugen; ~**ibility** [fleksɪ'bɪlɪtɪ] *n* Biegsamkeit *f*; *(fig)* Flexibilität *f*; ~**ible** *a* biegsam; *(plans)* flexibel.

flick [flɪk] *n* leichte(r) Schlag *m* // *vt* leicht schlagen; ~ **through** *vt* durchblättern.

flicker ['flɪkə*] *n* Flackern *nt* // *vi* flackern.

flier ['flaɪə*] *n* Flieger *m*.

flight [flaɪt] *n* Flug *m*; *(fleeing)* Flucht *f*; *(also:* ~ **of steps)** Treppe *f*; **to take** ~ die Flucht ergreifen; **to put to** ~ in die Flucht schlagen; ~ **attendant** *n* *(US)* Steward(eß *f*) *m*; ~ **deck** *n* Flugdeck *nt*.

flimsy ['flɪmzɪ] *a* *(thin)* hauchdünn; *(excuse)* fadenscheinig.

flinch [flɪntʃ] *vi* zurückschrecken *(away from* vor +*dat)*.

fling [flɪŋ], *pt, pp* **flung** *vt* schleudern.

flint [flɪnt] *n* Feuerstein *m*.

flip [flɪp] *vt* werfen.

flippant ['flɪpənt] *a* schnippisch.

flipper ['flɪpə*] *n* Flosse *f*.

flirt [flɜːt] *vi* flirten // *n*: he/she is a ~ er/ sie flirtet gern; ~**ation** [flɜː'teɪʃən] *n* Flirt *m*.

flit [flɪt] *vi* flitzen.

float [fləʊt] *n* *(FISHING)* Schwimmer *m*; *(esp in procession)* Plattformwagen *m* // *vi* schwimmen; *(in air)* schweben // *vt* *(COMM)* gründen; *(currency)* floaten.

flock [flɒk] *n* *(of sheep, REL)* Herde *f*; *(of birds)* Schwarm *m*; *(of people)* Schar *f*.

flog [flɒg] *vt* prügeln; *(col: sell)* verkaufen.

flood [flʌd] *n* Überschwemmung *f*; *(fig)* Flut *f* // *vt* überschwemmen; ~**ing** *n* Überschwemmung *f*; ~**light** *n* Flutlicht *nt*.

floor [flɔː*] *n* *(Fuß)*boden *m*; *(storey)* Stock *m*; *(person)* zu Boden schlagen; **ground** ~ *(Brit)*, **first** ~ *(US)* Erdgeschoß *nt*; **first** ~ *(Brit)*, **second** ~ *(US)* erste(r) Stock *m*; ~**board** *n* Diele *f*; ~ **show** *n* Kabarettvorstellung *f*.

flop [flɒp] *n* Plumps *m*; *(failure)* Reinfall *m* // *vi* *(fail)* durchfallen.

floppy ['flɒpɪ] *a* hängend; ~ **(disk)** *n* *(COMPUT)* Diskette *f*.

flora ['flɔːrə] *n* Flora *f*; ~**l** *a* Blumen-.

florid ['flɒrɪd] *a* *(style)* blumig.

florist ['flɒrɪst] *n* Blumenhändler(in *f*) *m*; ~**'s (shop)** *n* Blumengeschäft *nt*.

flounce [flaʊns] *vi*: **to** ~ **out** hinaus-

stürmen.

flounder ['flaʊndə*] *vi* *(fig)* ins Schleudern kommen // *n* *(ZOOL)* Flunder *f*.

flour ['flaʊə*] *n* Mehl *nt*.

flourish ['flʌrɪʃ] *vi* blühen; gedeihen // *n* *(waving)* Schwingen *nt*; *(of trumpets)* Tusch *m*, Fanfare *f*; ~**ing** *a* blühend.

flout [flaʊt] *vt* mißachten.

flow [fləʊ] *n* Fließen *nt*; *(of sea)* Flut *f* // *vi* fließen; ~ **chart** *n* Flußdiagramm *nt*.

flower ['flaʊə*] *n* Blume *f* // *vi* blühen; ~ **bed** *n* Blumenbeet *nt*; ~**pot** *n* Blumentopf *m*; ~**y** *a* *(style)* blumenreich.

flown [fləʊn] *pp of* **fly**.

flu [flu:] *n* Grippe *f*.

fluctuate ['flʌktjʊeɪt] *vi* schwanken.

fluctuation [flʌktjʊ'eɪʃən] *n* Schwankung *f*.

fluent *a*, ~**ly** *ad* ['flu:ənt, -lɪ] fließend.

fluff [flʌf] *n* Fussel *f*; ~**y** *a* flaumig.

fluid ['flu:ɪd] *n* Flüssigkeit *f* // *a* *(lit)* flüssig; *(fig: plans)* veränderbar.

fluke [flu:k] *n* *(col)* Dusel *m*.

flung [flʌŋ] *pt, pp of* **fling**.

fluoride ['flʊəraɪd] *n* Fluorid *nt*.

flurry ['flʌrɪ] *n* *(of activity)* Aufregung *f*; *(of snow)* Gestöber *nt*.

flush [flʌʃ] *n* Erröten *nt*; *(of excitement)* Glühen *nt* // *vt* *(aus)*spülen // *vi* erröten // *a* glatt; ~ **out** *vt* aufstöbern; ~**ed** *a* rot.

flustered ['flʌstəd] *a* verwirrt.

flute [flu:t] *n* Querflöte *f*.

flutter ['flʌtə*] *n* Flattern *nt* // *vi* flattern.

flux [flʌks] *n*: **in a state of** ~ im Fluß.

fly [flaɪ] *n* *(insect)* Fliege *f*; *(on trousers: also:* **flies)** *(Hosen)*schlitz *m* // *v* *(pt* **flew**, *pp* **flown)** *vt* fliegen // *vi* fliegen; *(flee)* fliehen; *(flag)* wehen; ~ **away** *or* **off** *vi* *(bird, insect)* wegfliegen; ~**ing** *n* Fliegen *nt* // *a*: **with** ~**ing colours** mit fliegenden Fahnen; ~**ing start** gute(r) Start *m*; ~**ing visit** Stippvisite *f*; ~**ing saucer** *n* fliegende Untertasse *f*; ~**over** *n* *(Brit)* Überführung *f*; ~**past** *n* Luftparade *f*; ~**sheet** *n* *(for tent)* Regendach *nt*.

foal [fəʊl] *n* Fohlen *nt*.

foam [fəʊm] *n* Schaum *m* // *vi* schäumen ~ **rubber** *n* Schaumgummi *m*.

fob [fɒb] *vt*: **to** ~ **off** andrehen *(sb with sth* jdm etw*)*; *(with promise)* abspeisen.

focal ['fəʊkəl] *a* Brenn-.

focus ['fəʊkəs] *n, pl* ~**es** Brennpunkt *m* // *vt* *(attention)* konzentrieren; *(camera)* scharf einstellen // *vi* sich konzentrieren *(on* auf +*acc)*; **in** ~ scharf eingestellt; **out of** ~ unscharf.

fodder ['fɒdə*] *n* Futter *nt*.

foe [fəʊ] *n* *(liter)* Feind *m*.

foetus ['fi:təs] *n* Fötus *m*.

fog [fɒg] *n* Nebel *m*; ~ **lamp** *n* *(AUT)*

Nebellampe f; **~gy** a neblig.

foil [fɔıl] vt vereiteln // n (metal, also fig) Folie f; (fencing) Florett nt.

fold [fəʊld] n (bend, crease) Falte f; (AGR) Pferch m // vt falten; **~ up** vt (map etc) zusammenfalten // vi (business) eingehen; **~er** n Schnellhefter m; **~ing** a (chair etc) Klapp-.

foliage ['fəʊlııdʒ] n Laubwerk nt.

folk [fəʊk] npl Volk nt // a Volks-; **~s** pl Leute pl; **~lore** ['fəʊklɔ:*] n (study) Volkskunde f; (tradition) Folklore f; **~song** n Volkslied nt; (modern) Folksong m.

follow ['fɒləʊ] vt folgen (+dat); (fashion) mitmachen // vi folgen; **~ up** vt verfolgen; **~er** n Anhänger(in f) m; **~ing** a folgend // n (people) Gefolgschaft f.

folly ['fɒlı] n Torheit f.

fond [fɒnd] a: to be **~ of** gern haben.

fondle ['fɒndl] vt streicheln.

font [fɒnt] n Taufbecken nt.

food [fu:d] n Essen nt, (for animals) Futter nt; **~ mixer** n Küchenmixer m; **~ poisoning** n Lebensmittelvergiftung f; **~ processor** n Küchenmaschine f; **~stuffs** npl Lebensmittel pl.

fool [fu:l] n Narr m, Närrin f // vt (deceive) hereinlegen // vi (also: **~ around**) (herum)albern; **~hardy** a tollkühn; **~ish** a albern; **~proof** a idiotensicher.

foot [fʊt] n, pl feet Fuß m // vt (bill) bezahlen; on **~** zu Fuß; **~age** n (CINE) Filmmaterial nt; **~ball** n Fußball m; (game: Brit) Fußball m; (: US) Football m; **~ball player** n (Brit: also: **~baller**) Fußball(spiel)er m; (US) Footballer m; **~brake** n Fußbremse f; **~bridge** n Fußgängerbrücke f; **~hills** npl Ausläufer pl; **~hold** n Halt m; **~ing** n (lit) Halt m; (fig) Verhältnis nt; **~lights** npl Rampenlicht nt; **~man** n Bedienstete(r) m; **~note** n Fußnote f; **~path** n Fußweg m; **~print** n Fußabdruck m; **~sore** a fußkrank; **~step** n Schritt m; **~wear** n Schuhzeug nt.

for [fɔ:*] ◆prep 1 für; is this **~** me? ist das für mich?; the train **~** London der Zug nach London; he went **~** the paper er ging die Zeitung holen; give it to me **—** what **~**? gib es mir **—** warum?

2 (because of) wegen; **~** this reason aus diesem Grunde

3 (referring to distance): there are roadworks **~** 5 km die Baustelle ist 5 km lang; we walked **~** miles wir sind meilenweit gegangen

4 (referring to time) seit; (: with future sense) für; he was away **~** 2 years er war zwei Jahre lang weg

5 (with infinitive clauses): it is not **~** me to decide das kann ich nicht ent-

scheiden; **~** this to be possible ... damit dies möglich wird/wurde ...

6 (in spite of) trotz (+gen or (col) +dat); **~** all his complaints obwohl er sich ständig beschwert

◆cj denn.

forage ['fɒrıdʒ] n (Vieh)futter nt.

foray ['fɒreı] n Raubzug m.

forbid [fə'bıd], pt forbad(e) [fə'bæd], pp forbidden [fə'bıdn] vt verbieten; **~ding** a einschüchternd.

force [fɔ:s] n Kraft f; (compulsion) Zwang m // vt zwingen; (lock) aufbrechen; in **~** (rule) gültig; (group) in großer Stärke; the F**~s** pl (Brit) die Streitkräfte; **~d** [fɔ:st] a (smile) gezwungen; (landing) Not-; **~-feed** vt zwangsernähren; **~ful** a (speech) kraftvoll; (personality) resolut.

forceps ['fɔ:seps] npl Zange f.

forcibly ['fɔ:səblı] ad zwangsweise.

ford [fɔ:d] n Furt f // vt durchwaten.

fore [fɔ:*] n: to the **~** in den Vordergrund.

forearm ['fɔ:rɑ:m] n Unterarm m.

foreboding [fɔ:'bəʊdıŋ] n Vorahnung f.

forecast ['fɔ:kɑ:st] n Vorhersage f // vt (irreg: like cast) voraussagen.

forecourt ['fɔ:kɔ:t] n (of garage) Vorplatz m.

forefathers ['fɔ:fɑ:ðəz] npl Vorfahren pl.

forefinger ['fɔ:fıŋgə*] n Zeigefinger m.

forefront ['fɔ:frʌnt] n Spitze f.

forego [fɔ:'gəʊ] (irreg: like go) vt verzichten auf (+acc).

foreground ['fɔ:graʊnd] n Vordergrund m.

forehead ['fɒrıd] n Stirn f.

foreign ['fɒrın] a Auslands-; (accent) ausländisch; (trade) ausländisch; (body) Fremd-; **~er** n Ausländer(in f) m; **~ exchange** n Devisen pl; F**~ Minister** n (Brit) Außenminister m; F**~ Office** n Außenministerium nt.

foreleg ['fɔ:leg] n Vorderbein nt.

foreman ['fɔ:mən] n Vorarbeiter m.

foremost ['fɔ:məʊst] a erste(r, s) // ad: first and **~** vor allem.

forensic [fə'rensık] a gerichtsmedizinisch.

forerunner ['fɔ:rʌnə*] n Vorläufer m.

foresee [fɔ:'si:] (irreg: like see) vt vorhersehen; **~able** a absehbar.

foreshadow [fɔ:'fædəʊ] vt andeuten.

foresight ['fɔ:saıt] n Voraussicht f.

forest ['fɒrıst] n Wald m.

forestall [fɔ:'stɔ:l] vt zuvorkommen (+dat).

forestry ['fɒrıstrı] n Forstwirtschaft f.

foretaste ['fɔ:teıst] n Vorgeschmack m.

foretell [fɔ:'tel] (irreg: like tell) vt vorhersagen.

forever [fə'revə*] ad für immer.

foreword ['fɔ:wɜ:d] n Vorwort nt.

forfeit ['fɔ:fɪt] n Einbuße f // vt verwirken.

forgave [fə'geɪv] pt of **forgive**.

forge [fɔ:dʒ] n Schmiede f // vt fälschen; (iron) schmieden; ~ **ahead** vi Fortschritte machen; ~r n Fälscher m; ~ry n Fälschung f.

forget [fə'get], pt **forgot**, pp **forgotten** vti vergessen; ~**ful** a vergeßlich; ~**me-not** n Vergißmeinnicht nt.

forgive [fə'gɪv], pt **forgave**, pp **forgiven** vt verzeihen (sb for sth jdm etw).

forgiveness [fə'gɪvnəs] n Verzeihung f.

forgo [fɔ:'gəʊ] see **forego**.

forgot [fə'gɒt] pt of **forget**.

forgotten [fə'gɒtn] pp of **forget**.

fork [fɔ:k] n Gabel f; (in road) Gabelung f // vi (road) sich gabeln; ~ **out** vt (col: pay) blechen; ~-**lift truck** n Gabelstapler m.

forlorn [fə'lɔ:n] a (person) verlassen; (hope) vergeblich.

form [fɔ:m] n Form f; (type) Art f; (figure) Gestalt f; (SCH) Klasse f; (bench) (Schul)bank f; (document) Formular nt // vt formen; (be part of) bilden.

formal ['fɔ:məl] a formell; (occasion) offiziell; ~**ity** [fɔ:'mælɪtɪ] n Förmlichkeit f; ~**ities** pl Formalitäten pl; ~**ly** ad (ceremoniously) formell; (officially) offiziell.

format ['fɔ:mæt] n Format nt // vt (COMPUT) formatieren.

formation [fɔ:'meɪʃən] n Bildung f; (AVIAT) Formation f.

formative ['fɔ:mətɪv] a (years) formend.

former ['fɔ:mə*] a früher; (opposite of latter) erstere(r, s); ~**ly** ad früher.

formidable ['fɔ:mɪdəbl] a furchtbar.

formula ['fɔ:mjulə] n Formel f; ~**te** ['fɔ:mjʊleɪt] vt formulieren.

forsake [fə'seɪk], pt **forsook** [fə'sʊk], pp **forsaken** [fə'seɪkən] vt verlassen.

fort [fɔ:t] n Feste f, Fort nt.

forte ['fɔ:tɪ] n Stärke f, starke Seite f.

forth [fɔ:θ] ad: **and so** ~ und so weiter; ~**coming** a kommend; (character) entgegenkommend; ~**right** a offen; ~**with** ad umgehend.

fortification [fɔ:tɪfɪ'keɪʃən] n Befestigung f.

fortify ['fɔ:tɪfaɪ] vt (ver)stärken; (protect) befestigen.

fortitude ['fɔ:tɪtjuːd] n Seelenstärke f.

fortnight ['fɔ:tnaɪt] n vierzehn Tage pl; ~**ly** a zweiwöchentlich // ad alle vierzehn Tage.

fortress ['fɔ:trɪs] n Festung f.

fortuitous [fɔ:'tjuːɪtəs] a zufällig.

fortunate ['fɔ:tʃənɪt] a glücklich; ~**ly** ad glücklicherweise, zum Glück.

fortune ['fɔ:tʃən] n Glück nt; (money) Vermögen nt; ~-**teller** n Wahrsager(in

f) m.

forty ['fɔ:tɪ] num vierzig.

forum ['fɔ:rəm] n Forum nt.

forward ['fɔ:wəd] a vordere(r, s); (movement) vorwärts; (person) vorlaut; (planning) Voraus- // ad vorwärts // n (SPORT) Stürmer m // vt (send) schicken; (help) fördern; ~(**s**) ad vorwärts.

forwent [fɔ:'went] pt of **forgo**.

fossil ['fɒsl] n Fossil nt, Versteinerung f.

foster ['fɒstə*] vt (talent) fördern; ~ **child** n Pflegekind nt; ~ **mother** n Pflegemutter f.

fought [fɔ:t] pt, pp of **fight**.

foul [faʊl] a schmutzig; (language) gemein; (weather) schlecht // n (SPORT) Foul nt // vt (mechanism) blockieren; (SPORT) foulen; ~ **play** n (SPORT) Foulspiel nt; (LAW) Verbrechen nt.

found [faʊnd] pt, pp of **find** // vt gründen; ~**ation** [faʊn'deɪʃən] n (act) Gründung f; (fig) Fundament nt; (also: ~ation **cream**) Grundierungscreme f; ~**ations** pl Fundament nt.

founder ['faʊndə*] n Gründer(in f) m // vi sinken.

foundry ['faʊndrɪ] n Gießerei f.

fountain [faʊntɪn] n (Spring)brunnen m; ~ **pen** n Füllfederhalter m.

four [fɔ:*] num vier; **on all** ~**s** auf allen vieren; ~-**poster** n Himmelbett nt; ~**some** n Quartett nt; ~**teen** num vierzehn; ~**teenth** a vierzehnte(r, s) ~**th** a vierte(r, s).

fowl [faʊl] n Huhn nt; (food) Geflügel nt.

fox [fɒks] n Fuchs m // vt täuschen; ~**trot** n Foxtrott m.

foyer ['fɔɪeɪ] n Foyer nt, Vorhalle f.

fraction ['frækʃən] n (MATH) Bruch m; (part) Bruchteil m.

fracture ['fræktʃə*] n (MED) Bruch m // vt brechen.

fragile ['frædʒaɪl] a zerbrechlich.

fragment ['frægmənt] n Bruchstück nt; (small part) Splitter m.

fragrance ['freɪɡrəns] n Duft m.

fragrant ['freɪɡrənt] a duftend.

frail [freɪl] a schwach, gebrechlich.

frame [freɪm] n Rahmen m; (of spectacles: also: ~**s**) Gestell nt; (body) Gestalt f // vt einrahmen; (col: incriminate): **to** ~ **sb** jdm etw anhängen; ~ **of mind** n Verfassung f; ~**work** n Rahmen m; (of society) Gefüge nt.

France [frɑːns] n Frankreich nt.

franchise ['fræntʃaɪz] n (POL) (aktives) Wahlrecht nt; (COMM) Lizenz f.

frank [fræŋk] a offen // vt (letter) frankieren; ~**ly** ad offen gesagt; ~**ness** n Offenheit f.

frantic ['fræntɪk] a verzweifelt.

fraternal [frə'tɜ:nl] a brüderlich.

fraternity [frə'tɜ:nɪtɪ] n (club) Vereini-

gung f; (spirit) Brüderlichkeit f; (US SCH) Studentenverbindung f.
fraternize ['frætənaɪz] vi fraternisieren.
fraud [frɔːd] n (trickery) Betrug m; (person) Schwindler(in f) m.
fraudulent ['frɔːdjʊlənt] a betrügerisch.
fraught [frɔːt] a voller (with gen).
fray [freɪ] n Rauferei f // vti ausfransen; tempers were ~ed die Gemüter waren erhitzt.
freak [friːk] n Monstrosität f; (storm etc) Ausnahmeerscheinung f.
freckle ['frekl] n Sommersprosse f.
free [friː] a frei; (loose) sich; (liberal) freigebig // vt (set free) befreien; (unblock) freimachen; ~ (of charge), for ~ ad gratis, umsonst; ~dom n Freiheit f; ~-for-all n (fight) allgemeine(s) Handgemenge nt; ~ gift n Geschenk nt; ~hold property n (freie(r)) Grundbesitz m; ~ kick n Freistoß m; ~lance a frei; (artist) freischaffend; ~ly ad frei; (admit) offen; ~mason n Freimaurer m; ~post n ≈ Gebühr zahlt Empfänger; ~-range a (hen) Farmhof-; (eggs) Land-; ~ trade n Freihandel m; ~way n (US) Autobahn f; ~wheel vi im Freilauf fahren; ~ will n: of one's own ~ will aus freien Stücken.
freeze [friːz] v (pt froze, pp frozen) vi gefrieren; (feel cold) frieren // vt (lit, fig) einfrieren // n (fig, FIN) Stopp m; ~r n Tiefkühltruhe f; (in fridge) Gefrierfach nt.
freezing ['friːzɪŋ] a eisig; (~ cold) eiskalt; ~ point n Gefrierpunkt m.
freight [freɪt] n Fracht f; ~ train n Güterzug m.
French [frentʃ] a französisch // n (LING) Französisch nt; the ~ pl die Franzosen; ~ bean n grüne Bohne f; ~ fried (potatoes) (Brit), ~ fries (US) npl Pommes frites pl; ~man/woman n Franzose m/Französin f; ~ window n Verandatür f.
frenzy ['frenzɪ] n Raserei f.
frequency ['friːkwənsɪ] n Häufigkeit f; (PHYS) Frequenz f.
frequent ['friːkwənt] a häufig // [frɪ'kwent] vt (regelmäßig) besuchen.
fresco ['freskəʊ] n Fresko nt.
fresh [freʃ] a frisch; ~en vi (also: ~en up) (sich) auffrischen; (person) sich frisch machen; ~er n (Brit UNIV: col) Erstsemester nt; ~ly ad gerade; ~man n (US) = ~er; ~ness n Frische f; ~water a (fish) Süßwasser-.
fret [fret] vi sich (dat) Sorgen machen.
friar ['fraɪə*] n Klosterbruder m.
friction ['frɪkʃən] n (lit, fig) Reibung f.
Friday ['fraɪdeɪ] n Freitag m.
fridge [frɪdʒ] n (Brit) Kühlschrank m.
fried [fraɪd] a gebraten.
friend [frend] n Freund(in f) m; ~liness n Freundlichkeit f; ~ly a

freundlich; (relations) freundschaftlich; ~ship n Freundschaft f.
frieze [friːz] n Fries m.
frigate ['frɪgɪt] n Fregatte f.
fright [fraɪt] n Schrecken m; to take ~ es mit der Angst zu tun bekommen; ~en vt erschrecken; to be ~ened Angst haben; ~ening a schrecklich; ~ful a, ~fully ad (col) furchtbar.
frigid ['frɪdʒɪd] a (woman) frigide.
frill [frɪl] n Rüsche f.
fringe [frɪndʒ] n Besatz m; (Brit: of hair) Pony m; (fig) Peripherie f; ~ benefits npl zusätzliche Leistungen pl.
frisk [frɪsk] vt durchsuchen.
frisky ['frɪskɪ] a lebendig, ausgelassen.
fritter ['frɪtə*] vt: to ~ away vergeuden.
frivolous ['frɪvələs] a frivol.
frizzy ['frɪzɪ] a kraus.
fro [frəʊ] see to.
frock [frɒk] n Kleid nt.
frog [frɒg] n Frosch m; ~man n Froschmann m.
frolic ['frɒlɪk] vi ausgelassen sein.
from [frɒm] prep 1 (indicating starting place) von; (indicating origin etc) aus (+dat); a letter/telephone call ~ my sister ein Brief/Anruf von meiner Schwester; where do you come ~? woher kommen Sie?; to drink ~ the bottle aus der Flasche trinken
2 (indicating time) von ... an; (: past) seit; ~ one o'clock to or until or till two von ein Uhr bis zwei; ~ January (on) ab Januar
3 (indicating distance) von ... (entfernt)
4 (indicating price, number etc) ab (+dat); ~ £10 ab £10; there were ~ 20 to 30 people there es waren zwischen 20 und 30 Leute da
5 (indicating difference): he can't tell red ~ green er kann nicht zwischen rot und grün unterscheiden; to be different ~ sb/sth anders sein als jd/etw
6 (because of, on the basis of): ~ what he says aus dem, was er sagt; weak ~ hunger schwach vor Hunger.
front [frʌnt] n Vorderseite f; (of house) Fassade f; (promenade: also: sea ~) Strandpromenade f; (MIL, POL, MET) Front f; (fig: appearances) Fassade f // a (forward) vordere(r, s), Vorder-; (first) vorderste(r, s); in ~ ad vorne; in ~ of vor; ~age n Vorderfront f; ~al a frontal, Vorder-; ~ier ['frʌntɪə*] n Grenze f; ~ door n Haustür f; ~ page n Titelseite f; ~ room n (Brit) Wohnzimmer nt; ~-wheel drive n Vorderradantrieb m.
frost [frɒst] n Frost m; ~bite n Erfrierung f; ~ed a (glass) Milch-; ~y a frostig.
froth [frɒθ] n Schaum m.
frown [fraʊn] n Stirnrunzeln nt // vi die Stirn runzeln.

froze [frəuz] *pt of* **freeze.**

frozen [ˈfrəuzn] *pp of* **freeze.**

frugal [ˈfruːgəl] *a* sparsam, bescheiden.

fruit [fruːt] *n, pl inv (as collective)* Obst *nt; (particular)* Frucht *f;* **~erer** *n* Obsthändler *m;* **~erer's (shop)** *n* Obsthandlung *f;* **~ful** *a* fruchtbar; **~ion** [fruːˈɪʃən] *n:* to come to **~ion** in Erfüllung gehen; **~ juice** *n* Fruchtsaft *m;* **~ machine** *n (Brit)* Spielautomat *m;* **~ salad** *n* Obstsalat *m.*

frustrate [frʌsˈtreɪt] *vt* vereiteln; **~d** *a* gehemmt; *(PSYCH)* frustriert.

fry [fraɪ], *pt, pp* **fried** *vt* braten; small **~** *pl* kleine Fische *pl;* **~ing pan** *n* Bratpfanne *f.*

ft. *abbr of* foot, feet.

fuddy-duddy [ˈfʌdɪdʌdɪ] *n* altmodische(r) Kauz *m.*

fudge [fʌdʒ] *n* Karamellen *pl.*

fuel [fjuəl] *n* Treibstoff *m; (for heating)* Brennstoff *m; (for lighter)* Benzin *nt;* **~ oil** *n (diesel fuel)* Heizöl *nt;* **~ tank** *n* Tank *m.*

fugitive [ˈfjuːdʒɪtɪv] *n* Flüchtling *m.*

fulfil [fulˈfɪl] *vt (duty)* erfüllen; *(promise)* einhalten; **~ment** *n* Erfüllung *f.*

full [ful] *a (box, bottle, price)* voll; *(person: satisfied)* satt; *(member, power, employment, moon)* Voll-; *(complete)* vollständig, Voll-; *(speed)* höchste(r, s); *(skirt)* weit // *ad:* **~ well** sehr wohl; **in ~** vollständig; **~-length** *a (portrait)* lebensgroß; **~ moon** *n* Vollmond *m;* **~-scale** *a (attack)* General-; *(drawing)* in Originalgröße; **~ stop** *n* Punkt *m;* **~-time** *a (job)* Ganztags- // *ad (work)* ganztags // *n (SPORT)* Spielschluß *nt;* **~y** *ad* völlig; **~y-fledged** *a (lit, fig)* flügge.

fulsome [ˈfulsəm] *a* übertrieben.

fumble [ˈfʌmbl] *vi* herumfummeln *(with an +dat).*

fume [fjuːm] *vi* qualmen; *(fig)* kochen *(col);* **~s** *pl* Abgase *pl.*

fumigate [ˈfjuːmɪgeɪt] *vt* ausräuchern.

fun [fʌn] *n* Spaß *m;* to make **~** of sich lustig machen über *(+acc).*

function [ˈfʌŋkʃən] *n* Funktion *f; (occasion)* Veranstaltung *f* // *vi* funktionieren; **~al** *a* funktionell.

fund [fʌnd] *n (money)* Geldmittel *pl,* Fonds *m; (store)* Vorrat *m;* **~s** *pl* Mittel *pl.*

fundamental [fʌndəˈmentl] *a* fundamental, grundlegend.

funeral [ˈfjuːnərəl] *n* Beerdigung *f;* **~ parlour** *n* Leichenhalle *f;* **~ service** *n* Trauergottesdienst *m.*

funfair [ˈfʌnfeə*] *n (Brit)* Jahrmarkt *m.*

fungus [ˈfʌŋgəs], *pl* **-gi** [ˈfʌŋgaɪ] *n* Pilz *m.*

funnel [ˈfʌnl] *n* Trichter *m; (NAUT)* Schornstein *m.*

funny [ˈfʌnɪ] *a* komisch.

fur [fɜː*] *n* Pelz *m;* **~ coat** *n* Pelzmantel *m.*

furious [ˈfjuərɪəs] *a* wütend; *(attempt)* heftig.

furlong [ˈfɜːlɒŋ] *n* = 220 yards.

furlough [ˈfɜːləu] *n (US MIL)* Urlaub *m.*

furnace [ˈfɜːnɪs] *n* (Brenn)ofen *m.*

furnish [ˈfɜːnɪʃ] *vt* einrichten; *(supply)* versehen; **~ings** *npl* Einrichtung *f.*

furniture [ˈfɜːnɪtʃə*] *n* Möbel *pl;* piece of **~** Möbelstück *nt.*

furrow [ˈfʌrəu] *n* Furche *f.*

furry [ˈfɜːrɪ] *a (tongue)* pelzig; *(animal)* Pelz-.

further [ˈfɜːðə*] *a* weitere(r, s) // *ad* weiter // *vt* fördern; **~ education** *n* Weiterbildung *f;* Erwachsenenbildung *f;* **~more** *ad* ferner.

furthest [ˈfɜːðɪst] *superl of* **far.**

furtive [ˈfɜːtɪv] *a* verstohlen.

fury [ˈfjuərɪ] *n* Wut *f,* Zorn *m.*

fuse [fjuːz] *n (ELEC)* Sicherung *f; (of bomb)* Zünder *m* // *vt* verschmelzen // *vi (Brit ELEC)* durchbrennen; **~ box** *n* Sicherungskasten *m.*

fuselage [ˈfjuːzəlɑːʒ] *n* Flugzeugrumpf *m.*

fusion [ˈfjuːʒən] *n* Verschmelzung *f.*

fuss [fʌs] *n* Theater *nt;* **~y** *a* kleinlich.

futile [ˈfjuːtaɪl] *a* zwecklos, sinnlos.

futility [fjuːˈtɪlɪtɪ] *n* Zwecklosigkeit *f.*

future [ˈfjuːtʃə*] *a* zukünftig // *n* Zukunft *f;* in (the) **~** in Zukunft.

fuze [fjuːz] *(US)* = **fuse.**

fuzzy [ˈfʌzɪ] *a (indistinct)* verschwommen; *(hair)* kraus.

G

G [dʒiː] *n (MUS)* G *nt.*

gabble [ˈgæbl] *vi* plappern.

gable [ˈgeɪbl] *n* Giebel *m.*

gadget [ˈgædʒɪt] *n* Vorrichtung *f.*

Gaelic [ˈgeɪlɪk] *a* gälisch // *n (LING)* Gälisch *nt.*

gaffe [gæf] *n* Fauxpas *m.*

gag [gæg] *n* Knebel *m; (THEAT)* Gag *m* // *vt* knebeln.

gaily [ˈgeɪlɪ] *ad* lustig, fröhlich.

gain [geɪn] *vt (obtain)* erhalten; *(win)* gewinnen // *vi (improve)* gewinnen *(in an +dat); (clock)* vorgehen // *n* Gewinn *m;* to **~ on** sb jdn einholen.

gait [geɪt] *n* Gang *m.*

gal. *abbr of* **gallon.**

gala [ˈgɑːlə] *n* Fest *nt.*

galaxy [ˈgæləksɪ] *n* Sternsystem *nt.*

gale [geɪl] *n* Sturm *m.*

gallant [ˈgælənt] *a* tapfer; *(polite)* galant; **~ry** *n* Tapferkeit *f;* Galanterie *f.*

gallbladder [ˈgɔːlblædə*] *n* Gallenblase *f.*

gallery [ˈgælərɪ] *n (also: art ~)* Galerie

f.

galley ['gælɪ] *n* (*ship's kitchen*) Kombüse *f*; (*ship*) Galeere *f*.

gallon ['gælən] *n* Gallone *f*.

gallop ['gæləp] *n* Galopp *m* // *vi* galoppieren.

gallows ['gæləʊz] *n* Galgen *m*.

gallstone ['gɔːlstəʊn] *n* Gallenstein *m*.

galore [gə'lɔː*] *ad* in Hülle und Fülle.

galvanize ['gælvənaɪz] *vt* (*metal*) galvanisieren; (*fig*) elektrisieren.

gamble ['gæmbl] *vi* (*um Geld*) spielen // *vt* (*risk*) aufs Spiel setzen // *n* Risiko *nt*; ~**r** *n* Spieler(in *f*) *m*.

gambling ['gæmblɪŋ] *n* Glücksspiel *nt*.

game [geɪm] *n* Spiel *nt*; (*hunting*) Wild *nt* // *a* bereit (*for* zu); ~**keeper** *n* Wildhüter *m*.

gammon ['gæmən] *n* geräucherte(r) Schinken *m*.

gamut ['gæmət] *n* Tonskala *f*.

gang [gæŋ] *n* (*of criminals, youths*) Bande *f*; (*of workmen*) Kolonne *f* // *vi*: to ~ up on sb sich gegen jdn verschwören.

gangrene ['gæŋgriːn] *n* Brand *m*.

gangster ['gæŋstə*] *n* Gangster *m*.

gangway ['gæŋweɪ] *n* (*NAUT*) Laufplanke *f*; (*aisle*) Gang *m*.

gaol [dʒeɪl] (*Brit*) = **jail**.

gap [gæp] *n* Lücke *f*.

gape [geɪp] *vi* glotzen.

gaping ['geɪpɪŋ] *a* (*wound*) klaffend; (*hole*) gähnend.

garage ['gærɑːʒ] *n* Garage *f*; (*for repair*) (Auto)reparaturwerkstatt *f*; (*for petrol*) Tankstelle *f*.

garbage ['gɑːbɪdʒ] *n* Abfall *m*; ~ can *n* (*US*) Mülltonne *f*.

garbled ['gɑːbld] *a* (*story*) verdreht.

garden ['gɑːdn] *n* Garten *m*; ~**er** *n* Gärtner(in *f*) *m*; ~**ing** *n* Gärtnern *nt*.

gargle ['gɑːgl] *vi* gurgeln.

gargoyle ['gɑːgɔɪl] *n* Wasserspeier *m*.

garish ['gɛərɪʃ] *a* grell.

garland ['gɑːlənd] *n* Girlande *f*.

garlic ['gɑːlɪk] *n* Knoblauch *m*.

garment ['gɑːmənt] *n* Kleidungsstück *nt*.

garnish ['gɑːnɪʃ] *vt* (*food*) garnieren.

garrison ['gærɪsən] *n* Garnison *f*.

garrulous ['gærʊləs] *a* geschwätzig.

garter ['gɑːtə*] *n* (*US*) Strumpfband *nt*.

gas [gæs] *n* Gas *nt*; (*esp US: petrol*) Benzin *nt* // *vt* vergasen; ~ **cooker** *n* (*Brit*) Gasherd *m*; ~ **cylinder** *n* Gasflasche *f*; ~ **fire** *n* Gasofen *m*.

gash [gæʃ] *n* klaffende Wunde *f* // *vt* tief verwunden.

gasket ['gæskɪt] *n* Dichtungsring *m*.

gas: ~**mask** *n* Gasmaske *f*; ~ **meter** *n* Gaszähler *m*.

gasoline ['gæsəliːn] *n* (*US*) Benzin *nt*.

gasp [gɑːsp] *vi* keuchen; (*in astonishment*) tief Luft holen // *n* Keu-

chen *nt*.

gas: ~ **ring** *n* Gasring *m*; ~**sy** *a* (*drink*) sprudelnd; ~ **tap** *n* Gashahn *m*.

gastric ['gæstrɪk] *a* Magen-.

gate [geɪt] *n* Tor *nt*; (*barrier*) Schranke *f*; ~**crash** *vt* (*Brit: party*) platzen in (+*acc*); ~**way** *n* Toreingang *m*.

gather ['gæðə*] *vt* (*people*) versammeln; (*things*) sammeln // *vi* (*understand*) annehmen; (*deduce*) schließen (*from* aus); (*assemble*) sich versammeln; to ~ speed schneller werden; ~**ing** *n* Versammlung *f*.

gauche [gəʊʃ] *a* linkisch.

gaudy ['gɔːdɪ] *a* schreiend.

gauge [geɪdʒ] *n* (*instrument*) Meßgerät *nt*; (*RAIL*) Spurweite *f*; (*dial*) Anzeiger *m*; (*measure*) Maß *nt* // *vt* (*lit*) (ab)messen; (*fig*) abschätzen.

gaunt [gɔːnt] *a* hager.

gauntlet ['gɔːntlɪt] *n* (*knight's*) (Fehde)handschuh *m*.

gauze [gɔːz] *n* Gaze *f*.

gave [geɪv] *pt of* **give**.

gay [geɪ] *a* (*homosexual*) schwul; (*lively*) lustig.

gaze [geɪz] *n* Blick *m* // *vi* (an)blicken (*at* acc).

gazelle [gə'zel] *n* Gazelle *f*.

gazetteer [gæzɪ'tɪə*] *n* geographische(s) Lexikon *nt*.

gazumping [gə'zʌmpɪŋ] *n* (*Brit*) Verkauf eines Hauses an einen zweiten Bieter trotz Zusage an den ersten.

GB *n abbr* (= *Great Britain*) GB.

GCE *n abbr* (*Brit*) of **General Certificate of Education**.

GCSE *n abbr* (*Brit*: = *General Certificate of Secondary Education*) ≈ Hauptschulabschluß *m*.

gear [gɪə*] *n* Getriebe *nt*; (*equipment*) Ausrüstung *f*; (*AUT*) Gang *m* // *vt* (*fig: adapt*): to be ~ed to ausgerichtet sein (*to* auf +*acc*); top or (*US*) high/low ~ höchste(r)/niedrige(r) Gang *m*; in ~ eingekuppelt; ~ box *n* Getriebe(gehäuse) *nt*; ~ lever, ~ shift (*US*) *n* Schalthebel *m*.

geese [giːs] *npl of* **goose**.

gel [dʒel] *n* Gel *nt*.

gelatin(e) ['dʒelətiːn] *n* Gelatine *f*.

gelignite ['dʒelɪgnaɪt] *n* Plastiksprengstoff *m*.

gem [dʒem] *n* Edelstein *m*; (*fig*) Juwel *nt*.

Gemini ['dʒemɪniː] *n* Zwillinge *pl*.

gender ['dʒendə*] *n* (*GRAM*) Geschlecht *nt*.

gene [dʒiːn] *n* Gen *nt*.

general ['dʒenərəl] *n* General *m* // *a* allgemein; ~ **delivery** *n* (*US*) Ausgabe(schalter *m*) *f* postlagernder Sendungen; ~ **election** *n* allgemeine Wahlen *pl*; ~**ization** [-aɪ'zeɪʃən] *n* Verallgemeinerung *f*; ~**ize** *vi* verallgemeinern; **~ly** *ad* allgemein, im allgemeinen; **~ practitioner (G.P.)** *n* praktische(r) Arzt *m*, praktische Ärztin *f*.

generate ['dʒenəreɪt] *vt* erzeugen.

generation [dʒenə'reɪʃən] *n* Generation *f*; (*act*) Erzeugung *f*.

generator ['dʒenəreɪtə*] *n* Generator *m*.

generosity [dʒenə'rɒsɪtɪ] *n* Großzügigkeit *f*.

generous ['dʒenərəs] *a* großzügig.

genetics [dʒɪ'netɪks] *n* Genetik *f*.

Geneva [dʒɪ'niːvə] *n* Genf *nt*.

genial ['dʒiːnɪəl] *a* freundlich, jovial.

genitals ['dʒenɪtlz] *npl* Genitalien *pl*.

genius ['dʒiːnɪəs] *n* Genie *nt*.

genocide ['dʒenəʊsaɪd] *n* Völkermord *m*.

gent [dʒent] *n abbr of* **gentleman**.

genteel [dʒen'tiːl] *a* (*polite*) wohlanständig; (*affected*) affektiert.

gentle ['dʒentl] *a* sanft, zart.

gentleman ['dʒentlmən] *n* Herr *m*; (*polite*) Gentleman *m*.

gentleness ['dʒentlnɪs] *n* Zartheit *f*, Milde *f*.

gently ['dʒentlɪ] *ad* zart, sanft.

gentry ['dʒentrɪ] *n* Landadel *m*.

gents [dʒents] *n*: G~ (*lavatory*) Herren.

genuine ['dʒenjʊɪn] *a* echt.

geographic(al) [dʒɪə'græfɪk(əl)] *a* geographisch.

geography [dʒɪ'ɒgrəfɪ] *n* Geographie *f*.

geological [dʒɪəʊ'lɒdʒɪkəl] *a* geologisch.

geologist [dʒɪ'ɒlədʒɪst] *n* Geologe *m*, Geologin *f*.

geology [dʒɪ'ɒlədʒɪ] *n* Geologie *f*.

geometry [dʒɪ'ɒmɪtrɪ] *n* Geometrie *f*.

geranium [dʒɪ'reɪnɪəm] *n* Geranie *f*.

geriatric [dʒerɪ'ætrɪk] *a* Alten- // *n* Greis(in *f*) *m*.

germ [dʒɜːm] *n* Keim *m*; (*MED*) Bazillus *m*.

German ['dʒɜːmən] *a* deutsch // *n* Deutsche(r) *mf*; (*LING*) Deutsch *nt*; **~ measles** *n* Röteln *pl*.

Germany ['dʒɜːmənɪ] *n* Deutschland *nt*.

germination [dʒɜːmɪ'neɪʃən] *n* Keimen *nt*.

gesticulate [dʒes'tɪkjʊleɪt] *vi* gestikulieren.

gesture ['dʒestʃə*] *n* Geste *f*.

get [get], *pt, pp* **got**, *pp* **gotten** (*US*) ◆*vi* **1** (*become, be*) werden; **to ~ old/tired** alt/müde werden; **to ~ married** heiraten

2 (*go*) (an)kommen, gehen

3 (*begin*): **to ~ to know sb** jdn kennenlernen; **let's ~ going** *or* **started** fangen wir an!

4 (*modal aux v*): **you've got to do it** du mußt es tun

◆*vt* **1**: **to ~ sth done** (*do*) etw machen;

(*have done*) etw machen lassen; **to ~ sth going** *or* **to go etw** in Gang bringen *or* bekommen; **to ~ sb to do sth** jdn dazu bringen, etw zu tun

2 (*obtain: money, permission, results*) erhalten; (*find: job, flat*) finden; (*catch: person, doctor, object*) holen; **to ~ sth for sb** jdm etw besorgen; **~ me Mr Jones, please** (*TEL*) verbinden Sie mich bitte mit Mr Jones

3 (*receive: present, letter*) bekommen, kriegen; (*acquire: reputation etc*) erwerben

4 (*catch*) bekommen, kriegen; (*hit: target etc*) treffen, erwischen; **~ him!** (*to dog*) faß!

5 (*take, move*) bringen; **to ~ sth to sb** jdm etw bringen

6 (*understand*) verstehen; (*hear*) mitbekommen; **I've got it!** ich hab's!

7 (*have, possess*): **to have got** etw haben.

get about *vi* herumkommen; (*news*) sich verbreiten

get along *vi* (*people*) (gut) zurechtkommen; (*depart*) sich (*acc*) auf den Weg machen

get at *vt* (*facts*) herausbekommen; **to ~ at sb** (*nag*) an jdm herumnörgeln

get away *vi* (*leave*) sich (*acc*) davonmachen; (*escape*) entkommen (*from dat*); **to ~ away with sth** mit etw davon kommen

get back *vi* (*return*) zurückkommen // *vt* zurückbekommen

get by *vi* (*pass*) vorbeikommen; (*manage*) zurechtkommen

get down *vi* (*her*)untergehen // *vt* (*depress*) fertigmachen; **to ~ down to** in Angriff nehmen; (*find time to do*) kommen zu

get in *vi* (*train*) ankommen; (*arrive home*) heimkommen

get into *vt* (*enter*) hinein-/ hereinkommen in (+*acc*); (: *car train etc*) einsteigen in (+*acc*); (*clothes*) anziehen

get off *vi* (*from train etc*) aussteigen; (*from horse*) absteigen // *vt* aussteigen aus; absteigen von

get on *vi* (*progress*) vorankommen; (*be friends*) auskommen; (*age*) alt werden; (*onto train etc*) einsteigen; (*onto horse*) aufsteigen // *vt* einsteigen in (+*acc*); aufsteigen auf (+*acc*)

get out *vi* (*of house*) herauskommen; (*of vehicle*) aussteigen // *vt* (*take out*) herausholen

get out of *vt* (*duty etc*) herumkommen um

get over *vt* (*illness*) sich (*acc*) erholen von; (*surprise*) verkraften; (*news*) fassen; (*loss*) sich abfinden mit

get round *vt* herumkommen; (*fig: person*) herumkriegen

get through to vt (TEL) durchkommen zu

get together vi zusammenkommen

get up vi aufstehen // vt hinaufbringen; (go up) hinaufgehen; (organize) auf die Beine stellen

get up to vt (reach) erreichen; (prank etc) anstellen.

getaway ['getəweɪ] n Flucht f.

geyser ['gi:zə*] n Geiser m; (heater) Durchlauferhitzer m.

ghastly ['ga:stlɪ] a (horrible) gräßlich.

gherkin ['gə:kɪn] n Gewürzgurke f.

ghetto ['getəʊ] n G(h)etto nt.

ghost [gəʊst] n Gespenst nt; ~ly a gespenstisch.

giant ['dʒaɪənt] n Riese m // a riesig, Riesen-.

gibberish ['dʒɪbərɪʃ] n dumme(s) Geschwätz nt.

gibe [dʒaɪb] n spöttische Bemerkung f.

giblets ['dʒɪblɪts] npl Geflügelinnereien pl.

giddiness ['gɪdɪnəs] n Schwindelgefühl nt.

giddy ['gɪdɪ] a schwindlig.

gift [gɪft] n Geschenk nt; (ability) Begabung f; ~ed a begabt; ~ token or **voucher** n Geschenkgutschein m.

gigantic [dʒaɪˈgæntɪk] a riesenhaft.

giggle ['gɪgl] vi kichern // n Gekicher nt.

gild [gɪld] vt vergolden.

gill [dʒɪl] n (1/4 pint) Viertelpinte f // n [gɪl] (of fish) Kieme f.

gilt [gɪlt] n Vergoldung f // a vergoldet; ~-edged a mündelsicher.

gimmick ['gɪmɪk] n Gag m.

gin [dʒɪn] n Gin m.

ginger ['dʒɪndʒə*] n Ingwer m; ~ **ale** n, ~ **beer** n Ingwerbier nt; ~**bread** n Pfefferkuchen m; ~-**haired** a rothaarig.

gingerly ['dʒɪndʒəlɪ] ad behutsam.

gipsy ['dʒɪpsɪ] n Zigeuner(in f) m.

giraffe [dʒɪˈrɑ:f] n Giraffe f.

girder ['gɜ:də*] n Eisenträger m.

girdle ['gɜ:dl] n Hüftgürtel m.

girl [gɜ:l] n Mädchen nt; ~**friend** n Freundin f; ~**ish** a mädchenhaft.

giro ['dʒaɪrəʊ] n (bank ~) Giro nt; (post office ~) Postscheckverkehr m.

girth [gɜ:θ] n (measure) Umfang m; (strap) Sattelgurt m.

gist [dʒɪst] n Wesentliche(s) nt.

give [gɪv], pt **gave**, pp **given** vt geben // vi (break) nachgeben; ~ **away** vt (give free) verschenken; (betray) verraten; ~ **back** vt zurückgeben; ~ **in** vi nachgeben // vt (hand in) abgeben; ~ **off** vt abgeben; ~ **out** vt verteilen; (announce) bekanntgeben; ~ **up** vti aufgeben; **to** ~ **o.s. up** sich stellen; (after siege) sich ergeben; ~ **way** vi (Brit: traffic) Vorfahrt lassen; (to feelings) nachgeben (+dat).

glacier ['glæsɪə*] n Gletscher m.

glad [glæd] a froh.

gladioli [glædɪˈəʊlaɪ] npl Gladiolen pl.

gladly ['glædlɪ] ad gern(e).

glamorous ['glæmərəs] a reizvoll.

glamour ['glæmə*] n Glanz m.

glance [glɑ:ns] n Blick m // vi (hin)blicken (at auf +acc); ~ **off** vi (fly off) abprallen von.

glancing ['glɑ:nsɪŋ] a (blow) Streif-.

gland [glænd] n Drüse f.

glare [glɛə*] n (light) grelle(s) Licht nt; (stare) wilde(r) Blick m // vi grell scheinen; (angrily) böse ansehen (at acc).

glaring ['glɛərɪŋ] a (injustice) schreiend; (mistake) kraß.

glass [glɑ:s] n Glas nt; (mirror: also: looking ~) Spiegel m; ~**es** pl Brille f; ~**house** n Gewächshaus nt; ~**ware** n Glaswaren pl; ~**y** a glasig.

glaze [gleɪz] vt verglasen; (finish with a ~) glasieren // n Glasur f; ~**d** a (eye) glasig; (pottery) glasiert.

glazier ['gleɪzɪə*] n Glaser m.

gleam [gli:m] n Schimmer m // vi schimmern; ~**ing** a schimmernd.

glean [gli:n] vt (fig) ausfindig machen.

glee [gli:] n Frohsinn m.

glen [glen] n Bergtal nt.

glib [glɪb] a oberflächlich.

glide [glaɪd] vi gleiten; ~**r** n (AVIAT) Segelflugzeug nt.

gliding ['glaɪdɪŋ] n Segelfliegen nt.

glimmer ['glɪmə*] n Schimmer m.

glimpse [glɪmps] n flüchtige(r) Blick m // vt flüchtig erblicken.

glint [glɪnt] n Glitzern nt // vi glitzern.

glisten ['glɪsn] vi glänzen.

glitter ['glɪtə*] vi funkeln // n Funkeln nt.

gloat [gləʊt] vi: **to** ~ **over** sich weiden an (+dat).

global ['gləʊbl] a global.

globe [gləʊb] n Erdball m; (sphere) Globus m.

gloom [glu:m] n (darkness) Dunkel nt; (depression) düstere Stimmung f; ~**y** a düster.

glorify ['glɔ:rɪfaɪ] vt verherrlichen.

glorious ['glɔ:rɪəs] a glorreich.

glory ['glɔ:rɪ] n Ruhm m.

gloss [glɒs] n (shine) Glanz m; ~ **over** vt übertünchen.

glossary ['glɒsərɪ] n Glossar nt.

glossy ['glɒsɪ] a (surface) glänzend.

glove [glʌv] n Handschuh m; ~ **compartment** n (AUT) Handschuhfach m.

glow [gləʊ] vi glühen // n Glühen nt.

glower ['glaʊə*] vi: **to** ~ **at** finster anblicken.

glucose ['glu:kəʊs] n Traubenzucker m.

glue [glu:] n Klebstoff m // vt kleben.

glum [glʌm] a bedrückt.

glut [glʌt] n Überfluß m.

glutton ['glʌtn] n Vielfraß m; a ~ **for** work ein Arbeitstier nt; ~**y** n Völlerei f.

glycerin(e) ['glɪsəriːn] *n* Glyzerin *nt*.

gnarled [nɑːld] *a* knorrig.

gnat [næt] *n* Stechmücke *f*.

gnaw [nɔː] *vt* nagen an (+*dat*).

gnome [nəʊm] *n* Gnom *m*.

go [gəʊ], *pt* went, *pp* gone *vi* gehen; (*travel*), reisen, fahren; (*depart: train*) (ab)fahren; (*be sold*) verkauft werden; (*work*) gehen, funktionieren; (*fit, suit*) passen (*with* zu); (*become*) werden; (*break etc*) nachgeben // *n* (*pl* ~es) (*energy*) Schwung *m*; (*attempt*) Versuch *m*; he's going to do it er wird es tun; to ~ **for a walk** spazieren gehen; to ~ **dancing** tanzen gehen; how did it ~? wie war's?; to have a ~ at sth etw versuchen; to be on the ~ auf Trab sein; whose ~ is it? wer ist dran?; ~ **about** *vi* (*rumour*) umgehen // *vt*: how do I ~ about this? wie packe ich das an?; ~ **ahead** *vi* (*proceed*) weitergehen; ~ **along** *vi* dahingehen, dahinfahren // *vt* entlanggehen, entlangfahren; to ~ **along with** (*agree to support*) zustimmen (+*dat*); ~ **away** *vi* (*depart*) weggehen; ~ **back** *vi* (*return*) zurückgehen; ~ **back on** *vt* (*promise*) nicht halten; ~ **by** *vi* (*years, time*) vergehen // *vt* sich richten nach; ~ **down** *vi* (*sun*) untergehen // *vt* hinuntergehen, hinunterfahren; ~ **for** *vt* (*fetch*) holen (gehen); (*like*) mögen; (*attack*) sich stürzen auf (+*acc*); ~ **in** *vi* hineingehen; ~ **in for** *vt* (*competition*) teilnehmen an; ~ **into** *vt* (*enter*) hineingehen in (+*acc*); (*study*) sich befassen mit; ~ **off** *vi* (*depart*) weggehen; (*lights*) ausgehen; (*milk etc*) sauer werden; (*explode*) losgehen // *vt* (*dislike*) nicht mehr mögen; ~ **on** *vi* (*continue*) weitergehen; (*col: complain*) meckern; (*lights*) angehen; to ~ **on with** sth mit etw weitermachen; ~ **out** *vi* (*fire, light*) ausgehen; (*of house*) hinausgehen; ~ **over** *vi* (*ship*) kentern // *vt* (*examine, check*) durchgehen; ~ **through** *vt* (*town etc*) durchgehen, durchfahren; ~ **up** *vi* (*price*) steigen; ~ **without** *vt* sich behelfen ohne; (*food*) entbehren.

goad [gəʊd] *vt* anstacheln.

go-ahead ['gəʊəhed] *a* zielstrebig; (*progressive*) fortschrittlich // *n* grüne(s) Licht *nt*.

goal [gəʊl] *n* Ziel *nt*; (*SPORT*) Tor *nt*; ~**keeper** *n* Torwart *m*; ~**post** *n* Torpfosten *m*.

goat [gəʊt] *n* Ziege *f*.

gobble ['gɒbl] *vt* (*also:* ~ **down**, ~ **up**) hinunterschlingen.

go-between ['gəʊbɪtwiːn] *n* Mittelsmann *m*.

goblet ['gɒblɪt] *n* Kelch(glas *nt*) *m*.

god [gɒd] *n* Gott *m*; **G~** *n* Gott *m*; ~**child** *n* Patenkind *nt*; ~**daughter** *n*

Patentochter *f*; ~**dess** *n* Göttin *f*; ~**father** *n* Pate *m*; ~**forsaken** *a* gottverlassen; ~**mother** *n* Patin *f*; ~**send** *n* Geschenk *nt* des Himmels; ~**son** *n* Patensohn *m*.

goggles ['gɒglz] *npl* Schutzbrille *f*.

going ['gəʊɪŋ] *n* (*horse-racing*) Bahn *f* // *a* (*rate*) gängig; (*concern*) gutgehend; it's hard ~ es ist schwierig.

gold [gəʊld] *n* Gold *nt* // *a* golden; ~**en** *a* golden, Gold-; ~**fish** *n* Goldfisch *m*; ~**mine** *n* Goldgrube *f*; ~**plated** *a* vergoldet; ~**smith** *n* Goldschmied (in *f*) *m*.

golf [gɒlf] *n* Golf *nt*; ~**ball** *n* (*also on typewriter*) Golfball *m*; ~ **club** *n* (*society*) Golfklub *m*; (*stick*) Golfschläger *m*; ~ **course** *n* Golfplatz *m*; ~**er** *n* Golfspieler (in *f*) *m*.

gondola ['gɒndələ] *n* Gondel *f*.

gone [gɒn] *pp* of **go**.

gong [gɒŋ] *n* Gong *m*.

good [gʊd] *a* (*benefit*) Wohl *nt*; (*moral excellence*) Güte *f* // *a* gut; ~**s** *pl* Waren *pl*, Güter *pl*; **a ~ deal** (*of*) ziemlich viel; **a ~ many** ziemlich viele; ~**bye!** *interj* auf Wiedersehen!; **G~ Friday** *n* Karfreitag *m*; ~**looking** *a* gutaussehend; ~ **morning!** *interj* guten Morgen!; ~**natured** *a* gutmütig; (*joke*) harmlos; ~**ness** *n* Güte *f*; (*virtue*) Tugend *f*; ~**s train** *n* (*Brit*) Güterzug; ~**will** *n* (*favour*) Wohlwollen *nt*; (*COMM*) Firmenansehen *nt*.

goose [guːs], *pl* **geese** *n* Gans *f*.

gooseberry ['gʊzbərɪ] *n* Stachelbeere *f*.

gooseflesh ['guːsfleʃ] *n*, **goose pimples** *npl* Gänsehaut *f*.

gore [gɔː*] *vt* aufspießen // *n* Blut *nt*.

gorge [gɔːdʒ] *n* Schlucht *f* // *vr*: to ~ **o.s.** (*sich voll*) fressen.

gorgeous ['gɔːdʒəs] *a* prächtig.

gorilla [gə'rɪlə] *n* Gorilla *m*.

gorse [gɔːs] *n* Stechginster *m*.

gory ['gɔːrɪ] *a* blutig.

go-slow ['gəʊ'sləʊ] *n* (*Brit*) Bummelstreik *m*.

gospel ['gɒspəl] *n* Evangelium *nt*.

gossip ['gɒsɪp] *n* Klatsch *m*; (*person*) Klatschbase *f* // *vi* klatschen.

got [gɒt] *pt, pp* of **get**; ~**ten** (*US*) *pp* of **get**.

gout [gaʊt] *n* Gicht *f*.

govern ['gʌvən] *vt* regieren; verwalten.

governess ['gʌvənɪs] *n* Gouvernante *f*.

government ['gʌvnmənt] *n* Regierung *f*.

governor ['gʌvənə*] *n* Gouverneur *m*.

gown [gaʊn] *n* Gewand *nt*; (*UNIV*) Robe *f*.

G.P. *n abbr of* **general practitioner**.

grab [græb] *vt* packen.

grace [greɪs] *n* Anmut *f*; (*blessing*) Gnade *f*; (*prayer*) Tischgebet *nt* // *vt* (*adorn*) zieren; (*honour*) auszeichnen; **5 days'** ~ 5 Tage Aufschub *m*; ~**ful** *a* an-

mutig.
gracious ['greɪʃəs] *a* gnädig; (*kind*) freundlich.

grade [greɪd] *n* Grad *m*; (*slope*) Gefälle *nt* // *vt* (*classify*) einstufen; ~ **crossing** *n* (*US*) Bahnübergang *m*; ~ **school** *n* (*US*) Grundschule *f*.

gradient ['greɪdɪənt] *n* Steigung *f*; Gefälle *nt*.

gradual ['grædjʊəl] *a* allmählich.

graduate ['grædjʊɪt] *n*: to be a ~ das Staatsexamen haben // *vi* ['grædjʊeɪt] das Staatsexamen machen.

graduation [grædjʊ'eɪʃən] *n* Erlangung *f* eines akademischen Grades.

graffiti [grə'fiːtɪ] *npl* Graffiti *pl*.

graft [grɑːft] *n* (*hard work*) Schufterei *f*; (*MED*) Verpflanzung *f* // *vt* propfen; (*fig*) aufpfropfen; (*MED*) verpflanzen.

grain [greɪn] *n* Korn *nt*; (*in wood*) Maserung *f*.

gram [græm] *n* Gramm *nt*.

grammar ['græmə*] *n* Grammatik *f*; ~ **school** *n* (*Brit*) Gymnasium *nt*.

gramme [græm] = **gram**.

granary ['grænərɪ] *n* Kornspeicher *m*.

grand [grænd] *a* großartig; ~**children** *npl* Enkel *pl*; ~**dad** *n* Opa *m*; ~**daughter** *n* Enkelin *f*; ~**eur** ['grændjə*] *n* Erhabenheit *f*; ~**father** *n* Großvater *m*; ~**iose** ['grændɪəʊs] *a* (*imposing*) großartig; (*pompous*) schwülstig; ~**ma** *n* Oma *f*; ~**mother** *n* Großmutter *f*; ~**pa** *n* = ~**dad**; ~**parents** *npl* Großeltern *pl*; ~ **piano** *n* Flügel *m*; ~**son** *n* Enkel *m*; ~**stand** *n* Haupttribüne *f*.

granite ['grænɪt] *n* Granit *m*.

granny ['grænɪ] *n* Oma *f*.

grant [grɑːnt] *vt* gewähren // *n* Unterstützung *f*; (*UNIV*) Stipendium *nt*; to take sth for ~ed etw als selbstverständlich (an)nehmen.

granulated sugar ['grænjʊleɪtɪd-] *n* Zuckerraffinade *f*.

granule ['grænjuːl] *n* Körnchen *nt*.

grape [greɪp] *n* (Wein)traube *f*.

grapefruit ['greɪpfruːt] *n* Pampelmuse *f*, Grapefruit *f*.

graph [grɑːf] *n* Schaubild *nt*; ~**ic** ['græfɪk] *a* (*descriptive*) anschaulich; (*drawing*) graphisch; ~**ics** ['græfɪks] *npl* Grafik *f*.

grapple ['græpl] *vi*: to ~ with kämpfen mit.

grasp [grɑːsp] *vt* ergreifen; (*understand*) begreifen // *n* Griff *m*; (*of subject*) Beherrschung *f*; ~**ing** *a* habgierig.

grass [grɑːs] *n* Gras *nt*; ~**hopper** *n* Heuschrecke *f*; ~**land** *n* Weideland *nt*; ~-**roots** *a* an der Basis; ~ **snake** *n* Ringelnatter *f*.

grate [greɪt] *n* Kamin *m* // *vi* (*sound*) knirschen; (*on nerves*) zerren (*on* an +*dat*) // *vt* (*cheese*) reiben.

grateful ['greɪtfʊl] *a* dankbar.

grater ['greɪtə*] *n* Reibe *f*.

gratify ['grætɪfaɪ] *vt* befriedigen.

gratifying ['grætɪfaɪɪŋ] *a* erfreulich.

grating ['greɪtɪŋ] *n* (*iron bars*) Gitter *nt* // *a* (*noise*) knirschend.

gratitude ['grætɪtjuːd] *n* Dankbarkeit *f*.

gratuity [grə'tjuːɪtɪ] *n* Gratifikation *f*.

grave [greɪv] *n* Grab *nt* // *a* (*serious*) ernst.

gravel ['grævəl] *n* Kies *m*.

grave: ~ **stone** *n* Grabstein *m*; ~**yard** *n* Friedhof *m*.

gravity ['grævɪtɪ] *n* Schwerkraft *f*; (*seriousness*) Schwere *f*.

gravy ['greɪvɪ] *n* (Braten)soße *f*.

gray [greɪ] *a* = **grey**.

graze [greɪz] *vi* grasen // *vt* (*touch*) streifen; (*MED*) abschürfen // *n* (*MED*) Abschürfung *f*.

grease [griːs] *n* (*fat*) Fett *nt*; (*lubricant*) Schmiere *f* // *vt* (ab)schmieren; ~**proof** *a* (*Brit: paper*) Butterbrot-.

greasy ['griːsɪ] *a* fettig.

great [greɪt] *a* groß; (*col: good*) prima; ~-**grandfather/mother** *m*/mutter *f*; ~**ly** *ad* sehr; ~**ness** *n* Größe *f*.

Greece [griːs] *n* Griechenland *nt*.

greed [griːd] *n* (*also*: ~**iness**) Gier *f* (*for* nach); (*meanness*) Geiz *m*; ~**y** *a* gierig.

Greek [griːk] *a* griechisch // *n* Grieche *m*, Griechin *f*; (*LING*) Griechisch *nt*.

green [griːn] *a* grün // *n* (*village* ~) Dorfwiese *f*; ~ **belt** *n* Grüngürtel *m*; ~ **card** *n* (*AUT*) grüne Versicherungskarte *f*; ~**ery** *n* Grün *nt*; grüne(s) Laub *nt*; ~**gage** *n* Reineclaude *f*; ~**grocer** *n* (*Brit*) Obst- und Gemüsehändler *m*; ~**house** *n* Gewächshaus *nt*; ~**ish** *a* grünlich.

Greenland ['griːnlənd] *n* Grönland *nt*.

greet [griːt] *vt* grüßen; ~**ing** *n* Gruß *m*; ~**ing(s) card** *n* Glückwunschkarte *f*.

gregarious [grɪ'gɛərɪəs] *a* gesellig.

grenade [grɪ'neɪd] *n* Granate *f*.

grew [gruː] *pt of* **grow**.

grey [greɪ] *a* grau; ~-**haired** *a* grauhaarig; ~**hound** *n* Windhund *m*; ~**ish** *a* gräulich.

grid [grɪd] *n* Gitter *nt*; (*ELEC*) Leitungsnetz *nt*; (*on map*) Gitternetz *nt*.

grief [griːf] *n* Gram *m*, Kummer *m*.

grievance ['griːvəns] *n* Beschwerde *f*.

grieve [griːv] *vi* sich grämen // *vt* betrüben.

grievous ['griːvəs] *a*: ~ **bodily harm** (*JUR*) schwere Körperverletzung *f*.

grill [grɪl] *n* Grill *m* // *vt* (*Brit*) grillen; (*question*) in die Mangel nehmen.

grille [grɪl] *n* (*on car etc*) (Kühler)gitter *nt*.

grim [grɪm] *a* grimmig; (*situation*) düster.

grimace [grɪ'meɪs] *n* Grimasse *f* // *vi*

Grimassen schneiden.
grime [graɪm] n Schmutz m.
grimy [ˈgraɪmɪ] a schmutzig.
grin [grɪn] n Grinsen nt // vi grinsen.
grind [graɪnd] vt, pt, pp **ground** mahlen; (US: meat) durch den Fleischwolf drehen; (sharpen) schleifen; (teeth) knirschen mit // n (bore) Plackerei f.
grip [grɪp] n Griff m; (suitcase) Handkoffer m // vt packen; ~**ping** a (exciting) spannend.
grisly [ˈgrɪzlɪ] a gräßlich.
gristle [ˈgrɪsl] n Knorpel m.
grit [grɪt] n Splitt m; (courage) Mut m // vt (teeth) knirschen mit; (road) (mit Splitt (be)streuen.
groan [grəʊn] n Stöhnen nt // vi stöhnen.
grocer [ˈgrəʊsə*] n Lebensmittelhändler m; ~**ies** pl Lebensmittel pl; ~**'s** (shop) n Lebensmittelgeschäft nt.
groggy [ˈgrɒgɪ] a benommen.
groin [grɔɪn] n Leistengegend f.
groom [gruːm] n (also: bride~) Bräutigam m; (for horses) Pferdeknecht m // vt (horse) striegeln; (well-)~ed gepflegt.
groove [gruːv] n Rille f, Furche f.
grope [grəʊp] vi tasten; ~ **for** vt suchen nach.
gross [grəʊs] a (coarse) dick, plump; (bad) grob, schwer; (COMM) brutto; ~**ly** ad höchst.
grotesque [grəʊˈtesk] a grotesk.
grotto [ˈgrɒtəʊ] n Grotte f.
ground [graʊnd] pt, pp of **grind** // n Boden m; (land) Grundbesitz m; (reason) Grund m; (US: also: ~ **wire**) Endleitung f; ~**s** pl (dregs) Bodensatz m; (around house) (Garten)anlagen pl // vi (run ashore) stranden, auflaufen; **on the** ~ am Boden; **to the** ~ zu Boden; **to gain/lose** ~ Boden gewinnen/verlieren; ~ **cloth** n (US) = ~ **sheet**; ~**ing** n (instruction) Anfangsunterricht m; ~**less** a grundlos; ~**sheet** n (Brit) Zeltboden m; ~ **staff** n Bodenpersonal nt; ~ **swell** n (of sea) Dünung; (fig) Zurnahme f; ~**work** n Grundlage f.
group [gruːp] n Gruppe f // vti (also: ~ **together**) (sich) gruppieren.
grouse [graʊs] n, pl inv (bird) schotti-sche(s) Moorhuhn nt // vi (complain) meckern.
grove [grəʊv] n Gehölz nt, Hain m.
grovel [ˈgrɒvl] vi (fig) kriechen.
grow [grəʊ], pt **grew**, pp **grown** vi wachsen; (become) werden // vt (raise) anbauen; ~ **up** vi aufwachsen; ~**er** n Züchter m; ~**ing** a zunehmend.
growl [graʊl] vi knurren.
grown [grəʊn] pp of **grow**; ~-**up** n Erwachsene(r) mf.
growth [grəʊθ] n Wachstum nt; (increase) Zunahme f; (of beard etc)

Wuchs m.
grub [grʌb] n Made f, Larve f; (col: food) Futter nt; ~**by** a schmutzig.
grudge [grʌdʒ] n Groll m // vt misgönnen (sb sth jdm etw); **to bear sb a** ~ einen Groll gegen jdn hegen.
gruelling [ˈgruəlɪŋ] a (climb, race) mörderisch.
gruesome [ˈgruːsəm] a grauenhaft.
gruff [grʌf] a barsch.
grumble [ˈgrʌmbl] vi murren.
grumpy [ˈgrʌmpɪ] a verdrießlich.
grunt [grʌnt] vi grunzen // n Grunzen nt.
G-string [ˈdʒiː-] n Minislip m.
guarantee [gærənˈtiː] n Garantie f // vt garantieren.
guard [gɑːd] n (sentry) Wache f; (Brit: RAIL) Zugbegleiter m // vt bewachen; ~**ed** a vorsichtig; ~**ian** n Vormund m; (keeper) Hüter m; ~**'s van** n (Brit RAIL) Dienstwagen m.
guerrilla [gəˈrɪlə] n Guerilla(kämpfer) m; ~ **warfare** n Guerillakrieg m.
guess [ges] vti (er)raten, schätzen // n Vermutung f; ~**work** n Raterei f.
guest [gest] n Gast m; ~-**house** n Pension f; ~ **room** n Gastzimmer nt.
guffaw [gʌˈfɔː] n schallend lachen.
guidance [ˈgaɪdəns] n (control) Leitung f; (advice) Beratung f.
guide [gaɪd] n Führer m // vt führen; (**girl**) ~ n Pfadfinderin f; ~**book** n Reiseführer m; ~ **dog** n Blindenhund m; ~**lines** npl Richtlinien pl.
guild [gɪld] n (HIST) Gilde f; ~**hall** n (Brit) Stadthalle f.
guile [gaɪl] n Arglist f.
guillotine [ˈgɪləˈtiːn] n Guillotine f.
guilt [gɪlt] n Schuld f; ~**y** a schuldig.
guinea pig [ˈgɪnɪ-] n Meerschweinchen nt; (fig) Versuchskaninchen nt.
guise [gaɪz] n: **in the** ~ of in der Form (+gen).
guitar [gɪˈtɑː*] n Gitarre f.
gulf [gʌlf] n Golf m; (fig) Abgrund m.
gull [gʌl] n Möwe f.
gullet [ˈgʌlɪt] n Schlund m.
gullible [ˈgʌlɪbl] a leichtgläubig.
gully [ˈgʌlɪ] n (Wasser)rinne f.
gulp [gʌlp] vt (also: ~ **down**) hinunter-schlucken // vi (gasp) schlucken.
gum [gʌm] n (around teeth) Zahnfleisch nt; (glue) Klebstoff m; (also: **chewing-**~) Kaugummi m // vt gummieren; ~**boots** npl (Brit) Gummistiefel pl.
gumption [ˈgʌmpʃən] n (col) Mumm m.
gun [gʌn] n Schußwaffe f; ~**boat** n Kanonenboot nt; ~**fire** n Geschützfeuer nt; ~**man** n bewaffnete(r) Verbrecher m; ~**ner** n Kanonier m, Artillerist m; ~**point** n: **at** ~**point** mit Waffengewalt; ~**powder** n Schießpulver nt; ~**shot** n Schuß m; ~**smith** n Büchsenmacher(in f) m.
gurgle [ˈgɜːgl] vi gluckern.

guru ['gʊruː] n Guru m.

gush [gʌʃ] vi (rush out) hervorströmen; (fig) schwärmen.

gusset ['gʌsɪt] n Keil m, Zwickel m.

gust [gʌst] n Windstoß m, Bö f.

gusto ['gʌstəʊ] n Genuß m, Lust f.

gut [gʌt] n (ANAT) Gedärme pl; (string) Darm m; ~s pl (fig) Schneid m.

gutter ['gʌtə*] n Dachrinne f; (in street) Gosse f.

guttural ['gʌtərəl] a guttural, Kehl-.

guy [gaɪ] n (also: ~rope) Halteseil nt; (man) Typ m, Kerl m.

guzzle ['gʌzl] vti (drink) saufen; (eat) fressen.

gym [dʒɪm] n (also: gymnasium) Turnhalle f; (also: gymnastics) Turnen nt; ~nast ['dʒɪmnæst] n Turner(in f) m; ~nastics [dʒɪm'næstɪks] n Turnen nt, Gymnastik f; ~ shoes npl Turnschuhe pl; ~ slip n (Brit) Schulträgerrock.

gynaecologist, (US) **gynecologist** [gaɪnɪ'kɒlədʒɪst] n Frauenarzt m/-ärztin f.

gynaecology, (US) **gynecology** [gaɪnɪ'kɒlədʒɪ] n Gynäkologie f, Frauenheilkunde f.

gypsy ['dʒɪpsɪ] n = gipsy.

gyrate [dʒaɪ'reɪt] vi kreisen.

H

haberdashery [hæbə'dæʃərɪ] n (Brit) Kurzwaren pl.

habit ['hæbɪt] n (An)gewohnheit f; (monk's) Habit nt or m.

habitable ['hæbɪtəbl] a bewohnbar.

habitat ['hæbɪtæt] n Lebensraum m.

habitual [hə'bɪtjʊəl] a gewohnheitsmäßig, ~ly ad gewöhnlich.

hack [hæk] vt hacken // n Hieb m; (writer) Schreiberling m.

hackneyed ['hæknɪd] a abgedroschen.

had [hæd] pt, pp of have.

haddock ['hædək], pl ~ or ~s n Schellfisch m.

hadn't ['hædnt] = had not.

haemorrhage, (US) **hemorrhage** ['hemərɪdʒ] n Blutung f.

haemorrhoids, (US) **hemorrhoids** ['hemərɔɪdz] npl Hämorrhoiden pl.

haggard ['hægəd] a abgekämpft.

haggle ['hægl] vi feilschen.

Hague [heɪg] n: The ~ Den Haag nt.

hail [heɪl] n Hagel m // vt umjubeln // vi hageln; ~stone n Hagelkorn nt.

hair [hɛə*] n Haar nt, Haare pl; (one ~) Haar nt; ~brush n Haarbürste f; ~cut n Haarschnitt m; to get a ~cut sich (dat) die Haare schneiden lassen; ~do n Frisur f; ~dresser n Friseur m, ~dresser's n Friseursalon m; ~ dryer n Trockenhaube f; (hand)

Fön m; ~grip n Klemme f; ~net n Haarnetz nt; ~pin n Haarnadel f; ~pin bend, (US) ~pin curve n Haarnadelkurve f; ~raising a haarsträubend; ~ remover n Enthaarungsmittel nt; ~ spray n Haarspray nt; ~style n Frisur f; ~y a haarig.

hake [heɪk] n Seehecht m.

half [hɑːf], pl halves n Hälfte f // a halb // ad halb, zur Hälfte; ~-an-hour eine halbe Stunde; two and a ~ zweieinhalb; to cut sth in ~ etw halbieren; ~-back n Läufer m; ~-breed n Mischling m; ~-caste n Mischling m; ~-hearted a lustlos; ~-hour n halbe Stunde f; ~-penny ['heɪpnɪ] n (Brit) halbe(r) Penny m; (at) ~-price zum halben Preis; ~ term n (Brit SCH) Ferien pl in der Mitte des Trimesters; ~-time n Halbzeit f; ~-way ad halbwegs, auf halbem Wege.

hall [hɔːl] n Saal m; (entrance ~) Hausflur m; (building) Halle f; ~ of residence n (Brit) Studentenwohnheim nt.

hallmark ['hɔːlmɑːk] n Stempel m.

hallo [hʌ'ləʊ] see hello.

Hallowe'en ['hæləʊ'iːn] n Tag m vor Allerheiligen.

hallucination [həluːsɪ'neɪʃən] n Halluzination f.

hallway ['hɔːlweɪ] n Korridor m.

halo ['heɪləʊ] n Heiligenschein m.

halt [hɔːlt] n Halt m // vti anhalten.

halve [hɑːv] vt halbieren.

halves [hɑːvz] pl of half.

ham [hæm] n Schinken m.

hamburger ['hæmbɜːgə*] n Hamburger m.

hamlet ['hæmlɪt] n Weiler m.

hammer ['hæmə*] n Hammer m // vt hämmern.

hammock ['hæmək] n Hängematte f.

hamper ['hæmpə*] vt (be)hindern // n Picknickkorb m.

hamster ['hæmstə*] n Hamster m.

hand [hænd] n Hand f; (of clock) (Uhr)zeiger m; (worker) Arbeiter m // vt (pass) geben; to give sb a ~ jdm helfen; at ~ nahe; to ~ zur Hand; in ~ (under control) unter Kontrolle; (being done) im Gange; (extra) übrig; on ~ zur Verfügung; on the one ~ ..., on the other ~ ... einerseits ..., andererseits ...; ~ in vt abgeben; (forms) einreichen; ~ out vt austeilen; ~ over vt (deliver) übergeben; (surrender) abgeben; (: prisoner) ausliefern; ~bag n Handtasche f; ~book n Handbuch nt; ~brake n Handbremse f; ~cuffs npl Handschellen pl; ~ful n Handvoll f; (col: person) Plage f.

handicap ['hændɪkæp] n Handikap nt // vt benachteiligen; mentally/physically ~ped geistig/körperlich behindert.

handicraft ['hændɪkrɑːft] n Kunsthandwerk *nt*.

handiwork ['hændɪwɜːk] *n* Arbeit *f*; (*fig*) Werk *nt*.

handkerchief ['hæŋkətʃɪf] *n* Taschentuch *nt*.

handle ['hændl] *n* (*of door etc*) Klinke *f*; (*of cup etc*) Henkel *m*; (*for winding*) Kurbel *f* // *vt* (*touch*) anfassen; (*deal with: things*) sich befassen mit; (: *people*) umgehen mit; **~bar(s)** *n(pl)* Lenkstange *f*.

hand: **~ luggage** *n* Handgepäck *nt*; **~made** *a* handgefertigt; **~out** *n* (*distribution*) Verteilung *f*; (*charity*) Geldzuwendung *f*; (*leaflet*) Flugblatt *nt*; **~rail** *n* Geländer *nt*; (*on ship*) Reling *f*; **~shake** *n* Händedruck *m*.

handsome ['hænsəm] *a* gutaussehend.

handwriting ['hændraɪtɪŋ] *n* Handschrift *f*.

handy ['hændɪ] *a* praktisch; (*shops*) leicht erreichbar.

handyman ['hændɪmən] *n* Bastler *m*.

hang [hæŋ] *v* (*pt, pp* **hung**) *vt* aufhängen; (*criminal: pt, pp* **hanged**) hängen // *vi* hängen // *n*: **to get the ~ of sth** (*col*) den richtigen Dreh bei etw herauskriegen; **~ about** *vi* sich herumtreiben; **~ on** *vi* (*wait*) warten; **~ up** *vi* (*TEL*) auflegen.

hanger ['hæŋə*] *n* Kleiderbügel *m*.

hanger-on ['hæŋər'ɒn] *n* Anhänger(in *f*) *m*.

hang-gliding ['hæŋglaɪdɪŋ] *n* Drachenfliegen *nt*.

hangover ['hæŋəʊvə*] *n* Kater *m*.

hang-up ['hæŋʌp] *n* Komplex *m*.

hanker ['hæŋkə*] *vi* sich sehnen (*for, after* nach).

hankie, hanky ['hæŋkɪ] *n abbr of* **handkerchief.**

haphazard ['hæp'hæzəd] *a* zufällig.

happen ['hæpən] *vi* sich ereignen, passieren; as it ~s I'm going there today zufällig(erweise) gehe ich heute (dort)hin; **~ing** *n* Ereignis *nt*.

happily ['hæpɪlɪ] *ad* glücklich; (*fortunately*) glücklicherweise.

happiness ['hæpɪnɪs] *n* Glück *nt*.

happy ['hæpɪ] *a* glücklich; **~ birthday!** alles Gute zum Geburtstag!; **~-go-lucky** *a* sorglos.

harass ['hærəs] *vt* plagen; **~ment** *n* Belästigung *f*.

harbour, (*US*) **harbor** ['hɑːbə*] *n* Hafen *m* // *vt* (*hope etc*) hegen; (*criminal etc*) Unterschlupf gewähren.

hard [hɑːd] *a* (*firm*) hart; (*difficult*) schwer; (*harsh*) hart(herzig) // *ad* (*work*) hart; (*try*) sehr; (*push, hit*) fest; **no ~ feelings!** ich nehme es dir nicht übel; **~ of hearing** schwerhörig; **to be ~ done by** übel dran sein; **~back** *n* kartonierte Ausgabe *f*; **~ cash** *n* Bargeld *nt*; **~ disk** *n* (*COMPUT*) Fest-

platte *f*; **~en** *vt* erhärten; (*fig*) verhärten // *vi* hart werden; (*fig*) sich verhärten; **~-headed** *a* nüchtern; **~ labour** *n* Zwangsarbeit *f*.

hardly ['hɑːdlɪ] *ad* kaum.

hard: **~ness** *n* Härte *f*; (*difficulty*) Schwierigkeit *f*; **~ship** *n* Not *f*; **~-up** *a* knapp bei Kasse; **~ware** *n* Eisenwaren *pl*; (*COMPUT*) Hardware *f*; **~ware shop** *n* Eisenwarenhandlung *f*; **~-wearing** *a* strapazierfähig; **~-working** *a* fleißig.

hardy ['hɑːdɪ] *a* widerstandsfähig.

hare [heə*] *n* Hase *m*; **~-brained** *a* schwachsinnig.

harm [hɑːm] *n* Schaden *m* // *vt* schaden (+*dat*); **out of ~'s way** in Sicherheit; **~ful** *a* schädlich; **~less** *a* harmlos.

harmonica [hɑː'mɒnɪkə] *n* Mundharmonika *f*.

harmonious [hɑː'məʊnɪəs] *a* harmonisch.

harmonize ['hɑːmənaɪz] *vt* abstimmen // *vi* harmonieren.

harmony ['hɑːmənɪ] *n* Harmonie *f*.

harness ['hɑːnɪs] *n* Geschirr *nt* // *vt* (*horse*) anschirren; (*fig*) nutzbar machen.

harp [hɑːp] *n* Harfe *f* // *vi*: **to ~ on about sth** auf etw (*dat*) herumreiten.

harpoon [hɑː'puːn] *n* Harpune *f*.

harrowing ['hærəʊɪŋ] *a* nervenaufreibend.

harsh [hɑːʃ] *a* (*rough*) rauh; (*severe*) streng; **~ness** *n* Härte *f*.

harvest ['hɑːvɪst] *n* Ernte *f* // *vti* ernten.

harvester ['hɑːvɪstə*] *n* Mähbinder *m*.

has [hæz] *v see* **have.**

hash [hæʃ] *vt* kleinhacken // *n* (*mess*) Kuddelmuddel *m*; (*meat*) Haschee *nt*.

hashish ['hæʃɪʃ] *n* Haschisch *nt*.

hasn't ['hæznt] = **has not.**

hassle ['hæsl] *n* (*col*) Theater *nt*.

haste [heɪst] *n* Eile *f*; **~n** ['heɪsn] *vt* beschleunigen // *vi* eilen.

hasty [heɪstɪ] *a* hastig; (*rash*) vorschnell.

hat [hæt] *n* Hut *m*.

hatch [hætʃ] *n* (*NAUT: also:* **~way**) Luke *f*; (*in house*) Durchreiche *f* // *vi* (*young*) ausschlüpfen // *vt* (*brood*) ausbrüten; (*plot*) aushecken.

hatchback ['hætʃbæk] *n* (*AUT*) (Auto *nt* mit) Heckklappe *f*.

hatchet ['hætʃɪt] *n* Beil *nt*.

hate [heɪt] *vt* hassen // *n* Haß *m*; **~ful** *a* verhaßt.

hatred ['heɪtrɪd] *n* Haß *m*.

haughty ['hɔːtɪ] *a* hochnäsig, überheblich.

haul [hɔːl] *vt* ziehen // *n* (*catch*) Fang *m*; **~age** *n* Spedition *f*; **~ier**, (*US*) **~er** *n* Spediteur *m*.

haunch [hɔːntʃ] *n* Lende *f*.

haunt [hɔːnt] *vt* (*ghost*) spuken in

(+*dat*); (*memory*) verfolgen; (*pub*) häufig besuchen // *n* Lieblingsplatz *m*; the castle is ~ed in dem Schloß spukt es.

have, *pt, pp* **had** [hæv, hæd] ◆ *aux v* **1** haben; (*esp with vs of motion*) sein; to ~ arrived/slept angekommen sein/ geschlafen haben; to ~ been gewesen sein; having eaten *or* when he had eaten, he left nachdem er gegessen hatte, ging er

2 (*in tag questions*): you've done it, ~n't you? du hast es doch gemacht, oder nicht?

3 (*in short answers and questions*): you've made a mistake — no I ~n't/so I ~ du hast einen Fehler gemacht — nein(, hab ich nicht)/ja, stimmt; we ~n't paid — yes we ~! wir haben nicht bezahlt — doch; I've been there before, ~ you? ich war schon einmal da, du auch?

◆ *modal aux v* (*be obliged*): to ~ (got) to do sth etw tun müssen; you ~n't to tell her du darfst es ihr nicht erzählen

◆ *vt* **1** (*possess*) haben; he has (got) blue eyes er hat blaue Augen; I ~ (got) an idea ich habe eine Idee

2 (*referring to meals etc*): to ~ breakfast/a cigarette frühstücken/eine Zigarette rauchen

3 (*receive, obtain etc*) haben; may I ~ your address? kann ich Ihre Adresse haben?; to ~ a baby ein Kind bekommen

4 (*maintain, allow*): he will ~ it that he is right er besteht darauf, daß er recht hat; I won't ~ it das lasse ich mir nicht bieten

5: to ~ sth done etw machen lassen; to ~ sb do sth jdn etw machen lassen; he soon had them all laughing er brachte sie alle zum Lachen

6 (*experience, suffer*): she had her bag stolen man hat ihr die Tasche gestohlen; he had his arm broken er hat sich den Arm gebrochen

7 (+ *noun: take, hold etc*): to ~ a walk/ rest spazierengehen/sich ausruhen; to ~ a meeting/party eine Besprechung/Party haben

have out *vt*: to ~ it out with sb (*settle a problem etc*) etw mit jdm bereden.

haven ['heɪvn] *n* Zufluchtsort *m*.

haven't ['hævnt] = **have not.**

haversack ['hævəsæk] *n* Rucksack *m*.

havoc ['hævək] *n* Verwüstung *f*.

Hawaii [hə'waɪiː] *n* Hawaii *nt*.

hawk [hɔːk] *n* Habicht *m*.

hay [heɪ] *n* Heu *nt*; ~ **fever** *n* Heuschnupfen *m*; ~**stack** *n* Heuschober *m*.

haywire ['heɪwaɪə*] *a* (*col*) durcheinander.

hazard ['hæzəd] *n* Risiko *nt* // *vt* aufs Spiel setzen; ~**ous** *a* gefährlich; ~ **(warning) lights** *npl* (*AUT*) Warnblinklicht *nt*.

haze [heɪz] *n* Dunst *m*.

hazelnut ['heɪzlnʌt] *n* Haselnuß *f*.

hazy ['heɪzɪ] *a* (*misty*) dunstig; (*vague*) verschwommen.

he [hiː] *pron er*.

head [hed] *n* Kopf *m*; (*leader*) Leiter *m* // *vt* (an)führen, leiten; (*ball*) köpfen; ~**s** (or tails) kopf (oder Zahl); ~ first mit dem Kopf nach unten; ~ over heels kopfüber; ~ for *vt* zugehen auf (+*acc*); ~**ache** *n* Kopfschmerzen *pl*; ~**dress** *n* Kopfschmuck *m*; ~**ing** *n* Überschrift *f*; ~**lamp** *n* (*Brit*) Scheinwerfer *m*; ~**land** *n* Landspitze *f*; ~**light** *n* = ~**lamp**; ~**line** *n* Schlagzeile *f*; ~**long** *ad* kopfüber; ~**master** *n* (*of primary school*) Rektor *m*; (*of secondary school*) Direktor *m*; ~**mistress** *n* Rektorin *f*; Direktorin *f*; ~ **office** *n* Zentrale *f*; ~-**on** *a* Frontal-; ~**phones** *npl* Kopfhörer *pl*; ~**quarters** (HQ) *npl* Zentrale *f*; (*MIL*) Hauptquartier *nt*; ~**rest** *n* Kopfstütze *f*; ~**room** *n* (*of bridges etc*) lichte Höhe *f*; ~**scarf** *n* Kopftuch *nt*; ~**strong** *a* eigenwillig; ~ **waiter** *n* Oberkellner *m*; ~**way** *n* Fortschritte *pl*; ~**wind** *n* Gegenwind *m*; ~**y** *a* berauschend.

heal [hiːl] *vt* heilen // *vi* verheilen.

health [helθ] *n* Gesundheit *f*; your ~! prost!; ~ **food** *n* Reformkost *f*; the H~ **Service** *n* (*Brit*) das Gesundheitswesen *nt*; ~**y** *a* gesund.

heap [hiːp] *n* Haufen *m* // *vt* häufen.

hear [hɪə*] *v* (*pt, pp* **heard** [hɜːd]) *vt* hören; (*listen to*) anhören // *vi* hören; ~**ing** *n* Gehör *nt*; (*JUR*) Verhandlung *f*; ~**ing aid** *n* Hörapparat *m*; ~**say** *n* Hörensagen *nt*.

hearse [hɜːs] *n* Leichenwagen *m*.

heart [hɑːt] *n* Herz *nt*; by ~ auswendig; ~**s** *pl* (*CARDS*) Herz *nt*; ~ **attack** *n* Herzanfall *m*; ~**beat** *n* Herzschlag *m*; ~**breaking** *a* herzzerbrechend; ~**broken** *a* (ganz)gebrochen; ~**burn** *n* Sodbrennen *nt*; ~ **failure** *n* Herzschlag *m*; ~**felt** *a* aufrichtig.

hearth [hɑːθ] *n* Herd *m*.

heartily ['hɑːtɪlɪ] *ad* herzlich; (*eat*) herzhaft.

heartless ['hɑːtlɪs] *a* herzlos.

hearty ['hɑːtɪ] *a* kräftig; (*friendly*) freundlich.

heat [hiːt] *n* Hitze *f*; (*of food, water etc*) Wärme *f*; (*SPORT: also*: qualifying ~) Ausscheidungsrunde *f* // *vt* (*house*) heizen; (*substance*) heiß machen, erhitzen; ~ **up** *vi* warm werden // *vt* aufwärmen; ~**ed** *a* erhitzt; (*fig*) hitzig; ~**er** *n* (Heiz)ofen *m*.

heath [hiːθ] *n* (*Brit*) Heide *f*.

heathen ['hiːðən] *n* Heide *m* // *a* heidnisch, Heiden-.

heather ['heðə*] *n* Heidekraut *nt*.

heating ['hiːtɪŋ] *n* Heizung *f*.

heatstroke ['hiːtstrəʊk] n Hitzschlag m.
heatwave ['hiːtweɪv] n Hitzewelle f.
heave [hiːv] vt hochheben; (sigh) ausstoßen // vi wogen; (breast) sich heben //
n Heben nt.
heaven [hevn] n Himmel m; **~ly** a
himmlisch.
heavily ['hevɪlɪ] ad schwer.
heavy ['hevɪ] a schwer; **~ goods vehicle (HGV)** n Lastkraftwagen (LKW) m;
~weight n (SPORT) Schwergewicht nt.
Hebrew ['hiːbruː] a hebräisch n
(LING) Hebräisch nt.
heckle ['hekl] vt unterbrechen.
hectic ['hektɪk] a hektisch.
he'd [hiːd] = he had; he would.
hedge [hedʒ] n Hecke f // vt einzäunen //
vi (fig) ausweichen; to **~** one's bets sich
absichern.
hedgehog ['hedʒhɒg] n Igel m.
heed [hiːd] vt (also: take **~** of) beachten
// n Beachtung f; **~less** a achtlos.
heel [hiːl] n Ferse f; (of shoe) Absatz m
// vt (shoes) mit Absätzen versehen.
hefty ['heftɪ] a (person) stämmig;
(portion) reichlich.
heifer ['hefə*] n Färse f.
height [haɪt] n (of person) Größe f; (of
object) Höhe f; **~en** vt erhöhen.
heir [eə*] n Erbe m; **~ess** ['ɛərɪs] n
Erbin f; **~loom** n Erbstück nt.
helicopter ['helɪkɒptə*] n Hubschrauber
m.
heliport ['helɪpɔːt] n Hubschrauber-
landeplatz m.
hell [hel] n Hölle f // interj verdammt!
he'll [hiːl] = he will, he shall.
hellish ['helɪʃ] a höllisch, verteufelt.
hello [hʌ'ləʊ] interj Hallo.
helm [helm] n Ruder nt, Steuer nt.
helmet ['helmɪt] n Helm m.
helmsman ['helmzmən] n Steuermann
m.
help [help] n Hilfe f // vt helfen (+dat); I
can't **~** it ich kann nichts dafür; **~** yourself bedienen Sie sich; **~er** n Helfer m;
~ful a hilfreich; **~ing** n Portion f;
~less a hilflos.
hem [hem] n Saum m // vt säumen; **~**
in vt einengen.
he-man ['hiːmæn] n (col) Macho m.
hemorrhage ['heməridʒ] n (US) =
haemorrhage.
hemorrhoids ['heməroɪdz] npl (US) =
haemorrhoids.
hen [hen] n Henne f.
hence [hens] ad von jetzt an; (therefore)
daher; **~forth** ad von nun an; (from
then on) von da an.
henchman ['hentʃmən] n Gefolgsmann
m.
henpecked ['henpekt] a: to be **~** unter
dem Pantoffel stehen; **~** husband n
Pantoffelheld m.
her [hɜː*] pron (acc) sie; (dat) ihr //

poss a ihr; see also me, my.
herald ['herəld] n (Vor)bote m // vt verkünden.
heraldry ['herəldrɪ] n Wappenkunde f.
herb [hɜːb] n Kraut nt.
herd [hɜːd] n Herde f.
here [hɪə*] ad hier; (to this place) hierher; **~after** ad hernach, künftig // n
Jenseits nt; **~by** ad hiermit.
hereditary [hɪ'redɪtərɪ] a erblich.
heredity [hɪ'redɪtɪ] n Vererbung f.
heresy ['herəsɪ] n Ketzerei f.
heretic ['herətɪk] n Ketzer m.
heritage ['herɪtɪdʒ] n Erbe nt.
hermetically [hɜː'metɪkəlɪ] ad: **~**
sealed hermetisch verschlossen.
hermit ['hɜːmɪt] n Einsiedler m.
hernia ['hɜːnɪə] n Bruch m.
hero ['hɪərəʊ], pl **~es** n Held m; **~ic**
[hɪ'rəʊɪk] a heroisch.
heroin ['herəʊɪn] n Heroin nt.
heroine ['herəʊɪn] n Heldin f.
heroism ['herəʊɪzəm] n Heldentum nt.
heron ['herən] n Reiher m.
herring ['herɪŋ] n Hering m.
hers [hɜːz] pron ihre(r, s); see also
mine.
herself [hɜː'self] pron sich (selbst); (emphatic) selbst; see also oneself.
he's [hiːz] = he is, he has.
hesitant ['hezɪtənt] a zögernd.
hesitate ['hezɪteɪt] vi zögern.
hesitation [hezɪ'teɪʃən] n Zögern nt.
hew [hjuː], pt hewed, pp hewn vt
hauen, hacken.
hexagon ['heksəgən] n Sechseck nt;
~al [hek'sægənəl] a sechseckig.
heyday ['heɪdeɪ] n Blüte f, Höhepunkt
m.
HGV n abbr of heavy goods vehicle.
hi [haɪ] interj he, hallo.
hiatus [haɪ'eɪtəs] n (gap) Lücke f.
hibernation [haɪbə'neɪʃən] n Winter-
schlaf m.
hiccough, hiccup ['hɪkʌp] vi den
Schluckauf haben; **~s** pl Schluckauf m.
hide [haɪd] n (skin) Haut f, Fell nt // v
(pt, hid [hɪd], pp hidden ['hɪdn]) vt
verstecken // vi sich verstecken; **~-and-
seek** n Versteckspiel nt; **~away** n Versteck nt.
hideous ['hɪdɪəs] a abscheulich.
hiding ['haɪdɪŋ] n (beating) Tracht f
Prügel; to be in **~** (concealed) sich ver-
steckt halten; **~ place** n Versteck nt.
hi-fi ['haɪfaɪ] n Hi-Fi nt // a Hi-Fi-.
high [haɪ] a hoch; (wind) stark // ad
hoch; **~boy** n (US: tallboy) hochbeinige
Kommode f; **~brow** a (betont)
intellektuell; **~chair** n Hochstuhl m;
~er education n Hochschulbildung f;
~-handed a eigenmächtig; **~-heeled** a
hochhackig; **~jack** vt = hijack; **~
jump** n (SPORT) Hochsprung m; **the
H~lands** npl das schottische Hochland;

~light n (fig) Höhepunkt m // vt hervorheben; **~ly** ad höchst; **~ly strung** a überempfindlich; **~ness** n Höhe f; **H~ness** n Hoheit f; **~-pitched** a hoch; **~-rise block** n Hochhaus nt; **~ school** n (US) Oberschule f; **~ season** n (Brit) Hochsaison f; **~ street** n (Brit) Hauptstraße f.

highway ['haɪweɪ] n Landstraße f; **H~ Code** n (Brit) Straßenverkehrsordnung f.

hijack ['haɪdʒæk] vt entführen; **~er** n Entführer(in f) m.

hike [haɪk] vi wandern // n Wanderung f; **~r** n Wanderer m.

hilarious [hɪ'lɛərɪəs] a lustig.

hill [hɪl] n Berg m; **~side** n (Berg)hang m; **~y** a hügelig.

hilt [hɪlt] n Heft nt; **up to the ~** ganz und gar.

him [hɪm] pron (acc) ihn; (dat) ihm; see also **me**.

himself [hɪm'self] pron sich (selbst); (emphatic) selbst; see also **oneself**.

hind [haɪnd] a hinter, Hinter-.

hinder ['hɪndə*] vt (stop) hindern; (delay) behindern.

hindrance ['hɪndrəns] n (delay) Behinderung f; (obstacle) Hindernis nt.

hindsight ['haɪndsaɪt] n: **with ~** im nachhinein.

Hindu ['hɪnduː] n Hindu m.

hinge [hɪndʒ] n Scharnier nt; (on door) Türangel f // vi (fig) abhängen (on von).

hint [hɪnt] n Tip m; (trace) Anflug m // vt: **to ~** that andeuten, daß // vi andeuten (at acc).

hip [hɪp] n Hüfte f.

hippopotamus [hɪpə'pɒtəməs], pl **~es** or **-mi** [-maɪ] n Nilpferd nt.

hire ['haɪə*] vt (worker) anstellen; (Brit: car) mieten // n Miete f; **for ~** (taxi) frei; **~ purchase (H.P.)** n (Brit) Teilzahlungskauf m.

his [hɪz] poss a sein // poss pron seine(r, s); see also **my, mine**.

hiss [hɪs] vi zischen // n Zischen nt.

historian [hɪs'tɔːrɪən] n Historiker m.

historic [hɪs'tɒrɪk] a historisch.

historical [hɪs'tɒrɪkəl] a historisch, geschichtlich.

history ['hɪstərɪ] n Geschichte f.

hit [hɪt] vt, pt, pp **hit** schlagen; (injure) treffen // n (blow) Schlag m; (success) Erfolg m (MUS) Hit m; **to ~ it off with** sb prima mit jdm auskommen; **~-and-run driver** n jd, der Fahrerflucht begeht.

hitch [hɪtʃ] vt festbinden; (also: ~ up) hochziehen // n (difficulty) Haken m; **to ~ a lift** trampen.

hitch-hike ['hɪtʃhaɪk] vi trampen, **~r** n Tramper m.

hitherto ['hɪðə'tuː] ad bislang.

hive [haɪv] n Bienenkorb m // vt: **to ~ off**

ausgliedern.

HMS abbr = *His(Her) Majesty's Ship*.

hoard [hɔːd] n Schatz m // vt horten, hamstern.

hoarding ['hɔːdɪŋ] n Bretterzaun m; (Brit: for advertising) Reklamewand f.

hoarfrost ['hɔː'frɒst] n (Rauh)reif m.

hoarse [hɔːs] a heiser, rauh.

hoax [həʊks] n Streich m.

hob [hɒb] n Kochmulde f.

hobble ['hɒbl] vi humpeln.

hobby ['hɒbɪ] n Hobby nt; **~-horse** n (fig) Steckenpferd nt.

hobo ['həʊbəʊ] n (US) Tippelbruder m.

hock [hɒk] n (wine) weiße(r) Rheinwein m.

hockey ['hɒkɪ] n Hockey nt.

hoe [həʊ] n Hacke f // vt hacken.

hog [hɒg] n Schlachtschwein nt // vt mit Beschlag belegen; **to go the whole ~** aufs Ganze gehen.

hoist [hɔɪst] n Winde f // vt hochziehen.

hold [həʊld] v (pt, pp **held**) vt halten; (contain) enthalten; (be able to contain) fassen; (breath) anhalten; (meeting) abhalten // vi (withstand pressure) aushalten // n (grasp) Halt m; (NAUT) Schiffsraum m; **~ the line!** (TEL) bleiben Sie am Apparat!; **to ~ one's own** sich behaupten; **~ back** vt zurückhalten; **~ down** vt niederhalten; (job) behalten; **~ off** vt (enemy) abwehren; **~ on** vi sich festhalten; (resist) durchhalten; (wait) warten; **~ on to** vt an etw (dat) festhalten; (keep) behalten; **~ out** vt hinhalten // vi aushalten; **~ up** vt (delay) aufhalten; (rob) überfallen; **~all** n (Brit) Reisetasche f; **~er** n Behälter m; **~ing** n (share) (Aktien)anteil m; **~up** n (Brit: in traffic) Stockung f; (robbery) Überfall m.

hole [həʊl] n Loch nt // vt durchlöchern.

holiday ['hɒlədɪ] n (day) Feiertag m; freie(r) Tag m; (vacation) Urlaub m; (SCH) Ferien pl; **~ camp** n Ferienlager nt; **~-maker** n (Brit) Urlauber(in f) m; **~ resort** n Ferienort m.

holiness ['həʊlɪnɪs] n Heiligkeit f.

Holland ['hɒlənd] n Holland nt.

hollow ['hɒləʊ] a hohl; (fig) leer // n Vertiefung f; **~ out** vt aushöhlen.

holly ['hɒlɪ] n Stechpalme f.

holocaust ['hɒləkɔːst] n Inferno nt.

holster ['həʊlstə*] n Pistolenhalfter m.

holy ['həʊlɪ] a heilig; **the H~ Ghost** or **Spirit** n der Heilige Geist.

homage ['hɒmɪdʒ] n Huldigung f; **to pay ~ to** huldigen (+dat).

home [həʊm] n Zuhause nt; (institution) Heim nt, Anstalt f // a einheimisch; (POL) inner // ad heim, nach Hause; **at ~** zu Hause; **~ address** n Heimatadresse f; **~coming** n Heimkehr f; **~ computer** n Heimcomputer m; **~land**

n Heimat(land *nt*) *f*; **~less** *a* obdachlos; **~ly** *a* häuslich; (*US: ugly*) unscheinbar; **~-made** *a* selbstgemacht; **H~ Office** *n* (*Brit*) Innenministerium *nt*; **~ rule** *n* Selbstverwaltung *f*; **H~ Secretary** *n* (*Brit*) Innenminister(in *f*) *m*; **~sick** *a*: to be **~sick** Heimweh haben; **~ town** *n* Heimatstadt *f*; **~ward** *a* heimwärts; **~work** *n* Hausaufgaben *pl*.

homicide ['hɒmɪsaɪd] *n* (*US*) Totschlag *m*.

homoeopathy [həʊmɪ'ɒpəθɪ] *n* Homöopathie *f*.

homogeneous [hɒmə'dʒiːnɪəs] *a* homogen.

homosexual ['hɒməʊ'seksjʊəl] *a* homosexuell // *n* Homosexuelle(r) *mf*.

honest ['ɒnɪst] *a* ehrlich; **~ly** *ad* ehrlich; **~y** *n* Ehrlichkeit *f*.

honey ['hʌnɪ] *n* Honig *m*; **~comb** *n* Honigwabe *f*; **~moon** *n* Flitterwochen *pl*, Hochzeitsreise *f*; **~suckle** *n* Geißblatt *nt*.

honk [hɒŋk] *vi* hupen.

honorary ['ɒnərərɪ] *a* Ehren-.

honour, (*US*) **honor** ['ɒnə*] *vt* ehren; (*cheque*) einlösen // *n* Ehre *f*; **~able** *a* ehrenwert; (*intention*) ehrenhaft; **~s degree** *n* (*SCH*) akademischer Grad mit Prüfung im Spezialfach.

hood [hʊd] *n* Kapuze *f*; (*Brit AUT*) Verdeck *nt*; (*US AUT*) Kühlerhaube *f*.

hoodlum ['huːdləm] *n* Rowdy *m*; (*member of gang*) Gangster *m*.

hoodwink ['hʊdwɪŋk] *vt* reinlegen.

hoof [huːf], *pl* **hooves** *n* Huf *m*.

hook [hʊk] *n* Haken *m* // *vt* einhaken.

hooligan ['huːlɪgən] *n* Rowdy *m*.

hoop [huːp] *n* Reifen *m*.

hoot [huːt] *vi* (*AUT*) hupen; **~er** *n* (*NAUT*) Dampfpfeife *f*; (*Brit AUT*) (Auto)hupe *f*.

hoover ['huːvə*] ® (*Brit*) *n* Staubsauger *m* // *vt* staubsaugen.

hooves [huːvz] *pl of* hoof.

hop [hɒp] *vi* hüpfen, hopsen // *n* (*jump*) Hopser *m*.

hope [həʊp] *vti* hoffen // *n* Hoffnung *f*; I hope so/not hoffentlich/hoffentlich nicht; **~ful** *a* hoffnungsvoll; (*promising*) vielversprechend; **~fully** *ad* hoffentlich; **~less** *a* hoffnungslos.

hops [hɒps] *npl* Hopfen *m*.

horizon [hə'raɪzn] *n* Horizont *m*; **~tal** [hɒrɪ'zɒntl] *a* horizontal.

hormone ['hɔːməʊn] *n* Hormon *nt*.

horn [hɔːn] *n* Horn *nt*; (*AUT*) Hupe *f*.

hornet ['hɔːnɪt] *n* Hornisse *f*.

horny ['hɔːnɪ] *a* schwielig; (*US col*) scharf.

horoscope ['hɒrəskəʊp] *n* Horoskop *nt*.

horrible ['hɒrɪbl] *a* fürchterlich.

horrid ['hɒrɪd] *a* scheußlich.

horrify ['hɒrɪfaɪ] *vt* entsetzen.

horror ['hɒrə*] *n* Schrecken *m*; **~ film**

n Horrorfilm *m*.

hors d'oeuvre [ɔː'dɜːvr] *n* Vorspeise *f*.

horse [hɔːs] *n* Pferd *nt*; on **~back** beritten; **~ chestnut** *n* Roßkastanie *f*; **~man/woman** *n* Reiter *m*/Reiterin *f*; **~power (h.p.)** *n* Pferdestärke *f*, PS *nt*; **~-racing** *n* Pferderennen *nt*; **~radish** *n* Meerrettich *m*; **~shoe** *n* Hufeisen *nt*.

horticulture ['hɔːtɪkʌltʃə*] *n* Gartenbau *m*.

hose(pipe) ['həʊz(paɪp)] *n* Schlauch *m*.

hosiery ['həʊzɪərɪ] *n* Strumpfwaren *pl*.

hospitable [hɒs'pɪtəbl] *a* gastfreundlich.

hospital ['hɒspɪtl] *n* Krankenhaus *nt*.

hospitality [hɒspɪ'tælɪtɪ] *n* Gastfreundschaft *f*.

host [həʊst] *n* Gastgeber *m*; (*innkeeper*) (Gast)wirt *m*; (*large number*) Heerschar *f*; (*ECCL*) Hostie *f*.

hostage ['hɒstɪdʒ] *n* Geisel *f*.

hostel ['hɒstəl] *n* Herberge *f*; **(youth) ~** *n* Jugendherberge *f*.

hostess ['həʊstes] *n* Gastgeberin *f*.

hostile ['hɒstaɪl] *a* feindlich.

hostility [hɒs'tɪlɪtɪ] *n* Feindschaft *f*; **hostilities** *pl* Feindseligkeiten *pl*.

hot [hɒt] *a* heiß; (*drink, food, water*) warm; (*spiced*) scharf; I'm **~** mir ist heiß; **~bed** *n* (*fig*) Nährboden *m*; **~ dog** *n* heiße(s) Würstchen *nt*.

hotel [həʊ'tel] *n* Hotel *nt*; **~ier** *n* Hotelier *m*.

hot: ~headed *a* hitzig; **~house** *n* Treibhaus *nt*; **~ line** *n* (*POL*) heiße(r) Draht *m*; **~ly** *ad* (*argue*) hitzig; **~plate** *n* Kochplatte *f*; **~-water bottle** *n* Wärmflasche *f*.

hound [haʊnd] *n* Jagdhund *m* // *vt* hetzen.

hour ['aʊə*] *n* Stunde *f*; (*time of day*) (Tages)zeit *f*; **~ly** *a*, *ad* stündlich.

house [haʊs] *n* Haus *nt* // *vt* [haʊz] unterbringen; on the **~** auf Kosten des Hauses; **~boat** *n* Hausboot *nt*; **~breaking** *n* Einbruch *m*; **~coat** *n* Morgenmantel *m*; **~hold** *n* Haushalt *m*; **~keeper** *n* Haushälterin *f*; **~keeping** *n* Haushaltung *f*; **~-warming party** *n* Einweihungsparty *f*; **~wife** *n* Hausfrau *f*; **~work** *n* Hausarbeit *f*.

housing ['haʊzɪŋ] *n* (*act*) Unterbringung *f*; (*houses*) Wohnungen *pl*; (*POL*) Wohnungsbau *m*; (*covering*) Gehäuse *nt*; **~ development**, (*Brit*) **~ estate** *n* (Wohn)siedlung *f*.

hovel ['hɒvəl] *n* elende Hütte *f*.

hover ['hɒvə*] *vi* (*bird*) schweben; (*person*) herumstehen; **~craft** *n* Luftkissenfahrzeug *nt*.

how [haʊ] *ad* wie; **~ are you?** wie geht es Ihnen?; **~ much milk?** wieviel Milch?; **~ many people?** wie viele Leute?

however [haʊ'evə*] *ad* (*but*) (je)doch, aber; **~ you phrase it** wie Sie es auch ausdrücken.

howl [haʊl] n Heulen nt // vi heulen.

h.p., H.P. abbr of **hire purchase; horse power.**

H.Q. abbr of **headquarters.**

hub [hʌb] n Radnabe f.

hubbub ['hʌbʌb] n Tumult m.

hubcap ['hʌbkæp] n Radkappe f.

huddle ['hʌdl] vi: to ~ **together** sich zusammendrängen.

hue [hju:] n Färbung f; ~ **and cry** n Zetergeschrei nt.

huff [hʌf] n: to go into a ~ einschnappen.

hug [hʌg] vt umarmen // n Umarmung f.

huge [hju:dʒ] a groß, riesig.

hulk [hʌlk] n (ship) abgetakelte(s) Schiff nt; (person) Koloß m.

hull [hʌl] n Schiffsrumpf m.

hullo [hʌ'ləʊ] see **hello.**

hum [hʌm] vti summen.

human ['hju:mən] a menschlich // n (also: ~ **being**) Mensch m.

humane [hju:'meɪn] a human.

humanity [hju:'mænɪtɪ] n Menschheit f; (kindliness) Menschlichkeit f.

humble ['hʌmbl] a demütig; (modest) bescheiden // vt demütigen.

humbug ['hʌmbʌg] n Humbug m; (Brit: sweet) Pfefferminzbonbon m.

humdrum ['hʌmdrʌm] a stumpfsinnig.

humid ['hju:mɪd] a feucht; ~**ity** [hju:'mɪdɪtɪ] n Feuchtigkeit f.

humiliate [hju:'mɪlɪeɪt] vt demütigen.

humiliation [hju:mɪlɪ'eɪʃən] n Demütigung f.

humility [hju:'mɪlɪtɪ] n Demut f.

humorous ['hju:mərəs] a humorvoll.

humour, (US) **humor** ['hju:mə*] n (fun) Humor m; (mood) Stimmung f // vt bei Stimmung halten.

hump [hʌmp] n Buckel m.

hunch [hʌntʃ] n (Vor)ahnung f; ~**back** n Bucklige(r) mf; ~**ed** a gekrümmt.

hundred ['hʌndrəd] num hundert; ~**weight** n Zentner m (Brit) = 50.8 kg; (US) = 45.3 kg.

hung [hʌŋ] pt, pp of **hang.**

Hungarian [hʌŋ'gɛərɪən] a ungarisch // n Ungar(in f) m; (LING) Ungarisch nt.

Hungary ['hʌŋgərɪ] n Ungarn nt.

hunger ['hʌŋgə*] n Hunger m // vi hungern; ~ **strike** n Hungerstreik m.

hungry ['hʌŋgrɪ] a hungrig; to be ~ Hunger haben.

hunk [hʌŋk] n (of bread) Stück nt.

hunt [hʌnt] vt jagen; (search) suchen (for acc) // vi jagen // n Jagd f; ~**er** n Jäger m; ~**ing** n Jagd f.

hurdle ['hɜ:dl] n (lit, fig) Hürde f.

hurl [hɜ:l] vt schleudern.

hurrah [hʊ'rɑ:], **hurray** [hʊ'reɪ] n Hurra nt.

hurricane ['hʌrɪkən] n Orkan m.

hurried ['hʌrɪd] a eilig; (hasty) übereilt; ~**ly** ad übereilt, hastig.

hurry ['hʌrɪ] n Eile f // vi sich beeilen // vt (an)treiben; (job) übereilen; to be in a ~ es eilig haben; ~ **up** vi sich beeilen // vt (person) zur Eile antreiben; (work) vorantreiben.

hurt [hɜ:t], pt, pp **hurt** vt weh tun (+dat); (injure, fig) verletzen // vi weh tun; ~**ful** a schädlich; (remark) verletzend.

hurtle ['hɜ:tl] vi sausen.

husband ['hʌzbənd] n (Ehe)mann m.

hush [hʌʃ] n Stille f // vt zur Ruhe bringen // interj pst, still.

husk [hʌsk] n Spelze f.

husky ['hʌskɪ] a (voice) rauh; (figure) stämmig // n Eskimohund m.

hustle ['hʌsl] vt (push) stoßen; (hurry) antreiben // n: ~ **and bustle** Geschäftigkeit f.

hut [hʌt] n Hütte f.

hutch [hʌtʃ] n (Kaninchen)stall m.

hyacinth ['haɪəsɪnθ] n Hyazinthe f.

hybrid ['haɪbrɪd] n Kreuzung f // a Misch-.

hydrant ['haɪdrənt] n (also: **fire** ~) Hydrant m.

hydraulic [haɪ'drɒlɪk] a hydraulisch.

hydrofoil ['haɪdrəʊfɔɪl] n Tragflügelboot nt.

hydrogen ['haɪdrɪdʒən] n Wasserstoff m.

hygiene ['haɪdʒi:n] n Hygiene f.

hygienic [haɪ'dʒi:nɪk] a hygienisch.

hymn [hɪm] n Kirchenlied nt.

hype [haɪp] n (col) Publicity f.

hypermarket ['haɪpə'mɑ:kɪt] n (Brit) Hypermarket m.

hyphen ['haɪfən] n Bindestrich m.

hypnosis [hɪp'nəʊsɪs] n Hypnose f.

hypnotic [hɪp'nɒtɪk] a hypnotisierend.

hypnotize ['hɪpnətaɪz] vt hypnotisieren.

hypocrisy [hɪ'pɒkrɪsɪ] n Heuchelei f.

hypocrite ['hɪpəkrɪt] n Heuchler m.

hypocritical [hɪpə'krɪtɪkəl] a scheinheilig, heuchlerisch.

hypothermia ['haɪpəʊ'θɜ:mɪə] n Unterkühlung f.

hypothetic(al) [haɪpəʊ'θetɪk(əl)] a hypothetisch.

hysterical [hɪs'terɪkəl] a hysterisch.

hysterics [hɪs'terɪks] npl hysterische(r) Anfall m.

I

I [aɪ] pron ich.

ice [aɪs] n Eis nt // vt (COOK) mit Zuckerguß überziehen // vi (also: ~ **up**) vereisen; ~ **axe** n Eispickel m; ~**berg** n Eisberg m; ~**box** n (US) Kühlschrank m; ~ **cream** n Eis nt; ~ **cube** n Eiswürfel m; ~ **hockey** n Eishockey nt.

Iceland ['aɪslənd] n Island nt.

ice: ~ **lolly** n (Brit) Eis nt am Stiel; ~

rink n (Kunst)eisbahn f; ~ **skating** n Schlittschuhlaufen nt.

icicle ['aɪsɪkl] n Eiszapfen m.

icing ['aɪsɪŋ] n (on cake) Zuckerguß m; (on window) Vereisung f; ~ **sugar** n (Brit) Puderzucker m.

icon ['aɪkɒn] n Ikone f.

icy ['aɪsɪ] a (slippery) vereist; (cold) eisig.

I'd [aɪd] = I would; I had.

idea [aɪ'dɪə] n Idee f.

ideal [aɪ'dɪəl] n Ideal nt // a ideal; ~**ist** n Idealist m.

identical [aɪ'dentɪkəl] a identisch; (twins) eineiig.

identification [aɪdentɪfɪ'keɪʃən] n Identifizierung f; **means of** ~ Ausweispapiere pl.

identify [aɪ'dentɪfaɪ] vt identifizieren; (regard as the same) gleichsetzen.

identikit picture [aɪ'dentɪkɪt-] n Phantombild nt.

identity [aɪ'dentɪtɪ] n Identität f; ~ **card** n Personalausweis m.

ideology [aɪdɪ'ɒlədʒɪ] n Ideologie f.

idiom ['ɪdɪəm] n (expression) Redewendung f; (dialect) Idiom nt; ~**atic** [-'mætɪk] a idiomatisch.

idiosyncrasy [ɪdɪə'sɪŋkrəsɪ] n Eigenart f.

idiot ['ɪdɪət] n Idiot(in f) m; ~**ic** [ɪdɪ'ɒtɪk] a idiotisch.

idle ['aɪdl] a (doing nothing) untätig; (lazy) faul; (useless) nutzlos; (machine) still(stehend); (threat, talk) leer // vi (machine) leerlaufen // vt: to ~ away the time die Zeit vertrödeln; ~**ness** n Müßiggang m; Faulheit f.

idol ['aɪdl] n Idol nt; ~**ize** vt vergöttern.

i.e. abbr (= that is) d.h.

if [ɪf] cj 1 wenn; (in case also) falls; ~ I were you wenn ich Sie wäre
2 (although): (even) ~ (selbst or auch) wenn
3 (whether) ob
4: ~ so/not wenn ja/nicht; ~ only ... wenn ... doch nur ...; ~ only I could wenn ich doch nur könnte; see also as.

ignite [ɪg'naɪt] vt (an)zünden // vi sich entzünden.

ignition [ɪg'nɪʃən] n Zündung f; to switch on/off the ~ den Motor anlassen/ abstellen; ~ **key** n (AUT) Zündschlüssel m.

ignorance ['ɪgnərəns] n Unwissenheit f.

ignorant ['ɪgnərənt] a unwissend; to be ~ of nicht wissen.

ignore [ɪg'nɔː*] vt ignorieren.

i'll [aɪl] = I will; I shall.

ill [ɪl] a krank // n Übel nt // ad schlecht; to take or be taken ~ krank werden; ~**-advised** a unklug; ~**-at-ease** a unbehaglich.

illegal a [ɪ'liːgəl] illegal.

illegible [ɪ'ledʒəbl] a unleserlich.

illegitimate [ɪlɪ'dʒɪtɪmət] a unehelich.

ill: ~**-fated** a unselig; ~ **feeling** n Verstimmung f.

illicit [ɪ'lɪsɪt] a verboten.

illiterate [ɪ'lɪtərət] a ungebildet.

ill-mannered ['ɪl'mænəd] a ungehobelt.

illness ['ɪlnəs] n Krankheit f.

illogical [ɪ'lɒdʒɪkəl] a unlogisch.

ill-treat ['ɪl'triːt] vt mißhandeln.

illuminate [ɪ'luːmɪneɪt] vt beleuchten.

illumination [ɪluːmɪ'neɪʃən] n Beleuchtung f; ~**s** pl festliche Beleuchtung f.

illusion [ɪ'luːʒən] n Illusion f; to be under the ~ that ... sich (dat) einbilden, daß ...

illusory [ɪ'luːsərɪ] a trügerisch.

illustrate ['ɪləstreɪt] vt (book) illustrieren; (explain) veranschaulichen.

illustration [ɪləs'treɪʃən] n Illustration f; (explanation) Veranschaulichung f.

illustrious [ɪ'lʌstrɪəs] a berühmt.

ill will ['ɪl'wɪl] n Groll m.

I'm [aɪm] = I am.

image ['ɪmɪdʒ] n Bild nt; (public ~) Image nt; ~**ry** n Symbolik f.

imaginary [ɪ'mædʒɪnərɪ] a eingebildet; (world) Phantasie-.

imagination [ɪmædʒɪ'neɪʃən] n Einbildung f; (creative) Phantasie f.

imaginative [ɪ'mædʒɪnətɪv] a phantasiereich, einfallsreich.

imagine [ɪ'mædʒɪn] vt sich vorstellen; (wrongly) sich einbilden.

imbalance [ɪm'bæləns] n Unausgeglichenheit f.

imbecile ['ɪmbəsiːl] n Schwachsinnige(r) mf.

imbue [ɪm'bjuː] vt: to ~ sth with etw erfüllen mit.

imitate ['ɪmɪteɪt] vt imitieren.

imitation [ɪmɪ'teɪʃən] n Imitation f.

immaculate [ɪ'mækjʊlɪt] a makellos; (dress) tadellos; (ECCL) unbefleckt.

immaterial [ɪmə'tɪərɪəl] a unwesentlich; it is ~ whether ... es ist unwichtig, ob ...

immature [ɪmə'tjʊə*] a unreif.

immediate [ɪ'miːdɪət] a (instant) sofortig; (near) unmittelbar; (relatives) nächste(r, s); (needs) dringlich; ~**ly** ad sofort; ~**ly** next to direkt neben.

immense [ɪ'mens] a unermeßlich.

immerse [ɪ'mɜːs] vt eintauchen; to be ~**d** in (fig) vertieft sein in (+acc).

immersion heater [ɪ'mɜːʃənhiːtə*] n (Brit) Boiler m.

immigrant ['ɪmɪgrənt] n Einwanderer m.

immigrate ['ɪmɪgreɪt] vi einwandern.

immigration [ɪmɪ'greɪʃən] n Einwanderung f.

imminent ['ɪmɪnənt] a bevorstehend.

immobile [ɪ'məʊbaɪl] a unbeweglich.

immobilize [ɪ'məʊbɪlaɪz] vt lähmen.

immoral [ɪ'mɒrəl] a unmoralisch; ~**ity** [ɪmə'rælɪtɪ] n Unsittlichkeit f.

immortal [ɪˈmɔːtl] *a* unsterblich; **~ize** *vt* unsterblich machen.

immune [ɪˈmjuːn] *a* (*secure*) sicher (*from* vor +*dat*); (*MED*) immun.

immunity [ɪˈmjuːnɪtɪ] *n* (*MED, JUR*) Immunität *f*; (*fig*) Freiheit *f*.

immunize [ˈɪmjʊnaɪz] *vt* immunisieren.

imp [ɪmp] *n* Kobold *m*.

impact [ˈɪmpækt] *n* (*lit*) Aufprall *m*; (*fig*) Wirkung *f*.

impair [ɪmˈpɛə*] *vt* beeinträchtigen.

impale [ɪmˈpeɪl] *vt* aufspießen.

impart [ɪmˈpɑːt] *vt* mitteilen; (*knowledge*) vermitteln; (*exude*) abgeben.

impartial [ɪmˈpɑːʃəl] *a* unparteiisch.

impassable [ɪmˈpɑːsəbl] *a* unpassierbar.

impasse [æmˈpɑːs] *n* Sackgasse *f*.

impassive [ɪmˈpæsɪv] *a* gelassen.

impatience [ɪmˈpeɪʃəns] *n* Ungeduld *f*.

impatient *a* [ɪmˈpeɪʃənt] ungeduldig.

impeccable [ɪmˈpekəbl] *a* tadellos.

impede [ɪmˈpiːd] *vt* (be)hindern.

impediment [ɪmˈpedɪmənt] *n* Hindernis *nt*; (*in speech*) Sprachfehler *m*.

impending [ɪmˈpendɪŋ] *a* bevorstehend.

impenetrable [ɪmˈpenɪtrəbl] *a* (*lit, fig*) undurchdringlich.

imperative [ɪmˈperətɪv] *a* (*necessary*) unbedingt erforderlich // *n* (*GRAM*) Imperativ *m*, Befehlsform *f*.

imperceptible [ɪmpəˈseptəbl] *a* nicht wahrnehmbar.

imperfect [ɪmˈpɜːfɪkt] *a* (*faulty*) fehlerhaft; **~ion** [-ˈfekʃən] *n* Unvollkommenheit *f*; (*fault*) Fehler *m*.

imperial [ɪmˈpɪərɪəl] *a* kaiserlich; **~ism** *n* Imperialismus *m*.

impersonal [ɪmˈpɜːsnl] *a* unpersönlich.

impersonate [ɪmˈpɜːsəneɪt] *vt* sich ausgeben als; (*for amusement*) imitieren.

impertinent [ɪmˈpɜːtɪnənt] *a* unverschämt, frech.

impervious [ɪmˈpɜːvɪəs] *a* (*fig*) unempfänglich (*to* für).

impetuous [ɪmˈpetjʊəs] *a* ungestüm.

impetus [ˈɪmpɪtəs] *n* Triebkraft *f*; (*fig*) Auftrieb *m*.

impinge [ɪmˈpɪndʒ]: **~ on** *vt* beeinträchtigen.

implacable [ɪmˈplækəbl] *a* unerbittlich.

implement [ˈɪmplɪmənt] *n* Werkzeug *nt* // [ˈɪmplɪment] *vi* ausführen.

implicate [ˈɪmplɪkeɪt] *vt* verwickeln.

implication [ɪmplɪˈkeɪʃən] *n* (*effect*) Auswirkung *f*; (*in crime*) Verwicklung *f*.

implicit [ɪmˈplɪsɪt] *a* (*suggested*) unausgesprochen; (*utter*) vorbehaltlos.

implore [ɪmˈplɔː*] *vt* anflehen.

imply [ɪmˈplaɪ] *vt* (*hint*) andeuten; (*be evidence for*) schließen lassen auf (+*acc*).

impolite [ɪmpəˈlaɪt] *a* unhöflich.

import [ɪmˈpɔːt] *vt* einführen // *n* [ˈɪmpɔːt] Einfuhr *f*; (*meaning*) Bedeutung *f*.

importance [ɪmˈpɔːtəns] *n* Bedeutung *f*.

important [ɪmˈpɔːtənt] *a* wichtig; it's not ~ es ist unwichtig.

importer [ɪmˈpɔːtə*] *n* Importeur *m*.

impose [ɪmˈpəʊz] *vti* auferlegen (*on dat*); (*penalty, sanctions*) verhängen (*on gegen*); to ~ (*o.s.*) **on sb** sich jdm aufdrängen.

imposing [ɪmˈpəʊzɪŋ] *a* eindrucksvoll.

imposition [ɪmpəˈzɪʃən] *n* (*of burden, fine*) Auferlegung *f*; (*SCH*) Strafarbeit *f*; to be an ~ (*on person*) eine Zumutung sein.

impossible *a* [ɪmˈpɒsəbl] unmöglich.

impostor [ɪmˈpɒstə*] *n* Hochstapler *m*.

impotence [ˈɪmpətəns] Impotenz *f*.

impotent [ˈɪmpətənt] *a* machtlos; (*sexually*) impotent.

impound [ɪmˈpaʊnd] *vt* beschlagnahmen.

impoverished [ɪmˈpɒvərɪʃt] *a* verarmt.

impracticable [ɪmˈpræktɪkəbl] *a* undurchführbar.

impractical [ɪmˈpræktɪkəl] *a* unpraktisch.

imprecise [ɪmprəˈsaɪs] *a* ungenau.

impregnable [ɪmˈpregnəbl] *a* (*castle*) uneinnehmbar.

impregnate [ˈɪmpregneɪt] *vt* (*saturate*) sättigen; (*fertilize*) befruchten.

impress [ɪmˈpres] *vt* (*influence*) beeindrucken; (*imprint*) (auf)drücken; to ~ **sth on sb** jdm etw einschärfen.

impression [ɪmˈpreʃən] *n* Eindruck *m*; (*on wax, footprint*) Abdruck *m*; (*of book*) Auflage *f*; (*take-off*) Nachahmung *f*; I was under the ~ ich hatte den Eindruck; **~able** *a* leicht zu beeindrucken; **~ist** *n* Impressionist *m*.

impressive [ɪmˈpresɪv] *a* eindrucksvoll.

imprint [ˈɪmprɪnt] *n* Abdruck *m*.

imprison [ɪmˈprɪzn] *vt* ins Gefängnis schicken; **~ment** *n* Inhaftierung *f*.

improbable [ɪmˈprɒbəbl] *a* unwahrscheinlich.

impromptu [ɪmˈprɒmptjuː] *a, ad* aus dem Stegreif, improvisiert.

improper [ɪmˈprɒpə*] *a* (*indecent*) unanständig; (*unsuitable*) unpassend.

improve [ɪmˈpruːv] *vt* verbessern // *vi* besser werden; **~ment** *n* (Ver)-besserung *f*.

improvise [ˈɪmprəvaɪz] *vti* improvisieren.

imprudent [ɪmˈpruːdənt] *a* unklug.

impudent [ˈɪmpjʊdənt] *a* unverschämt.

impulse [ˈɪmpʌls] *n* Impuls *m*; to act on ~ spontan handeln.

impulsive [ɪmˈpʌlsɪv] *a* impulsiv.

impunity [ɪmˈpjuːnɪtɪ] *n* Straflosigkeit *f*.

impure [ɪmˈpjʊə*] *a* (*dirty*) verunreinigt; (*bad*) unsauber.

impurity [ɪmˈpjʊərɪtɪ] *n* Unreinheit *f*;

(*TECH*) Verunreinigung *f*.

in [ɪn] ◆*prep* **1** (*indicating place, position*) in (+ *dat*); (*with motion*) in (+ *acc*); ~ **here/there** hier/dort; ~ **London** in London; ~ **the United States** in den Vereinigten Staaten **2** (*indicating time: during*) in (+ *dat*); ~ **summer** im Sommer; ~ **1988** (im Jahre) 1988; ~ **the afternoon** nachmittags, am Nachmittag **3** (*indicating time: in the space of*) innerhalb von; **I'll see you ~ 2 weeks** *or* ~ **2 weeks' time** ich sehe Sie in zwei Wochen **4** (*indicating manner, circumstances, state etc*) in (+ *dat*); ~ **the sun/rain** in der Sonne/im Regen; ~ **English/French** auf Englisch/Französisch; ~ **a loud/soft voice** mit lauter/leiser Stimme **5** (*with ratios, numbers*): **1 ~ 10** jeder zehnte; **20 pence ~ the pound** 20 Pence pro Pfund; **they lined up ~ twos** sie stellten sich in Zweierreihe auf **6** (*referring to people, works*): **the disease is common ~ children** die Krankheit ist bei Kindern häufig; ~ **Dickens** bei Dickens; **we have a loyal friend ~ him** er ist uns ein treuer Freund **7** (*indicating profession etc*): **to be ~ teaching/the army** Lehrer(in)/beim Militär sein; **to be ~ publishing** im Verlagswesen arbeiten **8** (*with present participle*): ~ **saying this, I ...** wenn ich das sage, ... ich; ~ **accepting this view, he ...** weil er diese Meinung akzeptierte, ... er ◆*ad*: **to be ~** (*person: at home, work*) dasein; (*train, ship, plane*) angekommen sein; (*in fashion*) in sein; **to ask sb ~** jdn hereinbitten; **to run/limp etc ~** hereingerannt/-gehumpelt *etc* kommen ◆*n*: **the ~s and outs** (*of proposal, situation etc*) die Feinheiten.

in., ins *abbr of* **inch(es)**.

inability [ɪnə'bɪlɪtɪ] *n* Unfähigkeit *f*.

inaccessible [ɪnæk'sesəbl] *a* unzugänglich.

inaccurate [ɪn'ækjʊrɪt] *a* ungenau; (*wrong*) unrichtig.

inactivity [ɪnæk'tɪvɪtɪ] *n* Untätigkeit *f*.

inadequate [ɪn'ædɪkwət] *a* unzulänglich.

inadvertently [ɪnəd'vɜːtəntlɪ] *ad* unabsichtlich.

inadvisable [ɪnəd'vaɪzəbl] *a* nicht ratsam.

inane [ɪ'neɪn] *a* dumm, albern.

inanimate [ɪn'ænɪmət] *a* leblos.

inappropriate [ɪnə'prəʊprɪət] *a* (*clothing*) ungeeignet; (*remark*) unangebracht.

inarticulate [ɪnɑː'tɪkjʊlət] *a* unklar.

inasmuch as [ɪnəz'mʌtʃəz] *ad* da; (*in so far as*) soweit.

inaudible [ɪn'ɔːdəbl] *a* unhörbar.

inaugural [ɪ'nɔːgjʊrəl] *a* Eröffnungs-.

inaugurate [ɪ'nɔːgjʊreɪt] *vt* (*open*) einweihen; (*admit to office*) (feierlich) einführen.

inauguration [ɪnɔːgjʊ'reɪʃən] *n* Eröffnung *f*; (feierliche) Amtseinführung *f*.

in-between [ɪnbɪ'twiːn] *a* Zwischen-.

inborn ['ɪn'bɔːn] *a* angeboren.

inbred ['ɪn'bred] *a* angeboren.

Inc. *abbr* (*US*) *of* **incorporated**.

incalculable [ɪn'kælkjʊləbl] *a* (*consequences*) unabsehbar.

incapable [ɪn'keɪpəbl] *a* unfähig (*of doing sth* etw zu tun).

incapacitate [ɪnkə'pæsɪteɪt] *vt* untauglich machen.

incapacity [ɪnkə'pæsɪtɪ] *n* Unfähigkeit *f*.

incarcerate [ɪn'kɑːsəreɪt] *vt* einkerkern.

incarnation [ɪnkɑː'neɪʃən] *n* (*ECCL*) Menschwerdung *f*; (*fig*) Inbegriff *m*.

incendiary [ɪn'sendɪərɪ] *a* Brand-.

incense ['ɪnsens] *n* Weihrauch *m* // *vt* [ɪn'sens] erzürnen.

incentive [ɪn'sentɪv] *n* Anreiz *m*.

incessant *a*, ~**ly** *ad* [ɪn'sesnt, -lɪ] unaufhörlich.

incest ['ɪnsest] *n* Inzest *m*.

inch [ɪntʃ] *n* Zoll *m*; **to be within an ~ of** kurz davor sein; **he didn't give an ~** er gab keinen Zentimeter nach; **to ~ forward** *vi* sich Stückchen für Stückchen vorwärts bewegen.

incidence ['ɪnsɪdəns] *n* Auftreten *nt*; (*of crime*) Quote *f*.

incident ['ɪnsɪdənt] *n* Vorfall *m*; (*disturbance*) Zwischenfall *m*.

incidental [ɪnsɪ'dentl] *a* (*music*) Begleit-; (*unimportant*) nebensächlich; (*remark*) beiläufig; ~**ly** [-'dentəlɪ] *ad* übrigens.

incinerator [ɪn'sɪnəreɪtə*] *n* Verbrennungsofen *m*.

incipient [ɪn'sɪpɪənt] *a* beginnend.

incision [ɪn'sɪʒən] *n* Einschnitt *m*.

incisive [ɪn'saɪsɪv] *a* (*style*) treffend; (*person*) scharfsinnig.

incite [ɪn'saɪt] *vt* anstacheln.

inclination [ɪnklɪ'neɪʃən] *n* Neigung *f*.

incline ['ɪnklaɪn] *n* Abhang *m* // [ɪn'klaɪn] *vt* neigen; (*fig*) veranlassen // *vi* sich neigen; **to be ~d to do sth** dazu neigen, etw zu tun.

include [ɪn'kluːd] *vt* einschließen; (*on list, in group*) aufnehmen.

including [ɪn'kluːdɪŋ] *prep*: ~ **X X** inbegriffen.

inclusion [ɪn'kluːʒən] *n* Aufnahme *f*.

inclusive [ɪn'kluːsɪv] *a* einschließlich; (*COMM*) inklusive; ~ **of** einschließlich (+ *gen*).

incoherent [ɪnkəʊ'hɪərənt] *a* zusammenhanglos.

income ['ɪnkʌm] *n* Einkommen *nt*; (*from business*) Einkünfte *pl*; ~ **tax** *n* Lohnsteuer *f*; (*of self-employed*) Einkommenssteuer *f*.

incoming ['ınkʌmıŋ] *a*: ~ **flight** eintreffende Maschine *f*.

incomparable [ın'kɒmpərəbl] *a* unvergleichlich.

incompatible [ınkəm'pætəbl] *a* unvereinbar; (*people*) unverträglich.

incompetence [ın'kɒmpıtəns] *n* Unfähigkeit *f*.

incompetent [ın'kɒmpıtənt] *a* unfähig.

incomplete [ınkəm'pli:t] *a* unvollständig.

incomprehensible [ınkɒmprı'hensəbl] *a* unverständlich.

inconceivable [ınkən'si:vəbl] *a* unvorstellbar.

incongruous [ın'kɒŋgruəs] *a* seltsam; (*remark*) unangebracht.

inconsiderate [ınkən'sıdərət] *a* rücksichtslos.

inconsistency [ınkən'sıstənsı] *n* Widersprüchlichkeit *f*; (*state*) Unbeständigkeit *f*.

inconsistent [ınkən'sıstənt] *a* (*action, speech*) widersprüchlich; (*person, work*) unbeständig; ~ **with** nicht übereinstimmend mit.

inconspicuous [ınkən'spıkjuəs] *a* unauffällig.

incontinent [ın'kɒntınənt] *a* (*MED*) nicht fähig, Stuhl und Harn zurückzuhalten.

inconvenience [ınkən'vi:nıəns] *n* Unbequemlichkeit *f*; (*trouble to others*) Unannehmlichkeiten *pl*.

inconvenient [ınkən'vi:nıənt] *a* ungelegen; (*journey*) unbequem.

incorporate [ın'kɔːrpɔreıt] *vt* (*include*) aufnehmen; (*contain*) enthalten.

incorporated [ın'kɔːpəreıtıd] *a*: ~**d company** (*US: abbr* Inc.) eingetragene Aktiengesellschaft *f*.

incorrect [ınkə'rekt] *a* unrichtig.

incorrigible [ın'kɒrıdʒəbl] *a* unverbesserlich.

incorruptible [ınkə'rʌptəbl] *a* unzerstörbar; (*person*) unbestechlich.

increase [ın'kri:s] *n* Zunahme *f*; (*pay* ~) Gehaltserhöhung *f*; (*in size*) Vergrößerung *f* // *vt* [ın'kri:s] erhöhen; (*wealth, rage*) vermehren; (*business*) erweitern // *vi* zunehmen; (*prices*) steigen; (*in size*) größer werden; (*in number*) sich vermehren.

increasing [ın'kri:sıŋ] *a* (*number*) steigend.

increasingly [ın'kri:sıŋlı] *ad* zunehmend.

incredible [ın'kredəbl] *a* unglaublich.

incredulous [ın'kredjuləs] *a* ungläubig.

increment ['ınkrımənt] *n* Zulage *f*.

incriminate [ın'krımıneıt] *vt* belasten.

incubation [ınkju'beıʃən] *n* Ausbrüten *nt*.

incubator ['ınkjubeıtə*] *n* Brutkasten

m.

incumbent [ın'kʌmbənt] *n* Amtsinhaber(in *f*) *m* // *a*: **it is** ~ **on him to** ... es obliegt ihm, ...

incur [ın'kɜː*] *vt* sich zuziehen; (*debts*) machen.

incurable [ın'kjuərəbl] *a* unheilbar; (*fig*) unverbesserlich.

incursion [ın'kɜːʃən] *n* Einfall *m*.

indebted [ın'detıd] *a* (*obliged*) verpflichtet (*to sb* jdm).

indecent [ın'di:snt] *a* unanständig; ~ **assault** *n* (*Brit*) Notzucht *f*; ~ **exposure** *n* Exhibitionismus *m*.

indecisive [ındı'saısıv] *a* (*battle*) nicht entscheidend; (*person*) unentschlossen.

indeed [ın'di:d] *ad* tatsächlich, in der Tat; **yes** ~! Allerdings!

indefinite [ın'defınıt] *a* unbestimmt; ~**ly** *ad* auf unbestimmte Zeit; (*wait*) unbegrenzt lange.

indelible [ın'deləbl] *a* unauslöschlich.

indemnify [ın'demnıfaı] *vt* entschädigen; (*safeguard*) versichern.

indemnity [ın'demnıtı] *n* (*insurance*) Versicherung *f*; (*compensation*) Schadenersatz *m*.

independence [ındı'pendəns] *n* Unabhängigkeit *f*.

independent [ındı'pendənt] *a* unabhängig.

indestructible [,ındıs'trʌktəbl] *a* unzerstörbar.

indeterminate [,ındı'tɜːmınıt] *a* unbestimmt.

index ['ındeks] *n* Index *m*; ~ **card** *n* Karteikarte *f*; ~ **finger** *n* Zeigefinger *m*; ~**-linked**, (*US*) ~**ed** *a* (*salaries*) der Inflationsrate (*dat*) angeglichen; (*pensions*) dynamisch.

India ['ındıə] *n* Indien *nt*; ~**n** *a* indisch // *n* Inder(in *f*) *m*; **Red** ~**n** Indianer(in *f*) *m*; **the** ~**n Ocean** *n* der Indische Ozean.

indicate ['ındıkeıt] *vt* anzeigen; (*hint*) andeuten.

indication [ındı'keıʃən] *n* Anzeichen *nt*; (*information*) Angabe *f*.

indicative [ın'dıkətıv] *a*: ~ **of** bezeichnend für // *n* (*GRAM*) Indikativ *m*.

indicator ['ındıkeıtə*] *n* (*sign*) (An)zeichen *nt*; (*AUT*) Richtungsanzeiger *m*.

indices ['ındısi:z] *pl of* **index**.

indict [ın'daıt] *vt* anklagen; ~**ment** *n* Anklage *f*.

indifference [ın'dıfrəns] *n* Gleichgültigkeit *f*; Unwichtigkeit *f*.

indifferent [ın'dıfrənt] *a* gleichgültig; (*mediocre*) mäßig.

indigenous [ın'dıdʒınəs] *a* einheimisch.

indigestion [ındı'dʒestʃən] *n* Verdauungsstörung *f*.

indignant [ın'dıgnənt] *a*: **to be** ~ **about**

sth über etw (*acc*) empört sein.

indignation [ɪndɪg'neɪʃən] *n* Entrüstung *f*.

indignity [ɪn'dɪgnɪtɪ] *n* Demütigung *f*.

indirect *a*, ~**ly** *ad* [ɪndɪ'rekt, -lɪ] indirekt.

indiscreet [ɪndɪs'kriːt] *a* (*insensitive*) taktlos; (*telling secrets*) indiskret.

indiscretion [ɪndɪs'kreʃən] *n* Taktlosigkeit *f*; Indiskretion *f*.

indiscriminate [ɪndɪs'krɪmɪnət] *a* wahllos; kritiklos.

indispensable [ɪndɪs'pensəbl] *a* unentbehrlich.

indisposed [ɪndɪs'pəʊzd] *a* unpäßlich.

indisputable [ɪndɪs'pjuːtəbl] *a* unbestreitbar; (*evidence*) unanfechtbar.

indistinct [ɪndɪs'tɪŋkt] *a* undeutlich.

individual [ɪndɪ'vɪdjʊəl] *n* Individuum *nt* // *a* individuell; (*case*) Einzel-; (*of, for one person*) eigen, individuell; (*characteristic*) eigentümlich; ~**ly** *ad* einzeln, individuell.

indivisible [ɪndɪ'vɪzəbl] *a* unteilbar.

indoctrinate [ɪn'dɒktrɪneɪt] *vt* indoktrinieren.

Indonesia [ɪndəʊ'niːzɪə] *n* Indonesien *nt*.

indoor ['ɪndɔː*] *a* Haus-; Zimmer-; Innen-; (*SPORT*) Hallen-; ~**s** [ɪn'dɔːz] *ad* drinnen, im Haus.

induce [ɪn'djuːs] *vt* dazu bewegen; (*reaction*) herbeiführen; ~**ment** *n* Veranlassung *f*; (*incentive*) Anreiz *m*.

induction [ɪn'dʌkʃən] *n* (*MED*: *of birth*) Einleitung *f*; ~ **course** *n* (*Brit*) Einführungskurs *m*.

indulge [ɪn'dʌldʒ] *vt* (*give way*) nachgeben (+*dat*); (*gratify*) frönen (+*dat*) // *vi* frönen (*in dat*); ~**nce** *n* Nachsicht *f*; (*enjoyment*) Genuß *m*; ~**nt** *a* nachsichtig; (*pej*) nachgiebig.

industrial [ɪn'dʌstrɪəl] *a* Industrie-, industriell; (*dispute, injury*) Arbeits-; ~ **action** *n* Arbeitskampfmaßnahmen *pl*; ~ **estate** *n* (*Brit*) Industriegebiet *nt*; ~**ist** *n* Industrielle(r) *mf*; ~**ize** *vt* industrialisieren; ~ **park** *n* (*US*) = ~ **estate**.

industrious [ɪn'dʌstrɪəs] *a* fleißig.

industry ['ɪndəstrɪ] *n* Industrie *f*; (*diligence*) Fleiß *m*.

inebriated [ɪ'niːbrɪeɪtɪd] *a* betrunken.

inedible [ɪn'edɪbl] *a* ungenießbar.

ineffective [ɪnɪ'fektɪv], **ineffectual** [ɪnɪ'fektjʊəl] *a* unwirksam; (*person*) untauglich.

inefficiency [ɪnɪ'fɪʃənsɪ] *n* Ineffizienz *f*.

inefficient [ɪnɪ'fɪʃənt] *a* ineffizient; (*ineffective*) unwirksam.

inept [ɪ'nept] *a* (*remark*) unpassend; (*person*) ungeeignet.

inequality [ɪnɪ'kwɒlɪtɪ] *n* Ungleichheit *f*.

inert [ɪ'nɜːt] *a* träge; (*CHEM*) inaktiv; (*motionless*) unbeweglich.

inertia [ɪ'nɜːʃə] *n* Trägheit *f*.

inescapable [ɪnɪs'keɪpəbl] *a* unvermeidbar.

inevitable [ɪn'evɪtəbl] *a* unvermeidlich.

inexcusable [ɪnɪks'kjuːzəbl] *a* unverzeihlich.

inexhaustible [ɪnɪg'zɔːstəbl] *a* unerschöpflich.

inexorable [ɪn'eksərəbl] *a* unerbittlich.

inexpensive [ɪnɪks'pensɪv] *a* preiswert.

inexperience [ɪnɪks'pɪərɪəns] *n* Unerfahrenheit *f*; ~**d** *a* unerfahren.

inexplicable [ɪnɪks'plɪkəbl] *a* unerklärlich.

inextricably [ɪnɪks'trɪkəblɪ] *ad* untrennbar.

infallible [ɪn'fæləbl] *a* unfehlbar.

infamous ['ɪnfəməs] *a* (*place*) verrufen; (*deed*) schändlich; (*person*) niederträchtig.

infamy ['ɪnfəmɪ] *n* Verrufenheit *f*; Niedertracht *f*; (*disgrace*) Schande *f*.

infancy ['ɪnfənsɪ] *n* frühe Kindheit *f*; (*fig*) Anfangsstadium *nt*.

infant ['ɪnfənt] *n* kleine(s) Kind *nt*, Säugling *m*; ~**ile** *a* kindisch, infantil; ~ **school** *n* (*Brit*) Grundschule *f* (*für die ersten beiden Jahrgänge*).

infantry ['ɪnfəntrɪ] *n* Infanterie *f*.

infatuated [ɪn'fætjʊeɪtɪd] *a* vernarrt; to become ~ with sich vernarren in (+*acc*).

infatuation [ɪnfætjʊ'eɪʃən] *n* Vernarrtheit *f* (*with* in +*acc*).

infect [ɪn'fekt] *vt* anstecken (*also fig*); ~**ed with** (*illness*) infiziert mit; ~**ion** *n* Infektion *f*; ~**ious** [ɪn'fekʃəs] *a* ansteckend.

infer [ɪn'fɜː*] *vt* schließen; ~**ence** ['ɪnfərəns] *n* Schlußfolgerung *f*.

inferior [ɪn'fɪərɪə*] *a* (*rank*) untergeordnet; (*quality*) minderwertig // *n* Untergebene(r) *m*; ~**ity** [ɪnfɪərɪ'ɒrɪtɪ] *n* Minderwertigkeit *f*; (*in rank*) untergeordnete Stellung *f*; ~**ity complex** *n* Minderwertigkeitskomplex *m*.

infernal [ɪn'fɜːnl] *a* höllisch.

infertile [ɪn'fɜːtaɪl] *a* unfruchtbar.

infertility [ɪnfɜː'tɪlɪtɪ] *n* Unfruchtbarkeit *f*.

infested [ɪn'festɪd] *a*: to be ~ with wimmeln von.

infidelity [ɪnfɪ'delɪtɪ] *n* Untreue *f*.

in-fighting ['ɪnfaɪtɪŋ] *n* Nahkampf *m*.

infiltrate ['ɪnfɪltreɪt] *vt* infiltrieren; (*spies*) einschleusen // *vi* (*MIL, liquid*) einsickern; (*POL*) unterwandern (*into acc*).

infinite ['ɪnfɪnɪt] *a* unendlich.

infinitive [ɪn'fɪnɪtɪv] *n* Infinitiv *m*.

infinity [ɪn'fɪnɪtɪ] *n* Unendlichkeit *f*.

infirm [ɪn'fɜːm] *a* gebrechlich.

infirmary [ɪn'fɜːmərɪ] *n* Krankenhaus *nt*.

infirmity [ɪn'fɜːmɪtɪ] *n* Schwäche *f*, Gebrechlichkeit *f*.

inflamed [ɪn'fleɪmd] *a* entzündet.

inflammable [ɪn'flæməbl] a (Brit) feuergefährlich.

inflammation [ɪnflə'meɪʃən] n Entzündung f.

inflatable [ɪn'fleɪtəbl] a aufblasbar.

inflate [ɪn'fleɪt] vt aufblasen; (tyre) aufpumpen; (prices) hochtreiben.

inflation [ɪn'fleɪʃən] n Inflation f; **~ary** a (increase) inflationistisch; (situation) inflationär.

inflexible [ɪn'fleksəbl] a (person) nicht flexibel; (opinion) starr; (thing) unbiegsam.

inflict [ɪn'flɪkt] vt zufügen (sth on sb jdm etw); (wound) beibringen (on dat).

influence ['ɪnfluəns] n Einfluß m // vt beeinflussen.

influential [ɪnflu'enʃəl] a einflußreich.

influenza [ɪnflu'enzə] n Grippe f.

influx ['ɪnflʌks] n (of people) Zustrom m; (of ideas) Eindringen nt.

inform [ɪn'fɔːm] vt informieren; to keep sb ~ed jdn auf dem laufenden halten // vi: to ~ on sb jdn denunzieren.

informal [ɪn'fɔːməl] a zwanglos; **~ity** [ɪnfɔː'mælɪtɪ] n Ungezwungenheit f.

informant [ɪn'fɔːmənt] n Informant(in f) m.

information [ɪnfə'meɪʃən] n Auskunft f, Information f; **a piece of ~** eine Auskunft, eine Information; **~ office** n Informationsbüro nt.

informative [ɪn'fɔːmətɪv] a informativ; (person) mitteilsam.

informer [ɪn'fɔːmə*] n Denunziant(in f) m.

infra-red ['ɪnfrə'red] a infrarot.

infrequent [ɪn'friːkwənt] a selten.

infringe [ɪn'frɪndʒ] vt (law) verstoßen gegen; **~ upon** vt verletzen; **~ment** n Verstoß m, Verletzung f.

infuriating [ɪn'fjuərɪeɪtɪŋ] a ärgerlich.

infusion [ɪn'fjuːʒən] n (tea etc) Aufguß m.

ingenious [ɪn'dʒiːnɪəs] a genial.

ingenuity [ɪndʒɪ'njuːɪtɪ] n Genialität f.

ingenuous [ɪn'dʒenjuəs] a aufrichtig; (naive) naiv.

ingot ['ɪŋgət] n Barren m.

ingrained [ɪn'greɪnd] a tiefsitzend (attr).

ingratiate [ɪn'greɪʃɪeɪt] vt einschmeicheln (o.s. with sb sich bei jdm).

ingratitude [ɪn'grætɪtjuːd] n Undankbarkeit f.

ingredient [ɪn'griːdɪənt] n Bestandteil m; (COOK) Zutat f.

inhabit [ɪn'hæbɪt] vt bewohnen; **~ant** n Bewohner(in f) m; (of island, town) Einwohner(in f) m.

inhale [ɪn'heɪl] vt einatmen; (MED, cigarettes) inhalieren.

inherent [ɪn'hɪərənt] a innewohnend (in dat).

inherit [ɪn'herɪt] vt erben; **~ance** n

Erbe nt, Erbschaft f.

inhibit [ɪn'hɪbɪt] vt hemmen; to ~ sb from doing sth jdn daran hindern, etw zu tun; **~ion** [ɪnhɪ'bɪʃən] n Hemmung f.

inhospitable [ɪnhɔs'pɪtəbl] a (person) ungastlich; (country) unwirtlich.

inhuman [ɪn'hjuːmən] a unmenschlich.

inimitable [ɪ'nɪmɪtəbl] a unnachahmlich.

iniquity [ɪ'nɪkwɪtɪ] n Ungerechtigkeit f.

initial [ɪ'nɪʃəl] a anfänglich, Anfangs- // n Initiale f // vt abzeichnen; (POL) paraphieren; **~s** pl Initialen pl; **~ly** ad anfangs.

initiate [ɪ'nɪʃɪeɪt] vt einführen; (negotiations) einleiten; to ~ sb into a secret jdn in ein Geheimnis einweihen; to ~ proceedings against sb (JUR) gerichtliche Schritte gegen jdn einleiten.

initiation [ɪnɪʃɪ'eɪʃən] n Einführung f; Einleitung f.

initiative [ɪ'nɪʃətɪv] n Initiative f.

inject [ɪn'dʒekt] vt einspritzen; (fig) einflößen; **~ion** n Spritze f.

injunction [ɪn'dʒʌŋkʃən] n Verfügung f.

injure ['ɪndʒə*] vt verletzen; **~d** a (person, arm) verletzt.

injury ['ɪndʒərɪ] n Verletzung f; to play ~ time (SPORT) nachspielen.

injustice [ɪn'dʒʌstɪs] n Ungerechtigkeit f.

ink [ɪŋk] n Tinte f.

inkling ['ɪŋklɪŋ] n (dunkle) Ahnung f.

inlaid ['ɪn'leɪd] a eingelegt, Einlege-.

inland ['ɪnlænd] a Binnen-; (domestic) Inlands- // ad landeinwärts; **~ revenue** n (Brit) Fiskus m.

in-laws ['ɪnlɔːz] npl (parents-in-law) Schwiegereltern pl; (others) angeheiratete Verwandte pl.

inlet ['ɪnlet] n Einlaß m; (bay) kleine Bucht f.

inmate ['ɪnmeɪt] n Insasse m.

inn [ɪn] n Gasthaus nt, Wirtshaus nt.

innate [ɪ'neɪt] a angeboren.

inner ['ɪnə*] a inner, Innen-; (fig) verborgen; **~ city** n Innenstadt f; **~ tube** n (of tyre) Schlauch m.

innings ['ɪnɪŋz] n (CRICKET) Innenrunde f.

innocence ['ɪnəsns] n Unschuld f; (ignorance) Unkenntnis f.

innocent ['ɪnəsnt] a unschuldig.

innocuous [ɪ'nɔkjuəs] a harmlos.

innovation [ɪnəʊ'veɪʃən] n Neuerung f.

innuendo [ɪnjʊ'endəʊ] n (versteckte) Anspielung f.

innumerable [ɪ'njuːmərəbl] a unzählig.

inoculation [ɪnɔkjʊ'leɪʃən] n Impfung f.

inopportune [ɪn'ɔpətjuːn] a (remark) unangebracht; (visit) ungelegen.

inordinately [ɪ'nɔːdɪnɪtlɪ] ad unmäßig.

in-patient ['ɪnpeɪʃənt] n stationäre(r) Patient(in f) m.

input ['ɪnput] n (COMPUT) Eingabe f;

(power ~) Energiezufuhr *f; (of energy, work)* Aufwand *m.*

inquest ['ɪnkwest] *n* gerichtliche Untersuchung *f.*

inquire [ɪn'kwaɪə*] *vi* sich erkundigen // *vt (price)* sich erkundigen nach; ~ **into** *vt* untersuchen.

inquiry [ɪn'kwaɪərɪ] *n (question)* Erkundigung *f; (investigation)* Untersuchung *f;* ~ **office** *n (Brit)* Auskunft(sbüro *nt) f.*

inquisitive [ɪn'kwɪzɪtɪv] *a* neugierig.

inroad ['ɪnrəʊd] *n (MIL)* Einfall *m; (fig)* Eingriff *m.*

insane [ɪn'seɪn] *a* wahnsinnig; *(MED)* geisteskrank.

insanity [ɪn'sænɪtɪ] *n* Wahnsinn *m.*

insatiable [ɪn'seɪʃəbl] *a* unersättlich.

inscribe [ɪn'skraɪb] *vt* eingravieren; *(book etc):* **to** ~ **(to sb)** (jdm) widmen.

inscription [ɪn'skrɪpʃən] *n (on stone)* Inschrift *f; (in book)* Widmung *f.*

inscrutable [ɪn'skru:təbl] *a* unergründlich.

insect ['ɪnsekt] *n* Insekt *nt;* ~**icide** [ɪn'sektɪsaɪd] *n* Insektenvertilgungsmittel *nt.*

insecure [ɪnsɪ'kjʊə*] *a (person)* unsicher; *(thing)* nicht fest *or* sicher.

insecurity [ɪnsɪ'kjʊərɪtɪ] *n* Unsicherheit *f.*

insemination [ɪnsemɪ'neɪʃən] *n:* artificial ~ künstliche Befruchtung *f.*

insensible [ɪn'sensɪbl] *a (unconscious)* bewußtlos.

insensitive [ɪn'sensɪtɪv] *a (to pain)* unempfindlich; *(without feelings)* gefühllos.

inseparable [ɪn'sepərəbl] *a (people)* unzertrennlich; *(word)* untrennbar.

insert [ɪn'sɜ:t] *vt* einfügen; *(coin)* einwerfen; *(stick into)* hineinstecken; *(advert)* aufgeben // *n* ['ɪnsɜ:t] *(in book)* Einlage *f; (in magazine)* Beilage *f;* ~**ion** *n* Einfügung *f; (PRESS)* Inserat *nt.*

in-service ['ɪn'sɜ:vɪs] *a (training)* berufsbegleitend.

inshore ['ɪn'ʃɔ:'] *a* Küsten- // *ad* ['ɪn'ʃɔ:*] an der Küste.

inside ['ɪn'saɪd] *n* Innenseite *f,* Innere(s) *nt* // *a* innere(r, s), Innen- // *ad (place)* innen; *(direction)* nach innen, hinein // *prep (place)* in (+*dat); (direction)* in (+*acc)* ... hinein; *(time)* innerhalb (+*gen);* ~ **10 minutes** in unter 10 Minuten; ~**s** *pl (col)* Eingeweide *nt;* ~ **forward** *n (SPORT)* Halbstürmer *m;* ~ **lane** *n (AUT: in Britain)* linke Spur; ~ **out** *ad* linksherum; *(know)* in- und auswendig.

insidious [ɪn'sɪdɪəs] *a* heimtückisch.

insight ['ɪnsaɪt] *n* Einsicht *f;* Einblick *m (into* in +*acc).*

insignificant [ɪnsɪg'nɪfɪkənt] *a* unbedeutend.

insincere [ɪnsɪn'sɪə*] *a* unaufrichtig.

insinuate [ɪn'sɪnjʊeɪt] *vt (hint)* andeuten.

insipid [ɪn'sɪpɪd] *a* fad(e).

insist [ɪn'sɪst] *vi* bestehen *(on* auf +*acc);* ~**ence** *nt* Bestehen *nt;* ~**ent** *a* hartnäckig; *(urgent)* dringend.

insole ['ɪnsəʊl] *n* Einlegesohle *f.*

insolence ['ɪnsələns] *n* Frechheit *f.*

insolent ['ɪnsələnt] *a* frech.

insoluble [ɪn'sɒljʊbl] *a* unlösbar; *(CHEM)* unlöslich.

insolvent [ɪn'sɒlvənt] *a* zahlungsunfähig.

insomnia [ɪn'sɒmnɪə] *n* Schlaflosigkeit *f.*

inspect [ɪn'spekt] *vt* prüfen; *(officially)* inspizieren; ~**or** *n* Inspektion *f;* ~**or** *n (official)* Inspektor *m; (police)* Polizeikommissar *m; (Brit: on buses, trains)* Kontrolleur *m.*

inspiration [ɪnspɪ'reɪʃən] *n* Inspiration *f.*

inspire [ɪn'spaɪə*] *vt (respect)* einflößen *(in dat); (hope)* wecken *(in* in +*dat); (person)* inspirieren.

instability [ɪnstə'bɪlɪtɪ] *n* Unbeständigkeit *f,* Labilität *f.*

install [ɪn'stɔ:l] *vt (put in)* installieren; *(telephone)* anschließen; *(establish)* einsetzen; ~**ation** [ɪnstə'leɪʃən] *n (of person)* (Amts)einsetzung *f; (of machinery)* Installierung *f; (machines etc)* Anlage *f.*

instalment, *(US)* **installment** [ɪn'stɔ:lmənt] *n* Rate *f; (of story)* Fortsetzung *f;* **to pay in** ~**s** auf Raten zahlen.

instance ['ɪnstəns] *n* Fall *m; (example)* Beispiel *nt;* **for** ~ zum Beispiel; **in the first** ~ zunächst.

instant ['ɪnstənt] *n* Augenblick *m* // *a* augenblicklich, sofortig; ~ **coffee** *n* Pulverkaffee *m.*

instantaneous [ɪnstən'teɪnɪəs] *a* unmittelbar.

instantly ['ɪnstəntlɪ] *ad* sofort.

instead [ɪn'sted] *ad* statt dessen; ~ **of** *prep* anstatt (+*gen).*

instep ['ɪnstep] *n* Spann *m; (of shoe)* Blatt *nt.*

instigation [ɪnstɪ'geɪʃən] *n* Veranlassung *f; (of crime etc)* Anstiftung *f.*

instil [ɪn'stɪl] *vt (fig)* beibringen *(in sb* jdm).

instinct ['ɪnstɪŋkt] *n* Instinkt *m;* ~**ive** [ɪn'stɪŋktɪv] *a* instinktiv.

institute ['ɪnstɪtju:t] *n* Institut *nt* // *vt* einführen; *(search)* einleiten.

institution [ɪnstɪ'tju:ʃən] *n* Institution *f; (home)* Anstalt *f.*

instruct [ɪn'strʌkt] *vt* anweisen; *(officially)* instruieren; ~**ion** [ɪn'strʌkʃən] *n* Unterricht *m;* ~**ions** *pl* Anweisungen *pl; (for use)* Gebrauchsanweisung *f;* ~**ive** *a* lehrreich; ~**or** *n* Lehrer *m; (MIL)* Ausbilder *m.*

instrument ['ɪnstrʊmənt] n Instrument nt; ~al [ɪnstrʊ'mentl] a (MUS) Instrumental-; (helpful) behilflich (in bei); ~ panel n Armaturenbrett nt.

insubordinate [ɪnsə'bɔːdənət] a aufsässig, widersetzlich.

insubordination ['ɪnsəbɔːdɪ'neɪʃən] n Gehorsamsverweigerung f.

insufferable [ɪn'sʌfərəbl] a unerträglich.

insufficient [ɪnsə'fɪʃənt] a ungenügend.

insular ['ɪnsjələ*] a (fig) engstirnig.

insulate ['ɪnsjʊleɪt] vt (ELEC) isolieren; (fig) abschirmen (from vor +dat).

insulating tape n Isolierband nt.

insulation [ɪnsjʊ'leɪʃən] n Isolierung f.

insulin ['ɪnsjʊlɪn] n Insulin nt.

insult ['ɪnsʌlt] n Beleidigung f // [ɪn'sʌlt] vt beleidigen; ~ing [ɪn'sʌltɪŋ] a beleidigend.

insuperable [ɪn'suːpərəbl] a unüberwindlich.

insurance [ɪn'ʃʊərəns] n Versicherung f; fire/life ~ Feuer-/Lebensversicherung; ~ agent n Versicherungsvertreter m; ~ policy n Versicherungspolice f.

insure [ɪn'ʃʊə*] vt versichern.

insurrection [ɪnsə'rekʃən] n Aufstand m.

intact [ɪn'tækt] a unversehrt.

intake ['ɪnteɪk] n (place) Einlaßöffnung f; (act) Aufnahme f; (Brit SCH): an ~ of 200 a year ein Neuzugang von 200 im Jahr.

intangible [ɪn'tændʒəbl] a nicht greifbar.

integral ['ɪntɪgrəl] a (essential) wesentlich; (complete) vollständig; (MATH) Integral-.

integrate ['ɪntɪgreɪt] vt integrieren // vi sich integrieren.

integrity [ɪn'tegrɪtɪ] n (honesty) Redlichkeit f, Integrität f.

intellect ['ɪntɪlekt] n Intellekt m; ~ual [ɪntɪ'lektjʊəl] a geistig, intellektuell // n Intellektuelle(r) mf.

intelligence [ɪn'telɪdʒəns] n (understanding) Intelligenz f; (news) Information f; (MIL) Geheimdienst m.

intelligent [ɪn'telɪdʒənt] a intelligent; ~ly ad klug; (write, speak) verständlich.

intelligentsia [ɪntelɪ'dʒentsɪə] n Intelligenz f.

intelligible [ɪn'telɪdʒəbl] a verständlich.

intend [ɪn'tend] vt beabsichtigen; that was ~ed for you das war für dich gedacht.

intense [ɪn'tens] a stark, intensiv; (person) ernsthaft; ~ly ad äußerst; (study) intensiv.

intensify [ɪn'tensɪfaɪ] vt verstärken, intensivieren.

intensity [ɪn'tensɪtɪ] n Intensität f.

intensive [ɪn'tensɪv] a intensiv; ~ care unit n Intensivstation f.

intent [ɪn'tent] n Absicht f; to all ~s and purposes praktisch; to be ~ on doing sth fest entschlossen sein, etw zu tun.

intention [ɪn'tenʃən] n Absicht f.

intentional a, ~ly ad [ɪn'tenʃənl, -nəlɪ] absichtlich.

intently [ɪn'tentlɪ] ad konzentriert.

inter [ɪn'tɜː*] vt beerdigen.

interact [ɪntər'ækt] vi aufeinander einwirken; ~ion n Wechselwirkung f.

intercede [ɪntə'siːd] vi sich verwenden.

intercept [ɪntə'sept] vt abfangen.

interchange n ['ɪntə'tʃeɪndʒ] n (exchange) Austausch m; (on roads) Verkehrskreuz nt // [ɪntə'tʃeɪndʒ] vt austauschen; ~able [ɪntə'tʃeɪndʒəbl] a austauschbar.

intercom ['ɪntəkɒm] n (Gegen-)sprechanlage f.

intercourse ['ɪntəkɔːs] n (exchange) Beziehungen pl; (sexual) Geschlechtsverkehr m.

interest ['ɪntrest] n Interesse nt; (FIN) Zinsen pl; (COMM: share) Anteil m; (group) Interessengruppe f // vt interessieren; ~ed a (having claims) beteiligt; (attentive) interessiert; to be ~ed in sich interessieren für; ~ing a interessant; ~ rate n Zinssatz m.

interface ['ɪntəfeɪs] n (COMPUT) Schnittstelle f, Interface nt.

interfere [ɪntə'fɪə*] vi (meddle) sich einmischen (with in +acc); (disrupt) stören (with acc).

interference [ɪntə'fɪərəns] n Einmischung f; (TV) Störung f.

interim ['ɪntərɪm] n: in the ~ inzwischen.

interior [ɪn'tɪərɪə*] n Innere(s) nt // a innere(r, s), Innen-; ~ designer n Innenarchitekt(in f) m.

interjection [ɪntə'dʒekʃən] n Ausruf m.

interlock [ɪntə'lɒk] vi ineinandergreifen.

interloper ['ɪntələʊpə*] n Eindringling m.

interlude ['ɪntəluːd] n Pause f.

intermarry [ɪntə'mærɪ] vi untereinander heiraten.

intermediary [ɪntə'miːdɪərɪ] n Vermittler m.

intermediate [ɪntə'miːdɪət] a Zwischen-, Mittel-.

interminable [ɪn'tɜːmɪnəbl] a endlos.

intermission [ɪntə'mɪʃən] n Pause f.

intermittent [ɪntə'mɪtənt] a periodisch, stoßweise.

intern [ɪn'tɜːn] vt internieren // ['ɪntɜːn] n (US) Assistenzarzt m/ -ärztin f.

internal [ɪn'tɜːnl] a (inside) innere(r, s); (domestic) Inlands-; (MED) innerlich; 'not to be taken ~ly' 'nur zur äußerlichen Anwendung'; I~ Revenue Service (IRS) n (US) Finanzamt nt.

international [intə'næʃnəl] *a* international // *n* (*SPORT*) Nationalspieler(in *f*) *m*; (: *match*) internationale(s) Spiel *nt*.

interplay ['intəpleɪ] *n* Wechselspiel *nt*.

interpret [in'tɜːprɪt] *vt* (*explain*) auslegen, interpretieren; (*translate*) dolmetschen; ~**ation** ['teɪʃən] *n* Interpretation *f*; ~**er** *n* Dolmetscher(in *f*) *m*.

interrelated [intərɪ'leɪtɪd] *a* untereinander zusammenhängend.

interrogate [in'terəgeɪt] *vt* verhören.

interrogation [intərə'geɪʃən] *n* Verhör *nt*.

interrogative [intə'rɒgətɪv] *a* Frage-.

interrupt [intə'rʌpt] *vt* unterbrechen; ~**ion** *n* Unterbrechung *f*.

intersect [intə'sekt] *vt* (durch)schneiden // *vi* sich schneiden; ~**ion** *n* (*of roads*) Kreuzung *f*; (*of lines*) Schnittpunkt *m*.

intersperse [intə'spɜːs] *vt*: to ~ sth with sth etw mit etw durchsetzen.

intertwine [intə'twaɪn] *vti* (sich) verflechten.

interval ['intəvəl] *n* Abstand *m*; (*Brit: SCH, THEAT, SPORT*) Pause *f*; at ~s in Abständen.

intervene [intə'viːn] *vi* dazwischenliegen; (*act*) einschreiten (*in gegen*).

intervention [intə'venʃən] *n* Eingreifen *nt*, Intervention *f*.

interview ['intəvjuː] *n* (*PRESS etc*) Interview *nt*; (*for job*) Vorstellungsgespräch *nt* // *vt* interviewen; ~**er** *n* Interviewer *m*.

intestine [in'testɪn] *n*: large/small ~ Dick-/Dünndarm *m*.

intimacy ['intɪməsɪ] *n* Intimität *f*.

intimate ['intɪmət] *a* (*inmost*) innerste(r, s); (*knowledge*) eingehend; (*familiar*) vertraut; (*friends*) eng // ['intɪmeɪt] *vt* andeuten.

intimidate [in'tɪmɪdeɪt] *vt* einschüchtern.

intimidation [intɪmɪ'deɪʃən] *n* Einschüchterung *f*.

into ['intu] *prep* (*motion*) in (+*acc*) ... hinein; 5 ~ 25 25 durch 5.

intolerable [in'tɒlərəbl] *a* unerträglich.

intolerant [in'tɒlərənt] *a*: ~ of unduldsam gegen (über).

intoxicate [in'tɒksɪkeɪt] *vt* berauschen; ~**d** *a* betrunken.

intoxication [intɒksɪ'keɪʃən] *n* Rausch *m*.

intractable [in'træktəbl] *a* schwer zu handhaben; (*problem*) schwer lösbar.

intransigent [in'trænsɪdʒənt] *a* unnachgiebig.

intravenous [intrə'viːnəs] *a* intravenös.

in-tray ['intreɪ] *n* Eingangskorb *m*.

intrepid [in'trepɪd] *a* unerschrocken.

intricate ['intrɪkət] *a* kompliziert.

intrigue [in'triːg] *n* Intrige *f* // *vt* faszinieren // *vi* intrigieren.

intriguing [in'triːgɪŋ] *a* faszinierend.

intrinsic [in'trinsik] *a* innere(r, s); (*difference*) wesentlich.

introduce [intrə'djuːs] *vt* (*person*) vorstellen (*to sb* jdm); (*sth new*) einführen; (*subject*) anschneiden; to ~ sb to sth jdn in etw (*acc*) einführen.

introduction [intrə'dʌkʃən] *n* Einführung *f*; (*to book*) Einleitung *f*.

introductory [intrə'dʌktərɪ] *a* Einführungs-, Vor-.

introspective [intrəʊ'spektɪv] *a* nach innen gekehrt.

introvert ['intrəʊvɜːt] *n* Introvertierte(r) *mf* // *a* introvertiert.

intrude [in'truːd] *vi* stören (*on acc*); ~**r** *n* Eindringling *m*.

intrusion [in'truːʒən] *n* Störung *f*.

intrusive [in'truːsɪv] *a* aufdringlich.

intuition [intjuː'ɪʃən] *n* Intuition *f*.

inundate ['inʌndeɪt] *vt* (*lit, fig*) überschwemmen.

invade [in'veɪd] *vt* einfallen in (+*acc*); ~**r** *n* Eindringling *m*.

invalid ['invəlɪd] *n* (*disabled*) Invalide *m* // *a* (*ill*) krank; (*disabled*) invalide; [in'vælɪd] (*not valid*) ungültig.

invaluable [in'væljuəbl] *a* unschätzbar.

invariable [in'vɛərɪəbl] *a* unveränderlich.

invariably [in'vɛərɪəblɪ] *ad* ausnahmslos.

invasion [in'veɪʒən] *n* Invasion *f*.

invent [in'vent] *vt* erfinden; ~**ion** [in'venʃən] *n* Erfindung *f*; ~**ive** *a* erfinderisch; ~**or** *n* Erfinder *m*.

inventory ['invəntrɪ] *n* Inventar *nt*.

inverse ['in'vɜːs] *n* Umkehrung *f* // *a* umgekehrt.

invert [in'vɜːt] *vt* umdrehen; ~**ed commas** *npl* (*Brit*) Anführungsstriche *pl*.

invertebrate [in'vɜːtɪbrət] *n* wirbellose(s) Tier *nt*.

invest [in'vest] *vt* investieren.

investigate [in'vestɪgeɪt] *vt* untersuchen.

investigation [investɪ'geɪʃən] *n* Untersuchung *f*.

investigator [in'vestɪgeɪtə*] *n* Untersuchungsbeamte(r) *m*.

investiture [in'vestɪtʃə*] *n* Amtseinsetzung *f*.

investment [in'vestmənt] *n* Investition *f*.

investor [in'vestə*] *n* (Geld)anleger *m*.

inveterate [in'vetərət] *a* unverbesserlich.

invidious [in'vɪdɪəs] *a* unangenehm; (*distinctions, remark*) ungerecht.

invigilate [in'vɪdʒɪleɪt] *vti* (*in exam*) Aufsicht führen (über).

invigorating [in'vɪgəreɪtɪŋ] *a* stärkend.

invincible [in'vɪnsəbl] *a* unbesiegbar.

inviolate [ɪn'vaɪələt] *a* unverletzt.
invisible [ɪn'vɪzəbl] *a* unsichtbar; ~ **ink** *n* Geheimtinte *f*.
invitation [ɪnvɪ'teɪʃən] *n* Einladung *f*.
invite [ɪn'vaɪt] *vt* einladen.
inviting [ɪn'vaɪtɪŋ] *a* einladend.
invoice ['ɪnvɔɪs] *n* Rechnung *f* // *vt* (*goods*) in Rechnung stellen (*sth for sb* jdm etw *acc*).
invoke [ɪn'vəʊk] *vt* anrufen.
involuntary [ɪn'vɒləntərɪ] *a* unabsichtlich.
involve [ɪn'vɒlv] *vt* (*entangle*) verwickeln; (*entail*) mit sich bringen; ~**d** *a* verwickelt; ~**ment** *n* Verwicklung *f*.
inward ['ɪnwəd] *a* innere(r, s); (*curve*) Innen-; ~(**s**) *ad* nach innen; ~**ly** *ad* im Innern.
I/O *abbr* (= *input/output*) I/O.
iodine ['aɪədiːn] *n* Jod *nt*.
iota [aɪ'əʊtə] *n* (*fig*) bißchen *nt*.
IOU *n abbr* of **I owe you.**
IQ *n abbr* (= *intelligence quotient*) IQ *m*.
IRA *n abbr* (= *Irish Republican Army*) IRA *f*.
Iran [ɪ'rɑːn] *n* Iran *nt*; ~**ian** [ɪ'reɪnɪən] *a* iranisch // *n* Iraner(in *f*) *m*; (*LING*) Iranisch *nt*.
Iraq [ɪ'rɑːk] *n* Irak; ~**i** *a* irakisch // *n* Iraker(in *f*) *m*; (*LING*) Irakisch *nt*.
irascible [ɪ'ræsɪbl] *a* reizbar.
irate [aɪ'reɪt] *a* zornig.
Ireland ['aɪələnd] *n* Irland *nt*.
irksome ['ɜːksəm] *a* lästig.
iron ['aɪən] *n* Eisen *nt*; (*for ironing*) Bügeleisen *nt* // *a* eisern // *vt* bügeln; ~ **out** *vt* (*lit, fig*) ausbügeln; **I~ Curtain** *n* Eiserne(r) Vorhang *m*.
ironic(al) [aɪ'rɒnɪk(əl)] *a* ironisch; (*coincidence etc*) witzig.
ironing ['aɪənɪŋ] *n* Bügeln *nt*; (*laundry*) Bügelwäsche *f*; ~ **board** *n* Bügelbrett *nt*.
ironmonger ['aɪənmʌŋgə*] *n* (*Brit*) Eisenwarenhändler *m*; ~'**s** (**shop**) *n* Eisenwarenhandlung *f*.
iron ore ['aɪənɔː*] *n* Eisenerz *nt*.
irony ['aɪərənɪ] *n* Ironie *f*.
irrational [ɪ'ræʃənl] *a* irrational.
irreconcilable [ɪrekən'saɪləbl] *a* unvereinbar.
irrefutable [ɪrɪ'fjuːtəbl] *a* unwiderlegbar.
irregular [ɪ'regjʊlə*] *a* unregelmäßig; (*shape*) ungleich(mäßig); (*fig*) unüblich; (*behaviour*) ungehörig; ~**ity** [ɪregjʊ'lærɪtɪ] *n* Unregelmäßigkeit *f*; Ungleichmäßigkeit *f*; (*fig*) Vergehen *nt*.
irrelevant [ɪ'reləvənt] *a* belanglos, irrelevant.
irreparable [ɪ'repərəbl] *a* nicht wiedergutzumachen.
irreplaceable [ɪrɪ'pleɪsəbl] *a* unersetzbar.
irrepressible [ɪrɪ'presəbl] *a* nicht zu

unterdrücken; (*joy*) unbändig.
irresistible [ɪrɪ'zɪstəbl] *a* unwiderstehlich.
irresolute [ɪ'rezəluːt] *a* unentschlossen.
irrespective [ɪrɪ'spektɪv]: ~ **of** *prep* ungeachtet (+*gen*).
irresponsible [ɪrɪ'spɒnsəbl] *a* verantwortungslos.
irreverent [ɪ'revərənt] *a* respektlos.
irrevocable [ɪ'revəkəbl] *a* unwiderrufbar.
irrigate ['ɪrɪgeɪt] *vt* bewässern.
irrigation [ɪrɪ'geɪʃən] *n* Bewässerung *f*.
irritable ['ɪrɪtəbl] *a* reizbar.
irritate ['ɪrɪteɪt] *vt* irritieren, reizen (*also MED*).
irritation [ɪrɪ'teɪʃən] *n* (*anger*) Ärger *m*; (*MED*) Reizung *f*.
IRS *n abbr* of **Internal Revenue Service.**
is [ɪz] *v see* **be.**
Islam ['ɪzlɑːm] *n* Islam *m*.
island ['aɪlənd] *n* Insel *f*; ~**er** *n* Inselbewohner(in *f*) *m*.
isle [aɪl] *n* (kleine) Insel *f*.
isn't ['ɪznt] = **is not.**
isolate ['aɪsəleɪt] *vt* isolieren; ~**d** *a* isoliert; (*case*) Einzel-.
isolation [aɪsəʊ'leɪʃən] *n* Isolierung *f*.
Israel ['ɪzreɪəl] *n* Israel *nt*; ~**i** [ɪz'reɪlɪ] *a* israelisch // *n* Israeli *mf*.
issue ['ɪʃuː] *n* (*matter*) Frage *f*; (*outcome*) Ausgang *m*; (*of newspaper, shares*) Ausgabe *f*; (*offspring*) Nachkommenschaft *f* // *vt* ausgeben; (*warrant*) erlassen; (*documents*) ausstellen; (*orders*) erteilen; (*books*) herausgeben; (*verdict*) aussprechen; **to be at ~** zur Debatte stehen; **to take ~ with sb over** sth jdm in etw (*dat*) widersprechen.
isthmus ['ɪsməs] *n* Landenge *f*.
it [ɪt] *pron* **1** (*specific: subject*) er/sie/es; (: *direct object*) ihn/sie/es; (: *indirect object*) ihm/ihr/ihm; **about/from/in/of** ~ darüber/davon/darin/davon
2 (*impersonal*) es; ~'s raining es regnet; **it's Friday tomorrow** morgen ist Freitag; **who is** ~? — ~'s **me** wer ist da? — es (bin's).
Italian [ɪ'tæljən] *a* italienisch // *n* Italiener(in *f*) *m*; (*LING*) Italienisch *nt*.
italic [ɪ'tælɪk] *a* kursiv; ~**s** *npl* Kursivschrift *f*.
Italy ['ɪtəlɪ] *n* Italien *nt*.
itch [ɪtʃ] *n* Juckreiz *m*; (*fig*) Lust *f* // *vi* jucken; **to be** ~**ing to do** sth darauf brennen, etw zu tun; ~**y** *a* juckend.
it'd ['ɪtd] = **it would; it had.**
item ['aɪtəm] *n* Gegenstand *m*; (*on list*) Posten *m*; (*in programme*) Nummer *f*; (*in agenda*) (Programm)punkt *m*; (*in newspaper*) (Zeitungs)notiz *f*; ~**ize** *vt* verzeichnen.
itinerant [ɪ'tɪnərənt] *a* (*person*) um-

herreisend.

itinerary [aɪ'tɪnərərɪ] n Reiseroute f.

it'll ['ɪtl] = **it will, it shall.**

its [ɪts] poss a (masculine, neuter) sein; (feminine) ihr.

it's [ɪts] = **it is; it has.**

itself [ɪt'self] pron sich (selbst); (emphatic) selbst.

ITV n abbr (Brit) of **Independent Television.**

I.U.D. n abbr (= intra-uterine device) Pessar nt.

I've [aɪv] = **I have.**

ivory ['aɪvərɪ] n Elfenbein nt; ~ **tower** n (fig) Elfenbeinturm m.

ivy ['aɪvɪ] n Efeu nt.

J

jab [dʒæb] vti (hinein)stechen // n Stich m, Stoß m; (col) Spritze f.

jabber ['dʒæbə*] vi plappern.

jack [dʒæk] n (AUT) (Wagen)heber m; (CARDS) Bube m; ~ **up** vt aufbocken.

jackal ['dʒækəl] n (ZOOL) Schakal m.

jackdaw ['dʒækdɔː] n Dohle f.

jacket ['dʒækɪt] n Jacke f; (of book) Schutzumschlag m; (TECH) Ummantelung f.

jack-knife ['dʒæknaɪf] vi (truck) sich zusammenschieben.

jack plug n (ELEC) Buchsenstecker m.

jackpot ['dʒækpɒt] n Haupttreffer m.

jade [dʒeɪd] n (stone) Jade m.

jaded ['dʒeɪdɪd] a ermattet.

jagged ['dʒægɪd] a zackig.

jail [dʒeɪl] n Gefängnis nt // vt einsperren; ~**er** n Gefängniswärter m.

jam [dʒæm] n Marmelade f; (also: traffic ~) (Verkehrs)stau m; (col: trouble) Klemme f // vt (wedge) einklemmen; (cram) hineinzwängen; (obstruct) blockieren // vi sich verklemmen; **to ~ sth into sth** etw in etw (acc) hineinstopfen.

Jamaica [dʒə'meɪkə] n Jamaika nt.

jangle ['dʒæŋgl] vti klimpern.

janitor ['dʒænɪtə*] n Hausmeister m.

January ['dʒænjʊərɪ] n Januar m.

Japan [dʒə'pæn] n Japan nt; ~**ese** [dʒæpə'niːz] a japanisch // n, pl inv Japaner(in f) m; (LING) Japanisch nt.

jar [dʒɑː*] n Glas nt // vi kreischen; (colours etc) nicht harmonieren.

jargon ['dʒɑːgən] n Fachsprache f, Jargon m.

jaundice ['dʒɔːndɪs] n Gelbsucht f; ~**d** a (fig) mißgünstig.

jaunt [dʒɔːnt] n Spritztour f; ~**y** a (lively) munter; (brisk) flott.

javelin ['dʒævlɪn] n Speer m.

jaw [dʒɔː] n Kiefer m.

jay [dʒeɪ] n (ZOOL) Eichelhäher m.

jaywalker ['dʒeɪwɔːkə*] n unvorsicht-

ige(r) Fußgänger m.

jazz [dʒæz] n Jazz m; ~ **up** vt (MUS) verjazzen; (enliven) aufpolieren; ~**y** a (colour) schreiend, auffallend.

jealous ['dʒeləs] a (envious) mißgünstig; (husband) eifersüchtig; ~**y** n Mißgunst f; Eifersucht f.

jeans [dʒiːnz] npl Jeans pl.

jeep [dʒiːp] n Jeep m.

jeer [dʒɪə*] vi höhnisch lachen (at über +acc), verspotten (at sb jdn).

jelly ['dʒelɪ] n Gelee nt; (dessert) Grütze f; ~**fish** n Qualle f.

jeopardize ['dʒepədaɪz] vt gefährden.

jeopardy ['dʒepədɪ] n: **to be in ~** in Gefahr sein.

jerk [dʒɜːk] n Ruck m; (col: idiot) Trottel m // vt ruckartig bewegen // vi sich ruckartig bewegen.

jerkin ['dʒɜːkɪn] n Wams nt.

jerky ['dʒɜːkɪ] a (movement) ruckartig; (ride) rüttelnd.

jersey ['dʒɜːzɪ] n Pullover m.

jest [dʒest] n Scherz m; **in ~** im Spaß // vi spaßen.

Jesus ['dʒiːzəs] n Jesus m.

jet [dʒet] n (stream: of water etc) Strahl m; (spout) Düse f; (AVIAT) Düsenflugzeug nt; ~-**black** a rabenschwarz; ~ **engine** n Düsenmotor m; ~-**lag** n Jet-lag m.

jettison ['dʒetɪsn] vt über Bord werfen.

jetty ['dʒetɪ] n Landesteg m, Mole f.

Jew [dʒuː] n Jude m.

jewel ['dʒuːəl] n (lit, fig) Juwel nt; ~**(l)er** n Juwelier m; ~**(l)er's (shop)** n Juwelier m; ~**(le)ry** n Schmuck m.

Jewess ['dʒuːɪs] n Jüdin f.

Jewish ['dʒuːɪʃ] a jüdisch.

jibe [dʒaɪb] n spöttische Bemerkung f.

jiffy ['dʒɪfɪ] n (col): **in a ~** sofort.

jigsaw (puzzle) ['dʒɪgsɔː(pʌzl)] n Puzzle(spiel) nt.

jilt [dʒɪlt] vt den Laufpaß geben (+dat).

jingle ['dʒɪŋgl] n (advertisement) Werbesong m // vti klimpern; (bells) bimmeln.

jinx [dʒɪŋks] n: **there's a ~ on it** es ist verhext.

jitters ['dʒɪtəz] npl (col): **to get the ~** einen Bammel kriegen.

job [dʒɒb] n (piece of work) Arbeit f; (position) Stellung f; (duty) Aufgabe f; (difficulty) Mühe f; **it's a good ~ he ...** es ist ein Glück, daß er ...; **just the ~** genau das Richtige; ~**centre** n (Brit) Arbeitsamt nt; ~**less** a arbeitslos.

jockey ['dʒɒkɪ] n Jockei m // vi: **to ~ for position** sich in eine gute Position drängeln.

jocular ['dʒɒkjʊlə*] a scherzhaft.

jog [dʒɒg] vt (an)stoßen // vi (run) joggen; **to ~ along** vor sich (acc) hinwursteln; (work) seinen Gang gehen; ~**ging** n Jogging nt.

join [dʒɔɪn] vt (put together) verbinden (to mit); (club) beitreten (+dat); (person) sich anschließen (+dat) // vi (unite) sich vereinigen // n Verbindungsstelle f, Naht f; ~ in vti mitmachen (sth bei etw); ~ up vi (MIL) zur Armee gehen.

joiner ['dʒɔɪnə*] n Schreiner m; ~y n Schreinerei f.

joint [dʒɔɪnt] n (TECH) Fuge f; (of bones) Gelenk nt; (of meat) Braten m; (col: place) Lokal nt // a gemeinsam; ~ **account** n (with bank etc) gemeinsame(s) Konto nt; ~ly ad gemeinsam.

joist [dʒɔɪst] n Träger m.

joke [dʒəʊk] n Witz m // vi Witze machen; to play a ~ on sb jdm einen Streich spielen; ~r n Witzbold m; (CARDS) Joker m.

jolly ['dʒɒlɪ] a lustig // ad (col) ganz schön.

jolt [dʒəʊlt] n (shock) Schock m; (jerk) Stoß m // vt (push) stoßen; (shake) durchschütteln; (fig) aufrütteln // vi holpern.

Jordan ['dʒɔːdən] n Jordanien nt; (river) Jordan m.

jostle ['dʒɒsl] vt anrempeln.

jot [dʒɒt] n: not one ~ kein Jota nt; ~ **down** vt notieren; ~ter n (Brit) Notizblock m.

journal ['dʒɜːnl] n (diary) Tagebuch nt; (magazine) Zeitschrift f; ~ese ['dʒɜːnə'liːz] n Zeitungsstil m; ~ism n Journalismus m; ~ist n Journalist(in f) m.

journey ['dʒɜːnɪ] n Reise f.

jovial ['dʒəʊvɪəl] a jovial.

joy [dʒɔɪ] n Freude f; ~ful, ~ous a freudig; ~ **ride** n Schwarzfahrt f; ~stick n Steuerknüppel m; (COMPUT) Joystick m.

J.P. n abbr of Justice of the Peace.

Jr abbr of junior.

jubilant ['dʒuːbɪlənt] a triumphierend.

jubilee ['dʒuːbɪliː] n Jubiläum nt.

judge [dʒʌdʒ] n Richter m; (fig) Kenner m // vt (JUR: person) die Verhandlung führen über (+acc); (case) verhandeln; (assess) beurteilen; (estimate) einschätzen; ~ment n (JUR) Urteil nt; (ECCL) Gericht nt; (ability) Urteilsvermögen nt.

judicial [dʒuː'dɪʃəl] a gerichtlich, Justiz-.

judiciary [dʒuː'dɪʃɪərɪ] n Gerichtsbehörden (pl) f; (judges) Richterstand m.

judicious [dʒuː'dɪʃəs] a weis(e).

judo ['dʒuːdəʊ] n Judo nt.

jug [dʒʌg] n Krug m.

juggernaut ['dʒʌgənɔːt] n (Brit: huge truck) Schwertransporter m.

juggle ['dʒʌgl] vti jonglieren; ~r n Jongleur m.

Jugoslav ['juːgəʊ'slɑːv] etc = **Yugoslav** etc.

juice [dʒuːs] n Saft m.

juicy ['dʒuːsɪ] a (lit, fig) saftig.

jukebox ['dʒuːkbɒks] n Musikautomat m.

July [dʒuː'laɪ] n Juli m.

jumble ['dʒʌmbl] n Durcheinander nt // vt (also: ~ up) durcheinanderwerfen; (facts) durcheinanderbringen; ~ **sale** n (Brit) Basar m, Flohmarkt m.

jumbo (jet) ['dʒʌmbəʊ-] n Jumbo(-Jet) m.

jump [dʒʌmp] vi springen; (nervously) zusammenzucken // vt überspringen // n Sprung m; to ~ **the queue** (Brit) sich vordrängeln.

jumper ['dʒʌmpə*] n (Brit: pullover) Pullover m; (US: dress) Trägerkleid nt; ~ **cables** npl (US) = **jump leads**.

jump leads npl (Brit) Überbrückungskabel nt.

jumpy ['dʒʌmpɪ] a nervös.

Jun abbr of junior.

junction ['dʒʌŋkʃən] n (Brit: of roads) (Straßen)kreuzung f; (RAIL) Knotenpunkt m.

juncture ['dʒʌŋktʃə*] n: at this ~ in diesem Augenblick.

June [dʒuːn] n Juni m.

jungle ['dʒʌŋgl] n Dschungel m.

junior ['dʒuːnɪə*] a (younger) jünger; (after name) junior; (SPORT) Junioren-; (lower position) untergeordnet; (for young people) Junioren- // n Jüngere(r) mf; ~ **school** n (Brit) Grundschule f.

junk [dʒʌŋk] n (rubbish) Plunder m; (ship) Dschunke f; ~ **food** n Plastikessen nt; ~shop n Ramschladen m.

Junr abbr of junior.

jurisdiction [dʒʊərɪs'dɪkʃən] n Gerichtsbarkeit f; (range of authority) Zuständigkeit(sbereich m) f.

juror ['dʒʊərə*] n Geschworene(r) mf; (in competition) Preisrichter m.

jury ['dʒʊərɪ] n (court) Geschworene pl; (in competition) Jury f.

just [dʒʌst] a gerecht // ad (recently, now) gerade, eben; (barely) gerade noch; (exactly) genau, gerade; (only) nur, bloß; (a small distance) gleich; (absolutely) einfach; ~ **as I arrived** gerade als ich ankam; ~ **as nice** genauso nett; ~ **as well** um so besser; ~ **now** soeben, gerade; ~ **try** versuch es mal.

justice ['dʒʌstɪs] n (fairness) Gerechtigkeit f; ~ **of the peace** n Friedensrichter m.

justifiable ['dʒʌstɪfaɪəbl] a berechtigt.

justification [dʒʌstɪfɪ'keɪʃən] n Rechtfertigung f.

justify ['dʒʌstɪfaɪ] vt rechtfertigen; (text) justieren.

justly ['dʒʌstlɪ] ad (say) mit Recht;

(*condemn*) gerecht.

jut [dʒʌt] *vi* (*also:* ~ **out**) herausragen, vorstehen.

juvenile ['dʒuːvənaɪl] *a* (*young*) jugendlich; (*for the young*) Jugend- // *n* Jugendliche(r) *mf*.

juxtapose ['dʒʌkstəpəʊz] *vt* nebeneinanderstellen.

K

K *abbr* (= *one thousand*) Tsd.; (= *Kilobyte*) K.

kangaroo [kæŋgə'ruː] *n* Känguruh *nt*.

karate [kə'rɑːtɪ] *n* Karate *nt*.

kebab [kə'bæb] *n* Kebab *m*.

keel [kiːl] *n* Kiel *m*; **on an even** ~ (*fig*) im Lot.

keen [kiːn] *a* begeistert; (*intelligence, wind, blade*) scharf; (*sight, hearing*) gut; **to be** ~ **to do** *or* **on doing sth** etw unbedingt tun wollen; **to be** ~ **on sth/sb** scharf auf etw/jdn sein.

keep [kiːp], *pt*, *pp* **kept** *vt* (*retain*) behalten; (*have*) haben; (*animals, one's word*) halten; (*support*) versorgen; (*maintain in state*) halten; (*preserve*) aufbewahren; (*restrain*) abhalten // *vi* (*continue in direction*) sich halten; (*food*) sich halten; (*remain: quiet etc*) bleiben // *n* Unterhalt *m*; (*tower*) Burgfried *m*; (*col*): **for** ~**s** für immer; **to** ~ **sth to o.s.** etw für sich behalten; **it** ~**s happening** es passiert immer wieder; ~ **back** *vt* fernhalten; (*secret*) verschweigen; ~ **on** *vi*: ~ **on doing sth** etw immer weiter tun; ~ **out** *vt* nicht hereinlassen; '~ **out**' 'Eintritt verboten!'; ~ **up** *vi* Schritt halten // *vt* aufrechterhalten; (*continue*) weitermachen; **to** ~ **up with** Schritt halten mit; ~**er** *n* Wärter(in *f*) *m*; (*goal-*) Torhüter(in *f*) *m*; ~**fit** *n* keep-fit *nt*; ~**ing** *n* (*care*) Obhut *f*; **in** ~**ing with** in Übereinstimmung mit; ~**sake** *n* Andenken *nt*.

keg [keg] *n* Faß *nt*.

kennel ['kenl] *n* Hundehütte *f*; ~**s** *pl*: **to put a dog in** ~**s** einen Hund in Pflege geben.

Kenya ['kenjə] *n* Kenia *nt*; ~**n** *a* kenianisch // *n* Kenianer(in *f*) *m*.

kept [kept] *pt*, *pp of* **keep.**

kerb [kɜːb] *n* (*Brit*) Bordstein *m*.

kernel ['kɜːnl] *n* Kern *m*.

kerosene ['kerəsiːn] *n* Kerosin *nt*.

ketchup ['ketʃəp] *n* Ketchup *nt* or *m*.

kettle ['ketl] *n* Kessel *m*; ~**drum** *n* Pauke *f*.

key [kiː] *n* Schlüssel *m*; (*of piano, typewriter*) Taste *f*; (*MUS*) Tonart *f* // *vt* (*also:* ~ **in**) eingeben; ~**board** *n* Tastatur *f*; ~**ed up** *a* (*person*) überdreht; ~**hole** *n* Schlüsselloch *nt*; ~**note** *n* Grundton *m*; ~ **ring** *n* Schlüsselring *m*.

khaki ['kɑːkɪ] *n* K(h)aki *nt* // *a* k(h)aki(farben).

kibbutz [kɪ'buts] *n* Kibbutz *m*.

kick [kɪk] *vt* einen Fußtritt geben (+*dat*) treten // *vi* treten; (*baby*) strampeln; (*horse*) ausschlagen // *n* (Fuß)tritt *m*; (*thrill*) Spaß *m*; **he does it for** ~**s** er macht das aus Jux; ~ **off** *vi* (*SPORT*) anstoßen; ~**-off** *n* (*SPORT*) Anstoß *m*.

kid [kɪd] *n* (*col: child*) Kind *nt*; (*goat*) Zicklein *nt*; (*leather*) Glacéleder *nt* // *vi* (*col*) Witze machen.

kidnap ['kɪdnæp] *vt* entführen; ~**per** *n* Entführer *m*; ~**ping** *n* Entführung *f*.

kidney ['kɪdnɪ] *n* Niere *f*.

kill [kɪl] *vt* töten, umbringen // *vi* töten // *n* Tötung *f*; (*hunting*) (Jagd)beute *f*; ~**er** *n* Mörder(in *f*) *m*; ~**ing** *n* Mord *m*; ~**joy** *n* Spaßverderber(in *f*) *m*.

kiln [kɪln] *n* Schottenrock *m*.

kilo ['kiːləʊ] *n* Kilo *nt*; ~**byte** *n* (*COMPUT*) Kilobyte *nt*; ~**gram(me)** *n* Kilogramm *nt*; ~**metre**, (*US*) ~**meter** *n* Kilometer *m*; ~**watt** *n* Kilowatt *nt*.

kilt [kɪlt] *n* Schottenrock *m*.

kin [kɪn] *n* Verwandtschaft *f*.

kind [kaɪnd] *a* freundlich // *n* Art *f*; **a** ~ **of eine Art von**; (**two**) **of a** ~ (zwei) von der gleichen Art; **in** ~ auf dieselbe Art; (*in goods*) in Naturalien.

kindergarten ['kɪndəgɑːtn] *n* Kindergarten *m*.

kind-hearted ['kaɪnd'hɑːtɪd] *a* gutherzig.

kindle ['kɪndl] *vt* (*set on fire*) anzünden; (*rouse*) reizen, (er)wecken.

kindly ['kaɪndlɪ] *a* freundlich // *ad* liebenswürdig(erweise); **would you** ~ ...? wären Sie so freundlich und ...?

kindness ['kaɪndnəs] *n* Freundlichkeit *f*.

kindred ['kɪndrɪd] *n* Verwandtschaft *f* // *a*: ~ **spirit** *n* Gleichgesinnte(r) *mf*.

king [kɪŋ] *n* König *m*; ~**dom** *n* Königreich *nt*; ~**fisher** *n* Eisvogel *m*; ~**-size** *a* (*cigarette*) Kingsize.

kinky ['kɪŋkɪ] *a* (*col*) (*person, ideas*) verrückt; (*sexual*) abartig.

kiosk ['kiːɒsk] *n* (*Brit TEL*) Telefonhäuschen *nt*.

kipper ['kɪpə*] *n* Räucherhering *m*.

kiss [kɪs] *n* Kuß *m* // *vt* küssen // *vi*: **they** ~**ed** sie küßten sich.

kit [kɪt] *n* Ausrüstung *f*; (*tools*) Werkzeug *nt*.

kitchen ['kɪtʃɪn] *n* Küche *f*; ~ **sink** *n* Spülbecken *nt*.

kite [kaɪt] *n* Drachen *m*.

kith [kɪθ] *n*: ~ **and kin** Blutsverwandte *pl*.

kitten ['kɪtn] *n* Kätzchen *nt*.

kitty ['kɪtɪ] *n* (*money*) Kasse *f*.

km *abbr* (= *kilometre*) km.

knack [næk] *n* Dreh *m*, Trick *m*.

knapsack ['næpsæk] *n* Rucksack *m*; (*MIL*) Tornister *m*.

knead [ni:d] vt kneten.
knee [ni:] n Knie nt; **~cap** n Kniescheibe f.
kneel [ni:l], pt, pp knelt vi (also: ~ down) knien.
knell [nel] n Grabgeläute nt.
knelt [nelt] pt, pp of kneel.
knew [nju:] pt of know.
knickers ['nɪkəz] npl (Brit) Schlüpfer m.
knife [naɪf], pl knives n Messer nt // vt erstechen.
knight [naɪt] n Ritter m; (chess) Springer m; **~hood** n (title): to get a ~hood zum Ritter geschlagen werden.
knit [nɪt] vti stricken // vi (bones) zusammenwachsen; **~ting** n (occupation) Stricken nt; (work) Strickzeug nt; **~ting machine** n Strickmaschine f; **~ting needle** n Stricknadel f; **~wear** n Strickwaren pl.
knives [naɪvz] pl of knife.
knob [nɒb] n Knauf m; (on instrument) Knopf m; (Brit: of butter etc) kleine(s) Stück nt.
knock [nɒk] vt schlagen; (criticize) heruntermachen // n Schlag m; (on door) Klopfen nt; to ~ at or on the door an die Tür klopfen; ~ **down** vt umwerfen; (with car) anfahren; ~ **off** vt (do quickly) hinhauen; (col: steal) klauen // vi (finish) Feierabend machen; ~ **out** vt ausschlagen; (BOXING) k.o. schlagen; ~ **over** vt (person, object) umwerfen; (with car) anfahren; **~er** n (on door) Türklopfer m; **~-kneed** a x-beinig; **~out** n (lit) K.o.-Schlag m; (fig) Sensation f.
knot [nɒt] n Knoten m // vt (ver)knoten.
knotty ['nɒtɪ] a (fig) kompliziert.
know [nəʊ], pt knew pp known vt wissen; (be able to) können; (be acquainted with) kennen; (recognize) erkennen; to ~ how to do sth wissen, wie man etw macht, etw tun können; to ~ about or of sth/sb etw/jdn kennen; **~-all** n Alleswisser m; **~-how** n Kenntnis f, Know-how nt; **~ing** a (look, smile) wissend; **~ingly** ad wissend; (intentionally) wissentlich.
knowledge ['nɒlɪdʒ] n Wissen nt, Kenntnis f; **~able** a informiert.
known [nəʊn] pp of know.
knuckle ['nʌkl] n Fingerknöchel m.
K.O. n abbr of Knockout.
Korea [kə'rɪə] n Korea nt.
kosher ['kəʊʃə*] a koscher.

L

l. abbr of litre.
lab [læb] n (col) Labor nt.
label ['leɪbl] n Etikett nt // vt etikettieren.
laboratory [lə'bɒrətərɪ] n Laboratorium nt.
laborious [lə'bɔːrɪəs] a mühsam.
labour, (US) **labor** ['leɪbə*] n Arbeit f; (workmen) Arbeitskräfte pl; (MED) Wehen pl // vi: to ~ (at) sich abmühen (mit) // vt breittreten (col); in ~ (MED) in den Wehen; L~, the L~ party (Brit) die Labour Party; hard ~ Zwangsarbeit f; **~ed** a (movement) gequält; (style) schwerfällig; **~er** n Arbeiter m.
lace [leɪs] n (fabric) Spitze f; (of shoe) Schnürsenkel m; (braid) Litze f // vt (also ~ up) (zu)schnüren.
lack [læk] n Mangel m // vt nicht haben; sb ~s sth jdm fehlt etw (nom); to be ~ing fehlen; sb is ~ing in sth es fehlt jdm an etw (dat); through or for ~ of aus Mangel an (+dat).
lackadaisical [lækə'deɪzɪkəl] a lasch.
lacquer ['lækə*] n Lack m.
lad [læd] n Junge m.
ladder ['lædə*] n Leiter f; (Brit: in tights) Laufmasche f // vt (Brit: tights) Laufmaschen bekommen in (+dat).
laden ['leɪdn] a beladen, voll.
ladle ['leɪdl] n Schöpfkelle f.
lady ['leɪdɪ] n Dame f; (title) Lady f; young ~ junge Dame; the ladies' (room) die Damentoilette; **~bird**, (US) **~bug** n Marienkäfer m; **~-in-waiting** n Hofdame f; **~like** a damenhaft, vornehm; **~ship** n: your ~ship Ihre Ladyschaft.
lag [læg] vi (also: ~ behind) zurückbleiben // vt (pipes) verkleiden.
lager ['lɑːgə*] n helle(s) Bier nt.
lagging ['lægɪŋ] n Isolierung f.
laid [leɪd] pt, pp of lay; ~ **back** a (col) cool.
lain [leɪn] pp of lie.
lair [lɛə*] n Lager nt.
laity ['leɪɪtɪ] n Laien pl.
lake [leɪk] n See m.
lamb [læm] n Lamm nt; (meat) Lammfleisch nt; ~ **chop** n Lammkotelett nt; **lambswool** n Lammwolle f.
lame [leɪm] a lahm; (excuse) faul.
lament [lə'ment] n Klage f // vt beklagen.
laminated ['læmɪneɪtɪd] a beschichtet.
lamp [læmp] n Lampe f; (in street) Straßenlaterne f.
lampoon [læm'puːn] vt verspotten.
lamp: **~post** n (Brit) Laternenpfahl m; **~shade** n Lampenschirm m.
lance [lɑːns] n Lanze f // vt (MED) aufschneiden; ~ **corporal** n (Brit) Obergefreite(r) m.
land [lænd] n Land nt // vi (from ship) an Land gehen; (AVIAT, end up) landen // vt (obtain) kriegen; (passengers) absetzen; (goods) abladen; (troops, space probe) landen; **~ing** n Landung f; (on stairs) (Treppen)absatz m; **~ing**

gear n Fahrgestell nt; **~ing stage** n (Brit) Landesteg m; **~ing strip** n Landebahn f; **~lady** n (Haus)wirtin f; **~locked** a landumschlossen, Binnen-; **~lord** n (of house) Hauswirt m, Besitzer m; (of pub) Gastwirt m; (of land) Grundbesitzer m; **~mark** n Wahrzeichen nt; (fig) Meilenstein m; **~owner** n Grundbesitzer m.

landscape ['lændskeıp] n Landschaft f.

landslide ['lændslaıd] n (GEOG) Erdrutsch m; (POL) überwältigende(r) Sieg m.

lane [leın] n (in town) Gasse f; (in country) Weg m; (of motorway) Fahrbahn f, Spur f; (SPORT) Bahn f.

language ['læŋgwıdʒ] n Sprache f; bad ~ unanständige Ausdrücke; ~ **laboratory** n Sprachlabor nt.

languid ['læŋgwıd] a schlaff, matt.

languish ['læŋgwıʃ] vi schmachten.

lank [læŋk] a dürr.

lanky ['læŋkı] a schlaksig.

lantern ['læntən] n Laterne f.

lap [læp] n Schoß m; (SPORT) Runde f // vt (also: ~ up) auflecken // vi (water) plätschern.

lapel [lə'pel] n Revers nt or m.

lapse [læps] n (moral) Fehltritt m // vi (decline) nachlassen; (expire) ablaufen; (claims) erlöschen; **to ~ into** bad habits sich schlechte Gewohnheiten angewöhnen.

larceny ['lɑːsənı] n Diebstahl m.

lard [lɑːd] n Schweineschmalz nt.

larder ['lɑːdə*] n Speisekammer f.

large [lɑːdʒ] a groß; **at ~** auf freiem Fuß; **~ly** ad zum größten Teil; **~-scale** a groß angelegt, Groß-.

largesse [lɑː'ʒes] n Freigebigkeit f.

lark [lɑːk] n (bird) Lerche f; (joke) Jux m; **~ about** vi (col) herumalbern.

laryngitis [lærın'dʒaıtıs] n Kehlkopfentzündung f.

larynx ['lærıŋks] n Kehlkopf m.

lascivious [lə'sıvıəs] a wollüstig.

laser ['leızə*] n Laser m; ~ **printer** n Laserdrucker m.

lash [læʃ] n Peitschenhieb m; (eye~) Wimper f // vt (rain) peitschen gegen; (whip) peitschen; (bind) festbinden; ~ **out** vi (with fists) um sich schlagen; (spend money) sich in Unkosten stürzen // vt (money etc) springen lassen.

lass [læs] n Mädchen nt.

lasso [læ'suː] n Lasso nt.

last [lɑːst] a letzte(r, s) // ad zuletzt; (last time) das letztemal // vi (continue) dauern; (remain good) sich halten; (money) ausreichen; **at ~** endlich; ~ **night** gestern abend; ~ **week** letzte Woche; ~ **but one** vorletzte(r, s); **~-ditch** a (attempt) in letzter Minute; **~ing** a dauerhaft; (shame etc) andauernd; **~ly** ad schließlich; **~-minute** a in letzter

Minute.

latch [lætʃ] n Riegel m.

late [leıt] a spät; (dead) verstorben // ad spät; (after proper time) zu spät; **to be ~** zu spät kommen; **of ~** in letzter Zeit; **in ~** May Ende Mai; **~comer** n Nachzügler(in f) m; **~ly** ad in letzter Zeit.

lateness ['leıtnəs] n (of person) Zuspätkommen nt; (of train) Verspätung f; ~ **of the hour** die vorgerückte Stunde.

later ['leıtə*] a (date etc) später; (version etc) neuer // ad später.

lateral ['lætərəl] a seitlich.

latest ['leıtıst] a (fashion) neueste(r, s) // n (news) Neu(e)ste(s) nt; **at the ~** spätestens.

lathe [leıð] n Drehbank f.

lather ['lɑːðə*] n (Seifen)schaum m; vt einschäumen // vi schäumen.

Latin ['lætın] n Latein nt // a lateinisch; (Roman) römisch; ~ **America** n Lateinamerika nt; **~-American** a lateinamerikanisch.

latitude ['lætıtjuːd] n (GEOG) Breite f; (freedom) Spielraum m.

latter ['lætə*] a (second of two) letztere; (coming at end) letzte(r, s), später // n: **the ~** der/die/das letztere, die letzteren; **~ly** ad in letzter Zeit.

lattice ['lætıs] n Gitter nt.

laudable ['lɔːdəbl] a löblich.

laugh [lɑːf] n Lachen nt // vi lachen; ~ **at** vt lachen über (+acc); ~ **off** vt lachend abtun; **~able** a lachhaft; **~ing stock** n Zielscheibe f des Spottes; **~ter** n Gelächter nt.

launch [lɔːntʃ] n (of ship) Stapellauf m; (of rocket) Abschuß m; (boat) Barkasse f; (of product) Einführung f // vt (set afloat) vom Stapel lassen; (rocket) (ab)schießen; (product) auf den Markt bringen; **~ing** n Stapellauf m; **~(ing) pad** n Abschußrampe f.

launder ['lɔːndə*] vt waschen.

launderette [lɔːn'dret], (US) **laundromat** ['lɔːndrəmæt] n Waschsalon m.

laundry ['lɔːndrı] n (place) Wäscherei f; (clothes) Wäsche f; **to do the ~** waschen.

laureate ['lɔːrıət] a see **poet**.

laurel ['lɔrəl] n Lorbeer m.

lavatory ['lævətrı] n Toilette f.

lavender ['lævındə*] n Lavendel m.

lavish ['lævıʃ] a (extravagant) verschwenderisch; (generous) großzügig // vt (money) verschwenden (**on** auf +acc); (attentions, gifts) überschütten mit (**on** sb jdn).

law [lɔː] n Gesetz nt; (system) Recht nt; (as studies) Jura no art; **~-abiding** a gesetzestreu; ~ **and order** n Recht nt und Ordnung f; **~ court** n Gerichtshof m; **~ful** a gesetzlich; **~less** a gesetzlos.

lawn [lɔːn] n Rasen m; **~mower** n Rasenmäher m; ~ **tennis** n

Rasentennis m.

law school n Rechtsakademie f.

lawsuit ['lɔ:su:t] n Prozeß m.

lawyer ['lɔ:jə*] n Rechtsanwalt m, Rechtsanwältin f.

laxative ['læksətɪv] n Abführmittel nt.

laxity ['læksɪtɪ] n Laxheit f.

lay [leɪ] pt of **lie** // a Laien- // vt, pt, pp **laid** (place) legen; (table) dekken; (egg) legen; (trap) stellen; (money) wetten; ~ **aside** vt zurücklegen; ~ **by** vt (set aside) beiseite legen; ~ **down** vt hinlegen; (rules) vorschreiben; (arms) strecken; **to** ~ **down the law** Vorschriften machen; ~ **off** vt (workers) (vorübergehend) entlassen; ~ **on** vt (water, gas) anschließen; (concert etc) veranstalten; ~ **out** vt (her)auslegen; (money) ausgeben; (corpse) aufbahren; ~ **up** vt (subj: illness) ans Bett fesseln; (supplies) anlegen; ~**about** n Faulenzer m; ~**by** n (Brit) Parkbucht f; (bigger) Rastplatz m.

layer ['leɪə*] n Schicht f.

layette [leɪ'et] n Babyausstattung f.

layman ['leɪmən] n Laie m.

layout ['leɪaʊt] n Anlage f; (ART) Layout m.

laze [leɪz] vi faulenzen.

laziness ['leɪzɪnəs] n Faulheit f.

lazy ['leɪzɪ] a faul; (slow-moving) träge.

lb. abbr of **pound** (weight).

lead [li:d] n (front position) Führung f; (distance, time ahead) Vorsprung f; (example) Vorbild nt; (clue) Tip m; (of police) Spur f; (THEAT) Hauptrolle f; (dog's) Leine f; [led] (chemical) Blei nt; (of pencil) (Bleistift)mine f // a [led] bleiern, Blei- // v [li:d] (pt, pp **led**) vt (guide) führen; (group etc) leiten // vi (be first) führen; **in the** ~ (SPORT, fig) in Führung; ~ **astray** vt irreführen; ~ **away** vt wegführen; (prisoner) abführen; ~ **back** vt zurückführen; ~ **on** vt anführen; ~ **on to** vt (induce) dazu bringen; ~ **to** vt (street) (hin)führen nach; (result in) führen zu; ~ **up to** vt (drive) führen zu; (speaker etc) hinführen auf (+acc).

leaden ['ledn] a (sky, sea) bleiern; (heavy: footsteps) bleischwer.

leader ['li:də*] n Führer m, Leiter m; (of party) Vorsitzende(r) m; (PRESS) Leitartikel m; ~**ship** n (office) Leitung f; (quality) Führerschaft f.

leading ['li:dɪŋ] a führend; ~ **lady** n (THEAT) Hauptdarstellerin f; ~ **light** n (person) führende(r) Geist m.

leaf [li:f], pl **leaves** n Blatt nt // vi: **to** ~ **through** durchblättern; **to turn over a new** ~ einen neuen Anfang nachen.

leaflet ['li:flɪt] n (advertisement) Prospekt m; (pamphlet) Flugblatt nt; (for information) Merkblatt nt.

league [li:g] n (union) Bund m; (SPORT)

Liga f; **to be in** ~ **with** unter einer Decke stecken mit.

leak [li:k] n undichte Stelle f; (in ship) Leck nt // vt (liquid etc) durchlassen // vi (pipe etc) undicht sein; (liquid etc) auslaufen; **the information was** ~**ed to the enemy** die Information wurde dem Feind zugespielt; ~ **out** vi (liquid etc) auslaufen; (information) durchsickern.

leaky ['li:kɪ] a undicht.

lean [li:n] a mager // (v: pt, pp **leaned** or **leant** [lent]) vi sich neigen // vt (an)lehnen; **to** ~ **against sth an etw** (dat) angelehnt sein; **sich an etw** (acc) anlehnen; ~ **back** vi sich zurücklehnen; ~ **forward** vi sich vorbeugen; **to** ~ **on** vi sich stützen auf (+acc); ~ **out** vi sich hinauslehnen; ~ **over** vi sich hinüberbeugen; ~**ing** n Neigung f // a schief; ~**to** n Anbau m.

leap [li:p] n Sprung m // vi, pt, pp **leaped** or **leapt** [lept] springen; ~**frog** n Bockspringen nt; ~ **year** n Schaltjahr nt.

learn [lɜ:n], pt, pp **learned** or **learnt** vti lernen; (find out) erfahren; **to** ~ **how to do sth etw** (er)lernen; ~**ed** ['lɜ:nɪd] a gelehrt; ~**er** n Anfänger(in f) m; (AUT) (Brit: also ~ **driver**) Fahrschüler(in f) m; ~**ing** n Gelehrsamkeit f.

lease [li:s] n (of property) Mietvertrag m // vt pachten.

leash [li:ʃ] n Leine f.

least [li:st] a geringste(r, s) // ad am wenigsten // n Mindeste(s) nt; **the** ~ **possible effort** möglichst geringer Aufwand; **at** ~ zumindest; **not in the** ~! durchaus nicht!

leather ['leðə*] n Leder nt.

leave [li:v], pt, pp **left** vt verlassen; (~ behind) zurücklassen; (forget) vergessen; (allow to remain) lassen; (after death) hinterlassen; (entrust) überlassen; (to sb jdm) // vi weggehen, wegfahren; (for journey) abreisen; (bus, train) abfahren // n Erlaubnis f; (MIL) Urlaub m; **to be left** (remain) übrigbleiben; **there's some milk left over** es ist noch etwas Milch übrig; **on** ~ auf Urlaub; ~ **behind** vt (person, object) dalassen; (: forget) liegenlassen, stehenlassen; ~ **out** vt auslassen; ~ **of absence** n Urlaub.

leaves [li:vz] pl of **leaf**.

Lebanon ['lebənən] n Libanon m.

lecherous ['letʃərəs] a lüstern.

lecture ['lektʃə*] n Vortrag m; (UNIV) Vorlesung f // vi einen Vortrag halten; (UNIV) lesen // vt (scold) abkanzeln; **to give a** ~ **on sth** einen Vortrag über etwas halten; ~**r** n Vortragende(r) mf; (Brit: UNIV) Dozent(in f) m.

led [led] pt, pp of **lead**.

ledge [ledʒ] n Leiste f; (window ~) Sims m or nt; (of mountain) (Fels)vorsprung

m.

ledger ['ledʒə*] n Hauptbuch nt.

lee [li:] n Windschatten m; (NAUT) Lee f.

leech [li:tʃ] n Blutegel m.

leek [li:k] n Lauch m.

leer [lɪə*] vi schielen (at nach).

leeway ['li:weɪ] n (fig): to have some ~ etwas Spielraum haben.

left [left] pt, pp of **leave** // linke(r, s) // n (side) linke Seite f // ad links; on the ~ links; to the ~ nach links; the L~ (POL) die Linke f; ~-**handed** a linkshändig; ~-**hand side** n linke Seite f; ~-**luggage (office)** n (Brit) Gepäckaufbewahrung f; ~-**overs** pl Reste pl; ~-**wing** a linke(r, s).

leg [leg] n Bein nt; (of meat) Keule f; (stage) Etappe f; 1st/2nd ~ (SPORT) 1./2. Etappe.

legacy ['legəsɪ] n Erbe nt, Erbschaft f.

legal ['li:gəl] a gesetzlich; (allowed) legal; ~ **holiday** n (US) gesetzlicher Feiertag; ~**ize** vt legalisieren; ~**ly** ad gesetzlich; legal; ~ **tender** n gesetzliche(s) Zahlungsmittel nt.

legend ['ledʒənd] n Legende f; ~**ary** a legendär.

legible ['ledʒəbl] a leserlich.

legislation [ledʒɪs'leɪʃən] n Gesetzgebung f.

legislative ['ledʒɪslətɪv] a gesetzgebend.

legislature ['ledʒɪslətʃə*] n Legislative f.

legitimate [lɪ'dʒɪtɪmət] a rechtmäßig, legitim; (child) ehelich.

legroom ['legrʊm] n Platz m für die Beine.

leisure ['leʒə*] n Freizeit f; to be at ~ Zeit haben; ~**ly** a gemächlich.

lemon ['lemən] n Zitrone f; (colour) Zitronengelb nt; ~**ade** [lemə'neɪd] n Limonade f.

lend [lend], pt, pp lent vt leihen; to ~ sb sth jdm etw leihen; ~**ing library** n Leihbibliothek f.

length [leŋθ] n Länge f; (section of road, pipe etc) Strecke f; (of material) Stück nt; at ~ (lengthily) ausführlich; (at last) schließlich; ~**en** vt verlängern // vi länger werden; ~**ways** ad längs; ~**y** a sehr lang, langatmig.

lenient ['li:nɪənt] a nachsichtig.

lens [lenz] n Linse f; (PHOT) Objektiv nt.

lent [lent] pt, pp of **lend**.

Lent [lent] n Fastenzeit f.

lentil ['lentl] n Linse f.

Leo ['li:əʊ] n Löwe m.

leotard ['li:ətɑ:d] n Trikot nt, Gymnastikanzug m.

leper ['lepə*] n Leprakranke(r) mf.

leprosy ['leprəsɪ] n Lepra f.

lesbian ['lezbɪən] a lesbisch // n Lesbierin f.

less [les] a, ad, pron weniger; ~ **than** half weniger als die Hälfte; ~ **than ever** weniger denn je; ~ **and** ~ immer weniger; **the** ~ **he works** je weniger er arbeitet.

lessen ['lesn] vi abnehmen // vt verringern, verkleinern.

lesser ['lesə*] a kleiner, geringer; to a ~ extent in geringerem Maße.

lesson ['lesn] n (SCH) Stunde f; (unit of study) Lektion f; (fig) Lehre f; (ECCL) Lesung f; a maths ~ eine Mathestunde.

lest [lest] cj: ~ it happen damit es nicht passiert.

let [let] vt, pt, pp let lassen; (Brit: lease) vermieten; to ~ sb do sth jdn etw tun lassen; to ~ sb know sth jdn etw wissen lassen; ~'s go! gehen wir!; ~ him come soll er doch kommen; ~ **down** vt hinunterlassen; (disappoint) enttäuschen; ~ **go** vi loslassen // vt (things) loslassen; (person) gehen lassen; ~ **in** vt hereinlassen; (water) durchlassen; ~ **off** vt (gun) abfeuern; (steam) ablassen; (forgive) laufen lassen; ~ **on** vi durchblicken lassen; (pretend) vorgeben; ~ **out** vt herauslassen; (scream) fahren lassen; ~ **up** vi nachlassen; (stop) aufhören.

lethal ['li:θəl] a tödlich.

letter ['letə*] n (of alphabet) Buchstabe m; (message) Brief m; ~ **bomb** n Briefbombe f; ~**box** n (Brit) Briefkasten m; ~ **of credit** n Akkreditiv m; ~**ing** n Beschriftung f.

lettuce ['letɪs] n (Kopf)salat m.

let-up ['letʌp] n (col) Nachlassen nt.

leukaemia, (US) **leukemia** [lu:'ki:mɪə] n Leukämie f.

level ['levl] a (ground) eben; (at same height) auf gleicher Höhe; (equal) gleich gut; (head) kühl // ad auf gleicher Höhe // n (instrument) Wasserwaage f; (altitude) Höhe f; (flat place) ebene Fläche f; (position on scale) Niveau nt; (amount, degree) Grad m; // vt (ground) einebnen; (blow) versetzen (at sb jdm); (remark) richten (at gegen); to draw ~ with gleichziehen mit; to be ~ **with** auf einer Höhe sein mit; '**A**' ~**s** npl (Brit) ≈ Abitur nt; '**O**' ~**s** npl (Brit) ≈ mittlere Reife f; on the ~ (fig: honest) ehrlich; ~ **off** or **out** vi flach or eben werden; (fig) sich ausgleichen; (plane) horizontal fliegen // vt (ground) planieren; (differences) ausgleichen; ~ **crossing** n (Brit) Bahnübergang m; ~-**headed** a vernünftig.

lever ['li:və*] n Hebel m; (fig) Druckmittel nt // vt (hoch)stemmen; ~**age** n Hebelkraft f; (fig) Einfluß m.

levity ['levɪtɪ] n Leichtfertigkeit f.

levy ['levɪ] n (of taxes) Erhebung f; (tax) Abgaben pl; (MIL) Aushebung f // vt erheben; (MIL) ausheben.

lewd [luːd] *a* unzüchtig, unanständig.

liability [laɪə'bɪlɪtɪ] *n* (*burden*) Belastung *f*; (*duty*) Pflicht *f*; (*debt*) Verpflichtung *f*; (*proneness*) Anfälligkeit *f*; (*responsibility*) Haftung *f*.

liable ['laɪəbl] *a* (*responsible*) haftbar; (*prone*) anfällig; **to be ~ for** etw (*dat*) unterliegen; **it's ~ to happen** es kann leicht vorkommen.

liaise [liː'eɪz] *vi* zusammenarbeiten (*with* mit).

liaison [liː'eɪzɒn] *n* Verbindung *f*.

liar ['laɪə*] *n* Lügner *m*.

libel ['laɪbəl] *n* Verleumdung *f* // *vt* verleumden.

liberal ['lɪbərəl] *a* (*generous*) großzügig; (*open-minded*) aufgeschlossen; (*POL*) liberal.

liberate ['lɪbəreɪt] *vt* befreien.

liberation [lɪbə'reɪʃən] *n* Befreiung *f*.

liberty ['lɪbətɪ] *n* Freiheit *f*; (*permission*) Erlaubnis *f*; **to be at ~ to** do sth etw tun dürfen; **to take the ~ of** doing sth sich (*dat*) erlauben, etw zu tun.

Libra ['liːbrə] *n* Waage *f*.

librarian [laɪbreərɪən] *n* Bibliothekar(in *f*) *m*.

library ['laɪbrərɪ] *n* Bibliothek *f*; (*lending* ~) Bücherei *f*.

Libya ['lɪbɪə] *n* Libyen *nt*; **~n** *a* libysch // *n* Libyer(in *f*) *m*.

lice [laɪs] *npl* of **louse**.

licence, (*US*) **license** ['laɪsəns] *n* (*permit*) Erlaubnis *f*; (*also*: **driving ~**, (*US*) **driver's ~**) Führerschein *m*; (*excess*) Zügellosigkeit *f*; **~ number** *n* (Kraftfahrzeug)kennzeichen *nt*; **~ plate** *n* (*US AUT*) Nummernschild *nt*.

license ['laɪsəns] *n* (*US*) = **licence** // *vt* genehmigen, konzessionieren; **~d** *a* (*for alcohol*) konzessioniert (*für den Ausschank von Alkohol*).

licentious [laɪ'senʃəs] *a* ausschweifend.

lichen ['laɪkən] *n* Flechte *f*.

lick [lɪk] *vt* lecken // *n* Lecken *nt*; **a ~ of** paint ein bißchen Farbe.

licorice ['lɪkərɪs] *n* = **liquorice**.

lid [lɪd] *n* Deckel *m*; (*eye*~) Lid *nt*.

lido ['liːdəʊ] *n* (*Brit*) Freibad *nt*.

lie [laɪ] *n* Lüge *f* // *vi* lügen // *vi*, *pt* **lay**, *pp* **lain** (*rest*, *be situated*) liegen; (*put o.s. in position*) sich legen; **to ~ low** (*fig*) untertauchen; **~ about** *vi* (*things*) herumliegen; (*people*) faulenzen; **~-down** *n*: **to have a ~-down** (*Brit*) ein Nickerchen machen; **~-in** *n*: **to have a ~-in** (*Brit*) sich ausschlafen.

lieu [luː] *n*: **in ~ of** anstatt (+*gen*)

lieutenant [lef'tenənt] *n* Leutnant *m*.

life [laɪf], *pl* **lives** *n* Leben *nt*; **~ assurance** (*Brit*) *n* Lebensversicherung *f*; **~belt** (*Brit*) *n* Rettungsring *m*; **~boat** *n* Rettungsboot *nt*; **~guard** *n* Rettungsschwimmer *m*; **~ insurance** *n* = **~ assurance**; **~ jacket** *n* Schwimmweste *f*; **~less** *a* (*dead*) leblos; (*dull*) langweilig; **~like** *a* lebenswahr, naturgetreu; **~line** *n* (*lit*) Rettungsleine *f*; (*fig*) Rettungsanker *m*; **~long** *a* lebenslang; **~ preserver** *n* (*US*) = **~belt**; **~saver** *n* Lebensretter(in *f*) *m*; **~ sentence** *n* lebenslängliche Freiheitsstrafe; **~-sized** *a* in Lebensgröße; **~ span** *n* Lebensspanne *f*; **~style** *n* Lebensstil *m*; **~ support system** *n* (*MED*) Lebenserhaltungssystem *nt*; **~time** *n*: **in his ~time** während er lebte; **once in a ~time** einmal im Leben.

lift [lɪft] *vt* hochheben // *vi* sich heben // *n* (*Brit*: *elevator*) Aufzug *m*, Lift *m*; **to give sb a ~** (*Brit*) jdn mitnehmen; **~-off** *n* Abheben *nt* (vom Boden).

ligament ['lɪgəmənt] *n* Band *nt*.

light [laɪt] *n* Licht *nt*; (*for cigarette etc*): **have you got a ~?** haben Sie Feuer?; **~s** *pl* (*AUT*) Beleuchtung *f* // *vt*, *pt*, *pp* **lighted** *or* **lit** beleuchten; (*lamp*) anmachen; (*fire*, *cigarette*) anzünden // *a* (*bright*) hell; (*pale*) hell-; (*not heavy*, *easy*) leicht; (*punishment*) milde; (*touch*) leicht; **~ up** *vi* (*lamp*) angehen; (*face*) aufleuchten // *vt* (*illuminate*) beleuchten; (*lights*) anmachen; **~ bulb** *n* Glühbirne *f*; **~en** *vi* (*brighten*) hell werden; (*lightning*) blitzen // *vt* (*give light to*) erhellen; (*hair*) aufhellen; (*gloom*) aufheitern; (*make less heavy*) leichter machen; (*fig*) erleichtern; **~er** *n* Feuerzeug *nt*; **~-headed** *a* (*thoughtless*) leichtsinnig; (*giddy*) schwindlig; **~-hearted** *a* leichtherzig, fröhlich; **~house** *n* Leuchtturm *m*; **~ing** *n* Beleuchtung *f*; **~ly** *ad* leicht; (*irresponsibly*) leichtfertig; **to get off ~ly** mit einem blauen Auge davonkommen; **~ness** *n* (*of weight*) Leichtigkeit *f*; (*of colour*) Helle *f*.

lightning ['laɪtnɪŋ] *n* Blitz *m*; **~ conductor**, (*US*) **~ rod** *n* Blitzableiter *m*.

light: **~ pen** *n* Lichtstift *m*; **~weight** *a* (*suit*) leicht; **~weight boxer** *n* Leichtgewichtler *m*; **~ year** *n* Lichtjahr *nt*.

like [laɪk] *vt* mögen, gernhaben // *prep* wie // *a* (*similar*) ähnlich; (*equal*) gleich // *n*: **the ~** dergleichen; **his ~s and dislikes** was er mag und was er nicht mag; **I would ~, I'd ~** ich möchte gern; **would you ~ a coffee?** möchten Sie einen Kaffee?; **to be** *or* **look ~** sb/sth jdm/etw ähneln; **that's just ~ him** das ist typisch für ihn; **do it ~ this** mach es so; **it is nothing ~ …** es ist nicht zu vergleichen mit …; **~able** *a* sympathisch.

likelihood ['laɪklɪhʊd] *n* Wahrscheinlichkeit *f*.

likely ['laɪklɪ] *a* wahrscheinlich; **he's ~ to leave** er geht möglicherweise; **not ~!**

wohl kaum.

likeness ['laiknis] n Ähnlichkeit f; (*portrait*) Bild nt.

likewise ['laikwaiz] ad ebenso.

liking ['laikiŋ] n Zuneigung f; (*taste for*) Vorliebe f.

lilac ['lailək] n Flieder m // a (*colour*) fliederfarben.

lily ['lili] n Lilie f; ~ **of the valley** n Maiglöckchen nt.

limb [lim] n Glied nt.

limber ['limbə*]: ~ **up** vi sich auflockern; (*fig*) sich vorbereiten.

limbo ['limbəu] n: **to be in** ~ (*fig*) in der Schwebe sein.

lime [laim] n (*tree*) Linde f; (*fruit*) Limone f; (*substance*) Kalk m.

limelight ['laimlait] n: **to be in the** ~ (*fig*) im Rampenlicht stehen.

limestone ['laimstəun] n Kalkstein m.

limit ['limit] n Grenze f; (*col*) Höhe f // vt begrenzen, einschränken; ~**ation** n Einschränkung f; ~**ed** a beschränkt; **to be** ~**ed to** sich beschränken auf (*acc*); ~**ed (liability) company (Ltd)** n (*Brit*) Gesellschaft f mit beschränkter Haftung, GmbH f.

limp [limp] n Hinken nt // vi hinken // a schlaff.

limpet ['limpit] n (*fig*) Klette f.

limpid ['limpid] a klar.

line [lain] n Linie f; (*rope*) Leine f; (*on face*) Falte f; (*row*) Reihe f; (*of hills*) Kette f; (*US: queue*) Schlange f; (*company*) Linie f, Gesellschaft f; (*RAIL*) Strecke f; (*pl*) Geleise pl; (*TEL*) Leitung f; (*written*) Zeile f; (*direction*) Richtung f; (*fig: business*) Branche f; (*range of items*) Kollektion f // vt (*coat*) füttern; (*border*) säumen; **in** ~ **with** in Übereinstimmung mit; ~ **up** vi sich aufstellen // vt aufstellen; (*prepare*) sorgen für; (*support*) mobilisieren; (*surprise*) planen.

linear ['liniə*] a gerade; (*measure*) Längen-.

lined [laind] a (*face*) faltig; (*paper*) liniert.

linen ['linin] n Leinen nt; (*sheets etc*) Wäsche f.

liner ['lainə*] n Überseedampfer m.

linesman ['lainzmən] n (*SPORT*) Linienrichter m.

line-up ['lainʌp] n Aufstellung f.

linger ['liŋgə*] vi (*remain long*) verweilen; (*taste*) (zurück)bleiben; (*delay*) zögern, verharren.

lingerie ['lænʒəri:] n Damenunterwäsche f.

lingering ['liŋgəriŋ] a (*doubt*) zurückbleibend; (*disease*) langwierig; (*taste*) nachhaltend; (*look*) lang.

lingo ['liŋgəu], pl ~**es** n (*col*) Sprache f.

linguist ['liŋgwist] n Sprachkundige(r) mf; (*UNIV*) Sprachwissenschaftler(in f) m.

linguistic [liŋ'gwistik] a sprachlich; sprachwissenschaftlich; ~**s** n Sprachwissenschaft f, Linguistik f.

lining ['lainiŋ] n (*of clothes*) Futter nt.

link [liŋk] n Glied nt; (*connection*) Verbindung f; ~**s** pl (*GOLF*) Golfplatz m // vt verbinden; ~ **up** vt verbinden // vi zusammenkommen; (*companies*) sich zusammenschließen; ~**-up** n (*TEL*) Verbindung f; (*of spaceships*) Kopplung f.

lino ['lainəu], **linoleum** [li'nəuliəm] n Linoleum nt.

linseed oil ['linsi:d'ɔil] n Leinöl nt.

lion ['laiən] n Löwe m; ~**ess** n Löwin f.

lip [lip] n Lippe f; (*of jug*) Schnabel m; ~**read** vi irreg von den Lippen ablesen; ~ **salve** n Lippenbalsam m; **to pay** ~ **service (to)** ein Lippenbekenntnis ablegen (zu); ~**stick** n Lippenstift m.

liqueur [li'kjuə*] n Likör m.

liquid ['likwid] n Flüssigkeit f // a flüssig.

liquidate ['likwideit] vt liquidieren.

liquidation [likwi'deiʃən] n Liquidation f.

liquidize ['likwidaiz] vt (*CULIN*) (im Mixer) pürieren.

liquidizer ['likwidaizə*] n Mixgerät nt.

liquor ['likə*] n Alkohol m.

liquorice ['likəris] n Lakritze f.

liquor store n (*US*) Spirituosengeschäft nt.

Lisbon ['lizbən] n Lissabon nt.

lisp [lisp] n Lispeln nt // vi lispeln.

list [list] n Liste f, Verzeichnis nt; (*of ship*) Schlagseite f // vt (*write down*) eine Liste machen von; (*verbally*) aufzählen // vi (*ship*) Schlagseite haben.

listen ['lisn] vi hören; ~ **to** vt zuhören (+dat); ~**er** n (Zu)hörer(in f) m.

listless ['listləs] a lustlos.

lit [lit] pt, pp of **light**.

literacy ['litərəsi] n Fähigkeit f zu lesen und zu schreiben.

literal ['litərəl] a buchstäblich; (*translation*) wortwörtlich; ~**ly** ad wörtlich; buchstäblich.

literary ['litərəri] a literarisch.

literate ['litərət] a des Lesens und Schreibens kundig.

literature ['litrətʃə*] n Literatur f.

lithe [laið] a geschmeidig.

litigation [liti'geiʃən] n Prozeß m.

litre, (US) liter ['li:tə*] n Liter m.

litter ['litə*] n (*rubbish*) Abfall m; (*of animals*) Wurf m // vt in Unordnung bringen; **to be** ~**ed with** übersät sein mit; ~ **bin** n (*Brit*) Abfalleimer m.

little ['litl] a klein // ad, n wenig; **a** ~ ein bißchen; ~ **by** ~ nach und nach.

live [liv] vi leben; (*dwell*) wohnen // vt (*life*) führen // a [laiv] lebendig; (*MIL*) scharf; (*ELEC*) geladen; (*broadcast*) live; ~ **down** vt: I'll never ~ it **down** das wird man mir nie vergessen; ~ **on**

vi weiterleben; **to ~ on** sth von etw leben; **to ~ together** *vi* zusammenleben; *(share a flat)* zusammenwohnen; **~ up to** *vt (standards)* gerecht werden (+*dat*); *(principles)* anstreben; *(hopes)* entsprechen (+*dat*).

livelihood ['laɪvlɪhʊd] *n* Lebensunterhalt *m*.

lively ['laɪvlɪ] *a* lebhaft, lebendig.

liven up [laɪvn-] *vt* beleben.

liver ['lɪvə*] *n (ANAT)* Leber *f*.

livery ['lɪvərɪ] *n* Livree *f*.

lives [laɪvz] *pl of* **life**.

livestock ['laɪvstɒk] *n* Vieh *nt*.

livid ['lɪvɪd] *a (lit)* bläulich; *(furious)* fuchsteufelswild.

living ['lɪvɪŋ] *n* (Lebens)unterhalt *m* // *a* lebendig; *(language etc)* lebend; **to earn** *or* **make a ~** sich (*dat*) seinen Lebensunterhalt verdienen; **~ conditions** *npl* Wohnverhältnisse *pl*; **~ room** *n* Wohnzimmer *nt*; **~ standards** *npl* Lebensstandard *m*; **~ wage** *n* ausreichender Lohn *m*.

lizard ['lɪzəd] *n* Eidechse *f*.

load [ləʊd] *n (burden)* Last *f*; *(amount)* Ladung *f* // *vt (also:* **~ up**)*:* **~ (with)** (be)laden (mit); *(COMPUT)* laden; *(camera)* Film einlegen in (+*acc*); *(gun)* laden; **a ~ of, ~s of** *(fig)* jede Menge; **~ed** *a* beladen; *(dice)* präpariert; *(question)* Fang-; *(col: rich)* steinreich; **~ing bay** *n* Ladeplatz *m*.

loaf [ləʊf] *n* Brot *nt* // *vi (also:* **~ about, ~ around**) herumlungern, faulenzen.

loan [ləʊn] *n* Leihgabe *f*; *(FIN)* Darlehen *nt* // *vt* leihen; **on ~** geliehen.

loath [ləʊθ] *a:* **to be ~ to do** sth etw ungern tun.

loathe [ləʊð] *vt* verabscheuen.

loathing ['ləʊðɪŋ] *n* Abscheu *f*.

loaves [ləʊvz] *pl of* **loaf**.

lobby ['lɒbɪ] *n* Vorhalle *f*; *(POL)* Lobby *f* // *vt* politisch beeinflussen (wollen).

lobe [ləʊb] *n* Ohrläppchen *nt*.

lobster ['lɒbstə*] *n* Hummer *m*.

local ['ləʊkəl] *a* ortsansässig, Orts- // *n (pub)* Stammwirtschaft *f*; **the ~s** *pl* die Ortsansässigen *pl*; **~ anaesthetic** *n (MED)* örtliche Betäubung *f*; **~ authority** *n* städtische Behörden *pl*; **~ call** *n (TEL)* Ortsgespräch *nt*; **~ government** *n* Gemeinde-/Kreisverwaltung *f*; **~ity** [ləʊ'kælɪtɪ] *n* Ort *m*; **~ly** *ad* örtlich, am Ort.

locate [ləʊ'keɪt] *vt* ausfindig machen; *(establish)* errichten.

location [ləʊ'keɪʃən] *n* Platz *m*, Lage *f*; **on ~** *(CINE)* auf Außenaufnahme.

loch [lɒx] *n (Scot)* See *m*.

lock [lɒk] *n* Schloß *nt*; *(NAUT)* Schleuse *f*; *(of hair)* Locke *f* // *vt (fasten)* (ver)schließen // *vi (door etc)* sich schließen (lassen); *(wheels)* blockieren.

locker ['lɒkə*] *n* Spind *m*.

locket ['lɒkɪt] *n* Medaillon *nt*.

lockout ['lɒkaʊt] *n* Aussperrung *f*.

locksmith ['lɒksmɪθ] *n* Schlosser(in *f*) *m*.

lock-up ['lɒkʌp] *n* Gefängnis *nt*.

locum ['ləʊkəm] *n (MED)* Vertreter(in *f*) *m*.

locust ['ləʊkəst] *n* Heuschrecke *f*.

lodge [lɒdʒ] *n (gatehouse)* Pförtnerhaus *nt*; *(freemasons')* Loge *f* // *vi* (in Untermiete) wohnen *(with* bei); *(get stuck)* stecken(bleiben) // *vt (protest)* einreichen; **~r** *n* (Unter)mieter *m*.

lodgings ['lɒdʒɪŋz] *n* (Miet)wohnung *f*.

loft [lɒft] *n* (Dach)boden *m*.

lofty ['lɒftɪ] *a* hoch(ragend); *(proud)* hochmütig.

log [lɒg] *n* Klotz *m*; *(book)* = **logbook**.

logbook ['lɒgbʊk] *n* Bordbuch *nt*; *(for lorry)* Fahrtenschreiber *m*; *(AUT)* Kraftfahrzeugbrief *m*.

loggerheads ['lɒgəhedz] *npl:* **to be at ~** sich in den Haaren liegen.

logic ['lɒdʒɪk] *n* Logik *f*; **~al** *a* logisch.

logistics [lɒ'dʒɪstɪks] *npl* Logistik *f*.

logo ['ləʊgəʊ] *n* Firmenzeichen *nt*.

loin [lɔɪn] *n* Lende *f*.

loiter ['lɔɪtə*] *vi* herumstehen.

loll [lɒl] *vi (also:* **~ about**) sich rekeln.

lollipop ['lɒlɪpɒp] *n* (Dauer)lutscher *m*; **~ man/lady** *n (Brit)* = Schülerlotse *m*.

London ['lʌndən] *n* London *nt*; **~er** *n* Londoner(in *f*) *m*.

lone [ləʊn] *a* einsam.

loneliness ['ləʊnlɪnəs] *n* Einsamkeit *f*.

lonely ['ləʊnlɪ] *a* einsam.

loner ['ləʊnə*] *n* Einzelgänger(in *f*) *m*.

long [lɒŋ] *a* lang; *(distance)* weit // *ad* lange // *vi* sich sehnen *(for* nach); **before ~** bald; **as ~ as** solange; **in the ~ run** auf die Dauer; **don't be ~!** beeil dich!; **how ~ is the street?** wie lang ist die Straße?; **how ~ is the lesson?** wie lange dauert die Stunde?; **6 metres ~** 6 Meter lang; **6 months ~** 6 Monate lang; **all night ~** die ganze Nacht; **he no ~er comes** er kommt nicht mehr; **~ ago** vor langer zeit; **~ before** lange vorher; **at ~ last** endlich; **~distance** *a* Fern-.

longevity [lɒn'dʒevɪtɪ] *n* Langlebigkeit *f*.

long: ~-haired *a* langhaarig; **~hand** *n* Langschrift *f*; **~ing** *n* Sehnsucht *f* // *a* sehnsüchtig.

longitude ['lɒŋgɪtjuːd] *n* Längengrad *m*.

long: ~ jump *n* Weitsprung *m*; **~-lost** *a* längst verloren geglaubt; **~-playing record** *n* Langspielplatte *f*; **~-range** *a* Langstrecken-, Fern-; **~-sighted** *a* weitsichtig; **~-standing** *a* alt, seit langer Zeit bestehend; **~-suffering** *a* schwer geprüft; **~-term** *a* langfristig; **~ wave** *n* Langwelle *f*; **~-winded** *a* langatmig.

loo [luː] n (Brit col) Klo nt.

look [luk] vi schauen; (seem) aussehen; (building etc): to ~ on to the sea aufs Meer gehen; // n Blick m; ~s pl Aussehen nt; ~ **after** vt (care for) sorgen für; (watch) aufpassen auf (+acc); ~ **at** vt ansehen; (consider) sich überlegen; ~ **back** vi sich umsehen; (fig) zurückblicken; ~ **down on** vt (fig) herabsehen auf (+acc); ~ **for** vt (seek) suchen; ~ **forward to** vt sich freuen auf (+acc); (in letters): we ~ forward to hearing from you wir hoffen, bald von Ihnen zu hören; ~ **into** vt untersuchen; ~ **on** vi zusehen; (take care) aufpassen; ~ **out** vi hinaussehen; ~ **out for** vt Ausschau halten nach; (be careful) achtgeben auf (+acc); ~ **round** vi sich umsehen; ~ **to** vt (take care of) achtgeben auf (+acc); (rely on) sich verlassen auf (+acc); ~ **up** vi aufblicken; (improve) sich bessern // vt (word) nachschlagen; (person) besuchen; ~ **up to** vt aufsehen zu; ~**out** n (watch) Ausschau f; (person) Wachposten m; (place) Ausguck m; (prospect) Aussichten pl; to be on the ~out for sth nach etw Ausschau halten.

loom [luːm] n Webstuhl m // vi sich abzeichnen.

loony ['luːnɪ] n (col) Verrückte(r) mf.

loop [luːp] n Schlaufe f; ~**hole** n (fig) Hintertürchen nt.

loose [luːs] a lose, locker; (free) frei; (inexact) unpräzise // vt lösen, losbinden; ~ **change** n Kleingeld nt; ~ **chippings** npl (on road) Rollsplit m; ~ **end** n: to be at a ~ end (Brit) or at ~ ends (US) nicht wissen, was man tun soll; ~**ly** ad locker, lose; ~**n** vt lockern, losmachen.

loot [luːt] n Beute f // vt plündern; ~**ing** n Plünderung f.

lop [lɒp]: ~ **off** vt abhacken.

lop-sided ['lɒp'saɪdɪd] a schief.

lord [lɔːd] n (ruler) Herr m; (Brit, title) Lord m; the L~ (Gott) der Herr m; the (House of) L~s das Oberhaus; ~**ship** n: your L~ship Eure Lordschaft.

lore [lɔː*] n Überlieferung f.

lorry ['lɒrɪ] n (Brit) Lastwagen m; ~ **driver** n (Brit) Lastwagenfahrer(in f) m.

lose [luːz] pt, pp **lost** vt verlieren; (chance) verpassen // vi verlieren; to ~ (time) (clock) nachgehen; ~**r** n Verlierer m.

loss [lɒs] n Verlust m; at a ~ (COMM) mit Verlust; (unable) außerratlos.

lost [lɒst] pt, pp of **lose** // a verloren; ~ **property**, (US) ~ **and found** n Fundsachen pl.

lot [lɒt] n (quantity) Menge f; (fate, at auction) Los nt; (col: people, things) Haufen m; the ~ alles; (people) alle; a

~ **of** sing viel // pl viele; ~**s of** massenhaft, viel(e); I read a ~ ich lese viel; to draw ~**s** for sth etw verlosen.

lotion ['ləʊʃən] n Lotion f.

lottery ['lɒtərɪ] n Lotterie f.

loud [laʊd] a laut; (showy) schreiend // ad laut; ~**hailer** n (Brit) Megaphon nt; ~**ly** ad laut; ~**speaker** n Lautsprecher m.

lounge [laʊndʒ] n (in hotel) Gesellschaftsraum m; (in house) Wohnzimmer nt // vi sich herumlümmeln; ~ **suit** n (Brit) Straßenanzug m.

louse [laʊs], pl **lice** n Laus f.

lousy ['laʊzɪ] a (fig) miserabel.

lout [laʊt] n Lümmel m.

louvre, (US) **louver** ['luːvə*] a (door, window) Jalousie-.

lovable ['lʌvəbl] a liebenswert.

love [lʌv] n Liebe f; (person) Liebling m; (SPORT) null // vt (person) lieben; (activity) gerne mögen; to ~ to do sth etw (sehr) gerne tun; to be in ~ with sb in jdn verliebt sein; to make ~ sich lieben; for the ~ of aus Liebe zu; '15 ~' (TENNIS) 15 null; ~ **affair** n (Liebes)verhältnis nt; ~ **letter** n Liebesbrief m; ~ **life** n Liebesleben nt.

lovely ['lʌvlɪ] a schön.

lover ['lʌvə*] n Liebhaber(in f) m.

loving ['lʌvɪŋ] a liebend, liebevoll.

low [ləʊ] a niedrig; (rank) niedere(r, s); (level, note, neckline) tief; (intelligence, density) gering; (vulgar) ordinär; (not loud) leise; (depressed) gedrückt // ad (not high) niedrig; (not loudly) leise // n (low point) Tiefstand m; (MET) Tief nt; to feel ~ sich mies fühlen; **turn (down)** ~ vt leiser stellen; ~-**cut** a (dress) tiefausgeschnitten.

lower ['ləʊə*] vt herunterlassen; (eyes, gun) senken; (reduce) herabsetzen, senken // vr: to ~ o.s. to (fig) sich herablassen zu.

low: ~-**fat** a fettarm, Mager-; ~ **lands** npl (GEO) Flachland nt; ~**ly** a bescheiden; ~-**lying** a tiefgelegen.

loyal ['lɔɪəl] a treu; ~**ty** n Treue f.

lozenge ['lɒzɪndʒ] n Pastille f.

L.P. n abbr of **long-playing record.**

L-plates ['elpleɪts] npl (Brit) L-Schild nt (für Fahrschüler).

Ltd abbr of **limited company.**

lubricant ['luːbrɪkənt] n Schmiermittel nt.

lubricate ['luːbrɪkeɪt] vt schmieren.

lucid ['luːsɪd] a klar; (sane) bei klarem Verstand; (moment) licht.

luck [lʌk] n Glück nt; **bad** ~ n Pech nt; **good** ~! viel Glück!; ~**ily** ad glücklicherweise, zum Glück; ~**y** a Glücks-; to be ~y Glück haben.

lucrative ['luːkrətɪv] a einträglich.

ludicrous ['luːdɪkrəs] a grotesk.

lug [lʌg] vt schleppen.

luggage ['lʌgɪdʒ] *n* Gepäck *nt*; ~ **rack** *n* Gepäcknetz *nt*.

lugubrious [luːˈguːbrɪəs] *a* traurig.

lukewarm ['luːkwɔːm] *a* lauwarm; (*indifferent*) lau.

lull [lʌl] *n* Flaute *f* // *vt* einlullen; (*calm*) beruhigen.

lullaby ['lʌləbaɪ] *n* Schlaflied *nt*.

lumbago [lʌmˈbeɪgəʊ] *n* Hexenschuß *m*.

lumber ['lʌmbə*] *n* Plunder *m*; (*wood*) Holz *nt*; ~**jack** *n* Holzfäller *m*.

luminous ['luːmɪnəs] *a* Leucht-.

lump [lʌmp] *n* Klumpen *m*; (*MED*) Schwellung *f*; (*in breast*) Knoten *m*; (*of sugar*) Stück *nt* // *vt* (*also*: ~ *together*) zusammentun; (*judge together*) in einen Topf werfen; ~ **sum** *n* Pauschalsumme *f*; ~**y** *a* klumpig.

lunacy ['luːnəsɪ] *n* Irrsinn *m*.

lunar ['luːnə*] *a* Mond-.

lunatic ['luːnətɪk] *n* Wahnsinnige(r) *mf* // *a* wahnsinnig, irr; ~ **asylum** *n* Irrenanstalt *f*.

lunch [lʌntʃ] *n* (*also* ~**eon** [-ən]) Mittagessen *nt*; ~**time** *n* Mittagszeit *f*; ~**eon meat** *n* Frühstücksfleisch *nt*; ~**eon voucher** *n* Essensmarke *f*.

lung [lʌŋ] *n* Lunge *f*.

lunge [lʌndʒ] *vi* (*also*: ~ *forward*) (los)stürzen; to ~ at sich stürzen auf (+*acc*).

lurch [lɜːtʃ] *vi* taumeln; (*NAUT*) schlingern // *n* Ruck *m*; (*NAUT*) Schlingern *nt*; to leave sb in the ~ jdn im Stich lassen.

lure [ljʊə*] *n* Köder *m*; (*fig*) Lockung *f* // *vt* (ver)locken.

lurid ['ljʊərɪd] *a* (*shocking*) grausig, widerlich; (*colour*) grell.

lurk [lɜːk] *vi* lauern.

luscious ['lʌʃəs] *a* köstlich.

lush [lʌʃ] *a* satt; (*vegetation*) üppig.

lust [lʌst] *n* (*sensation*) Wollust *f*; (*greed*) Gier *f* // *vi* gieren (*after* nach).

lustre, (*US*) **luster** ['lʌstə*] *n* Glanz *m*.

lusty ['lʌstɪ] *a* gesund und munter.

Luxembourg ['lʌksəmbɜːg] *n* Luxemburg *nt*.

luxuriant [lʌgˈzjʊərɪənt] *a* üppig.

luxurious [lʌgˈzjʊərɪəs] *a* luxuriös, Luxus-.

luxury ['lʌkʃərɪ] *n* Luxus *m* // *cpd* Luxus-.

lying ['laɪɪŋ] *n* Lügen *nt* // *a* verlogen.

lynx [lɪŋks] *n* Luchs *m*.

lyric ['lɪrɪk] *n* Lyrik *f*; (*pl*: *words for song*) (Lied)text *m* // *a* lyrisch; ~**al** *a* lyrisch, gefühlvoll.

M

M. *abbr of* metre; mile; million.

M.A. *abbr of* Master of Arts.

mac [mæk] *n* (*Brit col*) Regenmantel *m*.

macaroni [mækəˈrəʊnɪ] *n* Makkaroni *pl*.

mace [meɪs] *n* Amtsstab *m*; (*spice*) Muskat *m*.

machine [məˈʃiːn] *n* Maschine *f* // *vt* (*dress etc*) mit der Maschine nähen; ~ **gun** *n* Maschinengewehr *nt*; ~ **language** *n* (*COMPUT*) Maschinensprache *f*; ~**ry** [məˈʃiːnərɪ] *n* Maschinerie *f*.

macho ['mætʃəʊ] *a* macho.

mackerel ['mækrəl] *n* Makrele *f*.

mackintosh ['mækɪntɒʃ] *n* (*Brit*) Regenmantel *m*.

mad [mæd] *a* verrückt; (*dog*) tollwütig; (*angry*) wütend; ~ **about** (*fond of*) verrückt nach, versessen auf (+*acc*).

madam ['mædəm] *n* gnädige Frau *f*.

madden ['mædn] *vt* verrückt machen; (*make angry*) ärgern.

made [meɪd] *pt*, *pp of* **make**.

Madeira [məˈdɪərə] *n* (*GEOG*) Madeira *nt*; (*wine*) Madeira *m*.

made-to-measure ['meɪdtəˈmeʒə*] *a* (*Brit*) Maß-.

madly ['mædlɪ] *ad* wahnsinnig.

madman ['mædmən] *n* Verrückte(r) *m*, Irre(r) *m*.

madness ['mædnəs] *n* Wahnsinn *m*.

Madrid [məˈdrɪd] *n* Madrid *nt*.

Mafia ['mæfɪə] *n* Mafia *f*.

magazine ['mægəziːn] *n* Zeitschrift *f*; (*in gun*) Magazin *nt*.

maggot ['mægət] *n* Made *f*.

magic ['mædʒɪk] *n* Zauberei *f*, Magie *f*; (*fig*) Zauber *m* // *a* magisch, Zauber-; ~**al** *a* magisch; ~**ian** [məˈdʒɪʃən] *n* Zauberer *m*.

magistrate ['mædʒɪstreɪt] *n* (Friedens)richter *m*.

magnanimous [mægˈnænɪməs] *a* großmütig.

magnesium [mægˈniːzɪəm] *n* Magnesium *nt*.

magnet ['mægnɪt] *n* Magnet *m*; ~**ic** [mægˈnetɪk] *a* magnetisch; ~**ic tape** *n* Magnetband *nt*; ~**ism** *n* Magnetismus *m*; (*fig*) Ausstrahlungskraft *f*.

magnificence [mægˈnɪfɪsəns] *n* Großartigkeit *f*.

magnificent [mægˈnɪfɪsənt] *a* großartig.

magnify ['mægnɪfaɪ] *vt* vergrößern; ~**ing glass** *n* Lupe *f*.

magnitude ['mægnɪtjuːd] *n* (*size*) Größe *f*; (*importance*) Ausmaß *ni*.

magpie ['mægpaɪ] *n* Elster *f*.

mahogany [məˈhɒgənɪ] *n* Mahagoni *nt* // *cpd* Mahagoni-.

maid [meɪd] *n* Dienstmädchen *nt*; old ~ *n* alte Jungfer *f*.

maiden ['meɪdn] *n* (*liter*) Maid *f* // *a* (*flight, speech*) Jungfern-; ~ **name** *n* Mädchenname *m*.

mail [meɪl] *n* Post *f* // *vt* aufgeben; ~ **box** *n* (*US*) Briefkasten *m*; ~**ing list** *n* Anschreibeliste *f*; ~ **order** *n* Bestellung

f durch die Post; ~ **order firm** *n* Versandhaus *nt*.
maim [meɪm] *vt* verstümmeln.
main [meɪn] *a* hauptsächlich, Haupt // *n* (*pipe*) Hauptleitung *f*; **the** ~**s** (*ELEC*) das Stromnetz *nt*; **in the** ~ im großen und ganzen; ~**frame** *n* (*COMPUT*) Großrechner *m*; ~**land** *n* Festland *nt*; ~ **road** *n* Hauptstraße *f*; ~**stay** *n* (*fig*) Hauptstütze *f*; ~**stream** *n* Hauptrichtung *f*.
maintain [meɪnˈteɪn] *vt* (*machine, roads*) instand halten; (*support*) unterhalten; (*keep up*) aufrechterhalten; (*claim*) behaupten; (*innocence*) beteuern.
maintenance [ˈmeɪntənəns] *n* (*TECH*) Wartung *f*; (*of family*) Unterhalt *m*.
maize [meɪz] *n* Mais *m*.
majestic [məˈdʒestɪk] *a* majestätisch.
majesty [ˈmædʒɪstɪ] *n* Majestät *f*.
major [ˈmeɪdʒə*] *n* Major *m* // *a* (*MUS*) Dur; (*more important*) Haupt-; (*bigger*) größer.
Majorca [məˈjɔːkə] *n* Mallorca *nt*.
majority [məˈdʒɒrɪtɪ] *n* Mehrheit *f*; (*JUR*) Volljährigkeit *f*.
make [meɪk] *vt*, *pt*, *pp* **made** machen; (*appoint*) ernennen (zu); (*cause to do sth*) veranlassen; (*reach*) erreichen; (*in time*) schaffen; (*earn*) verdienen // *n* Marke *f*; **to** ~ **sth happen** etw geschehen lassen; **to** ~ **it** es schaffen; **what time do you** ~ **it?** wie spät hast du es? **to** ~ **do with** auskommen mit; ~ **for** *vi* gehen/fahren nach; ~ **out** *vt* (*write out*) ausstellen; (*understand*) verstehen; (*write: cheque*) ausstellen; ~ **up** *vt* (*make*) machen; (*face*) schminken; (*quarrel*) beilegen; (*story etc*) erfinden // *vi* sich versöhnen; ~ **up for** *vt* wiedergutmachen; (*COMM*) vergüten; ~**-believe** *n* Phantasie *f*; ~**r** *n* (*COMM*) Hersteller *m*; ~**shift** *a* behelfsmäßig, Not-; ~**-up** *n* Schminke *f*, Make-up *nt*; ~**-up remover** *n* Make-up-Entferner *m*.
making [ˈmeɪkɪŋ] *n*: **in the** ~ im Entstehen; **to have the** ~**s of** das Zeug haben zu.
malaise [mæˈleɪz] *n* Unbehagen *nt*.
Malaya [məˈleɪə] *n* Malaya *nt*.
Malaysia [məˈleɪzɪə] *n* Malaysia *nt*.
male [meɪl] *n* Mann *m*; (*animal*) Männchen *nt* // *a* männlich.
malevolent [məˈlevələnt] *a* übelwollend.
malfunction [mælˈfʌŋkʃən] *n* (*MED*) Funktionsstörung *f*; (*of machine*) Defekt *m*.
malice [ˈmælɪs] *n* Bosheit *f*.
malicious [məˈlɪʃəs] *a* böswillig, gehässig.
malign [məˈlaɪn] *vt* verleumden // *a* böse.
malignant [məˈlɪgnənt] *a* bösartig.
mall [mɔːl] *n* (*also:* **shopping** ~) Ein-

kaufszentrum *nt*.
malleable [ˈmælɪəbl] *a* formbar.
mallet [ˈmælɪt] *n* Holzhammer *m*.
malnutrition [ˈmælnjuˈtrɪʃən] *n* Unterernährung *f*.
malpractice [mælˈpræktɪs] *n* Amtsvergehen *nt*.
malt [mɔːlt] *n* Malz *nt*.
Malta [ˈmɔːltə] *n* Malta *nt*; **Maltese** [-ˈtiːz] *a* maltesisch // *n*, *pl inv* Malteser(in *f*) *m*.
maltreat [mælˈtriːt] *vt* mißhandeln.
mammal [ˈmæməl] *n* Säugetier *nt*.
mammoth [ˈmæməθ] *n* Mammut *nt* // *a* Mammut-.
man [mæn], *pl* **men** *n* Mann *m*; (*human race*) der Mensch, die Menschen *pl* // *vt* bemannen.
manage [ˈmænɪdʒ] *vi* zurechtkommen // *vt* (*control*) führen, leiten; (*cope with*) fertigwerden mit; ~**able** *a* (*person, animal*) fügsam; (*object*) handlich; ~**ment** *n* (*control*) Führung *f*, Leitung *f*; (*directors*) Management *nt*; ~**r** *n* Geschäftsführer *m*; ~**ress** [ˈmænɪdʒəˈres] *n* Geschäftsführerin *f*; ~**rial** [mænəˈdʒɪərɪəl] *a* (*post*) leitend; (*problem etc*) Management-.
managing [ˈmænɪdʒɪŋ] *a*: ~ **director** *n* Betriebsleiter *m*.
mandarin [ˈmændərɪn] *n* (*fruit*) Mandarine *f*.
mandatory [ˈmændətərɪ] *a* obligatorisch.
mane [meɪn] *n* Mähne *f*.
maneuver [məˈnuːvə*] (*US*) = **manoeuvre**.
manfully [ˈmænfulɪ] *ad* mannhaft.
mangle [ˈmæŋgl] *vt* verstümmeln // *n* Mangel *f*.
mango [ˈmæŋgəʊ], *pl* ~**es** *n* Mango(pflaume) *f*.
mangy [ˈmeɪndʒɪ] *a* (*dog*) räudig.
manhandle [ˈmænhændl] *vt* grob behandeln.
manhole [ˈmænhəʊl] *n* (Straßen)schacht *m*.
manhood [ˈmænhʊd] *n* Mannesalter *nt*; (*manliness*) Männlichkeit *f*.
man-hour [ˈmænˈaʊə*] *n* Arbeitsstunde *f*.
manhunt [ˈmænhʌnt] *n* Fahndung *f*.
mania [ˈmeɪnɪə] *n* Manie *f*; ~**c** [ˈmeɪnɪæk] *n* Wahnsinnige(r) *mf*.
manic [ˈmænɪk] *a* (*behaviour, activity*) hektisch; ~**-depressive** *n* Manisch-Depressive(r) *mf*.
manicure [ˈmænɪkjʊə*] *n* Maniküre *f*; ~ **set** *n* Necessaire *nt*.
manifest [ˈmænɪfest] *vt* offenbaren // *a* offenkundig; ~**ation** *n* (*sign*) Anzeichen *nt*.
manifesto [mænɪˈfestəʊ] *n* Manifest *nt*.
manipulate [məˈnɪpjʊleɪt] *vt* handhaben; (*fig*) manipulieren.

mankind [mæn'kaɪnd] n Menschheit f.

manly ['mænlɪ] a männlich; mannhaft.

man-made ['mæn'meɪd] a (fibre) künstlich.

manner ['mænə*] n Art f, Weise f; in a ~ of speaking sozusagen; ~s pl Manieren pl; ~ism n (of person) Angewohnheit f; (of style) Maniertheit f.

manoeuvre, (US) **maneuver** [mə'nu:və*] vti manövrieren // n (MIL) Feldzug m; (general) Manöver nt, Schachzug m.

manor ['mænə*] n Landgut nt; ~ house n Herrenhaus nt.

manpower ['mænpaʊə*] n Arbeitskräfte pl.

mansion ['mænʃən] n Villa f.

manslaughter ['mænslɔ:tə*] n Totschlag m.

mantelpiece ['mæntlpi:s] n Kaminsims m.

mantle ['mæntl] n (cloak) lange(r) Umhang m.

manual ['mænjʊəl] a manuell, Hand- // n Handbuch nt.

manufacture [mænjʊ'fæktʃə*] vt herstellen // n Herstellung f; ~r n Hersteller m.

manure [mə'njʊə*] n Dünger m.

manuscript ['mænjʊskrɪpt] n Manuskript nt.

Manx [mæŋks] a der Insel Man.

many ['menɪ] a, pron viele; a great ~ sehr viele; ~ a time oft.

map [mæp] n (Land)karte f; (of town) Stadtplan m // vt eine Karte machen von; ~ out vt (fig) ausarbeiten.

maple ['meɪpl] n Ahorn m.

mar [ma:*] vt verderben.

marathon ['mærəθən] n (SPORT) Marathonlauf m; (fig) Marathon m.

marauder [mə'rɔ:də*] n Plünderer m.

marble ['ma:bl] n Marmor m; (for game) Murmel f.

March [ma:tʃ] n März m.

march [ma:tʃ] vi marschieren // n Marsch m; ~-past n Vorbeimarsch m.

mare [mɛə*] n Stute f.

margarine [ma:dʒə'ri:n] n Margarine f.

margin ['ma:dʒɪn] n Rand m; (extra amount) Spielraum m; (COMM) Spanne f; ~al a (note) Rand-; (difference etc) geringfügig; ~ al (seat) n (POL) Wahlkreis, der nur mit knapper Mehrheit gehalten wird.

marigold ['mærɪgəʊld] n Ringelblume f.

marina [mə'ri:nə] n Yachthafen m.

marinate ['mærɪneɪt] vt marinieren.

marine [mə'ri:n] a Meeres-, See- // n (MIL) Marineinfanterist m.

marital ['mærɪtl] a ehelich, Ehe-; ~ status n Familienstand m.

maritime ['mærɪtaɪm] a See-.

mark [ma:k] n (coin) Mark f; (spot) Fleck m; (scar) Kratzer m; (sign) Zeichen nt; (target) Ziel nt; (SCH) Note f // vt (make mark) Flecken/Kratzer machen auf (+acc); (indicate) markieren; (exam) korrigieren; to ~ time (lit, fig) auf der Stelle treten; ~ out vt bestimmen; (area) abstecken; ~ed a deutlich; ~er n (in book) (Lese)zeichen nt; (on road) Schild nt.

market ['ma:kɪt] n Markt m; (stock ~) Börse f // vt (COMM: new product) auf den Markt bringen; (sell) vertreiben; ~ garden n (Brit) Handelsgärtnerei f; ~ing n Marketing nt; ~ place n Marktplatz m; ~ research n Marktforschung f; ~ value n Marktwert m.

marksman ['ma:ksmən] n Scharfschütze m.

marmalade ['ma:məleɪd] n Orangenmarmelade f.

maroon [mə'ru:n] vt aussetzen // a (colour) kastanienbraun.

marquee [ma:'ki:] n große(s) Zelt nt.

marriage ['mærɪdʒ] n Ehe f; (wedding) Heirat f; ~ bureau n Heiratsinstitut nt; ~ certificate n Heiratsurkunde f.

married ['mærɪd] a (person) verheiratet; (couple, life) Ehe-.

marrow ['mærəʊ] n (Knochen)mark nt; (vegetable) Kürbis m.

marry ['mærɪ] vt (join) trauen; (take as husband, wife) heiraten // vi (also: get married) heiraten.

Mars [ma:z] n (planet) Mars m.

marsh [ma:ʃ] n Sumpf m.

marshal ['ma:ʃəl] n (US) Bezirkspolizeichef m // vt (an)ordnen, arrangieren.

marshy ['ma:ʃɪ] a sumpfig.

martial ['ma:ʃəl] a kriegerisch; ~ law n Kriegsrecht nt.

martyr ['ma:tə*] n (lit, fig) Märtyrer(in f) m // vt zum Märtyrer machen; ~dom n Martyrium nt.

marvel ['ma:vəl] n Wunder nt // vi sich wundern (at über +acc); ~lous, (US) ~ous a wunderbar.

Marxist ['ma:ksɪst] n Marxist(in f) m.

marzipan [ma:zɪ'pæn] n Marzipan nt.

mascara [mæs'ka:rə] n Wimperntusche f.

mascot ['mæskət] n Maskottchen nt.

masculine ['mæskjʊlɪn] a männlich.

mash [mæʃ] n Brei m; ~ed potatoes npl Kartoffelbrei m or -püree nt.

mask [ma:sk] n (lit, fig) Maske f // vt maskieren, verdecken.

mason ['meɪsn] n (stone~) Steinmetz m; (free~) Freimaurer m; ~ic [mə'sɒnɪk] a Freimaurer-; ~ry n Mauerwerk nt.

masquerade [mæskə'reɪd] n Maskerade f // vi: to ~ as sich ausgeben als.

mass [mæs] n Masse f; (greater part) Mehrheit f; (REL) Messe f // vi sich sammeln; the ~es npl die Masse(n) f(pl).

massacre ['mæsəkə*] n Blutbad nt // vt niedermetzeln, massakrieren.
massage ['mæsɑːʒ] n Massage f // vt massieren.
massive ['mæsɪv] a gewaltig, massiv.
mass media ['mæs'miːdɪə] npl Massenmedien pl.
mass production n Massenproduktion f.
mast [mɑːst] n Mast m.
master ['mɑːstə*] n Herr m; (NAUT) Kapitän m; (teacher) Lehrer m; (artist) Meister m // vt meistern; (language etc) beherrschen; **M~ of Arts/Science (M.A./M.Sc.)** n Magister m der philosophischen/naturwissenschaftlichen Fakultät; **~ key** n Hauptschlüssel m; **~ly** a meisterhaft; **~mind** n Kapazität f // vt geschickt lenken; **~piece** n Meisterwerk nt; **~ plan** n kluge(r) Plan m; **~y** n Können nt.
masturbate ['mæstəbeɪt] vi masturbieren, onanieren.
mat [mæt] n Matte f; (for table) Untersetzer m // a = **mat(t)**.
match [mætʃ] n Streichholz nt; (sth corresponding) Pendant nt; (SPORT) Wettkampf m; (ball games) Spiel nt // vt (be alike, suit) passen zu; (equal) gleichkommen (+dat) // vi zusammenpassen; **it's a good ~** es paßt gut (for zu); **~box** n Streichholzschachtel f; **~ing** a passend.
mate [meɪt] n (companion) Kamerad m; (spouse) Lebensgefährte m; (of animal) Weibchen nt/Männchen nt; (NAUT) Schiffsoffizier m // vi (animals) sich paaren // vt (animals) paaren.
material [mə'tɪərɪəl] n Material nt; (for book, cloth) Stoff m // a (important) wesentlich; (damage) Sach-; (comforts etc) materiell; **~s** pl Materialien pl; **~istic** a materialistisch; **~ize** vi sich verwirklichen, zustande kommen.
maternal [mə'tɜːnl] a mütterlich, Mutter-.
maternity [mə'tɜːnɪtɪ] a (dress) Umstands-; (benefit) Wochen-; **~ hospital** n Entbindungsheim nt.
math [mæθ] n (US) = **maths**.
mathematics [mæθə'mætɪks] n Mathematik f.
maths [mæθs], (US) **math** [mæθ] n Mathe f.
matinée ['mætɪneɪ] n Matinee f.
mating ['meɪtɪŋ] n Paarung f; **~ call** n Lockruf m.
matrices ['meɪtrɪsiːz] pl of **matrix**.
matriculation [mətrɪkju'leɪʃən] n Immatrikulation f.
matrimonial [mætrɪ'məʊnɪəl] a ehelich, Ehe-.
matrimony ['mætrɪmənɪ] n Ehestand m.
matrix ['meɪtrɪks], pl **matrices** n Matrize f; (GEOL etc) Matrix f.

matron ['meɪtrən] n (MED) Oberin f; (SCH) Hausmutter f; **~ly** a matronenhaft.
mat(t) [mæt] a (paint) matt.
matted ['mætɪd] a verfilzt.
matter ['mætə*] n (substance) Materie f; (affair) Angelegenheit f // vi darauf ankommen; **it doesn't ~** es macht nichts; **no ~ how/what** egal wie/was; **what is the ~?** was ist los?; **as a ~ of course** selbstverständlich; **as a ~ of fact** eigentlich; **~-of-fact** a sachlich, nüchtern.
mattress ['mætrəs] n Matratze f.
mature [mə'tjʊə*] a reif // vi reif werden.
maturity [mə'tjʊərɪtɪ] n Reife f.
maudlin ['mɔːdlɪn] a gefühlsduselig.
maul [mɔːl] vt übel zurichten.
mauve [məʊv] a mauve.
maximum ['mæksɪməm] a Höchst-, Maximal- // n, pl **maxima** ['mæksɪmə] Maximum nt.
May [meɪ] n Mai m.
may [meɪ] vi (be possible) können; (have permission) dürfen; **he ~ come** er kommt vielleicht.
maybe ['meɪbiː] ad vielleicht.
Mayday ['meɪdeɪ] n (message) SOS nt.
mayhem ['meɪhem] n Chaos nt; (US) Körperverletzung f.
mayonnaise [meɪə'neɪz] n Mayonnaise f.
mayor [mɛə*] n Bürgermeister m; **~ess** (wife) (die) Frau f Bürgermeister; (lady ~) Bürgermeisterin f.
maypole ['meɪpəʊl] n Maibaum m.
maze [meɪz] n (lit) Irrgarten m; (fig) Wirrwarr nt.
M.D. abbr of **Doctor of Medicine.**
me [miː] pron **1** (direct) mich; **it's ~** ich bin's
2 (indirect) mir; **give them to ~** gib sie mir
3 (after prep: +acc) mich; (: +dat) mir; **with/without ~** mit mir/ohne mich.
meadow ['medəʊ] n Wiese f.
meagre, (US) **meager** ['miːgə*] a dürftig, spärlich.
meal [miːl] n Essen nt, Mahlzeit f; (grain) Schrotmehl nt; **to have a ~** essen (gehen); **~time** n Essenszeit f.
mean [miːn] a (stingy) geizig; (spiteful) gemein; (average) durchschnittlich, Durchschnitts- // vt, pt, pp **meant** (signify) bedeuten; (intend) vorhaben, beabsichtigen // n (average) Durchschnitt m; **~s** pl Mittel pl; (wealth) Vermögen nt; **by ~s of** durch; **by all ~s** selbstverständlich; **by no ~s** keineswegs; **do you ~ me?** meinst du mich?; **do you ~ it?** meinst du das ernst?; **what do you ~?** was willst du damit sagen?; **to be meant for sb/sth** für jdn/etw bestimmt sein.

meander ['mɪ'ændə*] vi sich schlängeln.
meaning ['mi:nɪŋ] n Bedeutung f; (of life) Sinn m; ~**ful** a bedeutungsvoll; (life) sinnvoll; ~**less** a sinnlos.
meanness ['mi:nnəs] n (stinginess) Geiz m; (spitefulness) Gemeinheit f.
meant [ment] pt, pp of **mean**.
meantime ['mi:n'taɪm], **meanwhile** ['mi:n'waɪl] ad inzwischen.
measles ['mi:zlz] n Masern pl.
measly ['mi:zlz] a (col) poplig.
measure ['meʒə*] vti messen // n Maß nt; (step) Maßnahme f; ~**d** a (slow) gemessen; ~**ments** npl Maße pl.
meat [mi:t] n Fleisch nt; **cold** ~ n Aufschnitt m; ~ **ball** n Fleischkloß m; ~ **pie** n Fleischpastete f; ~**y** a (lit) fleischig; (fig) gehaltvoll.
Mecca ['mekə] n Mekka nt (also fig).
mechanic [mɪ'kænɪk] n Mechaniker m; ~**s** n Mechanik f // npl Technik f; ~**al** a mechanisch.
mechanism ['mekənɪzəm] n Mechanismus m.
mechanize ['mekənaɪz] vt mechanisieren.
medal ['medl] n Medaille f; (decoration) Orden m; ~**list**, (US) ~**ist** n Medaillengewinner(in f) m.
meddle ['medl] vi sich einmischen (in in +acc); to ~ **with sth** sich an etw (dat) zu schaffen machen.
media ['mi:dɪə] npl Medien pl.
mediaeval [medɪ'i:vəl] a = **medieval**.
median ['mi:dɪən] n (US: also: ~ strip) Mittelstreifen m.
mediate ['mi:dɪeɪt] vi vermitteln.
mediation [mi:dɪ'eɪʃən] n Vermittlung f.
mediator ['mi:dɪeɪtə*] n Vermittler m.
Medicaid ['medɪkeɪd] n (US) medizinisches Versorgungsprogramm für Sozialschwache.
medical ['medɪkəl] a medizinisch; Medizin-; ärztlich // n (ärztliche) Untersuchung f.
Medicare ['medɪkeə*] n (US) staatliche Krankenversicherung besonders für Ältere.
medicated ['medɪkeɪtɪd] a medizinisch.
medication [medɪ'keɪʃən] n (drugs etc) Medikamente pl.
medicinal [me'dɪsɪnl] a medizinisch, Heil-.
medicine ['medsɪn] n Medizin f; (drugs) Arznei f.
medieval [medɪ'i:vəl] a mittelalterlich.
mediocre [mi:dɪ'əukə*] a mittelmäßig.
mediocrity [mi:dɪ'ɒkrɪtɪ] n Mittelmäßigkeit f.
meditate ['medɪteɪt] vi nachdenken (on über +acc); meditieren.
meditation [medɪ'teɪʃən] n Nachsinnen nt; Meditation f.
Mediterranean [medɪtə'reɪnɪən] a

Mittelmeer-; (person) südländisch; **the** ~ **(Sea)** das Mittelmeer.
medium ['mi:dɪəm] a mittlere(r, s), Mittel-, mittel- // n Mitte f; (means) Mittel nt; (person) Medium nt; **happy** ~ goldener Mittelweg; ~ **wave** n Mittelwelle f.
medley ['medlɪ] n Gemisch nt.
meek [mi:k] a sanft(mütig); (pej) duckmäuserisch.
meet [mi:t], pt, pp met vt (encounter) treffen, begegnen (+dat); (by arrangement) sich treffen mit; (difficulties) stoßen auf (+acc); (become acquainted with) kennenlernen; (fetch) abholen; (join) zusammentreffen mit; (satisfy) entsprechen (+dat) // vi sich treffen; (become acquainted) sich kennenlernen; ~ **with** vt (problems) stoßen auf (+acc); (US: people) zusammentreffen mit; ~**ing** n Treffen nt; (business ~) Besprechung f; (of committee) Sitzung f; (assembly) Versammlung f.
megabyte ['megəbaɪt] n (COMPUT) Megabyte nt.
melancholy ['melənkəlɪ] a (person) melancholisch; (sight, event) traurig.
mellow ['meləu] a mild, weich; (fruit) reif; (fig) gesetzt // vi reif werden.
melodious [mɪ'ləudɪəs] a wohlklingend.
melody ['melədɪ] n Melodie f.
melon ['melən] n Melone f.
melt [melt] vi schmelzen; (anger) verfliegen // vt schmelzen; ~ **away** vi dahinschmelzen; ~ **down** vt einschmelzen; ~**down** n (in nuclear reactor) Kernschmelze f; ~**ing point** n Schmelzpunkt m; ~**ing pot** n (fig) Schmelztiegel m.
member ['membə*] n Mitglied nt; (of tribe, species) Angehörige(r) m; (ANAT) Glied nt; **M~ of Parliament (MP)** n (Brit) Parlamentsmitglied nt; **M~ of the European Parliament (MEP)** n (Brit) Mitglied nt des Europäischen Parlaments; ~**ship** n Mitgliedschaft f; to seek ~**ship** of einen Antrag auf Mitgliedschaft stellen; ~**ship card** n Mitgliedskarte f.
memento [mə'mentəu] n Andenken nt.
memo ['meməu] n Mitteilung f.
memoirs ['memwɑ:z] npl Memoiren pl.
memorable ['memərəbl] a denkwürdig.
memorandum [memə'rændəm], pl **-da** [-də] n Mitteilung f.
memorial [mɪ'mɔ:rɪəl] n Denkmal nt // a Gedenk-.
memorize ['meməraɪz] vt sich einprägen.
memory ['memərɪ] n Gedächtnis nt; (of computer) Speicher m; (sth recalled) Erinnerung f.
men [men] pl of **man**.
menace ['menɪs] n Drohung f; Gefahr f

// vt bedrohen.
menacing ['menɪsɪŋ] a drohend.
menagerie [mɪ'nædʒərɪ] n Tierschau f.
mend [mend] vt reparieren, flicken // vi
(ver)heilen // n ausgebesserte Stelle f; on
the ~ auf dem Wege der Besserung;
~ing n (articles) Flickarbeit f.
menial ['miːnɪəl] a niedrig.
meningitis [menɪn'dʒaɪtɪs] n
Hirnhautentzündung f, Meningitis f.
menopause ['menəupɔːz] n
Wechseljahre pl, Menopause f.
menstruation [menstru'eɪʃən] n Menstruation f.
mental ['mentl] a geistig, Geistes-;
(arithmetic) Kopf-; (hospital) Nerven-;
(cruelty) seelisch; (col: abnormal) verrückt; ~ity [men'tælɪtɪ] n Mentalität f.
menthol ['menθəl] n Menthol nt.
mention ['menʃən] n Erwähnung f // vt
erwähnen; don't ~ it! bitte (sehr), gern
geschehen.
mentor ['mentɔː*] n Mentor m.
menu ['menjuː] n Speisekarte f.
MEP n abbr of **Member of the European Parliament**.
mercenary ['mɜːsɪnərɪ] a (person)
geldgierig; (MIL) Söldner- // n Söldner
m.
merchandise ['mɜːtʃəndaɪz] n
(Handels)ware f.
merchant ['mɜːtʃənt] n Kaufmann m;
~ **navy**, (US) ~ **marine** n
Handelsmarine f.
merciful ['mɜːsɪful] a gnädig.
merciless ['mɜːsɪləs] a erbarmungslos.
mercury ['mɜːkjurɪ] n Quecksilber nt.
mercy ['mɜːsɪ] n Erbarmen nt; Gnade f;
at the ~ of ausgeliefert (+dat).
mere a, ~ly ad [mɪə*, 'mɪəlɪ] bloß.
merge [mɜːdʒ] vt verbinden; (COMM)
fusionieren // vi verschmelzen; (roads)
zusammenlaufen; (COMM) fusionieren;
~r n (COMM) Fusion f.
meringue [mə'ræŋ] n Baiser nt.
merit ['merɪt] n Verdienst nt;
(advantage) Vorzug m // vt verdienen.
mermaid ['mɜːmeɪd] n Wassernixe f.
merry ['merɪ] a fröhlich; ~-go-round n
Karussell nt.
mesh [meʃ] n Masche f // vi (gears)
ineinandergreifen.
mesmerize ['mezməraɪz] vt hypnotisieren; (fig) faszinieren.
mess [mes] n Unordnung f; (dirt)
Schmutz m; (trouble) Schwierigkeiten
pl; (MIL) Messe f; ~ **about** or **around**
vi (tinker with) herummurksen (with an
+dat); (play the fool) herumalbern; (do
nothing in particular) herumgammeln;
~ **up** vt verpfuschen; (make untidy) in
Unordnung bringen.
message ['mesɪdʒ] n Mitteilung f; to get
the ~ kapieren.
messenger ['mesɪndʒə*] n Bote m.

Messrs ['mesəz] abbr (on letters) die
Herren.
messy ['mesɪ] a schmutzig; (untidy)
unordentlich.
met [met] pt, pp of **meet**.
metabolism [me'tæbəlɪzəm] n
Stoffwechsel m.
metal ['metl] n Metall nt.
metaphor ['metəfɔː*] n Metapher f.
mete [miːt]: **to ~ out** vt austeilen.
meteorology [miːtɪə'rɒlədʒɪ] n
Meteorologie f.
meter ['miːtə*] n Zähler m; (US) =
metre.
method ['meθəd] n Methode f; ~ical
[mɪ'θɒdɪkəl] a methodisch; **M~ist**
['meθədɪst] a methodistisch // n Metho-
dist(in f) m; ~ology [meθə'dɒlədʒɪ] n
Methodik f.
meths [meθs], **methylated spirit**
['meθɪleɪtɪd'spɪrɪt] n (Brit) (Brenn)-
spiritus m.
meticulous [mɪ'tɪkjuləs] a (über)genau.
metre, (US) **meter** ['miːtə*] n Meter m
or nt.
metric ['metrɪk] a (also: ~al) metrisch.
metropolitan [metrə'pɒlɪtən] a der
Großstadt; **the M~ Police** n (Brit) die
Londoner Polizei.
mettle ['metl] n Mut m.
mew [mjuː] vi (cat) miauen.
mews [mjuːz] n: ~ **cottage** n (Brit)
ehemaliges Kutscherhäuschen.
Mexican ['meksɪkən] a mexikanisch // n
Mexikaner(in f) m.
Mexico ['meksɪkəu] n Mexiko nt; ~
City n Mexiko City f.
miaow [miː'au] vi miauen.
mice [maɪs] pl of **mouse**.
microchip ['maɪkrəutʃɪp] n Mikrochip
m.
micro(computer)
['maɪkrəu(kəm'pjuːtə*)] n Mikro-
computer m.
microcosm ['maɪkrəukɒzəm] n Mikro-
kosmos m.
microfilm ['maɪkrəufɪlm] n Mikrofilm m
// vt auf Mikrofilm aufnehmen.
microphone ['maɪkrəfəun] n Mikrophon
nt.
microprocessor ['maɪkrəu'prəusesə*] n
Mikroprozessor m.
microscope ['maɪkrəskəup] n Mikro-
skop nt.
microwave ['maɪkrəuweɪv] n (also: ~
oven) Mikrowelle(nherd nt) f.
mid [mɪd] a: in ~ **afternoon** am
Nachmittag; in ~ **air** in der Luft; in ~
May Mitte Mai.
midday ['mɪd'deɪ] n Mittag m.
middle ['mɪdl] n Mitte f; (waist) Taille f
// a mittlere(r, s), Mittel-; in the ~ of
mitten in (+dat); ~-**aged** a mittleren
Alters; **the M~ Ages** npl das Mit-
telalter; ~-**class** a Mittelstands-; **the**

M~ East n der Nahe Osten; **~man** n (COMM) Zwischenhändler m; **~ name** n zweiter Vorname m; **~ weight** n (BOXING) Mittelgewicht nt.

middling ['mɪdlɪŋ] a mittelmäßig.

midge [mɪdʒ] n Mücke f.

midget ['mɪdʒɪt] n Liliputaner(in f) m.

Midlands ['mɪdləndz] npl die Midlands pl.

midnight ['mɪdnaɪt] n Mitternacht f.

midriff ['mɪdrɪf] n Taille f.

midst [mɪdst] n: in the ~ of (persons) mitten unter (+dat); (things) mitten in (+dat).

midsummer ['mɪdsʌmə*] n Hochsommer m.

midway ['mɪdweɪ] ad auf halbem Wege // a Mittel-.

midweek ['mɪdwi:k] ad in der Mitte der Woche.

midwife ['mɪdwaɪf], pl **-wives** [-waɪvz] n Hebamme f; **~ry** ['mɪdwɪfərɪ] n Geburtshilfe f.

midwinter ['mɪd'wɪntə*] n tiefste(r) Winter m.

might [maɪt] v pt of **may** // n Macht f, Kraft f; **I ~ come** ich komme vielleicht; **I ~ as well go** ich könnte genauso gut gehen; **you ~ like to try** du könntest vielleicht versuchen; **~y** a, ad mächtig.

migraine ['mi:greɪn] n Migräne f.

migrant ['maɪgrənt] a Wander-; (bird) Zug-.

migrate [maɪ'greɪt] vi (ab)wandern; (birds) (fort)ziehen.

migration [maɪ'greɪʃən] n Wanderung f, Zug m.

mike [maɪk] n = **microphone.**

Milan [mɪ'læn] n Mailand nt.

mild [maɪld] a mild; (medicine, interest) leicht; (person) sanft.

mildew ['mɪldju:] n (on plants) Mehltau m; (on food) Schimmel m.

mildly ['maɪldlɪ] ad leicht; **to put it ~** gelinde gesagt.

mile [maɪl] n Meile f; **~age** n Meilenzahl f; **~stone** n (lit, fig) Meilenstein m.

military ['mɪlɪtərɪ] a militärisch, Militär-, Wehr-.

militate ['mɪlɪteɪt] vi entgegenwirken (against dat).

militia [mɪ'lɪʃə] n Miliz f.

milk [mɪlk] n Milch f // vt (lit, fig) melken; **~ chocolate** n Milchschokolade f; **~man** n Milchmann m; **~ shake** n Milchmixgetränk nt; **~y** a milchig; **M~y Way** n Milchstraße f.

mill [mɪl] n Mühle f; (factory) Fabrik f // vt mahlen // vi (move around) umherlaufen.

millennium [mɪ'lenɪəm], pl **~s** or **-ia** [-nɪə] n Jahrtausend nt.

miller ['mɪlə*] n Müller m.

millet ['mɪlɪt] n Hirse f.

milligram(me) ['mɪlɪgræm] n Milligramm nt.

millimetre, (US) **millimeter** ['mɪlɪmi:tə*] n Millimeter m.

milliner ['mɪlɪnə*] n Hutmacher(in f) m; **~y** n (hats) Hüte pl.

million ['mɪljən] n Million f; **a ~ times** tausendmal; **~aire** [mɪljə'nɛə*] n Millionär(in f) m.

millstone ['mɪlstəun] n Mühlstein m.

milometer [maɪ'lɒmɪtə*] n Kilometerzähler m.

mime [maɪm] n Pantomime f // vti mimen.

mimic ['mɪmɪk] n Mimiker m // vti nachahmen; **~ry** ['mɪmɪkrɪ] n Nachahmung f; (BIOL) Mimikry f.

min. abbr (= minute(s); minimum) min.

minaret [mɪnə'ret] n Minarett n.

mince [mɪns] vt (zer)hacken // vi (walk) trippeln // n (meat) Hackfleisch nt; **~meat** n süße Pastetenfüllung f; **~ pie** n gefüllte (süße) Pastete f; **mincer** n Fleischwolf m.

mind [maɪnd] n Verstand m, Geist m; (opinion) Meinung f // vt aufpassen auf (+acc); (object to) etwas haben gegen; **on my ~** auf dem Herzen; **to my ~** meiner Meinung nach; **to be out of one's ~** wahnsinnig sein; **to bear** or **keep in ~** bedenken; **to change one's ~** es sich (dat) anders überlegen; **to make up one's ~** sich entschließen; **I don't ~** das macht mir nichts aus; **~ you, ...** allerdings ...; **never ~!** macht nichts!; **'~ the step'** 'Vorsicht Stufe'; **~ your own business** kümmern Sie sich um Ihre eigenen Angelegenheiten; **minder** n Aufpasser(in f) m; **~ful** a achtsam (of auf +acc); **~less** a sinnlos.

mine [maɪn] n (coal~) Bergwerk nt; (MIL) Mine f // vt abbauen; (MIL) verminen.

mine [maɪn] pron meine(r, s); **that book is ~** das Buch gehört mir; **a friend of ~** ein Freund von mir.

minefield ['maɪnfi:ld] n Minenfeld nt.

miner ['maɪnə*] n Bergarbeiter m.

mineral ['mɪnərəl] a mineralisch, Mineral- // n Mineral nt; **~s** pl (Brit: soft drinks) alkoholfreie Getränke pl; **~ water** n Mineralwasser nt.

minesweeper ['maɪnswi:pə*] n Minensuchboot nt.

mingle ['mɪŋgl] vi sich mischen (with unter +acc).

miniature ['mɪnɪtʃə*] a Miniatur- // n Miniatur f.

minibus ['mɪnɪbʌs] n Kleinbus m.

minim ['mɪnɪm] n halbe Note f.

minimal ['mɪnɪml] a minimal.

minimize ['mɪnɪmaɪz] vt auf das Mindestmaß beschränken.

minimum ['mɪnɪməm] n, pl **minima**

['mɪnɪmə] Minimum *nt* // *a* Mindest-.

mining ['maɪnɪŋ] *n* Bergbau *m* // *a* Bergbau-, Berg-.

miniskirt ['mɪnɪskɜːt] *n* Minirock *m*.

minister ['mɪnɪstə*] *n* (*Brit POL*) Minister *m*; (*ECCL*) Pfarrer *m* // *vi*: **to ~ to sb** sich um jdn kümmern; **~ial** [mɪnɪs'tɪərɪəl] *a* ministeriell, Minister-.

ministry ['mɪnɪstrɪ] *n* (*Brit POL*) Ministerium *nt*; (*ECCL*: *office*) geistliche(s) Amt *nt*.

mink [mɪŋk] *n* Nerz *m*; **~ coat** *n* Nerzmantel *m*.

minnow ['mɪnəʊ] *n* Elritze *f*.

minor ['maɪnə*] *a* kleiner; (*operation*) leicht; (*problem, poet*) unbedeutend; (*MUS*) Moll // *n* (*Brit: under 18*) Minderjährige(r) *mf*.

minority [maɪ'nɒrɪtɪ] *n* Minderheit *f*.

mint [mɪnt] *n* Minze *f*; (*sweet*) Pfefferminzbonbon *nt* // *vt* (*coins*) prägen; **the** (*Royal*) **M~**, (*US*) **the** (*US*) **M~** die Münzanstalt; **in ~ condition** in tadellosem Zustand.

minus ['maɪnəs] *n* Minuszeichen *nt*; (*amount*) Minusbetrag *m* // *prep* minus, weniger.

minuscule ['mɪnəskjuːl] *a* winzig.

minute [maɪ'njuːt] *a* winzig; (*detailed*) minuziös // *n* ['mɪnɪt] Minute *f*; (*moment*) Augenblick *m*; **~s** *pl* Protokoll *nt*.

miracle ['mɪrəkl] *n* Wunder *nt*.

miraculous [mɪ'rækjʊləs] *a* wunderbar.

mirage ['mɪrɑːʒ] *n* Fata Morgana *f*.

mire ['maɪə*] *n* Morast *m*.

mirror ['mɪrə*] *n* Spiegel *m* // *vt* (*wider*)spiegeln.

mirth [mɜːθ] *n* Heiterkeit *f*.

misadventure [mɪsəd'ventʃə*] *n* Mißgeschick *nt*, Unfall *m*.

misanthropist [mɪ'zænθrəpɪst] *n* Menschenfeind *m*.

misapprehension ['mɪsæprɪ'henʃən] *n* Mißverständnis *nt*.

misbehave ['mɪsbɪ'heɪv] *vi* sich schlecht benehmen.

miscalculate ['mɪs'kælkjʊleɪt] *vt* falsch berechnen.

miscarriage ['mɪskærɪdʒ] *n* (*MED*) Fehlgeburt *f*; **~ of justice** *n* Fehlurteil *nt*.

miscellaneous [mɪsɪ'leɪnɪəs] *a* verschieden.

mischance [mɪs'tʃɑːns] *n* Mißgeschick *nt*.

mischief ['mɪstʃɪf] *n* Unfug *m*.

mischievous ['mɪstʃɪvəs] *a* (*person*) durchtrieben; (*glance*) verschmitzt; (*rumour*) bösartig.

misconception ['mɪskən'sepʃən] *n* fälschliche Annahme *f*.

misconduct [mɪs'kɒndʌkt] *n* Vergehen *nt*; **professional ~** Berufsvergehen *nt*.

misconstrue ['mɪskən'struː] *vt* mißver-

stehen.

misdeed [mɪs'diːd] *n* Untat *f*.

misdemeanour, (*US*) **misdemeanor** [mɪsdɪ'miːnə*] *n* Vergehen *nt*.

miser ['maɪzə*] *n* Geizhals *m*.

miserable ['mɪzərəbl] *a* (*unhappy*) unglücklich; (*headache, weather*) fürchterlich; (*poor*) elend; (*contemptible*) erbärmlich.

miserly ['maɪzəlɪ] *a* geizig.

misery ['mɪzərɪ] *n* Elend *nt*, Qual *f*.

misfire ['mɪs'faɪə*] *vi* (*gun*) versagen; (*engine*) fehlzünden; (*plan*) fehlgehen.

misfit ['mɪsfɪt] *n* Außenseiter *m*.

misfortune [mɪs'fɔːtʃən] *n* Unglück *nt*.

misgiving(s) [mɪs'ɡɪvɪŋ(z)] *n(pl)* Bedenken *pl*.

misguided ['mɪs'ɡaɪdɪd] *a* fehlgeleitet; (*opinions*) irrig.

mishandle ['mɪs'hændl] *vt* falsch handhaben.

mishap ['mɪshæp] *n* Mißgeschick *nt*.

misinform ['mɪsɪn'fɔːm] *vt* falsch unterrichten.

misinterpret ['mɪsɪn'tɜːprɪt] *vt* falsch auffassen.

misjudge ['mɪs'dʒʌdʒ] *vt* falsch beurteilen.

mislay [mɪs'leɪ] (*irreg: like* lay) *vt* verlegen.

mislead [mɪs'liːd] (*irreg: like* lead) *vt* (*deceive*) irreführen; **~ing** *a* irreführend.

mismanage ['mɪs'mænɪdʒ] *vt* schlecht verwalten.

misnomer ['mɪs'nəʊmə*] *n* falsche Bezeichnung *f*.

misogynist [mɪ'sɒdʒɪnɪst] *n* Weiberfeind *m*.

misplace ['mɪs'pleɪs] *vt* verlegen.

misprint ['mɪsprɪnt] *n* Druckfehler *m*.

Miss [mɪs] *n* Fräulein *nt*.

miss [mɪs] *vt* (*fail to hit, catch*) verfehlen; (*not notice*) verpassen; (*be too late*) versäumen, verpassen; (*omit*) auslassen; (*regret the absence of*) vermissen // *vi* fehlen // *n* (*shot*) Fehlschuß *m*; (*failure*) Fehlschlag *m*; **that was a near ~** das war sehr knapp; **I ~ you** du fehlst mir; **~ out** *vt* auslassen.

missal ['mɪsəl] *n* Meßbuch *nt*.

misshapen ['mɪs'ʃeɪpən] *a* mißgestaltet.

missile ['mɪsaɪl] *n* Rakete *f*.

missing ['mɪsɪŋ] *a* (*person*) vermißt; (*thing*) fehlend; **to be ~** fehlen.

mission ['mɪʃən] *n* (*work*) Auftrag *m*; (*people*) Delegation *f*; (*REL*) Mission *f*; **~ary** *n* Missionar(in *f*) *m*.

misspell ['mɪs'spel] (*irreg: like* spell) *vt* falsch schreiben.

misspent ['mɪs'spent] *a* (*youth*) vergeudet.

mist [mɪst] *n* Dunst *m*, Nebel *m* // *vi* (*also:* **~ over**, **~ up**) sich trüben; (: *Brit: windows*) sich beschlagen.

mistake [mɪs'teɪk] n Fehler m // vt (irreg: like take) (misunderstand) mißverstehen; (mix up) verwechseln (for mit); to make a ~ einen Fehler machen; by ~ aus Versehen; to ~ A for B A mit B verwechseln; ~n a (idea) falsch; to be ~n sich irren.

mister ['mɪstə*] n (col) Herr m; see **Mr.**

mistletoe ['mɪsltəʊ] n Mistel f.

mistook [mɪs'tʊk] pt of **mistake.**

mistress ['mɪstrɪs] n (teacher) Lehrerin f; (in house) Herrin f; (lover) Geliebte f; see **Mrs.**

mistrust ['mɪs'trʌst] vt mißtrauen (+dat).

misty ['mɪstɪ] a neblig.

misunderstand ['mɪsʌndə'stænd] (irreg: like understand) vti mißverstehen, falsch verstehen; ~ing n Mißverständnis nt; (disagreement) Meinungsverschiedenheit f.

misuse [mɪs'juːs] n falsche(r) Gebrauch m // ['mɪs'juːz] vt falsch gebrauchen.

mitigate ['mɪtɪgeɪt] vt mildern.

mitt(en) ['mɪt(n)] n Fausthandschuh m.

mix [mɪks] vt (blend) (ver)mischen // vi (liquids) sich (ver)mischen lassen; (people: get on) sich vertragen; (: associate) Kontakt haben // n (mixture) Mischung f; ~ up vt (mix) zusammenmischen; (confuse) verwechseln; ~ed a gemischt; ~ed-up a durcheinander; ~er n (for food) Mixer m; ~ture n Mischung f; ~-up n Durcheinander nt

mm abbr (= millimetre) mm.

moan [məʊn] n Stöhnen nt; (complaint) Klage f // vi stöhnen; (complain) maulen.

moat [məʊt] n (Burg)graben m.

mob [mɒb] n Mob m; (the masses) Pöbel m // vt (star) herfallen über (+acc).

mobile ['məʊbaɪl] a beweglich; (library etc) fahrbar // n (decoration) Mobile nt; ~ home n Wohnwagen m.

mobility [məʊ'bɪlɪtɪ] n Beweglichkeit f.

mobilize ['məʊbɪlaɪz] vt mobilisieren.

moccasin ['mɒkəsɪn] n Mokassin m.

mock [mɒk] vt verspotten; (defy) trotzen (+dat) // a Schein-; ~ery n Spott m; (person) Gespött m.

mod [mɒd] a see **convenience.**

mode [məʊd] n (Art f und) Weise f.

model ['mɒdl] n Modell nt; (example) Vorbild nt; (in fashion) Mannequin nt // a (railway) Modell-; (perfect) Muster-; vorbildlich // vt (make) bilden; (clothes) vorführen // vi als Mannequin arbeiten.

modem ['məʊdem] n Modem nt.

moderate ['mɒdərət] a gemäßigt // n (POL) Gemäßigte(r) mf // ['mɒdəreɪt] vi sich mäßigen // vt mäßigen.

moderation [mɒdə'reɪʃən] n Mäßigung f; in ~ mit Maßen.

modern ['mɒdən] a modern; (history,

languages) neuere(r, s); (Greek etc) Neu-; ~ize vt modernisieren.

modest ['mɒdɪst] a bescheiden; ~y n Bescheidenheit f.

modicum ['mɒdɪkəm] n bißchen nt.

modification [mɒdɪfɪ'keɪʃən] n (Ab)änderung f.

modify ['mɒdɪfaɪ] vt abändern.

module ['mɒdjʊl] n (component) (Bau)element nt; (SPACE) (Raum)kapsel f.

mogul ['məʊgəl] n (fig) Mogul m.

mohair ['məʊhɛə*] n Mohair m.

moist [mɔɪst] a feucht; ~en ['mɔɪsn] vt befeuchten; ~ure n Feuchtigkeit f; ~urizer n Feuchtigkeitscreme f.

molar ['məʊlə*] n Backenzahn m.

molasses [mə'læsɪz] npl Melasse f.

mold [məʊld] n, vt (US) = **mould.**

mole [məʊl] n (spot) Leberfleck m; (animal) Maulwurf m; (pier) Mole f.

molest [məʊ'lest] vt belästigen.

mollycoddle ['mɒlɪkɒdl] vt verhätscheln.

molt [məʊlt] vi (US) = **moult.**

molten ['məʊltən] a geschmolzen.

mom [mɒm] n (US) = **mum.**

moment ['məʊmənt] n Moment m, Augenblick m; (importance) Tragweite f; at the ~ im Augenblick; ~ary a kurz; ~ous [məʊ'mentəs] a folgenschwer.

momentum [məʊ'mentəm] n Schwung m; to gather ~ in Fahrt kommen.

mommy ['mɒmɪ] n (US) = **mummy.**

Monaco ['mɒnəkəʊ] n Monaco nt.

monarch ['mɒnək] n Herrscher(in f) m; ~y n Monarchie f.

monastery ['mɒnəstrɪ] n Kloster nt.

monastic [mə'næstɪk] a klösterlich, Kloster-.

Monday ['mʌndeɪ] n Montag m.

monetary ['mʌnɪtərɪ] a Geld-; (of currency) Währungs-.

money ['mʌnɪ] n Geld nt; to make ~ Geld verdienen; ~lender n Geldverleiher m; ~ order n Postanweisung f; ~-spinner n (col) Verkaufsschlager m (col).

mongol ['mɒngəl] n (MED) mongoloide(s) Kind nt // a mongolisch; (MED) mongoloid.

mongrel ['mʌngrəl] n Promenadenmischung f.

monitor ['mɒnɪtə*] n (SCH) Klassenordner m; (television ~) Monitor m // vt (broadcasts) abhören; (control) überwachen.

monk [mʌŋk] n Mönch m.

monkey ['mʌŋkɪ] n Affe m; ~ nut n (Brit) Erdnuß f; ~ wrench n (TECH) Engländer m, Franzose m.

mono- ['mɒnəʊ] pref Mono-.

monochrome ['mɒnəkrəʊm] a schwarz-weiß.

monopolize [mə'nɒpəlaɪz] vt beherrschen.

monopoly [mə'nɒpəlı] n Monopol nt.

monosyllable ['mɒnəsıləbl] n ein-silbige(s) Wort nt.

monotone ['mɒnətəʊn] n gleich-bleibende(r) Ton(fall) m; **to speak in a ~** monoton sprechen.

monotonous [mə'nɒtənəs] a eintönig.

monotony [mə'nɒtənı] n Eintönigkeit f, Monotonie f.

monster ['mɒnstə*] n Ungeheuer nt; (person) Scheusal nt.

monstrosity [mɒns'trɒsıtı] n Unge-heuerlichkeit f; (thing) Monstrosität f.

monstrous ['mɒnstrəs] a (shocking) gräßlich, ungeheuerlich; (huge) riesig.

month [mʌnθ] n Monat m; **~ly** a monatlich, Monats- // ad einmal im Monat // n (magazine) Monatsschrift f.

monument ['mɒnjʊmənt] n Denkmal nt; **~al** [mɒnjʊ'mentl] a (huge) gewaltig; (ignorance) ungeheuer.

moo [mu:] vi muhen.

mood [mu:d] n Stimmung f, Laune f; **to be in a good/bad ~** gute/schlechte Laune haben; **~y** a launisch.

moon [mu:n] n Mond m; **~light** n Mondlicht nt; **~lighting** n Schwarzarbeit f; **~lit** a mondhell.

moor [mʊə*] n Heide f, Hochmoor nt // vt (ship) festmachen, verankern // vi an-legen; **~ings** npl Liegeplatz m.

moorland ['mʊələnd] n Heidemoor nt.

moose [mu:s] n Elch m.

mop [mɒp] n Mop m // vt (auf)wischen; **~ up** vt aufwischen.

mope [məʊp] vi Trübsal blasen.

moped ['məʊped] n Moped nt.

moral ['mɒrəl] a moralisch; (values) sittlich; (virtuous) tugendhaft // n Moral f; **~s** pl Moral f; **~e** [mɒ'rɑ:l] n Moral f; **~ity** [mə'rælıtı] n Sittlichkeit f.

morass [mə'ræs] n Sumpf m.

morbid ['mɔ:bıd] a krankhaft; (jokes) makaber.

more [mɔ:*] ◆ a (greater in number etc) mehr; (additional) noch mehr; **do you want (some) ~ tea?** möchten Sie noch etwas Tee?; **I have no** or **I don't have any ~** money ich habe kein Geld mehr ◆ pron (greater amount) mehr; (further or additional amount) noch mehr; **is there any ~?** gibt es noch mehr?; (left over) ist noch etwas da?; **there's no ~** es ist nichts mehr da ◆ ad mehr; **~ dangerous/easily** etc (than) gefährlicher/einfacher etc (als); **~ and ~** immer mehr; **~ and more ex-cited** immer aufgeregter; **~ or less** mehr oder weniger; **~ than ever** mehr denn je; **~ beautiful than ever** schöner denn je.

moreover [mɔ:'rəʊvə*] ad überdies.

morgue [mɔ:g] n Leichenschauhaus nt.

moribund ['mɒrıbʌnd] a aussterbend.

Mormon ['mɔ:mən] n Mormone m, Mormonin f.

morning ['mɔ:nıŋ] n Morgen; m in the **~ am** Morgen; **7 o'clock in the ~** 7 Uhr morgens.

Morocco [mə'rɒkəʊ] n Marokko nt.

moron ['mɔ:rɒn] n Schwachsinnige(r) mf.

morose [mə'rəʊs] a mürrisch.

morphine ['mɔ:fi:n] n Morphium nt.

Morse [mɔ:s] n (also: ~ code) Morseal-phabet nt.

morsel ['mɔ:sl] n Bissen m.

mortal ['mɔ:tl] a sterblich; (deadly) töd-lich; (very great) Todes- // n (human being) Sterbliche(r) mf; **~ity** [mɔ:'tælıtı] n Sterblichkeit f; (death rate) Sterblichkeitsziffer f.

mortar ['mɔ:tə*] n (for building) Mörtel m; (bowl) Mörser m; (MIL) Granatwerfer m.

mortgage ['mɔ:gıdʒ] n Hypothek f // vt eine Hypothek aufnehmen (+acc); **~ company** n (US) ≈ Bausparkasse f.

mortify ['mɔ:tıfaı] vt beschämen.

mortuary ['mɔ:tjʊərı] n Leichenhalle f.

Moscow ['mɒskəʊ] n Moskau nt.

Moslem ['mɒzləm] a, n = **Muslim**.

mosque [mɒsk] n Moschee f.

mosquito [mɒs'ki:təʊ], pl **~es** n Moskito m.

moss [mɒs] n Moos nt.

most [məʊst] a meiste(r, s) // ad am meisten; (very) höchst // n das meiste, der größte Teil; (people) die meisten; **~ men** die meisten Männer; **at the (very) ~** allerhöchstens; **to make the ~ of** das Beste machen aus; **a ~ interesting book** ein höchst interessantes Buch; **~ly** ad größtenteils.

MOT n abbr (Brit) (= Ministry of Transport): **the ~ (test)** ≈ der TÜV.

motel [məʊ'tel] n Motel nt.

moth [mɒθ] n Nachtfalter m; (wool-eating) Motte f; **~ball** n Mottenkugel f.

mother ['mʌðə*] n Mutter f // vt bemuttern; **~hood** n Mutterschaft f; **~-in-law** n Schwiegermutter f; **~ly** a mütterlich; **~-to-be** n werdende Mutter f; **~ tongue** n Muttersprache f.

motif [məʊ'ti:f] n Motiv nt.

motion ['məʊʃən] n Bewegung f; (in meeting) Antrag m // vti winken (+dat), zu verstehen geben (+dat); **~less** a regungslos; **~ picture** n Film m.

motivated ['məʊtıveıtıd] a motiviert.

motivation [məʊtı'veıʃən] n Motivie-rung f.

motive ['məʊtıv] n Motiv nt, Beweg-grund m // a treibend.

motley ['mɒtlı] a bunt.

motor ['məʊtə*] n Motor m; (Brit col: vehicle) Auto nt // a Motor-; **~bike** n Motorrad nt; **~boat** n Motorboot nt; **~car** n (Brit) Auto nt; **~cycle** n

Motorrad *nt*; **~cycle racing** *n* Motorradrennen *nt*; **~cyclist** *n* Motorradfahrer(in *f*) *m*; **~ing** *n* (*Brit*) Autofahren *nt* // *a* Auto-; **~ist** ['məʊtərɪst] *n* Autofahrer(in *f*) *m*; **~ racing** *n* (*Brit*) Autorennen *nt*; **~ scooter** *n* Motorroller *m*; **~ vehicle** *n* Kraftfahrzeug *nt*; **~way** *n* (*Brit*) Autobahn *f*.

mottled ['mɒtld] *a* gesprenkelt.

motto ['mɒtəʊ], *pl* **~es** *n* Motto *nt*.

mould, (*US*) **mold** [məʊld] *n* Form *f*; (*mildew*) Schimmel *m* // *vt* (*lit, fig*) formen; **~er** *vi* (*decay*) vermodern; **~y** *a* schimmelig.

moult, (*US*) **molt** [məʊlt] *vi* sich mausern.

mound [maʊnd] *n* (Erd)hügel *m*.

mount [maʊnt] *n* (*liter: hill*) Berg *m*; (*horse*) Pferd *nt*; (*for jewel etc*) Fassung *f* // *vt* (*horse*) steigen auf (+*acc*); (*put in setting*) fassen; (*exhibition*) veranstalten; (*attack*) unternehmen // *vi* (*also:* **~ up**) sich häufen; (*on horse*) aufsitzen.

mountain ['maʊntɪn] *n* Berg *m* // *cpd* Berg-; **~eer** [maʊntɪ'nɪə*] *n* Bergsteiger(in *f*) *m*; **~eering** *n* Bergsteigen *nt*; **~ous** *a* bergig; **~ rescue team** *n* Bergwacht *f*; **~side** *n* Berg(ab)hang *m*.

mourn [mɔːn] *vt* betrauen, beklagen // *vi* trauern (*for* um); **~er** *n* Trauernde(r) *mf*; **~ful** *a* traurig; **~ing** *n* (*grief*) Trauer *f* // *cpd* (*dress*) Trauer-; **in ~ing** (*period etc*) in Trauer; (*dress*) in Trauerkleidung *f*.

mouse [maʊs], *pl* **mice** *n* Maus *f*; **~trap** *n* Mausefalle *f*.

mousse [muːs] *n* (*CULIN*) Creme *f*; (*cosmetic*) Schaumfestiger *m*.

moustache [məs'taːʃ] *n* Schnurrbart *m*.

mousy ['maʊsɪ] *a* (*colour*) mausgrau; (*person*) schüchtern.

mouth [maʊθ], *pl* **~s** [maʊðz] *n* Mund *m*; (*general*) Öffnung *f*; (*of river*) Mündung *f*; **~ful** *n* Mundvoll *m*; **~ organ** *n* Mundharmonika *f*; **~piece** *n* (*lit*) Mundstück *nt*; (*fig*) Sprachrohr *nt*; **~wash** *n* Mundwasser *nt*; **~watering** *a* lecker, appetitlich.

movable ['muːvəbl] *a* beweglich.

move [muːv] *n* (*movement*) Bewegung *f*; (*in game*) Zug *m*; (*step*) Schritt *m*; (*of house*) Umzug *m* // *vt* bewegen; (*people*) transportieren; (*in job*) versetzen; (*emotionally*) bewegen // *vi* sich bewegen; (*vehicle, ship*) fahren; (*go to another house*) umziehen; **~ sb to do sth** jdn veranlassen, etw zu tun; **to get a ~ on** sich beeilen; **~ about** *or* **around** *vi* sich hin- und herbewegen; (*travel*) unterwegs sein; **~ along** *vi* weitergehen; (*cars*) weiterfahren; **~ away** *vi* weggehen; **~ back** *vi* zurückgehen; (*to the rear*) zurückwei-

chen; **~ forward** *vi* vorwärtsgehen, sich vorwärtsbewegen // *vt* vorschieben; (*time*) vorverlegen; **~ in** *vi* (*to house*) einziehen; (*troops*) einrücken; **~ on** *vi* weitergehen // *vt* weitergehen lassen; **~ out** *vi* (*of house*) ausziehen; (*troops*) abziehen; **~ over** *vi* zur Seite rücken; **~ up** *vi* aufsteigen; (*in job*) befördert werden // *vt* nach oben bewegen; (*in job*) befördern; **~ment** *n* Bewegung *f*.

movie ['muːvɪ] *n* Film *m*; **to go to the ~s** ins Kino gehen; **~ camera** *n* Filmkamera *f*.

moving ['muːvɪŋ] *a* beweglich; (*touching*) ergreifend.

mow [məʊ], *pt* **mowed**, *pp* **mowed** *or* **mown** *vt* mähen; **~ down** *vt* (*fig*) niedermähen; **~er** *n* (*machine*) Mähmaschine *f*; (*lawn~*) Rasenmäher *m*.

MP *n abbr of* **Member of Parliament**.

m.p.h. *abbr of* **miles per hour**.

Mr, Mr. [mɪstə*] Herr *m*.

Mrs, Mrs. ['mɪsɪz] Frau *f*.

Ms, Ms. [mɪz] *n* (= **Miss** *or* **Mrs**) Frau *f*.

M.Sc. *abbr of* **Master of Science**.

much [mʌtʃ] *a* viel // *ad* sehr; viel // *n* viel, eine Menge *f*; **how ~ is it?** wieviel kostet das?; **too ~** zuviel; **it's not ~** es ist nicht viel; **as ~ as** sosehr, soviel; **however ~ he tries** sosehr er es auch versucht.

muck [mʌk] *n* (*lit*) Mist *m*; (*fig*) Schmutz *m*; **~ about** *or* **around** *vi* (*col*) herumalbern (*with* an +*dat*); **~ up** *vt* (*col: ruin*) vermasseln; (*dirty*) dreckig machen; **~y** *a* (*dirty*) dreckig.

mucus ['mjuːkəs] *n* Schleim *m*.

mud [mʌd] *n* Schlamm *m*.

muddle ['mʌdl] *n* Durcheinander *nt* // *vt* (*also:* **~ up**) durcheinanderbringen; **~ through** *vi* sich durchwursteln.

muddy ['mʌdɪ] *a* schlammig.

mudguard ['mʌdgaːd] *n* Schutzblech *nt*.

mud-slinging ['mʌdslɪŋɪŋ] *n* (*col*) Verleumdung *f*.

muff [mʌf] *n* Muff *m* // *vt* (*chance*) verpassen; (*lines*) verpatzen (*col*).

muffin ['mʌfɪn] *n* süße(s) Teilchen *nt*.

muffle ['mʌfl] *vt* (*sound*) dämpfen; (*wrap up*) einhüllen; **~d** *a* gedämpft.

muffler ['mʌflə*] *n* (*US AUT*) Schalldämpfer *m*.

mug [mʌg] *n* (*cup*) Becher *m*; (*col: face*) Visage *f*; (*col: fool*) Trottel *m* // *vt* überfallen und ausrauben; **~ging** *n* Überfall *m*.

muggy ['mʌgɪ] *a* (*weather*) schwül.

mule [mjuːl] *n* Maulesel *m*.

mull [mʌl]: **~ over** *vt* nachdenken über (+*acc*).

mulled [mʌld] *a* (*wine*) Glüh-.

multi- ['mʌltɪ] *pref* Multi-, multi-.

multicoloured, (*US*) **multicolored**

['mʌltɪ'kʌləd] a mehrfarbig.
multifarious [mʌltɪ'feərɪəs] a
mannigfaltig.
multi-level ['mʌltɪlevl] a (US) = **multi-storey**.
multiple ['mʌltɪpl] n Vielfache(s) nt // a
mehrfach; (many) mehrere; ~ **sclerosis** n multiple Sklerose f.
multiply ['mʌltɪplaɪ] vt multiplizieren
(by mit) // vi (BIOL) sich vermehren.
multistorey ['mʌltɪ'stɔːrɪ] a (Brit:
building, car park) mehrstöckig.
multitude ['mʌltɪtjuːd] n Menge f.
mum [mʌm] a: to keep ~ den Mund
halten (about über +acc) // n (Brit col)
Mutti f.
mumble ['mʌmbl] vti murmeln // n
Gemurmel nt.
mummy ['mʌmɪ] n (dead body) Mumie
f; (Brit col) Mami f.
mumps [mʌmps] n Mumps m.
munch [mʌntʃ] vti mampfen.
mundane ['mʌn'deɪn] a banal.
municipal [mjuː'nɪsɪpəl] a städtisch,
Stadt-; ~**ity** [mjuːnɪsɪ'pælɪtɪ] n Stadt f
mit Selbstverwaltung.
mural ['mjuərəl] n Wandgemälde nt.
murder ['mɜːdə*] n Mord m // vt
ermorden; ~**er** n Mörder m; ~**ous** a
Mord-; (fig) mörderisch.
murky ['mɜːkɪ] a finster.
murmur ['mɜːmə*] n Murmeln nt; (of
water, wind) Rauschen nt // vti
murmeln.
muscle ['mʌsl] n Muskel m; ~ **in** vi
mitmischen.
muscular ['mʌskjulə*] a Muskel-;
(strong) muskulös.
muse [mjuːz] vi (nach)sinnen.
museum [mjuː'zɪəm] n Museum nt.
mushroom ['mʌʃruːm] n Champignon
m; Pilz m // vi (fig) emporschießen.
music ['mjuːzɪk] n Musik f; (printed)
Noten pl; ~**al** a (sound) melodisch;
(person) musikalisch // n (show) Musical
nt; ~**al instrument** n Musikinstrument
nt; ~ **hall** n (Brit) Varieté nt; ~**ian**
[mjuː'zɪʃən] n Musiker(in f) m.
musk [mʌsk] n Moschus m.
Muslim ['mʌzlɪm] a moslemisch // n
Moslem m.
muslin ['mʌzlɪn] n Musselin m.
mussel ['mʌsl] n Miesmuschel f.
must [mʌst] v aux müssen; (in negation)
dürfen // n Muß nt; the film is a ~ den
Film muß man einfach gesehen haben.
mustard ['mʌstəd] n Senf m.
muster ['mʌstə*] vt (MIL) antreten
lassen; (courage) zusammennehmen.
mustn't ['mʌsnt] = **must not**.
musty ['mʌstɪ] a muffig.
mute [mjuːt] a stumm // n (person)
Stumme(r) mf; (MUS) Dämpfer m.
muted ['mjuːtɪd] a gedämpft.
mutilate ['mjuːtɪleɪt] vt verstümmeln.

mutilation [mjuːtɪ'leɪʃən] n Verstümmelung f.
mutiny ['mjuːtɪnɪ] n Meuterei f // vi
meutern.
mutter ['mʌtə*] vti murmeln.
mutton ['mʌtn] n Hammelfleisch nt.
mutual ['mjuːtjuəl] a gegenseitig;
beiderseitig; ~**ly** ad gegenseitig; für
beide Seiten.
muzzle ['mʌzl] n (of animal) Schnauze
f; (for animal) Maulkorb m; (of gun)
Mündung f // vt einen Maulkorb anlegen
(+dat).
my [maɪ] a mein; this is ~ car das ist
mein Auto; I've washed ~ hair ich habe
mir die Haare gewaschen.
myopic [maɪ'ɒpɪk] a kurzsichtig.
myriad ['mɪrɪəd] n: a ~ of (people,
things) unzählige.
myself [maɪ'self] pron mich (acc); mir
(dat); (emphatic) selbst; see also **oneself**.
mysterious [mɪs'tɪərɪəs] a geheimnisvoll.
mystery ['mɪstərɪ] n (secret) Geheimnis
nt; (sth difficult) Rätsel nt.
mystify ['mɪstɪfaɪ] vt ein Rätsel sein
(+dat); verblüffen.
mystique [mɪs'tiːk] n geheimnisvolle
Natur f.
myth [mɪθ] n Mythos m; (fig) Erfindung
f; ~**ology** [mɪ'θɒlədʒɪ] n Mythologie f.

N

n/a abbr (= not applicable) nicht zutreffend.
nab [næb] vt (col) schnappen.
nag [næg] n (horse) Gaul m; (person)
Nörgler(in f) m // vti herumnörgeln (sb
an jdm); ~**ging** a (doubt) nagend // n
Nörgelei f.
nail [neɪl] n Nagel m // vt nageln; to ~ sb
down to doing sth jdn darauf festnageln,
etw zu tun; ~**brush** n Nagelbürste f;
~**file** n Nagelfeile f; ~ **polish** n
Nagellack m; ~ **polish remover** n
Nagellackentferner m; ~ **scissors** npl
Nagelschere f; ~ **varnish** n (Brit) = ~
polish.
naive [naɪ'iːv] a naiv.
naked ['neɪkɪd] a nackt.
name [neɪm] n Name m; (reputation)
Ruf m // vt nennen; (sth new) benennen;
(appoint) ernennen; by ~ mit Namen; I
know him only by ~ ich kenne ihn nur
dem Namen nach; maiden ~ Mädchenname m; what's your ~? wie heißen
Sie?; in the ~ of im Namen (+gen); (for
the sake of) um (+gen) willen; ~**less** a
namenlos; ~**ly** ad nämlich; ~**sake** n
Namensvetter m.
nanny ['nænɪ] n Kindermädchen nt.
nap [næp] n (sleep) Nickerchen nt; (on

cloth) Strich *m;* **to be caught ~ping** *(fig)* überrumpelt werden.

nape [neɪp] *n* Nacken *m.*

napkin ['næpkɪn] *n (at table)* Serviette *f; (Brit: for baby)* Windel *f.*

nappy ['næpɪ] *n (Brit: for baby)* Windel *f;* **~ liner** *n* Windeleinlage *f;* **~ rash** *n* wunde Stellen *pl.*

narcissus [nɑːˈsɪsəs], *pl* **-si** [-saɪ] *n (BOT)* Narzisse *f.*

narcotic [nɑːˈkɒtɪk] *a* betäubend // *n* Betäubungsmittel *nt.*

narrative ['nærətɪv] *n* Erzählung *f* // *a* erzählend.

narrator [nəˈreɪtə*] *n* Erzähler(in *f) m.*

narrow ['nærəʊ] *a* eng, schmal; *(limited)* beschränkt // *vi* sich verengen; **to have a ~ escape** mit knapper Not davonkommen; **to ~ sth down to sth** etw auf etw *(acc)* einschränken; **~ly** *ad (miss)* knapp; *(escape)* mit knapper Not; **~-minded** *a* engstirnig.

nasty ['nɑːstɪ] *a* ekelhaft, fies; *(business, wound)* schlimm.

nation ['neɪʃən] *n* Nation *f,* Volk *nt;* **~al** ['næʃnəl] *a* national, National-, Landes- // *n* Staatsangehörige(r) *mf;* **~al dress** *n* Tracht *f;* **N~al Health Service (NHS)** *n (Brit)* Staatliche(r) Gesundheitsdienst *m;* **N~al Insurance** *n (Brit)* Sozialversicherung *f;* **~alism** ['næʃnəlɪzəm] *n* Nationalismus *m;* **~alist** ['næʃnəlɪst] *n* Nationalist(in *f) m* // *a* nationalistisch; **~ality** [næʃəˈnælɪtɪ] *n* Staatsangehörigkeit *f;* **~alize** ['næʃnəlaɪz] *vt* verstaatlichen; **~ally** ['næʃnəlɪ] *ad* national, auf Staatsebene; **~-wide** *a, ad* allgemein, landesweit.

native ['neɪtɪv] *n (born in)* Einheimische(r) *mf; (original inhabitant)* Eingeborene(r) *mf* // *a (coming from a certain place)* einheimisch; *(of the original inhabitants)* Eingeborenen-; *(belonging by birth)* heimatlich, Heimat-; *(inborn)* angeboren, natürlich; **a ~ of Germany** ein gebürtiger Deutscher; **a ~ speaker of French** ein französischer Muttersprachler; **~ language** *n* Muttersprache *f.*

Nativity [nəˈtɪvɪtɪ] *n:* **the ~** Christi Geburt *no art.*

NATO ['neɪtəʊ] *n abbr* (*= North Atlantic Treaty Organization*) NATO *f.*

natter ['nætə*] *vi (Brit col)* quatschen // *n* Gequatsche *nt.*

natural ['nætʃrəl] *a* natürlich; Natur-; *(inborn)* (an)geboren; **~ gas** *n* Erdgas *nt;* **~ist** *n* Naturkundler(in *f) m;* **~ize** *vt (foreigner)* einbürgern; *(plant etc)* einführen; **~ly** *ad* natürlich.

nature ['neɪtʃə*] *n* Natur *f;* **by ~** von Natur (aus).

naught [nɔːt] *n =* **nought.**

naughty ['nɔːtɪ] *a (child)* unartig, ungezogen; *(action)* ungehörig.

nausea ['nɔːsɪə] *n (sickness)* Übelkeit *f; (disgust)* Ekel *m;* **~te** ['nɔːsɪeɪt] *vt* anekeln.

nautical ['nɔːtɪkəl] *a* nautisch; See-; *(expression)* seemännisch.

naval ['neɪvəl] *a* Marine-, Flotten-; **~ officer** *n* Marineoffizier *m.*

nave [neɪv] *n* Kirchen(haupt)schiff *nt.*

navel ['neɪvəl] *n* Nabel *m.*

navigate ['nævɪgeɪt] *vi* navigieren.

navigator ['nævɪgeɪtə*] *n* Steuermann *m; (AVIAT)* Navigator *m; (AUT)* Beifahrer(in *f) m.*

navvy ['nævɪ] *n (Brit)* Straßenarbeiter *m.*

navy ['neɪvɪ] *n* (Kriegs)marine *f;* **~(-blue)** *n* Marineblau *nt* // *a* marineblau.

NB *abbr* (*= nota bene*) NB.

near [nɪə*] *a* nah; // *ad* in der Nähe // *prep (also: ~ to: space)* in der Nähe (+*gen*); (: *time*) um (+*acc*) ... herum // *vt* sich nähern (+*dat*); **a ~ miss** knapp daneben; **~by** *a* nahe (gelegen) // *ad* in der Nähe; **~ly** *ad* fast; **I ~ly fell** ich wäre fast gefallen; **~side** *n (AUT)* Beifahrerseite *f* // *a* auf der Beifahrerseite.

neat *a,* **~ly** *ad* ['niːt, -lɪ] *(tidy)* ordentlich; *(solution)* sauber; *(pure)* pur.

nebulous ['nebjʊləs] *a* nebulös.

necessarily ['nesɪsərɪlɪ] *ad* unbedingt.

necessary ['nesɪsərɪ] *a* notwendig, nötig; **he did all that was ~** er erledigte alles, was nötig war.

necessitate [nɪˈsesɪteɪt] *vt* erforderlich machen.

necessity [nɪˈsesɪtɪ] *n (need)* Not *f; (compulsion)* Notwendigkeit *f;* **necessities** *pl* das Notwendigste.

neck [nek] *n* Hals *m* // *vi (col)* knutschen; **~ and ~** Kopf an Kopf.

necklace ['neklɪs] *n* Halskette *f.*

neckline ['neklaɪn] *n* Ausschnitt *m.*

necktie ['nektaɪ] *n (US)* Krawatte *f.*

née [neɪ] *a* geborene.

need [niːd] *n* Bedürfnis *nt (for* für); *(lack)* Mangel *m; (necessity)* Notwendigkeit *f; (poverty)* Not *f* // *vt* brauchen; **I ~ to do it** ich muß es tun; **you don't ~ to go** du brauchst nicht zu gehen.

needle ['niːdl] *n* Nadel *f* // *vt (fig: col)* ärgern.

needless ['niːdlɪs] *a* unnötig; **~ to say** natürlich.

needlework ['niːdlwɜːk] *n* Handarbeit *f.*

needn't ['niːdnt] *=* **need not.**

needy ['niːdɪ] *a* bedürftig.

negation [nɪˈgeɪʃən] *n* Verneinung *f.*

negative ['negətɪv] *n (PHOT)* Negativ *nt* // *a* negativ; *(answer)* abschlägig.

neglect [nɪˈglekt] *vt* vernachlässigen // *n* Vernachlässigung *f.*

negligence ['neglɪdʒəns] *n* Nachlässigkeit *f.*

negligible ['neglɪdʒəbl] *a* unbedeutend, geringfügig.

negotiable [nɪ'gəʊʃɪəbl] *a* (*cheque*) übertragbar, einlösbar.

negotiate [nɪ'gəʊʃɪeɪt] *vi* verhandeln // *vt* (*treaty*) abschließen; (*difficulty*) überwinden; (*corner*) nehmen; **negotiation** [-'eɪʃən] *n* Verhandlung *f*; **negotiator** *n* Unterhändler *m*.

Negress ['niːgres] *n* Negerin *f*.

Negro ['niːgrəʊ] *n* Neger *m* // *a* Neger-.

neigh [neɪ] *vi* wiehern.

neighbour, (*US*) **neighbor** ['neɪbə*] *n* Nachbar(in *f*) *m*; ~**hood** *n* Nachbarschaft *f*; Umgebung *f*; ~**ing** *a* benachbart, angrenzend.

neither ['naɪðə*] *a, pron* keine(r, s) (von beiden) // *cj*: he can't do it, and ~ can I er kann es nicht und ich auch nicht // *ad*: ~ good nor bad weder gut noch schlecht.

nephew ['nefjuː] *n* Neffe *m*.

nerve [nɜːv] *n* Nerv *m*; (*courage*) Mut *m*; (*impudence*) Frechheit *f*; to have a fit of ~s in Panik geraten; ~**-racking** *a* nervenaufreibend.

nervous ['nɜːvəs] *a* (*of the nerves*) Nerven-; (*timid*) nervös, ängstlich; ~ **breakdown** *n* Nervenzusammenbruch *m*; ~**ness** *n* Nervosität *f*.

nest [nest] *n* Nest *nt* // *vi* nisten; ~ **egg** *n* (*fig*) Notgroschen *m*.

nestle ['nesl] *vi* sich kuscheln.

net [net] *n* Netz *nt* // *a* netto, Netto- // *vt* netto einnehmen; ~**ball** *n* Netzball *m*; ~ **curtain** *n* Store *m*.

Netherlands ['neðələndz] *npl*: the ~ die Niederlande *pl*.

nett [net] *a* = **net**.

netting ['netɪŋ] *n* Netz(werk) *nt*.

nettle ['netl] *n* Nessel *f*.

network ['netwɜːk] *n* Netz *nt*.

neuter ['njuːtə*] *a* (*BIOL*) geschlechtslos; (*GRAM*) sächlich // *vt* kastrieren.

neutral ['njuːtrəl] *a* neutral // *n* (*AUT*) Leerlauf *m*; ~**ity** [njuː'trælɪtɪ] *n* Neutralität *f*; ~**ize** *vt* (*fig*) ausgleichen.

never ['nevə*] *ad* nie(mals); I ~ went ich bin gar nicht gegangen; ~ in my life nie im Leben; ~**-ending** *a* endlos; ~**theless** [nevəðə'les] *ad* trotzdem, dennoch.

new [njuː] *a* neu; ~**born** *a* neugeboren; ~**comer** *n* Neuankömmling *m*; ~**fangled** *a* (*pej*) neumodisch; ~**found** *a* neuentdeckt; ~**ly** *ad* frisch, neu; ~**lyweds** *npl* Frischvermählte *pl*; ~ **moon** *n* Neumond *m*.

news [njuːz] *n* Nachricht *f*; (*RAD, TV*) Nachrichten *pl*; a piece of ~ eine Nachricht; ~ **agency** *n* Nachrichtenagentur *f*; ~**agent** *n* (*Brit*) Zeitungshändler *m*; ~**caster** *n* Nachrichtensprecher(in *f*) *m*; ~ **dealer** *n*

(*US*) = ~**agent**; ~ **flash** *n* Kurzmeldung *f*; ~**letter** *n* Rundschreiben *nt*; ~**paper** *n* Zeitung *f*; ~**print** *n* Zeitungspapier *nt*; ~**reader** *n* = ~**caster**; ~**reel** *n* Wochenschau *f*; ~**stand** *n* Zeitungsstand *m*.

newt [njuːt] *n* Wassermolch *m*.

New Year *n* Neujahr *nt*; ~'s **Day** *n* Neujahrstag *m*; ~'s **Eve** *n* Silvester(abend *m*) *nt*.

New York [-'jɔːk] *n* New York *nt*.

New Zealand [-'ziːlənd] *n* Neuseeland *nt*; ~**er** *n* Neuseeländer(in *f*) *m*.

next [nekst] *a* nächste(r, s) // *ad* (*after*) dann, darauf; (*next time*) das nächstemal; the ~ day am nächsten *or* folgenden Tag; ~ **time** das nächste Mal; ~ **year** nächstes Jahr; ~ **door** *ad* nebenan // *a* (*neighbour, flat*) von nebenan; ~ **of kin** *n* Familienangehörige(r) *mf*; ~ **to** *prep* neben; ~ **to nothing** so gut wie nichts.

NHS *n abbr of* **National Health Service.**

nib [nɪb] *n* Spitze *f*.

nibble ['nɪbl] *vt* knabbern an (+*dat*).

nice [naɪs] *a* (*person*) nett; (*thing*) schön; (*subtle*) fein; ~**-looking** *a* gutaussehend; ~**ly** *ad* gut, nett; **niceties** ['naɪsɪtɪz] *npl* Feinheiten *pl*.

nick [nɪk] *n* Einkerbung *f* // *vt* (*col: steal*) klauen; in the ~ of time gerade rechtzeitig.

nickel ['nɪkl] *n* Nickel *nt*; (*US*) Nickel *m* (*5 cents*).

nickname ['nɪkneɪm] *n* Spitzname *m* // *vt* taufen.

Nigeria [naɪ'dʒɪərɪə] *n* Nigeria *nt*.

niece [niːs] *n* Nichte *f*.

niggardly ['nɪgədlɪ] *a* geizig.

niggling ['nɪglɪŋ] *a* pedantisch; (*doubt, worry*) quälend; (*detail*) kleinlich.

night [naɪt] *n* Nacht *f*; (*evening*) Abend *m*; the ~ before last vorletzte Nacht; at *or* by ~ (*after midnight*) nachts; (*before midnight*) abends; ~**cap** *n* (*drink*) Schlummertrunk *m*; ~**club** *n* Nachtlokal *nt*; ~**dress** *n* Nachthemd *nt*; ~**fall** *n* Einbruch *m* der Nacht; ~ **gown** *n* = ~**dress**; ~**ie** *n* (*col*) Nachthemd *nt*.

nightingale ['naɪtɪŋgeɪl] *n* Nachtigall *f*.

nightly ['naɪtlɪ] *a, ad* jeden Abend; jede Nacht.

nightmare ['naɪtmeə*] *n* Alptraum *m*.

night: ~ **porter** *n* Nachtportier *m*; ~ **school** *n* Abendschule *f*; ~ **shift** *n* Nachtschicht *f*; ~**time** *n* Nacht *f*.

nil [nɪl] *n* Null *f*.

Nile [naɪl] *n*: the ~ der Nil.

nimble ['nɪmbl] *a* beweglich.

nine [naɪn] *num* neun; ~**teen** *num* neunzehn; ~**ty** *num* neunzig.

ninth [naɪnθ] *a* neunte(r, s).

nip [nɪp] *vt* kneifen // *n* Kneifen *nt*.

nipple ['nɪpl] *n* Brustwarze *f*.

nippy ['nıpı] a (col: person) flink; (Brit col: car) flott; (: cold) frisch.

nitrogen ['naıtrədʒən] n Stickstoff m.

no [nəu] ♦ad (opposite of 'yes') nein; to answer ~ (to question) mit Nein antworten; (to request) nein sagen; ~ thank you nein, danke
♦a (not any) kein(e); I have ~ money/time ich habe kein Geld/keine Zeit; '~ smoking' 'Rauchen verboten'
♦n, pl ~es Nein nt; (~ vote) Neinstimme f.

nobility [nəu'bılıtı] n Adel m.

noble ['nəubl] a (rank) adlig; (splendid) nobel, edel.

nobody ['nəubədı] pron niemand, keiner.

nocturnal [nɒk'tɜ:nl] a (tour, visit) nächtlich; (animal) Nacht-.

nod [nɒd] vi nicken // vt nicken mit // n Nicken nt; ~ off vi einnicken.

noise [nɔız] n (sound) Geräusch nt; (unpleasant, loud) Lärm m.

noisy ['nɔızı] a laut; (crowd) lärmend.

nominal ['nɒmınl] a nominell.

nominate ['nɒmıneıt] vt (suggest) vorschlagen; (in election) aufstellen; (appoint) ernennen.

nomination [nɒmı'neıʃən] n (election) Nominierung f; (appointment) Ernennung f.

nominee [nɒmı'ni:] n Kandidat(in f) m.

non- [nɒn] pref Nicht-, un-; ~-alcoholic a alkoholfrei; ~-aligned a bündnisfrei.

nonchalant ['nɒnʃələnt] a lässig.

non-committal ['nɒnkə'mıtl] a (reserved) zurückhaltend; (uncommitted) unverbindlich.

nondescript ['nɒndıskrıpt] a mittelmäßig.

none [nʌn] a, pron kein(e, er, es) // ad: ~ of you keiner von euch; I've ~ left ich habe keine(n) mehr; he's ~ the worse for it es hat ihm nicht geschadet.

nonentity [nɒ'nentıtı] n Null f (col).

nonetheless ['nʌnðə'les] ad nichtsdestoweniger.

non: ~-existent a nicht vorhanden; ~-fiction n Sachbücher pl.

nonplussed ['nɒn'plʌst] a verdutzt.

nonsense ['nɒnsəns] n Unsinn m.

non: ~-smoker n Nichtraucher(in f) m; ~-stick a (pan, surface) Teflon- ®; ~-stop a Nonstop-.

noodles ['nu:dlz] npl Nudeln pl.

nook [nuk] n Winkel m; ~s and crannies Ecken und Winkel.

noon [nu:n] n (12 Uhr) Mittag m.

no one ['nəuwʌn] pron = nobody.

noose [nu:s] n Schlinge f.

nor [nɔ:*] cj = neither // ad see neither.

normal ['nɔ:məl] a normal; ~ly ad normal; (usually) normalerweise.

north [nɔ:θ] n Norden m // a nördlich, Nord- // ad nördlich, nach or im Norden;

~-east n Nordosten m; ~erly a nördlich, ['nɔːðəlı] a nördlich; ~ern ['nɔːðən] a nördlich, Nord-; N~ern Ireland n Nordirland nt; N~ Pole n Nordpole m; N~ Sea n Nordsee f; ~ward(s) ad nach Norden; ~-west n Nordwesten m.

Norway ['nɔːweı] n Norwegen nt; **Norwegian** [-'wiːdʒən] a norwegisch // n Norweger(in f) m; (LING) Norwegisch nt.

nose [nəuz] n Nase f // vi: to ~ about herumschnüffeln; ~bleed n Nasenbluten nt; ~-dive n Sturzflug m; ~y a = nosy.

nostril ['nɒstrıl] n Nasenloch nt.

nosy ['nəuzı] a (col) neugierig.

not [nɒt] ad nicht; he is ~ or isn't here er ist nicht hier; it's too late, isn't it? es ist zu spät, oder or nicht wahr?; ~ yet/now noch nicht/nicht jetzt; see also all, only.

notably ['nəutəblı] ad (especially) besonders; (noticeably) bemerkenswert.

notary ['nəutərı] n Notar(in f) m.

notch [nɒtʃ] n Kerbe f, Einschnitt m.

note [nəut] n (MUS) Note f, Ton m; (short letter) Nachricht f; (POL) Note f; (comment, attention) Notiz f; (of lecture etc) Aufzeichnung f; (bank~) Schein m; (fame) Ruf m // vt (observe) bemerken; (write down) notieren; ~book n Notizbuch nt; ~d a bekannt; ~pad n Notizblock m; ~paper n Briefpapier nt.

nothing ['nʌθıŋ] n nichts; ~ new/much nichts Neues/nicht viel; for ~ umsonst.

notice ['nəutıs] n (announcement) Bekanntmachung f; (warning) Ankündigung f; (dismissal) Kündigung f // vt bemerken; to take ~ of beachten; at short ~ kurzfristig; until further ~ bis auf weiteres; to hand in one's ~ kündigen; ~able a merklich; ~ board n Anschlagtafel f.

notify ['nəutıfaı] vt benachrichtigen.

notion ['nəuʃən] n Idee f.

notorious [nəu'tɔ:rıəs] a berüchtigt.

notwithstanding [nɒtwıθ'stændıŋ] ad trotzdem; ~ this ungeachtet dessen.

nought [nɔ:t] n Null f.

noun [naun] n Substantiv nt.

nourish ['nʌrıʃ] vt nähren; ~ing a nahrhaft; ~ment n Nahrung f.

novel ['nɒvl] n Roman m // a neu(artig); ~ist n Schriftsteller(in f) m; ~ty n Neuheit f.

November [nəu'vembə*] n November m.

novice ['nɒvıs] n Neuling m; (ECCL) Novize m.

now [nau] ad jetzt; right ~ jetzt, gerade; by ~ imzwischen; just ~ gerade; ~ and then, ~ and again ab und zu, manchmal; from ~ on von jetzt an; ~adays ad heutzutage.

nowhere ['nəuwɛə*] ad nirgends.

nozzle ['nɒzl] n Düse f.
nubile ['njuːbaɪl] a (woman) gut entwickelt.
nuclear ['njuːklɪə*] a (energy etc) Atom-, Kern-.
nucleus ['njuːklɪəs], pl ~lei [-lɪaɪ] n Kern m.
nude [njuːd] a nackt // n (ART) Akt m; **in the ~** nackt.
nudge [nʌdʒ] vt leicht anstoßen.
nudist ['njuːdɪst] n Nudist(in f) m.
nudity ['njuːdɪtɪ] n Nacktheit f.
nuisance ['njuːsns] n Ärgernis nt; **what a ~!** wie ärgerlich!
nuke [njuːk] (col) n Kernkraftwerk nt // vt atomar vernichten.
null [nʌl] a: **~ and void** null und nichtig.
numb [nʌm] a taub, gefühllos // vt betäuben.
number ['nʌmbə*] n Nummer f; (numeral also) Zahl f; (quantity) (An)zahl f // vt (give a number to) numerieren; (amount to) sein; **to be ~ed among** gezählt werden zu; **a ~ of** (several) einige; **they were ten in ~** sie waren zehn an der Zahl; **~ plate** n (Brit AUT) Nummernschild nt.
numeral ['njuːmərəl] n Ziffer f.
numerate ['njuːmərɪt] a rechenkundig.
numerical [njuː'merɪkəl] a (order) zahlenmäßig.
numerous ['njuːmərəs] a zahlreich.
nun [nʌn] n Nonne f.
nurse [nɜːs] n Krankenschwester f; (for children) Kindermädchen nt // vt (patient) pflegen; (doubt etc) hegen.
nursery ['nɜːsərɪ] n (for children) Kinderzimmer nt; (for plants) Gärtnerei f; (for trees) Baumschule f; **~ rhyme** n Kinderreim m; **~ school** n Kindergarten m; **~ slope** n (Brit SKI) Idiotenhügel m (col), Anfängerhügel m.
nursing ['nɜːsɪŋ] n (profession) Krankenpflege f; **~ home** n Privatklinik f.
nurture ['nɜːtʃə*] vt aufziehen.
nut [nʌt] n Nuß f; (screw) Schraubenmutter f; (col) Verrückte(r) mf; **~s** a (col: crazy) verrückt.
nutcrackers ['nʌtkrækəz] npl Nußknacker m.
nutmeg ['nʌtmeg] n Muskat(nuß f) m.
nutrient ['njuːtrɪənt] n Nährstoff m.
nutrition [njuː'trɪʃən] n Nahrung f.
nutritious [njuː'trɪʃəs] a nahrhaft.
nutshell ['nʌtʃel] n: **in a ~** in aller Kürze.
nylon ['naɪlɒn] n Nylon nt // a Nylon-.

O

oak [əʊk] n Eiche f // a Eichen(holz)-.
O.A.P. abbr of **old-age pensioner**.
oar [ɔː*] n Ruder nt.

oath [əʊθ] n (statement) Eid m, Schwur m; (swearword) Fluch m; **on** (Brit) or **under ~** unter Eid.
oatmeal ['əʊtmiːl] n Haferschrot m.
oats [əʊts] npl Hafer m.
obedience [ə'biːdɪəns] n Gehorsam m.
obedient [ə'biːdɪənt] a gehorsam.
obesity [əʊ'biːsɪtɪ] n Fettleibigkeit f.
obey [ə'beɪ] vti gehorchen (+dat).
obituary [ə'bɪtjʊərɪ] n Nachruf m.
object ['ɒbdʒɪkt] n (thing) Gegenstand m, Objekt nt; (purpose) Ziel nt // [əb'dʒekt] vi dagegen sein, Einwände haben (to gegen); (morally) Anstoß nehmen (to an +acc); **expense is no ~** Ausgaben spielen keine Rolle; **I ~!** ich protestiere!; **to ~ that** einwenden, daß; **~ion** [əb'dʒekʃən] n (reason against) Einwand m, Einspruch m; (dislike) Abneigung f; **I have no ~ion to ...** ich habe nichts gegen ... einzuwenden; **~ionable** [əb'dʒekʃnəbl] a nicht einwandfrei; (language) anstößig; **~ive** [əb'dʒektɪv] n Ziel nt // a objektiv.
obligation [ɒblɪ'geɪʃən] n Verpflichtung f; **without ~** unverbindlich.
obligatory [ɒ'blɪgətərɪ] a obligatorisch.
oblige [ə'blaɪdʒ] vt (compel) zwingen; (do a favour) einen Gefallen tun (+dat); **to be ~ed to sb for sth** jdm für etw verbunden sein.
obliging [ə'blaɪdʒɪŋ] a entgegenkommend.
oblique [ə'bliːk] a schräg, schief // n Schrägstrich m.
obliterate [ə'blɪtəreɪt] vt auslöschen.
oblivion [ə'blɪvɪən] n Vergessenheit f.
oblivious [ə'blɪvɪəs] a nicht bewußt (of gen).
oblong ['ɒblɒŋ] n Rechteck nt // a länglich.
obnoxious [əb'nɒkʃəs] a widerlich.
obscene [əb'siːn] a obszön.
obscenity [əb'senɪtɪ] n Obszönität f; **obscenities** pl Zoten pl.
obscure [əb'skjʊə*] a unklar; (indistinct) undeutlich; (unknown) unbekannt, obskur; (dark) düster // vt verdunkeln; (view) verbergen; (confuse) verwirren.
obscurity [əb'skjʊərɪtɪ] n Unklarheit f; (darkness) Dunkelheit f.
obsequious [əb'siːkwɪəs] a servil.
observance [əb'zɜːvəns] n Befolgung f.
observant [əb'zɜːvənt] a aufmerksam.
observation [ɒbzə'veɪʃən] n (noticing) Beobachtung f; (surveillance) Überwachung f; (remark) Bemerkung f.
observatory [əb'zɜːvətrɪ] n Sternwarte f, Observatorium nt.
observe [əb'zɜːv] vt (notice) bemerken; (watch) beobachten; (customs) einhalten; **~r** n Beobachter(in f) m.
obsess [əb'ses] vt verfolgen, quälen; **~ion** [əb'seʃən] n Besessenheit f, Wahn m; **~ive** a krankhaft.

obsolescence [ɒbsə'lesns] n Veralten nt.

obsolete ['ɒbsəli:t] a überholt, veraltet.

obstacle ['ɒbstəkl] n Hindernis nt; ~ **race** n Hindernisrennen nt.

obstetrics [ɒb'stetrɪks] n Geburtshilfe f.

obstinate a, ~**ly** ad ['ɒbstɪnət, -lɪ] hartnäckig, stur.

obstruct [əb'strʌkt] vt versperren; (pipe) verstopfen; (hinder) hemmen; ~**ion** [əb'strʌkʃən] n Versperrung f; Verstopfung f; (obstacle) Hindernis nt.

obtain [əb'teɪn] vt erhalten, bekommen; (result) erzielen.

obtrusive [əb'tru:sɪv] a aufdringlich.

obvious ['ɒbvɪəs] a offenbar, offensichtlich; ~**ly** ad offensichtlich.

occasion [ə'keɪʒən] n Gelegenheit f; (special event) Ereignis nt; (reason) Anlaß m // vt veranlassen; ~**al** a, ~**ally** ad gelegentlich.

occupant ['ɒkjupənt] n Inhaber(in f) m; (of house etc) Bewohner(in f) m.

occupation [ɒkju'peɪʃən] n (employment) Tätigkeit f, Beruf m; (pastime) Beschäftigung f; (of country) Besetzung f, Okkupation f; ~**al hazard** n Berufsrisiko nt.

occupier ['ɒkjupaɪə*] n Bewohner(in f) m.

occupy ['ɒkjupaɪ] vt (take possession of) besetzen; (seat) belegen; (live in) bewohnen; (position, office) bekleiden; (position in sb's life) einnehmen; (time) beanspruchen; to ~ o.s. with or by doing sich mit etw beschäftigen.

occur [ə'kɜ:*] vi vorkommen; to ~ to sb jdm einfallen; ~**rence** n (event) Ereignis nt; (appearing) Auftreten nt.

ocean ['əuʃən] n Ozean m, Meer nt; ~-**going** a Hochsee-.

o'clock [ə'klɒk] ad: it is 5 ~ es ist 5 Uhr.

OCR n abbr of **optical character reader.**

octagonal [ɒk'tægənl] a achteckig.

October [ɒk'təubə*] n Oktober m.

octopus ['ɒktəpəs] n Krake f; (small) Tintenfisch m.

odd [ɒd] a (strange) sonderbar; (not even) ungerade; (the other part missing) einzeln; (surplus) übrig; 60-~ so um die 60; at ~ times ab und zu; to be the ~ one out (person) das fünfte Rad am Wagen sein; (thing) nicht dazugehören; ~**s and ends** npl Krimskrams m; ~**ity** n (strangeness) Merkwürdigkeit f; (queer person) seltsame(r) Kauz m; (thing) Kuriosität f; ~-**job man** n Mädchen nt für alles; ~ **jobs** npl gelegentlich anfallende Arbeiten; ~**ly** ad seltsam; ~**ment** npl Reste pl; ~**s** pl Chancen pl; (betting) Gewinnchancen pl; it makes no ~s es spielt keine Rolle; at ~s uneinig.

odious ['əudɪəs] a verhaßt; (action) abscheulich.

odometer [əu'dɒmətə*] n (esp US) Tacho(meter) m.

odour, (US) **odor** ['əudə*] n Geruch m.

of [ɒv, əv] prep 1 von (+dat), use of gen; the history ~ Germany die Geschichte Deutschlands; a **friend** ~ **ours** ein Freund von uns; a **boy** ~ 10 ein 10-jähriger Junge; **that was kind** ~ **you** das war sehr freundlich von Ihnen
2 (expressing quantity, amount, dates etc): a kilo ~ flour ein Kilo Mehl; **how much** ~ **this do you need?** wieviel brauchen Sie (davon)?; **there were** 3 ~ **them** (people) sie waren zu dritt; (objects) es gab 3 (davon); a **cup** ~ **tea/vase** ~ **flow**ers eine Tasse Tee/Vase mit Blumen; **the** 5th ~ **July** der 5. Juli
3 (from, out of) aus; a **bridge made** ~ **wood** eine Holzbrücke, eine Brücke aus Holz.

off [ɒf] ad (absent) weg, fort; (switch) aus(geschaltet), ab(geschaltet); (Brit: food: bad) schlecht; to be ~ (to leave) gehen; to be ~ **sick** krank sein; a **day** ~ ein freier Tag; **to have an** ~ **day** einen schlechten Tag haben; **he had his coat** ~ er hatte seinen Mantel aus; 10% ~ (COMM) 10% Rabatt; 5 **km** ~ **(the road)** 5 km (von der Straße) entfernt; ~ **the coast** vor der Küste; **I'm** ~ **meat** (no longer eat it) ich esse kein Fleisch mehr; (no longer like it) ich mag kein Fleisch mehr; **on the** ~ **chance** auf gut Glück.

offal ['ɒfəl] n Innereien pl.

off-colour ['ɒf'kʌlə*] a nicht wohl.

offence, (US) **offense** [ə'fens] n (crime) Vergehen nt, Straftat f; (insult) Beleidigung f; **to take** ~ **at** gekränkt sein wegen.

offend [ə'fend] vt beleidigen; ~**er** n Gesetzesübertreter m.

offensive [ə'fensɪv] a (unpleasant) übel, abstoßend; (weapon) Kampf-; (remark) verletzend // n Angriff m.

offer ['ɒfə*] n Angebot f; on ~ zum Verkauf angeboten // vt anbieten; (opinion) äußern; (resistance) leisten; ~**ing** n Gabe f.

offhand ['ɒf'hænd] a lässig // ad ohne weiteres.

office ['ɒfɪs] n Büro nt; (position) Amt nt; **doctor's** ~ (US) Praxis f; **to take** ~ sein Amt antreten; (POL) die Regierung übernehmen; ~ **automation** n Büroautomatisierung f; ~ **block**, (US) ~ **building** n Büro(hoch)haus nt; ~ **hours** npl Dienstzeit f; (US MED) Sprechstunde f.

officer ['ɒfɪsə*] n (MIL) Offizier m; (public ~) Beamte(r) m.

official [ə'fɪʃl] a offiziell, amtlich // n Beamte(r) m; ~**dom** n Beamtentum nt.

officiate [ə'fɪʃɪeɪt] *vi* amtieren.
officious [ə'fɪʃəs] *a* aufdringlich.
offing ['ɒfɪŋ] *n*: in the ~ in (Aus)sicht.
off-licence ['ɒflaɪsəns] *n* (*Brit: shop*) Wein- und Spirituosenhandlung *f*.
off-peak ['ɒfpiːk] *a* (*charges*) verbilligt.
off-season ['ɒfsiːzn] *a* außer Saison.
offset ['ɒfset] *vt* (*irreg: like* set) ausgleichen // *n* (*also*: ~ **printing**) Offset(druck) *m*.
offshoot ['ɒfʃuːt] *n* (*fig*) (*of organization*) Zweig *m*; (*of discussion etc*) Randergebnis *nt*.
offshore ['ɒf'ʃɔː*] *ad* in einiger Entfernung von der Küste // *a* küstennah, Küsten-.
offside ['ɒf'saɪd] *a* (*SPORT*) im Abseits // *ad* abseits // *n* (*AUT*) Fahrerseite *f*.
offspring ['ɒfsprɪŋ] *n* Nachkommenschaft *f*; (*one*) Sprößling *m*.
offstage ['ɒf'steɪdʒ] *ad* hinter den Kulissen.
off: ~**-the-cuff** *a* unvorbereitet, aus dem Stegreif; ~**the-peg**, (*US*) ~**the-rack** *ad* von der Stange; ~**-white** *a* naturweiß.
often ['ɒfən] *ad* oft.
ogle ['əʊgl] *vt* liebäugeln mit.
oh [əʊ] *interj* oh, ach.
oil [ɔɪl] *n* Öl *nt* // *vt* ölen; ~**can** *n* Ölkännchen *nt*; ~**field** *n* Ölfeld *nt*; ~ **filter** *n* (*AUT*) Ölfilter *m*; ~**-fired** *a* Öl-; ~ **painting** *n* Ölgemälde *nt*; ~**-rig** *n* Ölplattform *f*; ~**skins** *npl* Ölzeug *nt*; ~ **tanker** *n* (Öl)tanker *m*; ~ **well** *n* Ölquelle *f*; ~**y** *a* ölig; (*dirty*) ölbeschmiert.
ointment ['ɔɪntmənt] *n* Salbe *f*.
O.K., okay ['əʊ'keɪ] *interj* in Ordnung, O.K. // *a* in Ordnung // *vt* genehmigen.
old [əʊld] *a* alt; **how** ~ **are you?** wie alt bist du?; **he's 10 years old** er ist 10 Jahre alt; ~ **age** *n* Alter *nt*; ~**-age pensioner (O.A.P.)** *n* (*Brit*) Rentner(in *f*) *m*; ~**-fashioned** *a* altmodisch.
olive ['ɒlɪv] *n* (*fruit*) Olive *f*; (*colour*) Olive *nt* // *a* Oliven-; (*coloured*) olivenfarbig; ~ **oil** *n* Olivenöl *nt*.
Olympic [əʊ'lɪmpɪk] *a* olympisch; ~ **Games**, ~**s** *pl* Olympische Spiele *pl*.
omelet(te) ['ɒmlət] *n* Omelett *nt*.
ominous ['ɒmɪnəs] *a* bedrohlich.
omission [əʊ'mɪʃən] *n* Auslassung *f*; (*neglect*) Versäumnis *nt*.
omit [əʊ'mɪt] *vt* auslassen; (*fail to do*) versäumen.
on [ɒn] ◆*prep* 1 (*indicating position*) auf (+*dat*); (*with v of motion*) auf(+*acc*); (*on vertical surface, part of body*) an (+*dat/acc*); **it's** ~ **the table** es ist auf dem Tisch; **she put the book** ~ **the table** sie legte das Buch auf den Tisch; ~ **the left** links
2 (*indicating means, method, condition etc*): ~ **foot** (*go, be*) zu Fuß; ~ **the**

train/plane (*go*) mit dem Zug/Flugzeug; (*be*) im Zug/Flugzeug; ~ **the telephone/ television** am Telefon/im Fernsehen; **to be** ~ **drugs** Drogen nehmen; **to be** ~ **holiday/business** im Urlaub/auf Geschäftsreise sein
3 (*referring to time*): ~ **Friday** (am) Freitag; ~ **Fridays** freitags; ~ **June 20th** am 20. Juni; **a week** ~ **Friday** Freitag in einer Woche;. ~ **arrival** he ... als er ankam, ... er ...
4 (*about, concerning*) über (+*acc*)
◆*ad see also* v + **on** 1 (*referring to dress*) an; **she put her boots/hat** ~ sie zog ihre Stiefel an/setzte ihren Hut auf
2 (*further, continuously*) weiter; **to walk** ~ weitergehen
◆*a* 1 (*functioning, in operation: machine, TV, light*) an; (: *tap*) aufgedreht; (: *brakes*) angezogen; **is the meeting still** ~? findet die Versammlung noch statt?; **there's a good film** ~ es läuft ein guter Film
2: **that's not** ~! (*col: of behaviour*) das liegt nicht drin!
once [wʌns] *ad* einmal // *cj* wenn ... einmal; ~ **he had left/it was done** nachdem er gegangen war/es fertig war; **at** ~ sofort; (*at the same time*) gleichzeitig; ~ **a week** einmal in der Woche; ~ **more** noch einmal; ~ **and for all** ein für allemal; ~ **upon a time** es war einmal.
oncoming ['ɒnkʌmɪŋ] *a* (*traffic*) Gegen-, entgegenkommend.
one [wʌn] ◆*num* eins; (*with noun, referring back to noun*) ein/eine/ein; **it is** ~ (o'clock) es ist eins, es ist ein Uhr; ~ **hundred and fifty** einhundertfünfzig
◆*a* 1 (*sole*) einzige(r, s); **the** ~ **book which** das einzige Buch, welches
2 (*same*) derselbe/dieselbe/dasselbe; **they came in the** ~ **car** sie kamen alle in dem einen Auto
3 (*indefinite*): ~ **day** I discovered ... eines Tages bemerkte ich ...
◆*pron* 1 eine(r, s); **do you have a red** ~? haben Sie einen roten/eine rote/ein rotes?; **this** ~ diese(r, s); **that** ~ der/ die/das; **which** ~? welche(r, s)?; ~ **by** ~ einzeln
2: ~ **another** einander; **do you two ever see** ~ **another?** seht ihr beide euch manchmal?
3 (*impersonal*) man; ~ **never knows** man kann nie wissen; **to cut** ~**'s finger** sich in den Finger schneiden.
one: ~**-armed bandit** *n* einarmiger Bandit *m*; ~**-day excursion** *n* (*US: day return*) Tagesrückfahrkarte *f*; ~**-man** *a* Einmann-; ~**-man band** *n* Einmannkapell *f*; (*fig*) Einmannbetrieb *m*; ~**-off** *n* (*Brit col*) Einzelfall *m*.
oneself [wʌn'self] *pron* (*reflexive; after prep*) sich; (~ *personally*) sich selbst *or* selber; (*emphatic*) (sich) selbst; **to hurt**

~ sich verletzen.

one: **~-sided** a (*argument*) einseitig; **~-to-~** a (*relationship*) eins-zu-eins; **~-upmanship** n die Kunst, anderen um eine Nasenlänge voraus zu sein; **~-way** a (*street*) Einbahn-.

ongoing ['ɒngəʊɪŋ] a momentan; (*progressing*) sich entwickelnd.

onion ['ʌnjən] n Zwiebel f.

onlooker ['ɒnlʊkə*] n Zuschauer(in f) m.

only ['əʊnlɪ] ad nur, bloß // a einzige(r, s) // cj nur, bloß; an ~ child ein Einzelkind; not ~ ... but also ... nicht nur ... sondern auch ...

onset ['ɒnset] n (*beginning*) Beginn m.

onslaught ['ɒnslɔːt] n Angriff m.

onto ['ɒntʊ] prep = **on to**.

onus ['əʊnəs] n Last f, Pflicht f.

onwards ['ɒnwədz] ad (*place*) voran, vorwärts; from that day ~ von dem Tag an; from today ~ ab heute.

ooze [uːz] vi sickern.

opaque [əʊ'peɪk] a undurchsichtig.

OPEC n abbr (= *Organization of Petroleum-Exporting Countries*) OPEC f.

open ['əʊpən] a offen; (*public*) öffentlich; (*mind*) aufgeschlossen // vt öffnen, aufmachen; (*trial, motorway, account*) eröffnen // vi (*begin*) anfangen; (*shop*) aufmachen; (*door, flower*) aufgehen; (*play*) Premiere haben; in the ~ (*air*) im Freien; to come ~ to sich öffnen auf (+ acc); ~ up vt (*route*) erschließen; (*shop, prospects*) eröffnen // vi öffnen; **~ing** n (*hole*) Öffnung f; (*beginning*) Anfang m; (*good chance*) Gelegenheit f; **~ly** ad offen; (*publicly*) öffentlich; **~-minded** a aufgeschlossen; **~-necked** a offen; **~-plan** a (*office*) Großraum-; (*flat etc*) offen angelegt.

opera ['ɒpərə] n Oper f; ~ **house** n Opernhaus nt.

operate ['ɒpəreɪt] vt (*machine*) bedienen; (*brakes, light*) betätigen // vi (*machine*) laufen, in Betrieb sein; (*person*) arbeiten; (*MED*): to ~ **on** operieren.

operatic [ɒpə'rætɪk] a Opern-.

operating ['ɒpəreɪtɪŋ]: ~ **table** n Operationstisch m; ~ **theatre** n Operationssaal m.

operation [ɒpə'reɪʃən] n (*working*) Betrieb m; (*MED*) Operation f; (*undertaking*) Unternehmen nt; (*MIL*) Einsatz m; to be in ~ (*JUR*) in Kraft sein; (*machine*) in Betrieb sein; to have an ~ (*MED*) operiert werden; **~al** a einsatzbereit.

operative ['ɒpərətɪv] a wirksam; (*MED*) operativ.

operator ['ɒpəreɪtə*] n (*of machine*) Arbeiter m; (*TEL*) Telefonist(in f) m.

ophthalmic [ɒf'θælmɪk] a Augen-.

opinion [ə'pɪnjən] n Meinung f; in my ~ meiner Meinung nach; **~ated** a starrsinnig; ~ **poll** n Meinungsumfrage f.

opponent [ə'pəʊnənt] n Gegner m.

opportunity [ɒpə'tjuːnɪtɪ] n Gelegenheit f, Möglichkeit f; to take the ~ of doing die Gelegenheit ergreifen, etw zu tun.

oppose [ə'pəʊz] vt entgegentreten (+dat); (*argument, idea*) ablehnen; (*plan*) bekämpfen; to be ~d to sth gegen etw sein; as ~d to im Gegensatz zu.

opposing [ə'pəʊzɪŋ] a gegnerisch; (*points of view*) entgegengesetzt.

opposite ['ɒpəzɪt] a (*house*) gegenüberliegend; (*direction*) entgegengesetzt // ad gegenüber // prep gegenüber // n Gegenteil nt.

opposition [ɒpə'zɪʃən] n (*resistance*) Widerstand m; (*POL*) Opposition f; (*contrast*) Gegensatz m.

oppress [ə'pres] vt unterdrücken; (*heat etc*) bedrücken; **~ion** [ə'preʃən] n Unterdrückung f; **~ive** a (*authority, law*) repressiv; (*burden, thought*) bedrückend; (*heat*) drückend.

opt [ɒpt] vi: to ~ **for** sich entscheiden für; to ~ **to do** sth sich entscheiden, etw zu tun; ~ **out of** vi sich drücken von (+dat); (*of society*) ausflippen aus (+dat).

optical ['ɒptɪkəl] a optisch; ~ **character reader (OCR)** n optische(s) Lesegerät nt (OCR m).

optician [ɒp'tɪʃən] n Optiker m.

optimist ['ɒptɪmɪst] n Optimist m; **~ic** [ɒptɪ'mɪstɪk] a optimistisch.

optimum ['ɒptɪməm] a optimal.

option ['ɒpʃən] n Wahl f; (*COMM*) Option f; to keep one's ~s open sich alle Möglichkeiten offenhalten; **~al** a freiwillig; (*subject*) wahlfrei; **~al extras** Extras auf Wunsch.

opulent ['ɒpjʊlənt] a sehr reich.

or [ɔː*] cj oder; he could not read ~ write er konnte weder lesen noch schreiben; ~ **else** sonst.

oral ['ɔːrəl] a mündlich // n (*exam*) mündliche Prüfung f.

orange ['ɒrɪndʒ] n (*fruit*) Apfelsine f, Orange f; (*colour*) Orange nt // a orange.

orator ['ɒrətə*] n Redner(in f) m.

orbit ['ɔːbɪt] n Umlaufbahn f.

orchard ['ɔːtʃəd] n Obstgarten m.

orchestra ['ɔːkɪstrə] n Orchester nt; (*US: seating*) Parkett nt.

orchid ['ɔːkɪd] n Orchidee f.

ordain [ɔː'deɪn] vt (*ECCL*) weihen; (*decide*) verfügen.

ordeal [ɔː'diːl] n Qual f.

order ['ɔːdə*] n (*sequence*) Reihenfolge f; (*good arrangement*) Ordnung f; (*command*) Befehl m; (*JUR*) Anordnung f; (*peace*) Ordnung f; (*condition*) Zustand m; (*rank*) Klasse f; (*COMM*) Bestellung f; (*ECCL, honour*) Orden m // vt (*also*: **put in** ~) ordnen; (*command*) befehlen (*sth* etw *acc*, *sb* jdm); (*COMM*) bestellen; **in** ~ in der Reihenfolge; **in (working)** ~ in gutem Zustand; **in** ~ **to do sth** um etw zu tun; **on** ~ (*COMM*) auf Bestellung; **to** ~ **sb to do sth** jdm befehlen, etw zu tun; ~ **form** *n* Bestellschein *m*; ~**ly** *n* (*MIL*) Sanitäter *m*; (*MED*) Pfleger *m* // *a* (*tidy*) ordentlich; (*well-behaved*) ruhig.

ordinary ['ɔːdnrɪ] *a* gewöhnlich; **out of the** ~ außergewöhnlich.

ordnance ['ɔːdnəns] *n* Artillerie *f*; **O~ Survey** *n* (*Brit*) amtlicher Kartographiedienst.

ore [ɔː*] *n* Erz *nt*.

organ ['ɔːgən] *n* (*MUS*) Orgel *f*; (*BIOL*, *fig*) Organ *nt*.

organization [ɔːgənarˈzeɪʃən] *n* Organisation *f*; (*make-up*) Struktur *f*.

organize ['ɔːgənaɪz] *vt* organisieren; ~**r** *n* Organisator *m*, Veranstalter *m*.

oriental [ɔːrɪˈentəl] *a* orientalisch.

origin ['ɒrɪdʒɪn] *n* Ursprung *m*; (*of the world*) Anfang *m*, Entstehung *f*.

original [əˈrɪdʒɪnl] *a* (*first*) ursprünglich; (*painting*) original; (*idea*) originell // *n* Original *nt*; ~**ly** *ad* ursprünglich; originell.

originate [əˈrɪdʒɪneɪt] *vi* entstehen // *vt* ins Leben rufen; **to** ~ **from** stammen aus.

ornament ['ɔːnəmənt] *n* Schmuck *m*; (*on mantelpiece*) Nippesfigur *f*; ~**al** [ɔːnəˈmentl] *a* Zier-.

ornate [ɔːˈneɪt] *a* reich verziert.

orphan ['ɔːfən] *n* Waise *f*, Waisenkind *nt* // *vt*: **to be** ~**ed** Waise werden; ~**age** *n* Waisenhaus *nt*.

orthodox ['ɔːθədɒks] *a* orthodox; ~**y** *n* Orthodoxie *f*; (*fig*) Konventionalität *f*.

orthopaedic, (*US*) **orthopedic** [ɔːθəʊˈpiːdɪk] *a* orthopädisch.

ostensibly [ɒsˈtensəblɪ] *ad* vorgeblich, angeblich.

ostentatious [ɒstenˈteɪʃəs] *a* großtuerisch, protzig.

ostracize ['ɒstrəsaɪz] *vt* ausstoßen.

ostrich ['ɒstrɪtʃ] *n* Strauß *m*.

other ['ʌðə*] *a* andere(r, s) // *pron* andere(r, s) // *ad*: ~ **than** anders als; **the** ~ **(one)** der, die, das andere; **the** ~ **day** neulich; ~**s** (~ *people*) andere; ~**wise** *ad* (*in a different way*) anders; (*or else*) sonst.

ouch [aʊtʃ] *interj* aua.

ought [ɔːt] *v aux* sollen; **I** ~ **to do it** ich sollte es tun; **this** ~ **to have been corrected** das hätte korrigiert werden sollen.

ounce [aʊns] *n* Unze *f*.

our [aʊə*] *poss a* unser; *see also* **my**; ~**s** *poss pron* unsere(r, s); *see also* **mine**; ~**selves** *pron* uns (selbst); (*emphatic*) (wir) selbst; *see also* **oneself**.

oust [aʊst] *vt* verdrängen.

out [aʊt] *ad* hinaus/heraus; (*not indoors*) draußen; (*not alight*) aus; (*unconscious*) bewußtlos; (*results*) bekanntgegeben; **to eat/go** ~ auswärts essen/ausgehen; ~ **there da draußen; he is** ~ (*absent*) er ist nicht da; **he was** ~ **in his calculations** seine Berechnungen waren nicht richtig; ~ **loud** *ad* laut; ~ **of** prep aus; (*away from*) außerhalb (+*gen*); **to be** ~ **of milk** *etc* keine Milch *etc* mehr haben; ~ **of order** außer Betrieb; ~**-and-**~ *a* (*liar*, *theft etc*) ausgemacht.

outback ['aʊtbæk] *n* Hinterland *nt*.

outboard (motor) ['aʊtbɔːd ('məʊtə*)] *n* Außenbordmotor *m*.

outbreak ['aʊtbreɪk] *n* Ausbruch *m*.

outburst ['aʊtbɜːst] *n* Ausbruch *m*.

outcast ['aʊtkɑːst] *n* Ausgestoßene(r) *mf*.

outcome ['aʊtkʌm] *n* Ergebnis *nt*.

outcrop ['aʊtkrɒp] *n* (*of rock*) Felsnase *f*.

outcry ['aʊtkraɪ] *n* Protest *m*.

outdated ['aʊtˈdeɪtɪd] *a* überholt.

outdo [aʊtˈduː] *vt* (*irreg: like* do) übertrumpfen.

outdoor ['aʊtdɔː*] *a* Außen-; (*SPORT*) im Freien; ~**s** *ad* im Freien.

outer ['aʊtə*] *a* äußere(r, s); ~ **space** *n* Weltraum *m*.

outfit ['aʊtfɪt] *n* Kleidung *f*; ~**ters** *n* (*Brit: for men's clothes*) Herrenausstatter *m*.

outgoing ['aʊtgəʊɪŋ] *a* (*character*) aufgeschlossen; ~**s** *npl* (*Brit*) Ausgaben *pl*.

outgrow [aʊtˈgrəʊ] *vt* (*irreg: like* grow) (*clothes*) herauswachsen aus; (*habit*) ablegen.

outhouse ['aʊthaʊs] *n* Nebengebäude *nt*.

outing ['aʊtɪŋ] *n* Ausflug *m*.

outlandish [aʊtˈlændɪʃ] *a* eigenartig.

outlaw ['aʊtlɔː] *n* Geächtete(r) *m* // *vt* ächten; (*thing*) verbieten.

outlay ['aʊtleɪ] *n* Auslage *f*.

outlet ['aʊtlet] *n* Auslaß *m*, Abfluß *m*; (*also*: **retail** ~) Absatzmarkt *m*; (*US ELEC*) Steckdose *f*; (*for emotions*) Ventil *nt*.

outline ['aʊtlaɪn] *n* Umriß *m*.

outlive [aʊtˈlɪv] *vt* überleben.

outlook ['aʊtlʊk] *n* (*lit, fig*) Aussicht *f*; (*attitude*) Einstellung *f*.

outlying ['aʊtlaɪɪŋ] *a* entlegen; (*district*) Außen-.

outmoded [aʊtˈməʊdɪd] *a* veraltet.

outnumber [aʊtˈnʌmbə*] *vt* zahlenmäßig überlegen sein (+*dat*).

out-: ~**-of-date** *a* (*passport*) abgelaufen; (*clothes etc*) altmodisch; (*ideas etc*) überholt; ~**-of-the-way** *a* abgelegen.

outpatient ['aʊtpeɪʃənt] *n* ambulante(r) Patient(in *f*) *m*.

outpost ['aʊtpəʊst] *n* (*MIL, fig*) Vorposten m.

output ['autput] n Leistung f, Produktion f; (COMPUT) Ausgabe f.

outrage ['autreɪdʒ] n (cruel deed) Ausschreitung f; (indecency) Skandal m // vt (morals) verstoßen gegen; (person) empören; **~ous** [aut'reɪdʒəs] a unerhört.

outright ['autraɪt] ad (at once) sofort; (openly) ohne Umschweife // a (denial) völlig; (sale) Total-; (winner) unbestritten.

outset ['autset] n Beginn m.

outside [aut'saɪd] n Außenseite f // a äußere(r, s), Außen-; (chance) gering // ad außen // prep außerhalb (+gen); at the ~ (fig) maximal; (time) spätestens; to go ~ nach draußen gehen; ~ **lane** n (AUT) äußere Spur f; **~left** n (FOOTBALL) Linksaußen m; ~ **line** n (TEL) Amtsanschluß m; ~**r** n Außenseiter(in f) m.

outsize ['autsaɪz] a übergroß.

outskirts ['autskɜːts] npl Stadtrand m.

outspoken [aut'spaukən] a freimütig.

outstanding [aut'stændɪŋ] a hervorragend; (debts etc) ausstehend.

outstay [aut'steɪ] vt: to ~ one's welcome länger bleiben als erwünscht.

outstretched ['autstretʃt] a ausgestreckt.

outstrip [aut'strɪp] vt übertreffen.

out-tray ['auttreɪ] n Ausgangskorb m.

outward ['autwəd] a äußere(r, s); (journey) Hin-; (freight) ausgehend // ad nach außen; **~ly** ad äußerlich.

outweigh [aut'weɪ] vt (fig) überwiegen.

outwit [aut'wɪt] vt überlisten.

oval ['auvəl] a oval // n Oval nt.

ovary ['auvərɪ] n Eierstock m.

ovation [au'veɪʃən] n Beifallssturm m.

oven ['ʌvn] n Backofen m; **~proof** a feuerfest.

over ['auvə*] ad (across) hinüber/herüber; (finished) vorbei; (left) übrig; (again) wieder, noch einmal // prep über; // pref (excessively) übermäßig; ~ here hier(hin), ~ there dort(hin); all ~ (everywhere) überall; (finished) vorbei; ~ **and** ~ immer wieder; ~ **and above** darüber hinaus; to ask sb ~ jdn einladen; to bend ~ sich bücken.

overall ['auvərɔːl] n (Brit) Kittel m // a (situation) allgemein; (length) Gesamt- // ad insgesamt; **~s** pl Overall m.

overawe [auvər'ɔː] vt (frighten) einschüchtern; (make impression) überwältigen.

overbalance [auvə'bæləns] vi Übergewicht bekommen.

overbearing [auvə'bɛərɪŋ] a aufdringlich.

overboard ['auvəbɔːd] ad über Bord.

overbook [auvə'buk] vi überbuchen.

overcast ['auvəkɑːst] a bedeckt.

overcharge [auvə'tʃɑːdʒ] vt: to ~ sb von jdm zuviel verlangen.

overcoat ['auvəkəut] n Mantel m.

overcome [auvə'kʌm] vt (irreg: like come) überwinden.

overcrowded [auvə'kraudɪd] a überfüllt.

overcrowding [auvə'kraudɪŋ] n Überfüllung f.

overdo [auvə'duː] vt (irreg: like do) (cook too much) verkochen; (exaggerate) übertreiben.

overdose ['auvədəus] n Überdosis f.

overdraft ['auvədrɑːft] n (Konto)-überziehung f.

overdrawn [auvə'drɔːn] a (account) überzogen.

overdue ['auvə'djuː] a überfällig.

overestimate ['auvər'estɪmeɪt] vt überschätzen.

overexcited [auvərɪk'saɪtɪd] a überreizt; (children) aufgeregt.

overflow [auvə'fləu] vi überfließen // n ['auvəfləu] (excess) Überschuß m; (also: ~ pipe) Überlaufrohr nt.

overgrown [auvə'grəun] a (garden) verwildert.

overhaul [auvə'hɔːl] vt (car) überholen; (plans) überprüfen // n ['auvəhɔːl] Überholung f.

overhead [auvə'hed] a Hoch-; (wire) oberirdisch; (lighting) Decken- // ad ['auvə'hed] oben; **~s** pl, (US) ~ n allgemeine Unkosten pl.

overhear [auvə'hɪə*] vt (irreg: like hear) (mit an)hören.

overheat [auvə'hiːt] vi (engine) heiß laufen.

overjoyed [auvə'dʒɔɪd] a überglücklich.

overkill ['auvəkɪl] n (fig) Rundumschlag m.

overland ['auvəlænd] a Überland- // ad [auvə'lænd] (travel) über Land.

overlap [auvə'læp] vi sich überschneiden; (objects) sich teilweise decken // n ['auvəlæp] Überschneidung f.

overleaf [auvə'liːf] ad umseitig.

overload ['auvə'ləud] vt überladen.

overlook [auvə'luk] vt (view from above) überblicken; (not notice) übersehen; (pardon) hinwegsehen über (+acc).

overnight ['auvə'naɪt] a (journey) Nacht- // ad über Nacht; ~ **stay** n Übernachtung f.

overpass ['auvəpɑːs] n Überführung f.

overpower [auvə'pauə*] vt überwältigen; **~ing** a überwältigend.

overrate [auvə'reɪt] vt überschätzen.

override [auvə'raɪd] vt (irreg: like ride) (order, decision) aufheben; (objection) übergehen.

overriding [auvə'raɪdɪŋ] a vorherrschend.

overrule [auvə'ruːl] vt verwerfen.

overrun [,ǝuvǝ'rʌn] vt (irreg: like run) (country) einfallen in; (time limit) überziehen.

overseas ['ǝuvǝ'si:z] ad nach/in.Übersee // a überseeisch, Übersee-.

overseer ['ǝuvǝsiǝ*] n Aufseher m.

overshadow [ǝuvǝ'ʃædǝu] vt überschatten.

overshoot ['ǝuvǝ'ʃu:t] vt (irreg: like shoot) (runway) hinausschießen über (+acc).

oversight ['ǝuvǝsait] n (mistake) Versehen nt.

oversleep ['ǝuvǝ'sli:p] vi (irreg: like sleep) verschlafen.

overspill ['ǝuvǝspil] n (Bevölkerungs)-überschuß m.

overstate [ǝuvǝ'steit] vt übertreiben.

overstep [ǝuvǝ'step] vt: to ~ the mark zu weit gehen.

overt [ǝu'vɜ:t] a offen(kundig).

overtake [ǝuvǝ'teik] vti (irreg: like take) überholen.

overthrow [ǝuvǝ'θrǝu] vt (irreg: like throw) (POL) stürzen.

overtime ['ǝuvǝtaim] n Überstunden pl.

overtone ['ǝuvǝtǝun] n (fig) Note f.

overturn [ǝuvǝ'tɜ:n] vti umkippen.

overweight ['ǝuvǝ'weit] a zu dick.

overwhelm [ǝuvǝ'welm] vt überwältigen; ~**ing** a überwältigend.

overwork ['ǝuvǝ'wɜ:k] n Überarbeitung f // vt überlasten // vi sich überarbeiten.

overwrought ['ǝuvǝ'rɔ:t] a überreizt.

owe [ǝu] vt schulden; to ~ sth to (money) jdm etw schulden; (favour etc) jdm etw verdanken; **owing to** prep wegen (+gen).

owl [aul] n Eule f.

own [ǝun] vt besitzen // a eigen; a room of my ~ mein eigenes Zimmer; to get one's ~ back sich rächen; on one's ~ allein; ~ **up** vi zugeben (to sth etw acc); ~**er** n Besitzer(in f) m; ~**ership** n Besitz m.

ox [ɒks], pl ~**en** ['ɒksn] n Ochse m.

oxtail ['ɒksteil] n: ~ **soup** n Ochsenschwanzsuppe f.

oxygen ['ɒksidʒǝn] n Sauerstoff m; ~ **mask** n Sauerstoffmaske f; ~ **tent** n Sauerstoffzelt nt.

oyster ['ɔistǝ*] n Auster f.

oz. abbr of **ounce(s)**.

P

p [pi:] abbr of **penny, pence**.

P.A. n abbr of **personal assistant; public address system**.

p.a. abbr of **per annum**.

pa [pɑ:] n (col) Papa m.

pace [peis] n Schritt m; (speed) Tempo nt // vi schreiten; to keep ~ with Schritt halten mit; ~-**maker** n Schrittmacher m.

pacific [pǝ'sifik] a pazifisch; // n: the P~ (Ocean) der Pazifik.

pacifist ['pæsifist] n Pazifist m.

pacify ['pæsifai] vt befrieden; (calm) beruhigen.

pack [pæk] n (of goods) Packung f; (of hounds) Meute f; (of cards) Spiel nt; (gang) Bande f // vi (case) packen; (clothes) einpacken; to ~ sb off to jdn nach ... schicken; ~ it in! laß es sein!

package ['pækidʒ] n Paket nt; ~ **tour** n Pauschalreise.

packed lunch ['pækt-] n Lunchpaket nt.

packet ['pækit] n Päckchen nt.

packing ['pækiŋ] n (action) Packen nt; (material) Verpackung f; ~ **case** n (Pack)kiste f.

pact [pækt] n Pakt m, Vertrag m.

pad [pæd] n (of paper) (Schreib)block m; (padding) Polster nt // vt polstern; ~**ding** n Polsterung f.

paddle ['pædl] n Paddel nt; (US: for table tennis) Schläger m // vt (boat) paddeln // vi (in sea) planschen; ~ **steamer** n Raddampfer m.

paddling pool ['pædliŋ-] n (Brit) Planschbecken nt.

paddock ['pædǝk] n Koppel f.

paddy field ['pædi-] n Reisfeld nt.

padlock ['pædlɒk] n Vorhängeschloß nt // vt verschließen.

paediatrics, (US) **pediatrics** [pi:di'ætriks] n Kinderheilkunde f.

pagan ['peigǝn] a heidnisch // n Heide m, Heidin f.

page [peidʒ] n Seite f; (person) Page m // vt (in hotel etc) ausrufen lassen.

pageant ['pædʒǝnt] n Festzug m; ~**ry** n Gepränge nt.

paid [peid] pt, pp of **pay** // a bezahlt; to put ~ to (Brit) zunichte machen.

pail [peil] n Eimer m.

pain [pein] n Schmerz m; to be in ~ Schmerzen haben; on ~ of death bei Todesstrafe; to take ~s to do sth sich (dat) Mühe geben, etw zu tun; ~**ed** a (expression) gequält; ~**ful** a (physically) schmerzhaft; (embarrassing) peinlich; (difficult) mühsam; ~**fully** ad (fig: very) schrecklich; ~**killer** n Schmerzmittel nt; ~**less** a schmerzlos; ~**staking** a gewissenhaft.

paint [peint] n Farbe f // vt anstreichen; (picture) malen; to ~ the door blue die Tür blau streichen; ~**brush** n Pinsel m; ~**er** n Maler m; ~**ing** n Malerei f; (picture) Gemälde nt; ~**work** n Anstrich m; (of car) Lack m.

pair [pɛǝ*] n Paar nt; ~ **of scissors** n Schere f; ~ **of trousers** n Hose f.

pajamas [pǝ'dʒɑ:mǝz] npl (US) Schlafanzug m.

Pakistan [pɑ:ki'stɑ:n] n Pakistan nt; ~**i**

a pakistanisch // *n* Pakistani *mf*.
pal [pæl] *n* (*col*) Kumpel *m*.
palace ['pæləs] *n* Palast *m*, Schloß *nt*.
palatable ['pælətəbl] *a* schmackhaft.
palate ['pælɪt] *n* Gaumen *m*.
palatial [pə'leɪʃəl] *a* palastartig.
palaver ['pɑːlɑːvə*] *n* (*col*) Theater *nt*.
pale [peɪl] *a* blaß, bleich; **to be beyond the ~** die Grenzen überschreiten.
Palestine ['pælɪstaɪn] *n* Palästina *nt*; **Palestinian** [-'tɪnɪən] *a* palästinensisch // *n* Palästinenser(in *f*) *m*.
paling ['peɪlɪŋ] *n* (*stake*) Zaunpfahl *m*; (*fence*) Lattenzaum *m*.
pall [pɔːl] *n* (*of smoke*) (Rauch)wolke *f* // *vi* jeden Reiz verlieren, verblassen; **~bearer** *n* Sargträger *m*.
pallet ['pælɪt] *n* (*for goods*) Palette *f*.
pallid ['pælɪd] *a* blaß, bleich.
pallor ['pælə*] *n* Blässe *f*.
palm [pɑːm] *n* (*of hand*) Handfläche *f*; (*also*: **~ tree**) Palme *f* // *vt*: **to ~ sth off on sb** jdm etw andrehen; **P~ Sunday** *n* Palmsonntag *m*.
palpable ['pælpəbl] *a* (*lit*, *fig*) greifbar.
palpitation [pælpɪ'teɪʃən] *n* Herzklopfen *nt*.
paltry ['pɔːltrɪ] *a* armselig.
pamper ['pæmpə*] *vt* verhätscheln.
pamphlet ['pæmflət] *n* Broschüre *f*.
pan [pæn] *n* Pfanne *f* // *vi* (*CINE*) schwenken.
panacea [pænə'sɪə] *n* (*fig*) Allheilmittel *nt*.
panache [pə'næʃ] *n* Schwung *m*.
pancake ['pænkeɪk] *n* Pfannkuchen *m*.
pancreas ['pæŋkrɪəs] *n* Bauchspeicheldrüse *f*.
panda ['pændə] *n* Panda *m*; **~ car** *n* (*Brit*) (Funk)streifenwagen *m*.
pandemonium [pændɪ'məunɪəm] *n* Hölle *f*; (*noise*) Höllenlärm *m*.
pander ['pændə*] *vi* sich richten (*to* nach).
pane [peɪn] *n* (Fenster)scheibe *f*.
panel ['pænl] *n* (*of wood*) Tafel *f*; (*TV*) Diskussionsrunde *f*; **~ling**, (*US*) **~ing** *n* Täfelung *f*.
pang [pæŋ] *n*: **~s of hunger** quälende(r) Hunger *m*; **~s of conscience** Gewissensbisse *pl*.
panic ['pænɪk] *n* Panik *f* // *vi* in Panik geraten; **don't ~** (nur) keine Panik; **~ky** *a* (*person*) überängstlich; **~-stricken** *a* von panischem Schrecken erfaßt; (*look*) panisch.
pansy ['pænzɪ] *n* (*flower*) Stiefmütterchen *nt*; (*col*) Schwule(r) *m*.
pant [pænt] *vi* keuchen; (*dog*) hecheln.
panties ['pæntɪz] *npl* (Damen)slip *m*.
pantihose ['pæntɪhəuz] *n* (*US*) Strumpfhose *f*.
pantomime ['pæntəmaɪm] *n* (*Brit*) Märchenkomödie *f* um Weihnachten.
pantry ['pæntrɪ] *n* Vorratskammer *f*.

pants [pænts] *npl* (*Brit*: *woman's*) Schlüpfer *m*; (: *man's*) Unterhose *f*; (*US*: *trousers*) Hose *f*.
papal ['peɪpəl] *a* päpstlich.
paper ['peɪpə*] *n* Papier *nt*; (*newspaper*) Zeitung *f*; (*essay*) Referat *nt* // *a* Papier-, aus Papier // *vt* (*wall*) tapezieren; **~s** *pl* (*identity*) Ausweis(papiere *pl*) *m*; **~back** *n* Taschenbuch *nt*; **~ bag** *n* Tüte *f*; **~ clip** *n* Büroklammer *f*; **~ hankie** *n* Tempotaschentuch ® *nt*; **~weight** *n* Briefbeschwerer *m*; **~work** *n* Schreibarbeit *f*.
par [pɑː*] *n* (*COMM*) Nennwert *m*; (*GOLF*) Par *nt*; **on a ~ with** ebenbürtig (+*dat*).
parable ['pærəbl] *n* (*REL*) Gleichnis *nt*.
parachute ['pærəʃuːt] *n* Fallschirm *m* // *vi* (mit dem Fallschirm) abspringen.
parade [pə'reɪd] *n* Parade *f* // *vt* aufmarschieren lassen // *vi* paradieren, vorbeimarschieren.
paradise ['pærədaɪs] *n* Paradies *nt*.
paradox ['pærədɒks] *n* Paradox *nt*; **~ically** [pærə'dɒksɪkəlɪ] *ad* paradoxerweise.
paraffin ['pærəfɪn] *n* (*Brit*) Paraffin *nt*.
paragon ['pærəgən] *n* Muster *nt*.
paragraph ['pærəgrɑːf] *n* Absatz *m*.
parallel ['pærəlel] *a* parallel // *n* Parallele *f*.
paralysis [pə'rælɪsɪs] *n* Lähmung *f*.
paralyze ['pærəlaɪz] *vt* lähmen.
parameter [pə'ræmɪtə*] *n* Parameter *m*; **~s** *pl* Rahmen *m*.
paramount ['pærəmaunt] *a* höchste(r, s), oberste(r, s).
parapet ['pærəpɪt] *n* Brüstung *f*.
paraphernalia ['pærəfə'neɪlɪə] *n* Zubehör *nt*, Utensilien *pl*.
paraphrase ['pærəfreɪz] *vt* umschreiben.
paraplegic [pærə'pliːdʒɪk] *n* Querschnittsgelähmte(r) *mf*.
parasite ['pærəsaɪt] *n* (*lit*, *fig*) Schmarotzer *m*, Parasit *m*.
parasol ['pærəsɒl] *n* Sonnenschirm *m*.
paratrooper ['pærətruːpə*] *n* Fallschirmjäger *m*.
parcel ['pɑːsl] *n* Paket *nt* // *vt* (*also*: **~ up**) einpacken.
parch [pɑːtʃ] *vt* (aus)dörren; **~ed** *a* ausgetrocknet; (*person*) am Verdursten.
parchment ['pɑːtʃmənt] *n* Pergament *nt*.
pardon ['pɑːdn] *n* Verzeihung *f* // *vt* (*JUR*) begnadigen; **~ me!, I beg your ~!** verzeihen Sie bitte!; **~ me?** (*US*), **(I beg your) ~?** wie bitte?
parent ['pɛərənt] *n* Elternteil *m*; **~s** *pl* Eltern *pl*; **~al** [pə'rentl] *a* elterlich, Eltern-.
parenthesis [pə'renθɪsɪs], *pl* **-theses** [-θɪsiːz] *n* Klammer *f*; (*sentence*) Parenthese *f*.
Paris ['pærɪs] *n* Paris *nt*.

parish ['pærɪʃ] n Gemeinde f.

parity ['pærɪtɪ] n (FIN) Umrechnungskurs m, Parität f.

park [pɑːk] n Park m // vti parken.

parking ['pɑːkɪŋ] n Parken nt; 'no ~' 'Parken verboten'; ~ **lot** n (US) Parkplatz m; ~ **meter** n Parkuhr f; ~ **ticket** n Strafzettel m.

parlance ['pɑːləns] n Sprachgebrauch m.

parliament ['pɑːləmənt] n Parlament nt; ~**ary** [pɑːlə'mentərɪ] a parlamentarisch, Parlaments-.

parlour, (US) **parlor** ['pɑːlə*] n Salon m, Wohnzimmer nt.

parochial [pə'rəʊkɪəl] a Gemeinde-; (narrow-minded) eng(stirnig).

parole [pə'rəʊl] n: on ~ (prisoner) auf Bewährung.

paroxysm ['pærəksɪzəm] n Anfall m.

parrot ['pærət] n Papagei m.

parry ['pærɪ] vt parieren, abwehren.

parsimonious [pɑːsɪ'məʊnɪəs] a knauserig.

parsley ['pɑːslɪ] n Petersilie m.

parsnip ['pɑːsnɪp] n Pastinake f.

parson ['pɑːsn] n Pfarrer m.

part [pɑːt] n (piece) Teil m; (THEAT) Rolle f; (of machine) Teil nt // ad = **partly** // vt trennen; (hair) scheiteln // vi (people) sich trennen; to take ~ in teilnehmen an (+dat); to take sth in good ~ etw nicht übelnehmen; to take sb's ~ sich auf jds Seite stellen; for my ~ ich für meinen Teil; for the most ~ meistens, größtenteils; in ~ exchange (Brit) in Zahlung; ~ **with** vt hergeben; (renounce) aufgeben; ~**ial** ['pɑːʃəl] a (incomplete) teilweise; (biased) parteiisch; to be ~**ial** to eine (besondere) Vorliebe haben für.

participant [pɑː'tɪsɪpənt] n Teilnehmer(in f) m.

participate [pɑː'tɪsɪpeɪt] vi teilnehmen (in an +dat).

participation [pɑːtɪsɪ'peɪʃən] n Teilnahme f; (sharing) Beteiligung f.

participle ['pɑːtɪsɪpl] n Partizip nt.

particle ['pɑːtɪkl] n Teilchen nt; (GRAM) Partikel m.

particular [pə'tɪkjʊlə*] a bestimmt; (exact) genau; (fussy) eigen; ~**s** pl (details) Einzelheiten pl; Personalien pl; in ~ ad, ~**ly** ad besonders.

parting ['pɑːtɪŋ] n (separation) Abschied m; (Brit: of hair) Scheitel m // a Abschieds-.

partition [pɑː'tɪʃən] n (wall) Trennwand f; (division) Teilung f // vt aufteilen.

partly ['pɑːtlɪ] ad zum Teil, teilweise.

partner ['pɑːtnə*] n Partner m // vt der Partner sein von; ~**ship** n Partnerschaft f; (COMM) Teilhaberschaft f.

partridge ['pɑːtrɪdʒ] n Rebhuhn nt.

part-time ['pɑːt'taɪm] a Teilzeit- // ad stundenweise.

party ['pɑːtɪ] n (POL, JUR) Partei f; (group) Gesellschaft f; (celebration) Party f // a (dress) Party-; (politics) Partei-; ~ **line** n (TEL) Gemeinschaftsanschluß m.

pass [pɑːs] vt (on foot) vorbeigehen an (+dat); (driving) vorbeifahren an (+dat); (surpass) übersteigen; (hand on) weitergeben; (approve) genehmigen; (time) verbringen; (exam) bestehen // vi (go by) vorbeigehen; vorbeifahren; (years) vergehen; (be successful) bestehen // n (in mountains) Paß m; (permission) Passierschein m; (SPORT) Paß m; (in exam): to get a ~ bestehen; to ~ sth through sth etw durch etw führen; to make a ~ at sb (col) bei jdm Annäherungsversuche machen; ~ **away** vi (euph) verscheiden; ~ **by** vi vorbeigehen; vorbeifahren; (years) vergehen; ~ **for** vi gehalten werden für; ~ **on** vt weitergeben; ~ **out** vi (faint) ohnmächtig werden; ~ **up** vt vorbeigehen lassen; ~**able** a (road) passierbar; (fairly good) passabel.

passage ['pæsɪdʒ] n (corridor) Gang m; (in book) (Text)stelle f; (voyage) Überfahrt f; ~**way** n Durchgang m.

passbook ['pɑːsbʊk] n Sparbuch nt.

passenger ['pæsɪndʒə*] n Passagier m; (on bus) Fahrgast m.

passer-by ['pɑːsə'baɪ] n Passant(in f) m.

passing ['pɑːsɪŋ] a (car) vorbeifahrend; (thought, affair) momentan; in ~ en passant; ~ **place** n (AUT) Ausweichstelle f.

passion ['pæʃən] n Leidenschaft f; ~**ate** a leidenschaftlich.

Passover ['pɑːsəʊvə*] n Passahfest nt.

passport ['pɑːspɔːt] n (Reise)paß m; ~ **control** n Paßkontrolle f.

password ['pɑːswɜːd] n Parole f, Kennwort nt, Losung f.

past [pɑːst] prep (motion) an (+dat) .... vorbei; (position) hinter (+dat); (later than) nach // a (years) vergangen; (president etc) ehemalig // n Vergangenheit f; he's ~ forty er ist über vierzig; for the ~ few/3 days in den letzten paar/3 Tagen; to run ~ vorbeilaufen.

pasta ['pæstə] n Teigwaren pl.

paste [peɪst] n (fish ~ etc) Paste f; (glue) Kleister m // vt kleben; (put ~ on) mit Kleister bestreichen.

pasteurized ['pæstəraɪzd] a pasteurisiert.

pastime ['pɑːstaɪm] n Zeitvertreib m.

pastor ['pɑːstə*] n Pfarrer m.

pastry ['peɪstrɪ] n Blätterteig m; (tarts etc) Stückchen pl.

pasture ['pɑːstʃə*] n Weide f.

pasty ['pæstɪ] n (Fleisch)pastete f // ['peɪstɪ] a bläßlich, käsig.

pat [pæt] n leichte(r) Schlag m, Klaps m

// vt tätscheln.

patch [pætʃ] n Fleck m // vt flicken; (to go through) a bad ~ eine Pechsträhne (haben); ~ **up** vt flicken; (quarrel) beilegen; ~**y** a (irregular) ungleichmäßig.

pâté ['pæteɪ] n Pastete f.

patent ['peɪtənt] n Patent nt // vt patentieren lassen; (by authorities) patentieren // a offenkundig; ~ **leather** n Lackleder nt.

paternal [pə'tɜ:nl] a väterlich.

paternity [pə'tɜ:nɪtɪ] n Vaterschaft f.

path [pɑ:θ] n Pfad m; Weg m; (of the sun) Bahn f.

pathetic [pə'θetɪk] a (very bad) kläglich.

pathology [pə'θɒlədʒɪ] n Pathologie f.

pathos ['peɪθɒs] n Rührseligkeit f.

pathway ['pɑ:θweɪ] n Weg m.

patience ['peɪʃəns] n Geduld f; (Brit: CARDS) Patience f.

patient ['peɪʃənt] n Patient(in f) m, Kranke(r) mf // a geduldig.

patio ['pætɪəʊ] n Innenhof m; (outside) Terrasse f.

patriotic [pætrɪ'ɒtɪk] a patriotisch.

patrol [pə'trəʊl] n Patrouille f; (police) Streife f // vt patrouillieren in (+dat) // vi (police) die Runde machen; (MIL) patrouillieren; ~ **car** n Streifenwagen m; ~**man** n (US) (Streifen)polizist m.

patron ['peɪtrən] n (in shop) (Stamm)kunde m; (in hotel) (Stamm)gast m; (supporter) Förderer m; ~ **of the arts** Mäzen m; ~**age** ['pætrənɪdʒ] n Schirmherrschaft f; ~**ize** ['pætrənaɪz] vt (support) unterstützen; (shop) besuchen; (treat condescendingly) von oben herab behandeln; ~ **saint** n Schutzpatron(in f) m.

patter ['pætə*] n (sound: of feet) Trappeln nt; (: of rain) Prasseln nt; (sales talk) Gerede nt // vi (feet) trappeln; (rain) prasseln.

pattern ['pætən] n Muster nt; (sewing) Schnittmuster nt; (knitting) Strickanleitung f.

paunch [pɔ:ntʃ] n Wanst m.

pauper ['pɔ:pə*] n Arme(r) mf.

pause [pɔ:z] n Pause f // vi innehalten.

pave [peɪv] vt pflastern; to ~ the way for den Weg bahnen für.

pavement ['peɪvmənt] n (Brit) Bürgersteig m.

pavilion [pə'vɪlɪən] n Pavillon m; (SPORT) Klubhaus nt.

paving ['peɪvɪŋ] n Straßenpflaster nt; ~ **stone** n Pflasterstein m.

paw [pɔ:] n Pfote f; (of big cats) Tatze f, Pranke f // vt (scrape) scharren; (handle) betatschen.

pawn [pɔ:n] n Pfand nt; (chess) Bauer m // vt verpfänden; ~**broker** n Pfandleiher m; ~**shop** n Pfandhaus nt.

pay [peɪ] n Bezahlung f, Lohn m // v (pt, pp **paid**) vt bezahlen // vi zahlen; (be profitable) sich bezahlt machen; to ~ attention achtgeben (to auf +acc); ~ **back** vt zurückzahlen; ~ **for** vt bezahlen; ~ **in** vt einzahlen; ~ **off** vt abzahlen // vi (scheme, decision) sich bezahlt machen; ~ **up** vi bezahlen; ~**able** a zahlbar, fällig; ~**ee** [peɪ'i:] n Zahlungsempfänger m; ~ **envelope** n (US) = ~ **packet**; ~**ment** n Bezahlung f; **advance** ~**ment** Vorauszahlung f; **monthly** ~**ment** monatliche Rate f; ~ **packet** n (Brit) Lohntüte f; ~ **phone** n Münzfernsprecher m; ~**roll** n Lohnliste f; ~ **slip** n Lohn-/Gehaltsstreifen m.

PC n abbr of **personal computer**.

p.c. abbr of **per cent**.

pea [pi:] n Erbse f.

peace [pi:s] n Friede(n) m; ~**able** a friedlich; ~**ful** a friedlich, ruhig; ~**keeping** a Friedens-.

peach [pi:tʃ] n Pfirsich m.

peacock ['pi:kɒk] n Pfau m.

peak [pi:k] n Spitze f; (of mountain) Gipfel m; (fig) Höhepunkt m; (of cap) (Mützen)schirm m; ~ **period** n Stoßzeit f, Hauptzeit f.

peal [pi:l] n (Glocken)läuten nt; ~**s** of laughter schallende(s) Gelächter nt.

peanut ['pi:nʌt] n Erdnuß f; ~ **butter** n Erdnußbutter f.

pear [pɛə*] n Birne f.

pearl [pɜ:l] n Perle f.

peasant ['pezənt] n Bauer m.

peat [pi:t] n Torf m.

pebble ['pebl] n Kiesel m.

peck [pek] vti picken // n (with beak) Schnabelhieb m; (kiss) flüchtige(r) Kuß m; ~**ing order** n Hackordnung f; ~**ish** a (Brit col) ein bißchen hungrig.

peculiar [pɪ'kju:lɪə*] a (odd) seltsam; ~ **to** charakteristisch für; ~**ity** [pɪkju:lɪ'ærɪtɪ] n (singular quality) Besonderheit f; (strangeness) Eigenartigkeit f.

pedal ['pedl] n Pedal nt // vti (cycle) fahren, radfahren.

peddler ['pedlə*] n Hausierer(in f) m; (of drugs) Drogenhändler(in f) m.

pedestal ['pedɪstl] n Sockel m.

pedestrian [pɪ'destrɪən] n Fußgänger m // a Fußgänger-; (humdrum) langweilig; ~ **crossing** n (Brit) Fußgängerüberweg m.

pediatrics [pi:dɪ'ætrɪks] n (US) = **paediatrics**.

pedigree ['pedɪgri:] n Stammbaum m // cpd (animal) reinrassig, Zucht-.

pedlar ['pedlə*] n = **peddler**.

pee [pi:] vi (col) pissen, pinkeln.

peek [pi:k] vi gucken.

peel [pi:l] n Schale f // vt schälen // vi (paint etc) abblättern; (skin) sich schälen.

peep [pi:p] *n* (*Brit*: *look*) neugierige(r) Blick *m*; (*sound*) Piepsen *nt* // *vi* (*Brit*: *look*) gucken; **~ out** *vi* herausgucken; **~hole** *n* Guckloch *nt*.

peer [pɪə*] *vi* starren; (*peep*) gucken // *n* (*nobleman*) Peer *m*; (*equal*) Ebenbürtige(r) *m*; **~age** *n* Peerswürde *f*.

peeved [pi:vd] *a* ärgerlich; (*person*) sauer.

peevish ['pi:vɪʃ] *a* verdrießlich.

peg [peg] *n* (*stake*) Pflock *m*; **clothes ~** *n* (*Brit*) Wäscheklammer *f*.

pelican ['pelɪkən] *n* Pelikan *m*; **~ crossing** *n* (*Brit AUT*) Ampelüberweg *m*.

pellet ['pelɪt] *n* Kügelchen *nt*.

pelmet ['pelmɪt] *n* Blende *f*.

pelt [pelt] *vt* bewerfen // *vi* (*rain*) schütten // *n* Pelz *m*, Fell *nt*.

pelvis ['pelvɪs] *n* Becken *nt*.

pen [pen] (*fountain ~*) Federhalter *m*; (*ball-point ~*) Kuli *m*; (*for sheep*) Pferch *m*.

penal ['pi:nl] *a* Straf-; **~ize** *vt* (*punish*) bestrafen; (*disadvantage*) benachteiligen; **~ty** ['penəltɪ] *n* Strafe *f*; (*FOOTBALL*) Elfmeter *m*; **~ty** (**kick**) *n* Elfmeter *m*.

penance ['penəns] *n* Buße *f*.

pence [pens] (*Brit*) *pl of* **penny**.

pencil ['pensl] *n* Bleistift *m*; **~ case** *n* Federmäppchen *nt*; **~ sharpener** *n* Bleistiftspitzer *m*.

pendant ['pendənt] *n* Anhänger *m*.

pending ['pendɪŋ] *prep* bis (zu) // *a* unentschieden, noch offen.

pendulum ['pendjuləm] *n* Pendel *nt*.

penetrate ['penɪtreɪt] *vt* durchdringen; (*enter into*) eindringen in (+*acc*).

penetration [penɪ'treɪʃən] *n* Durchdringen *nt*; Eindringen *nt*.

penfriend ['penfrend] *n* (*Brit*) Brieffreund(in *f*) *m*.

penguin ['pengwɪn] *n* Pinguin *m*.

penicillin [penɪ'sɪlɪn] *n* Penizillin *nt*.

peninsula [pɪ'nɪnsjʊlə] *n* Halbinsel *f*.

penis ['pi:nɪs] *n* Penis *m*.

penitence ['penɪtəns] *n* Reue *f*.

penitent ['penɪtənt] *a* reuig.

penitentiary [penɪ'tenʃərɪ] *n* (*US*) Zuchthaus *nt*.

penknife ['pennaɪf] *n* Federmesser *nt*.

pen name *n* Pseudonym *nt*.

penniless ['penɪləs] *a* mittellos.

penny ['penɪ] *n, pl* **pennies** ['penɪz] *or* (*Brit*) **pence** [pens] Penny *m*; (*US*) Centstück *nt*.

penpal ['penpæl] *n* Brieffreund(in *f*) *m*.

pension ['penʃən] *n* Rente *f*; **~er** *n* (*Brit*) Rentner(in *f*) *m*; **~ fund** *n* Rentenfonds *m*.

pensive ['pensɪv] *a* nachdenklich.

Pentecost ['pentɪkɒst] *n* Pfingsten *pl or* *nt*.

penthouse ['penthaʊs] *n* Dachterrassenwohnung *f*.

pent-up ['pentʌp] *a* (*feelings*) angestaut.

penultimate [pɪ'nʌltɪmət] *a* vorletzte(r, s).

people ['pi:pl] *n* (*nation*) Volk *nt* // *npl* (*persons*) Leute *pl*; (*inhabitants*) Bevölkerung *f* // *vt* besiedeln; **several ~ came** mehrere Leute kamen; **~ say that** ... man sagt, daß ...

pep [pep] *n* (*col*) Schwung *m*, Schmiß *m*; **~ up** *vt* aufmöbeln.

pepper ['pepə*] *n* Pfeffer *m*; (*vegetable*) Paprika *m* // *vt* (*pelt*) bombardieren; **~mint** *n* (*plant*) Pfefferminze *f*; (*sweet*) Pfefferminz *nt*.

peptalk ['peptɔ:k] *n* (*col*) Anstachelung *f*.

per [pɜ:*] *prep* pro; **~ day/person** pro Tag/Person; **~ annum** *ad* pro Jahr; **~ capita** *a* (*income*) Pro-Kopf- // *ad* pro Kopf.

perceive [pə'si:v] *vt* (*realize*) wahrnehmen; (*understand*) verstehen.

per cent [pə'sent] *n* Prozent *nt*.

percentage [pə'sentɪdʒ] *n* Prozentsatz *m*.

perception [pə'sepʃən] *n* Wahrnehmung *f*; (*insight*) Einsicht *f*.

perceptive [pə'septɪv] *a* (*person*) aufmerksam; (*analysis*) tiefgehend.

perch [pɜ:tʃ] *n* Stange *f*; (*fish*) Flußbarsch *m* // *vi* sitzen, hocken.

percolator ['pɜ:kəleɪtə*] *n* Kaffeemaschine *f*.

percussion [pɜ:'kʌʃən] *n* (*MUS*) Schlagzeug *nt*.

peremptory [pə'remptərɪ] *a* schroff.

perennial [pə'renɪəl] *a* wiederkehrend; (*everlasting*) unvergänglich.

perfect ['pɜ:fɪkt] *a* vollkommen; (*crime, solution*) perfekt // *n* (*GRAM*) Perfekt *nt* // [pə'fekt] *vt* vervollkommnen; **~ion** [pə'fekʃən] *n* Vollkommenheit *f*; **~ionist** [pə'fekʃənɪst] *n* Perfektionist *m*; **~ly** *ad* vollkommen, perfekt; (*quite*) ganz, einfach.

perforate ['pɜ:fəreɪt] *vt* durchlöchern.

perform [pə'fɔ:m] *vt* (*carry out*) durch- *or* ausführen; (*task*) verrichten; (*THEAT*) spielen, geben // *vi* (*THEAT*) auftreten; **~ance** *n* Durchführung *f*; (*efficiency*) Leistung *f*; (*show*) Vorstellung *f*; **~er** *n* Künstler(in *f*) *m*; **~ing** *a* (*animal*) dressiert.

perfume ['pɜ:fju:m] *n* Duft *m*; (*lady's*) Parfüm *nt*.

perfunctory [pə'fʌŋktərɪ] *a* oberflächlich, mechanisch.

perhaps [pə'hæps] *ad* vielleicht.

peril ['perɪl] *n* Gefahr *f*.

perimeter [pə'rɪmɪtə*] *n* Peripherie *f*; (*of circle etc*) Umfang *m*.

period ['pɪərɪəd] *n* Periode *f*; (*GRAM*

Punkt *m*; (*MED*) Periode *f* // *a* (*costume*) historisch; **~ic** [-'ɒdɪk] *a* periodisch; **~ical** [-'ɒdɪkəl] *n* Zeitschrift *f*; **~ically** [-'ɒdɪkəlɪ] *ad* periodisch.
peripheral [pə'rɪfərəl] *a* Rand-, peripher // *n* (*COMPUT*) Peripheriegerät *nt*.
perish ['perɪʃ] *vi* umkommen; (*fruit*) verderben; **~able** *a* (*fruit*) leicht verderblich.
perjury ['pɜ:dʒərɪ] *n* Meineid *m*.
perk [pɜ:k] *n* (*col: fringe benefit*) Vergünstigung *f*; **~ up** *vi* munter werden; **~y** *a* (*cheerful*) keck.
perm [pɜ:m] *n* Dauerwelle *f*.
permanent ['pɜ:mənənt] *a* dauernd, ständig.
permeate ['pɜ:mɪeɪt] *vti* durchdringen.
permissible [pə'mɪsəbl] *a* zulässig.
permission [pə'mɪʃən] *n* Erlaubnis *f*.
permit ['pɜ:mɪt] *n* Zulassung *f* // [pə'mɪt] *vt* erlauben, zulassen.
pernicious [pɜ:'nɪʃəs] *a* schädlich.
perpendicular [pɜ:pən'dɪkjʊlə*] *a* senkrecht.
perpetrate ['pɜ:pɪtreɪt] *vt* begehen.
perpetual [pə'petjʊəl] *a* dauernd, ständig.
perpetuate [pə'petjʊeɪt] *vt* verewigen, bewahren.
perplex [pə'pleks] *vt* verblüffen.
persecute ['pɜ:sɪkju:t] *vt* verfolgen.
persecution [pɜ:sɪ'kju:ʃən] *n* Verfolgung *f*.
perseverance [pɜ:sɪ'vɪərəns] *n* Ausdauer *f*.
persevere [pɜ:sɪ'vɪə*] *vi* durchhalten.
Persian ['pɜ:ʃən] *a* persisch // *n* Perser(in *f*) *m*; the (**~**) Gulf der Persische Golf.
persist [pə'sɪst] *vi* (*in belief etc*) bleiben (*in* bei); (*rain, smell*) andauern; (*continue*) nicht aufhören; **~ence** *n* Beharrlichkeit *f*; **~ent** *a* beharrlich; (*unending*) ständig.
person ['pɜ:sn] *n* Person *f*; in **~** persönlich; **~able** *a* gut aussehend; **~al** *a* persönlich; (*private*) privat; (*of body*) körperlich, Körper-; **~al assistant (P.A.)** *n* Assistent(in *f*) *m*; **~al computer (PC)** *n* Personalcomputer *m*; **~ality** [pɜ:sə'nælɪtɪ] *n* Persönlichkeit *f*; **~ally** *ad* persönlich; **~ify** [pɜ:'sɒnɪfaɪ] *vt* verkörpern.
personnel [pɜ:sə'nel] *n* Personal *nt*.
Perspex ['pɜ:speks] *n* ® Plexiglas *nt* ®.
perspiration [pɜ:spə'reɪʃən] *n* Transpiration *f*.
perspire [pəs'paɪə*] *vi* transpirieren.
persuade [pə'sweɪd] *vt* überreden; (*convince*) überzeugen.
persuasion [pə'sweɪʒən] *n* Überredung *f*; Überzeugung *f*.
persuasive [pə'sweɪsɪv] *a* überzeugend.
pert [pɜ:t] *a* keck.
pertaining [pɜ:'teɪnɪŋ]: **~ to** a betreffend (+*acc*).

pertinent ['pɜ:tɪnənt] *a* relevant.
perturb [pə'tɜ:b] *vt* beunruhigen.
peruse [pə'ru:z] *vt* lesen.
pervade [pɜ:'veɪd] *vt* erfüllen.
perverse [pə'vɜ:s] *a* pervers; (*obstinate*) eigensinnig.
pervert ['pɜ:vɜ:t] *n* perverse(r) Mensch *m* // [pə'vɜ:t] *vt* verdrehen; (*morally*) verderben.
pessimist ['pesɪmɪst] *n* Pessimist *m*; **~ic** [pesɪ'mɪstɪk] *a* pessimistisch.
pest [pest] *n* (*insect*) Schädling *m*; (*fig: person*) Nervensäge *f*; (*: thing*) Plage *f*.
pester ['pestə*] *vt* plagen.
pesticide ['pestɪsaɪd] *n* Insektenvertilgungsmittel *nt*.
pet [pet] *n* (*animal*) Haustier *nt* // *vt* liebkosen, streicheln // *vi* (*col*) Petting machen.
petal ['petl] *n* Blütenblatt *nt*.
peter out ['pi:tə-] *vi* allmählich zu Ende gehen.
petite [pə'ti:t] *a* zierlich.
petition [pə'tɪʃən] *n* Bittschrift *f*.
petrified ['petrɪfaɪd] *a* versteinert; (*person*) starr (vor Schreck).
petrify ['petrɪfaɪ] *vt* versteinern; (*person*) erstarren lassen.
petrol ['petrəl] (*Brit*) *n* Benzin *nt*, Kraftstoff *m*; **two-/four-star ~** ≈ Normal-/Superbenzin *nt*; **~ can** *n* Benzinkanister *m*.
petroleum [pɪ'trəʊlɪəm] *n* Petroleum *nt*.
petrol: ~pump *n* (*Brit: in car*) Benzinpumpe *f*; (*: at garage*) Zapfsäule *f*; **~ station** *n* (*Brit*) Tankstelle *f*; **~ tank** *n* (*Brit*) Benzintank *m*.
petty ['petɪ] *a* (*unimportant*) unbedeutend; (*mean*) kleinlich; **~ cash** *n* Portokasse *f*; **~ officer** *n* Maat *m*.
petulant ['petjʊlənt] *a* leicht reizbar.
pew [pju:] *n* Kirchenbank *f*.
pewter ['pju:tə*] *n* Zinn *nt*.
pharmacist ['fɑ:məsɪst] *n* Pharmazeut *m*; (*druggist*) Apotheker *m*.
pharmacy ['fɑ:məsɪ] *n* Pharmazie *f*; (*shop*) Apotheke *f*.
phase [feɪz] *n* Phase *f*; **~ out** *vt* langsam abbauen; (*model*) auslaufen lassen; (*person*) absetzen.
Ph.D. *abbr of* **Doctor of Philosophy.**
pheasant ['feznt] *n* Fasan *m*.
phenomenon [fɪ'nɒmɪnən], *pl* **-mena** [-mɪnə] *n* Phänomen *nt*.
philanthropist [fɪ'lænθrəpɪst] *n* Philanthrop *m*, Menschenfreund *m*.
Philippines ['fɪlɪpi:nz] *npl*: the **~** die Philippinen *pl*.
philosopher [fɪ'lɒsəfə*] *n* Philosoph *m*.
philosophy [fɪ'lɒsəfɪ] *n* Philosophie *f*.
phlegm [flem] *n* (*MED*) Schleim *m*; (*calmness*) Gelassenheit *f*; **~atic** [fleg'mætɪk] *a* gelassen.

phone [fəʊn] n Telefon nt // vti telefonieren, anrufen; **to be on the ~** telephonieren; **~ back** vti zurückrufen; **~ up** vti anrufen; **~ book** n Telefonbuch nt; **~ box** or **booth** n Telefonzelle f; **~ call** n Telefonanruf m; **~-in** n (RADIO, TV) Phone-in nt.

phoney ['fəʊnɪ] a (col) unecht // n (person) Schwindler m; (thing) Fälschung; (pound note) Blüte f.

phonograph ['fəʊnəɡrɑːf] n (US) Grammophon nt.

photo ['fəʊtəʊ] n Foto nt.

photocopier ['fəʊtəʊkɒpɪə*] n Kopiergerät nt.

photocopy ['fəʊtəʊkɒpɪ] n Fotokopie f // vt fotokopieren.

photogenic [fəʊtəʊ'dʒenɪk] a fotogen.

photograph ['fəʊtəɡrɑːf] n Fotografie f, Aufnahme f // vt fotografieren; **~er** [fə'tɒɡrəfə*] n Fotograf m; **~ic** [fəʊtə'ɡræfɪk] a fotografisch; **~y** [fə'tɒɡrəfɪ] n Fotografie f.

phrase [freɪz] n Satz m; (expression) Ausdruck m // vt ausdrücken, formulieren; **~ book** n Sprachführer m.

physical ['fɪzɪkəl] a physikalisch; (bodily) körperlich, physisch; **~ education** n Turnen nt; **~ly** ad physikalisch.

physician [fɪ'zɪʃən] n Arzt m.

physics ['fɪzɪks] n Physik f.

physiotherapy [fɪzɪə'θerəpɪ] n Heilgymnastik f, Physiotherapie f.

physique [fɪ'ziːk] n Körperbau m.

pianist ['pɪənɪst] n Pianist(in f) m.

piano ['pjɑːnəʊ] n Klavier nt.

pick [pɪk] n (tool) Pickel m; (choice) Auswahl f // vt (fruit) pflücken; (choose) aussuchen; **take your ~** such dir etwas aus; **to ~ sb's pocket** jdn bestehlen; **~ off** vt (kill) abschießen; **~ on** vt (person) herumhacken auf (+dat); **~ out** vt auswählen; **~ up** vi (improve) sich erholen // vt (lift up) aufheben; (learn) (schnell) mitbekommen; (collect) abholen; (girl) (sich dat) anlachen; (AUT: passenger) mitnehmen; (speed) gewinnen an (+dat); **to ~ o.s. up** aufstehen.

picket ['pɪkɪt] n (striker) Streikposten m // n (factory) (Streik)posten aufstellen vor (+dat) // vi (Streik)posten stehen.

pickle ['pɪkl] n (salty mixture) Pökel m; (col) Klemme f // vt (in Essig) einlegen; einpökeln.

pickpocket ['pɪkpɒkɪt] n Taschendieb m.

pickup ['pɪkʌp] n (Brit: on record player) Tonabnehmer m; (small truck) Lieferwagen m.

picnic ['pɪknɪk] n Picknick nt // vi picknicken.

pictorial [pɪk'tɔːrɪəl] a in Bildern.

picture ['pɪktʃə*] n Bild nt // vt (visualize) sich (dat) vorstellen; **in the ~** (fig) im Bild; **the ~s** pl (Brit) das Kino; **~ book** n Bilderbuch nt.

picturesque [pɪktʃə'resk] a malerisch.

pie [paɪ] n (meat) Pastete f; (fruit) Torte f.

piece [piːs] n Stück nt // vt: **to ~ together** zusammenstückeln; (fig) sich (dat) zusammenreimen; **to take to ~s** in Einzelteile zerlegen; **~meal** ad stückweise, Stück für Stück; **~work** n Akkordarbeit f.

pie chart n Kreisdiagramm nt.

pier [pɪə*] n Pier m, Mole f.

pierce [pɪəs] vt durchstechen, durchbohren (also look); durchdringen (also fig).

piercing ['pɪəsɪŋ] a durchdringend.

piety ['paɪətɪ] n Frömmigkeit f.

pig [pɪɡ] n Schwein nt.

pigeon ['pɪdʒən] n Taube f; **~hole** n (compartment) Ablegefach nt.

piggy bank ['pɪɡɪbæŋk] n Sparschwein nt.

pigheaded ['pɪɡ'hedɪd] a dickköpfig.

piglet ['pɪɡlət] n Ferkel nt.

pigskin ['pɪɡskɪn] n Schweinsleder nt.

pigsty ['pɪɡstaɪ] n (lit, fig) Schweinestall m.

pigtail ['pɪɡteɪl] n Zopf m.

pike [paɪk] n Pike f; (fish) Hecht m.

pilchard ['pɪltʃəd] n Sardine f.

pile [paɪl] n Haufen m; (of books, wood) Stapel m; (in ground) Pfahl m; (on carpet) Flausch m // vti (also: ~ up) sich anhäufen.

piles [paɪlz] n Hämorrhoiden pl.

pile-up ['paɪlʌp] n (AUT) Massenzusammenstoß m.

pilfering ['pɪlfərɪŋ] n Diebstahl m.

pilgrim ['pɪlɡrɪm] n Pilger(in f) m; **~age** n Wallfahrt f.

pill [pɪl] n Tablette f, Pille f; **the ~** die (Antibaby)pille.

pillage ['pɪlɪdʒ] vt plündern.

pillar ['pɪlə*] n Pfeiler m, Säule f (also fig); **~ box** n (Brit) Briefkasten m.

pillion ['pɪljən] n Soziussitz m.

pillory ['pɪlərɪ] vt (fig) anprangern.

pillow ['pɪləʊ] n Kissen nt; **~case** n Kissenbezug m.

pilot ['paɪlət] n Pilot m; (NAUT) Lotse m // a (scheme etc) Versuchs- // vt führen; (ship) lotsen; **~ light** n Zündflamme f.

pimp [pɪmp] n Zuhälter m.

pimple ['pɪmpl] n Pickel m.

pimply ['pɪmplɪ] a pick(e)lig.

pin [pɪn] n Nadel f; (for sewing) Stecknadel f; (TECH) Stift m, Bolzen m // vt stecken, heften (to an +acc); (keep in one position) pressen, drücken; **to ~ sth on sb** (fig) jdm etw anhängen; **~s and needles** n Kribbeln nt; **~ down** vt (fig: person) festnageln (to auf +acc).

pinafore ['pɪnəfɔ:*] n Schürze f; ~ **dress** n Kleiderrock m.

pinball ['pɪnbɔ:l] n Flipper m.

pincers ['pɪnsəz] npl Kneif- or Beißzange f; (MED) Pinzette f.

pinch [pɪntʃ] n Zwicken, Kneifen nt; (of salt) Prise f // vti zwicken, kneifen; (shoe) drücken // vt (col: steal) klauen; (arrest) schnappen; **at a ~** notfalls, zur Not.

pincushion ['pɪnkuʃən] n Nadelkissen nt.

pine [paɪn] n (also: ~ **tree**) Kiefer f // vi: ~ **for** sich sehnen nach; ~ **away** vi sich zu Tode sehnen.

pineapple ['paɪnæpl] n Ananas f.

ping [pɪŋ] n Klingeln nt; **~-pong** n Pingpong nt.

pink [pɪŋk] a rosa inv // n Rosa nt; (BOT) Nelke f.

pinnacle ['pɪnəkl] n Spitze f.

pinpoint ['pɪnpɔɪnt] vt festlegen.

pinstripe ['pɪnstraɪp] n Nadelstreifen m.

pint [paɪnt] n Pint nt; (Brit col: of beer) große(s) Bier nt.

pious ['paɪəs] a fromm.

pip [pɪp] n Kern m; (Brit: time signal on radio) Zeitzeichen nt.

pipe [paɪp] n (smoking) Pfeife f; (tube) Rohr nt; (in house) (Rohr)leitung f // vti (durch Rohre) leiten; (MUS) blasen; **~s** pl (also: bag**~s**) Dudelsack m; ~ **down** vi (be quiet) die Luft anhalten; ~ **cleaner** n Pfeifenreiniger m; **~-dream** n Luftschloß nt; **~line** n (for oil) Pipeline f; **~r** n Pfeifer m; (bagpipes) Dudelsackbläser m.

piping ['paɪpɪŋ] ad: ~ **hot** siedend heiß.

piquant ['pi:kənt] a pikant.

pique [pi:k] n gekränkte(r) Stolz m.

pirate ['paɪərɪt] n Pirat m, Seeräuber m; ~ **radio** n (Brit) Piratensender m.

Pisces ['paɪsɪz] n Fische pl.

piss [pɪs] vi (col) pissen; **~ed** a (col: drunk) voll.

pistol ['pɪstl] n Pistole f.

piston ['pɪstən] n Kolben m.

pit [pɪt] n Grube f; (THEAT) Parterre nt; (orchestra ~) Orchestergraben m // vt (mark with scars) zerfressen; (compare: o.s.) messen (against mit); (: sb/sth) messen (against an +dat); **the ~s** pl (motor racing) die Boxen.

pitch [pɪtʃ] n Wurf m; (of trader) Stand m; (SPORT) (Spiel)feld nt; (MUS) Tonlage f; (substance) Pech nt // vt werfen; (set up) aufschlagen // vi (NAUT) rollen; **to ~ a tent** ein Zelt aufbauen; **~-black** a pechschwarz; **~ed battle** n offene Schlacht f.

pitcher ['pɪtʃə*] n Krug m.

pitchfork ['pɪtʃfɔ:k] n Heugabel f.

piteous ['pɪtɪəs] a kläglich, erbärmlich.

pitfall ['pɪtfɔ:l] n (fig) Falle f.

pith [pɪθ] n Mark nt.

pithy ['pɪθɪ] a prägnant.

pitiful ['pɪtɪful] a (deserving pity) bedauernswert; (contemptible) jämmerlich.

pitiless ['pɪtɪləs] a erbarmungslos.

pittance ['pɪtəns] n Hungerlohn m.

pity ['pɪtɪ] n (sympathy) Mitleid nt // vt Mitleid haben mit; **what a ~!** wie schade!

pivot ['pɪvət] n Drehpunkt m // vi sich drehen (on um).

pixie ['pɪksɪ] n Elf(e f) m.

pizza ['pi:tsə] n Pizza f.

placard ['plækɑ:d] n Plakat nt, Anschlag m.

placate [plə'keɪt] vt beschwichtigen.

place [pleɪs] n Platz m; (spot) Stelle f; (town etc) Ort m // vt setzen, stellen, legen; (order) aufgeben; (SPORT) plazieren; (identify) unterbringen; **to take ~** stattfinden; **to be ~d third** (in race, exam) auf dem dritten Platz liegen; **out of ~** nicht am rechten Platz; (fig: remark) unangebracht; **in the first ~** erstens; **to change ~s with sb** mit jdm den Platz tauschen.

placid ['plæsɪd] a gelassen, ruhig.

plagiarism ['pleɪdʒɪərɪzəm] n Plagiat nt.

plague [pleɪg] n Pest f; (fig) Plage f // vt plagen.

plaice [pleɪs] n Scholle f.

plain [pleɪn] a (clear) klar, deutlich; (simple) einfach, schlicht; (not beautiful) alltäglich // n Ebene f; **in ~ clothes** (police) in Zivil(kleidung); ~ **chocolate** n Bitterschokolade f.

plaintiff ['pleɪntɪf] n Kläger m.

plaintive ['pleɪntɪv] a wehleidig.

plait [plæt] n Zopf m // vt flechten.

plan [plæn] n Plan m // vti planen; **according to ~** planmäßig; **to ~ to do sth** vorhaben, etw zu tun.

plane [pleɪn] n Ebene f; (AVIAT) Flugzeug nt; (tool) Hobel m; (tree) Platane f.

planet ['plænɪt] n Planet m.

plank [plæŋk] n Brett nt.

planning ['plænɪŋ] n Planung f; **family ~** Familienplanung f; ~ **permission** n Baugenehmigung f.

plant [plɑ:nt] n Pflanze f; (TECH) (Maschinen)anlage f; (factory) Fabrik f, Werk nt // vt pflanzen; (set firmly) stellen.

plantation [plæn'teɪʃən] n Plantage f.

plaque [plæk] n Gedenktafel f; (on teeth) (Zahn)belag m.

plaster ['plɑ:stə*] n Gips m; (in house) Verputz m; (Brit: also: sticking ~) Pflaster nt; (for fracture: also: ~ **of Paris**) Gipsverband m // vt gipsen; (hole) zugipsen; (ceiling) verputzen; (fig: with pictures etc) be- or verkleben; **~ed** a (col) besoffen; **~er** n Gipser m.

plastic ['plæstɪk] n Plastik nt or f // a (made of plastic) Plastik-; (ART) plastisch, bildend; ~ **bag** n Plastiktüte f.
plasticine ['plæstɪsiːn] n Plastilin nt.
plastic surgery n plastische Chirurgie f.
plate [pleɪt] n Teller m; (gold/silver) vergoldete(s)/versilberte(s) Tafelgeschirr nt; (flat sheet) Platte f; (in book) (Bild)tafel f.
plate glass n Tafelglas nt.
platform ['plætfɔːm] n (at meeting) Plattform f, Podium nt; (RAIL) Bahnsteig m; (POL) Parteiprogramm nt; ~ **ticket** n Bahnsteigkarte f.
platinum ['plætɪnəm] n Platin nt.
platoon [plə'tuːn] n (MIL) Zug m.
platter ['plætə*] n Platte f.
play [pleɪ] n Spiel m (also TECH); (THEAT) (Theater)stück nt // vti spielen; (another team) spielen gegen; **to ~ safe** auf Nummer sicher gehen; ~ **down** vt herunterspielen; ~ **up** vi (cause trouble) frech werden; (bad leg etc) weh tun // vt (person) plagen; **to ~ up to sb** jdm flattieren; ~-**acting** n Schauspielerei f; ~**boy** n Playboy m; ~**er** n Spieler(in f) m; ~**ful** a spielerisch; ~**ground** n Spielplatz m; ~**group** n Kindergarten m; ~**ing card** n Spielkarte f; ~**ing field** n Sportplatz m; ~**mate** n Spielkamerad m; ~**off** n (SPORT) Entscheidungsspiel nt; ~**pen** n Laufstall m; ~**school** n = ~**group**; ~**thing** n Spielzeug nt; ~**wright** n Theaterschriftsteller m.
plc abbr (= public limited company) AG.
plea [pliː] n Bitte f; (general appeal) Appell m; (JUR) Plädoyer nt.
plead [pliːd] vt (poverty) zur Entschuldigung anführen; (JUR: sb's case) vertreten // vi (beg) dringend bitten (with sb jdn); (JUR) plädieren.
pleasant ['pleznt] a angenehm; ~**ness** n Angenehme nt; (of person) Freundlichkeit f; ~**ries** npl (polite remarks) Nettigkeiten pl.
please [pliːz] vti (be agreeable to) gefallen (+dat); ~! bitte!; ~ **yourself!** wie du willst!; ~**d** a zufrieden; (glad) erfreut (with über +acc); ~**d to meet you** angenehm.
pleasing ['pliːzɪŋ] a erfreulich.
pleasure ['pleʒə*] n Freude f; (old: will) Wünsche pl // cpd Vergnügungs-; **'it's a ~'** 'gern geschehen'.
pleat [pliːt] n Falte f.
plectrum ['plektrəm] n Plektron nt.
pledge [pledʒ] n Pfand nt; (promise) Versprechen nt // vt verpfänden; (promise) geloben, versprechen.
plentiful ['plentɪfʊl] a reichlich.
plenty ['plentɪ] n Fülle f, Überfluß m; ~ **of** eine Menge, viel.

pleurisy ['plʊərɪsɪ] n Rippenfellentzündung f.
pliable ['plaɪəbl] a biegsam; (person) beeinflußbar.
pliers ['plaɪəz] npl (Kneif)zange f.
plight [plaɪt] n (Not)lage f.
plimsolls ['plɪmsəlz] npl (Brit) Turnschuhe pl.
plod [plɒd] vi (work) sich abplagen; (walk) trotten; ~**der** n Arbeitstier nt.
plonk [plɒŋk] n (Brit col: wine) billige(r) Wein m // vt: **to ~ sth down** etw hinknallen.
plot [plɒt] n Komplott nt; (story) Handlung f; (of land) Grundstück nt // vt markieren; (curve) zeichnen; (movements) nachzeichnen // vi (plan secretly) sich verschwören; ~**ter** n (instrument) Plotter m.
plough, (US) **plow** [plaʊ] n Pflug m // vt pflügen; ~ **back** vt (COMM) wieder in das Geschäft stecken; ~ **through** vt (water) durchpflügen; (book) sich kämpfen durch.
ploy [plɔɪ] n Masche f.
pluck [plʌk] vt (fruit) pflücken; (guitar) zupfen; (goose) rupfen // n Mut m; **to ~ up courage** all seinen Mut zusammennehmen; ~**y** a beherzt.
plug [plʌg] n Stöpsel m; (ELEC) Stecker m; (col: publicity) Schleichwerbung f; (AUT) Zündkerze f // vt (zu)stopfen; (col: advertise) Reklame machen für; ~ **in** vt (ELEC) anschließen.
plum [plʌm] n Pflaume f, Zwetschge f // a (job etc) Bomben-.
plumage ['pluːmɪdʒ] n Gefieder nt.
plumb [plʌm] a senkrecht // n Lot nt // ad (exactly) genau // vt ausloten; (fig) sondieren.
plumber ['plʌmə*] n Klempner m, Installateur m.
plumbing ['plʌmɪŋ] n (craft) Installieren nt; (fittings) Leitungen pl.
plume [pluːm] n Feder f; (of smoke etc) Fahne f.
plummet ['plʌmɪt] vi (ab)stürzen.
plump [plʌmp] a rundlich, füllig // vt plumpsen lassen; **to ~ for** (col: choose) sich entscheiden für.
plunder ['plʌndə*] n Plünderung f; (loot) Beute f // vt plündern.
plunge [plʌndʒ] n Sturz m // vt stoßen // vi (sich) stürzen; **to take the ~** den Sprung wagen.
plunging ['plʌndʒɪŋ] a (neckline) offenherzig.
pluperfect ['pluː'pɜːfɪkt] n Plusquamperfekt nt.
plural ['plʊərəl] n Plural m, Mehrzahl f.
plus [plʌs] n (also: ~ **sign**) Plus(zeichen) nt // prep plus, und; **ten/ twenty ~** mehr als zehn/zwanzig.
plush [plʌʃ] a (also ~**y**: col: luxurious) feudal.

ply [plaɪ] *vt* (*trade*) (be)treiben; (*with questions*) zusetzen (+*dat*); (*ship, taxi*) befahren // *vi* (*ship, taxi*) verkehren; **three-~** (*wool*) Dreifach-; **to ~ sb with drink** jdn zum Trinken animieren; **~wood** *n* Sperrholz *nt*.

P.M. *abbr of* **Prime Minister**.

p.m. *ad abbr* (= *post meridiem*) p.m.

pneumatic [nju:'mætɪk] *a* pneumatisch; (*TECH*) Luft-; **~ drill** *n* Preßluft-hammer *m*.

pneumonia [nju:'məʊnɪə] *n* Lungenentzündung *f*.

poach [pəʊtʃ] *vt* (*COOK*) pochieren; (*game*) stehlen // *vi* (*steal*) wildern (*for* nach); **~ed** *a* (*egg*) verloren; **~er** *n* Wilddieb *m*; **~ing** *n* Wildern *nt*.

P.O. Box *n abbr of* **Post Office Box**.

pocket ['pɒkɪt] *n* Tasche *f*; (*of resistance*) (Widerstands)nest *nt* // *vt* ein-stecken; **to be out of ~** (*Brit*) kein Geld haben; **~book** *n* Taschenbuch *nt*; **~ knife** *n* Taschenmesser *nt*; **~ money** *n* Taschengeld *nt*.

pod [pɒd] *n* Hülse *f*; (*of peas also*) Schote *f*.

podgy ['pɒdʒɪ] *a* pummelig.

podiatrist [pɒ'di:ətrɪst] *n* (*US*) Fußpfleger(in *f*) *m*.

poem ['pəʊəm] *n* Gedicht *nt*.

poet ['pəʊɪt] *n* Dichter *m*, Poet *m*; **~ic** [pəʊ'etɪk] *a* poetisch, dichterisch; **~ laureate** *n* Hofdichter *m*; **~ry** *n* Poesie *f*; (*poems*) Gedichte *pl*.

poignant ['pɔɪnjənt] *a* (*touching*) er-greifend.

point [pɔɪnt] *n* Punkt *m* (*also in discussion, scoring*); (*spot also*) Stelle *f*; (*sharpened tip*) Spitze *f*; (*moment*) (Zeit)punkt *m*; (*purpose*) Zweck *m*; (*idea*) Argument *nt*; (*decimal*) Dezimal-stelle *f*; (*personal characteristic*) Seite *f* // *vt* zeigen mit; (*gun*) richten // *vi* zeigen; **~s** *pl* (*RAIL*) Weichen *pl*; **to be on the ~ of doing sth** drauf und dran sein, etw zu tun; **to make a ~ of** Wert darauf legen; **to get the ~** verstehen, worum es geht; **to come to the ~** zur Sa-che kommen; **there's no ~** (in doing) es hat keinen Sinn (etw zu tun); **~ out** *vt* hinweisen auf (+*acc*); **~ to** *vt* zeigen auf (+*acc*); **~-blank** *ad* (*at close range*) aus nächster Entfernung; (*bluntly*) unverblümt; **~ed** *a*, **~edly** *ad* spitz, scharf; (*fig*) gezielt; **~er** *n* Zeige-stock *m*; (*on dial*) Zeiger *m*; **~less** *a* sinnlos; **~ of view** *n* Stand- *or* Gesichtspunkt *m*.

poise [pɔɪz] *n* Haltung *f*; (*fig*) Gelassen-heit *f*.

poison ['pɔɪzn] *n* (*lit, fig*) Gift *nt* // *vt* vergiften; **~ing** *n* Vergiftung *f*; **~ous** *a* giftig, Gift-.

poke [pəʊk] *vt* stoßen, (*put*) stecken; (*fire*) schüren; (*hole*) bohren; **~ about**

vi herumstochern; (*nose around*) her-umwühlen.

poker ['pəʊkə*] *n* Schürhaken *m*; (*CARDS*) Poker *nt*; **~-faced** *a* undurch-dringlich.

poky ['pəʊkɪ] *a* eng.

Poland ['pəʊlənd] *n* Polen *nt*.

polar ['pəʊlə*] *a* Polar-, polar; **~ bear** *n* Eisbär *m*; **~ize** *vt* polarisieren.

Pole [pəʊl] *n* Pole *m*, Polin *f*.

pole [pəʊl] *n* Stange *f*, Pfosten *m*; (*flag~, telegraph ~ also*) Mast *m*; (*ELEC, GEOG*) Pol *m*; (*SPORT*) (*vaulting ~*) Stab *m*; (*ski ~*) Stock *m*; **~ bean** *n* (*US: runner bean*) Stangenbohne *f*; **~ vault** *n* Stabhochsprung *m*.

police [pə'li:s] *n* Polizei *f* // *vt* kon-trollieren; **~ car** *n* Polizeiwagen *m*; **~man** *n* Polizist *m*; **~ state** *n* Polizei-staat *m*; **~ station** *n* (Polizei)revier *nt*, Wache *f*; **~woman** *n* Polizistin *f*.

policy ['pɒlɪsɪ] *n* Politik *f*; (*insurance*) (Versicherungs)police *f*.

polio ['pəʊlɪəʊ] *n* (spinale) Kinderläh-mung *f*, Polio *f*.

Polish ['pəʊlɪʃ] *a* polnisch // *n* Polnisch *nt*.

polish ['pɒlɪʃ] *n* Politur *f*; (*for floor*) Wachs *nt*; (*for shoes*) Creme *f*; (*nail ~*) Lack *m*; (*shine*) Glanz *m*; (*fig*) Schliff *m* // *vt* polieren; (*shoes*) putzen; (*fig*) den letzten Schliff geben (+*dat*); **~ off** *vt* (*col: work*) erledigen; (*food*) wegputzen; (*drink*) hinunterschütten; **~ed** *a* glänzend (*also fig*); (*manners*) verfeinert.

polite [pə'laɪt] *a* höflich; **~ness** *n* Höflichkeit *f*.

politic ['pɒlɪtɪk] *a* (*prudent*) di-plomatisch; **~al** *a*, **~ally** *ad* [pə'lɪtɪkəl, -ɪ] politisch; **~ian** [pɒlɪ'tɪʃən] *n* Politiker *m*; **~s** *pl* Politik *f*.

polka ['pɒlkə] *n* Polka *f*; **~ dot** *n* Tupfen *m*.

poll [pəʊl] *n* Abstimmung *f*; (*in election*) Wahl *f*; (*votes cast*) Wahlbeteiligung *f*; (*opinion ~*) Umfrage *f* // *vt* (*votes*) erhalten.

pollination [pɒlɪ'neɪʃən] *n* Befruchtung *f*.

polling ['pəʊlɪŋ]: **~ booth** *n* (*Brit*) Wahlkabine *f*; **~ day** *n* (*Brit*) Wahltag *m*; **~ station** *n* (*Brit*) Wahllokal *nt*.

pollute [pə'lu:t] *vt* verschmutzen, ver-unreinigen; **pollution** [pə'lu:ʃən] *n* Ver-schmutzung *f*.

polo ['pəʊləʊ] *n* Polo *nt*; **~-neck** *n* Roll-kragen(pullover) *m*.

polystyrene [pɒlɪ'staɪri:n] *n* Styropor *nt*.

polytechnic [pɒlɪ'teknɪk] *n* technische Hochschule *f*.

polythene ['pɒlɪθi:n] *n* Plastik *nt*.

pomegranate ['pɒməgrænɪt] *n* Granatapfel *m*.

pommel ['pʌml] *vt* mit den Fäusten bearbeiten // *n* Sattelknopf *m*.

pompom ['pɒmpɒm] *n*, **pompon** ['pɒmpɒn] *n* Troddel *f*; Pompon *m*.

pompous ['pɒmpəs] *a* aufgeblasen; (*language*) geschwollen.

pond [pɒnd] *n* Teich *m*, Weiher *m*.

ponder ['pɒndə*] *vt* nachdenken über (+*acc*); **~ous** *a* schwerfällig.

pong [pɒŋ] *n* (*Brit col*) Mief *m*.

pontiff ['pɒntɪf] *n* Pontifex *m*.

pontificate [pɒn'tɪfɪkeɪt] *vi* (*fig*) geschwollen reden.

pontoon [pɒn'tuːn] *n* Ponton *m*; (*CARDS*) 17-und-4 *nt*.

pony ['pəʊnɪ] *n* Pony *nt*; **~tail** *n* Pferdeschwanz *m*; **~ trekking** *n* (*Brit*) Ponyreiten *nt*.

poodle ['puːdl] *n* Pudel *m*.

pool [puːl] *n* (*swimming* ~) Schwimmbad *nt*; (*private*) Swimming pool *m*; (*of spilt liquid, blood*) Lache *f*; (*fund*) (gemeinsame) Kasse *f*; (*billiards*) Poolspiel *nt* // *vt* (*money etc*) zusammenlegen; (*typing*) ~ Schreibzentrale *f*; (*football*) ~s Toto *nt*.

poor [puə*] *a* arm; (*not good*) schlecht; **the ~** *pl* die Armen *pl*; **~ly** *ad* schlecht; (*dressed*) ärmlich // *a* schlecht.

pop [pɒp] *n* Knall *m*; (*music*) Popmusik *f*; (*drink*) Limo(nade) *f*; (*US col*) Pa *m* // *vt* (*put*) stecken; (*balloon*) platzen lassen // *vi* knallen; **~ in** *vi* kurz vorbeigehen; **~ out** *vi* (*person*) kurz rausgehen; (*thing*) herausspringen; **~ up** *vi* auftauchen; **~ concert** *n* Popkonzert *nt*; **~corn** *n* Puffmais *m*.

pope [pəʊp] *n* Papst *m*.

poplar ['pɒplə*] *n* Pappel *f*.

poppy ['pɒpɪ] *n* Mohn *m*.

Popsicle ['pɒpsɪkl] *n* ® (*US*: *ice lolly*) Eis *nt* am Stiel.

populace ['pɒpjʊləs] *n* Volk *nt*.

popular ['pɒpjʊlə*] *a* beliebt, populär; (*of the people*) volkstümlich; (*widespread*) allgemein; **~ity** [pɒpjʊ'lærɪtɪ] *n* Beliebtheit *f*, Popularität *f*; **~ize** *vt* popularisieren; **~ly** *ad* allgemein, überall.

population [pɒpjʊ'leɪʃən] *n* Bevölkerung *f*; (*of town*) Einwohner *pl*.

populous ['pɒpjʊləs] *a* dicht besiedelt.

porcelain ['pɔːslɪn] *n* Porzellan *nt*.

porch [pɔːtʃ] *n* Vorbau *m*, Veranda *f*.

porcupine ['pɔːkjʊpaɪn] *n* Stachelschwein *nt*.

pore [pɔː*] *n* Pore *f*; **~ over** *vt* brüten über (+*dat*).

pork [pɔːk] *n* Schweinefleisch *nt*.

pornography [pɔː'nɒgrəfɪ] *n* Pornographie *f*.

porous ['pɔːrəs] *a* porös; (*skin*) porig.

porpoise ['pɔːpəs] *n* Tümmler *m*.

porridge ['pɒrɪdʒ] *n* Haferbrei *m*.

port [pɔːt] *n* Hafen *m*; (*town*) Hafenstadt

f; (*NAUT*: *left side*) Backbord *nt*; (*wine*) Portwein *m*; **~ of call** Anlaufhafen *m*.

portable ['pɔːtəbl] *a* tragbar.

portent ['pɔːtent] *n* schlimme(s) Vorzeichen *nt*.

porter ['pɔːtə*] *n* Pförtner(in *f*) *m*; (*for luggage*) (Gepäck)träger *m*.

portfolio [pɔːt'fəʊlɪəʊ] *n* (*case*) Mappe *f*; (*POL*) Geschäftsbereich *m*; (*FIN*) Portefeuille *nt*; (*of artist*) Kollektion *f*.

porthole ['pɔːthəʊl] *n* Bullauge *nt*.

portion ['pɔːʃən] *n* Teil *m*, Stück *nt*; (*of food*) Portion *f*.

portly ['pɔːtlɪ] *a* korpulent, beleibt.

portrait ['pɔːtrɪt] *n* Porträt *nt*.

portray [pɔː'treɪ] *vt* darstellen; **~al** *n* Darstellung *f*.

Portugal ['pɔːtjʊgəl] *n* Portugal *nt*.

Portuguese [pɔːtjʊ'giːz] *a* portugiesisch // *n*, *pl inv* Portugiese *m*, Portugiesin *f*; (*LING*) Portugiesisch *nt*.

pose [pəʊz] *n* Stellung *f*, Pose *f* (*also affectation*) // *vi* posieren // *vt* stellen.

posh [pɒʃ] *a* (*col*) (piek)fein.

position [pə'zɪʃən] *n* Stellung *f*; (*place*) Lage *f*; (*job*) Stelle *f*; (*attitude*) Standpunkt *m* // *vt* aufstellen.

positive ['pɒzɪtɪv] *a* positiv; (*convinced*) sicher; (*definite*) eindeutig.

posse ['pɒsɪ] *n* (*US*) Aufgebot *nt*.

possess [pə'zes] *vt* besitzen; **~ion** [pə'zeʃən] *n* Besitz *m*; **~ive** *a* besitzergreifend, eigensüchtig.

possibility [pɒsə'bɪlɪtɪ] *n* Möglichkeit *f*.

possible ['pɒsəbl] *a* möglich; **as big as ~** so groß wie möglich, möglichst groß.

possibly ['pɒsəblɪ] *ad* möglicherweise, vielleicht; **I cannot ~ come** ich kann unmöglich kommen.

post [pəʊst] *n* (*Brit*: *letters, delivery*) Post *f*; (*pole*) Pfosten *m*, Pfahl *m*; (*place of duty*) Posten *m*; (*job*) Stelle *f* // *vt* (*notice*) anschlagen; (*Brit*: *letters*) aufgeben; (*Brit*: *appoint*) versetzen; (*soldiers*) aufstellen; **~age** *n* Postgebühr *f*, Porto *nt*; **~al** *a* Post-; **~al order** *n* Postanweisung *f*; **~box** *n* (*Brit*) Briefkasten *m*; **~card** *n* Postkarte *f*; **~code** *n* (*Brit*) Postleitzahl *f*.

postdate [pəʊst'deɪt] *vt* (*cheque*) nachdatieren.

poster ['pəʊstə*] *n* Plakat *nt*, Poster *nt*.

poste restante ['pəʊst'restãːnt] *n* Aufbewahrungsstelle *f* für postlagernde Sendungen.

posterior [pɒs'tɪərɪə*] *n* (*col*) Hintern *m*.

posterity [pɒs'terɪtɪ] *n* Nachwelt *f*.

postgraduate ['pəʊst'grædjuɪt] *n* Weiterstudierende(r) *mf*.

postman ['pəʊstmən] *n* Briefträger *m*.

postmark ['pəʊstmɑːk] *n* Poststempel *m*.

postmaster ['pəʊstmɑːstə*] *n* Postmeister *m*.

post-mortem ['pəust'mɔ:təm] *n* Autopsie *f*.

post office ['pəustɔfis] *n* Postamt *nt*, Post *f* (*also organization*); **Post Office Box (P.O. Box)** *n* Postfach *nt* (Postf.).

postpone [pə'spəun] *vt* verschieben; **~ment** *n* Verschiebung *f*.

postscript ['pəusskrıpt] *n* Postskript *nt*; (*to affair*) Nachspiel *nt*.

postulate ['pɔstjuleıt] *vt* voraussetzen; (*maintain*) behaupten.

posture ['pɔstʃə*] *n* Haltung *f* // *vi* posieren.

postwar ['pəust'wɔ:*] *a* Nachkriegs-.

posy ['pəuzı] *n* Blumenstrauß *m*.

pot [pɔt] *n* Topf *m*; (*tea~*) Kanne *f*; (*col: marijuana*) Hasch *m* // *vt* (*plant*) eintopfen; **to go to ~** (*col: work, performance*) auf den Hund kommen.

potato [pə'teıtəu] *pl* **~es** *n* Kartoffel *f*; **~ peeler** *n* Kartoffelschäler *m*.

potent ['pəutənt] *a* stark; (*argument*) zwingend.

potential [pəu'tenʃəl] *a* potentiell // *n* Potential *nt*; **~ly** *ad* potentiell.

pothole ['pɔthəul] *n* (*Brit: underground*) Höhle *f*; (*in road*) Schlagloch *nt*.

potholing ['pɔthəulıŋ] *n* (*Brit*): **to go ~** Höhlen erforschen.

potion ['pəuʃən] *n* Trank *m*.

potluck ['pɔt'lʌk] *n*: **to take ~ with** sth etw auf gut Glück nehmen.

potshot ['pɔtʃɔt] *n*: **to take a ~ at** sth auf etw (*acc*) ballern.

potted ['pɔtıd] *a* (*food*) eingelegt, eingemacht; (*plant*) Topf-; (*fig: book, version*) konzentriert.

potter ['pɔtə*] *n* Töpfer *m* // *vi* herumhantieren; **~y** *n* Töpferwaren *pl*; (*place*) Töpferei *f*.

potty ['pɔtı] *a* (*col*) verrückt // *n* Töpfchen *nt*.

pouch [pəutʃ] *n* Beutel *m*.

pouf(fe) [pu:f] *n* Sitzkissen *nt*.

poultry ['pəultrı] *n* Geflügel *nt*.

pounce [pəuns] *vi* sich stürzen (*on* auf +*acc*) // *n* Sprung *m*, Satz *m*.

pound [paund] *n* (*FIN, weight*) Pfund *nt*; (*for cars, animals*) Auslösestelle *f*; (*for stray animals*) (Tier)asyl *nt* // *vt* (*zer*)stampfen // *vi* klopfen, hämmern; **~ sterling** *n* Pfund Sterling *nt*.

pour [pɔ:*] *vt* gießen, schütten // *vi* gießen; (*crowds etc*) strömen; **~ away or off** *vt* abgießen; **~ in** *vi* (*people*) hereinströmen; **~ out** *vi* (*people*) herausströmen // *vt* (*drink*) einschenken; **~ing** *a*: **~ing rain** strömende(r) Regen *m*.

pout [paut] *vi* schmollen.

poverty ['pɔvətı] *n* Armut *f*; **~-stricken** *a* verarmt, sehr arm.

powder ['paudə*] *n* Pulver *nt*; (*cosmetic*) Puder *m* // *vt* pulverisieren; **to ~ one's nose** sich (*dat*) die Nase

pudern; **~ compact** *n* Puderdose *f*; **~ed milk** *n* Milchpulver *nt*; **~ room** *n* Damentoilette *f*; **~y** *a* pulverig.

power [pauə*] *n* Macht *f* (*also POL*); (*ability*) Fähigkeit *f*; (*strength*) Stärke *f*; (*MATH*) Potenz *f*; (*ELEC*) Strom *m* // *vt* betreiben, antreiben; **to be in ~** (*POL etc*) an der Macht sein; **~ cut**, (*US*) **~ failure** *n* Stromausfall *m*; **~ed** *a*: **~ed by** betrieben mit; **~ful** *a* (*person*) mächtig; (*engine, government*) stark; **~less** *a* machtlos; **~ point** *n* (*Brit*) elektrische(r) Anschluß *m*; **~ station** *n* Elektrizitätswerk *nt*.

p.p. *abbr* (= *per procurationem*): **~ J. Smith** i.A. J. Smith.

PR *abbr of* **public relations**.

practicable ['præktıkəbl] *a* durchführbar.

practical *a*, **~ly** *ad* ['præktıkəl, -ı] praktisch; **~ity** [-'kælıtı] *n* (*of person*) praktische Veranlagung *f*; (*of situation etc*) Durchführbarkeit *f*; **~ joke** *n* Streich *m*.

practice ['præktıs] *n* Übung *f*; (*reality*) Praxis *f*; (*custom*) Brauch *m*; (*in business*) Usus *m*; (*doctor's, lawyer's*) Praxis *f* // *vti* (*US*) = **practise**; **in ~** (*in reality*) in der Praxis; **out of ~** außer Übung.

practise, (*US*) **practice** ['præktıs] *vt* üben; (*profession*) ausüben // *vi* (*sich*) üben; (*doctor, lawyer*) praktizieren.

practising, (*US*) **practicing** ['præktısıŋ] *a* praktizierend; (*Christian etc*) aktiv.

practitioner [præk'tıʃənə*] *n* praktische(r) Arzt *m*.

pragmatic [præg'mætık] *a* pragmatisch.

prairie ['preərı] *n* Prärie *f*, Steppe *f*.

praise [preız] *n* Lob *nt* // *vt* loben; **~worthy** *a* lobenswert.

pram [præm] *n* (*Brit*) Kinderwagen *m*.

prance [prɑ:ns] *vi* (*horse*) tänzeln; (*person*) stolzieren; (*gaily*) herumhüpfen.

prank [præŋk] *n* Streich *m*.

prattle ['prætl] *vi* schwatzen, plappern.

prawn [prɔ:n] *n* Garnele *f*; Krabbe *f*.

pray [preı] *vi* beten; **~er** [preə*] *n* Gebet *nt*.

preach [pri:tʃ] *vi* predigen; **~er** *n* Prediger *m*.

preamble [pri:'æmbl] *n* Einleitung *f*.

precarious [prı'keərıəs] *a* prekär, unsicher.

precaution [prı'kɔ:ʃən] *n* (Vorsichts)maßnahme *f*.

precede [prı'si:d] *vti* vorausgehen (+*dat*); **~nce** ['presıdəns] *n* Vorrang *m*; **~nt** ['presıdənt] *n* Präzedenzfall *m*.

preceding [prı'si:dıŋ] *a* vorhergehend.

precept ['pri:sept] *n* Gebot *nt*, Regel *f*.

precinct ['pri:sıŋkt] *n* (*US: district*) Bezirk *m*; (*round building*): **~s** Gelände *nt*; (*area, environs*): **~s** Umgebung *f*;

pedestrian ~ Fußgängerzone *f*; shopping ~ Geschäftsviertel *nt*.

precious ['preʃəs] *a* kostbar, wertvoll; (*affected*) preziös, geziert.

precipice ['presɪpɪs] *n* Abgrund *m*.

precipitate [prɪ'sɪpɪtɪt] *a* überstürzt, übereilt // *vt* [prɪ'sɪpɪteɪt] hinunterstürzen; (*events*) heraufbeschwören.

precise *a*, ~**ly** *ad* [prɪ'saɪs, -lɪ] genau, präzis; **precision** [-'sɪʒən] *n* Präzision *f*.

preclude [prɪ'kluːd] *vt* ausschließen.

precocious [prɪ'kəuʃəs] *a* frühreif.

preconceived ['priːkən'siːvd] *a* (*idea*) vorgefaßt.

precondition ['priːkən'dɪʃən] *n* Vorbedingung *f*, Voraussetzung *f*.

precursor [priː'kɜːsə*] *n* Vorläufer *m*.

predator ['predətə*] *n* Raubtier *nt*.

predecessor ['priːdɪsesə*] *n* Vorgänger *m*.

predestination [priːdestɪ'neɪʃən] *n* Vorherbestimmung *f*.

predicament [prɪ'dɪkəmənt] *n* mißliche Lage *f*.

predict [prɪ'dɪkt] *vt* voraussagen; ~**able** *a* vorhersagbar; ~**ion** [prɪ'dɪkʃən] *n* Voraussage *f*.

predominantly [prɪ'dɒmɪnəntlɪ] *ad* überwiegend, hauptsächlich.

predominate [prɪ'dɒmɪneɪt] *vi* vorherrschen; (*fig also*) überwiegen.

pre-eminent [priː'emɪnənt] *a* hervorragend, herausragend.

pre-empt [priː'empt] *vt* (*action, decision*) vorwegnehmen.

preen [priːn] *vt* putzen; to ~ o.s. (*person*) sich herausputzen.

prefab ['priːfæb] *n* Fertighaus *nt*.

prefabricated ['priːfæbrɪkeɪtɪd] *a* vorgefertigt, Fertig-.

preface ['prefɪs] *n* Vorwort *nt*.

prefect ['priːfekt] *n* Präfekt *m*; (*SCH*) Aufsichtsschüler(in *f*) *m*.

prefer [prɪ'fɜː*] *vt* vorziehen, lieber mögen; to ~ to do sth etw lieber tun; ~**able** ['prefərəbl] *a* vorzuziehen(d) (*to dat*); ~**ably** ['prefərəblɪ] *ad* vorzugsweise, am liebsten; ~**ence** ['prefərəns] *n* Präferenz *f*, Vorzug *m*; ~**ential** [prefə'renʃəl] *a* bevorzugt, Vorzugs-.

prefix ['priːfɪks] *n* Vorsilbe *f*, Präfix *nt*.

pregnancy ['pregnənsɪ] *n* Schwangerschaft *f*.

pregnant ['pregnənt] *a* schwanger.

prejudice ['predʒʊdɪs] *n* (*opinion*) Vorurteil *nt*; (*bias*) Voreingenommenheit *f*; (*harm*) Schaden *m* // *vt* beeinträchtigen; ~**d** *a* (*person*) voreingenommen.

preliminary [prɪ'lɪmɪnərɪ] *a* einleitend, Vor-.

prelude ['preljuːd] *n* Vorspiel *nt*; (*fig also*) Auftakt *m*.

premarital ['priː'mærɪtl] *a* vorehelich.

premature ['premətʃʊə*] *a* vorzeitig, verfrüht; (*birth*) Früh-.

premeditated [priː'medɪteɪtɪd] *a* geplant; (*murder*) vorsätzlich.

premier ['premɪə*] *a* erste(r, s) // *n* Premier *m*.

première [premɪ'ɛə*] *n* Premiere *f*; Uraufführung *f*.

premise ['premɪs] *n* Voraussetzung *f*, Prämisse *f*; ~**s** *pl* Räumlichkeiten *pl*; (*grounds*) Gelände *nt*; on the ~s im Hause.

premium ['priːmɪəm] *n* Prämie *f*; to be at a ~ über pari stehen; ~ **bond** *n* (*Brit*) Prämienanleihe *f*.

premonition [premə'nɪʃən] *n* Vorahnung *f*.

preoccupation [priːɒkjʊ'peɪʃən] *n* Sorge *f*.

preoccupied [priː'ɒkjʊpaɪd] *a* (*look*) geistesabwesend.

prep [prep] *n* (*SCH: study*) Hausaufgabe *f*; ~ **school** *n* = **preparatory school**.

prepaid [priː'peɪd] *a* vorausbezahlt; (*letter*) frankiert.

preparation ['prepə'reɪʃən] *n* Vorbereitung *f*.

preparatory [prɪ'pærətərɪ] *a* Vor(bereitungs)-; ~ **school** *n* private Vorbereitungsschule für die Public School in Großbritannien oder die Hochschule in den USA.

prepare [prɪ'pɛə*] *vt* vorbereiten (*for* auf +*acc*) // *vi* sich vorbereiten; to be ~d to ... bereit sein zu ...

preponderance [prɪ'pɒndərəns] *n* Übergewicht *nt*.

preposition [prepə'zɪʃən] *n* Präposition *f*, Verhältniswort *nt*.

preposterous [prɪ'pɒstərəs] *a* absurd.

prerequisite [priː'rekwɪzɪt] *n* (unerläßliche) Voraussetzung *f*.

prerogative [prɪ'rɒgətɪv] *n* Vorrecht *nt*.

Presbyterian [prezbɪ'tɪərɪən] *a* presbyterianisch // *n* Presbyterier(in *f*) *m*.

preschool ['priːskuːl] *a* Vorschul-.

prescribe [prɪs'kraɪb] *vt* vorschreiben; (*MED*) verschreiben.

prescription [prɪs'krɪpʃən] *n* (*MED*) Rezept *nt*.

presence ['prezns] *n* Gegenwart *f*; ~ **of mind** *n* Geistesgegenwart *f*.

present ['preznt] *a* (*here*) anwesend; (*current*) gegenwärtig *n* Gegenwart *f*; (*gift*) Geschenk *nt* // *vt* [prɪ'zent] vorlegen; (*introduce*) vorstellen; (*show*) zeigen; (*give*): to ~ sb with sth jdm etw überreichen; at ~ im Augenblick; ~**able** [prɪ'zentəbl] *a* präsentabel; ~**ation** *n* Überreichung *f*; ~-**day** *a* heutig; ~**er** *n* (*RADIO, TV*) Moderator(in *f*) *m*; ~**ly** *ad* bald; (*at present*) im Augenblick.

preservation [prezə'veɪʃən] *n* Erhaltung *f*.

preservative [prɪ'zɜːvətɪv] n
Konservierungsmittel nt.

preserve [prɪ'zɜːv] vt erhalten; (food)
einmachen // n (jam) Eingemachte(s)
nt; (hunting) Schutzgebiet nt.

preside [prɪ'zaɪd] vi den Vorsitz haben.

presidency ['prezɪdənsɪ] n (POL)
Präsidentschaft f.

president ['prezɪdənt] n Präsident m;
~**ial** [prezɪ'denʃəl] a Präsidenten-;
(election) Präsidentschafts-; (system)
Präsidial-.

press [pres] n Presse f; (printing house)
Druckerei f // vt drücken; (iron) bügeln;
(urge) (be)drängen // vi (push) drücken;
to be ~ed for time unter Zeitdruck
stehen; to ~ for sth drängen auf etw
(acc); ~ on vi vorwärtsdrängen; ~
agency n Presseagentur f; ~ **conference** n Pressekonferenz f; ~**ing** a
dringend; ~**-stud** n (Brit) Druckknopf
m; ~**-up** n (Brit) Liegestütz m.

pressure [preʃə*] n Druck m; ~ **cooker** n Schnellkochtopf m; ~ **gauge** n
Druckmesser m.

pressurized ['preʃəraɪzd] a Druck-.

prestigious [pres'tɪdʒəs] a Prestige-.

presumably [prɪ'zjuːməblɪ] ad vermutlich.

presume [prɪ'zjuːm] vti annehmen; to ~
to do sth sich erlauben, etw zu tun.

presumption [prɪ'zʌmpʃən] n Annahme
f.

presumptuous [prɪ'zʌmptjuəs] a an-
maßend.

presuppose [priːsə'pəʊz] vt voraussetzen.

pretence, (US) **pretense** [prɪ'tens] n
Vorgabe f, Vortäuschung f; (false claim)
Vorwand m.

pretend [prɪ'tend] vt vorgeben, so tun
als ob ... // vi so tun; to ~ to sth Anspruch erheben auf etw (acc).

pretense [prɪ'tens] n (US) = **pretence.**

pretension [prɪ'tenʃən] n Anspruch m;
(impudent claim) Anmaßung f.

pretentious [prɪ'tenʃəs] a angeberisch.

pretext ['priːtekst] n Vorwand m.

pretty ['prɪtɪ] a hübsch // ad (col) ganz
schön.

prevail [prɪ'veɪl] vi siegen (against, over
über +acc); (custom) vorherrschen; to
~ (up)on sb to do sth jdn dazu bewegen,
etw zu tun; ~**ing** a vorherrschend.

prevalent ['prevələnt] a vorherrschend.

prevent [prɪ'vent] vt (stop) verhindern,
verhüten; to ~ sb from doing sth jdn
(daran) hindern, etw zu tun; ~**ative** n
Vorbeugungsmittel nt; ~**ion**
[prɪ'venʃən] n Verhütung f, Schutz m (of
gegen); ~**ive** a vorbeugend, Schutz-.

preview ['priːvjuː] n private Vorauffüh-
rung f; (trailer) Vorschau f.

previous ['priːvɪəs] a früher, vorherig;

~**ly** ad früher.

prewar ['priː'wɔː*] a Vorkriegs-.

prey [preɪ] n Beute f; ~ **on** vt Jagd machen auf (+acc); it was ~ing on his
mind es quälte sein Gewissen.

price [praɪs] n Preis m; (value) Wert m
// vt (label) auszeichnen; ~**less** a (lit,
fig) unbezahlbar; ~ **list** n Preisliste f.

prick [prɪk] n Stich m // vti stechen; to ~
up one's ears die Ohren spitzen.

prickle ['prɪkl] n Stachel m, Dorn m.

prickly ['prɪklɪ] a stachelig; (fig: person)
reizbar; ~ **heat** n Hitzebläschen pl.

pride [praɪd] n Stolz m; (arrogance)
Hochmut m // vt: to ~ o.s. on sth auf etw
(acc) stolz sein.

priest [priːst] n Priester m; ~**ess** n
Priesterin f; ~**hood** n Priesteramt nt.

prig [prɪg] n Selbstgefällige(r) mf.

prim [prɪm] a prüde.

primarily ['praɪmərɪlɪ] ad vorwiegend.

primary ['praɪmərɪ] a (main) Haupt-;
(SCH) Grund-; ~ **school** n (Brit)
Grundschule f.

prime [praɪm] a erste(r, s); (excellent)
erstklassig // vt vorbereiten; (gun)
laden; in the ~ of life in der Blüte der
Jahre; **P~ Minister (P.M.)** n
Premierminister m, Ministerpräsident
m; ~**r** n Fibel f.

primeval [praɪ'miːvəl] a vorzeitlich;
(forests) Ur-.

primitive ['prɪmɪtɪv] a primitiv.

primrose ['prɪmrəʊz] n (gelbe) Primel
f.

primus (stove) ['praɪməs (stəʊv)] n ®
(Brit) Primuskocher m.

prince [prɪns] n Prinz m; (ruler) Fürst
m; **princess** [prɪn'ses] n Prinzessin f;
Fürstin f.

principal ['prɪnsɪpəl] a Haupt- // n (SCH)
(Schul)direktor m, Rektor m; (money)
(Grund)kapital nt; ~**ity** [prɪnsɪ'pælɪtɪ] n
Fürstentum nt.

principle ['prɪnsɪpl] n Grundsatz m,
Prinzip nt; in ~ im Prinzip; on ~ aus
Prinzip, prinzipiell.

print [prɪnt] n Druck m; (made by feet,
fingers) Abdruck m; (PHOT) Abzug m //
vt drucken; (name) in Druckbuchstaben
schreiben; (Photo) abziehen; out of ~
vergriffen; ~**ed matter** n Drucksache
f; ~**er** n Drucker m; ~**ing** n Drucken
nt; (of photos) Abziehen nt; ~**out** n
(COMPUT) Ausdruck m.

prior ['praɪə*] a früher // n Prior m; ~ to
sth vor etw (dat); ~ to going abroad,
she had ... bevor sie ins Ausland ging,
hatte sie ...

priority [praɪ'ɒrɪtɪ] n Vorrang m;
Priorität f.

prise [praɪz] vt: to ~ open aufbrechen.

prison ['prɪzn] n Gefängnis nt // a
Gefängnis-; (system etc) Strafvollzugs-;
~**er** n Gefangene(r) mf.

pristine ['prɪstiːn] a makellos.

privacy ['prɪvəsɪ] n Ungestörtheit f, Ruhe f; Privatleben nt.

private ['praɪvɪt] a privat, Privat-; (secret) vertraulich, geheim // n einfache(r) Soldat m; '~' (on envelope) persönlich; in ~ privat, unter vier Augen; ~ **enterprise** n Privatunternehmen nt; ~ **eye** n Privatdetektiv m; ~**ly** ad privat; vertraulich, geheim; ~ **property** n Privatbesitz m; ~ **school** n Privatschule f; **privatize** vt privatisieren.

privet ['prɪvɪt] n Liguster m.

privilege ['prɪvɪlɪdʒ] n Privileg nt; ~d a bevorzugt, privilegiert.

privy ['prɪvɪ] a geheim, privat; **P~ Council** n Geheime(r) Staatsrat m.

prize [praɪz] n Preis m // a (example) erstklassig; (idiot) Voll- // vt (hoch)schätzen; ~ **giving** n Preisverteilung f; ~**winner** n Preisträger(in f) m.

pro [prəʊ] n (professional) Profi m; the ~s and cons pl das Für und Wider.

probability [prɒbə'bɪlɪtɪ] n Wahrscheinlichkeit f.

probable a, **probably** ad ['prɒbəbl, -blɪ] wahrscheinlich.

probation [prə'beɪʃən] n Probe(zeit) f; (JUR) Bewährung f; on ~ auf Probe; auf Bewährung.

probe [prəʊb] n Sonde f; (enquiry) Untersuchung f // vti erforschen.

problem ['prɒbləm] n Problem nt; ~**atic** [prɒblɪ'mætɪk] a problematisch.

procedure [prə'siːdʒə*] n Verfahren nt.

proceed [prə'siːd] vi (advance) vorrücken; (start) anfangen; (carry on) fortfahren; (set about) vorgehen; ~**ings** pl Verfahren nt; ~**s** ['prəʊsiːdz] pl Erlös m.

process ['prəʊses] n Prozeß m; (method) Verfahren nt // vt bearbeiten; (food) verarbeiten; (film) entwickeln; ~**ing** n (PHOT) Entwickeln nt.

procession [prə'seʃən] n Prozession f, Umzug m; funeral ~ Trauerprozession f.

proclaim [prə'kleɪm] vt verkünden.

proclamation [prɒklə'meɪʃən] n Verkündung f.

procrastinate [prəʊ'kræstɪneɪt] vi zaudern.

procreation [prəʊkrɪ'eɪʃən] n (Er)zeugung f.

procure [prə'kjʊə*] vt beschaffen.

prod [prɒd] vt stoßen // n Stoß m.

prodigal ['prɒdɪgəl] a verschwenderisch (of mit).

prodigious [prə'dɪdʒəs] a gewaltig; (wonderful) wunderbar.

prodigy ['prɒdɪdʒɪ] n Wunder nt.

produce ['prɒdjuːs] n (AGR) (Boden)produkte pl, (Natur)erzeugnis nt // vt [prə'djuːs] herstellen, produzieren; (cause) hervorrufen; (farmer) erzeugen;

(yield) liefern, bringen; (play) inszenieren; ~**r** n Erzeuger m, Hersteller m, Produzent m (also CINE).

product ['prɒdʌkt] n Produkt nt, Erzeugnis nt.

production [prə'dʌkʃən] n Produktion f, Herstellung f; (thing) Erzeugnis nt, Produkt nt; (THEAT) Inszenierung f; ~ **line** n Fließband nt.

productive [prə'dʌktɪv] a produktiv; (fertile) ertragreich, fruchtbar.

productivity [prɒdʌk'tɪvɪtɪ] n Produktivität f.

profess [prə'fes] vt bekennen; (show) zeigen; (claim to be) vorgeben.

profession [prə'feʃən] n Beruf m; (declaration) Bekenntnis nt; ~**al** [prə'feʃənl] n Fachmann m; (SPORT) Berufsspieler(in f) m // a (expert) fachlich; (player) professionell.

professor [prə'fesə*] n Professor m.

proficiency [prə'fɪʃənsɪ] n Können nt.

proficient [prə'fɪʃənt] a fähig.

profile ['prəʊfaɪl] n Profil nt; (fig: report) Kurzbiographie f.

profit ['prɒfɪt] n Gewinn m // vi profitieren (by, from von); ~**ability** [prɒfɪtə'bɪlɪtɪ] n Rentabilität f; ~**able** a einträglich, rentabel.

profiteering [prɒfɪ'tɪərɪŋ] n Profitmacherei f.

profound [prə'faʊnd] a tief.

profuse [prə'fjuːs] a überreich; ~**ly** ad überschwenglich; (sweat) reichlich.

profusion [prə'fjuːʒən] n Überfülle f, Überfluß m (of an +dat).

progeny ['prɒdʒɪnɪ] n Nachkommenschaft f.

programme, (US) **program** ['prəʊgræm] n Programm nt // vt planen; (computer) programmieren.

programmer ['prəʊgræmə*] n Programmierer(in f) m.

programming, (US) **programing** ['prəʊgræmɪŋ] n Programmieren nt.

progress ['prəʊgres] n Fortschritt m // vi [prə'gres] fortschreiten, weitergehen; in ~ im Gang; ~**ion** [prə'greʃən] n Folge f; ~**ive** [prə'gresɪv] a fortschrittlich, progressiv.

prohibit [prə'hɪbɪt] vt verbieten; to ~ sb from doing sth jdm untersagen, etw zu tun; ~**ion** [prəʊɪ'bɪʃən] n Verbot nt; (US) Alkoholverbot nt, Prohibition f; ~**ive** a (price etc) unerschwinglich.

project ['prɒdʒekt] n Projekt nt // v [prə'dʒekt] vt vorausplanen; (film etc) projizieren; (personality, voice) zum Tragen bringen // vi (stick out) hervorragen, (her)vortreten.

projectile [prə'dʒektaɪl] n Geschoß nt.

projection [prə'dʒekʃən] n Projektion f; (sth prominent) Vorsprung m.

projector [prə'dʒektə*] n Projektor m.

proletariat [prəʊlə'tɛərɪət] n Proletariat

nt.

proliferate [prə'lɪfəreɪt] *vi* sich vermehren.

prolific [prə'lɪfɪk] *a* fruchtbar; *(author etc)* produktiv.

prologue ['prəʊlɒg] *n* Prolog *m*; *(event)* Vorspiel *nt.*

prolong [prə'lɒŋ] *vt* verlängern.

prom [prɒm] *n abbr of* **promenade** *and* **promenade concert** *// n* (US: *college ball)* Studentenball *m.*

promenade [prɒmɪ'nɑːd] *n* Promenade *f*; ~ **concert** *n* Promenadenkonzert *nt.*

prominence ['prɒmɪnəns] *n* (große) Bedeutung *f.*

prominent ['prɒmɪnənt] *a* bedeutend; *(politician)* prominent; *(easily seen)* herausragend, auffallend.

promiscuous [prə'mɪskjʊəs] *a* lose.

promise ['prɒmɪs] *n* Versprechen *nt*; *(hope)* Aussicht *f (of* auf + *acc)* // *vti* versprechen.

promising ['prɒmɪsɪŋ] *a* vielversprechend.

promontory ['prɒməntrɪ] *n* Vorsprung *m.*

promote [prə'məʊt] *vt* befördern; *(help on)* fördern, unterstützen; ~**r** *n (in sport, entertainment)* Veranstalter *m*; *(for charity etc)* Organisator *m.*

promotion [prə'məʊʃən] *n (in rank)* Beförderung *f*; *(furtherance)* Förderung *f*; *(COMM)* Werbung *f (of* für).

prompt [prɒmpt] *a* prompt, schnell // *ad (punctually)* genau // *n (COMPUT)* Meldung *f* // *vt* veranlassen; *(THEAT)* soufflieren (+ *dat)*; **to ~ sb to do sth** jdn dazu veranlassen, etw zu tun; ~**ly** *ad* sofort.

prone [prəʊn] *a* hingestreckt; **to be ~ to** sth zu etw neigen.

prong [prɒŋ] *n* Zinke *f.*

pronoun ['prəʊnaʊn] *n* Fürwort *nt.*

pronounce [prə'naʊns] *vt* aussprechen; *(JUR)* verkünden // *vi (give an opinion)* sich äußern *(on* zu); ~**d** *a* ausgesprochen; ~**ment** *n* Erklärung *f.*

pronunciation [prənʌnsɪ'eɪʃən] *n* Aussprache *f.*

proof [pruːf] *n* Beweis *m*; *(PRINT)* Korrekturfahne *f*; *(of alcohol)* Alkoholgehalt *m* // *a* sicher.

prop [prɒp] *n* Stütze *f (also fig)*; *(THEAT)* Requisit *nt* // *vt (also:* ~ **up)** (ab)stützen.

propaganda [prɒpə'gændə] *n* Propaganda *f.*

propagate ['prɒpəgeɪt] *vt* fortpflanzen; *(news)* propagieren, verbreiten.

propel [prə'pel] *vt* (an)treiben; ~**ler** *n* Propeller *m*; ~**ling pencil** *n* Drehbleistift *m.*

propensity [prə'pensɪtɪ] *n* Tendenz *f.*

proper ['prɒpə*] *a* richtig; *(seemly)* schicklich; ~**ly** *ad* richtig; ~ **noun** *n*

Eigenname *m.*

property ['prɒpətɪ] *n* Eigentum *nt*; *(quality)* Eigenschaft *f*; *(land)* Grundbesitz *m*; ~ **owner** *n* Grundbesitzer *m.*

prophecy ['prɒfɪsɪ] *n* Prophezeiung *f.*

prophesy ['prɒfɪsaɪ] *vt* prophezeien.

prophet ['prɒfɪt] *n* Prophet *m.*

proportion [prə'pɔːʃən] *n* Verhältnis *nt*; *(share)* Teil *m* // *vt* abstimmen *(to* auf +*acc)*; ~**al** *a* proportional; ~**ate** *a* verhältnismäßig.

proposal [prə'pəʊzl] *n* Vorschlag *m*; *(of marriage)* Heiratsantrag *m.*

propose [prə'pəʊz] *vt* vorschlagen; *(toast)* ausbringen // *vi (offer marriage)* einen Heiratsantrag machen; **to ~ to do** sth beabsichtigen, etw zu tun.

proposition [prɒpə'zɪʃən] *n* Angebot *nt*; *(statement)* Satz *m.*

proprietor [prə'praɪətə*] *n* Besitzer *m*, Eigentümer *m.*

propriety [prə'praɪətɪ] *n* Anstand *m.*

pro rata [prəʊ'rɑːtə] *ad* anteilmäßig.

prose [prəʊz] *n* Prosa *f.*

prosecute ['prɒsɪkjuːt] *vt* (strafrechtlich) verfolgen.

prosecution [prɒsɪ'kjuːʃən] *n (JUR)* strafrechtliche Verfolgung *f*; *(party)* Anklage *f.*

prosecutor ['prɒsɪkjuːtə*] *n* Vertreter *m* der Anklage; **Public P~** *n* Staatsanwalt *m.*

prospect ['prɒspekt] *n* Aussicht *f* // *v* [prəs'pekt] *vt* auf Bodenschätze hin untersuchen // *vi* suchen *(for* nach); ~**ing** [prəs'pektɪŋ] *n (for minerals)* Suche *f*; ~**ive** [prəs'pektɪv] *a* möglich; ~**or** [prəs'pektə*] *n* (Gold)sucher *m*; ~**us** [prəs'pektəs] *n* (Werbe)prospekt *m.*

prosper ['prɒspə*] *vi* blühen, gedeihen; *(person)* erfolgreich sein; ~**ity** [prɒs'perɪtɪ] *n* Wohlstand *m*; ~**ous** *a* wohlhabend, reich.

prostitute ['prɒstɪtjuːt] *n* Prostituierte *f.*

prostrate ['prɒstreɪt] *a* ausgestreckt (liegend); ~ **with grief/exhaustion** *vor* Schmerz/Erschöpfung übermannt.

protagonist [prəʊ'tægənɪst] *n* Hauptperson *f*, Held *m.*

protect [prə'tekt] *vt* (be)schützen; ~**ion** [prə'tekʃən] *n* Schutz *m*; ~**ive** *a* Schutz-, (be)schützend.

protégé ['prɒteʒeɪ] *n* Schützling *m.*

protein ['prəʊtiːn] *n* Protein *nt*, Eiweiß *nt.*

protest ['prəʊtest] *n* Protest *m* // *v* [prə'test] *vi* protestieren *(against* gegen) // *vt (affirm)* beteuern.

Protestant ['prɒtɪstənt] *a* protestantisch // *n* Protestant(in *f*) *m.*

protracted [prə'træktɪd] *a* sich hinziehend.

protrude [prə'truːd] *vi* (her)vorstehen.

proud [praʊd] *a* stolz *(of* auf +*acc)*.

prove [pruːv] *vt* beweisen // *vi*: to ~ (to be) correct sich als richtig erweisen; to ~ o.s. sich bewähren.

proverb ['prɒvɜːb] *n* Sprichwort *nt*; ~ial [prə'vɜːbɪəl] *a* sprichwörtlich.

provide [prə'vaɪd] *vt* versehen; (*supply*) besorgen; to ~ sb with sth jdn mit etw versorgen; ~ **for** *vt* sorgen für; (*emergency*) Vorkehrungen treffen für; ~d (that) *cj* vorausgesetzt (, daß); **Providence** ['prɒvɪdəns] *n* die Vorsehung.

providing [prə'vaɪdɪŋ] *cj* vorausgesetzt (, daß).

province ['prɒvɪns] *n* Provinz *f*; (*division of work*) Bereich *m*.

provincial [prə'vɪnʃəl] *a* provinziell, Provinz-.

provision [prə'vɪʒən] *n* Vorkehrung *f*; (*condition*) Bestimmung *f*; ~s *pl* (*food*) Vorräte *pl*, Proviant *m*; ~al *a* provisorisch.

proviso [prə'vaɪzəu] *n* Bedingung *f*.

provoke [prə'vəuk] *vt* provozieren; (*cause*) hervorrufen.

prow [prau] *n* Bug *m*.

prowess ['prauɛs] *n* überragende(s) Können *nt*.

prowl [praul] *vi* herumstreichen; (*animal*) schleichen // *n*: on the ~ umherstreifend; ~er *n* Eindringling *m*.

proximity [prɒk'sɪmɪtɪ] *n* Nähe *f*.

proxy ['prɒksɪ] *n* (Stell)vertreter *m*; (*document*) Vollmacht *f*; by ~ durch einen Stellvertreter.

prudence ['pruːdəns] *n* Umsicht *f*.

prudent ['pruːdənt] *a* klug, umsichtig.

prudish ['pruːdɪʃ] *a* prüde.

prune [pruːn] *n* Backpflaume *f* // *vt* ausputzen; (*fig*) zurechtstutzen.

pry [praɪ] *vi* seine Nase stecken (*into* in +*acc*).

PS *abbr* (= *postscript*) PS.

pseudo- ['sjuːdəu] *pref* Pseudo-; **pseudonym** ['sjuːdənɪm] *n* Pseudonym *nt*, Deckname *m*.

psychiatrist [saɪ'kaɪətrɪst] *n* Psychiater *m*.

psychic ['saɪkɪk] *a* (*also:* ~al) übersinnlich; (*person*) paranormal begabt.

psychoanalyse, (*US*) **psychoanalyze** [saɪkəu'ænəlaɪz] *vt* psychoanalytisch behandeln.

psychoanalyst [saɪkəu'ænəlɪst] *n* Psychoanalytiker(in *f*) *m*.

psychological [saɪkə'lɒdʒɪkəl] *a* psychologisch.

psychologist [saɪ'kɒlədʒɪst] *n* Psychologe *m*, Psychologin *f*.

psychology [saɪ'kɒlədʒɪ] *n* Psychologie *f*.

PTO *abbr* (= *please turn over*).

pub [pʌb] *n* *abbr* (= *public house*) Kneipe *f*.

pubic ['pjuːbɪk] *a* Scham-.

public ['pʌblɪk] *a* öffentlich // *n* (*also:*

general ~) Öffentlichkeit *f*; in ~ in der Öffentlichkeit; ~ **address system (P.A.)** *n* Lautsprecheranlage *f*; ~**ly** *ad* öffentlich.

publican ['pʌblɪkən] *n* Wirt *m*.

publication [pʌblɪ'keɪʃən] *n* Veröffentlichung *f*.

public: ~ **company** *n* Aktiengesellschaft *f*; ~ **convenience** *n* (*Brit*) öffentliche Toiletten *pl*; ~ **holiday** *n* gesetzliche(r) Feiertag *m*; ~ **house** *n* (*Brit*) Lokal *nt*, Kneipe *f*.

publicity [pʌb'lɪsɪtɪ] *n* Publicity *f*, Werbung *f*.

publicize ['pʌblɪsaɪz] *vt* bekannt machen; (*advertise*) Publicity machen für.

public: ~ **opinion** *n* öffentliche Meinung *f*; ~ **relations (PR)** *pl* Public Relations *pl*; ~ **school** *n* (*Brit*) Privatschule *f*; (*US*) staatliche Schule *f*; ~-**spirited** *a* mit Gemeinschaftssinn; ~ **transport** *n* öffentliche Verkehrsmittel *pl*.

publish ['pʌblɪʃ] *vt* veröffentlichen; (*event*) bekanntgeben; ~**er** *n* Verleger *m*; ~**ing** *n* (*business*) Verlagswesen *nt*.

puce [pjuːs] *a* violettbraun.

pucker ['pʌkə*] *vt* (*face*) verziehen; (*lips*) kräuseln.

pudding ['pudɪŋ] *n* (*Brit:* *course*) Nachtisch *m*; Pudding *m*; **black** ~ ≈ Blutwurst *f*.

puddle ['pʌdl] *n* Pfütze *f*.

puff [pʌf] *n* (*of wind etc*) Stoß *m*; (*cosmetic*) Puderquaste *f* // *vt* blasen, pusten; (*pipe*) paffen // *vi* keuchen, schnaufen; (*smoke*) paffen; to ~ out smoke Rauch ausstoßen; ~ed *a* (*col:* *out of breath*) außer Puste.

puff pastry, (*US*) **puff paste** ['pʌf'peɪstrɪ, 'pʌf'peɪst] *n* Blätterteig *m*.

puffy ['pʌfɪ] *a* aufgedunsen.

pull [pul] *n* Ruck *m*; (*influence*) Beziehung *f* // *vt* ziehen; (*trigger*) abdrücken // *vi* ziehen; to ~ sb's leg jdn auf den Arm nehmen; to ~ to pieces (*lit*) in Stücke reißen; (*fig*) verreißen; to ~ one's punches sich zurückhalten; to ~ one's weight sich in die Riemen legen; to ~ o.s. together sich zusammenreißen; to ~ **apart** *vt* (*break*) zerreißen; (*dismantle*) auseinandernehmen; (*fighters*) trennen; ~ **down** *vt* (*house*) abreißen; ~ **in** *vi* hineinfahren; (*stop*) anhalten; (*RAIL*) einfahren; ~ **off** *vt* (*deal etc*) abschließen; ~ **out** *vi* (*car*) herausfahren; (*fig:* *partner*) aussteigen // *vt* herausziehen; ~ **over** *vi* (*AUT*) an die Seite fahren; ~ **round**, ~ **through** *vi* durchkommen; ~ **up** *vi* anhalten // *vt* (*uproot*) herausreißen; (*stop*) anhalten.

pulley ['pulɪ] *n* Rolle *f*, Flaschenzug *m*.

pullover ['puləuvə*] *n* Pullover *m*.

pulp [pʌlp] *n* Brei *m*; (*of fruit*) Fruchtfleisch *nt*.

pulpit ['pʊlpɪt] n Kanzel f.

pulsate [pʌl'seɪt] vi pulsieren.

pulse [pʌls] n Puls m.

pummel ['pʌml] vt mit den Fäusten bearbeiten.

pump [pʌmp] n Pumpe f; (shoe) leichter (Tanz)schuh m // vt pumpen; ~ up vt (tyre) aufpumpen.

pumpkin ['pʌmpkɪn] n Kürbis m.

pun [pʌn] n Wortspiel nt.

punch [pʌntʃ] n (tool) Locher m; (blow) (Faust)schlag m; (drink) Punsch m, Bowle f // vt lochen; (strike) schlagen, boxen; ~line n Pointe f; ~-up n (Brit col) Keilerei f.

punctual ['pʌŋktjʊəl] a pünktlich.

punctuate ['pʌŋktjʊeɪt] vt mit Satzzeichen versehen; (fig) unterbrechen.

punctuation [pʌŋktjʊ'eɪʃən] n Zeichensetzung f, Interpunktion f.

puncture ['pʌŋktʃə*] n Loch nt; (AUT) Reifenpanne f // vt durchbohren.

pundit ['pʌndɪt] n Gelehrte(r) m.

pungent ['pʌndʒənt] a scharf.

punish ['pʌnɪʃ] vt bestrafen; (in boxing etc) übel zurichten; ~ment n Strafe f; (action) Bestrafung f.

punk [pʌŋk] n (also: ~ rocker) Punker(in f) m; (also: ~ rock) Punk m; (US col: hoodlum) Ganove m.

punt [pʌnt] n Stechkahn m.

punter ['pʌntə*] n (Brit: better) Wetter m.

puny ['pjuːnɪ] a kümmerlich.

pup [pʌp] n = **puppy**.

pupil ['pjuːpl] n Schüler(in f) m; (in eye) Pupille f.

puppet ['pʌpɪt] n Puppe f; Marionette f.

puppy ['pʌpɪ] n junge(r) Hund m.

purchase ['pɜːtʃɪs] n Kauf m; (grip) Halt m // vt kaufen, erwerben; ~r n Käufer(in f) m.

pure [pjʊə*] a rein (also fig); ~ly ['pjʊəlɪ] ad rein.

purgatory ['pɜːgətərɪ] n Fegefeuer nt.

purge [pɜːdʒ] n Säuberung f (also POL); (medicine) Abführmittel nt // vt reinigen; (body) entschlacken.

purify ['pjʊərɪfaɪ] vt reinigen.

purity ['pjʊərɪtɪ] n Reinheit f.

purl [pɜːl] n linke Masche f.

purple ['pɜːpl] a violett; (face) dunkelrot.

purport [pɜː'pɔːt] vi vorgeben.

purpose ['pɜːpəs] n Zweck m, Ziel nt; (of person) Absicht f; on ~ absichtlich; ~ful a zielbewußt, entschlossen.

purr [pɜː*] n Schnurren nt // vi schnurren.

purse [pɜːs] n Portemonnaie nt, Geldbeutel m // vt (lips) zusammenpressen, schürzen.

purser ['pɜːsə*] n Zahlmeister m.

pursue [pə'sjuː] vt verfolgen; (study) nachgehen (+dat); ~r n Verfolger m.

pursuit [pə'sjuːt] n Verfolgung f; (occupation) Beschäftigung f.

purveyor [pɜː'veɪə*] n Lieferant m.

pus [pʌs] n Eiter m.

push [pʊʃ] n Stoß m, Schub m; (MIL) Vorstoß m // vt stoßen, schieben; (button) drücken; (idea) durchsetzen // vi stoßen, schieben; ~ aside vt beiseiteschieben; ~ off vi (col) abschieben; ~ on vi weitermachen; ~ through vt durchdrücken; (policy) durchsetzen; ~ up vt (total) erhöhen; (prices) hochtreiben; ~chair n (Brit) (Kinder)sportwagen m; ~over n (col) Kinderspiel nt; ~-up n (US: press-up) Liegestütz m; ~y a (col) aufdringlich.

puss [pʊs], **pussy(-cat)** ['pʊsɪ(kæt)] n Mieze(katze) f.

put [pʊt], pt, pp **put** vt setzen, stellen, legen; (express) ausdrücken, sagen; (write) schreiben; ~ about vi verbreiten; (back) wenden // vt (spread) verbreiten; ~ across vt (explain) erklären; ~ away vt weglegen; (store) beiseitelegen; ~ back vt zurückstellen or -legen; ~ by vt zurücklegen, sparen; ~ down vt hinstellen or -legen; (rebellion) niederschlagen; (animal) einschläfern; (in writing) niederschreiben; ~ forward vt (idea) vorbringen; (clock) vorstellen; ~ in vt (application, complaint) einreichen; ~ off vt verschieben; (discourage) abbringen von; ~ on vt (clothes etc) anziehen; (light etc) anschalten, anmachen; (play etc) aufführen; (brake) anziehen; ~ out vt (hand etc) (her)ausstrecken; (news, rumour) verbreiten; (light etc) ausschalten, ausmachen; ~ up vt (tent) aufstellen; (building) errichten; (price) erhöhen; (person) unterbringen; to ~ up with sich abfinden mit.

putrid ['pjuːtrɪd] a faul.

putt [pʌt] vt (golf) putten // n (golf) Putten nt; ~ing green n Rasenfläche f zum Putten.

putty ['pʌtɪ] n Kitt m; (fig) Wachs nt.

put-up ['pʊtʌp] a: ~ job abgekartete(s) Spiel nt.

puzzle ['pʌzl] n Rätsel nt; (toy) Geduldspiel nt // vt verwirren // vi sich den Kopf zerbrechen.

puzzling ['pʌzlɪŋ] a rätselhaft, verwirrend.

pyjamas [pɪ'dʒɑːməz] npl (Brit) Schlafanzug m, Pyjama m.

pylon ['paɪlən] n Mast m.

Q

quack [kwæk] n Quaken nt; (doctor) Quacksalber m // vi quaken.

quad [kwɒd] abbr of **quadrangle**; **quadruplet**.

quadrangle ['kwɒdræŋgl] n (court) Hof m; (MATH) Viereck nt.

quadruple ['kwɒ'dru:pl] a vierfach // vi sich vervierfachen // vt vervierfachen.

quadruplets [kwɒ'dru:plɪts] npl Vierlinge pl.

quagmire ['kwægmaɪə*] n Morast m.

quail [kweɪl] n (bird) Wachtel f // vi (vor Angst) zittern.

quaint [kweɪnt] a kurios; malerisch.

quake [kweɪk] vi beben, zittern // n abbr of **earthquake**.

Quaker ['kweɪkə*] n Quäker(in f) m.

qualification [kwɒlɪfɪ'keɪʃən] n Qualifikation f; (sth which limits) Einschränkung f.

qualified ['kwɒlɪfaɪd] a (competent) qualifiziert; (limited) bedingt.

qualify ['kwɒlɪfaɪ] vt (prepare) befähigen; (limit) einschränken // vi sich qualifizieren (for für); **to ~ as a doctor/ lawyer** sein juristisches/medizinisches Staatsexamen machen.

quality ['kwɒlɪtɪ] n Qualität f; (characteristic) Eigenschaft f.

qualm [kwɑ:m] n Bedenken nt.

quandary ['kwɒndərɪ] n: to be in a ~ in Verlegenheit sein.

quantity ['kwɒntɪtɪ] n Menge f; ~ **surveyor** n Baukostenkalkulator m.

quarantine ['kwɒrənti:n] n Quarantäne f.

quarrel ['kwɒrəl] n Streit m // vi sich streiten; **~some** a streitsüchtig.

quarry ['kwɒrɪ] n Steinbruch m; (animal) Wild nt; (fig) Opfer nt.

quart [kwɔ:t] n Quart nt.

quarter ['kwɔ:tə*] n Viertel nt; (of year) Quartal nt // vt (divide) vierteln; (MIL) einquartieren; **~s** pl (esp MIL) Quartier nt; **~ of an hour** n Viertelstunde f; **~ final** n Viertelfinale nt; **~ly** a vierteljährlich; **~master** n Quartiermeister m.

quash [kwɒʃ] vt (verdict) aufheben.

quasi- ['kwɑ:zɪ] pref Quasi-.

quaver ['kweɪvə*] n (Brit MUS) Achtelnote f // vi (tremble) zittern.

quay [ki:] n Kai m.

queasy ['kwi:zɪ] a übel.

queen [kwi:n] n Königin f; ~ **mother** n Königinmutter f.

queer [kwɪə*] a seltsam // n (col: homosexual) Schwule(r) m.

quell [kwel] vt unterdrücken.

quench [kwentʃ] vt (thirst) löschen.

querulous ['kwerʊləs] a nörglerisch.

query ['kwɪərɪ] n (question) (An)frage f; (question mark) Fragezeichen nt // vt in Zweifel ziehen, in Frage stellen.

quest [kwest] n Suche f.

question ['kwestʃən] n Frage f // vt (ask) (be)fragen; (suspect) verhören; (doubt) in Frage stellen, bezweifeln; **beyond** ~ ohne Frage; **out of the** ~ ausge-schlossen; **~able** a zweifelhaft; ~ **mark** n Fragezeichen nt.

questionnaire [kwestʃə'nɛə*] n Fragebogen m.

queue [kju:] (Brit) n Schlange f // vi (also: ~ up) Schlange stehen.

quibble ['kwɪbl] vi kleinlich sein.

quick [kwɪk] a schnell // n (of nail) Nagelhaut f; **cut to the** ~ (fig) tief getroffen; **be** ~! mach schnell!; **~en** vt (hasten) beschleunigen // vi sich beschleunigen; **~ly** a schnell; **~sand** n Treibsand m; **~-witted** a schlagfertig.

quid [kwɪd] n (Brit col: £1) Pfund nt.

quiet ['kwaɪət] a (without noise) leise; (peaceful, calm) still, ruhig // n Stille f, Ruhe f // vt, vi (US) = **~en**; **keep** ~! sei still!; **~en** (also: **~en down**) vi ruhig werden // vt beruhigen; **~ly** ad leise, ruhig; **~ness** n Ruhe f, Stille f.

quilt [kwɪlt] n (continental ~) Steppdecke f.

quin [kwɪn] abbr of **quintuplet**.

quinine [kwɪ'ni:n] n Chinin nt.

quintuplets [kwɪn'tju:plɪts] npl Fünflinge pl.

quip [kwɪp] n witzige Bemerkung f.

quirk [kw3:k] n (oddity) Eigenart f.

quit [kwɪt], pt, pp quit or quitted vt verlassen // vi aufhören.

quite [kwaɪt] ad (completely) ganz, völlig; (fairly) ziemlich; ~ **a few of them** ziemlich viele von ihnen; ~ **(so)!** richtig!

quits [kwɪts] a quitt; **let's call it** ~ lassen wir's gut sein.

quiver ['kwɪvə*] vi zittern // n (for arrows) Köcher m.

quiz [kwɪz] n (competition) Quiz nt // vt prüfen; **~zical** a fragend.

quorum ['kwɔ:rəm] n beschlußfähige Anzahl f.

quota ['kwəʊtə] n Anteil m; (COMM) Quote f.

quotation [kwəʊ'teɪʃən] n Zitat nt; (price) Kostenvoranschlag m; ~ **marks** pl Anführungszeichen pl.

quote [kwəʊt] n see **quotation** // vi (from book) zitieren // vt (from book) zitieren; (price) angeben.

R

rabbi ['ræbaɪ] n Rabbiner m; (title) Rabbi m.

rabbit ['ræbɪt] n Kaninchen nt; ~ **hole** n Kaninchenbau m; ~ **hutch** n Kaninchenstall m.

rabble ['ræbl] n Pöbel m.

rabies ['reɪbiːz] n Tollwut f.

RAC n abbr (Brit) of Royal Automobile Club.

raccoon [rə'ku:n] n Waschbär m.

race [reɪs] n (species) Rasse f;

(competition) Rennen nt; (on foot also) Wettlauf m; (rush) Hetze f // vt um die Wette laufen mit; (horses) laufen lassen // vi (run) rennen; (in contest) am Rennen teilnehmen; ~ **car** n (US) = **racing car**; ~ **car driver** n (US) = **racing driver**; ~**course** n (for horses) Rennbahn f; ~**horse** n Rennpferd nt; ~**track** n (for cars etc) Rennstrecke f.

racial ['reɪʃəl] a Rassen-; ~**ist** a rassistisch // n Rassist m.

racing ['reɪsɪŋ] n Rennen nt; ~ **car** n (Brit) Rennwagen m; ~ **driver** n (Brit) Rennfahrer m.

racism ['reɪsɪzəm] n Rassismus m.

racist ['reɪsɪst] n Rassist m // a rassistisch.

rack [ræk] n Ständer m, Gestell nt // vt plagen; **to go to** ~ **and ruin** verfallen; **to** ~ **one's brains** sich (dat) den Kopf zerbrechen.

racket ['rækɪt] n (din) Krach m; (scheme) (Schwindel)geschäft nt; (TENNIS) (Tennis)schläger m.

racoon [rə'ku:n] n = **raccoon**.

racquet ['rækɪt] n = **racket** (TENNIS).

racy ['reɪsɪ] a gewagt; (style) spritzig.

radar ['reɪdɑ:*] n Radar nt or m.

radial ['reɪdɪəl] a (also: US: ~-**ply**) radial.

radiance ['reɪdɪəns] n strahlende(r) Glanz m.

radiant ['reɪdɪənt] a strahlend; (giving out rays) Strahlungs-.

radiate ['reɪdɪeɪt] vti ausstrahlen; (roads, lines) strahlenförmig wegführen.

radiation [reɪdɪ'eɪʃən] n (Aus)strahlung f.

radiator ['reɪdɪeɪtə*] n (for heating) Heizkörper m; (AUT) Kühler m.

radical a, ~**ly** ad ['rædɪkəl, -ɪ] radikal.

radii ['reɪdɪaɪ] npl of **radius**.

radio ['reɪdɪəʊ] n Rundfunk m, Radio nt; (set) Radio nt, Radioapparat m; **on the** ~ im Radio.

radio... ['reɪdɪəʊ] pref Radio-; ~**active** a radioaktiv; ~**logy** [reɪdɪ'ɒlədʒɪ] n Strahlenkunde f.

radio station n Rundfunkstation f.

radiotherapy ['reɪdɪəʊ'θerəpɪ] n Röntgentherapie f.

radish ['rædɪʃ] n (big) Rettich m; (small) Radieschen nt.

radius ['reɪdɪəs], pl **radii** [-ɪaɪ] n Radius m; (area) Umkreis m.

RAF n abbr of **Royal Air Force**.

raffle ['ræfl] n Verlosung f, Tombola f // vt verlosen.

raft [rɑ:ft] n Floß nt.

rafter ['rɑ:ftə*] n Dachsparren m.

rag [ræg] n (cloth) Lumpen m, Lappen m; (col: newspaper) Käseblatt nt; (Univ: for charity) Sammelaktion f // vt (Brit) auf den Arm nehmen; ~**s** pl Lumpen pl; ~**-and-**

bone man n (Brit) = ~**man**; ~ **doll** n Flickenpuppe f.

rage [reɪdʒ] n Wut f; (fashion) große Mode f // vi wüten, toben.

ragged ['rægɪd] a (edge) gezackt; (clothes) zerlumpt.

ragman ['rægmæn] n Lumpensammler m.

raid [reɪd] n Überfall m; (MIL) Angriff m; (by police) Razzia f // vt überfallen; ~**er** n (person) (Bank)räuber m.

rail [reɪl] n Schiene f (on stair) Geländer nt; (of ship) Reling f; (RAIL) Schiene f; ~**s** pl Geleise pl; **by** ~ per Bahn; ~**ing(s)** n(pl) Geländer nt; ~**road** n (US), ~**way** n (Brit) Eisenbahn f; ~**way line** n (Brit) (Eisen)bahnlinie f; (: track) Gleis nt; ~**wayman** n (Brit) Eisenbahner m; ~**way station** n (Brit) Bahnhof m.

rain [reɪn] n Regen m // vti regnen; **in the** ~ im Regen; **it's** ~**ing** es regnet; ~**bow** n Regenbogen m; ~**coat** n Regenmantel m; ~**drop** n Regentropfen m; ~**fall** n Niederschlag m; ~**y** a (region, season) Regen-; (day) regnerisch, verregnet.

raisin ['reɪzən] n Rosine f.

rake [reɪk] n Rechen m, Harke f; (person) Wüstling m // vt rechen, harken; (with gun) (mit Feuer) bestreichen; (search) (durch)suchen.

rakish ['reɪkɪʃ] a verwegen.

rally ['rælɪ] n (POL etc) Kundgebung f; (AUT) Rallye f // vt (MIL) sammeln // vi Kräfte sammeln; ~ **round** vti (sich) scharen um; (help) zu Hilfe kommen (+dat).

RAM n abbr (= random access memory) RAM m.

ram [ræm] n Widder m; (instrument) Ramme f // vt (strike) rammen; (stuff) (hinein)stopfen.

ramble ['ræmbl] n Wanderung f // vi (talk) schwafeln; ~**r** n Wanderer m.

rambling ['ræmblɪŋ] a (speech) weitschweifig; (town) ausgedehnt.

ramp [ræmp] n Rampe f; **on/off** ~ (US AUT) Ein-/Ausfahrt f.

rampage [ræm'peɪdʒ] n: **to be on the** ~ (also ~ vi) randalieren.

rampant ['ræmpənt] a wild wuchernd.

rampart ['ræmpɑ:t] n (Schutz)wall m.

ramshackle ['ræmʃækl] a baufällig.

ran [ræn] pt of **run**.

ranch [rɑ:ntʃ] n Ranch f.

rancid ['rænsɪd] a ranzig.

rancour, (US) **rancor** ['ræŋkə*] n Verbitterung f, Groll m.

random ['rændəm] a ziellos, wahllos // n: at ~ aufs Geratewohl; ~ **access** n (COMPUT) wahlfreie(r) Zugriff m.

randy ['rændɪ] a (Brit col) geil, scharf.

rang [ræŋ] pt of **ring**.

range [reɪndʒ] n Reihe f; (of mountains) Kette f; (COMM) Sortiment nt; (selection) (große) Auswahl f (of an +dat); (reach) (Reich)weite f; (of gun) Schußweite f; (for shooting practice) Schießplatz m; (stove) (großer) Herd m // vt (set in row) anordnen, aufstellen; (roam) durchstreifen // vi: to ~ over (wander) umherstreifen in (+dat); (extend) sich erstrecken auf (+acc); **prices ranging from £5 to £10** Preise, die sich zwischen £5 und £10 bewegen; ~r n Förster m.

rank [ræŋk] n (row) Reihe f; (Brit: also: taxi ~) (Taxi)stand m; (MIL) Rang m; (social position) Stand m // vi (have ~) gehören (among zu) // a (strong-smelling) stinkend; (extreme) krass; the ~ and file (fig) die breite Masse.

rankle ['ræŋkl] vi nagen.

ransack ['rænsæk] vt (plunder) plündern; (search) durchwühlen.

ransom ['rænsəm] n Lösegeld nt; to hold sb to ~ jdn gegen Lösegeld festhalten.

rant [rænt] vi hochtrabend reden.

rap [ræp] n Schlag m // vt klopfen.

rape [reɪp] n Vergewaltigung f; (BOT) Raps m // vt vergewaltigen; ~ (seed) oil n Rapsöl nt.

rapid ['ræpɪd] a rasch, schnell; ~s npl Stromschnellen pl; ~ity [rə'pɪdɪtɪ] n Schnelligkeit f; ~ly ad schnell.

rapist ['reɪpɪst] n Vergewaltiger m.

rapport [ræ'pɔː*] n gute(s) Verhältnis nt.

rapture ['ræptʃə*] n Entzücken nt.

rapturous ['ræptʃərəs] a (applause) stürmisch; (expression) verzückt.

rare [reə*] a selten, rar; (underdone) nicht durchgebraten.

rarely ['reəlɪ] ad selten.

raring ['reərɪŋ] a: to be ~ to go (col) es kaum erwarten können, bis es losgeht.

rarity ['reərɪtɪ] n Seltenheit f.

rascal ['rɑːskəl] n Schuft m.

rash [ræʃ] a übereilt; (reckless) unbesonnen // n (Haut)ausschlag m.

rasher ['ræʃə*] n Speckscheibe f.

raspberry ['rɑːzbərɪ] n Himbeere f.

rasping ['rɑːspɪŋ] a (noise) kratzend; (voice) krächzend.

rat [ræt] n (animal) Ratte f; (person) Halunke m.

rate [reɪt] n (proportion) Rate f; (price) Tarif m; (speed) Tempo nt // vt (ein)schätzen; ~s pl (Brit) Grundsteuer f; to ~ as für etw halten; ~**able value** n (Brit) Einheitswert m (als Bemessungsgrundlage); ~**payer** n

(Brit) Steuerzahler(in f) m.

rather ['rɑːðə*] ad (in preference) lieber, eher; (to some extent) ziemlich; I would or I'd ~ go ich würde lieber gehen.

ratify ['rætɪfaɪ] vt bestätigen; (POL) ratifizieren.

rating ['reɪtɪŋ] n Klasse f; (Brit: sailor) Matrose m.

ratio ['reɪʃɪəʊ] n Verhältnis nt; in the ~ of 100 to 1 im Verhältnis 100 zu 1.

ration ['ræʃən] n (usually pl) Ration f // vt rationieren.

rational a, ~**ly** ad ['ræʃənl, -nəlɪ] rational; ~**e** [ræʃə'nɑːl] n Grundprinzip nt; ~**ize** ['ræʃnəlaɪz] vt rationalisieren.

rat race ['rætreɪs] n Konkurrenzkampf m.

rattle ['rætl] n (sound) Rasseln nt; (toy) Rassel f // vi ratteln, klappern // vt rasseln mit; ~**snake** n Klapperschlange f.

raucous ['rɔːkəs] a heiser, rauh.

ravage ['rævɪdʒ] vt verheeren; ~**s** pl verheerende Wirkungen pl.

rave [reɪv] vi (talk wildly) phantasieren; (rage) toben.

raven ['reɪvn] n Rabe m.

ravenous ['rævənəs] a heißhungrig.

ravine [rə'viːn] n Schlucht f.

raving ['reɪvɪŋ] a: ~ **lunatic** völlig Wahnsinnige(r) mf.

ravishing ['rævɪʃɪŋ] a atemberaubend.

raw [rɔː] a roh; (tender) wund(gerieben); (inexperienced) unerfahren; to get a ~ **deal** (col) schlecht wegkommen; ~ **material** n Rohmaterial nt.

ray [reɪ] n (of light) Strahl m; ~ **of hope** Hoffnungsschimmer m.

raze [reɪz] vt dem Erdboden gleichmachen.

razor ['reɪzə*] n Rasierapparat m; ~ **blade** n Rasierklinge f.

Rd abbr of **road**.

re [riː] prep (COMM) betreffs (+ gen).

reach [riːtʃ] n Reichweite f; (of river) Strecke f // vt (arrive at) erreichen; (give) reichen // vi (try to get) langen (for nach); (stretch) sich erstrecken; **within** ~ (shops etc) in erreichbarer Weite or Entfernung; **out** or außer Reichweite; ~ **out** vi die Hand ausstrecken; to ~ **out for sth** nach etw greifen.

react [riː'ækt] vi reagieren; ~**ion** [riː'ækʃən] n Reaktion f.

read [riːd] pt, pp **read** [red] vti lesen; (aloud) vorlesen; ~ **out** vt vorlesen; ~**able** a leserlich; (worth ~ing) lesenswert; ~**er** n (person) Leser(in f) m; (book) Lesebuch nt; ~**ership** n Leserschaft f.

readily ['redɪlɪ] ad (willingly) bereitwillig; (easily) prompt.

readiness ['redɪnəs] n (willingness) Bereitwilligkeit f; (being ready) Bereitschaft f; in ~ (prepared) bereit.

reading ['riːdɪŋ] n Lesen nt.

readjust ['riːə'dʒʌst] vt neu einstellen // vi (person): to ~ to sich wieder anpassen an (+acc).

ready ['redɪ] a (prepared, willing) bereit; // ad: ~-cooked vorgekocht // n: at the ~ bereit; ~-made a gebrauchsfertig, Fertig-; (clothes) Konfektions-; ~ money n Bargeld nt; ~ reckoner n Rechentabelle f; ~-to-wear a Konfektions-.

real [rɪəl] a wirklich; (actual) eigentlich; (not fake) echt; in ~ terms effektiv; ~ estate n Grundbesitz m; ~istic a, ~istically ad realistisch.

reality [rɪˈælɪtɪ] n Wirklichkeit f, Realität f; in ~ in Wirklichkeit.

realization [rɪəlaɪˈzeɪʃən] n (understanding) Erkenntnis f; (fulfilment) Verwirklichung f.

realize ['rɪəlaɪz] vt (understand) begreifen; (make real) verwirklichen; (money) einbringen; I didn't ~ ... ich wußte nicht, ...

really ['rɪəlɪ] ad wirklich.

realm [relm] n Reich nt.

realtor ['rɪəltɔːʳ] n (US) Grundstücksmakler(in f) m.

reap [riːp] vt ernten.

reappear ['riːəˈpɪəʳ] vi wieder erscheinen.

rear [rɪəʳ] a hintere(r, s), Rück- // n Rückseite f; (last part) Schluß m // vt (bring up) aufziehen // vi (horse) sich aufbäumen; ~guard n Nachhut f.

rearmament ['riːˈɑːməmənt] n Wiederaufrüstung f.

rearrange ['riːəˈreɪndʒ] vt umordnen.

rear-view mirror ['rɪəvjuː-] n Rückspiegel m.

reason ['riːzn] n (cause) Grund m; (ability to think) Verstand m; (sensible thoughts) Vernunft f // vi (think) denken; (use arguments) argumentieren; to ~ with sb mit jdm diskutieren; it stands to ~ that es ist logisch, daß; ~able a vernünftig; ~ably ad vernünftig; (fairly) ziemlich; ~ed a (argument) durchdacht; ~ing n Urteilen nt; (argumentation) Beweisführung f.

reassurance ['riːəˈʃʊərəns] n Beruhigung f; (confirmation) Bestätigung f.

reassure ['riːəˈʃʊəʳ] vt beruhigen; to ~ sb of sth jdm etw versichern.

reassuring ['riːəˈʃʊərɪŋ] a beruhigend.

rebate ['riːbeɪt] n Rückzahlung f.

rebel ['rebl] n Rebell m; ~lion [rɪˈbeljən] n Rebellion f, Aufstand m.

rebirth ['riːˈbɜːθ] n Wiedergeburt f.

rebound [rɪˈbaʊnd] vi zurückprallen // ['riːbaʊnd] n Rückprall m.

rebuff [rɪˈbʌf] n Abfuhr f // vt abblitzen

lassen.

rebuild ['riːˈbɪld] vt irreg wiederaufbauen; (fig) wiederherstellen.

rebuke [rɪˈbjuːk] n Tadel m // vt tadeln, rügen.

rebut [rɪˈbʌt] vt widerlegen.

recalcitrant [rɪˈkælsɪtrənt] a widerspenstig.

recall [rɪˈkɔːl] vt (call back) zurückrufen; (remember) sich erinnern an (+acc) // n Rückruf m.

recant [rɪˈkænt] vti widerrufen.

recap ['riːkæp] vti wiederholen.

recapitulate [ˌriːkəˈpɪtjuleɪt] vti = recap.

rec'd abbr (= received) Eing.

recede [rɪˈsiːd] vi zurückweichen.

receding [rɪˈsiːdɪŋ] a: ~ hair Stirnglatze f.

receipt [rɪˈsiːt] n (document) Quittung f; (receiving) Empfang m; ~s pl Einnahmen pl.

receive [rɪˈsiːv] vt erhalten; (visitors etc) empfangen; ~r n (TEL) Hörer m.

recent ['riːsnt] a vor kurzem (geschehen), neuerlich; (modern) neu; ~ly ad kürzlich, neulich.

receptacle [rɪˈseptəkl] n Behälter m.

reception [rɪˈsepʃən] n Empfang m; ~ desk n Empfang m; (in hotel) Rezeption f; ~ist n (in hotel) Empfangschef m/-dame f; (MED) Sprechstundenhilfe f.

receptive [rɪˈseptɪv] a aufnahmebereit.

recess [rɪˈses] n (break) Ferien pl; (hollow) Nische f; ~ion [rɪˈseʃən] n Rezession f.

recharge ['riːˈtʃɑːdʒ] vt (battery) aufladen.

recipe ['resɪpɪ] n Rezept nt.

recipient [rɪˈsɪpɪənt] n Empfänger m.

reciprocal [rɪˈsɪprəkəl] a gegenseitig; (mutual) wechselseitig.

recital [rɪˈsaɪtl] n Vortrag m.

recite [rɪˈsaɪt] vt vortragen, aufsagen.

reckless ['rekləs] a leichtsinnig; (driving) fahrlässig.

reckon ['rekən] vt (count) (be- or er)rechnen; (estimate) schätzen; (think) I ~ that ... ich nehme an, daß ...; ~ on vt rechnen mit; ~ing n (calculation) Rechnen nt.

reclaim [rɪˈkleɪm] vt (land) abgewinnen (from dat); (expenses) zurückverlangen.

reclamation [rekləˈmeɪʃən] n (of land) Gewinnung f.

recline [rɪˈklaɪn] vi sich zurücklehnen.

reclining [rɪˈklaɪnɪŋ] a Liege-.

recluse [rɪˈkluːs] n Einsiedler m.

recognition [rekəgˈnɪʃən] n (recognizing) Erkennen nt; (acknowledgement) Anerkennung f; transformed beyond ~ völlig verändert.

recognizable ['rekəgnaɪzəbl] a erkennbar.

recognize ['rekəgnaız] *vt* erkennen; *(POL, approve)* anerkennen; **to ~ as** anerkennen als; **to ~ by** erkennen an (+*dat*).

recoil [rı'kɔıl] *vi (in horror)* zurückschrecken; *(rebound)* zurückprallen; *(person)*: **to ~ from** doing sth davor zurückschrecken, etw zu tun.

recollect [rekə'lekt] *vt* sich erinnern an (+*acc*); **~ion** *n* Erinnerung *f*.

recommend [rekə'mend] *vt* empfehlen; **~ation** *n* Empfehlung *f*.

recompense ['rekəmpens] *n (compensation)* Entschädigung *f*; *(reward)* Belohnung *f* // *vt* entschädigen; belohnen.

reconcile ['rekənsaıl] *vt (facts)* vereinbaren; *(people)* versöhnen; **to ~ o.s. to sth** sich mit etw abfinden.

reconciliation [rekənsılı'eıʃən] *n* Versöhnung *f*.

recondition ['riːkən'dıʃən] *vt (machine)* generalüberholen.

reconnaissance [rı'kɒnısəns] *n* Aufklärung *f*.

reconnoitre, *(US)* **reconnoiter** [rekə'nɔıtə*] *vt* erkunden // *vi* aufklären.

reconsider ['riːkən'sıdə*] *vti* von neuem erwägen, (es) überdenken.

reconstruct ['riːkən'strʌkt] *vt* wiederaufbauen; *(crime)* rekonstruieren; **~ion** ['riːkən'strʌkʃən] *n* Rekonstruktion *f*.

record ['rekɔːd] *n* Aufzeichnung *f*; *(MUS)* Schallplatte *f*; *(best performance)* Rekord *m* // *a (time)* Rekord- // *vt* [rı'kɔːd] aufzeichnen; *(music etc)* aufnehmen; **in ~ time** in Rekordzeit; **off the ~** a vertraulich // *ad* im Vertrauen; **~ card** *n (in file)* Karteikarte *f*; **~ed delivery** [rı'kɔːdıd-] *n (Brit POST)* Einschreiben *nt*; **~er** [rı'kɔːdə*] *n (TECH)* Registriergerät *nt*; *(MUS)* Blockflöte *f*; **~ holder** *n (SPORT)* Rekordinhaber *m*; **~ing** [rı'kɔːdıŋ] *n (MUS)* Aufnahme *f*; **~ player** *n* Plattenspieler *m*.

recount ['riːkaunt] *n* Nachzählung *f* // *vt (count again)* nachzählen; [rı'kaunt] *(tell)* berichten.

recoup [rı'kuːp] *vt*: **to ~ one's losses** seinen Verlust wiedergutmachen.

recourse [rı'kɔːs] *n*: **to have ~ to** Zuflucht nehmen zu or bei.

recover [rı'kʌvə*] *vt (get back)* zurückerhalten; ['riː'kʌvə*] *(quilt etc)* neu überziehen // *vi* sich erholen; **~y** *n* Wiedererlangung *f*; *(of health)* Erholung *f*.

recreate ['riːkrı'eıt] *vt* wiederherstellen.

recreation [rekrı'eıʃən] *n* Erholung *f*; **~al** *a* Erholungs-.

recrimination [rıkrımı'neıʃən] *n* Gegenbeschuldigung *f*.

recruit [rı'kruːt] *n* Rekrut *m* // *vt* rekrutieren; **~ment** *n* Rekrutierung *f*.

rectangle ['rektæŋgl] *n* Rechteck *nt*.

rectangular [rek'tæŋgjulə*] *a* rechteckig, rechtwinklig.

rectify ['rektıfaı] *vt* berichtigen.

rector ['rektə*] *n (REL)* Pfarrer *m*; *(SCH)* Direktor(in *f*) *m*.

rectory ['rektərı] *n* Pfarrhaus *nt*.

recuperate [rı'kuːpəreıt] *vi* sich erholen.

recur [rı'kɜː*] *vi* sich wiederholen; **~rence** *n* Wiederholung *f*; **~rent** *a* wiederkehrend.

red [red] *n* Rot *nt*; *(POL)* Rote(r) *m* // *a* rot; **in the ~** in den roten Zahlen; **~ carpet treatment** *n* Sonderbehandlung *f*, große(r) Bahnhof *m*; **R~ Cross** *n* Rote(s) Kreuz *nt*; **~currant** *n* rote Johannisbeere *f*; **~den** *vti* (sich) röten; *(blush)* erröten; **~dish** *a* rötlich.

redeem [rı'diːm] *vt (COMM)* einlösen; *(save)* retten.

redeeming [rı'diːmıŋ] *a*: **~ feature** versöhnende(s) Moment *nt*.

redeploy ['riːdı'plɔı] *vt (resources)* umverteilen.

red-haired ['red'heəd] *a* rothaarig.

red-handed ['red'hændıd] *ad*: **to be caught ~** auf frischer Tat ertappt werden.

redhead ['redhed] *n* Rothaarige(r) *mf*.

red herring ['red'herıŋ] *n* Ablenkungsmanöver *nt*.

red-hot ['red'hɒt] *a* rotglühend.

redirect ['riːdaı'rekt] *vt* umleiten.

red light ['red'laıt] *n*: **to go through a ~** *(AUT)* bei Rot über die Ampel fahren; **red-light district** *n* Strichviertel *nt*.

redo ['riː'duː] *vt (irreg: like do)* nochmals machen.

redolent ['redəulənt] *a*: **~ of** riechend nach; *(fig)* erinnernd an (+*acc*).

redouble [riː'dʌbl] *vt*: **to ~ one's efforts** seine Anstrengungen verdoppeln.

redress [rı'dres] *n* Entschädigung *f* // *vt* wiedergutmachen.

Red Sea *n*: **the ~** das Rote Meer.

redskin ['redskın] *n* Rothaut *f*.

red tape *n* Bürokratismus *m*.

reduce [rı'djuːs] *vt (price)* herabsetzen *(to* auf +*acc*); *(speed, temperature)* vermindern; *(photo)* verkleinern; **'~ speed now'** *(AUT)* = 'langsam'; **at a ~d price** zum ermäßigten Preis.

reduction [rı'dʌkʃən] *n* Herabsetzung *f*; Verminderung *f*; Verkleinerung *f*; *(amount of money)* Nachlaß *m*.

redundancy [rı'dʌndənsı] *n* Überflüssigkeit *f*; *(of workers)* Entlassung *f*.

redundant [rı'dʌndənt] *a* überflüssig; *(workers)* ohne Arbeitsplatz; **to be made ~** arbeitslos werden.

reed [riːd] *n* Schilf *nt*; *(MUS)* Rohrblatt *nt*.

reef [riːf] *n* Riff *nt*.

reek [riːk] *vi* stinken *(of* nach).

reel [riːl] n Spule f, Rolle f // vt (also: ~ in) wickeln, spulen // vi (stagger) taumeln.

ref [ref] n abbr (col: = referee) Schiri m.

refectory [rɪ'fektərɪ] n (UNIV) Mensa f; (SCH) Speisesaal m; (ECCL) Refektorium nt.

refer [rɪ'fɜ:*] vt: to ~ sb to sb/sth jdn an jdn/etw verweisen // vi: to ~ to (to book) nachschlagen in (+dat); (mention) sich beziehen auf (+acc).

referee [refə'riː] n Schiedsrichter m; (Brit: for job) Referenz f // vt schiedsrichtern.

reference ['refrəns] n (allusion) Anspielung f (to auf +acc); (for job) Referenz f; (in book) Verweis m; (number, code) Aktenzeichen nt; with ~ to in bezug auf (+acc); ~ book n Nachschlagewerk nt; ~ number n Aktenzeichen nt.

referendum [refə'rendəm], pl -da [-də] n Volksabstimmung f.

refill ['riː'fɪl] vt nachfüllen // n ['riː'fɪl] (for pen) Ersatzmine f.

refine [rɪ'faɪn] vt (purify) raffinieren; ~d a kultiviert; ~ment n Kultiviertheit f.

reflect [rɪ'flekt] vt (light) reflektieren; (fig) (wider)spiegeln // vi (meditate) nachdenken (on über +acc); it ~s badly/well on him das stellt ihn in ein schlechtes/gutes Licht; ~ion f (image) Spiegelbild nt; (thought) Überlegung f; on ~ion wenn man sich (dat) das recht überlegt.

reform [rɪ'fɔːm] n Reform f // vt (person) bessern; ~atory n (US) Besserungsanstalt f.

refrain [rɪ'freɪn] vi unterlassen (from acc) // n Refrain m.

refresh [rɪ'freʃ] vt erfrischen; ~er course n (Brit) Wiederholungskurs m; ~ing a erfrischend; ~ments pl Erfrischungen pl.

refrigeration [rɪfrɪdʒə'reɪʃən] n Kühlung f.

refrigerator [rɪ'frɪdʒəreɪtə*] n Kühlschrank m.

refuel ['riː'fjuəl] vti auftanken.

refuge ['refjuːdʒ] n Zuflucht f; to take ~ in sich flüchten in (+acc).

refugee [refju'dʒiː] n Flüchtling m.

refund ['riːfʌnd] n Rückvergütung f // vt [rɪ'fʌnd] zurückerstatten.

refurbish ['riː'fɜːbɪʃ] vt aufpolieren.

refusal [rɪ'fjuːzəl] n (Ver)weigerung f; first ~ n Vorkaufsrecht nt.

refuse ['refjuːs] n Abfall m, Müll m // v [rɪ'fjuːz] vt abschlagen // vi sich weigern; ~ collection n Müllabfuhr f.

refute [rɪ'fjuːt] vt widerlegen.

regain [rɪ'geɪn] vt wiedergewinnen; (consciousness) wiedererlangen.

regal ['riːgəl] a königlich.

regalia [rɪ'geɪlɪə] npl Insignien pl.

regard [rɪ'gɑːd] n Achtung f // vt ansehen; to send one's ~s to sb jdn grüßen lassen; 'with kindest ~s' mit freundlichen Grüßen; ~ing, as ~s, with ~ to bezüglich (+gen), in bezug auf (+acc); ~less a ohne Rücksicht (of auf +acc) // ad trotzdem.

regenerate [rɪ'dʒenəreɪt] vt erneuern.

régime [reɪ'ʒiːm] n Regime nt.

regiment ['redʒɪmənt] n Regiment nt // vt (fig) reglementieren; ~al [redʒɪ'mentl] a Regiments-.

region ['riːdʒən] n Region f; in the ~ of (fig) so um; ~al a örtlich, regional.

register ['redʒɪstə*] n Register nt // vt (list) registrieren; (emotion) zeigen; (write down) eintragen // vi (at hotel) sich eintragen; (with police) sich melden (with bei); (make impression) wirken, ankommen; ~ed a (Brit: letter) Einschreibe-, eingeschrieben; ~ed trademark n eingetragene(s) Warenzeichen nt.

registrar [redʒɪs'trɑː*] n Standesbeamte(r) m.

registration [redʒɪs'treɪʃən] n (act) Registrierung f; (number) polizeiliche(s) Kennzeichen nt.

registry office ['redʒɪstrɪ'ɒfɪs] n (Brit) Standesamt nt; to get married in a ~ standesamtlich heiraten.

regret [rɪ'gret] n Bedauern nt // vt bedauern; ~fully ad mit Bedauern, ungern; ~table a bedauerlich.

regroup ['riː'gruːp] vt umgruppieren // vi sich umgruppieren.

regular ['regjulə*] a regelmäßig; (usual) üblich; (col) regelrecht // n (client etc) Stammkunde m; ~ity [regju'lærɪtɪ] n Regelmäßigkeit f; ~ly ad regelmäßig.

regulate ['regjuleɪt] vt regeln, regulieren.

regulation [regju'leɪʃən] n (rule) Vorschrift f; (control) Regulierung f.

rehabilitation ['riːhəbɪlɪ'teɪʃən] n (of criminal) Resozialisierung f.

rehearsal [rɪ'hɜːsəl] n Probe f.

rehearse [rɪ'hɜːs] vt proben.

reign [reɪn] n Herrschaft f // vi herrschen.

reimburse [riːɪm'bɜːs] vt entschädigen, zurückzahlen (sb for sth jdm etw).

rein [reɪn] n Zügel m.

reincarnation ['riːɪnkɑː'neɪʃən] n Wiedergeburt f.

reindeer ['reɪndɪə*] n Ren nt.

reinforce [riːɪn'fɔːs] vt verstärken; ~d concrete n Stahlbeton m; ~ment n Verstärkung f; ~ments pl (MIL) Verstärkungstruppen pl.

reinstate ['riːɪn'steɪt] vt wiedereinsetzen.

reissue ['riː'ɪʃuː] vt neu herausgeben.

reiterate [riː'ɪtəreɪt] vt wiederholen.

reject ['riːdʒekt] n (COMM) Aus-

schuß(artikel) *m* // [rɪ'dʒekt] *vt*
ablehnen; **~ion** [rɪ'dʒekʃən] *n*
Zurückweisung *f*.
rejoice [rɪ'dʒɔɪs] *vi*: to ~ at *or* over sich
freuen über.
rejuvenate [rɪ'dʒuːvɪneɪt] *vt* verjüngen.
rekindle ['riːkɪndl] *vt* wieder anfachen.
relapse [rɪ'læps] *n* Rückfall *m*.
relate [rɪ'leɪt] *vt* (*tell*) erzählen;
(*connect*) verbinden // *vi* zusammenhän-
gen (*to* mit); (*form relationship*) eine
Beziehung aufbauen (*to* zu); **~d** *a* verwandt (*to* mit).
relating [rɪ'leɪtɪŋ] *prep*: ~ to bezüglich
(+*gen*).
relation [rɪ'leɪʃən] *n* Verwandte(r) *mf*;
(*connection*) Beziehung *f*; **~ship** *n* Verhältnis *nt*, Beziehung *f*.
relative ['relətɪv] *n* Verwandte(r) *mf* // *a*
relativ; **~ly** *ad* verhältnismäßig.
relax [rɪ'læks] *vi* (*slacken*) sich lockern;
(*muscles*, *person*) sich entspannen // *vt*
(*ease*) lockern, entspannen; **~ation**
[riːlæk'seɪʃən] *n* Entspannung *f*; **~ed** *a*
entspannt, locker; **~ing** *a* entspannend.
relay ['riːleɪ] *n* (*SPORT*) Staffel *f* // *vt*
(*message*) weiterleiten; (*RAD, TV*) übertragen.
release [rɪ'liːs] *n* (*freedom*) Entlassung
f; (*TECH*) Auslöser *m* // *vt* befreien;
(*prisoner*) entlassen; (*report, news*) ver-
lautbaren, bekanntgeben.
relegate ['reləgeɪt] *vt* (*SPORT*): to be
~d absteigen.
relent [rɪ'lent] *vi* nachgeben; **~less** *a*,
~lessly *ad* unnachgiebig.
relevant ['reləvənt] *a* wichtig, relevant;
~ to relevant für.
reliability [rɪlaɪə'bɪlɪtɪ] *n* Zuverlässigkeit
f.
reliable *a*, **reliably** *ad* [rɪ'laɪəbl, -blɪ]
zuverlässig; **to be reliably informed that**
... aus zuverlässiger Quelle wissen, daß
...
reliance [rɪ'laɪəns] *n* Abhängigkeit *f* (*on*
von).
relic ['relɪk] *n* (*from past*) Überbleibsel
nt; (*REL*) Reliquie *f*.
relief [rɪ'liːf] *n* Erleichterung *f*; (*help*)
Hilfe *f*; (*person*) Ablösung *f*
relieve [rɪ'liːv] *vt* (*ease*) erleichtern;
(*bring help*) entlasten; (*person*) ablösen;
to ~ sb of sth jdm etw abnehmen; to ~
o.s. (*euph*) sich erleichtern (*euph*).
religion [rɪ'lɪdʒən] *n* Religion *f*.
religious [rɪ'lɪdʒəs] *a* religiös; **~ly** *ad*
religiös; (*conscientiously*) gewissenhaft.
relinquish [rɪ'lɪŋkwɪʃ] *vt* aufgeben.
relish ['relɪʃ] *n* Würze *f* // *vt* genießen; to
~ doing etw gern tun.
relocate ['riːləʊ'keɪt] *vt* verlegen // *vi*
umziehen.
reluctance [rɪ'lʌktəns] *n* Widerstreben
nt, Abneigung *f*.
reluctant [rɪ'lʌktənt] *a* widerwillig; **~ly**

ad ungern.
rely [rɪ'laɪ]: ~ on *vt* sich verlassen auf
(+*acc*).
remain [rɪ'meɪn] *vi* (*be left*) übrigbleiben; (*stay*) bleiben; **~der** *n* Rest
m; **~ing** *a* übrig(geblieben); **~s** *npl*
Überreste *pl*.
remand [rɪ'mɑːnd] *n*: on ~ in Untersuchungshaft // *vt*: to ~ in custody in
Untersuchungshaft schicken; ~ **home** *n*
(*Brit*) Untersuchungsgefängnis *nt* für
Jugendliche.
remark [rɪ'mɑːk] *n* Bemerkung *f* // *vt*
bemerken; **~able** *a*, **~ably** *ad*
bemerkenswert.
remarry ['riː'mærɪ] *vi* sich wieder ver-
heiraten.
remedial [rɪ'miːdɪəl] *a* Heil-; (*teaching*)
Hilfsschul-.
remedy ['remədɪ] *n* Mittel *nt* // *vt* (*pain*)
abhelfen (+*dat*); (*trouble*) in Ordnung
bringen.
remember [rɪ'membə*] *vt* sich erinnern
an (+*acc*).
remembrance [rɪ'membrəns] *n* Erinnerung *f*; (*official*) Gedenken *nt*.
remind [rɪ'maɪnd] *vt*: to ~ sb to do sth
jdn daran erinnern, etw zu tun; to ~ sb
of sth jdn an etw (*acc*) erinnern; she ~s
me of her mother sie erinnert mich an
ihre Mutter; **~er** *n* Mahnung *f*.
reminisce [remɪ'nɪs] *vi* in Erinnerungen
schwelgen.
reminiscent [remɪ'nɪsnt] *a*: be ~ of sth
an etw (*acc*) erinnern.
remiss [rɪ'mɪs] *a* nachlässig.
remission [rɪ'mɪʃən] *n* Nachlaß *m*; (*of
debt, sentence*) Erlaß *m*.
remit [rɪ'mɪt] *vt* (*money*) überweisen (*to
an* +*acc*); **~tance** *n* Geldanweisung *f*.
remnant ['remnənt] *n* Rest *m*; **~s** *pl*
(*COMM*) Einzelstücke *pl*.
remorse [rɪ'mɔːs] *n* Gewissensbisse *pl*;
~ful *a* reumütig; **~less** *a*, **~lessly** *ad*
unbarmherzig.
remote [rɪ'məʊt] *a* abgelegen; (*slight*)
gering; ~ **control** *n* Fernsteuerung *f*;
~ly *ad* entfernt.
remould ['riː'məʊld] *n* (*Brit*)
runderneuerte(r) Reifen *m*.
removable [rɪ'muːvəbl] *a* entfernbar.
removal [rɪ'muːvəl] *n* Beseitigung *f*; (*of
furniture*) Umzug *m*; (*from office*) Entlassung *f*; ~ **van** *n* (*Brit*) Möbelwagen
m.
remove [rɪ'muːv] *vt* beseitigen, entfernen; **~rs** *npl* Möbelspedition *f*.
remuneration [rɪmjuːnə'reɪʃən] *n* Vergütung *f*, Honorar *nt*.
render ['rendə*] *vt* machen; (*translate*)
übersetzen; **~ing** *n* (*MUS*) Wiedergabe
f.
renew [rɪ'njuː] *vt* erneuern; (*contract,
licence*) verlängern; (*replace*) ersetzen;
~al *n* Erneuerung *f*; Verlängerung *f*.

renounce [rɪ'nauns] vt (give up) verzichten auf (+acc); (disown) verstoßen.

renovate ['renəveɪt] vt renovieren; (building) restaurieren.

renown [rɪ'naun] n Ruf m; **~ed** a namhaft.

rent [rent] n Miete f; (for land) Pacht f // vt (hold as tenant) mieten; pachten; (let) vermieten; verpachten; (car etc) mieten; (firm) vermieten; **~al** n Miete f.

renunciation [rɪnʌnsɪ'eɪʃən] n Verzicht m (of auf +acc).

reorganize ['ri:'ɔːgənaɪz] vt umgestalten, reorganisieren.

rep [rep] n abbr of **representative**; **repertory**.

repair [rɪ'peə*] n Reparatur f // vt reparieren; (damage) wiedergutmachen; in good/bad **~** in gutem/schlechtem Zustand; **~ kit** n Werkzeugkasten m.

repartee [repɑː'tiː] n Witzeleien pl.

repatriate [riː'pætrɪeɪt] vt in die Heimat zurückschicken.

repay [riː'peɪ] vt (irreg: like pay) zurückzahlen; (reward) vergelten; **~ment** n Rückzahlung f; (fig) Vergeltung f.

repeal [rɪ'piːl] n Aufhebung f // vt aufheben.

repeat [rɪ'piːt] n (RAD, TV) Wiederholung(ssendung) f // vt wiederholen; **~edly** ad wiederholt.

repel [rɪ'pel] vt (drive back) zurückschlagen; (disgust) abstoßen; **~lent** a abstoßend // n: **insect ~lent** Insektenmittel nt.

repent [rɪ'pent] vti: to **~** (of) bereuen; **~ance** n Reue f.

repercussion [riːpə'kʌʃən] n Auswirkung f; to have **~s** ein Nachspiel haben.

repertory ['repətərɪ] n Repertoire nt.

repetition [repə'tɪʃən] n Wiederholung f.

repetitive [rɪ'petɪtɪv] a sich wiederholend.

replace [rɪ'pleɪs] vt ersetzen; (put back) zurückstellen; **~ment** n Ersatz m.

replay ['riːpleɪ] n (of match) Wiederholungsspiel nt; (of tape, film) Wiederholung f.

replenish [rɪ'plenɪʃ] vt ergänzen.

replete [rɪ'pliːt] a (zum Platzen) voll.

replica ['replɪkə] n Kopie f.

reply [rɪ'plaɪ] n Antwort f // vi antworten; **~ coupon** n Antwortschein m.

report [rɪ'pɔːt] n Bericht m; (Brit SCH) Zeugnis nt // vt (tell) berichten; (give information against) melden; (to police) anzeigen // vi (make report) Bericht erstatten; (present o.s.): to **~** (to sb) sich (bei jdm) melden; **~ card** n (US, Scot) Zeugnis nt; **~edly** ad wie verlautet; **~er** n Reporter m.

repose [rɪ'pəuz] n: in **~** (face, mouth) gelassen.

reprehensible [reprɪ'hensɪbl] a tadelnswert.

represent [reprɪ'zent] vt darstellen; (speak for) vertreten; **~ation** [-'teɪʃən] n Darstellung f; (being represented) Vertretung f; **~ations** pl (protest) Vorhaltungen pl; **~ative** n (person) Vertreter m; (US POL) Abgeordnete(r) mf // a repräsentativ.

repress [rɪ'pres] vt unterdrücken; **~ion** [rɪ'preʃən] n Unterdrückung f.

reprieve [rɪ'priːv] n (cancellation) Begnadigung f; (fig) Gnadenfrist f // vt (JUR) begnadigen.

reprimand ['reprɪmɑːnd] n Verweis m // vt einen Verweis erteilen (+dat).

reprint ['riːprɪnt] n Neudruck m // ['riː'prɪnt] vt wieder abdrucken.

reprisal [rɪ'praɪzəl] n Vergeltung f.

reproach [rɪ'prəutʃ] n Vorwurf m // vt Vorwürfe machen (+dat); to **~** sb with sth jdm etw vorwerfen; **~ful** a vorwurfsvoll.

reproduce [riːprə'djuːs] vt reproduzieren // vi (have offspring) sich vermehren.

reproduction [riːprə'dʌkʃən] n (ART, PHOT) Reproduktion f; (breeding) Fortpflanzung f.

reproductive [riːprə'dʌktɪv] a reproduktiv; (breeding) Fortpflanzungs-.

reprove [rɪ'pruːv] vt: to **~** sb for sth jdn für etw tadeln.

republic [rɪ'pʌblɪk] n Republik f.

repudiate [rɪ'pjuːdɪeɪt] vt zurückweisen.

repugnant [rɪ'pʌgnənt] a widerlich.

repulse [rɪ'pʌls] vt (drive back) zurückschlagen; (reject) abweisen.

repulsive [rɪ'pʌlsɪv] a abstoßend.

reputable ['repjutəbl] a angesehen.

reputation [repju'teɪʃən] n Ruf m.

repute [rɪ'pjuːt] n hohe(s) Ansehen nt; **~d** a, **~dly** ad angeblich.

request [rɪ'kwest] n (thing) Bitte f // vt (thing) erbitten; to **~** sth of or from sb jdn um etw bitten; (formally) jdn um etw ersuchen; **~ stop** n (Brit) Bedarfshaltestelle f.

require [rɪ'kwaɪə*] vt (need) brauchen; (demand) erfordern; **~ment** n (condition) Anforderung f; (need) Bedarf m.

requisite ['rekwɪzɪt] n Erfordernis nt // a erforderlich; **toilet ~s** (Brit) Toilettenartikel pl.

requisition [rekwɪ'zɪʃən] n Anforderung f // vt beschlagnahmen; to **~** (for sth) (etw) anfordern.

resale ['riːseɪl] n Weiterverkauf m.

rescind [rɪ'sɪnd] vt aufheben.

rescue ['reskjuː] n Rettung f // vt retten; **~ from** vt befreien aus; **~ party** n Rettungsmannschaft f; **~r** n Retter m.

research [rɪ'səːtʃ] n Forschung f // vi forschen // vt erforschen; **~er** n Forscher m.

resemblance [rɪ'zembləns] n Ähnlichkeit f.

resemble [rɪ'zembl] vt ähneln (+dat).

resent [rɪ'zent] vt übelnehmen; ~**ful** a nachtragend, empfindlich; ~**ment** n Verstimmung f, Unwille m.

reservation [rezə'veɪʃən] n (of seat) Reservierung f; (THEAT) Vorbestellung f; (doubt) Vorbehalt m; (land) Reservat nt.

reserve [rɪ'zɜːv] n (store) Vorrat m, Reserve f; (manner) Zurückhaltung f; (game ~) Naturschutzgebiet nt; (SPORT) Ersatzspieler(in f) m // vt reservieren; (judgement) sich (dat) vorbehalten; ~**s** pl (MIL) Reserve f; in ~ in Reserve; ~**d** a reserviert.

reshape [riː'ʃeɪp] vt umformen.

reshuffle [riː'ʃʌfl] n: cabinet ~ (POL) Kabinettsumbildung f // vt (POL) umbilden.

reside [rɪ'zaɪd] vi wohnen, ansässig sein.

residence ['rezɪdəns] n (house) Wohnsitz m; (living) Aufenthalt m.

resident ['rezɪdənt] n (in house) Bewohner m; (in area) Einwohner m // a wohnhaft, ansässig; ~**ial** [-'denʃəl] a Wohn-.

residue ['rezɪdjuː] n Rest m; (CHEM) Rückstand m; (fig) Bodensatz m.

resign [rɪ'zaɪn] vt (office) aufgeben, zurücktreten von // vi (from office) zurücktreten; (employee) kündigen; to be ~**ed** to sth, to ~ o.s. to sth sich mit etw abfinden; ~**ation** [rezɪg'neɪʃən] n (from job) Kündigung f; (POL) Rücktritt m; (submission) Resignation f; ~**ed** a resigniert.

resilience [rɪ'zɪlɪəns] n Spannkraft f; (of person) Unverwüstlichkeit f.

resilient [rɪ'zɪlɪənt] a unverwüstlich.

resin ['rezɪn] n Harz nt.

resist [rɪ'zɪst] vt widerstehen (+dat); ~**ance** n Widerstand m.

resolute a, ~**ly** ad ['rezəluːt, -lɪ] entschlossen, resolut.

resolution [rezə'luːʃən] n (firmness) Entschlossenheit f; (intention) Vorsatz m; (decision) Beschluß m.

resolve [rɪ'zɒlv] n Entschlossenheit f // vt (decide) beschließen // vi sich lösen; ~**d** a (fest) entschlossen.

resonant ['rezənənt] a voll.

resort [rɪ'zɔːt] n (holiday place) Erholungsort m; (help) Zuflucht f // vi Zuflucht nehmen (to zu); as a last ~ als letzter Ausweg.

resound [rɪ'zaʊnd] vi: to ~ (with) widerhallen von; ~**ing** a nachhallend; (success) groß.

resource [rɪ'sɔːs] n Findigkeit f; ~**s** pl (financial) Geldmittel pl; (natural) Bodenschätze pl; ~**ful** a findig.

respect [rɪs'pekt] n Respekt m // vt

achten, respektieren; ~**s** npl Grüße pl; with ~ to in bezug auf (+acc), hinsichtlich (+gen); in this ~ in dieser Hinsicht; ~**ability** [rɪspektə'bɪlɪtɪ] n Anständigkeit f; ~**able** a (decent) anständig; (fairly good) leidlich; ~**ful** a höflich.

respective [rɪs'pektɪv] a jeweilig; ~**ly** ad beziehungsweise.

respiration [respɪ'reɪʃən] n Atmung f.

respite ['respaɪt] n Ruhepause f.

resplendent [rɪs'plendənt] a strahlend.

respond [rɪs'pɒnd] vi antworten; (react) reagieren (to auf +acc).

response [rɪs'pɒns] n Antwort f; Reaktion f; (to advert etc) Resonanz f.

responsibility [rɪspɒnsə'bɪlɪtɪ] n Verantwortung f.

responsible [rɪs'pɒnsəbl] a (reliable) verantwortungsvoll; verantwortlich (for für).

responsive [rɪs'pɒnsɪv] a empfänglich.

rest [rest] n Ruhe f; (break) Pause f; (remainder) Rest m // vi sich ausruhen; (be supported) (auf)liegen // vt (lean): to ~ sth on/against sth etw gegen etw (acc) lehnen; the ~ of them die übrigen; it ~**s** with him to ... es liegt bei ihm, zu ....

restaurant ['restərɔ̃:ŋ] n Restaurant nt; ~ **car** n (Brit) Speisewagen m.

restful ['restful] a erholsam, ruhig.

rest home ['resthəʊm] n Erholungsheim nt.

restitution [restɪ'tjuːʃən] n Rückgabe f; to make ~ to sb for sth jdn für etw entschädigen.

restive ['restɪv] a unruhig.

restless ['restləs] a unruhig.

restore [rɪs'tɔː*] vt (order) wiederherstellen; (customs) wieder einführen; (person to position) wiedereinsetzen; (give back) zurückgeben; (paintings) restaurieren.

restrain [rɪs'treɪn] vt zurückhalten; (curiosity etc) beherrschen; (person): to ~ sb from doing sth jdn davon abhalten, etw zu tun; ~**ed** a (style etc) gedämpft, verhalten; ~**t** n (self-control) Zurückhaltung f.

restrict [rɪs'trɪkt] vt einschränken; ~**ion** [rɪs'trɪkʃən] n Einschränkung f; ~**ive** a einschränkend.

rest room ['restrʊm] n (US) Toilette f.

restructure ['riː'strʌktʃə*] vt umstrukturieren.

result [rɪ'zʌlt] n Resultat nt, Folge f; (of exam, game) Ergebnis nt // vi zur Folge haben (in acc); as a ~ of als Folge (+gen).

resume [rɪ'zjuːm] vt fortsetzen; (occupy again) wieder einnehmen // vi (work etc) wieder beginnen.

résumé ['reɪzjuːmeɪ] n Zusammenfassung f.

resumption [rɪ'zʌmpʃən] n Wiederaufnahme f.

resurgence [rɪ'sɜːdʒəns] n Wiedererwachen nt.

resurrection [rezə'rekʃən] n Auferstehung f.

resuscitate [rɪ'sʌsɪteɪt] vt wiederbeleben.

resuscitation [rɪsʌsɪ'teɪʃən] n Wiederbelebung f.

retail [ri:teɪl] n Einzelhandel m // a Einzelhandels- // v ['ri:teɪl] vt im kleinen verkaufen // vi im Einzelhandel kosten; ∼er ['ri:teɪlə*] n Einzelhändler m, Kleinhändler m; ∼ price n Ladenpreis m.

retain [rɪ'teɪn] vt (keep) (zurück)behalten; ∼er n (servant) Gefolgsmann m; (fee) (Honorar)vorschuß m.

retaliate [rɪ'tælɪeɪt] vi: to ∼ (against) zum Vergeltungsschlag (gegen +acc) ausholen.

retaliation [rɪtælɪ'eɪʃən] n Vergeltung f.

retarded [rɪ'tɑːdɪd] a zurückgeblieben.

retch [retʃ] vi würgen.

retentive [rɪ'tentɪv] a (memory) gut.

reticent ['retɪsənt] a schweigsam.

retina ['retɪnə] n Netzhaut f.

retinue ['retɪnjuː] n Gefolge nt.

retire [rɪ'taɪə*] vi (from work) in den Ruhestand treten; (withdraw) sich zurückziehen; (go to bed) schlafen gehen; ∼d a (person) pensioniert, im Ruhestand; ∼ment n Ruhestand m.

retiring [rɪ'taɪərɪŋ] a zurückhaltend.

retort [rɪ'tɔːt] n (reply) Erwiderung f; (sci) Retorte f // vi (scharf) erwidern.

retrace [rɪ'treɪs] vt zurückverfolgen; to ∼ one's steps denselben Weg zurückgehen.

retract [rɪ'trækt] vt (statement) zurücknehmen; (claws) einziehen // vi einen Rückzieher machen; ∼able a (aerial) ausziehbar.

retrain ['riː'treɪn] vt umschulen; ∼ing n Umschulung f.

retread ['riːtred] n (tyre) Reifen m mit erneuerter Lauffläche.

retreat [rɪ'triːt] n Rückzug m; (place) Zufluchtsort m // vi sich zurückziehen.

retribution [retrɪ'bjuːʃən] n Strafe f.

retrieval [rɪ'triːvəl] n Wiedergewinnung f.

retrieve [rɪ'triːv] vt wiederbekommen; (rescue) retten; ∼r n Apportierhund m.

retrograde ['retrəʊgreɪd] a (step) Rück-; (policy) rückschrittlich.

retrospect ['retrəʊspekt] n: in ∼ im Rückblick, rückblickend; ∼ive [retrəʊ'spektɪv] a (action) rückwirkend; (look) rückblickend.

return [rɪ'tɜːn] n Rückkehr f; (profits) Ertrag m (Brit: rail ticket etc) Rückfahrkarte f; (: plane) Rückflugkarte f // a (journey, match) Rück- // vi zurückkehren or -kommen //

vt zurückgeben, zurücksenden; (pay back) zurückzahlen; (elect) wählen; (verdict) aussprechen; ∼s npl (COMM) Gewinn m; (receipts) Einkünfte; in ∼ dafür; by ∼ of post postwendend; many happy ∼s (of the day)! herzlichen Glückwunsch zum Geburtstag.

reunion [riː'juːnjən] n Wiedervereinigung f; (SCH etc) Treffen nt.

reunite ['riːjuː'naɪt] vt wiedervereinigen.

rev [rev] n abbr (= revolution: AUT) Drehzahl f // vti (also: ∼ up) (den Motor) auf Touren bringen.

revamp ['riː'væmp] vt aufpolieren.

reveal [rɪ'viːl] vt enthüllen; ∼ing a aufschlußreich.

reveille [rɪ'vælɪ] n Wecken nt.

revel ['revl] vi: to ∼ in sth/in doing sth seine Freude an etw (dat) haben/daran haben, etw zu tun.

revelation [revə'leɪʃən] n Offenbarung f.

revelry ['revlrɪ] n Rummel m.

revenge [rɪ'vendʒ] n Rache f; to take ∼ on sich rächen an (+dat).

revenue ['revənjuː] n Einnahmen pl.

reverberate [rɪ'vɜːbəreɪt] vi widerhallen.

revere [rɪ'vɪə*] vt (ver)ehren; **reverence** ['revərəns] n Ehrfurcht f.

Reverend ['revərənd] a: the ∼ Robert Martin ≈ Pfarrer Robert Martin.

reverent ['revərənt] a ehrfurchtsvoll.

reverie ['revərɪ] n Träumerei f.

reversal [rɪ'vɜːsəl] n Umkehrung f.

reverse [rɪ'vɜːs] n Rückseite f; (AUT: gear) Rückwärtsgang m // a (order, direction) entgegengesetzt // vt umkehren // vi (Brit AUT) rückwärts fahren; ∼-charge call n (Brit) R-Gespräch nt; reversing lights npl (AUT) Rückfahrscheinwerfer pl.

revert [rɪ'vɜːt] vi zurückkehren; to ∼ to (to bad state) zurückfallen in (+acc).

review [rɪ'vjuː] n (MIL) Truppenschau f; (of book) Rezension f; (magazine) Zeitschrift f // vt Rückschau halten auf (+acc); (MIL) mustern; (book) rezensieren; (reexamine) von neuem untersuchen; ∼er n (critic) Rezensent m.

revile [rɪ'vaɪl] vt verunglimpfen.

revise [rɪ'vaɪz] vt (book) überarbeiten; (reconsider) ändern, revidieren.

revision [rɪ'vɪʒən] n Prüfung f; (COMM) Revision f; (SCH) Wiederholung f.

revitalize ['riː'vaɪtəlaɪz] vt neu beleben.

revival [rɪ'vaɪvəl] n Wiederbelebung f; (REL) Erweckung f; (THEAT) Wiederaufnahme f.

revive [rɪ'vaɪv] vt wiederbeleben; (fig) wieder auffrischen // vi wiedererwachen; (fig) wieder aufleben.

revoke [rɪ'vəʊk] vt aufheben.

revolt [rɪ'vəʊlt] n Aufstand m, Revolte f // vi sich auflehnen // vt entsetzen; ∼ing *a* widerlich.

revolution [revə'luːʃən] *n* (*turn*) Umdrehung *f*; (*POL*) Revolution *f*; ~**ary** *a* revolutionär // *n* Revolutionär *m*; ~**ize** *vt* revolutionieren.

revolve [rɪ'vɒlv] *vi* kreisen; (*on own axis*) sich drehen.

revulsion [rɪ'vʌlʃən] *n* Ekel *m*.

reward [rɪ'wɔːd] *n* Belohnung *f* // *vt* belohnen; ~**ing** *a* lohnend.

rewire ['riː'waɪə*] *vt* (*house*) neu verkabeln.

reword ['riː'wɜːd] *vt* anders formulieren.

rewrite ['riː'raɪt] (*irreg: like* write) *vt* umarbeiten, neu schreiben.

rheumatism ['ruːmətɪzəm] *n* Rheumatismus *m*, Rheuma *nt*.

Rhine [raɪn] *n*: the ~ der Rhein.

Rhone [rəʊn] *n*: the ~ die Rhone.

rhubarb ['ruːbɑːb] *n* Rhabarber *m*.

rhyme [raɪm] *n* Reim *m*.

rhythm ['rɪðəm] *n* Rhythmus *m*.

rib [rɪb] *n* Rippe *f* // *vt* (*mock*) hänseln, aufziehen.

ribald ['rɪbəld] *a* saftig.

ribbon ['rɪbən] *n* Band *nt*; **in** ~**s** (*torn*) in Fetzen.

rice [raɪs] *n* Reis *m*; ~ **pudding** *n* Milchreis *m*.

rich [rɪtʃ] *a* reich; (*food*) reichhaltig; **the** ~ die Reichen *pl*; ~**es** *npl* Reichtum *m*; ~**ly** *ad* reich; (*deserve*) völlig; ~**ness** *n* Reichtum *m*; (*of food*) Reichhaltigkeit *f*.

rickets ['rɪkɪts] *n* Rachitis *f*.

rickety ['rɪkɪtɪ] *a* wack(e)lig.

ricochet ['rɪkəʃeɪ] *n* Abprallen *nt*; (*shot*) Querschläger *m* // *vi* abprallen.

rid [rɪd], *pt, pp* rid *vt* befreien (*of* von); **to get** ~ **of** loswerden.

ridden ['rɪdn] *pp of* **ride**.

riddle ['rɪdl] *n* Rätsel *nt* // *vt*: **to be** ~**d with** völlig durchlöchert sein von.

ride [raɪd] *n* (*in vehicle*) Fahrt *f*; (*on horse*) Ritt *m* // (*v: pt* rode, *pp* ridden) *vt* (*horse*) reiten; (*bicycle*) fahren // *vi* fahren, reiten; **to take sb for a** ~ mit jdm eine Fahrt *etc* machen; (*fig*) jdn aufs Glatteis führen; **to** ~ **at anchor** (*NAUT*) vor Anker liegen; ~**r** *n* Reiter *m*; (*addition*) Zusatz *m*.

ridge [rɪdʒ] *n* Kamm *m*; (*of roof*) First *m*.

ridicule ['rɪdɪkjuːl] *n* Spott *m* // *vt* lächerlich machen.

ridiculous *a*, ~**ly** *ad* [rɪ'dɪkjʊləs, -lɪ] lächerlich.

riding ['raɪdɪŋ] *n* Reiten *nt*; ~ **school** *n* Reitschule *f*.

rife [raɪf] *a* weit verbreitet; **to be** ~ grassieren; **to be** ~ **with** voll sein von.

riffraff ['rɪfræf] *n* Pöbel *m*.

rifle ['raɪfl] *n* Gewehr *nt* // *vt* berauben; ~ **range** *n* Schießstand *m*.

rift [rɪft] *n* Spalte *f*; (*fig*) Bruch *m*.

rig [rɪg] *n* (*outfit*) Takelung *f*; (*fig*) Aufmachung *f*; (*oil* ~) Bohrinsel *f* // *vt* (*election etc*) manipulieren; ~ **out** *vt* (*Brit*) ausstatten; ~ **up** *vt* zusammenbasteln; ~**ging** *n* Takelage *f*.

right [raɪt] *a* (*correct, just*) richtig, recht; (*right side*) rechte(r, s) // *n* Recht *nt*; (*not left, POL*) Rechte *f* // *ad* (*on the right*) rechts; (*to the right*) nach rechts; (*look, work*) richtig, recht; (*directly*) gerade; (*exactly*) genau // *vt* in Ordnung bringen, korrigieren // *interj* gut; ~ **away** sofort; **to be** ~ recht haben; ~ **now** in diesem Augenblick, eben; ~ **in the middle** genau in der Mitte; **by** ~**s** von Rechts wegen; **on the** ~ rechts; **to be in the** ~ im Recht sein; ~ **angle** *n* rechte(r) Winkel *m*; ~**eous** ['raɪtʃəs] *a* rechtschaffen; ~**ful** *a* rechtmäßig; ~**handed** *a* rechtshändig; ~**hand man** *n* rechte Hand *f*; ~**hand side** *n* rechte Seite *f*; ~**ly** *ad* mit Recht; ~ **of way** *n* Vorfahrt *f*; ~**wing** *n* rechte(r) Flügel *m*.

rigid ['rɪdʒɪd] *a* (*stiff*) starr, steif; (*strict*) streng; ~**ity** [rɪ'dʒɪdɪtɪ] *n* Starrheit *f*; Strenge *f*.

rigmarole ['rɪgmərəʊl] *n* Gewäsch *nt*.

rigorous ['rɪgərəs] *a* streng.

rigour, (*US*) **rigor** ['rɪgə*] *n* Strenge *f*, Härte *f*.

rile [raɪl] *vt* ärgern.

rim [rɪm] *n* (*edge*) Rand *m*; (*of wheel*) Felge *f*.

rind [raɪnd] *n* Rinde *f*.

ring [rɪŋ] *n* Ring *m*; (*of people*) Kreis *m*; (*arena*) Manege *f*; (*of telephone*) Klingeln *nt* // *vti* (*pt* rang, *pp* rung) (*bell*) läuten; (*Brit: also:* ~ **up**) anrufen; ~ **back** *vti* zurückrufen; ~ **off** *vi* (*Brit*) aufhängen; ~**ing** *n* Klingeln *nt*; (*of large bell*) Läuten *nt*; (*in ears*) Klingen *nt*; ~**ing tone** *n* (*TEL*) Rufzeichen *nt*.

ringleader ['rɪŋliːdə*] *n* Anführer *m*, Rädelsführer *m*.

ringlets ['rɪŋlɪts] *npl* Ringellocken *pl*.

ring road ['rɪŋ'rəʊd] *n* (*Brit*) Umgehungsstraße *f*.

rink [rɪŋk] *n* (*ice* ~) Eisbahn *f*.

rinse [rɪns] *n* Spülen *nt* // *vt* spülen.

riot ['raɪət] *n* Aufruhr *m* // *vi* randalieren; **to run** ~ (*people*) randalieren; (*vegetation*) wuchern; ~**er** *n* Aufrührer *m*; ~**ous** *a*, ~**ously** *ad* aufrührerisch; (*noisy*) lärmend.

rip [rɪp] *n* Schlitz *m*, Riß *m* // *vti* (zer)reißen.

ripcord ['rɪpkɔːd] *n* Reißleine *f*.

ripe [raɪp] *a* reif; ~**n** *vti* reifen (lassen).

rip-off ['rɪpɒf] *n* (*col*): **it's a** ~! das ist Wucher!

ripple ['rɪpl] *n* kleine Welle *f* // *vt* kräuseln // *vi* sich kräuseln.

rise [raɪz] *n* (*slope*) Steigung *f*; (*esp in*

wages: Brit) Erhöhung *f*; (*growth*) Aufstieg *m* // *vi* (*pt* **rose**, *pp* **risen** ['rɪzn]) aufstehen; (*sun*) aufgehen; (*smoke*) aufsteigen; (*mountain*) sich erheben; (*ground*) ansteigen; (*prices*) steigen; (*in revolt*) sich erheben; **to give ~ to** Anlaß geben zu; **to ~ to** the occasion sich der Lage gewachsen zeigen; **rising** *a* (*increasing*: tide, numbers, prices) steigend; (*sun, moon*) aufgehend // *n* (*uprising*) Aufstand *m*.

risk [rɪsk] *n* Gefahr *f*, Risiko *nt* // *vt* (*venture*) wagen; (*chance loss of*) riskieren, aufs Spiel setzen; **to take** *or* **run the ~ of doing** das Risiko eingehen, zu tun; **at ~** in Gefahr; **at one's own ~** auf eigene Gefahr; **~y** *a* riskant.

risqué ['riːskeɪ] *a* gewagt.

rissole ['rɪsəʊl] *n* Fleischklößchen *nt*.

rite [raɪt] *n* Ritus *m*; **last ~s** *pl* Letzte Ölung *f*.

ritual ['rɪtjʊəl] *n* Ritual *nt* // *a* ritual, Ritual-; (*fig*) rituell.

rival ['raɪvəl] *n* Rivale *m*, Konkurrent *m* // *a* rivalisierend // *vt* rivalisieren mit; (*COMM*) konkurrieren mit; **~ry** *n* Rivalität *f*; Konkurrenz *f*.

river ['rɪvə*] *n* Fluß *m*, Strom *m* // *cpd* (*port, traffic*) Fluß-; **up/down ~** flußaufwärts/-abwärts; **~bank** *n* Flußufer *nt*; **~bed** *n* Flußbett *nt*.

rivet ['rɪvɪt] *n* Niete *f* // *vt* (*fasten*) (ver)nieten.

Riviera [rɪvɪ'eərə] *n*: **the ~** die Riviera.

road [rəʊd] *n* Straße *f* // *cpd* Straßen-; **major/minor ~** Haupt-/Nebenstraße *f*; **~block** *n* Straßensperre *f*; **~hog** *n* Verkehrsrowdy *m*; **~map** *n* Straßenkarte *f*; **~ safety** *n* Verkehrssicherheit *f*; **~side** *n* Straßenrand *m* // *a* an der Landstraße (gelegen); **~ sign** *n* Straßenschild *nt*; **~ user** *n* Verkehrsteilnehmer *m*; **~way** *n* Fahrbahn *f*; **~ works** *pl* Straßenbauarbeiten *pl*; **~worthy** *a* verkehrssicher.

roam [rəʊm] *vi* (umher)streifen // *vt* durchstreifen.

roar [rɔː*] *n* Brüllen *nt*, Gebrüll *nt* // *vi* brüllen; **to ~ with laughter** brüllen vor Lachen; **to do a ~ing trade** ein Riesengeschäft machen.

roast [rəʊst] *n* Braten *m* // *vt* braten, schmoren; **~ beef** *n* Roastbeef *nt*.

rob [rɒb] *vt* bestehlen, berauben; (*bank*) ausrauben; **to ~ sb of sth** jdm etw rauben; **~ber** *n* Räuber *m*; **~bery** *n* Raub *m*.

robe [rəʊb] *n* (*dress*) Gewand *nt*; (*US*) Hauskleid *nt*; (*judge's*) Robe *f*.

robin ['rɒbɪn] *n* Rotkehlchen *nt*.

robot ['rəʊbɒt] *n* Roboter *m*.

rock [rɒk] *n* Felsen *m*; (*Brit: sweet*) Zuckerstange *f* // *vt* wiegen, schaukeln; **on the ~s** (*drink*) mit Eis(würfeln); (*marriage*) gescheitert; (*ship*) aufgelaufen; **~ and roll** *n* Rock and Roll *m*; **~-bottom** *n* (*fig*) Tiefpunkt *m*; **~ery** *n* Steingarten *m*.

rocket ['rɒkɪt] *n* Rakete *f*.

rocking: **~chair** *n* Schaukelstuhl *m*; **~ horse** *n* Schaukelpferd *nt*.

rocky ['rɒkɪ] *a* felsig.

rod [rɒd] *n* (*bar*) Stange *f*; (*stick*) Rute *f*.

rode [rəʊd] *pt of* **ride**.

rodent ['rəʊdənt] *n* Nagetier *nt*.

roe [rəʊ] *n* (*deer*) Reh *nt*; (*of fish*) Rogen *m*; **hard/soft ~** Rogen *m*/Milch *f*.

rogue [rəʊg] *n* Schurke *m*.

role [rəʊl] *n* Rolle *f*.

roll [rəʊl] *n* Rolle *f*; (*bread*) Brötchen *nt*; (*list*) (Namens)liste *f*; (*of drum*) Wirbel *m* // *vt* (*turn*) rollen, (herum)wälzen; (*grass etc*) walzen // *vi* (*swing*) schlingern; (*sound*) (g)rollen; **~ about** *or* **around** *vi* (herum)schlingern; (*dog etc*) sich wälzen; **~ by** *vi* (*time*) verfließen; **~ in** *vi* (*mail*) hereinkommen; **~ over** *vi* sich (herum)drehen; **~ up** *vi* (*arrive*) kommen, auftauchen // *vt* (*carpet*) aufrollen; **~ call** *n* Namensaufruf *m*; **~er** *n* Rolle *f*, Walze *f*; (*road ~er*) Straßenwalze *f*; **~er coaster** *n* Achterbahn *f*; **~er skates** *pl* Rollschuhe *pl*.

rolling ['rəʊlɪŋ] *a* (*landscape*) wellig; **~ pin** *n* Nudel- *or* Wellholz *nt*; **~ stock** *n* Wagenmaterial *nt*.

ROM *n abbr* (= read only memory) ROM *m*.

Roman ['rəʊmən] *a* römisch // *n* Römer(in *f*) *m*; **~ Catholic** *a* römisch-katholisch // *n* Katholik(in *f*) *m*.

romance [rə'mæns] *n* Romanze *f*; (*story*) (Liebes)roman *m*.

Romania [rəʊ'meɪnɪə] *n* = **Rumania**.

Roman numeral *n* römische Ziffer.

romantic [rə'mæntɪk] *a* romantisch; **~ism** [rə'mæntɪsɪzəm] *n* Romantik *f*.

Rome [rəʊm] *n* Rom *nt*.

romp [rɒmp] *n* Tollen *nt* // *vi* (*also: ~ about*) herumtollen.

rompers ['rɒmpəz] *npl* Spielanzug *m*.

roof [ruːf] *n*, *pl* **~s** *n* Dach *nt*; (*of mouth*) Gaumen *m* // *vt* überdachen, überdecken; **~ing** *n* Deckmaterial *nt*; **~ rack** *n* (*AUT*) Dachgepäckträger *m*.

rook [rʊk] *n* (*bird*) Saatkrähe *f*; (*chess*) Turm *m*.

room [rʊm] *n* Zimmer *nt*, Raum *m*; (*space*) Platz *m*; (*fig*) Spielraum *m*; **~s** *pl* Wohnung *f*; **'~s to let'**, (*US*) **'~s for rent'** 'Zimmer zu vermieten'; **single/double ~** Einzel-/Doppelzimmer *nt*; **~ing house** *n* (*US*) Mietshaus *nt* (*mit möblierten Wohnungen*); **~-mate** *n* Mitbewohner(in *f*) *m*; **~ service** *n* Zimmerbedienung *f*; **~y** *a* geräumig.

roost [ruːst] *n* Hühnerstange *f* // *vi* auf der Stange hocken.

rooster ['ruːstə*] n Hahn m.

root [ruːt] n (lit, fig) Wurzel f // vi wurzeln; ~ **about** vi (fig) herumwühlen; ~ **for** vt Stimmung machen für; ~ **out** vt ausjäten; (fig) ausrotten.

rope [rəʊp] n Seil nt // vt (tie) festschnüren; **to know the ~s** sich auskennen; **to ~ sb in** jdn gewinnen; ~ **off** vt absperren; ~ **ladder** n Strickleiter f.

rosary ['rəʊzərɪ] n Rosenkranz m.

rose [rəʊz] pt of **rise** // n Rose f // a Rosen-, rosenrot.

rosé ['rəʊzeɪ] n Rosé m.

rosebud ['rəʊzbʌd] n Rosenknospe f.

rosebush ['rəʊzbʊʃ] n Rosenstock m.

rosemary ['rəʊzmərɪ] n Rosmarin m.

rosette [rəʊ'zet] n Rosette f.

roster ['rɒstə*] n Dienstplan m.

rostrum ['rɒstrəm] n Rednerbühne f.

rosy ['rəʊzɪ] a rosig.

rot [rɒt] n Fäulnis f; (nonsense) Quatsch m // vti verfaulen (lassen).

rota ['rəʊtə] n Dienstliste f.

rotary ['rəʊtərɪ] a rotierend.

rotate [rəʊ'teɪt] vt rotieren lassen; (two or more things in order) turnusmäßig wechseln // vi rotieren.

rotating [rəʊ'teɪtɪŋ] a rotierend.

rotation [rəʊ'teɪʃən] n Umdrehung f.

rote [rəʊt] n: **by ~** auswendig.

rotten ['rɒtn] a faul; (fig) schlecht, gemein; **to feel ~** (ill) sich elend fühlen.

rotund [rəʊ'tʌnd] a rundlich.

rouble, (US) **ruble** ['ruːbl] n Rubel m.

rough [rʌf] a (not smooth) rauh; (path) uneben; (violent) roh, grob; (crossing) stürmisch; (without comforts) hart, unbequem; (unfinished, makeshift) grob; (approximate) ungefähr // n (Brit: person) Rowdy m, Rohling m; (GOLF): **in the ~** im Rauh // vt: **to ~ it** primitiv leben; **to sleep ~** im Freien schlafen; **~age** n Ballaststoffe pl; **~-and-ready** a provisorisch; (work) zusammengehauen; **~cast** n Rauhputz m; ~ **copy** n, ~ **draft** n Entwurf m; **~en** vt aufrauhen; **~ly** ad grob; (about) ungefähr; **~ness** n Rauheit f; (of manner) Ungeschliffenheit f.

Roumania [ruː'meɪntə] n = **Rumania**.

round [raʊnd] a rund; (figures) aufgerundet // ad (in a circle) rundherum // prep um ... herum // n Runde f; (of ammunition) Magazin nt // vt (corner) biegen um; **all ~** überall; **the long way ~** der Umweg; **all the year ~** das ganze Jahr über; **it's just ~ the corner** (fig) es ist gerade um die Ecke; **~ the clock** ad rund um die Uhr; **to go ~** to sb's (house) jdn besuchen; **to go ~ the back** durch den Hintereingang gehen; **to go ~ a house** um ein Haus herumgehen; **enough to go ~** genug für alle; **to go the ~s** (story) die Runde machen; **a ~ of applause** ein Beifall m; **a ~ of drinks/**

sandwiches eine Runde Drinks/Sandwiches; ~ **off** vt abrunden; ~ **up** vt (end) abschließen; (figures) aufrunden; **~about** n (Brit: traffic) Kreisverkehr m; (: merry-go-round) Karussell nt // a auf Umwegen; **~ers** npl (game) ≃ Schlagball m; **~ly** ad (fig) gründlich; **~-shouldered** a mit abfallenden Schultern; ~ **trip** n Rundreise f; **~up** n Zusammentreiben nt, Sammeln nt.

rouse [raʊz] vt (waken) (auf)wecken; (stir up) erregen.

rousing ['raʊzɪŋ] a (welcome) stürmisch; (speech) zündend.

route [ruːt] n Weg m, Route f; ~ **map** n (Brit: for journey) Streckenkarte f.

routine [ruː'tiːn] n Routine f // a Routine-.

roving ['rəʊvɪŋ] a (reporter) im Außendienst.

row [rəʊ] n (line) Reihe f // vti (boat) rudern; **in a ~** (fig) hintereinander.

row [raʊ] n (noise) Lärm m; (dispute) Streit m // vi sich streiten.

rowboat ['rəʊbəʊt] n (US) Ruderboot nt.

rowdy ['raʊdɪ] a rüpelhaft // n (person) Rowdy m.

rowing ['rəʊɪŋ] n Rudern nt; (SPORT) Rudersport m; ~ **boat** n (Brit) Ruderboot nt.

royal ['rɔɪəl] a königlich, Königs-; ~ **Air Force (RAF)** n Königliche Luftwaffe f.

royalty ['rɔɪəltɪ] n (family) königliche Familie f; (for book) Tantieme f.

rpm abbr (= revs per minute) U/min.

R.S.V.P. abbr (= répondez s'il vous plaît) u.A.w.g.

Rt Hon. abbr (Brit: = Right Honourable) Abgeordnete(r) mf.

rub [rʌb] n (problem) Haken m // vt reiben; **to ~ sb up** or (US) ~ **sb the wrong way** jdn aufreizen; ~ **off** vi (lit, fig) abfärben (on auf +acc); ~ **out** vt herausreiben; (with eraser) ausradieren.

rubber ['rʌbə*] n Gummi m; (Brit) Radiergummi m; ~ **band** n Gummiband nt; ~ **plant** n Gummibaum m; **~y** a gummiartig.

rubbish ['rʌbɪʃ] n (waste) Abfall m; (nonsense) Blödsinn m, Quatsch m; ~ **bin** n (Brit) Mülleimer m; ~ **dump** n Müllablageplatz m.

rubble ['rʌbl] n (Stein)schutt m.

ruby ['ruːbɪ] n Rubin m // a rubinrot.

rucksack ['rʌksæk] n Rucksack m.

ructions ['rʌkʃənz] npl Krach m.

rudder ['rʌdə*] n Steuerruder nt.

ruddy ['rʌdɪ] a (colour) rötlich; (col: bloody) verdammt.

rude [ruːd] a unverschämt; (shock) hart; (awakening) unsanft; (unrefined, rough) grob; **~ness** n Unverschämtheit f; Grobheit f.

rudiment ['ru:dɪmənt] n Grundlage f.
rueful ['ru:fʊl] a reuevoll; (situation) beklagenswert.
ruffian ['rʌfɪən] n Rohling m.
ruffle ['rʌfl] vt kräuseln.
rug [rʌg] n Brücke f; (in bedroom) Bettvorleger m; (Brit: for knees) (Reise)decke f.
rugby ['rʌgbɪ] n (also: ~ football) Rugby nt.
rugged ['rʌgɪd] a (coastline) zerklüftet; (features) markig.
rugger ['rʌgə*] n (Brit col) Rugby nt.
ruin ['ru:ɪn] n Ruine f; (downfall) Ruin m // vt ruinieren; ~s pl Trümmer pl; ~ous a ruinierend.
rule [ru:l] n Regel f; (government) Regierung f; (for measuring) Lineal nt // vti (govern) herrschen über (+acc), regieren; (decide) anordnen, entscheiden; (make lines) linieren; as a ~ in der Regel; ~ out vt ausschließen; ~d a (paper) liniert; ~r n Lineal nt; Herrscher m.
ruling ['ru:lɪŋ] a (party) Regierungs-; (class) herrschend // n (JUR) Entscheid m.
rum [rʌm] n Rum m.
Rumania [ru:'meɪnɪə] n Rumänien nt; ~n a rumänisch // n Rumäne m, Rumänin f; (LING) Rumänisch nt.
rumble ['rʌmbl] n Rumpeln nt; (of thunder) Rollen nt // vi rumpeln; grollen.
rummage ['rʌmɪdʒ] vi durchstöbern.
rumour, (US) **rumor** ['ru:mə*] n Gerücht nt // vt: it is ~ed that man sagt or man munkelt, daß.
rump [rʌmp] n Hinterteil nt; ~ **steak** n Rumpsteak nt.
rumpus ['rʌmpəs] n Spektakel m.
run [rʌn] n Lauf m; (in car) (Spazier)fahrt f; (series) Serie f, Reihe f; (ski ~) (Ski)abfahrt f; (in stocking) Laufmasche f // a (pt ran, pp run) vt (cause to run) laufen lassen; (car, train, bus) fahren; (race, distance) laufen, rennen; (manage) leiten; (COMPUT) laufen lassen; (pass: hand, eye) gleiten lassen // vi laufen; (move quickly also) rennen; (bus, train) fahren; (flow) fließen, laufen; (colours) (ab)färben; there was a ~ on (meat, tickets) es gab einen Ansturm auf (+acc); on the ~ auf der Flucht; in the long ~ auf die Dauer; I'll ~ you to the station ich fahre dich zum Bahnhof; to ~ a risk ein Risiko eingehen; ~ **about** or **around** vi (children) umherspringen; ~ **across** vt (find) stoßen auf (+acc); ~ **away** vi weglaufen; ~ **down** vi (clock) ablaufen // vt (production, factory) allmählich auflösen; (with car) überfahren; (talk against) heruntermachen; to be ~ down erschöpft or abgespannt sein; ~ **in** vt (Brit: car) einfahren; ~ **into** vt (meet:

person) zufällig treffen; (: trouble) bekommen; (collide with) rennen/fahren gegen; ~ **off** vi fortlaufen; ~ **out** vi (person) hinausrennen; (liquid) auslaufen; (lease) ablaufen; (money) ausgehen; he ran out of money/petrol ihm ging das Geld/Benzin aus; ~ **over** vt (in accident) überfahren; ~ **through** vt (instructions) durchgehen; ~ **up** vt (debt, bill) machen; ~ **up against** vt (difficulties) stoßen auf (+acc); ~**away** a (horse) ausgebrochen; (person) flüchtig.
rung [rʌŋ] pp of **ring** // n Sprosse f.
runner ['rʌnə*] n Läufer(in f) m; (for sleigh) Kufe f; ~ **bean** n (Brit) Stangenbohne f; ~-**up** n Zweite(r) mf.
running ['rʌnɪŋ] n (of business) Leitung f; (of machine) Betrieb m // a (water) fließend; (commentary) laufend; to be in/out of the ~ for sth im/aus dem Rennen für etw sein; 3 days ~ 3 Tage lang or hintereinander.
runny ['rʌnɪ] a dünn.
run-of-the-mill ['rʌnəvðə'mɪl] a gewöhnlich, alltäglich.
run-up ['rʌnʌp] n: ~ **to** (election etc) Endphase vor (+dat).
runway ['rʌnweɪ] n Startbahn f.
rupee [ru:'pi:] n Rupie f.
rupture ['rʌptʃə*] n (MED) Bruch m // vt: to ~ **o.s.** sich (dat) einen Bruch zuziehen.
rural ['rʊərəl] a ländlich, Land-.
ruse [ru:z] n Kniff m, List f.
rush [rʌʃ] n Eile f, Hetze f; (FIN) starke Nachfrage f // vt (carry along) auf dem schnellsten Wege schaffen or transportieren; (attack) losstürmen auf (+acc); don't ~ me dräng mich nicht // vi (hurry) eilen, stürzen; ~ **hour** n Hauptverkehrszeit f.
rusk [rʌsk] n Zwieback m.
Russia ['rʌʃə] n Rußland nt; ~n a russisch // n Russe m, Russin f; (LING) Russisch nt.
rust [rʌst] n Rost m // vi rosten.
rustic ['rʌstɪk] a bäuerlich, ländlich.
rustle ['rʌsl] n rauschen, rascheln // vt rascheln lassen; (cattle) stehlen.
rustproof ['rʌstpru:f] a rostfrei.
rusty ['rʌstɪ] a rostig.
rut [rʌt] n (in track) Radspur f; to be in a ~ im Trott stecken.
ruthless ['ru:θlɪs] a rücksichtslos.
rye [raɪ] n Roggen m; ~ **bread** n Roggenbrot nt.

S

sabbatical [sə'bætɪkəl] a: ~ **year** n Beurlaubungs- or Forschungsjahr nt.
sabotage ['sæbətɑ:ʒ] n Sabotage f // vt sabotieren.

saccharin(e) ['sækərɪn] n Saccharin nt.

sachet ['sæʃeɪ] n (of shampoo) Briefchen nt, Kissen nt.

sack [sæk] n Sack m // vt (col) hinauswerfen; (pillage) plündern; **to get the ~** rausfliegen; **~ing** n (material) Sackleinen nt; (col) Rausschmiß m.

sacred ['seɪkrɪd] a heilig.

sacrifice ['sækrɪfaɪs] n Opfer nt // vt (lit, fig) opfern.

sacrilege ['sækrɪlɪdʒ] n Schändung f.

sad [sæd] a traurig; **~den** vt traurig machen, betrüben.

saddle ['sædl] n Sattel m // vt (burden) aufhalsen (sb with sth jdm etw); **~bag** n Satteltasche f.

sadly ['sædlɪ] ad traurig; (unfortunately) leider; **she is ~ lacking (in)** ... ihr fehlt es leider ...

sadness ['sædnəs] n Traurigkeit f.

sae abbr (= stamped addressed envelope) adressierte(r) Rückumschlag m.

safe [seɪf] a (free from danger) sicher; (careful) vorsichtig // n Safe m; **~ and sound** gesund und wohl; **(just) to be on the ~ side** um ganz sicher zu gehen; **~- conduct** n freie(s) Geleit nt; **~-deposit** n (vault) Tresorraum m; (box) Banksafe m; **~-guard** n Sicherung f // vt sichern, schützen; **~-keeping** n sichere Verwahrung f; **~ly** ad sicher; (arrive) wohlbehalten.

safety ['seɪftɪ] n Sicherheit f; **~ belt** n Sicherheitsgurt m; **~ pin** n Sicherheitsnadel f; **~ valve** n Sicherheitsventil nt.

sag [sæg] vi (durch)sacken.

sage [seɪdʒ] n (herb) Salbei m; (man) Weise(r) m.

Sagittarius [sædʒɪ'teərɪəs] n Schütze m.

Sahara [sə'hɑːrə] n: **the ~ (Desert)** die (Wüste) Sahara.

said [sed] pt, pp of **say**.

sail [seɪl] n Segel nt; (trip) Fahrt f // vt segeln // vi segeln; (begin voyage: person) abfahren; (: ship) auslaufen; (fig: cloud etc) dahinsegeln; **to go for a ~** segeln gehen; **they ~ed into Copenhagen** sie liefen in Kopenhagen ein; **to ~ through** vti (fig) spielend schaffen; **~boat** n (US) Segelboot nt; **~ing** n Segeln nt; **~ing ship** n Segelschiff nt; **~or** n Matrose m, Seemann m.

saint [seɪnt] n Heilige(r) mf; **~ly** a heilig, fromm.

sake [seɪk] n: **for the ~ of** um (+gen) willen.

salad ['sæləd] n Salat m; **~ bowl** n Salatschüssel f; **~ cream** n (Brit) gewürzte Mayonnaise f; **~ dressing** n Salatsoße f.

salami [sə'lɑːmɪ] n Salami f.

salary ['sælərɪ] n Gehalt nt.

sale [seɪl] n Verkauf m; (reduced prices)

Schlußverkauf m; **'for ~'** zu verkaufen; **on ~** zu verkaufen; **~room** n Verkaufsraum m; **~s assistant**, (US) **~s clerk** n Verkäufer(in f) m; **salesman** n Verkäufer m; (representative) Vertreter m; **saleswoman** n Verkäuferin f.

salient ['seɪlɪənt] a bemerkenswert.

saliva [sə'laɪvə] n Speichel m.

sallow ['sæləʊ] a fahl; (face) bleich.

salmon ['sæmən] n Lachs m.

saloon [sə'luːn] n (Brit AUT) Limousine f; (ship's lounge) Salon m.

salt [sɔːlt] n Salz nt // vt (cure) einsalzen; (flavour) salzen; **~ away** n (col: money) auf die hohe Kante legen; **~cellar** n Salzfaß nt; **~ water** a Salzwasser-; **~y** a salzig.

salutary ['sæljʊtərɪ] a nützlich.

salute [sə'luːt] n (MIL) Gruß m; (with guns) Salutschüsse pl // vt (MIL) salutieren.

salvage ['sælvɪdʒ] n (from ship) Bergung f; (property) Rettung f // vt bergen; retten.

salvation [sæl'veɪʃən] n Rettung f; **S-Army** n Heilsarmee f.

same [seɪm] a, pron (similar) gleiche(r, s); (identical) derselbe/dieselbe/ dasselbe; **the ~ book** as das gleiche Buch wie; **at the ~ time** zur gleichen Zeit, gleichzeitig; (however) zugleich, andererseits; **all or just the ~** trotzdem; **the ~ to you!** gleichfalls.

sample ['sɑːmpl] n Probe f // vt probieren.

sanctify ['sæŋktɪfaɪ] vt weihen.

sanctimonious [sæŋktɪ'məʊnɪəs] a scheinheilig.

sanctity ['sæŋktɪtɪ] n Heiligkeit f; (fig) Unverletzlichkeit f.

sanctuary ['sæŋktjʊərɪ] n (for fugitive) Asyl nt; (refuge) Zufluchtsort m; (for animals) Schutzgebiet nt.

sand [sænd] n Sand m // vt (furniture) schmirgeln; **~s** pl Sand m.

sandal ['sændl] n Sandale f.

sand-: ~box n (US) = **~pit**; **~castle** n Sandburg f; **~ dune** n (Sand)düne f; **~paper** n Sandpapier nt; **~pit** n Sandkasten m; **~stone** n Sandstein m.

sandwich ['sænwɪdʒ] n Sandwich m or nt // vt (also: **~ in**) einklemmen; **~ed between** eingeklemmt zwischen; **cheese/ ham ~** Käse-/Schinkenbrot; **~ board** n Reklametafel f; **~ course** n (Brit) Ausbildungsgang m mit abwechselnden Theorie- und Praxisteilen.

sandy ['sændɪ] a sandig; (hair) rotblond.

sane [seɪn] a geistig gesund or normal; (sensible) vernünftig, gescheit.

sang [sæŋ] pt of **sing**.

sanitary ['sænɪtərɪ] a hygienisch; **~ towel**, (US) **~ napkin** n (Monats)binde f.

sanitation [sænɪ'teɪʃən] n sanitäre Ein-

richtungen *pl*; ~ **department** *n* (*US*)
Stadtreinigung *f*.
sanity ['sænɪtɪ] *n* geistige Gesundheit *f*;
(*good sense*) Vernunft *f*.
sank [sæŋk] *pt of* **sink**.
Santa Claus [sæntə'klɔːz] *n* Nikolaus
m, Weihnachtsmann *m*.
sap [sæp] *n* (*of plants*) Saft *m* // *vt*
(*strength*) schwächen.
sapling ['sæplɪŋ] *n* junge(r) Baum *m*.
sapphire ['sæfaɪə*] *n* Saphir *m*.
sarcastic [sɑː'kæstɪk] *a* sarkastisch.
sardine [sɑː'diːn] *n* Sardine *f*.
Sardinia [sɑː'dɪnɪə] *n* Sardinien *nt*.
sardonic [sɑː'dɒnɪk] *a* zynisch.
sash [sæʃ] *n* Schärpe *f*.
sat [sæt] *pt*, *pp of* **sit**.
Satan ['seɪtn] *n* Satan *m*.
satchel ['sætʃəl] *n* (*SCH*) Schulmappe *f*.
sated ['seɪtɪd] *a* (*appetite*, *person*)
gesättigt.
satin ['sætɪn] *n* Satin *m* // *a* Satin-.
satisfaction [sætɪs'fækʃən] *n* Befriedigung *f*, Genugtuung *f*.
satisfactory [sætɪs'fæktərɪ] *a* zufrieden-
stellend, befriedigend.
satisfy ['sætɪsfaɪ] *vt* befriedigen, zu-
friedenstellen; (*convince*) überzeugen;
(*conditions*) erfüllen; ~**ing** *a* befriedigend; (*meal*) sättigend.
saturate ['sætʃəreɪt] *vt* (durch)tränken.
saturation [sætʃə'reɪʃən] *n* Durchträn-
kung *f*; (*CHEM*, *fig*) Sättigung *f*.
Saturday ['sætədeɪ] *n* Samstag *m*,
Sonnabend *m*.
sauce [sɔːs] *n* Soße *f*, Sauce *f*; ~**pan** *n*
Kasserolle *f*.
saucer ['sɔːsə*] *n* Untertasse *f*.
saucy ['sɔːsɪ] *a* frech, keck.
Saudi ['saʊdɪ]: ~ **Arabia** *n* Saudi-
Arabien *nt*; ~ (**Arabian**) *a*
saudiarabisch // *n* Saudiaraber(in *f*) *m*.
sauna ['sɔːnə] *n* Sauna *f*.
saunter ['sɔːntə*] *vi* schlendern.
sausage ['sɒsɪdʒ] *n* Wurst *f*; ~ **roll** *n*
Wurst *f* im Schlafrock, Wurstpastete *f*.
sauté ['səʊteɪ] *a* Röst-.
savage ['sævɪdʒ] *a* wild // *n* Wilde(r) *mf*
// *vt* (*animals*) zerfleischen; ~**ry** *n* Ro-
heit *f*, Grausamkeit *f*.
save [seɪv] *vt* retten; (*money*, *electricity*
etc) sparen; (*strength etc*) aufsparen;
(*COMPUT*) speichern // *vi* (*also*: ~ **up**)
sparen // *n* (*SPORT*) (Ball)abwehr *f* //
prep, *cj* außer, ausgenommen.
saving ['seɪvɪŋ] *a*: the ~ **grace** of das
Versöhnende an (+ *dat*) // *n* Sparen *nt*,
Ersparnis *f*; ~**s** *pl* Ersparnisse *pl*; ~**s**
bank *n* Sparkasse *f*; ~**s account** *n*
Sparkonto *nt*.
saviour, (*US*) **savior** ['seɪvjə*] *n*
(*ECCL*) Erlöser *m*.
savour, (*US*) **savor** ['seɪvə*] *vt* (*taste*)
schmecken; (*fig*) genießen; ~**y** *a* pikant,
würzig.

saw [sɔː] *pt of* **see** // *n* (*tool*) Säge *f* //
vti, *pt* **sawed**, *pp* **sawed** *or* **sawn**
sägen; ~**dust** *n* Sägemehl *nt*; ~**mill** *n*
Sägewerk *nt*; ~**n-off shotgun** *n*
Gewehr *nt* mit abgesägtem Lauf.
say [seɪ] *n*: to have no/a ~ in sth (kein)
Mitspracherecht bei etw haben; let him
have his ~ laß ihn doch reden // *vti*, *pt*,
pp **said** sagen; to ~ yes/no ja/nein
sagen; that goes without ~ing das Versteht sich von selbst; that is to ~ das
heißt; ~**ing** *n* Sprichwort *nt*.
scab [skæb] *n* Schorf *m*; (*pej*) Streikbre-
cher *m*.
scaffold ['skæfəʊld] *n* (*for execution*)
Schafott *nt*; ~**ing** *n* (Bau)gerüst *nt*.
scald [skɔːld] *n* Verbrühung *f* // *vt* (*burn*)
verbrühen; (*clean*) ausbrühen.
scale [skeɪl] *n* (*of fish*) Schuppe *f*; (*MUS*)
Tonleiter *f*; (*on map*, *size*) Maßstab *m*;
(*gradation*) Skala *f* // *vt* (*climb*) er-
klimmen; ~**s** *pl* (*balance*) Waage *f*; on
a large ~ (*fig*) im großen, in großem
Umfang; ~ **of charges** Gebührenordnung
f; ~ **down** *vt* verkleinern; ~ **model** *n*
maßstabgetreue(s) Modell *nt*.
scallop ['skɒləp] *n* Kammuschel *f*.
scalp [skælp] *n* Kopfhaut *f*.
scamper ['skæmpə*] *vi*: ~ **away**, ~
off verschwinden.
scampi ['skæmpɪ] *npl* Scampi *pl*.
scan [skæn] *vt* (*examine*) genau prüfen;
(*quickly*) überfliegen; (*horizon*) absuchen; (*poetry*) skandieren.
Scandinavia [skændɪ'neɪvɪə] *n*
Skandinavien *nt*; ~**n** *a* skandinavisch //
n Skandinavier(in *f*) *m*.
scant [skænt] *a* knapp; ~**ily** *ad* knapp,
dürftig; ~**iness** *n* Knappheit *f*; ~**y** *a*
knapp, unzureichend.
scapegoat ['skeɪpgəʊt] *n* Sündenbock
m.
scar [skɑː*] *n* Narbe *f* // *vt* durch Narben
entstellen.
scarce ['skɛəs] *a* selten, rar; (*goods*)
knapp; ~**ly** *ad* kaum.
scarcity ['skɛəsɪtɪ] *n* Mangel *m*.
scare {'skɛə*] *n* Schrecken *m* // *vt*
erschrecken; to ~ sb stiff jdn zu Tode
erschrecken; to be ~d Angst haben;
bomb ~ Bombendrohung *f*; ~**crow** *n*
Vogelscheuche *f*.
scarf [skɑːf], *pl* **scarves** *n* Schal *m*;
(*head*~) Kopftuch *nt*.
scarlet ['skɑːlət] *a* scharlachrot // *n*
Scharlachrot *nt*; ~ **fever** *n* Scharlach
m.
scarves [skɑːvz] *pl of* **scarf**.
scary ['skɛərɪ] *a* (*col*) schaurig.
scathing ['skeɪðɪŋ] *a* scharf, vernichtend.
scatter ['skætə*] *vt* (*sprinkle*)
(ver)streuen; (*disperse*) zerstreuen // *vi*
sich zerstreuen; ~**brained** *a* flatterhaft,
schusselig.

scavenger ['skævɪndʒə*] n (animal) Aasfresser m.

scenario [sɪ'nɑːrɪəʊ] n (THEAT, CINE) Szenarium nt; (fig) Szenario nt.

scene [siːn] n (of happening) Ort m; (of play, incident) Szene f; (view) Anblick m; (argument) Szene f, Auftritt m; **~ry** ['siːnərɪ] n (THEAT) Bühnenbild nt; (landscape) Landschaft f.

scenic ['siːnɪk] a landschaftlich.

scent [sent] n Parfüm nt; (smell) Duft m // vt parfümieren.

schedule ['ʃedjuːl] n (list) Liste f; (plan) Programm nt; (of work) Zeitplan m // vt planen; on ~ pünktlich; to be ahead of/behind ~ dem Zeitplan voraus/im Rückstand sein; **~d flight** n (not charter) Linienflug m.

scheme [skiːm] n Schema nt; (dishonest) Intrige f; (plan of action) Plan m // vi intrigieren // vt planen.

scheming ['skiːmɪŋ] a intrigierend.

scholar ['skɒlə*] n Gelehrte(r) m; (holding scholarship) Stipendiat m; **~ly** a gelehrt; **~ship** n Gelehrsamkeit f; (grant) Stipendium nt.

school [skuːl] n Schule f; (UNIV) Fakultät f // vt schulen; (dog) trainieren; ~ **age** n schulpflichtige(s) Alter nt; **~book** n Schulbuch nt; **~boy** n Schüler m; ~ **children** npl Schüler pl, Schulkinder pl; **~days** pl (alte) Schulzeit f; **~girl** n Schülerin f; **~ing** n Schulung f, Ausbildung f; **~master** n Lehrer m; **~mistress** n Lehrerin f; **~teacher** n Lehrer(in f) m.

sciatica [saɪ'ætɪkə] n Ischias m or nt.

science ['saɪəns] n Wissenschaft f; (natural ~) Naturwissenschaft f.

scientific [saɪən'tɪfɪk] a wissenschaftlich; (natural sciences) naturwissenschaftlich.

scientist ['saɪəntɪst] n Wissenschaftler(in f) m.

scintillating ['sɪntɪleɪtɪŋ] a sprühend.

scissors ['sɪzəz] npl Schere f; a pair of ~ eine Schere.

scoff [skɒf] vt (Brit col: eat) fressen // vi (mock) spotten (at über +acc).

scold [skəʊld] vt schimpfen.

scone [skɒn] n weiche(s) Teegebäck nt.

scoop [skuːp] n Schaufel f; (news) sensationelle Erstmeldung f // vt (also: ~ out or up) schaufeln.

scooter ['skuːtə*] n Motorroller m; (child's) Roller m.

scope [skəʊp] n Ausmaß nt; (opportunity) (Spiel)raum m.

scorch [skɔːtʃ] n Brandstelle f // vt versengen; **~ing** a brennend.

score [skɔː*] n (in game) Punktzahl f; (final ~) (Spiel)ergebnis nt; (MUS) Partitur f; (line) Kratzer m; (twenty) 20, 20 Stück // vt (goal) schießen; (points) machen; (mark) einritzen // vi

(keep record) Punkte zählen; on that ~ in dieser Hinsicht; what's the ~? wie steht's? ~ out vt ausstreichen; **~board** n Anschreibetafel f; **~r** n Torschütze m; (recorder) (Auf)schreiber m.

scorn ['skɔːn] n Verachtung f // vt verhöhnen; **~ful** a verächtlich.

Scorpio ['skɔːpɪəʊ] n Skorpion m.

Scot [skɒt] n Schotte m, Schottin f.

scotch [skɒtʃ] vt (end) unterbinden; **S~** n Scotch m.

scot-free ['skɒt'friː] ad: to get off ~ (unpunished) ungeschoren davonkommen.

Scotland ['skɒtlənd] n Schottland nt.

Scots [skɒts] a schottisch; **~man/-woman** n Schotte m/Schottin f.

Scottish ['skɒtɪʃ] a schottisch.

scoundrel ['skaʊndrəl] n Schuft m.

scour ['skaʊə*] vt (search) absuchen; (clean) schrubben.

scourge [skɜːdʒ] n (whip) Geißel f; (plague) Qual f.

scout [skaʊt] n (MIL) Späher m; (also: boy ~) Pfadfinder m // vi: ~ **around** vi sich umsehen (for nach).

scowl [skaʊl] n finstere(r) Blick m // vi finster blicken.

scrabble ['skræbl] vi (claw) kratzen (at an + dat); (also: ~ **around**: search) (herum)tasten // n: S~ ® Scrabble nt ®.

scraggy ['skrægɪ] a dürr, hager.

scram [skræm] vi (col) abhauen.

scramble ['skræmbl] n (climb) Kletterei f; (struggle) Kampf m // vi klettern; (fight) sich schlagen; to ~ out/through krabbeln ausdurch; to ~ **for** sth sich um etw raufen; **~d eggs** npl Rührei nt.

scrap [skræp] n (bit) Stückchen nt; (fight) Keilerei f; (also: ~ **iron**) Schrott m // vt verwerfen // vi (fight) streiten, sich prügeln; **~book** n Einklebealbum nt; ~ **dealer** n Schrotthändler(in f) m; **~s** pl Reste pl; (waste) Abfall m.

scrape [skreɪp] n Kratzen nt; (trouble) Klemme f // vt kratzen; (car) zerkratzen; (clean) abkratzen // vi (make harsh noise) kratzen; to ~ **through** gerade noch durchkommen; **~r** n Kratzer m.

scrap heap ['skræphiːp] n Schrotthaufen m; on the ~ (fig) beim alten Eisen.

scrap merchant ['skræpmɜːtʃənt] n (Brit) Altwarenhändler(in f) m.

scrappy ['skræpɪ] a zusammengestoppelt.

scratch [skrætʃ] n (wound) Kratzer m, Schramme f // a: ~ **team** zusammengewürfelte Mannschaft // vt kratzen; (car) zerkratzen // vi (sich) kratzen; to start from ~ ganz von vorne anfangen; to be up to ~ den Anforderungen entsprechen.

scrawl [skrɔːl] n Gekritzel nt // vti kritzeln.

scrawny ['skrɔ:nɪ] a (*person, neck*) dürr.

scream [skri:m] n Schrei m // vi schreien.

scree [skri:] n Geröll(halde f) nt.

screech [skri:tʃ] n Schrei m // vi kreischen.

screen [skri:n] n (*protective*) Schutzschirm m; (*film*) Leinwand f; (*TV*) Bildschirm m // vt (*shelter*) (be)schirmen; (*film*) zeigen, vorführen; **~ing** n (*MED*) Untersuchung f; **~play** n Drehbuch nt.

screw [skru:] n Schraube f // vt (*fasten*) schrauben; (*vulgar*) bumsen; **~ up** vt (*paper etc*) zerknüllen; (*col: ruin*) vermasseln (*col*); **~driver** n Schraubenzieher m.

scribble ['skrɪbl] n Gekritzel nt // vt kritzeln.

script [skrɪpt] n (*handwriting*) Handschrift f; (*for film*) Drehbuch nt; (*THEAT*) Manuskript nt, Text m.

Scripture ['skrɪptʃə*] n Heilige Schrift f.

scroll [skrəʊl] n Schriftrolle f.

scrounge [skraʊndʒ] vt (*col*): **to ~ sth off** or **from sb** etw bei jdm abstauben // n: **on the ~** beim Schnorren.

scrub [skrʌb] n (*clean*) Schrubben nt; (*in countryside*) Gestrüpp nt // vt (*clean*) schrubben; (*reject*) fallenlassen.

scruff [skrʌf] n: **by the ~ of the neck** am Genick.

scruffy ['skrʌfɪ] a unordentlich, vergammelt.

scrum(mage) ['skrʌm(ɪdʒ)] n Getümmel nt.

scruple ['skru:pl] n Skrupel m, Bedenken nt.

scrupulous ['skru:pjʊləs] a peinlich genau, gewissenhaft.

scrutinize ['skru:tɪnaɪz] vt genau prüfen.

scrutiny ['skru:tɪnɪ] n genaue Untersuchung f.

scuff [skʌf] vt (*shoes*) abstoßen.

scuffle ['skʌfl] n Handgemenge nt.

scullery ['skʌlərɪ] n Spülküche f.

sculptor ['skʌlptə*] n Bildhauer(in f) m.

sculpture ['skʌlptʃə*] n (*ART*) Bildhauerei f; (*statue*) Skulptur f.

scum [skʌm] n (*lit, fig*) Abschaum m.

scupper ['skʌpə*] vt (*NAUT*) versenken; (*fig*) zerstören.

scurrilous ['skʌrɪləs] a unflätig.

scurry ['skʌrɪ] vi huschen.

scuttle ['skʌtl] n (*also: coal ~*) Kohleneimer m // vt (*ship*) versenken // vi (*scamper*): **to ~ away** or **off** sich davonmachen.

scythe [saɪð] n Sense f.

SDP n abbr (*Brit: = Social Democratic Party*) Sozialdemokratische Partei f.

sea [si:] n Meer nt (*also fig*), See f // a Meeres-, See-; **by ~** (*travel*) auf dem Seeweg; **on the ~** (*boat*) auf dem Meer;

(*town*) am Meer; **to be all at ~** (*fig*) nicht durchblicken; **out to** or **at ~** aufs Meer (hinaus); **~board** n Küste f; **~ breeze** n Seewind m; **~food** n Meeresfrüchte pl; **~ front** n Strandpromenade f; **~going** a seetüchtig, Hochsee-; **~gull** n Möwe f.

seal [si:l] n (*animal*) Robbe f, Seehund m; (*stamp, impression*) Siegel nt // vt versiegeln.

sea level ['si:levl] n Meeresspiegel m.

sea lion ['si:laɪən] n Seelöwe m.

seam [si:m] n Saum m; (*edges joining*) Naht f; (*of coal*) Flöz nt.

seaman ['si:mən] n Seemann m.

seamy ['si:mɪ] a (*people, café*) zwielichtig; (*life*) anrüchig.

seaplane ['si:pleɪn] n Wasserflugzeug nt.

seaport ['si:pɔ:t] n Seehafen m.

search [sɜ:tʃ] n Suche f (*for* nach) // vi suchen // vt (*examine*) durchsuchen; **in ~ of** auf der Suche nach; **~ for** vt suchen nach; **~ through** vt durchsuchen; **~ing** a (*look*) forschend; **~light** n Scheinwerfer m; **~ party** n Suchmannschaft f; **~ warrant** n Durchsuchungsbefehl m.

seashore ['si:ʃɔ:*] n Meeresküste f.

seasick ['si:sɪk] a seekrank; **~ness** n Seekrankheit f.

seaside ['si:saɪd] n Küste f; **~ resort** n Badeort m.

season ['si:zn] n Jahreszeit f; (*e.g. Christmas*) Zeit f, Saison f // vt (*flavour*) würzen; **~al** a Saison-; **~ed** a (*fig*) erfahren; **~ing** n Gewürz nt, Würze f; **~ ticket** n (*RAIL*) Zeitkarte f; (*THEAT*) Abonnement nt.

seat [si:t] n Sitz m, Platz m; (*in Parliament*) Sitz m; (*part of body*) Gesäß nt; (*part of garment*) Hosenboden m // vt (*place*) setzen; (*have space for*) Sitzplätze bieten für; **to be ~ed** sitzen; **~ belt** n Sicherheitsgurt m.

sea water ['si:wɔ:tə*] n Meerwasser nt.

seaweed ['si:wi:d] n (See)tang m.

seaworthy ['si:wɜ:ðɪ] a seetüchtig.

sec. abbr (= second(s)) Sek.

secluded [sɪ'klu:dɪd] a abgelegen.

seclusion [sɪ'klu:ʒən] n Zurückgezogenheit f.

second ['sekənd] a zweite(r, s) // ad (*in ~ position*) an zweiter Stelle // n Sekunde f; (*person*) Zweite(r) m; (*COMM: imperfect*) zweite Wahl f; (*SPORT*) Sekundant m (*AUT: also: ~ gear*) zweiter Gang; (*Brit SCOL: degree*) mittlere Note bei Prüfungen // vt (*support*) unterstützen; **~ary** a zweitrangig; **~ary school** n höhere Schule f, Mittelschule f; **~class** a zweiter Klasse; **~hand** a aus zweiter Hand; (*car etc*) gebraucht; **~ hand** n (*on clock*) Sekundenzeiger m; **~ly** ad zweitens; **~ment** [sɪ'kɔndmənt] n (*Brit*) Abordnung f; **~-**

rate *a* mittelmäßig; ~ **thoughts** *npl*: to have ~ thoughts es sich (*dat*) anders überlegen; **on** ~ **thoughts** *or* (*US*) thought or lieber (nicht).

secrecy ['si:krəsɪ] *n* Geheimhaltung *f*.

secret ['si:krət] *n* Geheimnis *nt* // *a* geheim, Geheim-; **in** ~, ~**ly** *ad* geheim.

secretarial [sekrə'tɛərɪəl] *a* Sekretärinnen-.

secretary ['sekrɪtrɪ] *n* Sekretär(in *f*) *m*; (*government*) Minister *m*.

secretion [sɪ'kri:ʃən] *n* Absonderung *f*.

secretive ['si:krətɪv] *a* geheimtuerisch.

section ['sekʃən] *n* Teil *m*; (*department*) Abteilung *f*; (*of document*) Abschnitt *m*.

sector ['sektə*] *n* Sektor *m*.

secular ['sekjulə*] *a* weltlich, profan.

secure [sɪ'kjuə*] *a* (*safe*) sicher; (*firmly fixed*) fest // *vt* (*make firm*) befestigen, sichern; (*obtain*) sichern.

security [sɪ'kjuərɪtɪ] *n* Sicherheit *f*; (*pledge*) Pfand *nt*; (*document*) Wertpapier *nt*; (*national* ~) Staatssicherheit *f*.

sedan [sɪ'dæn] *n* (*US AUT*) Limousine *f*.

sedate [sɪ'deɪt] *a* gesetzt // *vt* (*MED*) ein Beruhigungsmittel geben (+*dat*).

sedation [sɪ'deɪʃən] *n* (*MED*) Einfluß *m* von Beruhigungsmitteln.

sedative ['sedətɪv] *n* Beruhigungsmittel *nt* // *a* beruhigend, einschläfernd.

sedentary ['sedntrɪ] *a* (*job*) sitzend.

sediment ['sedɪmənt] *n* (Boden)satz *m*.

sedition [sə'dɪʃən] *n* Aufwiegelung *f*.

seduce [sɪ'dju:s] *vt* verführen.

seduction [sɪ'dʌkʃən] *n* Verführung *f*.

seductive [sɪ'dʌktɪv] *a* verführerisch.

see [si:] *v* (*pt* **saw**, *pp* **seen**) *vt* sehen; (*understand*) (ein)sehen, erkennen; (*visit*) besuchen // *vi* (*be aware*) sehen; (*find out*) nachsehen // *n* (*ECCL: R.C.*) Bistum *nt*; (: *Protestant*) Kirchenkreis *m*; **to** ~ **sb to the door** jdn hinausbegleiten; **to** ~ **that** (*ensure*) dafür sorgen, daß; **to** ~ **about** sich kümmern um; ~ **you soon!** bis bald!; **to** ~ **sth through** etw durchfechten; **to** ~ **through sb/sth** jdn/etw durchschauen; **to** ~ **to it** dafür sorgen; **to** ~ **sb off** jdn zum Zug *etc* begleiten.

seed [si:d] *n* Samen *m* // *vt* (*Tennis*) plazieren; **to go to** ~ (*plant*) schießen; (*fig*) herunterkommen; ~**ling** *n* Setzling *m*; ~**y** *a* (*café*) übel; (*person*) zweifelhaft.

seeing ['si:ɪŋ] *cj*: ~ (**that**) da.

seek [si:k], *pt, pp* **sought** *vt* suchen.

seem [si:m] *vi* scheinen; there ~s to be ... es scheint, ...; ~**ingly** *ad* anscheinend.

seen [si:n] *pp of* **see.**

seep [si:p] *vi* sickern.

seesaw ['si:sɔ:] *n* Wippe *f*.

seethe [si:ð] *vi*: **to** ~ **with anger** vor Wut

kochen.

see-through ['si:θru:] *a* (*dress*) durchsichtig.

segment ['segmənt] *n* Teil *m*; (*of circle*) Ausschnitt *m*.

segregate ['segrɪgeɪt] *vt* trennen.

seize [si:z] *vt* (*grasp*) (er)greifen, packen; (*power*) ergreifen; (*take legally*) beschlagnahmen; ~ (**up**)**on** *vt* sich stürzen auf (+*acc*); ~ **up** *vi* (*TECH*) sich festfressen.

seizure ['si:ʒə*] *n* (*illness*) Anfall *m*.

seldom ['seldəm] *ad* selten.

select [sɪ'lekt] *a* ausgewählt // *vt* auswählen; ~**ion** [sɪ'lekʃən] *n* Auswahl *f*; ~**ive** *a* (*person*) wählerisch.

self [self] *pron* selbst // *n, pl* **selves** Selbst *nt*, Ich *nt*; **the** ~ das Ich; ~**assured** *a* selbstbewußt; ~**catering** *a* (*Brit*) für Selbstversorger; ~**centred**, (*US*) ~**centered** *a* egozentrisch; ~**confidence** *n* Selbstvertrauen *nt*, Selbstbewußtsein *nt*; ~**conscious** *a* gehemmt, befangen; ~**contained** *a* (*complete*) (in sich) geschlossen; (*person*) verschlossen; (*Brit*: *flat*) separat; ~**control** *n* Selbstbeherrschung *f*; ~**defence**, (*US*) ~**defense** *n* Selbstverteidigung *f*; (*JUR*) Notwehr *f*; ~**discipline** *n* Selbstdisziplin *f*; ~**employed** *a* frei(schaffend); ~**evident** *a* offensichtlich; ~**governing** *a* selbstverwaltet; ~**indulgent** *a* zügellos; ~**interest** *n* Eigennutz *m*; ~**ish** *a* egoistisch, selbstsüchtig; ~**ishness** *n* Egoismus *m*, Selbstsucht *f*; ~**lessly** *ad* selbstlos; ~**pity** *n* Selbstmitleid *nt*; ~**portrait** *n* Selbstbildnis *nt*; ~**possessed** *a* selbstbeherrscht; ~**preservation** *n* Selbsterhaltung *f*; ~**reliant** *a* unabhängig; ~**respect** *n* Selbstachtung *f*; ~**righteous** *a* selbstgerecht; ~**sacrifice** *n* Selbstaufopferung *f*; ~**satisfied** *a* selbstzufrieden; ~**service** *a* Selbstbedienungs-; ~**sufficient** *a* selbstgenügsam; ~**taught** *a* selbstlernt; a ~**taught** person ein Autodidakt.

sell [sel] *v* (*pt, pp* **sold**) *vt* verkaufen // *vi* verkaufen; (*goods*) sich verkaufen; **to** ~ **at** *or* **for £10** für £10 verkaufen; ~ **off** *vt* verkaufen; ~ **out** *vi* alles verkaufen; ~-**by date** *n* Verfalldatum *nt*; ~**er** *n* Verkäufer *m*; ~**ing price** *n* Verkaufspreis *m*.

Sellotape ['seləuteɪp] *n* ® (*Brit*) Tesafilm *m* ®.

sellout ['selaut] *n* (*of tickets*): it was a ~ es war ausverkauft.

selves [selvz] *pl of* **self.**

semaphore ['seməfɔ:*] *n* Winkzeichen *pl*.

semblance ['sembləns] *n* Anschein *m*.

semen ['si:mən] *n* Sperma *nt*.

semester [sɪ'mestə*] *n* (*US*) Semester

nt.

semi ['semɪ] n = ~detached house;
~circle n Halbkreis m; ~colon n
Semikolon nt; ~conductor n Halbleiter
m; ~detached house n (Brit)
Doppelhaus nt; ~final n Halbfinale nt.

seminary ['semɪnərɪ] n (REL) Prie-
sterseminar nt.

semiskilled ['semɪ'skɪld] a angelernt.

send [send] v (pt, pp sent) vt senden,
schicken; (col: inspire) hinreißen; ~
away vt wegschicken; ~ **away for** vt
anfordern; ~ **back** vt zurückschicken;
~ **for** vt holen lassen; ~ **off** vt (goods)
abschicken; (Brit SPORT: player) vom
Feld schicken; ~ **out** vt (invitation)
aussenden; ~ **up** vt hinaufsenden;
(Brit: parody) verulken; ~**er** n
Absender m; ~**off** n: a good ~-off eine
Abschiedsparty.

senior ['si:nɪə*] a (older) älter; (higher
rank) Ober- (in (older person) Ältere(r)
m; (higher ranking) Rangälteste(r) m;
~ **citizen** n älterer(r) Mitbürger(in f)
m; ~**ity** [si:nɪ'ɒrɪtɪ] n (of age)
höhere(s) Alter nt; (in rank) höhere(r)
Dienstgrad m.

sensation [sen'seɪʃən] n Gefühl nt;
(excitement) Sensation f, Aufsehen nt.

sense [sens] n Sinn m; (understanding)
Verstand m, Vernunft f; (feeling) Gefühl
nt // vt fühlen, spüren; ~ of humour
Humor m; to make ~ Sinn ergeben;
~**less** a sinnlos; (unconscious)
besinnungslos.

sensibility [sensɪ'bɪlɪtɪ] n Empfindsam-
keit f; (feeling hurt) Empfindlichkeit f;
sensibilities npl Zartgefühl nt.

sensible ['sensəbl] a vernünftig.

sensitive ['sensɪtɪv] a empfindlich (to
gegen).

sensitivity [sensɪ'tɪvɪtɪ] n Empfindlichkeit f; (artistic) Feingefühl nt; (tact)
Feinfühligkeit f.

sensual ['sensjuəl] a sinnlich.

sensuous ['sensjuəs] a sinnlich.

sent [sent] pt, pp of **send**.

sentence ['sentəns] n Satz m; (JUR)
Strafe f; Urteil nt // vt: to ~ sb to death/
to 5 years jdn zum Tode/zu 5 Jahren verurteilen.

sentiment ['sentɪmənt] n Gefühl nt;
(thought) Gedanke m; ~**al** [sentɪ'mentl]
a sentimental; (of feelings rather than
reason) gefühlsmäßig.

sentry ['sentrɪ] n (Schild)wache f.

separate ['seprət] a getrennt, separat //
['sepəreɪt] vt trennen // vi sich trennen;
~**ly** ad getrennt; ~**s** npl (clothes)
Röcke, Pullover etc.

separation [sepə'reɪʃən] n Trennung f.

September [sep'tembə*] n September
m.

septic ['septɪk] a vereitert, septisch; ~
tank n Klärbehälter m.

sequel ['si:kwəl] n Folge f.

sequence ['si:kwəns] n (Reihen)folge f.

sequin ['si:kwɪn] n Paillette f.

serene [sə'ri:n] a heiter.

serenity [sɪ'renɪtɪ] n Heiterkeit f.

sergeant ['sɑ:dʒənt] n Feldwebel m;
(police) (Polizei)wachtmeister m.

serial ['sɪərɪəl] n Fortsetzungsroman m;
(TV) Fernsehserie f // a (number)
(fort)laufend; ~**ize** vt in Fortsetzungen
veröffentlichen/senden.

series ['sɪərɪz] n, pl inv Serie f, Reihe f.

serious ['sɪərɪəs] a ernst; (injury)
schwer; ~**ly** ad ernst(haft); (hurt)
schwer; ~**ness** n Ernst m, Ernsthaftig-
keit f.

sermon ['sɜ:mən] n Predigt f.

serrated [se'reɪtɪd] a gezackt.

servant ['sɜ:vənt] n Diener(in f) m.

serve [sɜ:v] vt dienen (+dat); (guest, customer) bedienen; (food) servieren;
(writ) zustellen (on sb jdm) // vi dienen,
nützen; (at table) servieren; (TENNIS)
geben, aufschlagen; it ~s him right das
geschieht ihm recht; that'll ~ as a table
das geht als Tisch; ~ **out** or **up** vt
(food) auftragen, servieren.

service ['sɜ:vɪs] n (help) Dienst m;
(trains etc) Verbindung f; (hotel)
Service m, Bedienung f; (set of dishes)
Service nt; (REL) Gottesdienst m; (car)
Inspektion f; (for TVs etc) Kundendienst
m; (TENNIS) Aufschlag m // vt (AUT,
TECH) warten, überholen; the S~s pl
(armed forces) die Streitkräfte pl; to be
of ~ to sb jdm einen großen Dienst
erweisen; ~**able** a brauchbar; ~ **area**
n (on motorway) Raststätte f; ~
charge n (Brit) Bedienung f; ~**man** n
(soldier etc) Soldat m; ~ **station** n
(Groß)tankstelle f.

serviette [sɜ:vɪ'et] n Serviette f.

servile ['sɜ:vaɪl] a unterwürfig.

session ['seʃən] n Sitzung f; (POL)
Sitzungsperiode f; to be in ~ tagen.

set [set] n (collection of things) Satz m,
Set nt; (RAD, TV) Apparat m; (TENNIS)
Satz m; (group of people) Kreis m;
(CINE) Szene f; (THEAT) Bühnenbild nt
// a festgelegt; (ready) bereit // v (pt, pp
set) vt (place) setzen, stellen, legen;
(arrange) (an)ordnen; (table) decken;
(time, price) festsetzen; (alarm, watch)
stellen; (jewels) (ein)fassen; (task)
stellen; (exam) ausarbeiten // vi (sun)
untergehen; (become hard) fest werden;
(bone) zusammenwachsen; to be ~ on
doing sth etw unbedingt tun wollen; to ~
to music vertonen; to ~ on fire anstecken; to ~ free freilassen; to ~ sth
going etw in Gang bringen; to ~ sail
losfahren; ~ **about** vt (task) anpacken;
~ **aside** vt beiseitelegen; ~ **back** vt
zurückwerfen; (in time): to ~ **back** vt
zurückwerfen (um); ~ **off** vi aufbrechen

// vt (*explode*) sprengen; (*alarm*) losgehen lassen; (*show up well*) hervorheben; **~ out** vi: to ~ out to do sth vorhaben, etw zu tun // vt (*arrange*) anlegen, arrangieren; (*state*) darlegen; **~ up** vt (*organization*) aufziehen; (*record*) aufstellen; (*monument*) erstellen; **~back** n Rückschlag m; **~ menu** n Tageskarte f.

settee [se'ti:] n Sofa nt.

setting ['setɪŋ] n Hintergrund m.

settle ['setl] vt beruhigen; (*pay*) begleichen, bezahlen; (*agree*) regeln // vi (*also*: **~ down**) sich einleben; (*come to rest*) sich niederlassen; (*sink*) sich setzen; (*calm down*) sich beruhigen; to **~ for** sich mit etw zufriedengeben; **~ in** vi sich eingewöhnen; to **~ on** sth sich für etw entscheiden; to **~ up with** sb mit jdm abrechnen; **~ment** n Regelung f; (*payment*) Begleichung f; (*colony*) Siedlung f; **~r** n Siedler m.

setup ['setʌp] n (*situation*) Lage f.

seven ['sevn] num sieben; **~teen** num siebzehn; **~th** a siebte(r, s) // n Siebtel nt; **~ty** num siebzig.

sever ['sevə*] vt abtrennen.

several ['sevrəl] a mehrere, verschiedene // pron mehrere; **~ of us** einige von uns.

severance ['sevərəns] n: **~ pay** Abfindung f.

severe [sɪ'vɪə*] a (*strict*) streng; (*serious*) schwer; (*climate*) rauh.

severity [sɪ'verɪtɪ] n Strenge f; Schwere f; Ernst m.

sew [səu], pt **sewed**, pp **sewn** vti nähen; **~ up** vt zunähen.

sewage ['sju:ɪdʒ] n Abwässer pl.

sewer ['sjuə*] n (Abwasser)kanal m.

sewing ['səuɪŋ] n Näharbeit f; **~ machine** n Nähmaschine f.

sewn [səun] pp of **sew**.

sex [seks] n Sex m; (*gender*) Geschlecht nt; to **have ~ with** sb mit jdm Geschlechtsverkehr haben; **~ist** a sexistisch // n Sexist(in f) m.

sexual ['seksjuəl] a sexuell, geschlecht-lich, Geschlechts-.

sexy ['seksɪ] a sexy.

shabby ['ʃæbɪ] a (*lit, fig*) schäbig.

shack [ʃæk] n Hütte f.

shackles ['ʃæklz] npl (*lit, fig*) Fesseln pl, Ketten pl.

shade [ʃeɪd] n Schatten m; (*for lamp*) Lampenschirm m; (*colour*) Farbton m // vt abschirmen; **in the ~** im Schatten; **a ~ smaller** ein bißchen kleiner.

shadow ['ʃædəu] n Schatten m // vt (*follow*) beschatten // a: **~ cabinet** n (*Brit POL*) Schattenkabinett nt; **~y** a schattig.

shady ['ʃeɪdɪ] a schattig; (*fig*) zwielichtig.

shaft [ʃɑːft] n (*of spear etc*) Schaft m;

(*in mine*) Schacht m; (*TECH*) Welle f; (*of light*) Strahl m.

shaggy ['ʃægɪ] a struppig.

shake [ʃeɪk] v (pt **shook**, pp **shaken**) vt schütteln, rütteln; (*shock*) erschüttern // vi (*move*) schwanken; (*tremble*) zittern, beben // n (*jerk*) Schütteln nt, Rütteln nt; to **~ hands** die Hand geben (*with dat*); to **~ one's head** den Kopf schütteln; **~ off** vt abschütteln; **~ up** vt (*lit*) aufschütteln; (*fig*) aufrütteln.

shaky ['ʃeɪkɪ] a zittrig; (*weak*) unsicher.

shall [ʃæl] v aux: **I ~ go** ich werde gehen.

shallow ['ʃæləu] a seicht.

sham [ʃæm] n Schein m // a unecht, falsch.

shambles ['ʃæmblz] n sing Durcheinander nt.

shame [ʃeɪm] n Scham f; (*disgrace, pity*) Schande f // vt beschämen; it is a **~** that es ist schade, daß; it is a **~ to do** ... es ist eine Schande, ... zu tun; **what a ~!** wie schade!; **~faced** a beschämt; **~ful** a schändlich; **~less** a schamlos.

shampoo [ʃæm'pu:] n Shampoo(n) nt // vt (*hair*) waschen; **~ and set** n Waschen und Legen.

shamrock ['ʃæmrɒk] n Kleeblatt nt.

shandy ['ʃændɪ] n Bier nt mit Limonade.

shan't [ʃɑːnt] = **shall not**.

shanty town ['ʃæntɪ-] n Elendsviertel nt.

shape [ʃeɪp] n Form f // vt formen, gestalten // vi (*also*: **~ up**) sich entwickeln; to **take ~** Gestalt annehmen; **-shaped** suff: heart-shaped herzförmig; **~less** a formlos; **~ly** a wohlproportioniert.

share [ʃeə*] n (An)teil m; (*FIN*) Aktie f // vt teilen; to **~ out** (*among or between*) verteilen (*unter or zwischen*); **~holder** n Aktionär(in f) m.

shark [ʃɑːk] n Hai(fisch) m; (*swindler*) Gauner m.

sharp [ʃɑːp] a scharf; (*pin*) spitz; (*person*) clever; (*MUS*) erhöht // n (*MUS*) Kreuz nt // ad (*MUS*) zu hoch; **nine o'clock ~** Punkt neun; **~en** vt schärfen; (*pencil*) spitzen; **~ener** n (*also*: pencil ~ener) Anspitzer m; **~eyed** a scharfsichtig; **~ly** ad (*turn, stop*) plötzlich; (*stand out, contrast*) deutlich; (*criticize, retort*) scharf.

shatter ['ʃætə*] vt zerschmettern; (*fig*) zerstören // vi zerspringen.

shave [ʃeɪv] n Rasur f // vt rasieren // vi sich rasieren; to **have a ~** sich rasieren (lassen); **~r** n (*also*: electric shaver) Rasierapparat m.

shaving ['ʃeɪvɪŋ] n (*action*) Rasieren nt; **~s** pl (*of wood etc*) Späne pl; **~ brush** n Rasierpinsel m; **~ cream** n Rasierkrem f.

shawl [ʃɔːl] n Schal m, Umhang m.

she [ʃiː] pron sie // a weiblich; **~-bear** n

Bärenweibchen nt.

sheaf [ʃiːf], pl **sheaves** n Garbe f.

shear [ʃɪə*], pt **sheared**, pp **sheared** or **shorn** vt scheren; ~ **off** vi abbrechen; ~**s** pl Heckenschere f.

sheath [ʃiːθ] n Scheide f; (condom) Kondom m or nt.

sheaves [ʃiːvz] pl of **sheaf**.

shed [ʃed] n Schuppen m; (for animals) Stall m // vt, pt, pp **shed** (leaves etc) verlieren; (tears) vergießen.

she'd [ʃiːd] = **she had**; **she would**.

sheen [ʃiːn] n Glanz m.

sheep [ʃiːp] n Schaf nt; ~**dog** n Schäferhund m; ~**ish** a verlegen; ~**skin** n Schaffell nt.

sheer [ʃɪə*] a bloß, rein; (steep) steil; (transparent) (hauch)dünn // ad (directly) direkt.

sheet [ʃiːt] n Bettuch nt, Bettlaken nt; (of paper) Blatt nt; (of metal etc) Platte f; (of ice) Fläche f.

shelf [ʃelf], pl **shelves** n Bord nt, Regal nt.

she'll [ʃiːl] = **she will**; **she shall**.

shell [ʃel] n Schale f; (sea~) Muschel f; (explosive) Granate f // vt (peas) schälen; (fire on) beschießen.

shellfish [ˈʃelfɪʃ] n Schalentier nt; (as food) Meeresfrüchte pl.

shelter [ˈʃeltə*] n Schutz m; (air-raid ~) Bunker m // vt schützen, bedecken; (refugees) aufnehmen // vi sich unterstellen; ~**ed** a (life) behütet; (spot) geschützt.

shelve [ʃelv] vt aufschieben // vi abfallen.

shelves [ʃelvz] pl of **shelf**.

shepherd [ˈʃepəd] n Schäfer m // vt treiben, führen; ~'**s pie** n Auflauf m aus Hackfleisch und Kartoffelbrei.

sherry [ˈʃerɪ] n Sherry m.

she's [ʃiːz] = **she is**; **she has**.

Shetland [ˈʃetlənd] n (also: **the ~s**, **the ~ Isles**) die Shetlandinseln pl.

shield [ʃiːld] n Schild m; (fig) Schirm m // vt (be)schirmen; (TECH) abschirmen.

shift [ʃɪft] n Verschiebung f; (work) Schicht f // vt (ver)rücken, verschieben; (arm) wegnehmen // vi sich verschieben; ~**less** a (person) träge; ~ **work** n Schichtarbeit f; ~**y** a verschlagen.

shilly-shally [ˈʃɪlɪʃælɪ] vi zögern.

shin [ʃɪn] n Schienbein nt.

shine [ʃaɪn] n Glanz m, Schein m // v (pt, pp **shone**) vt polieren // vi scheinen; (fig) glänzen; **to ~ a torch on sb** jdn (mit einer Lampe) anleuchten.

shingle [ˈʃɪŋgl] n Strandkies m; ~**s** pl (MED) Gürtelrose f.

shiny [ˈʃaɪnɪ] a glänzend.

ship [ʃɪp] n Schiff nt // vt verschiffen; ~**building** n Schiffbau m; ~**ment** n Schiffsladung f; ~**per** n Verschiffer m; ~**ping** n (act) Verschiffung f; (ships)

Schiffahrt f; ~**shape** a in Ordnung; ~**wreck** n Schiffbruch m; (destroyed ship) Wrack nt // vt: **to be ~wrecked** Schiffbruch erleiden; ~**yard** n Werft f.

shire [ˈʃaɪə*] n (Brit) Grafschaft f.

shirk [ʃɜːk] vt ausweichen (+dat).

shirt [ʃɜːt] n (Ober)hemd nt; **in ~sleeves** in Hemdsärmeln; ~**y** a (col) mürrisch.

shit [ʃɪt] interj (col!) Scheiße f (!).

shiver [ˈʃɪvə*] n Schauer m // vi frösteln, zittern.

shoal [ʃəul] n (Fisch)schwarm m.

shock [ʃɔk] n Erschütterung f; (mental) Schock m; (ELEC) Schlag m // vt erschüttern; (offend) schockieren; ~ **absorber** n Stoßdämpfer m; ~**ing** a unerhört.

shod [ʃɔd] pt, pp of **shoe** // a beschuht.

shoddy [ˈʃɔdɪ] a schäbig.

shoe [ʃuː] n Schuh m; (of horse) Hufeisen nt // vt, pt, pp **shod** (horse) beschlagen; ~**brush** n Schuhbürste f; ~**horn** n Schuhlöffel m; ~**lace** n Schnürsenkel m; ~ **polish** n Schuhcreme f; ~ **shop** n Schuhgeschäft nt; ~**string** n (fig): **on a ~string** mit sehr wenig Geld.

shone [ʃɔn] pt, pp of **shine**.

shoo [ʃuː] interj sch!; (to dog etc) pfui!

shook [ʃuk] pt of **shake**.

shoot [ʃuːt] n (branch) Schößling m // v (pt, pp **shot**) vt (gun) abfeuern; (goal, arrow) schießen; (kill) erschießen; (film) drehen // vi (gun, move quickly) schießen; ~ **(at)** schießen (auf) (+acc); ~ **down** vt abschießen; ~ **in/out** vi hinein-/hinausschießen; ~ **up** vi (fig) aus dem Boden schießen; ~**ing** n Schießerei f; ~**ing star** n Sternschnuppe f.

shop [ʃɔp] n (esp Brit) Geschäft nt, Laden m; (workshop) Werkstatt f // vi (also: **go ~ping**) einkaufen gehen; ~ **assistant** n (Brit) Verkäufer(in f) m; ~ **floor** n (Brit) Werkstatt f; ~**keeper** n Geschäftsinhaber m; ~**lifting** n Ladendiebstahl m; ~**per** n Käufer(in f) m; ~**ping** n Einkaufen nt, Einkauf m; ~**ping bag** n Einkaufstasche f; ~**ping centre**, (US) ~**ping center** n Einkaufszentrum nt; ~-**soiled** a angeschmutzt; ~ **steward** n (Brit INDUSTRY) Betriebsrat m; ~ **window** n Schaufenster nt.

shore [ʃɔː*] n Ufer nt; (of sea) Strand m // vt: ~ **up** abstützen.

shorn [ʃɔːn] pp of **shear**.

short [ʃɔːt] a kurz; (person) klein; (curt) kurz angebunden; (measure) zu knapp // n (also: ~ **film**) Kurzfilm m // ad (suddenly) plötzlich // vi (ELEC) einen Kurzschluß haben; **to be ~ of sth** nicht genug von etw haben; **in ~** kurz gesagt; ~ **of doing sth** ohne so weit zu

gehen, etw zu tun; **everything ~ of ...**
alles außer ...; **it is ~ for** das ist die
Kurzform von; **to cut ~** abkürzen; **to fall
~ of** sth etw nicht erreichen; **to stop ~**
plötzlich anhalten; **to stop ~ of** haltmachen vor; **~age** n Knappheit f, Mangel
m; **~bread** n Mürbegebäck nt; **~-
change** vt: to **~change sb** jdm zuwenig
herausgeben; **~circuit** n Kurzschluß m
// vi einen Kurzschluß haben // vt kurz-
schließen; **~coming** n Mangel m;
~(crust) pastry n (Brit) Mürbeteig m;
~ cut n Abkürzung f; **~en** vt
(ab)kürzen; (clothes) kürzer machen;
~fall n Defizit nt; **~hand** n (Brit)
Stenographie f; **~hand typist** n (Brit)
Stenotypistin f; **~list** n (Brit: for job)
engere Wahl f; **~lived** a kurzlebig; **~ly**
ad bald; **~ness** n Kürze f; **~s** npl
Shorts pl; **~sighted** a (Brit: lit, fig)
kurzsichtig; **~staffed** a: to be **~-
staffed** zu wenig Personal haben; **~
story** n Kurzgeschichte f; **~tempered**
a leicht aufbrausend; **~-term** a (effect)
kurzfristig; **~ wave** n (RAD) Kurzwelle
f.
shot [ʃɒt] pt, pp of **shoot** // n (from
gun) Schuß m; (person) Schütze m;
(try) Versuch m; (injection) Spritze f;
(PHOT) Aufnahme f; **like a ~** wie der
Blitz; **~gun** n Schrotflinte f.
should [ʃʊd] v aux: **I ~** go now ich
sollte jetzt gehen; **he ~ be** there now er
sollte eigentlich schon hier sein; **I ~** go
if I were you ich würde gehen, wenn ich
du wäre; **I ~** like to ich möchte gerne.
shoulder [ʃəʊldə*] n Schulter f; (Brit:
of road): **hard ~** Seitenstreifen m // vt
(rifle) schultern; (fig) auf sich nehmen;
~ blade n Schulterblatt nt; **~ bag** n
Umhängetasche f; **~ strap** n (MIL)
Schulterklappe; (of dress etc) Träger m.
shouldn't [ʃʊdnt] = **should not**.
shout [ʃaʊt] n Schrei m; (call) Ruf m //
vt rufen // vi schreien; **~ down** vt
niederbrüllen; **~ing** n Geschrei nt.
shove [ʃʌv] n Schubs m, Stoß m // vt
schieben, stoßen, schubsen; (col: put):
to ~ sth in(to) sth etw in etw (acc) hin-
einschieben; **~ off** vi (NAUT) abstoßen;
(fig col) abhauen.
shovel [ʃʌvl] n Schaufel f // vt
schaufeln.
show [ʃəʊ] n (display) Schau f;
(exhibition) Ausstellung f; (CINE,
THEAT) Vorstellung f, Show f // vi (pt
showed, pp **shown**) vt zeigen;
(kindness) erweisen // vi zu sehen sein;
to be on ~ (exhibits etc) ausgestellt
sein; **to ~ sb in** jdn hereinführen; **to ~
sb out** jdn hinausbegleiten; **~ off** vi
(pej) angeben // vt (display) ausstellen;
~ up vi (stand out) sich abheben; (arrive)
erscheinen // vt aufzeigen;
(unmask) bloßstellen; **~ business** n

Showbusineß nt; **~down** n Kraftprobe f.
shower [ʃaʊə*] n Schauer m; (of
stones) (Stein)hagel m; (~ bath) Dusche
f // vi duschen // vt: **to ~ sb with** sth jdn
mit etw überschütten; **~proof** a
wasserabstoßend.
showing [ʃəʊɪŋ] n Vorführung f.
show jumping [ʃəʊdʒʌmpɪŋ] n
Turnierreiten nt.
shown [ʃəʊn] pp of **show**.
show-off [ʃəʊɒf] n Angeber(in f) m.
showpiece [ʃəʊpiːs] n Paradestück nt.
showroom [ʃəʊrʊm] n Aus-
stellungsraum m.
shrank [ʃræŋk] pt of **shrink**.
shred [ʃred] n Fetzen m // vt zerfetzen;
(COOK) raspeln; **~der** n (vegetable ~)
Gemüseschneider m; (document)
Reißwolf m.
shrewd [ʃruːd] a clever.
shriek [ʃriːk] n Schrei m // vti kreischen,
schreien.
shrimp [ʃrɪmp] n Krabbe f, Garnele f.
shrink [ʃrɪŋk] v (pt shrank, pp shrunk)
vi schrumpfen, eingehen // vt ein-
schrumpfen lassen; **to ~ from** doing sth
davor zurückschrecken, etw zu tun;
~age n Schrumpfung f; **~ wrap** vt
einschweißen.
shrivel [ʃrɪvl] vti (also: **~ up**)
schrumpfen, schrumpeln.
shroud [ʃraʊd] n Leichentuch nt // vt:
~ed in mystery mit einem Geheimnis
umgeben.
Shrove Tuesday [ʃrəʊvtjuːzdeɪ] n
Fastnachtsdienstag m.
shrub [ʃrʌb] n Busch m, Strauch m;
~bery n Gebüsch nt.
shrug [ʃrʌg] n Achselzucken nt // vi: **to
~** (one's shoulders) die Achseln zucken;
~ off vt auf die leichte Schulter
nehmen.
shrunk [ʃrʌŋk] pp of **shrink**.
shudder [ʃʌdə*] n Schauder m // vi
schaudern.
shuffle [ʃʌfl] n (CARDS) (Karten)-
mischen nt // vt (cards) mischen; **to ~**
(one's feet) schlurfen.
shun [ʃʌn] vt scheuen, (ver)meiden.
shunt [ʃʌnt] vt rangieren.
shut [ʃʌt] v (pt, pp shut) vt schließen,
zumachen // vi sich schließen (lassen);
~ down vti schließen; **~ off** vt (supply) abdrehen; **~ up** vi (keep quiet) den
Mund halten // vt (close) zuschließen;
~ter n Fensterladen m; (PHOT) Verschluß m.
shuttle [ʃʌtl] n (plane, train etc)
Pendelflugzeug nt/-zug m etc; (space ~)
Raumtransporter m; (also: **~ service**)
Pendelverkehr m.
shuttlecock [ʃʌtlkɒk] n Federball m.
shy [ʃaɪ] a schüchtern; **~ness** n
Schüchternheit f.
Siamese [saɪəmiːz] a: **~ cat** n

Siamkatze f.
Siberia [saɪˈbɪərɪə] n Sibirien nt.
sibling [ˈsɪblɪŋ] n Geschwister nt.
Sicily [ˈsɪsɪlɪ] n Sizilien nt.
sick [sɪk] a krank; (joke) makaber; I feel ~ mir ist schlecht; I was ~ ich habe gebrochen; to be ~ of sb/sth jdn/etw satt haben; ~ **bay** n (Schiffs)lazarett nt; **~en** vt (disgust) krankmachen // vi krank werden; **~ening** a (sight) widerlich; (annoying) zum Weinen.
sickle [ˈsɪkl] n Sichel f.
sick leave [ˈsɪkliːv] n: to be on ~ krank geschrieben sein.
sickly [ˈsɪklɪ] a kränklich, blaß; (causing nausea) widerlich.
sickness [ˈsɪknəs] n Krankheit f; (vomiting) Übelkeit f, Erbrechen nt.
sick pay [ˈsɪkpeɪ] n Krankengeld nt.
side [saɪd] n Seite f // a (door, entrance) Seiten-, Neben- // vi: to ~ with sb jds Partei ergreifen; by the ~ of neben; ~ by ~ nebeneinander; on all ~s von allen Seiten; to take ~s (with) Partei nehmen (für); **~boards** (Brit), **~burns** pl Koteletten pl; **~car** n Beiwagen m; ~ **drum** n (MUS) kleine Trommel; ~ **effect** n Nebenwirkung f; **~light** n (AUT) Parkleuchte f; **~line** n (SPORT) Seitenlinie f; (fig: hobby) Nebenbeschäftigung f; **~long** a Seiten-; **~saddle** ad im Damensattel; ~ **show** n Nebenausstellung f; **~step** vt (fig) ausweichen; ~ **street** n Seitenstraße f; **~track** vt (fig) ablenken; **~walk** n (US) Bürgersteig m; **~ways** ad seitwärts.
siding [ˈsaɪdɪŋ] n Nebengleis nt.
sidle [ˈsaɪdl] vi: to ~ up sich heranmachen (to an +acc).
siege [siːdʒ] n Belagerung f.
sieve [sɪv] n Sieb nt // vt sieben.
sift [sɪft] vt sieben; (fig) sichten.
sigh [saɪ] n Seufzer m // vi seufzen.
sight [saɪt] n (power of seeing) Sehvermögen nt; (look) Blick m; (fact of seeing) Anblick m; (of gun) Visier nt // vt sichten; in ~ in Sicht; out of ~ außer Sicht; **~seeing** n Besuch m von Sehenswürdigkeiten; to go **~seeing** Sehenswürdigkeiten besichtigen.
sign [saɪn] n Zeichen nt; (notice, road ~ etc) Schild nt // vt unterschreiben; to ~ sth over to sb jdm etw überschreiben; ~ **on** vi (MIL) sich verpflichten; (as unemployed) sich (arbeitslos) melden // vt (MIL) verpflichten; (employee) anstellen; ~ **up** vi (MIL) sich verpflichten // vt verpflichten.
signal [ˈsɪgnl] n Signal nt // vt ein Zeichen geben (+dat); **~man** n (RAIL) Stellwerkswärter(in f) m.
signature [ˈsɪgnətʃə*] n Unterschrift f; ~ **tune** n Erkennungsmelodie f.
signet ring [ˈsɪgnətrɪŋ] n Siegelring m.

significance [sɪgˈnɪfɪkəns] n Bedeutung f.
significant [sɪgˈnɪfɪkənt] a (meaning sth) bedeutsam; (important) bedeutend.
signify [ˈsɪgnɪfaɪ] vt bedeuten; (show) andeuten, zu verstehen geben.
sign language [ˈsaɪnlæŋgwɪdʒ] n Zeichensprache f, Fingersprache f.
signpost [ˈsaɪnpəʊst] n Wegweiser m.
silence [ˈsaɪləns] n Stille f; (of person) Schweigen nt // vt zum Schweigen bringen; **~r** n (on gun) Schalldämpfer m; (Brit AUT) Auspufftopf m.
silent [ˈsaɪlənt] a still; (person) schweigsam; to remain ~ schweigen; ~ **partner** n (COMM) stille(r) Teilhaber m.
silk [sɪlk] n Seide f // a seiden, Seiden-; **~y** a seidig.
silly [ˈsɪlɪ] a dumm, albern.
silt [sɪlt] n Schlamm m, Schlick m.
silver [ˈsɪlvə*] n Silber nt // a silbern, Silber-; ~ **paper** n (Brit) Silberpapier nt; **~-plated** a versilbert; **~smith** n Silberschmied m; **~ware** n Silber nt; **~y** a silbern.
similar [ˈsɪmɪlə*] a ähnlich (to dat); **~ity** [sɪmɪˈlærɪtɪ] n Ähnlichkeit f; **~ly** ad in ähnlicher Weise.
simile [ˈsɪmɪlɪ] n Vergleich m.
simmer [ˈsɪmə*] vti sieden (lassen).
simpering [ˈsɪmpərɪŋ] a albern.
simple [ˈsɪmpl] a einfach; **~(-minded)** a einfältig; **~ton** n Einfaltspinsel m.
simplicity [sɪmˈplɪsɪtɪ] n Einfachheit f; (of person) Einfältigkeit f.
simplify [ˈsɪmplɪfaɪ] vt vereinfachen.
simply [ˈsɪmplɪ] ad einfach.
simulate [ˈsɪmjʊleɪt] vt simulieren.
simultaneous [sɪməlˈteɪnɪəs] a gleichzeitig.
sin [sɪn] n Sünde f // vi sündigen.
since [sɪns] ad seither // prep seit, seitdem // cj (time) seit; (because) da, weil; ~ **then** seitdem.
sincere [sɪnˈsɪə*] a aufrichtig; yours **~ly** mit freundlichen Grüßen.
sincerity [sɪnˈserɪtɪ] n Aufrichtigkeit f.
sinew [ˈsɪnjuː] n Sehne f.
sinful [ˈsɪnful] a sündig, sündhaft.
sing [sɪŋ], pt **sang**, pp **sung** vti singen.
Singapore [sɪŋgəˈpɔː*] n Singapur nt.
singe [sɪndʒ] vt versengen.
singer [ˈsɪŋə*] n Sänger(in f) m.
single [ˈsɪŋgl] a (one only) einzig; (bed, room) Einzel-, einzeln; (unmarried) ledig; (Brit: ticket) einfach; (having one part only) einzeln // n (Brit: also: ~ ticket) einfache Fahrkarte f; **~s** n (TENNIS) Einzel nt; ~ **out** vt aussuchen, auswählen; ~ **bed** n Einzelbett nt; **~-breasted** a einreihig; in ~ **file** hintereinander; **~-handed** a allein; **~-minded** a zielstrebig; ~ **room** n Einzelzimmer nt.

singlet ['sɪŋglət] n Unterhemd nt.

singly ['sɪŋglɪ] ad einzeln, allein.

singular ['sɪŋgjulə*] a (GRAM) Singular-; (odd) merkwürdig, seltsam // n (GRAM) Einzahl f, Singular m.

sinister ['sɪnɪstə*] a (evil) böse; (ghostly) unheimlich.

sink [sɪŋk] n Spülbecken nt // v (pt **sank**, pp **sunk**) vt (ship) versenken // vi sinken; **to ~ sth into** (teeth, claws) etw schlagen in (+acc); **~ in** vi (news etc) eingehen (+dat).

sinner ['sɪnə*] n Sünder(in f) m.

sip [sɪp] n Schlückchen nt // vt nippen an (+dat).

siphon ['saɪfən] n Siphon(flasche f) m; **~ off** vt absaugen; (fig) abschöpfen.

sir [sɜ:*] n (respect) Herr m; (knight) Sir m; **S~ John Smith** Sir John Smith; **yes ~** ja(wohl, mein Herr).

siren ['saɪərən] n Sirene f.

sirloin ['sɜ:lɔɪn] n Lendenstück nt.

sissy ['sɪsɪ] n (col) Waschlappen m.

sister ['sɪstə*] n Schwester f; (Brit: nurse) Oberschwester f; (nun) Ordensschwester f; **~-in-law** n Schwägerin f.

sit [sɪt] v (pt, pp **sat**) vi sitzen; (hold session) tagen // vt (exam) machen; **~ down** vi sich hinsetzen; **~ in on** vt dabeisein bei; **~ up** vi (after lying) sich aufsetzen; (straight) sich gerade setzen; (at night) aufbleiben.

sitcom ['sɪtkɒm] n abbr (= situation comedy) Situationskomödie f.

site [saɪt] n Platz m; (also: building ~) Baustelle f // vt legen.

sitting ['sɪtɪŋ] n (meeting) Sitzung f; **~ room** n Wohnzimmer nt.

situated ['sɪtjueɪtɪd] a: **to be ~** liegen.

situation [sɪtju'eɪʃən] n Situation f, Lage f; (place) Lage f; (employment) Stelle f; **~s vacant** (Brit) Stellenangebote pl.

six [sɪks] num sechs; **~teen** num sechzehn; **~th** a sechste(r, s) // n Sechstel nt; **~ty** num sechzig.

size [saɪz] n Größe f; (of project) Umfang m; **~ up** vt (assess) abschätzen, einschätzen; **~able** a ziemlich groß, ansehnlich.

sizzle ['sɪzl] vi zischen; (COOK) brutzeln.

skate [skeɪt] n Schlittschuh m; (fish: pl inv) Rochen m // vi Schlittschuh laufen; **~r** n Schlittschuhläufer(in f) m.

skating ['skeɪtɪŋ] n Eislauf m; **to go ~** Eislaufen gehen; **~ rink** n Eisbahn f.

skeleton ['skelɪtn] n Skelett nt; (fig) Gerüst nt; **~ key** n Dietrich m; **~ staff** n Notbesetzung f.

sketch [sketʃ] n Skizze f; (THEAT) Sketch m // vt skizzieren; **~book** n Skizzenbuch nt; **~y** a skizzenhaft.

skewer ['skjuə*] n Fleischspieß m.

ski [ski:] n Ski m, Schi m // vi Ski or Schi laufen; **~ boot** n Skistiefel m.

skid [skɪd] n (AUT) Schleudern nt // vi rutschen; (AUT) schleudern.

skier ['ski:ə*] n Skiläufer(in f) m.

skiing ['ski:ɪŋ] n: **to go ~** Skilaufen gehen.

ski-jump ['ski:dʒʌmp] n Sprungschanze f // vi Ski springen.

skilful ['skɪlful] a geschickt.

ski-lift ['ski:lɪft] n Skilift m.

skill [skɪl] n Können nt; **~ed** a geschickt; (worker) Fach-, gelernt.

skim [skɪm] vt (liquid) abschöpfen; (glide over) gleiten über (+acc) // vi: **~ through** (book) überfliegen; **~med milk** n Magermilch f.

skimp [skɪmp] vt (do carelessly) oberflächlich tun; **~y** a (work) schlecht gemacht; (dress) knapp.

skin [skɪn] n Haut f; (peel) Schale f // vt abhäuten; schälen; **~-deep** a oberflächlich; **~ diving** n Schwimmtauchen nt; **~ny** a dünn; **~tight** a (dress etc) hauteng.

skip [skɪp] n Sprung m // vi hüpfen; (with rope) Seil springen // vt (pass over) übergehen.

ski: **~ pants** npl Skihosen pl; **~ pole** n Skistock m.

skipper ['skɪpə*] n Kapitän m // vt führen.

skipping rope ['skɪpɪŋrəup] n (Brit) Hüpfseil nt.

skirmish ['skɜ:mɪʃ] n Scharmützel nt.

skirt [skɜ:t] n Rock m // vt herumgehen um; (fig) umgehen; **~ing board** n (Brit) Fußleiste f.

ski suit n Skianzug m.

skit [skɪt] n Parodie f.

skittle ['skɪtl] n Kegel m; **~s** n (game) Kegeln nt.

skive [skaɪv] vi (Brit col) schwänzen.

skulk [skʌlk] vi sich herumdrücken.

skull [skʌl] n Schädel m.

skunk [skʌŋk] n Stinktier nt.

sky [skaɪ] n Himmel m; **~light** n Oberlicht nt; **~scraper** n Wolkenkratzer m.

slab [slæb] n (of stone) Platte f.

slack [slæk] a (loose) locker; (business) flau; (careless) nachlässig, lasch // n nachlässig sein // n: **to take up the ~** straffziehen; **~s** pl Hose(n pl) f; **~en** (also: **~en off**) vi locker werden; (become slower) nachlassen, stocken // vt (loosen) lockern.

slag [slæg] n Schlacke f; **~ heap** n Halde f.

slain [sleɪn] pp of **slay**.

slam [slæm] n Knall m // vt (door) zuschlagen; (throw down) knallen // vi zuschlagen.

slander ['slɑ:ndə*] n Verleumdung f // vt verleumden.

slant [slɑ:nt] n (lit) Schräge f; (fig) Tendenz f // vt schräg legen // vi schräg liegen; **~ed**, **~ing** a schräg.

slap [slæp] n Klaps m // vt einen Klaps geben (+dat) // ad (directly) geradewegs; **~dash** a salopp; **~stick** (comedy) Klamauk m; **~-up** a (Brit: meal) erstklassig, prima.

slash [slæʃ] n Schnittwunde f // vt (auf)schlitzen; (expenditure) radikal kürzen.

slat [slæt] n (of wood, plastic) Leiste f.

slate [sleɪt] n (stone) Schiefer m; (roofing) Dachziegel m // vt (criticize) verreißen.

slaughter ['slɔːtə*] n (of animals) Schlachten nt; (of people) Gemetzel nt // vt schlachten; (people) niedermetzeln; **~house** n Schlachthof m.

Slav [slɑːv] a slawisch.

slave [sleɪv] n Sklave m, Sklavin f // vi schuften, sich schinden; **~ry** n Sklaverei f; (work) Schinderei f.

slay [sleɪ], pt slew, pp slain vt ermorden.

sleazy ['sliːzɪ] a (place) schmierig.

sledge ['sledʒ] n Schlitten m; **~hammer** n Schmiedehammer m.

sleek [sliːk] a glatt; (shape) rassig.

sleep [sliːp] n Schlaf m // vi, pt, pp slept schlafen; **to go to ~** einschlafen; **~ in** vi ausschlafen; (oversleep) verschlafen; **~er** n (person) Schläfer m; (Brit RAIL) Schlafwagen m; (beam) Schwelle f; **~ing bag** n Schlafsack m; **~ing car** n Schlafwagen m; **~ing pill** n Schlaftablette f; **~less** a (night) schlaflos; **~walker** n Schlafwandler(in) m; **~y** a schläfrig.

sleet [sliːt] n Schneeregen m.

sleeve [sliːv] n Ärmel m; (of record) Umschlag m; **~less** a ärmellos.

sleigh [sleɪ] n Pferdeschlitten m.

sleight [slaɪt] n: **~ of hand** Fingerfertigkeit f.

slender ['slendə*] a schlank; (fig) gering.

slept [slept] pt, pp of sleep.

slew [sluː] vi (veer) (herum)schwenken // pt of slay.

slice [slaɪs] n Scheibe f // vt in Scheiben schneiden.

slick [slɪk] a (clever) raffiniert, aalglatt // n Ölteppich m.

slide [slaɪd] n Rutschbahn f; (PHOT) Dia(positiv) nt; (Brit: for hair) (Haar)spange f // v (pt, pp slid) vt schieben // vi (slip) gleiten, rutschen; **~rule** n Rechenschieber m.

sliding ['slaɪdɪŋ] a (door) Schiebe-; **~ scale** n gleitende Skala f.

slight [slaɪt] a zierlich; (trivial) geringfügig; (small) gering // n Kränkung f // vt (offend) kränken; **not in the ~est** nicht im geringsten; **~ly** ad etwas, ein bißchen.

slim [slɪm] a schlank; (book) dünn;

(chance) gering // vi eine Schlankheitskur machen.

slime [slaɪm] n Schleim m.

slimming ['slɪmɪŋ] n Schlankheitskur f.

slimy ['slaɪmɪ] a glitschig; (dirty) schlammig; (person) schmierig.

sling [slɪŋ] n Schlinge f; (weapon) Schleuder f // vt, pt, pp slung schleudern.

slip [slɪp] n (mistake) Flüchtigkeitsfehler m; (petticoat) Unterrock m; (of paper) Zettel m // vt (put) stecken, schieben // vi (lose balance) ausrutschen; (move) gleiten, rutschen; (decline) nachlassen; (move smoothly): **to ~ into/out of** (room etc) hinein-/hinausschlüpfen; **to give sb the ~** jdm entwischen; **~ of the tongue** Versprecher m; **it ~ped my mind** das ist mir entfallen; **to ~ sth on/off** etw über-/abstreifen; **~ away** vi sich wegstehlen; **~ by** vi (time) verstreichen; **~ in** vt hineingleiten lassen // vi (errors) sich einschleichen; **~ped disc** n Bandscheibenschaden m.

slipper ['slɪpə*] n Hausschuh m.

slippery ['slɪpərɪ] a glatt.

slip: **~-road** n (Brit) Auffahrt f/Ausfahrt f; **~shod** a schlampig; **~-up** n Panne f; **~way** n Auslaufbahn f.

slit [slɪt] n Schlitz m // vt, pt, pp slit aufschlitzen.

slither ['slɪðə*] vi schlittern; (snake) sich schlängeln.

sliver ['slɪvə*] n (of glass, wood) Splitter m; (of cheese etc) Scheibchen nt.

slob [slɒb] n (col) Klotz m.

slog [slɒg] vi (work hard) schuften // n: **it was a ~** es war eine Plackerei.

slogan ['sləʊgən] n Schlagwort nt; (COMM) Werbespruch m.

slop [slɒp] vi (also: **~ over**) überschwappen // vt verschütten.

slope [sləʊp] n Neigung f; (of mountains) (Ab)hang m // vi: **~ down** sich senken; **~ up** ansteigen.

sloping ['sləʊpɪŋ] a schräg.

sloppy ['slɒpɪ] a schlampig.

slot [slɒt] n Schlitz m // vt: **to ~ sth in** etw einlegen; **~ machine** n (Brit: vending machine) Automat m; (for gambling) Spielautomat m.

sloth [sləʊθ] n (laziness) Faulheit f.

slouch [slaʊtʃ] vi: **to ~ about** (laze) herumhängen (col).

slovenly ['slʌvnlɪ] a schlampig; (speech) salopp.

slow [sləʊ] a langsam; **to be ~** (clock) nachgehen; (stupid) begriffsstutzig sein // ad langsam; **~ down** vi langsamer werden // vt verlangsamen; **~ up** vi sich verlangsamen, sich verzögern // vt aufhalten, langsamer machen; **'~'** (road sign) 'Langsam'; **~ly** ad langsam; **in ~ motion** in Zeitlupe.

sludge [slʌdʒ] n Schlamm m.

slug [slʌg] n Nacktschnecke f; (col: bullet) Kugel f; **~gish** a träge; (COMM) schleppend.
sluice [slu:s] n Schleuse f.
slumber ['slʌmbə*] n Schlummer m.
slump [slʌmp] n Rückgang m // vi fallen, stürzen.
slung [slʌŋ] pt, pp of **sling**.
slur [slɜ:*] n Undeutlichkeit f; (insult) Verleumdung f // vt (words) verschlucken **~red** [slɜ:d] a (pronunciation) undeutlich.
slush [slʌʃ] n (snow) Schneematsch m; **~ fund** n Schmiergeldfonds m.
slut [slʌt] n Schlampe f.
sly [slaɪ] a schlau.
smack [smæk] n Klaps m // vt einen Klaps geben (+dat); **to ~ one's lips** schmatzen, sich (dat) die Lippen lecken; **~ of** vi riechen nach.
small [smɔ:l] a klein; **~ ads** npl (Brit) Kleinanzeigen pl; **in the ~ hours** in den frühen Morgenstunden; **~ change** n Kleingeld nt; **~ holder** n (Brit) Kleinbauer m; **~pox** n Pocken pl; **~ talk** n Geplauder nt.
smart [sma:t] a (fashionable) elegant, schick; (neat) adrett; (clever) clever; (quick) scharf // vi brennen, schmerzen; **~en up** vi sich in Schale werfen // vt herausputzen.
smash [smæʃ] n Zusammenstoß m; (TENNIS) Schmetterball m // vt (break) zerschmettern; (destroy) vernichten // vi (break) zersplittern, zerspringen; **~ing** a (col) toll.
smattering ['smætərɪŋ] n oberflächliche Kenntnis f.
smear [smɪə*] n Fleck m // vt beschmieren.
smell [smel] n Geruch m; (sense) Geruchssinn m // vti, pt, pp **smelt** or **smelled** riechen (of nach); **~y** a übelriechend.
smelt [smelt] vt (ore) schmelzen.
smile [smaɪl] n Lächeln nt // vi lächeln; **smiling** a lächelnd.
smirk [smɜ:k] n blöde(s) Grinsen nt.
smith [smɪθ] n Schmied m; **~y** ['smɪðɪ] n Schmiede f.
smock [smɒk] n Kittel m.
smoke [sməʊk] n Rauch m // vt rauchen; (food) räuchern // vi rauchen; **~d** a (bacon) geräuchert; (glass) Rauch-; **~r** n Raucher(in f) m; (RAIL) Raucherabteil nt; **~ screen** n Rauchwand f.
smoking ['sməʊkɪŋ] n: '**no ~**' 'Rauchen verboten'.
smoky ['sməʊkɪ] a rauchig; (room) verraucht; (taste) geräuchert.
smolder ['sməʊldə*] vi (US) = **smoulder**.
smooth [smu:ð] a glatt // vt (also: **~ out**) glätten, glattstreichen.
smother ['smʌðə*] vt ersticken.

smoulder, (US) **smolder** ['sməʊldə*] vi schwelen.
smudge [smʌdʒ] n Schmutzfleck m // vt beschmieren.
smug [smʌg] a selbstgefällig.
smuggle ['smʌgl] vt schmuggeln; **~r** n Schmuggler m.
smuggling ['smʌglɪŋ] n Schmuggel m.
smutty ['smʌtɪ] a schmutzig.
snack [snæk] n Imbiß m; **~ bar** n Imbißstube f.
snag [snæg] n Haken m.
snail [sneɪl] n Schnecke f.
snake [sneɪk] n Schlange f.
snap [snæp] n Schnappen nt; (photograph) Schnappschuß m // a (decision) schnell // vt (break) zerbrechen; (PHOT) knipsen // vi (break) brechen; (speak) anfauchen; **to ~ shut** zuschnappen; **~ at** vt schnappen nach; **~ off** vt (break) abbrechen; **~ up** vt aufschnappen; **~py** a flott; **~shot** n Schnappschuß m.
snare [snɛə*] n Schlinge f // vt mit einer Schlinge fangen.
snarl [sna:l] n Zähnefletschen nt // vi (dog) knurren.
snatch [snætʃ] n (small amount) Bruchteil m // vt schnappen, packen.
sneak [sni:k] vi schleichen // n (col) Petze(r) mf.
sneakers ['sni:kəz] npl (US) Freizeitschuhe pl.
sneaky ['sni:kɪ] a raffiniert.
sneer [snɪə*] n Hohnlächeln nt // vi spötteln.
sneeze [sni:z] n Niesen nt // vi niesen.
sniff [snɪf] n Schnüffeln nt // vi schnieben; (smell) schnüffeln // vt schnuppern.
snigger ['snɪgə*] n Kichern nt // vi hämisch kichern.
snip [snɪp] n Schnippel m, Schnipsel m // vt schnippeln.
sniper ['snaɪpə*] n Heckenschütze m.
snippet ['snɪpɪt] n Schnipsel m; (of conversation) Fetzen m.
snivelling ['snɪvlɪŋ] a weinerlich.
snooker ['snu:kə*] n Snooker nt.
snoop [snu:p] vi: **to ~ about** herumschnüffeln.
snooty ['snu:tɪ] a (col) hochnäsig.
snooze [snu:z] n Nickerchen nt // vi ein Nickerchen machen, dösen.
snore [snɔ:*] vi schnarchen // n Schnarchen nt.
snorkel ['snɔ:kl] n Schnorchel m.
snort [snɔ:t] n Schnauben nt // vi schnauben.
snout [snaʊt] n Schnauze f.
snow [snəʊ] n Schnee m // vi schneien; **~ball** n Schneeball m // vi eskalieren; **~bound** a eingeschneit; **~drift** n Schneewehe f; **~drop** n Schneeglöckchen nt; **~fall** n Schneefall m; **~flake** n Schneeflocke f; **~man** n Schneemann

m; **~plough,** (US) **~plow** n
Schneepflug m; ~ **shoe** n Schneeschuh
m; **~storm** n Schneesturm m.

snub [snʌb] vt schroff abfertigen // n
Verweis m; **~-nosed** a stupsnasig.

snuff [snʌf] n Schnupftabak m.

snug [snʌg] a gemütlich, behaglich.

snuggle ['snʌgl] vi: to ~ up to sb sich
an jdn kuscheln.

so [səʊ] ◆ ad 1 (thus) so; (likewise)
auch; ~ saying he walked away indem
er das sagte, ging er; if ~ wenn ja; I
didn't do it — you did ~! ich hab das
nicht gemacht — hast du wohl! ~ do I,
~ am I etc ich auch; ~ it is! tatsächlich!; I hope/think ~ hoffentlich/ich
glaube schon; ~ far bis jetzt
2 (in comparisons etc: to such a degree)
so; ~ quickly/big (that) so schnell/groß,
daß; I'm ~ glad to see you ich freue
mich so, dich zu sehen
3: ~ much a so viel // ad so sehr; ~
many a so viele
4 (phrases): 10 or ~ etwa 10; ~ long!
(col: goodbye) tschüs!
◆conj **1** (expressing purpose): ~ as to
um nicht; ~ (that) damit
2 (expressing result) also; ~ I was right
after all ich hatte ja also doch recht; ~ you
see ... wie du siehst ...

soak [səʊk] vt durchnässen; (leave in
liquid) einweichen // vi (ein)weichen; ~
in vi einsickern; ~ **up** vt aufsaugen.

so-and-so ['səʊənsəʊ] n (somebody)
soundso m.

soap [səʊp] n Seife f; **~flakes** pl
Seifenflocken pl; ~ **opera** n
Familienserie f (im Fernsehen, Radio);
~ **powder** n Waschpulver nt; **~y** a
seifig, Seifen-.

soar [sɔː*] vi aufsteigen; (prices) in die
Höhe schnellen.

sob [sɔb] n Schluchzen nt // vi
schluchzen.

sober ['səʊbə*] a (lit, fig) nüchtern; ~
up vi nüchtern werden.

so-called ['səʊ'kɔːld] a sogenannt.

soccer ['sɔkə*] n Fußball m.

sociable ['səʊʃəbl] a gesellig.

social ['səʊʃəl] a sozial; (friendly, living
with others) gesellig // n gesellige(r)
Abend m; ~ **club** n Verein m (für
Freizeitgestaltung); **~ism** n Sozialismus
m; **~ist** n Sozialist(in f) m // a soziali-
stisch; **~ize** vi: to ~ (with) gesellschaft-
lich verkehren (mit); **~ly** ad gesell-
schaftlich, privat; ~ **security** n
Sozialversicherung f; ~ **work** n
Sozialarbeit f; ~ **worker** n
Sozialarbeiter(in f) m.

society [sə'saɪətɪ] n Gesellschaft f;
(fashionable world) die große Welt.

sock [sɔk] n Socke f.

socket ['sɔkɪt] n (ELEC) Steckdose f;
(of eye) Augenhöhle f; (TECH)

Rohransatz m.

sod [sɔd] n Rasenstück nt; (col!)
Saukerl m (!).

soda ['səʊdə] n Soda f; (also: ~ water)
Soda(wasser) nt; (US: also: ~ pop)
Limonade f.

sodden ['sɔdn] a durchweicht.

sodium ['səʊdɪəm] n Natrium nt.

sofa ['səʊfə] n Sofa nt.

soft [sɔft] a weich; (not loud) leise;
(weak) nachgiebig; ~ **drink** n alkohol-
freie(s) Getränk nt; **~en** ['sɔfn] vt
weich machen; (blow) abschwächen,
mildern // vi weich werden; **~ly** ad
sanft; leise; **~ness** n Weichheit f; (fig)
Sanftheit f.

software ['sɔftwɛə*] n (COMPUT)
Software f.

soggy ['sɔgɪ] a (ground) sumpfig;
(bread) aufgeweicht.

soil [sɔɪl] n Erde f // vt beschmutzen;
~ed a beschmutzt.

solace ['sɔləs] n Trost m.

solar ['səʊlə*] a Sonnen-.

sold [səʊld] pt, pp of **sell**; ~ **out** a
(COMM) ausverkauft.

solder ['səʊldə*] vt löten // n Lötmetall
nt.

soldier ['səʊldʒə*] n Soldat m.

sole [səʊl] n Sohle f; (fish) Seezunge f //
a alleinig, Allein-; **~ly** ad ausschließlich; ~ **trader** n (COMM) Ein-
zelunternehmen nt.

solemn ['sɔləm] a feierlich.

solicit [sə'lɪsɪt] vt (request) bitten um //
vi (prostitute) Kunden anwerben.

solicitor [sə'lɪsɪtə*] n Rechtsanwalt m/
-anwältin f.

solid ['sɔlɪd] a (hard) fest; (of same
material) massiv; (not hollow) massiv;
(without break) voll, ganz; (reliable,
sensible) solide // n Feste(s) nt.

solidarity [sɔlɪ'dærɪtɪ] n Solidarität f.

solidify [sə'lɪdɪfaɪ] fest werden.

solitary ['sɔlɪtərɪ] a einsam, einzeln; ~
confinement n Einzelhaft f.

solitude ['sɔlɪtjuːd] n Einsamkeit f.

soluble ['sɔljʊbl] a (substance) löslich;
(problem) (auf)lösbar.

solution [sə'luːʃən] n (lit, fig) Lösung f;
(of mystery) Erklärung f.

solve [sɔlv] vt (auf)lösen.

solvent ['sɔlvənt] a (FIN) zahlungsfähig
// n (CHEM) Lösungsmittel nt.

sombre, (US) **somber** ['sɔmbə*] a düster.

some [sʌm] ◆ a 1 (a certain amount or
number of) einige; (a few) ein paar;
(with singular nouns) etwas; ~ tea/
biscuits etwas Tee/ein paar Plätzchen;
I've got ~ money, but not much ich habe
ein bißchen Geld, aber nicht viel
2 (certain: in contrasts) manche(r, s);
~ **people say that** ... manche Leute
sagen, daß ...

3 (*unspecified*) irgendein(e); ~ **woman was asking for you** da hat eine Frau nach Ihnen gefragt; ~ **day** eines Tages; ~ **day next week** irgendwann nächste Woche

♦*pron* **1** (*a certain number*) einige; **have you got ~?** Haben Sie welche?

2 (*a certain amount*) etwas; **I've read ~ of the book** ich habe das Buch teilweise gelesen

♦*ad:* ~ **10 people** etwa 10 Leute.

somebody ['sʌmbədɪ] *pron*, **someone** ['sʌmwʌn] *pron* jemand; (*direct obj*) jemand(en); (*indirect obj*) jemandem.

somersault ['sʌməsɔːlt] *n* Salto *m* // *vi* einen Salto machen.

something ['sʌmθɪŋ] *pron* etwas.

sometime ['sʌmtaɪm] *ad* (irgend) einmal.

sometimes ['sʌmtaɪmz] *ad* manchmal.

somewhat ['sʌmwɒt] *ad* etwas.

somewhere ['sʌmwɛə*] *ad* irgendwo; (*to a place*) irgendwohin; ~ **else** irgendwo anders.

son [sʌn] *n* Sohn *m*.

sonar ['səʊnɑː*] *n* Echolot *nt*.

song [sɒŋ] *n* Lied *nt*.

sonic ['sɒnɪk] *a* Schall-; ~ **boom** *n* Überschallknall *m*.

son-in-law ['sʌnɪnlɔː] *n* Schwiegersohn *m*.

sonny ['sʌnɪ] *n* (col) Kleine(r) *m*.

soon [suːn] *ad* bald; ~ **afterwards** kurz danach; ~**er** *ad* (*time*) früher; (*for preference*) lieber; ~**er or later** früher oder später.

soot [sʊt] *n* Ruß *m*.

soothe [suːð] *vt* (*person*) beruhigen; (*pain*) lindern.

sophisticated [sə'fɪstɪkeɪtɪd] *a* (*person*) kultiviert; (*machinery*) hochentwickelt.

sophomore ['sɒfəmɔː*] *n* (*US*) College-Student *m* im 2. Jahr.

soporific [sɒpə'rɪfɪk] *a* einschläfernd.

sopping ['sɒpɪŋ] *a* patschnaß.

soppy ['sɒpɪ] *a* (col) schmalzig.

sorcerer ['sɔːsərə*] *n* Hexenmeister *m*.

sordid ['sɔːdɪd] *a* erbärmlich.

sore [sɔː*] *a* schmerzend; (*point*) wund // *n* Wunde *f*; ~**ly** *ad* (*tempted*) stark, sehr.

sorrow ['sɒrəʊ] *n* Kummer *m*, Leid *nt*; ~**ful** *a* sorgenvoll.

sorry ['sɒrɪ] *a* traurig, erbärmlich; ~! Entschuldigung!; **to feel ~ for sb** jdn bemitleiden; **I feel ~ for him** er tut mir leid.

sort [sɔːt] *n* Art *f*, Sorte *f* // *vt* (*also:* ~ **out**) (*papers*) sortieren, sichten; (*problems*) in Ordnung bringen; ~**ing office** *n* Sortierstelle *f*.

SOS *n* SOS *nt*.

so-so ['səʊ'səʊ] *ad* so(-so) la-la.

sought [sɔːt] *pt, pp of* **seek**.

soul [səʊl] *n* Seele *f*; (*music*) Soul *m*;

~-**destroying** *a* trostlos; ~**ful** *a* seelenvoll.

sound [saʊnd] *a* (*healthy*) gesund; (*safe*) sicher; (*sensible*) vernünftig; (*theory*) stichhaltig; (*thorough*) tüchtig, gehörig // *ad:* **to be** ~ **asleep** fest schlafen // *n* (*noise*) Geräusch *nt*, Laut *m*; (*GEOG*) Sund *m* // *vt* erschallen lassen; (*alarm*) (Alarm) schlagen; (*MED*) abhorchen // *vi* (*make a sound*) schallen, tönen; (*seem*) klingen; **to ~ like** sich anhören wie; ~ **out** *vt* (*opinion*) erforschen; (*person*) auf den Zahn fühlen (+*dat*); ~ **barrier** *n* Schallmauer *f*; ~ **effects** *npl* Toneffekte *pl*; ~**ing** *n* (*NAUT etc*) Lotung *f*; ~**ly** *ad* (*sleep*) fest; (*beat*) tüchtig; ~**proof** *a* (*room*) schalldicht; ~-**track** *n* Tonstreifen *m*; (*music*) Filmmusik *f*.

soup [suːp] *n* Suppe *f*; **in the ~** (col) in der Tinte; ~ **plate** *n* Suppenteller *m*; ~**spoon** *n* Suppenlöffel *m*.

sour ['saʊə*] *a* (*lit, fig*) sauer; **it's ~ grapes** (*fig*) die Trauben hängen zu hoch.

source [sɔːs] *n* (*lit, fig*) Quelle *f*.

south [saʊθ] *n* Süden *m* // *a* Süd-, südlich // *ad* nach Süden, südwärts; **S~ Africa** *n* Südafrika *nt*; **S~ African** *a* südafrikanisch // *n* Südafrikaner(in *f*) *m*; **S~ America** *n* Südamerika *nt*; **S~ American** *a* südamerikanisch // *n* Südamerikaner(in *f*) *m*; ~-**east** *n* Südosten *m*; ~**erly** ['sʌðəlɪ] *a* südlich; ~**ern** ['sʌðən] *a* südlich, Süd-; **S~ Pole** *n* Südpol *m*; ~-**ward(s)** *ad* südwärts, nach Süden; ~-**west** *n* Südwesten *m*.

souvenir [suːvə'nɪə*] *n* Souvenir *nt*.

sovereign ['sɒvrɪn] *n* (*ruler*) Herrscher(in *f*) *m* // *a* (*independent*) souverän.

soviet ['səʊvɪət] *a* sowjetisch; **the S~ Union** die Sowjetunion.

sow [saʊ] *n* Sau *f* // *vt* [səʊ], *pt* **sowed**, *pp* **sown** [səʊn] (*lit, fig*) säen.

soy [sɔɪ] *n:* ~ **sauce** Sojasauce *f*.

soya bean ['sɔɪə'biːn] *n* Sojabohne *f*.

spa [spɑː] *n* (*place*) Kurort *m*.

space [speɪs] *n* Platz *m*, Raum *m*; (*universe*) Weltraum *m*, All *nt*; (*length of time*) Abstand *m* // *vt* (*also:* ~ **out**) verteilen; ~**craft** ~ **ship** *n* Raumschiff *nt*; ~**man** *n* Raumfahrer *m*; **spacing** *n* Abstand *m*; (*also:* **spacing out**) Verteilung *f*.

spacious ['speɪʃəs] *a* geräumig, weit.

spade [speɪd] *n* Spaten *m*; ~**s** *n* (*CARDS*) Pik *nt*.

Spain [speɪn] *n* Spanien *nt*.

span [spæn] *n* Spanne *f*; (*of bridge etc*) Spannweite *f* // *vt* überspannen.

Spaniard ['spænjəd] *n* Spanier(in *f*) *m*.

Spanish ['spænɪʃ] *a* spanisch *n* (*LING*) Spanisch *nt*; **the ~** *npl* die Spanier.

spank [spæŋk] *vt* verhauen, versohlen.

spanner ['spænə*] *n* (*Brit*) Schrauben-

schlüssel *m*.
spar [spɑː*] *n* (*NAUT*) Sparren *m* // *vi*
(*BOXING*) einen Sparring machen.
spare [spɛə*] *a* Ersatz- // *n* = ~ **part** //
vt (*lives*, *feelings*) verschonen; (*trouble*)
ersparen; **to** ~ (*surplus*) übrig; ~ **part**
n Ersatzteil *nt*; ~ **time** *n* Freizeit *f*; ~
wheel *n* (*AUT*) Reservereifen *m*.
sparing ['spɛərɪŋ] *a*: **to be** ~ **with** geizen
mit; ~**ly** *ad* sparsam; (*eat*, *spend etc*)
in Maßen.
spark [spɑːk] *n* Funken *m*; ~(**ing**) **plug**
n Zündkerze *f*.
sparkle ['spɑːkl] *n* Funkeln *nt*; (*gaiety*)
Schwung *m* // *vi* funkeln.
sparkling ['spɑːklɪŋ] *a* funkelnd; (*wine*)
Schaum-; (*conversation*) spritzig, geistreich.
sparrow ['spærəu] *n* Spatz *m*.
sparse [spɑːs] *a* spärlich.
spasm ['spæzəm] *n* (*MED*) Krampf *m*;
(*fig*) Anfall *m*; ~**odic** [spæz'mɒdɪk] *a*
(*fig*) sprunghaft.
spat [spæt] *pt*, *pp* of **spit**.
spate [speɪt] *n* (*fig*) Flut *f*, Schwall *m*;
in ~ (*river*) angeschwollen.
spatter ['spætə*] *vt* bespritzen, ver-
spritzen.
spatula ['spætjulə] *n* Spatel *m*.
spawn [spɔːn] *vi* laichen // *n* Laich *m*.
speak [spiːk] *v* (*pt* **spoke**, *pp* **spoken**)
vt sprechen, reden; (*truth*) sagen; (*language*) sprechen // *vi* sprechen (*to mit or
zu*); ~ **to sb of or about sth** mit jdm
über etw (*acc*) sprechen; ~ **up!** sprich
lauter!; ~**er** *n* Sprecher(in *f*) *m*,
Redner(in *f*) *m*; (*loud*~**er**) Lautsprecher
m; (*POL*): **the S~er** der Vorsitzende
(*Brit*) des Parlaments *or* (*US*) des Kon-
gresses.
spear [spɪə*] *n* Speer *m* // *vt* aufspießen;
~**head** *vt* (*attack etc*) anführen.
spec [spek] *n* (*col*): **on** ~ auf gut Glück.
special ['speʃəl] *a* besondere(r, s); ~**ist**
n (*TECH*) Fachmann *m*; (*MED*)
Facharzt *m*, Fachärztin *f*; ~**ity**
[speʃɪ'ælɪtɪ] *n* Spezialität *f*; (*study*)
Spezialgebiet *nt*; ~**ize** *vi* sich
spezialisieren (*in auf* +*acc*); ~**ly** *ad*
besonders; (*explicitly*) extra.
species ['spiːʃiːz] *n* Art *f*.
specific [spə'sɪfɪk] *a* spezifisch; ~**ally**
ad spezifisch.
specification [spesɪfɪ'keɪʃən] *n* Angabe
f; (*stipulation*) Bedingung; ~**s** *pl*
(*TECH*) technische Daten *pl*.
specify ['spesɪfaɪ] *vt* genau angeben.
specimen ['spesɪmɪn] *n* Probe *f*.
speck [spek] *n* Fleckchen *nt*.
speckled ['spekld] *a* gesprenkelt.
specs [speks] *npl* (*col*) Brille *f*.
spectacle ['spektəkl] *n* Schauspiel *nt*;
~**s** *pl* Brille *f*.
spectator [spek'teɪtə*] *n* Zuschauer(in
f) *m*.

spectre, (*US*) **specter** ['spektə*] *n* Geist
m, Gespenst *n*.
speculate ['spekjuleɪt] *vi* spekulieren.
speech [spiːtʃ] *n* Sprache *f*; (*address*)
Rede *f*; (*manner of speaking*)
Sprechweise *f*; ~**less** *a* sprachlos.
speed [spiːd] *n* Geschwindigkeit *f*;
(*gear*) Gang *m* // (*JUR*) (*zu*) schnell
fahren; **at full** *or* **top** ~ mit Höchstge-
schwindigkeit; ~ **up** *vt* beschleunigen //
vi schneller werden/fahren; ~**boat** *n*
Schnellboot *nt*; ~**ily** *ad* schleunigst;
~**ing** *n* zu schnelles Fahren; ~ **limit** *n*
Geschwindigkeitsbegrenzung *f*;
~**ometer** [spɪ'dɒmɪtə*] *n* Tachometer
m; ~**way** *n* (*bike racing*) Motor-
radrennstrecke *f*; ~**y** *a* schnell.
spell [spel] *n* (*magic*) Bann *m*; (*period
of time*) Zeitlang *f* // *vt*, *pp* **spelt**
(*Brit*) *or* **spelled** buchstabieren; (*imply*) bedeuten; **to cast a** ~ **on sb** jdn ver-
zaubern; ~**bound** *a* (*wie*) gebannt;
~**ing** *n* Rechtschreibung *f*.
spend [spend], *pt*, *pp* **spent** [spent] *vt*
(*money*) ausgeben; (*time*) verbringen;
~**thrift** *n* Verschwender(in *f*) *m*.
sperm [spɜːm] *n* (*BIOL*) Samenflüssig-
keit *f*.
spew [spjuː] *vt* (er)brechen.
sphere [sfɪə*] *n* (*globe*) Kugel *f*; (*fig*)
Sphäre *f*, Gebiet *nt*.
spherical ['sferɪkəl] *a* kugelförmig.
spice [spaɪs] *n* Gewürz *nt* // *vt* würzen.
spick-and-span ['spɪkən'spæn] *a* blitz-
blank.
spider ['spaɪdə*] *n* Spinne *f*.
spike [spaɪk] *n* Dorn *m*, Spitze *f*.
spill [spɪl] *v* (*pt*, *pp* **spilt** [spɪlt] *or*
spilled) *vt* verschütten // *vi* sich
ergießen; ~ **over** *vi* überlaufen; (*fig*)
sich ausbreiten.
spin [spɪn] *n* (*trip in car*) Spazierfahrt *f*;
(*AVIAT*) (Ab)trudeln *nt*; (*on ball*) Drall
m // *v* (*pt*, *pp* **spun**) *vt* (*thread*)
spinnen; (*like top*) (herum)wirbeln // *vi*
sich drehen; ~ **out** *vt* in die Länge
ziehen.
spinach ['spɪnɪtʃ] *n* Spinat *m*.
spinal ['spaɪnl] *a* Rückgrat-; ~ **cord** *n*
Rückenmark *nt*.
spindly ['spɪndlɪ] *a* spindeldürr.
spin-dryer ['spɪn'draɪə*] *n* (*Brit*) Wä-
scheschleuder *f*.
spine [spaɪn] *n* Rückgrat *nt*; (*thorn*) Stachel *m*; ~**less** *a* (*lit*, *fig*) rückgratlos.
spinning ['spɪnɪŋ] *n* Spinnen *nt*; ~ **top**
n Kreisel *m*; ~ **wheel** *n* Spinnrad *nt*.
spin-off ['spɪnɒf] *n* Nebenprodukt *nt*.
spinster ['spɪnstə*] *n* unverheiratete
Frau *f*; (*pej*) alte Jungfer *f*.
spire [spaɪə*] *n* Turm *m*.
spirit ['spɪrɪt] *n* Geist *m*; (*humour*,
mood) Stimmung *f*; (*courage*) Mut *m*;
(*verve*) Elan *m*; (*alcohol*) Alkohol *m*;
~**s** *pl* Spirituosen *pl*; **in good** ~**s** gut auf-

gelegt; ~ed a beherzt; ~ level n Wasserwaage f.

spiritual ['spɪrɪtjuəl] a geistig, seelisch; (REL) geistlich // n Spiritual nt.

spit [spɪt] n (for roasting) (Brat)spieß m; (saliva) Spucke f // vi, pt, pp **spat** spucken; (rain) sprühen; (make a sound) zischen; (cat) fauchen.

spite [spaɪt] n Gehässigkeit f // vt kränken; in ~ of trotz (+gen or dat); ~ful a gehässig.

spittle ['spɪtl] n Speichel m, Spucke f.

splash [splæʃ] n Spritzer m; (of colour) (Farb)fleck m // vt bespritzen // vi spritzen.

spleen [splɪ:n] n (ANAT) Milz f.

splendid ['splendɪd] a glänzend.

splendour, (US) **splendor** ['splendə*] n Pracht f.

splint [splɪnt] n Schiene f.

splinter ['splɪntə*] n Splitter m // vi (zer)splittern.

split [splɪt] n Spalte f; (fig) Spaltung f; (division) Trennung f // v (pt, pp **split**) vt spalten // vi (divide) reißen; ~ up vi sich trennen.

splutter ['splʌtə*] vi stottern.

spoil [spɔɪl], pt, pp **spoilt** or **spoiled** vt (ruin) verderben; (child) verwöhnen; ~s npl Beute f; ~**sport** n Spielverderber m.

spoke [spəʊk] pt of **speak** // n Speiche f.

spoken ['spəʊkn] pp of **speak**.

spokesman ['spəʊksmən] n Sprecher m.

spokeswoman ['spəʊkswʊmən] n Sprecherin f.

sponge [spʌndʒ] n Schwamm m // vt abwaschen // vi auf Kosten leben (on gen); ~ bag n (Brit) Kulturbeutel m; ~ cake n Rührkuchen m.

sponsor ['spɒnsə*] n Sponsor m // vt fördern; ~**ship** n Finanzierung f; (public) Schirmherrschaft f.

spontaneous [spɒn'teɪnɪəs] a spontan.

spooky ['spu:kɪ] a (col) gespenstisch.

spool [spu:l] n Spule f, Rolle f.

spoon [spu:n] n Löffel m; ~**feed** vt irreg (lit) mit dem Löffel füttern; (fig) hochpäppeln; ~**ful** n Löffel(voll) m.

sport [spɔ:t] n Sport m; (person) feine(r) Kerl m; ~**ing** a (fair) sportlich, fair; to give sb a ~ing chance jdm eine faire Chance geben; ~s car n Sportwagen m; ~s jacket, (US) ~ jacket Sportjackett m; **sportsman** n Sportler m; **sportsmanship** n Sportlichkeit f; **sportswear** n Sportkleidung f; **sportswoman** n Sportlerin f; ~y a sportlich.

spot [spɒt] n Punkt m; (dirty) Fleck(en) m; (place) Stelle f; (MED) Pickel m // vt erspähen; (mistake) bemerken; on the ~ an Ort und Stelle; (at once) auf der Stelle; ~ check n Stichprobe f;

~**less** a fleckenlos; ~**light** n Scheinwerferlicht nt; (lamp) Scheinwerfer m; ~**ted** a gefleckt; ~**ty** a (face) pickelig.

spouse [spauz] n Gatte m/Gattin f.

spout [spaʊt] n (of pot) Tülle f; (jet) Wasserstrahl m // vi speien.

sprain [spreɪn] n Verrenkung f // vt verrenken.

sprang [spræŋ] pt of **spring**.

sprawl [sprɔ:l] vi sich strecken.

spray [spreɪ] n Spray nt; (off sea) Gischt f; (of flowers) Zweig m // vt besprühen, sprayen.

spread [spred] n (extent) Verbreitung f; (col: meal) Schmaus m; (for bread) Aufstrich m // v (pt, pp **spread**) vt ausbreiten; (scatter) verbreiten; (butter) streichen // vi sich ausbreiten; ~**eagled** a: to be ~-eagled alle viere von sich strecken.

spree [spri:] n (shopping) Einkaufsbummel m; to go on a ~ einen draufmachen.

sprightly ['spraɪtlɪ] a munter, lebhaft.

spring [sprɪŋ] n (leap) Sprung m; (metal) Feder f; (season) Frühling m; (water) Quelle f // vi, pt sprang, pp sprung (leap) springen; ~ up vi (problem) auftauchen; ~**board** n Sprungbrett nt; ~**clean** n (also: ~-cleaning) n Frühjahrsputz m; ~**time** n Frühling m; ~y a federnd, elastisch.

sprinkle ['sprɪŋkl] vt (salt) streuen; (liquid) sprenkeln; to ~ water on, ~ with water mit Wasser besprengen.

sprinkler ['sprɪŋklə*] n (for lawn) Sprenger m; (for fire fighting) Sprinkler m.

sprite [spraɪt] n Elfe f; Kobold m.

sprout [spraʊt] vi sprießen; (Brussels) ~s npl Rosenkohl m.

spruce [spru:s] n Fichte f // a schmuck, adrett.

sprung [sprʌŋ] pp of **spring**.

spry [spraɪ] a flink, rege.

spun [spʌn] pt, pp of **spin**.

spur [spɜ:*] n Sporn m; (fig) Ansporn m // vt (also: ~ on) (fig) anspornen; on the ~ of the moment spontan.

spurious ['spjʊərɪəs] a falsch.

spurn [spɜ:n] vt verschmähen.

spurt [spɜ:t] n (jet) Strahl m; (acceleration) Spurt m // vi (liquid) schießen.

spy [spaɪ] n Spion (in f) m // vi spionieren // vt erspähen; ~**ing** n Spionage f.

sq. abbr of **square**.

squabble ['skwɒbl] n Zank m // vi sich zanken.

squad [skwɒd] n (MIL) Abteilung f; (police) Kommando nt.

squadron ['skwɒdrən] n (cavalry) Schwadron f; (NAUT) Geschwader nt; (air force) Staffel f.

squalid ['skwɒlɪd] *a* verkommen.

squall [skwɔːl] *n* Bö *f*, Windstoß *m*.

squalor ['skwɒlə*] *n* Verwahrlosung *f*.

squander ['skwɒndə*] *vt* verschwenden.

square [skweə*] *n* Quadrat *nt*; (*open space*) Platz *m*; (*instrument*) Winkel *m*; (*col: person*) Spießer *m* // *a* viereckig; (*col: ideas, tastes*) spießig // *vt* (*arrange*) ausmachen; (*MATH*) ins Quadrat erheben // *vi* (*agree*) übereinstimmen; **all ~** quitt; **a ~ meal** eine ordentliche Mahlzeit; **2 metres ~** 2 Meter im Quadrat; **1 ~ metre** 1 Quadratmeter; **~ly** *ad* fest, gerade.

squash [skwɒʃ] *n* (*Brit: drink*) Saft *m* // *vt* zerquetschen.

squat [skwɒt] *a* untersetzt // *vi* hocken; **~ter** *n* Hausbesetzer *m*.

squawk [skwɔːk] *vi* kreischen.

squeak [skwiːk] *vi* quiek(s)en; (*spring, door etc*) quietschen.

squeal [skwiːl] *vi* schrill schreien.

squeamish ['skwiːmɪʃ] *a* empfindlich.

squeeze [skwiːz] *n* (*POL*) Geldknappheit *f* // *vt* pressen, drücken; (*orange*) auspressen; **~ out** *vt* ausquetschen.

squelch [skweltʃ] *vi* platschen.

squid [skwɪd] *n* Tintenfisch *m*.

squiggle ['skwɪgl] *n* Schnörkel *m*.

squint [skwɪnt] *vi* schielen (*at* nach) // *n*: **to have a ~** schielen.

squire ['skwaɪə*] *n* (*Brit*) Gutsherr *m*.

squirm [skwɜːm] *vi* sich winden.

squirrel ['skwɪrəl] *n* Eichhörnchen *nt*.

squirt [skwɜːt] *vti* spritzen.

Sr *abbr* (= *senior*) sen.

St *abbr* (= *saint*) hl., St.; (= *street*) Str.

stab [stæb] *n* (*blow*) Stich *m*; (*col: try*) Versuch *m* // *vt* erstechen.

stabilize ['steɪbəlaɪz] *vt* stabilisieren // *vi* sich stabilisieren.

stable ['steɪbl] *a* stabil // *n* Stall *m*.

stack [stæk] *n* Stapel *m* // *vt* stapeln.

stadium ['steɪdɪəm] *n* Stadion *nt*.

staff [stɑːf] *n* (*stick*, *MIL*) Stab *m*; (*personnel*) Personal *nt*; (*Brit SCH*) Lehrkräfte *pl* // *vt* (*with people*) besetzen.

stag [stæg] *n* Hirsch *m*.

stage [steɪdʒ] *n* Bühne *f*; (*of journey*) Etappe *f*; (*degree*) Stufe *f*; (*point*) Stadium *nt* // *vt* (*put on*) aufführen; (*simulate*) inszenieren; (*demonstration*) veranstalten; **in ~s** etappenweise; **~coach** *n* Postkutsche *f*; **~ door** *n* Bühneneingang *m*; **~ manager** *n* Intendant *m*.

stagger ['stægə*] *vi* wanken, taumeln // *vt* (*amaze*) verblüffen; (*hours*) staffeln; **~ing** *a* unglaublich.

stagnant ['stægnənt] *a* stagnierend; (*water*) stehend.

stagnate [stæg'neɪt] *vi* stagnieren.

stag party *n* Männerabend *m* (vom Bräutigam vor der Hochzeit gegeben).

staid [steɪd] *a* gesetzt.

stain [steɪn] *n* Fleck *m* // *vt* beflecken; **~ed glass window** buntes Glasfenster *nt*; **~less** *a* (*steel*) rostfrei; **~ remover** *n* Fleckentferner *m*.

stair [steə*] *n* (Treppen)stufe *f*; **~case** *n* Treppenhaus *nt*, Treppe *f*; **~s** *pl* Treppe *f*; **~way** *n* Treppenaufgang *m*.

stake [steɪk] *n* (*post*) Pfahl *m*; (*money*) Einsatz *m* // *vt* (*bet money*) setzen; **to be at ~** auf dem Spiel stehen.

stale [steɪl] *a* alt; (*bread*) altbacken.

stalemate ['steɪlmeɪt] *n* (*CHESS*) Patt *nt*; (*fig*) Stillstand *m*.

stalk [stɔːk] *n* Stengel *m*, Stiel *m* // *vt* (*game*) jagen; **~ off** *vi* abstolzieren.

stall [stɔːl] *n* (*in stable*) Stand *m*, Box *f*; (*in market*) (Verkaufs)stand *m* // *vt* (*AUT*) (den Motor) abwürgen // *vi* (*AUT*) stehenbleiben; (*avoid*) Ausflüchte machen; **~s** *npl* (*Brit THEAT*) Parkett *nt*.

stallion ['stælɪən] *n* Zuchthengst *m*.

stalwart ['stɔːlwət] *n* treue(r) Anhänger *m*.

stamina ['stæmɪnə] *n* Durchhaltevermögen *nt*, Zähigkeit *f*.

stammer ['stæmə*] *n* Stottern *nt* // *vti* stottern, stammeln.

stamp [stæmp] *n* Briefmarke *f*; (*for document*) Stempel *m* // *vi* stampfen // *vt* (*mark*) stempeln; (*mail*) frankieren; (*foot*) stampfen *mit*; **~ album** *n* Briefmarkenalbum *nt*; **~ collecting** *n* Briefmarkensammeln *nt*.

stampede [stæm'piːd] *n* panische Flucht *f*.

stance [stæns] *n* Haltung *f*.

stand [stænd] *n* (*for objects*) Gestell *nt*; (*seats*) Tribüne *f* // *v* (*pt, pp* **stood**) *vi* stehen; (*rise*) aufstehen; (*decision*) feststehen // *vt* setzen, stellen; (*endure*) aushalten; (*person*) ausstehen; (*nonsense*) dulden; **to make a ~** Widerstand leisten; **to ~ for parliament** (*Brit*) für das Parlament kandidieren; **~ by** *vi* (*be ready*) bereitstehen // *vt* (*opinion*) treu bleiben (+*dat*); **~ down** *vi* (*withdraw*) zurücktreten; **~ for** *vt* (*signify*) stehen für; (*permit, tolerate*) hinnehmen; **~ in for** *vt* einspringen für; **~ out** *vi* (*be prominent*) hervorstechen; **~ up** *vi* (*rise*) aufstehen; **~ up for** *vi* sich einsetzen für; **~ up to** *vt*: **~ up to sth/sb** *vt* einer Sache gewachsen sein/sich jdm gegenüber behaupten.

standard ['stændəd] *n* (*measure*) Norm *f*; (*flag*) Fahne *f* // *a* (*size etc*) Normal-; **~s** *npl* (*morals*) Maßstäbe *pl*; **~ize** *vt* vereinheitlichen; **~ lamp** *n* (*Brit*) Stehlampe *f*; **~ of living** *n* Lebensstandard *m*.

stand-by ['stændbaɪ] *n* Reserve *f*; **to be on ~** in Bereitschaft sein; **~ ticket** *n* (*AVIAT*) Standby-Ticket *nt*.

stand-in ['stændɪn] n Ersatz m.

standing ['stændɪŋ] a (erect) stehend; (permanent) ständig; (invitation) offen // n (duration) Dauer f; (reputation) Ansehen nt; of many years' ~ langjährig; ~ order a (Brit: at bank) Dauerauftrag m; ~ orders pl (MIL) Vorschrift; ~ room n Stehplatz m.

stand-offish ['stænd'ɒfɪʃ] a zurückhaltend, sehr reserviert.

standpoint ['stændpɔɪnt] n Standpunkt m.

standstill ['stændstɪl] n: to be at a ~ stillstehen; to come to a ~ zum Stillstand kommen.

stank [stæŋk] pt of stink.

staple ['steɪpl] n (in paper) Heftklamme f; (article) Haupterzeugnis nt // a Grund-, Haupt- // vt (fest)klammern; ~r n Heftmaschine f.

star [stɑ:*] n Stern m; (person) Star m // vi die Hauptrolle spielen.

starboard ['stɑ:bəd] n Steuerbord nt.

starch [stɑ:tʃ] n Stärke f.

stardom ['stɑ:dəm] n Berühmtheit f.

stare [stɛə*] n starre(r) Blick m // vi starren (at auf +acc); ~ at vt anstarren.

starfish ['stɑ:fɪʃ] n Seestern m.

stark [stɑ:k] a öde // ad: ~ naked splitternackt.

starling ['stɑ:lɪŋ] n Star m.

starry ['stɑ:rɪ] a Sternen-; ~-eyed a (innocent) blauäugig.

start [stɑ:t] n Anfang m; (SPORT) Start m; (lead) Vorsprung m // vt in Gang setzen; (car) anlassen // vi anfangen; (car) anspringen; (on journey) aufbrechen; (SPORT) starten; (with fright) zusammenfahren; to ~ doing or to do sth anfangen, etw zu tun; ~ off vi anfangen; (begin moving) losgehen/-fahren; ~ up vi anfangen; (startled) auffahren // vt beginnen; (car) anlassen; (engine) starten; ~er n (AUT) Anlasser m; (for race) Starter m; (Brit COOK) Vorspeise f; ~ing point n Ausgangspunkt m.

startle ['stɑ:tl] vt erschrecken.

startling ['stɑ:tlɪŋ] a erschreckend.

starvation [stɑ:'veɪʃən] n Verhungern nt.

starve [stɑ:v] vi verhungern // vt verhungern lassen; I'm starving ich sterbe vor Hunger.

state [steɪt] n (condition) Zustand m; (POL) Staat m // vt erklären; (facts) angeben; the S~s die Staaten; to be in a ~ durchdrehen; ~ly a würdevoll; ~ment n Aussage f; (POL) Erklärung f; **statesman** n Staatsmann m.

static ['stætɪk] n: ~ electricity n Reibungselektrizität f.

station ['steɪʃən] n (RAIL etc) Bahnhof m; (police etc) Wache f; (in society)

Stand m // vt stationieren.

stationary ['steɪʃənərɪ] a stillstehend; (car) parkend.

stationer ['steɪʃənə*] n Schreibwarenhändler m; ~'s n (shop) Schreibwarengeschäft nt; ~y n Schreibwaren pl.

station master ['steɪʃənmɑ:stə*] n Bahnhofsvorsteher m.

station wagon ['steɪʃənwægən] n Kombiwagen m.

statistics [stə'tɪstɪks] n Statistik f.

statue ['stætju:] n Statue f.

stature ['stætʃə*] n Größe f.

status ['steɪtəs] n Status m.

statute ['stætju:t] n Gesetz nt.

statutory ['stætjutərɪ] a gesetzlich.

staunch [stɔ:ntʃ] a standhaft.

stave [steɪv]: ~ off vt (attack) abwehren; (threat) abwenden.

stay [steɪ] n Aufenthalt m // vi bleiben; (reside) wohnen; to ~ put an Ort und Stelle bleiben; to ~ the night übernachten; ~ behind vi zurückbleiben; ~ in vi (at home) zu Hause bleiben; ~ on vi (continue) länger bleiben; ~ out vi (of house) wegbleiben; ~ up vi (at night) aufbleiben; ~ing power n Durchhaltevermögen nt.

stead [sted] n: in sb's ~ an jds Stelle; to stand sb in good ~ jdm zugute kommen.

steadfast ['stedfəst] a standhaft, treu.

steadily ['stedɪlɪ] ad stetig, regelmäßig.

steady ['stedɪ] a (firm) fest, stabil; (regular) gleichmäßig; (reliable) beständig; (hand) ruhig; (job, boyfriend) fest // vt festigen; to ~ o.s. on or against sth sich stützen auf or gegen etw (acc).

steak [steɪk] n Steak nt; (fish) Filet nt.

steal [sti:l] v (pt stole, pp stolen) vti stehlen // vi sich stehlen.

stealth [stelθ] n Heimlichkeit f; ~y ['stelθɪ] a verstohlen, heimlich.

steam [sti:m] n Dampf m // vt (COOK) im Dampfbad erhitzen // vi dampfen; ~ engine n Dampfmaschine f; ~er n Dampfer m; ~roller n Dampfwalze f; ~ship n = ~er; ~y a dampfig.

steel [sti:l] n Stahl m // a Stahl-; (fig) stählern; ~works n Stahlwerke pl.

steep [sti:p] a steil; (price) gepfeffert // vt einweichen.

steeple ['sti:pl] n Kirchturm m; ~chase n Hindernisrennen nt.

steer [stɪə*] vti steuern; (car etc) lenken; ~ing n (AUT) Steuerung f; ~ing wheel n Steuer- or Lenkrad nt.

stellar ['stelə*] a Stern(en)-.

stem [stem] n Stiel m // vt aufhalten; ~ from vt abstammen von.

stench [stentʃ] n Gestank m.

stencil ['stensl] n Schablone f // vt (auf)drucken.

stenographer [ste'nɒgrəfə*] n (US) Stenograph(in f) m.

step [stɛp] n Schritt m; (stair) Stufe f //
vi treten, schreiten; **to take ~s** Schritte
unternehmen; **~s** pl = **~ladder**; **in/out
of ~ (with)** im/nicht im Gleichklang
(mit); **~daughter** n Stieftochter f; **~
down** vi (fig) abtreten; **~ off** vt aussteigen aus (+dat); **~ up** vt steigern;
~brother n Stiefbruder m; **~father** n
Stiefvater m; **~ladder** n Trittleiter f;
~mother n Stiefmutter f; **~ping stone**
n Stein m; (fig) Sprungbrett nt;
~sister n Stiefschwester f; **~son** n
Stiefsohn m.

stereo ['stɛrɪəʊ] n Stereoanlage f // a
(also: **~phonic**) stereophonisch.

stereotype ['stɪərɪətaɪp] n Prototyp m;
(fig) Klischee nt // vt stereotypieren;
(fig) stereotyp machen.

sterile ['stɛraɪl] a steril; (person) unfruchtbar.

sterling ['stɜːlɪŋ] a (FIN) Sterling-;
(character) gediegen // n (ECON) Pfund
Sterling; **a pound ~** ein Pfund Sterling.

stern [stɜːn] a streng // n Heck nt,
Achterschiff nt.

stew [stjuː] n Eintopf m // vti schmoren.

steward ['stjuːəd] n Steward m; **~ess** n
Stewardess f.

stick [stɪk] n Stock m; (of chalk etc)
Stück nt // v (pt, pp **stuck**) vt (stab) stechen; (fix) stecken; (put) stellen; (gum)
(an)kleben; (col: tolerate) vertragen //
vi (stop) steckenbleiben; (get stuck)
klemmen; (hold fast) kleben, haften; **~
out** vi (project) hervorstehen aus; **~ up**
vi (project) in die Höhe stehen; **~ up
for** vt (defend) eintreten für; **~er** n Aufkleber m; **~ing plaster** n Heftpflaster
nt.

stickler ['stɪklə*] n Pedant m (for in
+acc).

stick-up ['stɪkʌp] n (col) (Raub)überfall
m.

sticky ['stɪkɪ] a klebrig; (atmosphere)
stickig.

stiff [stɪf] a steif; (difficult) hart; (paste)
dick; (drink) stark; **~en** vt versteifen,
(ver)stärken // vi sich versteifen; **~ness**
n Steifheit f.

stifle ['staɪfl] vt unterdrücken.

stifling ['staɪflɪŋ] a drückend.

stigma ['stɪgmə], pl (BOT, MED, REL)
~ta [-tə], (fig) **~s** n Stigma nt.

stile [staɪl] n Steige f.

stiletto [stɪ'lɛtəʊ] n (Brit: also: **~ heel**)
Pfennigabsatz m.

still [stɪl] n a still // ad (immer) noch;
(anyhow) immerhin; **~born** a tot-
geboren; **~ life** n Stilleben nt.

stilt [stɪlt] n Stelze f.

stilted ['stɪltɪd] a gestelzt.

stimulate ['stɪmjʊleɪt] vt anregen,
stimulieren.

stimulus ['stɪmjʊləs], pl **-li** [-laɪ] n Anregung f, Reiz m.

sting [stɪŋ] n Stich m; (organ) Stachel m
// vti, pt, pp **stung** stechen; (on skin)
brennen.

stingy ['stɪndʒɪ] a geizig, knauserig.

stink [stɪŋk] n Gestank m // vi, pt **stank**,
pp **stunk** stinken; **~ing** a (fig) widerlich.

stint [stɪnt] n Pensum nt; (period)
Betätigung f // vi knausern; **to do one's
~** seine Arbeit tun; (share) seinen Teil
beitragen.

stipulate ['stɪpjʊleɪt] vt festsetzen.

stir [stɜː*] n Bewegung f; (COOK)
Rühren nt; (sensation) Aufsehen nt // vt
(um)rühren // vi sich rühren; **~ up** vt
mob aufhetzen; (mixture) umrühren;
(dust) aufwirbeln.

stirrup ['stɪrəp] n Steigbügel m.

stitch [stɪtʃ] n (with needle) Stich m;
(MED) Faden m; (of knitting) Masche f;
(pain) Stich m // vt nähen.

stoat [stəʊt] n Wiesel nt.

stock [stɒk] n Vorrat m; (COMM) (Waren)lager nt; (live~) Vieh nt; (COOK)
Brühe f; (FIN) Grundkapital nt // a stets
vorrätig; (standard) Normal- // vt (in
shop) führen; **in/out of ~** vorrätig/nicht
vorrätig; **to take ~ of** Inventur machen
von; (fig) Bilanz ziehen aus; **~s** npl
Aktien pl; **~s and shares** Effekten pl; **to
~ up with** Reserven anlegen von.

stockbroker ['stɒkbrəʊkə*] n
Börsenmakler m.

stock cube n Brühwürfel m.

stock exchange n Börse f.

stocking ['stɒkɪŋ] n Strumpf m.

stockist ['stɒkɪst] n Händler m.

stock market ['stɒkmɑːkɪt] n Börse f.

stock phrase n Standardsatz m.

stockpile ['stɒkpaɪl] n Vorrat m // vt
aufstapeln.

stocktaking ['stɒkteɪkɪŋ] n (Brit
COMM) Inventur f, Bestandsaufnahme f.

stocky ['stɒkɪ] a untersetzt.

stodgy ['stɒdʒɪ] a pampig; (fig) trocken.

stoke [stəʊk] vt schüren.

stole [stəʊl] pt of **steal** // n Stola f.

stolen ['stəʊlən] pp of **steal**.

stolid ['stɒlɪd] a stur.

stomach ['stʌmək] n Bauch m, Magen
m // vt vertragen; **~ache** n Magen- or
Bauchschmerzen pl.

stone [stəʊn] n Stein m; (Brit: weight)
Gewichtseinheit f = 6.35 kg // vt (olive)
entkernen; (kill) steinigen; **~-cold** a
eiskalt; **~-deaf** a stocktaub; **~work** n
Mauerwerk nt.

stony ['stəʊnɪ] a steinig.

stood [stʊd] pt, pp of **stand**.

stool [stuːl] n Hocker m.

stoop [stuːp] vi sich bücken.

stop [stɒp] n Halt m; (bus~) Haltestelle
f; (punctuation) Punkt m // vt anhalten;
(bring to end) aufhören (mit), sein
lassen // vi aufhören; (clock) stehen-

bleiben; (*remain*) bleiben; **to ~ doing sth** aufhören, etw zu tun; **~ dead** *vi* innehalten; **~ off** *vi* kurz haltmachen; **~ up** *vt* (*hole*) zustopfen, verstopfen; **~gap** *n* Notlösung *f*; **~lights** *npl* (*AUT*) Bremslichter *pl*; **~over** *n* (*on journey*) Zwischenaufenthalt *m*.

stoppage ['stɒpɪdʒ] *n* (An)halten *nt*; (*traffic*) Verkehrsstockung *f*; (*strike*) Arbeitseinstellung *f*.

stopper ['stɒpə*] *n* Propfen *m*, Stöpsel *m*.

stop press *n* letzte Meldung *f*.

stopwatch ['stɒpwɒtʃ] *n* Stoppuhr *f*.

storage ['stɔːrɪdʒ] *n* Lagerung *f*; **~ heater** *n* (Nachtstrom)speicherofen *m*.

store [stɔː*] *n* Vorrat *m*; (*place*) Lager *nt*, Warenhaus *nt*; (*Brit: large shop*) Kaufhaus *nt*; (*US*) Laden *m*; **~s** *pl* Vorräte *pl* // *vt* lagern; **~ up** *vt* sich eindecken mit; **~room** *n* Lagerraum *m*, Vorratsraum *m*.

storey, (*US*) **story** ['stɔːrɪ] *n* Stock *m*.

stork [stɔːk] *n* Storch *m*.

storm [stɔːm] *n* (*lit, fig*) Sturm *m* // *vti* stürmen; **~y** *a* stürmisch.

story ['stɔːrɪ] *n* Geschichte *f*; (*lie*) Märchen *nt*; (*US*) = **storey**; **~book** *n* Geschichtenbuch *nt*; **~teller** *n* Geschichtenerzähler *m*.

stout [staʊt] *a* (*bold*) tapfer; (*too fat*) beleibt // *n* Starkbier *nt*; (*also: sweet ~*) ≃ Malzbier *nt*.

stove [staʊv] *n* (Koch)herd *m*; (*for heating*) Ofen *m*.

stow [staʊ] *vt* verstauen; **~away** *n* blinde(r) Passagier *m*.

straddle ['strædl] *vt* (*horse, fence*) rittlings sitzen auf (+*dat*); (*fig*) überbrücken.

straggle ['strægl] *vi* (*branches etc*) wuchern; (*people*) nachhinken; **~r** *n* Nachzügler *m*; **straggling**, **straggly** *a* (*hair*) zottig.

straight [streɪt] *a* gerade; (*honest*) offen, ehrlich; (*drink*) pur // *ad* (*direct*) direkt, geradewegs; **to put** *or* **get sth ~** etw in Ordnung bringen; **~away** *ad* sofort; **~ off** *ad* sofort; **~en** *vt* (*also:* **~en up**) (*lit*) gerade machen; (*fig*) klarstellen; **~-faced** *ad* ohne die Miene zu verziehen // *a*: **to be ~-faced** keine Miene verziehen; **~forward** *a* einfach, unkompliziert.

strain [streɪn] *n* Belastung *f*; (*streak, trace*) Zug *m*; (*of music*) Fetzen *m* // *vt* überanstrengen; (*stretch*) anspannen; (*muscle*) zerren; (*filter*) (durch)seihen // *vi* sich anstrengen; **~ed** *a* (*laugh*) gezwungen; (*relations*) gespannt; **~er** *n* Sieb *nt*.

strait [streɪt] *n* Straße *f*, Meerenge *f*; **~-jacket** *n* Zwangsjacke *f*; **~-laced** *a* engherzig, streng.

strand [strænd] *n* (*lit, fig*) Faden *m*; (*of hair*) Strähne *f*; **~ed** (*lit, fig*) gestrandet.

strange [streɪndʒ] *a* fremd; (*unusual*) seltsam; **~r** *n* Fremde(r) *m/f*.

strangle ['stræŋgl] *vt* erwürgen; **~hold** *n* (*fig*) Umklammerung *f*.

strap [stræp] *n* Riemen *m*; (*on clothes*) Träger *m* // *vt* (*fasten*) festschnallen.

strapping ['stræpɪŋ] *a* stramm.

strata ['strɑːtə] *pl of* **stratum**.

stratagem ['strætədʒəm] *n* (Kriegs)list *f*.

strategic [strə'tiːdʒɪk] *a* strategisch.

strategy ['strætədʒɪ] *n* (*fig*) Strategie *f*.

stratum ['strɑːtəm], *pl* **-ta** *n* Schicht *f*.

straw [strɔː] *n* Stroh *nt*; (*single stalk, drinking ~*) Strohhalm *m*; **that's the last ~!** das ist der Gipfel!

strawberry ['strɔːbərɪ] *n* Erdbeere *f*.

stray [streɪ] *a* (*animal*) verirrt; (*thought*) zufällig // *vi* herumstreunen.

streak ['striːk] *n* Streifen *m*; (*in character*) Einschlag *m*; (*in hair*) Strähne *f* // *vt* streifen // *vi* zucken; (*move quickly*) flitzen; **~ of bad luck** Pechsträhne *f*; **~y** *a* gestreift; (*bacon*) durchwachsen.

stream [striːm] *n* (*brook*) Bach *m*; (*fig*) Strom *m* // *vt* (*SCH*) in (Leistungs)gruppen einteilen // *vi* strömen; **to ~ in/out** (*people*) hinein-/hinausströmen.

streamer ['striːmə*] *n* (*pennon*) Wimpel *m*; (*of paper*) Luftschlange *f*.

streamlined ['striːmlaɪnd] *a* stromlinienförmig; (*effective*) rationell.

street [striːt] *n* Straße *f* // *a* Straßen-; **~car** *n* (*US*) Straßenbahn *f*; **~ lamp** *n* Straßenlaterne *f*; **~ plan** *n* Stadtplan *m*; **~wise** *a* (*col*): **to be ~wise** wissen, wo es lang geht.

strength [streŋθ] *n* Stärke *f* (*also fig*); Kraft *f*; **~en** *vt* (ver)stärken.

strenuous ['strenjʊəs] *a* anstrengend.

stress [stres] *n* Druck *m*; (*mental*) Streß *m*; (*GRAM*) Betonung *f* // *vt* betonen.

stretch [stretʃ] *n* Strecke *f* // *vt* ausdehnen, strecken // *vi* sich erstrecken; (*person*) sich strecken; **~ out** *vi* sich ausstrecken // *vt* ausstrecken.

stretcher ['stretʃə*] *n* Tragbahre *f*.

strewn [struːn] *a*: **~ with** übersät mit.

stricken ['strɪkən] *a* (*person*) ergriffen; (*city, country*) heimgesucht; **~ with** (*arthritis, disease*) leidend unter.

strict [strɪkt] *a* (*exact*) genau; (*severe*) streng; **~ly** *ad* streng, genau.

stride [straɪd] *n* lange(r) Schritt *m* // *vi*, *pt* **strode**, *pp* **stridden** ['strɪdn] schreiten.

strident ['straɪdənt] *a* schneidend, durchdringend.

strife [straɪf] *n* Streit *m*.

strike [straɪk] *n* Streik *m*; (*attack*) Schlag *m* // *v* (*pt, pp* **struck**) *vt* (*hit*) schlagen; (collide) stoßen gegen; (come to mind) einfallen (+dat); (find) finden // vi (stop work) streiken; (attack) zuschlagen; (clock) schlagen; on ~ (workers) im Streik; to ~ a match ein Streichholz anzünden; ~ **down** vt (lay low) niederschlagen; ~ **out** vt (cross out) ausstreichen; ~ **up** vt (music) anstimmen; (friendship) schließen; ~**r** n Streikende(r) mf.

striking ['straɪkɪŋ] a auffallend.

string [strɪŋ] n Schnur f; (row) Reihe f; (MUS) Saite f // v (pt, pp **strung**) vt: to ~ **together** aneinanderreihen // vi: to ~ **out** (sich)verteilen; **the** ~**s** pl (MUS) die Streichinstrumente pl; to **pull** ~**s** (fig) Fäden ziehen; ~ **bean** n grüne Bohne f; ~(**ed**) **instrument** n (MUS) Saiteninstrument nt.

stringent ['strɪndʒənt] a streng.

strip [strɪp] n Streifen m // vt (uncover) abstreifen, abziehen; (clothes) ausziehen; (TECH) auseinandernehmen // vi (undress) sich ausziehen; ~ **cartoon** n Bildserie f.

stripe [straɪp] n Streifen m; ~**d** a gestreift.

strip lighting n Neonlicht nt.

stripper ['strɪpə*] n Stripteasetänzerin f.

strive [straɪv] vi, pt **strove**, pp **striven** ['strɪvn] streben (for nach).

strode [strəud] pt of **stride**.

stroke [strəuk] n Schlag m; (swim, row) Stoß m; (TECH) Hub m; (MED) Schlaganfall m; (caress) Streicheln nt // vt streicheln; at a ~ mit einem Schlag.

stroll [strəul] n Spaziergang m // vi schlendern; ~**er** n (US: pushchair) Sportwagen m.

strong [strɔŋ] a stark; (firm) fest; they are 50 ~ sie sind 50 Mann stark; ~**box** n Kassette f; ~**hold** n Hochburg f; ~**ly** ad stark; ~**room** n Tresor m.

strove [strəuv] pt of **strive**.

struck [strʌk] pt, pp of **strike**.

structure ['strʌktʃə*] n Struktur f, Aufbau m; (building) Bau m.

struggle ['strʌgl] n Kampf m // vi (fight) kämpfen.

strum [strʌm] vt (guitar) klimpern auf (+dat).

strung [strʌŋ] pt, pp of **string**.

strut [strʌt] n Strebe f, Stütze f // vi stolzieren.

stub [stʌb] n Stummel m; (of cigarette) Kippe f // vt: to ~ **one's toe** sich (dat) den Zeh anstoßen; ~ **out** vt ausdrücken.

stubble ['stʌbl] n Stoppel f.

stubborn ['stʌbən] a hartnäckig.

stuck [stʌk] pt, pp of **stick** // a (jammed) klemmend; ~**-up** a hochnäsig.

stud [stʌd] n (button) Kragenknopf m; (place) Gestüt nt // vt (fig): ~**ded with**

übersät mit.

student ['stjuːdənt] n Student(in f) m; (US also) Schüler(in f) m // a Studenten-; ~ **driver** n (US) Fahrschüler(in f) m.

studio ['stjuːdɪəu] n Studio nt; (for artist) Atelier nt; ~ **flat**, (US) ~ **apartment** n Appartement nt.

studious ['stjuːdɪəs] a lernbegierig.

study ['stʌdɪ] n Studium nt; (investigation also) Untersuchung f; (room) Arbeitszimmer nt; (essay etc) Studie f // vt studieren; (face) erforschen; (evidence) prüfen // vi studieren.

stuff [stʌf] n Stoff m; (col) Zeug nt // vt stopfen, füllen; (animal) ausstopfen; ~**ing** n Füllung f; ~**y** a (room) schwül; (person) spießig.

stumble ['stʌmbl] vi stolpern; to ~ **across** (fig) zufällig stoßen auf (+acc).

stumbling block ['stʌmblɪŋblɔk] n Hindernis nt.

stump [stʌmp] n Stumpf m // vt umwerfen.

stun [stʌn] vt betäuben; (shock) niederschmettern.

stung [stʌŋ] pt, pp of **sting**.

stunk [stʌŋk] pp of **stink**.

stunning ['stʌnɪŋ] a betäubend; (news) überwältigend, umwerfend.

stunt [stʌnt] n Kunststück nt, Trick m; ~**ed** a verkümmert; ~**man** n Stuntman m.

stupefy ['stjuːpɪfaɪ] vt betäuben; (by news) bestürzen.

stupendous [stjuˈpɛndəs] a erstaunlich, enorm.

stupid ['stjuːpɪd] a dumm; ~**ity** [stjuːˈpɪdɪtɪ] n Dummheit f.

stupor ['stjuːpə*] n Betäubung f.

sturdy ['stɜːdɪ] a kräftig, robust.

stutter ['stʌtə*] n Stottern nt // vi stottern.

sty [staɪ] n Schweinestall m.

stye [staɪ] n Gerstenkorn nt.

style [staɪl] n Stil m; (fashion) Mode f.

stylish ['staɪlɪʃ] a modisch.

stylist ['staɪlɪst] n (hair ~) Friseur m, Friseuse f.

stylus ['staɪləs] n (Grammophon)nadel f.

suave [swɑːv] a zuvorkommend.

sub- [sʌb] pref Unter-.

subconscious ['sʌbˈkɔnʃəs] a unterbewußt // n: **the** ~ das Unterbewußte.

subcontract ['sʌbənˈtrækt] vt (vertraglich) untervermitteln.

subdivide ['sʌbdɪˈvaɪd] vt unterteilen.

subdue [səbˈdjuː] vt unterwerfen; ~**d** a (lighting) gedämpft; (person) still.

subject ['sʌbdʒɪkt] n (of kingdom) Untertan m; (citizen) Staatsangehörige(r) mf; (topic) Thema nt; (SCH) Fach nt; (GRAM) Subjekt nt // [səbˈdʒɛkt] (subdue) unterwerfen; (expose) aussetzen // a ['sʌbdʒɪkt]: to be

~ to unterworfen sein (+*dat*); (*exposed*) ausgesetzt sein (+*dat*); ~**ive** [səb'dʒɛktɪv] *a* subjektiv; ~ **matter** *n* Thema *nt*.

subjugate ['sʌbdʒʊgeɪt] *vt* unterjochen.

subjunctive [səb'dʒʌŋktɪv] *a* Konjunktiv- // *n* Konjunktiv *m*.

sublet ['sʌb'let] (*irreg: like* let) *vt* untervermieten.

sublime [sə'blaɪm] *a* erhaben.

submachine gun ['sʌbmə'ʃiːn-] *n* Maschinenpistole *f*.

submarine [sʌbmə'riːn] *n* Unterseeboot *nt*, U-Boot *nt*.

submerge [səb'mɜːdʒ] *vt* untertauchen; (*flood*) überschwemmen // *vi* untertauchen.

submission [səb'mɪʃən] *n* (*obedience*) Gehorsam *m*; (*claim*) Behauptung *f*; (*of plan*) Unterbreitung *f*.

submissive [səb'mɪsɪv] *a* . demütig, unterwürfig (*pej*).

submit [səb'mɪt] *vt* behaupten; (*plan*) unterbreiten // *vi* (*give in*) sich ergeben.

subnormal ['sʌb'nɔːməl] *a* minderbegabt.

subordinate [sə'bɔːdɪnət] *a* untergeordnet // *n* Untergebene(r) *mf*.

subpoena [sə'piːnə] *n* Vorladung *f* // *vt* vorladen.

subscribe [səb'skraɪb] *vi* (*to view etc*) unterstützen; (*to newspaper*) abonnieren (*to acc*); ~**r** *n* (*to periodical*) Abonnent *m*; (*TEL*) Telefonteilnehmer *m*.

subscription [səb'skrɪpʃən] *n* Abonnement *nt*; (*money subscribed*) (Mitglieds)beitrag *m*.

subsequent ['sʌbsɪkwənt] *a* folgend, später; ~**ly** *ad* später.

subside [səb'saɪd] *vi* sich senken; **subsidence** [sʌb'saɪdəns] *n* Senkung *f*.

subsidiary [səb'sɪdɪərɪ] *a* Neben- // *n* (*company*) Tochtergesellschaft *f*.

subsidize ['sʌbsɪdaɪz] *vt* subventionieren.

subsidy ['sʌbsɪdɪ] *n* Subvention *f*.

subsistence [səb'sɪstəns] *n* Unterhalt *m*.

substance ['sʌbstəns] *n* Substanz *f*.

substantial [səb'stænʃəl] *a* (*strong*) fest, kräftig; (*important*) wesentlich; ~**ly** *ad* erheblich.

substantiate [səb'stænʃɪeɪt] *vt* begründen, belegen.

substitute ['sʌbstɪtjuːt] *n* Ersatz *m* // *vt* ersetzen.

substitution [sʌbstɪ'tjuːʃən] *n* Ersetzung *f*.

subterfuge ['sʌbtəfjuːdʒ] *n* Vorwand *m*; (*trick*) Trick *m*.

subterranean [sʌbtə'reɪnɪən] *a* unterirdisch.

subtitle ['sʌbtaɪtl] *n* Untertitel *m*.

subtle ['sʌtl] *a* fein; ~**ty** *n* Feinheit *f*.

subtotal [sʌb'təʊtl] *n* Zwischensumme *f*.

subtract [səb'trækt] *vt* abziehen; ~**ion** [səb'trækʃən] *n* Abziehen *nt*, Subtraktion *f*.

suburb ['sʌbɜːb] *n* Vorort *m*; **the** ~**s** die Außenbezirke; (*to town*) [sə'bɜːbən] *a* Vorort(s)-, Stadtrand-; ~**ia** [sə'bɜːbɪə] *n* Vorstadt *f*.

subversive [səb'vɜːsɪv] *a* subversiv.

subway ['sʌbweɪ] *n* (*US*) U-Bahn *f*; (*Brit*) Unterführung *f*.

succeed [sək'siːd] *vi* gelingen (+*dat*), Erfolg haben // *vt* (nach)folgen (+*dat*); he ~**ed** in doing it es gelang ihm, es zu tun; ~**ing** *a* (nach)folgend.

success [sək'ses] *n* Erfolg *m*; ~**ful** *a*, ~**fully** *ad* erfolgreich; **to be** ~**ful** (**in doing sth**) Erfolg haben (bei etw).

succession [sək'seʃən] *n* (Aufeinander)folge *f*; (*to throne*) Nachfolge *f*.

successive *a* [sək'sesɪv] aufeinanderfolgend.

successor [sək'sesə*] *n* Nachfolger(in *f*) *m*.

succinct [sək'sɪŋkt] *a* knapp.

succulent ['sʌkjʊlənt] *a* saftig.

succumb [sə'kʌm] *vi* erliegen (**to** *dat*); (*yield*) nachgeben.

such [sʌtʃ] *a* solche(r, s); ~ **a book** so ein Buch; ~ **books** solche Bücher; ~ **courage** so ein Mut; ~ **a long trip** so eine lange Reise; ~ **a lot of** so viel(e); ~ **as** wie; **a noise** ~ **as** to ein derartiger Lärm, daß; **as** ~ **an sich**; ~**and**~ **a** time/town die und die Zeit/Stadt.

suck [sʌk] *vt* saugen; (*ice cream etc*) lutschen; ~**er** *n* (*col*) Idiot *m*.

suction ['sʌkʃən] *n* Saugkraft *f*.

sudden ['sʌdn] *a* plötzlich; **all of a** ~ auf einmal; ~**ly** *ad* plötzlich.

suds [sʌdz] *npl* Seifenlauge *f*; (*lather*) Seifenschaum *m*.

sue [suː] *vt* verklagen.

suede [sweɪd] *n* Wildleder *nt*.

suet ['suːɪt] *n* Nierenfett *nt*.

Suez ['suːɪz] *n*: **the** ~ **Canal** der Suezkanal *m*.

suffer ['sʌfə*] *vt* (er)leiden // *vi* leiden; ~**er** *n* Leidende(r) *mf*; ~**ing** *n* Leiden *nt*.

suffice [sə'faɪs] *vi* genügen.

sufficient *a*, ~**ly** *ad* [sə'fɪʃənt, -lɪ] ausreichend.

suffix ['sʌfɪks] *n* Nachsilbe *f*.

suffocate ['sʌfəkeɪt] *vti* ersticken.

suffocation [sʌfə'keɪʃən] *n* Ersticken *nt*.

suffrage ['sʌfrɪdʒ] *n* Wahlrecht *nt*.

sugar ['ʃʊgə*] *n* Zucker *m* // *vt* zuckern; ~ **beet** *n* Zuckerrübe *f*; ~ **cane** *n* Zuckerrohr *nt*; ~**y** *a* süß.

suggest [sə'dʒest] *vt* vorschlagen; (*show*) schließen lassen auf (+*acc*); ~**ion** [sə'dʒestʃən] *n* Vorschlag *m*; ~**ive** *a* anregend; (*indecent*) zweideutig.

suicide ['sʊɪsaɪd] *n* Selbstmord *m*; **to**

commit ~ Selbstmord begehen.

suit [su:t] *n* Anzug *m*; (*CARDS*) Farbe *f* // *vt* passen (+*dat*); (*clothes*) stehen (+*dat*); **well ~ed** (*well matched: couple*) gut zusammenpassend; **~able** *a* geeignet, passend; **~ably** *ad* passend, angemessen.

suitcase ['su:tkeɪs] *n* (Hand)koffer *m*.

suite [swi:t] *n* (*of rooms*) Zimmerflucht *f*; (*of furniture*) Einrichtung *f*; (*MUS*) Suite *f*.

suitor ['su:tə*] *n* (*JUR*) Kläger(in *f*) *m*.

sulfur ['sʌlfə*] *n* (*US*) = **sulphur**.

sulk [sʌlk] *vi* schmollen; **~y** *a* schmollend.

sullen ['sʌlən] *a* mürrisch.

sulphur, (*US*) **sulfur** ['sʌlfə*] *n* Schwefel *m*.

sultry ['sʌltrɪ] *a* schwül.

sum [sʌm] *n* Summe *f*; (*money also*) Betrag *m*; (*arithmetic*) Rechenaufgabe *f*; **~ up** *vti* zusammenfassen.

summarize ['sʌməraɪz] *vt* kurz zusammenfassen.

summary ['sʌmərɪ] *n* Zusammenfassung *f* // *a* (*justice*) kurzerhand erteilt.

summer ['sʌmə*] *n* Sommer *m* // *a* Sommer-; **~house** *n* (*in garden*) Gartenhaus *nt*; **~time** *n* Sommerzeit *f*.

summit ['sʌmɪt] *n* Gipfel *m*; **~ (conference)** *n* Gipfelkonferenz *f*.

summon ['sʌmən] *vt* herbeirufen; (*JUR*) vorladen; (*gather up*) aufbringen; **~s** *n* (*JUR*) Vorladung *f* // *vt* vorladen.

sump [sʌmp] *n* (*Brit AUT*) Ölwanne *f*.

sumptuous ['sʌmptjʊəs] *a* prächtig.

sun [sʌn] *n* Sonne *f*; **~bathe** *vi* sich sonnen; **~burn** *n* Sonnenbrand *m*.

Sunday ['sʌndɪ] *n* Sonntag *m*; **~ school** *n* Sonntagsschule *f*.

sundial ['sʌndaɪəl] *n* Sonnenuhr *f*.

sundown ['sʌndaʊn] *n* Sonnenuntergang *m*.

sundry ['sʌndrɪ] *a* verschieden; **all and ~** alle; **sundries** *npl* Verschiedene(s) *nt*.

sunflower ['sʌnflaʊə*] *n* Sonnenblume *f*.

sung [sʌŋ] *pp of* **sing**.

sunglasses ['sʌnglɑ:sɪz] *npl* Sonnenbrille *f*.

sunk [sʌŋk] *pp of* **sink**.

sunlight ['sʌnlaɪt] *n* Sonnenlicht *nt*.

sunlit ['sʌnlɪt] *a* sonnenbeschienen.

sunny ['sʌnɪ] *a* sonnig.

sunrise ['sʌnraɪz] *n* Sonnenaufgang *m*.

sunset ['sʌnset] *n* Sonnenuntergang *m*.

sunshade ['sʌnʃeɪd] *n* Sonnenschirm *m*.

sunshine ['sʌnʃaɪn] *n* Sonnenschein *m*.

sunstroke ['sʌnstrəʊk] *n* Hitzschlag *m*.

suntan ['sʌntæn] *n* (Sonnen)bräune *f*; **~ oil** *n* Sonnenöl *nt*.

super ['su:pə*] *a* (*col*) prima, klasse; Super-, Über-.

superannuation ['su:pərænjʊ'eɪʃən] *n* Pension *f*.

superb [su:'pɜ:b] *a* ausgezeichnet, hervorragend.

supercilious [su:pə'sɪlɪəs] *a* herablassend.

superficial [su:pə'fɪʃəl] *a* oberflächlich.

superfluous [su'pɜ:fluəs] *a* überflüssig.

superhuman [su:pə'hju:mən] *a* (*effort*) übermenschlich.

superimpose ['su:pərɪm'pəʊz] *vt* übereinanderlegen.

superintendent [su:pərɪn'tendənt] *n* Polizeichef *m*.

superior [su'pɪərɪə*] *a* überlegen; (*better*) besser // *n* Vorgesetzte(r) *mf*; **~ity** [supɪərɪ'ɒrɪtɪ] *n* Überlegenheit *f*.

superlative [su'pɜ:lətɪv] *a* überragend.

superman ['su:pəmæn] *n* Übermensch *m*.

supermarket ['su:pəmɑ:kɪt] *n* Supermarkt *m*.

supernatural [su:pə'nætʃərəl] *a* übernatürlich.

superpower ['su:pəpaʊə*] *n* Weltmacht *f*.

supersede [su:pə'si:d] *vt* ersetzen.

supersonic ['su:pə'sɒnɪk] *n* Überschall-.

superstition [su:pə'stɪʃən] *n* Aberglaube *m*.

superstitious [su:pə'stɪʃəs] *a* abergläubisch.

supervise ['su:pəvaɪz] *vt* beaufsichtigen, kontrollieren.

supervision [su:pə'vɪʒən] *n* Aufsicht *f*.

supervisor ['su:pəvaɪzə*] *n* Aufsichtsperson *f*; **~y** *a* Aufsichts-.

supine ['su:paɪn] *a* auf dem Rücken liegend.

supper ['sʌpə*] *n* Abendessen *nt*.

supplant [sə'plɑ:nt] *vt* (*person, thing*) ersetzen.

supple ['sʌpl] *a* geschmeidig.

supplement ['sʌplɪmənt] *n* Ergänzung *f*; (*in book*) Nachtrag *m* // *vt* [sʌplɪ'ment] ergänzen; **~ary** [sʌplɪ'mentərɪ] *a* ergänzend.

supplier [sə'plaɪə*] *n* Lieferant *m*.

supply [sə'plaɪ] *vt* liefern // *n* Vorrat *m*; (*supplying*) Lieferung *f* // *a* (*teacher etc*) Aushilfs-; **supplies** *npl* (*food*) Vorräte *pl*; (*MIL*) Nachschub *m*.

support [sə'pɔ:t] *n* Unterstützung *f*; (*TECH*) Stütze *f* // *vt* (*hold up*) stützen, tragen; (*provide for*) ernähren; (*be in favour of*) unterstützen; **~er** *n* Anhänger(in *f*) *m*.

suppose [sə'pəʊz] *vti* annehmen; **to be ~d** to **do sth** etw tun sollen; **~dly** [sə'pəʊzɪdlɪ] *ad* angeblich.

supposing [sə'pəʊzɪŋ] *cj* angenommen.

supposition [sʌpə'zɪʃən] *n* Voraussetzung *f*.

suppress [sə'pres] *vt* unterdrücken; **~ion** [sə'preʃən] *n* Unterdrückung *f*.

supremacy [su'preməsɪ] *n* Vorherrschaft *f*, Oberhoheit *f*.

supreme [su'pri:m] *a* oberste(r, s),

höchste(r, s).

surcharge ['sɜːtʃɑːdʒ] n Zuschlag m.

sure [ʃuə*] a sicher, gewiß; ~! (of course) klar!; **to make ~ of sth/that** sich einer Sache vergewissern/vergewissern, daß; ~ **enough** (with past) tatsächlich; (with future) ganz bestimmt; ~**footed** a sicher (auf den Füßen); ~**ly** ad (certainly) sicherlich, gewiß; ~**ly it's wrong** das ist doch wohl falsch.

surety ['ʃuərətɪ] n Sicherheit f; (person) Bürge m.

surf [sɜːf] n Brandung f.

surface ['sɜːfɪs] n Oberfläche f // vt (roadway) teeren // vi auftauchen; ~ **mail** n gewöhnliche Post f.

surfboard ['sɜːfbɔːd] n Wellenreiterbrett nt.

surfeit ['sɜːfɪt] n Übermaß nt.

surfing ['sɜːfɪŋ] n Wellenreiten nt.

surge [sɜːdʒ] n Woge f // vi wogen.

surgeon ['sɜːdʒən] n Chirurg(in f) m.

surgery ['sɜːdʒərɪ] n (Brit: place) Praxis f; (time) Sprechstunde f; (treatment) Operation f; **to undergo ~** operiert werden; ~ **hours** npl (Brit) Sprechstunde pl.

surgical ['sɜːdʒɪkəl] a chirurgisch; ~ **spirit** n (Brit) Wundbenzin nt.

surly ['sɜːlɪ] a verdrießlich, grob.

surmount [sɜːˈmaunt] vt überwinden.

surname ['sɜːneɪm] n Zuname m.

surpass [sɜːˈpɑːs] vt übertreffen.

surplus ['sɜːpləs] n Überschuß m // a überschüssig, Über(schuß)-.

surprise [səˈpraɪz] n Überraschung f // vt überraschen.

surprising [səˈpraɪzɪŋ] a überraschend; ~**ly** ad überraschend(erweise).

surrender [səˈrendə*] n Kapitulation f // vi sich ergeben.

surreptitious [sʌrəpˈtɪʃəs] a verstohlen.

surrogate ['sʌrəgɪt] n Ersatz m; ~ **mother** n Leihmutter f.

surround [səˈraund] vt umgeben; ~**ing** a (countryside) umliegend // n: ~**ings** pl Umgebung f; (environment) Umwelt f.

surveillance [sɜːˈveɪləns] n Überwachung f.

survey ['sɜːveɪ] n Übersicht f // [sɜːˈveɪ] vt überblicken; (land) vermessen; ~**or** [səˈveɪə*] n Land(ver)messer(in f) m.

survival [səˈvaɪvəl] n Überleben nt.

survive [səˈvaɪv] vti überleben.

survivor [səˈvaɪvə*] n Überlebende(r) mf.

susceptible [səˈseptəbl] a empfindlich (to gegen); (to charms etc) empfänglich (to für).

suspect ['sʌspekt] n Verdächtige(r) mf // a verdächtig // vt [səsˈpekt] verdächtigen; (think) vermuten.

suspend [səsˈpend] vt verschieben; (from work) suspendieren; (hang up) aufhängen; (SPORT) sperren; ~**ed sen-**

tence n (LAW) zur Bewährung ausgesetzte Strafe; ~**er belt** n Strumpf(halter)gürtel m; ~**ers** npl (Brit) Strumpfhalter m; (men's) Sokkenhalter m; (US) Hosenträger m.

suspense [səsˈpens] n Spannung f.

suspension [səsˈpenʃən] n (from work) Suspendierung f; (SPORT) Sperrung f; (AUT) Federung f; ~ **bridge** n Hängebrücke f.

suspicion [səsˈpɪʃən] n Mißtrauen nt; Verdacht m.

suspicious [səsˈpɪʃəs] a mißtrauisch; (causing suspicion) verdächtig.

sustain [səsˈteɪn] vt (maintain) aufrechterhalten; (confirm) bestätigen; (JUR) anerkennen; (injury) davontragen; ~**ed** a (effort) anhaltend.

sustenance ['sʌstɪnəns] n Nahrung f.

swab [swɒb] n (MED) Tupfer m.

swagger ['swægə*] vi stolzieren.

swallow ['swɒləu] n (bird) Schwalbe f; (of food etc) Schluck m // vt (ver)schlucken; ~ **up** vt verschlingen.

swam [swæm] pt of **swim.**

swamp [swɒmp] n Sumpf m // vt überschwemmen.

swan [swɒn] n Schwan m.

swap [swɒp] n Tausch m // vt (ein)tauschen (for gegen).

swarm [swɔːm] n Schwarm m // vi wimmeln (with von).

swarthy ['swɔːðɪ] a dunkel, braun.

swastika ['swɒstɪkə] n Hakenkreuz nt.

swat [swɒt] vt totschlagen.

sway [sweɪ] vi schwanken; (branches) schaukeln, sich wiegen // vt schwenken; (influence) beeinflussen.

swear [sweə*] vi, pt **swore,** pp **sworn** vi (promise) schwören; (curse) fluchen; **to ~ to sth** schwören auf etw (acc); ~**word** n Fluch m.

sweat [swet] n Schweiß m // vi schwitzen.

sweater ['swetə*] n Pullover m.

sweatshirt ['swetʃɜːt] n Sweatshirt nt.

sweaty ['swetɪ] a verschwitzt.

swede [swiːd] n (Brit) Steckrübe f.

Swede [swiːd] n Schwede m, Schwedin f.

Sweden ['swiːdn] n Schweden nt.

Swedish ['swiːdɪʃ] a schwedisch // n (LING) Schwedisch nt.

sweep [swiːp] n (chimney ~) Schornsteinfeger m // vt (pt, pp **swept**) vt fegen, kehren // vi (go quickly) rauschen; ~ **away** vt wegfegen; ~ **past** vi vorbeisausen; ~ **up** vt zusammenkehren; ~**ing** a (gesture) schwungvoll; (statement) verallgemeinernd.

sweet [swiːt] n (course) Nachtisch m; (candy) Bonbon nt // a süß; ~**corn** n Zuckermais m; ~**en** vt süßen; (fig) versüßen; ~**heart** n Liebste(r) mf; ~**ness** n Süße f; ~ **pea** n Gartenwicke f.

swell [swel] n Seegang m // a (col) todschick // v (pt **swelled**, pp **swollen** or **swelled**) vt (numbers) vermehren // vi (also: ~ **up**) (an)schwellen; ~**ing** n Schwellung f.

sweltering ['swelterɪŋ] a drückend.

swept [swept] pt, pp of **sweep**.

swerve [swɜːv] vti ausscheren.

swift [swɪft] n Mauersegler m // a, ~**ly** ad geschwind, schnell, rasch.

swig [swɪg] n Zug m.

swill [swɪl] n (for pigs) Schweinefutter nt // vt spülen.

swim [swɪm] n: to go for a ~ schwimmen gehen // v (pt **swam**, pp **swum**) vi schwimmen // vt (cross) (durch)schwimmen; ~**mer** n Schwimmer(in f) m; ~**ming** n Schwimmen nt; ~**ming cap** n Badehaube f, Badekappe f; ~**ming costume** n (Brit) Badeanzug m; ~**ming pool** n Schwimmbecken nt; (private) Swimming-Pool m; ~**suit** n Badeanzug m.

swindle ['swɪndl] n Schwindel m, Betrug m // vt betrügen.

swine [swaɪn] n (lit, fig) Schwein nt.

swing [swɪŋ] n (child's) Schaukel f; (swinging) Schwung m; (MUS) Swing m // v (pt, pp **swung**) vt schwingen // vi schwingen, schaukeln; (turn quickly) schwenken; in full ~ in vollem Gange; ~ **bridge** n Drehbrücke f; ~ **door**, (US) ~**ing door** n Schwingtür f.

swingeing ['swɪndʒɪŋ] a (Brit) hart; (taxation, cuts) extrem.

swipe [swaɪp] n Hieb m // vt (col) (hit) hart schlagen; (steal) klauen.

swirl [swɜːl] vi wirbeln.

swish [swɪʃ] a (col: smart) schick // vi zischen; (grass, skirts) rascheln.

Swiss [swɪs] a Schweizer, schweizerisch // n Schweizer(in f) m; the ~ die Schweizer pl.

switch [swɪtʃ] n (ELEC) Schalter m; (change) Wechsel m // vti (ELEC) schalten; (change) wechseln; ~ **off** vt ab- or ausschalten; ~ **on** vt an- or einschalten; ~**board** n Zentrale f; (board) Schaltbrett nt.

Switzerland ['swɪtsələnd] n die Schweiz f.

swivel ['swɪvl] vti (also: ~ **round**) (sich) drehen.

swollen ['swəʊlən] pp of **swell**.

swoon [swuːn] vi (old) in Ohnmacht fallen.

swoop [swuːp] n Sturzflug m; (esp by police) Razzia f // vi (also: ~ **down**) stürzen.

swop [swɒp] = **swap**.

sword [sɔːd] n Schwert nt; ~**fish** n Schwertfisch m.

swore [swɔː*] pt of **swear**.

sworn [swɔːn] pp of **swear**.

swot [swɒt] vti pauken.

swum [swʌm] pp of **swim**.

swung [swʌŋ] pt, pp of **swing**.

sycamore ['sɪkəmɔː*] n (US) Platane f; (Brit) Bergahorn m.

syllable ['sɪləbl] n Silbe f.

syllabus ['sɪləbəs] n Lehrplan m.

symbol ['sɪmbəl] n Symbol nt; ~**ic(al)** [sɪm'bɒlɪk(əl)] a symbolisch.

symmetry ['sɪmɪtrɪ] n Symmetrie f.

sympathetic [sɪmpə'θetɪk] a mitfühlend.

sympathize ['sɪmpəθaɪz] vi mitfühlen; ~**r** n Mitfühlende(r) mf; (POL) Sympathisant(in f) m.

sympathy ['sɪmpəθɪ] n Mitleid nt, Mitgefühl nt; (condolence) Beileid nt; **with our deepest** ~ mit tiefempfundenem Beileid.

symphony ['sɪmfənɪ] n Sinfonie f.

symposium [sɪm'pəʊzɪəm] n Tagung f.

symptom ['sɪmptəm] n Symptom nt; ~**atic** [sɪmptə'mætɪk] a (fig) bezeichnend (of für).

synagogue ['sɪnəgɒg] n Synagoge f.

synchronize ['sɪŋkrənaɪz] vt synchronisieren // vi gleichzeitig sein or ablaufen.

syncopated ['sɪŋkəpeɪtɪd] a synkopiert.

syndicate ['sɪndɪkət] n Konsortium nt.

synonym ['sɪnənɪm] n Synonym nt.

synonymous [sɪ'nɒnɪməs] a: ~ (with) gleichbedeutend (mit).

synopsis [sɪ'nɒpsɪs] n Zusammenfassung f.

syphon ['saɪfən] = **siphon**.

Syria ['sɪrɪə] n Syrien nt.

syringe [sɪ'rɪndʒ] n Spritze f.

syrup ['sɪrəp] n Sirup m; (of sugar) Melasse f.

system ['sɪstəm] n System nt; ~**atic** [sɪstə'mætɪk] a systematisch; ~ **disk** n (COMPUT) Systemdiskette f; ~**s analyst** n Systemanalytiker(in f) m.

T

ta [tɑː] interj (Brit col) danke.

tab [tæb] n Aufhänger m; (name ~) Schild nt; **to keep** ~**s on** (fig) genau im Auge behalten.

table ['teɪbl] n Tisch m; (list) Tabelle f // vt (Parl: propose) vorlegen, einbringen; **to lay** or **set the** ~ den Tisch decken; ~ **of contents** n Inhaltsverzeichnis nt; ~ **lamp** n Tischlampe f.

tablecloth ['teɪblklɒθ] n Tischtuch nt.

table d'hôte ['tɑːbl'dəʊt] n Tagesmenü nt.

tablemat ['teɪblmæt] n Untersatz m.

tablespoon ['teɪblspuːn] n Eßlöffel m; ~**ful** n Eßlöffel(voll) m.

tablet ['tæblət] n (MED) Tablette f; (for writing) Täfelchen nt.

table tennis ['teɪbltenɪs] n Tischtennis

nt.

table wine ['teɪblwaɪn] *n* Tafelwein *m*.

tabloid ['tæblɔɪd] *n* Zeitung *f* in kleinem Formal; (*pej*) Boulevardzeitung.

tabulate ['tæbjʊleɪt] *vt* tabellarisch ordnen.

tacit *a*, ~**ly** *ad* ['tæsɪt, -lɪ] stillschweigend.

taciturn ['tæsɪtɜːn] *a* wortkarg.

tack [tæk] *n* (*small nail*) Stift *m*; (*US: thumb~*) Reißzwecke *f*; (*stitch*) Heftstich *m*; (*NAUT*) Lavieren *nt*; (*course*) Kurs *m* // *vt* (*nail*) nageln; (*stitch*) heften // *vi* aufkreuzen.

tackle ['tækl] *n* (*for lifting*) Flaschenzug *m*; (*NAUT*) Takelage *f*; (*SPORT*) Tackling *nt* // *vt* (*deal with*) anpacken, in Angriff nehmen; (*person*) festhalten; (*player*) angehen.

tacky ['tækɪ] *a* klebrig.

tact [tækt] *n* Takt *m*; ~**ful** *a*, ~**fully** *ad* taktvoll.

tactical ['tæktɪkəl] *a* taktisch.

tactics ['tæktɪks] *npl* Taktik *f*.

tactless *a*, ~**ly** *ad* ['tæktlɪs, -lɪ] taktlos.

tadpole ['tædpəʊl] *n* Kaulquappe *f*.

taffy ['tæfɪ] *n* (*US*) Sahnebonbon *nt*.

tag [tæg] *n* (*label*) Schild *nt*, Anhänger *m*; (*maker's name*) Etikett *nt*; (*phrase*) Floskel *f*; ~ **along** *vi* mitkommen.

tail [teɪl] *n* Schwanz *m*; (*of coin*) Schluß *m* // *vt* folgen (+*dat*); ~ **away**, ~ **off** *vi* abfallen, schwinden; ~**back** *n* (*Brit AUT*) (Rück)stau *m*; ~ **coat** *n* Frack *m*; ~ **end** *n* Schluß *m*, Ende *nt*; ~**gate** *n* (*AUT*) Heckklappe *f*.

tailor ['teɪlə*] *n* Schneider *m*; ~**ing** *n* Schneidern *nt*; ~**made** *a* (*lit*) maßgeschneidert; (*fig*) wie auf den Leib geschnitten (*for sb* jdm).

tailwind ['teɪlwɪnd] *n* Rückenwind *m*.

tainted ['teɪntɪd] *a* verdorben.

take [teɪk], *pt* **took**, *pp* **taken** *vt* nehmen; (*trip*, *exam*) machen; (*capture: person*) fassen; (: *town*) einnehmen; (*carry to a place*) bringen; (*MATH: subtract*) abziehen (*from* von); (*extract*, *quotation*) entnehmen (*from dat*); (*get for o.s.*) sich (*dat*) nehmen; (*gain*, *obtain*) bekommen; (*FIN*, *COMM*) einnehmen; (*PHOT*) machen; (*put up with*) hinnehmen; (*respond to*) aufnehmen; (*interpret*) auffassen; (*assume*) annehmen; (*contain*) Platz haben für; (*GRAM*) stehen mit; **to ~ sth from sb** jdm etw wegnehmen; ~ **after** *vt* ähnlich sein (+*dat*); ~ **apart** *vt* auseinandernehmen; ~ **away** *vt* (*remove*) wegnehmen; (*carry off*) wegbringen; ~ **back** *vt* (*return*) zurückbringen; (*retract*) zurücknehmen; ~ **down** *vt* (*pull down*) abreißen; (*write down*) aufschreiben; ~ **in** *vt* (*deceive*) hereinlegen; (*understand*) begreifen; (*include*) einschließen; ~ **off** *vi* (*plane*)

starten // *vt* (*remove*) wegnehmen; (*clothing*) ausziehen; (*imitate*) nachmachen; ~ **on** *vt* (*undertake*) übernehmen; (*engage*) einstellen; (*opponent*) antreten gegen; ~ **out** *vt* (*girl*, *dog*) ausführen; (*extract*) herausnehmen; (*insurance*) abschließen; (*licence*) sich (*dat*) geben lassen; (*book*) ausleihen; (*remove*) entfernen; **to ~ sth out of sth** (*drawer*, *pocket etc*) etw aus etw herausnehmen; ~ **over** *vt* übernehmen // *vi* ablösen (*from acc*); ~ **to** *vt* (*like*) mögen; (*adopt as practice*) sich (*dat*) angewöhnen; ~ **up** *vt* (*raise*) aufnehmen; (*hem*) kürzer machen; (*occupy*) in Anspruch nehmen; (*engage in*) sich befassen mit; ~**away**, (*US*) ~**out** *a* zum Mitnehmen; ~**home pay** *n* Nettolohn *m*; ~**off** *n* (*AVIAT*) Start *m*; (*imitation*) Nachahmung *f*; ~**over** *n* (*COMM*) Übernahme *f*.

takings ['teɪkɪŋz] *npl* (*COMM*) Einnahmen *pl*.

talc [tælk] *n* (*also*: ~**um powder**) Talkumpuder *m*.

tale [teɪl] *n* Geschichte *f*, Erzählung *f*; **to tell ~s** (*fig*: *lie*) Geschichten erfinden.

talent ['tælənt] *n* Talent *nt*; ~**ed** *a* begabt.

talk [tɔːk] *n* (*conversation*) Gespräch *nt*; (*rumour*) Gerede *nt*; (*speech*) Vortrag *m* // *vi* sprechen, reden; ~**s** *pl* (*POL etc*) Gespräche *pl*; **to ~ sb into doing sth** jdn überreden, etw zu tun; **to ~ sb out of doing sth** jdm ausreden, etw zu tun; **to ~ shop** fachsimpeln; ~ **about** *vi* sprechen von (+*dat*) or über (+*acc*); ~ **over** *vt* besprechen; ~**ative** *a* gesprächig.

tall [tɔːl] *a* groß; (*building*) hoch; **to be 1 m 80** – 1,80 m groß sein; ~**boy** *n* (*Brit*) Kommode *f*; ~ **story** *n* übertriebene Geschichte *f*.

tally ['tælɪ] *n* Abrechnung *f* // *vi* übereinstimmen (*with* mit).

talon ['tælən] *n* Kralle *f*.

tame [teɪm] *a* zahm; (*fig*) fade.

tamper ['tæmpə*]: ~ **with** *vt* herumpfuschen an (+*dat*).

tampon ['tæmpən] *n* Tampon *m*.

tan [tæn] *n* (*on skin*) (Sonnen)bräune *f*; (*colour*) Gelbbraun *nt* // *a* (*colour*) (gelb)braun // *vt* bräunen; (*skins*) gerben // *vi* braun werden.

tang [tæŋ] *n* Schärfe *f*.

tangent ['tændʒənt] *n* Tangente *f*; **to go off at a ~** (*fig*) vom Thema abkommen.

tangerine [tændʒə'riːn] *n* Mandarine *f*.

tangible ['tændʒəbl] *a* greifbar.

tangle ['tæŋgl] *n* Durcheinander *nt*; (*trouble*) Schwierigkeiten *pl*; **to get in(to) a ~** sich verheddern.

tank [tæŋk] *n* (*container*) Tank *m*, Behälter *m*; (*MIL*) Panzer *m*.

tanker ['tæŋkə*] *n* (*ship*) Tanker *m*; (*vehicle*) Tankwagen *m*.

tanned [tænd] a (skin) gebräunt.

tantalizing ['tæntəlaızıŋ] a verlockend; (annoying) quälend.

tantamount ['tæntəmaʊnt] a gleichbedeutend (to mit).

tantrum ['tæntrəm] n Wutanfall m.

tap [tæp] n Hahn m; (gentle blow) Klopfen nt // vt (strike) klopfen; (supply) anzapfen; (telephone) abhören; on ~ (fig: resources) zur Hand.

tap-dancing ['tæpdɑːnsıŋ] n Steppen nt.

tape [teıp] n Band nt; (magnetic) (Ton)band nt; (adhesive) Klebstreifen m // vt (record) aufnehmen; ~ measure n Maßband nt.

taper ['teıpə*] n (dünne) Wachskerze f // vi spitz zulaufen.

tape recorder n Tonbandgerät nt.

tapestry ['tæpıstrı] n Wandteppich m.

tar [tɑː*] n Teer m.

target ['tɑːgıt] n Ziel nt; (board) Zielscheibe f; ~ **practice** n Zielschießen nt.

tariff ['tærıf] n (duty paid) Zoll m; (list) Tarif m.

tarmac ['tɑːmæk] n (AVIAT) Rollfeld nt.

tarnish ['tɑːnıʃ] vt (lit) matt machen; (fig) beflecken.

tarpaulin [tɑː'pɔːlın] n Plane f.

tarragon ['tærəgən] n Estragon m.

tart [tɑːt] n (Obst)torte f; (col) Nutte f // a scharf; ~ **up** vt (col) aufmachen (col); (person) auftakeln (col).

tartan ['tɑːtən] n Schottenkaro nt // a mit Schottenkaro.

tartar ['tɑːtə*] n Zahnstein m; ~(e) **sauce** n Remouladensoße f.

task [tɑːsk] n Aufgabe f; to take sb to ~ sich (dat) jdn vornehmen; ~ **force** n Sondertrupp m.

tassel ['tæsəl] n Quaste f.

taste [teıst] n Geschmack m; (sense) Geschmackssinn m; (small quantity) Kostprobe f; (liking) Vorliebe f // vt schmecken; (try) probieren // vi schmecken (of nach); you can ~ the garlic (in it) man kann den Knoblauch herausschmecken; **can I have a ~ of this wine?** kann ich diesen Wein probieren?; to have a ~ for sth etw mögen; in good/bad ~ geschmackvoll/geschmacklos; ~**ful** a, ~**fully** ad geschmackvoll; ~**less** a (insipid) fade; (in bad taste) geschmacklos; ~**lessly** ad geschmacklos.

tasty ['teıstı] a schmackhaft.

tatters ['tætəz] npl: in ~ in Fetzen.

tattoo [tə'tuː] n (MIL) Zapfenstreich m; (on skin) Tätowierung f // vt tätowieren.

tatty ['tætı] a (Brit col) schäbig.

taught [tɔːt] pt, pp of **teach**.

taunt [tɔːnt] n höhnische Bemerkung f // vt verhöhnen.

Taurus ['tɔːrəs] n Stier m.

taut [tɔːt] a straff.

tawdry ['tɔːdrı] a (bunt und) billig.

tawny ['tɔːnı] a gelbbraun.

tax [tæks] n Steuer f // vt besteuern; (strain) strapazieren; (strength) angreifen; ~**able** a (income) steuerpflichtig; ~**ation** [tæk'seıʃən] n Besteuerung f; ~ **avoidance** n Steuerumgehung f; ~ **collector** n Steuereinnehmer m; ~ **disc** n (Brit AUT) Kraftfahrzeugsteuerplakette f (, die an der Windschutzscheibe angebracht wird); ~ **evasion** n Steuerhinterziehung f; ~**free** a steuerfrei.

taxi ['tæksı] n Taxi nt // vi (plane) rollen; ~ **driver** n Taxifahrer m; ~ **rank** (Brit), ~ **stand** n Taxistand m.

taxpayer ['tækspeıə*] n Steuerzahler m.

tax relief n Steuerermäßigung f.

tax return n Steuererklärung f.

TB abbr (= tuberculosis) Tb f, Tbc f.

tea [tiː] n Tee m; (meal) (frühes) Abendessen nt; **high** ~ n (Brit) Abendessen nt; ~ **bag** n Teebeutel m; ~ **break** n (Brit) Teepause f.

teach [tiːtʃ], pt, pp **taught** vti lehren; (SCH also) unterrichten; (show) beibringen (sb sth jdm etw); ~**er** n Lehrer(in f) m; ~**ing** n (teacher's work) Unterricht m; (doctrine) Lehre f.

tea cosy n Teewärmer m.

teacup ['tiːkʌp] n Teetasse f.

tea leaves ['tiːliːvz] npl Teeblätter pl.

team [tiːm] n (workers) Team nt; (SPORT) Mannschaft f; (animals) Gespann nt.

teapot ['tiːpɒt] n Teekanne f.

tear [tɛə*] n Riß m; [tıə*] Träne f // v [tɛə*] (pt **tore**, pp **torn**) vt zerreißen; (muscle) zerren // vi (zer)reißen; (rush) rasen; ~ **along** vi (rush) entlangrasen; ~ **up** vt (sheet of paper etc) zerreißen; ~**ful** ['tıəful] a weinend; (voice) weinerlich; ~ **gas** ['tıəgæs] n Tränengas nt.

tearoom ['tiːrʊm] n Teestube f.

tease [tiːz] n Hänsler m // vt necken.

tea set n Teeservice nt.

teaspoon ['tiːspuːn] n Teelöffel m.

teat [tiːt] n (of woman) Brustwarze f; (of animal) Zitze f; (of bottle) Sauger m.

tea time n (in the afternoon) Teestunde f; (mealtime) Abendessen nt.

tea towel n Küchenhandtuch nt.

technical ['teknıkəl] a technisch; (knowledge, terms) Fach-; ~**ity** [teknı'kælıtı] n technische Einzelheit f; (JUR) Formsache f; ~**ly** ad technisch; (speak) spezialisiert; (fig) genau genommen.

technician [tek'nıʃən] n Techniker m.

technique [tek'niːk] n Technik f.

technological [teknə'lɒdʒıkəl] a technologisch.

technology [tek'nɒlədʒı] n Technologie f.

teddy (bear) ['tedı(bɛə*)] n Teddybär m.

tedious a, ~**ly** ad ['tiːdıəs, -lı] langweilig, ermüdend.

tee [ti:] n (GOLF) Abschlagstelle f; (object) Tee m.

teem [ti:m] vi (swarm) wimmeln (with von); it is ~ing (with rain) es gießt in Strömen.

teenage ['ti:neɪdʒ] a (fashions etc) Teenager-, jugendlich; ~r n Teenager m, Jugendliche(r) mf.

teens [ti:nz] npl Teenageralter nt; to be in one's ~ im Teenageralter sein.

tee-shirt ['ti:ʃɜ:t] n T-Shirt nt.

teeter ['ti:tə*] vi schwanken.

teeth [ti:θ] npl of tooth.

teethe [ti:ð] vi zahnen.

teething ['ti:ðɪŋ]: ~ ring n Beißring m; ~ troubles npl (fig) Kinderkrankheiten pl.

teetotal ['ti:'təʊtl] a abstinent.

telecommunications ['telɪkəmju:nɪ-'keɪʃənz] npl Fernmeldewesen nt.

telegram ['telɪgræm] n Telegramm nt.

telephone ['telɪfəʊn] n Telefon nt, Fernsprecher m // vt anrufen; (message) telefonisch mitteilen; ~ **booth**, (Brit) ~ **box** n Telefonzelle f; ~ **call** n Telefongespräch nt, Anruf m; ~ **directory** n Telefonbuch nt; ~ **number** n Telefonnummer f.

telephoto lens ['telɪfəʊtəʊ'lenz] n Teleobjektiv nt.

telescope ['telɪskəʊp] n Teleskop nt, Fernrohr nt // vt ineinanderschieben.

televise ['telɪvaɪz] vt durch das Fernsehen übertragen.

television ['telɪvɪʒən] n Fernsehen nt; ~ **(set)** n Fernsehapparat m, Fernseher m.

telex ['teleks] n Telex nt // vt per Telex schicken.

tell [tel], pt, pp **told** vt (story) erzählen; (secret) ausplaudern; (say, make known) sagen (sth to sb jdm etw); (distinguish) erkennen (sb by sth jdn an etw dat); (be sure) wissen // vi (talk) sprechen (of von); (be sure) wissen; (divulge) es verraten; (have effect) sich auswirken; (distinguish): to ~ sth from etw unterscheiden von; to ~ sb to do sth jdm sagen, daß er etw tun soll; to ~ sb off jdn ausschimpfen; ~**er** n Kassenbeamte(r) mf; ~**ing** a verräterisch; (blow) hart; ~**tale** a verräterisch.

telly ['telɪ] n (Brit col) abbr of **television**.

temerity [tɪ'merɪtɪ] n (Toll)kühnheit f.

temp [temp] n abbr (= temporary) f // vi Aushilfskraft f // vi als Aushilfskraft arbeiten.

temper ['tempə*] n (disposition) Temperament nt; (anger) Zorn m // vt (tone down) mildern; (metal) härten; to be in a (bad) ~ wütend sein; to lose one's ~ die Beherrschung verlieren.

temperament ['tempramənt] n Temperament nt; ~**al** [tempərə'mentl] a (moody) launisch.

temperance ['tempərəns] n Mäßigung f; (abstinence) Enthaltsamkeit f.

temperate ['tempərət] a gemäßigt.

temperature ['temprɪtʃə*] n Temperatur f; (Med: high ~) Fieber nt; to have or run a ~ Fieber haben.

tempest ['tempɪst] n (wilder) Sturm m.

tempi ['tempi:] npl of **tempo**.

template ['templət] n Schablone f.

temple ['templ] n Tempel m; (ANAT) Schläfe f.

temporal ['tempərəl] a (of time) zeitlich; (worldly) irdisch, weltlich.

temporarily ['tempərərɪlɪ] ad zeitweilig, vorübergehend.

temporary ['tempərərɪ] a vorläufig; (road, building) provisorisch.

tempt [tempt] vt (persuade) verleiten; (attract) reizen, (ver)locken; to ~ sb into doing sth jdn dazu verleiten, etw zu tun; ~**ation** [temp'teɪʃən] n Versuchung f; ~**ing** a (person) verführerisch; (object, situation) verlockend.

ten [ten] num zehn.

tenable ['tenəbl] a haltbar.

tenacious a, ~**ly** ad [tə'neɪʃəs, -lɪ] zäh, hartnäckig.

tenacity [tə'næsɪtɪ] n Zähigkeit f, Hartnäckigkeit f.

tenancy ['tenənsɪ] n Mietverhältnis nt.

tenant ['tenənt] n Mieter m; (of larger property) Pächter m.

tend [tend] vt (look after) sich kümmern um // vi neigen (to zu); to ~ to do sth (things) etw gewöhnlich tun.

tendency ['tendənsɪ] n Tendenz f; (person also) Neigung f.

tender ['tendə*] a zart; (loving) zärtlich // n (COMM: offer) Kostenanschlag m // vt (an)bieten; (resignation) einreichen; (money): **legal** ~ n gesetzliche(s) Zahlungsmittel nt; ~**ness** n Zartheit f; (being loving) Zärtlichkeit f.

tendon ['tendən] n Sehne f.

tenement ['tenəmənt] n Mietshaus nt.

tenet ['tenət] n Lehre f.

tennis ['tenɪs] n Tennis nt; ~ **ball** n Tennisball m; ~ **court** n Tennisplatz m; ~ **player** n Tennisspieler(in f) m; ~ **racket** n Tennisschläger m; ~ **shoes** npl Tennisschuhe pl.

tenpin bowling ['tenpɪn-] n Bowling nt.

tense [tens] a angespannt // n Zeitform f.

tension ['tenʃən] n Spannung f.

tent [tent] n Zelt nt.

tentacle ['tentəkl] n Fühler m; (of sea animals) Fangarm m.

tentative ['tentətɪv] a (movement) unsicher; (offer) Probe-; (arrangement) vorläufig; (suggestion) unverbindlich; ~**ly** ad versuchsweise; (try, move) vorsichtig.

tenterhooks ['tentəhʊks] *npl*: to be on ~ auf die Folter gespannt sein.

tenth [tenθ] *a* zehnte(r, s).

tent peg *n* Hering *m*.

tent pole *n* Zeltstange *f*.

tenuous ['tenjʊəs] *a* schwach.

tenure ['tenjʊə*] *n* (*of land*) Besitz *m*; (*of office*) Amtszeit *f*.

tepid ['tepɪd] *a* lauwarm.

term [tɜːm] *n* (*period of time*) Zeit(raum *m*) *f*; (*limit*) Frist *f*; (*SCH*) Quartal *nt*; (*UNIV*) Trimester *nt*; (*expression*) Ausdruck *m* // *vt* (be)nennen; ~s *pl* (*conditions*) Bedingungen *pl*; in the short/long ~ auf kurze/lange Sicht; to be on good ~s with sb gut mit jdm auskommen; to come to ~s with (*person*) sich einigen mit; (*problem*) sich abfinden mit.

terminal ['tɜːmɪnl] *n* (*Brit: also:* coach ~) Endstation *f*; (*AVIAT*) Terminal *m*; (*COMPUT*) Terminal *nt* or *m* // *a* Schluß-; (*MED*) unheilbar.

terminate ['tɜːmɪneɪt] *vt* beenden // *vi* enden, aufhören (in auf +*dat*).

terminus ['tɜːmɪnəs], *pl* -mini [-mɪnaɪ] *n* Endstation *f*.

terrace ['terəs] *n* (*Brit: row of houses*) Häuserreihe *f*; (*in garden etc*) Terrasse *f*; the ~s (*Brit SPORT*) die Ränge; ~d *a* (*garden*) terrassenförmig angelegt; (*house*) Reihen-.

terrible ['terəbl] *a* schrecklich, entsetzlich, fürchterlich.

terribly ['terəblɪ] *ad* fürchterlich.

terrific [tə'rɪfɪk] *a* unwahrscheinlich; ~! klasse!

terrify ['terɪfaɪ] *vt* erschrecken.

territorial [terɪ'tɔːrɪəl] *a* Gebiets-, territorial.

territory ['terɪtərɪ] *n* Gebiet *nt*.

terror ['terə*] *n* Schrecken *m*; (*POL*) Terror *m*; ~ist *n* Terrorist(in *f*) *m*; ~ize *vt* terrorisieren.

terse [tɜːs] *a* knapp, kurz, bündig.

test [test] *n* Probe *f*; (*examination*) Prüfung *f*; (*PSYCH, TECH*) Test *m* // *vt* prüfen; (*PSYCH*) testen.

testicle ['testɪkl] *n* Hoden *m*.

testify ['testɪfaɪ] *vi* aussagen; bezeugen (*to acc*); to ~ to sth etw bezeugen.

testimony ['testɪmənɪ] *n* (*JUR*) Zeugenaussage *f*; (*fig*) Zeugnis *nt*.

test match *n* (*SPORT*) Länderkampf *m*.

test tube *n* Reagenzglas *nt*.

testy ['testɪ] *a* gereizt; reizbar.

tetanus ['tetənəs] *n* Wundstarrkrampf *m*, Tetanus *m*.

tetchy ['tetʃɪ] *a* empfindlich.

tether ['teðə*] *vt* anbinden // *n*: at the end of one's ~ völlig am Ende.

text [tekst] *n* Text *m*; (*of document*) Wortlaut *m*; ~book *n* Lehrbuch *nt*.

textiles ['tekstaɪlz] *npl* Textilien *pl*.

texture ['tekstʃə*] *n* Beschaffenheit *f*.

Thai [taɪ] *a* thailändisch // *n* Thailänder(in *f*) *m*; (*LING*) Thailändisch *nt*; ~land *n* Thailand *nt*.

Thames [temz] *n*: the ~ die Themse.

than [ðæn] *prep* (*in comparisons*) als.

thank [θæŋk] *vt* danken (+*dat*); you've him to ~ for your success Sie haben Ihren Erfolg ihm zu verdanken; ~ful *a* dankbar; ~less *a* undankbar; ~s *npl* Dank *m* // *interj* danke; ~s to conj (+*gen*); ~ you (very much) danke (vielmals), danke schön; **T~sgiving (Day)** *n* (*US*) Thanksgiving Day *m*.

that [ðæt] ◆ *a* (*demonstrative: pl* those) der/die/das, jene(r, s); ~ one das da

◆ *pron* **1** (*demonstrative: pl* those) das; who's/what's ~? wer ist da/was ist das?; is ~ you? bist du das?; ~'s what he said genau das hat er gesagt; what happened after ~? was passierte danach?; ~ is das heißt

2 (*relative: subject*) der/die/das, die; (: *direct obj*) den/die/das, die; (: *indirect obj*) dem/der/dem, denen; all (~) I have alles, was ich habe

3 (*relative: of time*): the day (~) an dem Tag, als; the winter (~) he came in dem Winter, in dem er kam

◆ *cj* daß; he thought ~ I was ill er dachte, daß ich krank sei or er dachte, ich sei krank

◆ *ad* (*demonstrative*) so; I can't work ~ much ich kann nicht soviel arbeiten

thatched [θætʃt] *a* strohgedeckt; (*cottage*) mit Strohdach.

thaw [θɔː] *n* Tauwetter *nt* // *vi* tauen; (*frozen foods, fig: people*) auftauen // *vt* (auf)tauen lassen.

the [ðiː, ðə] *definite art* **1** der/die/das; to play ~ piano/violin Klavier/Geige spielen; I'm going to ~ butcher's/~ cinema ich gehe zum Fleischer/ins Kino; Elizabeth ~ First Elisabeth die Erste

2 (+ *adjective to form noun*) das, die; ~ rich and ~ poor die Reichen und die Armen

3 (*in comparisons*): ~ more he works ~ more he earns je mehr er arbeitet, desto mehr verdient er.

theatre, (*US*) **theater** ['θɪətə*] *n* Theater *nt*; (*for lectures etc*) Saal *m*; (*MED*) Operationssaal *m*; ~goer *n* Theaterbesucher(in *f*) *m*.

theatrical [θɪ'ætrɪkəl] *a* Theater-; (*career*) Schauspieler-; (*showy*) theatralisch.

theft [θeft] *n* Diebstahl *m*.

their [ðeə*] *poss a* ihr; ~s *poss pron* ihre(r, s); *see also* **my, mine.**

them [ðem, ðəm] *pron* (*acc*) sie; (*dat*) ihnen; *see also* **me.**

theme [θiːm] *n* Thema *nt*; (*MUS*) Motiv *nt*; ~ song *n* Titelmusik *f*.

themselves [ðəm'selvz] *pl pron*

(*reflexive*) sich (selbst); (*emphatic*) selbst; *see also* **oneself.**

then [ðɛn] *ad* (*at that time*) damals; (*next*) dann // *cj* also, folglich; (*furthermore*) ferner // *a* damalig; **the ~ president** der damalige Präsident; **from ~ on** von da an; **by ~** bis dahin.

theology [θɪ'ɒlədʒɪ] *n* Theologie *f*.

theoretical *a*, **~ly** *ad* [θɪə'retɪkəl, -ɪ] theoretisch.

theory ['θɪərɪ] *n* Theorie *f*.

therapist ['θerəpɪst] *a* Therapeut(in *f*) *m*.

therapy ['θerəpɪ] *n* Therapie *f*.

there [ðɛə*] *ad* **1:** **~ is, ~ are** es *or* da ist/sind; (*~ exists/exist also*) es gibt; **~ are 3 of them** (*people, things*) es gibt drei davon; **~ has been an accident** da war ein Unfall **2** (*referring to place*) da, dort; (*with v of movement*) dahin, dorthin; **put it in/on ~** leg es dahinein/dorthinauf **3: ~, ~** (*esp to child*) na, na.

thermometer [θə'mɒmɪtə*] *n* Thermometer *nt*.

Thermos ['θɜːməs] *n* ® Thermosflasche *f*.

thesaurus [θɪ'sɔːrəs] *n* Synonymwörterbuch *nt*.

these [ðiːz] *pl pron*, *a* diese.

thesis ['θiːsɪs] *n* (*for discussion*) These *f*; (*UNIV*) Dissertation *f*, Doktorarbeit *f*.

they [ðeɪ] *pl pron* sie; (*people in general*) man; **~ say that ...** (*it is said that*) es wird gesagt, daß ...; **~'d** = they had; they would; **~'ll** = they shall, they will; **~'re** = they are; **~'ve** = they have.

thick [θɪk] *a* dick; (*forest*) dicht; (*liquid*) dickflüssig; (*slow, stupid*) dumm, schwer von Begriff // *n*: **in the ~ of** mitten in (+*dat*); **it's 20 cm ~** es ist 20 cm dick *or* stark; **~en** *vi* (*fog*) dichter werden // *vt* (*sauce etc*) verdicken; **~ness** *n* (*of object*) Dicke *f*; Dichte *f*; Dickflüssigkeit *f*; **~set** *a* untersetzt; **~skinned** *a* dickhäutig.

thief [θiːf], *pl* **thieves** [θiːvz] *n* Dieb(in *f*) *m*.

thieving ['θiːvɪŋ] *n* Stehlen *nt* // *a* diebisch.

thigh [θaɪ] *n* Oberschenkel *m*.

thimble ['θɪmbl] *n* Fingerhut *m*.

thin [θɪn] *a* dünn; (*person also*) mager; (*excuse*) schwach // *vt*: **to ~ (down)** (*sauce, paint*) verdünnen.

thing [θɪŋ] *n* Ding *nt*; (*affair*) Sache *f*; **my ~s** meine Sachen *pl*; **the best ~ would be to ...** das beste wäre, ...; **how are ~s?** wie geht's?

think [θɪŋk], *pt, pp* **thought** *vti* denken; **what did you ~ of them?** was halten Sie von ihnen?; **to ~ about** sth/jdn nachdenken über etw/jdn; **I'll ~ about it** ich überlege es mir; **to ~ of doing sth**

vorhaben *or* beabsichtigen, etw zu tun; **I ~ so/not** ich glaube (schon)/glaube nicht; **to ~ well of sb** viel von jdm halten; **~ over** *vt* überdenken; **~ up** *vt* sich (*dat*) ausdenken; **~ tank** *n* Experten-gruppe *f*.

thinly ['θɪnlɪ] *ad* dünn; (*disguised*) kaum.

third [θɜːd] *a* dritte(r, s) // *n* (*person*) Dritte(r) *mf*; (*part*) Drittel *nt*; **~ly** *ad* drittens; **~ party insurance** *n* (*Brit*) Haftpflichtversicherung *f*; **~-rate** *a* minderwertig; **the T~ World** *n* die Dritte Welt *f*.

thirst [θɜːst] *n* (*lit, fig*) Durst *m*; **~y** *a* (*person*) durstig; (*work*) durstig machend; **to be ~y** Durst haben.

thirteen ['θɜː'tiːn] *num* dreizehn.

thirty ['θɜːtɪ] *num* dreißig.

this [ðɪs] ◆*a* (*demonstrative: pl* **these**) diese(r, s); **~ evening** heute abend; **~ one** diese(r, s) (da) ◆*pronoun* (*demonstrative: pl* **these**) dies, das; **who/what is ~?** wer/was ist das?; **~ is where I live** hier wohne ich; **~ is what he said** das hat er gesagt; **~ is Mr Brown** (*in introductions/photo*) dies ist Mr Brown; (*on telephone*) hier ist Mr Brown ◆*ad* (*demonstrative*): **~ high/long** *etc* so groß/lang *etc*.

thistle ['θɪsl] *n* Distel *f*.

thong [θɒŋ] *n* (Leder)riemen *m*.

thorn [θɔːn] *n* Dorn *m*; **~y** *a* dornig; (*problem*) schwierig.

thorough ['θʌrə] *a* gründlich; **~bred** *n* Vollblut *nt* // *a* reinrassig, Vollblut-; **~fare** *n* Straße *f*; **'no ~fare'** 'Durchfahrt verboten'; **~ly** *ad* gründlich; (*extremely*) äußerst.

those [ðəʊz] *pl pron* die (da), jene // *a* die, jene.

though [ðəʊ] *cj* obwohl // *ad* trotzdem.

thought [θɔːt] *pt, pp of* **think** // *n* (*idea*) Gedanke *m*; (*thinking*) Denken *nt*, Denkvermögen *nt*; **~ful** *a* (*thinking*) gedankenvoll, nachdenklich; (*kind*) rücksichtsvoll, aufmerksam; **~less** *a* gedankenlos, unbesonnen; (*unkind*) rücksichtslos.

thousand ['θaʊzənd] *num* tausend; **two ~** zweitausend; **~s of** Tausende (von); **~th** *a* tausendste(r, s).

thrash [θræʃ] *vt* (*lit*) verdreschen; (*fig*) (vernichtend) schlagen; **~ about** *vi* um sich schlagen; **~ out** *vt* ausdiskutieren.

thread [θred] *n* Faden *m*, Garn *nt*; (*on screw*) Gewinde *nt*; (*in story*) Faden *m* // *vt* (*needle*) einfädeln; **~bare** *a* (*lit, fig*) fadenscheinig.

threat [θret] *n* Drohung *f*; (*danger*) Gefahr *f*; **~en** *vt* bedrohen // *vi* drohen; **to ~en sb with sth** jdm etw androhen.

three [θriː] *num* drei; **~-dimensional** *a* dreidimensional; **~-piece suit** *n* dreiteilige(r) Anzug m; **~-piece suite** n dreiteilige Polstergarnitur f; **~-ply** a (wool) dreifach; (wood) dreischichtig; **~-wheeler** n Dreiradwagen m.

thresh [θreʃ] vti dreschen.

threshold ['θreʃhəʊld] n Schwelle f.

threw [θru:] pt of throw.

thrift [θrɪft] n Sparsamkeit f; **~y** a sparsam.

thrill [θrɪl] n Reiz m, Erregung f || vt begeistern, packen; to be ~ed (with glad etc) sich unheimlich freuen über (+acc); ~er n Krimi m; **~ing** a spannend; (news) aufregend.

thrive [θraɪv], pt throve [θrəʊv], pp thrived or thriven ['θrɪvn] vi gedeihen (on bei).

thriving ['θraɪvɪŋ] a blühend.

throat [θrəʊt] n Hals m, Kehle f; to have a sore ~ Halsschmerzen haben.

throb [θrɒb] n Pochen nt || vi klopfen, pochen.

throes [θrəʊz] npl: in the ~ of mitten in (+dat).

throng [θrɒŋ] n (Menschen)schar f || vt sich drängen in (+dat).

throttle ['θrɒtl] n Gashebel m || vt erdrosseln.

through [θru:] prep durch; (time) während (+gen); (because of) aus, durch || ad durch || a (ticket, train) durchgehend; (finished) fertig; to put sb ~ (TEL) jdn verbinden (to mit) to be ~ (TEL) eine Verbindung haben; (have finished) fertig sein; 'no ~ way' (Brit) Sackgasse f; **~out** [θru'aʊt] prep (place) überall in (+dat); (time) während (+gen) || ad überall; die ganze Zeit.

throve [θrəʊv] pt of thrive.

throw [θrəʊ] n Wurf m || vt, pt threw, pp thrown werfen; to ~ a party eine Party geben; ~ **away** vt wegwerfen; (waste) verschenken; (money) verschwenden; ~ **off** vt abwerfen; (pursuer) abschütteln; ~ **out** vt hinauswerfen; (rubbish) wegwerfen; (plan) verwerfen; ~ **up** vti (vomit) speien; **~away** a Wegwerf-; **~-in** n Einwurf m.

thru [θru:] (US) = through.

thrush [θrʌʃ] n Drossel f.

thrust [θrʌst] n (TECH) Schubkraft f || vti, pt, pp thrust (push) stoßen.

thud [θʌd] n dumpfe(r) (Auf)schlag m.

thug [θʌg] n Schlägertyp m.

thumb [θʌm] n Daumen m || vt (book) durchblättern; to ~ a lift per Anhalter fahren (wollen); **~tack** n (US) Reißzwecke f.

thump [θʌmp] n (blow) Schlag m; (noise) Bums m || vi hämmern, pochen || vt schlagen auf (+acc).

thunder ['θʌndə*] n Donner m || vi donnern; (train etc): to ~ past vorbeidonnern || vt brüllen; **~bolt** n Blitz

nt; **~clap** n Donnerschlag m; **~storm** n Gewitter nt, Unwetter nt; **~y** a gewitterschwül.

Thursday ['θɜ:zdeɪ] n Donnerstag m.

thus [ðʌs] ad (in this way) so; (therefore) somit, also, folglich.

thwart [θwɔ:t] vt vereiteln, durchkreuzen; (person) hindern.

thyme [taɪm] n Thymian m.

thyroid ['θaɪrɔɪd] n Schilddrüse f.

tic [tɪk] n Tick m.

tick [tɪk] n (sound) Ticken nt; (mark) Häkchen nt || vi ticken || vt abhaken; in a ~ (Brit col) sofort; ~ **off** vt abhaken; (person) ausschimpfen; ~ **over** vi (engine) im Leerlauf laufen; (fig) auf Sparflamme laufen.

ticket ['tɪkɪt] n (for travel) Fahrkarte f; (for entrance) (Eintritts)karte f; (price ~) Preisschild nt; (luggage ~) (Gepäck)schein m; (raffle ~) Los nt; (parking ~) Strafzettel m; (permission) Parkschein m; ~ **collector** n Fahrkartenkontrolleur m; ~ **office** n (RAIL etc) Fahrkartenschalter m; (THEAT etc) Kasse f.

tickle ['tɪkl] n Kitzeln nt || vt kitzeln; (amuse) amüsieren.

ticklish ['tɪklɪʃ] a (lit, fig) kitzlig.

tidal ['taɪdl] a Flut-, Tide-; ~ **wave** n Flutwelle f.

tidbit ['tɪdbɪt] n (US) Leckerbissen m.

tiddlywinks ['tɪdlɪwɪŋks] n Floh(hüpf)spiel nt.

tide [taɪd] n Gezeiten pl; high/low ~ Flut f/Ebbe f.

tidy ['taɪdɪ] a ordentlich || vt aufräumen, in Ordnung bringen.

tie [taɪ] n (Brit: necktie) Kravatte f, Schlips m; (sth connecting) Band nt; (SPORT) Unentschieden nt || vt (fasten, restrict) binden || vi (SPORT) unentschieden spielen; (in competition) punktgleich sein; to ~ in a bow zur Schleife binden; to ~ a knot in sth einen Knoten in etw (acc) machen; ~ **down** vt (lit) festbinden; to ~ sb **down** to jdn binden an (+acc); ~ **up** vt (dog) anbinden; (parcel) verschnüren; (boat) festmachen; (person) fesseln; to be ~d **up** (busy) beschäftigt sein.

tier [tɪə*] n Rang m; (of cake) Etage f.

tight [taɪt] a (close) eng, knapp; (schedule) gedrängt; (firm) fest; (control) streng; (stretched) stramm, (an)gespannt; (col) blau, stramm || ad (squeeze) fest; **~s** pl (Brit) Strumpfhose f; **~en** vt anziehen, anspannen; (restrictions) verschärfen || vi sich spannen; **~-fisted** a knauserig; **~ly** ad eng; fest; (stretched) straff; **~-rope** n Seil nt.

tile [taɪl] n (in roof) Dachziegel m; (on wall or floor) Fliese f; **~d** a (roof) gedeckt, Ziegel-; (floor, wall) mit Fliesen belegt.

till [tɪl] *n* Kasse *f* // *vt* bestellen // *prep, cj* = **until**.

tiller ['tɪlə*] *n* Ruderpinne *f*.

tilt [tɪlt] *vt* kippen, neigen // *vi* sich neigen.

timber ['tɪmbə*] *n* Holz *nt*; (*trees*) Baumbestand *m*.

time [taɪm] *n* Zeit *f*; (*occasion*) Mal *nt*; (*rhythm*) Takt *m* // *vt* zur rechten Zeit tun, zeitlich einrichten; (*SPORT*) stoppen; in 2 weeks' ~ in 2 Wochen; a long ~ lange; for the ~ being vorläufig; 4 at a ~ zu jeweils 4; from ~ to ~ gelegentlich; to have a good ~ sich amüsieren; in ~ (*soon enough*) rechtzeitig; (*after some time*) mit der Zeit; (*MUS*) im Takt; in no ~ im Handumdrehen; any ~ jederzeit; on ~ pünktlich, rechtzeitig; five ~s 5 fünfmal 5; what ~ is it? wieviel Uhr ist es?, wie spät ist es?; ~ **bomb** *n* Zeitbombe *f*; ~**lag** *n* (*in travel*) Verzögerung *f*; (*difference*) Zeitunterschied *m*; ~**less** *a* (*beauty*) zeitlos; ~ **limit** *n* Frist *f*; ~**ly** *a* rechtzeitig; günstig; ~ **off** *n* freie Zeit *f*; **timer** *n* (~ *switch: in kitchen*) Schaltuhr *f*; ~ **scale** *n* Zeitspanne *f*; ~ **switch** *n* (*Brit*) Zeitschalter *m*; ~**table** *n* Fahrplan *m*; (*SCH*) Stundenplan *m*; ~ **zone** *n* Zeitzone *f*.

timid ['tɪmɪd] *a* ängstlich, schüchtern.

timing ['taɪmɪŋ] *n* Wahl *f* des richtigen Zeitpunkts, Timing *nt*; (*AUT*) Einstellung *f*.

timpani ['tɪmpənɪ] *npl* Kesselpauken *pl*.

tin [tɪn] *n* (*metal*) Blech *nt*; (*container*) Büchse *f*, Dose *f*; ~**foil** *n* Staniolpapier *nt*.

tinge [tɪndʒ] *n* (*colour*) Färbung *f*; (*fig*) Anflug *m* // *vt* färben; ~**d with** mit einer Spur von.

tingle ['tɪŋgl] *n* Prickeln *nt* // *vi* prickeln.

tinker ['tɪŋkə*] *n* Kesselflicker *m*; ~ **with** *vt* herumpfuschen an (+*dat*).

tinkle ['tɪŋkl] *vi* klingeln.

tinned [tɪnd] *a* (*Bri: food*) Dosen-, Büchsen-.

tin opener ['tɪnəʊpnə*] *n* (*Brit*) Dosen- *or* Büchsenöffner *m*.

tinsel ['tɪnsəl] *n* Rauschgold *nt*.

tint [tɪnt] *n* Farbton *m*; (*slight colour*) Anflug *m*; (*hair*) Tönung *f*; ~**ed** *a* getönt.

tiny ['taɪnɪ] *a* winzig.

tip [tɪp] *n* (*pointed end*) Spitze *f*; (*money*) Trinkgeld *nt*; (*hint*) Wink *m*, Tip *m* // *vt* (*slant*) kippen; (*hat*) antippen; (~ *over*) umkippen; (*waiter*) ein Trinkgeld geben (+*dat*); ~**off** *n* Hinweis *m*, Tip *m*; ~**ped** *a* (*Brit: cigarette*) Filter-.

tipsy ['tɪpsɪ] *a* beschwipst.

tiptoe ['tɪptəʊ] *n*: on ~ auf Zehenspitzen.

tiptop ['tɪp'tɒp] *a*: in ~ condition

tipptopp, erstklassig.

tire ['taɪə*] *n* (*US*) = **tyre** // *vti* ermüden, müde machen/werden; ~**d** *a* müde; to be ~**d of** sth etw satt haben; ~**less** *a*, ~**lessly** *ad* unermüdlich; ~**some** *a* lästig.

tiring ['taɪərɪŋ] *a* ermüdend.

tissue ['tɪʃuː] *n* Gewebe *nt*; (*paper handkerchief*) Papiertaschentuch *nt*; ~ **paper** *n* Seidenpapier *nt*.

tit [tɪt] *n* (*bird*) Meise *f*; ~**s** *pl* (*col: breasts*) Busen *m*; ~ **for tat** wie du mir, so ich dir.

titbit ['tɪtbɪt], (*US*) **tidbit** ['tɪdbɪt] *n* Leckerbissen *m*.

titillate ['tɪtɪleɪt] *vt* kitzeln.

titivate ['tɪtɪveɪt] *vt* schniegeln.

title ['taɪtl] *n* Titel *m*; ~ **deed** *n* Eigentumsurkunde *f*; ~ **role** *n* Hauptrolle *f*.

titter ['tɪtə*] *vi* kichern.

TM *abbr* (= *trademark*) Wz.

to [tuː, tə] ◆*prep* 1 (*direction*) zu; nach; to go ~ France/school nach Frankreich/ zur Schule gehen; ~ the left nach links

2 (*as far as*) bis

3 (*with expressions of time*) vor; a quarter ~ 5 Viertel vor 5

4 (*for, of*) für; secretary ~ the director Sekretärin des Direktors

5 (*expressing indirect object*): to give sth ~ sb jdm etw geben; to talk ~ sb mit jdm sprechen; I sold it ~ a friend ich habe es einem Freund verkauft

6 (*in relation to*) zu; 30 miles ~ the gallon 30 Meilen pro Gallone

7 (*purpose, result*) zu; my surprise zu meiner Überraschung

◆*with v* 1 (*infinitive*): ~ go/eat trinken/ essen; to want ~ do sth etw tun wollen/ try/start ~ do sth etw versuchen/anfangen, etw zu tun; he has a lot ~ lose er hat viel zu verlieren

2 (*with v omitted*): I don't want ~ ich will (es) nicht

3 (*purpose, result*) um; I did it ~ help you ich tat es, um dir zu helfen

4 (*after adjective etc*): ready ~ use gebrauchsfertig; too old/young ~ ... zu alt/ jung, um ...

◆*ad*: push/pull the door ~ die Tür zuschieben/zuziehen.

toad [təʊd] *n* Kröte *f*; ~**stool** *n* Giftpilz *m*.

toast [təʊst] *n* (*bread*) Toast *m*; (*drinking*) Trinkspruch *m* // *vt* trinken auf (+*acc*); (*bread*) toasten; (*warm*) wärmen; ~**er** *n* Toaster *m*.

tobacco [tə'bækəʊ] *n* Tabak *m*; ~**nist** [tə'bækənɪst] *n* Tabakhändler *m*; ~**nist's (shop)** *n* Tabakladen *m*.

toboggan [tə'bɒgən] *n* (Rodel)schlitten *m*.

today [tə'deɪ] *ad* heute; (*at the present time*) heutzutage.

toddler ['tɒdlə*] *n* Kleinkind *nt.*
toddy ['tɒdı] *n* (Whisky) grog *m.*
to-do [tə'duː] *n* Theater *nt.*
toe [təʊ] *n* Zehe *f*; (of sock, shoe) Spitze *f* || *vt*: to ~ the line (fig) sich einfügen; ~nail *n* Zehennagel *m.*
toffee ['tɒfı] *n* Sahnebonbon *nt*; ~ apple *n* (Brit) kandierte(r) Apfel *m.*
together [tə'geðə*] *ad* zusammen; (at the same time) gleichzeitig; ~ with *prep* zusammen/gleichzeitig mit; ~ness *n* (company) Beisammensein *nt.*
toil [tɔıl] *n* harte Arbeit *f*, Plackerei *f* || *vi* sich abmühen, sich plagen.
toilet ['tɔılət] *n* Toilette *f* || *cpd* Toiletten-; ~ bag *n* Waschbeutel *m*; ~ paper *n* Toilettenpapier *nt*; ~ries ['tɔılətrız] *npl* Toilettenartikel *pl*; ~ roll *n* Rolle *f* Toilettenpapier; ~ water *n* Toilettenwasser *nt.*
token ['təʊkən] *n* Zeichen *nt*; (gift ~) Gutschein *m*; book/record ~ (Brit) Bücher-/Plattengutschein *m.*
Tokyo ['təʊkjəʊ] *n* Tokio *nt.*
told [təʊld] *pt*, *pp of* tell.
tolerable ['tɒlərəbl] *a* (bearable) erträglich; (fairly good) leidlich.
tolerate ['tɒləreıt] *vt* dulden; (noise) ertragen.
toll [təʊl] *n* Gebühr *f* || *vi* (bell) läuten.
tomato [tə'mɑːtəʊ] *n*, *pl* ~es Tomate *f.*
tomb [tuːm] *n* Grab(mal) *nt.*
tomboy ['tɒmbɔı] *n* Wildfang *m.*
tombstone ['tuːmstəʊn] *n* Grabstein *m.*
tomcat ['tɒmkæt] *n* Kater *m.*
tomorrow [tə'mɒrəʊ] *n* Morgen *nt* || *ad* morgen; the day after ~ übermorgen; ~ morning morgen früh; a week ~ morgen in einer Woche.
ton [tʌn] *n* (Brit) Tonne *f*; (US: also: short ~) 907,18 kg; (metric ~) Tonne *f*; ~s of (col) eine Unmenge von.
tone [təʊn] *n* Ton *m*; ~ down *vt* (criticism, demands) mäßigen; (colours) abtonen; ~ up *vt* in Form bringen; ~-deaf *a* ohne musikalisches Gehör.
tongs [tɒŋz] *npl* Zange *f*; (curling ~) Lockenstab *m.*
tongue [tʌŋ] *n* Zunge *f*; (language) Sprache *f*; with ~ in cheek scherzhaft; ~-tied *a* stumm, sprachlos; ~-twister *n* Zungenbrecher *m.*
tonic ['tɒnık] *n* (MED) Stärkungsmittel *nt*; (drink) Tonic *m.*
tonight [tə'naıt] *ad* heute abend.
tonsil ['tɒnsl] *n* Mandel *f*; ~litis [tɒnsı'laıtıs] *n* Mandelentzündung *f.*
too [tuː] *ad* zu; (also) auch; ~ bad! Pech!
took [tʊk] *pt of* take.
tool [tuːl] *n* (lit, fig) Werkzeug *nt*; ~box *n* Werkzeugkasten *m.*
toot [tuːt] *n* Hupen *nt* || *vi* tuten; (AUT) hupen.
tooth [tuːθ] *n*, *pl* teeth Zahn *m*; ~ache

n Zahnschmerzen *pl*, Zahnweh *nt*; ~brush *n* Zahnbürste *f*; ~paste *n* Zahnpasta *f*; ~pick *n* Zahnstocher *m.*
top [tɒp] *n* Spitze *f*; (of mountain) Gipfel *m*; (of tree) Wipfel *m*; (toy) Kreisel *m*; (~ gear) vierte(r) Gang *m* || *a* oberste(r, s) || *vt* (list) an erster Stelle stehen auf (+dat); on ~ of oben auf (+dat); from ~ to bottom von oben bis unten; ~ up, (US) ~ off *vt* auffüllen; ~ floor *n* oberste Stockwerk *nt*; ~ hat *n* Zylinder *m*; ~-heavy *a* kopflastig.
topic ['tɒpık] *n* Thema *nt*, Gesprächsgegenstand *m*; ~al *a* aktuell.
topless ['tɒpləs] *a* (dress) oben ohne.
top-level ['tɒp'levl] *a* auf höchster Ebene.
topmost ['tɒpməʊst] *a* oberste(r, s).
topple ['tɒpl] *vti* stürzen, kippen.
top-secret ['tɒp'siːkrət] *a* streng geheim.
topsy-turvy ['tɒpsı'tɜːvı] *ad* durcheinander || *a* auf den Kopf gestellt.
torch [tɔːtʃ] *n* (Brit ELEC) Taschenlampe *f*; (with flame) Fackel *f.*
tore [tɔː*] *pt of* tear.
torment ['tɔːment] *n* Qual *f* || [tɔː'ment] *vt* (distress) quälen.
torn [tɔːn] *pp of* tear || *a* hin- und hergerissen.
torrent ['tɒrənt] *n* Sturzbach *m*; ~ial [tə'renʃəl] *a* wolkenbruchartig.
torrid ['tɒrıd] *a* heiß.
tortoise ['tɔːtəs] *n* Schildkröte *f*; ~shell ['tɔːtəʃel] *n* Schildpatt *nt.*
tortuous ['tɔːtjʊəs] *a* gewunden.
torture ['tɔːtʃə*] *n* Folter *f* || *vt* foltern.
Tory ['tɔːrı] *n* (Brit POL) Tory *m* || *a* Tory-, konservativ.
toss [tɒs] *vt* schleudern; to ~ a coin, to ~ up for sth etw mit einer Münze entscheiden; to ~ and turn (in bed) sich hin und her werfen.
tot [tɒt] *n* (small quantity) bißchen *nt*; (small child) Knirps *m.*
total ['təʊtl] *n* Gesamtheit *f*; (money) Endsumme *f* || *a* Gesamt-, total || *vt* (add up) zusammenzählen; (amount to) sich belaufen auf.
totalitarian [təʊtælı'teərıən] *a* totalitär.
totally ['təʊtəlı] *ad* total.
totter [tɒtə*] *vi* wanken, schwanken.
touch [tʌtʃ] *n* Berührung *f*; (sense of feeling) Tastsinn *m* || *vt* (feel) berühren; (come against) leicht anstoßen; (emotionally) rühren; a ~ of (fig) eine Spur von; to get in ~ with sb sich mit jdm in Verbindung setzen; to lose ~ (friends) Kontakt verlieren; ~ on *vt* (topic) berühren, erwähnen; ~ up *vt* (paint) auffrischen; ~-and-go *a* riskant, knapp; ~down *n* Landen *nt*, Niedergehen *nt*; ~ing *a* rührend; ~line *n* Seitenlinie *f*; ~y *a* empfindlich, reizbar.

tough [tʌf] a zäh; (difficult) schwierig // n Schläger(typ) m; ~**en** vt zäh machen; (make strong) abhärten.

toupée ['tu:peɪ] n Toupet nt.

tour ['tuə*] n Tour f // vi umherreisen; (THEAT) auf Tour sein/gehen; ~**ing** n Umherreisen nt; (THEAT) Tournee f.

tourism ['tuərɪzm] n Fremdenverkehr m, Tourismus m.

tourist ['tuərɪst] n Tourist(in f) // cpd (class) Touristen-; ~ **office** n Verkehrsamt nt.

tournament ['tuənəmənt] n Turnier nt.

tousled ['tauzld] a zerzaust.

tout [taut] vi: to ~ **for** auf Kundenfang gehen für // n: **ticket** ~ Kundenschlepper(in f) m.

tow [təu] vt (ab)schleppen; on or (US) in ~ (AUT) im Schlepp.

toward(s) [tə'wɔːd(z)] prep (with time) gegen; (in direction of) nach.

towel ['tauəl] n Handtuch nt; ~**ling** n (fabric) Frottee nt or m; ~ **rail**, (US) ~ **rack** n Handtuchstange f.

tower ['tauə*] n Turm m; ~ **block** n (Brit) Hochhaus nt; ~**ing** a hochragend.

town [taun] n Stadt f; to go to ~ (fig) sich ins Zeug legen; ~ **centre** n Stadtzentrum nt; ~ **clerk** n Stadtdirektor m; ~ **council** n Stadtrat m; ~ **hall** n Rathaus nt ~ **plan** n Stadtplan m; ~ **planning** n Stadtplanung f.

towrope ['təurəup] n Abschlepptau nt.

tow truck n (US): breakdown lorry) Abschleppwagen m.

toxic ['tɒksɪk] a giftig, Gift-.

toy [tɔɪ] n Spielzeug nt; ~ **with** vt spielen mit; ~**shop** n Spielwarengeschäft nt.

trace [treɪs] n Spur f // vt (follow a course) nachspüren (+dat); (find out) aufspüren; (copy) durchpausen; **tracing paper** n Pauspapier nt.

track [træk] n (mark) Spur f; (path) Weg m; (race-~) Rennbahn f; (RAIL) Gleis nt // vt verfolgen; to keep ~ of sb jdn im Auge behalten; ~ **down** vt aufspüren; ~ **suit** n Trainingsanzug m.

tract [trækt] n (of land) Gebiet nt; (booklet) Traktat nt.

traction ['trækʃən] n (power) Zugkraft f; (AUT: grip) Bodenhaftung f; (MED): **in** ~ im Streckverband.

trade [treɪd] n (commerce) Handel m; (business) Geschäft nt, Gewerbe nt; (people) Geschäftsleute pl; (skilled manual work) Handwerk nt // vi handeln (in mit) // vt tauschen; ~ **in** vt in Zahlung geben; ~ **fair** n Messe nt; ~-**in price** n Preis m, zu dem etw in Zahlung genommen wird; ~**mark** n Warenzeichen nt; ~ **name** n Handelsbezeichnung f; ~**r** n Händler m; **tradesman** n (shopkeeper) Geschäftsmann m; (work-

man) Handwerker m; (delivery man) Lieferant m; ~ **union** n Gewerkschaft f; ~ **unionist** n Gewerkschaftler(in f) m.

trading ['treɪdɪŋ] n Handel m; ~ **estate** n (Brit) Industriegelände nt.

tradition [trə'dɪʃən] n Tradition f; ~**al** a traditionell, herkömmlich.

traffic ['træfɪk] n Verkehr m; (esp in drugs) Handel m (in mit) // vi: to ~ **in** (esp drugs) handeln mit; ~ **circle** n (US) Kreisverkehr m; ~ **jam** n Verkehrsstauung f; ~ **lights** npl Verkehrsampeln pl; ~ **warden** n ≈ Verkehrspolizist m, Politesse f (ohne amtliche Befugnisse).

tragedy ['trædʒədɪ] n Tragödie f.

tragic ['trædʒɪk] a tragisch.

trail [treɪl] n (track) Spur f; (of smoke) Rauchfahne f; (of dust) Staubwolke f; (road) Pfad m, Weg m // vt (animal) verfolgen; (person) folgen (+dat); (drag) schleppen // vi (hang loosely) schleifen; (plants) sich ranken; (be behind) hinterherhinken; (SPORT) weit zurückliegen; (walk) zuckeln; ~ **behind** vi zurückbleiben; ~**er** n Anhänger m; (US: caravan) Wohnwagen m; (for film) Vorschau f; ~ **truck** n (US) Sattelschlepper m.

train [treɪn] n Zug m; (of dress) Schleppe f; (series) Folge f // vt (teach: person) ausbilden; (: animal) abrichten; (: mind) schulen; (SPORT) trainieren; (aim) richten (on auf +acc) // vi (exercise) trainieren; (study) ausgebildet werden; ~ **of thought** Gedankengang m; ~**ed** a (eye) geschult; (person, voice) ausgebildet; ~**ee** n Lehrling m; Praktikant(in f) m; ~**er** n (SPORT) Trainer m; Ausbilder m; ~**ing** n (for occupation) Ausbildung f; (SPORT) Training nt; **in** ~**ing** im Training; ~**ing college** n Pädagogische Hochschule f, Lehrerseminar nt; ~**ing shoes** npl Turnschuhe pl.

traipse [treɪps] vi latschen.

trait [treɪ(t)] n Zug m, Merkmal nt.

traitor ['treɪtə*] n Verräter m.

trajectory [trə'dʒektərɪ] n Flugbahn f.

tram(car) ['træm(kɑː*)] n Straßenbahn f.

tramp [træmp] n Landstreicher m // vi (walk heavily) stampfen, stapfen; (travel on foot) wandern.

trample ['træmpl] vt (nieder)trampeln // vi (herum)trampeln; to ~ (underfoot) herumtrampeln auf (+dat).

tranquil ['træŋkwɪl] a ruhig, friedlich; ~**ity** [træŋ'kwɪlɪtɪ] n Ruhe f; ~**izer** n Beruhigungsmittel nt.

transact [træn'zækt] vt abwickeln; ~**ion** n Abwicklung f; (piece of business) Geschäft nt, Transaktion f.

transcend [træn'send] vt übersteigen.

transcript ['trænskrɪpt] n Abschrift f, Kopie f; (JUR) Protokoll nt; **~ion** [træn'skrɪpʃən] n Transkription f; (product) Abschrift f.

transfer ['trænsfə*] n (transferring) Übertragung f; (of business) Umzug m; (being transferred) Versetzung f; (design) Abziehbild nt; (SPORT) Transfer m // [træns'fɜ:*] vt (business) verlegen; (person) versetzen; (prisoner) überführen; (drawing) übertragen; (money) überweisen; to ~ the charges (Brit TEL) ein R-Gespräch führen.

transform [træns'fɔ:m] vt umwandeln; **~ation** [trænsfə'meɪʃən] n Umwandlung f, Verwandlung f; **~er** n (ELEC) Transformator m.

transfusion [træns'fju:ʒən] n Blutübertragung f, Transfusion f.

transient ['trænzɪənt] a kurz(lebig).

transistor [træn'zɪstə*] n (ELEC) Transistor m; (radio) Transistorradio nt.

transit ['trænzɪt] n: in ~ unterwegs.

transition [træn'zɪʃən] n Übergang m; **~al** a Übergangs-.

transitory ['trænzɪtərɪ] a vorübergehend.

translate [trænz'leɪt] vti übersetzen.

translation [trænz'leɪʃən] n Übersetzung f.

translator [trænz'leɪtə*] n Übersetzer(in f) m.

transmission [trænz'mɪʃən] n (of information) Übermittlung f; (ELEC, MED, TV) Übertragung f; (AUT) Getriebe nt.

transmit [trænz'mɪt] vt (message) übermitteln; (ELEC, MED, TV) übertragen; **~ter** n Sender m.

transparency [træns'pɛərənsɪ] n Durchsichtigkeit f; (Brit PHOT) Dia(positiv) nt.

transparent [træns'pærənt] a (lit) durchsichtig; (fig) offenkundig.

transpire [træns'paɪə*] vi (turn out) sich herausstellen; (happen) passieren.

transplant [træns'plɑ:nt] vt umpflanzen; (MED) verpflanzen; (fig: person) verpflanzen // ['trænsplɑ:nt] n (MED) Transplantation f; (organ) Transplantat nt.

transport ['trænspɔ:t] n Transport m, Beförderung f // vt [træns'pɔ:t] befördern; transportieren; means of ~ Transportmittel nt; **~ation** [trænspɔ:-'teɪʃən] n Transport m, Beförderung f; (means) Beförderungsmittel nt; (cost) Transportkosten pl; ~ **café** n (Brit) Fernfahrerlokal nt.

transverse ['trænzvɜ:s] a Quer-; (position) horizontal; (engine) querliegend.

trap [træp] n Falle f; (carriage) zweirädrige(r) Einspänner m; (col: mouth) Klappe f // vt fangen; (person) in eine Falle locken; **~door** n Falltür f.

trappings ['træpɪŋz] npl Aufmachung f.

trash [træʃ] n (rubbish) Plunder m; (nonsense) Mist m; ~ **can** n (US) Mülleimer m.

travel ['trævl] n Reisen nt // vi reisen // vt (distance) zurücklegen; (country) bereisen; ~ **agency** n Reisebüro nt; ~ **agent** n Reisebürokaufmann m; Reisebürokauffrau f; **~ler**, (US) **~er** n Reisende(r) mf; (salesman) Handlungsreisende(r) m; **~ler's cheque**, (US) **~er's check** n Reisescheck m; **~ling**, (US) **~ing** n Reisen nt; ~ **sickness** n Reisekrankheit f.

tray [treɪ] n (tea ~) Tablett nt; (receptacle) Schale f; (for mail) Ablage f.

treacherous ['tretʃərəs] a verräterisch; (road) tückisch.

treachery ['tretʃərɪ] n Verrat m.

treacle ['tri:kl] n Sirup m, Melasse f.

tread [tred] n Schritt m, Tritt m; (of stair) Stufe f; (on tyre) Profil nt // vi, pt **trod**, pp **trodden** treten; ~ **on** vt treten auf (+acc).

treason ['tri:zn] n Verrat m.

treasure ['treʒə*] n Schatz m // vt schätzen.

treasurer ['treʒərə*] n Kassenverwalter m, Schatzmeister m.

treasury ['treʒərɪ] n (POL) Finanzministerium nt.

treat [tri:t] n besondere Freude f // vt (deal with) behandeln; to ~ sb to sth jdn zu etw einladen.

treatise ['tri:tɪz] n Abhandlung f.

treatment ['tri:tmənt] n Behandlung f.

treaty ['tri:tɪ] n Vertrag m.

treble ['trebl] a dreifach // vt verdreifachen; ~ **clef** n Violinschlüssel m.

tree [tri:] n Baum m; ~ **trunk** n Baumstamm m.

trellis ['trelɪs] n Gitter nt; (for gardening) Spalier nt.

tremble ['trembl] vi zittern; (ground) beben.

trembling ['tremblɪŋ] n Zittern nt // a zitternd.

tremendous [trə'mendəs] a gewaltig, kolossal; (col: very good) prima.

tremor ['tremə*] n Zittern nt; (of earth) Beben nt.

trench [trentʃ] n Graben m; (MIL) Schützengraben m.

trend [trend] n Tendenz f; **~y** a (col) modisch.

trepidation [trepɪ'deɪʃən] n Beklommenheit f.

trespass ['trespəs] vi widerrechtlich betreten (on acc); 'no **~ing**' 'Betreten verboten.'

tress [tres] n Locke f.

trestle ['tresl] n Bock m; ~ **table** n Klapptisch m.

trial ['traɪəl] n (JUR) Prozeß m; (test)

Versuch *m*, Probe *f*; (*hardship*) Prüfung *f*; by ~ and error durch Ausprobieren.

triangle ['traɪæŋgl] *n* Dreieck *nt*; (*MUS*) Triangel *f*.

triangular [traɪ'æŋgjʊlə*] *a* dreieckig.

tribal ['traɪbəl] *a* Stammes-.

tribe [traɪb] *n* Stamm *m*; **tribesman** *n* Stammesangehörige(r) *m*.

tribulation [trɪbjʊ'leɪʃən] *n* Not *f*, Mühsal *f*.

tribunal [traɪ'bjuːnl] *n* Gericht *nt*; (*inquiry*) Untersuchungsausschuß *m*.

tributary ['trɪbjʊtərɪ] *n* Nebenfluß *m*.

tribute ['trɪbjuːt] *n* (*admiration*) Zeichen *nt* der Hochachtung; **to pay ~ to** jdm/ einer Sache Tribut zollen.

trice [traɪs] *n*: **in a ~** im Nu.

trick [trɪk] *n* Trick *m*; (*CARDS*) Stich *m* // *vt* überlisten, beschwindeln; **to play a ~ on sb** jdm einen Streich spielen; **that should do the ~** das müßte eigentlich klappen; **~ery** *n* Tricks *pl*.

trickle ['trɪkl] *n* Tröpfeln *nt*; (*small river*) Rinnsal *nt* // *vi* tröpfeln; (*seep*) sickern.

tricky ['trɪkɪ] *a* (*problem*) schwierig; (*situation*) kitzlig.

tricycle ['traɪsɪkl] *n* Dreirad *nt*.

trifle ['traɪfl] *n* Kleinigkeit *f*; (*COOK*) Trifle *m* // *ad*: **a ~** ein bißchen.

trifling ['traɪflɪŋ] *a* geringfügig.

trigger ['trɪgə*] *n* Drücker *m*; **~ off** *vt* auslösen.

trim [trɪm] *a* gepflegt; (*figure*) schlank // *n* (gute) Verfassung *f*; (*embellishment, on car*) Verzierung *f* // *vt* (*clip*) schneiden; (*trees*) stutzen; (*decorate*) besetzen; (*sails*) trimmen; **~mings** *npl* (*decorations*) Verzierung(en *pl*) *f*; (*extras*) Zubehör *nt*.

Trinity ['trɪnɪtɪ] *n*: **the ~** die Dreieinigkeit.

trinket ['trɪŋkɪt] *n* kleine(s) Schmuckstück *nt*.

trip [trɪp] *n* (kurze) Reise *f*; (*outing*) Ausflug *m*; (*stumble*) Stolpern *nt* // *vi* (*walk quickly*) trippeln; (*stumble*) stolpern; **on a ~** auf Reisen; **~ up** *vi* stolpern; (*fig also*) einen Fehler machen // *vt* zu Fall bringen; (*fig*) hereinlegen.

tripe [traɪp] *n* (*food*) Kutteln *pl*; (*rubbish*) Mist *m*.

triple ['trɪpl] *a* dreifach.

triplets ['trɪplɪts] *npl* Drillinge *pl*.

triplicate ['trɪplɪkət] *n*: **in ~** in dreifacher Ausfertigung.

tripod ['traɪpɒd] *n* (*PHOT*) Stativ *nt*.

trite [traɪt] *a* banal.

triumph ['traɪʌmf] *n* Triumph *m* // *vi* triumphieren; **to ~ (over)** triumphieren (über (+*acc*)) **~ant** [traɪ'ʌmfənt] *a* triumphierend.

trivia ['trɪvɪə] *npl* Trivialitäten *pl*.

trivial ['trɪvɪəl] *a* gering(fügig), trivial.

trod [trɒd], **trodden** ['trɒdn] *pt*, *pp* of

tread.

trolley ['trɒlɪ] *n* Handwagen *m*; (*in shop*) Einkaufswagen; (*for luggage*) Kofferkuli *m*; (*table*) Teewagen *m*; **~ bus** *n* O(berleitungs)bus *m*.

troop [truːp] *n* Schar *f*; (*MIL*) Trupp *m*; **~s** *pl* Truppen *pl*; **~ in/out** *vi* hinein-/ hinausströmen; **~er** *n* Kavallerist *m*; **~ing the colour** *n* (*ceremony*) Fahnenparade *f*.

tropic ['trɒpɪk] *n* Wendekreis *m*; **~al** *a* tropisch.

trot [trɒt] *n* Trott *m* // *vi* trotten; **on the ~** (*Brit fig: col*) in einer Tour.

trouble ['trʌbl] *n* (*problems*) Ärger *m*; (*worry*) Sorge *f*, (*in country, industry*) Unruhen *pl*; (*effort*) Mühe *f*; (*MED*): **stomach ~** Magenbeschwerden *pl*; // *vt* (*disturb*) stören; **to ~ to do sth** sich bemühen, etw zu tun; **to be in ~** Probleme or Ärger haben; **~s** *pl* (*POL etc*) Unruhen *pl*; **to go to the ~ of doing sth** sich die Mühe machen, etw zu tun; **what's the ~?** was ist los?; (*to sick person*) wo fehlt's?; **~d** *a* (*person*) beunruhigt; (*country*) geplagt; **~-free** *a* sorglos; **~maker** *n* Unruhestifter *m*; **~shooter** *n* Vermittler *m*; **~some** *a* lästig, unangenehm; (*child*) schwierig.

trough [trɒf] *n* (*vessel*) Trog *m*; (*channel*) Rinne *f*, Kanal *m*; (*MET*) Tief *nt*.

trounce [traʊns] *vt* (*esp SPORT*) vernichtend schlagen.

trousers ['traʊzəz] *npl* Hose *f*.

trousseau ['truːsəʊ], *pl* **~x** or **~s** [-z] *n* Aussteuer *f*.

trout [traʊt] *n* Forelle *f*.

trowel ['traʊəl] *n* Kelle *f*.

truant ['truːənt] *n*: **to play ~** (*Brit*) (die Schule) schwänzen.

truce [truːs] *n* Waffenstillstand *m*.

truck [trʌk] *n* Lastwagen *m*; (*RAIL*) offene(r) Güterwagen *m*; **~ driver** *n* Lastwagenfahrer *m*; **~ farm** *n* (*US*) Gemüsegärtnerei *f*.

truculent ['trʌkjʊlənt] *a* trotzig.

trudge [trʌdʒ] *vi* sich (mühselig) dahinschleppen.

true [truː] *a* (*exact*) wahr; (*genuine*) echt; (*friend*) treu.

truly ['truːlɪ] *ad* wirklich; **yours ~** Ihr sehr ergebener.

trump [trʌmp] *n* (*CARDS*) Trumpf *m*; **~ed-up** *a* erfunden.

trumpet ['trʌmpɪt] *n* Trompete *f*.

truncheon ['trʌntʃən] *n* Gummiknüppel *m*.

trundle ['trʌndl] *vt* schieben // *vi*: **~ along** entlangrollen.

trunk [trʌŋk] *n* (*of tree*) (Baum)stamm *m*; (*ANAT*) Rumpf *m*; (*box*) Truhe *f*, Überseekoffer *m*; (*of elephant*) Rüssel *m*; (*US AUT*) Kofferraum; **~s** *pl* Badehose *f*; **~ (up)** *vt* fesseln.

truss [trʌs] n (MED) Bruchband nt.

trust [trʌst] n (confidence) Vertrauen nt; (for property etc) Treuhandvermögen nt // vt (rely on) vertrauen (+dat), sich verlassen auf (+acc); (hope) hoffen; (entrust); to ~ sth to sb jdm etw anvertrauen; **~ed** a treu; **~ee** [trʌs'ti:] n Vermögensverwalter m; **~ful** a, **~ing** a vertrauensvoll; **~worthy** a vertrauenswürdig; (account) glaubwürdig; **~y** a treu, zuverlässig.

truth [tru:θ], pl **~s** [tru:ðz] n Wahrheit f; **~ful** a ehrlich.

try [trai] n Versuch m; to have a ~ es versuchen // vt (attempt) versuchen; (test) (aus)probieren; (JUR: person) unter Anklage stellen; (: case) verhandeln; (courage, patience) auf die Probe stellen // vi (make effort) versuchen, sich bemühen; to ~ to do sth versuchen, etw zu tun; ~ **on** vt (dress) anprobieren; (hat) aufprobieren; ~ **out** vt ausprobieren; **~ing** a schwierig.

T-shirt ['ti:ʃə:t] n T-shirt nt.

T-square ['ti:skweə*] n Reißschiene f.

tub [tʌb] n Wanne f, Kübel m; (for margarine etc) Becher m.

tubby ['tʌbi] a rundlich.

tube [tju:b] n (pipe) Röhre f, Rohr nt; (for toothpaste etc) Tube f; (in London) U-Bahn f; (AUT: for tyre) Schlauch m.

tube station ['tju:bsteiʃən] n (Brit) U-Bahnstation f.

tubing ['tju:biŋ] n Schlauch m; a piece of ~ ein (Stück) Schlauch.

tubular ['tju:bjulə*] a röhrenförmig.

TUC n abbr (Brit) of **Trades Union Congress.**

tuck [tʌk] n (fold) Falte f, Einschlag m // vt (put) stecken; (gather) fälteln, einschlagen; ~ **away** vt wegstecken; ~ **in** vt hineinstecken; (blanket etc) feststecken; (person) zudecken // vi (eat) hineinhauen, zulangen; ~ **up** vt (child) warm zudecken; ~ **shop** n Süßwarenladen m.

Tuesday ['tju:zdei] n Dienstag m.

tuft [tʌft] n Büschel m.

tug [tʌg] n (jerk) Zerren nt, Ruck m; (NAUT) Schleppdampfer m // vti zerren, ziehen; (boat) schleppen; **~-of-war** n Tauziehen nt.

tuition [tju:'iʃən] n (Brit) Unterricht m; (: private ~) Privatunterricht m; (US: school fees) Schulgeld nt.

tulip ['tju:lip] n Tulpe f.

tumble ['tʌmbl] n (fall) Sturz m // vi (fall) fallen, stürzen; ~ **to** vt kapieren; **~down** a baufällig; ~ **dryer** n (Brit) Trockner m; **tumbler** n (glass) Trinkglas nt.

tummy ['tʌmi] n (col) Bauch m.

tuna ['tju:nə] n Thunfisch m.

tune [tju:n] n Melodie f // vt (put in tune) stimmen; (AUT) richtig einstellen; to

sing in ~/out of ~ richtig/falsch singen; to be out of ~ with nicht harmonieren mit; ~ **in** vi einstellen (to acc); ~ **up** vi (MUS) stimmen; **tuner** n (person) (Instrumenten)stimmer m; (part) Tuner m; **piano tuner** n Klavierstimmer(in f) m; **~ful** a melodisch.

tunic ['tju:nik] n Waffenrock m; (loose garment) lange Bluse f.

tuning ['tju:niŋ] n (RAD, AUT) Einstellen nt; (MUS) Stimmen nt; ~ **fork** n Stimmgabel f.

Tunisia [tju:'niziə] n Tunesien nt.

tunnel ['tʌnl] n Tunnel m, Unterführung f // vi einen Tunnel anlegen.

turbulent ['tɜ:bjulənt] a stürmisch.

tureen [tjʊ'ri:n] n Terrine f.

turf [tɜ:f] n Rasen m; (piece) Sode f // vt mit Grassoden belegen; ~ **out** vt (col) rauswerfen.

turgid ['tɜ:dʒid] a geschwollen.

Turk [tɜ:k] n Türke m, Türkin f.

turkey ['tɜ:ki] n Puter m, Truthahn m.

Turkey ['tɜ:ki] n Türkei f; **Turkish** a türkisch // n (LING) Türkisch nt.

turmoil ['tɜ:moil] n Aufruhr m, Tumult m.

turn [tɜ:n] n (rotation) (Um)drehung f; (performance) (Programm)nummer f; (MED) Schock m // vt (rotate) drehen; (change position of) umdrehen, wenden; (page) umblättern; (transform): to ~ sth into sth etw in etw (acc) verwandeln; (direct) zuwenden // vi (rotate) sich drehen; (change direction: in car) abbiegen; (: wind) drehen; (~ round) umdrehen, wenden; (become) werden; (leaves) sich verfärben; (milk) sauer werden; (weather) umschlagen; to do sb a good ~ jdm etw Gutes tun; it's your ~ du bist dran or an der Reihe; in ~, by ~s abwechseln; to take ~s abwechseln; it gave me quite a ~ das hat mich schön erschreckt; 'no left ~' (AUT) 'Linksabbiegen verboten'; ~ **away** vi sich abwenden; ~ **back** vt umdrehen; (person) zurückschicken; (clock) zurückstellen // vi umkehren; ~ **down** vt (refuse) ablehnen; (fold down) umschlagen; ~ **in** vi (go to bed) ins Bett gehen // vt (fold inwards) einwärts biegen; ~ **off** vi abbiegen // vt ausschalten; (tap) zudrehen; (machine, electricity) abstellen; ~ **on** vt (light) anschalten, einschalten; (tap) aufdrehen; (machine) anstellen; ~ **out** vt (prove to be) sich erweisen; (people) sich entwickeln; how did the cake ~ out? wie ist der Kuchen geworden? // vt (light) ausschalten; (gas) abstellen; (produce) produzieren; ~ **round** vi (person, vehicle) sich herumdrehen; (rotate) sich drehen; ~ **up** vi auftauchen; (happen) passieren, sich ereignen // vt (collar) hochklappen, hochstellen;

turnip (*nose*) rümpfen; (*increase: radio*) lauter stellen; (: *heat*) höher drehen; **~ing** *n* (*in road*) Abzweigung *f*; **~ing point** *n* Wendepunkt *m*.

turnip ['tɜːnɪp] *n* Steckrübe *f*.

turnout ['tɜːnaʊt] *n* (Besucher)zahl *f*; (COMM) Produktion *f*.

turnover ['tɜːnəʊvə*] *n* Umsatz *m*; (*of staff*) Wechsel *m*.

turnpike ['tɜːnpaɪk] *n* (US) gebührenpflichtige Straße *f*.

turnstile ['tɜːnstaɪl] *n* Drehkreuz *nt*.

turntable ['tɜːnteɪbl] *n* (*of record-player*) Plattenteller *m*; (RAIL) Drehscheibe *f*.

turn-up ['tɜːnʌp] *n* (*Brit: on trousers*) Aufschlag *m*.

turpentine ['tɜːpəntaɪn] *n* Terpentin *nt*.

turquoise ['tɜːkwɔɪz] *n* (*gem*) Türkis *m*; (*colour*) Türkis *nt* // *a* türkisfarben.

turret ['tʌrɪt] *n* Turm *m*.

turtle ['tɜːtl] *n* Schildkröte *f*; **~ neck (sweater)** *n* (Pullover *m* mit) Schildkrötkragen *m*.

tusk [tʌsk] *n* Stoßzahn *m*.

tussle ['tʌsl] *n* Balgerei *f*.

tutor ['tjuːtə*] *n* (*teacher*) Privatlehrer *m*; (*college instructor*) Tutor *m*; **~ial** [tjuː'tɔːrɪəl] *n* (UNIV) Kolloquium *nt*, Seminarübung *f*.

tuxedo [tʌk'siːdəʊ] *n* (US) Smoking *m*.

TV ['tiː'viː] *n abbr* (= *television*) TV *nt*.

twang [twæŋ] *n* scharfe(r) Ton *m*; (*of voice*) Näseln *nt*.

tweezers ['twiːzəz] *npl* Pinzette *f*.

twelfth [twelfθ] *a* zwölfte(r, s).

twelve [twelv] *num a* zwölf; **at ~ o'clock** (*midday*) um 12 Uhr; (*midnight*) um Null Uhr.

twentieth ['twentɪɪθ] *a* zwanzigste(r, s).

twenty ['twentɪ] *num a* zwanzig.

twice [twaɪs] *ad* zweimal; **~ as much** doppelt soviel.

twiddle ['twɪdl] *vti*: **to ~ (with)** sth an etw (*dat*) herumdrehen; **to ~ one's thumbs** (*fig*) Däumchen drehen.

twig [twɪg] *n* dünne(r) Zweig *m* // *vt* (*col*) kapieren, merken.

twilight ['twaɪlaɪt] *n* Zwielicht *nt*.

twin [twɪn] *n* Zwilling *m* // *a* Zwillings-; (*very similar*) Doppel- // *vt* (*towns*) zu Partnerstädten machen; **~-bedded room** *n* Zimmer *nt* mit zwei Einzelbetten.

twine [twaɪn] *n* Bindfaden *m* // *vi* binden.

twinge [twɪndʒ] *n* stechende(r) Schmerz *m*, Stechen *nt*.

twinkle ['twɪŋkl] *n* Funkeln *nt*, Blitzen *nt* // *vi* funkeln.

twirl [twɜːl] *n* Wirbel *m* // *vti* (herum)wirbeln.

twist [twɪst] *n* (*twisting*), Drehung *f*; (*bend*) Kurve *f* // *vt* (*turn*) drehen; (*make crooked*) verbiegen; (*distort*) ver-

drehen // *vi* (*wind*) sich drehen; (*curve*) sich winden.

twit [twɪt] *n* (*col*) Idiot *m*.

twitch [twɪtʃ] *n* Zucken *nt* // *vi* zucken.

two [tuː] *num* zwei; **to put ~ and ~ together** seine Schlüsse ziehen; **~-door** *a* zweitürig; **~-faced** *a* falsch; **~-fold** *a*, *ad* zweifach, doppelt; **to increase ~fold** verdoppeln; **~-piece** *a* zweiteilig; **~-piece (suit)** *n* Zweiteiler *m*; **~-piece (swimsuit)** *n* zweiteilige(r) Badeanzug *m*; **~-seater** *n* (*plane, car*) Zweisitzer *m*; **~-some** *n* Paar *nt*; **~-way** *a* (*traffic*) Gegen-.

tycoon [taɪ'kuːn] *n*: (*business*) **~** (Industrie)magnat *m*.

type [taɪp] *n* Typ *m*, Art *f*; (PRINT) Type *f* // *vti* maschineschreiben, tippen; **~-cast** *a* (THEAT, TV) auf eine Rolle festgelegt; **~-face** *n* Schrift *f*; **~-script** *n* maschinegeschriebene(r) Text *m*; **~-writer** *n* Schreibmaschine *f*; **~-written** *a* maschinegeschrieben.

typhoid ['taɪfɔɪd] *n* Typhus *m*.

typical *a*, **~-ly** *ad* ['tɪpɪkəl, -klɪ] typisch (*of* für).

typify ['tɪpɪfaɪ] *vt* typisch sein für.

typing ['taɪpɪŋ] *n* Maschineschreiben *nt*.

typist ['taɪpɪst] *n* Maschinenschreiber(in *f*) *m*, Tippse *f* (*col*).

tyre, (US) tire [taɪə*] *n* Reifen *m*; **~ pressure** *n* Reifendruck *m*.

U

U-bend ['juː'bend] *n* (*in pipe*) U-Bogen *m*.

ubiquitous [juː'bɪkwɪtəs] *adj* überall zu findend, allgegenwärtig.

udder ['ʌdə*] *n* Euter *nt*.

UFO ['juːfəʊ] *n abbr* (= *unidentified flying object*) UFO *nt*.

ugh [ɜːh] *interj* hu.

ugliness ['ʌglɪnəs] *n* Häßlichkeit *f*.

ugly ['ʌglɪ] *a* häßlich; (*bad*) böse, schlimm.

U.K. *n abbr of* United Kingdom.

ulcer ['ʌlsə*] *n* Geschwür *nt*.

Ulster ['ʌlstə*] *n* Ulster *nt*.

ulterior [ʌl'tɪərɪə*] *a*: **~ motive** *n* Hintergedanke *m*.

ultimate ['ʌltɪmət] *a* äußerste(r, s), allerletzte(r, s); **~-ly** *ad* schließlich, letzten Endes.

ultrasound ['ʌltrə'saʊnd] *n* (MED) Ultraschall *m*.

umbilical cord [ʌm'bɪlɪkl kɔːd] *n* Nabelschnur *f*.

umbrella [ʌm'brelə] *n* Schirm *m*.

umpire ['ʌmpaɪə*] *n* Schiedsrichter *m* // *vti* schiedsrichtern.

umpteen ['ʌmptiːn] *num* (*col*) zig; **for the ~th time** zum X-ten Mal.

UN, UNO *n abbr* (= *United Nations*

(*Organization*)) UN *f*, UNO *f*.

unable ['ʌn'eɪbl] *a*: to be ~ to do sth etw nicht tun können.

unaccompanied ['ʌnə'kʌmpənɪd] *a* ohne Begleitung.

unaccountably ['ʌnə'kaʊntəblɪ] *ad* unerklärlich.

unaccustomed ['ʌnə'kʌstəmd] *a* nicht gewöhnt (*to* an +*acc*); (*unusual*) ungewohnt.

unanimous *a*, ~ly *ad* [juː'nænɪməs, -lɪ] einmütig; (*vote*) einstimmig.

unarmed [ʌn'ɑːmd] *a* unbewaffnet.

unashamed ['ʌnə'ʃeɪmd] *a* schamlos.

unassuming [ʌnə'sjuːmɪŋ] *a* bescheiden.

unattached ['ʌnə'tætʃt] *a* ungebunden.

unattended ['ʌnə'tendɪd] *a* (*person*) unbeaufsichtigt; (*thing*) unbewacht.

unauthorized ['ʌn'ɔːθəraɪzd] *a* unbefugt.

unavoidable [ʌnə'vɔɪdəbl] *a* unvermeidlich.

unaware ['ʌnə'wɛə*] *a*: to be ~ of sth sich (*dat*) einer Sache nicht bewußt sein; ~s *ad* unversehens.

unbalanced ['ʌn'bælənst] *a* unausgeglichen; (*mentally*) gestört.

unbearable [ʌn'bɛərəbl] *a* unerträglich.

unbeatable ['ʌn'biːtəbl] *a* unschlagbar.

unbeknown(st) ['ʌnbɪ'nəʊn(st)] *ad*: ~ to me ohne mein Wissen.

unbelievable [ʌnbɪ'liːvəbl] *a* unglaublich.

unbend ['ʌn'bend] (*irreg: like* bend) *vt* geradebiegen // *vi* aus sich herausgehen.

unbiased ['ʌn'baɪəst] *a* unparteiisch.

unbreakable ['ʌn'breɪkəbl] *a* unzerbrechlich.

unbridled [ʌn'braɪdld] *a* ungezügelt.

unbroken ['ʌn'brəʊkən] *a* (*period*) ununterbrochen; (*spirit*) ungebrochen; (*record*) unübertroffen.

unburden [ʌn'bɜːdn] *vt*: ~ o.s. (jdm) sein Herz ausschütten.

unbutton [ʌn'bʌtn] *vt* aufknöpfen.

uncalled-for [ʌn'kɔːldfɔː*] *a* unnötig.

uncanny [ʌn'kænɪ] *a* unheimlich.

unceasing [ʌn'siːsɪŋ] *a* unaufhörlich.

unceremonious ['ʌnserɪ'məʊnɪəs] *a* (*abrupt*, *rude*) brüsk; (*exit*, *departure*) überstürzt.

uncertain [ʌn'sɜːtn] *a* unsicher; (*doubtful*) ungewiß; (*unreliable*) unbeständig; (*vague*) undeutlich, vage; ~ty *n* Ungewißheit *f*.

unchanged ['ʌn'tʃeɪndʒd] *a* unverändert.

unchecked ['ʌn'tʃekt] *a* ungeprüft; (*not stopped*: *advance*) ungehindert.

uncivilized ['ʌn'sɪvɪlaɪzd] *a* unzivilisiert.

uncle ['ʌŋkl] *n* Onkel *m*.

uncomfortable [ʌn'kʌmfətəbl] *a* unbequem, ungemütlich.

uncommon [ʌn'kɒmən] *a* ungewöhn-

lich; (*outstanding*) außergewöhnlich.

uncompromising [ʌn'kɒmprəmaɪzɪŋ] *a* kompromißlos, unnachgiebig.

unconcerned [ʌnkən'sɜːnd] *a* unbekümmert; (*indifferent*) gleichgültig.

unconditional ['ʌnkən'dɪʃənl] *a* bedingungslos.

uncongenial ['ʌnkən'dʒiːnɪəl] *a* unangenehm.

unconscious [ʌn'kɒnʃəs] *a* (MED) bewußtlos; (*not meant*) unbeabsichtigt; the ~ das Unbewußte; ~ly *ad* unbewußt.

uncontrollable ['ʌnkən'trəʊləbl] *a* unkontrollierbar, unbändig.

unconventional [ʌnkən'venʃənl] *a* unkonventionell.

uncouth [ʌn'kuːθ] *a* grob.

uncover [ʌn'kʌvə*] *vt* aufdecken.

undecided ['ʌndɪ'saɪdd] *a* unschlüssig.

undeniable [ʌndɪ'naɪəbl] *a* unleugbar.

under ['ʌndə*] *prep* unter // *ad* darunter; ~ there da drunter; ~ repair in Reparatur; ~-age *a* minderjährig.

undercarriage ['ʌndəkærɪdʒ] *n* (Brit AVIAT) Fahrgestell *nt*.

undercharge [ʌndə'tʃɑːdʒ] *vt* jdm zu wenig berechnen.

underclothes ['ʌndəkləʊðz] *npl* Unterwäsche *f*.

undercoat ['ʌndəkəʊt] *n* (*paint*) Grundierung *f*.

undercover ['ʌndəkʌvə*] *a* Geheim-.

undercurrent ['ʌndəkʌrənt] *n* Unterströmung *f*.

undercut ['ʌndəkʌt] *vt* (*irreg: like* cut) unterbieten.

underdeveloped ['ʌndədɪ'veləpt] *a* Entwicklungs-, unterentwickelt.

underdog ['ʌndədɒg] *n* Unterlegene(r) *mf*.

underdone ['ʌndə'dʌn] *a* (COOK) nicht gar, nicht durchgebraten.

underestimate ['ʌndər'estɪmeɪt] *vt* unterschätzen.

underexposed ['ʌndərɪks'pəʊzd] *a* unterbelichtet.

underfed ['ʌndə'fed] *a* unterernährt.

underfoot ['ʌndə'fʊt] *ad* am Boden.

undergo ['ʌndə'gəʊ] *vt* (*irreg: like* go) (*experience*) durchmachen; (*operation*, *test*) sich unterziehen (+*dat*).

undergraduate ['ʌndə'grædjʊət] *n* Student(in *f*) *m*.

underground ['ʌndəgraʊnd] *n* U-Bahn *f* // *a* Untergrund-.

undergrowth ['ʌndəgrəʊθ] *n* Gestrüpp *nt*, Unterholz *nt*.

underhand(ed) ['ʌndə'hænd(ɪd)] *a* hinterhältig.

underlie [ʌndə'laɪ] *vt* (*irreg: like* lie) (*form the basis of*) zugrundeliegen (+*dat*).

underline [ʌndə'laɪn] *vt* unterstreichen; (*emphasize*) betonen.

underling ['ʌndəlɪŋ] *n* Handlanger *m*.

undermine [ʌndə'maɪn] *vt* untergraben.

underneath ['ʌndə'niːθ] *ad* darunter // *prep* unter.

underpaid ['ʌndə'peɪd] *a* unterbezahlt.

underpants ['ʌndəpænts] *npl* Unterhose *f*.

underpass ['ʌndəpɑːs] *n* (*Brit*) Unterführung *f*.

underprivileged ['ʌndə'prɪvɪlɪdʒd] *a* benachteiligt, unterprivilegiert.

underrate [ʌndə'reɪt] *vt* unterschätzen.

undershirt ['ʌndəʃɜːt] *n* (*US*) Unterhemd *nt*.

undershorts ['ʌndəʃɔːts] *npl* (*US*) Unterhose *f*.

underside ['ʌndəsaɪd] *n* Unterseite *f*.

underskirt ['ʌndəskɜːt] *n* (*Brit*) Unterrock *m*.

understand [ʌndə'stænd] *vti* (*irreg: like stand*) verstehen; I ~ that ... ich habe gehört, daß ...; am I to ~ that ...? soll das (etwa) heißen, daß ...?; what do you ~ by that? was verstehen Sie darunter?; it is understood that ... es wurde vereinbart, daß ...; to make o.s. understood sich verständlich machen; is that understood? ist das klar?; ~able *a* verständlich; ~ing *n* Verständnis *nt* // *a* verständnisvoll.

understood [ʌndə'stud] *pt, pp of* **understand** // *a* klar; (*implied*) angenommen.

understudy ['ʌndəstʌdɪ] *n* Ersatz-(schau)spieler(in *f*) *m*.

undertake [ʌndə'teɪk] (*irreg: like take*) *vt* unternehmen // *vi* : to ~ to do sth sich verpflichten, etw zu tun.

undertaker ['ʌndəteɪkə*] *n* Leichenbestatter *m*.

undertaking [ʌndə'teɪkɪŋ] *n* (*enterprise*) Unternehmen *nt*; (*promise*) Verpflichtung *f*.

undertone ['ʌndətəʊn] *n*: in an ~ mit gedämpfter Stimme.

underwater ['ʌndə'wɔːtə*] *ad* unter Wasser // *a* Unterwasser-.

underwear ['ʌndəwεə*] *n* Unterwäsche *f*.

underworld ['ʌndəwɜːld] *n* (*of crime*) Unterwelt *f*.

underwriter ['ʌndəraɪtə*] *n* Assekurant *m*.

undesirable [ʌndɪ'zaɪərəbl] *a* unerwünscht.

undies ['ʌndɪz] *npl* (*col*) (Damen)-unterwäsche *f*.

undisputed ['ʌndɪs'pjuːtɪd] *a* unbestritten.

undo ['ʌn'duː] *vt* (*irreg: like* **do**) (*unfasten*) öffnen, aufmachen; (*work*) zunichte machen; ~ing *n* Verderben *nt*.

undoubted [ʌn'daʊtɪd] *a* unbezweifelt; ~ly *ad* zweifellos, ohne Zweifel.

undress ['ʌn'dres] *vti* (sich) ausziehen.

undue ['ʌndjuː] *a* übermäßig.

undulating ['ʌndjʊleɪtɪŋ] *a* wellenförmig; (*country*) wellig.

unduly ['ʌn'djuːlɪ] *ad* übermäßig.

unearth ['ʌn'ɜːθ] *vt* (*dig up*) ausgraben; (*discover*) ans Licht bringen.

unearthly [ʌn'ɜːθlɪ] *a* (*hour*) nachtschlafen.

uneasy [ʌn'iːzɪ] *a* (*worried*) unruhig; (*feeling*) ungut.

uneconomic(al) ['ʌniːkə'nɒmɪk(əl)] *a* unwirtschaftlich.

uneducated ['ʌn'edjʊkeɪtɪd] *a* ungebildet.

unemployed ['ʌnɪm'plɔɪd] *a* arbeitslos; the ~ die Arbeitslosen *pl*.

unemployment ['ʌnɪm'plɔɪmənt] *n* Arbeitslosigkeit *f*.

unending [ʌn'endɪŋ] *a* endlos.

unerring ['ʌn'ɜːrɪŋ] *a* unfehlbar.

uneven ['ʌn'iːvən] *a* (*surface*) uneben; (*quality*) ungleichmäßig.

unexpected *a*, ~ly *ad* [ʌnɪk'spektɪd,-lɪ] unerwartet.

unfailing [ʌn'feɪlɪŋ] *a* nie versagend.

unfair ['ʌn'fεə*] *a* ungerecht, unfair.

unfaithful ['ʌn'feɪθfʊl] *a* untreu.

unfamiliar [ʌnfə'mɪlɪə*] *a* ungewohnt; (*person, subject*) unbekannt.

unfashionable [ʌn'fæʃnəbl] *a* unmodern; (*area, hotel etc*) nicht in Mode.

unfasten ['ʌn'fɑːsn] *vt* öffnen, aufmachen.

unfavourable, (*US*) **unfavorable** ['ʌn'feɪvərəbl] *a* ungünstig.

unfeeling [ʌn'fiːlɪŋ] *a* gefühllos, kalt.

unfinished ['ʌn'fɪnɪʃt] *a* unvollendet.

unfit ['ʌn'fɪt] *a* ungeeignet (*for* zu, für); (*in bad health*) nicht fit.

unfold [ʌn'fəʊld] *vt* entfalten; (*paper*) auseinanderfalten // *vi* (*develop*) sich entfalten.

unforeseen ['ʌnfɔː'siːn] *a* unvorhergesehen.

unforgettable [ʌnfə'getəbl] *a* unvergeßlich.

unforgivable ['ʌnfə'gɪvəbl] *a* unverzeihlich.

unfortunate [ʌn'fɔːtʃnət] *a* unglücklich, bedauerlich; ~ly *ad* leider.

unfounded ['ʌn'faʊndɪd] *a* unbegründet.

unfriendly ['ʌn'frendlɪ] *a* unfreundlich.

ungainly [ʌn'geɪnlɪ] *a* linkisch.

ungodly [ʌn'gɒdlɪ] *a* (*hour*) nachtschlafend; (*row*) heillos.

ungrateful [ʌn'greɪtfʊl] *a* undankbar.

unhappiness [ʌn'hæpɪnəs] *n* Unglück *nt*, Unglückseligkeit *f*.

unhappy [ʌn'hæpɪ] *a* unglücklich; ~ with (*arrangements etc*) unzufrieden mit.

unharmed ['ʌn'hɑːmd] *a* wohlbehalten, unversehrt.

unhealthy [ʌn'helθɪ] *a* ungesund.

unheard-of [ʌnˈhɜːdɒv] a unerhört.
unhook [ʌnˈhʊk] vt (from wall) vom Haken nehmen; (dress) loshaken.
unhurt [ʌnˈhɜːt] a unverletzt.
unidentified [ˈʌnaɪˈdentɪfaɪd] a unbekannt, nicht identifiziert.
uniform [ˈjuːnɪfɔːm] n Uniform f // a einheitlich; **~ity** [juːnɪˈfɔːmɪti] n Einheitlichkeit f.
unify [ˈjuːnɪfaɪ] vt vereinigen.
unilateral [ˈjuːnɪˈlætərəl] a einseitig.
uninhabited [ʌnɪnˈhæbɪtɪd] a unbewohnt.
unintentional [ˈʌnɪnˈtenʃənl] a unabsichtlich.
union [ˈjuːnjən] n (uniting) Vereinigung f; (alliance) Bund m, Union f; (trade ~) Gewerkschaft f; **U~ Jack** n Union Jack m.
unique [juːˈniːk] a einzig(artig).
unison [ˈjuːnɪzn] n Einstimmigkeit f; in ~ einstimmig.
unit [ˈjuːnɪt] n Einheit f; **kitchen ~** Küchenelement nt.
unite [juːˈnaɪt] vt vereinigen // vi sich vereinigen; **~d** a vereinigt; (together) vereint; **U~d Kingdom (U.K.)** n Vereinigtes Königreich; **U~d Nations (Organization) (UN, UNO)** n Vereinte Nationen pl; **U~d States (of America) (US, USA)** n Vereinigte Staaten pl (von Amerika) (US, USA f).
unit trust [ˈjuːnɪtˈtrʌst] n (Brit) Treuhandgesellschaft f.
unity [ˈjuːnɪti] n Einheit f; (agreement) Einigkeit f.
universal [juːnɪˈvɜːsəl] a allgemein.
universe [ˈjuːnɪvɜːs] n (Welt)all nt.
university [juːnɪˈvɜːsɪti] n Universität f.
unjust [ˈʌnˈdʒʌst] a ungerecht.
unkempt [ˈʌnˈkempt] a ungepflegt.
unkind [ʌnˈkaɪnd] a unfreundlich.
unknown [ˈʌnˈnəʊn] a unbekannt (to dat).
unlawful [ʌnˈlɔːfʊl] a illegal.
unleash [ˈʌnˈliːʃ] vt entfesseln.
unless [ənˈles] cj wenn nicht, es sei denn ...; ~ **he comes** es sei denn, er kommt; ~ **otherwise stated** sofern nicht anders angegeben.
unlike [ˈʌnˈlaɪk] a unähnlich // prep im Gegensatz zu.
unlimited [ʌnˈlɪmɪtɪd] a unbegrenzt.
unlisted [ʌnˈlɪstɪd] a (US) nicht im Telefonbuch stehend.
unload [ˈʌnˈləʊd] vt entladen.
unlock [ˈʌnˈlɒk] vt aufschließen.
unlucky [ʌnˈlʌkɪ] a unglücklich; (person) unglückselig; **to be ~** Pech haben.
unmarried [ˈʌnˈmærɪd] a unverheiratet, ledig.
unmask [ˈʌnˈmɑːsk] vt entlarven.
unmistakable [ˈʌnmɪsˈteɪkəbl] a unverkennbar.

unmitigated [ʌnˈmɪtɪgeɪtɪd] a ungemildert, ganz.
unnatural [ʌnˈnætʃrəl] a unnatürlich.
unnecessary [ˈʌnˈnesəsərɪ] a unnötig.
unnoticed [ʌnˈnəʊtɪst] a: **to go ~** unbemerkt bleiben.
UNO [ˈjuːnəʊ] n abbr of **United Nations Organization**.
unobtainable [ˈʌnəbˈteɪnəbl] a: **this number is ~** kein Anschluß unter dieser Nummer.
unobtrusive [ʌnəbˈtruːsɪv] a unauffällig.
unofficial [ʌnəˈfɪʃl] a inoffiziell.
unpack [ˈʌnˈpæk] vti auspacken.
unpalatable [ʌnˈpælətəbl] a (truth) bitter.
unparalleled [ʌnˈpærəleld] a beispiellos.
unpleasant [ʌnˈplezɪnt] a unangenehm.
unplug [ˈʌnˈplʌg] vt den Stecker herausziehen von.
unprecedented [ʌnˈpresɪdəntɪd] a beispiellos.
unpredictable [ʌnprɪˈdɪktəbl] a unvorhersehbar; (weather, person) unberechenbar.
unprofessional [ʌnprəˈfeʃənl] a unprofessionell.
unqualified [ˈʌnˈkwɒlɪfaɪd] a (success) uneingeschränkt, voll; (person) unqualifiziert.
unquestionably [ʌnˈkwestʃənəblɪ] ad fraglos.
unravel [ʌnˈrævəl] vt (disentangle) auffasern, entwirren; (solve) lösen.
unreal [ˈʌnˈrɪəl] a unwirklich.
unrealistic [ʌnrɪəˈlɪstɪk] a unrealistisch.
unreasonable [ʌnˈriːznəbl] a unvernünftig; (demand) übertrieben.
unrelated [ʌnrɪˈleɪtɪd] a ohne Beziehung; (family) nicht verwandt.
unrelenting [ʌnrɪˈlentɪŋ] a unerbittlich.
unreliable [ʌnrɪˈlaɪəbl] a unzuverlässig.
unremitting [ʌnrɪˈmɪtɪŋ] a (efforts, attempts) unermüdlich.
unreservedly [ʌnrɪzɜːˈvɪdlɪ] ad offen; (believe, trust) uneingeschränkt; (cry) rückhaltlos.
unrest [ʌnˈrest] n (discontent) Unruhe f; (fighting) Unruhen pl.
unroll [ˈʌnˈrəʊl] vt aufrollen.
unruly [ʌnˈruːlɪ] a (child) undiszipliniert; schwer lenkbar.
unsafe [ˈʌnˈseɪf] a nicht sicher.
unsaid [ˈʌnˈsed] a: **to leave sth ~** etw ungesagt sein lassen.
unsatisfactory [ˈʌnsætɪsˈfæktərɪ] a unbefriedigend; unzulänglich.
unsavoury, (US) **unsavory** [ˈʌnˈseɪvərɪ] a (fig) widerwärtig.
unscathed [ʌnˈskeɪðd] a unversehrt.
unscrew [ˈʌnˈskruː] vt aufschrauben.
unscrupulous [ʌnˈskruːpjʊləs] a skrupellos.
unsettled [ˈʌnˈsetld] a (person) rastlos;

(weather) wechselhaft.

unshaven [ˈʌnˈʃeɪvn] a unrasiert.

unsightly [ʌnˈsaɪtlɪ] a unansehnlich.

unskilled [ˈʌnˈskɪld] a ungelernt.

unspeakable [ʌnˈspiːkəbl] a *(joy)* unsagbar; *(crime)* scheußlich.

unstable [ʌnˈsteɪbl] a instabil; *(mentally)* labil.

unsteady [ʌnˈstedɪ] a unsicher; *(growth)* unregelmäßig.

unstuck [ˈʌnˈstʌk] a: to come ~ *(lit)* sich lösen; *(fig)* ins Wasser fallen.

unsuccessful [ˈʌnsəkˈsesful] a erfolglos.

unsuitable [ˈʌnˈsuːtəbl] a unpassend.

unsuspecting [ˈʌnsəsˈpektɪŋ] a nichtsahnend.

unsympathetic [ˈʌnsɪmpəˈθetɪk] a gefühllos; *(response)* abweisend; *(unlikeable)* unsympathisch.

untapped [ˈʌnˈtæpt] a *(resources)* ungenützt.

unthinkable [ʌnˈθɪŋkəbl] a unvorstellbar.

untidy [ʌnˈtaɪdɪ] a unordentlich.

untie [ˈʌnˈtaɪ] vt aufschnüren.

until [ənˈtɪl] prep, cj bis; ~ he comes bis er kommt; ~ then bis dann.

untimely [ʌnˈtaɪmlɪ] a *(death)* vorzeitig.

untold [ˈʌnˈtəʊld] a unermeßlich.

untoward [ʌntəˈwɔːd] a widrig.

unused [ˈʌnˈjuːzd] a unbenutzt.

unusual [ʌnˈjuːʒʊəl] a ungewöhnlich.

unveil [ʌnˈveɪl] vt enthüllen.

unwavering [ʌnˈweɪvərɪŋ] a standhaft, unerschütterlich.

unwelcome [ʌnˈwelkəm] a *(at a bad time)* unwillkommen; *(unpleasant)* unerfreulich.

unwell [ˈʌnˈwel] a: to feel or be ~ sich nicht wohl fühlen.

unwieldy [ʌnˈwiːldɪ] a sperrig.

unwilling [ˈʌnˈwɪlɪŋ] a: to be ~ to do sth nicht bereit sein, etw zu tun; ~ly ad widerwillig.

unwind [ˈʌnˈwaɪnd] *(irreg: like wind)* vt *(lit)* abwickeln // vi *(relax)* sich entspannen.

unwise [ʌnˈwaɪz] a unklug.

unwitting [ʌnˈwɪtɪŋ] a unwissentlich.

unworkable [ʌnˈwɜːkəbl] a *(plan)* undurchführbar.

unworthy [ʌnˈwɜːðɪ] a *(person)* nicht wert *(of gen)*.

unwrap [ˈʌnˈræp] vt auspacken.

unwritten [ˈʌnˈrɪtn] a ungeschrieben.

up [ʌp] ♦ prep: to be ~ sth oben auf etw *(dat)* sein; to go ~ sth etw *(acc)* hinauf gehen; go ~ that road gehen Sie die Straße hinauf

♦ ad 1 *(upwards, higher)* oben; put it a bit higher ~ stell es etwas weiter nach oben; ~ there da oben, dort oben; ~ above hoch oben

2: to be ~ *(out of bed)* auf; *(prices, level)* gestiegen; *(building, tent)* stehen

3: ~ to *(as far as)* bis; ~ to now bis jetzt

4: to be ~ to *(depending on)*: it's ~ to you das hängt von dir ab; it's not ~ to me to decide die Entscheidung liegt nicht bei mir; *(equal to)*: he's not ~ to it *(job, task etc)* er ist dem nicht gewachsen; his work is not ~ to the required standard seine Arbeit entspricht nicht dem geforderten Niveau; *(col: be doing)*: what is he ~ to? *(showing disapproval, suspicion)* was führt er im Schilde?

♦ ~s and downs npl *(in life, career)* Höhen und Tiefen pl.

upbringing [ˈʌpbrɪŋɪŋ] n Erziehung f.

update [ʌpˈdeɪt] vt auf den neuesten Stand bringen.

upgrade [ʌpˈgreɪd] vt höher einstufen.

upheaval [ʌpˈhiːvəl] n Umbruch m.

uphill [ˈʌpˈhɪl] a ansteigend; *(fig)* mühsam // ad: to go ~ bergauf gehen/fahren.

uphold [ʌpˈhəʊld] vt *(irreg: like hold)* unterstützen.

upholstery [ʌpˈhəʊlstərɪ] n Polster nt; Polsterung f.

upkeep [ˈʌpkiːp] n Instandhaltung f.

upon [əˈpɒn] prep auf.

upper [ˈʌpə*] n *(on shoe)* Oberleder nt // a obere(r, s), höhere(r, s); to have the ~ hand die Oberhand haben; ~-class a vornehm; ~most a oberste(r, s), höchste(r, s); what was ~most in my mind was mich in erster Linie beschäftigte.

upright [ˈʌpraɪt] a aufrecht.

uprising [ˈʌpˈraɪzɪŋ] n Aufstand m.

uproar [ˈʌprɔː*] n Aufruhr m.

uproot [ʌpˈruːt] vt ausreißen.

upset [ˈʌpset] n Aufregung f // vt [ʌpˈset] *(irreg: like set)* *(overturn)* umwerfen; *(disturb)* aufregen, bestürzen; *(plans)* durcheinanderbringen // a [ʌpˈset] *(person)* aufgeregt; *(stomach)* verdorben.

upshot [ˈʌpʃɒt] n *(End)*ergebnis nt.

upside-down [ˈʌpsaɪdˈdaʊn] ad verkehrt herum; *(fig)* drunter und drüber.

upstairs [ˈʌpˈsteəz] ad oben; *(go)* nach oben // a *(room)* obere(r, s), Ober- // n obere(s) Stockwerk nt.

upstart [ˈʌpstaːt] n Emporkömmling m.

upstream [ˈʌpˈstriːm] ad stromaufwärts.

uptake [ˈʌpteɪk] n: to be quick on the ~ schnell begreifen; to be slow on the ~ schwer von Begriff sein.

uptight [ˈʌpˈtaɪt] a *(col: nervous)* nervös; *(: inhibited)* verklemmt.

up-to-date [ˈʌptəˈdeɪt] a *(clothes)* modisch, modern; *(information)* neueste(r, s); to bring sth up to date etw auf den neuesten Stand bringen.

upturn [ˈʌptɜːn] n Aufschwung m.

upward [ˈʌpwəd] a nach oben gerichtet; ~(s) ad aufwärts.

uranium [juəˈreɪnɪəm] n Uran nt.

urban ['ɜːbən] a städtisch, Stadt-.

urbane [ɜːˈbeɪn] a höflich.

urchin ['ɜːtʃɪn] n (boy) Schlingel m; (sea ~) Seeigel m.

urge [ɜːdʒ] n Drang m // vt: to ~ sb to do sth jdn (dazu) drängen, etw zu tun.

urgency ['ɜːdʒənsɪ] n Dringlichkeit f.

urgent ['ɜːdʒənt] a dringend.

urinal ['jʊərɪnl] n (MED) Urinflasche f; (public) Pissoir nt.

urinate ['jʊərɪneɪt] vi urinieren.

urine ['jʊərɪn] n Urin m, Harn m.

urn [ɜːn] n Urne f; (tea ~) Teemaschine f.

us [ʌs] pron uns; see also **me.**

US, USA n abbr of **United States (of America).**

usage ['juːzɪdʒ] n Gebrauch m; (esp LING) Sprachgebrauch m.

use [juːs] n (employment) Gebrauch m; (point) Zweck m // vt [juːz] gebrauchen; in ~ in Gebrauch; out of ~ außer Gebrauch; to be of ~ nützlich sein; it's no ~ es hat keinen Zweck; what's the ~? was soll's?; ~d to [juːst] gewöhnt an (+acc); she ~d to live here sie hat früher mal hier gewohnt; ~ up [juːz] vt aufbrauchen, verbrauchen; ~d [juːzd] a (car) Gebraucht-; ~ful a nützlich; ~fulness n Nützlichkeit f; ~less a nutzlos, unnütz; ~r ['juːzə*] n Benutzer m; ~r-friendly a (computer) benutzerfreundlich.

usher ['ʌʃə*] n Platzanweiser m; ~ette [ʌʃəˈret] n Platzanweiserin f.

USSR n: the ~ die UdSSR.

usual ['juːʒʊəl] a gewöhnlich, üblich; as ~ wie üblich; ~ly ad gewöhnlich.

usurp [juːˈzɜːp] vt an sich reißen.

utensil [juːˈtensl] n Gerät nt; kitchen ~s Küchengeräte pl.

utilitarian [juːtɪlɪˈtɛərɪən] a Nützlichkeits-.

utility [juːˈtɪlɪtɪ] n (usefulness) Nützlichkeit f; (also public ~) öffentliche(r) Versorgungsbetrieb m; ~ room n Hauswirtschaftsraum m.

utilize ['juːtɪlaɪz] vt benützen.

utmost ['ʌtməʊst] a äußerste(r, s) // n: to do one's ~ sein möglichstes tun.

utter ['ʌtə*] a äußerste(r, s) höchste(r, s), völlig // vt äußern, aussprechen; ~ance n Äußerung f; ~ly ad äußerst, absolut, völlig.

U-turn ['juːˈtɜːn] n (AUT) Kehrtwendung f.

V

v. abbr of **verse; versus; volt; vide.**

vacancy ['veɪkənsɪ] n (Brit: job) offene Stelle f; (room) freies Zimmer nt.

vacant ['veɪkənt] a leer; (unoccupied) frei; (house) leerstehend, unbewohnt;

(stupid) (gedanken)leer; ~ lot n (US) unbebaute(s) Grundstück nt.

vacate [vəˈkeɪt] vt (seat) frei machen; (room) räumen.

vacation [vəˈkeɪʃən] n Ferien pl, Urlaub m; ~ist n (US) Ferienreisende(r) mf.

vaccinate ['væksɪneɪt] vt impfen.

vaccine ['væksiːn] n Impfstoff m.

vacuum ['vækjʊm] n Vakuum nt; ~ bottle (US), ~ flask (Brit) n Thermosflasche f; ~ cleaner n Staubsauger m; ~-packed a vakuumversiegelt.

vagina [vəˈdʒaɪnə] n Scheide f.

vagrant ['veɪɡrənt] n Landstreicher m.

vague [veɪɡ] a vage; (absent-minded) geistesabwesend; ~ly ad unbestimmt, vage.

vain [veɪn] a eitel; (attempt) vergeblich; in ~ vergebens, umsonst.

valentine ['væləntaɪn] n (also: ~ card) Valentinsgruß m.

valet ['væleɪ] n Kammerdiener m.

valiant a, ~ly ad ['væliənt, -lɪ] tapfer.

valid ['vælɪd] a gültig; (argument) stichhaltig; (objection) berechtigt; ~ity [vəˈlɪdɪtɪ] n Gültigkeit f.

valley ['vælɪ] n Tal nt.

valour, (US) **valor** ['vælə*] n Tapferkeit f.

valuable ['væljʊəbl] a wertvoll; (time) kostbar; ~s npl Wertsachen pl.

valuation [væljʊˈeɪʃən] n (FIN) Schätzung f; Beurteilung f.

value ['væljuː] n Wert m; (usefulness) Nutzen m // vt (prize) (hoch)schätzen, werthalten; (estimate) schätzen; ~ added tax (VAT) n (Brit) Mehrwertsteuer f (MwSt); ~d a (hoch)geschätzt.

valve [vælv] n Ventil nt; (BIOL) Klappe f; (RAD) Röhre f.

van [væn] n Lieferwagen m (Brit: RAIL) Waggon m.

vandalize ['vændəlaɪz] vt mutwillig beschädigen.

vanguard ['væŋɡɑːd] n (fig) Spitze f.

vanilla [vəˈnɪlə] n Vanille f.

vanish ['vænɪʃ] vi verschwinden.

vanity ['vænɪtɪ] n Eitelkeit f; ~ case n Schminkkoffer m.

vantage ['vɑːntɪdʒ] n: ~ point gute(r) Aussichtspunkt m.

vapour, (US) **vapor** ['veɪpə*] n (mist) Dunst m; (gas) Dampf m.

variable ['vɛərɪəbl] a wechselhaft, veränderlich; (speed, height) regulierbar.

variance ['vɛərɪəns] n: to be at ~ (with) nicht übereinstimmen (mit).

variation [vɛərɪˈeɪʃən] n Variation f; (of temperature, prices) Schwankung f.

varicose ['værɪkəʊs] a: ~ veins npl Krampfadern pl.

varied ['vɛərɪd] a unterschiedlich; (life) abwechslungsreich.

variety [vəˈraɪətɪ] n (difference)

Abwechslung *f;* *(varied collection)* Vielfalt *f;* *(COMM)* Auswahl *f;* *(sort)* Sorte *f,* Art *f;* ~ **show** *n* Varieté *nt.*

various ['vɛərɪəs] *a* verschieden; *(several)* mehrere.

varnish ['vɑːnɪʃ] *n* Lack *m;* *(on pottery)* Glasur *f* // *vt* lackieren.

vary ['vɛərɪ] *vt* *(alter)* verändern; *(give variety to)* abwechslungsreicher gestalten // *vi* sich (ver)ändern; *(prices)* schwanken; *(weather)* unterschiedlich sein.

vase [vɑːz] *n* Vase *f.*

Vaseline ['væsɪliːn] *n* ® Vaseline *f.*

vast [vɑːst] *a* weit, groß, riesig.

VAT [væt] *n abbr of* **Value Added Tax.**

vat [væt] *n* große(s) Faß *nt.*

vault [vɔːlt] *n* *(of roof)* Gewölbe *nt;* *(tomb)* Gruft *f;* *(in bank)* Tresorraum *m;* *(leap)* Sprung *m* // *vt* *(also:* ~ **over)** überspringen.

vaunted ['vɔːntɪd] *a:* **much-~** vielgerühmt.

VCR *n abbr of* **video cassette recorder.**

VD *n abbr of* **venereal disease.**

VDU *n abbr of* **visual display unit.**

veal [viːl] *n* Kalbfleisch *nt.*

veer [vɪə*] *vi* sich drehen; *(of car)* ausscheren.

vegetable ['vedʒətəbl] *n* Gemüse *nt* // *a* Gemüse-; ~**s** *pl* Gemüse *nt.*

vegetarian [vedʒɪˈtɛərɪən] *n* Vegetarier(in *f*) *m* // *a* vegetarisch.

vegetate ['vedʒɪteɪt] *vi* (dahin)vegetieren.

vehemence ['viːɪməns] *n* Heftigkeit *f.*

vehement ['viːɪmənt] *a* heftig.

vehicle ['viːɪkl] *n* Fahrzeug *nt;* *(fig)* Mittel *nt.*

veil [veɪl] *n* *(lit, fig)* Schleier *m* // *vt* verschleiern.

vein [veɪn] *n* Ader *f;* *(mood)* Stimmung *f.*

velocity [vɪˈlɒsɪtɪ] *n* Geschwindigkeit *f.*

velvet ['velvɪt] *n* Samt *m* // *a* Samt-.

vendetta [venˈdetə] *n* Fehde *f;* *(in family)* Blutrache *f.*

vending machine ['vendɪŋməʃiːn] *n* Automat *m.*

vendor ['vendɔː*] *n* Verkäufer *m.*

veneer [vəˈnɪə*] *n* *(lit)* Furnier(holz) *nt;* *(fig)* äußere(r) Anstrich *m.*

venereal [vɪˈnɪərɪəl] *a:* ~ **disease (VD)** Geschlechtskrankheit *f.*

Venetian blind [vɪˈniːʃən-] *n* Jalousie *f.*

vengeance ['vendʒəns] *n* Rache *f;* **with a** ~ gewaltig.

venison ['venɪsn] *n* Reh(fleisch) *nt.*

venom ['venəm] *n* Gift *nt.*

vent [vent] *n* Öffnung *f;* *(in coat)* Schlitz *m;* *(fig)* Ventil *nt* // *vt* *(emotion)* abreagieren.

ventilate ['ventɪleɪt] *vt* belüften.

ventilator ['ventɪleɪtə*] *n* Ventilator *m.*

ventriloquist [venˈtrɪləkwɪst] *n* Bauchredner *m.*

venture ['ventʃə*] *n* Unternehmung *f,* Projekt *nt* // *vt* wagen; *(life)* aufs Spiel setzen // *vi* sich wagen.

venue ['venjuː] *n* Schauplatz *m.*

verb [vɜːb] *n* Zeitwort *nt,* Verb *nt;* ~**al** *a* *(spoken)* mündlich; *(translation)* wörtlich; *(of a verb)* verbal, Verbal-; ~**ally** *ad* mündlich; *(as a verb)* verbal.

verbatim [vɜːˈbeɪtɪm] *ad* Wort für Wort // *a* wortwörtlich.

verbose [vɜːˈbəʊs] *a* wortreich.

verdict ['vɜːdɪkt] *n* Urteil *nt.*

verge [vɜːdʒ] *n* *(Brit)* Rand *m;* 'soft ~s' *(Brit AUT)* 'Seitenstreifen nicht befahrbar'; **on the** ~ **of doing sth im Begriff, etw zu tun //** *vi:* ~ **on** grenzen an *(+acc).*

verify ['verɪfaɪ] *vt* (über)prüfen; *(confirm)* bestätigen; *(theory)* beweisen.

veritable ['verɪtəbl] *a* wirklich, echt.

vermin ['vɜːmɪn] *npl* Ungeziefer *nt.*

vermouth ['vɜːməθ] *n* Wermut *m.*

vernacular [vəˈnækjʊlə*] *n* Landessprache *f.*

versatile ['vɜːsətaɪl] *a* vielseitig.

versatility [vɜːsəˈtɪlɪtɪ] *n* Vielseitigkeit *f.*

verse [vɜːs] *n* *(poetry)* Poesie *f;* *(stanza)* Strophe *f;* *(of Bible)* Vers *m;* **in** ~ in Versform.

versed [vɜːst] *a:* **(well-)~ in** bewandert in *(+dat),* beschlagen in *(+dat).*

version ['vɜːʃən] *n* Version *f;* *(of car)* Modell *nt.*

versus ['vɜːsəs] *prep* gegen.

vertebra ['vɜːtɪbrə] *n, pl* ~**e** [-briː] (Rücken)wirbel *m.*

vertebrate ['vɜːtɪbrət] *a* *(animal)* Wirbel-.

vertical ['vɜːtɪkəl] *a* senkrecht.

vertigo ['vɜːtɪɡəʊ] *n* Schwindel *m.*

verve [vɜːv] *n* Schwung *m.*

very ['verɪ] *ad* sehr // *a* *(extreme)* äußerste(r, s); **the** ~ **book which** genau das Buch, welches; **the** ~ **last** die/das allerletzte; **at the** ~ **least** allerwenigstens; ~ **much** sehr.

vessel ['vesl] *n* *(ship)* Schiff *nt;* *(container)* Gefäß *nt.*

vest [vest] *n* *(Brit)* Unterhemd *nt;* *(US: waistcoat)* Weste *f;* ~**ed interests** *npl* finanzielle Beteiligung *f;* *(people)* finanziell Beteiligte *pl;* *(fig)* persönliche(s) Interesse *nt.*

vestige ['vestɪdʒ] *n* Spur *f.*

vestry ['vestrɪ] *n* Sakristei *f.*

vet [vet] *n abbr* (= *veterinary surgeon*) Tierarzt *m*/-ärztin *f* // *vt* überprüfen.

veterinary ['vetrɪnərɪ] *a* Veterinär-; ~ **surgeon,** *(US)* **veterinarian** *n* Tierarzt *m*/-ärztin *f.*

veto ['viːtəʊ] *n, pl* ~**es** Veto *nt* // *vt* sein Veto einlegen gegen.

vex [veks] *vt* ärgern; ~**ed** *a* verärgert;

~ed question umstrittene Frage *f*.

VHF *abbr* (= *very high frequency*) UKW *f*.

via ['vaɪə] *prep* über (+*acc*).

viable ['vaɪəbl] *a* (*plan*) durchführbar; (*company*) rentabel.

vibrant ['vaɪbrənt] *a* (*lively*) lebhaft; (*bright*) leuchtend; (*full of emotion*: *voice*) bebend.

vibrate [vaɪ'breɪt] *vi* zittern, beben; (*machine, string*) vibrieren.

vibration [vaɪ'breɪʃən] *n* Schwingung *f*; (*of machine*) Vibrieren *nt*.

vicar ['vɪkə*] *n* Pfarrer *m*; ~**age** *n* Pfarrhaus *nt*.

vicarious [vɪ'kɛərɪəs] *a* nachempfunden.

vice [vaɪs] *n* (*evil*) Laster *nt*; (*TECH*) Schraubstock *m* // *pref*: ~-**chairman** *n* stellvertretende(r) Vorsitzende(r) *m*; ~-**president** *n* Vizepräsident *m*.

vice squad *n* ≈ Sittenpolizei *f*.

vice versa ['vaɪsɪ'vɜːsə] *ad* umgekehrt.

vicinity [vɪ'sɪnɪtɪ] *n* Umgebung *f*; (*closeness*) Nähe *f*.

vicious ['vɪʃəs] *a* gemein, böse; ~ **circle** *n* Teufelskreis *m*.

victim ['vɪktɪm] *n* Opfer *nt*; ~**ize** *vt* benachteiligen.

victor ['vɪktə*] *n* Sieger *m*.

Victorian [vɪk'tɔːrɪən] *a* viktorianisch; (*fig*) (sitten)streng.

victorious [vɪk'tɔːrɪəs] *a* siegreich.

victory ['vɪktərɪ] *n* Sieg *m*.

video ['vɪdɪəʊ] *a* Fernseh-, Bild- // *n* (~ *film*) Video *nt*; (*also*: ~ **cassette**) Videocassette *f*; (*also*: ~ **cassette recorder**) Videorekorder *m*; ~ **tape** *n* Videoband *nt*.

vie [vaɪ] *vi* wetteifern.

Vienna [vɪ'enə] *n* Wien *nt*.

view [vjuː] *n* (*sight*) Sicht *f*, Blick *m*; (*scene*) Aussicht *f*; (*opinion*) Ansicht *f*; (*intention*) Absicht *f* // *vt* (*situation*) betrachten; (*house*) besichtigen; **to have sth in** ~ etw beabsichtigen; **on** ~ ausgestellt; **in** ~ **of** wegen (+*gen*), angesichts (+*gen*); ~**er** *n* (*viewfinder*) Sucher *m*; (*Phot: small projector*) Gucki *m*; (*TV*) Fernsehzuschauer(in *f*) *m*; ~**finder** *n* Sucher *m*; ~**point** *n* Standpunkt *m*.

vigil ['vɪdʒɪl] *n* (Nacht)wache *f*; ~**ance** *n* Wachsamkeit *f*; ~**ant** *a* wachsam.

vigorous *a*, ~**ly** *ad* ['vɪgərəs, -lɪ] kräftig; (*protest*) energisch, heftig.

vigour, (*US*) **vigor** ['vɪgə*] *n* Vitalität *f*; (*of protest*) Heftigkeit *f*.

vile [vaɪl] *a* (*mean*) gemein; (*foul*) abscheulich.

vilify ['vɪlɪfaɪ] *vt* verleumden.

villa ['vɪlə] *n* Villa *f*.

village ['vɪlɪdʒ] *n* Dorf *nt*; ~**r** *n* Dorfbewohner(in *f*) *m*.

villain ['vɪlən] *n* Schurke *m*.

vindicate ['vɪndɪkeɪt] *vt* rechtfertigen.

vindictive [vɪn'dɪktɪv] *a* nachtragend, rachsüchtig.

vine [vaɪn] *n* Rebstock *m*, Rebe *f*.

vinegar ['vɪnɪgə*] *n* Essig *m*.

vineyard ['vɪnjəd] *n* Weinberg *m*.

vintage ['vɪntɪdʒ] *n* (*of wine*) Jahrgang *m*; ~ **wine** *n* edle(r) Wein *m*.

viola [vɪ'əʊlə] *n* Bratsche *f*.

violate ['vaɪəleɪt] *vt* (*law*) übertreten; (*rights, rule, neutrality*) verletzen; (*sanctity, woman*) schänden.

violation [vaɪə'leɪʃən] *n* Verletzung *f*; Übertretung *f*.

violence ['vaɪələns] *n* (*force*) Heftigkeit *f*; (*brutality*) Gewalttätigkeit *f*.

violent *a*, ~**ly** *ad* ['vaɪələnt, -lɪ] (*strong*) heftig; (*brutal*) gewalttätig, brutal; (*contrast*) kraß; (*death*) gewaltsam.

violet ['vaɪələt] *n* Veilchen *nt* // *a* veilchenblau, violett.

violin [vaɪə'lɪn] *n* Geige *f*, Violine *f*; ~**ist** *n* Geiger(in *f*) *m*.

VIP *n abbr* (= *very important person*) VIP *m*.

virgin ['vɜːdʒɪn] *n* Jungfrau *f* // *a* jungfräulich, unberührt; **the Blessed V~** die heilige Jungfrau Maria; ~**ity** [vɜː'dʒɪnɪtɪ] *n* Unschuld *f*.

Virgo ['vɜːgəʊ] *n* Jungfrau *f*.

virile ['vɪraɪl] *a* männlich.

virility [vɪ'rɪlɪtɪ] *n* Männlichkeit *f*.

virtually ['vɜːtjʊəlɪ] *ad* praktisch, fast.

virtue ['vɜːtjuː] *n* (*moral goodness*) Tugend *f*; (*good quality*) Vorteil *m*, Vorzug *m*; **by** ~ **of** aufgrund (+*gen*).

virtuous ['vɜːtjʊəs] *a* tugendhaft.

virulent ['vɪrjʊlənt] *a* (*poisonous*) bösartig; (*bitter*) scharf, geharnischt.

virus ['vaɪərəs] *n* Virus *m*.

visa ['viːzə] *n* Visum *nt*.

vis-à-vis ['viːzəviː] *prep* gegenüber.

viscous ['vɪskəs] *a* zähflüssig.

visibility [vɪzɪ'bɪlɪtɪ] *n* (*MET*) Sicht(weite) *f*.

visible ['vɪzəbl] *a* sichtbar.

visibly ['vɪzəblɪ] *ad* sichtlich.

vision ['vɪʒən] *n* (*ability*) Sehvermögen *nt*; (*foresight*) Weitblick *m*; (*in dream, image*) Vision *f*.

visit ['vɪzɪt] *n* Besuch *m* // *vt* besuchen; (*town, country*) fahren nach; ~**ing** *a* (*professor*) Gast-; ~**ing card** *n* Visitenkarte *f*; ~**ing hours** *npl* (*in hospital etc*) Besuchszeiten *pl*; ~**or** *n* (*in house*) Besucher(in *f*) *m*; (*in hotel*) Gast *m*; ~**or's book** *n* Gästebuch *nt*.

visor ['vaɪzə*] *n* Visier *nt*; (*on cap*) Schirm *m*; (*AUT*) Blende *f*.

vista ['vɪstə] *n* Aussicht *f*.

visual ['vɪzjʊəl] *a* Seh-, visuell; ~ **aid** *n* Anschauungsmaterial *nt*; ~ **display unit** (**VDU**) *n* Bildschirm(gerät *nt*) *m*; ~**ize** *vt* sich (*dat*) vorstellen.

vital ['vaɪtl] *a* (*important*) unerläßlich; (*necessary for life*) Lebens-, lebenswichtig; (*lively*) vital; ~**ity**

[vaɪˈtælɪtɪ] n Vitalität f; ~ly ad: ~ly
important äußerst wichtig; ~ statistics
npl (fig) Maße pl.
vitamin ['vɪtəmɪn] n Vitamin nt.
vivacious [vɪˈveɪʃəs] a lebhaft.
vivid a, ~ly ad ['vɪvɪd, -lɪ] (graphic)
lebendig; (memory) lebhaft; (bright)
leuchtend.
V-neck ['viːˈnek] n V-Ausschnitt m.
vocabulary [vəʊˈkæbjʊlərɪ] n Wort-
schatz m, Vokabular nt.
vocal ['vəʊkəl] a Vokal-, Gesang-; (fig)
lautstark; ~ cords npl Stimmbänder pl.
vocation [vəʊˈkeɪʃən] n (calling) Berufung f; ~al a Berufs-.
vociferous a, ~ly ad [vəʊˈsɪfərəs, -lɪ]
lautstark.
vodka ['vɒdkə] n Wodka m.
vogue [vəʊg] n Mode f.
voice [vɔɪs] n (lit) Stimme f; (fig) Mitspracherecht nt // vt äußern.
void [vɔɪd] n Leere f // a (invalid)
nichtig, ungültig; (empty): ~ of ohne,
bar (+ gen); see null.
volatile ['vɒlətaɪl] a (gas) flüchtig;
(person) impulsiv; (situation) brisant.
volcano [vɒlˈkeɪnəʊ] n Vulkan m.
volition [vəˈlɪʃən] n Wille m; of one's
own ~ aus freiem Willen.
volley ['vɒlɪ] n (of guns) Salve f; (of
stones) Hagel m; (of words) Schwall m;
(tennis) Flugball m; ~ball n Volleyball
m.
volt [vəʊlt] n Volt nt; ~age n
(Volt)spannung f.
voluble ['vɒljʊbl] a redselig.
volume ['vɒljuːm] n (book) Band m;
(size) Umfang m; (space) Rauminhalt
m; (of sound) Lautstärke f.
voluminous [vəˈluːmɪnəs] a üppig;
(clothes) wallend; (correspondence,
notes) umfangreich.
voluntary a, **voluntarily** ad ['vɒləntərɪ,
-lɪ] freiwillig.
volunteer [vɒlənˈtɪə*] n Freiwillige(r)
mf // vi sich freiwillig melden; to ~ to do
sth sich anbieten, etw zu tun.
voluptuous [vəˈlʌptjʊəs] a sinnlich.
vomit ['vɒmɪt] n Erbrochene(s) nt // vt
spucken // vi sich übergeben.
vote [vəʊt] n Stimme f; (ballot) Abstimmung f; (result) Abstimmungs-
ergebnis nt; (right to vote) Wahlrecht nt
// vti wählen; ~ of thanks n
Dankesworte pl; ~r n Wähler(in f) m.
voting ['vəʊtɪŋ] n Wahl f.
vouch [vaʊtʃ]: ~ for vi bürgen für.
voucher ['vaʊtʃə*] n Gutschein m.
vow [vaʊ] n Versprechen nt; (REL)
Gelübde nt // vt geloben.
vowel ['vaʊəl] n Vokal m.
voyage ['vɔɪɪdʒ] n Reise f.
vulgar ['vʌlgə*] a (rude) vulgär; (of
common people) allgemein, Volks-; ~ity
[vʌlˈgærɪtɪ] n Vulgarität f.

vulnerable ['vʌlnərəbl] a (easily
injured) verwundbar; (sensitive) verletz-
lich.
vulture ['vʌltʃə*] n Geier m.

W

wad [wɒd] n (bundle) Bündel nt; (of
paper) Stoß m; (of money) Packen m.
waddle ['wɒdl] vi watscheln.
wade [weɪd] vi: to ~ through waten
durch.
wafer ['weɪfə*] n Waffel f; (ECCL) Hostie f; (COMPUT) Wafer f.
waffle ['wɒfl] n Waffel f; (col: empty
talk) Geschwafel nt // vi (col) schwafeln.
waft [wɑːft] vti wehen.
wag [wæg] vt (tail) wedeln mit // vi
(tail) wedeln.
wage [weɪdʒ] n (also: ~s) (Arbeits)lohn
m // vt: to ~ war Krieg führen; ~ earner n Lohnempfänger(in f) m; ~ packet
n Lohntüte f.
wager ['weɪdʒə*] n Wette f // vti wetten.
waggle ['wægl] vt (tail) wedeln mit // vi
wedeln.
wag(g)on ['wægən] n (horse-drawn)
Fuhrwerk nt; (US AUT) Wagen m; (Brit
RAIL) Waggon m.
wail [weɪl] n Wehgeschrei nt // vi weh-
klagen, jammern.
waist [weɪst] n Taille f; ~coat n (Brit)
Weste f; ~line n Taille f.
wait [weɪt] n Wartezeit f // vi warten; lie
in ~ for sb jdm auflauern; I can't ~ to
see him ich kann's kaum erwarten, ihn
zu sehen; no ~ing (Brit AUT)
Halteverbot nt; ~ behind vi zurückbleiben; ~ for vt warten auf (+acc); ~
on vt bedienen; ~er n Kellner m; (as
address) Herr Ober m; ~ing list n Warte-
liste f; ~ing room n (MED) War-
tezimmer nt; (RAIL) Wartesaal m;
~ress n Kellnerin f; (as address)
Fräulein nt.
waive [weɪv] vt verzichten auf (+acc).
wake [weɪk] v (pt woke or waked, pp
woken or waked) vt wecken // vi
(also: ~ up) aufwachen; to ~ up to (fig)
sich bewußt werden (+gen) // n (NAUT)
Kielwasser nt; (for dead) Totenwache f.
waken ['weɪkən] vt aufwecken.
Wales [weɪlz] n Wales nt.
walk [wɔːk] n Spaziergang m; (way of
walking) Gang m; (route) Weg m // vi
gehen; (stroll) spazierengehen; (longer)
wandern; ~s of life Sphären pl; a 10-
minute ~ 10 Minuten zu Fuß; to ~ out on
sb (col) jdn sitzenlassen; ~er n
Spaziergänger m; (hiker) Wanderer m;
~ie-talkie n tragbare(s) Sprechfunk-
gerät nt; ~ing n Gehen nt; (hiking)
Wandern nt // a Wander-; ~ing shoes
npl Wanderschuhe pl; ~ing stick n

Spazierstock *m*; **~out** *n* Streik *m*;
~over *n* (*col*) leichte(r) Sieg *m*; **~**
way *n* Fußweg *m*.
wall [wɔːl] *n* (*inside*) Wand *f*; (*outside*)
Mauer *f*; **~ed** *a* von Mauern umgeben.
wallet [ˈwɔlɪt] *n* Brieftasche *f*.
wallflower [ˈwɔːlflauə*] *n* Goldlack *m*;
to be a ~ (*fig*) ein Mauerblümchen sein.
wallop [ˈwɔləp] *vt* (*col*) schlagen, verprügeln.
wallow [ˈwɔləu] *vi* sich wälzen.
wallpaper [ˈwɔːlpeɪpə*] *n* Tapete *f*.
wally [ˈwɔlɪ] *n* (*col*) Idiot *m*.
walnut [ˈwɔːlnʌt] *n* Walnuß *f*.
waltz [wɔːlts] *n* Walzer *m* // *vi* Walzer
tanzen.
wan [wɔn] *a* bleich.
wand [wɔnd] *n* (*also*: **magic ~**) Zauber-
stab *m*.
wander [ˈwɔndə*] *vi* (*roam*) (herum)wandern; (*fig*) abschweifen.
wane [weɪn] *vi* abnehmen; (*fig*)
schwinden.
wangle [ˈwæŋgl] *vt* (*Brit col*): to ~ sth
etw richtig hindreisen.
want [wɔnt] *n* (*lack*) Mangel *m* (*of* an
+*dat*); **for ~ of** aus Mangel an (+*dat*);
mangels (+*gen*); **~s** *pl* (*needs*)
Bedürfnisse *pl* // *vt* (*need*) brauchen;
(*desire*) wollen; (*lack*) nicht haben; to ~
to do sth etw tun wollen; to ~ sb to do
sth wollen, daß jd etw tut; **~ing** *a*: to be
found ~ing sich als unzulänglich
erweisen.
wanton [ˈwɔntən] *a* mutwillig, zügellos.
war [wɔː*] *n* Krieg *m*; **to make ~** Krieg
führen.
ward [wɔːd] *n* (*in hospital*) Station *f*;
(*child*) Mündel *nt*; (*of city*) Bezirk *m*; **~**
off *vt* abwenden, abwehren.
warden [ˈwɔːdən] *n* (*guard*) Wächter *m*,
Aufseher *m*; (*Brit: in youth hostel*) Herbergsvater *m*; (*UNIV*) Heimleiter *m*;
(*Brit: also*: **traffic ~**) ≃ Verkehrspolizist
m, Politesse *f*.
warder [ˈwɔːdə*] *n* (*Brit*) Gefängniswärter *m*.
wardrobe [ˈwɔːdrəub] *n* Kleiderschrank
m; (*clothes*) Garderobe *f*.
warehouse [ˈwɛəhaus] *n* Lagerhaus *nt*.
wares [wɛəz] *npl* Ware *f*.
warfare [ˈwɔːfɛə*] *n* Krieg *m*;
Kriegsführung *f*.
warhead [ˈwɔːhed] *n* Sprengkopf *m*.
warily [ˈwɛərɪlɪ] *ad* vorsichtig.
warlike [ˈwɔːlaɪk] *a* kriegerisch.
warm [wɔːm] *a* warm; (*welcome*) herzlich; **I'm ~** mir ist warm // *vti* wärmen;
~ up *vt* aufwärmen // *vi* warm werden;
~-hearted *a* warmherzig; **~ly** *ad*
warm; herzlich; **warmth** *n* Wärme *f*;
Herzlichkeit *f*.
warn [wɔːn] *vt* warnen (*of, against* vor
+*dat*); **~ing** *n* Warnung *f*; **without ~ing**
unerwartet; **~ing light** *n* Warnlicht *nt*;

~ing triangle *n* (*AUT*) Warndreieck *nt*.
warp [wɔːp] *vt* verziehen; **~ed** *a* (*lit*)
wellig; (*fig*) pervers.
warrant [ˈwɔrənt] *n* Haftbefehl *m*.
warranty [ˈwɔrəntɪ] *n* Garantie *f*.
warren [ˈwɔrən] *n* Labyrinth *nt*.
warrior [ˈwɔrɪə*] *n* Krieger *m*.
Warsaw [ˈwɔːsɔː] *n* Warschau *nt*.
warship [ˈwɔːʃɪp] *n* Kriegsschiff *nt*.
wart [wɔːt] *n* Warze *f*.
wartime [ˈwɔːtaɪm] *n* Krieg *m*.
wary [ˈwɛərɪ] *a* mißtrauisch.
was [wɔz, wəz] *pt* of **be**.
wash [wɔʃ] *n* Wäsche *f* // *vt* waschen;
(*dishes*) abwaschen // *vi* sich waschen;
(*do washing*) waschen; **to have a ~** sich
waschen; **~ away** *vt* abwaschen,
wegspülen; **~ off** *vt* abwaschen; **~ up**
vi (*Brit*) spülen; (*US*) sich waschen;
~able *a* waschbar; **~basin**, (*US*) **~**
bowl *n* Waschbecken *nt*; **~ cloth** *n*
(*US: face cloth*) Waschlappen *m*; **~er** *n*
(*TECH*) Dichtungsring *m*; (*machine*)
Waschmaschine *f*; **~ing** *n* Wäsche *f*;
~ing machine *n* Waschmaschine *f*;
~ing powder *n* (*Brit*) Waschpulver *nt*;
~ing-up *n* Abwasch *m*; **~ing-up liquid**
n Spülmittel *nt*; **~out** *n* (*col: event*)
Reinfall *m*; (: *person*) Niete *f*; **~room**
n Waschraum *m*.
wasn't [ˈwɔznt] = **was not**.
wasp [wɔsp] *n* Wespe *f*.
wastage [ˈweɪstɪdʒ] *n* Verlust *m*; natural ~ Verschleiß *m*.
waste [weɪst] *n* (*wasting*) Verschwendung *f*; (*what is wasted*) Abfall *m*; **~s** *pl*
Einöde *f* // *a* (*useless*) überschüssig,
Abfall- // *vt* (*object*) verschwenden;
(*time, life*) vergeuden // *vi*: **~ away** verfallen; **to lay ~** verwüsten; **~ disposal**
unit *n* (*Brit*) Müllschlucker *m*; **~ful** *a*
verschwenderisch; (*process*) aufwendig;
~ ground *n* (*Brit*) unbebautes Grundstück *nt*; **~land** *n* Ödland *nt*; **~paper**
basket *n* Papierkorb *m*; **~ pipe** *n*
Abflußrohr *nt*.
watch [wɔtʃ] *n* Wache *f*; (*for time*) Uhr
f // *vt* ansehen; (*observe*) beobachten;
(*be careful of*) aufpassen auf (+*acc*);
(*guard*) bewachen // *vi* zusehen; **to be on**
the ~ (*for sth*) (auf etw *acc*) aufpassen;
to ~ TV fernsehen; **to ~ sb doing sth**
jdm bei der etw zuschauen; **~ out** *vi* Ausschau halten; (*be careful*) aufpassen; **~**
out! paß auf!; **~dog** *n* (*lit*) Wachthund
m; (*fig*) Wächter *m*; **~ful** *a* wachsam;
~maker *n* Uhrmacher *m*; **~man** *n* (*also*:
night ~man) (Nacht)wächter *m*; **~**
strap *n* Uhrarmband *nt*.
water [ˈwɔːtə*] *n* Wasser *nt*; **~s** *pl*
Gewässer *nt* // *vt* (be)gießen; (*river*)
bewässern; (*horses*) tränken // *vi* (*eye*)
tränen; **~ down** *vt* verwässern; **~**
closet *n* (*Brit*) (Wasser)klosett *nt*;
~colour, (*US*) **~color** *n* (*painting*)

Aquarell *nt*; (*paint*) Wasserfarbe *f*; **~cress** *n* (Brunnen)kresse *f*; **~fall** *n* Wasserfall *m*; **~ heater** *n* Heißwassergerät *nt*; **~ing can** *n* Gießkanne *f*; **~ level** *n* Wasserstand *m*; **~lily** *n* Seerose *f*; **~line** *n* Wasserlinie *f*; **~logged** *a* (*ground*) voll Wasser; (*wood*) mit Wasser vollgesogen; **~ main** *n* Haupt(wasser)leitung *f*; **~mark** *n* Wasserzeichen *nt*; (*on wall*) Wasserstandsmarke *f*; **~melon** *n* Wassermelone *f*; **~ polo** *n* Wasserball(spiel) *nt*; **~proof** *a* wasserdicht; **~shed** *n* Wasserscheide *f*; **~skiing** *n* Wasserschilaufen *nt*; **~ tank** *n* Wassertank *m*; **~tight** *a* wasserdicht; **~ way** *n* Wasserweg *m*; **~works** *npl* Wasserwerk *nt*; **~y** *a* wäss(e)rig.

wave [weɪv] *n* Welle *f*; (*with hand*) Winken *nt* // *vt* (*move to and fro*) schwenken; (*hand, flag*) winken mit; (*hair*) wellen // *vi* (*person*) winken; (*flag*) wehen; **~length** *n* (*lit, fig*) Wellenlänge *f*.

waver ['weɪvə*] *vi* schwanken.

wavy ['weɪvɪ] *a* wellig.

wax [wæks] *n* Wachs *nt*; (*sealing ~*) Siegellack *m*; (*in ear*) Ohrenschmalz *m* // *vt* (*floor*) (ein)wachsen // *vi* (*moon*) zunehmen; **~works** *npl* Wachsfigurenkabinett *nt*.

way [weɪ] *n* Weg *m*; (*method*) Art und Weise *f*; (*direction*) Richtung *f*; (*habit*) Gewohnheit *f*; (*distance*) Entfernung *f*; (*condition*) Zustand *m*; which ~? — this ~ welche Richtung? — hier entlang; on the ~ (*en route*) unterwegs; to be in the ~ im Weg sein; to go out of one's ~ to do sth sich besonders anstrengen, um etw zu tun; to lose one's ~ sich verirren; give ~ (*Brit* AUT) Vorfahrt achten!; in a ~ in gewisser Weise; by the ~ übrigens; in some ~s in gewisser Hinsicht; '~ in' (*Brit*) 'Eingang'; '~ out' (*Brit*) 'Ausgang'.

waylay ['weɪleɪ] *vt* (*irreg: like* lay) auflauern (+*dat*).

wayward ['weɪwəd] *a* eigensinnig.

W.C. ['dʌbljuː'siː] *n* (*Brit*) WC *nt*.

we [wiː] *pl pron* wir.

weak [wiːk] *a* schwach; **~en** *vt* schwächen // *vi* schwächer werden; **~ling** *n* Schwächling *m*; **~ly** *ad* schwach; **~ness** *n* Schwäche *f*.

wealth [welθ] *n* Reichtum *m*; (*abundance*) Fülle *f*; **~y** *a* reich.

wean [wiːn] *vt* entwöhnen.

weapon ['wepən] *n* Waffe *f*.

wear [weə*] *n* (*clothing*): sports/baby ~ Sport-/Babykleidung *f*; (*use*) Verschleiß *m* // *v* (*pt* **wore**, *pp* **worn**) *vt* (*have on*) tragen; (*smile etc*) haben; (*use*) abnutzen // *vi* (*last*) halten; (*become old*) (sich) verschleißen; evening ~ Abendkleidung *f*; **~ and tear** Verschleiß

m; **~ away** *vt* verbrauchen // *vi* schwinden; **~ down** *vt* (*people*) zermürben; **~ off** *vi* sich verlieren; **~ out** *vt* verschleißen; (*person*) erschöpfen.

weary ['wɪərɪ] *a* müde // *vt* ermüden // *vi* überdrüssig werden (*of gen*).

weather ['weðə*] *n* Wetter *nt* // *vt* verwittern lassen; (*resist*) überstehen; under the ~ (*fig: ill*) angeschlagen (*col*); **~-beaten** *a* verwittert; **~cock** *n* Wetterhahn *m*; **~ forecast** *n* Wettervorhersage *f*; **~ vane** *n* Wetterfahne *f*.

weave [wiːv], *pt* **wove**, *pp* **woven** *vt* weben; (*~r*) *n* Weber(in *f*) *m*; **weaving** *n* (*craft*) Webkunst *f*.

web [web] *n* Netz *nt*; (*membrane*) Schwimmhaut *f*.

wed [wed], *pt*, *pp* **wedded** *vt* heiraten // *n*: the newly-~s die Frischvermählten.

we'd [wiːd] = **we had; we would**.

wedding ['wedɪŋ] *n* Hochzeit *f*; silver/golden ~ (*Brit*), silver/golden ~ anniversary Silberhochzeit *f*/Goldene Hochzeit; **~ day** *n* Hochzeitstag *m*; **~ dress** *n* Hochzeitskleid *nt*; **~ present** *n* Hochzeitsgeschenk *nt*; **~ ring** *n* Trau- or Ehering *m*.

wedge [wedʒ] *n* Keil *m*; (*of cheese etc*) Stück *nt* // *vt* (*fasten*) festklemmen; (*pack tightly*) einkeilen.

wedlock ['wedlɒk] *n* Ehe *f*.

Wednesday ['wenzdeɪ] *n* Mittwoch *m*.

wee [wiː] *a* (*esp Scot*) klein, winzig.

weed [wiːd] *n* Unkraut *nt* // *vt* jäten; **~killer** *n* Unkrautvertilgungsmittel *nt*; **~y** *a* (*person*) schmächtig.

week [wiːk] *n* Woche *f*; a ~ today/on Friday heute/Freitag in einer Woche; **~day** *n* Wochentag *m*; **~end** *n* Wochenende *nt*; **~ly** *a*, *ad* wöchentlich; (*wages, magazine*) Wochen-.

weep [wiːp], *pt*, *pp* **wept** *vi* weinen; **~ing willow** *n* Trauerweide *f*.

weigh [weɪ] *vti* wiegen; to ~ anchor den Anker lichten; **~ down** *vt* niederdrücken; **~ up** *vt* abschätzen.

weight [weɪt] *n* Gewicht *nt*; to lose/put on ~ abnehmen/zunehmen; **~ing** *n* (*allowance*) Zulage *f*; **~-lifter** *n* Gewichtheber *m*; **~y** *a* (*heavy*) gewichtig; (*important*) schwerwiegend.

weir [wɪə*] *n* (Stau)wehr *nt*.

weird [wɪəd] *a* seltsam.

welcome ['welkəm] *n* Willkommen *nt*, Empfang *m* // *vt* begrüßen; thank you — you're ~! danke — nichts zu danken.

weld [weld] *n* Schweißnaht *f* // *vt* schweißen; **~ing** *n* Schweißen *nt*.

welfare ['welfeə*] *n* Wohl *nt*; (*social*) Fürsorge *f*; **~ state** *n* Wohlfahrtsstaat *m*; **~ work** *n* Fürsorge *f*.

well [wel] *n* Brunnen *m*; (*oil* ~) Quelle *f* // *a* (*in good health*) gesund // *ad* gut //

interj nun, na schön; I'm ~ es geht mir gut; as ~ auch; as ~ as sowohl als auch; ~ done! gut gemacht!; get ~ soon! gute Besserung; to do ~ (*person*) gut zurechtkommen; (*business*) gut gehen; ~ up *vi* emporsteigen; (*fig*) aufsteigen.

we'll [wiːl] = **we will, we shall.**

well-behaved ['welbɪ'heɪvd] *a* wohlerzogen.

well-being ['welbiːɪŋ] *n* Wohl *nt*.

well-built ['wel'bɪlt] *a* kräftig gebaut.

well-deserved ['weldɪ'zɜːvd] *a* wohlverdient.

well-dressed ['wel'drest] *a* gut gekleidet.

well-heeled ['wel'hiːld] *a* (*col: wealthy*) gut gepolstert.

wellingtons ['welɪŋtənz] *npl* (*also:* wellington boots) Gummistiefel *pl*.

well-known ['wel'nəʊn] *a* bekannt.

well-mannered ['wel'mænəd] *a* wohlerzogen.

well-meaning ['wel'miːnɪŋ] *a* (*person*) wohlmeinend; (*action*) gutgemeint.

well-off ['wel'ɒf] *a* gut situiert.

well-read ['wel'red] *a* (sehr) belesen.

well-to-do ['weltə'duː] *a* wohlhabend.

well-wisher ['welwɪʃə•] *n* Gönner *m*.

Welsh [welʃ] *a* walisisch; **the ~** *npl* die Waliser; **~man/woman** *n* Waliser *m*/ Waliserin *f*; **~ rarebit** *n* überbackene Käseschnitte *pl*.

went [went] *pt of* **go.**

wept [wept] *pt, pp of* **weep.**

were [wɜː•] *pt pl of* **be.**

we're [wɪə•] = **we are.**

weren't [wɜːnt] = **were not.**

west [west] *a* Westen *m* // *a* West-, westlich // *ad* westwärts, nach Westen; **the W~** *n* der Westen; **the W~ Country** *n* (*Brit*) der Südwesten Englands; **~erly** *a* westlich; **~ern** *a* westlich, West- // *n* (*CINE*) Western *m*; **W~ Germany** *n* Westdeutschland *nt*, Bundesrepublik Deutschland *f*; **W~ Indian** *a* westindisch // *n* Westindier(in *f*) *m*; **W~ Indies** *npl* Westindische Inseln *pl*; **~ward(s)** *ad* westwärts.

wet [wet] *a* naß; **to get ~** naß werden; **'~ paint** 'frisch gestrichen'; **~ blanket** *n* (*fig*) Triefel *m*; **~ suit** *n* Tauchanzug *m*.

we've [wiːv] = **we have.**

whack [wæk] *n* Schlag *m* // *vt* schlagen.

whale [weɪl] *n* Wal *m*.

wharf [wɔːf] *n* Kai *m*.

what [wɒt] ◆ *a* 1 (*in direct/indirect questions*) welche(r, s), was für ein(e); ~ size is it? welche Größe ist das?
2 (*in exclamations*) was für ein(e); ~ a mess! was für ein Durcheinander!
◆ *pron* (*interrogative/relative*) was; ~ are you doing? was machst du gerade?; ~ are you talking about? wovon reden

Sie?; ~ is it called? wie heißt das?; ~ about ...? wie wär's mit ...?; I saw ~ you did ich habe gesehen, was du gemacht hast
◆ *interj* (*disbelieving*) wie, was; ~, no coffee! wie, kein Kaffee?; I've crashed the car — ~! ich hatte einen Autounfall — was!

wheat [wiːt] *n* Weizen *m*; ~ **germ** *n* Weizenkeim *m*.

wheedle ['wiːdl] *vt*: to ~ sb into doing sth jdn dazu überreden, etw zu tun; to ~ sth out of sb jdm etw abluchsen.

wheel [wiːl] *n* Rad *nt*; (*steering* ~) Lenkrad *nt*; (*disc*) Scheibe *f* // *vt* schieben; **~barrow** *n* Schubkarren *m*; **~chair** *n* Rollstuhl *m*; **~ clamp** *n* (*AUT*) Radblockierung *f* (*von der Polizei an falschparkenden Autos angebracht*).

wheeze [wiːz] *vi* keuchen.

when [wen] ◆ *ad* wenn
◆ *cj* 1 (*at, during, after the time that*) wenn; (*with past reference*) als; she was reading ~ I came in sie las, als ich hereinkam; be careful ~ you cross the road seien Sie vorsichtig, wenn Sie über die Straße gehen
2 (*on, at which*) als; on the day ~ I met him am Tag, an dem ich ihn traf.
3 (*whereas*) wo ... doch.

where [weə•] *ad* (*place*) wo; (*direction*) wohin; ~ **from** woher; **~abouts** ['weərə'baʊts] *ad* wo // *n* Aufenthaltsort *m*; nobody knows his ~abouts niemand weiß, wo er ist; **~as** [weər'æz] *cj* während, wo ... doch; **whereby** *pron* woran, wodurch, womit, wovon; **whereupon** *cj* worauf, wonach; (*at beginning of sentence*) daraufhin.

wherever [weər'evə•] *ad* wo (immer).

wherewithal ['weəwɪðɔːl] *n* nötige (Geld)mittel *pl*.

whet [wet] *vt* (*appetite*) anregen.

whether ['weðə•] *cj* ob; I don't know ~ to accept or not ich weiß nicht, ob ich es annehmen soll oder nicht; ~ you go or not ob du gehst oder nicht.

which [wɪtʃ] ◆ *a* 1 (*interrogative: direct, indirect*) welche(r, s); ~ one? welche(r, s)?
2: in ~ case in diesem Fall; by ~ time zu dieser Zeit
◆ *pron* 1 (*interrogative*) welche(r, s); (*of people also*) wer
2 (*relative*) der/die/das; (*referring to clause*) was; the apple ~ you ate/~ is on the table der Apfel, den du gegessen hast/der auf dem Tisch liegt; he said he saw her, ~ is true er sagte, er habe sie gesehen, was auch stimmt.

whiff [wɪf] *n* Hauch *m*.

while [waɪl] *n* Weile *f* // *cj* während; for a ~ eine Zeitlang; ~ **away** *vt* (*time*) sich (*dat*) vertreiben.

whim [wɪm] *n* Laune *f*.

whimper ['wɪmpə*] n Wimmern nt // vi wimmern.

whimsical ['wɪmzɪkəl] a launisch.

whine [waɪn] n Gewinsel nt, Gejammer nt // vi heulen, winseln.

whip [wɪp] n Peitsche f; (POL) Fraktionsführer m // vt (beat) peitschen; (snatch) reißen; n ~ped cream n Schlagsahne; ~round n (Brit col) Geldsammlung f.

whirl [wɜːl] n Wirbel m // vti (herum)wirbeln; ~pool n Wirbel m; ~wind n Wirbelwind m.

whirr [wɜː*] vi schwirren, surren.

whisk [wɪsk] n Schneebesen m // vt (cream etc) schlagen; to ~ sb away or off mit jdm davon sausen.

whisker ['wɪskə*] n (of animal) Barthaare pl; ~s pl (of man) Backenbart m.

whisky, (US, Ireland) whiskey ['wɪskɪ] n Whisky m.

whisper ['wɪspə*] n Flüstern nt // vti flüstern.

whistle ['wɪsl] n Pfiff m; (instrument) Pfeife f // vti pfeifen.

white [waɪt] n Weiß nt; (of egg) Eiweiß nt // a weiß; ~ coffee n (Brit) Kaffee m mit Milch; ~collar worker n Angestellte(r) m; ~ elephant n (fig) Fehlinvestition f; ~ lie n Notlüge f; ~ness n Weiß nt; ~ paper n (POL) Weißbuch nt; ~wash n (paint) Tünche f; (fig) Ehrenrettung f // vt weißen, tünchen; (fig) reinwaschen.

whiting ['waɪtɪŋ] n Weißfisch m.

Whitsun ['wɪtsn] n Pfingsten nt.

whittle ['wɪtl] vt: to ~ away or down stutzen, verringern.

whizz [wɪz] vi: to ~ past or by vorbeizischen, vorbeischwirren; ~ kid n (col) Kanone f.

who [huː] pron 1 (interrogative) wer; (acc) wen; (dat) wem; ~ is it?, ~'s there? wer ist da?
2 (relative) der/die/das; the man/woman ~ spoke to me der Mann/die Frau, der/die mit mir sprach.

whole [həʊl] a ganz // n Ganze(s) nt; the ~ of the town die ganze Stadt; on the ~, as a ~ im großen und ganzen; ~hearted a rückhaltlos; ~heartedly ad von ganzem Herzen; ~meal n (bread, flour) Vollkorn-; ~sale n Großhandel m // a (trade) Großhandels-; (destruction) Massen-; ~saler n Großhändler m; ~some a bekömmlich, gesund; ~wheat a = ~meal.

wholly ['həʊlɪ] ad ganz, völlig.

whom [huːm] pron 1 (interrogative: acc) wen; (: dat) wem; ~ did you see? wen haben Sie gesehen?; to ~ did you give it? wem haben Sie es gegeben?
2 (relative: acc) den/die/das; (: dat) dem/der/dem; the man ~ I saw/to ~ I

spoke der Mann, den ich sah/mit dem ich sprach.

whooping cough ['huːpɪŋkɒf] n Keuchhusten m.

whore ['hɔː*] n Hure f.

whose [huːz] a (poss: interrog) wessen; ~ book is this?, ~ is this book? wessen Buch ist das?; (: rel) dessen; (after f and pl) deren // pron wessen; ~ is this? wem gehört das?

why [waɪ] ◆ ad warum, weshalb
◆ cj warum, weshalb; that's not ~ I'm here ich bin nicht deswegen hier; that's the reason ~ deshalb
◆ interj (expressing surprise, shock, annoyance) na so was; (explaining) also dann; ~, it's you! na so was, du bist es!

wick [wɪk] n Docht m.

wicked ['wɪkɪd] a böse.

wicker ['wɪkə*] n (also: ~work) Korbgeflecht nt.

wicket ['wɪkɪt] n Tor nt, Dreistab m.

wide [waɪd] a breit; (plain) weit; (in firing) daneben // ad: open ~ weit offen; to shoot ~ daneben schießen; ~angle lens n Weitwinkelobjektiv nt; ~awake a hellwach; ~ly ad weit; (known) allgemein; ~n vt erweitern; ~open a weit geöffnet; ~spread a weitverbreitet.

widow ['wɪdəʊ] n Witwe f; ~ed a verwitwet; ~er n Witwer m.

width [wɪdθ] n Breite f, Weite f.

wield [wiːld] vt schwingen, handhaben.

wife [waɪf] n (Ehe)frau f, Gattin f.

wig [wɪg] n Perücke f.

wiggle ['wɪgl] n Wackeln nt // vt wackeln mit // vi wackeln.

wild [waɪld] a wild; (violent) heftig; (plan, idea) verrückt; the ~s die Wildnis; ~erness ['wɪldənəs] n Wildnis f, Wüste f; ~goose chase n (fig) fruchtlose(s) Unternehmen nt; ~life n Tierwelt f; ~ly ad wild, ungestüm; (exaggerated) irrsinnig.

wilful ['wɪlful] a (intended) vorsätzlich; (obstinate) eigensinnig.

will [wɪl] ◆ v aux 1 (forming future tense) werden; I ~ finish it tomorrow ich mache es morgen zu Ende
2 (in conjectures, predictions): he ~ or he'll be there by now er dürfte jetzt da sein; that ~ be the postman das wird der Postbote sein
3 (in commands, requests, offers): ~ you be quiet! sei endlich still!; ~ you help me? hilfst du mir?; ~ you have a cup of tea? Trinken Sie eine Tasse Tee?; I won't put up with it! das lasse ich mir nicht gefallen!
◆ vt wollen; ~ing a gewillt, bereit; ~ingly ad bereitwillig, gern; ~ingness n (Bereit)willigkeit f.

willow ['wɪləʊ] n Weide f.

willpower ['wɪl'paʊə*] n Willenskraft f.

willy-nilly ['wɪlɪ'nɪlɪ] *ad* einfach so.
wilt [wɪlt] *vi* (ver)welken.
wily ['waɪlɪ] *a* gerissen.
win [wɪn] *n* Sieg *m* // *vti, pt, pp* **won**
gewinnen; **to ~ sb over** *or* (*Brit*) **round**
jdn gewinnen, jdn dazu bringen.
wince [wɪns] *n* Zusammenzucken *nt* // *vi*
zusammenzucken.
winch [wɪntʃ] *n* Winde *f*.
wind [waɪnd] *v* (*pt, pp* **wound**) *vt*
(*rope*) winden; (*bandage*) wickeln // *vi*
(*turn*) sich winden; **~ up** *vt* (*clock*) aufziehen; (*debate*) (ab)schließen.
wind [wɪnd] *n* Wind *m*; (*MED*)
Blähungen *pl*; **~fall** *n* unverhoffte(r)
Glücksfall *m*.
winding ['waɪndɪŋ] *a* (*road*) gewunden.
wind instrument ['wɪndɪnstrʊmənt] *n*
Blasinstrument *nt*.
windmill ['wɪndmɪl] *n* Windmühle *f*.
window ['wɪndəʊ] *n* Fenster *nt*; **~ box**
n Blumenkasten *m*; **~ cleaner** *n* Fen-
sterputzer *m*; **~ envelope** *n* Fenster-
briefumschlag *m*; **~ ledge** *n* Fen-
stersims *m*; **~ pane** *n* Fensterscheibe *f*;
~sill *n* Fensterbank *f*.
windpipe ['wɪndpaɪp] *n* Luftröhre *f*.
windscreen ['wɪndskriːn], (*US*) **windshield** ['wɪndʃiːld] *n* Windschutzscheibe
f; **~ washer** *n* Scheibenwaschanlage *f*;
~ wiper *n* Scheibenwischer *m*.
windswept ['wɪndswept] *a* vom Wind
gepeitscht; (*person*) zerzaust.
windy ['wɪndɪ] *a* windig.
wine [waɪn] *n* Wein *m*; **~ cellar** *n*
Weinkeller *m*; **~glass** *n* Weinglas *nt*;
~ list *n* Weinkarte *f*; **~ merchant** *n*
Weinhändler *m*; **~ tasting** *n* Weinprobe
f; **~ waiter** *n* Weinkellner *m*.
wing [wɪŋ] *n* Flügel *m*; (*MIL*) Gruppe *f*;
~s *pl* (*THEAT*) Seitenkulisse *f*; **~er** *n*
(*SPORT*) Flügelstürmer *m*.
wink [wɪŋk] *n* Zwinkern *nt* // *vi*
zwinkern, blinzeln.
winner ['wɪnə*] *n* Gewinner *m*;
(*SPORT*) Sieger *m*.
winning ['wɪnɪŋ] *a* (*team*) siegreich,
Sieger-; (*goal*) entscheidend // *n:* **~s** *pl*
Gewinn *m*; **~ post** *n* Ziel *nt*.
winter ['wɪntə*] *n* Winter *m* // *a*
(*clothes*) Winter- // *vi* überwintern;
~ sports *npl* Wintersport *m*.
wintry ['wɪntrɪ] *a* Winter-, winterlich.
wipe [waɪp] *n:* **to give sth a ~** etw
(ab)wischen; **~ off** *vt* abwischen; **~
out** *vt* (*debt*) löschen; (*destroy*) auslöschen; **~ up** *vt* aufwischen.
wire [waɪə*] *n* Draht *m*; (*telegram*)
Telegramm *nt* // *vt* telegrafieren (*sb*
jdm, *sth* etw).
wireless ['waɪəlɪs] *n* (*Brit*)
Radio(apparat *m*) *nt*.
wiring ['waɪərɪŋ] *n* elektrische Leitungen
pl.
wiry ['waɪərɪ] *a* drahtig.

wisdom ['wɪzdəm] *n* Weisheit *f*; (*of
decision*) Klugheit *f*; **~ tooth** *n*
Weisheitszahn *m*.
wise [waɪz] *a* klug, weise.
...wise [waɪz] *suff:* **time~** zeitlich
gesehen.
wisecrack ['waɪzkræk] *n* Witzelei *f*.
wish [wɪʃ] *n* Wunsch *m* // *vt* wünschen;
best ~es (*on birthday etc*) alles Gute;
with best ~es herzliche Grüße; **to ~ sb
goodbye** jdn verabschieden; **he ~ed me
well** er wünschte mir Glück; **to ~ to do
sth** etw tun wollen; **~ for** *vt* sich (*dat*)
wünschen; **~ful thinking** *n*
Wunschdenken *nt*.
wishy-washy ['wɪʃɪ'wɒʃɪ] *a* (*col:
colour*) verwaschen; (*: ideas, argument*)
verschwommen.
wisp [wɪsp] *n* (Haar)strähne *f*; (*of
smoke*) Wölkchen *nt*.
wistful ['wɪstfʊl] *a* sehnsüchtig.
wit [wɪt] *n* (*also:* **~s**) Verstand *m no pl*;
(*amusing ideas*) Witz *m*; (*person*)
Witzbold *m*.
witch [wɪtʃ] *n* Hexe *f*; **~craft** *n* Hexerei
f.
with [wɪð, wɪθ] *prep* **1** (*accompanying,
in the company of*) mit; **we stayed ~
friends** wir übernachteten bei Freunden;
I'll be ~ you in a minute einen Augenblick, ich bin sofort da; **I'm not ~ you** (*I
don't understand*) das verstehe ich nicht;
to be ~ it (*col: up-to-date*) auf dem
laufenden sein; (*: alert*) (voll) da sein
(*col*)
2 (*descriptive, indicating manner etc*)
mit; **the man ~ the grey hat** der Mann
mit dem grauen Hut; **red ~ anger** rot
vor Wut.
withdraw [wɪθ'drɔː] (*irreg: like draw*)
vt zurückziehen; (*money*) abheben;
(*remark*) zurücknehmen // *vi* sich
zurückziehen; **~al** *n* Zurückziehung *f*;
Abheben *nt*; Zurücknahme *f*; **~n** *a*
(*person*) verschlossen.
wither ['wɪðə*] *vi* (ver)welken.
withhold [wɪθ'həʊld] *vt* (*irreg: like
hold*) vorenthalten (*from sb* jdm).
within [wɪð'ɪn] *prep* innerhalb (+*gen*) //
ad: **~ reach** in Reichweite; **~ sight of** in
Sichtweite von; **~ the week** innerhalb
dieser Woche.
without [wɪð'aʊt] *prep* ohne.
withstand [wɪθ'stænd] *vt* (*irreg: like
stand*) widerstehen (+*dat*).
witness ['wɪtnəs] *n* Zeuge *m*, Zeugin *f* //
vt (*see*) sehen, miterleben; (*sign
document*) beglaubigen; **~ box**, (*US*) **~
stand** *n* Zeugenstand *m*.
witticism ['wɪtɪsɪzəm] *n* witzige
Bemerkung *f*.
witty ['wɪtɪ] *a* witzig, geistreich.
wives [waɪvz] *pl of* **wife**.
wizard ['wɪzəd] *n* Zauberer *m*.
wk *abbr of* **week**.

wobble ['wɒbl] *vi* wackeln.
woe [wəʊ] *n* Kummer *m.*
woke [wəʊk], **woken** ['wəʊkən] *pt, pp of* **wake.**
woman ['wʊmən] *n, pl* **women** Frau *f*; ~ **doctor** *n* Ärztin *f*; **women's lib** *n* (*col*) Frauenrechtsbewegung *f*; ~**ly** *a* weiblich.
womb [wu:m] *n* Gebärmutter *f.*
women ['wɪmɪn] *pl of* **woman.**
wonder ['wʌndə*] *n* (*marvel*) Wunder *nt*; (*surprise*) Staunen *nt*, Verwunderung *f* // *vi* sich wundern // *vt*: **I ~ whether ...** ich frage mich, ob ...; **it's no ~ that** es ist kein Wunder, daß; **to ~ at** sich wundern über (+*acc*); **to ~ about** sich Gedanken machen über (+*acc*); ~**ful** *a* wunderbar, herrlich; ~**fully** *ad* wunderbar.
won't [wəʊnt] = **will not.**
wood [wʊd] *n* Holz *nt*; (*forest*) Wald *m*; ~ **carving** *n* Holzschnitzerei *f*; ~**ed** *a* bewaldet; ~**en** *a* (*lit, fig*) hölzern; ~**pecker** *n* Specht *m*; ~**wind** *n* Blasinstrumente *pl*; ~**work** *n* Holzwerk *nt*; (*craft*) Holzarbeiten *pl*; ~**worm** *n* Holzwurm *m.*
wool [wʊl] *n* Wolle *f*; **to pull the ~ over sb's eyes** (*fig*) jdm Sand in die Augen streuen; ~**len,** (*US*) ~**en** *a* Woll-; ~**lens** *npl* Wollsachen *pl*; ~**ly,** (*US*) ~**y** *a* wollig; (*fig*) schwammig.
word [wɜ:d] *n* Wort *nt*; (*news*) Bescheid *m* // *vt* formulieren; **in other ~s** anders gesagt; **to break/keep one's ~** sein Wort brechen/halten; ~ **processing** *n* Textverarbeitung *f*; ~ **processor** *n* Textverarbeitungsgerät *nt*; ~**ing** *n* Wortlaut *m.*
work [wɜ:k] *n* Arbeit *f*; (ART, LITER) Werk *nt* // *vi* arbeiten; (*machine*) funktionieren; (*medicine*) wirken; (*succeed*) klappen; **to be out of ~** arbeitslos sein; ~**s** *n sing* (*Brit: factory*) Fabrik *f*, Werk *nt*; *pl* (*of watch*) Werk *nt*; ~ **loose** *vi* sich lockern; ~ **on** *vi* weiterarbeiten // *vt* (*be engaged in*) arbeiten an (+*dat*); (*influence*) bearbeiten; ~ **out** *vi* (*sum*) aufgehen; (*plan*) klappen // *vt* (*problem*) lösen; (*plan*) ausarbeiten; **it ~s out at £100** das gibt *or* macht £100; ~ **up** *vt*: **to get ~ed up** sich aufregen; ~**able** *a* (*soil*) bearbeitbar; (*plan*) ausführbar; **workaholic** *n* Arbeitssüchtige(r) *mf*; ~**er** *n* Arbeiter(in *f*) *m*; ~**force** *n* Arbeiterschaft *f*; ~**ing class** *n* Arbeiterklasse *f*; ~**ing-class** *a* Arbeiter-; **in ~ing order** in betriebsfähigem Zustand; ~**man** *n* Arbeiter *m*; ~**manship** *n* Arbeit *f*, Ausführung *f*; ~**sheet** *n* Arbeitsblatt *nt*; ~**shop** *n* Werkstatt *f*; ~ **station** *n* Arbeitsplatz *m*; ~**-to-rule** *n* (*Brit*) Dienst *m* nach Vorschrift.
world [wɜ:ld] *n* Welt *f*; **to think the ~ of sb** große Stücke auf jdn halten; ~**ly** *a* weltlich, irdisch; ~**-wide** *a* weltweit.
worm [wɜ:m] *n* Wurm *m.*
worn [wɔ:n] *pp of* **wear** // *a* (*clothes*) abgetragen; ~**-out** *a* (*object*) abgenutzt; (*person*) völlig erschöpft.
worried ['wʌrɪd] *a* besorgt, beunruhigt.
worry ['wʌrɪ] *n* Sorge *f* // *vt* beunruhigen // *vi* (*feel uneasy*) sich sorgen, sich (*dat*) Gedanken machen; ~**ing** *a* beunruhigend.
worse [wɜ:s] *a comp of* **bad** schlechter, schlimmer // *ad comp of* **badly** schlimmer, ärger // *n* Schlimmere(s) *nt*, Schlechtere(s) *nt*; **a change for the ~** eine Verschlechterung; ~**n** *vt* verschlimmern // *vi* sich verschlechtern; ~ **off** *a* (*fig*) schlechter dran.
worship ['wɜ:ʃɪp] *n* Verehrung *f* // *vt* anbeten; **Your W~** (*Brit: to mayor*) Herr/Frau Bürgermeister; (*: to judge*) Euer Ehren.
worst [wɜ:st] *a superl of* **bad** schlimmste(r, s), schlechteste(r, s) // *ad superl of* **badly** am schlimmsten, am ärgsten // *n* Schlimmste(s) *nt*, Ärgste(s) *nt*; **at ~** schlimmstenfalls.
worsted ['wʊstɪd] *n* Kammgarn *nt.*
worth [wɜ:θ] *n* Wert *m* // *a* wert; **it's ~ it** es lohnt sich; **to be ~ one's while (to do)** die Mühe wert sein (, etw zu tun); ~**less** *a* wertlos; (*person*) nichtsnutzig; ~**while** *a* lohnend, der Mühe wert.
worthy [wɜ:ðɪ] *a* wert (*of gen*), würdig (*of gen*).
would [wʊd] *v aux* **1** (*conditional tense*): **if you asked him he ~ do it** wenn du ihn fragtest, würde er es tun; **if you had asked him he ~ have done it** wenn du ihn gefragt hättest, hätte er es getan
2 (*in offers, invitations, requests*): **~ you like a biscuit?** möchten Sie ein Plätzchen?; **~ you ask him to come in?** würden Sie ihn bitte hineinbitten?
3 (*in indirect speech*): **I said I ~ do it** ich sagte, ich würde es tun
4 (*emphatic*): **it WOULD have to snow today!** es mußte ja ausgerechnet heute schneien!
5 (*insistence*): **she ~n't behave** sie wollte sich partout nicht anständig benehmen
6 (*conjecture*): **it ~ have been midnight** es ungefähr Mitternacht gewesen sein; **it ~ seem so** es sieht wohl so aus
7 (*indicating habit*): **he ~ go there on Mondays** er ging jeden Montag dorthin.
wouldn't ['wʊdnt] = **would not.**
wound [waʊnd] *pt, pp of* **wind** // *n* [wu:nd] (*lit, fig*) Wunde *f* // *vt* [wu:nd] verwunden, verletzen (*also fig*).
wove [wəʊv], **woven** ['wəʊvən] *pt, pp of* **weave.**
wrangle ['ræŋgl] *n* Streit *m* // *vi* sich zanken.

wrap [ræp] *n* (*stole*) Schal *m* // *vt* (*also*: ~ up) einwickeln; ~ **up** *vt* (*deal*) abschließen; ~**per** *n* Umschlag *m*, Schutzhülle *f*; ~**ping paper** *n* Einwickelpapier *nt*.

wrath [rɒθ] *n* Zorn *m*.

wreak [riːk] *vt* (*havoc*) anrichten; (*vengeance*) üben.

wreath [riːθ] *n* Kranz *m*.

wreck [rek] *n* (*ship*) Wrack *nt*; (*sth ruined*) Ruine *f* // *vt* zerstören; ~**age** *n* Trümmer *pl*.

wren [ren] *n* Zaunkönig *m*.

wrench [rentʃ] *n* (*spanner*) Schraubenschlüssel *m*; (*twist*) Ruck *m* // *vt* reißen, zerren; **to** ~ **sth from sb** jdm etw entreißen *or* entwinden.

wrestle ['resl] *vi*: **to** ~ (**with sb**) mit jdm ringen; **wrestler** *n* Ringer(in *f*); **wrestling** *n* Ringen *nt*.

wretched ['retʃɪd] *a* (*hovel*) elend; (*col*) verflixt; **I feel** ~ mir ist es elend.

wriggle ['rɪgl] *n* Schlängeln *n* // *vi* sich winden.

wring [rɪŋ], *pt*, *pp* **wrung** *vt* wringen.

wrinkle ['rɪŋkl] *n* Falte *f*, Runzel *f* // *vt* runzeln // *vi* sich runzeln; (*material*) knittern.

wrist [rɪst] *n* Handgelenk *nt*; ~**watch** *n* Armbanduhr *f*.

writ [rɪt] *n* gerichtliche(r) Befehl *m*.

write [raɪt], *pt* **wrote**, *pp* **written** *vti* schreiben; ~ **down** *vt* aufschreiben; ~ **off** *vt* (*dismiss*) abschreiben; ~ **out** *vt* (*essay*) abschreiben; (*cheque*) ausstellen; ~ **up** *vt* schreiben; ~**-off** *n*: **it is a** ~**-off das kann man abschreiben**; ~**r** *n* Schriftsteller *m*.

writhe [raɪð] *vi* sich winden.

writing ['raɪtɪŋ] *n* (*act*) Schreiben *nt*; (*hand*~) (Hand)schrift *f*; **in** ~ schriftlich; ~ **paper** *n* Schreibpapier *nt*.

written ['rɪtn] *pp* of **write**.

wrong [rɒŋ] *a* (*incorrect*) falsch; (*morally*) unrecht; **he was** ~ **in doing that** es war nicht recht von ihm, das zu tun; **you are** ~ **about that, you've got it** ~ da hast du unrecht; **be in the** ~ im Unrecht sein; **what's** ~ **with your leg?** was ist mit deinem Bein los?; **to go** ~ (*plan*) schiefgehen; (*person*) einen Fehler machen // *n* Unrecht *nt* // *vt* Unrecht tun (+*dat*); ~**ful** *a* unrechtmäßig; ~**ly** *ad* falsch; (*accuse*) zu Unrecht.

wrote [rəʊt] *pt* of **write**.

wrought [rɔːt] *a*: ~ **iron** *n* Schmiedeeisen *nt*.

wrung [rʌŋ] *pt*, *pp* of **wring**.

wry [raɪ] *a* ironisch.

wt. *abbr* of **weight**.

X

Xmas ['eksməs] *n abbr of* **Christmas**.

X-ray ['eks'reɪ] *n* Röntgenaufnahme *f* // *vt* röntgen; ~**s** *npl* Rontgenstrahlen *pl*.

Y

yacht [jɒt] *n* Jacht *f*; ~**ing** *n* (Sport)segeln *nt*; ~**sman** *n* Sportsegler *m*.

Yank [jæŋk], **Yankee** ['jæŋkɪ] *n* (*col*) Ami *m*.

yap [jæp] *vi* (*dog*) kläffen.

yard [jɑːd] *n* Hof *m*; (*measure*) (englische) Elle *f*, Yard *nt*, 0,91 *m*; ~**stick** *n* (*fig*) Maßstab *m*.

yarn [jɑːn] *n* (*thread*) Garn *nt*; (*story*) (Seemanns)garn *nt*.

yawn [jɔːn] *n* Gähnen *nt* // *vi* gähnen; ~**ing** *a* (*gap*) gähnend.

yd. *abbr of* **yard(s)**.

yeah [jeə] *ad* (*col*) ja.

year [jɪə*] *n* Jahr *nt*; **be 8** ~**s old** acht Jahre alt sein; **an eight-**~**-old child** *n* achtjähriges Kind; ~**ly** *a*, *ad* jährlich.

yearn [jɜːn] *vi* sich sehnen (*for* nach); ~**ing** *n* Verlangen *nt*, Sehnsucht *f*.

yeast [jiːst] *n* Hefe *f*.

yell [jel] *n* gellende(r) Schrei *m* // *vi* laut schreien.

yellow ['jeləʊ] *a* gelb // *n* Gelb *nt*.

yelp [jelp] *n* Gekläff *nt* // *vi* kläffen.

yeoman ['jəʊmən] *n*: **Y**~ **of the Guard** Leibgardist *m*.

yes [jes] *ad* ja // *n* Ja *nt*, Jawort *nt*; **to say/answer** ~ ja sagen/mit Ja antworten.

yesterday ['jestədeɪ] *ad* gestern // *n* Gestern *nt*; ~ **morning/evening** gestern morgen/abend; **all day** ~ gestern den ganzen Tag; **the day before** ~ vorgestern.

yet [jet] *ad* noch; (*in question*) schon; (*up to now*) bis jetzt; **it is not finished** ~ es ist noch nicht fertig; **the best** ~ das bisher beste; **as** ~ bis jetzt; (*in past*) bis dahin // *cj* doch, dennoch.

yew [juː] *n* Eibe *f*.

yield [jiːld] *n* Ertrag *m* // *vt* (*result*, *crop*) hervorbringen; (*interest*, *profit*) abwerfen; (*concede*) abtreten // *vi* nachgeben; (*MIL*) sich ergeben, '~' (*US AUT*) 'Vorfahrt gewähren'.

YMCA *n abbr* (= *Young Men's Christian Association*) CVJM *m*.

yoga ['jəʊgə] *n* Joga *m*.

yog(h)ourt, **yog(h)urt** ['jɒgət] *n* Joghurt *m*.

yoke [jəʊk] *n* (*lit*, *fig*) Joch *nt*.

yolk [jəʊk] *n* Eidotter *m*, Eigelb *nt*.

yonder ['jɒndə*] *ad* dort drüben, da drüben // *a* jene(r, s) dort.

you [ju:] *pron* **1** (*subject, in comparisons: German familiar form: sing*) du; (: *pl*) ihr; (*in letters also*) Du, Ihr; (: *German polite form*) Sie; ~ Germans ihr Deutschen; **she's younger than ~** sie ist jünger als du/Sie **2** (*direct object, after prep + acc: German familiar form: sing*) dich; (: *pl*) euch; (*in letters also*) Dich, Euch; (: *German polite form*) Sie; **I know ~** ich kenne dich/euch/Sie. **3** (*indirect object, after prep + dat: German familiar form: sing*) dir; (: *pl*) euch (*in letters also*) Dir, Euch; (: *German polite form*) Ihnen; **I gave it to ~** ich gab es dir/euch/Ihnen **4** (*impersonal: one: subject*) man; (: *direct object*) einen; (: *indirect object*) einem; **fresh air does ~ good** frische Luft tut gut.

you'd [ju:d] = **you had; you would.**

you'll [ju:l] = **you will, you shall.**

young [jʌŋ] *a* jung // *npl* **die Jungen**; **~ish** *a* ziemlich jung; **~ster** *n* Junge *m*, junge(r) Bursche *m*/junge(s) Mädchen *nt*.

your [jɔ:*] *poss a* (*familiar: sing*) dein; (: *pl*) euer, eure *pl*; (*polite*) Ihr; *see also* **my.**

you're [jʊə*] = **you are.**

yours [jɔ:z] *poss pron* (*familiar: sing*) deine(r, s); (: *pl*) eure(r, s); (*polite*) Ihre(r, s); **~ sincerely/faithfully** mit freundlichen Grüßen; *see also* **mine.**

yourself [jɔ:'self] *pron* (*emphatic*) selbst; (*familiar: sing*) (*acc*) dich (selbst); (*dat*) dir (selbst); (: *pl*) euch (selbst); (*polite*) sich (selbst); *see also* **oneself.**

youth [ju:θ] *n* Jugend *f*; (*young man*) junge(r) Mann *m*; **~s** *pl* Jugendliche *pl*;

~ club *n* Jugendzentrum *nt*; **~ful** *a* jugendlich; **~ hostel** *n* Jugendherberge *f.*

you've [ju:v] = **you have.**

YTS *n abbr* (*Brit*: = *Youth Training Scheme*) staatliches Förderprogramm für arbeitslose Jugendliche.

Yugoslav ['ju:gəʊ'slɑ:v] *a* jugoslawisch // *n* Jugoslawe *m*, Jugoslawin *f.*

Yugoslavia ['ju:gəʊ'slɑ:vɪə] *n* Jugoslawien *nt.*

YWCA *n abbr* (= *Young Women's Christian Association*) CVJF *m.*

Z

zap [zæp] *vt* (*COMPUT*) löschen.

zeal [zi:l] *n* Eifer *m*; **~ous** ['zeləs] *a* eifrig.

zebra ['zi:brə] *n* Zebra *nt*; **~ crossing** ['zi:brə'krɒsɪŋ] *n* (*Brit*) Zebrastreifen *m.*

zero ['zɪərəʊ] *n* Null *f*; (*on scale*) Nullpunkt *m.*

zest [zest] *n* Begeisterung *f.*

zigzag ['zɪgzæg] *n* Zickzack *m.*

zip [zɪp] *n* (*also*: ~ **fastener**, (*US*) **~per**) Reißverschluß *m* // *vt* (*also*: ~ **up**) den Reißverschluß zumachen (+*gen*); **~ code** *n* (*US*) Postleitzahl *f.*

zodiac ['zəʊdɪæk] *n* Tierkreis *m.*

zombie ['zɒmbɪ] *n*: **like a ~** (*fig*) wie im Tran.

zoo [zu:] *n* Zoo *m.*

zoology [zəʊ'ɒlədʒɪ] *n* Zoologie *f.*

zoom [zu:m] *vi*: **to ~ past** vorbeisausen; **~ lens** *n* Zoomobjektiv *nt.*

zucchini [zu:'ki:nɪ] *npl* (*US*: *courgettes*) Zucchini *f.*

GERMAN IRREGULAR VERBS
*with 'sein'

infinitive	present indicative (2nd, 3rd sing.)	preterite	past participle
aufschrecken*	schrickst auf, schrickt auf	schrak or schreckte auf	aufgeschreckt
ausbedingen	bedingst aus, bedingt aus	bedang or bedingte aus	ausbedungen
backen	bäckst, bäckt	backte or buk	gebacken
befehlen	befiehlst, befiehlt	befahl	befohlen
beginnen	beginnst, beginnt	begann	begonnen
beißen	beißt, beißt	biß	gebissen
bergen	birgst, birgt	barg	geborgen
bersten*	birst, birst	barst	geborsten
bescheißen*	bescheißt, bescheißt	beschiß	beschissen
bewegen	bewegst, bewegt	bewog	bewogen
biegen	biegst, biegt	bog	gebogen
bieten	bietest, bietet	bot	geboten
binden	bindest, bindet	band	gebunden
bitten	bittest, bittet	bat	gebeten
blasen	bläst, bläst	blies	geblasen
bleiben*	bleibst, bleibt	blieb	geblieben
braten	brätst, brät	briet	gebraten
brechen*	brichst, bricht	brach	gebrochen
brennen	brennst, brennt	brannte	gebrannt
bringen	bringst, bringt	brachte	gebracht
denken	denkst, denkt	dachte	gedacht
dreschen	drisch(e)st, drischt	drasch	gedroschen
dringen*	dringst, dringt	drang	gedrungen
dürfen	darfst, darf	durfte	gedurft
empfehlen	empfiehlst, empfiehlt	empfahl	empfohlen
erbleichen*	erbleichst, erbleicht	erbleichte	erblichen
erlöschen*	erlischst, erlischt	erlosch	erloschen
erschrecken*	erschrickst, erschrickt	erschrak	erschrocken
essen	ißt, ißt	aß	gegessen
fahren*	fährst, fährt	fuhr	gefahren
fallen*	fällst, fällt	fiel	gefallen
fangen	fängst, fängt	fing	gefangen
fechten	fichtst, ficht	focht	gefochten
finden	findest, findet	fand	gefunden
flechten	flichtst, flicht	flocht	geflochten
fliegen*	fliegst, fliegt	flog	geflogen
fliehen*	fliehst, flieht	floh	geflohen
fließen*	fließt, fließt	floß	geflossen
fressen	frißt, frißt	fraß	gefressen
frieren	frierst, friert	fror	gefroren
gären*	gärst, gärt	gor	gegoren
gebären	gebierst, gebiert	gebar	geboren
geben	gibst, gibt	gab	gegeben
gedeihen*	gedeihst, gedeiht	gedieh	gediehen
gehen*	gehst, geht	ging	gegangen
gelingen*	——, gelingt	gelang	gelungen
gelten	giltst, gilt	galt	gegolten
genesen*	gene(se)st, genest	genas	genesen
genießen	genießt, genießt	genoß	genossen
geraten*	gerätst, gerät	geriet	geraten
geschehen*	——, geschieht	geschah	geschehen

infinitive	present indicative (2nd, 3rd sing.)	preterite	past participle
gewinnen	gewinnst, gewinnt	gewann	gewonnen
gießen	gießt, gießt	goß	gegossen
gleichen	gleichst, gleicht	glich	geglichen
gleiten*	gleitest, gleitet	glitt	geglitten
glimmen	glimmst, glimmt	glomm	geglommen
graben	gräbst, gräbt	grub	gegraben
greifen	greifst, greift	griff	gegriffen
haben	hast, hat	hatte	gehabt
halten	hältst, hält	hielt	gehalten
hängen	hängst, hängt	hing	gehangen
hauen	haust, haut	haute	gehauen
heben	hebst, hebt	hob	gehoben
heißen	heißt, heißt	hieß	geheißen
helfen	hilfst, hilft	half	geholfen
kennen	kennst, kennt	kannte	gekannt
klimmen*	klimmst, klimmt	klomm	geklommen
klingen	klingst, klingt	klang	geklungen
kneifen	kneifst, kneift	kniff	gekniffen
kommen*	kommst, kommt	kam	gekommen
können	kannst, kann	konnte	gekonnt
kriechen*	kriechst, kriecht	kroch	gekrochen
laden	lädst, lädt	lud	geladen
lassen	läßt, läßt	ließ	gelassen
laufen*	läufst, läuft	lief	gelaufen
leiden	leidest, leidet	litt	gelitten
leihen	leihst, leiht	lieh	geliehen
lesen	liest, liest	las	gelesen
liegen*	liegst, liegt	lag	gelegen
lügen	lügst, lügt	log	gelogen
mahlen	mahlst, mahlt	mahlte	gemahlen
meiden	meidest, meidet	mied	gemieden
melken	melkst, melkt	melkte	gemolken
messen	mißt, mißt	maß	gemessen
mißlingen*	——, mißlingt	mißlang	mißlungen
mögen	magst, mag	mochte	gemocht
müssen	mußt, muß	mußte	gemußt
nehmen	nimmst, nimmt	nahm	genommen
nennen	nennst, nennt	nannte	genannt
pfeifen	pfeifst, pfeift	pfiff	gepfiffen
preisen	preist, preist	pries	gepriesen
quellen*	quillst, quillt	quoll	gequollen
raten	rätst, rät	riet	geraten
reiben	reibst, reibt	rieb	gerieben
reißen*	reißt, reißt	riß	gerissen
reiten*	reitest, reitet	ritt	geritten
rennen*	rennst, rennt	rannte	gerannt
riechen	riechst, riecht	roch	gerochen
ringen	ringst, ringt	rang	gerungen
rinnen*	rinnst, rinnt	rann	geronnen
rufen	rufst, ruft	rief	gerufen
salzen	salzt, salzt	salzte	gesalzen
saufen	säufst, säuft	soff	gesoffen
saugen	saugst, saugt	sog	gesogen
schaffen	schaffst, schafft	schuf	geschaffen
scheiden	scheidest, scheidet	schied	geschieden
scheinen	scheinst, scheint	schien	geschienen
schelten	schiltst, schilt	schalt	gescholten

infinitive	present indicative (2nd, 3rd sing.)	preterite	past participle
scheren	scherst, schert	schor	geschoren
schieben	schiebst, schiebt	schob	geschoben
schießen	schießt, schießt	schoß	geschossen
schinden	schindest, schindet	schindete	geschunden
schlafen	schläfst, schläft	schlief	geschlafen
schlagen	schlägst, schlägt	schlug	geschlagen
schleichen*	schleichst, schleicht	schlich	geschlichen
schleifen	schleifst, schleift	schliff	geschliffen
schließen	schließt, schließt	schloß	geschlossen
schlingen	schlingst, schlingt	schlang	geschlungen
schmeißen	schmeißt, schmeißt	schmiß	geschmissen
schmelzen*	schmilzt, schmilzt	schmolz	geschmolzen
schneiden	schneidest, schneidet	schnitt	geschnitten
schreiben	schreibst, schreibt	schrieb	geschrieben
schreien	schreist, schreit	schrie	geschrie(e)n
schreiten	schreitest, schreitet	schritt	geschritten
schweigen	schweigst, schweigt	schwieg	geschwiegen
schwellen*	schwillst, schwillt	schwoll	geschwollen
schwimmen*	schwimmst, schwimmt	schwamm	geschwommen
schwinden*	schwindest, schwindet	schwand	geschwunden
schwingen	schwingst, schwingt	schwang	geschwungen
schwören	schwörst, schwört	schwor	geschworen
sehen	siehst, sieht	sah	gesehen
sein*	bist, ist	war	gewesen
senden	sendest, sendet	sandte	gesandt
singen	singst, singt	sang	gesungen
sinken*	sinkst, sinkt	sank	gesunken
sinnen	sinnst, sinnt	sann	gesonnen
sitzen*	sitzt, sitzt	saß	gesessen
sollen	sollst, soll	sollte	gesollt
speien	speist, speit	spie	gespie(e)n
spinnen	spinnst, spinnt	spann	gesponnen
sprechen	sprichst, spricht	sprach	gesprochen
sprießen*	sprießt, sprießt	sproß	gesprossen
springen*	springst, springt	sprang	gesprungen
stechen	stichst, sticht	stach	gestochen
stecken	steckst, steckt	steckte or stak	gesteckt
stehen	stehst, steht	stand	gestanden
stehlen	stiehlst, stiehlt	stahl	gestohlen
steigen*	steigst, steigt	stieg	gestiegen
sterben*	stirbst, stirbt	starb	gestorben
stinken	stinkst, stinkt	stank	gestunken
stoßen	stößt, stößt	stieß	gestoßen
streichen	streichst, streicht	strich	gestrichen
streiten*	streitest, streitet	stritt	gestritten
tragen	trägst, trägt	trug	getragen
treffen	triffst, trifft	traf	getroffen
treiben*	treibst, treibt	trieb	getrieben
treten*	trittst, tritt	trat	getreten
trinken	trinkst, trinkt	trank	getrunken
trügen	trügst, trügt	trog	getrogen
tun	tust, tut	tat	getan
verderben	verdirbst, verdirbt	verdarb	verdorben
verdrießen	verdrießt, verdrießt	verdroß	verdrossen
vergessen	vergißt, vergißt	vergaß	vergessen
verlieren	verlierst, verliert	verlor	verloren

infinitive	present indicative (2nd, 3rd sing.)	preterite	past participle
verschleißen	verschleißt, verschleißt	verschliß	verschlissen
wachsen*	wächst, wächst	wuchs	gewachsen
wägen	wägst, wägt	wog	gewogen
waschen	wäschst, wäscht	wusch	gewaschen
weben	webst, webt	webte *or* wob	gewoben
weichen*	weichst, weicht	wich	gewichen
weisen	weist, weist	wies	gewiesen
wenden	wendest, wendet	wandte	gewandt
werben	wirbst, wirbt	warb	geworben
werden*	wirst, wird	wurde	geworden
werfen	wirfst, wirft	warf	geworfen
wiegen	wiegst, wiegt	wog	gewogen
winden	windest, windet	wand	gewunden
wissen	weißt, weiß	wußte	gewußt
wollen	willst, will	wollte	gewollt
wringen	wringst, wringt	wrang	gewrungen
zeihen	zeihst, zeiht	zieh	geziehen
ziehen*	ziehst, zieht	zog	gezogen
zwingen	zwingst, zwingt	zwang	gezwungen

UNREGELMÄSSIGE ENGLISCHE VERBEN

present	pt	pp	present	pt	pp
arise	arose	arisen	fling	flung	flung
awake	awoke	awaked	fly (flies)	flew	flown
be (am, is, are; being)	was, were	been	forbid	forbade	forbidden
			forecast	forecast	forecast
bear	bore	born(e)	forego	forewent	foregone
beat	beat	beaten	foresee	foresaw	foreseen
become	became	become	foretell	foretold	foretold
begin	began	begun	forget	forgot	forgotten
behold	beheld	beheld	forgive	forgave	forgiven
bend	bent	bent	forsake	forsook	forsaken
beseech	besought	besought	freeze	froze	frozen
beset	beset	beset	get	got	got, (US) gotten
bet	bet, betted	bet, betted	give	gave	given
bid	bid, bade	bid, bidden	go (goes)	went	gone
bind	bound	bound	grind	ground	ground
bite	bit	bitten	grow	grew	grown
bleed	bled	bled	hang	hung, hanged	hung, hanged
blow	blew	blown			
break	broke	broken	have (has; having)	had	had
breed	bred	bred			
bring	brought	brought	hear	heard	heard
build	built	built	hide	hid	hidden
burn	burnt, burned	burnt, burned	hit	hit	hit
			hold	held	held
burst	burst	burst	hurt	hurt	hurt
buy	bought	bought	keep	kept	kept
can	could	(been able)	kneel	knelt, kneeled	knelt, kneeled
cast	cast	cast			
catch	caught	caught	know	knew	known
choose	chose	chosen	lay	laid	laid
cling	clung	clung	lead	led	led
come	came	come	lean	leant, leaned	leant, leaned
cost	cost	cost			
creep	crept	crept	leap	leapt, leaped	leapt, leaped
cut	cut	cut			
deal	dealt	dealt	learn	learnt, learned	learnt, learned
dig	dug	dug			
do (3rd person: he/she/it does)	did	done	leave	left	left
			lend	lent	lent
			let	let	let
			lie (lying)	lay	lain
draw	drew	drawn	light	lit, lighted	lit, lighted
dream	dreamed, dreamt	dreamed, dreamt	lose	lost	lost
			make	made	made
drink	drank	drunk	may	might	—
drive	drove	driven	mean	meant	meant
dwell	dwelt	dwelt	meet	met	met
eat	ate	eaten	mistake	mistook	mistaken
fall	fell	fallen	mow	mowed	mown, mowed
feed	fed	fed	must	(had to)	(had to)
feel	felt	felt	pay	paid	paid
fight	fought	fought	put	put	put
find	found	found	quit	quit, quitted	quit, quitted
flee	fled	fled	read	read	read

present	pt	pp	present	pt	pp
rid	rid	rid	split	split	split
ride	rode	ridden	spoil	spoiled, spoilt	spoiled, spoilt
ring	rang	rung			
rise	rose	risen	spread	spread	spread
run	ran	run	spring	sprang	sprung
saw	sawed	sawn	stand	stood	stood
say	said	said	steal	stole	stolen
see	saw	seen	stick	stuck	stuck
seek	sought	sought	sting	stung	stung
sell	sold	sold	stink	stank	stunk
send	sent	sent	stride	strode	stridden
set	set	set	strike	struck	struck, stricken
shake	shook	shaken	strive	strove	striven
shall	should	—	swear	swore	sworn
shear	sheared	shorn, sheared	sweep	swept	swept
shed	shed	shed	swell	swelled	swollen, swelled
shine	shone	shone	swim	swam	swum
shoot	shot	shot	swing	swung	swung
show	showed	shown	take	took	taken
shrink	shrank	shrunk	teach	taught	taught
shut	shut	shut	tear	tore	torn
sing	sang	sung	tell	told	told
sink	sank	sunk	think	thought	thought
sit	sat	sat	throw	threw	thrown
slay	slew	slain	thrust	thrust	thrust
sleep	slept	slept	tread	trod	trodden
slide	slid	slid	wake	woke, waked	woken, waked
sling	slung	slung			
slit	slit	slit	waylay	waylaid	waylaid
smell	smelt, smelled	smelt, smelled	wear	wore	worn
			weave	wove, weaved	woven, weaved
sow	sowed	sown, sowed			
speak	spoke	spoken	wed	wedded, wed	wedded, wed
speed	sped, speeded	sped, speeded			
			weep	wept	wept
spell	spelt, spelled	spelt, spelled	win	won	won
			wind	wound	wound
spend	spent	spent	withdraw	withdrew	withdrawn
spill	spilt, spilled	spilt, spilled	withhold	withheld	withheld
			withstand	withstood	withstood
spin	spun	spun	wring	wrung	wrung
spit	spat	spat	write	wrote	written

NUMMER

NUMBERS

ein(s)	1	one	
zwei	2	two	
drei	3	three	
vier	4	four	
fünf	5	five	
sechs	6	six	
sieben	7	seven	
acht	8	eight	
neun	9	nine	
zehn	10	ten	
elf	11	eleven	
zwölf	12	twelve	
dreizehn	13	thirteen	
vierzehn	14	fourteen	
fünfzehn	15	fifteen	
sechzehn	16	sixteen	
siebzehn	17	seventeen	
achtzehn	18	eighteen	
neunzehn	19	nineteen	
zwanzig	20	twenty	
einundzwanzig	21	twenty-one	
zweiundzwanzig	22	twenty-two	
dreißig	30	thirty	
vierzig	40	forty	
fünfzig	50	fifty	
sechzig	60	sixty	
siebzig	70	seventy	
achtzig	80	eighty	
neunzig	90	ninety	
hundert	100	a hundred	
hunderteins	101	a hundred and one	
zweihundert	200	two hundred	
zweihunderteins	201	two hundred and one	
dreihundert	300	three hundred	
dreihunderteins	301	three hundred and one	
tausend	1000	a thousand	
tausend(und)eins	1001	a thousand and one	
fünftausend	5000	five thousand	
eine Million	1000000	a million	
erste(r,s)	1.	first	1st
zweite(r,s)	2.	second	2nd
dritte(r,s)	3.	third	3rd
vierte(r,s)	4.	fourth	4th
fünfte(r,s)	5.	fifth	5th
sechste(r,s)	6.	sixth	6th
siebte(r,s)	7.	seventh	7th
achte(r,s)	8.	eighth	8th
neunte(r,s)	9.	ninth	9th
zehnte(r,s)	10.	tenth	10th

elfte (r,s)	11.	eleventh	11th
zwölfte (r,s)	12.	twelfth	12th
dreizehnte (r,s)	13.	thirteenth	13th
vierzehnte (r,s)	14.	fourteenth	14th
fünfzehnte (r,s)	15.	fifteenth	15th
sechzehnte (r,s)	16.	sixteenth	16th
siebzehnte (r,s)	17.	seventeenth	17th
achtzehnte (r,s)	18.	eighteenth	18th
neunzehnte (r,s)	19.	nineteenth	19th
zwanzigste (r,s)	20.	twentieth	20th
einundzwanzigste (r,s)	21.	twenty-first	21st
dreißigste (r,s)	30.	thirtieth	30th
hundertste (r,s)	100.	hundredth	100th
hunderterste (r,s)	101.	hundred-and-first	101st
tausendste (r,s)	1000.	thousandth	1000th

Bruche usw.

Fractions etc.

ein Halb	½	a half	
ein Drittel	⅓	a third	
ein Viertel	¼	a quarter	
ein Fünftel	⅕	a fifth	
null Komma fünf	0,5	(nought) point five	0.5
drei Komma vier	3,4	three point four	3.4
sechs Komma acht neun	6,89	six point eight nine	6.89
zehn Prozent	10%	ten per cent	
hundert Prozent	100%	a hundred per cent	

Beispiele

Examples

er wohnt in Nummer 10 — he lives at number 10
es steht in Kapitel 7 — it's in chapter 7
auf Seite 7 — on page 7
er wohnt im 7. Stock — he lives on the 7th floor
er wurde 7. — he came in 7th
im Maßstab eins zu zwanzigtausend — scale one to twenty thousand

UHRZEIT

THE TIME

wieviel Uhr ist es?, wie spät ist es?

es ist ...

Mitternacht, zwölf Uhr nachts
ein Uhr (morgens *or* früh)

fünf nach eins, ein Uhr fünf
zehn nach eins, ein Uhr zehn
viertel nach eins, ein Uhr fünfzehn
fünf vor halb zwei, ein Uhr fünfundzwanzig
halb zwei, ein Uhr dreißig
fünf nach halb zwei, ein Uhr fünfunddreißig
zwanzig vor zwei, ein Uhr vierzig
viertel vor zwei, ein Uhr fünfundvierzig
zehn vor zwei, ein Uhr fünfzig
zwölf Uhr (mittags), Mittag
halb eins (mittags *or* nachmittags), zwölf Uhr dreißig
zwei Uhr (nachmittags)

halb acht (abends)

um wieviel Uhr?
um Mitternacht
um sieben Uhr

in zwanzig Minuten
vor fünfzehn Minuten

THE TIME

what time is it?

it's ...

midnight, twelve p.m.
one o'clock (in the morning), one (a.m.)

five past one
ten past one
a quarter past one, one fifteen
twenty-five past one, one twenty-five
half past one, one thirty
twenty-five to two, one thirty-five

twenty to two, one forty
a quarter to two, one forty-five

ten to two, one fifty
twelve o'clock, midday, noon
half past twelve, twelve thirty (p.m.)
two o'clock (in the afternoon), two (p.m.)
half past seven (in the evening), seven thirty (p.m.)

at what time?
at midnight
at seven o'clock

in twenty minutes
fifteen minutes ago